FOREWORD BY THE SECRETARY OF STATE FOR EDUCATION AND SCIENCE

This report is about a complex and important subject. The response of the education service to ethnic diversity concerns all who have responsibilities in education as well as all parents and their children.

The Government is firmly committed to the principle that all children, irrespective of race, colour or ethnic origin, should have a good education which develops their abilities and aptitudes to the full and brings about a true sense of belonging to Britain. The Committee's report explores in detail how this principle may be made good, marshalling in the process a mass of evidence. At my request Lord Swann himself has written a brief guide which draws the reader's attention to the main issues in the report and to its central findings.

We can all be grateful to Lord Swann and his colleagues for their hard work over a long period of time. They have done a great service in drawing the issues affecting ethnic minority pupils to public attention.

March 1985   KEITH JOSEPH

19th February 1985

Dear Secretary of State

I have the honour to present the Final Report of the Committee set up in 1979 to inquire into the Education of Children from Ethnic Minority Groups. I should like to take this opportunity of expressing our warmest thanks to a number of your staff, in particular to our Secretariat: Mr David Halladay, Miss Christina Bienkowska, Mr Peter Connell and Mrs Angela Craig, as well as to our Assessors at various stages, namely Mr Brian Baish, Mr Eric Bolton HMI and Mr John Singh HMI. All of them have been of inestimable help to the Committee and to me, in our long drawn-out endeavours.

Yours sincerely

Michael Swann

(Chairman)

The Rt Hon Sir Keith Joseph Bt MP

Education For All

Chairman: Lord Swann FRS, FRSE

The Report of the Committee of Inquiry into the Education of Children from Ethnic Minority Groups

Presented to Parliament by the Secretary of State for Education and Science by Command of Her Majesty

March 1985

LONDON

HER MAJESTY'S STATIONERY OFFICE

Reprinted 1986

£25.00 net

Cmnd. 9453

THE COMMITTEE*

Chairman

Mr A Rampton, OBE   Until May 1981.

Lord Swann, FRSE   From May 1981.

Members

Mr J P Athisayam	Behavioural Scientist.
Mr T Carter	Senior Education Liaison Officer, ILEA.
Mrs L Chapman	Adviser for the Education of Children in Early Years, Bradford Metropolitan Council.
Ms Y Collymore	Freelance Writer.
Mr G L Cooksey (appointed June 1981)	Principal, Greenhead College, Huddersfield, West Yorkshire.
Mr J P Cornford (appointed August 1981)	Director, Nuffield Foundation.
Mrs A Dummett (resigned November 1984)	Research Worker, Joint Council for the Welfare of Immigrants.
Mr C G Duncan	Head, Wyke Manor Upper School, Wyke, Bradford.
Mr D B Evans	Inspector, ILEA.
Mr J G Evans (appointed June 1981)	Director of Education, Derbyshire County Council.
Baroness Faithfull, OBE	Formerly Director of Social Services, Oxford City Council.
Mr M Feeley (resigned November 1980)	Adviser for Multicultural Education, Coventry Education Authority.
Mrs S Flather, JP	Councillor, Windsor and Maidenhead, Commissioner, Commission for Racial Equality.
Dr F S Hashmi, OBE (appointed May 1982)	Consultant Psychiatrist, All Saints Hospital, Birmingham. Commissioner, Commission for Racial Equality.
Professor E W Hawkins, CBE (resigned May 1981)	Formerly Director of Language Teaching Centre, University of York.

* Appointments shown are those held by members at the time of submission of the report to the Secretary of State or at the time of their resignation from the Committee.

iii

Professor P H Hirst (appointed November 1981)	Professor of Education, University of Cambridge.
Father M Hollings (resigned November 1984)	Parish Priest, Bayswater, Notting Hill, London.
Mr M A Khan-Cheema (appointed June 1981)	General Adviser in Education with special responsibility for Multicultural Education, Bradford Metropolitan Council.
Mrs D E McAuslan	SRN; SCM; Health Visitor Certificate, Lecturer in Health Education, Northamptonshire County Council.
Mr P K C Millins, CBE (resigned May 1981)	Formerly Director of Edge Hill College of Higher Education, Ormskirk, Lancashire.
Mr P A Newsam (resigned July 1982 on appointment as Chairman of the Commission for Racial Equality)	Education Officer, Inner London Education Authority.
Mr R Pal (resigned October 1979)	Managing Director CTS Leasing Ltd., Reading, Berkshire.
Dr B Parekh (resigned November 1981 to become Vice Chancellor, University of Baroda)	Senior Lecturer, Department of Political Studies, University of Hull.
Mr J Phillips, CBE	Formerly Chairman, Distributive Industry Training Board.
Mr E J B Rose, CBE (resigned June 1981)	Chairman, Penguin Books.
Mr A J B Rowe	Member of Parliament for Mid Kent.
Mrs Y Sheikh (resigned January 1981)	Peripatetic Teacher of English as a Second Language, London Borough of Croydon.
Dr G K Verma (appointed May 1982)	Reader in Education, University of Bradford.
Mr D Wong (appointed June 1981)	Research Officer, Special Projects (Ethnic Minorities), Education Department, Manchester City Council.

Assessors:

| Mr B L Baish | Department of Education and Science. |

Mr E J Bolton (until September 1981)	Her Majesty's Inspectorate.
Mr P Singh (from October 1981)	Her Majesty's Inspectorate.

Secretariat:

Mr D G Halladay	Department of Education and Science.
Miss C A Bienkowska	Department of Education and Science.
Mr P A Connell	Department of Education and Science.
Mrs A E Craig	Department of Education and Science.

Costs of Committee

The estimated cost of the production of the report is £692,618, of which £127,815 represents the estimated cost of printing and publication. £477,000 the cost of administration and research and £87,803 the travelling and other expenses of members.

TERMINOLOGY

We refer throughout this report, to a number of different ethnic minorities, as well as to the (white) ethnic majority. Following common usage, and in the interests of brevity, we refer to "West Indians" and "Asians" as shorthand for the more accurate, but more cumbersome "British citizens of West Indian or Asian origin". It should be borne in mind that virtually all of the "West Indian" children about whom this report is concerned and the vast majority of "Asian" children were in fact born in this country. The term "Asian", unless otherwise specified is also used as a collective term to cover a range of ethnic minorities whose cultural roots emanate from the Indian sub-continent, India, Pakistan and Bangladesh, although some came to Britain from East Africa and elsewhere. The religious affiliations of these groups include Islam, Hinduism, Sikhism and others and their languages include Urdu, Punjabi, Gujerati, Bengali, Pushtu, Sindhi and others.

In addition we refer to the ethnic majority as the "white" or "indigenous" majority. None of these terms is wholly satisfactory. There are white minorities within the white majority, while some of the white minorities have lived long enough in Britain to be regarded as indigenous. Nevertheless we think, given these warnings, that our use of the different terms will not cause confusion.

PREFACE

Origins of this Committee

1. The origins of this Committee can be traced back to the concern expressed by the West Indian Community during the late 1960s and early 1970s about the academic performance of their children. This concern was recognised by the Select Committee on Race Relations and Immigration and in their report on the West Indian Community in 1977 they recommended that:

> *". . . . as a matter of urgency the Government (should) institute a high level and independent inquiry into the causes of the underachievement of children of West Indian origin in maintained schools and the remedial action required".*

2. The then Government accepted the need for an inquiry but felt that it should be concerned with the needs of pupils from all ethnic minority groups with priority being given to children of West Indian origin[2]. In consequence this Committee was established in 1979 with the following terms of reference:

> *"Recognising the contribution of schools in preparing all pupils for life in a society which is both multi-racial and culturally diverse, the Committee is required to:*

Terms of Reference

> *review in relation to schools the educational needs and attainments of children from ethnic minority groups taking account, as necessary, of factors outside the formal education system relevant to school performance, including influences in early childhood and prospects for school leavers;*
>
> *consider the potential value of instituting arrangements for keeping under review the educational performance of different ethnic minority groups, and what those arrangements might be;*
>
> *consider the most effective use of resources for these purposes; and to make recommendations.*
>
> *In carrying out its programme of work, the Committee is to give early and particular attention to the educational needs and attainments of pupils of West Indian origin and to make interim recommendations as soon as possible on action which might be taken in the interests of this group."*

NB: The Committee's terms of reference relate only to England.

---

[1] "The West Indian Community." Select Committee on Race Relations and Immigration. February 1977. HMSO. HC 180 I.
[2] "The West Indian Community." Cmnd 7186. HMSO. April 1978.

**Interim
Report**

3. Our interim report, fulfilling the requirement in our terms of reference to give particular attention to the situation of West Indian children, was submitted to the Secretary of State on 27 February 1981 and was published on 17 June 1981[3]. In that report we concluded that West Indian children as a group were:

> *". . . . underachieving in relation to their peers."*

We then went on to consider the various factors, both within the education system and more generally, which had been said to contribute to this underachievement and identified:

> *". . . . no single cause . . . . but rather a network of widely differing attitudes and expectations on the part of teachers and the education system as a whole, and on the part of West Indian parents, which lead the West Indian child to have particular difficulties and face particular hurdles in achieving his or her full potential."*

In calling for urgent measures to remedy West Indian underachievement we put forward a programme for action and set out in some detail the part which various agencies could play in bringing about the changes in attitude and practice which we believed to be necessary. We prepared a summary of our interim report, attached as an annex to this preface, drawing together our main findings and recommendations, which was given a very wide distribution. In this report we seek to follow up the findings and conclusions of our interim report and to respond fully to our terms of reference.

**Modus
Operandi**

4. Throughout our work we have adopted a structure of specialist sub-committees and sub-groups to consider the range of issues encompassed by our remit. Although our membership covered a wide range of interest and expertise, we felt that we would benefit from the presence on our sub-committees of additional members with particular knowledge and experience. We therefore co-opted a number of individuals to whom we are particularly grateful for their help and advice. Whilst this report owes much to the contributions of our co-opted members, they are not however responsible for the conclusions and recommendations which we put forward here. Details of these co-options are given in Appendix A of this report.

**Reviews of
Research**

5. In order to enable us to make the best possible use of the relevant research evidence available, we commissioned the National Foundation for Educational Research (NFER) to prepare a series of

---

[3] "West Indian Children in our Schools." Cmnd 8273. HMSO. June 1981.

evaluative reviews of research. These reviews are or will be available publicly, as follows:

● "Caught Between: A Review of Research into the Education of pupils of West Indian origin." Monica J Taylor. NFER-Nelson. 1981;

● "The Best of Both Worlds . . . . ?: A Review of Research into the Education of pupils of South Asian origin." Monica J Taylor and Seamus Hegarty (forthcoming); and

● Third Review of Research (relating to the "other" minorities considered by the Committee): Monica J Taylor and Seamus Hegarty (forthcoming).

Research Studies

As well as proving particularly helpful to us in our work – and we have indeed drawn on the conclusions of these reviews throughout this report – the NFER reviews provide a wealth of material on the educational experiences of ethnic minority pupils, as well as describing the backgrounds of the various ethnic minority communities in our society, which will, we are sure, be of considerable interest to those working in this field. In the course of our work we have ourselves commissioned a number of studies relating to particular issues or areas of concern. References to the findings of these studies are included in the relevant chapters of this report.

Evidence-Gathering

6. During our lifetime we have issued two main invitations for evidence – firstly at the start of our work, when we were seeking evidence relating particularly to the situation of pupils of West Indian origin, and then again, after the publication of our interim report, when we invited both comments on that report together with further evidence relating to other ethnic minority groups and to the broader issues encompassed by our remit. On both occasions our invitations for evidence were given a very wide distribution and we also supplemented these general requests for evidence by approaching a range of educational organisations and ethnic minority community organisations, for evidence on their specific concerns. The summary of our interim report's findings and conclusions was also sent to every maintained school and teacher training institution in England, inviting comments and further evidence. In addition to these requests for evidence, our sub-committees have also, on a number of occasions, requested information relating to more specialist matters within their remits. The response to our various invitations for evidence and requests for information has been quite overwhelming; we estimate that we have received almost 1000 submissions of

evidence, all of which have proved immensely helpful to us in our work, as well as indicating the amount of interest and, in some cases, concern about the whole field of "multicultural education". We also called together representatives of several "interested organisations" to discuss particular issues in greater depth and organised oral evidence sessions, for both the full Committee and at sub-committee level. Lists of those who submitted evidence to us are included as Appendices to this report.

Forums   7.   We decided early on in our work that we wished to extend our consultations beyond the traditional education interest groups and the leading national ethnic minority organisations to involve also parents and young people, particularly from the various ethnic minority communities, who might otherwise have been unlikely to make their voices heard through formal channels. We therefore organised some 30 open meetings or "forums" around the country, which took place in schools or community centres, in the evening or at weekends, usually under the auspices of local community relations councils, at which we could discuss the major issues of concern to the communities in these areas. These forums provided a very valuable further source of evidence to us and lent added immediacy to our understanding of the communities' concerns, particularly about the influence of racism on their everyday lives. Details of the various forums are given in Appendix E.

National   8.   As well as inviting written comments on our interim report, we
Conference   also convened a one day national conference, in November 1981, to discuss its findings. There were over 250 participants, including representatives of both Houses of Parliament, local authority members and officers, Heads and teachers and community representatives from a range of ethnic minority groups, and the conference was opened by the Secretary of State for Education and Science. This conference enabled us to discuss, with representatives of a very wide range of interest groups, the broader implications of the conclusions which we had reached in our interim report, as well as to hear their views on the specific issues to which they felt we should devote attention for this report.

Visits   9.   Throughout our work we have endeavoured to visit as many LEAs, schools and other educational institutions, of as many differing types and in as many parts of the country as possible. We have received evidence from nearly one third of LEAs and have investigated in rather more detail the work of 20 of them. Members or representatives of this Committee have visited over 150 schools and

x

other institutions – these are listed in Appendix B. On our visits to primary schools we have made particular efforts to talk to parents about their expectations of schools and their aspirations for their children. In secondary schools we have taken every opportunity to meet and talk with groups of senior pupils, especially but not exclusively from ethnic minority groups, in order to seek their views on the various issues within our remit – bearing in mind that in many ways it is *their* attitudes, as the citizens and parents of the future, which offer a crucial insight into the future nature of our society.

Acknowledge-
ment

10.   We are grateful to all the local authorities, schools, organisations and individuals who took the time and trouble to prepare written evidence for us or to participate in discussions about aspects of our work. We are particularly grateful to those schools which we visited both for their hospitality and the open and frank way in which the teachers and indeed the pupils were prepared to discuss their anxieties and concerns with us.

PLAN OF THE REPORT

We hope that this report will be considered as a whole by all those concerned about the role of education in relation to the changed and changing nature of our society. Although we devote individual chapters to considering various specific issues within our remit, these chapters are invariably inter-related and the conclusions reached within them depend for their proper understanding on the broad context and underlying aims and objectives on which the whole of our work has been based. These chapters are themselves grouped to form several distinct parts of the report, reflecting different aspects of our deliberations.

In *Part One* of the report – *"Setting the Scene"* – we set the context for our work by discussing the relationship between the education system and the nature of present day British society. We begin by considering the various ways in which our multi-racial society could evolve and then put forward our own view of the role which we believe education can and must play in laying the foundations for a society based on genuinely pluralist principles. We go on to discuss the controversial issue of racism, and its influence on both schools and the wider society, on which so much of our evidence has focussed. We consider both the broad concept of prejudice and the particular roots of racism as well as looking at the various ways in which racism, at both individual and institutional level, can manifest itself and, more importantly, can be countered. Finally we return to the issue of the achievement and underachievement of pupils of ethnic minority origin, which was of course central to our interim report.

In *Part Two* of the report – *"Education for All"* – we review the evolution of policies and practice, at both central and local level, in the field of "multicultural education" from the early days of large scale immigration up to the present day. We reflect in particular on the way in which the aims and objectives of policy making in this field have changed over the years, in relation to changing circumstances and the concerns of ethnic minority communities and educationists. We also draw together here the findings of some of the research studies which we have ourselves commissioned in the course of our work. We then go on to put forward, in Chapter Six, our own view of the task for education in meeting the needs of ethnic minority pupils and preparing *all* pupils, both ethnic majority and ethnic minority, for life in a society which is both multi-racial and culturally diverse. Having set out the broad principles which we believe should underlie our philosophy of "Education for All" and considered the practical implications of such an approach for the curriculum, we conclude by putting forward an overall strategy for the management of change needed in order to achieve the objectives we have advocated.

In *Part Three* of the report – *"Major Areas of Concern"* – we devote chapters to considering those aspects of education which emerged clearly from our evidence as arousing the greatest interest and anxieties amongst both the ethnic minority communities and educationists: language and language education, and religion and the role of the school. In both chapters we put forward specific conclusions and recommendations for progress, reflecting the principles of "Education for All". We also devote a chapter to considering the implications of our view of the task facing education, for teacher training at all levels and set out a distinct strategy for change within the teacher training field to complement and support the development of "Education for All".

In these three parts of the report we focus primarily, but not exclusively, on the needs and concerns of the two most numerous ethnic communities in this country – the West Indian community[4], which was the subject of our interim report, and the Asian community[5]. Our terms of reference required us however to consider

---

[4] According to data from the Ethnic Statistics Unit of the Office of Population Censuses and Surveys, the West Indian population of Great Britain in 1981 (the most recent year for which figures are available – from the 1981 Labour Force Survey) numbered some 604,000.
[5] According to OPCS data the Asian population of Great Britain in 1981 numbered 1,114,000.

the needs of children from the whole range of ethnic minority groups. In *Part Four* of the report – *"Other" Ethnic Minority Groups* – we therefore consider the needs and problems of several of the numerically smaller ethnic minority communities which are also now an integral part of British society, ranging from the Chinese community to the Vietnamese refugees and the Travelling community. Here again we seek to relate our specific findings to the broader debate about the response of the education system to the experiences and aspirations of ethnic minority communities and more broadly to the emergence of an increasingly complex and diverse multi-racial society.

In *Part Five* of the report we draw together, for ease of reference, our *Main Conclusions and Recommendations.* It must be recognised however that several of our most important chapters do not in fact contain detailed recommendations of this kind and we would therefore emphasise again that we hope this report will be read in full by educationists and others in positions of responsibility and influence.

Throughout our report, we have sought to draw together, both in the text of the chapters and as annexes, examples of attitude and practice drawn from the wealth of evidence we have received, both in order to illustrate and highlight the overall message which we wish to convey to both policy makers and practitioners.

WEST INDIAN CHILDREN
IN OUR SCHOOLS

A brief guide to the
interim report of the Committee of Inquiry
into the Education of Children from
Ethnic Minority Groups

BACKGROUND

1.   The Committee of Inquiry into the Education of Children from Ethnic Minority Groups was established by the then Government in March 1979 as part of its response to the report of the Select Committee on Race Relations and Immigration on "The West Indian Community"[1] which highlighted concern about the academic performance of West Indian children. The present Government confirmed the Committee's establishment and completed the appointment of members. The Committee was asked to look at the educational needs and attainments of children from the whole range of ethnic minority groups bearing in mind factors relating to pre-school experiences and prospects for school leavers. As a first step, however, the Committee was required to prepare an interim report on the particular needs and attainments of West Indian children.

2.   The Committee's interim report "West Indian Children in our Schools" was published on 17 June 1981[2]. This leaflet sets out the main findings of the report and summarises the recommendations offered in it.

---

[1] House of Commons HC 180 I–III February 1977.
[2] Cmnd. 8273 HMSO June 1981 Price £5.30.

INTRODUCTION

3.   In the absence of any nationally agreed definition of "West Indian" the Committee has dealt in its report with "children who are black, whose families came originally from the group of islands known as the West Indies, and who are generally speaking regarded as West Indian by teachers and the community at large". The report stresses that virtually all these children are British-born.

4.   In preparing its interim report, the Committee received written and oral evidence from a wide range of individuals and organisations including many representatives of the West Indian community and between January and July 1980 members spent over 100 days visiting schools and other institutions around the country.

5.   The report stresses that "the education of West Indian children cannot be seen in isolation and must be considered as part of the education of all children". As well as discussing the major issues in the education of West Indian children, the Committee's interim report also therefore considers the much broader question of what schools in general should be attempting to provide for all their pupils in today's "multiracial and culturally diverse" society.

CHAPTER ONE
The Evidence of Underachievement

6. The Committee summarises briefly the various studies which over recent years have appeared to show considerable underachievement by West Indian pupils in relation to their white peers. For example in 1966 and 1968 Little's studies of the reading standards of 9 year olds in ILEA showed that West Indian children were performing less well than their contemporaries and the 1980 ILEA Literacy Survey showed that at 15+ this was still the case. In order to obtain some up to date statistical information on the academic performance of West Indian children the DES Statistics Branch included, at the Committee's request, in their School Leavers Survey for 1978/79, for six LEAs (covering approximately half of the school leavers from ethnic minorities) a question on the ethnic origin of the leavers.

7. The results of the School Leavers Survey Exercise show:

– **In all CSE and GCE 'O' level examinations** only 3% of West Indians obtained 5 or more higher grades[3] compared with 18% of Asians and 16% of all other leavers in these LEAs;

– **In CSE English and GCE 'O' level English Language** only 9% of West Indians obtained higher grades compared with 21% of Asians and 29% of all other leavers in these LEAs;

– **In CSE and GCE 'O' level in Mathematics** only 5% of West Indians obtained higher grades compared with 20% of Asians and 19% of all other leavers in these LEAs;

– **At GCE 'A' level** only 2% of West Indians gained one or more pass compared with 13% Asians and 12% of all other leavers in these LEAs;

– Only 1% of West Indians **went on to University** compared with 3% of Asians and 3% of all other leavers in these LEAs; and

– Only 1% of West Indians went on to **full time degree courses in further education** compared with 5% of Asians and 4% of all other leavers in these LEAs.

8. The Committee concludes that although there will "always be some children who will underachieve and for various reasons will fail to reach their full potential" their concern is that West Indian children **as a group** are "underachieving in relation to their peers, not least in obtaining the examination qualifications needed to give them equality of opportunity in the employment market and to enable them to take advantage of the range of post school opportunities available".

---

[3] Grades A–C at 'O' level and Grade 1 CSE.

CHAPTER TWO

The Factors Contributing to Underachievement

9. The report considers in some detail the various factors, both within the education system and outside it, which have been said to lead West Indian children to underachieve:

Racism

Many West Indians who gave evidence to the Committee saw racism as the major reason for their children's underachievement and other people mentioned this as a contributory factor. The Committee believes that only a very small minority of teachers could be said to be racist in the commonly accepted sense. However it claims that a teacher's attitude towards, and expectations of, West Indian pupils may be subconsciously influenced by stereotyped, negative or patronising views of their abilities and potential, which may prove a self-fulfilling prophecy, and can be seen as a form of 'unintentional racism'. The Committee concludes that, whilst racism, whether intentional or unintentional, cannot be said alone to account for the underachievement of West Indian children, it can and does have an important bearing on their performance at school. The report therefore urges teachers to be prepared to examine and reappraise their attitudes and behaviour, to challenge all manifestations of racism and to play a leading role in seeking to change the attitudes of society as a whole towards ethnic minority communities.

Pre-school Provision

The Committee feels that the existing provision for the under fives, both in terms of day care and nursery education, is generally inadequate to meet the needs of the population as a whole, and may be particularly ill-suited to the needs of West Indian families. It believes that evidence "points to the cycle of West Indian underachievement having its roots in the pre-school years and . . . . that measures relating to primary and secondary education must be accompanied by improvements in the pre-school field". The report recommends that local authorities should make greater efforts to ensure that West Indian parents are aware of the pre-school facilities available and that LEAs should do more to help parents appreciate the contribution which they can make to the progress of their child, before he enters school. Other recommendations relate to the need for better co-ordination within local authorities of services for the under-fives, the conversion of former primary school premises for nursery use, the extension of the opening hours of nursery schools and units, the need for those who work with under-fives to be made aware of the particular difficulties faced by West Indian families, and the need for there to be more nursery nurses and health visitors from ethnic minority groups.

Reading and Language
Reading
The report summarises the findings and conclusions of the 1980 ILEA Literacy Survey on the low reading attainment of West Indian children and discusses briefly

the methods and materials used by schools for teaching reading. It focuses on a recent study of the benefits derived by schools from involving parents more directly in helping their children to learn to read and recommends that all LEAs and schools should consider ways of building on this work.

Language
The report summarises current views on the nature of the language of West Indian children, the various approaches adopted by schools and teachers to this language and the attitudes of West Indian parents. It concludes that "for the majority of West Indian children in our schools, who were born and brought up in this country, linguistic factors play (no) part in underachievement". It feels however that "the attitudes towards West Indian children's language held by some teachers . . . . may have an important bearing on their motivation and achievement" and recommends a range of measures designed to encourage teachers' understanding and appreciation of the nature of West Indian language.

Curriculum
The report argues strongly that a broadly-based, "multi-cultural" approach to the curriculum should be adopted by all schools, both those with ethnic minority pupils and all white schools, and offers some examples, at both primary and secondary level, of what it sees as 'good practice' in this respect. The Committee does not "believe that education should seek to iron out the differences between cultures, nor attempt to draw everyone into the dominant culture" but rather should "draw upon the experiences of the many cultures that make up our society and thus broaden the cultural horizons of every child". The Committee's recommendations to the DES, HM Inspectorate and the Schools Council are designed to encourage a multi-cultural approach throughout education and within schools, headteachers and teachers, especially those from ethnic minority groups, are seen as having particular roles to play in bringing this about.

Books and Teaching Materials
The Committee's call for a multi-cultural approach in education is reiterated in relation to the books and teaching materials used by schools. The Committee felt that some of these still presented an inaccurate and negative picture of ethnic minority groups and of other cultures, and calls upon teachers and librarians, with advice from their LEAs, to examine the books they use and to take account of their appropriateness to today's multi-racial society.

Examinations
The Committee feels that "examinations have a major part to play in complementing and reflecting a multi-cultural approach to the curriculum in schools and the multi-racial nature of today's society". It believes that the examining boards have shown themselves inflexible and, in some cases, dismissive both of the particular needs which ethnic minority pupils may have, and of the need for their syllabuses and papers to be more relevant to the actual experiences of the pupils in schools today. It therefore recommends that all GCE and CSE boards should review their policies in

this respect and, looking towards the restructuring of the examinations system, that the DES should take account of these considerations in any new arrangements.

School Pastoral Arrangements
The report emphasises that the Committee "believe(s) that all teachers have a pastoral role in schools and that it cannot be separated from their overall teaching duties" and that "pastoral care cannot be seen as being solely the concern of those staff expressly designated as having pastoral responsibilities". It recommends that headteachers should ensure all their staff are aware of their pastoral responsibilities; that LEAs should provide appropriate in-service courses on the particular needs of ethnic minority pupils and that teachers should be encouraged to attend these courses.

Links between Schools and the Community
The Committee highlights here one of the main themes running throughout its report – the gulf in trust and understanding between schools and West Indian parents. The failure of some schools to understand the particular social and economic pressures which West Indian parents may face, together with the failure of some West Indian parents to appreciate the contribution which they can make to their child's education, are both seen as factors in the underachievement of West Indian children. The Committee urges schools to 'reach out' to parents by, for example, more teachers undertaking home visiting and by making information on the school's policies and on children's progress more easily accessible to parents. In turn West Indian parents and the West Indian community are encouraged to respond positively to approaches from schools and to seek ways of being actively involved in the school's work. The report offers a range of recommendations designed to foster closer links between schools and the community they serve.

Special Provision
Much of the concern which originally led to the Committee's establishment centred around West Indians' fears that their children were being wrongly placed in ESN(M) schools. The Committee attempted to ascertain whether West Indian children were disproportionately represented in ESN(M) schools but the absence of ethnically based statistics on the school population meant that they were unable "to confirm or deny this belief". The report therefore recommends strongly that the DES should carry out its undertaking[4] to collect statistics on the ethnic mix of ESN(M) schools in order to establish the facts clearly and (in chapter three) recommends that further ethnically based educational statistics should be collected. The committee welcomes the Education Bill 1981 which proposes wide-ranging changes in current arrangements for children with 'special educational needs' and in particular new rights for parents. The report recommends measures designed to ensure that West Indian children are not incorrectly assessed for special education by, for example, asking LEAs to "take full account of the particular factors, such as cultural differences and the effects of discrimination, which may have a bearing on the educational progress of West Indian pupils". The report refers briefly to the anxiety frequently voiced by parents about

[4] Home Office White Paper "The West Indian Community." Cmnd. 7186 April 1978.

the number of West Indian children who are suspended or excluded from school. It therefore recommends that procedures after a pupil is suspended or excluded should be tightened up. The Committee expresses its concern at the increase in the number of special behavioural or 'disruptive' units established in recent years, especially since West Indians believe that their children are often wrongly referred to these units. Again the absence of statistics meant that it was not possible for the Committee to establish whether West Indians were over-represented although in the units the members visited this did not seem to be the case. The report offers a number of recommendations concerning referral to the units and recommends that the DES should "consider the legal position of units serving more than one school and which cater on a full-time basis for disruptive pupils".

Preparation for Adult Life
The Committee devotes considerable attention to issues relating to the transition from school to work and the particular needs of West Indian pupils since this is an area "which probably worries West Indians more than any other covered by our remit". The report points out that unemployment is disproportionately high among young West Indians, not least because discrimination is still widespread in the jobs market. It calls upon those concerned to bring about equality of opportunity for all school leavers. Poor employment prospects, combined with low teacher expectations, are said to have a demotivating effect on West Indian pupils and to discourage them from achieving their full potential. Although many West Indians believe that some careers teachers and careers officers discriminate against West Indian pupils and tend to channel them into certain low-level occupations, the Committee does not accept that in the vast majority of cases this is so. It suggests however that, as with the teaching profession as a whole, there may be instances of 'unintentional racism' resulting from stereo-typed views of West Indian children. The report offers a range of recommendations designed to make school careers education and the work of the careers service more effective and responsive to the particular needs of West Indian youngsters by, for example, suggesting that training courses for careers officers should include reference to their needs and that more West Indians and people from other ethnic minority groups should be involved in careers work. It also recommends that schools should monitor on an ethnic basis the destination of their leavers to "allow schools to identify any worrying patterns in the achievement or lack of achievement of any ethnic minority group".

CHAPTER THREE

Support for Schools and Teachers

10.   In this chapter the Committee considers the support available for schools and teachers through teacher education, LEA advisory services, statistics and funding:

Teacher Education

Throughout its report the Committee has emphasised the key role which it sees teachers and headteachers playing in making the education system, and particularly the curriculum, more responsive to the needs of ethnic minority pupils and genuinely multi-cultural in character. In the field of **inital training** the Committee concludes that no teacher training institution "appears to have succeeded in providing a satisfactory grounding in multi-cultural education for all of its students" and that "the great majority of students are thus entering teaching having received little or no guidance on how to adopt a broadly-based approach to education which takes full account of the presence of ethnic minorities in our society". It recommends that all teacher training institutions should review their policies in this respect. The Committee also urges LEAs and schools to establish effective **induction programmes**. Whilst developments in the field of **in-service education** are seen as more positive especially in terms of school-based work, the report recommends various ways in which provision relating to the needs of ethnic minority pupils and the theory and practice of a multi-cultural approach to education should be extended and encouraged. The Committee attaches considerable importance to developments in in-service education as "the most effective means of directly affecting teaching in our schools in the immediate future". The Committee reiterates its call for there to be more West Indian teachers and professionals at all levels in the education service and presses for there to be more 'special access' courses designed to enable ethnic minority people and others to train for teaching.

The Advisory Services

The Committee believes that all LEA advisers "have a role to play in increasing awareness and understanding of the needs of ethnic minority pupils and in fostering the development of a curriculum relevant to the needs of society today". Where LEAs have advisers with specific responsibility for multi-cultural education — and the Commitee recommends that all LEAs with substantial ethnic minority populations should consider making such an appointment — the report stresses that the person concerned "needs to have a genuine understanding of ethnic minority pupils and a knowledge of the minority communities' cultures and concerns".

Statistics

The Committee points out that its task in preparing its report has been continually hampered by the absence of ethnically-based educational statistics and goes further to say that "the absence of ethnically-based statistics throughout the education system has contributed to the lack of positive action at both national and local level to identify and seek to remedy the underachievement of West Indian children".

It declares itself "wholly in favour of the collection of educational statistics on an ethnic basis where they are to be used in establishing facts about how members of the ethnic minorities are faring in the education system" and therefore recommends a range of statistics should be recorded and collected with effect from 1 September 1982. In recognition of the concerns which have been voiced in the past about the use of ethnic classifications and the confidentiality of the information obtained, it recommends that as a first step the DES should consult the local authority associations, the teacher unions, the Society of Education Officers and representatives of the ethnic minority communities.

Funding

The Committee acknowledges that it has received evidence about the possibility of establishing a Central Fund to meet the educational needs of ethnic minority children but defers consideration on this until its main report. The Committee discusses the various criticisms which have been voiced about the current arrangements for the provision of funds to local authorities under Section 11 of the Local Government Act 1966. It concludes that "Section 11 provides a valuable source of funding to local authorities" but there is a "need for the government to revise its provisions to make it more appropriate to the needs of the ethnic minority communities in our society". It recommends therefore that the Government should undertake a review of the provisions and operation of Section 11.

CHAPTER FOUR

Programme for Action

11.   In the final chapter of its report the Committee summarises briefly the various factors which it has discussed relating to the underachievement of West Indian children. It reiterates that West Indian children are indeed underachieving and that "urgent action is needed to remedy this". As far as the reasons for this underachievement are concerned the Committee says it has identified "no single cause . . . but rather a network of widely differing attitudes and expectations on the part of teachers and the education system as a whole, and on the part of West Indian parents, which lead the West Indian child to have particular difficulties and face particular hurdles in achieving his or her full potential".

12.   The Committee then considers in some detail the part which various 'agencies of change' can play in bringing about the overall changes for which the report calls. It discusses the roles of central government (particularly the DES), local government (particularly LEAs), and a range of interested organisations and institutions including teacher unions, examining boards and the CRE and local CRCs.

13.   The Committee then considers the cost implications of its recommendations. It emphasises that the majority call for no additional funds but rather "a reordering of the priorities under which resources are at present allocated so as to bring about a fundamental change in attitude towards the ethnic minorities in our society and in particular towards ethnic minority pupils in our schools". It recognises however that there will be some additional costs for example associated with staff time in establishing links between schools and parents and reviewing the curriculum. Some of the recommendations which call for schools to review the extent to which they take account of the multi-racial nature of society will have 'psychological' rather than 'financial' costs since "all concerned — teachers, pupils and parents — will need to be prepared to reappraise in some cases long-accepted views of the "British education system" and of their roles within it".

14.   Having listed all the specific recommendations it has offered, the Committee then summarises a number of issues which have been raised in the report which, in the time available, it has not yet considered fully or which affect **all** ethnic minority groups and will therefore be considered in the main report. The Committee concludes with a call for comments on this report and further evidence for its main report.

TABLE OF CONTENTS

PART 1—SETTING THE SCENE

Chapter 3   Achievement and Underachievement

PART II—"EDUCATION FOR ALL"

Chapter 4   Ethnic Minorities and Education: A Historical Perspective

Chapter 5 Multicultural Education: Further Studies

Chapter 6   "Education For All":
A New Approach

Annexes

Annex A: "Education for Racial Equality": Policy document from Berkshire LEA.

Annex B: Examples of Anti-Racist Policy Statements adopted by Two Multi-Racial Secondary Schools.

PART III—MAJOR AREAS OF CONCERN

Chapter Seven   Language and Language Education

Annexes

Chapter 8   Religion and the Role of the School: Religious Education and the "Separate" Schools Debate

I.   Religious Education

II. The "Separate" Schools Debate

Annexes

Annex A: Extracts from the Education Act 1944.

Annex B: Extract from Religious Heritage and Personal Quest—Guidelines for Religious Education—Berkshire LEA 1982.

Annex C: Extract from evidence from a Primary School setting out its aims of Religious Education and describing a number of Projects which had been undertaken.

Annex D: Extracts from evidence submitted by Multi-Racial Secondary Schools setting out their aims and objectives of Religious Education.

Annex E: The Establishment of Voluntary Aided Schools—Background Explanatory Notes by the DES.

Chapter 9   Teacher Education and the Employment of Ethnic Minority Teachers

Annexes
Annex A: Paper by Derek Cherrington and Ray Giles summarising the Findings of
a National Survey of Multicultural Aspects of Teacher Training.
Annex B: Paper by HMI Ivor Ambrose summarising the Findings of an Inspection
Exercise to Investigate the Coverage of Multicultural Education in Initial
and In-Service Teacher Training courses.
Annex C: Extracts from Evidence received from Two Teacher Training Institutions
reflecting the underlying principles of Permeation.
Annex D: Extracts from Evidence illustrating the ways in which Multicultural Issues
have been incorporated in the Core Studies of various Teacher Training
Institutions.
Annex E: Extracts from Evidence relating to Optional Courses offered by various
Teacher Training Institutions.
Annex F: Extract from Evidence describing the work undertaken in a PGCE Option
Course in Multicultural Education at a University Department of
Education.

PART IV—"OTHER" ETHNIC MINORITY GROUPS

Chapter 10   The Educational Needs of Children of Chinese Origin

Annex: Extracts from "Community Education: The Unknown Perspective—
Chinese Mother Tongue Classes". Ming Tsow.

Chapter 11   The Educational Needs of Children of Cypriot Origin

Chapter 12   The Educational Needs of Children of Italian Origin

Annex: Outline of the EC-Sponsored Project "Mother Tongue and Culture in Bedfordshire".

Chapter 13   The Educational Needs of Children of Ukranian Origin

Chapter 14   The Educational Needs of Vietnamese Children

Chapter 15   The Educational Needs of "Liverpool Blacks"

Chapter 16   The Educational Needs of Travellers' Children

Annex: Extract from "The Education of Travellers' Children"—An HMI Discussion Document. DES. 1983.

Reflections and Conclusions

PART V—MAIN CONCLUSIONS AND RECOMMENDATIONS

APPENDICES TO THE REPORT

Appendix A Co-opted members to Sub Committees.

Appendix B List of Educational Institutions which have submitted evidence to the Committee.

Appendix C List of LEAs and organisations which have submitted evidence to the Committee.

Appendix D List of individuals who have submitted evidence to the Committee.

Appendix E List of open meetings or "forums" arranged to hear the views of parents and young people.

PART I

Setting the Scene

CHAPTER 1

The Nature of Society

Education and the Nature of Society

1. The relationship between the education offered in our schools and the broader nature of society has of course long been the subject of considerable debate and discussion in educational circles. In drawing up our terms of reference the then Government set the context for our work in a society which they described as:

"both multi-racial and culturally diverse."

In considering the broader and longer term implications of the various specific issues to which we have devoted attention in this report, we have increasingly been led to reflect upon the nature of British society today, and particularly the relationship within it between the ethnic majority community and the ethnic minority groups with whose needs we have been chiefly concerned. In order to set the overall context for our work we feel it is important to begin by setting out clearly our view of the kind of multi-racial society for which we believe the education system should be preparing all youngsters, and the extent to which the reality of life in Britain today is at variance with this ideal.

"Ethnic Identity"

2. By birth, choice or chance we are all members of a variety of different "groups", the members of which share characteristics which distinguish them from other groups. Our "membership" of particular groups may be based on characteristics, such as age or gender, which are easily perceived and over which we have no control, or on less obvious characteristics, such as occupation or religion, which can derive from social circumstances and may to some extent be based on choice and which may vary over time. Membership of a particular **ethnic** group is however one of the most important aspects of an individual's identity – in how he or she perceives him or herself and in how he or she is perceived by others. A particular ethnic group may be characterised both by shared physical attributes such as skin colour, which are constant and which are not a matter of choice, and also by certain shared cultural attributes, which may be open to change or choice but which can also serve as powerful forces in maintaining that group's distinctiveness. We believe it would be entirely wrong to overestimate the extent to which an individual's character, lifestyle or abilities can in any sense be fully understood simply on the

3

basis of the ethnic group to which he or she may belong. It would nevertheless be similarly naive in our opinion to deny the crucial role which ethnicity, perhaps particularly in the "eye of the beholder", can play in determining an individual's place in this society. Whilst individuals may belong to different groups of various kinds they are in addition also part of the wider national society by virtue of a range of common shared characteristics, such as a common language and a common political and legal system, which, taken together, give that society a degree of unity and its members a form of "corporate identity". A **democratic** society can in general terms be seen to be further united by a shared commitment to certain essential freedoms and to fundamental values such as a belief in justice and equality.

Assimilation or Separatism

3. In Britain today, there are members of many diverse and numerically smaller ethnic minority groups living alongside a majority group which, though far from homogeneous in its actual composition, history and origins, is nevertheless regarded as, and tends to regard itself as, sharing a common ethnic identity. A number of important and fundamental issues arise however over the relationship which can and should exist between the ethnic majority group and the various ethnic minority groups and it is on the resolution of these issues that the future of our multi-racial society depends. In theory there are two extreme forms which the relationship between ethnic minority groups and ethnic majority group can take in a society. On the one hand, there is full assimilation – where the minority group loses all the distinctive characteristics of its identity and is ultimately absorbed and subsumed within the majority group. On the other hand, there is separatism – where minority and majority groups continue to live in the same society but each effectively operating within their own separate "compartment", with the minimum interaction needed in order to coexist. In our view neither of these "solutions" offers a just or indeed practicable basis for a multi-racial society. A deliberate social policy of assimilation would, we believe, be a denial of the fundamental freedom of all individuals to differ on aspects of their lives where no single way can justifiably be presented as universally appropriate. The sense of "ethnic identity" amongst many members of ethnic minority groups, as we have indeed found time and time again throughout our work, is very strong and there is little indication that this will simply dissolve in the face of the influence of the majority group's way of life. Even if minority groups were prepared to lose some aspects of their identity in this way, there are, as we have already observed, certain features of the ethnic identity of some minority groups, most notably perhaps skin colour, which individuals cannot change even if they so wish and which are likely therefore to continue to distinguish them from other

4

members of society and thus prevent full assimilation. Equally we consider that a policy of enforced "separate development" of different groups would be unlikely to offer equality or justice to the members of all groups, least of all the numerically smaller minorities. Indeed, a society based, in this way, on the enforcement of rigid divisions between different groups within it could be said to be almost a contradiction in terms, since a degree of shared experience can be seen as one of the major factors in maintaining a cohesive society.

The Concept of Pluralism

4.   We consider that a multi-racial society such as ours would in fact function most effectively and harmoniously on the basis of pluralism which enables, expects and encourages members of all ethnic groups, both minority and majority, to participate fully in shaping the society as a whole within a framework of commonly accepted values, practices and procedures, whilst also allowing and, where necessary, assisting the ethnic minority communities in maintaining their distinct ethnic identities within this common framework. Clearly the balance between the shared common identity of society as a whole and the distinct identities of different ethnic groups is crucial in establishing and maintaining a pluralist society, and it must be recognised that such a society places obligations on both the minority and majority groups within it, if it is to offer them all a full range of benefits and opportunities. In a democratic pluralist society, we believe all members of that society, regardless of ethnic origin, have an obligation to abide by the current laws of the country and to seek to change them only through peaceful and democratic means, but there is also an obligation on Government to ensure equal treatment and protection by the law for members of all groups, together with equality of access to education and employment, equal freedom and opportunity to participate fully in social and political life, both locally and nationally, equal freedom of cultural expression and equal freedom of conscience for all. The ethnic majority community in a truly pluralist society cannot expect to remain untouched and unchanged by the presence of ethnic minority groups – indeed the concept of pluralism implies seeing the very diversity of such a society, in terms for example of the range of religious experience and the variety of languages and language forms, as an enrichment of the experience of all those within it. Similarly, however, the ethnic minority communities cannot in practice preserve all elements of their cultures and lifestyles unchanged and in their entirety – indeed if they were to wish to do so it would in many cases be impossible for them then to take on the shared values of the wider pluralist society. In order to retain their identities when faced with the pervasive influences of the lifestyle of the majority community, ethnic

5

minority groups must nevertheless be free within the democratic framework to maintain those elements which they themselves consider to be the most essential to their sense of ethnic identity – whether these take the form of adherence to a particular religious faith or the maintenance of their own language for use within the home and their ethnic community – without fear of prejudice or persecution by other groups. It is important to emphasize here free choice for individuals, so that all may move and develop as they wish within the structure of the pluralist society. We would thus regard a democratic pluralist society as seeking to achieve a balance between, on the one hand, the maintenance and active support of the essential elements of the cultures and lifestyles of all the ethnic groups within it, and, on the other, the acceptance by all groups of a set of shared values distinctive of the society as a whole. This then is our view of a genuinely pluralist society, as both socially cohesive and culturally diverse.

Variance with Reality

5. In looking at the relationship which exists in Britain today between the ethnic majority and the various ethnic minority groups, which are now an integral part of our society, we believe that the pluralist ideal which we have put forward is far from being realised. Many within the majority community appear to be largely oblivious to the significance of the multi-racial nature of society, tending to regard the members of ethnic minority groups very much as "immigrants" and "outsiders" even though almost all have either been born in this country or belong to groups which have been established here for many years. Where the ethnic minority communities are accepted as belonging here it frequently seems to be very much on the understanding that there is an onus on them to adapt their lifestyles to conform to the traditional British way of life so as to cause as little disruption as possible to the lives of the majority community and even the suggestion that the presence of these groups might have a bearing on the lives of the majority community appears to be dismissed. Thus in many respects the majority community appears to favour the development of a multi-racial society along assimilationist lines in which the ethnic minority communities in due course merge with an unchanged ethnic majority group. As we have already pointed out however, such a "solution" is, in our view, both unrealistic and unjust and would make quite unreasonable demands on the ethnic minority communities. In contrast to, and to some extent in consequence of, these views within the ethnic majority community, there are growing signs within some ethnic minority communities of a trend towards a separatist philosophy – a tendency to begin to look inwards to reinforcing their separate group identities at the expense of looking outwards to the wider community which, having rejected

6

them, they are now in turn choosing to reject. We believe that unless major efforts are made to reconcile the concerns and aspirations of both the majority and minority communities along more genuinely pluralist lines, there is a real risk of the fragmentation of our society along ethnic lines which would seriously threaten the stability and cohesion of society as a whole.

Diversity within Unity

6. It is essential, we feel, to acknowledge the reality of the multi-racial context in which we all now live, to recognise the positive benefits and opportunities which this offers all of us and to seek to build together a society which both values the diversity within it, whilst united by the cohesive force of the common aims, attributes and values which we all share. In advocating the development of our society along ethnically pluralist lines we are conscious that Britain can in principle be seen as already pluralist in other respects, for example in terms of the regional variations and various cultural groupings which are readily accepted as part of the overall British "way of life". We are not therefore seeking a radically different social structure, but rather looking for an extension of this existing pluralism to embrace ethnic minority communities. We realise that some people when faced with our aim of a more genuinely pluralist society may challenge this as in some way seeking to undermine an ill-defined and nebulous concept of "true Britishness". The identity of our society however represents an amalgam of all the various forces which have been and indeed are still at work within it and the many influences which have impinged upon it from outside. Thus to seek to represent "being British" as something long established and immutable fails to acknowledge that the concept is in fact dynamic and ever changing, adapting and absorbing new ideas and influences. As put in evidence to us:

> "Britain has always been a multi-cultural society. Over four centuries of Empire and Commonwealth it has become a multi-racial society. This process is irreversible – a legacy of British history."

and, as the Home Secretary himself has asserted[1]:

> "It is no longer appropriate to speak of the ethnic minorities in this country as immigrants. Already almost half of Britain's population whose origins lie in the New Commonwealth or Pakistan were born here. Many more were brought up in this country and, for practical purposes, know no other. Britain is their home. They belong here; they are here to stay and to play their part in the life of their country."

[1] Speech at the Hindu Cultural Centre and Temple, Bradford. 22 July 1983.

We believe that a genuinely pluralist society cannot be achieved without the social integration of ethnic minority communities and the ethnic majority community within a common whole. Whilst we are *not* looking for the assimilation of the minority communities within an unchanged dominant way of life, we are perhaps looking for the "assimilation" of *all* groups within a redefined concept of what it means to live in British society today. We are not seeking to fit ethnic minorities into a mould which was originally cast for a society, relatively homogeneous in language, religion and culture, nor to break this mould completely and replace it with one which is in all senses "foreign" to our established way of life. We are instead looking to recast the mould into a form which retains the fundamental principles of the original but within a broader pluralist conspectus – diversity within unity.

Influence of Racism

7.   This then is our view of the kind of pluralist multi-racial society for which we believe the education system should help to lay the foundations – a theme which we go on to develop further in this report. Before doing so however it is essential to discuss the influence of the racism faced by many ethnic minority communities, both in terms of its influence on individual attitudes and behaviour and its less obvious but in many respects more pervasive influence on institutional policies and practices – which can be seen as the major obstacle to the realisation of the kind of society which we have envisaged here. We devote our next chapter therefore to considering this controversial and difficult area of concern.

CHAPTER 2

Racism: Theory and Practice

As we said in our interim report:

"Very few people can be said to be entirely without prejudice of one kind or another and in this country, due in part at least to the influence of history, these prejudices may be directed against West Indians and other non-white ethnic minority groups. A well-intentioned and apparently sympathetic person may, as a result of his education, experiences or environment, have negative, patronising or stereotyped views about ethnic minority groups which may subconsciously affect his attitude and behaviour towards members of those groups . . . . We see such attitudes and behaviour as a form of 'unintentional' racism.

Although genuine misunderstandings can sometimes lead people, both black and white, to believe mistakenly that racism lies behind certain behaviour or situations, we are convinced from the evidence that we have obtained that racism, both intentional and unintentional, has a direct and important bearing on the performance of West Indian children in our schools.

The suggestion that teachers are in any way racist understandably arouses very strong reactions from the profession and is often simply rejected out of hand as entirely unjustified and malicious. Since a profession of nearly half a million people must to a great extent reflect the attitudes of society at large there must inevitably be some teachers who hold explicitly racist views. Such teachers are very much in the minority. We have, however, found some evidence of what we have described as unintentional racism in the behaviour and attitudes of other teachers whom it would be misleading to describe as racist in the commonly accepted sense. They firmly believe that any prejudices they may have, can do no harm since they are not translated into any openly discriminatory behaviour. Nevertheless, if their attitudes are influenced in any way by prejudices against ethnic minority groups, this can and does, we believe, have a detrimental effect on all children whom they encounter."

Extract from our Interim Report
"West Indian Children in our Schools".

9

The Changing Climate of the Debate

1. **Introduction**

1.1 Since we referred in these terms in our interim report to the role which racism could play in the educational experience of ethnic minority children, we believe that there has been a quite marked shift in opinion, both within the education system and society at large, on the propriety of openly discussing this issue. Views may still differ on the nature of racism, the extent of its influence and how best to overcome its effects. Even those people who would challenge its very existence in this country however now seem to accept it as a concept which justifies full and careful consideration and are willing to consider the possibility that certain attitudes and procedures may work against particular ethnic minority groups in society. Whereas in the early part of our work the mere mention of the word racism, in meetings and discussions with educationists and others, was sometimes sufficient to provoke extreme reactions of anger, distress and defensiveness, more recently we have found a far greater willingness to explore this issue in a balanced and dispassionate manner. The considerable attention devoted by the media to considering racial disadvantage and discrimination in the wake of the disturbances in some inner city areas during 1981, and subsequently Lord Scarman's well-publicised report,[1] have clearly done much in bringing about this new climate of opinion and it seems that in education circles at least our interim report has also contributed to the debate. Since we believe that the key to understanding the concept of racism lies in creating a situation where people are willing and able to examine and appraise attitudes and practices, both their own and other people's, free from preconceived notions of superiority and inferiority, or "guilt" and "innocence", we are greatly encouraged by this heightened level of awareness.

Reactions to Our Interim Report

1.2 The conclusions which we drew in our interim report on the issue of racism provoked a good deal of reaction and comment at the time and many people welcomed the fact that we had sought to tackle an issue which they felt had in the past often tended to be overlooked in consideration of the educational needs of ethnic minorities. There was a general indication however, especially in the comments we received from individual Heads and teachers, that some people felt that we had not dealt with this complex and difficult issue in sufficient depth and had in some respects therefore failed to present convincing and fully substantiated arguments to justify the conclusions we had reached. Some of our readers felt that we had taken our consideration or racism too far, whilst others felt that we

[1] "The Brixton Disorders"–Report of an Inquiry by the Rt. Hon. the Lord Scarman OBE. Cmnd 8427. HMSO. November 1981.

had not gone far enough in considering the wide-ranging influence of racism in all its forms and how this should be challenged. From some of the misunderstandings which arose in discussions about our views on what we termed "unintentional" racism, it seemed in particular that the distinctions which we had sought to draw between this and the more overt manifestations of "intentional" racism still remained unclear in some people's minds. The following extracts from responses to our interim report illustrate vividly the wide variety of feelings inspired by our comments on racism:

> "This (racism) is a very unhelpful term. Unless you are applying it to the extremes of racial prejudice then it has no real meaning . . . . suffice it to say the Scarman found no evidence of institutional prejudice in Britain. Moreover in my 21 years in the (teaching) profession, spread across five schools and four authorities, I have not met a single teacher who can be described as prejudiced against his or her pupils on the grounds of race. What I have observed, overwhelmingly, is a goodwill and a tolerance towards all children which has never failed to impress me. The English teaching profession has a very pronounced tendency to perceive children as unique individuals–regardless of the colour of their skins."

> "(We are) appalled that without giving details of the supportive evidence, the Committee felt impelled to say ". . . . racism, both intentional and unintentional, has a direct and important bearing on the performance of West Indian children in our schools". We do not deny, however, that schools contain pupils who are growing up in a prejudiced world, or that some teachers may have formed stereotyped ideas of West Indian children and of their abilities which are insensitive. Despite this the vast majority of teachers are determined to combat the prejudices which children may bring to school from outside and which may reflect society's attitudes."

> "The Interim Report rightly calls attention to racism as one of the significant factors bearing on the "achievement" of "West Indian" children. We would go further and suggest that racism, in various forms, exists in our schools, that it affects the development of all our children, and that one of the school's fundamental tasks is to prepare its pupils to live constructively in a multi-racial society . . . . we . . . . believe that it is a priority for our schools. We would hope that the Final Report will give an equally central place to an acknowledgement that racism exists and an analysis of how it works and how it affects children

11

(white and black) and teachers. It has become conventional (and the Interim Report echoes this tendency) to speak of most racism as "unintentional". However, we believe this is too innocent a description. Racism in fact has many faces–there is semi-conscious racism, rationalised racism, covert racism, and many forms of silent collusion. It is important that teachers and heads understand racism in all its depth and complexity, rather than allow themselves to believe simplistically that all racism in schools is "unintentional"."

In view of the wide range of reaction illustrated by these comments we make no apologies for returning in this report to the issue of racism.

Our Approach to Racism

1.3   In this chapter we seek not only to take up some of the specific points relating to racism which have been made in evidence to us but also to correct some of the misunderstandings which may have arisen from our interim report. Since the issue of racism is clearly so emotive, in an effort to analyse its causes and effects, we begin by looking at the broad concept of prejudice and then move on to consider the ethnic minority dimension of prejudice – racism – and its influence on the educational experience of both ethnic minority and ethnic majority pupils. In so doing, we attempt to set out our view of how the overall climate of racism which exists in Britain today has arisen and the various ways in which this bears on the lives of all members of this society – thus setting the scene for our consideration, later in this report, of the contribution which we believe the education system can and should make to challenging racism and laying the foundations for the kind of genuinely pluralist society which we envisaged in our opening chapter.

The Mechanism of Prejudice

2.   The Concept of Prejudice

2.1   The concept of prejudice – a preconceived opinion or bias for or against someone or something – is a fact of life in this society. We could all be said to have "prejudices" in the sense of likes and dislikes and these are inevitably determined to a greater or lesser extent by our own upbringing and experiences, by the climate of opinion at the time, and by the facts or at least the version of them, however tenuous, that we receive from "influential others", be they family, friend, teacher, church-leader or the media. Where prejudice, we believe, often goes beyond simple likes and dislikes however is in the very literal sense that something or, more importantly, someone is being prejudged ie. evaluated on the basis of assumed characteristics in advance, and, by implication, without adequate information on which to base a rational judgment. Whereas people's straightforward preferences are generally open to reason and thus to change, if these attitudes have become hardened and more deeply ingrained as "prejudices" they can be seen as no longer open to question or discussion and thus as rigid, immutable and irreversible.[2] Because prejudice in its very nature overlooks the actual qualities or merits of an individual person, it is often directed against, (and, less frequently, in favour of), groups of people who are assumed to share common attributes and behaviour patterns. Prejudice thus requires that one has formed a stereotype of a particular "group" of people, be they women drivers, trade unionists or "immigrants", which then allows one to judge a member of this group, and in particular their actions, according to an established set of expectations. This clearly leaves little room for flexibility in forming opinions of people and even if, on closer acquaintance, a member of a particular group is found not to conform to the code of behaviour expected of him or her, this can all to easily be seen simply as an exception to the rule rather than as a reason to question the validity of the established stereotype of their group. There seem thus to be two factors which are essential for prejudices initially to be formed and subsequently maintained and even reinforced – firstly, ignorance, in the literal sense of lack of knowledge on which to base informed opinions and judgments, and, secondly, the existence and promulgation of stereotypes of particular groups of people as conveyed by the major informers of public opinion most notably the media and the education process.

The Task for Education
2.2   The role of education in relation to prejudice is surely therefore clear – to equip a pupil with knowledge and understanding in place of ignorance and to develop his or her ability to formulate views and attitudes and to assess and judge situations on the basis of this knowledge. In thus encouraging a child to think critically and to make increasingly rational judgments, education should seek to counter any mistaken impressions or inaccurate, hearsay evidence which he or she may have acquired within the family, peer group or, more broadly, from the local community or the media. In seeking to correct misunderstandings, it is however essential that under no circumstances does education become simply a process of

---

[2] As explained by Professor Michael Banton in his book "White and Coloured":

"the word 'prejudice' is derived from the Latin 'praejudicium', which meant a precedent, a judgment based on previous decisions and experiences. In English the word came to mean a prejudgment and it is still sometimes understood in this sense, though it will be clear upon reflection that this is not its normal meaning, for prejudgments are necessary in almost everything we do, whereas no one could claim the same for prejudices. Prejudgments become prejudices only if they are not subject to modification in the light of new experience. One of the major characteristics of prejudice is this mental rigidity which the prejudiced individual maintains by twisting new information to accord with his stereotyped preconceptions."

indoctrinating[3] a child into one particular way of thinking as the only 'right and proper' view, since in so doing, his or her capacity to make reasoned and rational judgments may, in effect, again be undermined by simply replacing one stereotype with another. In this respect we would see it as no more desirable or defensible for the education system to seek to create or perpetuate **positive** prejudices in favour of a particular group than to countenance negative views.

Negative Prejudice

2.3 From looking at the many forms of prejudice which exist it is clear that one of the major catalysts in a group becoming subject to prejudice is that its members are seen as in some way outside the mainstream of society and aberrant from an accepted code of behaviour. In many respects this perceived "strangeness" or "difference", whilst perhaps an inevitable consequence of ignorance, seems to arouse suspicion, hostility and even fear, as constituting an ill-defined threat to the values and traditions of the majority community. Thus negative prejudice – where the members of a particular group are themselves resented or rejected – seems regrettably to be more commonplace than prejudice of a positive nature.

Ethnic Minorities as Outsiders

3. **The Ethnic Minority Dimension of Prejudice**

3.1 In view of the elements of prejudice which we have identified, it is perhaps inevitable that ethnic minority groups, who are relative newcomers to this country, should find themselves subject to possibly the most insidious and pernicious form of negative prejudice in our society – racism. Although ethnic minority groups are an integral part of this society and indeed almost all the ethnic minority children in this country are now British-born, from the continual references both in evidence to us and more generally, to ethnic minorities as "immigrants", and "foreigners", this seems to be far from generally accepted by the majority community. One of the most vivid illustrations of how even long established ethnic minority communities can find themselves still regarded as "outsiders" is possibly the situation of the "black" community in Liverpool (and some other seaports in this country such as Cardiff and Bristol) which, although established over several generations, still suffer from extremes of racial prejudice. The prejudice encountered by members of ethnic minority groups can take a range of different forms and may for example manifest itself as linguistic prejudice – against non-English speakers – or religious prejudice – against those whose religion differs from that

---

[3] By the term "indoctrination" we have in mind what I A Snook ("Indoctrination and Education." 1972) described as:

"(suggesting) that someone is taking advantage of a privileged role to influence those under his charge in a manner which is likely to distort their ability to assess the evidence on its own merits."

14

of the majority community. In addition, where the members of a particular ethnic minority group share an indentifiably different skin colour from the majority community this can of course provide one of the most obvious manifestations of "difference" which can serve as a basis for irrational prejudice. Negative prejudice against ethnic minority groups can however extend beyond the "colour divide" and may be experienced, albeit to a lesser extent, by the "white" ethnic minorities in this country – as we explain, later in this report, in our chapters relating to the Italian, Cypriot and Travelling communities.

3.2   On a broader level we feel it is important to bear in mind that the arrival of sizeable and visible ethnic minority communities, especially in some northern industrial centres, coincided with the decline of long established traditional industries and the consequent rising unemployment. It is perhaps understandable that, in the absence of an effective explanation of the background to these developments both in schools and the media, this coincidence was all too readily seen as "cause and effect" and the "newcomers" simply blamed, quite unjustly, for the effects of the recession. In these circumstances, growing competition for housing and jobs has created particular tensions which have undoubtedly exacerbated negative prejudices against ethnic minorities.

Stereotyping of Ethnic Minorities

3.3   An equally influential factor in the growth of racial prejudice in this country has been the general lack of knowledge amongst the ethnic majority community of ethnic minority communities which in turn has allowed inaccurate stereotypes to flourish. This ignorance extends to virtually every aspect of the background of ethnic minority communities – their countries of origin, the languages they speak and their religious and cultural traditions. We ourselves have now ceased to be surprised when even in multi-racial areas and schools, pupils and teachers refer to all non-white ethnic minorities collectively as "Pakis" and to their language as "Indian" or "African", or regard the wearing of a turban or not eating meat as simply matters of personal preference, which can be altered by "gentle persuasion." We have encountered in the course of our work a vast range of myths and stereotypes of different ethnic minority groups. The most immediately relevant in our context are clearly those which relate to the expectations which the education system appears to have of ethnic minority pupils, such as "West Indian children will be good at sports but 'not academic' "; "Asian children will be hard working and well motivated but likely to have unrealistically high career aspirations"; "Chinese children will be reserved, well behaved, and likely to be 'under pressure' at home from having to help in the family business in the evenings."

15

3.4 Ethnic minorities also appear to be placed in an "order of merit" in terms of the groups generally considered most/least desirable to have in a school – teachers, on the one hand, for example, praising Chinese pupils for the lack of trouble they cause and expressing the wish that they could have "a class full of them", and, on the other hand, explaining that they were "fortunate" to have only a few West Indian pupils. This situation may be further complicated where stereotypes already exist of particular areas of a town or city which have traditionally been seen as "depressed" and "deprived", with all the assumed concomitant educational needs amongst the children, and these stereotypes – which are regrettable in themselves – are simply transferred to recently-established ethnic minority communities living in the same areas, who may in fact have an entirely different set of attitudes and expectations from the local "white" community.

3.5 Some of the stereotypes of certain ethnic minority groups can be seen as a legacy of history – from the days of the British Empire – and as a consequence of the view of other nations and peoples as in some sense "inferior", which was until relatively recently promulgated through the curriculum offered by many schools. A striking example of the powerful influence of such stereotypes was the marked difference which we ourselves found between the relative perceptions which some teachers have of the Greek Cypriot and Turkish Cypriot communities. Youngsters from the Greek Cypriot community were generally seen very much in a positive light as enriching the cultural wealth of the classroom whilst those from the Turkish Cypriot community tended to be viewed negatively as potential underachievers and disruptive elements. In discussions with representatives of both communities there was general agreement that the causes for this surprising variation lay firstly in the difference in skin colour – Greek Cypriot children tending to be lighter skinned than their Turkish Cypriot peers, this seemingly being equated, in the minds of some teachers, with greater academic ability – and secondly in the very different historical stereotypes which exist of the Greeks and the Turks – the former being seen as a major influence on the evolution of Western civilisation and culture, and the latter as "barbarians."

Influence of the Media

3.6 Much of the responsibility for the creation and continuance of stereotypes of ethnic minority youngsters within the education system can we believe be seen to derive from inadequate or even misleading attempts to explain the background of ethnic minorities which may in fact serve to resurrect and perpetuate inaccurate stereotypes. In discussing stereotypes of ethnic minority communities it is impossible not to take account of the pervasive influence of

16

all branches of the media in today's society. A report[4] by a group of
teachers in 1983 emphasised the generally negative way in which
ethnic minority groups were treated in a range of television
programmes and concluded that:

> ".... *there was a distinct under-representation in the selected
> programmes of the (ethnic minority) groups we studied, with
> too few positive and realistic images of them made available.
> There was little suggestion of the part they were playing, or
> might play, in contemporary society, and such treatment as
> there was in the selected programmes tended to reinforce
> stereotypes, or link members of these groups to a problem. In
> giving insufficient coverage to these groups, television is not
> only giving a distorted view of the society in which it operates;
> it is also missing opportunities to provide a richer, more varied
> coverage of human experience ....*"

A background paper prepared by one of our members, reviewing the
literature on the role of the media in relation to race relations, is
attached as Annex A to this Chapter, and shows that this negative
and unhelpful stance on the part of the media is by no means new.
It is clear that images, whether on television or in newspapers, can
influence greatly an individual's outlook or perception of events,
especially where they have no knowledge or personal experience to
weigh against the general impression presented. In our own discussions with groups of white youngsters in schools well away from areas
of ethnic minority settlement, it was notable that the mere mention
of Brixton or Liverpool evoked common "knowledge" of these areas,
based almost exclusively on the television reports of the disturbances
which had taken place there, although few if any of them had actually
visited parts of the country away from their own localities.

3.7   A further dimension which we found in our visits to "all white"
areas – which clearly illustrates the irrationality of some aspects of
racism – is the confusion which can arise where there are **conflicting**
stereotypes, for example, where youngsters from the majority
community may be prejudiced against Asians on the grounds that,
on the one hand, "they all live on Social Security", and on the other,
that "they're all taking our jobs." Several teachers whom we met felt
that such attitudes could only be countered effectively by a balanced
and open consideration of the multi-racial nature of society today,
throughout the school curriculum so that youngsters were led to
hold more rational opinions about ethnic minority communities and
adopt a more positive view of today's society. We ourselves believe

---

[4] "Popular TV and School Children." The report of a group of teachers. DES. April 1983.

17

that the education system can and must play a major part in challenging the stereotyping of ethnic minority communities in order to counter the pervasive influence of racism.

4.   The Roots of Racism

Reasons for Migration

4.1   Before considering the influence of racism in practice we believe it is important to look at the particular background factors relating to the original migration of different ethnic minorities to this country and the reactions and responses which the emergence of an increasingly complex multi-racial society has evoked from both the minority and majority communities. In general terms a clear distinction can be drawn between, on the one hand, those communities where the majority of the original immigrants can be seen as refugees from conflict and internal strife in their own countries, and on the other those who chose to migrate to this country for economic betterment, in some cases actively encouraged by the British Government or by British employers. In the case of refugees, the initial reaction of the majority community can be seen as welcoming, arising from a genuine desire to aid a group of people under threat, taking pride in the view of Britain as a traditional haven for those in need. Such sentiments seem however in practice often to have been superficial and short-lived since as soon as the refugees ceased to be perceived as a special case and as "front page news" and attempted to move from their settlement camps into the wider community they were seen simply as "just more immigrants" in competition with the majority population for jobs and housing. They thus often became increasingly subject to resentment and even open hostility in the form of racism. This was certainly true for the Vietnamese community (whose situation we discuss in Chapter Fourteen) where the initial wave of public goodwill towards the "boat people" has now been dissipated to a point where reports of racial harassment and attacks on Vietnamese families have sadly become more frequent.

4.2   For those communities who were actively encouraged to come to this country the situation was to some extent comparable to that of refugees: they were intially welcomed, albeit grudgingly, as meeting an economic need and their presence was not resented as a threat to the indigenous work force since the jobs which they were recruited to take were those at the lower end of the employment market which could not be filled from within the majority community who, at a time of economic growth in the 1960s, had many other more attractive avenues of employment open to them. Little if any thought seems however to have been given to the wider social implications of meeting a short term need in this way and it seems to have been assumed that the ethnic minority workers would be content to remain in the jobs for which they had been recruited thus constituting an artificial economic sub-class at the traditional working class end of the employment spectrum. Such a view took no account of the pressures for upward social mobility and career advancement amongst the ethnic minority workers themselves nor did it foresee the situation of recent years where the British-born children of the original immigrants quite justifiably expect to find the whole range of career opportunities open to them and are certainly not content merely to "follow in their father's footsteps". In the face of such aspirations the majority community seem not only to resent moves by these ethnic minority groups to advance beyond their "prescribed place" in this society but more recently, with rising unemployment, have come to resist and actively challenge their employment even in the areas of work for which they were originally recruited. It is almost as though having made use of workers who were prepared to work for lower wages and in worse conditions than indigenous workers at a time of apparent prosperity, the time has now come for them to "go back where they came from" since their services are no longer needed and they are seen as competing for jobs against indigenous workers. The cycle of racism once again is thus brought to bear on ethnic minority groups who originally met with some acceptance here.

Expectations of this Country 4.3 As important, if not more so than the question of how ethnic minority groups were viewed when they came to this country is the variety of expectations which the group themselves had of their likely reception here. Whilst recognising the risks inherent in ascribing views, expectations and aspirations to ethnic minority groups as though they were homogeneous entities, it is possible to discern a variation in how different groups have perceived their position in this country, according to the circumstances of their arrival here. In the case of refugees, two particular factors have clearly been influential – firstly, the option of returning to their countries of origin has generally speaking been unavailable and so they have a particularly strong will to succeed here, and secondly, having found "sanctuary" here, their will to succeed is tempered somewhat by a wish to conform to society as it is and not therefore to seek to bring about any changes. (Such attitudes are of course less likely to be held by the children of the original refugees who may feel more secure in living in this country as a right rather than as a matter of "privilege"). On the other hand, those immigrants who came here for economic betterment and to enhance the prospects for their children, came on the understanding that they had every right to come to this country and, once they and their families were established here, they would not only be entitled to full equality of opportunity in terms of housing, jobs and education but would also be in a position to seek changes in existing systems and procedures where these took no account of their presence here. When ethnic minority groups actually encounter racism in our society it is clear therefore that, whilst those who have come here as refugees may simply accept this as the price to be paid for being allowed to remain in this country, many will not only be disillusioned and resentful of such a denial of their place here but likely in reaction to become alienated from a society which they see as rejecting them.

The Myth of an Alternative

4.4   With certain groups, perhaps particularly the European minorities such as the Italians (see Chapter Twelve) and the Hong Kong Chinese (see Chapter Ten), their close links with their countries of origin are evidenced by an established pattern of regular visits to see relatives and also a tradition of some children travelling "home" for part of their education or subsequently to work. Such direct links inevitably serve to reinforce a sense of indentity at the individual level and also to heighten the community's awareness of its roots and thus to enhance its sense of self esteem. Of even greater importance however is the point made to us repeatedly by representatives of these ethnic minority groups that retaining such close ties with their countries of origin cushions them in a sense against the harsher realities of life in this country especially the influence of racism, and provides them with an alternative view of themselves and their futures – for example British-born Italian and Chinese youngsters have explained to us that if they are unable to find employment in this country they feel they could always consider seeking their fortunes in their family's countries of origin. The fact that in reality "return" might be prevented by the immigration rules of the countries of origin, that employment may be no easier to find there and that "returning" to live in a country may be very different from simply visiting it on holiday, in no way seems to undermine what could be described as the "myth of an alternative" which to a certain extent can offset or at least distance them from the direct influence of racism.

The Myth of Return

4.5   With some ethnic minority communities, especially some Asian groups, the sense of having an alternative to life in this country has tended to be taken further and constitutes what has been described as a "myth of return" – many of the original immigrants believed that after a period of work in this country they would return to their countries of origin. Much of the evidence which we have received has suggested that this myth of return may also have helped to sustain these first immigrants in the face of some of the worst manifestations of overt racism. Since the original immigrants have now however become established here, have been joined by their families and their children have actually been born here, there seems to have been a weakening of this myth altough it still seems to provide a fall back position when faced with extremes of racism.

The Myth of Belonging

4.6   Within the West Indian community ties with the home country seem to be less close than for other ethnic minority groups, despite an undoubted nostalgia for the West Indies amongst the original immigrants and a certain amount of actual return by older immigrants on their retirement. From the evidence we have received it seems that the major reason for this apparent difference in outlook is the extent to which the majority of West Indians originally came to this country believing that they were already British, since, unlike many other immigrants, they spoke English, they were Christian, and they had been brought up in an English style education system which through its curriculum, examinations and teaching methods had imbued them with the British culture and way of life. They therefore came assuming not only that they would be welcomed on equal terms as coming home to the "mother country" but that their social integration within British society would be a matter of course. On arrival they found their initial "welcome" at best grudging or even openly hostile and it is hardly suprising that they found the experience traumatic in the extreme. This "myth of belonging" and the impact of seeing it in effect punctured by the experience of racism has been described graphically in the following terms by a West Indian mother[5]:

> *"Many of us came here with a myth in our minds, the myth of belonging. We have also raised our children to believe that they belong in these societies and cultures (simply because they were born here) only to find that as they grew older, they were seen in the eyes of the host community as a new nation of intruders. Our children are then faced with great traumatic and psychological problems, since they are made to feel that they do not belong here, also they feel that because they were not born in the West Indies they do not belong there either ...".*

The sense of despair and frustration thus engendered within the West Indian community over the years, heightened perhaps by the absence of the illusory safety valve of returning "home", found with other communities, has we believe contributed to growing alienation within this particular group. The sense of rejection experienced by many of the original West Indian immigrants seems to have led some West Indian youngsters to expect that they will be faced with racism at every stage of their lives. Despite the evident grounds for such

[5] Extract from a letter published in "The Caribbean Times". 8 April 1983.

anxieties, we are concerned about the possible consequences of such an emphasis on the inevitability of racism, seeming in effect to deny the possibility of a West Indian youngster ever succeeding.

4.7   In contrast, it seems that many of the original immigrants from other ethnic minority communities, whilst not being prepared for the degree of antagonism they would face in this country, were not perhaps looking for the same degree of social integration as were West Indians. The major reasons for this difference in outlook can we believe be traced back to the fact that, as we have observed, many of the members of these groups did not necessarily see their long term futures in this country. These communities were also characterised by strong cultural and, more importantly religious traditions which necessitated a degree of separateness, and the existence of strong community ties both here and with the countries of origin, which, combined with a strong extended family system, tended to encourage a sense of self sufficiency and to discourage the development of contacts with the wider community. Members of these groups, unlike West Indians, were more likely to live and work within their own communities and they were therefore in a sense sheltered from the full effects of racism. As the economic situation in this country has worsened however the capacity of these communities to remain self contained in this way has been increasingly undermined – for example more Chinese youngsters are now having to enter the main-stream employment market as the traditional Chinese catering trade has come under pressure – and there are increasing numbers of British born youngsters who see themselves as part of the wider community and are not content to see their futures exclusively within the confines of their ethnic community. In recent years communities such as these have come more directly under pressure from racism and in many respects have found themselves subject to some of the worst manifestations of overt racism in the form of harassment and racial attacks. This situation is increasingly leading youngsters from the whole range of ethnic minority groups to share the West Indian community's sense of frustration and scepticism that any meaningful progress will ever be made in combatting and overcoming racism in all its forms.

5.   Racism in Practice

Research   5.1   Having considered the origins and roots of racism we now turn to racism in practice and in particular the bearing which it may have on the education of ethnic minority pupils. As the authors of the NFER reviews of research point out, comparatively little research has in fact been carried out on teachers' attitudes towards ethnic

22

minority pupils or on the more controversial question of the extent to which a teacher's expectations of a pupil can directly affect that pupil's achievement or behaviour. They were nevertheless able to cite a number of studies, albeit some rather limited in scale, which have been undertaken on the existence of teacher stereotypes, in both Britain and the United States, going back as far as Rosenthal and Jacobson's famous study in 1968 "Pygmalion in the Classroom". The other main research studies identified by the NFER can be summarised as follows:

– Townsend and Brittan's survey (1972)[6] reported that a majority of the secondary heads involved commented favourably on the manners, courtesy, keeness to learn and industrious application of the Indian and Pakistani pupils.

– Brittan's study (1976)[7] revealed a high degree of consensus of opinion concerning the academic and social behaviour of pupils of West Indian origin, with more than two-thirds of the teachers in the sample indicating unfavourable opinions of West Indians.

– Stewart's study (1978)[8] showed the teachers interviewed as having a positive stereotype of the Asian pupil as industrious, responsible, keen to learn and having none of the behaviour problems associated with West Indian pupils.

– Tomlinson's study (1979)[9] showed that the heads interviewed were more likely to respond at length about West Indian pupils and to have generalised views about them than in the case of Asian pupils. The heads expressed strong feelings that the learning process was slower for West Indian pupils, that they lacked long term concentration and that they would tend to underachieve and be remedial.

The broad consensus of the findings of the studies reviewed by the NFER was that some teachers did have clear stereotypes of the West Indian pupil and the Asian pupil, that these stereotypes were quite different – that of the former being generally negative and that of the latter generally positive – and that the stereotypes of West Indian pupils tended to be more uniform, more firmly established and more strongly held.

---

[6] "Organisation in Multi-Racial Schools." H E R Townsend and E M Brittan. NFER. 1972.
[7] "Multiracial Education – Teacher Opinion on Aspects of Schoo Life." E M Brittan. Educ Research 18.3. 1976.
[8] "The role of ethnicity in teachers' accounts of their interaction with pupils in multicultural classrooms." O F Stewart. Unpublished MSc. University of Aston. 1978.
[9] "Decision making in Special Education ESN(M) with some reference to children of immigrant parentage." S Tomlinson. Unpublished PhD thesis. University of Warwick. 1979.

5.2   The paucity of research data in this field seems to result not from any lack of interest on the part of the research community – although race-related issues have often in the past been regarded as the preserve of sociological rather than educational researchers – but rather from the daunting problems of attempting to investigate whether teachers' attitudes towards ethnic minority pupils may, however unintentionally, be influenced by racism. Also, as the authors of the second NFER review of research have explained:

> *"Apart from the difficulties of obtaining permission to carry out research into prejudice it is quite likely that an awareness on the part of those being researched of the nature of the research will distort findings. There is, moreover, the question of criteria of judgement of prejudice, especially when this is not tested by some supposedly calibrated measuring instrument, but depends, as much anecdotal evidence of racism must do, on the perceptions of the observer."*

5.3   **Studies on the extent to which such stereotyped attitudes affect school achievement, however, have often been inconclusive and sometimes conflicting see (Chapter 3). The NFER authors do however highlight a study by Dr Peter Green of the University of Durham[10] as in their opinion the first real attempt to look in detail at the influence of teachers' attitudes towards pupils from different ethnic minority groups and as having:**

> *".... redressed the balance of previous research by shifting the focus from the child who has been seen at the centre of the 'problem' of his 'under-achievement' and the consequent emphasis placed on his inter-ethnic attitudes, with the corresponding lack of stress on studies of teachers' ethnocentricism, because of professional sensitivity, to a proper consideration of the relationships which obtain between teachers and pupils."*

Dr Green's research investigated the general style of teaching employed by different teachers in relation to pupils of European, Asian and West Indian origin, focussing in particular on the influence which the personal characteristics of the teachers, most notably their level of "ethnocentrism", appeared to have on their interaction with pupils from the different groups. Dr Green defines "ethnocentrism" as:

---

[10] "Teachers' influence on the self concept of pupils of different ethnic origins". P A Green. Unpublished PhD thesis. 1983.

". . . . the tendency to consider the characteristics and attributes of ethnic groups other than one's own to be inferior."

This definition is of course very close to the view which we ourselves have taken of racism and the measures used by Dr Green to determine the degree of ethnocentrism of the teachers relate very much to issues which would commonly be accepted as "racial". Dr Green's major reason for using the term ethnocentrism appears to be his wish to avoid the emotive and negative connotations of the term racism rather than any clear distinction which he has drawn between the two types of attitude. We believe however that in the context of Dr Green's work the term ethnocentrism can in fact be seen as synonymous with racism. Quite apart from the interesting points which Dr Green's findings raise in relation to the extent to which some teachers may be unaware of the way in which they teach, and about the different approaches which different teachers may use in similar contexts, of greatest significance to us is his central conclusion that:

"children of different ethnic origins, taught in the same multi-ethnic class by the same teacher, are likely to receive widely different educational experiences."

Moreover there seems to be a strong indication that whereas Asian pupils may be more likely to receive praise and encouragement from teachers, West Indian pupils, particularly boys, appeared to receive a fair amount of individual attention – but mainly in the form of criticism! Whilst care must clearly be exercised in seeking to base firm conclusions on the findings of a single study, itself somewhat limited in scale and scope, we believe that Dr Green's study offers an interesting and valuable insight into the influences of teachers' attitudes towards ethnic minority pupils. We therefore attach as Annex B to this chapter a summary prepared by Dr Green of his work since we believe that further such studies would be both valuable and worthwhile.

5.4   In our interim report we explained that we believed there to be two rather different forms which racism could take in our society – on the one hand, overt and intentional racism, and on the other, covert and unintentional racism. We stressed that in the educational context it was the latter – unintentional racism – which caused us the greatest concern. From the further work we have done since the preparation of our interim report we find ourselves all the more convinced of the major role which the particular expectations and attitudes which many teachers have, not only of West Indian pupils but indeed of pupils from the whole range of ethnic minority groups, can and do play in the educational experience and perhaps the academic achievement of these pupils. We believe that if teachers allow themselves to be influenced by, and even to perpetuate, stereotypes of different ethnic minority groups, their ability to educate an individual pupil from such a group according to his or her actual "age, aptitude and ability" may, however unwittingly, be undermined and it can become all too easy to ascribe the pupil's behaviour or performance to the assumed stereotype rather than to exercise professional judgment. As we have already indicated, research findings and our own evidence have indicated that the stereotypes teachers tend to have of West Indian children are often related directly to a particular, and generally negative, expectation of academic performance. By contrast, although there seems to be a more generally positive **educational** stereotype of Asian pupils, they may be subject to racism in more direct and overt ways. The fear or indeed the actual experience of racial harassment and attack may also have an indirect bearing on the motivation and achievement of an Asian pupil. Racism, both intentional and unintentional, can we believe also influence negatively the educational experience of pupils from other ethnic minority groups as we discuss later in this report. A Chinese pupil for example, who is sitting at the back of the class, not taking an active part in the lesson, may be seen simply as conforming to the stereotype of his group – as "reserved and well behaved" – rather than this behaviour being interpreted, as it would be with an indigenous pupil, as showing that he or she might be in difficulties with the work and therefore need some extra attention and encouragement.

"Colour Blindness"

5.5 As we explained in the section on racism in our interim report:

> "... many of the teachers to whom we spoke on our visits were at pains to assert that they deliberately made no distinction between "black" pupils and others: they were "colour-blind". In this way, they claimed to fulfil the first duty of a teacher which they saw as regarding all pupils equally, as having particular strengths and weaknesses, and individual educational needs."

In our evidence gathering for this report we have again found this to be a very widespread attitude amongst teachers and it is clear that there is a substantial body of opinion within the teaching profession which firmly believes that to recognise differences between people of various ethnic origins is divisive and can in fact constitute a major obstacle to creating a harmonious multi-racial society. We ourselves regard "colour-blindness" however as potentially just as negative as

26

a straightforward rejection of people with a different skin colour since both types of attitude seek to deny the validity of an important aspect of a person's identity. This concern was shared by many of those who gave evidence to us, amongst them the Head of a multi-racial school who reflected thus:

"It is interesting to record that the reaction of teachers . . . . was to aver that all pupils in the school were treated alike and to deny that any distinction is made between their cultural differences. Sadly, this initial reaction, if perpetuated, could deny the school the opportunity of developing potentially rich cultural resources. In such an event there would be a real danger that, through a determination not to discriminate ("discriminate" in the sense of recognising differences), the school would in time become culturally impoverished."

We feel that the fundamental issues which lie at the heart of the phenomenon of "colour-blindness" are encapsulated in the following observation by the Dean of Liverpool, quoted in evidence to us:

"'God is colour-blind', I once saw on a wayside pulpit in Liverpool. But as is the habit of such religious graffiti, it was wrong. The God who made the rainbow and who made the whole kaleidoscope of creation, culminating in men and women of such rich variety – it is not He who is colour-blind but we who find life easier to cope with if we treat it as monochrome."

A "White British" Problem?

5.6 In recent years there has been a growing tendency to suggest that racism is in some way unique to the "white" majority and to this country. On the latter point, we believe that racism cannot be seen as a uniquely British phenomenon in view of the inter-racial prejudices which clearly exist in other countries, for example in America (against Blacks), in France (against North Africans) and in West Germany (against Turkish Guest Workers). We also believe that to describe racism simply as a "white" problem is similarly misconceived. Feelings of negative prejudice against ethnic groups other than one's own can be found both within and between minority communities as well as between minority and majority groups, although this in no way of course excuses or justifies the attitudes of some members of the majority community in this country towards ethnic minorities. In the course of our own work we have come across a number of instances of racist attitudes between ethnic minority groups, for example the attitudes of Chinese and Vietnamese pupils towards "black" children, the animosity of certain Asian groups towards other ethnic minority communities, conflicts between

27

African and West Indian pupils and instances of West Indian youngsters becoming involved alongside their white school fellows in actual racial attacks on Asians. It has been suggested to use that such prejudices as exist within and between ethnic minority groups are not truly comparable with prejudices between the majority and minority communities since even if members of a particular ethnic minority group are prejudiced against another group they are extremely unlikely to be in a position to put their prejudice into practice in such a way as to have a detrimental effect on members of the other group. Since, on straightforward numerical grounds alone, it is only the "white" majority which has the power to give expression to its prejudices by using its inherent dominance of all walks of life to deny opportunity and access to other minority communities, "white racism" is considered to be the only area to be tackled. We firmly believe however that **all** forms of prejudice against groups of people on racial grounds are wrong – as Lord Scarman put it in his report:

> *"Pride in being Black is one thing, but black racialism is no more acceptable than white. A vigorous rejection of discriminatory and racialist views is as important among black people as among white if social harmony is to be ensured."*

Institutional Racism

5.7 Reference to the role of power in racism leads us directly on to a dimension of the influence of racism within our society – what has generally come to be referred to as "institutional" racism. As with so many other terms within our field of interest, we believe that this term is used by different people to cover a range of circumstances and, being thus ill-defined, discussion of the extent of its influence and indeed even its existence is often both confused and confusing. We see institutional racism as describing the way in which a range of long established systems, practices and procedures, both within education and the wider society, whch were originally conceived and devised to meet the needs and aspirations of a relatively homogeneous society, can now be seen not only to fail to take account of the multi-racial nature of Britain today but may also ignore or even actively work against the interests of ethnic minority communities. The kind of practices about which we are concerned include many which, whilst clearly originally well-intentioned and in no way racist in **intent,** can now be seen as racist in **effect,** in depriving members of ethnic minority groups of equality of access to the full range of opportunities which the majority community can take for granted or denying their right to have a say in the future of the society of which they are an integral part. These include, for example, the provision of separate language centres for children whose first

28

language is not English (see Chapter Seven), and the arrangements for the appointment of members to governing bodies of schools and other institutions which take no account of the changed and changing nature of the local population. Institutional racism can thus we believe be seen as visibly demonstrating the extent to which our society has continued to define itself according to criteria prescribed to meet the needs of a homogeneous whole, and which inevitably does not recognise and therefore cannot take account of the far more complex network of aims and aspirations present in Britain today.

5.8   We believe that institutional racism is just as much a cause for concern as the prejudiced attitudes which some individuals may hold since the establishment, in this way, of racism within the "system" itself can serve to reinforce, to magnify and to perpetuate such attitudes even where individual attitudes may be open to change. It is, for example, harder to convince individuals of the damaging effects which their actions may have on particular groups of children if they can argue that they are simply "following the normal procedure" and therefore cannot in any way be said to be prejudiced against a particular group. A complex inter-relationship thus exists between individual attitudes and the influence of institutionalised practices and procedures. It is undeniably true that both long established practices and procedures which are seen as following the traditional "way things are done here", and the conventional policy making processes and power structures of institutions can all too often override individual attitudes, which may be submerged in simply "running the system." Similarly however it must be recognised that institutionalised forms are themselves in no small measure sustained by attitudes. The extent to which changing the attitudes of individuals can directly influence the way in which established procedures, systems and institutions function is thus difficult to assess and some people have argued that change can only be brought about through legislation or the revision of traditional "rules and regulations" which in turn requires individuals to appraise and where necessary revise their behaviour accordingly. Whilst a realisation amongst the staff of an institution that the policies which they are following may work against some members of our society may lead them to question and even actively challenge and seek to change the rules which govern their institution, in order to effect change in a more rapid and direct way it may nevertheless be necessary to prescribe institutional change from the "top" downwards in order to complement and foster any such shift in grass roots opinion. We believe that institutional change of this kind and changing individual attitudes are of equal importance and have complementary roles to play in achieving the overall shift in emphasis and outlook which we believe to be essential in relation to today's multi-racial society.

5.9   Within the education system, power is of course exercised at many different levels from the Secretary of State to the major national academic institutions and the individual teacher or parent. It is important to recognise therefore that, in overcoming institutional racism, different approaches and emphases may be more appropriate than others for different types of educational institution. For example in a primary school, with fewer staff and and more informal ethos and flexible style of work, the emphasis might best be on encouraging individual teachers to review their own attitudes and practices and thus to effect any necessary changes themselves. In a large secondary school, however, with its compartmentalised curricular organisation and its clearly defined tiers of responsibility, in a Local Education Authority with its complex bureaucracy or a university with its long established traditions, a more determined effort may need to be made to revise and restructure the actual systems in order for there to be any hope of the policies pursued offering true equality of opportunity.

Climate of Racism

5.10   In considering the influence which racism whether intentional or unintentional can have on the education process we feel that it is essential to recognise the very direct and acute bearing which the general "climate" of racism in this country has on what takes place in the school classroom. By this we mean the way in which the confidence of ethnic minority groups to see themselves as an integral part of our society and thus as having equal claim to shaping their own futures within it, has been undermined and to some extent lost entirely. The extent of racial disadvantage in this country has of course been well documented in a number of studies of recent years – for example the Policy Studies Institute's seminal studies on Racial Disadvantage[11] surveyed the position of ethnic minority groups in fields such as housing, social services and employment. The continuing influence of racism in the employment field has also been documented in the report "Half a Chance"[12] and the influence of racism in relation to housing in a multi-racial area in a report[13] published last year – both by the Commission for Racial Equality. There are two other aspects of the pressures to which ethnic minority communities find themselves subject, which have been raised repeatedly with us by parents and young people, particularly from the Asian community, and which have undoubtedly contributed greatly to the overall climate of racism: the fear of radical harassment and attack, and the uncertainty created by the policies of successive

---

[11] "Racial Discrimination in England." W W Daniel. Penguin 1968;
   "Racial Disadvantage in Britain." David J Smith. Penguin 1977;
   "Black and White Britain." Colin Brown. PSI 1984.
[12] "A report on job discrimination against young blacks in Nottingham." CRE November 1980.
[13] "Race and Council Housing in Hackney – Report of a Formal Investigation into the allocation of housing in the London Borough of Hackney." CRE January 1984.

Immigration and Nationality

Governments on immigration and nationality. On the latter issue we believe that it is deplorable that children who have been born in this country or whose families have chosen to make their homes here should be made to feel that they are not accepted in their own right and have no role to play in the future of this country. Those ethnic minority groups who have more recently settled here, now, through no fault of their own, find their position questioned and indeed in their eyes under threat and their very peace of mind disrupted by the prevailing climate of uncertainty. (We review the development of Government policies in relation to immigration and nationality in Chapter Four, see paragraphs 3.3.18 to 3.3.21.)

Racial Attacks

5.11 A considerable amount of attention has been devoted over recent years to the issue of racial attacks culminating in the publication, in 1981, of a report by a Home Office Study Group investigating this situation.[14] The Group offered the following vivid portrait of the situation which they found:

"The views expressed by ethnic minority representatives about racial attacks reflected a general feeling of fear and apprehension for the future. In all the places we visited, we were given accounts of racial violence, abuse and harassment. . . . Assaults, jostling in the streets, abusive remarks, broken windows, slogans daubed on walls – these were among the less serious kinds of racial harassment which many members of the ethnic minorities (particularly Asians) experience, sometimes on repeated occasions. The fact that they are interleaved with far more serious racially-motivated offences (murders, serious assaults, systematic attacks by gangs on people's homes at night) increases the feeling of fear experienced by the ethnic minorities. It was clear to us that the Asian community widely believes that is is the object of a campaign of unremitting racial harassment which it fears will grow worse in the future. In many places we were told that Asian families were too frightened to leave their homes at night or to visit the main shopping centre in town at weekends when gangs of young skinheads regularly congregate. Even in places where comparatively few racial incidents have occurred, the awareness of what is happening in other parts of the country induces a widespread apprehension that the climate locally is likely to deteriorate and that more serious incidents are likely in the future. In some places there was a sense of uncomplaining acceptance among some Asians to manifestations of racial violence: the problem was thought to be so widespread that they regarded it as little more than an unwelcome feature of contemporary British life."

---

[14] "Racial Attacks" – Report of a Home Office Study. November 1981.

The Study Group drew three main conclusions from their investigations:

> *"(there was) a significantly high number of racially motivated attacks on persons and property by one ethnic group on another . . . . compared with white people, both blacks and Asians suffer disproportionately from racially motivated attacks, and the Asians worst of all . . . . the absolute number of racial attacks appears to have increased."*

Thus, in the Study Group's own words, racial attacks must be recognised as:

> *" . . . . a matter of fact not of opinion."*

We believe that the fear of racial attack has a very profound effect on the ethnic minority communities who find themselves subject to this particularly vicious form of overt and intentional racism and its influence has been brought home to us on numerous occasions in our discussions with Asian parents and particularly mothers, when matter such as their apparent unwillingness to become involved in the work of the school, by for example responding to invitations to visit a school to discuss a child's work or to participate in after-school activities, are raised.

5.12   The Home Office Study Group also raised an issue to which we have already referred (see paragraph 3.6 and Annex A to this Chapter) – the role of the media – as follows:

> *"The Study Group were also persuaded that the media – newspapers and broadcasting – played a powerful role in shaping people's perceptions of the problem. This is particularly true of reports in many local newspapers which appear to sensationalise apparently racial incidents. But it is also true nationally since, as close-knit communities, ethnic minorities are very conscious of what happens elsewhere in the country. Attacks on Asians in one place can cause great concern in Asian communities elsewhere; similarly the response of the police in one area can directly affect the ethnic minority view of the local police several hundred miles away. A single television interview with a prominent public figure who puts forward a view which appears hostile to the ethnic minority communities can, in its impact, be out of proportion to its significance, and can unreasonably create the impression that that view is held by the authorities generally."*

Relationship with the Police Whilst it refers primarily to the situation of the Asian community, the above quotation draws attention to the relationship between the police and ethnic minority communities generally. This is an issue which has and continues to be an area of public concern and debate in relation particularly to the West Indian community, and was of course central to the Scarman report. Here again the essential element seems to us to be not so much the actual facts of the situation, although there is considerable evidence in some cases to justify communities' concerns, but equally the wide gulf in trust and understanding which exists between ethnic minority communities and "establishment figures" which is itself symptomatic of the overall climate of racism which we believe exists.

Inter-Racial Tension 5.13 We believe that this climate of racism can impinge on an individual school in a range of different ways. The impact of racism on ethnic minority pupils may be particularly strong when they are present in relatively small numbers in schools and are thus less able to be mutually supportive in the face of racial abuse. This point was brought out in the following terms in evidence we received from a Community Relations Council:

> "Direct Racism is tragically too common in this area. Rarely a week passes without at least one case being reported to this Council . . . .it is no exaggeration to state that for some young Asian people particularly, being racially harassed is a way of life. This ranges from direct violence upon the person to verbal abuse and threats. They are daily confronted with racist graffiti in and out of school premises, which remain for months and, in some cases, years. The situation for those pupils in schools with 1%–5% black students is unenviable. Their isolation makes them particularly vulnerable . . . . The unwillingness of schools to tackle the issues, the graffiti remaining unchallenged, the insistence of some teaching staff on regarding the attacks as "part of the rough and tumble of youngsters round here" and that "boys will be boys" all encourage a climate where racism is acceptable."

Impact on Schools This broader and immediate impact of racism on schools is illustrated by the following extract from a report prepared by the Head of a multi-racial school we visited where the influence of "National Front style extremists" was particularly pronounced:

> "We have over the past 7/8 months had an increase in tension "from the outside." Examples of this are:

33

a. *invasion of a summer leavers' disco by outsiders, some ex-pupils. It was not quite clear how far this had racial overtones. It led to "gate" trouble after school on several days thereafter.*

b. *intruders (youths, some ex-pupils) coming on to the premises during the school day. Again it is not clear how far there are racial overtones.*

c. *at least 3 instances of unprovoked attacks by "outsiders" on coloured pupils who were members of official school visits to places in the Borough.*

d. *one serious attack by "outsiders" on coloured pupils playing table tennis in a school hall just after school.*

e. *many instances of "outsiders" congregating at the gate at about the end of afternoon school with definite anti-coloured actions, some physical. On at least one occasion this involved youths armed with sticks.*

f. *several attacks on coloured youngsters outside the school after normal school hours."*

Influence on Ethnic Minority Pupils

5.14   A disturbing picture of the way in which a school may appear to be entirely oblivious to the impact of racism on the day to day experiences of an ethnic minority pupil is portrayed in the following extract from an essay written for us by an Asian fifth former:

". . . . I attended a middle school where approximately 90% of the pupils were white. The results of this situation were terrifying. The group of black children were bussed to the school and then isolated from their neighbourhood. At home they were again isolated from any school contacts. During the four years I spent in that school, not one person attended any after-school activities for fear of walking through the neighbourhood where about ninety-two % of the population were white. It would be literally true to say that there was a physical barrier between our homes and our school and the only way in or out was on the coach. At school the situation was the same. The Asians were constantly in fear of being attacked by the several gangs of white boys. As we ran towards the staff room a teacher would come out and disperse the white gang, throw us back into the playground and then walk back in as if nothing had happened. The teachers had no idea of what we were experiencing."

The Role of the School If in the face of such forms of racism, or indeed in the face of ignorance and inaccurate statements about ethnic minorities, the school seeks simply to remain neutral and uninvolved we would see this as not only a failure in terms of its educational responsibilities but also as in effect condoning and thereby encouraging the persistence of such occurrences. Certainly it is difficult for ethnic minority communities to have full confidence and trust in an institution which they see as simply ignoring or dismissing what is in fact an ever present and all pervasive shadow over their everyday lives.

Racist Name-Calling 5.15 One particular manifestation of racism within schools on which we have received a considerable amount of evidence is racist name-calling. Some teachers have argued that this is no different from the normal name-calling in which even young children may indulge and which is entirely harmless both in intent and long-term effect. On the other hand many ethnic minority representatives, including some older ethnic minority pupils, have stressed to us the very damaging effects which they believe being subject to racist abuse can have on the self-image and motivation of an ethnic minority pupil — as one Asian mother put it to us:

> *"These remarks can be very traumatic and hurtful to young children who often come home very upset by this. One tries to forget it and hope it will die down, but all too often the same thing recurs. School authorities try to play it down so as to keep the school atmosphere calm. However, this does not resolve the hurt that registers very forcefully in a young child's mind".*

We believe the essential difference between racist name-calling and other forms of name-calling is that whereas the latter may be related only to the individual characteristics of a child, the former is a reference not only to the child but also by extension to their family and indeed more broadly their ethnic community as a whole. Racist name-calling, and its frequent companion racist graffiti, can thus convey to a child the accepted value judgement which the majority community has passed on his or her group and, as we have explained earlier in this chapter, where this value judgement is internalised by an individual and in time by a community this can only serve to strengthen and perpetuate the overall climate of racism in which they find themselves.

35

"All-White"
Schools

5.16   Whilst most people would accept that there may be a degree of inter-racial tension between groups in schools with substantial ethnic minority populations, it might generally be felt that racist attitudes and behaviour would be less common in schools with few or no ethnic minority pupils. As we go on to discuss later in this report we believe this is regrettably far from the case — see for example the findings of the study carried out in "all-white" schools — detailed in Chapter Five — which illustrates very clearly the points which we have made in this chapter about the pervasive influence of racism which, through ignorance and ill-informed stereotyping and the negative influence of the media, has a quite definite effect on the attitudes of youngsters in these areas. Even though the opportunities for these attitudes being put into practice may be limited, as we have already pointed out the very existence of such attitudes, with, in most cases, little real attempt being made by schools either to challenge or counteract them, can of itself contribute to the overall climate of racism.

6. Conclusion

6.1   We believe that racism is an insidious evil which, for the sake of the future unity and stability of our society, must be countered. A clear distinction can be drawn between what can be seen as "individual" racism and the broader and more pervasive "climate" of racism and within that the way institutions and established practices and procedures may serve to reinforce, perpetuate and extend this. Racism, in all these forms, however needs to be tackled, we believe, in the interests of our community as a whole, since it damages not only the groups seen and treated as in some way inferior or manipulable, but also the more powerful groups in that it feeds them with a totally false sense of superiority and thus distorts their understanding of themselves and the world around them. All members of a racist society suffer from feelings of fear and insecurity and, as we have seen, it takes little to fan the flames of suspicion and mistrust into open hatred and violence.

6.2   We believe that for schools to allow racist attitudes to persist unchecked in fact constitutes a fundamental **mis**-education for their pupils. All youngsters need to be provided with the necessary knowledge and the ability for reasoned and rational thought and judgment. Whilst schools may not therefore be able to lead change directly they should be capable of leading **to** change by creating an overall unity of purpose which will encompass the concept that to be British you do not have to have a white skin nor to have family origins only in this country.

6.3   We are convinced that the policies we put forward in this report will, if put into practice, mark a major change in the way in which ethnic minorities are perceived and perceive themselves in relation to the education system. Much of what we recommend will require a fundamental shift in attitude and, as we acknowledged in our interim report, which also focussed on the need for attitude change, this will involve expenditure in "psychological" terms over and above the direct financial outlay needed. Quite apart from any specific recommendations which we offer, we sincerely hope that a full and careful reading of this report as a whole will contribute to a greater understanding of the issues involved in considering an education appropriate to today's multi-racial society and which will help to lay the foundations for a genuinely pluralist society in the future.

ANNEX A

The Role of the Media
A background paper by Dr G K Verma

The use of the broad term 'the media' in this paper applies to both the press and broadcasting.

The question is often asked as to the extent to which the media foster, reinforce or counteract attitudes in the field of race relations. This is a complex question to which the literature offers no conclusive answers. At one level it can be shown, for example, that the views of most American adults about Russia are derived from newspapers, radio and television (Mackinnon and Centers, 1958). But from which sources are the views of the mass media derived? From Government sources or from the people themselves? The process of cause and effect is extremely difficult to unravel.

Some studies in America have shown that the mass media may influence racialist attitudes (or reinforce and thus strengthen existing attitudes) on relatively non-controversial issues (Colfax and Steinberg, 1972; Johnson et al 1971). It is probably fair to say that the less controversial the issue, and the more there is some consensus in society in that issue, the more likely it is that the mass media will support, and reinforce such racial attitudes. Again, cause and effect are interwoven.

Rose and his associates (1969), reviewing race relations in Britain, commented that:

> "The role of the press and of the broadcasting authorities .... can be crucial. In the last five years immigration and race relations have rivalled almost any other subject except natural disasters for prominence in newspapers and on television. They have an irresistible appeal for news and features editors and for those who produce discussion programmes. They bulk largely in the cockpit of the correspondence columns, especially in local newspapers. Whenever a politician speaks on the subject he knows that he will almost certainly be reported; some do not even trouble to speak: they pick up the telephone and dictate a statement to the Press Association".

It should be mentioned that Rose and his colleagues produced no evidence to support the statement. They were making a general statement about the crucial nature of the press in the field of race relations.

A number of writers have stressed that the press has no desire or impetus to engage in campaigning on issues which do not reflect the interests of, or the wishes of, their readers. Newspapers are entrepreneurial institutions which depend for their survival on the goodwill of their readers and advertisers. Writing about American communities Breed (1964) suggests that the press maintains socio-cultural consensus and therefore protects the existing power and class structure. Other studies support this view (Olien et al, 1968). Similarly, opinions prevail that television is biassed in favour of the existing power structure of society.

There is also evidence that the press can foster and support alarmist views about ethnic minorities. In such situations the press is again probably merely reflecting the views of dominant power groups. Examples of this kind of effect were given to the International Seminar on the Press in Davao City, Phillipines, in April 1969. A number of papers were presented which indicated that partial, emotive or inaccurate reports had helped to make existing racial tensions worse. Evidence was given on American riots, on Malay-Chinese riots in Kuala Lumpur, on Sinhalese-Tamil riots in Ceylon and on Hindu-Moslem conflicts in India. (A minor skirmish took place outside a Hindu temple in Ahmedabad. The next day Indian language newspapers carried headlines with emotive content such as "Fanatics attack Jagannath temple". Other newspapers also inflated the incident.)

A detailed content analysis of press and television reporting of a British demonstration against the Vietnam war has been made by Halloran and his colleagues (1970). A large but overwhelmingly peaceful demonstration in London in October 1968 was treated by the press in terms of a basic issue – that of violence and threat to public order. This treatment served to distort news, since all events were analysed and reported to the extent which they fitted the media's conceptual framework of this issue.

A study by Hartmann and Husband (1970) argues that the British mass media, including television, handle race relations material in a way that both perpetuates negative perceptions of blacks and also defines the race relations situation as one of intergroup conflict. A test of a hypothesis about the possible effect of the media on the attitudes of 208 teenagers was made by comparing attitudes of youngsters with varying degrees of contact with New Commonwealth immigrants. Significantly more youngsters in low contact areas cited media sources for their information about black people than those in high contact areas, where information was more likely to be based on personal contact. Moreover, teenagers who cited conflict themes (when questioned about their knowledge of black people in Britain) were significantly more likely to cite the media as a source of information. Conflict themes were much more often mentioned by young people in low contact areas. There is an obvious inference from these findings that teenagers who rely on the mass media for their information about New Commonwealth people have to some extent internalised the image of New Commonwealth people presented to them by these media.

A detailed content analysis of the treatment of race over the period 1963 to 1970 in four British national newspapers – The Times, The Guardian, Daily Express and Daily Mirror – was undertaken by Hartmann and Husband (1974). The researchers found that the four papers proved to be similar in the kind of subject matter they carried. The kinds of news concerning race relations which these four papers thought was worth printing, and the amount of space they gave to different kinds of material turned out to be very similar indeed. The amount of race related material appearing in the press increased over the period of analysis. According to the researchers, this was due entirely to an increase in material about the British situation, for which there was nearly twice as much in the second half of the period as in the first. This indicates that with the increased number of Blacks press attention to race relations increased. It is difficult to explain the increasing attention in terms of "more black people make more black news". It is interesting to point out that issues of black people's housing, education and employment did not receive increased attention by the press. Rather the emphasis was on salient questions such as immigration, inter-group hostility, the relationships between white and black, the views of Enoch Powell and so on. The researchers analysed the material and found that 39 per cent was signalled as race related by words such as race, colour, immigrant, negroes in the headlines; 10 per cent of headings contained words like murder, kill, shoot or burn; 12 per cent included words like hate, crisis, row, clash and threat, showing conflict and disagreement; 6 per cent of headlines contained restrictive words like stop, curb, out, ban and bar.

Rex (1970 and 1972) argues that the mass media, including the press, reinforce existing cultural stereotypes about ethnic minorities. Thus 'stories' which represent blacks and Asians as stupid or unclean are seized upon and exaggerated, while events which represent minorities in ways contrary to popular stereotypes are played down. The same process has operated in the treatment by American mass media of minorities (Ehrlich, 1973).

Influence of the press on attitudes
The literature shows that there may be three complementary models which can account for the connections between mass media and racial attitudes and actions. First, the primary influence of the press is to act as a support for opinions which already exist in the general population – probably in a semi-articulated way. The press operates to articulate, legitimise and support the opinions held by the large majority of their readers. Second, the press conforms to its own stereotype of how news in the particular field should be handled (a number of studies provide evidence for this view – e.g. Halloran et al, Hartmann and Husband). This conception may distort news of events and is likely to be a negative one.

The third model is one in which the press plays a role in supporting or initiating social movement. The massive anxiety in the host community over the entry of British Asians is an example.

In our empirical studies we were concerned with aspects of the first model. The hypotheses derived from this model are:

a. The press can most easily influence attitudes in race relations by influencing attitudes in the direction in which they are already well advanced. For example, if the majority of the population hold racially prejudiced attitudes, the press can be successful in making people more prejudiced, but it is unlikely to be able to make people less prejudiced.

b. Press attitudes to specific issues reflect the underlying attitudes of the public; press attitudes serve to reinforce and strengthen public attitudes in this sphere, and increase their intensity.

It is not possible to employ any direct test of these hypotheses. However, we have tried to provide answers to a number of questions which bear on these hypotheses. (See Bagley and Verma, 1979, for a more detailed discussion.)

Racial attitudes and the press
It is true, of course, that attitudes and ways of communicating are affected to a great extent by what is seen, heard, read and assimilated from the individual's environment. Young children in particular are more susceptible to these outside factors. Unfortunately, the impression of non-western cultures portrayed by the media is often unfavourable. Our experience based on interviews with children suggests that the negative description by the media of ethnic minorities contributes to the low self-esteem of the minority-culture child. Such children and their parents may also obtain a view of British life as a permissive society. In such circumstances children over-estimate the degree of 'freedom' enjoyed by their contemporaries, and this stiffens the resolve of their parents to adhere to their standards and expectations. Thus, inter-generational conflict is heightened.

Data from a random sample survey of 2,490 individuals living in five English boroughs with an average proportion of black people (Lambeth, Ealing, Wolverhampton, Nottingham, Bradford) have been analysed to indicate the prevalence of prejudiced attitudes, the kinds of sources which those sampled use for information on race relations and the extent to which prejudiced people say that they obtain information about race relations from the press. The results showed that nearly half of the population sampled manifested a marked degree of prejudice, and only 14 per cent of the population sampled did not manifest prejudiced attitudes (Bagley, 1970).

The researcher posed the following questions: to what extent do the members of the population sampled use the press as a source of information about black people; to what extent are individuals using various sources of information prejudiced, and to what extent are various institutions, including mass media, seen as favourable to black people?

Analysis of the data showed that the large majority of respondents obtained their information from more than one source. The most frequently cited source of information was 'personal contact' with black people (54 per cent). 34 per cent of the respondents said that they used the press as a source of such information. The tabulation of the percentage of those prejudiced against sources of information suggested that significantly fewer of those who got information about black people from personal contact or from the radio were prejudiced than the remainder of the individuals in the sample. The number of respondents who obtained their information from the press alone was small (n = 127). 70 of these individuals (55 per cent) had prejudiced scores above the median level.

The conclusions drawn by the researcher are that a third of the population in the areas surveyed obtained information about New Commonwealth people from the press; 46 per cent of those individuals were prejudiced. This percentage is close to the prejudice in the population as a whole. However, individuals who rely on the press alone as a source of information are significantly more prejudiced than the rest of the population. This does not, of course, logically imply any causal link between readership of the press and prejudice. Both the local and the national press are seen as holding favourable attitudes to black people by a little under 40 per cent of respondents. Some 14 per cent see the local and national press as being hostile to black people.

Bagley (1973) conducted an analysis of the content of all reports in the provicial press in Britain published in the first four months of 1968. It was in the middle of this period that Powell's first major speech on race was made, and he attempted to assess the impact of this on newspapers' attitudes in race relations by comparing three periods – before the Powell speech, immediately after the Powell speech and some months after the speech.

By utilising rigorous methods of analysis the researcher classified 2,235 reports on race relations which appeared in some 200 British provincial newspapers in January, February, March and April 1968. The selection of material was made by the staff of a press cuttings agency.

The main issues in race relations which occupied the press during the four months were; in January, the problems of illegal entry; in February, the entry of East African Asians, and the government bill to restrict their entry; the announcement of the forthcoming Race Relations Act; Wolverhampton's ban on turbanned Sikhs on their corporation buses; the black power movement, and Powell's first major speech on immigration. In March the press were concerned mainly with the passage of the Race Relations Act, and the establishment of community relations officers, while in April the main issues were the debate on the Race Relations Bill, and Powell's second major speech on 20 April, 1968.

The classification of the press cuttings indicated that the most hostile area was crime, and the next most hostile area was those reports which concerned Powell's speeches. The areas where the press reports were least hostile were concerned with the personal activities of immigrants, employment, housing and education.

Letters to the editor were markedly more hostile than either editorials or articles written by regular contributors. The majority of the letters (64 per cent) were either critical of, or hostile to blacks and Asians. Letters on the general area of race relations were definitely more favourable than letters on the Kenyan Asian issue.

A classification of individual newspapers indicated that the most unfavourable or hostile newspapers (to black immigrants) were the Preston Lancashire Evening Post, the Portsmouth Evening News, the Oldham Chronicle, the Manchester Evening News, the South London Press, the Coventry Evening Telegraph and the Middlesbrough Evening Gazette. The papers with the highest proportion of 'favourable' reports were the Darlington Northern Echo (50 per cent) and the Kensington Post (52 per cent).

It is interesting to mention that the amount of negative items reported in the press increased quite markedly from January to February as the number of press reports on race relations increased. The researcher concluded that the reason for this increase could be attributed to the press reactions in February to Powell's first major speech on 9 February, and the actions and debates resulting from it. The level of hostility to coloured people was largely maintained in press reports of November of the same year.

One important way in which the provincial press conveys opinion in the race relations field is by printing readers' letters. The bulk of these letters – both those received and those printed – were hostile to coloured immigrants.

An interesting example of how the press can create race relations 'news' out of nothing has been provided by reports in national newspapers about the action of the Race Relations Board (Race Relations Bulletin, 1970). In April 1970, Gentleshaw and Cannock Wood Women's Institute entered a local talent competition and chose to sing an old fashioned song called 'Ten Little Nigger Boys'. However they had second thoughts, believing that the title might offend some people, so changed the words to 'Ten Little Golliwogs' instead. The day afterwards a journalist rang the chairman of the West Midlands branch of the Race Relations Board and asked his personal view on the substitution. The spokesman said he thought either words would offend some people. Next day, the Daily Telegraph ran a story under the headline, "Race Board ban Women's Institute's Ten Little Nigger Boys". The Leicester Mercury headline declared, "Race Relations Board rebuke of some Women's Institute Singers". The Birmingham Post carried the

41

opinion of a politician that "the decision was pettifogging interference with ordinary pleasures of decent people".

The Race Relations Board itself had no power to ban anything, and it had no formal complaint about the song whatever, nor had it contacted any of the parties involved. The initiative in the case, and the distortion involved, was entirely journalistic. Indeed, a week later, the President of the Woman's Institute involved wrote to the Birmingham Post that "The Race Relations Board did not in any way interfere with our singing 'Ten Little Nigger Boys'. They did not even know about it then".

The chairman of the Race Relations Board commented on this matter that a period of positive neglect by the mass media of the more lurid aspects of race relations would be helpful.

The brief review of the literature suggests that the press may have a profound effect in the sphere of race relations. The influence that it has had has been largely negative, and has been related to the propensity of populations to be unfavourable or negative to ethnic minorities. The press in so far as it has been innovative has acted as a support or catalyst of existing propensities in the community. In particular, the press has frequently served to maintain socio-cultural integration. The model examined concerning the connection of race relations and the British press is one in which the press initially reflects opinion of leaders in the race relations field to the degree to which such individuals have large and popular support. Since the press, both national and local, depend for their survival on the goodwill of readers and advertisers, it is unlikely that they will pursue an editorial policy in the field of race relations which is too far removed from the will of the majority.

Overall, the recent effects of the press on race relations have not been liberal (as the earlier influence of the press in this field was not liberal), and its effects have also not been benign.

Race and the press in Britain – a developing pattern

The phenomenon of the 'racialist letter' to the local press has fluctuated according to the salience of particular issues (Priestley, 1972). It is also possible that as editors and editorial policy changes, some of the newspapers identified as hostile to coloured immigrants in 1968 will become less hostile (and vice versa). Following editorial changes, the South London Press, for example, became less hostile in its attacks on black and Asian settlers in South London. Nevertheless, it continued to publish a variety of readers' letters, including ones expressing great hostility as regards matters affecting race relations. The National Front, for example, gave a special award to a member for a letter published in the South London Press (Wall, 1976).

A detailed analysis of the role of the mass media in fostering and supporting attitudes during the arrival of British Asian refugees from Uganda in 1972 has been made by Humphry and Ward (1974). From the inception of the 'crisis' in August, 1972: "Newspapers carried pages of letters of protest which voiced people's fear of a fundamental change in British society which they thought the coming of the Asians would cause".

The Daily Express was particularly active in a campaign of 'feeding people's fears' with stories of villages and towns which would shortly be over-run with Asians. By September, both the Daily Express and the Daily Telegraph were conducting vigorous campaigns, with the Express using 'large cartoons featuring Asians which at other times would have been considered an offence to good taste'.

Peter Harland, editor of the Bradford 'Telegraph and Argus' has commented:

> "It would be a mistake however to assume that, because the media's attention has passed on to such new excitements as inflation and kidnapping, racialism has disappeared altogether. It is merely latent. There is no evidence that the prejudice freely expressed in 1972–73 has evaporated miraculously. Its strength then was shown vividly by Derek Humphrey and Michael Ward in their 1974 Penguin Special – Passports and Politics. Perhaps because they chose to concentrate on one particular area – Basildon in Essex – their book was criticised as being both exaggerated and untypical. But everything that Humphrey and Ward found in Basildon, I experienced, and more, at the same time in Bradford, although Bradford was not an area designated to receive more than a handful of Ugandan Asians" (Harland, 1976).

The effects of television upon attitudes

A leading television broadcaster (Gillard, 1975) has claimed that the role of television in maintaining national spirit and morale in times of crisis and difficulty is crucial. He may be right. The role of television clearly stands above that of other forms of mass media. Hartmann and Husband (1974) found that for the children and adolescents they interviewed, television was undoubtedly the most important source of information about the world. They argue that the important effect of the mass media is not that watching television makes us more violent or permissive or racist, but that the media throw some features into sharp relief, obliterate others, select and limit the issues which are worthy of consideration or recall. The mass media do not determine attitudes, but they do structure and select information we may use on which to base decisions about what attitude is appropriate. For the mass of people, of course, this process is hardly rational or conscious. Attitudes themselves are ill-formed and may be focussed by the images and attitudes of the mass media. It is posssible, too, as Halloran and his colleagues have argued (1974) that television and other news media serve to support already formed prejudiced opinions, in that adults and children who are already prejudiced recall more readily news items and programmes whose content is racial. The same programme can also mean different things to different observers. The influence of television programmes may be both subtle and indirect.

Television becomes important as children grow older. In a study of 11 national and cultural groups Lambert and Klineberg (1967) found that six year old children report a primary dependence on their parents for attitudes about other ethnic groups. Children of ten and older, however, report a greater dependence on television and reading materials. What this implies is that children can learn racial concepts, and racial terms of abuse which they would otherwise have been ignorant of. A case in point is the influence of the TV series 'Love Thy Neighbour" which portrays a white bigot who heaps racial abuse upon his neighbour. The programme is meant to be funny. The Area Round-Up Column of 'Race Today' reported in May 1973 that a primary school headteacher in Fife, Scotland, said 'that children in his school had made a coloured worker's life a misery, calling him names like 'coon' and 'Sambo', having picked them up from the programme 'Love Thy Neighbour'. A Thames TV spokesman said that all the evidence they had showed that people were overwhelmingly in favour of the programme both as entertainment and as good race relations – "by using humour it takes the heat out of the colour question". It could be said that the programme created a 'colour question' in Fife and in other areas where there are very few coloured immigrants.

Carlin (1975) has noted that, "Racial clowning is the classic defence against humiliation and physical attack . . . there is the Latin American clown, who is always smiling; there is, as Conor Cruise O'Brien again has pointed out, the Irish clown, who is always drunk; there is the Asian clown, the Babu; there is the Negro clown – we know him well. There is – or was – a Jewish clown. All racial clowns are sooner or later celebrated on the musical comedy stage". These clowns are celebrated too, on our TV screens, and serve to reinforce the stereotypes of the majority. In recent years television's treatment of other cultures concerns the Arabs. Characters are either wealthy stumblebums in situation comedies or unprincipled terrorists in so-called dramas.

Both BBC and ITV continue to show a variety of old films, which portray Africans and American Indians as untrustworthy savages, fit peoples for subjugation and civilisation by the white man. A new genre of TV programmes has appeared on British screens in recent years – specially produced fictional programmes for TV which have been made in America in a new era of apparent racial enlightenment. A detailed content analysis of these programmes has been made by a group of American researchers (Donagher *et al*, 1975). A number of programmes analysed have been shown on British TV. The formal roles assigned to the characters varied considerably. Males, both white and black, were represented as professionals or semi-professionals e.g. educators, policemen, firemen, detectives, ranchers. Females of both races were portrayed as teachers, secretaries and housewives, whereas white females also took on such roles as nurses, counsellors, detectives and newspaper owners. Formal role-status, say the researchers, was not completely equitable but represented a substantial movement toward equality compared to role assignment during the earlier years of television. Citing research which shows that children's positive and negative attitudes toward their own and other races can be influenced by the specific ways in which racial characters are portrayed on television, Donagher *et al* conclude that the new wave of television dramas may have served to transmit a new wave of stereotypes, but these stereotypes are still ones of black inferiority.

Current statistics show that children spend a great deal of time watching television. A piece of research was conducted to ascertain the effects of a television series specifically designed to influence racial attitudes (Kemelfield, 1972). Kemelfield evaluated the effects of programmes transmitted in schools TV service for 9 to 12 year olds on the lives of children in other cultures. The programmes were shown to two groups of children, one in an area of immigrant settlement, and one in an area without immigrants. In general, the programme was well received, and also effective in achieving its aims of 'encouraging appreciation and tolerance of people of different creeds and races now living in Britain'. For example, of the subjects in the low contact area, 39 per cent thought that 'Pakistanis are usually as clean as English people', before seeing the programme, compared with 75 per cent of those questioned after seeing it. There was one exception to these results, in white children in one school in an area of high immigrant settlement, where 28 per cent of pupils were, in fact from Pakistan. Here, all the children's pre-programme knowledge was generally greater, but their post-programme answers suggested that in certain areas they were reacting to their own knowledge of their Pakistani peers rather than to the programme content. After viewing the programme, white pupils in this high contact school appeared to be more sensitive to the possibilities of culture clashes (e.g. over different diets) with Pakistani children. Clearly the effects of television are complex as are the effects of teaching about race relations in schools (Verma and MacDonald, 1971; Verma and Bagley, 1973; Verma and Bagley, 1979; Stenhouse, Verma and Wild, 1982), but TV programmes can have, in certain circumstances, a considerable influence on attitudes. If programmes transmitted by school television can affect attitudes in positive ways, it seems probable that programmes transmitted at other times can also affect attitudes. Unfortunately, there is not as much research on the issues as would be desirable.

References

Bagley, C. (1970d): 'Social Structure and Prejudice in Fiv. London Institute of Race Relations

Bagley, C. (1973b): 'Race Relations and the British press: an empirical study'. Race, 15, 60-89

Bagley, C and Verma, G. K. (1979): 'Racial Prejudice, the Individual and Society'. Farnborough: Saxon House

Breed, W. (1964): 'Mass communication and socio-cultural integration' in L. Dexter and D. White (eds) 'People, Society and Mass Communications'. New York; The Free Press

Carlin, M (1975): 'Clowns for all races'. New Society, January 9, 75-6

Cofax, J. and Sternberg, S. (1972): 'The perpetuation of racial stereotypes: blacks in mass circulation magazine advertisements'. Public Opinion Quarterly, 36, 8-18

Donagher, P., Paulos, R., Leibert, R. and Davidson, E. (1975): 'Race, sex and social example: an analysis of character portrayals on inter-racial television entertainment'. Psychological Reports, 37, 1023-34

Ehrlich, H. (1973): 'The Social Psychology of Prejudice'. New York: Wiley

Gillard, F. (1975): Quoted in The Times, 19 September, 1975

Halloran, J., Elliott, P. and Murdock G. (1970): 'Demonstrations and Communication. A Case Study'. London: Penguin Books

Halloran, J., Hartmann, P. and Husband, C. (1974): 'Mass media and social attitudes'. SSRC Newsletter, 23, 18

Harland, P. (1976): 'The media and race relations today'. New Community, 4, 435-60

Hartmann, P. and Husband, C. (1970): 'The mass media and racial conflict'. Race, 12, 267-82

Hartmann, P., and Husband, C. (1974): 'Racism and the Mass Media'. London: Davis-Poynter

Humphry, D. and Ward, M. (1974): 'Passports and Politics'. London: Penguin Books

Johnson, P., Sears, D. and McConahay, J. (1971): 'Black invisibility, the press and the Los Angeles Riot'. American Journal of Sociology, 76, 698-721

Kemelfield, G. (1972): 'The evaluation of schools' broadcasting: piloting a new approach'. New Society, June 1, 472-73

MacKinnon, W. and Centers, R. (1958): 'Social-psychological factors in public orientation toward an out-group'. American Journal of Sociology, 63, 415-19

Olien, C. et al (1968) 'The Community editor's power and the reporting conflict'. Journalism Quarterly, 45, 243-52

Race Relations Bulletin (1970): 'Frivolity and the Race Relations Act'. Race Relations Bulletin (London) May

Rex, J. (1970): 'Race Relations in Sociological Theory'. London: Weidenfeld and Nicolson

Rex, J. (1972): 'Nature versus nurture: the significance of the revived debate'. In W. Richardson and D. Spears (eds) 'Race, Culture and Intelligence'. London: Penguin Books

Rose, J. and others (1969): 'Colour and Citizenship'. London: Oxford University Press.

Stenhouse, L., Verma, G. K. and Wild, R. (1982) 'Teaching About Race Relations: Problems and Effects'. London: Routledge

Verma, G. K. and Bagley, C. (1973): 'Changing racial attitudes'. International Journal of Psychology, 8, 55-8

Verma, G. K. and Bagley, C. (1979): 'The evaluation of three strategies in teaching about race relations'. In G. K. Verma and C. Bagley (eds) 'Race, Education and Identity'. London: Macmillan

Verma, G. K. and MacDonald, B. (1971): 'Teaching race in schools: some effects on the attitudinal and sociometric patterns of adolescents'. Race, 13, No. 2

Wall, M. (1976): 'Caution or credibility'. New Community, 4, 463-64

ANNEX B

Multi-Ethnic Teaching and the Pupils' Self-Concepts
A paper by Peter A Green

The sudden influx of immigrants during the nineteen-fifties and nineteen-sixties introduced into Britain a whole generation of Commonwealth citizens who tended to settle in a limited number of large towns and cities where they found accommodation available only in severely restricted areas with the consequence that schools serving those areas had to admit large numbers of immigrant children who then formed a substantial proportion of the pupils in any one school. Very little was known about educating immigrant minorities[1] (in some schools they were *majorities*) alongside indigenous children for whom the educational system was developed and even as late as 1969 Vernon, commenting about immigrant children wrote, "it is widely recognised that children of school age have considerable difficulties in adjusting to the unfamiliar conditions of English schooling"[2]. Understandably teachers were concerned with immediate problems and researchers responded with a number of important studies[3,4]. However, these problems were generally interpreted as being solely related to, and centred upon, the immigrant pupil's weaknesses, inabilities and failures which resulted in children of Asian and of West Indian origins being seen as the cause of the difficulties confronting the teacher in the multi-ethnic classroom. Black children were expected to fit into white schools and educational difficulties were almost invariably identified as immigrant problems.

The rapidly imposed changes threatened established educational practices and in their train induced feelings of insecurity[5] which tended to accentuate the significance of the white teacher's attitude towards black children of West Indian or Asian origin. The relationship between pupils and their teacher in the multi-ethnic classroom emerged as a major factor since "any successful classroom has to be based upon a dialogue between students and teachers"[6] and because "in many respects a child is taught what he is by being told what his actions 'mean', by their 'effect' on the others"[7]. This awareness, once assimilated into the child's concept of himself, is likely to become an influential element in learning[8] and may be a significant factor in low levels of academic achievement. In the research on which this paper is based[9] the self-concept was viewed as a mental image established as a result of the knowledge the child has of himself and which is subject to modification through further learning. The malleable nature of the self-concept is widely recognised[e.g. 10,11] and such flexibility surrounding the relatively stable core of the self[12] places a formidable burden of responsibility upon the professional shoulders of the schoolteacher especially when "the school is second only to the home in determining an individual's attitudes of self-acceptance and self-rejection"[13]. As a learned structure it follows that, to some extent, it is taught by those people who are dominant in the life of the child. Few people can be more dominant than the child's teacher who, with an aura of authority, projects appraisals based on personally selected criteria which will be affected by the white teacher's attitude towards the black child and towards the educational task in which they are mutually engaged. Despite the development of new strategies in recent years the processes of education and social control in the classroom are still orally dominated by the teacher and the language of interaction becomes a means of appraisal by the teacher and a guide for self-evaluation by the child for as Laing points out "identity is reached and sustained two-dimensionally, it requires recognition of oneself by others as well as the simple recognition one accords oneself"[14]. In the course of this interaction the child himself will engage in making comparative appraisals

46

comparing his own skills, attributes and performance with those of his peers and assessing his degree of success or failure. Davidson and Lang[15] showed that during the Primary School years there is a positive correlation between the child's self-concept and the child's perception of his teacher's feelings towards him. Other studies clearly indicate that the perception of behaviour surrounding a child is interpreted and internalized to become part of the child's evaluation of himself[16,17] so whilst still in its very formative state the self is partially a product of formal education and as a learned structure becomes "a condition of subsequent learning"[18]. In America Rubovits and Maehr observed in their research that "in general, black students were treated less positively than whites"[19] and "were given less attention, ignored more, praised less and criticized more"[20]. The interaction which takes place in the multi-ethnic classroom between the teacher and individual boys and girls of European, Asian and West Indian origins is, therefore, likely to be influential in the development of the self-concept, which itself has been consistently shown to be associated with the child's level of academic achievement[21].

The behaviour of the teacher in the multi-ethnic classroom, unless it is modified to produce a spurious behavioural pattern for some particular reason, is likely to reflect those attitudes which are stimulated by ethnic factors and because an attitude predisposes "one to respond in some preferential manner"[22] the level of the teachers' ethnocentrism assumes considerable significance. By ethnocentrism we mean the tendency to consider the characteristics and attributes of ethnic groups other than one's own to be inferior. As it is derived from a basis of the individual's knowledge, or assumed knowledge, it tends to avoid the more emotive and active connotations associated with notions such as racial prejudice and racism which are usually based on predominantly negative and subjective beliefs. As a major influence on the behaviour a teacher exhibits in the multi-ethnic classroom it may be an influential factor in reaching the numerous professional decisions required of a teacher during the course of a working day. There have been few investigations in British schools into either the extent or the effect of ethnocentrism amongst teachers. Thus the present lack of objective evidence from empirical studies enforces a heavy reliance upon subjective comment from a number of observers of the multi-ethnic scene who, themselves, will not be completely immune from the effects of the phenomenon. The importance of classroom atmosphere is referred to by Davey when he asks, "If self-esteem is dependent on the appraisal of others will not the prejudice of the dominant group enter into the stigmatised group member's perception of himself?"[23]. What comes through quite clearly from a number of studies is that the quality of contact is likely to be an influential factor in the development of the child's self-concept especially in a multi-ethnic classroom dominated by the authority of a white teacher[24].

Any manifestation of the teacher's ethnocentrism in the multi-ethnic classroom takes place in the context of professional activity so the teacher's attitude towards that activity ought not to be disregarded. Goldman comments that "the attitudes of teachers and educational administrators are important formative influences on how the ethnically different child generates his self-image"[25] and from the American scene Yamamoto expresses a similar view when writing about the teacher's role in the nurture of the self-concept in children of Primary School age[26]. Following the work of Oliver[27] the research reported here distinguishes the presence in the sample of toughminded/tenderminded, idealistic/naturalistic and conservative/radical attitudes towards education.

The toughminded/tenderminded dimension is sensitive to practical as against theoretical viewpoints indicating the teacher's attitude towards the methods used to achieve educational objectives; the idealistic/naturalistic dimension distinguishes the advocates of teacher-controlled education exercising an instilling function from those preferring child-centred education exercising a guiding function[28]; and the conservative/radical dimension shows the teacher's attitude towards conservation or change in education. The different types of attitudes teachers have towards some fundamental aspects of teaching and learning are likely to influence their style of teaching and the type of teacher/pupil relationship which is encouraged. Additionally teachers carry into the multi-ethnic class their own degree of ethnocentrism which will find accentuated or diminished expression within the context of their teaching. The activity which takes place in the form of interaction is likely to influence the development of the child's self-concept as a learner which, in turn, may have a bearing on the level of scholastic achievement.

47

To study the influence which teachers may have on the development of the self-concept of pupils of different ethnic origins the research investigated whether teachers' gender, their ethnocentrism and the types of attitudes they have towards education are associated with the use they make of different modes of teaching and whether that teaching is correlated to the child's level of self-concept. The sample consisted of seventy full-time qualified teachers and their 1,814 pupils in three Middle and three Junior co-educational schools drawn from two Local Education Authority areas. The teachers, twenty-eight male and forty-two female white British nationals, were predominantly in their twenties and thirties with 43% of the sample having had five or more years experience of teaching in multi-ethnic schools. Of the pupil sample those of European origin comprised 28% boys and 24% girls; of Asian origin 12% boys and 13% girls and of West Indian origin 12% boys and 11% girls. Two schools served the central districts of their Authority's area with the children living in older type privately owned property. Away from the central districts two schools had catchment areas which included modern council and owner-occupied housing in roughly equal proportions. The remaining two schools were situated in older council estates with mainly poor housing conditions. The field work for the study was carried out during the latter half of the school year so that teachers and children had been in lengthy contract with each other by the time the data was collected.

To assess and record the classroom interaction the ten-category schedule devised by Flanders[29] was used distinguishing the acceptance of the pupils' feelings (Category 1), praise and encouragement (C2), the acceptance or use of pupils' ideas (C3), the teacher asking questions (C4), direct teaching of a didactic type (C5), the teacher's directions (C6), the teacher's criticism or justification of authority (C7), pupil talk in response to the teacher (C8), pupil initiatory talk (C9) and silence during teaching sequences (C10). The system of recording the interaction enabled the amount of time spent by the teacher in using any one category with the class as a whole or with individual boys and girls of each ethnic group to be calculated for each class for a complete day[a]. To measure the extent to which ethnocentrism was present in the sample of teachers a revised form of 'A British Ethnocentrism Scale'[30] was used and this revealed four main groups of teachers whose levels of ethnocentrism were significantly different. The two extreme groups, with twelve teachers in each, were designated as highly intolerant and highly tolerant teachers. The teachers' attitudes towards education were measured by the 'Survey of Opinions about Education'[31] which showed women teachers in the sample to be predominantly idealistic-toughminded-radicals whilst men teachers were idealistic-radicals with a tendency towards tendermindedness. Translating these theoretical constructs into a description of the probable behaviour of teachers in the multi-ethnic classroom we would expect both men and women in the sample to accept changes in education whilst seeking, from all children, a high level of performance emphasizing the importance of subject matter. The main difference between men and women teachers in the sample is most likely to be evident in the manner in which they accept the changes and strive for excellence. Women are likely to be more authoritarian establishing a fairly inflexible classroom routine in contrast to men teachers who will tend to allow children a greater degree of freedom imposing their ideas less frequently than women teachers in a more relaxed classroom atmosphere. The level of the children's self-concepts were measured by three scales orally administered in the absence of their teacher: a modified form of the Bledsoe Self-Concept Scale[32], a modified form of the Coopersmith Self-Esteem Inventory[33] and the Waetjen Self-Concept as a Learner Scale[34].

Before focusing on the detail of multi-ethnic classroom interaction the general pattern of the teaching observed is described by the use of four indices. The first of these, the teacher response ratio, is an index corresponding to the teacher's tendency to react positively to the ideas and feelings expressed by the children. The second index, the teacher question ratio, illustrates the tendency of a teacher to emphasize questioning in preference to direct teaching of the didactic

---

a. The expected frequency of any teaching mode was calculated according to the percentage number of children of each ethnic group being taught. Thus girls of Asian origin, who constituted 12.96% of the children taught by male teachers, would be expected to receive 12.96% of the total time given to any mode of teaching during individual teaching. The difference between observed and expected frequency provides a measure of the excess or deficit teaching in relation to boys and girls of each ethnic group.

type. Thirdly, a pupil initiation ratio illustrates pupil's initiatory talk as a proprtion of all talking and, lastly, the teacher authority ratio is an index representing that proportion of the teacher's direct teaching activity used for giving directions, criticizing and justifying his authority. Relating these indices to the types of attitudes the teachers held about education shows that both tough and tenderminded teachers responded more positively to the ideas and feelings expressed by girls than they did to those of boys in each ethnic group. Both groups of teachers tended to respond more negatively to the contributions made by boys of West Indian origin than they did to those made by any other children. The responses of both groups of teachers, whilst similar in pattern are, nevertheless, at different levels: tenderminded teachers reacted more positively with boys and girls of Asian and of West Indian origins than their toughminded colleagues who responded more positively with boys and girls of European origin. The teacher question ratio shows that all teachers, irrespective of whether they held tough or tenderminded attitudes towards their task, spent a higher proportion of time asking questions of children of Asian and of West Indian origins than they did with children of European origin. In other words, the teaching of children of European origin, especially boys, tended to emphasize direct teaching in preference to questioning. With the exception of girls of Asian origin all black children received a higher proportion of questioning from toughminded teachers than from those holding tender-minded attitudes. Whereas girls spent most of their talking-time responding to these questions, boys, taught by toughminded teachers, when compared with girls of the same ethnic group, spent most time using initiatory talk. When exercising their authority in the multi-ethnic classroom both tough and tenderminded teachers spent proportionately least time doing so with pupils of European origin and most time with children of West Indian origin. Within the context of this teaching girls of Asian origin and boys of West Indian origin taught by tenderminded teachers recorded a significantly higher level of self-concept than those girls and boys of the same ethnic group taught by teachers holding toughminded attitudes towards their work. **Within** those classes taught by tenderminded teachers there was no significant difference between the levels of self-concept of boys and girls in each ethnic group but when taught by toughminded teachers girls of Asian origin and boys of West Indian origin recorded significantly lower levels of self-concept than all other children in the same classes.

Turning to the conservative/radical dimension, no significant differences were found between the self-concept levels of children taught by either group of teachers. However, within classes some distinct differences emerged. Boys of European origin in classes taught by teachers holding conservative attitudes towards education recorded a significantly higher level of self-concept than boys and girls of Asian and of West Indian origins in the same classes. They received more positive responses from their conservative teachers and more time for initiatory talking than children of Asian and of West Indian origins and they were subjected to less questioning and less authoritarian comment. In those classes taught by teachers holding predominantly radical attitudes towards education girls of Asian origin and boys of West Indian origin recorded significantly lower levels of self-concept than boys and girls of European origin and girls of West Indian origin. Girls of Asian origin received a high level of positive response from their radically minded teachers but a very low level of questioning, little opportunity for initiatory talking and only minimal authoritarian comment. Although teachers holding radical views about their work responded to girls of Asian origin in a strongly positive manner the general picture which emerges is one in which these pupils are relatively ignored. That is not the case with boys of West Indian origin who received from radically minded teachers an almost exactly opposite style of teaching which emphasized questioning and authoritarian statements and gave a lot of time to the boys' initiatory talking but only minimal time for responding positively to their ideas and feelings.

Teachers inclined toward naturalism recorded a significantly higher response ratio than those inclined towards idealism. This more positive response of naturalistic teachers is evident in their work with boys and girls of each ethnic group. There is also a gender distinction in that girls, irrespective of whether they were taught by teachers inclined towards idealism or naturalism, received more positive responses from their teachers than boys of the same ethnic group. The pattern of responses within those classes taught by idealistic teachers is one in which they responded less frequently to the ideas and feelings of boys and girls of Asian and of West Indian origins than to those of European origin. Likewise with girls, the idealistic teachers' responses were less frequent with girls of Asian and of West Indian origins than with girls of European origin . In the other classes those teachers inclined towards naturalism had a tendency to respond more positively to pupils of Asian origin than to those of European or of West Indian origin. These same teachers also spent more time than their idealistic counterparts in questioning pupils and both groups of teachers questioned black pupils more extensively than white. It is not surprising to find that teachers holding naturalistic attitudes about education tend to allow greater scope for their pupils to initiate contributions in the multi-ethnic classroom than the more formally and traditionally centred teachers holding idealistic attitudes about education who allow white pupils more time than they allow black pupils for initiating their ideas. Authoritarian comment from idealistic teachers tended to be directed towards boys rather than girls and towards black rather than white pupils. At the other end of the attitude scale naturalistic teachers used less authoritarian comment with children of Asian origin and most with children of West Indian origin. The level of self-concept of girls of Asian origin taught by idealistic teachers is significantly lower than that of girls of the same ethnic group taught by teachers inclined towards naturalism. Idealistic teachers responded to girls of Asian origin much less positively than their naturalistic colleagues, spent less time asking questions of these pupils, allowed them considerably less time for initiatory talking and spent slightly less time making authoritarian comments. Within classes taught by teachers holding idealistic attitudes towards education, girls of Asian origin and boys of West Indian origin recorded a significantly lower level of self-concept than boys and girls of European origin.

The evidence of our study[9] suggests that the attitudes which teachers of multi-ethnic classes hold about education may foster, through the teaching styles generated by them, educational environments to which the self-concept of some children is differentially sensitive. It is within these educational environments that teachers also manifest their differing degrees of ethnocentrism so the pertinent question is, "What is it like to be on the receiving end if your teacher is ethnically highly tolerant or highly intolerant?".

Boys of European origin, taught by highly tolerant teachers, received less attention than their numbers warranted in respect of nine of the ten modes of teaching (described earlier in this paper). Very minimal extra time was given to the negative criticism of the boys' work and behaviour but it was the most frequently used mode in a pattern which emphasized direct teaching supported by the opportunity for initiatory talking. These boys are given very little praise for their efforts receiving some 44% less than would have been the case in an equitable distribution. In a multi-ethnic class taught by a teacher who is ethnically highly intolerant, boys of European origin received additional time in nine modes with only directives taking less than expected time. A positive approach gives some 35% extra time to these boys in which to initiate their own ideas and provides substantial additional time (+32%) for silence during teaching sequences suggesting a fairly relaxed atmosphere with boys of European origin. Their initiatives find ready acceptance and are reinforced by additional time given to praise and encouragement (+20%) but they are not, however, immune from criticism (+21%). These boys, taught by highly tolerant teachers, have a significantly lower level of self-concept than those taught by highly intolerant teachers. Furthermore, within those classes taught by highly intolerant teachers, boys of European origin recorded a level of self-concept which is very significantly higher than those of boys and girls of Asian and of West Indian origins but which is not significantly different from that of girls of European origin. Within those classes taught by highly tolerant teachers there are no statistically significant differences in self-concept levels.

Girls of European origin when taught by teachers who are highly tolerant are not likely to be slow in perceiving that, compared with pupils in other ethnic groups but like boys in their own, they are relatively disregarded. When they do receive the teacher's attention they will find themselves subjected, again like boys of European origin, mainly to criticism and a style of teaching which emphasizes direct teaching. Less parsimonious in their use of some modes of teaching, highly intolerant teachers allocated to these girls slightly more than their fair share of time in respect of direct teaching, the opportunity to express their own ideas and opinions and the use of these contributions in classroom activity. The efforts of these girls are given more praise and encouragement than their numbers warrant but the most conspicuous excess of time is given to the acceptance of their feelings and responding to them. Highly intolerant teachers use a very mild level of criticism (-37%) with girls of European origin and this is positively and significantly correlated to their level of self-concept which, coupled with an association discovered between direct teaching and the level of self-concept of these girls, may be an influential factor in the positive self-concept recorded by these girls when they are taught by highly intolerant teachers.

Boys of Asian origin received from highly tolerant teachers all modes of teaching in excess of what would normally be expected. This is the only group of pupils to receive such concentrated attention although boys of West Indian origin are not far behind when taught by the same category of teachers. The most distinctive feature is the lowest possible priority[b] given to the direct teaching of these boys by highly tolerant teachers: highly intolerant teachers give less priority only to the acceptance of the boys' feelings. The teaching profile of highly tolerant teachers working with boys of Asian origin is one, with high priority given to pupil responses and praise and low priority given to criticism, which suggests a pupil-orientated approach although somewhat surprisingly the pupils' initiatives, whilst attracting excess time, nevertheless command only low priority. Despite their exceptionally high level of ethnocentrism, highly intolerant teachers give considerable excess time to the responses ($+50\%$) and initiatives ($+49\%$) made by boys of Asian origin. These teachers not only give the highest priority to these two forms of pupil-talk but support also comes from excess time allowed for silence which occurs predominantly during the pupil-talk sequences. Although there is no significant difference between the level of self-concept of boys of Asian origin taught by highly tolerant and those taught by highly intolerant teachers, within individual classes, where differences of emphasis may be readily perceived by the children, boys of Asian origin taught by highly intolerant teachers record a level of self-concept which is significantly lower than that of boys and girls of European origin.

Girls of Asian origin received from teachers who are highly tolerant a relatively even allocation of time in respect of most modes of teaching with a tendency to err on the side of excess time except for direct teaching, criticism and the acceptance of the pupils' feelings. The emphasis that these teachers give to silence, the use of the girls' ideas coupled with substantial praise and encouragement suggests a positive and supportive style of teaching. The tendency for these teachers to give extra time to the girls' talking, both in response and initiation, is indicative of a child-orientated approach which finds further support in the minimal time which is given to direct teaching and criticism. Highly intolerant teachers, whilst also giving additional time and a high priority to praise, tend to emphasize questioning and direct teaching giving a very low priority to the responses and the initiatory talk of girls of Asian origin. The high priority given to praise contrasts sharply with the low priority given to the girls' talking in response and initiation both of which are the most common activators of the teachers' use of praise.

The wide difference, not evident with other pupil groups, between the length of time given to the pupils' talking and the extent of the teacher's praise suggests an abnormally excessive and, perhaps, spurious use of praise with girls of Asian origin when being taught by highly intolerant teachers. In classes taught by these highly ethnocentric teachers, the self-concept of girls of Asian origin is at a significantly lower level than that of boys and girls of European origin but there is not, however, any significant difference between the self-concept levels of girls of Asian origin taught by highly tolerant teachers and those girls of the same ethnic group taught by highly intolerant teachers.

Boys of West Indian origin are given more individual teaching time by highly tolerant teachers than their numbers would justify in respect of every teaching mode except for the even balance achieved when responding to the boys' feelings. The order of precedence given to the teaching modes, $(+)$ $7 - 6 - 4 - 10 - 2 - 5 - 9 - 8 - 3/1$ (o), illustrates the importance that these teachers attach to maintaining control of the interaction through criticism (C7) and directives (C6) supported by excessive ($+76\%$) questioning (C4) which is a form of control accentuated by the low priority given to the responses (C8) evoked by the questions. The '9 – 8 – 3' pattern at the

---

b. By 'order of priority' or 'precedence' we mean that the interaction categories, 1 to 10, are ranked according to the use made of any one category by a particular teacher group with a particular pupil group *as a proportion of its total use with all children.*

lower end of the order of precedence is a classic example of the teacher's limited use of the pupils' contributions (C3) inhibiting further contribution in the form of responses (C8) and initiatives (C9). The combination of the high priority given by highly tolerant teachers to categories '7 – 6 – 4' and the low priority given to categories '9 – 8 – 3' is indicative of tight teacher control dominating the work with boys of West Indian origin. With no other pupil group do these teachers give the acceptance and use of contributions such a low prioity. Highly intolerant teachers differ only slightly from their more tolerant colleagues in the order of priority they give to the ten modes of teaching with boys of West Indian origin but they utilize each mode at a much lower level of frequency. Every mode, except criticism, is used less than would be expected in an equitable distribution giving a profile (+) 7/6 – 4 – 5 – 2 – 8 – 10 – 3 – 9 – 1 (−) which reflects the emphasis on criticism (C7), directives (C6) and questioning (C4) already observed in the work of highly tolerant teachers with these boys. At the lower end of the order of precedence we again find a low priority being given to the boy's initiatives (C9) and only minimal use being made of their contributions (C3). Although highly intolerant teachers give less attention to boys of West Indian origin than their numbers warrant, these teachers give a higher priority to direct teaching (C5) than those who are highly tolerant, which may suggest a greater concern with the process of imparting information to these boys. Although the priorities given to the modes of teaching by both groups of teachers are very similar, the differences in levels of frequency are considerable and may contribute to the significantly lower level of self-concept recorded by these boys when they are taught by teachers who are highly intolerant. In those classes taught by these teachers, boys of West Indian origin record a level of self-concept which is significantly lower than that of boys and girls of European origin.

Girls of West Indian origin in classes taught by highly tolerant teachers can expect to receive more than their fair share of individual attention during the use of six of the ten modes of teaching. Least time is spent criticizing them and giving them directives which suggests that these teachers tend to adopt a positive approach to their work with girls of West Indian origin. The teaching profile emphasizes, with high priority and excess time, the acceptance of the girls' feelings and the initiation of their contributions to the work of the class. The highly tolerant teacher gives additional time to the use of the girls' contributions, to direct teaching and to the use of questions. Uncharacteristic of the general tenor of the work with these girls is the minimal time given to their responses to questions which, since there is some evidence to suggest that questioning is used by some teachers as a control mechanism, might not be unrelated to the infrequent use made of directives and criticism. The highly intolerant teacher employs these latter two modes more frequently than any others with girls of West Indian origin and they are the only two given excess time. It is interesting to note that questioning also occupies a high priority ranking fourth in order of precedence. When this pattern is contrasted to the very minimal amount of time given to the initiatives of these girls and the very low priority accorded to their praise and encouragement the restrictive nature of the teaching they receive becomes clear. Unlike their highly tolerant colleagues, highly intolerant teachers tend to use a similar pattern of teaching whether they are teaching boys or girls of West Indian origin. Girls of West Indian origin, taught by highly tolerant teachers using a (+) 1-9-4-3-5-2/10-8-6-7 (−) order of teaching priority, have a significantly higher level of self-concept than girls of the same ethnic origin taught by highly intolerant teachers using a (+) 6-7/3-8-10-5-4-2-9-1 (−) order of teaching priority. In classes taught by highly tolerant teachers, girls of West Indian origin record a level of self-concept which is not significantly different from that of other children in the class. The situation is different, however, in those classes taught by highly intolerant teachers where these girls record a level of self-concept which is significantly lower than that of boys and girls of European origin.

Within multi-ethnic classes taught by highly intolerant teachers, significant differences have been discovered between the self-concept levels of children of European origin and children of Asian and of West Indian origins so we conclude by reviewing the style of teaching used by highly intolerant teachers. Our evidence suggests that when teaching pupils individually, teachers who are ethnically highly intolerant use a style of teaching within which they respond less positively to the ideas and feelings expressed by their pupils than highly tolerant teachers. This lack of responsiveness is particularly noticeable when highly intolerant teachers work with individual girls of West Indian origin and, to a lesser extent, with boys of the same ethnic group. During the more content orientated sequences of teaching with individual children, the use of questions figures prominently in the work of highly intolerant teachers and is very conspicuous when they are teaching boys of Asian origin and girls of West Indian origin whilst the balance of direct teaching is weighted very much towards boys and girls of European origin. Another feature of the teaching style of these teachers which seems to favour children of European origin is the greater opportunity which they are given during their talking to initiate ideas and opinions and to introduce questions and new topics into the interaction of the multi-ethnic classroom. The limited opportunity for initiatory talk given to black pupils by highly intolerant teachers is particularly evident in the case of girls of West Indian origin whose white classmates, when they are talking, receive over three times as much opportunity to engage in this type of activity. When girls of West Indian origin contribute to the interaction of the multi-ethnic classroom they do so mainly in direct response to the highly intolerant teacher's questions and, being given very little freedom to express their own ideas, seem to be subjected to a style of teaching which maintains a tight controlling influence. This restrictive feature in the style of teaching of the highly intolerant teacher is displayed in a more explicit fashion in the emphasis these teachers place on projecting their authority. This is illustrated most markedly when individual work takes place with boys and girls of West Indian origin with whom highly intolerant teachers use a balance of teaching which strongly emphasizes directives, criticism and the authority of the teacher at the expense of direct teaching.

During less personal work with the class as a whole, highly intolerant teachers respond to their pupils' ideas and feelings even less positively than during individual teaching which seems to indicate an almost overriding concern with maintaining class control through criticism and directives. This tight teacher control tends to generate an authoritarian atmosphere within which direct teaching to the class as a whole takes place. However, the teacher authority ratio for working with the class as a whole is substantially lower than that when teaching children individually which highlights the emphasis that highly intolerant teachers give to controlling and regulating the behaviour of indiviual pupils. This style of teaching the class as a whole conflated with the style of teaching used during periods of individual teaching by highly intolerant teachers emphasizes the use of questions, directives, criticism and authority statements at the expense of direct teaching. This style of teaching is accentuated by a lack of positive response from the teacher to the contributions of the pupils who are given only minimal opportunity to introduce their initiatives. In those classes taught by teachers who are ethnically highly intolerant it is children of West Indian origin who are most seriously affected by this style of teaching and it is these children who record the lowest levels of self-concept.

The research on which this paper is based [9] was conducted against a backcloth of public concern about the apparent lack of educational progress amongst children of ethnic minority groups. Since the pupil's failure may be seen as a reflection of the teacher's failure the need to reveal something of the dynamics of teaching and learning in the multi-ethnic classroom was considered to be important so the veil of obscurity, which inevitably conceals much of any teacher's work, was raised, albeit very slightly, to expose some elements of the teacher's influence on the self-concept of pupils of different ethnic origins. We conclude that boys and girls of different ethnic origins taught in the same multi-ethnic classroom by the same teacher are likely to receive widely different educational experiences some elements of which may be differentially related to the teacher's gender[35], the types of attitudes held about education and, when present, extreme levels of ethnocentrism. That there is no all-embracing explanation of, or solution to, underachievement in the multi-ethnic classroom seems to be axiomatic especially since the range of influential factors is unknown and makes elusive any simple aetiology of the problem. Bearing in mind that this cross-sectional study investigated what obtained in a relatively small sample and that correlation is not causality the findings should be interpreted with caution, assessed with discretion and ascribed with prudence but they ought not to be disregarded as they contain indications of ways in which multi-ethnic teaching might be modified to the benefit of multi-ethnic learning which is not unimportant as underachievement is a mutual failing.

REFERENCES

1.	Goldman, R. J.	Coloured immigrant children; a survey of research studies and literature on their education and problems in Britain. *Educational Research,* 8; 3; 1966, pp.163-183.
2.	Vernon, P. E.	*Intelligence and Cultural Environment.* Methuen, 1969, p.169.
3.	Derrick, June.	*Teaching English to Immigrants.* Longmans, 1966.
4.	Wight, James, Worsley, F. J. and Norris, R. A.	*Concept 7 – 9,* Arnold for Schools Council, 1972.
5.	Green, Peter A.	*Attitudes of Teachers of West Indian Immigrant Children.* Unpub. M.Phil. thesis, Univ. of Nottingham, 1972, p.67.
6.	Kohl, Herbert.	*36 Children.* Penguin Books, 1973, p.111.
7.	Laing, R. D.	*Self and Others.* Penguin Books, 1975, p.156.
8.	Purkey, W. W.	*Inviting School Success: a self-concept approach to teaching and learning.* Wadsworth Publishing Co. Inc., 1978, pp.22-33.
9.	Green, Peter A.	*Teachers' Influence on the Self-concept of Pupils of Different Ethnic Origins.* Unpub. Ph.D. thesis, Univ. of Durham, 1983.
10.	Piaget, Jean.	*The Origin of Intelligence in the Child.* Penguin Books, 1977, p.157-158.
11.	Rogers, C.	*On Becoming a Person.* Houghton Mifflin, 1961, pp.163-198.
12.	Brehm, J. W. and Cohen, A. R.	*Explorations in Cognitive Dissonance.* Wiley, 1962.
13.	Mistry, Z. D.	*A Study of the self-picture as held by groups of adolescent girls, prior to, and after school leaving age.* Unpub. M.A. thesis, Univ. of London, 1960.
14.	Laing, R. D.	*The Divided Self.* Penguin Books, 1965, p.138.
15.	Davidson, Helen and Lang, Gerhard.	Children's perceptions of their teachers' feelings towards them related to self perception, school achievement and behaviour. *Jnl. Exper. Educ.,* 29, 1960, pp.107-118.
16.	Wylie, Ruth.	*The Self-Concept.* University of Nebraska Press, 1961, p.121.

17.	Mead, G. H.	*'Self'. George Herbert Mead on Social Psychology.* (ed. Strauss, A.), University of Chicago Press, 1964, p.246.
18.	Staines, J. W.	The Self-picture as a Factor in the Classroom. *Brit. Jnl. Educ. Psychol.* 28, 1958, pp.97-111.
19.	Rubovits, Pamela and Maehr, Martin L.	Pygmalion Black and White. *Jnl. of Pers. and Soc. Psychol,* 25, 2, 1973, p.210.
20.	Rubovits, Pamela and Maehr, Martin L.	Op. cit., p.217.
21.	Brownfain, John J.	Stability of the Self-concept as a Dimension of Personality. *Jnl. Ab. and Soc. Psychol.,* 47, July, 1952, pp.597-606.
22.	Rokeach, Milton.	The Nature of Attitudes. *International Encyclopaedia of the Social Sciences.* Macmillan and Free Press, 1968, p.449.
23.	Davey, A.	Racial Awareness in Children and Teacher Education. *Education for Teaching,* Summer 1975, 97, p.29.
24.	Parker, Bob.	Will it happen here? *The Times Educational Supplement,* 3145, 12th September, 1975, p.23.
25.	Goldman, Ronald.	Education and Immigrants, *Psychology and Race,* (ed. Watson, Peter), Penguin Books, 1973, p.350.
26.	Yamamoto, K.	*The Child and His Image.* Houghton Mifflin, 1972, p.60.
27.	Oliver, R. A. C.	Attitudes to Education. *Brit. Jnl. Educ. Studies,* 2, 1, Nov. 1953, p.35.
28.	Peters, R. S.	*Ethics and Education,* Allen and Unwin, 1966, p.100.
29.	Flanders, N. A.	*Analysing Teaching Behaviour.* Addison-Wesley, 1970, p.34.
30.	Warr, P. B. Faust, J. and Harrison, G. J.	A British Ethnocentrism Scale. *Brit. Jnl. soc. clin. Psychol.* 1, 1967, pp.267-277.
31.	Oliver, R. A. C. and Butcher, H. J.	Teachers' attitudes to education. The structure of educational attitudes. *Brit. Jnl. soc. clin. Psychol.* 1, 1962, pp.56-59.
32.	Bledsoe, J. C.	Self-concepts of children and their intelligence, achievement, interests and anxiety. *Jnl. of Individual Psychol.* 20, 1964, pp.55-58.
33.	Coopersmith, S.	*The Antecedents of Self-esteem.* W. H. Freeman and Co., 1967, pp.265-6.

34.   Waetjen, Walter.   ·   (Self-concept as a Learner Scale, University of Maryland, 1963),
                                        Quoted in: *'Social Relationships'* (E.281), The Open University Press, 1972, pp.165-167.

35.   Green, Peter A.   Male and Female Created He Them . . . . . . *Multicultural Teaching,* 2, 1, Autumn, 1983, pp.4-7.

CHAPTER 3

Achievement and Underachievement

1. **Introduction**

2. **The Achievement of West Indian Pupils**

3. **The Achievement of Asian Pupils**

4 **Factors involved in School Performance**
   4.1   Our Interim Report
   4.6   The range of factors involved in achievement and underachievement
   4.10   The IQ Question
   4.15   The inter-relationship of Racial discrimination, socio-economic status, social class and Region.
   4.23   Educational and other factors

5. **Our Conclusions – West Indians**

6. **Our Conclusions – Asians**

7. **The Implications of our Findings**

8. **Summary of Main Conclusions**

9. **References**

Annexes

Annex A – Achievement and Underachievement: Evidence from Young People of Afro-Caribbean and Asian origin

Annex B – Results from the School Leavers' Survey 1981/82: A Paper by DES Statistics Branch

Annex C – The Education of Bangladeshi Children in Tower Hamlets: A Background Paper by the Education Officer, Inner London Education Authority

Annex D – The IQ Question: A Paper by Professor N J Mackintosh and Dr C G N Mascie-Taylor

Annex E – Revised Research Proposal on "Academically Successful Black Pupils", submitted by the Research and Statistics Branch of the Inner London Education Authority.

Annex F – Summary of Main Findings of a Longitudinal Study undertaken by Dr G K Verma

Annex G – A Note on Research: A Paper by Mr J Cornford.

CHAPTER 3

Achievement and Underachievement

1. **Introduction**
1.1   Our terms of reference required us to ".. review .... the educational needs and attainments of children from ethnic minority groups ...." They also required us to ".. give early and particular attention .... to pupils of West Indian origin and to make interim recommendations...." While we considered the attainment of West Indian children at some length in our interim report, we left a number of matters for further investigation in this, our final report, where in addition we examine the attainments of children from other minority groups.

1.2   In our interim report we discussed at length the evidence we received on the factors involved in achievement and under-achievement, from the ethnic minorities themselves, from those in the educational system and from others. This revealed a wide consensus that focused on racial intolerance, prejudice and discrimination as a prime cause, with the emphasis on these factors as they operate within the educational system. To give something of the flavour of this evidence we have included in Annex A to this chapter quotations from the evidence given to the Committee in November 1980 by a group of students assembled by the NUS and from interviews with young people between 15 and 18 years of age, conducted in the Leeds and Bradford area between 1980 and 1983.

1.3   This chapter is concerned with a different type of evidence, namely research and statistics, and any such investigation is beset with difficulties. The evidence is incomplete and sometimes conflicting; in addition there is the immediate problem of deciding what we mean by achievement and underachievement. These are not absolute terms, only relative ones. But relative to what? Moreover, they are terms that are often used indiscriminately in two crucially different senses.

1.4   Turning to the first sense, we have, throughout this report, and in our interim report, made the comparison between the achievement of particular ethnic minorities **and their school-fellows in the White majority.** For the most part this simple comparison is the only one that we can make, but it is not as simple a one as might appear at first sight, mainly because of the complexities of the effects of racial discrimination, social class and socio-economic status, matters we deal with in paras. 4.15 onwards. This comparison is also unsatisfactory in that it gives little indication of the extent to which individuals or groups are achieving **their full potential**—namely achieving in the second sense. It is often supposed, naively, that there is a true measure of innate potential, namely a child's IQ (Intelligence Quotient), but this, as we shall see, is not the case. It may be the best measure of potential that has yet been devised, but it is far from perfect and is influenced by a variety of factors. In short, there is no really reliable indicator of a child's academic potential. Nevertheless, we are clear that many ethnic minority children are not achieving their full potential, regardless of how they compare with the white majority. The problem is further complicated by the fact that many white children are not achieving their full potential either.

1.5 A further point cannot be stressed too often. In our data on achievement and underachievement we frequently quote average performances for different groups. West Indian averages, for instance, tend to be lower than White averages. This however does not mean that all West Indian pupils are achieving less well than whites. Far from it; as Figueroa[1] has recently pointed out, some West Indian children do very well in this country. A statistical average conceals a wide range of scores, some very high, some very low, a fair number on the high side, a fair number on the low side, and most somewhere in the middle, clustering around the average, ie the group mean. In fact there are greater differences **within a group**, where achievement is concerned, than between groups, no matter what their ethnic identity may be. To complicate matters yet further, unexpected differences within groups have often been noted. In some studies, for example, West Indian girls have been found to be performing at a higher level than West Indian boys[2].

2. The achievement of West Indian Pupils

2.1 The origins of this Committee can be traced back to a widespread concern about the level of achievement of West Indian pupils in British schools. In preparing our interim report, however, we were much hampered by the absence of ethnically based examination statistics at a national level. We had therefore to rely in large measure on a variety of research evidence already available on the academic performance of West Indian pupils. This evidence was identified and analysed for us by the National Foundation for Educational Research in their first review[3].
They concluded:

". . . there is an overwhelming consensus: that research evidence shows a strong trend to underachievement of pupils of West Indian origin on the main indicators of academic performance

59

.... Depressing though it is to relate, it appears inescapable that by any standard of comparison, the pupil of West Indian origin is underachieving."

2.2　For the interim report we were able to obtain, through the DES Statistics Branch, some information on examination results on an ethnic basis, using the Department's annual school leavers' survey. This showed that on every measure used, West Indian school leavers were doing markedly less well than White school leavers (see pages 6 – 9 of the interim report). These findings were echoed in much of the evidence we received in the first stage of our work. The overall message was clear. Whatever the reasons, and they are certainly complex, West Indian children are not doing at all well in the educational system.

2.3　Since our interim report and the first NFER review of research were published, a range of other studies have confirmed this picture of West Indian underachievement, including for example, a recent study by Craft and Craft[4] carried out in an Outer London Borough, which showed clearly that, irrespective of social class, West Indian children are markedly under-represented amongst high achievers, and markedly over-represented amongst low achievers. We reproduce a Table from this paper below:

Fifth-form Examination Performance by Ethnicity and Social Class

Examination Performance	White (%)		Asian (%)		West Indian (%)		Other (%)		All (%)		Totals (%)
	MC	WC	MC	WC	MC	WC	MC	WC	MC	WC[a]	
High[b]	31	18	32	16	20	9	26	16	30	16	21
Medium	55	62	58	64	49	51	59	63	56	61	59
Low	14	20	10	21	31	41	16	21	14	23	20
Total (Number)	445	786	165	359	31	176	114	155	761	1476	2237

[a]MC = Middle Class, WC = Working Class. These categories are based on OPCS classification. See original paper for further details.

[b]High, Medium, Low. These categories are based on number of GCE 'O' level and/or CSE passes. See original paper for details.

2.4　When our interim report was published, many Heads and teachers offered further evidence to support our view that West Indian children were indeed underachieving in the educational system. Some however questioned the existence of West Indian underachievement by offering instances from their own experience of children who had been academically successful (in the light of our earlier comments this is in no way surprising), or commented on what they regarded as the shortcomings of the data from the school leavers' survey exercise. The major criticism which was levelled at these data was the absence of any attempt to take account of socio-economic variables and the bearing which these might have had on the findings. We would be the first to acknowledge that such background information would have added to the completeness of the picture and indeed at the time we explored with the DES Statistics Branch whether this additional information could be collected. We were informed however that the nature of the school leavers' survey precluded this being done, most notably because at the time the information is collected, many of the pupils concerned had left school several months previously. It was also suggested that the value of the school leavers' survey exercise data would have been enhanced by the inclusion of more specific and clearly defined ethnic classifications for the groups studied, rather than simply the broad divisions of "Asian", "West Indian" and "all others". In fact those schools which participated in the school leavers' survey exercise were asked to place their leavers in one of **ten** ethnic categories:

West Indian   Subsequently shown as
                                                "WEST INDIAN"

Indian
Pakistani
Bangladeshi   Subsequently aggregated as
East African   "ASIAN"
Other Asian

African
African or West Indian   Subsequently aggregated as
All other descriptions   "ALL OTHER LEAVERS"
Not recorded

The numbers in the sub-categories of "Asian" and "All Other Leavers" were, we were informed, too small to be statistically significant and the findings were therefore aggregated under the general heading—thus permitting a broad comparison to be made on the basis of figures which were statistically significant.

2.5   A further comment which was made by a number of people in relation to the school leavers' survey exercise data in our interim report was that too much reliance should not be placed on information relating to examination results for just one year and that the evidence for West Indian underachievement would be considerably strengthened if it could be shown, by repeating this exercise over several years, that the results for 1978/79 were not atypical but part of a continuing pattern. One of the principal recommendations of our interim report was that steps should be taken to collect a range of educational statistics on an ethnic basis and *inter alia* we recommended that the DES should, with effect from 1 September 1982, introduce ethnic classifications into its school leavers' survey. When it became clear that this recommendation was not going to be implemented by the date we had specified, we asked the DES Statistics Branch to repeat the school leavers' survey exercise for us to enable us to see whether, within the limitations already acknowledged, the relative performance of the groups had altered in any way in the intervening three years. They kindly agreed to assist us again and we reproduce at Annex B their paper summarising the findings of the exercise carried out in relation to the 1981/1982 school leavers' survey and incorporating some statistical comparisons with the previous exercise.

2.6   What is most immediately apparent from the findings of the more recent school leavers' survey exercise is that, as in the previous exercise, West Indian children are again shown to be performing markedly less well than their fellows from other groups on all the measures used:

– In all CSE and GCE 'O' level examinations 6 per cent of West Indians obtained five or more higher grades compared with 17 per cent of Asians and 19 per cent of "all other leavers" in these LEAs;

– In CSE English and GCE 'O' level English Language 15 per cent of West Indians obtained higher grades compared with 21 per cent of Asians and 29 per cent of "all other leavers" in these LEAs;

– In CSE and GCE 'O' level Mathematics 8 per cent of West Indians obtained higher grades compared with 21 per cent of Asians and 21 per cent of "all other leavers" in these LEAs;

– At GCE 'A' Level 5 per cent of West Indians gained one or more pass compared with 13 per cent of Asians and 13 per cent of "all other leavers" in these LEAs;

– 1 per cent of West Indians went on to University compared with 4 per cent of Asians and 4 per cent of "all other leavers" in these LEAs; and

– 1 per cent of West Indians went on to full-time degree courses in further education compared with 5 per cent of Asians and 5 per cent of "all other leavers" in these LEAs.

Less marked but equally clear from the figures however is that there have been some statistically significant improvements in the relative performance of the West Indian leavers in each of the areas highlighted above, when compared with the findings of the previous exercise:

– In all CSE and GCE 'O' level examinations, the percentage of West Indians obtaining five or more higher grades has increased from 3 per cent in 1978/79 to 6 per cent in 1981/82;

– In CSE English and CSE 'O' Level English Language, not only has the percentage of West Indians obtaining no graded result fallen from 31 per cent in 1978/79 to 25 per cent in 1981/82, but the percentage obtaining higher grades has also increased from 9 per cent in 1978/79 to 15 per cent in 1981/82;

– In CSE and GCE 'O' level Mathematics, not only has the percentage of West Indians obtaining no graded result fallen from 47 per cent in 1978/79 to 45 per cent in 1981/82, but the percentage obtaining higher grades has also increased from 5 per cent in 1978/79 to 8 per cent in 1981/82; and

– At GCE 'A' level, the percentage of West Indians obtaining at least one 'A' level pass has increased from 2 per cent in 1978/79 to 5 per cent in 1981/82.

We are of course encouraged by these signs, albeit limited, of a narrowing in the gap between the performance of West Indians and their school fellows from other groups. Such improvements have been noted in a number of studies over the last two decades, and have been related to length of stay and length of schooling in Britain – see for example Tomlinson[5] and [6]; also Fogelman[7]. We would hope that they may also be due to increased sensitivity on the part of schools. Be this as it may, we believe they offer scant grounds for complacency and we hope that no one will be tempted to interpret them as an indication that there is no longer any need for concern about the performance of West Indian pupils. On the contrary, these further data strengthen our belief that, as we stated in our interim report:

> *"West Indian children as a group are underachieving in our education system . . . . (and) . . . . this should be a matter of deep concern not only to all those involved in education but also the whole community."*

63

3. The Achievement of Asian Pupils

3.1 In considering the performance of Asian pupils we have again been hampered by the absence of ethnically based statistics at a national level. A considerable amount of research has however been undertaken on their performance, and the broad consensus of these studies was described in the following terms by the NFER in their second review of research[8]:

> *"Asians do not in general perform worse at public examinations than indigenous peers from the same schools and neighbourhoods . . . . Most of the studies point to performance levels on the part of Asians that either match or exceed those of indigenous peers. Findings usually relate to overall examination performance; when individual subject breakdowns are given, English often stands out as the area of weakness."*

School Leavers' Survey Exercise Data

3.2 Both the initial school leavers' survey exercise (1978/79) and the further exercise (1981/82) obtained data relating to Asian leavers[1]. In general terms the findings of the two exercises (see Annex B), taken together, show Asian leavers to be achieving very much on a par with, and in some cases marginally better than, their school fellows from all other groups in the same LEAs in terms of the various measures used:

– At GCE 'A' level the percentage of Asians gaining one or more pass, in both years studied, mirrored exactly the "all other leavers" figures: 12 per cent in 1978/79 and 13 per cent in 1981/82;

– In CSE and GCE 'O' level Mathematics the percentage of Asians obtaining higher grades in the 1981/82 exercise was the same as for "all other leavers" 21 per cent;

– The same percentage of Asian leavers as "all other leavers" went on to University in both 1978/79: 3 per cent, and 1981/82: 4 per cent.

The major divergence from this pattern of achievement was in relation to CSE and GCE 'O' level English Language – see Table 5 in Annex B – with a significantly higher percentage of Asian leavers obtaining no graded result compared with "all other leavers" in the same LEA's, and the percentage obtaining higher grades being also significantly lower. The marked difference in performance in this

---

[1] As explained in paragraph 3.4 above, the exercises in fact collected data relating to five Asian categories – Indian, Pakistani, Bangladeshi, East African Asian and "Other Asian" but, in order for the group size to be statistically significant, the sub group figures were subsequently aggregated under the overall category Asian.

particular subject may well, of course, be a major contributory factor in the lower percentage of Asian leavers obtaining "5 or more higher grades" in the Table of overall 'O' level and CSE achievements – see Table 4 in Annex A.

3.3   While the evidence about school performance of Asian pupils is not unanimous, the majority of studies, in common with the School Leavers Survey exercises, show an average level of performance, other than in English Language, that is generally on a par with that of indigenous White children. Recently Craft and Craft[4], for instance, in an extensive study (see para 2.3 above), have shown that the examination performance of Asian pupils at fifth form level, whether categorised as middle class or working class, compares quite closely with that of their White School fellows. And a smaller study by Brooks and Singh[9] reaches the interesting conclusion that:

> *"It is the similarities between White and Asian performance which are impressive, rather than any differences."*

3.4   Although there is an absence of ethnically based statistics at a national level in the education field, many multi-racial schools collect information about the performance of their ethnic minority pupils as part of their normal self-evaluation. When, therefore, we came to consider the academic performance of Asian pupils, a number of schools were able to supply us with information about the relative achievement of different groups. In the absence of nationally agreed categories, the classifications used by the schools varied widely, from a straightforward division between "ethnic minority" and "White", or "Asian" and "West Indian", to breakdowns between Asian sub-groups on a country of origin basis (Pakistan, East Africa, India), a religious basis (Muslim, Sikh, Hindu) or on the basis of home language (Punjabi, Gujerati). This lack of a common approach to classification meant that we were unable to base any firm conclusions on the data we received as to the relative performance of the Asian sub-categories. In by far the majority of the schools which provided us with information however, it was clear that pupils of Asian origin as a group were achieving in examination terms, very much on a par with their school fellows from other groups, except where they were suffering from linguistic difficulties. The following extract from the evidence of one school is typical of the responses received:

> *"Asians as a group tend to do well in examinations . . . . there appears to be no special trend in examination success . . . . different from those of the indigenous population."*

3.5   This may not however be the full story, and one matter has frequently been raised with us, namely the extent to which statistics on the performance of Asians as a group, may mask considerable variations in the performance of different sub-groups. As we have explained earlier, although the School Leavers' surveys exercise collected data relating to some of the sub-groups, the numbers were too small to provide conclusions that were statistically significant. In their second review of research[8], however, the NFER do draw attention to evidence which bears on this question as does Tomlinson[2]. Despite limitations, both in terms of sample size and research design, there **are** indications of differences in performance between some of the sub-groups, but with one exception these differences are not great. Children of Bangladeshi origin, however, have been shown in a number of instances to be performing markedly less well than their school fellows in other groups, both minority and majority. We discuss this matter later on, and reproduce in full as Annex C a paper by the Education Officer of the Inner London Education Authority.

4.   Factors involved in School Performance

Our Interim Report

4.1   Diagnosing and evaluating the factors involved in achievement and underachievement is full of difficulties, and we turn first to the conclusions of our interim report. The factor most frequently and forcibly put to our Committee was undoubtedly racism within schools, mainly centring around teachers' low expectations of West Indian children; this we accepted as significant. But as we pointed out in our conclusions (p70):

> *"Whilst we cannot accept that racism, intentional or unintentional, alone accounts for the underachievement of West Indian children in our schools we believe that when taken together with, for example, negative teacher attitudes and an inappropriate curriculum, racism does play a major part in their underachievement."*

4.2   In the course of our interim report we listed a number of other factors that needed further consideration. In particular we discussed (p15) the pressures on West Indian families and concluded that West Indian parents are caught up in a cycle of cumulative disadvantage and went on to quote the well-known and significant statement in the Government White Paper "Racial Discrimination 1975"[10] which pointed out:

> *". . . .relatively low paid or low status jobs for the first generation of immigrants go hand in hand with poor overcrowded living*

conditions and a depressed environment. If for example, job opportunities, educational facilities, housing and environmental conditions are all poor, the next generation will grow up less well equipped to deal with difficulties facing them. The wheel comes full circle, as the second generation find themselves trapped in poor jobs and poor housing."

It is significant that the Scarman Inquiry of 1981[11] which followed the disturbances of that time, argued forcibly that racial prejudice and discrimination, particularly in the areas of housing, education and employment, contributed extensively to this cumulative disadvantage.

4.3   On page 20 we went on to consider the 1980 ILEA Literacy Survey(12), which showed that reading attainment of West Indian children was low at eight years, and remained low at school leaving age. The survey examines a number of possible factors which might have led to this result – length of education in this country, social deprivation, linguistic handicaps, teacher expectations and the self image of the child. It finds that each of these factors plays some part in the overall picture of underachievement, and concludes:

"A major contributory factor would seem to be adverse environmental circumstances. When factors of social deprivation . . . . were taken into account the difference in the average attainment of West Indians and Whites . . . . was halved. The possible effects of linguistic interference and teacher attitudes and expectations could not be measured directly but it seems probable that they have an adverse effect on West Indians, particularly when coupled with adverse social circumstances."

4.4   Our interim report was widely represented as putting forward racism **in the education system** as the sole cause of underachievement, in spite of the fact that we considered racism in the wider social context as well, and concluded that all these aspects of racism, put together, were the major factor. Despite this misunderstanding of our conclusions, the report did, we believe, give encouragement and support to teachers and others concerned about West Indian underachievement, though it has to be said that elsewhere it was subjected to some sharp criticism.

4.5   Since we presented figures that showed Asians on average to be performing very much on a par with whites, and since it was argued by our critics that Asians were no less subject to racism than West Indians, it was said that the prominence we had given to this factor must be misplaced and that other factors must therefore be at the root of the problem. Low West Indian IQ scores were mentioned as the real cause, and, as we have noted earlier, the absence of any consideration of socio-economic factors was also criticised. It became clear to us that we must examine these criticisms in detail in the final report, as indeed we had, in our interim report, declared our intention of doing.

The range of factors involved in Achievement and Underachievement
4.6   Many research workers who have studied the matter in depth, have listed the wide range of factors that may be involved, and have gone out of their way to emphasise that the problem is a very complex one with no single cause, but rather a large number of inter-related causes – see for example Jeffcoate,[13] and[14] Mabey[15] and the ILEA Report on Race, Sex and Class[16] as well as the study by Tomlinson[2] and both NFER Reports[3] and[8]. The same point emerges in the study we commissioned from one of our members, Dr. Verma, which we consider later in this chapter – see also Annex F. The argument has recently been put particularly succinctly and readably by Dr. Bhikhu Parekh, formerly a member of our Committee[17].

4.7   Under the heading "Some explanations of underachievement" Dr Parekh lists the following:

"First, the low attainment of West Indian children is, according to some commentators, easily and adequately explained in terms of their genetic intellectual inferiority. This view of Eysenck and others is far more widely held than is realised . . . ."

"A second explanation accounts for West Indian children's low attainment in terms of the structure of their family . . . ."

"Third, some commentators explain the fact of low attainment in terms of the materially and culturally disadvantaged West Indian home. While the previous explanation blames the parent and the traditional structure of the family, this one blames their economic conditions and the character of the wider social structure . . . ."

"Fourth, some explain . . . . low attainment in terms of racism both in society at large and in the school . . . ."

"Fifth, some hold the structure and ethos of the school responsible . . . . because many a school has renounced its traditional task of educating its pupils and helping them achieve

basic intellectual skills, in favour of dabbling in social work and psychotherapy . . . . they underplay the value of formal methods of teaching, hard work and discipline . . . ."

"Sixth, some explain the low attainment of the West Indian child in terms of the failure of the educational authorities to identify and meet his educational needs . . . ."

"In addition to the above, several other explanations are also advanced from time to time . . . ."

4.8 Dr Parekh goes on, under the heading "The underlying assumptions" to explain why the debate has been so confused and unsatisfactory:

"First, the debate is vitiated by what I might call the fallacy of the single factor. The participants tend to look for one specific factor, be it class, racism, West Indian family, West Indian culture, the school or educational system, to explain the fact of underachievement. This is obviously an inherently impossible enterprise. Not even a relatively simple natural phenomenon like the falling of an apple or the dropping of a stone can be explained in terms of a single cause . . . ."

"Second the debate is led astray by two false assumptions, namely that all West Indian children fail and all Asian children succeed . . . . thanks to these assumptions, some have argued that the reasons for West Indian children's underachievement cannot be found in the factors they share in common with the Asians . . . . thus racism, either in the society at large or in the school, is dismissed as an important factor on the ground that otherwise we would not be able to explain Asian success . . . . as we saw, the assumptions are false . . . . (the argument) is invalid also because it wrongly assumes that the same factor must always produce the same results.

"Third, much of the debate is conducted at too abstract a level to connect with the reality of the school or the child, or to permit sensible discussion, or to have clear policy implications . . . ."

"Fourth, with few notable exceptions, the participants are deeply committed to specific theories and either ignore others or dismiss them with a bundle of sweeping generalisations . . . ."

Fifth, as we would expect, a debate on so sensitive an issue . . . can hardly remain apolitical. By its very nature every

69

*explanation points an accusatory finger at a particular target
.... Not surprisingly, the group which suspects that it might be
blamed.... tends to marshal whatever arguments it can against
the threatening explanation, or to demand impossible standards
of proof and conceptual rigour, while not bothering to provide
these for its own alternative explanation.... Like every political
debate, the debate has an ideological character...."*

4.9   It is not to be expected that this or any Committee of Inquiry
could disentangle all the many threads of this complex web. But we
are very conscious, as Dr Parekh also points out, that too often
society has "sought ideological shelter behind the unsatisfactory
character of the debate and used it as an excuse for inaction, arguing
against every proposed course of action that the factors involved are
not the only ones, the evidence is not conclusive, and so on". We
therefore add what evidence we can to the debate, and put forward
our collective opinion in the sections that follow.

The IQ Question

4.10   Scores in IQ (Intelligence Quotient) Tests were for a long time
used as a measure of academic potential, and a pupil's score in such
tests undoubtedly played a part in determining the set, stream or
band in which he was placed, and this in turn was liable to condition
the expectations of individual teachers, and indeed of the educational
system as a whole. The high proportion of West Indian children
placed in ESN schools as a result of such tests was first pointed
out by Coard[18] in 1971. Present practice, however, has changed
markedly, and the limitations of IQ tests are now much more clearly
appreciated within the educational system. Nevertheless, there
remains in society at large a view, quite widely but as we shall see
incorrectly held, namely that West Indian underachievement is the
result of low IQs. To what extent this misconception has contributed
to racist attitudes in general and a feeling in particular that West
Indian underachievement is inevitable, is a matter for conjecture.
But it is, as we said in our interim report, a matter that we decided
we must examine, and this we have now done.

4.11   Interest in the differences in IQ scores between different ethnic
groups stems from the United States, where it was discovered, a long
time ago, that US Blacks scored substantially below US Whites.
There has been less research in this country, but a similar, if less
pronounced difference, has been found between children of West
Indian origin and the indigenous population. It must be emphasised
here that the argument only centres round **average** scores. **Individual**
scores vary greatly, both within the West Indian community, and
within the White one. It follows that many West Indian children

have higher IQ scores than many White children. It is when the averages are calculated that West Indians are rather consistently seen to be scoring less highly than Whites.

4.12   The heated debate that has followed these findings, has centred round the cause of the difference. Jensen, in the US, and Eysenck, in this country, amongst others, have argued that it is little more than a reflection of the respective difference in average intelligence, and that a significant part of this difference is due to genetic inheritance. Others, for a variety of reasons, have disagreed.

4.13   This is a complex, difficult and sensitive area, and we have been very fortunate in getting a distinguished psychologist, Professor Nicholas Mackintosh of the University of Cambridge to review the field for us, and to carry out some fresh investigations. His paper, prepared in association with his colleague Dr Mascie-Taylor, is reproduced in full as Annex D to this chapter. The paper is a lucid and cogent exposition of the different arguments involved in the controversy, and we would urge that it be widely and carefully read. The authors are duly cautious about the evidence, but they have, we believe, disposed of the idea that West Indian underachievement can be explained away by reference to IQ scores.

4.14   We have not attempted to summarise Professor Mackintosh's and Dr Mascie-Taylor's rigorous and balanced argument, if only because they summarise it very clearly themselves (pp48-52, Annex D to the Chapter). In brief they show that much of the difference in IQ scores between West Indian and indigenous children appears to be related to differences between them in such factors as parental occupation, income, size of family, degree of overcrowding, and neighbourhood. All of these factors are related to IQ among Whites, and when they are taken into account, the difference between West Indian and indigenous children is sharply reduced.

The inter-relationship of Racial discrimination, Socio-economic status, Social class and Region.
4.15   Racial discrimination, in a variety of ways, affects Socio-economic status, Social class and Region, and some explanation of these terms, which may not be universally familiar, is necessary before we go any further. Socio-economic status, or SES for short, and often referred to as socio-economic circumstances or socio-economic variables, is an umbrella for a variety of reasonably precise measures of the degree of affluence or deprivation of an individual, a family or a group. What is the level of income, what is the level of

unemployment, is there overcrowding or ill-health, are they living in an unfavourable environment, and so on? Social class is a more blanket way of referring to the same thing, and is based on categories of employment eg professional, intermediate, skilled non-manual, skilled manual, partly skilled manual and unskilled manual. These categories are often grouped together in various ways eg middle class and working class, descriptions which, it should be mentioned, do not carry all the overtones of everyday usage. Finally there is the term region, which refers to the sort of neighbourhood in which people live eg inner city, suburban etc. Socio-economic status, social class and region, for the White majority, are determined, without doubt, by a great many factors, ranging from parental circumstances to educational qualifications. But where ethnic minorities are concerned, there is a further crucial factor, racial discrimination, which, as we discuss in later sections of this chapter, can, and frequently does, lead to poorer jobs, higher levels of unemployment, poorer housing in poorer areas, and in many instances poorer school achievement and fewer qualifications, than are to be found in the White majority.

4.16 Thanks to the pioneering work of J W B Douglas and many others, it has long been known, where White children are concerned, that poor school performance is closely correlated with low socio-economic status. It is also well known, as Professor Mackintosh points out, that IQ scores and low SES are similarly related. The precise interplay of cause and effect in these correlations is by no means fully understood, but is generally accepted as involving a great many factors, including level of employment, quality of housing, and level of parental education, see for example Rutter and Madge[19] and Mortimore and Blackstone[20]. Nevertheless the **phenomenon** is so marked and so consistent as to leave no doubt about its significance. The fact that two things are correlated, however, does not prove that one is the cause of the other. It could be that both are caused by one or more quite other factors. At the same time it does not take much imagination to see why poor socio-economic circumstances might have a marked effect on school performance. There are first, of all, **material** reasons. It has long been realised that they can lead to poorer health and nutrition, and that they can lead to overcrowding, and little space and quiet for children to work. There are also **psychological** reasons. Families where parents have to work long or unsocial hours, and have to be out when children are at home, with the best will in the world cannot readily provide as much adult talk, or as much interest and encouragement in schooling as, say, a more affluent home. Region introduces a further complication. The poorest socio-economic circumstances are usually to be found in (often decaying) inner city areas, and here again the interplay of cause and effect is complex. On the one hand the poorest people are only likely to be able to afford to buy or rent in such areas, or, if they seek local authority housing, to find it in such areas. They therefore gravitate to these neighbourhoods, and having arrived there, they find an extra dimension of deprivation in terms of social amenities and available work.

4.17   As with almost all sociological problems, it is not possible to reach unchallengeable conclusions, and it may be that all the factors we have discussed play some part. Nevertheless, the weight of evidence about the direct effects of socio-economic deprivation make it likely that this is a very important factor (see references in para 4.19). In any case, the fact that it clearly operates across ethnic lines, revealing a marked correlation with school performance for Whites as well as all ethnic minorities (see again para 4.19), means that we must take account of it before reaching conclusions about achievement and underachievement, defined either as a comparison with White peers or with potential.

4.18   There is, of course, a very wide spectrum of socio-economic circumstances in the White population as a whole, but in the light of our comments above, we would expect to find the lowest socio-economic circumstances and the poorest school performance figures amongst children living in inner urban areas. This, indeed, is the case. A close examination of the school leavers' survey exercise tables in our interim report, and in Annex B of this chapter, shows, for instance, that the performance of "all other leavers" (mainly White children) is noticeably poorer than the national average. Since the school leavers' survey exercise was conducted in inner urban LEA's (where the largest amount of deprivation is to be found), this is exactly what would be expected. Had the comparison been with leavers in areas more affluent than the national average, the disparity would have been greater still. It follows that a large number of white as well as of minority children, are not achieving all they might, given more favourable circumstances. So much is common knowledge, and emerges very clearly from a recent Statistical Bulletin published by DES(21).

4.19   We turn now to the more complex question of socio-economic circumstances in relation to ethnic minority children. It would be surprising if social and economic deprivation did not affect them as it affects White children, and there is indeed clear evidence that it does. Professor Mackintosh, having discussed this effect as it shows up with IQ, analysed some of the same data in relation to school performance, and concluded:

*".... not surprisingly, they show that much, but by no means
all of the initial difference between either West Indian or Asian
and White children is accounted for by the differences in their
social circumstances."*

The data in question are not extensive, and the studies from which
they are derived were carried out some years ago. There is however
much other evidence besides. We have quoted the work of Craft and
Craft(4) earlier in this chapter, and an examination of the Table in
para 2.3, taken from the summary of their findings, shows the effect
of social class (as defined earlier) with striking clarity. Whether White,
Asian or West Indian, the percentage of children in the high
achievement category is about twice as high for the middle class as
for the working class. In the low achievement category, the situation
is reversed. We referred in our interim report, and again in this report
(para 4.3) to the ILEA Literacy Survey[12] which showed that half
of the discrepancy between West Indian and White children was
explicable in terms of these same factors. Fogelman,[7] in an interesting paper referred to earlier, finds socio-economic effects to be
important, and much other research points in the same
direction—see reviews by NFER[3] and[8], Tomlinson[2] and
Mortimore and Blackstone[20]. **How** important these effects may be,
is not precisely answerable, and we leave the question to a later
section. For the time being we only reiterate the view of those who
have studied the matter in detail, namely that social class, socio-
economic circumstances and region **are** very important. Indeed, the
major and influential reports by Coleman[22] and Jencks[23] in the
United States several years ago, placed considerably greater weight
on the signficance of social background than on school factors, in
terms of educational outcome.

4.21   At this stage in the argument we need to look at the extent to
which ethnic minorities are economically and socially deprived. If
they were no more deprived, on average, than the White majority
then any underachievement by comparison with their White peers
in similar circumstances, could only be due to factors other than
social class, socio-economic circumstances, or region. But in fact
there is a great deal of evidence that many minority groups **are**
substantially more deprived than Whites, and this must increase the
significance of these factors. This evidence is collected together in
the masterly third PSI (formerly PEP) Survey[24]. The Employment
Gazette[25] also provides much recent evidence. We do not attempt
to summarise the massive PSI report in any detail, and would refer
the reader to the work itself, in particular to the last chapter. Suffice
it to say that though there are many differences of detail, ethnic

74

minorities in general suffer from higher levels of unemployment than Whites, and when employed have lower incomes. Their housing, in addition, is poorer than White housing. Moreover the survey finds that although there have been a few improvements, there has been depressingly little change since the previous survey (1974).

4.22 The PSI report goes a considerable way towards analysing why there should be this marked level of ethnic minority social and economic deprivation, over and above that of the majority White population. As they point out:

"One purpose of this type of Survey is to obtain information on the total impact of racial disadvantage on the black population (the Report uses the term black to include all non-white minorities). This requires a detailed survey because it is important that our comparisons between white people and black people take into account the other differences that presently exist between them: for example in this study the analysis of job levels can be adjusted for any differences of qualifications and English fluency. It is also important to understand from the outset that no direct evidence of racial discrimination is available from a survey like this, except in the reports of individuals who have reason to suspect that they have been its victims. For objective evidence about the levels of discrimination we must look to other studies, and in particular the research carried out by making test applications to employers and other bodies and observing the responses to black and white applicants."

(A number of these studies are listed on page 15 of the PSI Report, and we would add to this list the recent CRE Report[26] on Race and Council Housing in Hackney.)

Despite these caveats, the report leaves us in no doubt that a substantial part of ethnic minority deprivation is, in fact, due to racial discrimination of various sorts. It is of some interest to learn where the minorities themselves laid the blame for this treatment.[24]

"Several bodies stand out from the others, however, with a significant proportion of Asians and West Indians claiming they discriminated: those were employers, private landlords and the police. Among West Indians, concern is also expressed, though to a lesser extent, about the Courts, Housing Department and Schools."

4.22 In conclusion, then, we are left in no doubt that the ethnic minority communities are, on average, markedly more socially and economically deprived than the White majority, though to an extent and in a manner that varies as between different groups. Secondly this extra deprivation is almost certainly due, in substantial part, to racial prejudice and discrimination. And lastly, this extra level of deprivation in turn contributes substantially to underachievement at school. The range of special programmes supported by successive Governments to provide additional resources to counter the effects of deprivation and to foster equality of opportunity, indicates clearly the significance that society has attached to socio-economic factors. Nevertheless we are clear that it would be quite wrong to assume that low socio-economic status must lead **inevitably** to low school attainment. Clearly it does not, since many children in such circumstances do well. Any teacher who sought to explain away, or who **expected** low achievement as the inevitable result of poor circumstances, would be failing in his task as an educator, and thereby seriously letting down the children and young people in his care.

Educational and other factors

4.23 It will be recalled that in preparing our interim report we received a great deal of written and oral comment, especially from the West Indian community, pointing to racism within schools as an important factor in the underachievement of West Indian children. We concluded that:

> *". . . . there seemed to be a fairly widespread opinion among teachers to whom we spoke that West Indian pupils inevitably caused difficulties. These pupils were, therefore, seen either as problems to be put up with or, at best, deserving sympathy. Such negative and patronising attitudes, focusing as they do on West Indian children as problems, cannot lead to a constructive or balanced approach to their education . . . ."*

> *"Teachers should be prepared to examine and reappraise their own attitudes and actions in an effort to ensure that their behaviour towards and expectations of ethnic minority pupils are not influenced by stereotyped and negative views."*

> *". . . . discrimination, both intentional and unintentional, can have an adverse effect on how a West Indian child sees himself and his ethnic group in relation to majority White society which in turn can have a bearing on his motivation and achievement. This is clearly a complex and difficult issue . . . . We shall be looking further at this whole issue, in relation to all ethnic minority children, for our main Report."*

4.24   We have not found it easy to take these matters much further. Professor Mackintosh in his Report (Annex D) looked for research evidence that might point to any effects of teacher expectations on IQ scores:

> *"Intuitively one can readily see how constant denigration, whether overt or more subtle, might sap a child's confidence in his own abilities, and cause him to fail."*

But he comes to the conclusion that such research on West Indian children as there is, does not, on balance, and perhaps surprisingly, seem to indicate such an effect. This, however, is not necessarily unexpected. IQ tests are designed to be as free from outside influences as possible. When, however, we turn to the large volume of research that bears on the effect of teacher stereotyping and expectations on school performance, the evidence can only be described as confusing. The problem is reviewed at length by Tomlinson[2], and Taylor in her first NFER survey[3]. Taylor concludes:

> *"Overall the evidence on teacher expectation and attitudes does not really permit firm conclusions as to whether teacher expectations for black children are a determining influence on their school life and performance. Whilst it is most likely that some teachers do have negative perceptions of and attitudes towards (some) black pupils, it would also appear that many teachers are sensitively and actively concerned to evolve a consistent and fair policy towards and treatment of their black pupils . . . ."*

A further interesting comment is to be found in a rigorous critique of the whole teacher expectancy argument by Nash[27]:

> *"We know that expectancy effects can be found and that they cannot always be replicated, we know that the most subtle experiment may fail to show expectancy effects and we know that they will turn up (contrarily) in quite unexpected contexts."*

In short, some teachers hold stereotype attitudes and some do not, while sometimes the teacher expectancy effect works and sometimes it does not. This is hardly surprising; the educational process involves a complicated interaction between teacher and taught, teacher attitudes and stereotypes no doubt vary greatly, as do pupil attitudes. Clearly we are faced with a very complex and ill-understood phenomenon.

4.25 This conflict of evidence is nevertheless puzzling, for it is not only West Indian parents who believe that schools are not bringing out the best from their children. There can hardly be any parent anywhere who does not think that some teachers bring out the best in their children, while others do not. We come therefore to the tentative conclusion that we ourselves, those who give evidence to us, and those who have researched into the question, may perhaps be taking too simplistic a view of the matter. It is for this reason that we touched on the work of Green and reproduced his paper in Annex B of Chapter 2. Despite the cautious disclaimers at the end of his paper, we think his work suggests an interesting new approach to the problem. We also think the vebatim remarks quoted by two researchers (see Annex G to this Chapter), give much food for thought. In short, while we do not retreat from our earlier conclusions about the influence of teachers, we do think the problem is complex and subtle, and needs much more research if it is ever to be understood in full. To use a medical metaphor, until it **is** understood, it will be difficult to prescribe with certainty the treatment that is likely to be most effective.

4.26 Where teacher attitudes and expectancy effects are concerned, the research evidence is clearly conflicting and confusing. In many other areas where comparable factors have been thought to be important, in the school, in the home or elsewhere, the research evidence, is, once again, all too often confusing. The question, for instance, of whether underachievement can be attributed to low self-esteem, generated by racist treatment in school or elsewhere, has been much disputed and much researched – see references and comments in Taylor[3], Tomlinson[2], Figueroa[1] and Jeffcoate[14] as well as Thomas[28]. We can only conclude that the issues involved are certainly complex and that there is now a good deal of evidence that low self-esteem amongst ethnic minority children is not, contrary to what one might expect, the widespread phenomenon that has often been supposed. The related question of motivation is equally complex and as Verma[29] and Verma and Ashworth[30] have shown, depends on attitudes in school, in society and in the family.

4.27 The extent of the conflict and confusion that prevails in so many areas of research on the achievement of ethnic minorities has, no doubt, many causes. Some of it is simply not very good research and suffers from some or even all of the defects vividly listed by Parekh—(see para 4.9). But above all, we believe, it must be attributed to the complexity of the problems, and the fact that there are many underlying causes. We have emphasised this point repeatedly, and do so again. Nevertheless, we believe that the message is slowly getting across, and not only in the world of research. In this context we draw attention to a paper that has reached us recently, and which makes the point very clearly. Blatchford *et al* [31], examining the influence of ethnic origin, gender and home on entry skills (literacy and numeracy) into infant schools, looked at a large number of possible factors, and by means of multiple regression analysis separated out those that were important and those that were not. In this case three factors stood out—parental teaching, the extent of parental education (particularly maternal) and parental views on education. But even these three only accounted for one quarter of the variation in children's entry skill scores. The conclusions are interesting and important in themselves, but the clear demonstration of the complexity of the problem is perhaps even more striking.

4.28   In the light of the difficulty in reaching helpful conclusions from existing research about the factors, other than socio-economic status, which are involved in achievement and underachievement, we decided that a major study was needed to unravel further the many issues involved, believing them to consist of a complex **combination of factors**, operating differentially both **in school and out of school**. We were fortunate that Dr Mortimore, the Director of Research and Statistics at the Inner London Education Authority (ILEA) approached us about undertaking such a study on our behalf, designed to provide information on the factors— in the school, in the community and at home—which had enabled West Indian pupils in a range of ILEA schools to be successful in GCE 'O' level and CSE examinations. The proposed study closely resembled that suggested by the NFER in their first review of research [3]:

> "A major in-depth investigation . . . . to study and compare the relation between the performance of West Indian pupils, their family background and factors internal to school. The emphasis in such a study would be on home—school interaction and type, size and atmosphere of school, necessitating carefully matched samples for detailed study, focusing particularly on those children who were comparatively high achievers."

At our suggestion, the ILEA proposal was enlarged to include Asian as well as West Indian and White pupils, and to give greater attention to the influence of racism. A copy of the revised research proposal is attached as Annex E. We were also concerned that a study which was wholly London-based might not be properly representative. We therefore explored the possibility of replicating the work in LEA's in the Midlands and the North of England, thereby increasing the sample to well over 1000 pupils.

4.29 The researchers embarked on informal consultations about the project with interested organisations, communities and individuals, but it soon became evident that there were serious reservations, and since the research team felt that the co-operation of teachers and the ethnic minority communities was essential to the success of the project, they decided that they had no option but to abandon it. Some members of the Committee regret the loss of this study, believing that it might have provided valuable insights into a difficult problem. Others were sceptical about its value and feasibility.

4.30 With the loss of this research project, we were anxious to find other data concerned with the factors influencing the performance of ethnic minority pupils, including those of West Indian origin. We were fortunate that one of our members, Dr G K Verma, had already collected some relevant data in the connection with a longitudinal study he was undertaking in the Leeds and Bradford area on "Ethnicity and Achievement in British Schools", and that he was able to draw out for us from this data some broad conclusions on the main factors influencing the examination achievement of children from the different ethnic groups. A summary by Dr Verma of the main findings of his study is attached as Annex F of this chapter. As the summary makes clear, the study was not intended to compare directly the levels of achievement of different ethnic groups, but rather to identify the way in which different factors influenced the high and the low achievers within each group. The findings raise a number of interesting points, and highlight yet again the complexity of the factors involved and the need for further research in this area.

4.31 Finally, this Chapter would be incomplete if we were not to note the changing response of schools to the presence of ethnic minority pupils, and the relevance of this to underachievement. At the outset, as we discuss in detail later in our report, the aim was assimilation, and LEA's concentrated their efforts on E2L work. But in the past few years, and in part, we would like to think, as a result of our interim report, things have begun to change. More pluralist aims have come to the fore, more positive attitudes towards pupil bilingualism and dialect differences are apparent, and there are stronger moves towards respect for diversity through curriculum permeation. We have noted, in Paragraph 2.6 that there are signs of improved pupil performance, and we would like to think that these are the result of changing school attitudes. But there is a long way to go, and only time will tell.

5. Our Conclusions—West Indians

5.1 There is no doubt that West Indian children, as a group, and on average, are underachieving, both by comparison with their school fellows in the White majority, as well as in terms of their potential, notwithstanding that some are doing well. In our interim report we laid particular stress on teachers' stereotyped attitudes and negative expectations as likely to be an important factor in this under-achievement. But we also listed a whole range of other factors to be examined in more detail in our final report. This, as best we can, we have now done, and we are led, not so much to revise our earlier conclusions, as to add to them. This is not surprising—we originally pointed out that we were dealing with a complex problem and that there were likely to be a variety of factors involved.

5.2 Our interim report was criticised on two grounds in particular, first, that it failed to consider IQ, held by many to be responsible for West Indian underachievement, and second that we paid altogether too little attention to social class and socio-economic factors, long known to be closely related to achievement amongst White children. We turn first to IQ where, we believe, we have been able to make an important contribution, thanks to an impressive research paper which we commissioned from Professor Mackintosh and Dr Mascie-Taylor. The authors show that the often quoted gap between West Indian and White IQ scores is sharply reduced when account is taken of socio-economic factors—contrary to general belief, IQ scores, like school performance, are related to these factors. It follows from their work that low West Indian average IQ scores are not a major factor in underachievement, and as the authors point out, may well be of no more significance than the well-known average difference in IQ scores between twins and singletons within a family. As the authors put it:

> "We do not think that this matters and we should rightly question the good sense or good will of anyone who claimed that it did."

5.3 IQ has long been a sensitive and emotive issue. We hope that it can now cease to be so, and we turn to another matter which has tended to be only slightly less emotive, namely social class and socio-economic status (we use both terms in the technical sense, as measures of deprivation, and we have discussed them in more detail in the previous section). It has long been known, where White children are concerned, that poverty and poor housing are associated with underachievement at school, in all probability for a range of perfectly understandable reasons that we have discussed in the previous section. It is now clear, as one would expect, that ethnic minority children suffer in a similar way. But, as we have seen, members of the ethnic minorities suffer from an **extra** element of social and economic deprivation, over and above that of the White majority—due, as we discussed in the last section, mainly to prejudice and discrimination in the employment and housing markets, together, in the case of relatively recent arrivals, with language difficulties and incompatibility in qualifications. It is hardly surprising, therefore, that ethnic minority children may underachieve by comparison with their White school fellows.

5.4 Having reached this stage in the argument, it is natural to ask the question: what proportion of West Indian underachievement is due to these social and environmental factors? There is no easy answer, but where achievement is recorded as a straight score, as for instance IQ, or literacy, then the answer seems to be something like a half (see Annex D, and the ILEA Literacy Survey, mentioned in our interim report and in Para 4.3 of this chapter). Where we are dealing with other measures of achievement, such as percentages of children obtaining various numbers of CSE, O Level or A Level grades, which cannot be expressed so simply, then the answer is less sure. We can however get an idea of the importance of these social class and socio-economic factors by looking in detail at the paper by Craft and Craft, discussed earlier, and in particular at their Table in Paragraph 2.3. Though the percentages with high achievement are markedly different as between Whites and West Indians, there is in both cases a **two-fold** difference between middle class children and working class children. We can, however look at these figures in another way and calculate from them the difference between White and West Indian high-scoring percentages with the class adjustment removed. It turns out that 22.7% of White children are high achievers, as against 10.6% of West Indian children, that is to say about a **two-fold** difference. If however we look at the original figures for middle-class children in the Table, we see that 31% of Whites are high achievers, as against 20% of West Indians. In other words, a two-fold difference has been sharply reduced to only a **one and a half fold difference.** Returning to our question, how much of West Indian underachievement is attributable to social class and socio-economic factors, it is clearly difficult to give a precise figure. Perhaps, a substantial amount is the best answer. But there is no doubt that these factors do not explain all of West Indian underachievement, so that we are left with an important element still unaccounted for, to which we now turn.

5.5 Having concluded that the complex of factors involved in social class, socio-economic status and region account for a substantial part of West Indian underachievement, but not all of it, and having

82

concluded that IQ is not a major factor, and possibly not even a minor one, we are left with a large number of other factors that have been suggested in explanation. These are summarised briefly in our quotation from Parekh (Para 4.8). All of them involve the interaction of the school and society at large with the West Indian child, the West Indian family and the West Indian community, with, running through the whole complex, the influences of prejudice and discrimination in one form or another. We had hoped to get further than we have in disentangling this web of possible factors, but the research evidence is often lacking, and where it exists it is often sketchy or conflicting, or both. Moreover our own research project on the factors making for success, which many of us believe could have pointed the surest ways forward, had, as we explained earlier, to be abandoned. In this context current research being carried out jointly by the Policy Studies Institute and the University of Lancaster by Dr David Smith and Professor Sally Tomlinson[32] will, we believe, prove helpful. Meanwhile we seek to draw a few conclusions in this particularly difficult area:

We and many others offer views on where solutions lie, and it may be that society, mainly by hunch, will light on what prove to be the key ones. But there is a serious need for more research, and especially more good and innovative research in this ill defined area. There is, in some quarters, an uneasy suspicion of scientific enquiry, but as Sir Peter Medawar has put it:

> "the purpose of scientific enquiry is not to compile an inventory of factual information . . . . it begins as a story about a Possible World—a story which we invent and criticise and modify as we go along, so that it ends by being, as nearly as we can make it, a story about real life."

Research into our present problem has by no means reached the end of this road, but as it goes along it will gradually increase our understanding and indicate, with increasing certainty, as it has done in so many other areas, how best to solve the problems. With this in mind we asked James Cornford, one of our members, to write a paper for us on possible ways ahead in research, and this we reproduce as Annex G to the present chapter. We are also glad to report that the Economic and Social Research Council has expressed its interest in supporting good research in this area.

Secondly, and in this same context, we have seen in the previous section, that even such familiar explanations as the effects of teacher stereotyping and teacher expectations, are likely to be more complex and subtle than has usually been supposed. It would not be surprising if other current explanations also turned out to be too simplistic.

83

Thirdly, even if it were to be shown beyond any doubt that some particular factor related to ethnicity played a large part in under-achievement, we would not expect that we could alter it by exhortation of the individual or group concerned. Shy people are not turned into extroverts by telling them to be more talkative; nor are teachers, advisers or administrators whose educational practices need to be liberalised and made more aware of the multi-ethnic context, likely to change without considerable encouragement, advice and in-service assistance. If we want to help, we have to do what we can to reduce ethnocentrism and racism in the educational system, and where the educational system can help to reduce this in the next generation, it must do so. As we discuss at length elsewhere in our report, there is now a good deal of material available, produced by the former Schools Council and the School Curriculum Development Committee, as well as by many LEAs and others, designed to help teachers and advisers to produce a curriculum appropriate for **all** children in a plural society, as well as meeting the particular needs of minority children. We conclude that the message of the interim report still stands: we should do all we can to diminish prejudice and discrimination within the educational system, and, through the next generation, outside it; and, simultaneously, we should give every help and encouragement within the educational system to enable minority children to overcome their disadvantages.

6. Our Conclusions—Asians

6.1 Incomplete as our conclusions on West Indian achievement may be, we have to admit that our conclusions on Asian achievement are even more incomplete. Moreover the statistical and research evidence on the many smaller minorities is so lacking that we do not even attempt an analysis where they are concerned, though it seems certain that some at least of them are seriously underachieving—see Part IV of this Report and the third NFER Survey[33].

6.2 Much evidence, as we have seen, leaves no doubt that the performance of the totality of Asian children resembles on average the performance of White children. This has not always been the case, since new immigrant children with language difficulties, not surprisingly, did not do well; but this effect has faded away in recent years with the decline in immigration. Averages, however, as we have pointed out earlier, conceal much variability, and statistics have often shown differences in achievement between the various Asian sub-groups. These differences, however, are not always consistent, and are not great, with the exception of the Bangladeshis, whom we discuss in Paragraph 6.8. They, it is clear, are seriously underachieving.

6.3   The close resemblance between the performance of most Asian and White children is not easily explained. It will be recalled that our remarks in the interim report about racism in general, and racism in schools especially, as being an important factor in West Indian underachievement, were much criticised in some quarters, on the grounds that Asians also are subject to these influences, but do not seem to be affected by them, at least where school performance is concerned. We have more to say about this later, but it is not the only puzzling feature of Asian achievement. We have seen earlier that the performance of **all** children, White, West Indian and Asian, varies with social class, socio-economic circumstances and region; moreover that Asians as well as West Indians are, on average, **more** deprived than Whites, for reasons we have discussed earlier. Once again, therefore, one might expect to find Asian performance to be poorer than White performance. But in general it is not.

6.4   We examined earlier the question of IQ, to see whether this might be the cause of West Indian underachievement, but concluded that it was not. Is it possible, on the other hand, that Asians have rather high IQ's? If so we might have an explanation of their achievement. But as is apparent from Professor Mackintosh's Report (Annex D), there is no reason to suppose that their scores differ much from those of the White majority, when adjusted for social class.

6.5   There is, as we have seen earlier, no doubt that Asians **are** affected by social and economic deprivation, as are West Indians (and Whites) but it would seem that it cannot be to quite the same extent, or in quite the same way. When, moreover, we turn to the educational and other factors which, as we saw in paragraphs 4.23—4.29, seem to be substantially involved in the under-achievement of West Indians, we have to conclude that they can only be having, at most, a slight effect on Asians. Notwithstanding the criticisms made of the interim report on this very point, we need not be surprised. As we have made clear earlier in this chapter, we are dealing with a very complex interaction between social class, ethnicity and race. White attitudes towards the different ethnic minorities vary, no doubt in association with social class perceptions and racial frames of reference. There are, in consequence, likely to be different forms of prejudice and discrimination directed at the different ethnic minorities, while the cultures of the ethnic minorities are the product of very different histories, which have led to very different attitudes, beliefs and assumptions on the part of the community, the family and the individual, a point that comes out very clearly from Dr Verma's study. Given the infinite variability of mankind, it is not surprising that different groups should evoke different reactions from the White majority, and themselves react differently to this complex of factors. On the contrary, it would be surprising if they did not. **We would remind anyone who thinks that racial prejudice and discrimination must have identical effects on every minority, of Parekh's perceptive second comment in Paragraph 4.8.**

6.6   Nevertheless, as we examine school performance, we are bound to ask what it is about Asians that somehow enables them to surmount in some degree the influences of social and economic deprivation, to an extent that seemingly West Indians do not; and what it is that enables them either to surmount direct racial prejudice, discrimination and harassment, to an extent that West Indians seemingly do not, or causes them to attract such prejudice and discrimination to a lesser extent, or in a different form. We do not know the answers, though a number of suggestions have been put to us. Some of these we find contrived and unconvincing, but two of them seem to us to have a certain plausibility. We put them forward tentatively, since there is little objective evidence:

> Asians, it has been put to us, are given to "keeping their heads down" and adopting "a low profile", thereby making it easier to succeed in a hostile environment. West Indians, by contrast, are given to "protest" and "a high profile", with the reverse effect. Given the very different histories of the two groups, it is not an improbable explanation. But it is a stereotype judgement, and as with all stereotype judgements it must be viewed with caution—it is certainly not true of all Asians or all West Indians.

> It has also been put to us that the explanation lies in the particularly tightly knit nature of the Asian community and the Asian family, more tightly knit than is the case either with Whites or West Indians. Since parental and family influences on speed of learning to read, and educational success in general have long been recognised—see the Plowden Report[34], Johnson[35] and Douglas[36] this also seems to us to be a factor to be borne in mind.

6.7   On a more general note, it should be recalled that the nature of the West Indian and Asian migrations were significantly different, the one arising from the largely rural, colonial hierarchy of island economies, the other deriving from the more diversified labour market of a colonial administration run more in partnership with the established social system. It would therefore be no surprise if attitudes to education and the acquisition of qualifications were to vary as between West Indians and Asians, and a number of commentators have seen this as significant. Wherever the truth may lie, the reasons for the very different school performances of Asians and West Indians seem likely to lie deep within their respective cultures. It should also be said that the British school system has perceived the needs of these different groups of children rather differently. As we have noted elsewhere in this report, Asian children were seen on arrival to present, primarily, a language problem, which was readily identifiable and manageable through an elaborate E2L provision. The needs of West Indian children on the other hand seem to have been less easily understood, and have, arguably, attracted altogether insufficient attention and resources, e.g. via Section II of the Local Government Act 1966.

6.8   We mentioned earlier that the Bangladeshis were the one Asian sub-group whose school achievement was very low indeed, and we reproduce an ILEA Report on the large Bangladeshi community in Tower Hamlets in Annex C of this chapter. We have no relevant research on this particular minority group, but it will be evident that their degree of social and economic deprivation, not to mention racial harassment, is so high that we are not surprised at their marked level of underachievement. We are glad that ILEA is well aware of their special problems.

7.   The implications of our findings

7.1   We have seen that school performance depends in substantial part, for ethnic minority groups, just as it does for Whites, on social class, socio-economic circumstances and region. To this extent any minority underachievement is part of the universal problem of social deprivation. But as we have also seen, the ethnic minorities, to varying extents, are, on average, significantly **more** deprived than Whites. And again, as we have seen, there can be no doubt that a substantial part of this extra deprivation is due to prejudice and discrimination by the White majority. Other factors may enter in—there may be an element of the "cycle of deprivation", and in the case of Asians, lack of fluency in English may also be involved, though with the slowing down of immigration, to a decreasing extent. Nevertheless, the fact remains that racism in society at large, and operating through employers, trade unions, landlords and Housing Authorities, not to mention racial harassment and violence, contributes to this extra element of deprivation, which in turn may generate an extra element of underachievement.

7.2   In the short term, countering racism within society at large must be a matter for the Law, for Government, Local Authorities,

Employers, Trade Unions, the Commission for Racial Equality and indeed many others, individually and collectively. But in the long term, teachers have a crucial role to play. Though they may sometimes weary at being expected so often to put society to rights, the fact remains that education is a powerful instrument when it comes to changing social attitudes. And our conclusions so far leave us in no doubt that the educational system is perhaps the most promising instrument for bringing forward future generations of children who will grow up knowing about the nature of our plural society, about its many minority cultures, as well as about the diverse origins and many borrowings of its dominant, white culture. "Prejudice," it has been said by Hazlitt "is the child of ignorance", and teachers have a unique opportunity to dispel present ignorance, and with it, present prejudices. The logic behind the emphasis we have laid on educating all children to this end, and behind the phrase we have used to describe the sort of education we look forward to, namely "Education for All", will be obvious.

7.3   As we have seen in earlier sections of this chapter, social and economic deprivation, exacerbated in the case of the ethnic minorities by racial prejudice and discrimination on the part of society at large, accounts for a substantial part of school underachievement, where this occurs. But it does not account for all of it. There is a further part, the causes of which must be sought elsewhere. As we have pointed out, a large number of factors have been suggested as being responsible. Moreover, throughout the large amount of oral and written evidence we have had from individuals and groups within the ethnic minorities and elsewhere, a special emphasis has frequently been laid on racial prejudice and discrimination within the educational system, and particularly on the low expectations that teachers may have about the achievement of West Indian children. Disappointingly, research evidence does not, so far, point decisively to which factors are the most important. Rather, as we have said earlier, it points to the complexity of the issues involved, and the likelihood that many different factors are involved. This is not the first time that research and common wisdom have been at odds. Research tends to take a long time to reach a fair degree of certainty, and neither it, nor any human endeavour, can achieve complete certainty. But wherever truth may ultimately seem to lie, all the factors which have been suggested are ones that impinge on ethnic minority children. Teachers, therefore, more than anyone else, have the opportunity to help be it in the way they teach, in their relations with parents and families, and in their relations with minority communities. As James Cornord, one of our members, points out in his perceptive "Note on Research" (Annex G):

"Many of the recommendations of this Report are, as it were, acts of faith, based upon experience and commonsense. If, as we hope, they are implemented, they will become hypotheses to be tested to see whether or not they have the good results we expect."

It follows that our conclusions and recommendations about what schools should do, constitute what we believe to be the most hopeful way forward, in the light of the evidence now available to us. They represent the other half of our conception of "Education for All", and much of the rest of this report is concerned with suggesting how best this aim can be achieved.

8. Summary of main conclusions

8.1 West Indian children on average are underachieving at school (Section 2). Asian children, by contrast, show on average a pattern of achievement which resembles that of White children, though there is some evidence of variation between different sub-groups (Section 3). Bangladeshis in particular are seriously underachieving (Annex C). Such evidence as there is suggests that of the smaller ethnic minorities, some are underachieving and some are not (Part IV). Averages, of course, conceal much variation. There are West Indian children who do well, as well as Asian children who are underachieving. We discuss possible causes for the difference in **average** achievement between Asian and West Indian children in Section 6.

8.2 Low average IQ has often been suggested as a cause of underachievement, particularly in the case of West Indians. This has long been disputed, and our own investigations leave us in no doubt that IQ is **not** a significant factor in underachievement (Paragraphs 4.10—4.14 and Annex D).

8.3 School performance has long been known to show a close correlation with socio-economic status and social class, in the case of all children. The ethnic minorities, however, are particularly disadvantaged in social and economic terms, and there can no longer be any doubt that this extra deprivation is the result of racial prejudice and discrimination, especially in the areas of employment and housing. This extra deprivation, over and above that of disadvantaged Whites, leads in many instances to an **extra** element of underachievement. A substantial part of ethnic minority underachievement, where it occurs, is thus the result of racial prejudice and discrimination on the part of society at large, bearing on ethnic minority homes and families, and hence, **indirectly,** on children (Paragraphs 4.15 to 4.22).

8.4   Not all of underachievement, where it occurs, is to be accounted for in these terms, and the rest, we believe, is due in large measure to prejudice and discrimination bearing **directly** on children, within the educational system, as well as outside it. We have received much oral and written evidence on this score, referring in particular to stereotyped attitudes amongst teachers as well as other factors, and these we discussed in our interim report. See also Chapter Two and Annex A.

8.5   We have examined the research evidence about racial prejudice and discrimination in the educational system and their effects on ethnic minority children. We can only say that the findings are inconclusive when it comes to deciding which factors may be import-ant (Paragraphs 4.23—4.31). We are left in no doubt, however, that the issues involved are complex and ill-understood, and that much more research is needed if we are to understand the problems. We include a section on future research at Annex G.

8.6   It will be evident that society is faced with a dual problem: eradicating the discriminatory attitudes of the white majority on the one hand, and on the other, evolving an educational system which ensures that **all** pupils achieve their full potential.

8.7   In the short term, the first of these problems is a matter for the Law, the Government, Housing Authorities, Employers' Unions, the Commission for Racial Equality, and many others. But in the long run we believe that it is a matter for schools to bring about this much-needed change in attitudes amongst coming generations.

8.8   The second problem is specifically one for the educational system. A start has been made in recent years, but there is still a long way to go before schools bring out the full potential of all their pupils, and in this context, particularly their ethnic minority pupils.

8.9   This dual approach to one of Britain's most serious social concerns, leads us to the concept that we have called "Education for All"—an attempt simultaneously to change attitudes amongst the White majority, and to develop a pattern of education that enables **all** pupils to give of their best.

9.   **References**
1.   Figueroa, P (1984). "Minority Pupil Progress," in Craft, M: (Ed). **Education and Cultural Pluralism.** Falmer Press
2.   Tomlinson, S (1983). **Ethnic Minorities in British Schools.** Heinemann
3.   Taylor, M (1981). **Caught Between.** NFER-Nelson
4.   Craft, M and Craft A (1983). The Participation of Ethnic Minority Pupils in Further and Higher Education. Education Research 25.1
5.   Tomlinson, S (1983). "The Educational Performance of Minority Children." **New Community** 8.3
6.   Tomlinson, S (1983). "The Education Performance of Children of Asian origin." **New Community** 10.3
7.   Fogelman, K (Ed) (1983). **Growing up in Great Britain: papers from the National Child Development Study.** Macmillan
8.   Taylor, M and Hegarty, S (forthcoming) **Between Two Cultures.** NFER
9.   Brooks, D and Singh, K, (1978). "Aspirations Versus Opportunities—Asian and White school leavers in the Midlands." Walsall CRC and Leicester CRC
10.   HMSO (1975) "Racial Discrimination." Cmnd 6234
11.   HMSO (1981) "The Brixton Disorders." Cmnd 8427
12.   ILEA Literacy Survey. (1980) London: ILEA
13.   Jeffcoate, R (1984) "Ideologies and Multicultural Education." In Craft, M (Ed). **Education and Cultural Pluralism.** Falmer Press
14.   Jeffcoate, R (1984). **Ethnic Minorities and Education.** Harper and Row
15.   Mabey, C (1981). "Black British Literacy." Educational Research 23.2
16.   ILEA (1983) Race, Sex and Class:1. Achievement in Schools. ILEA, London
17.   Parekh, B (1983). "Educational Opportunity in Multi-Ethnic Britain." In: **Ethnic Pluralism and Public Policy.** (Ed Glazer, N and Young, K.) Heinemann
18.   Coard, B (1971). "How the West Indian Child was made educationally subnormal in the British School System." New Beacon Books
19.   Rutter, M and Madge N (1976). **Cycles of Deprivation.** Heineman
20.   Mortimore, J and Blackstone, T (1982) **Disadvantage and Education.** Heineman
21.   DES (1984) "School Standards and Spending: Statistical Analysis." DES Statistical Bulletin 13/84
22.   Coleman, J S (1966) **Equality of Educational Opportunity.** Washington: US Government Printing Office
23.   Jencks, C (1972) **Inequality: a Reassessment of the Effect of Family and Schooling in America.** Allen Lane
24.   Brown, C (1984) **Black and White Britain: The Third PSI Survey.** Heineman
25.   **Employment Gazette** (October 1983 and June 1984)
26.   CRE (1984) "Race and Council Housing in Hackney: Report of a Formal Investigation." CRE
27.   Nash, R (1976) **Teacher Expectations and Pupil Learning.** Routledge and Kegan Paul
28.   Thomas, K C (1984) "A Study of Stereotyping in a Multicultural Comprehensive School." Educational Studies 10.1

29. Verma, G K (1980) **The Impact of Innovation: An Evaluation of the Humanities Curriculum Project.** University of East Anglia Press
30. Verma, G K and Ashworth, B (forthcoming) **Ethnicity and Educational Achievement.** Macmillan
31. Blatchford, P Burke, J, Farquhar, C Plewis, I and Tizard, B (1984) Educational Research
32. Smith, D and Tomlinson, S (forthcoming) Factors Associated with success in Multi Ethnic Secondary Schools PSI/University of Lancaster
33. Taylor, M and Hegarty, S. Third Review of Research NFER (forthcoming)
34. HMSO (1967). **Children and their Primary Schools:** Report of the Central Advisory Council for Education in England. HMSO
35. Johnson, D (1982) "Educational Research and Development in Britain." Ed. Cohen, L. Thomas, J and Manion, L. NFER-Nelson
36. Douglas, J W B (1964) **The Home and the School.** MacGibbon and Kee

ANNEX A

Achievement and Underachievement: Evidence from Young People of Afro-Caribbean and Asian Origin

Introduction

1. It has to be borne in mind when looking at achievement and underachievement that conclusions drawn from statistical evidence are only one side of the argument. The conclusions drawn in Chapter 3 may offer scant comfort to the individual pupil or parent, who feels the issue acutely as 'what is happening to me (or my child)'. The perceptions of individuals give the human dimension of the argument. While those perceptions cannot be added up and set out neatly in tabular form, they provide a reminder of the expectations held of education by individuals and of the realities they see themselves as having to wrestle with to make sense of their world.

2. We want to consider some of these realities now, in order that as wide an audience as possible has the opportunity to share them and to understand that there is much still to do, if ethnic minority children are to be given a 'fair deal'.

Part One: Evidence from Students of Caribbean and African Origin

1. The quotations which follow are selected from the oral evidence of 18 students brought together by the National Union of Students from universities in different parts of the country and following a variety of degree courses including law, anthropology and education. They had been educated in state schools as far apart as Harlesden and Huddersfield, Birmingham and Croydon, Leeds and Newham. Some had progressed from the lower streams of comprehensives in inner urban areas, others through the A streams of suburban areas where 11-plus selection for grammar schools still exists, and at least one student had attended an otherwise all-white rural school. The value of this evidence, we believe, is that it comes from academically successful students in universities, polytechnics and colleges of education; not from pupils who might be expected to bear a grudge against the education system. These students were particularly well placed to compare their experiences with those of their peers who had not 'made it' in education and to assess the range of factors that influenced their own educational progress. Their perceptions of the reasons underlying 'success' or 'failure' present another dimension of evidence — the human reality behind the statistical research.

2. Headings and a linking commentary are added to group the quotations into some of the many factors raised in the discussion.

I   School Factors

a. *Experiences of School — The Situation of Black Children*
"... I was the only one with a hint of a tint in an A stream in my year and the majority of black children were in the bottom stream ... but why was it that all these black children were in lower classes, there must be something wrong ..."

"The same thing happened with me, I went to a ... comprehensive ... and ... all the children that passed 11-plus were in the top stream ... the majority of the black kids were in the bottom two streams and that obviously affects their whole performance through the school."

93

"I also think it affects the children's self-image . . . I am a classic example because I was put in a low stream when I started school and when I came first in class I was quite amazed because I thought the teacher was doing me a favour because he liked me. And when it happened on numerous occasions and I eventually reached the top stream, all the time I kept thinking I should be in the bottom stream because I still haven't got that capability because all the black kids up to then were all in the lower stream . . . Like on prizegiving I still never got in coming first [in class] any kind of recognition in terms of prize, but I got prizes for sport and dance."

". . . Those children in the lower streams end up unemployed or on the dole and other kids see that and think, well, that's what will happen to me."

"The type of education that the black kids are given is so limited it is usually in the direction of the arts, that they can never have the chance to become doctors or scientists . . ."

"I feel my education is lacking. I have got a whole bunch of O Levels which are all commerce, history, social studies, but no maths no science . . ."

"I think that's down to the streaming because when I was at school I couldn't do the science because the sciences were taught to the top groups and all the blacks were in the bottom groups. So your education is restricted in that sense."

"I feel that a lot of black kids lose out in terms of the kind of science (or) maths teacher they get. I know this is a problem that happens to white kids as well. But since money and prestige in the science department is far greater than in social studies, where most of the black people tend to tail off into. There is a lot lacking in the primary schools towards black kids."

"You are holding back the black society from going further . . . to become part of an industrialised society."

Asked why Asian children were not associated with low streams and underachievement, one student replied:

"It is expectation again because Asians have always been recognised as having a valid civilisation whereas people from the Caribbean have not, so it is a racial expectation which is different."

There are many comments on teacher expectation of black pupils, and very strong feelings on the teaching of history and the content of the curriculum in history and language, including the selection of books and materials.

b.   *School Experience — Teacher Expectation and Teacher Attitudes*

"People like us who make it through the system . . . the teachers will say . . . 'But you are different', instead of changing their attitudes about black people they make an exception of you . . . They don't make an assessment that . . . perhaps we might be a bit wrong about this."

". . . The teachers expect very little of coloured children and that is why they are put in the lower streams."

There are several examples in which students had observed, or experienced, different treatment of black children by teachers to that given to white pupils.

"I was in the top set in school but even . . . I was excluded from school, and to this day I am not sure why, you see, because I didn't turn out for a voluntary lesson after school or because they said I was rude. I was excluded for a whole week . . . I missed all my classes and I stood outside the office, and it was at that time that I realised that some of these children are having a hard time. Because you stand outside the office, teachers pass you and you hear 'This is another rude boy'. You just stand there, you don't have to do anything, you have your lunch and come back and stand there, day after day after day. That sort of thing should not happen."

"In my sixth form there were a lot of white children who would play truant just as much, the point is that . . . they get a letter from their parents, their parents say they were ill or whatever and that letter will go straight through. On the other hand it is always the black child who did it, the point being that you have written this letter and have signed it, and they will probably ring home to see if your parent has agreed to this. It's a sort of suspicious attitude which they show towards you."

"If you want particular instances, I was sitting in the sixth form once . . . white children had truanted — they had missed an entire lecture . . . and some black kids had been playing cards during a free period. The ones who had truanted were just told off, the black kids had letters sent home, had threats about what was going to be done."

There were several examples of teachers' expectations being influenced by pupils' involvement with the police whether or not they had been convicted.

"I think once they get involved with the police . . . it creates a bad feeling in school because the teachers reinforce certain ideas they have about black children . . . once the police have arrested you they assume you are guilty . . . and the teacher will go on that premise that you are a crook, therefore . . . you can't be trusted."

"Yes . . . when my brother was picked up he was then accused at school by the teacher for stealing something out of her bag. That was about two weeks after he had been picked up."

"Yes, when I went to a school to observe, I was in the staff room and one teacher came in and said, 'Oh, so and so was causing a lot of trouble — she pinched someone's book, as a joke.' So the other teacher said to her, 'Oh, you have got to be careful of her you know, she was picked up the other day by the police and she is a bloody kleptomaniac.' Already they had labelled her."

The point was made that teachers' references could make a difference to the outcome of a court case, and an example was given of a reference which had had favourable results. The effects on family life and on schoolwork of being arrested, and on pupils' attitudes to school, were also stressed.

". . . if the kids are spending so much time in prison and police custody they have very little time to pay attention to school, I mean that affects them if they think they're going to be hassled — that disillusions them with the whole school system, because often the teachers when they come up to give reports they are going to give 'Oh, yes, that kid used to be so disruptive in school and so naughty' — that's just the kind of back-up the kid doesn't need. So it works both ways, the school could help black kids who get into trouble much more. I mean — a lot of black kids get into trouble because they are truanting because often the lessons are so boring, the teachers are not giving them any stimulation . . ."

95

"My brother and some of his friends were picked up . . . and that sort of destroyed the whole family atmosphere for a year and when the court case actually came up the police were unable to come . . . hence went another six months . . . at the end of it the judge says 'I can't see any evidence that these boys did these things, they seem to be reasonably intelligent and respectable boys.' And all because they got very good references from school and my mum made a lot of fuss."

There were examples of the positive expectations of some teachers in contrast:

"I went to a comprehensive school which was quite small, 600, and I went there the year after it opened . . . and I was the only black pupil in the top stream. My sister came in the year afterwards. Because I was doing so well, obviously she was going to do well . . . and all the attention was put on her. When she got to her A Levels the teacher was taking bets on what grade she was going to get and which university she was going to go (to)."

". . . in my first year I had a black form master and his attitude was always to get all the black guys around and counsel us as to our work . . . push us forward to work . . . all the black boys although we were in the A stream we all came in the first ten . . . but we had another teacher, he took us for chemistry . . . in the fifth form . . . (and) was also my form master, now he wasn't really bothered whether or not we got on, . . . he didn't really help us."

Asked whether there was a need for more black teachers, the students replied:

"Yes we need them in the teaching profession, but we need them as black people not as black in colour . . . There is an important difference . . ."

"You find a lot of black teachers who go into the school system they end up teaching on the same sort of basis as a white teacher, because they haven't got much choice right, because they are not in a position of authority. That's how they have been trained. When they try to do anything different, they just get called up before the headmaster and he says you are not teaching by our curriculum that we have set out so you have to curb what you are doing. He hasn't much choice if he wants to keep his job . . ."

The students had clear expectations of teachers white or black, and additional expectations of black teachers that related to their perception of being black. The effects of schooling on their own identity as black people emerged quite frequently in relation to the curriculum and with reference to parental attitudes.

c.   *School Experience – Identity, Race and Culture*

". . . I'm not West Indian . . . but I consider myself black now, and I am half and half. But I made it, absolutely perfectly through the system, through grammar school, 11-plus, university ok . . . I personally denied my blackness, because that is how I made it in the system . . . I wasn't taught anything about myself as a black child or a child that was not necessarily white, except I was sometimes held up as the nicest token coloured girl. I lived in a nice middle class, country rural area . . . It wasn't until I left university and actually faced the reality of going out and getting a job and things like that did I actually recognise that there was something wrong . . . I couldn't now go and get a really good job unless it's . . . to be a teacher or get involved with the race relations industry, because I am not going to make it in a successful sense as whites are supposed to make it . . . and the way I was brought up to think I could achieve."

". . . in secondary school, . . . up to about the third year I was white minded in so far as I didn't know anything about being black and I came to realize when I was about 18 and these guys started throwing these Black books at me and assuming that I knew them, and I didn't and I felt so ashamed. And then it was that I knew that my background and my education had been very limited, because I knew nothing about it. Yet all the time within myself I thought I was very Black, I mean I went to Black parties and none of my friends outside school were white . . . I had considered myself Black. Here I was at 18 and didn't know anything about Africa or the West Indies or anything."

There was quite a discussion on the role that books used in school played in culturally alienating black children:

"also it is a matter of materials, the kinds of books used in primary schools for black children, and the kind of cultural references they have are totally inadequate and alienating for a black child."

"In a lot of books you will find lovely pretty pictures, but the pictures are white postmen, white businessmen. You never see a black postman, you never read about a black family, you never read about black scientists, black whatever. It is always white. If you can't really identify yourself with something that you are learning then it is going to kill the incentive in you to learn or go further."

In response to the argument that books are a relatively small influence among the many other influences in society, and that they had succeeded in spite of the kind of books described, the students commented:

". . . the books are the first stage of your learning, the primary school plays a big part in what (children) conceive as the society . . ."

". . . things like Noddy where the little black boy goes and nicks his car, what a terrible little black boy, poor Noddy all sympathy for Noddy because this little black boy comes and nicks his car. All black boys must be naughty, they do bad and terrible things."

"the kids don't have a choice of the books they look at anyway."

"Self image is very important and the point is that ok a few people make it through the system, but then you can say ok there will be other factors that have helped us . . . but look at the majority of others that haven't."

"Also you say that we . . . have succeeded . . . , but I look back . . . at the years that I have wasted and that's what makes me really angry . . . I could have been learning so much more . . . spending hours with things which are totally irrelevant to me and to what I want to do with my life as a black person."

"It is of special importance to us because we are West Indian but . . . why the system should be changed is not just for black people but white kids are getting a biased impression as well; it could help towards a multi-racial society, truly multi-racial . . . to start to understand each other . . ."

The students expanded on the way in which the multi-racial society is reflected in schools, and their own concepts of multi-racial and multi-cultural.

"I'm doing this post graduate teacher training course and we do a multi-cultural education option. And the headmaster has got a school in the North of London and his school is all white . . . he said up until recently he didn't see any reason why he should have a multi-cultural prospectus, curriculum, there was no reason to 'We haven't got a problem we have got no Black or Asian kids' . . . He was seeing the school as a sort of autonomous body and totally divorced from society as a whole, until one day he was walking down the corridor and he heard one of the boys come out with what he thought was a particularly racist comment. And he suddenly thought something has got to be done, because they are going to go into the outside world and . . . mix with black people, whether they like it or not. So it is relevant for both black and white children."

"The problem here is this idea of multi-culturalism which has been brought down from above somewhere and the idea blacks were still supposed to be interested in Rastas, in reggae, and mangoes and coconuts. They do not see the correlation between the other cultures in this country. In terms of Asians, they are here for the same reasons that West Indians are here, they have different cultures but they have a common struggle. That is, multi-culturalism is not recognised, they are recognising the difference but they are not recognising the common struggle which is the problem of housing, education, police and the society. And if teachers were to be sensitive to that I think they could go a lot further . . ."

d.   *Experiences of School – The History Curriculum*

"We hear about (our) history as slavery . . ."

". . . it's like Africa never existed until . . . the white man came and civilised everybody."

"That phrase 'the Europeans brought civilisation', that phrase should be cut off, it should never be taught at school, it implies heavily that their ancestors were inferior."

". . . they should be careful what kind of books they have and the use of words like 'primitive' and 'tribal' and 'civilisation', I mean those continue to reflect or give the black kids inferior concepts of themselves."

"You want to point out to children really that the black contribution to the world is just as valuable as the white contribution. We just get it from the white angle all the time."

". . . the slant, . . . it affects not just blacks but the whites as well. Whites get an inferior sort of feel towards black children. My class at school, and I was at the top of the class, but when we did history and the slave trade, it was embarrassing. I felt as if I shouldn't be there, even though on paper I was as good as the person sitting next to me. It was the slant not so much as the history itself, you know."

"Exactly, I think the slant of it is very important and . . . looking where history books come from and the kind of people that teach them, it goes right through to university level. Even . . . where special courses arranged for African history to be taught it was always white ex-colonial lecturers . . ."

". . . looking at the curriculum as it stands now . . . Egypt is in the curriculum for all first years in most of England . . . look at the way Egypt is taught and you would get the impression that all Egyptians are white."

". . . If I had put down that the majority of Egyptians in the early stages of the Egyptian dynasty were black in an exam, that would have been marked wrong. So what do I put? That is a denial of my identity."

"... nobody ever correlates ... that Egypt was black ... the correlation between African and Egypt, and Egypt and Greece, and in Greece the Western civilisation, and nobody ever makes that correlation that Africa has contributed to the western civilisations and is probably the basis of it."

"Who is teaching the teachers? My degree was in anthropology and I was taught by an ex-colonialist and it was primitive tribes in the Sudan. It's the university lecturers and the lecturers in the teacher training colleges they are the ones who are teaching ... the teachers and the subsequent lecture lecturers ... so not only is it the course content but it is also the teachers themselves and who is writing the textbooks."

"If you are looking for people who are going to be creating resources for black people to be using, those people will have gone to those universities and if they have been dealt rubbish like that then the amount of work that they have got to do to overcome that miseducation is massive ..."

"... if there were special courses in African whatever, or West Indian, it must also be introduced into the curriculum when it is valid, and not just something special that black people can have as an option, so that they can take it as an exam and it is a valid piece of paper."

"And it goes right across the board in things like geography as well."

"... they are teaching like multi-cultural education but in such a passive way ... it's lip-service to it really."

"Like yesterday we were discussing language and the fact that language in the classroom can be very racist and sexist ... most of the students could not understand why this lecturer was making such a big deal about ... certain words such as blackmail, ... although they can be taken at this very simplistic level, there are other words which do have much deeper meanings that do affect the self image of the black child. There was so much debate going on ... people couldn't see the implicit assumptions and sometimes the explicit assumptions that are being made by teachers in the type of books they use. You can take the word golliwog which is a figure on a jam jar but when a racist calls you a wog they are not calling you a bottle of marmalade, they are calling you something more, ... yet here were these 200 people who are going on to be teachers and they were totally unaware that there was a problem."

e. *Experience of School – Language and Reading*

One student introduced the question of reading as basic requirement for education, and this led to a discussion of the language of West Indians.

"When I finished my O Levels we were helping some of the children to read in class and some of them were black ... one particular child ... was 11 or 12, he had a reading age of 5. As far as I could see, not being a doctor, he wasn't mentally sub-normal ... quite a few of them have passed through the system without being able to read — a basic necessity ..."

"That's dedication on the part of the teachers. Teachers have such an amount of time to spend on each individual child, ... if a child is very slow with reading, the teacher is not going to spend the time in my experience. So it means I couldn't read ... it was in the West Indies. Another teacher went out of her way to show me basics ... now that is what is needed in schools for any child ..."

"I would also say it's a question of language as well, I mean that West Indian is faced with two dialects which they have to overcome, and sometimes you get a teacher who categorizes a child who speaks with let us say a Jamaican accent, or pronounces words in a Jamaican way . . ."

". . . I had such a low self-image because I had a bad primary school education where I came last the whole time, because I had just come to England and my Jamaican accent was very pronounced and most of the teachers didn't understand me."

When asked what view teachers should take of West Indian language in school, the students replied:

". . . English and speaking it reasonably correctly is a necessary thing, therefore I think that that should be basic, I don't think you should ban patois . . . but we live in this country right, therefore in order to succeed it's no good talking patois when you are going for a job and if you are not dealing basically with black people . . ."

"I don't think it ought to be denied, I mean if a child starts to speak in the classroom, not on his essay, but in the classroom to the teacher in a Jamaican way or whatever, it shouldn't be put down . . ."

". . . language is part of the curriculum . . . and in terms of dialect in Creole that we speak, in terms of English in the English Department, in my experience I wanted to speak in dialect and I was stopped and dialect should be part and parcel of the curriculum because it is a question of recognising the cultures within the school and how they want to express themselves, and how they perceive themselves . . . so if we actually deny the existence of dialect or patois or Creole in school we are denying (the culture) . . . and I feel that a lot of teachers feel inadequate in terms of . . . all the cultures that exist in school and they find difficulty in trying to cope with it . . ."

"I think in drama you could find patois or Creole could be very effective in the English teacher understanding the West Indian Creole . . ."

It was pointed out that parents, in evidence to the Committee, had spoken out very strongly against the use of Creole in the school, and the students responded:

". . . they want their children to get through the educational system within Britain . . . the only way . . . is by becoming as anglicised as possible and that means denying all your sort of cultural connections and that means speaking in a way that everybody else will recognise as standard English . . ."

". . . it seems to me a sad state of affairs when even in the West Indian home kids are discouraged from speaking patois, I mean my parents they were concerned about getting me through the system. If I broke out speaking patois in the home they'd tell me 'No, you have got to learn to speak this way automatically because that's the way people speak to get on.'"

"They force white middle class values on you, that's the only way they think you can succeed."

II Home Factors

a. *Parental Attitudes*

"One thing we felt was very important is the sort of different attitudes that West Indian parents have to schooling. Like, for instance, in the West Indies parents consider that you should send your child to school and it is the duty of the teachers to teach children . . . Therefore perhaps they don't really expect the problems that occur . . . like if you are in school here and you are not working, . . . quite often teachers just let you get on with it . . ."

". . . Working class parents, particularly West Indian, put all their trust in the educational system for their children. They think that the teacher will educate the child and we are not really involved in that, we get them to the school, you teach them . . ."

". . . I had what I reckon to be very good parents who knew the way through the system and were willing to fight for me."

". . . my mother . . . knows a certain amount about the system and therefore she isn't going to sit down and watch anything happen to any of us. She will go down there and will tell them what's what."

"If the parents are very very persistent they will get something done, but if the parents don't know the system . . . they don't know how to get around it."

". . . I know of two incidents where parents have been told that their children need special schooling, . . . in the end it turns out to be an ESN school . . . it was put into such luxury language that the parents were totally blinded . . ."

Asked about the difficulties of transferring from home to school at the age of five, or pre-school influences, one student commented:

"The thing is that there are certain housing policies which put black people into certain areas, thus they go to these certain schools, that is the point."

". . . you can see very clearly not just in high immigrant areas . . . the majority of black kids will be sent to one school . . . and white kids go to the other schools and the educational facilities at some schools are decidedly better than the others . . ."

". . . I know . . . you write down on the list of where you want your children to go first, second, third choice. But then if you don't get your choice, well bad luck."

"The policy of these schools, you see a lot of children do CSEs they don't push O Levels . . ."

The students were asked the reasons for their success and mentioned the following:

"In my case it is due to my parents, and in a lot of cases it is due to the child losing its identity as a black child and sitting down keeping quiet, taking everything that is put to him or her . . . because their fighting ability has been killed as they grow up. So (they) just do the work. And when they get to the top if they do . . . , they are only black in face. They haven't tended to look back and to pick up their brothers and sisters, they are only there as a figure head."

"There are some people that just learn to play the game, you realise how it works and you think well, if I want to get on, . . . this is how I have got to do it, you don't have to become totally Anglicised . . . you don't have to lose all identity, some people do. You don't have to, you learn to switch the system to how you want it. I met a lot of people at university who said, 'We are doing this because we want to prove that we are better than the white person.''

"It means you have to work ten times harder if you are not conforming to get through, if you want your own identity you have to work that much harder."

". . . many black students who make it to university make it through evening classes and . . . college, not necessarily from the school they went to."

"Another thing . . . a certain number of people would like to get back into the system . . . into education and they find it very difficult to get into it again because of lack of grants . . . Therefore to do evening classes . . . would take a sacrifice on somebody's part and working and trying to support yourself is difficult."

"You should get data from schools, if you were to ask your headmasters to write down how many blacks go up to university, directly from school . . . you will have your data there straight away . . ."

"I know teachers know how many blacks there are in the sixth form and how many go to university because there are very few, I was one. They are usually outstanding in a sense because everyone knows them — this is the prize black boy, he will go far, . . . so people will remember them."

"I tend to feel that we are exceptions to the rule therefore it is more important for us to say why we think the others won't make it . . . because I had what I reckon to be very good parents who knew the way through the system and were willing to fight for me. I had brothers . . . who had been through the system already, had been to grammar school . . . to university. You can't hope to make the environment of every child the same as ours was."

"That's why individual statements from all of us would be useless, because the most important thing is to identify the areas that need to be changed . . ."

"We are black, we have made it. We have made it at a loss in many cases or we have made it with a fight and usually since we were young children the fight wasn't ours . . . in my case it was my mum, in a lot of cases probably the parents, in a lot of cases probably older brothers and sisters."

"And it might just be sheer motivation, you might think well I'm going to prove that I can do just as well as the next person . . ."

"If you look for a clue or a common factor, you can see that the common factor is self realization among everyone that the system works against you. And whether that self realization is given by your parents or your brother, anything, you realize it sooner or later and you work."

". . . we have a pretty realistic attitude to what's going on in society therefore we attempt . . . to use the system to our advantage."

One thing that the students were quite clear had not been a positive factor in motivating them or influencing their decisions about their future careers was the advice on careers which they had received in school.

"The type of advice I was given by my careers teacher at school . . . when I started to become a lawyer was 'Work in Woolworths where you can meet people' . . . I was so amazed I couldn't be bothered to say anything else to her."

"I had the same thing, when I went to see my careers adviser I said I wanted to apply to university and before that I had wanted to go to teacher training college and he told me not to run before I could walk, no sort of encouragement at all . . ."

"I didn't have (encouragement) to go to university either, I was told to do something like HND or something that would far better suit my ability."

". . . I was leaving comprehensive school and I wanted to go to sixth form college. I was pushed into lots of different jobs — building, welding, car mechanic, . . . it just wasn't on that I should go, they felt I should leave and get a job."

"I think it is that careers officers tend to say to a black person "We all know black people are good with their hands so you find yourself something to do with your hands.""

"I didn't have that experience because . . . I just asked him about universities, I didn't bother to ask him anything else because I knew what I was going to do therefore I didn't ask him for any advice."

"I feel I didn't really want to go to them because I heard so many stories about them like one guy he wanted to be an engineer, and they put him in a factory as a machine operator. And other people wanted to go to university and the careers office just laughed at them. I didn't go . . ."

When asked the question "What would be the main recommendations you would want to see?", the students replied in unison:

"Change the system."

One student then added:

"That is generally what we want, we want the system changed. Barring that we want the curriculum changed by the schools at a young age."

". . . I wouldn't want positive discrimination in a way that made black kids somehow special, so that they are seen as targets by their white classmates. I mean, that is bad positive discrimination where the two kids are getting on well together. Not problems, not similar to Head Start or the compensatory education . . ."

"Like positive discrimination in the sense that you are actively making teachers aware of other cultural things, like that type of positive discrimination — where you actually decide to spend money on educating teachers."

Part Two: Evidence from Young People of Asian Origin

1. The quotations that follow are taken from a series of over 200 individual interviews conducted with youngsters in the Leeds/Bradford area, in the course of Dr G K Verma's longitudinal study of ethnic minority adolescents. The quotations are not taken exclusively from interviews with Asian youngsters, although the sex and ethnicity of each youngster accompanies each quotation. We should point out here that the term 'Asian', which is used as a general category in the statistical evidence, can be misleading in view of the widely differing religious, linguistic, social and cultural traditions and the different experiences of the various groups from the Asian sub-continent. The interviews from which these quotations are taken were recorded during the period 1980-83 and were fully transcribed. The perceptions and attitudes displayed in these quotations were similar to the ones given at a number of forums conducted during the course of this Committee's work.

2. These quotations are offered with the minimum of editorial comment but have been set out under three main headings: Home and Family, School and (Un)employment/Further Education.

I. Home and Family

a. *Parental support expectations*

>   i. **Indian Boy.** "Well the only reason he (his father) came over was to get a better education for his children. I don't want to let my father down — his sole ambition was to come over here and educate his children because the education in India is non-existent."

>   ii. **Indian Girl.** "To do well you need a good relationship with your parents — good relationships with the family as a whole. I think if you have got your parents and the family you can face anything in the world. That's my belief."

>   iii. **Pakistani Boy.** "The only reason anyone comes here is that education is better, it's free and in Pakistan pupils have to cross rivers and walk miles a day. Here there is the luxury of buses. So we come here for education so we can go home and say we have got a qualification and get a job and settle down and that's it. That's the whole point in coming here, I think." (NB This boy's intention to return home was atypical).

>   iv. **Pakistani Boy.** "Asian parents are really looking towards a good future for their sons, they are the base of the family. Actually the girls do the housework, but it would help if they are educated, but they don't rely as much on them as they do on sons."

b. *Pressures of ethnic minority cultural norms*

>   i. **Indian Boy.** "I am proud of being English, but I am more proud of being Indian. I don't agree with my Mum and Dad hardly ever, but if it comes to the crunch I am more Indian than I am English. I think that my kids will be very western but they will never forget their own culture."

>   ii. **Indian Boy.** "There is the stuff like arranged marriages and so on. I disagree with that, but that doesn't mean that I am totally 100% against it — I am against it 90% but because of my parents you know — like, say you found a girl and fell in love, well I'd ask my parents about it first if I did want to get married."

iii. **Pakistani Boy.** (asked whether he'd seen any changes in the community) "It just depends on what type of families you look at. 'Cos my Dad gives me more freedom, you know he doesn't care if neighbours say something or talk about something. He sort of argues against them and he sticks up for me, whether I am wrong or right. But the next door neighbours, if there is anything their family does wrong and somebody tells them about it they get really angry. Like my friends, when they see all these ladies and women and all this English sort coming down to our house, they start getting funny ideas about what we are doing."

iv. **Indian Girl.** "I'd do exactly what my parents have done to me because I think it's very important to keep one's culture; to be identified because when you live in a society it's very important to belong to a society. If you don't belong to something, then you are cast out and get lonely and it's very bad for you."

v. **Pakistani Girl.** "I had two interviews with the careers teacher and they asked me what I wanted to do. I said helping old people and nursery nursing and so on. Then they told me to go on work experience. My parents don't allow that, they say work experience is mixed for girls and boys and my parents say it's no good thing being with boys because boys are . . . , boys are different than girls."

vi. **Pakistani Girl.** "I could have been a nurse — there are girls who take City and Guilds who go to different hospitals in Bradford. But if I took on nursing I would have to wear a skirt which is against my religion. I'd like that very much."

vii. **English Girl.** "Obviously Asians don't get as far as we do because of their families and religions — especially the girls — the girls marry at an early age. Their parents say to them that you should get married and have a family and stay at home. You don't see many Asian women at work as you do English. You tend to see them more with children just staying at home. I think some of them have got used to the English culture. I think they must have felt a lot of resentment."

II. School

a. *Perceptions of their Teachers*

i. **Pakistani Girl.** "The teacher didn't get on well with me neither, 'cos I was Asian and we only had about two or three Asians in our group. She always picked on us or something."

ii. **Sikh Boy.** "Things which should hold me back in life are being . . . because I am Indian, that is a disadvantage. Some teachers have very poor expectations of all Asians."

iii. **Pakistani Girl.** "You try to humour them (teachers) . . . they treat you as though you are from another planet or something. If you get on well with them they stop hating you . . . but you have got to try first. If you start putting a barrier between them and you, they hate you more, so you have always got to try to be on your best side for them."

b.   *Careers education/advice*

i.   **Pakistani Boy.** "The careers teachers were trying to get me into engineering and forcing me, and they were saying don't stay on at school, it's bad for you, you will never make 'A' levels and discouraged like hell they did. You really got put off and the only thing that keeps you going is your friends who say 'don't listen to them, you'll do all right.'"

ii.   **Asian Boy.** "Nobody really bothered about the careers teacher, to be quite honest; because what she said was a load of codswallop anyway."

iii. **Pakistani Boy.** "The Careers Officers asked me why I don't want to take up agriculture as my career. He said that my father comes from a rural area of Pakistan."

iv.   **English Boy.** "Yes there was a weekly careers. They had a careers teacher there and you had a careers interview. I don't know how often it was, I can't remember. But to be quite honest I thought they were a waste of money, they were no help at all — I suppose to others they may be — but to me they weren't."

v.   **English Girl.** "Well there was a careers teacher at school and we used to go and see her about once a week. But every kind of job we said we wanted, she would try and put us off."

c.   *Racial prejudice/attack*

i.   **Indian Girl.** "When I was in junior school I never bothered about my colour . . . Since I have come to this school I have encountered a lot of racial prejudice and I realised that I was this colour, and it was this colour that was making them so horrible to me."

ii.   **Tanzanian Girl.** "Well some people, that's what I don't like, some people are really against you, racialist mostly here (at this school) . . . and it's just that I don't like it. It's just people's attitudes . . . Being Indian, I think that is a disadvantage."

iii. **Indian Girl.** "One girl in the fifth form, she picked on me and she kept on picking on me every day. I just kept on ignoring her and then she pushed me down the steps. I told the Headteacher and he took her and told her off. She said if you tell the Headteacher again I'll kick you in again. And she kept on doing that to me again. So I told my parents and they went up to school and told the Headmaster."

d.   *Teachers' Stereotypes*

This section on school would be incomplete if it were to be confined to illustrations of pupils' perceptions. Therefore, the following quotations, taken from interviews with teachers, are presented to offer an illustration of the type of stereotyping of ethnic minority pupils, which some teachers engage in, either consciously or unconsciously. Such stereotyping, as epitomised by these examples, is likely to have an adverse effect on teachers' interactions with pupils, with all sorts of attendant consequences for the latters' educational achievement and, ultimately, life chances.

i.   **Teacher.** "There is a certain tendency amongst some of them (Asians), to believe that knowledge and ability can be boxed and taken down from a shelf, and the

106

ingredients of that box can be put in front of them and all that they need to do is to soak it up, recharge themselves like a battery with academic standing; that's very sad because there's a great tendency to believe among the Asian community — to think sheer diligence is sufficient, and it is not."

ii. **Teacher.** "They (Asians) approach their ambitions with the hopes of obtaining a particular post or particular places, and yet academically they are not bright enough, so that they set their aims too high, and although a school will try very often to indicate this to them, they don't really want to know and therefore they switch off."

iii. **Teacher.** "We have no distinction in this school between pupil and pupil, that's our first objective ... I should have put it — if all the Asians ... evaporated tomorrow, it would not make a scrap of difference to the curriculum."

iv. **Teacher.** ". . . the people (Asians) you are talking about, their sons and daughters, finish up in this school in classes which are non-examinations or bottom CSE. They rarely have sons and daughters who are going to be bright GCE candidates, and it isn't the fault of the education system, and it isn't the fault of Western civilization — it's inherent in life."

III. (Un)employment/Further Education/Sixth Form?

a. *Jobless*

i. **Indian Boy.** "Now I have been rejected from so many jobs, all I want to do now is get a job. I am asking people what is the fault with me: why can't I get a job?

ii. **Pakistani Girl.** "Yes — I feel really funny now, like going down to the Job Centre. I don't even like to meet my friends sometimes because they all know what they're doing, don't they. Look at me, I'm here, I've done nothing really. Before in school I used to be the one who knew everything, but now I feel as though I don't know anything. I don't like to meet them a lot."

b. *Discrimination*

i. **Indian Boy.** "I remember seeing some of the applicants, and prior to that my Mum and Dad used to say that racial prejudice exists and I used not to believe them because of my friends and the teachers. As soon as I started to experience this situation where I was short-listed and did not get the job, I started feeling sort of rejected and bitter."

ii. **Pakistani Girl.** "You see they offered this work at . . . . You know, at school, there were five of us who applied for it. Three Asian girls applied for it, including me, and two English girls. And . . . . accepted the two English ones and said no to us and I don't think that's fair."

107

c.   *Do qualifications lead to jobs?*

Although a substantial proportion of youngsters interviewed held the belief that better examination results lead to better job opportunities, a number who had left school and found work discovered that academic qualifications were not the only criteria used by employers during employee selection.

    i.   **Pakistani Boy.** "I have been reading all the papers you see. You need experience, you have got the qualifications, then you need five year's experience behind you. Experience is vital really, apart from qualifications as well."

    ii.   **Pakistani Boy.** "Well, first is that I don't have any experience. Secondly is that they wanted someone who knows about the thing, and sometimes is a matter of age. Sometimes they make you take a test; you might pass or fail. You don't know; but they say you haven't succeeded."

d.   *Sixth form or seek work?*

    i.   **West Indian Boy.** "A year is quite enough in the sixth form. I don't think I would stop on two years because when you are 18 — they would want experience, and in some jobs it's not brains you want, they wouldn't want you at all. Experience — it's experience what counts, in some jobs. And besides, they would want you at 16 if they want brains or such. That's what I think anyway."

    ii.   **Indian Boy.** "Basically what I am trying to do now is staying on in the sixth form so that people think the lad's not losing interest, and so that when I go for a job I can say 'Well look I am in the sixth form!' I am in a situation whereby I am willing to leave if I am offered a good job, but I'm not going to be too choosy. So I stayed on in the sixth form so as not to be regarded as a 16 year old who had left school with virtually no education. 'Cos people who leave school with 5 'O' levels get a job, it is very seldom that they don't, and that is why I stayed on in the sixth form. And also I took 'A' level economics, history, geography and general studies."

    iii.   **West Indian Girl.** "I think a lot of people choose the sixth form because of the job situation, because they didn't want to go through the dole and things. I think it's depressing seeing your friends on the dole anyway — you don't want that to happen to you. Stay on, even if it's just for the year. You do it 'cos you think you might as well, because you are not given anything else."

    iv.   **Pakistani Girl.** "I could have stayed on but you see the way things are with Asian people at school, with girls — they have been baddies at school really. You know, my parents — some people told my parents about girls, how they have been at school. So my parents have got the idea you see, of girls, how they are at school and how they are at home you see. So my parents; that's why they didn't tell me to stay on a bit further with my courses you see. That's why really. It's one of the main reasons."

    v.   **Pakistani Girl.** "They (her parents) think that you know there's no jobs nowadays for us so they said that you might as well stay on at school and get a higher grade or, you know, get a higher qualification for a better job."

    vi.   **Pakistani Boy.** "I want a job where my academic effort is valid . . . I don't want to be regarded as a shopkeeper; I would do that anytime. If I had known that, I could have messed about in the fifth form, no effort whatsoever. And they are in jobs — they are in good jobs — which makes me feel degraded when I stand next to them and yet they have not got any 'O' levels."

vii.   **West Indian Boy.** "Most of my friends who have got jobs are English — well, white — they've got the jobs probably because they are white. 'Cos all my mates who are Asian or Black as it were, they have gone back to sixth form."

Conclusions

1.   It is evident from these quotations that the struggle of young people of Asian and West Indian origin in British Society has many dimensions; it is closely bound up with many social, educational and institutional factors which impose numerous disadvantages. Under-achievement may have its origins in the very beginnings of schooling — whether in nursery school or infant school — where pre-conceived attitudes to children's ability, racist or ethno-centric reading books and the treatment of misdemeanours can give a child a negative picture of himself and his place in the wider world. And these disadvantages become cumulative as the child progresses through the system.

2.   The dilemma in which these young people are placed is an extremely difficult one. Their parents have by and large found themselves on the lowest rungs of the ladder of British Society. This has led to great pressure from the family for success in the second generation. Prejudice and discrimination both in school and in the wider society add to this pressure. In order to overcome these adverse factors, many of these young people stressed their determination and need to do exceptionally well in school. But even success in the educational system is not without its problems: it does not necessarily lead to social and economic success, and if teachers' perceptions of ethnic minority pupils often appear to be a hindrance to effective educational practice, the discouragement or suppression of aspirations by teachers and careers advisers may result in a profound alienation between these pupils and the educational system.

ANNEX B

Results from the School Leavers Survey 1981/82
A Paper by DES Statistics Branch

Introduction

1.   This paper presents a summary of the results obtained from the Department of Education and Science's School Leavers Survey for 1981/82 on the educational qualifications, age on leaving school and destination in respect of a sample of children from specified ethnic groups. The survey collects data on the age, sex and numbers of all young people who leave school during a given academic year and, for a 10 per cent sample of such leavers, information relating to their educational (academic) qualifications and their intended destination on leaving school.

2.   This latest exercise, presented here, broadly replicates that which was conducted in respect of the School Leavers Survey for 1978/79, the results of which were published by the Committee in its interim report "West Indian children in our schools"[1]. For the earlier inquiry, six LEAs with high concentrations of children from ethnic minority groups who, between them, were believed to account for approximately one half of the school leavers of ethnic minorities in this country, agreed to co-operate with the committee and ask all maintained secondary schools in their areas to complete an ethnicity question contained in the School Leavers Survey questionnaire relating to the 10 per cent sample of leavers.

3.   Because of the degree of interest accorded to these results, the Committee asked for the renewed co-operation of the authorities in carrying out a repeat exercise to be conducted under the auspices of the 1981/82 School Leavers Survey. The main teacher unions, local authority association and the Chief Education Officers of the LEAs concerned were again consulted and all but one of the LEAs agreed to cooperate. The results contained in this paper thus relate to five authorities.

4.   The response to the School Leavers Survey was again of a high order with approximately 99 per cent of the school leavers from the 5 LEAs being allocated to one of the nine specified ethnic group classifications. As a result, information on qualification and destination was obtained on 1317 Asian, African or West Indian school leavers. The Asian category was composed of five sub-groups: Indian, Pakistani, Bangladeshi, East African Asian and "other" Asian; the last sub-group included children for whom a more precise category was either not appropriate or was not known. None of these sub-groups contained a large number of school leavers and consequently the results for individual sub-groups are subject to considerable sampling error. In general, because of the small sample sizes involved differences between sub-groups in their characteristics are not likely to be statistically significant and therefore the results presented in this paper refer solely to the combined Asian group.

5.   The West Indian group contained 653 school leavers and constitutes a group which is referred to in the tables and commented on in the text. The small numbers of African or undifferentiated West Indian/African leavers have been combined with those leavers whose ethnicity was not recorded to form a third, specified, group under the heading "all other." The following paragraphs accordingly present results for these three Asian, West Indian and "other" category groups and compare them individually with, firstly, their combination – which forms a group of all leavers from the 5 LEAs – and with the overall results for all children leaving maintained schools in England for 1981/82.

---

[1]Cmnd 8273 June 1981

6. In order to maximise the usefulness of the data collected by both School Leaver Surveys, the results put forward in this paper show the information collected by the 1978/79 survey reworked onto the five LEA basis. Only very small differences have occurred between these summary results and those previously published.

7. A note on the compilation of sampling errors and of the likely statistical significance of any changes in proportion between the results of the two surveys is given in the Appendix to this paper.

Main Results

Age of School Leavers

8. Table 1 shows the percentage distribution by age – at the beginning of the academic year during which the children left school – by sex and differentiated between the specified categories of school leaver. Those aged 15 at the beginning of the academic year are normally in the fifth form and attain school leaving age during that year and those aged 16 are normally in the first year sixth, and so forth.

9. The Table shows that girls, noticably those from ethnic minorities, are more likely to stay on at school past the school leaving age than boys. Half of Asian school leavers do so after completing at least one year in the sixth form. These results suggest that West Indian children, more especially the boys, increased their propensity to stay on into the sixth form and that for this group they are now almost as likely to stay on to the sixth form as the group formed by the broad range of non-specified ethnic leavers. However, only 12 per cent of West Indian children stay on into the second year sixth, or later, compared with 25 per cent of Asian children and 17 per cent of all English school leavers. For all school leavers from the five LEAs, taken as a group, compared with the average for all school leavers in England, both boys and girls tend to leave school at the school leaving age with less frequency but then to participate to a greater degree in only one more year of study taken in the sixth form. The proportion of children staying-on to the second year sixth and beyond is very nearly the same in the five LEAs as it is in England generally.

Destination and Type of Course to be followed

10. Table 2 shows the percentage distribution by destination of school leavers. It shows that only 1 per cent of West Indians went to University compared with 5 per cent of all maintained school leavers.

11. There was a statistically significant increase between the two surveys in the proportions of each ethnic group pursuing some form of full-time further education on leaving school (other than a degree course). This was more marked for ethnic minority school leavers than for other leavers. Asians and West Indian children were much more likely to leave school to follow full-time further education in 1981/82 than were the "other" leavers within the five LEAs and as compared with all maintained school leavers generally. Accompanying this rise there was an offsetting, and statistically significant, decrease in the proportion of children in all school leaver categories leaving for employment.

12. Whereas 10 per cent of all children in England leave school to a destination not known by their Headteacher, one fifth of leavers from the 5 LEAs exhibit this characteristic. For Asian school leavers, the proportion was 28 per cent.

111

TABLE 1.   Age of School Leavers from Maintained Secondary Schools

	BOYS										GIRLS										BOYS AND GIRLS									
	Asians		West Indians		All Other Leavers		Total School Leavers from 5 LEA's		All Maintained School Leavers in England		Asians		West Indians		All Other Leavers		Total School Leavers from 5 LEA's		All Maintained School Leavers in England		Asians		West Indians		All Other Leavers		Total School Leavers from 5 LEA's		All Maintained School Leavers in England	
Age at 31 August	1978/79	1981/82	1978/79	1981/82	1978/79	1981/82	1978/79	1981/82	1978/79	1981/82	1978/79	1981/82	1978/79	1981/82	1978/79	1981/82	1978/79	1981/82	1978/79	1981/82	1978/79	1981/82	1978/79	1981/82	1978/79	1981/82	1978/79	1981/82	1978/79	1981/82
	%	%	%	%	%	%	%	%	%	%	%	%	%	%	%	%	%	%	%	%	%	%	%	%	%	%	%	%	%	%
15	51	54	79	68	74	70	73	68	77	73	36	46	59	56	71	64	67	61	74	69	44	50	69	62	72	67	70	64	75	71
16	21	24	16	23	12	14	13	16	8	10	34	25	32	31	13	19	16	21	11	13	27	25	24	27	12	16	15	18	10	12
17	19	14	4	6	12	14	12	14	13	15	21	22	9	11	15	16	15	16	14	16	20	18	6	9	14	15	13	15	14	15
18+	9	8	1	3	2	2	3	3	2	2	9	7	1	3	2	2	2	2	1	2	9	7	1	3	2	2	2	3	2	2
Total (Number)	262/ 319		378/ 315		2,487/ 2,363		3,127/ 2,997		352,580/ 357,440		204/ 252		340/ 338		2,525/ 2,355		3,069/ 2,945		341,260/ 349,240		466/ 571		718/ 653		5,012/ 4,718		6,196/ 5,942		693,840/ 706,690	

TABLE 2.   **Destinations of School Leavers from Maintained Secondary Schools**

	Asians		West Indians		All Other Leavers		Total School Leavers from 5 LEA's		All Maintained School Leavers in England	
	1978/79	1981/82	1978/79	1981/82	1978/79	1981/82	1978/79	1981/82	1978/79	1981/82
	%	%	%	%	%	%	%	%	%	%
University	3	4	—	1	3	4	3	4	5	4
Other full-time Further Education	17	30	16	27	9	14	11	17	14	21
Employment	55	39	66	51	76	64	73	60	73	64
Not Known	25	28	18	22	12	18	13	20	8	11
Total Leavers (Numbers)	466	571	718	653	5,012	4,718	6,196	5,942	693,840	706,690

— Denotes less than ½%

Full-time Further Education Courses

13.   Table 3 shows the type of course followed by those entering full-time further education. Only 1 per cent of West Indians were intending to enter degree courses in 1982/83 compared with 6 per cent nationally in 1981/82. There were small increases in the number of Asian and West Indian children leaving school to study 'A' levels as a full-time course. There was a statistically significant increase across all categories of school leavers in the five LEAs in the proportion leaving school to follow courses other than those leading to 'A' levels or degrees. Approximately 25 per cent of Asian leavers falling within this category were intending to take 'O' level courses with a further one fifth BEC/TEC courses compared with one tenth of West Indian children respectively.

TABLE 3.   **Further Education Courses (Full-time)**

	Asians		West Indians		All Other Leavers		Total School Leavers from 5 LEA's		All Maintained School Leavers in England	
	1978/79	1981/82	1978/79	1981/82	1978/79	1981/82	1978/79	1981/82	1978/79	1981/82
	%	%	%	%	%	%	%	%	%	%
Degree	5	5	—	1	4	5	4	5	6	6
'A' Level	5	8	1	2	1	2	1	3	2	3
Any other Course	11	21	15	24	7	10	8	13	11	17
No Course (Including unknown Destination)	80	67	83	72	88	83	87	80	81	74
Total Leavers (Number)	466	571	718	653	5,012	4,718	6,196	5,942	693,840	706,690

GCE 'O' Level and CSE Achievements

14.   Table 4 shows the percentage distribution by broad levels of 'O' level and CSE achievement. It shows that there is no significant difference between the school leaver categories within the five LEAs in terms of the proportion who achieved no graded results but that this proportion is significantly higher, statistically, than the national figure. The major difference between the achievements of West Indians, Asians and other leavers lies in the proportions obtaining five or more higher grades (grades A–C at 'O' level or CSE Grade 1). Only 6 per cent of West Indian leavers in 1981/82 had obtained this level of qualification compared with 17 per cent of Asians and 19 per cent of all other leavers in the five LEAs. However the increase in proportion for West Indian children between the two surveys is statistically significant.

TABLE 4.   'O' Level and CSE Achievement

	Asians		West Indians		All Other Leavers		Total School Leavers from 5 LEA's		All Maintained School Leavers in England	
	1978/ 79	1981/ 82	1978/ 79	1981/ 82	1978/ 79	1981/ 82	1978/ 79	1981/ 82	1978/ 79	1981/ 82
	%	%	%	%	%	%	%	%	%	%
No Graded Results (including those who attempted no examinations)	20	19	17	19	22	19	21	19	14	11
At least 1 Graded Result but less than 5 Higher Graded Results	63	64	80	75	62	62	64	63	66	66
5 or more Higher Graded Results	17	17	3	6	16	19	15	18	21	23
Total Leavers (Number)	466	571	718	653	5,012	4,718	6,196	5,942	693,840	706,690

'O' Level and CSE Achievements in English Language and Mathematics

15.   Tables 5 and 6 show the percentage distributions by broad level of achievement at CSE or 'O' level in English language and Mathematics. In English language, 15 per cent of West Indians achieve a higher grade pass compared with 21 per cent of Asians and 29 per cent of all other leavers in the five LEAs. These differences are statistically significant. Further, the proportions for the five LEAs are significantly different from the national average. However the table shows that the proportion of West Indian children achieving no graded result decreased between the two survey periods, matched by an increase in proportion achieving higher grades. These changes are also statistically significant.

114

16.   In mathematics only 8 per cent of West Indian leavers had achieved a higher grade pass in 1981/82, but this represented a statistically significant increase from the 5 per cent that achieved this level of qualification observed in the previous survey. There was no difference between the proportion of Asian or "other" leavers obtaining higher grades, but this level of achievement was significantly lower than the national average.

17.   The proportions achieving lower grade passes, just under half of all school leavers, did not vary significantly between ethnic categories or from the national figure. As a consequence, since only 8 per cent of West Indian children achieved higher grade passes, the proportion achieving no graded result also represented nearly one half of all West Indian school leavers in 1981/82, a proportion significantly higher, statistically, than the proportion of Asian or "other" leavers.

TABLE 5.   English Language ('O' Level and CSE)

	Asians		West Indians		All Other Leavers		Total School Leavers from 5 LEA's		All Maintained School Leavers in England	
	1978/ 79	1981/ 82	1978/ 79	1981/ 82	1978/ 79	1981/ 82	1978/ 79	1981/ 82	1978/ 79	1981/ 82
	%	%	%	%	%	%	%	%	%	%
No Graded Result	31	28	31	25	30	25	30	25	21	18
Lower Grades Only	47	51	61	60	41	46	44	48	45	47
Higher Grades	22	21	9	15	29	29	26	26	34	36
Total Leavers (Number)	466	571	718	653	5,012	4,718	6,196	5,942	693,840	706,690

TABLE 6.   Mathematics ('O' Level and CSE)

	Asians		West Indians		All Other Leavers		Total School Leavers from 5 LEA's		All Maintained School Leavers in England	
	1978/ 79	1981/ 82	1978/ 79	1981/ 82	1978/ 79	1981/ 82	1978/ 79	1981/ 82	1978/ 79	1981/ 82
	%	%	%	%	%	%	%	%	%	%
No Graded Result	38	33	47	45	40	32	40	34	32	27
Lower Grades Only	41	46	47	47	42	47	42	46	45	47
Higher Grades	21	21	5	8	19	21	17	20	23	26
Total Leavers (Number)	466	571	718	653	5,012	4,718	6,196	5,942	693,840	706,690

'A' Level Achievements

18.   Table 7 shows the percentage of school leavers achieving an 'A' level pass. 5 per cent of West Indian leavers in 1981/82 compared with 13 per cent of Asians and as compared with the 13 per cent which is the national average figure, obtained at least one 'A' level pass. The increase in the proportion of West Indian school leavers gaining this level of achievement from that recorded by the previous survey was statistically significant.

TABLE 7.   'A' Level Achievements

	Asians		West Indians		All Other Leavers		Total School Leavers from 5 LEA's		All Maintained School Leavers in England	
	1978/ 79	1981/ 82	1978/ 79	1981/ 82	1978/ 79	1981/ 82	1978/ 79	1981/ 82	1978/ 79	1981/ 82
	%	%	%	%	%	%	%	%	%	%
No 'A' Level Pass	88	87	98	95	88	87	90	88	87	86
At least 1 'A' level Pass	12	13	2	5	12	13	10	12	13	14
Total Leavers (Numbers)	466	571	718	653	5,012	4,718	6,196	5,942	693,840	706,690

Summary of Results

19.   Asian children stay on longer at school than other children, and achieve slightly below the national average in overall levels of academic achievement. They exhibit a greater propensity to leave school to follow some form of full-time further education and are only slightly less likely to go to university or sit a degree course.

20.   West Indian children, more especially the girls, also tend to stay on at school longer than other children (excluding Asian children). They also tend to go more frequently than the average child from school to some form of full-time education course – but not to university or to pursue a degree course – and to have obtained a lower general level of academic achievement at school.

APPENDIX

Sampling Errors

1. The information contained in the paper is drawn from the School Leavers Sample Surveys for 1978/79 and 1981/82 for five LEAs with high levels of ethnic minority school leavers. Because the data was not collected from a random selection of LEAs in England no probability statements concerning the characteristics shown by ethnic minority school leavers in England as a whole can be made from the sample. All statements in the text refer solely to the characteristics shown by the sample of ethnic school leavers within the purposively selected LEAs and all comparisons between sub-groups are subject also to this limitation.

2. Because the data was collected through a sample survey (approximately a 10 per cent sample), the proportions shown in the tables are subject to randomsampling error. The effect of this is that a difference between estimates obtained from the sample and the 'true' population value being estimated can be expected. (Here the population is limited to the leavers from the five LEAs for the reason given in paragraph 1). However, since the sample was randomly drawn, confidence limits within which we would expect the 'true' population value to lie can be calculated and hence a probability statement regarding how likely it is two sample estimates reflect different population values can be made. The method by which this is achieved, together with an example, is demonstrated at paragraph 4.

3. It is usual to present confidence limits of the population value at the 95 per cent level. This means that it is expected that the 'true' population value lies outside the range given by the confidence limits on average only once in twenty times. Other confidence limits are equally possible; narrower limits, eg 90 per cent, indicating a reduced degree of belief that the smaller range will encompass the 'true' value, and wider limits eg 99 per cent indicating that it would be expected that the 'true' value would lie outside them on 1 per cent of occasions. Where the term 'statistical significance' has been used in the text, 95 per cent confidence limits have been used but this does not imply that other limits are inappropriate.

4. The variance in simple random sampling of attributes is denoted by $\frac{pq}{n}$ where p represents the proportion of the sample exhibiting any desired characteristic, and q represents the proportion who do <u>not</u> exhibit this characteristic ie $q = 1-p$, and n is the sample size. The standard error of the sample estimate is denoted by the square root of the variance, namely:

$$^6(p) \quad = \quad \sqrt{\frac{pq}{n}}$$

In order to test whether the sample proportions from two samples (eg p_a and p_b) are 'significantly' different then the standard error of the difference in proportion is calculated and compared with the actual difference in proportion between the samples. That is;

$$^6(p_1\text{-}p_2) \quad = \quad \sqrt{p_o q_o \left(\frac{1}{n_1} + \frac{1}{n_2}\right)}$$

where p_o is the pooled estimate of proportion from the 2 samples of assumed common population proportion,

$$p_o \quad = \quad \frac{n_1 p_1 + n_2 p_2}{n_1 + n_2}$$

By calculating the standard error of the difference in proportions and by dividing the actual difference by this factor provides an estimate of how likely it is that the sample estimates reflect a difference in the appropriate population values.

117

5.   For example, from Table 4 consider the proportions of West Indians achieving 5 or more higher grade 'O' level/CSE passes. From the 1978/79 survey sample size is 718 and proportion exhibiting characteristics is 3 per cent and from the 1981/82 survey sample size is 653 and proportion exhibiting characteristic is 6 per cent. Hence, standard error of difference in proportion is:

$$^6(p_1\_p_2) \quad = \quad \sqrt{p_o q_o \left(\frac{1}{n_1} + \frac{1}{n_2}\right)}$$

$$\text{where } p_o \quad = \quad \frac{(0.03 \times 718) + (0.06 \times 653)}{718 + 653} \quad = \quad 4.4\%$$

$$\text{or } \underline{{}^6(p_1\_p_2)} \;=\; \sqrt{0.44 \times 0.956 \left(\frac{1}{718} + \frac{1}{653}\right)} \quad = \quad 1.1\%$$

A difference between the estimates of proportion exceeding (1.96 x 1.1 per cent) = 2.2 per cent would be statistically significant at the 95 per cent level of confidence. Since the actual difference in proportion is 3 per cent it can be concluded that there was a significant increase in the proportion of West Indians achieving 5 or more higher grade 'O' level/CSE passes between the two surveys.

ANNEX C

THE EDUCATION OF BANGLADESHI CHILDREN IN TOWER HAMLETS

A background paper by the Education Officer, Inner London Education Authority

A General Background

1.   Although Tower Hamlets has received immigrants from Bangladesh (formerly East Pakistan) for many years, the arrival of Bangladeshis in significant numbers dates from the early 70s. Initially, almost all those who came to Tower Hamlets settled in the western part of the Borough, mainly in the Spitalfields area. Despite the gradual increase in the number of Bangladeshi children admitted to the primary schools serving that area, there was no real pressure on school places at that stage. Declining school rolls throughout Tower Hamlets ensured that there were generally sufficient places for these children in the schools nearest to where they were living. By the mid-70s the school population in a small number of schools in Spitalfields had already become predominantly Bangladeshi.

2.   Up to 1975 the majority of the children of school age coming to Tower Hamlets from Bangladesh were of secondary age, mainly teenage boys who came to join older male relatives already settled and working in the Borough. Most of these new arrivals attended the one secondary school serving Spitalfields. From the mid-70's onwards, however, the pattern of immigration began to change, with more and more of the men already here being joined by their wives and younger children. Since most of these families settled in the western part of the Borough, pressure on places in those primary schools which already had most Bangladeshi pupils became increasingly evident and difficulties in placing children occurred more frequently.

3.   Although there were alternative schools with vacancies in adjoining areas fairly close to Spitalfields, Bangladeshi parents were clearly reluctant to send their children other than to the nearest schools to their home. This was perhaps not surprising bearing in mind that the children did not speak English, had only just arrived from Bangladesh from a rural community and often had no previous experience of school. In addition, there was evident fear on the part of the Bangladeshi community of women and young children being subjected to harassment and physical and verbal attack on the way to and from school. Some alternative schools – often little more than half a mile from their homes – involved journeys through areas which were viewed by the community as 'hostile territory' or involved crossing busy major roads, especially frightening for women and children who had no previous experience of an urban environment and of heavy motor traffic.

4.   In the past three years more and more Bangladeshi families have been rehoused in other parts of Tower Hamlets outside the Spitalfields area and the number of schools which have admitted increasing numbers of Bangladeshi children has correspondingly grown. The recent language survey (June 1983) indicated that pupils for whom English was a second language, the majority of whom are Bengali speakers represented 80% or more of the roll in 6 schools and more than 40% of the roll in a further 21 schools. Although the heaviest concentration of Bangladeshis remains in the western part of Tower Hamlets, the community is now settled in significant numbers both in the centre and eastern parts of the Borough.

119

5. The Bangladeshi community is affected by racism in many ways. Some of these are quite outside the responsibilities or powers of an education authority. The areas where the ILEA does have responsibility are to do with the security of Asian pupils from various forms of harassment and abuse in school; with ensuring equality in the employment and promotion of staff from this and other minority groups; with the attitudes and low expectations teachers sometimes have towards the educational potential of Bangladeshi children and towards the quality and validity of Bengali culture. The authority's initiative on multi-ethnic education and racial equality throughout the ILEA area is a positive move to make major changes both structural and attitudinal to improve the position.

B Language/Communication/School Placements
1. Many of the Bangladeshi children in primary schools and a growing proportion of those entering secondary schools, speak a Sylheti variety of Bengali, but relatively little English. The 1981 Language Survey showed that Tower Hamlets had 3,200 Bengali speakers, which was 15 times as many as the average number in the other Divisions. Tower Hamlets also had 1,530 children who were complete beginners in English. Twenty per cent (2,440) of all the pupils in the Division were either at the beginner or intermediate stage in their mastery of English. The average for the other divisions was six per cent. The great majority of the pupils at these early stages of English learning are Bengali speakers and are in schools in Spitalfields and adjacent districts. Over twenty schools in this area have a majority of Bengali speakers and several have over 90 per cent.

2. Very few staff, whether teaching or non-teaching, in schools with a large proportion of Bengali speaking pupils actually speak Bengali themselves. This linguistic disparity greatly impairs the quality of communication in the classroom and other forms of communication, such as liaison with the parents, which are essential to the running of successful schools. Hence the major thrust and concentration on language within the authority's initiatives in this area.

3. One of the major obstacles in dealing with the placing of children in schools has been the difficulties encountered by schools and the Education Welfare Service (EWS) in communicating with members of the Bangladeshi community, for the most part non-English speaking. In recent years efforts have been made to recruit Bengali speakers to teaching and non-teaching posts in schools and to posts in the EWS. In May 1981 a Bengali speaker was recruited as an interpreter for the EWS in Tower Hamlets and subsequently an Asian Team, comprising a Senior Education Welfare Officer, 3 Education Welfare Officers and a team clerk – all Bangladeshis – was established. In addition a further 3 Bengali speakers have also been recruited to the basic EWS posts in Tower Hamlets and a second interpreter post, already authorised, will shortly be filled.

4. The addition of these Bengali speakers has ensured that the EWS is able to give more support to the Bangladeshi community in Tower Hamlets. However, school placements still remain a critical issue, because of the demand from the community for places in a relatively small number of schools, which are generally full and because of the mobility of the Bangladeshi community. There are no institutional means by which EWS can know of children out of school: they are dependent for this information on parents presenting themselves at the school of their choice to request a place. In these circumstances and especially bearing in mind the very short stay of some families at their first address in Tower Hamlets, the task of following up children out of school is a particularly heavy one. The figure of primary children 'out of school' known to EWS is about 100 at any one time, although the majority of these will be very recent arrivals. There remains, nevertheless, a number of children who remain out of school for at least a term because of the refusal of parents to consider suitable vacancies in alternative schools and where negotiations between EWS and the families are inevitably protracted.

5. Although there are sufficient secondary school places overall, there have nevertheless been some difficulties in placing pupils, particularly those who arrive in Tower Hamlets during the course of the school year when the number of schools with vacancies in the appropriate year

group may be very restricted. Additionally the demand for single-sex schools, especially for girls on religious grounds has resulted in some pressure on girls-only schools and has led to a situation where the sex balance in some mixed schools has become distorted.

C   Growth of Pupil Numbers and Provision of Additional School Accommodation

1.   As the pressure on primary schools increased from 1978 onwards as a result of the continuing, growing immigration from Bangladesh, action was taken by the authority to make extra places available, particularly in Spitalfields and the adjoining area south of Commerical Road to meet the needs of the Bangladeshi community. The additional places have been provided by:

(a)   bringing into use existing spare accommodation;

(b)   releasing accommodation on primary school sites by re-locating other educational users;

(c)   the minor adaptations of buildings or the provision of hutted accommodation.

2.   Despite these measures there have, nevertheless, been considerable problems in the past 2 years, in meeting the wishes of many Bangladeshi parents, who generally remain reluctant to agree to their children going to other than the nearest school. There is no longer scope for providing further extra places in the existing schools in Spitalfields and the area to the south of Commercial Road. In the light of the continuing demand for primary places in these areas and of future roll projections, new schools are now being planned for the western part of the Borough.

3.   As far as secondary schools are concerned there has not been the same pressure on places. Overall there are sufficient secondary places available to meet current needs, bearing in mind that it is accepted that secondary pupils will normally travel further to schools.

4.   The following points are important when considering the provision of additional school accommodation:

(a)   **Primary Schools**

   (i)   **Reluctance of Asians to travel**
   Asian mothers are reluctant to take their children any distance to school. This is of critical importance in the planning of primary school provision in areas like Spitalfields in that the planning has to be based on a smaller area than would normally be the case. The Department of Education and Science normally require LEAs to calculate the basic need for primary school places on a three mile radius. Experience in Tower Hamlets is that Asians will travel less than ¼ mile if the journey involved is through what they consider to be an unsafe area. This means that a detailed knowledge of the relevant geographical and social factors is essential in order to ensure that the school accommodation needs of the Asian community are met. The willingness of the Department of Education and Science to consider a relaxation of normal requirements in recognition of the particular needs of the Asian community in this respect has been welcomed.

   (ii)   **Need for small group spaces**
   Non-English speaking children need more intensive teaching in small groups and this has accommodation implications. A recent brief for a new 210 place primary school includes 4 small group rooms each of $12m^2$. In addition existing buildings are being examined with a view to providing extra small group spaces in schools with a large number of Asian children. Care needs to be taken that the small group rooms are quiet and in the design of new accommodation generally Architects

need to ensure that the children will feel secure. Infant play areas, for instance, need to be well protected and segregated from the more boisterous juniors whilst being closely linked to the infants' classrooms.

(iii) **Size of classes**

The Authority normally bases primary school planning on class sizes of 30. In open plan schools or in small schools which lack small group spaces, class sizes of 30 are not considered adequate for teaching non-English speaking children. In assessing the capacity of primary schools in Spitalfields, class sizes of 25 rather than 30 are used for those schools with a high proportion of non-English speaking children. This gives a capacity for the schools in Spitalfields of 1,105 compared with 1,470 by conventional planning methods, thus illustrating the considerable extra space requirements for the teaching of non-English speaking children.

(iv) **Sanitary Provision**

Separate boys' and girls' toilet facilities need to be provided for infants as well as juniors in schools with a high percentage of Asians as well as separate boys' and girls' changing areas.

(b) **Secondary Schools**

The most important consideration is the marked preference amongst Asians for single sex schools particularly for girls. This needs to be taken into account in planning secondary school accommodation in Tower Hamlets.

D   Resourcing of Schools' Curriculum and Language Needs

1.   In addition to the language factors in the curriculum referred to above, there is a need to change aspects of the curriculum as well. At present most Bangladeshi children study a school curriculum that has not been designed with them primarily in mind. This is not to imply that Bengali children or children of any other ethnic group, should follow a curriculum that is unique to them; nor that Bangladeshi parents are asking for anything special or separate for their children. Nor is it suggested that teachers and lecturers in schools and colleges have not already made many adaptations, both in the content and in the linguistic presentation of the curriculum. But the Authority recognises that there is still much to be done to ensure that the school curriculum engages adequately with the social reality and the cultural strengths of Bangladeshi children's lives. Much work is actively in hand.

2.   The additional needs of the Bangladeshis in Tower Hamlets have been recognised in the resourcing of schools. Although the basic resourcing of all schools is roll related, additional resources are allocated according to needs, determined by the Authority's primary and secondary school indices (which place schools in a ranking order on the basis of a number of measures of deprivation, eg, fluency in English, ethnic family background, free meals eligibility, large families, one parent families, parental occupation, mobility, behaviour and by the Language Survey (which records the number of pupils for whom English is a second language (E2L) and the stages of pupils' language development). From 1983, indices have been altered to include for the first time a specific E2L measure which has resulted in a further shift, within overall allocations, of resources from parts of London with fewer E2L pupils to Divisions like Tower Hamlets with high numbers of E2L pupils. In terms of teaching posts, Tower Hamlets had an additional 60 full time equivalent Special Needs Posts for primary and secondary schools for 1983/84 over the allocations for 1982/83 (the 1982/83 allocations, in turn, showed an increase of 57.2 posts over the allocation for the previous year). Since the cash allocations to schools under the Authority's Alternative Use of Resources Scheme (ie money which can be used to purchase additional teaching or non-teaching staff or capitation items) are based on roll and schools ranking in the primary and secondary schools indices, Tower Hamlets schools overall received more than £250,000 additional resourcing for 1983/84 in real terms over the allocations for 1982/83. The following table shows the level of English fluency of Bengali speakers:–

English fluency of Bengali, Gujerati, Punjabi and Urdu speakers
Tnot fluent in English*

Age in years	Bengali	Gujerati	Punjabi	Urdu
5 and under	96.9	86.3	87.4	83.8
6	93.2	73.6	79.2	69.2
7	89.5	67.3	70.8	61.0
8	86.7	56.8	64.3	50.8
9	86.9	53.5	61.0	52.7
10	80.9	46.6	55.4	42.1
11	74.4	40.4	47.6	42.4
12	77.1	36.2	43.8	33.6
13	70.2	28.6	25.2	27.7
14	73.7	27.6	35.6	27.1
15	74.0	21.2	26.3	22.5
16+	36.5	17.1	17.3	18.1

*Pupils in primary and secondary schools only – nursery and Special schools not included.
(Taken from the 1983 ILEA Language Survey.)

E   Tower Hamlets Initiative

1.   Conscious of the need to improve education support to the community in Tower Hamlets the authority made provision in its 1983/84 Budget for a major new initiative. This was seen as having two main objectives:

(a)   To link the process of education to the needs of families and young children, providing increased opportunities for learning English language skills, developing mother-tongue teaching and involving the parents in the education of their children.

(b)   To provide increased opportunities for young people and adults, through in-service training and curriculum development support for work in E2L and mother-tongue teaching, piloting skill-based courses in mother-tongue, developing general access courses and in partnership with local youth organisations, making a significant extension of youth provision.

2.   A Project Co-ordinator was appointed, to ensure that there was full and speedy consultation with the local community. The Authority encouraged members of the local community in the establishment of a body (Bangladeshi Education Needs in Tower Hamlets – BENTH) to articulate their own needs for discussion in a joint body with elected members of the Authority on which they enjoy full voting rights.

F   Careers and Unemployment

1.   The needs for early identification of potential E2L candidates in secondary schools is a major factor in Careers Service work as it has far reaching effects on employment prospects. Even the highly qualified are less likely to find employment if English is their second language. Sometimes accent rather than command of the English language constitutes a handicap.

2.   There is a need to develop language tuition for the older teenager. Since many Asians do not arrive in this country until the teens and may have sporadic attendance at school the problem persists into adulthood. As a result, language is a major obstacle to effective Careers Service work. Although the Authority has both Asian careers officers and support staff there are none who speak Bengali or more particularly the Sylheti dialect. This hampers good communication with some youngsters and even with parents. To help in overcoming this language problem certain careers service literature is printed in Asian languages.

3.   The absorption of young leavers into the extended family and family business reduces the number of unemployed registered with careers offices. The size of the unemployment problem is thus hidden and the extent of under-employment becomes immeasurable. Female unemployment is almost entirely hidden with many young Asian women becoming isolated within their traditional cultural role in the home. The traditional approach to finance, with money set aside for dowry and/or higher education is breaking down as funds are diverted to support growing unemployment throughout families. Girls in particular tend to suffer because of this.

4.   While Bangladeshis suffer from the same problems as other Asian groups, they also face added difficulties. As a generalisation, fewer attain the better academic qualifications normally expected of Asian youngsters as illustrated in the following table:

Achievement in Public Examinations (1981/82)

An analysis of a sample of school-leavers in ILEA shows marked differences in the achievements of the Asian groups. The numbers are relatively small and have been divided into two broad categories comprising the following groups:

Lower: not entered
no grades
one or more CSE grades 4 or 5

Higher: one or more CSE grades 2 or 3 or 'O' level D or E
one to four CSE grade 1 or 'O' level A to C
five or more CSE grade 1 or 'O' level A to C

Percentages achieving in the two groups are:

	Indian	Pakistani	Bangladeshi	African Asian	Other Asian
Lower	9	16	79	24	20
Higher	91	84	21	76	80

5.   There is a high absentee rate from interviews at school with careers officers. The explanation appears to be that many return to Bangladesh for extended stays, while some are believed to be working on family contracts, usually in the garment trade, restaurants or shops. Those who do find jobs outside the traditional openings are often restricted to unskilled manual jobs (of which there are fewer and fewer available) as they are hampered by language.

6.   While language seems to be the biggest disadvantage in employment it is equally true to say the cultural differences in the Moslem community create the severest problems for Asian girls.

G   General Comment

As full ethnically based statistics of pupil performance do not exist, it is difficult to assess Bangladeshi pupils performance as compared to pupils from other ethnic groups. Nonetheless, it would be unrealistic to claim that Bangladeshi pupils in this area generally, leave school for example with exam results comparable to those of their indigenous peers. That is not surprising as a substantial number of those factors which are generally accepted as adversely influencing educational performance are present in relatively extreme forms in Tower Hamlets. In addition, the length of time spent by pupils from Bangladesh in schools is often quite short and even those pupils who have been in primary schools before transferring to secondary have often had their schooling considerably disrupted by extended 'holidays' in Bangladesh. Many 'new arrival' entrants to secondary schools from Bangladesh have had no formal schooling whatsoever up to that point. These factors are obviously exacerbated by these pupils' lack of competence in English. Statements about 'poor performance' (often allied with claims about how schools are 'failing') tend to be made too readily. This is said in full recognition of the dangers of 'low expectations' of such pupils' performance and without seeking to deny that further special efforts need to be made to help them make up ground on their peers, against the background of their extreme disadvantage. It is in recognition of the need of such special efforts that the Authority is taking the exceptional measures shown in this paper.

October 1983.

ANNEX D

The IQ Question: A Paper by Professor N J Mackintosh and Dr C G N Mascie-Taylor

Introduction: The Nature of IQ Tests

If a child does badly at school, lagging behind other children in learning to read, being assigned to lower streams or classes, failing exams and finally leaving school at 16 with few if any educational qualifications, it may seem only natural to say that the child was not good at schoolwork, perhaps that he was not academically minded or was just not very bright. We may thus think that we have explained the child's performance at school by reference to his ability or capacity (or lack thereof). And if it could further be shown that the child also obtained low scores on standard intelligence or IQ tests, it might seem that this explanation had been confirmed: science would have documented the fact that the child lacked the intellectual ability needed for success at school.

Even when we are dealing with an individual child, there are reasons for questioning several of the steps in this argument. When we are dealing with large groups of children, the doubts multiply. It has long been known that children from working-class families are, on average, academically less succesful than those from middle-class families.[1] Is this really because they are naturally less intelligent? And it has also been apparent for some time that children in this country from certain ethnic minorities tend to perform less well at school than do indigenous children.[2] Is this because they too, as a group, are on average less intelligent?

Even to pose the question will seem repugnant or insulting to many people. But it would be idle to pretend that no one has ever taken such possibilities seriously. In a celebrated article published in 1969, the American educational psychologist, A. R. Jensen noted that blacks in the USA were not only less successful at school than whites, but also scored significantly lower on standard IQ tests, and concluded that it is "a not unreasonable hypothesis that genetic factors are strongly implicated in the average Negro-White intelligence difference."[3] The British psychologist H. J. Eysenck is characteristically blunter: "All the evidence to date" he has written, "suggests the strong and indeed overwhelming importance of genetic factors in producing the great variety of intellectual differences which we observe in our culture, and much of the difference between certain racial groups."[4]

There is a whole network of assumptions underlying these arguments, some reasonable enough, others distinctly more questionable. Before considering some of the evidence, it will be as well to make clear what some of these assumptions are. The first, and one of the more questionable, is that there is something called "intelligence" which can be accurately measured by an IQ test; more especially, that a child's IQ reflects a single capacity or even a set of abilities with which he is endowed by nature and which determines, or sets limits to, what he will achieve at school. The distinction is sometimes drawn between ability or potential, measured by an IQ test, and achievement or performance, measured by school exams.

This is no place for a detailed discussion of IQ tests,[5] and to be brief it will be necessary to be dogmatic. It is important to insist at the outset that an IQ test simply measures a sample of a person's behaviour at a given point in time, what he knows or has learned, how well he can solve certain kinds of problem. But school exams also purport to measure a child's knowledge and what he has learned, and will often test the ability to solve certain kinds of problem (consider a mathematics exam). The distinction between an IQ test and a school exam is not trivial, for the former is more likely than the latter to test knowledge that has not been formally taught at school

126

and to require the child to solve problems rather different from any that he may have come across before. But it is a difference of degree, not of kind. An IQ score does not, indeed could not, provide any magically direct insight into a child's intellectual capacity divorced of all he has been taught or learned for himself. It measures his potential only in much the same way that (even if more accurately than) school exams also measure potential. Teachers and examiners assume that an exam result tells them not only what a child has learned, but also how well he is likely to do in the future. Scores on IQ tests will also predict a child's likely performance in other situations – for example how well he will do at school. In that sense, but in no other, they may be said to measure the child's potential.

A common assumption is that an IQ score reflects a child's potential in the sense that it measures a fixed, innate ability. It is true that IQ scores are **relatively** stable: a child's IQ at the age of 6 or 7 will predict quite well his IQ at 16 or 17.[6] But large changes are quite common. It is also probable that inheritance plays some part in determining IQ. That is to say, it seems probable that some of the differences in IQ observed in the population of the U.S. or the U.K. are caused by genetic differences between members of these populations. How important genetic factors may be cannot be realistically determined from any available data. The claim of Jensen and Eysenck that no less than 80% of the variation in IQ is genetically caused is not justified on the basis of published evidence, and recent estimates, based on more recent and better data, have given estimates of the order of 50%.[7] But the most reasonable conclusion is that there are far too many problems inherent in all the data to justify this sort of precise, quantitative statement; the safest claim is that probably somewhere between one quarter and three quarters of the variation seen in IQ in most Western societies is due to genetic difference between members of those societies.

Perhaps the most contentious assumption underlying the whole argument, however, is that IQ tests could ever provide a fair measure of the intelligence of children from working-class families, let alone those from ethnic or racial minorities. Devised by white, middle-class psychologists, standardized on white children, validated by their ability to predict performance in white schools, IQ tests, it is argued, will inevitably reflect white, middle-class values, must be biased against other groups, and could not possibly provide a realistic assessment of their abilities. The argument may seem reasonable and persuasive. But it needs examination to disentangle what is possibly true from what is probably misleading. As has been justly remarked, criticizing IQ tests "for reflecting class differences is rather like blaming the weighing machine when it shows an undernourished child to be below weight."[8] If a child has been deprived of intellectual stimulation or educational opportunity, it is small wonder that his intellectual performance will reflect this fact. An IQ test is no more able to gauge a child's true innate potential regardless of the circumstances of his upbringing than is a pair of scales to measure his true potential weight regardless of what he has been fed. To repeat: IQ tests measure a sample of a child's actual behaviour, what he knows and has learned. Some children may have lacked the opportunity to acquire the knowledge crucial for answering certain questions, just as a starved child may have been fed a diet lacking critical nutrients. To claim that IQ tests are biased is often only a misleading way of making the point that IQ tests measure skills and knowledge which not all children may have been able to acquire; in other words, that differences in IQ scores are partly due to differences in the environmental experiences of different children. But we already knew that.

What is commonly meant by the claim that an IQ test is biased against a particular group of children is that it does not reveal their true intelligence. But if this assertion is to carry any weight, it must mean that the IQ test provides a lower estimate of their intellectual performance than does some alternative measure. Bias is now a relative term. For example, one IQ test might be more biased against, say, children from working-class families than was another IQ test. Psychologists have indeed tried valiantly to construct "culture-fair" tests which require less specialised knowledge, but no one would seriously argue that there could ever exist a test that required no such knowledge at all. Nevertheless there is reasonably good evidence that tests depending heavily on vocabulary produce larger differences between the scores of working-class and middle-class children and between those from large and small families than do so-called nonverbal IQ tests.[9] In other words, verbal tests are, by this criterion, more biased against working-class children than are nonverbal tests. But, contrary to widespread opinion, the differences between the IQ scores of blacks and whites in the U.S. are, at least usually, no greater on verbal tests than on nonverbal tests.[10] Whether the same is true of any differences between West Indian and white children in this country is a question addressed below.

It is, of course, possible that all IQ tests are biased against working-class or black children – by comparison with some other measure. The problem, then, is to find the other measure. An obvious candidate might be performance on school tests or exams. But, again contrary to widespread opinion, there is no evidence that IQ tests are more biased against working-class children either in this country or in the U.S., or against black children in the U.S., than are conventional exams or measures of school peformance.[11] The question whether they are biased against ethnic minorities in this country is considered below. But for these other groups, where any differences have been found they have almost invariably been in the opposite direction. That is to say, if a working-class and middle-class child have similar IQs, the chances are that the middle-class child will do better on school exams: the IQ test gives the working-class child a higher score than does the exam. Of course, one could argue, this shows only that exams are even more biased against working-class children. In this limited sense, it certainly suggests that by comparison with IQ tests, school exams are biased against working-class children. But that does not tell us whether IQ tests themselves are biased in their favour or against them.

The critic who claims that IQ tests do not give a true measure of the intelligence of, say, working-class children, must find some other, better measure of their intelligence. We have already argued that IQ tests cannot provide any magical insight into a child's true innate potential. There is no reason to believe that any other measure could achieve this miracle. Indeed, those who claim that IQ tests do not **really** measure intelligence must face up to the problem that is has proved remarkably difficult to find any other test that looks as if it might be measuring intellectual abilities but does not also give results that agree rather closely with existing IQ tests. To this extent, IQ tests, although no doubt very far from perfect, are as good a measure of intelligence or cognitive ability as we have.

Black-White Differences in IQ

With no further preamble, then, let us turn to the question of immediate concern. Children from ethnic minorities do not necessarily do so well at school in this country as do indigenous children. Might this be because they are naturally less intelligent? More specifically, for example, is there any evidence that the average IQ of West Indian children in this country is lower than that of whites?[12]

In the U.S. there has been substantial evidence available for 50 years or more that blacks on average obtain significantly lower scores than whites on standard IQ tests.[13] The differences is usually said to average about 15 points, although it varies considerably from study to study.[14] But this tells us little or nothing about the standing of West Indian children in this country: there have been, not surprisingly, far fewer studies comparing the IQ scores of West Indians and whites in the U.K. and they go back for not much more than 10 to 15 years. The results of four studies are shown in Table 1. The largest, by Yule, Berger, Rutter & Yule[15] which was published in 1975 (but for which the data was collected about 5 years earlier), obtained scores on nonverbal group IQ tests from approximately 14,000 white and 350 West Indian children in their last year at LEA primary schools. In addition, 105 white children and 100 West Indians were given individual IQ tests. These latter results are shown with the West Indian children divided into those born in the West Indies and those born in this country. It is apparent that the West Indian children have lower scores than the whites, although equally apparent that the differences diminish when the West Indian children are born, and therefore receive all their education, in this country. A second, smaller published study, by McFie and Thompson,[16] reported individual IQ scores for a group of West Indian children, aged 5–15 years and a group of white children matched by age and sex to the West Indian sample. The results are very similar, and again show that the longer the West Indian children have been in this country, the better they perform.

The final two sets of data shown in the Table have not previously been published; they come from two large national surveys. The National Child Development Study[17] has provided an exhaustive survey of all children born in a particular week in 1958. There are data for over 10,000 white children and for smaller numbers of various ethnic minorities. At the age of 11, these children were given various educational tests, including verbal and nonverbal IQ tests. The results show that the scores of the West Indian children for whom data are available are significantly lower than those of the white majority, being particularly low for those children resident in this country for less than 4 years. The Child Health and Education Study has provided a similar survey of all children born in a particular week in 1970; the children were given a variety of tests at the age of 10, including four sub-tests from the recently developed British Ability Scales.[18] All but one of the West Indian children identified in the survey had been born in this country, so the results are not broken down by length of residence in the U.K. The results show that West Indian children obtained signficantly lower scores than white children, but it is notable that the difference is rather smaller than in earlier studies, being less than 10 points on the two main verbal tests (definitions and similarities), just over 6 points on the nonverbal matrices test and only 3 points on the digit span.

There are differences between these various studies, both in the extent to which West Indian children lag behind whites and in whether the lag is greater on verbal or nonverbal tests. Such differences are hardly surprising, for the studies have differed widely not only in the samples of children studied, and the date when they were studied, but also in the type of tests employed. For example, the West Indian children in CHES are doing rather better that those in earlier studies. Their total IQ score of 92.4 is only 8 points below the white mean. This cannot be simply because they were all born in this country (compare their scores with those of the U.K. born children in the Yule, Berger, Rutter and Yule study). It may imply that the position of West Indian children has indeed improved in the 10 years since the other studies were undertaken. But it is equally possible that it is the change in tests that is responsible for this apparent improvement. As it happens, the British Ability Scales, unlike the other tests employed in these studies, were standardized on a sample of children that would have included some children of West Indian and Asian origin. Although it does not follow that such children will necessarily do better on this test than on others, it is obvious enough that the only way to find out whether there really have been changes since 1970 in the standing of West Indian children is to administer the same test to random samples of children born in different years over the period between 1960 and 1974. Unfortunately no study has done this.

The differences between the studies reported in Table 1, however, should not be exaggerated. There is also a fair degree of consistency between them. There can be little doubt that on average West Indian children in this country obtain signficantly lower scores on a variety of IQ tests than do white children. There is no suggestion that this poor peformance is confined to verbal tests, although in three of the four studies it was certainly larger on the verbal than on the nonverbal tests. The overall difference is usually not as large as the 15-point difference said to hold between American blacks and whites and it is considerbly smaller than this when the West Indian child has been resident in this country for any length of time. This is not entirely surprising, for there is evidence that blacks from the West Indies are more successful than other blacks in the U.S.[19] It is important, therefore, not to generalize too readily from the American case. Nevertheless, when all is said and done, there is usually still a difference of about 5 to 12 points on a variety of tests between West Indian and white children in this country even when all children have been born here.

129

Genetic Interpretations

Given that there does appear to be a real difference between the IQ scores of West Indian and indigenous children in this country, is there any reason to believe that it might be due to genetic differences between the two groups? How could one set about finding the answer to this question? It seems obvious that the only evidence that would be sufficient to **prove** that black-white differences in IQ, either here or for that matter in the U.S., were genetic in origin would be the demonstration of a difference in IQ scores between randomly selected groups of black and white children brought up in strictly comparable conditions. Given the nature of American and British societies, the experiment seems hardly feasible. It is difficult to believe that black and white children could ever experience truly comparable environments, and it would always be possible to appeal to some uncontrolled differences in their experience to explain away any remaining differences in their IQ scores. What is striking, however, is that in the three studies that have attemped to approximate these ideal conditions (albeit not very successfully), such differences have been extremely small. Unfortunately, only one of these studies is British. It looked at 4-to 5-year old children living in residential nurseries.[20] At this age, it is important to acknowledge, "IQ" scores do not predict later IQ particularly well; it is not clear, therefore, whether the several measures taken of the children will have had much bearing on their IQ when they were older. It is also clear that neither the black nor the white children were a representative sample of the black and white populations of this country, since the occupations of their natural parents were more likely to be non-manual than is true of the population as a whole. In other words, the study is very far from ideal. Nevertheless, its outcome is impressive: the test scores of the 30 children, one or both of whose parents were black, were somewhat **higher** than those of the 24 children who had two white parents.

The two other studies are both concerned with American blacks. One looked at illegitimate children born to, and brought up by, German women, but fathered by American (and a small proportion of French) servicemen between 1945 and 1952.[21] Some of these servicemen were black, others white. This had no effect, however, on the IQ score of the children. The more recent study looked at children brought up by white adoptive families in Minnesota:[22] some of the children had two white natural parents, some had two black parents, some one black and one white. The difference between the IQ scores of the white and mixed-race children was small and statistically insignificant. The black children did have significantly lower scores (approximately 12 points lower) than either of the other groups, and this might suggest a genetic effect. But they had also been adopted at a later age than the mixed-race children and had been with their adoptive families for a significantly shorter period of time before IQ scores were obtained. Moreover, their adoptive parents were less well educated than those adopting the mixed-race children. In combination, as the authors noted, these environmental factors may be sufficient to account for the observed differences in IQ.

All three studies have numerous flaws: the samples are small and sometimes seriously unrepresentative; in the one British study, the IQ scores are questionable; in each case, some or all of the children are of mixed parentage, and in the Minnesota adoption study, the results from the children with two black parents are distinctly equivocal. Nevertheless, these are the only studies that even approximate to the ideal, and on balance there is little doubt which way they point: measured differences in IQ scores between black and white children in the U.S. and between West Indian and white children in this country are probably largely environmental in origin. The data do not compel this conclusion, for they are very imperfect. But there is no other **direct** evidence to contradict it. So why should anyone have concluded otherwise? Why, for example, should Jensen have argued that the difference in average IQ between blacks and whites in the U.S. is partly caused by genetic differences between the two groups?[23] Although there is no guarantee that his conclusions would apply to the difference between West Indians and whites in this country, they should not, for that reason alone, simply be dismissed out of hand. It is important to see what his arguments are and whether there is any reason to accept them. They are, in fact, largely indirect and amount to the assertion that there are no plausible environmental factors which could account for the observed differences in IQ. In particular, Jensen has stressed three points:–

130

1.   Differences in IQ between American blacks and whites are not just due to differences in "socio-economic status" (SES), since even when one compares children from families of similar SES, there is still a large difference in IQ. In California, indeed, Jensen has claimed that black children from high SES families have marginally lower IQs than white children from low SES families.

2.   The difference between American blacks and whites is very much larger than that observed between whites and other ethnic minorities in the U.S. (e.g. American Indians and Mexicans) who are on average even poorer and hold worse jobs than blacks; while some ethnic minorities (notably people of Japanese or Chinese origin) obtain higher scores than the white majority on nonverbal IQ tests.

3.   The difference is not just due to bias in the tests. In the first place, it holds up, and indeed is often greater, on supposedly unbiased non-verbal IQ tests than on possibly biased verbal tests of intelligence. Secondly, Jensen argues, there is no evidence that IQ tests in general are particularly biased against blacks in the U.S., for they predict academic achievement for blacks just as well as they do for whites.

Whether these arguments are persuasive is perhaps a matter of opinion. They are surely not conclusive, and in the light of the direct evidence from adoption studies cited above, it might be argued that they should be rejected. But that direct evidence was itself far from conclusive and a more sensible response is surely to take Jensen's arguments seriously and consider whether there is any force to them – in particular whether they should be applied to the British case. If for no other reason, it is important to consider what might be the environmental factors that produce such large differences between the average IQ scores of blacks and whites. All too often, environmentalists have been content to mount an onslaught on hereditarian positions, but have refused to accept the obligation to provide any explanation themselves of the observed facts. Such explanations, moreover, may have practical consequences: if it is really true that environmental factors are depressing the IQ scores, and perhaps therefore also the school performance, of West Indian children in this country, a more precise understanding of these factors may help to improve their performance.

The Environment
Little enough is known about the environmental factors that affect IQ in any population – let alone those that might be responsible for differences between ethnic groups or classes within that population. It is known, for example, that differences in IQ are correlated with differences in social class or SES, but many psychologists (Jensen and Eysenck to name but two) have argued that these may partly reflect genetic rather than environmental differences between the classes. It is known that certain demographic variables, such as family size, and other related factors such as birth order, are correlated with IQ, but although these effects are almost certainly environmental in origin, it is not certain just how they are produced.[24]

For our purposes, one critical question is whether differences **between** ethnic groups may be accounted for by appeal to the same sorts of factors as those supposedly responsible for differences **within**, say, the majority group, or whether it is necessary to appeal to some unique factors affecting the cognitive or scholastic performance of an ethnic minority. It is perfectly clear, for example, that West Indians in this country and blacks in the U.S. are, on average, poorer and occupy jobs of lower status that the white majority;[25] since these factors affect IQ in the white population, it seems entirely probable that they may also help to explain the lower test scores of West Indian children. There are other, equally well established, differences in their backgrounds. A higher proportion of West Indian that of white families contain only a single parent; a higher proportion of West Indian than of white mothers go out to work; and a higher proportion of West Indian than of white children are looked after by child-minders.[26] Is it not possible that some of these differences are related to, perhaps even cause, the observed differences in the children's IQ scores?

131

Jensen's first argument was that differences in IQ between blacks and whites in the U.S. cannot be explained this way. Paradoxically enough, his fiercest critics accept this initial premise, although clearly not the conclusions he draws from it. A number of writers, both in this country and in the U.S., have rejected all attempts to explain differences between blacks and whites by appeal to the family background of the blacks.[27] Such explanations are said to imply that there is something "pathological" about black family life or culture, and are seen as no less insulting than Jensen's own suggestion that differences in IQ are genetic in origin. These writers have seen a racist society rather than a pathological family background as the major cause of these differences. Black children are said to lack self-esteem: constant exposure to racial slurs and low expectations (for example from teachers) eventually ensures that black children will live down to these expectations and peform poorly both in IQ tests and in school in general. The argument, in other words, is that there is something unique about the experience of children from some ethnic minorities that is directly responsible for their relatively poor performance on a variety of tests.

That certain ethnic minorities in this country (and in the U.S.) suffer from racial discrimination will probably not be disputed. The question is whether such discrimination has a direct effect on a child's performance in school. An alternative possibility is that racial discrimination is a major cause of the impoverished social circumstances of their parents and affects the children's IQ scores only indirectly, by ensuring that they grow up in the sorts of circumstances that contribute to a low IQ score in the indigenous majority also. In what follows , therefore, we shall attempt to see first, how far differences between blacks and whites can be accounted for in terms of the sorts of environmental factors that are thought to affect IQ in the white population; secondly, whether any of Jensen's other indirect arguments have any force when applied to the British case; and finally, whether there is any evidence to support the argument that racial discrimination provides a unique factor directly affecting the IQ scores of black children in this country.

Class and family background
Jensen's first argument was that black-white differences in IQ are not simply a consequence of differences in SES, for high-SES blacks actually have rather lower scores than low-SES whites. Equating for SES, he has claimed, reduces what is otherwise a 15-point or greater difference in IQ by no more than 2 or 3 points.[28] This is consistent with data surveyed by Shuey in 1966:[29] from 13 studies undertaken between 1921 and 1964, she concluded that the average difference in IQ between blacks and whites of similar SES was 12.80 points. But many of these studies are too flawed to be taken seriously: the attempts to equate socio-economic status were frequently crude and clearly unsuccessful.[30] Moreover, Shuey also analysed a further 14 studies carried out between 1922 and 1958 which had looked at blacks and whites living in similar neighbourhoods, and found that the average difference was now reduced to 8 points. And there are other more recent American studies which have obtained results wholly at variance with Jensen's claim and Shuey's summaries. In one large and careful survey carried out in Boston, Philadelphia and Baltimore,[31] individual IQ tests were given to a total of over 15,000 black and white children from either high or low SES families: differences between blacks and whites of similar SES averaged between 4 and 6 IQ points – considerably less than the 9 or 10 points separating children from the high and low SES backgrounds.

Much the same appears to be true in this country. The data from the National Child Development Study, shown in Table 2, reveal a 15-point difference between West Indian and white children in total IQ. But, as can be seen, this difference is immediately reduced to 11 points by adjusting for the fact that a very much smaller proportion of West Indian than of white children have fathers with non-manual jobs (the actual proportions are shown in Table 3). Table 2 also shows the results of a second British study by Grace who gave IQ tests to 11-year old indigenous and West Indian children attending the same, inner-city schools, and therefore approximately equated for the neighbourhood in which they lived.[32] It is clear that the difference in IQ scores is very much less than most of those shown in Table 1.

Father's occupation and neighbourhood are hardly the only factors known to be related to a child's IQ. If equating black and white children on variables as simple as these has such an effect on the difference in their IQs, it seems possible that a more comprehensive attempt to match them for potentially important environmental variables might well reduce the difference to quite trivial proportions. And so it has seemed.[33] Two studies published over 10 years ago found essentially no differences between the IQ scores of West Indian and white children when some of the more obvious disparities in social circumstances between them were reduced or controlled.[34] Their results are also shown in Table 2. Houghton studied 5-year old West Indian and white children living in a decaying city centre, attending the same schools and with similar nursery school experience. All but two of the West Indian children had either been born or lived at least two years in this country. Although the average IQ scores were low, the difference between the two groups of children was trivial and statistically insignificant. Bagley deliberately selected West Indian children from relatively advantageous backgrounds, by excluding those whose father was absent or unemployed, those with three or more brothers and sisters or living in crowded conditions, and by requiring that the child should have attended British schools since the age of 5 (the children were 7-10 years old at the time of the study). He matched the 50 West Indian children so obtained with 50 English children in terms of age, sex and father's occupation. As can be seen, both groups of children had slightly above average IQs, with the West Indians doing very slightly better.

Neither of these studies is very large and their conclusions should not necessarily be accepted without question. In Houghton's study, for example, the children were only 5 years old at the time of testing, and one can wonder about the social composition of a white population left behind in a decaying city centre. Bagley's West Indian children were an admittedly highly selected and unrepresentative sample. In order to obtain more evidence on this crucial question, we have undertaken analyses of the National Child Development and Child Health and Education studies whose summary data were shown in Table 1. Although neither study contains particularly large groups of West Indian children, they have one virtue almost unique in this area. The children were selected, on the sole basis of the date of their birth, from the entire country. They constitute, therefore, a reasonably representative and, for our purposes, randomly chosen sample of the population. Both studies, moreover, provide information on the child's family and social circumstances and thus enable one to form some idea of the relationship between social circumstances and test scores. There are numerous factors besides parental occupation that correlate with IQ scores in the white samples and in terms of many of these factors West Indian children can be said to suffer disadvantage. Our analyses suggest indeed that much, although by no means all, of the original differences in overall IQ between West Indian and white children can be accounted for in terms of a relatively small number of social variables.

A measure of the social disadvantage suffered by the West Indian children is shown in Table 3.[35] In the NCDS sample, for example, a signficantly higher proportion of West Indian than of white households contain four or more children, occupy crowded accommodation that involves sharing basic amenities and suffer from serious financial problems; West Indian fathers are more likely than white fathers to have manual rather than non-manual jobs or to have been unemployed for part of the preceding year, and more families have no male head. In the CHES sample, not suprisingly, data are not always available for exactly the same set of factors, but as can be seen from the table, West Indian fathers are still more likely to have manual rather than non-manual occupations; West Indian families are larger and poorer than white families, more likely to have no male head, and to live in inner cities or council estates.

In each study, all of the factors listed in Table 3 are significantly related to children's IQ scores in the population as a whole and are likely therefore to be related to the average difference in IQ scores between West Indian and white children. Many of them, of course, tend to go together: other things equal, households with large numbers of children are more likely to be overcrowded; unemployment tends to produce financial difficulties. It is obviously inappropriate therefore to

133

add the contribution for each factor independently. But the statistical technique of multiple regression allows one to take account of the effect of one variable having made allowance for that part of its effect which it shares with other variables.

The results of a series of multiple regression analyses of the NCDS and CHES data are shown in Table 4. The data are broken down by sex and by type of IQ score (verbal and nonverbal in NCDS and the four sub-tests in CHES), and for the NCDS data there is a separate analysis for those children who had been in the UK for four years or more. Several points are immediately apparent. When the factors listed in Table 3 are taken into account, the differences between West Indian and indigenous IQ scores are considerably reduced, although they are not completely eliminated. Moreover, this general conclusion covers a great deal of variation within and between each of the two studies.

In the NCDS analyses, differences of over 10 points in both verbal and nonverbal IQ between West Indian and indigenous males are reduced to differences of less than 5 points; in the case of females, however, the residual difference, especially in nonverbal IQ scores, is considerably larger. If the analysis is confined to those children who had been in the country for four or more years before being tested, all these differences are reduced without much change in the general pattern. In the CHES data, the original unadjusted differences between West Indian and indigenous children are rather smaller than in the NCDS data, at least for the matrices and digit span tests. And the regression analysis, although accounting for a somewhat smaller proportion of the overall differences, thus leaves rather smaller residual differences, at least for these tests. The differences between the sexes that was so apparent in the NCDS data have essentially disappeared in the CHES data – indeed girls do rather better than boys on the matrices test.

Another way of looking at the effect of these social variables, and one that takes advantage of the very much larger number of indigenous than of West Indian children in these studies, is to select individual white children who match individual West Indian children in terms of the factors listed in Table 3. Thus if a particular West Indian boy lives in a household containing more than four children, has a father with a manual job who has been unemployed for part of the past year, has attended more than two schools etc., one searches for a white boy in the sample with the same set of characteristics. We have undertaken such an analysis for both the NCDS and CHES samples. In neither case is it in fact possible to find matches for all West Indian children for whom complete data were available (an indication, perhaps, of the discrepancy between the social circumstances of West Indian and white children). In NCDS it was possible to match only 50 of the 72 West Indian children; in CHES, 77 out of 92 children were matched. In NCDS, the average total IQ score of the matched indigenous children is only 5.6 points greater than that of the West Indian children, a difference that reduces to 5.2 points if the analysis is confined to the 40 West Indian children who entered the country before the age of 7. In CHES, the difference in total IQ between the West Indian and matched indigenous children is only 2.6 points.

These various analyses show that it is possible to account for a significant proportion of the difference in IQ scores betwen West Indian and white children. But in no case was the difference completely abolished. This may cast some doubt on the generality of the conclusions suggested by the Houghton and Bagley studies shown in Table 2. It may even suggest the possibility that the differences unaccounted for by the analyses must be of genetic origin. One immediate problem with that conclusion is to decide which, if any, of these differences is to be accepted. The suggestion that there is a residual core of genetically determined difference in the intelligence of West Indian and white children hardly prepares one for the way this difference varies in such a capricious manner from less than 3 points in some cases to nearly 10 in others. If one were to argue, for example, that nonverbal tests provide a potentially less biased measure of intelligence than verbal tests, then in the CHES data at least, the residual differences in the digit span and matrices tests were small and statistically not significant.

There are, however, rather more general reasons why the conclusions that can be drawn from a multiple regression analysis of this sort are strictly limited. It is obvious enough that large-scale surveys will probably neither identify all the social and environmental factors that can affect IQ (why should they be only social, economic or demographic?), nor measure the ones that have been identified very precisely. It is entirely possible that the residual differences in Table 4 could be reduced yet further by including more variables in the regression analysis. For example, in the NCDS sample, one additional factor that has a highly significant effect on IQ scores is the teacher's rating of the child's "social adjustment". West Indian children obtain significantly lower ratings than white children, and when this factor is included in the analysis it reduces the residual differences in Table 4 by between 2 and 3 IQ points. Similarly, in the CHES survey, children were asked to complete questionnaires designed to measure the extent to which they attributed success or failure to their own efforts (or lack of them) or to external factors beyond their control. Here too, there were significant differences between the scores obtained by West Indian and white children, and since these scores were related to IQ scores in the sample as a whole, their inclusion in the regression analysis again reduces the residual differences in Table 4 by anything up to 2 points.

If this suggests that Table 4 may be overestimating the importance of genetic factors, there are equally good reasons for supposing that it might underestimate them. It is one thing to show that differences in IQ scores between two groups are related to differences in social circumstances between them. But is is quite another matter to show that the differences in social circumstances **cause** the differences in IQ. The discovery of a correlation between the two variables does not prove that one causes the other. Consider, for example, the effect of the teacher's assessment of a child's social adjustment in the NCDS data. Low ratings of social adjustment go with low IQ scores, and West Indian children obtain lower ratings than do white children. Have we therefore identified one cause of the difference between West Indian and white IQ scores? It is not difficult to think of other explanations of the observed pattern of correlations. Perhaps, for example, some teachers are inclined to label children as maladjusted (a euphemism for behaving badly in school) simply because they are West Indian. The label does not cause a low IQ independently of skin colour. It is simply a reflection of skin colour and in itself irrelevant to IQ.

There is, moreover, reason to believe that genetic factors contribute to differences in IQ within the white population. Perhaps, then, unfortunate social circumstances do not cause a low IQ; they are themselves a consequence of a genetically determined low IQ. The possibility that such genetic effects contribute to the observed correlation between social circumstances and IQ cannot be dismissed. But the importance of this contribution depends, among other things, on one's guess as to the heritability of IQ in the population as a whole. There is good reason to believe that this may be very much less than the figure of 80% espoused by Jensen and Eysenck, and this would mean that the genetic contribution to the correlation between social circumstances and IQ was unlikely to be of overriding significance. Its importance, moreover, is likely to be greater for some circumstances than for others. Parental education, for example, is correlated with a child's IQ score, but it will also be related to the parent's own IQ score, and parent's IQ is surely the one factor most likely to be genetically related to a child's IQ. But parental education was **not** one of the variables entered into these regression analyses. Father's occupation was, of course, entered and both Jensen and Eysenck (in common with many other psychologists) have argued that differences between occupations or social classes are a consequence of genetic differences in IQ. They may be right, although it is worth insisting that there is virtually no direct evidence to support this assumption. And it does not take much imagination to see that the reason why many West Indian adults hold poor jobs is at least as likely to be discrimination on the part of the employers as genetic inferiority on the part of West Indians.[36]

The importance of the analyses shown in Tables 2 and 4, therefore, does not lie so much in the absolute size of any residual, unexplained difference between West Indian and white scores. In some cases, that difference remains quite large; in others it has vanished completely. But it is impossible to be certain whether the role of social factors has been underestimated, because the analysis failed to measure all relevant variables, or whether their importance has been overestimated, because the analysis included factors which themselves reflect genetic differences. The real importance of these analyses is that they suggest that there are indeed social circumstances which predict a significant proportion of the difference between average West Indian and white IQ scores and that they are exactly the same as those which predict differences within the white population. This simultaneously undermines both Jensen's position and that of his sternest critics. It cannot disprove a genetic hypothesis, but when combined with the direct evidence considered earlier it makes it even less likely that genetic factors are an overriding cause of black-white differences in IQ: whatever may be the case in the U.S., it is simply not true to claim that no known environmental factors can account for more than a small fraction of the difference between West Indian and white IQ scores in this country. And since the factors which have been identified are those that contribute to differences within the white population, there is that much less reason to believe that there is something unique about the experience of West Indian children in this country which causes their low IQ scores. If racial discrimination is responsible for their poor performance it seems more likely that this is due to its effects on their parents' social circumstances.

Comparison with other ethnic minorities
Jensen's second argument was that the poor performance of American blacks on IQ tests cannot be attributed to their social circumstances, since other ethnic groups such as Mexican immigrants or American Indians, who are even more impoverished, obtain higher IQ scores. Without examining this claim in more detail, it is worth asking whether there are relevant comparisons to be made between West Indian children in this country and children from other ethnic minorities.

The second major group of recent immigrants to the U.K. has been that from the Indian sub-continent. If only because of the obvious problems raised by their not all speaking English as a first language, there has been for a long time a concern for the educational attainment of their children. But evidence becoming available in the mid-1970s suggested that, although they might find considerable initial difficulties, these children rapidly adapted to British schools and performed relatively well on standard tests of reading and mathematics, as well as on public examinations such as CSE and O-levels.[37] There is rather less information available on their performance on IQ tests, but Table 5 shows the results of two earlier studies, along with analyses of the NCDS and CHES surveys.[38] Yet again, there is considerable variability from one study to another, but some common trends can be discerned.

The most notable conclusion is that length of stay in this country has a very marked effect on performance. In the three studies where data are available, there is a striking and consistent improvement in the scores obtained when children have been resident in this country for a reasonable length of time and, presumably, have received most of their education here. This is as true for a supposedly "culture-fair" test like Raven's Matrices as it is for verbal tests. The second impression is that children who have been long resident in the U.K. usually obtain scores well within the normal British range. In several cases, indeed, there is essentially no difference between the scores obtained by long-resident Asian children and those of indigenous children. The most serious exception to this generalization is to be found in the CHES data where children from Pakistan obtain consistently low scores, and both Indian and Pakistani children do particularly badly on the two verbal tests (definitions and similarities).[39]

The CHES data suggest that earlier complacency about the performance of Asian children may have been somewhat misplaced. As a comparison with Table 1 will reveal, these CHES data show that Pakistani children do not obtain average scores any higher than those of West Indian children, and even Indian children are not consistently better. In this, they contrast rather strikingly with data from the NCDS survey, where long-resident Asian children scored some 8 to 10 points above the West Indian children. It is not at all easy to say why this might be. The number of long-resident Asian children in NCDS is very small and they may have, by chance, been an unrepresentative sample. This does not seem entirely likely, for the NCDS data agree tolerably well with those of the other studies shown in Table 5. It should also be remembered that CHES and NCDS employed quite different sets of tests, and that the two studies tested the children at slightly different ages (10 in CHES and 11 in NCDS). The possible importance of the former factor should not need emphasis: this is not the first time that we have seen differences between various groups come and go depending on the type of test employed. Although there was only a one year difference in the age at which children were tested, it is conceivable that this might have been important. There is evidence that both Indian and Pakistani children may improve by comparison with West Indians between the ages of 8 and 12.[40]

A final possibility is that the social circumstances of Asian immigrants have changed over the 12 years separating the two studies. There is some evidence to support this. The data for the NCDS sample have been analysed by others.[41] In terms of the sorts of factors considered in Table 3, the families of Asian children born in this country were substantially more advantaged than those of West Indian children and did not suffer by comparison with indigenous families. The CHES data tell a different story. Although there are some differences between Indian and Pakistani families, the general tendency is for both groups to resemble West Indian rather than indigenous families in terms of the proportion of fathers in manual occupation, number of children in the family, family income, free school meals and neighbourhood. The actual proportions are shown in Table 6.[42]

The importance of these factors is suggested by the results of a series of regression analyses, similar to those undertaken on the West Indian data, whose results are also shown in Table 6. The effects of these analyses are in general more marked for Pakistani than for Indian children, since their social circumstances are in general poorer. From having started with scores lower on average than those of the Indian children, the Pakistanis often end up, after the regression analysis, with slightly higher scores. But the more important comparison is with the West Indian children whose results were shown in Table 4. By and large, the two Asian groups produce a pattern of results very similar to that observed in the West Indian case. The regression analysis significantly reduces the gap separating all three groups from the indigenous majority, and although the residual differences for the two verbal tests remain considerable, those for the digit span and matrices tests are small and statistically insignificant. The only notable departure from the West Indian results is that the sex difference observed in the matrices scores in West Indian children is reversed: in the present case it is the males, rather than females, who do better. One could speculate about the cultural factors that might be responsible for this difference, but in the absence of further data it would remain speculation. It does not, however, seem likely that the difference reflects any genetic, sex-related differences between the different ethnic groups.

Two conclusions can perhaps be drawn from this discussion. First, there is some suggestion that children of Indian and Pakistani immigrants may no longer be obtaining higher test scores than those of West Indian immigrants, and if true this might be because their social circumstances are no longer as markedly superior as they used to be. This must be a tentative conclusion, to be regarded with considerable suspicion unless it can be confirmed by other, larger surveys. Secondly, however, one can assert with some confidence that the comparison of West Indian and Asian children in this country provides little support for the sort of argument proposed by Jensen on the basis of his comparisons of blacks with other ethnic minorities in the U.S. The present comparison suggests that where there is a difference in the IQ scores of West Indian and Asian children, there is also a demonstrable difference in their social circumstances. Where their circumstances are similar, there is no significant difference in measured IQ. There is no evidence for the combination of superior IQ and poorer circumstances which Jensen claims to find in his American comparisons.[43]

Test bias

Jensen's final argument was that the poor performance of American blacks on IQ tests cannot be due to bias in the tests themselves. The argument rests on two claims. The first is that blacks, unlike other minority groups, obtain low scores not only on possibly biased verbal IQ tests, but also on less biased nonverbal tests such as Raven's Matrices, sometimes indeed performing even worse on the latter than on the former. The second is that there is no reason to accept that IQ tests are in general biased against blacks for they predict school achievement as well for blacks as they do for whites. Indeed, he has argued, if there is any difference it is that IQ tests **over**estimate the scholastic attainment of blacks. The relationship between IQ and school performance among ethnic minorities in this country raises a number of wider issues which it will be more convenient to discuss at a later point in this paper. We can anticipate one of the conclusions of that discussion here by noting that the picture is on the whole fairly similar to that reported by Jensen for the U.S. By and large, IQ scores do not seriously **under**estimate the performance of West Indian or Asian children at school. In some cases, the reverse is true.

This is worth noting, but it may not be sufficient to establish the conclusion which Jensen wishes to draw. The fact that blacks do at least as badly at school as their IQ scores would lead one to expect may prove that IQ tests are not more biased than are other measures of school achievement. But it is surely possible that both sets of measures might be biased against blacks. It is this possibility that Jensen seeks to dispute by arguing that in the U.S. blacks perform badly not only on verbal IQ tests which clearly require knowledge of the majority culture, but also on a variety of nonverbal or "culture-fair" IQ tests which, it is to be supposed, do not require such knowledge.

The argument will not convince everyone, for it rests on the unproven assumption that because a particular IQ test employs nonverbal, diagrammatic and abstract material, it no longer requires culturally specific knowledge or skills. Jensen's favourite example of such a test is Raven's Matrices. But two of the studies reported in Table 5 show differences of between 10 and 20 points on this test between Asian children who have and those who have not resided for any length of time in this country. The ability to solve abstract nonverbal problems may depend as much on education and experience of a particular type as does the ability to answer questions about the meanings of English words. It is only a rather simple-minded view of intelligence and of differences in cultural tradition that could blind one to this possibility.

But it is not necessary to rely on these general arguments. The question at issue is whether there is any evidence that West Indian children in this country, unlike other ethnic minorities, obtain low scores not only on verbal but also on nonverbal IQ tests. As usual the data are fragmentary and somewhat less clear than one might wish. But the answer they suggest is surely no. In the two previously published studies shown in Table 1 (Yule, Berger, Rutter & Yule; McFie & Thompson), West Indian children obtained rather higher scores on nonverbal than on verbal tests, regardless of their length of stay in this country. In the one previously published study shown in Table 5 (Ashby, Morrison & Butcher) Asian children resident less than 4 years in the U.K. obtained higher nonverbal than verbal scores, but those here more than 4 years obtained slightly higher verbal scores. The only two studies that permit a direct comparison between West Indian and Asian children are the National Child Development and Child Health and Education Studies. The former found no difference between verbal and nonverbal IQ scores in either group. In the latter, both groups did better on the nonverbal matrices test than on the two main verbal tests (and best of all on the recall of digits).

Relative performance on verbal and nonverbal tests clearly depends on the precise tests employed. The most common result appears to be for ethnic minorities to obtain lower scores on verbal tests, a finding entirely consistent with the suggestion that they are more biased than nonverbal tests against minority groups. But the difference is neither large nor consistent. And there is certainly no suggestion that it is confined to Asian children. If recently arrived in this country, such children will often not speak English as a first language (if at all). It would hardly be surprising if they were at a particular disadvantage on verbal tests. The fact that there is no good evidence of any difference between the relative performance of West Indian and Asian children on verbal and nonverbal tests, therefore, provides striking disconfirmation of Jensen's supposition that blacks necessarily differ from other ethnic minorities by scoring poorly on both kinds of test.[44]

Conclusions
We have considered the three types of indirect argument put forward by Jensen to support his claim that the difference between black and white IQ scores in the U.S. is probably largely genetic in origin, without finding much reason to accept that any of them applies to the case of West Indian children in the U.K. First, it turns out to be quite easy to find social and environmental factors that account for a significant part of the average difference between West Indian and white IQ scores in this country. Secondly, there is no evidence that West Indian children obtain lower IQ scores than other ethnic minorities suffering from comparable levels of social and economic deprivation. Finally, there is no reason to suppose that West Indian children differ from Asian children in the pattern of their scores on verbal and nonverbal tests, for both tend, if anything, to obtain rather lower scores on verbal tests. If nonverbal scores are taken as the less biased measure of intelligence, the differences between both minority groups and the indigenous majority are often quite small. The implication of this indirect evidence, then, is much the same as that of the direct evidence considered earlier. If there are genetic differences for IQ between various ethnic groups in this country, they are likely to be extremely small.

Racial Discrimination
It is time to turn to Jensen's critics, to those who have argued that the poor performance of black children on IQ tests cannot be attributed to their family background, but would rather lay the blame directly on their experience of a racist society. As we have already seen, to the extent that social variables related to differences in IQ within the white population are also related to differences in IQ between West Indian and white children, it is unnecessary to appeal to factors unique to the experience of West Indian children to explain their low IQ scores. If racial discrimination is affecting their test scores, it must be doing so indirectly through its effects on the social status and circumstances of their parents.

In practice, however, the regression analyses reported above did not completely abolish the differences in IQ scores between West Indian and white children, but left some sizeable differences unaccounted for. It is possible that some of these further differences are due to the direct effects of discrimination on the children themselves. It is certainly not unreasonable in principle to suggest that the attitudes of a hostile and contemptuous white majority have so affected the self-confidence and ambitions of West Indian children that they are unable or unwilling to succeed in school or obtain high scores on IQ tests. The question is whether there is any evidence for this.

The first requirement of any comprehensive account of ethnic differences in scholastic performance is that it should be able to explain why children of Asian origin by and large do better than those of West Indian.[45] On the face of it, the suggestion that the Asian community in this country suffers less racial discrimination than the West Indian might seem hard to defend. But it is obviously necessary to distinguish between different forms of discrimination: our present concern is with attitudes towards the intelligence of an ethnic group, not whether they are attacked in the streets by hooligans. And there can be little doubt that teachers have markedly different views of the abilities of Asian and West Indian children – as the following unguarded remarks show:–

> *"West Indians are boisterous and less keen on education than Asians. This is well known obviously."*
>
> *"They are slower than Asian children – not as bright."*[46]

It is, of course, one thing to show that many people, including perhaps many teachers, believe that West Indian children are unlikely to succeed at school. It is a rather different matter to prove this attitude is the **cause** of their relatively poor performance: it is conceivable after all, that teachers' attitudes are no more than an accurate reflection of the fact that West Indian children do, as a matter of fact, tend to perform less well than others.

Teachers' expectations
But the suggestion that the attitudes of society at large and of teachers in particular may have deleterious effects on the performance of West Indian children is quite plausible. Intuitively, one can readily see how constant denigration, whether overt or more subtle, might sap a child's confidence in his own abilities and cause him to fail. And the suggestion has the backing of received, or at least of popular, psychological opinion. The notion of the self-fulfilling prophecy was given wide currency by Rosenthal and Jacobson's study, "Pygmalion in the Classroom".[47] Rosenthal and Jacobson claimed to have shown that children's IQ scores could increase dramatically if their teachers were led to believe that a special test administered to all children in class had indentified these particular children as "late bloomers" due to show a marked spurt. Although the study has achieved widespread fame, most of those who have examined it closely have remained unconvinced.[48] The increase in IQ scores occurred in only two of the six grades tested (that is, in only 19 children). The IQ tests were administered by the teachers themselves rather than by a trained tester – leading one to wonder who was fulfilling the prophecy. And some of the scores obtained, which ranged from zero to 300, must mean either that it was not being administered properly or that the test itself was an absurd one. Moreover, although several ingenious and better-controlled studies have established quite clearly that a teacher's expectations can have a significant effect on a child's general performance, no subsequent study has replicated Rosenthal and Jacobson's finding that **IQ scores** can be so affected.[49] This is an important conclusion, for it suggests that although one might be able to blame teachers' attitudes for the generally poor school performance of West Indian children, it is less likely that such attitudes are responsible for their low IQ scores. And to the extent that IQ is related to school performance, of course, this in turn suggests that prejudice is in fact unlikely to be the **sole** cause of their poor school peformance.

This conclusion is based on the failure of several, no doubt somewhat contrived, experimental studies to demonstrate a direct effect of teachers' attitudes and expectations on their pupils' IQ scores. It is possible, of course, that the attitudes towards West Indian children actually held by teachers in British schools and the expectations they develop are both subtler and more powerful determinants of their pupils' performance. All one can say is that there is relatively little direct evidence that convincingly establishes such an effect. Measured IQ scores may be rather less malleable than is sometimes supposed. Certainly, in the U.S., there is now a considerable body of evidence to contradict the common assertion that blacks obtain low scores on IQ tests because they are tested by white testers. Although a few studies have found that children obtain higher IQ scores when tested by an examiner of their own race, others have reported exactly the opposite result, and the majority have found no difference either way.[50]

Motivation and self-esteem
But there are still other possibilities. A person's performance on an IQ test can be significantly affected by his attitudes and motivation. There is evidence from the U.S. that blacks and whites alike obtain lower scores if they are too anxious (they may also perform less than optimally if they are too relaxed and do not take the task seriously). It would hardly be surprising if some black children perceived some situations as more threatening than white children do. They might therefore feel too anxious in a situation where white children are performing at their best. But although these effects are sometimes statistically significant, they are rarely large, and invariably insufficient to eliminate differences between black and white children.[50] One can only conclude that if this sort of factor really is important in the real world, then it has not been

satisfactorily captured in the artificial setting of an experimental study. That is not, perhaps, too surprising, but it follows that it is only an act of faith that allows anyone to assert that "test anxiety" is the real cause of blacks' poor performance.

Anxiety is not the only motivational factor which has been thought to contribute to poor performance. It has been suggested by some writers in this country that West Indian children lack confidence in their own abilities, have low expectations or, in psychological jargon, poor "self-esteem". More particularly, it is possible that West Indian children who do badly at school have especially low self-esteem. One study identified a group of West Indian children whose scores on standardized reading tests were as good as those of white, middle-class children, and showed that their family background and attitudes were markedly more independent, self-reliant and indeed hostile towards white society than were those of other West Indian families.[51] Unfortunately, the two groups of families also differed in social class, the former being distinctly more middle-class than the latter, and it is at least possible that other attributes of middle-class family life were responsible for the superior performance of their children. Another study reported that differences in self-esteem between West Indians and whites were confined to boys: West Indian girls were as self-confident as their white counterparts.[52] It is sometimes claimed that West Indian girls do better at school than boys – and even that they achieve higher scores on IQ tests, but there are numerous studies which have found no such effect, and some which have not confirmed the original differences in self-esteem.[53]

The evidence is far from persuasive, and the picture looks even less convincing when other studies are considered. It has been shown that West Indian children born in the West Indies may have higher self-esteem than those born in this country.[54] But we have seen that it is the latter group who score higher on IQ tests and do better at school. There is some evidence that increases in the proportion of immigrant pupils in a school may improve the self-esteem of immigrant pupils, but no evidence that it will improve their scholastic record.[55]

It is not even clear that West Indian children in general have lower self-esteem than whites. Some studies have shown such a difference, others the reverse.[56] The numerous conflicts in evidence in this area of research may reflect genuine differences in attitude between different groups: attitudes may well have changed, for example, over the last 20 years; some West Indian children, in some circumstances, may well be more self-confident than others placed in different circumstances. But one suspects that part of the problem may arise from the ill-defined nature of the concept of self-esteem.

Even if the relationship between measures of self-esteem and IQ or scholastic performance were very much clearer than they are, we could still not assert that low self-esteem had been shown to be the cause of poor performance. Once again it might simply be a reflection of that performance. The child who, for whatever reason, is doing badly at school may well be inclined to agree with such statements as "I'm not doing as well in school as I'd like to" or "I often get discouraged at school". These are two of the items to be found in the most widely used self-esteem inventory.

Very much the same could be said about attitudes to school itself. It seems probable that children who are successful at school might also like school more than those who are not. This would not be surprising but would hardly prove that their success was caused by their favourable attitude. In fact, there is little reason to believe that West Indian children do have particularly unfavourable attitudes to school. Certainly, their parents commonly show significantly more interest in, and concern for, their children's education than do white parents of comparable socio-economic status.[57] And there have been several reports showing that West Indian children themselves express attitudes to school at least as favourable as those held by indigenous children.[58] As we shall show below, they obtain rather more total CSE and O-level passes than indigenous children with comparable IQ scores or in comparable social circumstances, and it is possible that this partly reflects the greater value they place on school achievement.

Changes in performance over time

Although it seems entirely plausible to suppose that a child's IQ score and performance at school should be affected both by his own attitude to school and by his teachers' attitudes towards him, it is difficult, particularly in the case of IQ scores, to find evidence to prove that such an effect is operating to depress the achievement of West Indian children in this country. There remains one further line of evidence that may bear on this issue. It has been suggested that West Indian children, unlike those from other ethnic minorities, fall progressively further behind their white contemporaries as they go through school. What starts as a relatively small difference between the various groups at the age of 7 or 8 it has been claimed, increases, in the case of West Indian children, to a much larger difference at the age of 12 to 16. Such a failure to keep pace with their contemporaries would suggest that West Indian children suffer from some environmental disadvantage: an obvious possibility is that this disadvantage is the prejudiced attitude of school and society. If there were widespread evidence of such a relative decline in the performance of West Indian children, therefore, this might strengthen the case for believing that they suffer from discrimination, for example at the hands of their teachers, and that this discrimination is one factor directly contributing to their poor performance. In fact, the evidence, particularly in the case of IQ scores, is far from convincing.

One recent study, widely reported in the press, is said to have shown that "West Indian children are failing in school to such an extent that their intelligence scores go into a sharp decline between the ages of 8 and 12".[59] This is a remarkable interpretation to put on the findings actually reported. At the age of 8, the IQ scores of West Indian and white children from the same schools were 98.3 and 106.7 respectively, while at the age of 12 they were 98.7 and 107.8. There is no suggestion that West Indian IQ scores have declined and the gap between them and white children has increased by a trivial 0.7 points. The claim that they have declined is based on the results of a somewhat misleading regression analysis which also included data from Indian and Pakistani children in the same schools. These children, although initially doing no better than the West Indians, did indeed show striking gains in IQ scores, of 10 and 8 points respectively, from the ages of 8 to 12. Their inclusion means that, **on average,** children with low IQ scores at 8 had higher scores at 12 and it is, in effect, by comparison with this average that West Indian children are being said to show a decline. But this decline appears to be only by comparison with Asian children, who are making striking gains (the importance of which has already been alluded to) not by comparison with whites.[60]

The results of an analysis of scores obtained on tests of reading by children in the Inner London Education Authority are also said to show serious evidence of a progressive decline by West Indian children.[61] Indigenous children obtained scores of 98.1 and 97.8 at age 8 and 15 respectively, while the comparable scores for West Indian children were 88.1 and 85.9, a decline of 2.2 points and an increase in the gap between indigenous and West Indian children of 1.9 points (Indian and Pakistani children showed gains). Here the decline is real, if small, but once again it is increased by a statistical analysis which is said to show that the increase in the gap at age 15 is really as large as 3.7 points.[62]

Comparison with the ILEA data can be obtained by analysing the scores on reading tests given at age 11 and 16 in the National Child Development Study. Here the gap between West Indian and indigenous children is 14.3 points at age 11 and 14.1 points at age 16. The size of the gap is somewhat larger than in the ILEA data, presumably because there the indigenous children scored about 2 points below the national average. But there is no suggestion that West Indian children are falling further behind their white contemporaries. This may, of course be partly because some of the decline occurs before the age of 11 (this is certainly true in the ILEA survey). But it is also possible that the statistical analysis of the ILEA data has exaggerated the extent of the decline. If that is true, then the overall picture, from the relatively small number of studies available, is one of, at most, relatively trivial declines in West Indian performance over time.

There is little justification, particularly in the case of IQ scores, for the claim that West Indian children fall seriously further behind their white contemporaries as they progress through school.

It was difficult, if not impossible, to find convincing evidence that the school achievements, let alone IQ scores, of West Indian children in this country are adversely affected by such psychological factors as their attitudes to school, society and themselves, or directly by society's or their teachers' attitudes to them. The fact that West Indian children do not appear to fall seriously further behind white children in school as they grow older, although surely welcome in itself, tends to undermine one final possible reason for accepting this explanation of their relatively poor performance. It does not, of course, prove that such an explanation is wrong. The idea that a child's achievements at school, and perhaps even his IQ, could be affected by psychological factors is by no means unreasonable. It is surely more unreasonable to suppose that the only environmental factors to affect IQ should be economic and demographic – just because there are the variables most readily measured in large-scale social surveys. But the fact remains that the evidence for other, more psychological factors is almost totally lacking.

IQ, Social Circumstances and School Performance

The question which we originally set out to answer was whether differences in school performance between indigenous children and those from any ethnic minority should be attributed in whole or in part to differences in their natural intelligence. Although children from some ethnic minorities certainly obtain, on average, lower scores on standard IQ tests than do indigenous children, we have found rather little reason to believe that this reflects genetic differences for intelligence. On the contrary, such differences in IQ scores as we have found are clearly related to the same sort of differences in social circumstances that are associated with differences in IQ among the indigenous majority. If we could show that children's IQ scores were related to school performance in much the same way whether they are white, West Indian or Asian, the implication would be that any differences between groups in school performance were also related to differences in their social circumstances.

IQ and school performance.

How well do IQ scores predict the school performance of children from ethnic minorities? The question is, in part, one concerned with potential bias in IQ tests. If it turned out that IQ scores seriously underestimated the performance of which, say, West Indian children proved capable in school, in the sense that a West Indian child with an IQ of 90 did very much better in school than a white child with the same IQ score, this would imply that IQ tests were biased against West Indians. In the U.S., Jensen has claimed, there is no evidence that IQ tests are biased against blacks in this way. What is the position in this country?

There are several reports on the performance of West Indian and Asian children on standard tests of reading and mathematical ability. Their general findings are broadly comparable to those that have looked at IQ scores: both West Indian and Asian children, but particularly the former, tend to obtain lower scores than do indigenous children.[63] This suggests that average differences between groups in IQ scores are related to the average differences found when children are directly tested for what they have learnt in school. But it is also important to know whether, within each group. children who obtain higher IQ scores also do better on these other tests. If this were not true, we should be inclined to doubt that IQ had the same meaning for each group. The National Child Development and Child Health and Education Studies gave both IQ and reading and mathematics tests to children, and we have calculated, for each ethnic group, the correlation between IQ scores and scores on these other tests.[64] The results are shown in Part A of Table 7. As can be seen, the correlations are all high, and there is no serious suggestion that their size differs systematically between groups (statistically, none of the differences is significant). By this measure, then, IQ scores do mean much the same in each group.

But there is a further question which we can ask, for these correlations tell us only that, for

143

example, a West Indian child with an IQ of 105 is likely to obtain higher scores on reading and mathematics tests than one with an IQ of 85. They do not say whether he will obtain the same scores as a white child with an IQ of 105. It is possible that West Indian and white children with similar IQ scores obtain systematically different scores on reading and mathematics tests. In order to answer this question, it is necessary to perform another regression analysis which, in effect, compares the reading and mathematics scores actually obtained by West Indian children with the scores they would have obtained, given their IQ, if the relationship between reading or mathematics and IQ scores were exactly the same in West Indian children as it is in white children. The results of these regression analyses are shown in Part B of Table 7. It is clear that the actual scores obtained by both West Indian and Asian children, in both studies, are not only lower than the average white scores (approximately 100 on both tests in both studies), their scores are also, in virtually all cases, lower than the scores one would have predicted on the basis of their IQ. In other words, IQ scores tend, if anything, to **over**estimate the performance of both West Indian and Asian children on these standard tests of school achievement.

Many of these discrepancies are extremely small and statistically not significant. But some are too large to be ignored and require some explanation. The discrepancies between obtained and predicted scores for the Asian children in NCDS, although quite sizeable in the case of reading, are largely due to the inclusion of children who had been in the country for less than 4 years. The scores obtained by Asian children who entered the U.K. before the age of 7 are as good as those of indigenous children, on both reading and mathematics tests, and do not differ from the scores one would have expected on the basis of their IQ. In CHES, there is essentially no discrepancy between predicted and obtained scores for Indian children, while Pakistani children, although doing worse on reading tests, do slightly better on mathematics tests, than their IQ scores would have led one to expect. Possibly more serious discrepancies are to be found in the West Indian children in CHES, for they perform at a significantly lower level on both reading and mathematics tests, particularly the latter, than their IQ scores would predict. Why this should be so is not clear. Perhaps their IQ scores are misleadingly high. But an alternative possibility is suggested by the arguments we considered in the previous section. If West Indian children are not doing as well at reading and mathematics as one might have expected, this might be because of the way they are taught or the preconceptions teachers have about their abilities. There is some evidence, as we have seen, that teachers' expectations can have a greater impact on measures of school achievement than on IQ scores. There is, of course, no evidence to show that this is what has actually been happening to the children in question. Moreover, other studies have not reported such discrepancies between IQ scores and measures of school achievement in West Indian children. In the NCDS data, shown in Table 7, the discrepancies are quite small. And in another study, which reported IQ and reading scores for indigenous, West Indian and Asian children, at age 12 the West Indian children were reading as well as the Asian children in spite of obtaining significantly lower IQ scores.[65] In this case, therefore, it was the Asian children who read less well than their IQ would have led one to expect.

Perhaps of even more interest than the scores obtained on reading and mathematics tests are the results of public examinations such as CSE and O-levels taken at the age of 16+. How well do West Indian and Asian children do on such exams and how well is their performance predicted by the scores they obtain on IQ tests? Published evidence suggests that West Indian children obtain significantly fewer "good" passes (O-levels A-C and CSE 1) than indigenous children, but that Asian children are probably doing just as well as the indigenous majority.[66] There are, however, no published data on the relationship between IQ scores and examination performance and we have therefore analysed data from NCDS to provide some preliminary information. The results of our analyses are shown in Table 8. The picture is distinctly complex.

Since a sizeable minority of children, whether white, West Indian or Asian, obtained no graded passes in CSE or O-levels at all (either because they did not enter or because they failed), the data are analysed first to see whether there is any difference in IQ scores between children with at least one graded pass and those with none. As can be seen from Part A of the table, indigenous children with at least one pass have, unsurprisingly, a higher IQ score than those with none. But although the same is true for Asian children, in West Indian children there is virtually no difference between the two groups. In West Indians alone, for reasons which are not immediately apparent, IQ scores do not seem to predict which children will have some success in these exams and which will have none.

Part B of the table gives the correlation, in those children with at least one passing grade, between IQ scores and two measures of success: the total number of passes achieved at any age, and the number of good passes achieved by the age of 16. Both of these measures of examination performance show moderately high correlations with IQ in all ethnic groups. Although the correlations for West Indian children are slightly lower than those for the other children, the differences are not large. In all groups, children with higher IQ scores tend to do better than those with lower scores.

But, as with the reading and mathematics tests, we also need to know whether a West Indian or Asian child with a high IQ obtained as many passes as a white child with a similar IQ score. Once again, therefore, we need to perform a regression analysis which compares the number of passes obtained and the number predicted on the basis of IQ. This information is given in Part C of the table. It is clear that both West Indian and Asian children actually obtain rather **more** total CSE and O-level passes than would have been expected, given their IQ scores, if they had been white. In the case of Indian children this underestimate of examination performance is statistically significant. It should be noted, however, that both groups of children have rather fewer "good" CSE or O-level passes by the age of 16 than their IQ scores would have predicted (although these differences are not significant).

The number of children involved in these analyses is relatively small and, yet again therefore, their results should be treated with some caution. For example, the data for the Asian children do not accord with more recent, published data which suggest that Asian children obtain as many good passes as white children, and thus considerably more than in this study. But in the case of West Indian children there are now some other fragments of evidence to suggest that they may be obtaining rather better examination results than is sometimes supposed.[67] There is no room for complacency, for there seems to be no question but that they obtain significantly fewer good examination passes than white or Asian children, but the picture is not one of unrelieved gloom.

What then can we say about the relationship between IQ scores and these measures of school achievement? There is no simple answer. While IQ scores tended to overestimate the performance of Asian, and perhaps more strikingly of West Indian, children on tests of reading and mathematics, there is equally good evidence that they can underestimate the performance of both groups, again more particularly of West Indians, on public examinations. Yet again, we can only speculate why this should be so. It is at least possible that both West Indian and Asian children and their parents place a higher value on examination credentials than their white contemporaries and are more willing to stay on at school or to attend a college of further education in order to obtain such credentials.

But we should not exaggerate the discrepancies between IQ and school achievement in ethnic minorities. The fact is that many of the relationships between the two are very similar in West Indian, Asian and indigenous children. The correlations between IQ and reading, mathematics and examination passes are reasonably high and of much the same value in all three groups. Although some studies have reported discrepancies between IQ scores and some measures of school achievement, they have not always been confirmed, and the discrepancy between IQ and a different index of school achievement may be in exactly the opposite direction. It would surely be unreasonable to argue, on the basis of this evidence, that IQ tests systematically underestimate the academic potential of West Indian or Asian children in this country. If the criterion of bias is that one test gives a lower estimate of performance than another, there is no more reason to suppose that IQ tests are invariably biased against West Indians in this country than against blacks in the U.S. More important, if high and low IQ scores have much the same implication for school performance in other ethnic groups as they do in whites, then one might expect to find that factors that affected West Indian or Asian IQ scores would also affect their school achievements.

Social circumstances and school performance.
If IQ scores are related to school achievement in much the same way in West Indian, Asian and white children, and if the differences between the IQ scores of the three groups of children are related to differences in their social circumstances, it seems at least possible that differences in their school achievement will also be related to these differences in social circumstances.

A final set of regression analyses, similar to those whose results are shown in Tables 4 and 6, were conducted to examine this possibility. The measures of school achievement we used were the results of the reading and mathematics tests from NCDS (at both 11 and 16) and CHES (at age 10), and the examinations results from NCDS. Performance on all of these was correlated, in the indigenous population, with the same set of social circumstances that were related to variations in IQ scores. The results of the regression analyses are given in Table 9; not surprisingly, they show that much, although by no means all, of the initial difference between either West Indian or Asian and white children is accounted for by the differences in their social circumstances.

Several comments on these results are in order. The data from NCDS are for all available children regardless of how recently they had entered the country. This certainly explains the particularly poor performance of the Asian children at age 11. As can be seen, by age 16 they have made significant gains, particularly in the mathematics test; and if the analysis is confined to those children who entered the country before the age of 7, the residual differences at age 11 are trivially small, and by age 16 Asian children obtain higher scores than white children even before the regression analysis is carried out. As with IQ tests, the West Indian children do not show such a marked effect of length of residence in this country, and show relatively little improvement from 11 to 16. The data from CHES indicate that West Indian children obtain lower scores on reading and mathematics tests than do either Indian or Pakistani children and that the residual differences between their scores and those of the white children, i.e. the differences unaccounted for by differences in their social circumstances are considerably larger than in these other groups. The results shown in Table 7 should have prepared one for this finding, since there we saw that West Indian children, unlike Asians, obtained lower scores on these tests than their IQ scores would have led one to expect. Once again, we can offer no more than speculation why this should be so, and must stress that it is an isolated result to be treated with the same caution.

But the overall pattern of results is as we might have expected. Differences in their social circumstance can account for a significant part of the differences in school performance observed between ethnic minorities and white children. In the case of the examination data from NCDS, it can be seen that both West Indian and Asian children obtain more total passes than do white children in comparable social circumstances, just as they obtained more passes than white children with comparable IQ scores. And the difference in the number of good grades obtained is very small once social circumstances have been taken into account. Although it is important to remember that regression analyses such as these can never prove that differences in test scores are actually caused by differences in social circumstance, it is at least worth considering the possibility that elimination of some of the more glaring instances of social inequality might significantly affect differences in school achievement.

146

Summary and Conclusions

At the risk of seeming unduly pedantic, it is necessary to reiterate that the evidence available to answer any of the important questions about the attainments and abilities of ethnic minorities is very imperfect. There are relatively few studies providing information about their performance on standard IQ tests; in most of these the data were collected 10 or more years ago; their results do not always agree with one another; and in virtually no case is there any information that would make it possible to disentangle possible causes of differences between different ethnic groups. It has been necessary from time to time to call upon American data to answer certain questions, but there is no guarantee that such data are relevant to the British case. The only safe conclusion is that few secure conclusions can be drawn — and that many of those most confidently asserted reflect preconception and prejudice rather than sober evaluation of the evidence. With that proviso, it is worth seeing in what direction the evidence seems to point.

1. Several studies undertaken in this country over the past 10 to 15 years have shown that children from ethnic minorities on average attain somewhat lower scores on standard IQ tests than indigenous children.

2. Much of this difference has been due to the particularly poor performance of children who have only recently immigrated into this country. This is particularly true in the case of the Asian community, where children of Indian or Pakistani origin born in this country have in some, although by no means all, studies both achieved IQ scores well within the range of the indigenous population and also performed equally well on school exams. Whether this is still true, or true of all groups of Asian children, may be open to question.

3. In the case of children of West Indian origin, this does not seem to be the whole story: while those born in this country have higher scores than recent immigrants, they still score, on average, about 5 to 12 points below the population mean. Despite claims to the contrary, however, there is little reason to believe that the size of this gap increases as children progress through school. Indeed, there is some evidence that West Indian children may do rather better at CSE and O-level examinations than the gap in IQ scores might lead one to expect.

4. Much of this difference in IQ scores between West Indian and indigenous children appears to be related to differences between them in such factors as parental occupation, income, size of family, degree of overcrowding, and neighbourhood. All of these factors are related to IQ among whites, and when they are taken into account, the difference between West Indian and indigenous children is sharply reduced, to somewhere between 1 and 7 points.

5. These findings tend to argue against those who would seek to provide a predominantly genetic explanation of ethnic differences in IQ, but they equally imply that such differences are not due to a special set of factors unique to the West Indian experience. Although discrimination against West Indian families in this country may have an important indirect effect on their children's IQ scores by ensuring that they live in impoverished circumstances, there is less reason to believe that such discrimination, whether by society as a whole or by teachers and IQ testers in particular, has any **direct** effect on the West Indian child's performance. There is, moreover, relatively little evidence that specifically supports either this or the genetic position. Such imperfect attempts as have been made to study the intellectual development of black and white children brought up in comparable surroundings have found few if any differences in their IQ scores. Conversely, there is not much reason to believe that teachers' expectations have any large effects on their pupils' IQ scores (although they may affect other aspects of their performance at school), and although motivational and attitudinal factors have sometimes been found to have significant effects on IQ scores, the effects are neither consistent nor large. At best such factors may make a modest contribution to observed ethnic differences in IQ scores; they are unlikely to be the most important cause.

147

6.   The evidence is not compelling, then, but on balance it does seem to point one way rather than others: ethnic differences in IQ scores are probably largely caused by the same factors as are responsible for differences in IQ within the white population as a whole. And much the same conclusion probably applies to ethnic differences in more specific measures of school performance such as tests of reading or mathematics or public examinations. Here too, such differences as there are between different ethnic groups seem to be largely related to the same social factors that are related to differences within the indigenous populations. If, therefore, we wish to affect the IQ scores of children from ethnic minorities in our society, or indeed their school performance, we might make a start by improving the social and economic circumstances of their families.

Finally, it seems worth stressing that the possibility that such a programme might have beneficial effects on IQ scores is surely not the best reason for wishing to improve the conditions in which a substantial minority of the community is forced to live. By the same token, even if it turns out that racial prejudice is not a direct cause of the low IQ scores obtained by many West Indian children, this is no reason to countenance such prejudice. There are many things in life substantially more important than IQ. Even in a narrow educational context, no one should be particularly interested in IQ scores. Educationalists should be concerned rather with how well children do at school, how adequately they master certain basic skills and, if need be, with their examination results — since these results will affect their future chances in life in a multitude of ways. They should ask, for example, why West Indian children do not read as well as white children, and rather than wondering whether this is due to a difference in IQ, they would be better advised to tackle the problem directly — by relying on those factors (such as parental involvement[68]) actually shown to be capable of affecting a child's ability to read.

The only reason for being concerned with IQ scores is that they tend to predict educational attainment (and even that not particularly well). Attempts to invest a child's IQ score with greater importance usually rest on one of two assumptions: that it provides a direct measure of his true worth, or that it predicts his later success in life significantly more accurately than other measures of educational attainment. Neither assumption is justified. There is a third fact that, in some minds at least, has inflated the importance of IQ scores: the possibility that there might be significant and ineradicable differences in the **average** IQ of different social, ethnic or racial groups has been thought by some to justify prejudice or discrimination against all members of the groups with lower scores. But the justification is spurious. As has often been pointed out, an average difference between two groups, even one as large as the 15-point difference claimed to hold between blacks and whites in the U.S., conceals even larger differences within each group and therefore a very large degree of overlap between the two. Indeed, even with this 15-point difference, it has been argued, the chances are that the difference in IQ between a randomly selected black child in the U.S. and a similarly chosen white child from the same social class will be only 1 point larger than the difference one would expect to find between a brother and sister brought up in the same family.[69] And the fact of the matter is that we do not discriminate against all groups with lower than average IQ scores. No one has ever suggested that we should discriminate against twins; but there is excellent evidence that the average IQ of twins is about 5 points below that of the rest of the population.[70] We do not think that this matters, and we should rightly question the good sense or good will of anyone who claimed that it did.

TABLE 1

Summary of Four Studies Comparing IQ Scores of Indigenous Children and Children of West Indian Origin

	Yule, Berger, Rutter and Yule[15] Wechsler Tests		McFie and Thompson[16] Wechsler Tests		National Child Development Study[17] NFER Tests		Child Health and Education Study[18] British Ability Scales			
	Verbal	Perfor-mance	Verbal	Perfor-mance	Verbal	Non-Verbal	Word definitions	Simi-larities	Mat-rices	Recall of digits
Indigenous	(N=105)* 101·3	103·9	(N=61) 95	102	(N=10,299) 100·6	100·5	(N=10,812) 100·6	100·6	100·4	100·1
West Indian	Total (N=100) 86·9	90·4	Total (N=61) 87	90	Total (N=113) 87·7	86·3	Total (N=125) 93·2	90·9	93·9	99·2
	UK born (N=51) 88·4	93·6	Arrived in UK before age of 5 91	94	In UK 4 or more years (N=74) 89·8	89·3				
	WI born (N=48) 85·4	87·1	Arrived in UK at age 5 or over 85	84	In UK less than 4 years (N=39) 83·7	81·0				

*These numbers in brackets refer to the number of children (where known), included in the study in various categories.

TABLE 2

Summary of Four Studies Showing IQ Scores of West Indian and Indigenous Children Approximately Matched for Father's Occupation or Neighbourhood

	NCDS		Grace[32]		Houghton[34]	Bagley[34]
	Unadjusted Total IQ	IQ Adjusted for Father's Occupation*	Matched for School Class		Matched for School and Neighbourhood	Matched for Father's Occupation, Presence of both Parents, Family Size
	NFER Tests		Vocabulary	Ravens Matrices‡	Stanford-Binet Test	Stanford-Binet Test
Indigenous	(N=9,940) 101·6	101·6	(N=76) 86	90	(N=71) 92·0	(N=50) 103·2
West Indian	(N=108) 86·3	90·5	(N=76) 82	87	(N=71) 90·1	(N=50) 105·7

* These adjusted IQ scores were obtained by assuming that the same proportion of West Indian fathers were in each of the various occupational categories, and then weighting the mean IQ of the West Indian population accordingly. Since in West Indian children as in whites, IQ was positively related to father's occupation, and since more white than West Indian fathers had occupations of higher status, the effect is to increase the IQ of the West Indian sample.

‡ The IQ scores shown for Grace's study have been converted from the raw scores reported by her in accordance with published tables of norms for the tests she used. The exact numbers should therefore be treated with some caution, but the differences between West Indian and white children can be taken as reasonably accurate.

150

TABLE 3

Percentage of Indigenous and of West Indian Families Living in Various Social Circumstances

	NCDS		CHES	
	Indigenous	West Indian	Indigenous	West Indian
Father in manual occupation	56·8	70·6	54·5	71·5
Father unemployed for part of preceding year	7·0	11·8		
No male head of household	4·1	9·8	4·4	16·2
Four or more children in household or family	29·0	57·5	14·8	43·5
Overcrowded (1·5 or more people per room)	10·0	32·1		
Child sharing bed	16·3	43·7		
Family sharing bathroom, hot water and lavatory	2·5	16·1		
Family income less than £100 per week			36·6	51·8
Serious financial hardship	10·1	27·4		
Child receiving free school meals			15·4	32·5
Child attended more than two schools	14·8	29·1		
Neighbourhood: inner city or council estate			34·7	72·9

Where there is no entry, this is either because the data are not available in that study or because there is no significant difference between West Indian and Indigenous children.

TABLE 4

Results of Multiple Regression Analyses of West Indian and Indigenous Children's IQ Scores Using Variables Listed in Table 3

		NCDS				CHES (N=92)			
		Entered UK any time (N=72)		Four or more years in UK (N=54)					
		Verbal	Non-Verbal	Verbal	Non-Verbal	Word definitions	Similarities	Matrices	Recall of digits
Male	Unadjusted	10·2	10·9	8·1	9·2	8·2	10·5	8·9	2·6
	Residual	4·2	4·9	3·0	3·9	3·7	6·5	4·6	1·2
Female	Unadjusted	11·5	14·9	11·7	14·2	8·1	11·0	5·6	3·4
	Residual	7·2	10·6	7·5	9·8	3·9	7·1	2·9	1·9

The data shown are the differences in IQ scores between West Indian and indigenous children before (unadjusted) and after (residual) the multiple regression analysis.

TABLE 5

Summary of Four Studies Comparing IQ Scores of Indigenous Children and Children of Indian or Pakistani Origin

	Ashby, Morrison and Butcher[38]			Sharma[38]			National Child Development Study[17]			Child Health and Education Study[18]				
	Condition	Verbal Reasoning*	Raven's Matrices	Condition	Wechsler Performance	Raven's Matrices	Condition	Verbal	Non-Verbal	Condition	Word definitions	Similarities	Matrices	Recall of Digits
Indigenous		100·5	102	(N=43)	107·9	109·8	(N=10,299)	100·6	100·5	(N=10,812)	100·6	100·6	100·4	100·1
Asian†	9 or more years in UK	100·4	100	7 or more years in UK (N=43)	99·0	104·4	4 or more years in UK (N=25)	99·9	97·5	Indian (N=170)	91·3	89·6	97·1	97·3
	4–8 years in UK	93·9	92	Less than 2 years in UK (N=43)	84·2	83·7	Less than 4 years in UK (N=37)	82·6	83·3	Pakistani (N=91)	89·3	86·9	93·0	98·5
	Less than 4 years in UK	82·5	87	Living in India (N=43)	75·7	81·1								

* Average of score on two separate tests — Glasgow and Moray House Verbal Reasoning Tests.

† Ashby, Morrison and Butcher and NCDS report data for both Indian and Pakistani children without the possibility of further breakdown. The children in Sharma's study were all Indian. Only in CHES is it possible to present data for Indian and Pakistani children separately. The latter group includes 10 children from Bangladesh.

TABLE 6

Social Circumstances of Indian and Pakistani Families and Results of Regression Analyses of Children's IQ Scores Taking these Factors into Account. Data from CHES

A.

Percentage of Indian and Pakistani Families in Various Circumstances

	Indian	Pakistani
Father in manual occupation	72·4	71·0
No male head	2·8	4·3
Four or more children	43·4	77·5
Income less than £100 per week	47·5	68·0
Child receiving free school meals	9·4	31·0
Inner city or council estate	48·4	77·1

B. Regression Analyses

		Indian (N=123)				Pakistani (N=58)			
		Word defini-tion	Similari-ties	Mat-rices	Recall of digits	Word defini-tion	Similari-ties	Mat-rices	Recall of digits
Male	Unadjusted	8·6	11·5	3·0	2·8	11·1	12·5	4·3	+1·5
	Residual	5·2	8·6	1·6	2·1	5·4	6·6	1·1	+2·4
Female	Unadjusted	8·5	9·7	3·7	4·2	12·5	12·5	7·3	3·0
	Residual	5·8	7·4	2·5	3·3	5·7	5·3	4·4	0·9

The data shown are the differences in IQ scores between Asian and indigenous children before (unadjusted) and after (residual) the regression analysis. The + before the scores for Pakistani makes on recall of digits indicates that they had higher scores than indigenous children on this sub-test.

TABLE 7

Prediction of Performance on Tests of Reading and Mathematics by IQ Scores. (Total IQ)

A.   Correlations of IQ with Reading and Mathematics Scores

	NCDS			CHES			
	Indigenous (N=7597)	West Indian (N=74)	Asian (N=36)	Indigenous (N=10748)	West Indian (N=93)	Indian (N=136)	Pakistani (N=61)
Reading	·73	·60	·78	·74	·75	·77	·75
Mathematics	·80	·78	·85	·74	·72	·72	·74

B.   Predicted and obtained Reading and Mathematics Scores*

		NCDS			CHES			
		Indigenous	West Indian	Asian	Indigenous	West Indian	Indian	Pakistani
Reading	Obtained	100·6	88·2	85·6	100·8	90·0	94·0	89·6
	Predicted	—	89·1	92·3	—	93·8	94·3	92·8
Mathematics	Obtained	100·9	86·2	86·7	100·8	87·6	94·5	91·4
	Predicted	—	88·4	90·3	—	93·8	94·7	90·5

* Reading and Mathematics scores as predicted by IQ scores if the relationship between IQ and reading and mathematics scores were exactly the same in West Indian and Asian children as it is in indigenous children.

TABLE 8

Prediction of Examination Performance at Age 16+ by IQ Score at Age 11 for Indigenous, West Indian and Asian Children.

Data from National Child Development Study.

		Indigenous	West Indian	Asian
A.	**IQ Scores**			
	Children with at least 1 pass at CSE or O-level	103·6 (N=7491)	86·5 (N=74)	92·0 (N=42)
	Children with no pass	86·5 (N=1258)	85·3 (N=15)	77·1 (N=5)
B.	**Correlations of IQ with Exam Scores**			
	Total number of CSE and O-level passes	·47	·41	·57
	O-level (A-C) and CSE (1) by age 16	·54	·40	·63
C.	**Predicted and Obtained Examination Passes***			
	Total Passes — Obtained	4·66	3·95	4·09
	Total Passes — Predicted	—	3·20	3·66
	O-level (A-C) and CSE (1) — Obtained	2·10	0·55	1·05
	O-level (A-C) and CSE (1) — Predicted	—	0·71	1·14

* Examination performance as predicted by IQ scores if the relationship between IQ and examination results were exactly the same in West Indian and Asian children as it is in indigenous children.

TABLE 9

Results of Multiple Regression Analyses of West Indian, Asian and Indigenous Scores on Reading and Mathematics Tests and Public Examinations Using Social Variables Listed in Table 3

A.   Reading and Mathematics Tests

	NCDS			
Age 11	West Indian (N=72)		Asian (N=40)	
	Reading	Mathematics	Reading	Mathematics
Unadjusted	10·6	12·6	15·7	13·3
Residual	4·4	7·1	10·6	8·8
Age 16	(N=54)		(N=27)	
Unadjusted	12·0	9·9	10·1	6·1
Residual	5·2	4·4	5·3	1·2

	CHES					
Age 10	West Indian (N=92)		Indian (N=133)		Pakistani (N=58)	
	Reading	Mathematics	Reading	Mathematics	Reading	Mathematics
Unadjusted	10·8	13·2	6·8	6·3	11·0	9·4
Residual	6·4	9·0	3·8	3·6	4·3	2·7

B.   CSE and O-Level Examinations

	NCDS			
	West Indian (N=58)		Asian (N=30)	
	Total Passes	O-level (A-C) and CSE (1)	Total Passes	O-level (A-C) and CSE (1)
Unadjusted	1·13	1·70	0·90	1·31
Residual	+0·70	0·52	+0·66	0·27

Plus scores indicate that both West Indian and Asian children obtained more total passes than indigenous children once differences in their social circumstances are taken into account.

157

FOOTNOTES

1. J W B Douglas, **The Home and the School,** MacGibbon & Kee, 1964; C Jencks, **Inequality,** Basic Books, 1972; M Rutter & N Madge, **Cycles of Disadvantage,** Heinemann, 1976.
2. See, for example: **Interim Report of Committee of Inquiry into the Education of Children from Ethnic Minority Groups,** HMSO, 1981, pp. 6-8; M J Taylor **Caught Between,** NFER-Nelson, 1981, pp. 111-122; S Scarr, B K Caparulo, B M Ferdman & R B Tower, **Brit. J Develop. Psychol.,** 1983,**1,** 31-48.
3. A R Jensen, **Harvard Educ. Rev.,** 1969, 39, 1-129.
4. H J Eysenck, **Race, Intelligence and Education,** Temple Smith, 1971, p. 130.
5. There is not even complete agreement on what is to count as an IQ test, although the traditional distinction between them and tests of achievement (e.g., of reading or mathematics) is followed here. IQ tests are usually divided into individual or group tests, depending on whether they are administered to one person at a time, as are the Stanford-Binet or Wechsler tests, or to a large group at the same time. A more important distinction is between "verbal" and "non-verbal" tests, the former concentrating (not necessarily exclusively) on tests of vocabulary, meanings of phrases, verbal analogies and the like; while the latter may use numerical, pictorial or diagrammatic material, as in Raven's Matrices test which can be administered to a group with only minimal instructions. The Wechsler test is divided into two parts, verbal and performance, the former including tests of general knowledge and mathematics as well as vocabulary, and the latter comprising typical non-verbal pictorial and diagrammatic material.
6. See, for example: A R Jensen, **Bias in Mental Testing,** Methuen, 1980, pp. 277-281.
7. The proportion of the total variation in any characteristic found in a given population that can be attributed to genetic differences between members of that population is termed the "heritability" of the characteristic.
   Heritability can, in principle, be calculated for any characteristic that can be measured, whether it be height, weight, colour of hair or of skin, musical ability or IQ. Two points should be stressed. First, heritability is a statistic applicable only to a particular population at a particular time. Secondly, high heritability does not mean that the characteristic in question is genetically fixed and therefore unamenable to environmental influence. The heritability of height, for example, is generally taken to be very high, of the order of .90, in most modern populations. But changes in the diet of a particular population can still produce large increases in average height: that of the Japanese, for example, has increased by over 5 cm. since 1945.
   Both Jensen and Eysenck have repeatedly argued that the heritability of IQ is about .80, i.e., that 80% of the observed variation in IQ in modern Western populations is due to genetic variation within these populations. Relatively few other authorities would now agree with them. N D Henderson **(Ann. Rev. Psychol.,** 1982, **33,** p. 413) states that "an estimate of 50% seems more in vogue" or "between .4 and .7." S Scarr and L Carter-Saltzman in **Handbook of Human Intelligence,** (Ed. R J Sternberg), Cambridge University Press, 1982, p. 792) write: "Most investigators in behavior genetics conclude from the evidence that about half ($\pm$.1) of the current differences among individuals in U.S. and European white populations in measured intelligence result from genetic differences among them."
8. P E Vernon, **Intelligence and Cultural Environment,** Methuen, 1969, p.70.
9. R S MacArthur & W B Elley, **Brit. J. Educ. Psychol.,** 1963, **33,** 107-119; J D Nisbet & N J Entwhistle, **Brit. J. Educ. Psychol.,** 1967, **37** 188-193.
10. J C Loehlin, G Lindzey & J N Spuhler, **Race Differences in Intelligence,** Freeman, 1975, pp. 177-195.
11. L A Messé, W D Crane, S R Messé & W Rice, **J. Educe. Psychol.,** 1979, **71,** 233-241; A R Jensen, **Bias in Mental Testing,** pp. 465-515; S Scarr & D Yee, **Educ. Psychologist,** 1980, **15,** 1-22.
12. It is clearly somewhat inappropriate to refer to U.K. citizens as West Indian children. In earlier studies, many children so characterized may have been born there, but this is not true of more recent studies. We use the term, somewhat hesitantly, and later the term

Asian, Indian or Pakistani to refer to children whose families have recently migrated from the West Indies or Indian sub-continents. Where we report the results of original analyses of The National Child Development Study, the criterion for counting a child as West Indian or Asian was that he should be described as of the appropriate ethnic appearance, and that both his parents should have been born in the West Indies or in India, Pakistan or Bangladesh. This is, obviously, a rather conservative criterion. For the more recent Child Health and Education Study, where data on parental place of birth were not available, the criterion was simply that the child be described in the parental interview as of West Indian, Indian or Pakistani (including Bangladeshi) ethnic groups.

13. A M Shuey, **The Testing of Negro Intelligence,** Social Sciences Press, 1966; J C Loehlin, G Lindzey & J N Spuhler, **Race Differences in Intelligence.**

14. IQ tests are normally "standardized" to give a mean or average score for the population as a whole of 100, with a "standard deviation" of 15 points. That is to say, approximately two thirds of the population will obtain IQ scores between 85 and 115, or one standard deviation on either side of the mean. If, therefore, there is a 15-point difference between the mean IQ scores of blacks and whites in the U.S., this would imply that whereas about 50% of whites obtained IQ scores of 100 or more, only about 15 to 20% of blacks will do so.

15. W Yule, M Berger, M Rutter & B Yule, **J. Child Psychol. Psychiat.,** 1975. **16,** 1-17.

16. J McFie & J A Thompson, **Brit. J. Educ. Psychol.,** 1970, **40,** 348-351.

17. The National Child Development Study is organized by the National Children's Bureau, 8 Wakley Street, London, E.C.1. We are very grateful to the Bureau for making the data available and in particular to K Fogelman for all his help. The raw scores on the two IQ tests have been converted to IQ scores with a mean of 100 and standard deviation of 15.

18. The Child Health and Education Study is directed by Professor N R Butler, University of Bristol. We are very grateful to him and to his colleagues Dr Mary Haslam and Mr B Howlett for making the data available and for all their help. Our analyses of the data from this and the National Child Development Study were financially supported by a grant from the Economic and Social Research Council.

The British Ability Scales (C D Elliott, NFER-Nelson, 1979) consist of a set of 23 separate sub-tests or scales, only four of which were used in this study: word definitions, similarities, matrices and recall of digits. The first is a test of vocabulary, and the second a test of conceptual grouping or categorisation; by any criterion, these would be regarded as verbal IQ tests. The matrices sub-test is similar to Raven's Matrices, requiring the child to complete diagrammatic sequences, and is equally clearly a non-verbal IQ test. In the recall of digits sub-test or digit span, the child listens to a sequence of numbers and simply has to repeat them back to the tester; it is a test used in many other IQ tests (in the Wechsler tests and some versions of the Stanford-Binet test), where it is usually classified as a verbal test (as it is in the British Ability Scales). The basis for such classification is that factor analysis reveals that the digits test tends to agree with other verbal tests more than with non-verbal tests, although it is acknowledged that it usually correlates less strongly with other verbal tests than they do with one another. We have calculated the inter-correlations between these four sub-tests in the unusually large sample provided by this study. The correlation between definitions and similarities was twice as large as that between either of these sub-tests and recall of digits, and these were, in turn, no larger than the correlation between recall of digits and matrices. We also performed a factor analysis (varimax rotation) on these scores: the first factor was one on which definitions and similarities loaded more strongly than digits or matrices; the second was one on which the latter two tests loaded more strongly than the first two. By this criterion, the similarities and definitions sub-tests go together as a measure of verbal IQ, while the recall of digits and matrices tests go together as a measure of non-verbal IQ. Rather than insist on this grouping, however, we have chosen to present the results of the four sub-tests separately, allowing readers to make up their own minds.

19. N Foner, **Internat. Migration Rev.,** 1979 **13,** 284-297.

20, B Tizard, O Cooperman, A Joseph & J Tizard, **Child Development,** 1972 **43,** 337-358.

21. K Eyferth, **Archiv. Gesamte Psychol.**, 1961, **113**, 222-241.
22. S Scarr & R A Weinberg, **Amer. Psychologist**, 1976, **31**, 726-739.
23. See, for example: A R Jensen, **Straight Talk about Mental Tests,** Methuen, 1981, pp. 207-232. An excellent discussion of Jensen's data and arguments is provided by J R Flynn, **Race, IQ and Jensen,** Routledge, 1980. It will be obvious to the reader of Flynn's book that our own discussion owes a great deal to his painstaking and scrupulously honest account.
24. For a good discussion, see: M Rutter & N Madge, **Cycles of Disadvantage,** pp. 110-123.
25. M J Taylor, **Caught Between,** pp. 27-35; M Ghodsian, J Essen & K Richardson, **New Community,** 1980, 8, 195-205; S Scarr *et al.,* **Brit. J. Develop. Psychol.,** 1983, **1,** 31-48; A R Jensen, **Educability and Group Differences,** Methuen, 1973, pp. 168-169.
26. M J Taylor, **Caught Between,** pp. 35-45; M Rutter, B Yule, J Morton & C Bagley, **J. Child Psychol. Psychiat.,** 1975, **16,** 105-124; S Scarr *et al.,* **Brit. J. Develop. Psychol.,** 1983, **1,** 32-48.
27. For example: S S Baratz & J C Baratz, **Harvard Educ. Rev.,** 1970, **40,** 34-36; Black People's Progressive Association and Redbridge Community Relations Council, **Cause for Concern: West Indian Pupils in Redbridge,** 1978.
28. A R Jensen, **Straight Talk about Mental Tests,** p.192.
29. A M Shuey, **The Testing of Negro Intelligence.**
30. For a critical analysis of the studies relied on by Shuey, see: P M Green, **Dissent,** 1976, 284-297.
31. P L Nichols & V E Anderson, **Soc. Biol.,** 1973, **20,** 367-374.
32. A M Grace, Unpublished M.Ed. Thesis, University of Nottingham, 1972.
33. One relevant study in California (J R Mercer & W C Brown, In **The Fallacy of IQ** (Ed. C. Senna), The Third Press, 1973) found that a relatively small number of factors, father's occupation and education, type of neighbourhood, home ownership, mother's participation in various local organizations, and family structure, were able to account for most of the difference between the IQ scores of black and white children. It is important to note that to "account for" such a difference in terms of a particular set of social factors does not mean that the social factors have been shown to **cause** the difference, but only that they were correlated with it and when allowance is made for them the IQ difference disappears. Whether this implies a direct causal relationship is another matter, discussed on p. 22.
34. V P Houghton, **Race,** 1968, 147-156; C Bagley, **Soc. Econ. Studies,** 1971 **10.**
35. It must be stressed that the information provided in Table 3 comes from two independent studies which asked rather different questions and collected and tabulated data in rather different ways. Even information seemingly as straightforward as the number of children, for example, is not comparable, for in NCDS this item refers to the number of children in the household (which might contain more than one family) while in CHES, it refers to the number of children in the family. In no sense, therefore, should the table be used to infer whether or not there has been any change in the social circumstances of West Indian (or indigenous) children over the 12 years separating the two studies.

A similar analysis of NCDS data has been published by C Bagley in **Self-Concept, Achievement and Multicultural Education** (ed. G Verma & C Bagley), Macmillan, 1982. One problem with this sort of analysis is that data on all the variables may not be available for all the children in the original sample. In the NCDS sample, for example, complete data for the variables listed in Table 3 are available for only 72 of the original 113 West Indian children, of whom only 54 had been in the U.K. for more than 4 years. It is difficult to know whether they are a random sample from the initial set of 113, but the mean IQ score of 88.4 for these 72 does not differ greatly from the mean of 86.3 for all 113 children, while the mean of 89.7 for the 54 who had been in the U.K. for more than 4 years hardly differs at all from the mean of 89.0 for the 74 children in the entire sample who had been in this country for this length of time. In the CHES sample, complete data are available for 92 of the original West Indian children, with a mean IQ score of 91.5 compared to that of 92.4 for the entire sample. Although this difference in total IQ is trivially small, by an odd chance it is largely made up of a difference in scores on the recall of digits. The 92 children in the regression analysis had a mean score of 97.3 on this sub-test compared with a score of 99.2 for the entire sample.

36. M J Taylor, **Caught Between,** pp. 27-35. Runnymede Trust, **Britain's Black Population,** Heinemann, 1980, pp. 55-72.

37. **Interim Report of the Committee of Inquiry into the Education of Children from Ethnic Minority Groups,** pp. 6-8; J Essen & M Ghodsian, **New Community,** 1979, **7,** 422-429.

38. B Ashby, A Morrison & H J Butcher, **Res. Educ.,** 1970, **4,** 73-80; R Sharma, unpublished Ph. D. Thesis, University of London, 1971; other data on the performance of Asian children on IQ tests and in school are discussed in the report prepared for this committee by M J Taylor.

39. As was true for the West Indian children in CHES, the large majority of Indian and Pakistani children in this study had lived in the U.K. for at least 5 years by the time of these tests – 159 of 170 Indian children and 79 of 91 Pakistani children. Exclusion of the small number of recent immigrants makes very little difference to the results shown in Table 5: they did obtain rather lower scores on the two verbal sub-tests, but actually obtained slightly higher scores on the matrices and recall of digits sub-tests.

40. S Scarr **et al. Brit. J. Develop. Psychol.,** 1983, **1,** 31-48.

41. M Ghodsian **et al., New Community,** 1980, **8,** 195-205.

42. The data shown in Table 6 are from all Indian and Pakistani children regardless of their date of entry into the U.K. Exclusion of the small numbers who were not born here makes virtually no difference to the results of the analyses. Statistical analyses of the data on the social circumstances of West Indian, Indian and Pakistani children given in Tables 3 and 6 confirms, what is evident from the figures, that both Indian and Pakistani families are significantly less likely than West Indian families to have no male head, and that Indian children are significantly less likely than West Indians to receive free school meals or to live in inner cities or council estates. The only other significant differences are those where Pakistani families are actually worse off than West Indians.

43. There are, of course, numerous other minority groups now resident in the U.K. They are mostly too small to provide significant numbers of children in national surveys like NCDS and CHES. But some thorough local studies have occasionally turned up enough children to provide meaningful data. One such is W Yule **et al., J. Child Psychol. Psychiat.,** 1975, **16,** 1-17. This found, for example, that Turkish Cypriot children obtained scores on IQ tests lower than those of West Indian children.

44. We have found one British study where West Indian children, selected to have similar scores to white children on verbal tasks, obtained reliably lower scores on Raven's Matrices (J F Payne, unpublished M A Thesis, University of Keele, 1967). But there were no data on any other ethnic group and it is impossible to know whether the results have any generality. American studies, on which of course Jensen's arguments were originally based, give little reason to believe so. Although some have reported particularly poor performance by American blacks on this test (C Higgins & C Sivers, **J. Consult. Psychol.,** 1958, **22,** 465-468; A R Jensen, **Educability and Group Differences,** pp. 309-312), others have found no such deficit (I J Semler & I Iscoe, **J. Educ. Psychol.,** 1966, **57,** 326-336; J M Mandler & N L Stein, **J. Exp. Psychol.,** 1974, **102,** 657-669). There is some evidence that blacks in the U.S. find particular difficulty with the "Blocks Design" sub-test of the Wechsler tests: this requires one to manipulate diagrammatic, spatial relationships possibly similar to those called for in the Matrices test. The evidence is discussed by J C Loehlin, G Lindzey and J N Spuhler, **Race Differences in Intelligence,** pp. 186-187; see also G R Reynolds & A R Jensen, **J. Educ. Psychol.,** 1983, **75,** 207-214. J M Mandler & N L Stein, **Psychol. Bull.,** 1977, **84,** 173-192, have published a thorough, critical review of this whole issue, entitled "The myth of perceptual defect"; their conclusion is that there is no good reason to believe that blacks in the U.S. perform especially poorly on nonverbal, perceptual or spatial tests.

45. We are assuming here that there probably is a difference between the IQ scores of West Indian and of Asian children, and that their relatively similar performance at age 10 in CHES should be taken as the exception rather than the rule. The evidence from various measures of school achievement, tests of reading and mathematics and public examinations, tends to support this. Provided thay have been living in this country for a reasonable

length of time, Asian children do better at school than West Indian children (see below, pp. 41-48). Even in CHES, West Indian children obtain lower scores on tests of reading and mathematics than Indian children, and lower mathematics scores than Pakistani children.

46. Cited by: S Tomlinson, **Educational Subnormality: A Study in Decision Making,** Routledge & Kegan Paul, 1981, pp. 146-147.

47. R Rosenthal & L Jacobson, **Pygmalion in the Classrooom,** Holt, Rinehart & Winston, 1968.

48. See: J D Elashoff & R E Snow, **Pygmalion Reconsidered,** Jones Publishing Company, 1971.

49. Elashoff & Snow, op. cit.,; see also W B Seaver **J. Pers. Soc. Psychol.,** 1973, **28,** 333-342; W D Crane & P M Mellon, **J. Educ. Psychol.,** 1978, **70,** 39-49.

50. See: A R Jensen, **Bias in Mental Testing,** pp. 596-618; W Samuel, D J Soto, M Parks, P Ngissah & B Jones, **J. Educ. Psychol.,** 1976, **68,** 273-285; W Samuel, **J. Educ. Psychol.,** 1977, **69,** 593-604.

51. C Bagley, M Bart & J Wong, In **Race, Education and Identity** (ed. G K Verma and C Bagley), Macmillan, 1979.

52. C Bagley, K Mallick & G K Verma. In **Race, Education and Identity.**

53. W Yule **et al., J. Child Psychol. Psychiat.,** 1975, **16,** 1-17, found that West Indian girls performed better on IQ tests than West Indian boys, but neither the NCDS nor the CHES data show such differences: in NCDS the total IQ for boys is 86.7, for girls 85.5; in CHES, the comparable scores are 92.6 and 92.1. A M Grace (see footnote 32) also found no evidence that West Indian girls obtained higher scores than boys. One study which has reported higher self-esteem in West Indian boys than girls is: D M Louden, **New Community,** 1978, **6,** 218-234.

54. P Lomax, **Educ. Rev., 1977, 29,** 107-119.

55. C Bagley **et al.** In **Race, Education and Identity.**

56. D Milner, **Children and Race,** Penguin, 1975; A G Davey & P N Mullin, **J. Child Psychol. Psychiat.,** 1980, **21,** 241-251; P Lomax, **Educ. Rev.,** 1977, **29,** 107-119; M Stone, **The Education of the Black Child in Britain,** Fontana, 1981.

57. A M Grace, M Ed. Thesis, University of Nottingham, 1972: Community Relations Commission, **Education of Ethnic Minority Children from the Perspecives of Parents, Teachers and Education Authorities,** 1977.

58. A Dawson, In **Youth in contemporary Society** (ed. C Murray), NFER, 1978.

59. S Scarr **et al., Brit. J. Develop, Psychol.,** 1938, **1,** 31-48. The quotation is from **The Sunday Times.**

60. Data from Inner London, analysed by M Rutter, have shown that at the age of 10, West Indian children obtain nonverbal scores nearly 11 points below the indigenous mean, while at the age of 14 the difference is only 9 points.

61. C Mabey, **Educ. Research,** 1981, **23,** 83-95. The reading scores reported by Mabey have been standardized, just like IQ scores, to give a mean of 100 and a standard deviation of 15. We have adopted the same procedure with the reading and mathematics scores from NCDS and CHES reported below.

62. The problem with the statistical analysis of the ILEA data (an analysis of co-variance) is that it assumes that the relationship between scores on the first reading test and scores on the second is a strictly linear one. Since West Indian children's scores tend to cluster together at one end of the scale on the first test, any deviation from linearity could lead to a mistaken estimate of their expected scores on the second test. Our own analysis of the scores on the two reading tests in NCDS revealed just such a departure from linearity, the consequence of which was that a linear regression analysis indicated a spurious decline in West Indian scores from one age to another.

63. A Little, **Oxford Rev. Educ.,** 1975, **1,** 117-135; W Yule **et al., J. Child Psychol. Psychol. Psychiat.,** 1975, **16,** 1-17; C Mabey, **Educ. Research,** 1981, **23,** 83-95; S Scarr **et al., Brit. J. Develop. Psychol.,** 1983, **1,** 31-48.

64. The simplest measure of the relationship between two sets of scores is a correlation coefficient, which will have the value of 1.0 if the two sets of scores agree perfectly (i.e., the

child with the highest score on one test has the highest score on the other and so on down to the child with the lowest score on both tests) and a value of zero if there is no agreement between them. S Scarr **et al., (Brit. J. Develop. Psychol.,** 1983, **1,** 31-48) also report similar correlations between IQ and reading scores in West Indian, Asian and white children.

65. S Scarr **et al., Brit. J. Develop. Psychol.,** 1983, **1,** 31-48.
66. Interim Report of Committee of Inquiry into the Education of Children from Ethnic Minority Groups, H.M.S.O., 1981.
67. The data presented in Table C of the **Interim Report of Committee of Inquiry into the Education of Children from Ethnic Minority Groups,** confirm that although West Indian children obtain fewer "good " CSE and O-level passes than whites, they are less likely to leave school with no passes at all. Data from the Inner London Education Authority also indicate that a smaller proportion of West Indian than of white children have no CSE or O-level passes by the age of 16 (17% versus 28%), although a much smaller proportion (2% versus 11%) obtain 5 or more "good" passes (C Mabey, personal communication). An analysis of a smaller group of West Indians and whites in Inner London suggests that if examinations passed at the 6th form level are included, the proportion of West Indian children obtaining 5 or more O-levels is 19% compared to only 16% in whites (M Rutter, G Gray, B Maughan & A Smith, **School experience and achievements and the first year of employment,** Final report to Department of Education and Science, 1982).
68. J Tizard, W N Schofield & J Hewison, **Brit. J. Educ. Psychol.,** 1982, **52,** 1-15.
69. A R Jensen, **Straight Talk about Mental Tests,** pp. 192-193.
70. R G Record, T McKeown & J H Edwards, **Annals Human Genetics,** 1970, **34,** 11-20.

ANNEX E

Revised Research Proposal on "Academically Successful Black Pupils", submitted by the Research and Statistics Branch of the Inner London Education Authority July 1981

Synopsis

The proposed study is an investigation into the environmental factors – both at school and home – which enable Black students to succeed in CSE and 'O' level examinations[1]. Three groups of seventy-five students: Black students with family backgrounds from the West Indies[2]; Black students with Asian family backgrounds; and White students, who have obtained at least five CSE Grade 1 or 'O' level Grades A-C awards are to be interviewed in depth. Control groups of equal numbers of students of similar backgrounds – without qualifications – will also be interviewed. The information obtained from these interviews will be analysed in order to identify the factors which contribute towards the academic success of Black students in the British Educational System and to answer questions concerning the differences and similarities of these groups to the control groups.

Location of Study

The study is to be located in the Research and Statistics Branch of the ILEA.

Proposed Investigation

The recently published interim report of the Committee of Inquiry into the Education of Children from Ethnic Minority Groups recognised that some students with West Indian family backgrounds are achieving results 'comparable with, or indeed higher than, those of their peers'[1]. This report identified the need for research evidence about particular factors which have led some Black pupils to succeed in their secondary schooling.

The need for such evidence arises because much research on children of West Indian family origin has tended to concentrate on overall levels of attainment and to compare these with that of other groups. (Yule *et al* 1975, Redbridge 1978, Essen and Ghodsian 1980 and Mabey 1981). Such studies, though vitally important in providing information, may, in some ways, have contributed to a negative view of Black school pupils. (One exception is the study by Driver (1980) which claims a superior performance by West Indian pupils, but is methodologically flawed – Taylor 1981). The APU study which sought to repeat an investigation of the average attainment of children of West Indian family backgound was rejected by the minority ethnic groups and the teachers' associations on such grounds. Furthermore, a recent review of literature in this area (Mortimore 1981) argued that current research findings were inadequate to explain differences in attainment between different ethnic groups and that further detailed research was needed.

---

[1]We do recognise, of course, that educational success cannot be measured solely in terms of examination results. Nevertheless, success at public examinations is important for enabling the school leaver to compete in the employment market and to take advantage of the post-school educational opportunities available.

[2]In this proposal we have adopted a terminology used by, amongst others, the Catholic Commission for Racial Justice. The term 'Black' is used to refer to all those people who are identifiable by skin colour and share the experience of being the objects of racism at the hands of the white majority.

The term 'racism' is difficult to define. (See Tierney in "Race, Migration and Schooling.") In this proposal we have used the definition given in paragraph 2 Chapter 2 of the Rampton Report: "In our view racism describes a set of attitudes and behaviour towards people of another race which is based on the belief that races are distinct and can be graded as 'superior' or 'inferior'. A racist is therefore someone who believes that people of a particular race, colour or national origin are inherently inferior, so that their identity, culture, self-esteem, views and feelings are of less value than his or her own and can be disregarded or treated as less important."

A study of school and other factors which enable pupils to be academically successful could contribute to a positive view of Black pupils. Such a study would be in tune with other work which has developed around the concept of 'coping skills'. The study by Quinton *et al* (forthcoming) and the work of Rutter (1981) have both focussed on the strategies by which people who have experienced social disadvantage manage to overcome their difficulties and achieve success. The proposed study would attempt similar tasks by focussing on, and investigating in detail the experiences – both positive and negative – of Black pupils of West Indian family background, Black pupils of Asian family background and White pupils, all of whom are already known to be "academically" successful. Examining and contrasting these same experiences with those of less academically successful pupils from the same ethnic groups will provide data to answer a number of key questions and indicate how school and classroom environments may be modified to suit the needs and demands of Black pupils.

Research Aims

The main aim of the study will be to answer the following questions:

1. What difference do the pupils' school and classroom experiences make to their success or failure?

2. What contribution does the pupils' home environment make to their success (or failure)?

3. What effects, if any, do peer influences have on success (and failure)?

It should be noted that it is impossible to tackle successfully any one of these questions without, at the same time, answering the others. For example, in order to determine and measure with any confidence the contribution of schooling experiences to success, it is necessary first to identify, control and allow for the effects of home and peer group, as well as a host of other relevant factors.

To answer these three questions it is, therefore, necessary to collect detailed information covering the following areas:

1. **School experience**

   (a) **Pre-school and primary school experiences:**
   Attainment, referrals to and contact with any agencies; ethnic and social composition of the schools attended; experiences of racism.

   (b) **Secondary school experience:**
   Verbal reasoning band placement, school organisation (streamed/banded/mixed-ability), option choice advice, options taken up, extra coaching, career advice, participation in school life, attainment at different ages, responsibilities, participation, use of counselling, ethnic and social composition of school, experience of racism, supplementary schooling.

   (c) **Organisation and structure of secondary school attended:**
   Multi-ethnic policy/anti-racist policy, multi-ethnic curriculum, departmental policy statements on multi-ethnic education, number of Black teachers, Black parental involvement, use of multi-ethnic advisory teachers, staff attitudes/opinions regarding race/multi-ethnic education, school participation in local Black activities and events, language policy, E2L provision, in-service training, library policy and resources, relationship with supplementary schools.

2. **Home environment**

   (a) **Family backgrounds:**
   Origins, length of stay of parents in UK, family composition, economic status, number of siblings, respondent's position in family, religious affiliations, type of housing.

---

[1]'West Indian children in our schools' (Interim Report of the Committee of Inquiry into the Education of Children from Ethnic Minority Groups)

(b) **Style of family life:**
Levels of supervision, existence of and type of family activities, parents' ambitions for their children, parents' attitude to schooling.

3. **Individual characteristics attitudes and experiences**
Physical description[1], health, interests, ambitions, attitudes to school, to other ethnic groups, to British society, command of English, languages spoken, (for students with West Indian family backgrounds, command of Creole, attitude towards Creole speaking), experience of paid employment and/or voluntary community work, contact with institutional or direct racism in life outside school.

4. **Peer influences**
School peers, ethnicity of school peers, influence of peers, leisure activities, existence of key friend.

5. **Existence of 'significant others'**
Scouts/guides, church, youth club, family friends, teachers, social workers.

6. **Present activity and future plans**
Whether in employment, education or training, aspirations, and long-term plans.

7. **Racism**
This is clearly a complex, difficult, and sensitive issue. However as the above makes clear, we intend to look at racism and its effects on Black pupils' attainment both within school and in Society.

Research Design
Three groups of 75 pupils for each of the ethnic groups as described above are to be identified. These young people will have gained at least five CSE Grade 1/'O' level Grades A–C by Summer 1981. In addition three equal-sized control groups of similar ethnic background but without the academic qualifications are also to be identified.

All pupils will be interviewed by trained interviewers. It is important that interviewers should not be aware before the interviews of the identity of young people from the target groups and from the control groups.

Research Instruments
An interview schedule designed to elicit answers to the questions on the themes noted above will be developed. Parallel versions for each of the groups will also be prepared as appropriate. It is hoped, with the respondents' permission, to approach secondary schools for supplementary information.

---

[1]The relevance of some of the areas included (such as physical characteristics) may not be immediately apparent. There is some evidence to suggest that pupils of the same ethnic origin are treated differently by peers and teachers depending on their physical appearance.

ANNEX F

Summary of the main findings of a longitudinal study undertaken by Dr G K Verma

1. The study, based at the University of Bradford, was conducted in three phases. The first phase was designed to explore the determinants of the vocational aspirations, choices and achievements of ethnic minority adolescents in the Leeds/Bradford area of West Yorkshire. The second phase examined the occupational experience of a cohort of adolescents and attempted to set this experience in the context of achievement aspirations, scholastic achievement and expectations of working life. (The findings of these first two stages of the study are detailed in the project reports: "Problems of Vocational Adaptation of South Asian Adolescents in Britain, with special reference to the role of the school"—November 1981 and "The Occupational Adaptation of Ethnic Minority Adolescents in early Working Life"—March 1982.) The final phase, which was funded by the DES to assist the Swann Committee in its work, was specifically concerned with the academic achievement of ethnic minority adolescents and sought to establish profiles of high and low achievers among adolescents within different ethnic groups. In this phase of the research, the findings of which are summarised in this paper, no attempt was made to compare directly the overall levels of achievement of different ethnic groups; instead the factors which appeared to be associated with high and low achievers within each group were analysed separately, ie the study was concerned primarily with *intra-* rather than *inter-* ethnic comparisons. The full findings of the study are being published separately.[1]

2. In the final phase of the study, profiles of high and low achievers within ethnic groups were subjected to analysis on three levels:

Cultural Factors

a. composition of various cultures

b. the "core values" of each culture

c. actual and perceived differences

d. the individual's perception of his/her group membership and others' views of this.

Immediate Environment of the Individual

Family, school, peers and other environmental variables were studied, and how they interacted to produce cultural factors.

Individual Factors

Analysis for this level included self-esteem, motivation and attitude.

3. The study drew its sample from nine schools in West Yorkshire. In total some 1,224 pupils (694 boys, 530 girls) were studied, made up as follows:

	Whites	Indians	Pakistani	Bangladeshi	West Indian	Others
Girls	290	66	78	36	38	22
Boys	366	90	92	44	54	48
Total	656	156	170	80	92	70

In relation to South Asian youngsters, the religious breakdown was as follows:

Hindus	84
Muslims	250
Sikhs	72

Over 80% of the ethnic minority pupils studied were born in this country.

[1] "Ethnicity and Educational Achievement". Verma, G K and Ashworth, B. Macmillan.

4. The main findings of the study are as follows:

    i. **Views on Education**

    South Asian youngsters (Indian, Pakistani and Bangladeshi) appeared to have a high regard for education and usually gave overall approval to school, school work and teaching. Youngsters from other groups (whites and West Indians) tended to be more selective in their likes and dislikes and to offer more judgment on schools and teachers. About half the South Asians commented that they enjoyed or liked school. There also appeared to be a number of differences between the ethnic groups studied in terms of educational motivation. The South Asian youngsters' motivation in particular appeared to be centred around a commitment to school and examination success, possibly in the hope of social mobility, or, more likely, to avoid the damaging effect of failure. Over two-thirds of the total sample studied believed that examination success led to success in obtaining employment. West Indian youngsters on the other hand were less inclined to see a firm relationship between examination success and obtaining employment—possibly the knowledge that brothers and sisters and other West Indian youngsters with good qualifications are still discriminated against is a factor here. However South Asian youngsters who also experienced discrimination appeared to respond by reaffirming their commitment to educational qualifications as a means of social mobility

    Youngsters staying on at school did so to enter higher education later, to obtain better qualifications for work or to avoid unemployment. White pupils—particularly, able girls—tended to decide early to stay on at school and try to enter higher education, but a number of boys stayed on to improve previous examination results. Although South Asian pupils staying on generally thought that increased qualifications would lead to better job prospects the boys were beginning to show some doubts. The girls believed this as a result of leaving school and unsuccessfully searching for work before returning to the sixth form. A greater proportion of Pakistani and Indian youngsters expressed the intention of re-taking examinations which they had failed than that in any other group. The proportion intending to re-take was lowest for the White group. Many Muslim girls had their own difficulties, for parental control was strong and this led to some uncertainty over plans for work and assumptions about arranged marriages. West Indian girls had clearer reasons for staying on than boys. Like the South Asian and White girls they either needed more qualifications to enter further or higher education or could not find work. Unemployed South Asians who were not high achievers tended to regret their previous school performance. They attached no blame to the school, however, and took personal responsibility for being unable to find work. Many who had left school and found work realised that educational qualifications were not the only criteria used by employers in selecting employees. The intention to seek entry to further or higher education was most frequently expressed by South Asian pupils. In contrast, two-thirds of the White pupils intended to leave school to seek employment; in the South Asian and West Indian groups only approximately one-third expressed such an intention.

    ii. **Self-Esteem**

    No significant inter-ethnic differences were found in levels of self-esteem. However, factors contributing to self-esteem varied in their importance for different ethnic groups. West Indian youngsters, for example, derived much of their self-esteem from peer group sources; school sources made little contribution. In contrast South Asian youngsters derived most of their self-esteem from family and school sources. Youngsters unable to obtain employment had significantly lower levels of self-esteem than either those who had found employment or those who had stayed on at school beyond the age of 16. In the South Asian groups girls tended to have lower levels of self-esteem than boys. The reverse was true in the White and West Indian groups.

iii. **The Cultural Context of Achievement**

Although aware of their cultural heritage many South Asians had adopted some English cultural ways and ideas, and as a result faced many dilemmas which varied in intensity from family to family. South Asian youth's attitude presented the paradox of family loyalty and integration (with traditional values) with a materialistic and resentful attitude to British society. Some South Asian girls in particular faced family alienation in their search for independence. There were families, however, who had modified their own ideas of their culture in the light of English circumstances. Cultural adaptation was of less concern to White youngsters, however. For them it was more a question of other ethnic groups assimilating or adapting to the indigenous culture.

iv. **Family Influences on Achievement**

The family, particularly parents, appeared to be a major source of influence and help for all youngsters, but did not perform the same role for each ethnic group. In terms of perceived parental interest in their child's education, there was one significant inter-ethnic difference. High maternal and lower paternal interest were characteristic of West Indian youngsters; with other ethnic groups, perceived levels of maternal and paternal interest were more equally rated. The influence of the mother in West Indian families was particularly strong and this seemed to provide a dynamic model for girls. They had clearer ideas than boys about what they wanted to achieve and the means of doing so. South Asians tended to have clear guidance about schooling and careers and a number had well-educated relatives. Such families usually were supportive to the child and a number had come to England to increase their family's educational opportunities.

v. **Sources of Information about Jobs**

White youngsters tended to obtain their information about jobs from family and friends. Ethnic minority youngsters tended to obtain most information about jobs from 'formal' sources—from careers education at school or the Careers Office. 'Informal' sources for gaining employment were rated significantly more highly by White youngsters. 'Knowing the right people' was considered important by approximately 4 White youngsters in every 10; for Pakistani youngsters the proportion was just below 2 in 10. In terms of gaining employment, West Indian pupils tended to believe that having a 'good school record' was particularly important, while rating the acquisition of educational qualifications less highly.

Factors Affecting Examination Achievement

5.   To sum up therefore, the major factors discriminating between 'high' and 'low' examination achievement were not the same for every ethnic group.

i.   For **White** adolescents, such factors appeared to be:

— level of self-esteem, including its general-self, peer group and school-academic dimensions

— social class

— perceived level of maternal interest

— perceived level of help from the following sources: teachers, school, parents, siblings and friends

— enjoyment of school

— school attendance/absence

ii. For **Pakistani** adolescents, the main factors were:

— use of mother tongue at home

— social class

— perceived level of paternal *and* maternal interest

— perceived level of help from: school and siblings

— enjoyment of school

— school attendance/absence

iii. For **Bangladeshi** adolescents the factors discriminating between 'high' and 'low' achievement were:

— perceived level of paternal interest

— school attendance/absence

iv. For **Indian** adolescents, those factors appeared to be:

— perceived level of paternal interest

— enjoyment of school

— school attendance/absence

v. For **West Indian** adolescents, the factors discriminating between 'high' and 'low' achievement were:

— level of self-esteem, including its general-self and school-academic dimensions

— perceived level of maternal interest

— perceived level of help from school

— school attendance/absence

All the factors reported were significant at or above the 5% level. Given the nature of the data and the method by which it was analysed, it would be inappropriate and inadvisable to attempt to weight the factors. The factors listed above, although found to discriminate between high and low achievement, represent only part of a complex interaction which is different for each ethnic group. Other factors, despite not reaching statistical significance, also mediated on each interaction complex, making each unique. Thus, school attendance/absence, a discriminating factor in **all** ethnic groups has a separate value for **each** group. It cannot therefore be considered as having equal value in characterising high and low achievement in all ethnic groups.

6. The results obtained from this study, although confined to only one area of the country, suggest that the process of examination achievement is ethnically specific; factors affecting the achievement of one ethnic group may not necessarily affect the achievement of another one. It may be fallacious, therefore, to attempt to explain the 'underachievement' of a particular ethnic minority group from an understanding of the achievement process of the majority group. The examination of the interplay of social, education, cultural, familial and psychological factors mediating on achievement by intra-ethnic analysis shows distinct variation between high and low achievers of one ethnic group when compared with those of the other groups. To produce a definitive list of how the process of achievement differs with the ethnicity of the individual would be a fruitful area for further research that was specifically designed for this task.

ANNEX G

A Note on Research: by James Cornford

1. Introduction

The committee has faced a number of difficulties in finding satisfactory research to supplement and support the evidence it has received from teachers, parents, local education authorities, and the many other individuals and groups listed in the Appendices to this report. The first difficulty was that the Committee was not able to consider at length a comprehensive research strategy, given the requirement to produce quickly an interim report. The second difficulty, reflected clearly in the interim report, was the inadequacy of official statistics to provide anything but the crudest indications of the extent of differences between ethnic groups in academic achievement. This is regrettable but not surprising. The School Leavers Survey, onto which additional ethnic questions were piggy backed with the collaboration of a number of LEAs, is an administrative exercise. It was not designed for the Committee's purposes and not capable of adaptation to include the large number of additional questions about pupils, their backgrounds and the schools themselves, which would have been necessary to get behind crude ethnic categories and to give some idea of the causes as well as the extent of differences of achievement. This is not the fault of the Statistics Branch of the Department of Education and Science for whose help we are grateful. The Branch was indeed quick to point out the limitations of the survey. But it is a comment on the failure of the Department to keep itself adequately informed on what has for many years been acknowledged to be an urgent problem. We can only repeat once again the recommendation of our interim report that the Department should institute a programme for monitoring the educational progress of children from ethnic minorities. If this should prove too complex and too sensitive to handle as a routine administrative exercise, as may well prove to be the case, then the Department should establish a research programme to examine these problems in a regular and systematic way. Research undertaken by individual initiative in universities, colleges and research institutes has for the most part been on a small scale, not replicated or cumulative and often indifferent in quality.

That has been our third difficulty. The most important step taken by the Committee was to commission from the National Foundation for Educational Research three reviews of research into the education of pupils of West Indian, Asian and other origins: the first of these has been published as **Caught Between** by Monica J Taylor (NFER—Nelson 1981), and it is anticipated that the others, co-authored by Monica Taylor and Seamus Hegarty, will be published in due course. In the main body of our report we have drawn wherever possible on the findings of the research reviewed. And it must be said that whatever its shortcomings the cumulative effect of the research is to confirm and underline the seriousness and complexity of the educational problems facing ethnic minorities. The point to make again here however is the inadequacy of the past *ad hoc* research effort as a basis for policy and the need for the Department to make the fullest use of the small number of first-rate research workers in the field.

The fourth difficulty facing the Committee has been the sheer sensitivity of the issues it wanted to examine. This may be illustrated by a brief account of the major research initiative attempted by the Committee in response to criticisms of its interim report. This initiative originated with a proposal from the Research and Statistics Branch of the Inner London Education Authority for a project on **Black Students and educational success.** The idea was to interview about their home background and school experience two groups of black pupils, one of which would have achieved a certain level of success in public examinations at sixteen plus and the other not. Matching groups of white pupils were to be interviewed at the same time. It was hoped in this way not only to shift the focus of attention from factors associated with failure to those associated with success, but to get at the pupils' own perceptions of their schooling and in particular of the influence of racial attitudes on their performance. The major limitation of the research design, of which the proponents were well aware, was that to get groups of an adequate size the sample had to be drawn from a large number of schools. This would have precluded independent examination and assessment of the policies and practices of the schools themselves which are widely recognised to be a critical factor in pupils' achievement. Despite this limitation, the Committee saw this as a promising proposal, but wished to extend its scope to include both Asian pupils and places outside London. Negotiations to modify the research design and to conduct linked projects in Birmingham and Bradford were making progress when the project had to be abandoned.

The project was criticised at a conference of the National Association for Multiracial Education (NAME) and subsequent meetings between members of the Committee, of the research team and members of the Caribbean Teachers Association, NAME, the Afro-Caribbean Education Research Project (ACER) and other teachers and community workers revealed grave doubts about the value of the project and serious criticism of its design. The central issues were the emphasis on social and cultural factors and the weakness in relation to the schools. Whatever view one took about the force of these criticisms, there could be no mistaking the strength of the conviction behind them, and without the goodwill and cooperation of the critics the project had no chance of success. It was therefore withdrawn.

The Committee agreed with its critics about the lack of research about what goes on in schools and asked the ILEA team to design an alternative project to look at such factors as streaming, subject choice, examination entry and curriculum content as they affected children from ethnic minorities. The most illuminating studies of ethnic factors in schools have been based on direct observation, carried out in particular schools and classrooms, often highly perceptive and suggestive but necessarily limited for purposes of generalisation. The question is whether, drawing on these perceptions, measures can be developed which are methodologically sound, capable of replication and acceptable to LEAs, teachers, parents and pupils. This was the question to which the ILEA team now addressed itself. Unfortunately the earlier delays and the time taken to develop the feasibility study pushed the timetable beyond the anticipated life of the Committee. It was not therefore possible to fund this study from the Committee's budget and the Committee strongly recommended that the DES should fund it. The Department however delayed a decision beyond the point where the ILEA team could be kept together and thus lost the opportunity to build directly on the work already done. We regret this and believe that direct research on school policy and practice is essential if progress is to be made towards understanding the dynamics of ethnic relations in schools and towards improving performance. It is also necessary to reassure ethnic minorities that serious attention is given to their complaints and that research will be conducted which is not so designed as to throw the whole burden of responsibility for low academic achievement on pupils and their families. For these reasons we particularly welcome the joint research project of the Policy Studies Institute and the University of Lancaster, funded by the DES, on 'Factors associated with success in multi-ethnic schools'. This study concentrates on the relation between school policies and practices and the achievement of pupils. It has not however been found possible to focus directly on the influence of racial factors, as some direct observational studies have done. The problem addressed by the ILEA feasibility study remains to be tackled.

2. Commissioned Work
The upshot of this sorry tale was that, apart from the review of existing research, the Committee was able to commission new research on a modest scale only. Its major commissions were not indeed of new research, but were subventions to current programmes to enable research teams to complete work in progress in time to be of use to the Committee. The first of these was to the ESRC's Research Unit on Ethnic Relations, at the University of Aston, for a study of the definition and implementation of multicultural education policy by four local education authorities, by Professor John Rex and colleagues (**The Development of Multi-Cultural Education Policy in Four Local Education Authority Areas,** Research Unit on Ethnic Relations, April 1983).

172

The second commission was to the Postgraduate School of Studies in Research in Education of the University of Bradford to enable the Committee to draw on the findings of a longitudinal study of academic achievement under the direction of Dr G K Verma for which the fieldwork had been carried out in 1977-1982 **(Ethnicity and Achievement in British Schools,** University of Bradford, 1984).

Two other studies were directly commissioned on matters of particular concern to the Committee: a survey of present provision and capacity for training teachers in ethnic minority community languages **(Training of Teachers of Ethnic Minority Community Languages** by Professor Maurice Craft and Dr Madelaine Atkins, School of Education, University of Nottingham); and a study of provision for multicultural education in "all-white" schools (A Report of visits to schools with few or no Ethnic Minority Pupils by Arnold Matthews and Laurie Fallows). Each of these studies has produced useful information and interesting argument which are reflected at the appropriate places in the main body of our report.

We also commissioned from Eglon Whittingham a report on "Language and its relation to achievement among children of West Indian origin". In this report Mr Whittingham reviews the published research on the subject of creole and patois. He also draws on a small research project of his own to give detailed examples of children's use of creole linguistic forms in the classroom and the problems to which they may give rise, and demonstrates the need for further investigation. The report is available from the DES.

3.   Agenda for Research
There are three steps which we see as essential to provide a sound basis for future policy:
1.   the establishment of an adequate statistical base;
2.   the setting up of a programme of longitudinal studies to monitor in greater depth the progress of ethnic minority children; and
3.   the support of research projects which concentrate on the educational process, particularly policies and practices within schools, the relationship between home and school, and the transition from school to work.

4.   The Statistical Base
1.   In our interim report we argued for the value of ethnically based statistics as follows:

"Ethnically based statistics can, we believe, be of value at all levels and to all parties within education: to central government, in determining policy; to LEAs in quantifying and locating particular needs; to schools so that they can take full account of the cultural and linguistic backgrounds of pupils and see whether any groups are under-achieving or are disproportionately represented in any subject or class and to make an appropriate response; and to parents so that they can assess their child's performance in relation to his peers. We are therefore wholly in favour of the collection of educational statistics on an ethnic basis where they are to be used in establishing facts about how members of the ethnic minorities are faring in the educational system".

And we made specific recommendations about pupils and teachers including:

"i.   All schools should record the ethnic origin of a child's family, along with the normal standard data, when a child first enters school, on the basis of discussion with parents.

ii.   The DES should reincorporate the collection of information on the ethnic origin of all pupils in schools into its annual statistical exercise and should introduce ethnic classifications into its school leavers survey."

173

2. We are aware that there are strong objections to the collection of ethnically based statistics including:

  a. that the information is not and will not be used to the advantage of the groups concerned: a more probable result is the perpetuation of negative stereotypes. Monitoring in the past has not led to improvements;

  b. that ethnic classifications are unsatisfactory and have no educational relevance; and

  c. that information on ethnic origin may be used in conjunction with the British Nationality Act 1981 to determine individual citizenship.

3. Although we understand the fears that lie behind these objections, we continue to believe that the collection of ethnically based statistics is necessary both for planning the policies we have recommended in this report and for making sure that they are being implemented. We agree however that:

  a. it is necessary to arrive at a commonly agreed set of classifications that can be seen to have a definite **educational** relevance because they correspond to real social and cultural differences which affect the relationships between schools and pupils; and

  b. that we must distinguish between information which it is in the direct interest of individual pupils and their families to have collected (eg language, religion) and more general information, including ethnic origins, which may be of importance for LEA or DES policy, but which does not need to be collected from each pupil or recorded individually.

4. The first thing to establish is the purpose for which statistics should be collected. The following have been suggested:

  a. The assessment of special education need (pupil).

  b. The allocation of staffing and other resources to meet such need (LEA/School).

  c. Monitoring of performance (LEA/DES).

5. The second thing to determine is what information is required and from whom, for example:

  a. **Pupils**
    i. Mother tongue and whether used at home.
    ii. Special dietary needs.
    iii. Religion.

  b. **Schools** in addition to (a)(i)—(iii) above
    i. English Language proficiency.
    ii. Standardised test results at various ages.
    iii. Admission to selective schools, composition of bands or streams.
    iv. Suspensions, referrals to special agencies outside school.
    v. External examinations: entries and results.
    vi. Staying on into full-time education post 16.
    vii. Success in obtaining employment.
    viii. Entry into higher education.

  c. **LEA/DES** in addition to above
    i. Ethnic origin

6. This information may be collected as follows:

  a. **Pupil** information: from parents on entering school.

174

b. **School** information: compiled by school as pupil progresses through school.

c. **LEA/DES:** the important point is that information on ethnic origin need not be collected from every individual pupil at all: the information is being collected primarily for a **political** purpose, namely to monitor the performance of ethnic groups, not to help with the problems of individual pupils or to allocate resources which must be done on the basis of need, ie the numbers of pupils actually experiencing language difficulties.

7. Information on ethnic origins could of course be collected from parents when children first enter schools as we originally recommended. Given the fears that have been expressed and the fact that this information is required for general policy purposes and not for direct educational decisions about individual pupils, there is a case for collecting this information by sample survey. The major problem about information collected from individuals is **confidentiality:** that information may be used for purposes other than that for which it was originally required (eg fears about nationality). The advantages of using a social survey for monitoring as against the collection of information from each and every individual include:

   i. the guarantee of anonymity and confidentiality to those questioned: the survey is a separate exercise and the information is not recorded on the individual's record card;

   ii. greater accuracy: it is much easier to collect accurate information from a sample than from routine administrative enquiry to a whole population;

   iii. greater flexibility: information sought can be adjusted in the light of experience, an administrative system is cumbersome, and expensive to alter;

   iv. more scope for gathering additional information which may be pertinent to monitoring including information on institutional factors. A regular survey could have a core of questions on ethnic background, but study in addition specific problems like the school allocation problems of an LEA or placement in special schools.

5. **Monitoring**

   a. What is proposed in effect is to include the collection of information on ethnic origins within a programme of research rather than through the administrative procedures of the school, in the belief that the survey interview is more searching, more sensitive and more secure for the informant and will avoid raising delicate issues between schools and parents. It is also likely to yield more accurate, detailed and meaningful information than that which would emerge from the necessarily rough classifications which would have to be adopted for administrative record keeping.

   We believe in any event that the monitoring of performance should not be left to *ad hoc* investigation but should be the subject of a continuing research programme. The main elements of such a programme would be as follows:

   i. To obtain data on all categories of children, but with particular care to see that ethnic minority children are adequately represented in the samples.

   ii. To collect contextual data on teachers, peers and schools to ensure adequate interpretation.

   iii. To ensure acceptable measures of minority status, that is agreed definitions or classifications of ethnic origin.

   iv. As a large part of the purpose is to establish trends, to maintain consistency and comparability of definitions.

   v. The progress of children through the system and from one point to another will be of central interest, which implies longitudinal studies following cohorts of children in the manner of the National Child Development Study and the Child Health and Education Study.

vi.   It will be necessary to include parents in the surveys in order to obtain adequate data on key background factors such as social class.

vii.   Consideration will need to be given to the measures used to assess the outcomes or achievements of children. The use of public examination results alone is unlikely to be adequate.

viii.   There will need to be a guarantee of long-term funding to ensure continuity, to enable research procedures to be progressively improved and to allow for an adequate judgement of the success of the programme.

b.   Any such programme will need to be the responsibility of a specially designated research unit or group, either within the DES itself or in some research institute or university. To the extent that it needs to acquire the confidence and cooperation of a number of groups, parental, professional and official, there would be something to be said for a position independent of the DES and for the involvement of the various groups in the work of the unit. Its staff would need to have experience of work in ethnic relations and particular skills in the area of educational survey research. There are likely to be difficult issues both of classification and of survey design, which will need to be tackled with a combination of technical competence, imagination and political sensitivity. This will not be a routine research assignment.

The main responsibility of the unit would be to set up and run a series of overlapping longitudinal studies, perhaps three or four, covering the age ranges of interest, from infant through to post compulsory school age, and including further education and training. The main purpose of these studies would be to compare the progress of minorities and other groups through the crucial stages of the system. Thus a study from age 13 to age 16 would look at how comparable pupils aged 13 from different groups had made out by the time of their examination year. It would be important to report these studies every two or three years to monitor change. It would be equally important to include in the design of such studies as much data as possible on the character and composition of schools.

6. Specific Research

Here we indicate the areas of research which we think should enjoy priority. We have not devised and do not propose particular projects. There is a limited number of first rate research workers and it is seldom possible and never wise to tell them what to do. Nevertheless we think the DES and other funding bodies should give priority, other things being equal, to research in the following areas:

1.   Policy and practice in schools.
2.   Multicultural policies.
3.   Language.
4.   The transition from school to work.
5.   Pre-school learning.

7. Schools

In her review of research from 1960 to 1982 (**Ethnic Minorities in British Schools,** Policy Studies Institute/Heinemann Educational Books, London 1983, p4) Sally Tomlinson comments:

"The literature has largely documented underachievement among minority group children, particularly children of West Indian origin, and there has been an obsessive concern with

'explaining' this rather than focusing on factors which might make for children's improved education. There is very little positive literature documenting factors in and out of school which might make for more success among minority children within the existing school system, and there is no literature at all documenting particular factors within schools which might make for more effective education for the children."

To this we might add that there is precious little research which throws light on factors within schools which may help to explain the difficulties which children encounter, whether matters of school policy, organisation or classroom practice. To do so requires a different approach and a different kind of research from most of what has been done to date. As a perceptive critique of our own aborted project on successful black students put it:

"... the sponsors appear to want a particular kind of evidence, ie quantified information which can be quoted with ease and treated as 'proof' yet without examining internal school dynamics.

Surely it seems reasonable to put the case for research of a more qualitative, interactive nature. Though this type of evidence may be less suited to 'proving' what makes a successful black student, it can give much greater insight into the complex range of variables which affect the educational life-changes of Black British children[1]."

The report goes on to suggest that eight factors should figure prominently in any research designed to look at school dynamics, namely: discipline policy, school policy on examination procedures, non-examination procedures, teachers, school management, home/school liaison, links with the community, and post-16 curriculum and opportunities. (Further specification of these factors as set out in the report is given in Appendix 1.)

We agree that there is an urgent need to look at these factors in schools and it is for that reason that we have already welcomed the PSI/Lancaster study. Experience of that project however suggests that there are major difficulties in carrying out an ambitious programme covering a large number of schools and that it may be necessary to restrict future research either to a relatively small number of schools, to be studied in depth, or to concentrate on a few aspects of policy and practice across a larger sample of schools. If the second approach were to be adopted, the PSI/Lancaster researchers themselves would be inclined to concentrate on home/school liaison, the curriculum in the humanities and the pastoral system.

More sensitive yet are the questions raised by research on classroom practice; and here we may have fallen foul of our own usage. 'Racism' has been used by us to describe a wide range of attitudes and behaviour, in a way which makes perfectly good sense to those who experience it, but is puzzling and alienating to those who do not. Experience and research (see for example the second review of research by the NFER and the study by Peter Green noted in Chapter Two) both show that teachers hold marked stereotypes of children from different ethnic groups and have different expectations of them, just as they do of boys and girls and of children from different social backgrounds. Some of these prejudices may be open and some unconscious. Their effect in a mixed classroom must be complex and can only be teased out by patient and scrupulous observation. Nothing can be done without the cooperation of the teachers themselves and we cannot emphasise too strongly that the purpose of such research is not to find another scapegoat for the shortcomings of the schools, but to help teachers to be more aware of the influence of their attitudes on the learning of their pupils and the extent to which unexamined prejudices can lead to self fulfilling prophecies, whether of success or failure. It is important to know whether or not there are regular patterns in the way teachers deal with the children from

---

[1] ACER Project: Racism and the Black Child: Report of Follow Up Groups on the Interim Rampton Report. May 1982, p 57.

different ethnic groups, how far these patterns reflect conscious or unconscious assumptions on the part of the teachers about the character and capabilities of the children, and how far these assumptions reflect the differences of language, culture and experience which children bring with them to school. These subtle and complex problems deserve at least as much attention as, for instance, the question of mixed ability teaching has received. (In Appendix 2 we quote comments from two researchers which throw light on the problems and possibilities of 'classroom research'.)

8. Multicultural Policies

It is clear from the researches of the Economic and Social Research Council's Research Unit on Ethnic Relations reported in Chapter Five that multicultural educational policies have been adopted piecemeal by LEAs in response to a variety of pressures. It is not clear exactly what these policies mean in principle and still less what their implications will be in practice. The RUER is following up the question of implementation in the school as part of its programme. It is not surprising, and perhaps not regrettable, that public policy should develop in a haphazard and muddled fashion. There are nevertheless some sharp and difficult choices which cannot be resolved by the application of the panacea of 'multiculturalism', which have already surfaced in the field of religious education and which are going to become increasingly pressing in the field of languages and the humanities curriculum in general.

These choices are thrown into relief by our own report whose emphasis has shifted from a primary concern with the academic achievement of children from ethnic minority groups to a wider and more fundamental prescription about the kind of society for which schools should be trying to prepare all children. We have referred frequently to a commitment to a 'truly pluralist society' to justify various policy recommendations. But it is not at all clear what 'pluralist' means. Taylor and Hegarty in their review of research on 'Asian' children comment sharply:

> *"What for example is really meant by cultural pluralism? How are the cultures and their representatives to coexist? At what level, for example, are the cultures to be integrated? Would there, for instance, be a separation of public and private cultures? What implications does cultural pluralism have for social cohesion? Does cultural pluralism imply greater individuality or segregation? What links are there between cultural pluralism and equal opportunities or racial harmony?"*

These questions need to be further explored both generally and in relation to education. Different interpretations of pluralism have different political and educational implications, and it is likely that not only the majority and minorities may differ over which one they prefer but that both majority and minorities may also differ among themselves. Compare for the sake of argument two crudely characterised versions of pluralism:

1. **Individualist**

    This view starts from the assumption of the modern, universalist, nation state in which the rights of individual citizens to life, liberty, property, association, worship and political participation are guaranteed. It is assumed that there are core values—loyalty to the regime and support for those civil rights—to which all citizens subscribe, but that beyond this there is a limited need for conformity: many things which in the past were thought to require common agreement can now be regarded as "things indifferent". There may need to be common road traffic regulations, but there is freedom of religious belief and worship. This view requires assimilation on the part both of majority and minorities. Minorities have to accept the political regime; the majority should in logic modify that regime to exclude "things indifferent" from state regulation, for example disestablish the Church of England and end compulsory religious education in maintained schools. 'Assimilation' is to a common core with everything else left to private choice and action.

2. **Communitarian**

    This view differs in that in addition to a common core of public values to which majority and minorities adhere, it demands that public recognition and support be given to separate values and activities of majority and minorities. Public resources should be made available for activities specific to particular groups: for example public money for compulsory religious education of whatever kind parents demand, or possibly for special provision for teaching minority languages. Separate maintained schools for Muslims are a logical consequence of adhering to the present support for compulsory religious education.

The individualist assumes that in essentials (and the essentials are liberal) there will be conformity, but limits essentials and omits some very important aspects, like religion, from the core. The communitarian assumes that in some essentials groups will differ and can be enabled and encouraged to do so. To take the example of language: for the individualist English only may be essential. There is no official recognition of other languages, only optional study on the same basis as foreign languages. For the communitarian other community languages would be afforded some official recognition and encouragement, including provision in the curriculum as a medium of instruction.

The essential distinction in this example is between the recognition of individuals with equal rights and the recognition of groups with particular claims. Other distinctions could be made with different implications. The point of the example is that it would be useful to have spelt out the implications of various definitions of pluralism, so that policy makers in the midst of their piecemeal accommodations can have a better idea of where their decisions may lead them.

There are at least three ways in which research may help:

1. By establishing what public attitudes to multicultural issues are, not because these necessarily dictate what policies should be adopted, but because it should be helpful to know what reactions to anticipate and how much persuasion may be necessary to win general acceptance for innovation. Such evidence as we have suggests that there is a long way to go on some issues of pressing importance to minorities (See Table 1.)

2. By looking abroad at the policies and experience of other countries with substantial ethnic minorities. Policies can seldom be transplanted wholesale, but detached observation of other people's problems can often throw light on our own and will certainly provide warnings against exaggerated expectations of fashionable nostrums. Such research to be useful requires detailed first hand knowledge of the countries concerned: there is nothing useful to be gained from tourism. For this reason there is much to be said in favour of comparative research by cross national teams. It would, for example, be of great interest to compare the development of multicultural education in Holland and the United Kingdom, preferably by a detailed case study of what is actually happening in schools.

3. By monitoring developments in the curriculum. In the absence of a centrally ordained curriculum, changes in examination syllabuses and still more changes in the content and emphasis of what is taught in schools take place piecemeal. No doubt HM Inspectorate are aware of what is going on and can and will draw attention to significant changes. But it may also be useful to have a deliberate look at how 'multiculturalism' is affecting the teaching of history, which conveys what one might call the authorised version of the society children are members of and how it came to be as it is. Changes in the teaching of history and related studies are bound to be contentious and for that reason alone deserve to be widely understood and debated. We are not likely to become a truly pluralist society by stealth.

TABLE 1
Attitudes to Multi-Cultural Education*

. . . . respondents were asked whether or not they thought that schools containing many children whose parents came from other countries and cultures should adopt special policies. Such policies included:

	% Agreeing
Providing special classes in English if required;	77
Teaching **all** children about the history and culture of these countries	74
Allowing those for whom it is important to wear traditional dress;	43
Teaching children (from different backgrounds) about the history and culture of their parents' countries or origin;	40
Providing separate religious instruction if their parents request it; and	32
Allowing these children to study their mother tongue in school hours	16

9. Language
There has been a great deal of research and experiment on various aspects of language on which we have drawn in this report. Problems remain to be investigated, but there are two points which have a general application but seem to us to be particularly worth making in the context of language:

1. The first is that special attention should be given to communicating the results of research both to those who commission it and to those who are its subjects but often also active collaborators in carrying out the projects. **The Language Information Network Coordination,** which grew out of the Linguistic Minorities Project (LMP), is an example of an attempt to build dissemination on to a research project and to maintain the impetus and interest which the original project generated. This example should be imitated: both researchers and funding bodies need to recognise this and allow for it in their initial planning. (For further information relating to the LMP see paragraph 3.2 and Annex D of Chapter Seven of this report).

2. It has been usual to look on ethnic minorities as presenting language problems, first because they require special teaching in English in order to participate fully in education, and secondly because they make demands for special recognition for their community languages. Both have been and remain serious problems, but they should not be allowed to obscure the fact that a large British bi-lingual population is an asset and a resource, which ought to be welcomed and exploited. The recent DES Consultative Paper **Foreign Languages in the School Curriculum** (1983) gives scant recognition to the possibilities. We hope that a more radical reappraisal of language policies will in future include the mother tongue of linguistic minority pupils within the compass of languages available to all pupils, as well as making greater provision for their academic study by bi-lingual pupils.

   Some LEAs have already embarked on experiments with Faculties of Communication which bring together the various aspects of language learning. These experiments should be monitored and the results made as widely available as possible.

10. The transition from school to work, further education and training
It has to be faced that changes in the curriculum, however desirable in themselves, will not necessarily translate into improved academic achievement narrowly defined; nor will academic

*British Social Attitudes—The 1984 Report. Edited by Roger Jowell and Colin Airey, SCPR, Gower 1984, p 112.

success necessarily translate into career opportunities, given the prevalence of discrimination in the labour market. As children from ethnic minorities are likely to remain disproportionately represented in non-examination classes, it will be important to monitor:

1.   new developments in the secondary school curriculum, especially those that involve a move towards more practical or less academic subjects. Will ethnic minority pupils do newer, less academic and less well regarded subjects, and if so how will it affect their chances of employment?

2.   the Technical and Vocational Educational Initiative, now being piloted in several LEAs and about to be adopted by many more. The curriculum being developed under TVEI seems to be designed to develop the sort of skills in which many minority pupils, particularly West Indians, have expressed an interest. Are they aware of the scheme and getting a chance to participate, and if so to what effect?

3.   the experience of minority pupils on youth training schemes and in further educa-tion. A comparatively high proportion of minority pupils attend further education colleges, and this, along with youth training schemes, may be the most important substitute for the education that some of them are not getting at school. How far is this the case?

4.   the number and progress of minority students in higher education. This is a matter of critical importance, particularly for the future recruitment of teachers, and there is precious little information about it. There has been some monitoring of the initial stages of access courses, but we understand that the DES does not itself propose to follow this through to ascertain whether or not the policy is working. As these courses have been widely adopted, this seems to us a mistake, which should not need to be made good by others.

5.   Finally there is a case, given the shortage of information on the post school experience of ethnic minority pupils, to exploit the data of the National Child Development Study. The proportion of ethnic minority subjects in the sample is small but the data are rich and now extend from birth to age twenty-three, and thus include a full educational history of training and early work experience, as well as much else. At the least this would provide a basis for comparison with subsequent generations. Similar use might be made of the Child Health and Education Study at Bristol University.

11.   Pre-School Learning

It is well established that by the age of seven the level of children's academic achievement is strongly related to family background factors, particularly social class and ethnicity. Research by the Thomas Coram Unit in London and the Community Education Development Centre in Coventry suggest that there is an important link between reading attainment and direct parental teaching. The Thomas Coram Unit is at present trying to tease out the effects of parental and teacher influence on children's achievement in the infant school for a sample of white British children and black British children of Caribbean descent in 33 ILEA infant schools.* If this research emphasises the importance of pre-school learning, as well as parental involvement, it will reinforce the case for looking at pre-school provision for ethnic minority children. It is already known that working mothers from ethnic minority groups make disproportionate use of child minders (CRC Who Minds? 1975) and that the marked variations in the use of services by different ethnic groups are not simply reflections of different patterns of maternal employment (ILEA: Pre-School Survey, 1982). We need to know how far these differences may be determined by practical difficulties, such as hours of opening of nursery schools, and how much by more

*Thomas Coram Research Unit. Current Research. (October 1983)

sensitive factors such as differences of views over child rearing, which may effect the willingness of ethnic minority mothers either to leave their children in nursery schools or to become involved with the education they are receiving there. Perhaps the most useful and important thing would be to find examples of successful provision of pre-school education for ethnic minority children and how they have been organised and funded.

12. Conclusion

In conclusion three points:

1. We have stressed the importance of systematic monitoring and the collection of an adequate statistical base for policy. But we must also emphasise that to grasp what is actually going on in the schools small scale research, often in the form of demonstration projects or experiments, is essential and that the involvement of teachers, parents and pupils in such projects is often the most effective means to change.

2. We have also emphasised the importance of direct research in the schools themselves: it is equally important to relate what is happening in schools to the communities in which they operate, and especially from our point of view the ethnic minority communities, which like the rest of society are continuously changing. Stereotypes of these communities are as dangerous and misleading as stereotypes of pupils.

3. Many of the recommendations of this Report are as it were acts of faith, based upon experience and commonsense. If, as we hope, they are implemented, they will become hypotheses to be tested to see whether or not they have the good results we expect.

APPENDIX 1

ACER suggestions for variables to be included in study of school dynamics.

1. **Discipline Policy**
   a. Suspension.
   b. Expulsion.
   c. Referral procedures, eg assessment centres, intermediate treatment centres, discipline units.
   d. Home tuition: what is taught.

2. **School Policy on Examination Procedures**
   a. Streaming and setting.
   b. Mixed ability teaching:
      1. Maths and English and how these subjects are taught.
      2. Remedial education: withdrawal procedures and who goes where and when.
      3. Does the school have a policy of combining mixed ability teaching methods with streaming procedures?
   c. Option choice procedures:
      1. Does the timetable restrict flexibility of choice?
      2. Guidance on option choice: careers/pastoral advice and parental involvement/consultation.

3. **Non-Examination Procedures**
   a. What curriculum is available for pupils not entered for exams?
   b. Does the school provide school leavers with a record of their studies?
      1. Does this record indicate what subjects the pupil studied?
   c. Pupils' incentive to attend non-examinable subjects.

4. **Teachers**
   a. How does the teacher see his/her role within the school?
      1. Managerial, subject oriented, pastoral, counselling and careers advice throughout the pupil's school life.
   b. Does the teacher see the child as a whole person or is the child simply studying English, maths, history, etc?
   c. Teachers' expectation of pupils and pupils' expectations of teachers.

5. **School Management**

   a. Does the Head delegate? In what ways is the Head involved in the whole life of the school?

   b. Role of Deputy Head/s and Senior Teachers and Pastoral Heads.

   c. Role of Governors in decision making.

6. **Home-school Liaison**

   a. Role of Parent-Teachers Association:
      1. To what extent do parents influence school policy?
      2. Is the PTA's function purely extra curricular?

   b. Parents' Evenings: school reports and option choice?
      1. How much consultation is there between parents and teachers?

   c. Open evenings and cultural evenings.

7. **Links with the Community**

   a. Advice centres.

   b. Supplementary schools.

   c. Youth clubs.

   d. Community centres.

8. **Post-16 Curriculum and Opportunities**

   a. Work experience.

   b. Counselling.

   c. 6th Form curriculum: academic, vocational, non-vocational.

APPENDIX 2

Two Quotations on the Multi-Ethnic Classroom

1. **Alf Davey** (having just described the findings of a study which showed early ethnocentricity among primary school children, the reluctance of parents to deal with it and their willingness to leave responsibility to the schools).

:So here you could say that the schools have a sort of implicit mandate to do more than they are actually doing in community relations. Now thinking about these parents, it seems to me that one of the things we ought to be investigating is how to get the parents involved in school planning, so you not only get the benefit of the different teacher-parent approaches, but you get the opportunity for parent to parent education, which seems to us to be so appropriate. As regard to the children's ethnocentricity, what I have been thinking of are ways children could be put together in some sort of interdependence of one another. One of the things that came up in the study was that, if you could get some kids into some sort of interdependence, their contribution to problem solving tasks or whatever, or their ability to contribute in this situation, becomes more important than their ethnicity. But it seems to me that it must be a whole school approach. There's a limit to what two or three teachers can do in a school, it is a problem that must be recognised by the school as a whole to be successful; and this applies even in a primary school where the teachers have got their kids most of the day. If the head teacher is not with them or the school is not with them, you get a dichotomy between the sort of structure of the school, which might be an authoritarian structure, and therefore has conflict built into its structure, and what teachers are trying to do. It seems to me that if you have conflict in the structure of your school, it doesn't matter how long you talk about children from other lands, it isn't going to alter the situation. We have got to start looking at teachers' styles, and the extent to which teachers are prepared to negotiate with children, to share authority with children, and the marrying together of the content and the structure of multicultural education.

2. **Geoffrey Driver** (on the multi-ethnic classroom and teachers' strategies).
:I think the issue that arises here though, is that if we're conscious of ethnicity in the classroom, and I've sat at the back of so many classrooms and been aware of this, one is aware of a cultural collision of some kind, where perceptions and expectations do not match. If you have ever been in a traditional secondary modern school in a place like Birkenhead, where there are probably not too many ethnic minority kids, you'll find that there is a tradition of teacher-hood if you like that can cope with those youngsters; you may not admire them (the teachers) academically, but their social skills in meeting the youngsters, and the youngsters' expectations of them, are such that there is a basic respect. There is no sort of sense that people are being sold short. They may think sometimes that they are roughly treated but in terms of

their confidence in one another, it's all there. Now what's happening in multi-racial classrooms is that very often because of the cultural wavebands, you can't get that kind of expectation now with young children; and I think this is the problem, they don't fight the battle, they immediately go over on to the (teacher's) wavelength. They are very adaptable, as I see it, to the power that is built into the dominant culture. Now what happens as you go up through the school, especially if there is negative reinforcement for what you're doing as a teacher, there is gradually a hardening of resistance, as there is in all schools, even in the working class ones I'm talking about. But it comes earlier, and in a way which much more bewilders teachers, with minority youngsters. That seems to me to be the nub of the issue of what you call ethnocentrism. It isn't in fact a static factor. It is situational and it can be negotiated. Nobody lacks respect for a teacher who is a racist if he is doing a good job of teaching maths, oddly enough. I mean I've seen it. The complexity of the situation is that the teacher is just one man, with perhaps not two groups but three or four or five groups. The whole thing then becomes at that level an impossible task. I don't think it is realistic somehow to expect teachers to be non-ethnocentric. They can only be who they are, and especially faced with that situation, they pray to God that they'll get through by being who they are; and some of them make it because they are nice generous people, who in the end of the day the kids will forgive for everything. You go into the staffroom and after those classes it is like a bloody air raid shelter.

APPENDIX 3

In preparing this paper we have to thank for informal discussions and advice:

Brandon Ashworth
Roger Ballard
Allan Beattie
Godfrey Brandt

Verity Saifullah Khan

Alan Little
Miriam Lloyd

Alf Davey
Steven Delsol
Geoffrey Driver

Peter Mortimore

Ken Fogelman

John Rex
Harold Rosen

Len Garrison
Peter Green
Jagdish Gundara

George Skinner
David Smith

Bryan Hargreaves
Hilary Hester
Roger Hewitt

Monica Taylor
Sally Tomlinson
Barry Troyna

Crispin Jones

Andreas Varlaam

Bev Woodroffe

PART II

"Education For All"

CHAPTER 4

Ethnic Minorities and Education:
A Historical Perspective

1. Introduction

1.1 In this chapter we attempt to offer an overview of the way in which the range of specialist measures, approaches to teaching and educational principles which have come to be known collectively as "multicultural" education have evolved over the last twenty years or so and then to reflect on the state of multicultural education today. In so doing we seek to identify the various strands of the debate and the concerns of the ethnic minority communities, as well as examining central Government policies and pronouncements and the response of LEAs and individual schools. We have sought to stand back from the tide of often-heated argument, debate and invective which today surrounds the whole area of the educational needs of ethnic minority children, and the issue of how schools in "all-white" areas should be preparing their pupils for life in a multi-racial society, and examine critically some of the basic assumptions which have influenced and to some extent still underlie policy making from central Government and local government level to the individual school and the individual teacher in the classroom.

2. Early Educational Responses to Immigration

2.1 Although children from a range of different ethnic backgrounds have long been present in this country, it is only since the early 1950s, with the sharp rise in immigration from Commonwealth countries, that the changing nature of British society and the fact that this might have particular implications for education has been seen as an issue. It is generally accepted that attitudes towards the educational needs of ethnic minority pupils fall into a clearly defined chronological pattern, moving from the early days of what is usually termed "assimilation", through attempts to give at least some recognition in schools to the backgrounds of ethnic minority children – usually known as "integration" – to the more recent moves towards multicultural education. We deal with each of these phases in turn.

191

Assimilation

**Language
Needs and
"Culture
Shock"**

2.2   The initial response of the education system to the arrival of increasing numbers of immigrant children in schools during the late 1950s and early 1960s was to focus on absorbing them into the majority pupil population as rapidly as possible. The major obstacles to achieving this were seen as first and foremost the children's lack of expertise in the English language, coupled with the disorientation which they were felt to experience on arrival in a new country: commonly known as "culture shock". It is interesting to recall that in view of this focus on language as the major "problem", children from the West Indies were considered to have no particular educational needs. For other immigrant children, from non-English speaking families, as the DES Circular 7/65[1] put it:

> *"From the beginning the major educational task is the teaching of English."*

The emphasis was therefore on the teaching of English as a second language to immigrant children, often in specialist language or reception centres which also provided some basic pastoral support to counter "culture shock", apparently in the belief that once these problems had been remedied the children might then be subsumed within the overall school population.

Dispersal

2.3   Another major concern of the assimilationist phase of the educational response to immigrant children, which appears to have arisen as much for political as educational reasons, was the officially sanctioned and indeed encouraged attempts at "dispersing" these children between different schools in an attempt to "spread the problem" and avoid any school becoming predominantly immigrant in character (mirroring of course the thinking behind moves in the United States towards bussing "black" children in certain areas). The 1964 report of the Commonwealth Immigrants Advisory Council (CIAC)[2] expressed the concerns of many in education at the time about the possible effects of a school having large numbers of immigrant pupils, as follows:

> *"The presence of a high proportion of immigrant children in one class slows down the general routine of working and hampers the progress of the whole class, especially where the immigrants do not speak or write English fluently. This is clearly in itself undesirable and unfair to all the children in the class . . . . The*

---

[1] "The Education of Immigrants". DES Circular 7/65 (14 June 1965).
[2] Second Report by The Commonwealth Immigrants Advisory Council. Cmnd 2266. HMSO. February 1964.

evidence we have received strongly suggests that if a school has more than a certain percentage of immigrant children among its pupils the whole character and ethos of the school is altered. Immigrant pupils in such a school will not get as good an introduction to British life as they would get in a normal school, and we think their education in the widest sense must suffer as a result . . . . we were concerned by the evidence we received that there were schools in certain parts of the country containing an extremely high proportion of immigrant children. Moreover, the evidence from one or two areas showed something a good deal more disturbing than a rise in the proportion of immigrant children in certain schools; it showed a tendency towards the creation of predominantly immigrant schools, partly because of the increase in the number of immigrant children in certain neighbourhoods, but also partly because some parents tend to take native-born children away from schools when the proportion of immigrant pupils exceeds a level which suggests to them that the school is becoming an immigrant school. If this trend continues, both the social and the educational consequences might be very grave."

In expressing these concerns the CIAC clearly had in mind events in the Southall area of London where a group of parents from the majority community had protested against the presence of large numbers of immigrant children in their children's schools. In response, the then Minister of Education set the tone for the emergence of an official dispersal policy when he expressed the view, to the House of Commons in 1963[3] that:

"If possible, it is desirable on education grounds that no one school should have more than about 30% of immigrants . . . . I must regretfully tell the House that one school must be regarded now as irretrievably an immigrant school. The important thing to do is to prevent this happening elsewhere."

2.4   The policy of dispersal was confirmed and developed in the DES Circular 7/65 which, under the heading "Spreading the Children", said:

"It is inevitable that, as the proportion of immigrant children in a school or class increases, the problems will become more difficult to solve, and the chances of assimilation more remote. How far any given proportion of immigrant children can be absorbed with benefit to both sides depends on, among other

---

[3] Hansard Vol. 685 Cols 433-4. 27 November 1963.

of immigrant children who are proficient in English; the dividing line cannot be precisely defined. Experience suggests, however, that . . . . up to a fifth of immigrant children in any group fit in with reasonable ease, but that, if the proportion goes over about one third either in the school as a whole or in any one class, serious strains arise. It is therefore desirable that the catchment areas of schools should, wherever possible, be arranged to avoid undue concentrations of immigrant children. Where this proves impracticable simply because the school serves an area which is occupied largely by immigrants, every effort should be made to disperse the immigrant children round a greater number of schools and to meet such problems of transport as may arise."

Possibly the most telling part of this Circular, as far as it reveals the thinking which lay behind the Government's policy, was the following section which was italicised, presumably for emphasis:

"It will be helpful if the parents of non-immigrant children can see that practical measures have been taken to deal with the problems in the schools, and that the progress of their own children is not being restricted by the undue preoccupation of the teaching staff with the linguistic and other difficulties of immigrant children."

2.5   It is difficult to avoid the conclusion that such pronouncements by Government served to confirm and reinforce the belief of many in the majority community that immigrant pupils merely caused problems and posed a threat to the well-being of indigenous children and to traditional educational standards. The "problem-centred" approach to the education of ethnic minority pupils – which has we believe continued to underlie thinking and policy making in this field ever since, was thus officially sanctioned and articulated for the first time. As the authors of the Institute of Race Relations 1969 report[4] observed:

"The whole question of the educational effect of dispersal schemes was given only cursory attention when the policy was first proposed. For some, the point of the policy was to make life easier for teachers in schools which would normally have large intakes of children of immigrants. For others, the policy was a way of preventing the development of 'all immigrant' schools, which were per se undesirable. For still others, dispersal was an

---

[4] "Colour and Citizenship – A Report on British Race Relations." Institute of Race Relations. 1969.

essential basis for cultural assimilation, including the learning of English . . . . Little or no thought had been devoted to a clear analysis of the nature and the extent of the educational needs of the immigrants. It was wrongly assumed that an influx of immigrant pupils into a school automatically hampered the chances of native English children in the school and that the children were competitors for the teacher's attention under all circumstances . . . . Official policy gave the accurate impression of having been devised under the pressure of circumstances and based on received ideas. Central to both was the concept that, as a result of the coming of immigrant pupils, the schools were changing for the worse . . . . The official dispersal policy, with its emphasis on preserving the normal routine of a school, was in a sense a Canute-like attempt to prevent change."

Form 7(i) and Section 11

2.6   In order to provide the statistical basis for the dispersal policy and also to quantify the degree of language need, the DES initiated, in 1966, the collection of statistics on "immigrant" children, through Form 7(i) returns, which sought information on children who were themselves immigrants or had been born in this country to immigrant parents who had arrived in the previous ten years. By implication these statistics suggested that after ten years in Britain an immigrant family would cease to suffer from any educational difficulties that could be attributed to immigration and racial difference. Financial support for the Government's overall strategy at this time was made under Section 11 of the Local Government Act 1966 whereby the Home Office provided a 50% (later to become 75%) grant to local authorities who were required to make special provision in the exercise of any of their functions in consequence of the presence within their areas of substantial numbers of immigrants from the Commonwealth:

"whose language or customs differ from those of the community."

Since the claim was based solely on the presence of immigrant children in a school, rather than on the number of these children felt to be in need of additional educational support, the problem-centred perception of ethnic minority pupils, referred to above, was further emphasised.

2.7   The assimilationist phase can thus be seen as characterised by *ad hoc* responses to the educational needs of immigrant pupils designed on the one hand to "compensate" for their assumed "deficiencies" – primarily in being non-English speaking – and on the other hand to disrupt the education of indigenous children as little as possible. Above all the assimilationist approach seems to have recognised the existence of a single cultural criterion which was "white", Christian and English-speaking, and to have failed to acknowledge any wider implications of the changing nature of British society. Despite subsequent developments in policy making in this field the two most tangible manifestations of this approach: separate language centres and the policy of the dispersal or bussing of ethnic minority pupils continued long after policy makers would claim that the days of assimilationist thinking were behind them – language centres still being in existence in some parts of the country today, and bussing having continued in one LEA until 1979. The major source of funding for educational activities in relation to the needs of ethnic minorities also remains Section 11, which as we have seen not only took a somewhat limited view of the extent of educational need but was also designed to support the overall policy of assimilation.

Integration

2.8   Even while the official focus remained on the need to assimilate ethnic minority pupils as quickly as possible into majority society, many of the teachers who were working in multi-racial schools had come to feel that the education process should give some recognition to the differences in lifestyle and cultural and religious background of ethnic minority children – what became known as integration. As HMI Eric Bolton has recalled[5]:

> *"Contrary to the assimilationist belief that, given English language fluency, the immigrant would disappear into the crowd, those arguing for integration claimed that a much more planned and detailed education and social programme needed to be undertaken if immigrants were to be able to integrate with the majority society. The emphasis was still upon integrating the minorities with the majority society and culture so that a culturally homogeneous society would be created. This meant that it was up to the minorities to change and adapt, and there was little or no pressure upon the majority society to modify or change its prevailing attitudes or practices. However, to enable integration to take place, it was argued that the majority society needed to be more aware of historical and cultural factors affecting different minorities. Knowledge and awareness would enable the majority society to make allowances for differences in lifestyle, culture and religion that might make it difficult for some immigrant groups to integrate with British society and would help to avoid the embarrassing mistakes that could arise from ignorance."*

[5] "Education in a Multi-racial Society." E J Bolton. Trends in Education. Winter 1979.

The need for teachers to have an awareness of the backgrounds of ethnic minority pupils was acknowledged in official policies and publications from the late 1960s onwards. In order to foster this increased awareness, the integrationist phase was characterised by a proliferation of "relevant information" in the form of in-service courses on "life in the countries of origin", visits to India or the West Indies and an increase in the number of books and other materials depicting ethnic minorities in their "native surroundings". The emphasis was almost exclusively upon ethnic minority pupils as immigrants from other countries rather than as an integral part of British society (although there were by this time increasing numbers of British-born second-generation children), and in many cases inaccurate or damaging stereotypes, which still persist today, were perpetuated or even created.

2.9   In practice there was little real difference between the assimilationist and integrationist viewpoints in that they shared the common aim of absorbing ethnic minority communities within society with as little disruption to the life of the majority community as possible. Whilst the integrationist stance went at least some way towards acknowledging that the life-styles of the ethnic minority communities were valid in their own right, it failed to consider the broader implications for the traditional perception of the "British way of life" which the presence of communities with such diverse backgrounds might have in the longer term. Indeed, looking back some ten years later on its policies during the 1960s, the Government itself summarised[6] its objectives in the following rather limited and negative terms:

"i.   to help create a climate in schools in which colour and race were not divisive and which would give all immigrant children opportunities for personal development in their new environment;

ii.   to ensure that building programmes and teacher quotas reflected the needs of areas with large numbers of immigrant pupils;

iii.   to offer advice and practical help to teachers faced with the challenge of teaching immigrant children;

iv.   to safeguard against any lowering of standards, due to the presence of large numbers of non-English speaking children, which might adversely affect the progress of other children;

v.   to encourage and promote relevant research."

[6] "The Education of Immigrants."   Education Survey 13. DES. 1971.

Our View   2.10   In view of the philosophy which we put forward at the opening of this report, for the development of a pluralist society and our rejection of the notion of the assimilation of ethnic minority groups within the majority community as both undesirable and unworkable, it is hardly surprising that we regard both the assimilationist and integrationist educational responses to the needs of ethnic minority pupils as, in retrospect, misguided and ill-founded. Regrettably, however, many of the legacies of these early days still underlie much of the thinking and discussion about the educational needs of ethnic minority groups and have also, we believe, distorted the nature and development of the broader concept of multicultural education, quite apart from the residual physical manifestations of the period such as separate language centres. For example, the negative stereotypes of certain ethnic minority groups which were established and which still persist, the seemingly automatic assumption by some teachers that an ethnic minority pupil will experience, and may well cause, problems, and, above all perhaps, the underlying suspicion that the arrival of ethnic minority pupils has meant that schools have changed for the worse and that their presence poses a threat both to traditional educational standards and to the educational wellbeing of ethnic majority pupils.

3.   The Emergence of Multicultural Education

Widely Varying Interpretations   3.1   We now look at the various factors which have influenced the emergence, over the past decade or so, of what has generally been termed "multicultural" education. This concept is far from being clearly defined and explained, and although many people have attempted to put forward their own widely-varying definitions of multicultural education none of these can be said to have gained universal acceptance in the education world, especially in the absence of any detailed guidance from Government. Although many teachers, especially those in multi-racial schools have increasingly come to accept that multicultural education is a valid concept, we have found in our own visits and discussions, that interpretations as to what changes in policy or teaching practices are actually required, vary enormously and it seems clear that, despite the proliferation in recent years of books, courses and conferences concerned with this issue, in the words of the second NFER review of research:

> *"In a very real and pressing sense the aims of education await to be rewritten . . . . the very lack of a definition of multi-cultural education has permitted not only the widest theoretical interpretations and broadest policy objectives, but also a considerable mis-match between these and educational practices."*

198

**Two
Distinct
Themes**

3.2   The most obvious difference between the early days of assimilation and integration, and the concept of multicultural education is that, whereas the former focused primarily on seeking to "remedy" the perceived "problems" of ethnic minority children and to "compensate" for their perceived "disabilities", multicultural education has usually tended to have two distinct themes – firstly, meeting the particular educational needs of ethnic minority children and secondly, the broader issue of preparing **all** pupils for life in a multiracial society. These two themes are of course very much inter-related and indeed in our view, inter-dependent, but in order to seek to disentangle the developments which have taken place in the field of multicultural education, we shall consider each of them in turn.

3.3   The Educational Needs of Ethnic Minority Children

The Changing Nature of the Debate

**The
"Failure" of
Assimilation**

3.3.1   By the late 1960s and early 1970s there was a growing realisation that the policies of assimilation and integration had failed to achieve their objectives – many ethnic minority pupils clearly still had educational needs which existing policies were proving unable to meet. On the broader level ethnic minority groups as a whole had not "disappeared", as seems to have been hoped, by being absorbed by the majority community and the essential naivety of expecting the immigrant communities to be accepted by the indigenous majority as equal citizens of this country had been exposed by the rising tide of racial prejudice and hostility. Efforts by the Government to stem this tide had proved largely ineffective, especially since successive Governments had also passed Immigration Acts and Rules which were clearly intended to, and had the effect of, excluding people of non-European descent from this country. The Race Relations Acts of 1965 and 1968 and the establishment of the Race Relations Board and the Community Relations Commission (the forerunners of today's Commission for Racial Equality) – see paragraphs 3.3.19 and 3.3.20 below – whilst providing an indication of the Government's growing concern about racial disharmony and racial prejudice, did not have the same impact on public opinion at the time as did Enoch Powell's "rivers of blood" speech in the Spring of 1968.

**Communities'
Concerns**

3.3.2   Meanwhile, there was growing concern about the apparent underachievement of West Indian pupils who, according to assimilationist beliefs, should have had little difficulty in "settling down". The concern of some educationists about the generally low performance of West Indian pupils was matched if not exceeded by mounting concern in the West Indian community itself about this

199

issue and about the specific question of the allegedly disproportionately high number of West Indian children who were finding themselves in schools for the educationally sub-normal. This latter concern was given fervent expression in 1971 in the polemical pamphlet "How the West Indian Child is Made Educationally Sub-normal in the British School System"[7]. Thus a new dimension had entered the debate on ethnic minority education – the ethnic minority communities themselves, now established in this country, had begun to voice their own concerns about their children's education, which in some cases differed from the concerns of the education system.

Curriculum Content

3.3.3   The West Indian community's concerns covered a range of different issues amongst these a belief that the language needs of West Indian pupils were not sufficiently catered for or understood, which was seen as a major factor in their misclassification as educationally sub-normal or "remedial". Concern was also felt about the curriculum content of subjects such as history and geography and the need to avoid negative or offensive references to "black people". The following extract from evidence presented to the Select Committee on Race Relations and Immigration (SCORRI)[8] in 1972/73 by a West Indian community organisation illustrates these concerns:

> "In educational terms a lot has been said of teaching in a multi-racial school, but not enough thought has been given to the way in which such a school should be organised, the books used, the type of teachers, the type of material read in the schools. Are multi-racial schools to continue to be English schools which let in Black children? We believe that such a school should reflect the contribution by and participation of all ethnic groups. Through the teaching of geography, history, drama, music, literature, West Indians could be seen as contributing to the school curriculum. Books used now not only ignore the presence of such children, but some, like "Black Sambo" are in our estimation racist and help to perpetuate the stereotyping that could only be divisive in a school community."

"Black Studies"

3.3.4   At this time there were also calls from the West Indian community, influenced perhaps by developments in the USA, for the introduction of "Black Studies" as a discrete subject within the curriculum, primarily as a means of reinforcing West Indian pupils' self-image – as illustrated by the following further extract from the SCORRI evidence:

---

[7] "How the West Indian Child is Made Educationally Sub-normal in the British School System." B Coard. New Beacon Books. 1971.
[8] "Education." Report of the Select Committee on Race Relations and Immigration. 1972-3. HMSO. HC 405 I-III.

".... many of the difficulties experienced by black people, particularly the youth in this country, are either caused through or exacerbated by what some of us would like to think of as a crisis of identity. This in turn is motivated by an inadequate knowledge of their past history and a lack of proper visual inspirational aid, current in the educational process of the United Kingdom .... the inclusion of Black Study Courses in the school curriculum would be of inestimable value .... The black child goes to a white school, he is taught by white teachers, he sees pictures of white persons, he uses books written by white craftsmen, he hears and sings songs about white people, he learns poems written by white people about white people. All this necessarily accustoms him to appreciation of white values only. This largely accounts for the obvious gap in mutual appreciation between black and white in Britain today. The primary purpose of Black Studies is the adjustment of this imbalance, and to help black people in this country, particularly the children who try desperately, as one writer puts it, to escape from the "prisons of their skins."

West Indian Teachers

3.3.5 Calls for "Black Studies" were often coupled with calls for more teachers who were themselves of West Indian origin since it was felt that they would be better able to understand the needs of West Indian pupils and to further reinforce the pupils' self-image and motivation by acting as models of "successful" West Indians. From the late 1960s onwards there was also a proliferation of West Indian "supplementary" schools – community-based classes held in the evenings or at weekends where West Indian pupils could not only receive additional help from West Indian teachers with their mainstream school work, but could also learn about their community's background and cultural heritage in what was seen as a "supportive" environment.

"Supple-mentary" Schools

3.3.6 During the 1970s the emphasis shifted from advocating specific "separate" provision within mainstream schools – in the form of Black Studies – to a greater desire to see aspects of West Indian language and culture included within the existing curriculum. This changing emphasis was reflected in much of the evidence submitted to the SCORRI when it devoted its 1976–7 session to considering the West Indian community[9]. One of the major recommendations of the Select Committee's report was for an inquiry into the education of West Indian pupils which in turn of course led to the establishment of this Committee, with a rather wider brief but still with the needs of West Indian pupils foremost amongst our concerns.

---

[9] "The West Indian Community." Report of the Select Committee on Race Relations and Immigration. 1976/7. HMSO. HC 180-I.

Concerns of the Asian Community

3.3.7 During the lifetime of this Committee, there has been a marked shift in emphasis from the previous focus on the West Indian situation, to greater concern about aspects of the educational experience of pupils from the various Asian groups. Since the Asian community became established in this country rather later than the West Indian community, it is hardly surprising that only in recent years have Asian parents, teachers and community representatives begun to make known their concerns about their children's education. Whilst sharing some of the concerns already voiced by the West Indian community about, for example, the balance and content of the curriculum, the need for more teachers drawn from their own community, and above all, the pervasive influence of racism both within schools and in the wider society, the Asian community has also broadened the debate considerably by raising two further issues: firstly, the responsibility of the education system for the maintenance and teaching of the children's "mother tongue" languages; and, secondly, whether existing schools can provide an educational environment which parents will find acceptable in terms of their religious beliefs – for example in relation to religious education and pastoral matters.

"Mother Tongue"

3.3.8 Interest within education circles about the first of these issues – "mother tongue" – can be seen to date back to the discussion in the Bullock Report[10] of the language needs of "children from families of overseas origin", which as well as stressing the need for a positive attitude to West Indian dialect, also emphasised the significance of there being large numbers of pupils in British schools with "mother tongues" other than English, thus:

> *"Their bilingualism is of great importance to the children and their families, and also to society as a whole. In a linguistically conscious nation in the modern world we should see it as an asset, as something to be nurtured, and one of the agencies which should nurture it is the school. Certainly the school should adopt a positive attitude to its pupils' bilingualism and wherever possible should help maintain and deepen their knowledge of their mother tongues."*

The growing concern of many Asian parents, together with parents from some "European" ethnic minorities notably Italians, at their children losing touch with their cultural heritages through the absence of any form of "support" for their home languages and the risk of their children's ethnic identity being "submerged" by the influence of English, did not however receive wide attention until the EC

---

[10] "A Language for Life." Report of a Committee of Inquiry Chaired by Sir Alan Bullock. HMSO. 1975.

Directive on the Education of Children of Migrant Workers in 1977 which was seen by many community leaders as entitling ethnic minority children to "mother tongue teaching". In recent years therefore the "mother tongue" issue has come to be seen as a central issue in the debate on multicultural education and we therefore discuss this issue in some detail in our Chapter on Language.

Pastoral Matters

3.3.9   Concern about what can broadly be termed pastoral matters has been felt by Asian parents and particularly Muslims since the early days of their arrival in this country when their children first entered school and were confronted with facilities for meals and dress which brought them into direct conflict with the requirements of their religious beliefs. Strength of feeling about such matters has increased as the size of the Asian pupil population has grown and as the concentration of Asian pupils in particular schools and areas has become more marked. The world-wide resurgence of Islam and the accompanying emphasis on fundamental Islamic principles since the beginning of the decade has also clearly had a direct bearing on the Muslim community in this country, causing them to be more vociferous and determined in their efforts to bring about changes in the "rules and regulations" affecting such matters within schools and encouraging parents to recognise and respect their religious "rights and duties" in relation to their children's education. The logical conclusion of such moves has been seen by some sections of these communities as the establishment of their own voluntary or independent schools and we discuss the implications of this trend –

"Separate" Schools

which has received considerable publicity in recent months – in our Chapter on Religion and the Role of the School later in this report.

3.3.10   It is important to recognise that neither West Indian nor Asian parents, as distinct from some teachers and community workers from these groups, have pressed for what could be described as "multicultural" education involving all pupils. In expressing their concerns about specific issues, such as a school's treatment of West Indian language or its policies with regard to meals or uniform, the parents have simply sought to improve the educational provision which **their** children receive. Certainly our own discussions with parents have tended to focus on specific issues such as "mother tongue" or racism in school textbooks, rather than on the educational experience as a whole. Multicultural education can thus perhaps be seen as the response of the education system – educational theorists, educational administrators and teachers – to the wide range of concerns expressed by ethnic minority communities, as well as to the "problems" experienced by multi-racial schools in catering for the needs of their pupils. In seeking to encompass such a wide and varied range of concerns and interests it is perhaps hardly surprising that firm definitions and analyses of multicultural education prove so elusive.

203

Criticisms of Multi-cultural Education

3.3.11   The concept of multicultural education has of course had its critics, quite apart from those people who have simply rejected it out of hand as "progressive, left-wing, trendy nonsense". One of the major criticisms has been of the emphasis on "culture" – a term which is itself rarely clearly defined and is thus open to a myriad of interpretations – and which is often seen as avoiding the more central issues of race, prejudice and power. Multicultural education has also been criticised for failing to face up to or challenge what is regarded as the most fundamental influence on the situation of ethnic minorities in this country i.e. racism. Adherents of this view have argued that a consideration of the origins and influence of racism should be integral features of an education process which truly seeks to prepare all pupils for life in a multi-racial society. As one writer has put it[11]:

> *"Racist attitudes and low teacher expectations arising from negative and demeaning stereotypes do exist and have to be come to terms with and changed. This, in turn, will require fundamental changes of attitude, the first step along the road to which is the recognition of the social and ethnic discrimination legitimized by the educational system which we have constructed. To make such a statement is not to place in question the immense good will of the vast majority of teachers, not to label them as racists, but rather to draw attention to their role in servicing a system which has institutionalized racial and social discrimination so effectively."*

3.3.12   Other critics of multicultural education have argued that it is in fact little more than a form of subtle racism itself, and that by seeking to "co-opt" aspects of a particular ethnic group's culture or life-style, by drawing on them in the curriculum, schools are attempting to "take over" and thereby destroy ethnic minority communities' sense of identity and group cohesiveness. As one writer has put it[12]:

> *"As interpreted and practised by many, multi-racial education has appeared to become an instrument of control and stability rather than one of change, of the subordination rather than the freedom of blacks in schools and or society as a whole. In the context of schools and against a wider societal background of institutionalized racism, multi-racial education programmes, from the assimilationist's view on English teaching to the integrationist's stance on multicultural and black studies, have in fact integrally contributed to the increased alienation of black*

---

[11] Chapter on "Educational theory and practice of Multi-Cultural education." by James Lynch from "Teaching in the Multi-Cultural School." ed. J Lynch. Ward Lock Educational. 1981.
[12] Chapter on "Multiracial Education in Britain: "From Assimilation to Cultural Pluralism" by Dr C Mullard from "Race Migration and Schooling." ed. J Tierney. Holt Education. 1982.

youth. To be told, however politely and cleverly, that your culture and history count for nothing is to invoke responses ranging from low self esteem and lack of confidence . . . . , to political opposition and resistance. To be told that your culture and history count for something only within the pedagogic boundaries of the school curriculum and not outside the school gates in the white dominated world of work and politics is to foster the response of a 'blacks only for the black studies class'. To be goaded to integrate politically and then in practice to take up your place at the bottom of society with as much of your culture intact as is permitted is, to extend Gus John's conclusion, a madness that not even a mad and subordinated black can any longer contemplate. Simply, what multiracial education, as viewed in British schools, is teaching black pupils is that they will always remain second-class citizens; and, ironically, that in order to survive or exist as blacks it is necessary to resist racist authority within and outside school."

3.3.13   Another line of criticism of multicultural education, which represents a rather different viewpoint is that it constitutes simply another form of "compensatory" education, essentially no different from assimilationist programmes, designed to counter the assumed "disadvantages" of ethnic minority children, and particularly West Indians, through "special provision" which is inherently inferior, and which has visibly failed to achieve its objectives. As one West Indian researcher[13] has put it:

" . . . . MRE (Multiracial education) is conceptually unsound, ... its theoretical and practical implications have not been worked out and . . . . it represents a developing feature of urban education aimed at 'watering down' the curriculum and 'cooling out' black city children while at the same time creating for teachers, both radical and liberal, the illusion that they are doing something special for a particularly disadvantaged group. Many of the ideas of MRE draw upon the social-pathology analysis of the black personality, lifestyle and family arrangements. Although explicitly rejecting labels of inferiority it argues instead for 'difference' – meaning exactly the same thing . . . . The aims of multiracial education are tied in with the cultural deprivation theory which aims to compensate working-class children for being culturally deprived (of middle-class culture) and black children for not being white . . . . it takes schools and teachers away from their central concern which is basically teaching or instructing children in the knowledge and skills essential to life in this society. It effectively reduces choice and creates dependence on experts and professionals which undermines the individual's own capacity to cope."

---

[13] "The Education of the Black Child in Britain – The Myth of Multi-racial Education." Maureen Stone. Fontana. 1981.

3.3.14   In our interim report we noted the tendency of some schools to regard multicultural education simply as a separate "module" added on to the existing formal curriculum and as catering solely for ethnic minority pupils. This approach has been described as the "steel band syndrome" since, in schools with West Indian pupils, it often takes the form of encouraging these pupils to establish their own steel band thus, in theory at least, respecting their cultural identity and manifesting the "multicultural awareness" of the school. To some extent, such a response can be seen to derive from the West Indian community's own calls, in the 1960s, for "Black Studies", although as we have seen, the community has now moved away from advocating such separate provision. In relation to the Asian community however the situation is rather more complex since some of the educational measures for which they have pressed – most notably religious instruction and the maintenance of "mother tongue" languages – can in some respects be seen to necessitate such "separate" provision. On the general level, however, the inherent attractiveness of relying on such "special" provision to meet the needs of ethnic minority pupils can easily be discerned in view of the continuing desire of many in education to adhere to one of the fundamental principles of the assimilationist philosophy – that whatever provision is made for ethnic minority pupils, there should be as little disturbance as possible of the education of their indigenous peers. This view is summed up in the following quotation from the 1973 Report of the Select Committee on Race Relations and Immigration:

> "... in understanding and providing for the difficulties of minorities, care has to be taken not to overcome them by reversing well-tried policies or, in deference to real or imagined susceptibilities, by bending a system evolved to suit the majority so far as to unhinge it altogether."

Concern About Racism

3.3.15   During the last few years the debate on multicultural education has begun to shift again, towards a greater emphasis on the role of education in challenging and countering racism, both within schools and in the wider society. This change in emphasis can be seen as one aspect of the generally increasing level of awareness of the existence of racism combined with the greater willingness to discuss its possible effects, which we noted at the beginning of our Chapter on Racism. Our own interim report and Lord Scarman's report have of course also helped to focus attention on this issue, as have the activities of "concerned" organisations such as the National Union of Teachers, which, in its booklet "Combating Racism in Schools" [14], made the following comments:

---

[14] "Combating Racism in Schools. A Union Policy Statement: guidance for members." NUT. March 1983 (revised edition).

"Teachers in schools have a responsibility to educate their pupils for life in a multi-racial, culturally diverse society. Their task is hampered by racial attitudes and prejudices present in society which affect pupils in schools and the climate in which they learn. The Union believes that a positive approach to multicultural education will be strengthened by a firm stand on the part of teachers in combating racism in schools . . . ."

This concern with racism is not yet however regarded by the majority of teachers as a valid part of multicultural education as they perceive it, and this omission has often led to criticism of the concept of multicultural education as such and a demand for "anti racist" education in its stead.

The Role of Teachers

3.3.16   Another of the major focuses of multicultural education has increasingly been the role of teachers and the extent to which the teaching force as a whole is equipped both to cater for the particular needs of ethnic minority pupils and also to prepare all children for life in a multi-racial society. As HMI Eric Bolton has observed however, again in his article on the development of multicultural education (see paragraph 2.8):

"The complexity of the educational and social issues involved gives teachers a very onerous and difficult task to perform – a task most of them were not prepared for in their teacher training nor in their own experiences of life."

As early as 1964, the Commonwealth Immigrants Advisory Council had observed, in its second report, that:

"Not all teachers have immigrant children in their classes but all teachers should have some knowledge of the problems and opportunities of a multi-racial society . . . . Those responsible for planning the social studies undertaken in training colleges will, we hope, bear in mind that future British society is going to contain citizens of many races."

We discuss in our Chapter on Teacher Education, later in this report, the contribution of the teacher training system to the development of multicultural education over the years. Another dimension of the role of teachers in relation to multicultural education which has also long been the subject of concern, especially among the ethnic minority communities themselves, has been the limited number of teachers who are themselves from these communities, and who might therefore be able to offer particular help and support to ethnic minority pupils – an issue which we also discuss in our Teachers Chapter.

207

Policies of Central Government

General
Policies
Relating to
Immigration
and
Nationality

3.3.17 Having looked briefly at the way in which the focus of multicultural education has changed over the past decade or so and the various factors which have influenced the debate about its aims and objectives, we now need to consider the way in which the policies of central Government relating to ethnic minorities during this period have responded to and reflected these various needs and concerns. Before considering the specifically "educational" aspects of central Government's policies in relation to the needs of ethnic minority groups, it may be worthwhile recalling briefly the development of successive Governments' overall policies towards "immigrants" on the broader level.

3.3.18 From 1947 onwards the general welfare of what were then perceived as "colonial" peoples coming to work and settle in Britain was the responsibility of the Colonial Office Welfare Service. In 1956, the Colonial Office set up the British Caribbean Welfare Service, which subsequently moved out of the Colonial Office and assumed an independent existence. The Home Office then became responsible for colonial, or Commonwealth immigrants' affairs, since the policies being proposed, but not yet implemented, for tackling "immigration" fell into two categories: control over entry, and laws against racial discrimination. Very little positive action of any kind was undertaken at this time by central Government to inform or assist the ethnic minorities. The Commonwealth Immigrants Act 1962 was concerned entirely with controlling the entry and settlement of colonial and Commonwealth citizens, and no attempt was made at the time to legislate against discrimination: the only positive step was to establish a Commonwealth Immigrants Advisory Council to review the situation. Positive action was thus left entirely to voluntary effort.

3.3.19 In 1964 the then Government established a Department of Economic Affairs with a Minister with specific responsibility for co-ordinating policy on immigrants. But in 1965 a White Paper on immigration[15], despite including a section on the positive economic benefits of immigration and the lack of problems caused by it, introduced proposals for limiting Commonwealth immigration much more closely than before by a system of work-vouchers and by new limitations on dependent relatives. Positive action was however taken to re-shape the former Advisory Council into a National Committee for Commonwealth Immigrants (NCCI), which saw its role as the promotion and coordination of harmonious community

---

[15] "Immigration from the Commonwealth." Cmnd. 2739. HMSO. August 1965.

relations. In the same year, the first Race Relations Act became law, and established a Race Relations Board, with virtually no powers except powers to "conciliate" if it could, on receiving a complaint of discrimination within a very limited field which did not include housing, employment, or education. The Act also made racial incitement a criminal offence, but one where only the Attorney-General could initiate a prosecution.

3.3.20   In 1968, two new laws were passed: a Commonwealth Immigrants Act which removed right of entry from British Asians in East Africa and a Race Relations Act, greatly widened in scope, to include housing, employment and many services, but again with very limited powers for the Board. The Act also established a new statutory body, the Community Relations Commission, to replace the NCCI. The new Commission was given a larger budget and wider powers to grant-aid voluntary bodies on its own terms and to initiate projects. It developed some of the work already begun by the NCCI but unlike the NCCI, which had been appointed to advise the Prime Minister, it advised the Home Secretary on matters relating to Commonwealth immigrants, and "community relations" in general. In 1969, an Immigration Appeals Act was passed, establishing a structure under which immigrants could appeal against refusal of entry, refusal to vary conditions of stay and, in some circumstances, against deportation. The provisions of this Act, with a few changes, were incorporated into the 1971 Immigration Act, which established a single regime of control on entry and after entry over aliens and Commonwealth citizens and also empowered the Home Secretary to make Immigration Rules at any time. From around 1970, by which time the entry of Commonwealth immigrants for work had virtually ceased under the increasingly strict requirements which the Department of Employment had established for work vouchers, ethnic minority affairs became almost entirely the responsibility of the Home Office. The emphasis of central Government policy, and the bulk of expenditure, was on immigration control rather than upon community relations work and anti-discrimination initiatives. Wide though the theoretical scope of the bodies set up to deal with the latter two was, the positive achievements they could point to were small in comparison with the impact of successive Immigration Acts and Rules on the lives of ethnic minorities and upon public perceptions of "immigration" and "race". As has been observed[16]:

".... the effectiveness of the Race Relations Act is and will continue to be undermined by discriminatory immigration

---

[16] "Race and Law." A Lester and G Bindman. Penguin. 1972.

'laws. The use of such laws to prevent immigration to Britain from the coloured Commonwealth inevitably impairs the Race Relations Board's endeavours to persuade employers, trade unions, local authorities and commercial undertakings to treat people regardless of colour or race, and encourages profound insecurity among Commonwealth immigrants in Britain."

3.3.21   The Race Relations Act 1976 extended the scope of anti-discrimination coverage and amalgamated the Race Relations Board and Community Relations Commission into a new Commission for Racial Equality, responsible to, and funded by, the Home Office. In April 1977 a Green Paper was published proposing changes to British nationality law, which would leave the existing immigration control structure untouched but would remove the possibility of transmission of British nationality to wives and children from male citizens of the colonies and from the remaining British Asians in East Africa. In 1981 the British Nationality Act was passed amid considerable controversy and there was some confusion about whether it was really a nationality measure or rather an immigration law "in disguise". Logically however it marked a further step on the same road that immigration laws had followed since 1962.

Educational Policies

3.3.22   Turning to education, the development of Government thinking can, we feel, best be traced through a consideration of some of the major reports and publications which appeared at various times. DES Survey 13 "The Education of Immigrants", which was published in 1971, can be seen as following very closely the assumptions and objectives of central Government pronouncements of the 1960s, with its continuing emphasis on the teaching of English, as:

"the most urgent single challenge facing the schools";

DES Survey 13

This report also, however, in seeking to emphasise the need for schools to have some knowledge of a pupil's home background, inadvertently included some of the clearest manifestations of stereotypes of different groups, most notably perhaps the following picture of a West Indian child and his home and family background which can in many respects, as we have already emphasised in our Racism Chapter, be seen to persist in the minds of many teachers even today:

"For the West Indian child the change can be more radical. He is accustomed to living together with two or three generations in the same house, dependent not so much on his mother as upon a number of adults among whom his grandmother holds a special place. The environment is one in which marriage is

210

not always considered important in providing a secure basis for raising children, whilst family discipline may be strict and physical punishment for mis-behaviour all too familiar. He leaves behind this often repressive, but affectionate and known home environment to join his mother from whom he may have been separated for several years, almost a stranger among new unknown brothers and sisters, possibly disliking and not fully accepted by the unknown father with whom his mother may be living, and perhaps, if very young, sent out to child-minders while his parents go out to work. Little wonder that the sense of insecurity these conditions create often brings in its train emotional disturbance and mal-adjustment and that in school such a child will often exhibit behaviour problems. He may be restless and boisterous, displaying hostility towards adults and other children, showing little ability to concentrate or to apply himself for long to the job in hand – or else retreat depressed and uncommunicative into a withdrawn world."

There were however some signs in this report of a growing realisation on the part of central Government that the issue of "immigrant education" might be rather more complex than had been previously admitted. For example, in relation to its earlier advocacy of dispersal, the Government now took the somewhat equivocal view that:

"It is difficult to measure the contribution of dispersal or non-dispersal to the success or otherwise of an authority's policy for the education of immigrant children . . . . It remains for each local education authority to decide what its policy for the education of immigrant children should be, and it is hoped that authorities will keep their arrangements (including any dispersal arrangements) under review in the light of local developments and the changing educational needs of pupils."

Influence of Racism

Whilst this line represented a marked lessening in the Government's previous enthusiasm for dispersal, the report did not, as has been claimed, state that dispersal was wrong, and indeed, as we have already recalled, several LEAs continued to "bus" ethnic minority children well into the 1970s. This report was also significant in that it acknowledged the existence of racism in society and the influence which this might have on teachers' attitudes:

"The (immigrant) child is very much a stranger in a strange land and may encounter hostility from members of the white community" . . . . "Teachers and others in education need to recognise that they are no less prone than anyone else to feelings

211

of prejudice or even acts of discrimination and to realise that their attitudes, their interests and their example to a very great extent shape the personalities of those in whose hands lies the fate of coming generations."

Perception of Ethnic Minorities as "Disad- vantaged"

– and also raised the question which was subsequently to dominate much of the thinking on ethnic minority education during the 1970s: whether the problems faced by immigrant children were in essence any different from those facing children from the majority community regarded as coming from "disadvantaged" backgrounds. As the report observed:

"Some argue that where there are immigrant educational difficulties these differ in no way from those encountered in educating native-born children living in socially and culturally deprived areas. It is in such areas that very many immigrant children live – in the ugly, bare, built-up 'twilight areas' – badly housed, lacking social, cultural and recreational amenities, attending schools with frequent staff changes, in poor buildings. They share all the difficulties of environmental deprivation known to native-born children living in these same areas. They frequently appear to suffer the same emotional disturbance the same inarticulateness and difficulty with language, the same insecure approach to school and school work, the same unsatis- factory attitudes in social relationships – all of which affect their life and general progress in school."

The assimilationist view had, as we have seen, tended to regard immigrant children as, by definition, "remedial" but had nevertheless felt that their very particular needs could be remedied by short-term, ad hoc measures. Now that it was becoming clear that the educational needs of ethnic minority pupils were not so easily met, the report was thus lending weight to a new stereotype which was emerging of ethnic minority pupils as suffering from what was traditionally termed the "cycle of cumulative disadvantage". This move towards seeing ethnic minority groups simply as "disadvan- taged" was in general resented and resisted by the ethnic minority communities themselves since as the Open University coursebook "Ethnic Minorities and Education"[17] has put it:

"To them it implied that 'immigrants' could be lumped together in a crude, undifferentiated way with the most unfortunate members of the indigenous community."

---

[17] "Ethnic Minorities and Education." (E354 – Block 4 Units 13 and 14.) The Open University Press. 1982.

"Inner City" Dimension

Since the education system had not succeeded in devising an education appropriate to the needs of the disadvantaged indigenous communities, it was therefore suggested by implication that the needs of ethnic minority pupils were simply another aspect of this wider problem. A further dimension of this new stereotype of ethnic minorities as, by definition, disadvantaged was the correlation which was increasingly drawn between their situation and the "plight" of the inner-cities which was the subject of increasing public concern during the 1970s. As the 1975 White Paper on "Racial Discrimination"[18] put it:

> ".... the problems of racial disadvantage can be seen to occur typically in the context of an urban problem whose nature is only imperfectly understood. There is no modern industrial society which has not experienced a similar difficulty. None has so far succeeded in resolving it."

The tendency to see the need of ethnic minority groups, and particularly the educational needs of ethnic minority pupils, as simply part of a far broader, and to some extent insoluble, problem of inner city disadvantage. This is still often put forward today as in some way explaining and excusing lack of progress in developing multicultural education and combating the underachievement of particular ethnic minority groups, but as we shall see in Chapter 3, the problem is more complex. Whilst, as we have emphasised in the previous Chapter, ethnic minority communities can in general be seen to suffer from a considerable degree of deprivation in a number of fields such as employment and housing, the very particular circumstances which have exacerbated this situation, notably the influence of racism, must we feel be taken into account and it is therefore a considerable oversimplification of a complex situation to ascribe the same motives, aspirations, expectations and general outlook to ethnic minority communities as to deprived indigenous communities simply by reason of their outwardly similar circumstances. It is also misleading to regard ethnic minorities solely in the context of the inner city problem since they were in fact already to be found in many parts of the country outside the major inner city areas – in for example many smaller towns in the rural North of England and the Midlands.

SCORRI Report 1972-1973

3.3.23 The SCORRI report of 1972-1973 on Education expressed concern about a number of aspects of the education of ethnic minority children and put forward three main recommendations:

---

[18] "Racial Discrimination," Cmnd 6234. HMSO. September 1975.

"First, that consideration be given to the establishment of a central fund to which local education authorities could apply for resources to meet the special educational needs of immigrant children and adults; second, the local education authorities should be required, as a condition of using the Department's resources and services, to report regularly and fully on the situation in their area and what they are doing about it; third, that an immigrant education advisory unit should be set up in the Department of Education and Science."

Government White Paper 1974

The Government's response to the SCORRI report[19] reaffirmed the trend towards seeing ethnic minority needs within the overall context of disadvantage, as follows:

"Where immigrants and their descendants live in the older urban and industrial areas, the majority of their children are likely to share with the indigenous children of those areas the educational disadvantages associated with an impoverished environment. The Government believe that immigrant pupils will accordingly benefit increasingly from special help given to all those suffering from educational disadvantage. They accept the Select Committee's view that many of those born here, of all minority ethnic groups, will experience continuing difficulties, which must receive special attention from the education service. But others, including many children and adults of indigenous origin, also have particular problems to which the education service must respond; and in large, if not in complete, measure much the same effort and attention will be called for. The pattern of special help must thus provide for all those suffering educational disadvantage, taking account of the distinct needs of different ethnic groups and of individuals, whatever their origin . . . . The Government believe that it is necessary to make more formal arrangements for the development of the work which is now being done on the education of immigrants and education for a multi-racial society. But they also see a need to provide for all those suffering from educational disadvantage, and . . . . they have decided that the arrangements which they create, while allowing for any distinct educational needs of different ethnic groups, should have this broader concern."

Establishment of EDU and CED

The Government accordingly set up a specialist Educational Disadvantage Unit (EDU) within the DES to oversee " . . . . matters, at all stages of education, connected with educational disadvantage and

[19] "Educational Disadvantage and the Educational Needs of Immigrants." Cmnd 5720. HMSO. August 1974.

the education of immigrants" and charged it with setting up an "information centre" relating to its field of interest – subsequently established as the Centre for Information and Advice on Educational Disadvantage (CED). The Select Committee's recommendation for a "central fund" was rejected on the grounds that Section 11 (which as we have already seen was firmly rooted in the assimilationist tradition) and the Urban Aid programme (again identifying ethnic minorities simply as "inner-city dwellers") already catered for the needs of "immigrants" and that the concept of a central fund might undermine local authorities' autonomy. It is perhaps hardly surprising that these further indications of the Government's view of ethnic minority needs under the overall heading of "disadvantage" were opposed by many ethnic minority representatives at the time. The **Ethnically** Select Committee report had discussed the appropriateness and val-**Based** idity of the 7(i) statistics of "immigrant" children which the DES **Statistics** had continued to collect (see paragraph 2.6 above). They had concluded that the definitions used were unsatisfactory and that the data obtained did not accordingly reflect the multi-racial mix of school populations and had recommended therefore that:

> *"The collection of statistics under the present formula should cease forthwith."*

In its response, the Government confirmed that it had already discontinued the collection of the 7(i) statistics but, because of the failure of consultations with interested parties to produce any more satisfactory basis for statistical returns, no alternative arrangements for the collection of ethnically-based educational statistics had been made in their stead.

SCORRI
Report
1976/1977

3.3.24 SCORRI devoted its 1976/77 session to considering the West Indian community.[20] In its evidence to them, the DES reiterated the view that the needs of the West Indian community had much in common with those of the disadvantaged sections of the indigenous community:

> *".... the West Indian community suffers disproportionately from some disadvantages which can be seen to depress the educational performance of indigenous children too – such as high proportions of families with the main breadwinner in unskilled work or in poor housing.... the phenomenon of low average attainment will not disappear with the ending of*

---

[20] "The West Indian Community." Select Committee on Race Relations and Immigration. February 1977. HMSO. HC 180 I-III.

immigration from the Caribbean . . . . For (immigrants) from the West Indies . . . . it is generally argued that in many respects they need not so much discrete provision as better opportunities to benefit from educational services, which should also be open to indigenous people with similar needs . . . . ."

The Select Committee was unconvinced that the educational problems of West Indian pupils were simply a symptom of their community's degree of "disadvantage" and concluded that:

". . . . the relative underachievement of West Indian children seriously affects their future employment prospects and is a matter of major importance both in educational terms and in the context of race relations. They (i.e. the Select Committee) regard the assumption of its continuance as unacceptable."

**Establish-
ment of this
Committee**

Accordingly they recommended the establishment of "a high level and independent inquiry into the causes of the underachievement of children of West Indian origin". In response to this recommendation the Government of course established this Committee with a broader remit than originally proposed, in response to the concerns expressed about the educational needs of children from the whole range of ethnic minority groups, as well as about the preparation of **all** pupils for life in a multi-racial and culturally diverse society.

**Closure
of CED**

3.3.25   We now turn to considering Government policies during our own lifetime and although in some respects the very existence of this Committee had led to something of a hiatus in policy making in this field there have been several developments which it may be helpful to recall here. In November 1979 the Secretary of State announced his intention to close the Centre for Educational Disadvantage (CED), (see paragraph 3.3.23 above), on the grounds that it had:

"not wholly fulfilled the expectations raised at its foundation and continued grant aid would not provide value for money in meeting the needs of the educationally disadvantaged."[21]

This announcement caused considerable controversy and it was not until May 1980 that the closure was confirmed. The fate of CED was

[20] "The West Indian Community." Select Committee on Race Relations and Immigration. February 1977. HMSO. HC 180 I-III.
[21] House of Commons Hansard Fifth Series Vol 973 Col 729 15 November 1979.

subsequently raised on the floor of the House of Commons[22] when the proposed closure was challenged as "not being on educational grounds" and the capacity of HM Inspectorate and the Department's Educational Disadvantage Unit (EDU) – see paragraph 3.3.23 above – to "fill the void" created by the closure, as the Secretary of State hoped, was questioned. The then joint Parliamentary Under Secretary of State, replying to the debate, asserted that:

"the closure of the centre does not mean that the Government have lost interest in work to combat educational disadvantage – far from it. Through the work of the Inspectorate and the Educational Disadvantage Unit in the Department, we shall continue to be involved in these matters . . . . at national level we shall remain involved in and concerned about all aspects of work to combat educational disadvantage."

The extent to which the education of ethnic minority pupils was by this time seen by the Government as synonymous with educational disadvantage was clearly manifested by the following reference by the Minister to **this** Committee in the course of the debate:

"the existence of the Committee is a clear indication of our continuing concern for those who face educational disadvantage."

Our Interim Report and the Government's Response

3.3.26 Our interim report was submitted to the Secretary of State in February 1981 and was published in June that year. In July 1981 the Home Affairs Committee published its report[23] on Racial Disadvantage which also included a section on education (see paragraph 3.3.25). In October 1981 the DES issued to the local authority associations, teacher unions and other interested organisations, a consultative document relating both to our recommendations and to those on educational issues in the Home Affairs Committee's report. The Government's response to the Home Affairs Committee's report, drawing on the findings of the consultation exercise, was published in January 1982[24] and in this the Government undertook to respond to our interim report:

"in the early part of 1982."

---

[22] House of Commons Hansard 11 June 1980 Cols 757-772.
[23] Fifth Report from the Home Affairs Committee. 1980/1981. "Racial Disadvantage." HC 424 I-III.
[24] Racial Disadvantage – The Government Reply to the Fifth Report from the Home Affairs Committee Session 1980-81 HC 424 Cmnd 8476.

In November 1982 the Home Office issued revised guidelines[25] on the administration of grants under Section 11 thus implementing the recommendation we had made in this area in our interim report. The only one of our recommendations addressed to the DES to which there has as yet been a formal response is in relation to the collection of educational statistics on an ethnic basis on which, in evidence to the Home Affairs Committee in July 1982[26] the Secretary of State stated his intention:

> ". . . . to explore, on the basis of the cautious approbation from consultation, with the local education authorities and the teachers and the ethnic minorities, how statistics might be collected so as to avoid the bureaucratic dangers, so as to respect confidentiality . . . . and so as to try to achieve the monitoring that is sought without damaging consequences, or worrying consequences."

We understand that in October 1983 a Working Group was established by the DES, with membership drawn from the ethnic minorities, the Commission for Racial Equality, local authority associations and teacher unions, to consider how the Secretary of State's undertaking might be put into practice. (The Group's terms of reference relate only to the collection of statistics within schools however and do not therefore concern the other recommendations which we put forward in our interim report concerning the collection of ethnically based statistics by teacher training institutions, universities, polytechnics and colleges of higher education and by the DES in its school leavers survey and in relation to teachers in employment.) The outcome of the Group's deliberations are still awaited.

Home Affairs Committee Report 1981

3.3.27   The Home Affairs Committee in its 1981 Report on "Racial Disadvantage" found the efforts being made to meet the educational need of ethnic minority pupils "unimpressive". They expressed particular concern about the effectiveness of the DES Educational Disadvantage Unit (EDU) – see paragraph 3.3.23 above – in the field of multicultural education thus:

> "We are not convinced that the Unit has in the past achieved much beyond "informal discussion and talk" with the Inspectorate and within the Department. Its only positive achievement referred to in evidence was the establishment of

---

[25] Home Office Circular 97/82.
[26] Minutes of evidence. Home Affairs Committee Sub-Committee on Race Relations and Immigration. 12 July 1982 HC 405-(i)-(iv).

the Rampton Committee, which was of course the result of a recommendation made in 1977 by the former Select Committee. A unit concerned exclusively with multi-racial education rather than with the whole range of educational disadvantage arising from social deprivation would be better placed to advise the Secretary of State on questions such as mother tongue teaching or the language problems of West Indian children."

Above all, the Home Affairs Committee focussed attention on the risks inherent in viewing ethnic minority educational needs strictly in the context of educational disadvantage which they regarded as "typified" by the establishment of the CED and the EDU – a tendency which, as we have seen, has characterised the Government's approach to multicultural education since the early 1970s. The Home Affairs Committee observed:

"many of the disadvantages suffered by ethnic minority children are shared by other children from socially deprived backgrounds. Some ethnic minority children do not suffer these disadvantages, and others achieve well in spite of them. There is indeed a danger of ethnic minority pupils being stereotyped as problems ... ethnic minority underachievement is not inherent in ethnic minority pupils."

To counter this danger, the Home Affairs Committee recommended that:

"the Department of Education and Science review their administrative arrangements with a view to setting up a Unit concerned solely with multi-racial education."

In their White Paper on Racial Disadvantage in response to the Home Affairs Committee Report, the Government stated that they had:

"carefully considered this recommendation (and had) concluded that, within existing manpower constraints, the present arrangements within the Department of Education and Science are the most effective means of co-ordinating its policy in relation to multi-ethnic education. Under these arrangements, the Educational Disadvantage Unit, acting with and through the other branches of the Department and with the advice of HM Inspectorate, is involved not only with disadvantage but also with multi-ethnic education. The fact that the work of the Unit covers both aspects does not lessen the ability of the Department as a whole to consider issues related to multi-ethnic education."

Broad Conclusions on Central Government Policy

3.3.28 A number of broad conclusions can we believe be drawn about central Government's role in the emergence of multicultural education over the past decade or so. In the early days, Government pronouncements appear to have been much influenced by assimilationist thinking with little real attempt to give a lead to a more positive view of ethnic minority pupil's educational needs. To some extent at least, policy making in this field seems also to have been unduly distorted by political considerations and particularly by concern at the possible impact on majority public opinion of appearing to adopt a more constructive approach to ethnic minority needs. The subsequent attempts to relegate multicultural education to an aspect of "educational disadvantage" and to subsume ethnic minority needs within the wider "inner city problem", seem difficult to comprehend on educational grounds and in many ways appear to belie the public pronouncements of a commitment to a broader concept of multiculturalism. It is important to recall that the establishment of this Committee, which could be seen as an attempt to give due recognition to the need for positive progress in the field of multicultural education, came only in response to a Select Committee recommendation and not as part of a central Government strategy. The absence of a full response to our interim report, which was specifically requested by the Government, can also perhaps be regarded as evidence of the extent of genuine concern and commitment to this field of work and indeed this view was expressed by many of the organisations which submitted evidence to us for this report, for example the National Union of Teachers, in their published evidence[27], observed that:

> *". . . the so far lukewarm (or even non-existent) response on the part of the Government to the Rampton interim report . . . does not inspire confidence among teachers working in schools that the measures they deem necessary have official support and backing."*

The various criticisms voiced by Select Committees as to the appropriateness and effectiveness of arrangements within the DES itself to give a lead in the development of multicultural education do not appear to have been fully answered. All in all, central Government appears to have lacked a coherent strategy for fostering the development of multicultural education and thus to have been unable to play a leading role in co-ordinating or encouraging progress in this field.

---

[27]"Education for a Multicultural Society – Evidence to the Swann Committee of Inquiry. Submitted by the NUT." Published May 1982.

LEA and School Policies

3.3.29   In considering the evolution of multicultural education it is also essential to look at the way in which policies have been developed and put into practice at LEA level and with individual schools. Whilst there are similarities between central and local government attitudes, and in several respects, policy at the centre, for example in relation to funding arrangements, has directly conditioned local government's practices, it is noticeable that there have been a number of occasions when policies in particular LEAs and schools have varied considerably from the line of Government thinking. In some cases, as with the rejection by some LEAs of the policy of dispersal, this has been because broad policy approaches have been considered to be impracticable or unworkable, or because individual teachers or LEA officials have felt national policies to be inappropriate to the actual school situation.

Varying Approaches to Multicultural Education

3.3.30   In the absence of any detailed guidance from the centre about what actually constitutes "multicultural education", many of the most important initiatives in this field have arisen from the effort and commitment of individuals or small groups of people around the country, for example devising their own guidelines for reviewing the curriculum or establishing working parties to discuss issues of concern. Whilst such local initiatives have clearly contributed greatly to thinking on multicultural education they have also led to the very wide variation in approaches to this area of work which are to be found between different LEAs and between schools within the same LEA. This has contributed to the general confusion as to the precise meaning and content of multicultural education. Also, where initiatives in this field can be seen as the direct result of perhaps one teacher's particular enthusiasm and interest, this has also meant that the basis of such work and the extent to which it is built into a school or LEA "strategy" can be rather tenuous. There is always a risk that if the key personality or group of people move elsewhere that their work will simply "fade away" without them. It is also apparent from the variety of approaches to multicultural education in different LEAs that developments in this field are often related to the presence of ethnic minority pupils in schools, with, in effect, the greater the number of ethnic minority pupils, the greater the efforts on multicultural education. This apparent belief that multicultural education is relevant only **because** of the presence of ethnic minority pupils, and by implication therefore, not otherwise, was clearly demonstrated to us by those LEAs we consulted, where ethnic minority settlement was confined to one particular area within the Authority who stressed that multicultural education was therefore "only of relevance to" or "only practised in" **that** area and was a matter therefore not for "County Hall" but for a particular district/area/divisional education office.

221

3.3.31   It is also noticeable that the "type" of multicultural education found in a particular LEA seems determined by the nature of the ethnic minority communities there – for example in LEAs where pupils of West Indian origin form a substantial part of the school population, the emphasis tends to have been on measures to overcome West Indian underachievement, encouraging the use of West Indian Language and the employment of more West Indian teachers etc, whereas in other LEAs with large Asian populations, particularly Muslims, the focus has instead been on measures to meet the community's concerns over matters such as religious education, single sex provision, "pastoral" issues and "mother tongue teaching". This "tailoring" of multicultural education according to the ethnic minority community in a particular area can we believe be seen as further evidence that the overall objectives and philosophy of multiculturalism have been insufficiently thought out and that what provision is made, is very much in the form of a response to perceived "problems" or to direct requests from schools or from certain communities for action on particular issues, rather than as part of a coherent and planned strategy. In many respects therefore, multicultural education at local level can be said to have evolved as a range of *ad hoc* measures which have been "lumped together" under a common heading but are essentially unrelated. In fact, no less a collection of *ad hoc* "emergency" and "compensatory" measures than characterised the assimilationist phase.

Conclusions of Main Research Studies

3.3.32   The variety of approaches adopted by LEAs and schools to multicultural education has been illustrated by a number of research studies undertaken since the early 1970s. The second NFER review of research discusses the findings of these studies in some detail, but in considering the development of policies relating to multicultural education we ourselves looked at four of the most important such studies, spanning the dacade:

– Townsend and Brittan's studies: "Immigrant Pupils in England: The LEA Response" (1971) and "Organisation in Multiracial Schools" (1972);

– DES Education Survey 14: "The Continuing Needs of Immigrants" (1972) (based on a survey of LEAs and schools undertaken by HM Inspectorate);

– Little and Willey's report on "Studies in the Multi-ethnic Curriculum" (1983) Schools Council, (based on a project carried out in 1979/80);

– Young and Connelly's report on "Policy and Practice in the Multi-Racial City" (1981) Policy Studies Institute, (based on a project carried out in 1979/81).

The development of multicultural education in multi-racial areas, between the early 1970s and early 1980s, as illustrated by these research studies, can be summarised as follows:

– At the beginning of the 1970s there was a wide variation between LEAs in both their priorities and practices in the multicultural field. The only common factor appeared to be an overwhelming emphasis on meeting the linguistic needs of children for whom English was not a first language – E2L needs. The type of E2L provision made by different authorities varied widely however from full-time separate language centres to part-time language classes on a withdrawal basis within pupils' own schools. Some LEAs were beginning to appoint advisers or administrators with specific responsibilities for "immigrants" but again the emphasis was chiefly on co-ordinating efforts in relation to language needs rather than any wider considerations. LEAs also varied in the in-service provision which they offered to their teachers in relation to multicultural issues and there was a tendency for such courses as were available to attract only specialists, such as E2L teachers, who were working directly with ethnic minority pupils. Within schools, the main emphasis was again on E2L provision with varying approaches being adopted. Where children with language needs were withdrawn to attend a separate language centre there were generally few links between the staff of the two institutions. The second stage language needs of E2L learners in general received little attention and were, as Townsend and Brittan put it, "imperfectly understood". The possible language needs of West Indian pupils tended to be "equally misunderstood". There was consequently felt to be a risk for all ethnic minority pupils, but especially West Indians, that their academic ability might be incorrectly assessed and that they might therefore be misplaced in remedial streams or classes. Although the "pastoral" needs of ethnic minority pupils, for example in relation to school meals or uniform, were not yet found to be a major issue – possibly because schools were only just beginning to find themselves with large numbers of Asian pupils – there were nevertheless already indications of the need for schools and ethnic minority parents to have a better understanding of each other's concerns and for improved home/school links. As far as the curriculum was concerned, as the authors of Education Survey 14 put it, "very little modification has taken place" and there was indeed little evidence that even the possibility of changes to reflect the multi-racial nature of society had even been considered. Teachers were found to have had little or no preparation, through

223

either their initial or in-service training, for the multi-racial context, and to have little background knowledge of ethnic minority groups. Multicultural considerations were rarely considered formally by schools and much reliance was placed on the enthusiasm and initiative of individual teachers. Where relevant courses were available, they were often undersubscribed and few teachers other than specialists attended them. The trend of policies at both LEA and school level at this time therefore seemed to be very much in the assimilationist tradition – that once ethnic minority children had mastered English, their needs would have been fully met and they would then "settle down" and cease to experience, or cause, educational problems. Little or no attention was given at this time to reaching an understanding of the social and cultural needs of the children or of the wider implications of the changing nature of society. The practices of this period were described by Townsend and Brittan as:

> *"(an) adaptation of tried and tested procedures to untried and untested circumstances."*

In seeking to build however on earlier educational practices in relation to ethnic minority pupils, which, as we have seen, had very clear and very limited objectives, there was little scope for positive or constructive thinking about the true needs of a genuinely "multicultural" society.

– By the turn of the decade one might have expected considerable progress to have been made but many of the same problems and difficulties mentioned above were revealed by the two later surveys. Indeed Little and Willey's study concluded that LEAs were still:

> *"at an early stage in beginning the difficult process of adapting a pattern of organizational arrangements established to meet particular needs ... to the wider task of fulfilling the educational needs of all children in a multi-ethnic society."*

Only a minority of LEAs were found to have clear strategies for multicultural education, and E2L teaching was still widely regarded as the central priority. A variety of approaches were adopted to E2L provision but there had been a general move away from separate language centres towards the use of teams of peripatetic E2L teachers working within normal schools. There seemed however to be growing dissatisfaction amongst E2L specialists with the type of language provision which they were able to offer, with a feeling that second stage language needs were still largely neglected and that there needed to be improved language education as a whole – along the lines recommended by the Bullock report. West Indian language needs remained a subject for concern in some areas and there was a more general feeling that the needs of West Indian pupils were still not fully understood nor catered for. Also in the language field, there was an increasing awareness at both LEA and school level of issues relating to "mother tongue" provision – presumably partly as a result of pressure from the Asian community – and some provision in the form of "mother tongue teaching", although views varied widely as to the desirability of developing or extending such provision. Various approaches had been adopted by LEAs to co-ordinate their efforts in the "multicultural" field through specialist advisers or administrators and the actual impact of such specialists on schools also varied considerably. More relevant in-service courses seemed to be available than earlier in the decade but there was still concern that they tended to reach only those staff who were already "converted" to the cause of "multiculturalism". Within schools, there seemed to be a growing acceptance, in theory at least, of the need to permeate the whole curriculum with an awareness of the multi-racial nature of society, but little progress seemed yet to have been made in practice in achieving this aim. Indeed there appeared to be a good deal of uncertainty amongst teachers as to how they might revise their work, combined with a residual resistance amongst some to the need to change at all. Although some multi-racial schools were now considering multicultural issues in a structured way, and some had, for example, established staff working parties to review policy. There still seemed to be however a marked lack of clarity as to the precise policy aims to be achieved and a desire for guidance and leadership from the centre. Some changes had taken place in various areas of the curriculum, notably religious education – perhaps because of the particular concern about this subject amongst certain Asian groups – and there had been some attempts to seek to identify and counter racism within the school, but elsewhere efforts had tended to be at best, as Young and Connelly put it, "cautious". Some efforts had been made to improve home/school links with ethnic minority parents but it was still felt that much more remained to be done in this respect. Over "pastoral" matters, there had been "problems", but attempts had been made to issue guidance and advice to schools and teachers and there was now at least a greater awareness of the difficulties which could arise. Teachers generally were still felt to have been inadequately prepared by their training for dealing with the situation which faced them and although it was often acknowledged that the presence of more ethnic minority teachers might be particularly valuable, there were found to be very few such teachers actually in schools. When compared with the position some ten years previously it can be seen that whilst some of the underlying legacies of the assimilationist tradition still persisted, especially at LEA level, there was by the beginning of this decade a growing feeling that multicultural education might in fact involve far more wide ranging and fundamental changes in attitude and practice than had previously

225

been envisaged. It is also clear that there was a considerable "credibility gap" between actual practices at LEA and school level, and the pronouncements at national level of the advocates of multicultural education, and there was therefore an urgent need for the formulation of clear policy guidelines and an overall strategy for change – both of which had so far been lacking – in order to direct energies towards nationally-agreed objectives.

3.4   The Relevance of Multicultural Education to All Children

Government Approach

3.4.1   At the beginning of this consideration of the development of multicultural education (see paragraph 3.2 above) we noted that one of the major aspects of the debate on multicultural education which distinguishes it most clearly from the early days of assimilation, is the recognition that the multi-racial nature of today's society has implications for the education of **all** children, including those from the ethnic majority community. In recent years this view of multicultural education has extended beyond pupils attending multi-racial schools, to embrace **all** children in this country, including those living and being educated in "all-white" areas. The emergence of this broader view can also be traced through the public pronouncements of the Government over the years. As early as 1963 there was some recognition, albeit in rather guarded terms and in the context of the "problems" they pose, that the presence of ethnic minority pupils in a school might offer some positive benefits to the other pupils, as the following extract from the report "English for Immigrants"[28] shows:

> "... it is certainly true that the presence of ... immigrant children can give an added immediacy and meaning to many of our geography and history lessons; their contributions from the arts of their countries can add interest and variety to many school occasions; their differing religions, customs, dress and food can provide most useful and immediate materials for the inculcation of at least some measure of international understanding. The presence of our visitors from overseas can cause problems, especially if they come with little English and more especially if they come to any one school in very large numbers; but they also present challenging opportunities which a great many schools, both primary and secondary, have been quick to recognise and to accept with mutual advantage to British and immigrant pupils."

This theme was fully articulated in rather more positive terms in the 1971 Education Survey, as follows:

> "The arrival of immigrant pupils ... (has) ... given the schools a unique opportunity to get to know something at first-hand

---

[28]"English for Immigrants." Ministry of Education Pamphlet No. 43. HMSO. 1963.

226

about how peoples in other parts of the world live, and, perhaps more significantly, have provided the opportunity for everyone in their school, themselves included, to experience a multi-racial society in miniature. In this special situation, the schools can demonstrate how people from different ethnic groups and cultural backgrounds can live together happily and successfully, and can help to create the kind of cohesive, multi-cultural society on which the future of this country – and possibly the world – depends."

3.4.2   The theme of the potential for ethnic minority pupils to positively "enrich" the life of a school was reiterated in subsequent reports and by the latter half of the 1970s, this had been broadened to embrace the need for the education of **all** pupils whether ethnic minority or majority, or in multi-racial or "all-white" schools, to reflect the range of cultures present in British society today. For example the Government's 1977 Consultative Document "Education in Schools"[29] emphasised this "broader view" of multicultural education in stressing that:

"Our society is a multicultural, muti-racial one and the curriculum should reflect a sympathetic understanding of the different cultures and races that now make up our society . . . The curriculum of schools . . . must reflect the needs of this new Britain."

and in addressing a conference on multicultural education in 1980, the then Minister of State observed[30]:

"It is just as important in schools where there are no ethnic minority pupils for the teaching there to refer to the different cultures now present in Britain, as it is for the teaching in schools in the inner areas of cities like Birmingham and London. It is a question of developing a curriculum which draws positive advantage from the different cultures."

3.4.3   There has however rarely been any specific guidance from central Government as to how such sentiments should actually be put into practice in 'all-white' areas and schools. Although central Government refers to "the need for **all** children to be educated for life in a multi-racial society" as though this were already a widely-accepted and long-established principle of the British education system, as we have seen from our review of central Government's policies over the years, it is in fact a relatively recent feature and

---

[29]"Education in Schools – A Consultative Document." Cmnd 6869. HMSO. July 1977.
[30]Address to the CRE's conference on Education for a Multicultural Society by Baroness Young. 19 April 1980.

many of the previous policies on "ethnic minority education" were in fact explicitly designed to ensure that the multi-racial nature of the pupil populations in some schools impinged as little as possible on the educational experience of pupils from the majority community. It seems almost as though central Government, having decided to shift the emphasis of multicultural education to embrace "all" schools feels that by constant reiteration and exhortation to this effect, the message will somehow "permeate" the "all-white" schools, with no further efforts or resources.

Research   3.4.4   This broader dimension of multicultural education has been little researched, in terms of actual practice at school level and individual teacher attitudes; the only major project to have really attempted to review developments in this field, carried out under the auspices of the Schools Council has been Little and Willey's 1983 report "Studies in the Multi-ethnic Curriculum". Some broad conclusions can we feel be drawn from the findings of this project and indeed from the other limited work which has been undertaken in this field: first and foremost there appears to be little evidence of efforts in LEAs and schools with few or no ethnic minorities to reappraise or revise their practices to reflect the multi-racial nature of the wider society; indeed multicultural education tends to be largely dismissed as "not our concern", "a very low priority" or "likely to be divisive and counterproductive". The concept of multicultural education being of relevance to **all** children, including those attending "all-white" schools, appears to have failed to impinge in practice on non-multi-racial areas, which still seemingly equate multicultural education with the actual presence of ethnic minority pupils and therefore tend to explain their lack of concern with such developments by simply pointing out that they have no ethnic minority pupils. Those schools which do feel that they should be attempting to develop policies in this respect, profess themselves uncertain of how to tackle this, in the absence of clear guidance from LEA or central Government level – as Little and Willey put it, there appears to be "little effort beyond exhortation" put into encouraging developments in such schools.

CHAPTER 5

Multicultural Education: Further Research Studies

1. Introduction

1.1   In the previous chapter we reviewed the state of multicultural education by reference to the development of policies at both central and local level and the concerns of different ethnic minority communities. Clearly the whole of this Committee's work, for both of our reports, has been concerned with various aspects of multicultural education and the particular educational needs of ethnic minority pupils. The sheer volume of material which we have received and the wide-ranging opinions which have been expressed to us in our various meetings and visits are impossible to summarise briefly. We have however sought to draw on and reflect, thoughout this report, the range of evidence which we have received, and have indeed already referred at some length to some aspects of our evidence in our Achievement and Racism chapters. In addition to this general evidence, we commissioned several small-scale studies to investigate particular issues or concerns. Where these related to specific areas of work, such as language education, we have drawn on the findings in the appropriate chapters, as we have of course also drawn extensively on the conclusions of the NFER reviews of research.

1.2   We have not sought to review in depth current practice at a national level in each and every specific subject area. We were fortunate in being able to draw on the wealth of material collected by Alan Little and Richard Willey for the Schools Council for their project "Studies in a Multi-ethnic Curriculum[1]." We were also conscious that the various subject specific studies within the Schools Council's project on "Assessment in a Multicultural Society" were in progress and we have drawn on some of these reports in finalising this report. We commissioned two projects which related to particular aspects of the overall development of multicultural education, which we feel it is important to describe here, before going on, in the next chapter, to set out our own views on the extent to which multicultural education as presently conceived is preparing youngsters from all groups to live in and to shape the kind of pluralist society which we envisaged at the opening of this report.

---

[1] "Studies in the Multi-ethnic Curriculum." Little and Willey. Schools Council. 1983.

2. Project A: The Development of Multicultural Education Policyin Four Local Education Authority Areas

2.1 We have already referred, in Chapter Four, to several of the research projects which have been undertaken to investigate provision for multicultural education in various LEAs. These have in general surveyed the range of provision made at a given point in time and only rarely was there any attempt to relate "current" provision to earlier developments or to examine the past pressures which might have influenced the present-day policies of an LEA towards ethnic minority education. We were therefore pleased to receive a proposal, from the Social Science Research Council Research Unit on Ethnic Relations based at the University of Aston in Birmingham, to prepare a series of reports for us on the way in which policy had emerged in four LEAs around the country, to be undertaken as part of the Unit's ongoing research programme on "Ethnicity and Education[2]."

2.2 The detailed reports on the four LEAs which were the subject of the study – Manchester, Walsall, Bradford and the Inner London Education Authority – are published separately and we have not therefore reproduced their findings in full here. We attach as Annex A to this chapter however some extracts from the introduction to the research reports, writeen by Professor John Rex, who led the study team. These not only set the context for the reports but also raise a number of interesting and thought-provoking issues relating to policy-making in this field. We should stress that both Professor Rex's comments here and the views taken in the individual research reports are the opinions of the researchers themselves and do not necessarily reflect the thinking of this Committee – indeed, as will become apparent, some of the views expressed are somewhat at variance with the line we have taken in this report. Nevertheless we feel that the findings of this project offer a valuable and intriguing insight into the varying ways in which educational policy-making can evolve in very different ways in different parts of the country.

2.3 While it is not for us to comment on the conclusions of the reports on the individual LEAs, there are clearly a number of general conclusions which can be drawn from the project's findings as a whole about the development of multicultural education at local

---

[2] The Ethnicity and Education Programme began in 1981 under the direction of Professor John Rex, Director of the Research Unit on Ethnic Relations. The aim of the programme is described as "an account of the demands made by ethnic minorities on the education system and the ways in which the education system has responded to these demands." The programme has four phases. The first is an anthropological study of the minority communities and the demands being made by minority parents and children on the education system. The second phase, which gave rise to the study reported here, is concerned with the reasons for and the content of multicultural educational policy as it has developed in four local authority areas. The third phase will be concerned with a study of the response by teachers to the policies developed by their local education authorities, and, in the final phase, this will be followed by detailed in-school studies.

level. Professor Rex himself highlights the following broad conclusions which can be made on the basis of this project, many of which echo the findings of other studies of multicultural education:–

> *"– There is no consensus on what multicultural education actually means, the actual specification of the policy having been the consequence of whatever political pressures happen to be dominant.*
>
> *– There will always be uncertainty and doubts about the legitimacy of the whole idea of multiculturalism until clear commitments are made at the highest political level.*
>
> *– Multicultural Education appears . . . . to be too often divorced from the whole complex of issues concerned with equality of opportunity for the minority child . . . . The two ideals of promoting equality of opportunity for the minority child and that of developing education for a multicultural and non-racist society are complementary rather than contradictory.*
>
> *– The ideal of Equality of Opportunity has to be conceived in much wider terms than has been the case when policy has been concentrated on the narrow question of West Indian underachievement.*
>
> *– The question of underachievement by an ethnic group or class is a real one in our schools, but its practical solution must lie in better educational practice rather than in emphasising the cultural and environmental differences between children outside the school.*
>
> *– Many policy decisions taken in the past have rested on dogmatic beliefs about the desirability of assimilation or separatism.*
>
> *– Too many decisions in the past have been taken against the wishes of minority communities.*
>
> *– Finally we should notice that the whole business of multicultural education is in an experimental stage. So far policies have been formulated, but hardly implemented."*

2.4 These general findings serve to reinforce some of our own conclusions about the overall state of multicultural education today; most notably perhaps the absence of a clearly agreed and accepted definition of the aims and objectives involved. It is also interesting to note that Professor Rex sees as one of the major factors which has contributed to this lack of a consensus on multicultural education, the vagaries of political pressures in this field, at both central and local level, over the years – a view which we ourselves have also previously expressed.

3. Project B: "All-White" Schools

3.1 One of the aspects of multicultural education which we were particularly anxious to investigate further was the extent to which an awareness of the multi-racial nature of Britain today had influenced the thinking of schools which themselves had few or no ethnic minority pupils. More importantly, we were concerned with the extent to which such schools saw it as part of their overall responsibility to inform their pupils about different ethnic minority groups and to encourage a positive view of their role within our society. As we recalled in Chapter Four, such limited research as there has been in this field shows that the situation on both these fronts still leaves much to be desired, and in our own interim report we highlighted comments made to us by ethnic majority pupils about "immigrants" which we felt also gave considerable cause for concern. In view of the major part which, as we explained in Chapter Two, we believe misleading stereotypes can play in reinforcing and perpetuating the overall climate of racism, we endeavoured to investigate further the extent of such views within "all-white schools," and what, if anything, was being done by the schools to counter them.

3.2 We were fortunate in this respect to obtain the assistance once again of Arnold Matthews – who had worked with us on our interim report and who had visited some "all-white" schools on our behalf – and also Laurie Fallows, who had also been co-opted to one of our sub-committees during the first stage of our work. As we have already acknowledged, people's attitudes are a particularly difficult area for research. The most satisfactory approach to our task therefore seemed to be to undertake "case studies" of the views and practices found within a number of "all-white" schools and this therefore was the approach adopted by Mr Matthews and Mr Fallows. During the winter of 1982/1983 they visited a total of 26 schools, both primary and secondary, and county and voluntary, drawn from six LEAs – three in the North of England and three in the South. The particular issues which they endeavoured to investigate for us are listed at Annex B, and the reports which they prepared on the schools they visited are attached as Annexes C and D. Following their visits to schools, Mr Matthews and Mr Fallows met representatives of the six authorities concerned to discuss their findings. Brief summaries of these discussions are included in the respective reports.

3.3   In our view, these reports provide a valuable insight into the attitudes and behaviour found in "all-white" areas and schools in relation to ethnic minorities and illustrate vividly the gap which exists between the pronouncements and exhortations made at national level about the need to educate all pupils for life in a multi-racial society, and the extent to which such an aim is accepted and acted upon. We commend the detailed reports to our readers as portraying the actual situation in the schools and areas visited. There are however a number of broad conclusions[3] which we feel can be drawn from the findings of this project:

Curriculum Content

Almost without exception, the schools visited saw the concept of multicultural education as remote and irrelevant to their own needs and responsibilities, taking the view that such an approach was needed only where there were substantial numbers of ethnic minority pupils. The concept of being part of a multi-racial society appeared to have impinged little on the consciousness of the schools, which were in many respects inward-looking and concerned primarily with immediate local issues. Whilst there was a greater awareness of the multi-racial "dimension" in the schools which were close to areas of ethnic minority settlement, or where there were ethnic minority pupils, little consideration had been given to the need to amend their work to take account of cultural diversity; indeed such moves were often seen as being too controversial and too inflammatory to contemplate. However there were indications from several of the schools that teachers would welcome and respond to a positive lead, with appropriate definition and guidance, from the DES and LEAs about "education for life in a multicultural society." It seemed that an emphasis on providing "good" education, rather than on concepts like "multi-racial" or "multicultural," which had little immediate reality in such areas, would be most likely to have an impact.

In relation to particular curriculum areas:

Religious Education – with one or two exceptions RE was found to be very much the "poor relation" subject, regarded as of little status by the schools, the teachers and the pupils. Several of the schools were attempting to provide a "multi-faith" style syllabus covering world religions in addition to Christianity, with varying degrees of success. A major obstacle to such developments in areas with no ethnic minority settlement was the lack of opportunities to visit the places of worship of other faiths or to meet adherents of other religions, which were available in multi-racial areas. Many of the RE

---

[3] We should emphasise that these represent the conclusions of **this Committee,** although based on the findings of Mr Matthews and Mr Fallows.

teachers claimed they lacked the necessary knowledge of other faiths to deal with them effectively or to select from the various course materials available. Although a few schools felt that their attempts to teach about the faiths of ethnic minority communities were well-received by pupils and served to broaden their horizons, in those schools where overt racial views were already present, such initiatives were seen as of little value in altering attitudes. RE courses in some schools sought to deal with issues relating to 'Race and Prejudice', again with varying degrees of commitment and success. Where such topics formed part of an integrated studies or a social studies course they were, in several schools, viewed with open hostility by parents, pupils and some staff members.

English – despite some teachers' expressed desire to offer their pupils experience of a wider range of literature, the majority of books studied and to be found in the school libraries reflected a narrow and outdated view of Britain and the world. A number of teachers pleaded their unfamiliarity with recent books drawing on a wider cultural framework and uncertainty about their authenticity or quality, despite the increasing number of multicultural booklists. Again, in schools where racist feelings were strong, attempts to introduce books by, or referring to, members of ethnic minority communities were generally rejected by both pupils and their parents.

History and Geography – in the majority of schools there was little attempt to reflect the multi-racial nature of society or to teach pupils about the origins and background of the various communities which are now a part of Britain. In Geography, one of the most disconcerting aspects of present provision was that, where they attempted to discuss developing countries, schools frequently projected inaccurate, outdated and stereotyped views of the "Third World", thus confirming any negative prejudices which pupils might have, rather than seeking to counter them.

Racism
The project revealed widespread evidence of racism in all the areas covered – ranging from unintentional racism and patronising and stereotyped ideas about ethnic minority groups combined with an appalling ignorance of their cultural backgrounds and life-styles and of the facts of race and immigration, to extremes of overt racial hatred and "National Front" – style attitudes. Asian pupils, usually viewed collectively as "Pakis", seemed to be most frequently the object of animosity, dislike and hatred, apparently because of their greater perceived "strangeness" and "difference" from the accepted cultural, religious and linguistic norms. Racial prejudice appeared to be most prevalent amongst the lower ability pupils who might feel

most threatened by a sense of intellectual and social inferiority aroused by "successful" ethnic minority communities, and incipient racism was clearly present in urban areas where there was increasing competition for housing and jobs. There were however some indications that youngsters might be more prepared than their elders to adopt a more positive view of the multicultural society, provided they were given the opportunity to learn more about other communities – pupils' attitudes generally appeared to harden as they grew older. It is interesting to note that in some cases, even where negative views about ethnic minority groups were expressed, pupils were anxious to exempt any ethnic minority school friends or acquaintances suggesting that the original antagonism was based on unfamiliarity and accepted stereotypes rather than deep-seated feelings.

Influences on Pupils' Attitudes

Many of the pupils had had little or no direct contact with ethnic minorities on which to formulate their own views, and the major influence on their outlook appeared to be the attitudes of their parents and local community. Where the community was generally antipathetic towards "outsiders" – a term which could be applied particularly to ethnic minorities – this outlook was shared by the pupils. Other major influences were the media – television, for example in its coverage of the Brixton "disturbances," and in its protrayal of ethnic minority characters in comedy programmes, and the local press, some of which was clearly biased against "immigrants" – and the school curriculum – especially history and geography lessons and textbooks which emphasised an Anglocentric and Imperialist view of the world as well as portraying developing countries in an outdated manner.

Teachers

Teachers were generally found to reflect the attitudes of their local communities even where they themselves had originated elsewhere, and, apart from a few committed "multiculturalists", the majority remained preoccupied with the immediate concerns of their day-to-day teaching activities and believed that "multicultural" considerations were irrelevant both to them and to their pupils. Primary school teachers seemed in general to be more willing to consider that the changing nature of British society might have implications for their pupils, than were their secondary school counterparts who were chiefly concerned with their own subject specialisms and with meeting the constraints imposed by the public examinations system. Many teachers felt that they lacked the knowledge and confidence to revise their practices and blamed the training which they had received for failing even to raise the issues and principles involved in the concept of multicultural education. Even those teachers who had only recently qualified commented on the inadequacy of the coverage of this field in their courses. As far as their attitudes towards ethnic minority groups were concerned, in the words of one of our researchers:

"the whole gamut of racial misunderstandings and folk mythology was revealed, racial stereotypes were common and attitudes ranged from the unveiled hostility of a few, through the apathy of many and the condescension of others, to total acceptance and respect by a minority."

Where there were clear instances of overt racism amongst pupils within their schools, many teachers were uncertain, reluctant or quite determined that nothing could or should be done by the school to challenge these attitudes. It was often stressed that emphasising "differences" between various groups could only be counter-productive and divisive, and that attempting to tackle "racial" issues openly could exacerbate the situation.

3.4   We believe that two major conclusions can be drawn from the findings of this project. Firstly, the concept of multicultural education involving and having implications for **all** schools, whether or not they have ethnic minority pupils, is far from accepted and indeed appears to be rejected by many "all-white" schools, despite national pronouncements to the contrary. Indeed the attitudes of many of those in the schools visited by Mr Matthews and Mr Fallows appeared to echo the narrow and insular view of one "all-white" school quoted in the Little and Willey study referred to earlier.

"we do not have a multi-ethnic society in this school."

The second major conclusion which we feel must regrettably be drawn from the findings of this project, is in relation to the widespread existence of racism, whether unintentional and "latent", or overt and aggressive, in the schools visited. The extent to which myths and stereotypes of ethnic minority groups are established and reinforced by parental attitudes, by the influence of the media and through institutional practices within the schools, is we believe all too apparent. On a positive note it was however encouraging to find that in a number of schools, the teachers professed themselves ready and willing to reappraise their own work and prepared to consider the need for a broader approach to their pupils' learning, provided a clear lead was given as to how this might be achieved, together with any necessary on-going support and guidance to put this into effect.

3.5   In relation to the follow up meetings with the LEAs in whose areas the schools were located, there were also a number of broad conclusions which we feel can be drawn out. All but one of the authorities visited expressed their belief in the **principle** of educating **all** children for life in a multi-racial society, but there was a good deal of caution about putting this into practice, influenced to some extent at least by the possible "political" repercussions of taking action in what was seen as a controversial field. Several of the LEAs emphasised their "good intentions" towards developing activities in relation to multicultural education, pointing for example to various initiatives in the field of in-service training or guidance to schools which were "in the pipeline" or "under consideration." There appeared in general however to be very little which had actually taken place in such areas to lend credibility to these authorities' professed allegiance to multicultural principles. Even in LEAs which had some areas of ethnic minority settlement, it seemed that any provision which was made was limited to those schools which actually had multi-racial pupil populations – and was generally concerned only with language teaching or religious education – and little attempt had been made to broaden such provision to encompass the "all-white" schools as well. It is interesting that in several of the LEAs, the advisory staff professed a lack of understanding of the principles involved in preparing all pupils for life in a multi-racial society and it was therefore perhaps hardly surprising that they had seemingly not ventured to seek to convince "all-white" schools of the need to appraise and possibly revise their work. From these various discussions with LEAs it would therefore seem that the degree of public commitment to multicultural education for **all** pupils expressed by central Government has as yet impinged only marginally on the thinking of LEAs with few or no ethnic minority pupils, and even less on their actual practices. Once again the most encouraging feature of the LEAs' attitudes was a general desire for guidance and advice on how they might implement policies in relation to multicultural education – at present it seemed that the majority of them were largely unaware of where to turn for such assistance.

ANNEX A

Extracts from Professor John Rex's introduction to the Report on the Development of Multicultural Education Policy in four local Education Authority Areas

The Issues in Multicultural Education

In order to understand the four reports . . . . . . as more than a merely descriptive account it will be necessary to consider what some of the major issues in the so-called multicultural field are. Only against this background will it become evident what choices are being made in the various authorities and what options have, in fact been discarded.

One way of approaching the problem, and one which will inform the final report of the Education and Ethnicity Programme, is to begin with the demands actually being made by parents, children and the representatives of minority communities. Another is to set out systematically the implications of the related, and yet distinct, policy goals of promoting equality of opportunity for minority children, and of developing an appropriate education for a multicultural society.

From what we know so far from our colleagues' work on parents demands and attitudes, four things seem to be important. First there is a demand of a quite simple and direct kind that education should be as good as possible an education, so that children entering the world of employment or higher education should have the best opportunities possible. Secondly, there appears to be widespread demand for mother tongue instruction. Thirdly, there are some specific demands arising most strongly amongst Muslim parents for appropriate recognition of minority customs. Finally, there is a concern that the schools should play a supportive role in the moral education of children, supportive, that is, of the kind of morality which parents see themselves as trying to inculcate in their homes.

Not included in this list, it will be noted, is a specific demand for something called multicultural education. There may be in the minority communities a commitment to cultural pluralism, it is true, but this does not usually lead to general demands on teachers and the school as distinct from the specific demands mentioned above. Minority parents expect that their language, culture and religion should be treated with respect and that it should not become the object of racist denigration and abuse, but there is widespread recognition of the schools as agencies which can promote or restrict equality of opportunity, and a fear that the provision of special education designed for minorities might hold children back from academic achievement.

Minority organisations, even when they are consulted only through official local Community Relations Councils, express similar demands. They tend to be dissatisfied with the provision for English teaching, to want specific mother tongue classes, to require special consideration on specific issues relating to school assemblies, food, dress, sex segregation and generally on questions of morality, and they are often much concerned about equality of opportunity for teachers from their own communities. There is a considerable record of dissatisfaction being expressed with actual policies adopted by LEAs on these matters, but also on the more general policies which have arisen from the successive stands taken by the authorities which result from their general philosophy on the question of pluralism and integration. Thus, when local authorities considered proposals for dispersal through bussing they rarely had any support from the minority community. Nor is there enthusiastic support for published policies on multicultural education.

Necessarily, of course, it is to be expected that local authorities will wish to pursue what they believe to be the best educational policies whether or not these represent a response to consumer demand. One does not expect therefore that any local authority will simply do all that parents ask. Nonetheless, if one looks at the way in which provision for minority children has been made since 1960 two things stand out. One is that, in the first phase, many of the policies which were adopted on such matters as E2L teaching, dealing with low achievers and discipline, had more to do with keeping the system running with the minimal disruption rather than with dealing with the needs of minority children. The other is that when minority-specific policies were developed they were often based upon incoherent and conflicting assumptions about the problems of a multicultural society.

We have thought it useful at all times to judge local authority policies not simply as a more or less adequate response to parent's or children's demands, but in terms of the adequacy as a means of implementing certain social, educational and political ideals to which Britain is supposed to be formally committed. Two such ideals are important. One is the recognition of the right to equality of educational opportunity for all children. The other is the attempt to create a multicultural society. These two ideals have to be taken together. To claim to be creating a multicultural society, when there is no guarantee of equality of opportunity, is to risk offering minority children an education which is different and inferior. To promote equality of opportunity without allowing for cultural pluralism is to move towards a policy of forced assimilation.

In an earlier paper one of us[1] has sought to set out some of the specific policy implications in education of the notion of equal opportunity for the minority child. These include the following:

1. Instruction of non-English speaking children in their own language at the point of their entry into the system, not in order to segregate them permanently, but in order that they should not be prevented at an early stage from learning to learn by a situation of linguistic and cultural shock.

2. Instruction in the mother tongue so that children should not have to pay the price of not being able to communicate with their parents for any success which they may have in education.

3. The early introduction to English as a second language, with adequate arrangements to ensure that the time spent on acquiring English does not prevent progress in normal school subjects.

4. Second stage English instruction to ensure that children are given not merely minimal English, but sufficient command of the language to enable them to cope with study at whatever level they are otherwise capable of reaching.

5. The inclusion in the syllabus of subject matter relating to their own culture, so that they are not deprived of their own inheritance, and can see that it has recognition within the curriculum and within the value system of British society (this requirement not being met by paternalistic teaching at a low level, which could have the effect of denigrating rather than strengthening minority cultures).

6. The teaching of minority languages, history and culture up to the highest level and not merely in the low-status and uncertificated parts of the syllabus, so that these subjects have equality of status with, say, French language, literature and history.

7. The elimination from the syllabus in all subjects of all those elements derived from an earlier historical period in which the culture of minorities is denigrated and a positive emphasis in the syllabus on the histories and cultures of their countries as an important part of the education of all children.

---

[1] John Rex, "Equality of Opportunity and the Minority Child." To be published by the London Institute of Education.

8. A positive commitment on the part of the school to the elimination of racism through the syllabus as a whole, through specific teaching against racism and through school practices which treat racism as a disciplinary offence.

9. The employment of qualified school-teachers from the minority groups in all subjects and a guarantee that they will be promoted on merit.

This check-list of items appears to us to provide a standard against which existing provision should be judged. It needs, however, to be accompanied by other measures designed to foster rather than suppress cultural pluralism.

It is often said, and it is said too glibly, that Britain is now a multicultural society and that education should reflect this fact. But the statement is misleading. Britain is not and is unlikely to become a multicultural society in the sense that Quebec or Brussels is. There two ethnic groups actually share political power and their languages may equally be used in Parliament and the Civil Service. What we should mean by it in Britain is that, while British culture and language albeit in changing and developing forms, remain dominant, British society is nonetheless committed to fostering minority languages and cultures and regards them as a source of enrichment rather than as something to be repressed or only tolerated.

In some respects, the United States has moved towards recognising Spanish in this way. Canada is also committed to a policy of multiculturalism and there are other precedents which could be followed in Britain.

Crucial to a multicultural policy of this kind is the notion that multicultural education concerns the whole syllabus and the syllabus of the "White" suburban child, as much as that of the minority child in inner city schools with a high minority concentration. Such a policy has a deliberate political objective. It seeks to eliminate fear of minority cultures and people and the notion that the continued existence of these cultures means the "swamping" of Britain by alien forces. Of course the implementation of such a policy would contribute to increasing equality of opportunity to minority children by improving the political and social climate in which they have to live, but it has to be mentioned in its own right because it is all too often assumed that multiculturalism in education is solely a matter of making special provision for minority children. The kind of emphasis which we are placing here **excludes** the kind of token provision for minority children which is expressed in encouraging West Indian children to organise steel bands or giving Asian children special lessons on rice-growing. It implies a radical policy of encouraging respect for Caribbean and Asian culture by British children as a part of their education. It is also designed to create a non-racist society.

It was not perhaps to be expected that the two ideals of equality of educational opportunity and the creation of a multicultural society would have been systematically applied to the million immigrants and their children from South Asia and the Caribbean who settled in Britain betweeen 1950 and 1970. Such immigration was accepted as a matter of economic expediency rather as something which provide new challenges to social policy. What one saw, therefore, was at best a series of ad hoc responses concerned with preventing the problems of the newcomers from disrupting the system and at worst a racist panic in which minority children were expected to become Anglicised as quickly as possible or somehow to go away. It was only in the mid-seventies, in fact, that British educationalists began to think more systematically about these problems. By then there was much suspicion amongst the minorities of the newer policies which were proposed and, in any case, the problems were doubly difficult because the education system had to deal not simply with the children of immigrants but with a generation who had been the victims of racism, discrimination and disadvantage.

The two major policy responses in the sixties had been the proposal for dispersing by bussing and the ad hoc development of language teaching for non-English speaking children. Bussing was not, as in the United States a policy developed in response to minority demands for equality of opportunity. It was developed out of fear that the presence of Black children in large numbers would lower standards and children were to be bussed regardless of whether they could speak English or not or whether they had special problems or not, but only if or because they were Black. If the policy was not widely adopted, moreover, it was not because minorities opposed it, but because White suburban schools did not want minority children and certainly didn't want their children bussed as a *quid pro quo* to Black schools. What was hardly noticed however was that there was virtually no support for the policy in the minority communities, because any slight advantages which it might have for some children were greatly outweighed by its disadvantages for all of them.

Language provision for the non-English speaking was of an equally primitive kind. The main point about it was that the immigrant child had to be withdrawn from the class-room because his presence there was likely to hold up the other children's progress. In some way therefore they had to be withdrawn, whether to special centres or to classes conducted by peripatetic teachers. In these centres they were given enough English to enable them to communicate and be communicated with by their teachers, but with little attempt being made to ensure that they could catch up with their main subject work or that they went on improving their English so that they could achieve at the highest level. All too often the language teaching itself or the problems of the "re-inserted" child were seen to belong to those of the Remedial Department along with those of other backward children.

The tendency to incorporate provision for minority children under the heading of remedial work reflected a wider tendency in social policy on the national as well as the local level. This was to deal with minority problems in a non-specific way under the more general heading of deprivation and disadvantage. The main central government provision for expenditure on minorities took the form of grants under Section 11 of the Local Government Act. It was always unclear, however, whether these grants were given for the benefit of minorities and immigrants or whether they were simply to help local authorities faced with problems consequent upon the arrival of immigrants. The confusion over this issue was compounded by the fact that simultaneously with seeking Section 11 grants, local authorities were called upon to adopt a policy of positive discrimination towards schools which had high indices for deprivation. Local authorities in these circumstances were all too likely to claim that their expenditure on deprived schools was their way of meeting minority needs. Many, indeed, argued, prior to the early 70s, that it was desirable in principle to deal with minority needs in this way as part of a general integrationist policy.

By 1970, however, the question of the education of the minority child came to have a new focus. This was that of the failure of West Indian children. In our view this problem has hardly been understood because the statistics have been presented in the crudest possible way in terms of gross comparisons between English, Asian and West Indian children. Had elementary statistical controls been introduced for the occupation, education and socio-economic group of parents the differences might well have virtually disappeared and any unexplained differences could quite as easily have been explained by the child's experience from an early age of British racism as it could by his cultural background. Since, however, it might still be asked why children from poor lower-class backgrounds do so badly, a problem might still remain. The more serious problem for us seems to be why it is that British schools so largely succeed in imposing on children the same social and economic status as their parents. If this happens for English working class children, is it not far more likely to happen for children from poor post-colonial societies.

Unfortunately questions like this have not been asked. Instead report after report has drawn attention to West Indian failure as an intractable problem, and if, fortunately, hereditarian ideas have not to any large extent been invoked by way of explanation, the explanation which has been sought has usually been in terms of some deficiency of the West Indian child, whether because of some deficiency in his self concept or because of his or her poor material or social

241

home environment. What has not been discussed is whether something might not be going wrong in the child's encounters with White society, not least in the school itself. In fact the debate about West Indian failure, like those about numbers and about language deficiency are not really understandable unless one realises that it has been informed as much as by anything else by racist panic.

Against the background of these ad hoc and panicky responses the emergence of a debate about multicultural education suggests something of a new start and as such it is to be welcomed. Certainly it involves a deliberate move away from the notion that minorities are to be provided for simply as part of a general programme for the disadvantaged. Nonetheless, although "Multicultural Education" became a widely accepted slogan, there was considerable uncertainty as to what it actually meant. To some it meant the whole set of policies to provide for the immigrant or minority child. To others it was seen as something more specific being concerned with bringing minority cultures into the curriculum. Within these two options, moreover, there were many alternative possibilities. Multicultural education might be thought of as something which applied to the curriculum of all children or it might be thought of as something which was to be provided for minority children only. If it was taken to mean the latter, it might or might not be seen as something whose main function was to improve performance and achievement. In some cases, moreover, the central meaning which was attached to the term was that it referred to the set of policies designed to deal with West Indian underachievement.

The problems of Asian children and those of West Indians, or more correctly, the problems of the children of Asian and West Indian immigrants, were likely to be systematically confused in this debate. On the one hand some local authorities were likely to be preoccupied with West Indian underachievement. On the other there were those who were concerned primarily with Asians. General policy discussions therefore often assumed a child who combined the problems of both and who in addition was assumed to share all the characteristics of the inner city poor.

Finally, one should note another overriding factor in these debates. This is that while there were those who were concerned with removing for the minority child all the obstacles which stood in the way of the highest possible achievement, there were certainly others who saw the problem as part of a wider problem of providing education of a relevant kind for the less able child. If, therefore, there was less than total enthusiasm on the part of minority communities for the new policies, it was probably because they saw them as offering less than the best to their children. One of the problems which we have had to face therefore in analysing the debates which went on before an apparent consensus about multicultural education was arrived at is whether some of the parties to that consensus and some of the agents who would have to carry it out only gave their consent on the assumption that what the policy was referring to was simply the provision of alternative provision for minorities in the low-status parts of the curriculum.

ANNEX B

"All-White" Schools Project: Outline

1. Overall Aim
To look at the ways in which a small sample of schools with few or no ethnic minorities are responding to the mulit-racial nature of Britain today.

2. Method
Interviews/discussions with Headteachers, teachers, non-teaching staff, parents and governors (where possible) and pupils.

3. Issues to be Investigated

i. The extent to which the school (Head, teachers, parents and pupils) feels it has a responsibility to inform and prepare its pupils for life in a multi-racial society (or whether this is seen as a "problem" faced only by multi-racial schools).

ii. The varying perceptions of what is meant by "multicultural" education – whether this is seen as:–
   - simply "celebrating" Eid or Diwali;
   - "Black Studies" where there are black pupils;
   - the latest "trendy bandwagons";
   - the education of all our children to a greater appreciation of the linguistic, cultural and religious diversity of Britain today.

iii. The extent to which the school (a). attempts and (b). succeeds to inform its pupils about ethnic minority groups in this country – their religions, cultures etc – and about the facts of immigration – numbers and distribution of ethnic minority groups and numbers of ethnic minority children now born in this country. Where schools are making progress in this field, to what extent are they receiving support and encouragement from their LEAs through the advisory services, resources centres or inservice courses.

iv. The perceptions and reactions of pupils, teachers and parents towards ethnic minority groups and how these have originated.

v. Whether the school has any explicit anti-racism curriculum content – eg dealing with racial discrimination within social studies – or a more general policy for eradicating racism eg "exchange" schemes with multi-racial schools and/or a policy on racist name calling;

vi. The extent to which Heads and teachers feel that their training has prepared them to adopt a "multi-cultural" approach to their work and what more they feel could be done in the teacher education field in this respect;

vii. The views of pupils, teachers and parents on the potential value of ethnic minority teachers. Also, where there are any ethnic minority teachers, how they themselves see their role in an "all white" school.

243

A Report of visits to Schools with few or no ethnic minority pupils by Arnold Matthews MBE (formerly adviser for multicultural education, London Borough of Ealing)

I   Introduction

1.   Background

1.1   During the winter of 1982/1983 I visited 13 schools with few or no ethnic minority pupils with a brief to find out how they were responding to the need to prepare **all** pupils for life in multi-racial Britain. The schools were situated in three local education authorities – LEA A, a rural county, LEA B, a largely rural county and LEA C, a metropolitan district – and were chosen from a short list provided by each of the LEAs. Two full days were spent in each secondary school and one full day in each primary school.

1.2   The notes which follow are presented largely in the form of anecdotes, written extracts from pupils' work or verbatim notes of conversations with head-teachers, teachers and pupils. They have not been selected or structured to either support or conflict with any pre-conceived view of the school or the area and they represent an honest and true reflection of what I found. They are not indended to portray a complete picture of the schools and LEAs concerned and I have not sought to pass judgement on their work but rather to give a flavour of the underlying attitudes present in each.

1.3   On completion of the visits to the schools, I met representatives of the three LEAs to inform them of my findings. Notes of these meetings are included in my report.

2.   Why Us? – We have No Problems. – Some Early Misunderstandings

2.1   A letter from the Committee Secretary to three local education authorities expressed a desire to obtain information about the views held by pupils and teachers in schools with few or no ethnic minority pupils about ethnic minority groups. Yet when these visits were carried out it was usually found that Headteachers expressed surprise that their schools had been chosen since they had few or no ethnic minority pupils; the multi-racial character of society in Britain was not considered to have much relevance for schools which themselves were not confronted with compelling racial problems. The predominant question in the minds of most of those occupying responsible positions in schools was how they were treating ethnic minority pupils within their administration: and in almost every case the claim was 'no differently to other children' because they presented 'no problem' and so were not thought of as being 'different'.

II   Attitudes found within the Schools

LEA A

1.   The schools in LEA A were characterised by a persistent insularity of outlook and this was very apparent amongst members of staff who tended to remain near to their places of origin. Those who had been trained or who had taught in other parts of the country had returned to the area at the first opportunity. One teacher, locally born, who had been trained and taught out of the region, pointed out that people had traditionally remained in the locality and even people with ability would deny themselves opportunities for rewarding work and accept a lower standard of living to stay at home. She commented that people were relaxed and easy-going and there were no pressures from the few ethnic minorities in the areas of jobs or housing and in her view since those children who would move away from the area on leaving school would be the more able children who would be going to situations where they would meet educated ethnic minorities there would be no "serious problems". Another teacher with experience of teaching in Africa felt angry about the prejudice which was very prevalent in Britain. This was particularly suffered by a highly-qualified African teacher-friend of hers in his search for a post in Britain which took four unremitting years.

2.   Experience gained by some teachers elsewhere was not necessarily profitable in terms of race relations. One teacher had served in a multi-racial school for twelve years prior to moving to this area. The practice at that time had been to treat West Indian pupils as if they were white: "They were part of us and so we treated them exactly like white children; for example, we had a black lad who misbehaved so we belted him; it didn't do any harm at all". He pointed out that many West Indians were good-humoured about their colour and he recalled rubbing down a black boy after a shower-bath. The boy joked, "It's no use, sir, it won't come off"! The teacher claimed to have happy memories of that time but admitted being angry when reading in the Rampton Report[1] of West Indian discontent and protest. "Have the immigrants been got at politically"? he asked. "Perhaps the media hadn't got on to race at that time". In another school a teacher referring to some of her colleagues said, "a number of staff here have never moved outside the region". She herself had, for many years, regularly travelled to various parts of the world, but she rejected as "outrageous" the suggestion that there should be a re-ordering of priorities in the allocation of resources in British education so as to give emphasis to the correction of disadvantages suffered by ethnic minorities. "We've got a damn-sight better use for our money", she asserted.

3.   Teachers in this area generally admitted to being preoccupied with their curricula and with immediate problems; considerations of the multi-racial society and the preparation of pupils' attitudes towards that society occupied a very slight part in the practice of only a few teachers and none at all in that of the great majority. One teacher, who had previously taught and had served as a community worker in two large cities, described his colleagues at his present school as having very limited experience of other cultures and being only concerned with academic aspects of their subjects which he saw "in this day and age like burying one's head in the sand". Another admitted, "we are very geared to exams here but we really ought to get the multi-racial thing in". One remedial teacher said, "teachers here don't appreciate the value of other cultures. If a child doesn't do French, he's remedial". Another teacher claimed, "I love all children but if my daughter came home with a black boy, I don't think I'd like it". A regional representative of a teachers' association who had been many years in his school confessed, "We've never given multi-racial education a thought".

4.   Not surprisingly the pupils in this area were also very insular in their outlook and understanding. Teachers frequently talked of the pupils' ignorance and inability to understand urban life. Some children had never been to the city and for the great majority it was a rare experience. "An inner city is for these children as remote as a very distant land". They had little or no experience of a multi-racial society and without exception, in the secondary schools, there were clear indications of racial prejudice in the attitudes of some of the pupils towards people from other ethnic groups regardless of whether they had had any personal knowledge of them.

School A1
1.   This small "all-white" primary school was situated in a village in which there were a few young families some of whom had moved from London and other cities. Its catchment area included a few hamlets which were dotted around the village.

2.   When asked what they knew about 'immigrants', a word they did not know and which had to be explained, some of the children said they had visited cities on family excursions and had seen but not met black people on these occasions. They were interested in people's differences in colour, language, dress and said they would like to make friends with black people and live next door to them. The sister of one child had a black friend, who was liked because "she is very kind". A boy on a visit to London spoke to and played with some Indian boys. "I liked them but they went," he said. "People don't like them, but they're no different; I would like them to come to this school".

---

[1] Interim report of the Committee of Inquiry into the Education of Children from Ethnic Minority Groups.

3.   Learning that many of the black children living in this country were born here, one little boy asked, "How can they be black if they were born in England? In India there are black skins because it's hot, but in England it's cold". "They might keep the heat on in the house", another boy answered.

4.   This school was of special interest because it had accommodated for some six months (on an exchange with some British service families) the children of two or three Argentinian servicemen. The Spanish speaking children had no knowledge of English and were objects of great interest to the school and community. The English children responded to them as individuals with differing characteristics many of which were rather endearing and they were very popular. The Argentinians were still living in the area when their forces invaded the Falkland Islands but the event appeared to make little difference to relationships between children or adults in the village. A birthday party was given at school to one of the visiting children and there was an objection from one English mother on the grounds that "some things are more important than friendship". The remaining parents disagreed and deliberately placed emphasis on friendship. When the British Task Force set sail the Argentines were moved to France as a first stage to returning home. The local children and their teachers were sad at their departure. Subsequently, in the course of military action against the British Forces one of these servicemen was killed. Asked what they thought about it the school children's feelings were summed up by "We are not happy for our friend".

5.   A travelling theatre company of four players had visited the school and performed for the children. Two of the actors were black and were described by the children as "nice", "interesting" and "we liked them". It may be significant here that their teacher had a history of positive friendship with black people in her home neighbourhood and at a Youth Club in her teenage years.

6.   The Head was also positive in his aim of developing an educational curriculum "within a moral framework". His creative approach drew on the immediate experience of the children. He felt he could effectively deal with abstractions eg relationships with minority groups, such as the handicapped, but only when the opportunity presented itself and came from the children. For this reason he welcomed visitors to the school and invited them to talk with the children – if they were black or of another culture then so much the better.

School A2

1.   School A2, a medium sized co-educational comprehensive secondary school, was situated in a market town. Teachers with long service at the school could recollect only having a few black families during the last dozen years. There was, I was told only one "dark child" at present. The reaction to this fact was "We are very lucky: we've had very few coloureds here. There are no problems of that kind in this area".

2.   Very little attention had been paid in the curriculum to preparing pupils for life in a multi-racial society. In Religious Education the LEA Agreed Syllabus pays slight attention to World religions and the Head of RE stressed "it's one of the priorities in my subject that pupils should at least know about other religions". When dealing with Judaism, a Rabbi visits the school to talk to pupils. Attempts to deal with race and immigration are made in the Integrated Studies Course for the lower ability groups of the first two years, when stories about Africa and India are a part of the reading programme used to teach reading skills. Prejudice was a topic which occupied half a day for unemployed girls who returned to school for a M.S.C. course. The Duke of Edinburgh Award Scheme at the school provided an opportunity for some senior girls to spend time in a multi-racial area of a nearby City.

3.   Although the shortage of money for new books coupled with a lack of knowledge of suitable materials were put forward as reasons for not attempting a multicultural approach to the curriculum, there was also the situation of one teacher who read "To Sir with Love" with three

fourth year classes; they did not understand it and treated it as a 'huge joke'. Similar attempts by this teacher at introducing serious discussion had failed and a study of other cultures in a course of Religious and Social Education was described by a sixth former reminiscently as 'just another lesson and so boring'. In the same group other students considered the members of a class by drawing attention to their differences. A teacher summed up the views of many members of staff when he said "we don't get any prejudiced views because we hardly get any ethnic minority children".

4.   The Drama teacher sees her work as an overt commitment to the preparation of pupils for life in which tolerance, understanding and harmony amongst people of all kinds are essential attributes. She teaches every pupil during their third year and so has an opportunity to contribute something to the lives of all pupils during their stay at school. She is convinced that children in the region who like herself during her schooldays and in her home locality 'never saw a non-white person', should be made aware of a multi-racial society. She uses role play as the most effective medium for treatment of the topic of 'Barriers' during which children have suggested the barriers of language and culture (for example the wearing of the turban in school). Another valuable experience mentioned at this school was a performance by a visiting company for fourth year pupils of a play about Hitler, Jews and Moseley followed by discussions by the company of the National Front and the treatment of ethnic minorities. This teacher also uses role play with her tutor group as a means of 'sorting out' attitudes on various questions including those of race.

5.   There were clear indications of racial prejudice in the attitudes of some pupils: this was illustrated by an incident which took place when a group of senior pupils were being prepared for a visit to London. The teacher invited the group to tell her what they wanted to see in London. "Can we go to Brixton, Miss"? one boy asked. "Why Brixton"? queried the teacher. "We might see some Pakis" he said. "And his intention was not for them to make friends", observed the Deputy Head who narrated the story.

6.   One teacher with pastoral responsibility expressed anxiety about racist gestures which were seen in the school, for example, National Front slogans written on notebooks and symbols drawn on the person, such as on the back of boys' hands. When informed about these signs one father replied, "We've got to get rid of these racials". This teacher who had made efforts to deal with these incidents effectively when they arose, expressed his conviction that in predominantly white areas, bigoted views were often held in the community and it was therefore very important for the school to get pupils to examine prejudices. "Out of ignorance, the worst side of human nature is bred", the teacher said, "and I don't accept the excuse that these youngsters don't know better. In fact I find that they are fairly open-minded". This teacher was convinced that the school should be more concerned about racial prejudice and felt frustrated by the attitudes and views of some colleagues.

7.   Another teacher pointed out the record of the one black boy at present attending the school – a very pleasant personality, outstanding in games and successful in his work. "Nobody takes any notice of his colour." This picture of success relating to one individual child was offered as evidence of good practice in the field of race relations in the school.

8.   This school had experience of Gypsy children. They came from a permanent site, described as tidy and well organised, and the families were employed by farmers in vegetable picking. The present generation of children is the first to enter the school system and they have not created much difficulty. Problems arose when a boy was old enough to do useful work and therefore unlikely to attend school. An arrangement was then made between the authority and the Gypsy community that the boy would be allowed to work in the fields although he would be retained on the school register and would be visited by a social worker. The parents had no formal education themselves, no knowledge of the school system and therefore no confidence in dealing with the school. The Gypsy children were described by a senior teacher as 'usually delightful'.

They enjoyed school as a social experience and were particularly at their ease with adults with whom they loved to chat. They had enjoyed particularly good relations with the school secretaries. The few who briefly aspired to other occupations abandoned them later and remained with their families in the field. The work ethic was strong in their make-up and they played no games; the mores of their community were firmly retained; they observed strict norms of sexual behaviour and had no dealings with non-Gypsy children of the opposite sex; they cared openly for each other, supporting one another strongly in adversity such as when they were called names by other children.

School A3

1.   This voluntary aided co-educational secondary school was situated in a large market town and was "all-white" with the exception of two Vietnamese, one Iranian, two half-Chinese and two half-Indian pupils who were, in the words of the headmaster "treated as pets". A Sikh teacher was held in high esteem by staff and pupils and was held up to pupils by colleagues as a symbol of his race.

2.   The Head of RE commented "Although we are a friendly staff and look after the ethnic minority children, we've never discussed the question of the multi-racial society". This was confirmed in writings of a fourth year class which were extraordinarily free from prejudice, were remarkably fair and often naive about racial questions – for example, "I think that when a black person is caught committing a crime, the police are more harsh on them than if it were a white person, police often pick up black people for no reason because they are just suspicious if that person is black. I think that there is not this trouble in this town because we have accepted to live with blacks instead of treating them as someone or something which is unlike us", and "Employers are slightly racial, they would rather give a white man a job behind a desk rather than a black man. Although blacks are just as intelligent, an employer seems to have more trust in a white person. A lot of black people seem to be unemployed and spend their time walking the streets, this could be a reason why they get a bad name. Housing – most ethnic minorities seem to live in one area of a town or city, and that area always seems to be a dirty place. I'm not sure if the blacks make it that way or if the local councils deliberately house the coloured people together in a bad area".

3.   Another fourth year pupil who had previously lived in a large urban centre had a more realistic awareness of the racial scene: "I don't feel that the West Indians, Asians, Greeks, Chinese get as good an education as the white people in this country, this in my view is very unfair. I lived in a city for a while. People who are colour prejudiced are just plain stupid. I mean we're all human, and coloured people have just as much right to make a success of their lives as white people. Therefore they should have an education equal to what white people have".

4.   To date, little thought had been given by the school to a multicultural approach to the curriculum although the Head felt that the "warm atmosphere" noticeable in the staff room might mean that the staff would now be ready to spend time discussing education for a multi-racial society. Classroom discussions exposed prejudiced views but some greater understanding is achieved by the playing of tape-recorded accounts of ethnic minorities who talk about their experiences of prejudice which has been directed against them.

School A4

1.   School A4, a large co-educational comprehensive school, was situated in what was once a market town but which now has engineering and food processing industries. It was described by a member of staff as an "an industrial town with a rural mentality" and "an industrialised village".

2.   Again, only limited thought had been given to the possibility of a multi-cultural approach to the curriculum. The Head of English lamented the tendency in English teaching to drift away from an emphasis on sociological English to one on technical language. He stressed that literature and its values were his department's concern. 'We in the English Department teach a liberal

concensus view'. He illustrated this from 'To Kill a Mocking Bird'. He referred to prejudice amongst some fourth year pupils and added 'The rest of the department and I loathe the National Front and I make my views clear to the kids'. He found a book entitled 'Invisible Man' about the negro's position in America, 'a vitriolic statement on racism' and the writings of the African Chinowa Achebe to make effective reading in the sixth form. The LEA's Agreed Syllabus in RE includes World Religions but the treatment is rather slight which has led one RE teacher to use the more extensive Birmingham Syllabus and to introduce five major world faiths. He believes that this region should not be allowed to separate itself from the rest of Britain. The ideas conveyed by other religions however appear very strange to his pupils who find it difficult to take them seriously and, since few attend any church, are disinclined to give RE much status.

3. The Drama teacher uses role play to encourage children to see other people's points of view or experiences of life. He sets theoretical situations removed from contemporary experience eg an unknown tribe in an Amazon jungle into which a parachutist descends; this is balanced with a small village community in a remote part of Britain at which a non-English speaking yachtsman is driven in for shelter. This teacher has not postulated racial problems for role play but agreed that they would be very suitable topics for the method the aim of which is to explore ideas, arrive at conclusions and discover principles.

4. One teacher at the school was a recent appointment having just completed a post-graduate Teaching Diploma course which included an Urban Studies option. This course included multicultural education but the options he chose with teaching practice in the region did not. The college, he said, had a firm policy of recruiting students from Africa and the Students' Union was keen to advance the welfare of overseas students; there were good race relations and this experience was helpful in preparing the attitudes of future teachers. He did not however see much value in privileged middle-class Africans teaching the children of immigrants in Britain. Perhaps their impact on the white school population might be more valuable.

5. The one black family represented in the school were said by the Head to 'have an interest value' and to be 'well received – the Chinese less so, but the staff will say there are no problems here'. There had clearly been very little experience of ethnic minority people in the community or at school. The Deputy Head mentioned an East African Asian family which had met with prejudice and unpleasantness and so left the area to live in another town. "A group of children here could be very unpleasant – there are clear undertones of the National Front" he said. News coverage of racial matters tended to inflame antagonism towards minorities.

6. A particularly interesting person at the school was a young Indian employed as a member of the non-teaching staff. His parents had come to England from the Punjab but he was born in London and had attended school there. He not only spoke English but Punjabi with a cockney accent! He had thoroughly enjoyed his time at school and had obtained three 'O' levels. He had developed confidence in himself and was therefore well accepted and had made white friends. "Groups of all Indians become targets for racialism", he said. "Some of my closest friends were racialist but fine with me. Some other Indians didn't like me for this, but others respected me for it". He had come to the town to visit friends and remained for a while and had then decided to take a job at the school. He felt he wanted to "drop out from the pace of London". When he first came to the town he was suspicious of everyone; people regarded him with curiosity and stared at him. At last to one woman who stood gaping at him at the entrance to a shop he asked, "Have you never seen a wog before"? When the woman had recovered her breath she spluttered in indignation, "Another Londoner come here causing trouble!" He said that the children at school were curious at first and had taken some time to make up their minds about him, but he now had no problems. His confidence and competence made him an impressive representative of his ethnic group; the value of his contribution to this school and the community far exceeded that of his role as a staff member.

7. The Head of History said, "In every class some children would pack all immigrants back home" and the Head of Humanities illustrated the irrelevant prejudice by reference to a

gratuitous answer written to an internal examination question about population in London. The fifth year pupil wrote: "The only real solution in London is to chuck out all non-British citizens and cut immigration drastically to reduce the risk of more street violence in years to come".

8.   The Head of English agreed that some of the classes were strongly prejudiced against ethnic minorities although a written exercise which I gave to a top set of fourth years revealed some good understanding. Of 26 pupils in this class, 12 showed a good appraisal of what had happened in the public disturbances in Brixton and elsewhere and were in the main sympathetic to ethnic minorities. Five expressed some antipathy and nine were neutral or uncertain (sometimes anxious) in their reactions. The following are examples of their writing:—

"These disturbances involved in the main black youths in conflict with the police. Their protest was that they were tired of the unjust treatment and racial discrimination they had received from the local police forces. Their resentment had been brewing for a long while, and their patience finally snapped over another incident of unfair treatment, which made it finally too much".

"There were occasional outbreaks of fighting between blacks and whites but mostly it was young black people rioting in order to try and make people see how they felt. They smashed cars, looting of shops took place and 'crowd fever', made the riots swell until finally special police forces were called in to stop the disturbances".

"These disturbances called to the public's attention the conditions in which many blacks had to live and the resentment which they felt as a result. Blacks were encouraged to air their views and community policing was introduced to try and get the police closer to the black community".

"I would hope that in the future all races and religions would be treated as equally as possible, and I would try to treat other races as the same as me. Although I would hope for this I would not really expect it.

People will always regard a different-coloured skin as different, and perhaps this is a good thing. Interest in other religions is good, but to be prejudiced against them is not".

"I believe that in the future racial minorities will become less unusual and as a result people will become more accepting of them. I do think that there will always be people who resent the presence of other races in Britain, but I hope this will become a smaller and smaller minority".

"In the future more of the black population will have been born here and so they will have greater knowledge and greater acceptance of the British way of life. If they receive equal education they will, hopefully, not be prejudiced against in jobs, and for young white people to grow up with, be educated with, and finally to work with blacks is the best way to teach them to accept each other".

"When coloured people applied for jobs they were probably often refused work just because of their colour. It didn't seem to make any difference how many qualifications the black youths had, they were almost always turned away in favour of white people".

"If I was working with black people it wouldn't make an awful lot of difference to me, as I wouldn't have anything to do with them anyway".

"Under no circumstances would I live next door to a black family. I would be worried sick in case one of my children went out with a coloured child. That would really embarrass me".

"I don't really like any foreigners at all, it is nothing personal about just coloured people".

"I would avoid any situation where I might have to be included in a racial community".

250

"I don't like the way of life of black people, they ought to keep their opinions to themselves".

"I wouldn't want to live in a mixed race. I'd rather be away from coloured people".

"The ethnic minorities would not accept British law and justice and they would not accept that the police represented this".

"If in the future I had to live within a multi-racial community, I wouldn't mind as long as they accept our laws and customs. If they got a job instead of me, as long as they were more qualified or better suited for the job, then I wouldn't complain. Different coloured people can get on, if they want to".

"At first I would be wary of black people and probably be a bit squeamish of touching them, but would probably get used to them, hoping that I didn't embarrass too many people by my embarrassment. I wouldn't treat them any different after I got used to them and would look for the people inside them not to judge them on what you hear about them. I would still be wary of a group of blacks together as some of them still think they are badly treated by the police and employers etc".

"I don't think that all blacks etc should be carted off back to their own countries as most of them are British and if we did that we would have to send any French, German and any other immigrants who weren't coloured as well. We imported them to do our dirty work, cheap labour so we're stuck with them".

9.   The local black sportsmen were popular heroes in the eyes of the young locally; they were seen in public and liked as indiiduals as well as fine sportsmen. One boy wrote: 'Although people like coloured sportsmen they still think other coloured people are troublemakers' and 'coloured sportsmen are treated kindly whereas others are treated harshly'.

LEA B

1.   In many ways the attitudes I encountered during my visits to schools in LEA B were similar to those encountered in LEA A. The same insularity of outlook was reflected in the schools; teachers were equally preoccupied with their curricula and little attention was paid to the need to prepare pupils for life in a multi-racial society. Indeed, the major difference was that there tended to be a rather more visible ethnic minority presence both within school and in the surrounding area and thus a more readily identifiable "target" for racist attitudes.

School B1

1.   This large infants school was an example of a resourceful, adaptable school in an area of growing population. The headteacher was supported wholeheartedly by a deeply caring and conscientious staff. In keeping with the general picture of great care and attention being devoted to the needs of all pupils there was evidence of the few ethnic minority children being given a warm welcome and favourable provision.

2.   The Head emphasised that the hidden curriculum fosters positive attitudes of tolerance and goodwill amongst all kinds and groups of people including the application of the Good Samaritan story to a foreigner "without having to underline it". The teaching staff included a former white African who had accepted the 'racial divide' without question but is now totally converted in her attitudes towards black people and expressed positive ideas about multicultural education. Teacher after teacher confidently expressed the conviction that no racial prejudice had been found from parents or children.

3.   Arrangements were made for a group of about ten of the most articulate older children to join me in the Head's room during the afternoon. they were confident and talkative and the

conversation flitted briefly from topic to topic. Suddenly one child described a holiday spent in Wales where she had seen some black children peeping at her out of a caravan. Asked whether she talked or played with them she answered, "Oh no. I didn't want to play with black children". Another little girl then blurted out "I don't like black people, only Sarah" (one of the group present). Other children spontaneously chimed in "Nor I". I narrated this incident to the Head afterwards and she was deeply shocked by the revelation. The Deputy Head, however admitted that she had had a similar experience with children in her class some months before. She had not however reported it to the Head.

School B2

1.   School B2 – a formal, strictly disciplined co-educational comprehensive school – had a largely all-white pupil population apart from a few West Indian, Asian, Iranian and Chinese pupils. Potential incidents between ethnic groups were, as far as possible, avoided. There was some concern that a group of Kenyan Asian girls had suffered from name calling and were unhappy. The Chinese children were reported to be experiencing difficulty with English and were felt to be "probably misinterpreted in their behaviour". The formality of the school, according to a senior member of staff made it easier for 'outsiders' – eg Asians – to get lost, to accept the system quietly and so to remain unnoticed and neglected. Collective worship was conducted as a distinct policy but no account was taken of faiths other than Christianity.

2.   A multicultural approach to the curriculum was not considered necessary. The Deputy Head, who had previously taught in a multi-racial school observed "there is little apparent need here for a multicultural curriculum so very little is being done". Great stress was however placed by the school on RE which is provided for all pupils using the agreed syllabus for the LEA which devoted substantial time to World faiths. According to one teacher, "other faiths are regarded with interest and are well received. It is the only subject in the school curriculum which deals with the cultivation of attitudes towards other cultures". Another teacher commented "Junior schools do little in RE. This school has to start from scratch. We have to deal with shocking ignorance about Christian teaching". Ethics is taught in the sixth form and this subject includes the discussion of Race. The general impression conveyed is that there is a strong feeling against discrimination. An exhibition on World Faiths was presented at one Parents' Evening and parents were impressed by what they saw (and smelt – they were drawn to it by the smell of incense).

3.   No concessions are made to other cultures in English teaching but it was pointed out that some standard text books contain references to coloured children. Some reading books raised occasional points about race, eg 'Hucklebury Finn'. The published aim of the English department was 'to help children towards awareness of self and others'. In the modern languages department all children study at least one foreign language for three years. Visits are arranged each year to several European countries and an exchange system is run between pupils at the school and those of a French school. The school was careful in pairing West Indian children with French children, ensuring that families knew about one another in advance. Generally, ethnic minority children did not wish to take part in the exchanges, but those who did enjoyed the experience and there were no serious problems. The Head of Department said "There is an antipathy to foreigners in this region; there is resistance about the children going abroad and families jib at receiving foreign children into their homes".

4.   All the teachers reported that the school had experienced racialist incidents when the National Front was depicted in the news. Several boys were punished and one was expelled. Asian girls in the school had been the objects of attacks. One teacher said "I've taken great pains to explain Pakistani girls' dress and behaviour as a part of their religion but they are still laughed at by the others". The Head of History had met prejudice amongst the upper school pupils who attended local football matches. There were also supporters who visited the grounds of other clubs where they obtained National Front "indoctrination". Racialist literature was handed out

252

locally. A senior member of staff said, "Kids have an inbuilt racial prejudice here", whilst, at the other end of the academic scale, the teacher in charge of the Special Unit expressed his worry about "agitators", because incidents were usually provoked. "Incidents here could easily arise – a few hot-heads shooting their mouth off and others following like sheep". He was worried that too much attention might be shown to ethnic minorities and that they might be given favoured treatment. "I must watch that I don't take the side of the ethnic minorities and be seen to favour the underdog".

5.   A class of mixed ability fourth year pupils was asked to write on some aspects of immigration into Britain – numbers, languages, religions, food, housing, jobs and the public disturbances. Their statements revealed appalling ignorance – for example, estimates of numbers ranged from six million to half the population of the country (five answers) and twenty million (three answers). Of the twenty pupils the writings of eight were antagonistic and some strongly racist, two were mildly sympathetic and ten were neutral, confining themselves to the factual statements which were asked for – (opinions were given gratuitously). Here are examples of pupil writings:—

- "We take everybody in because we're mugs. Also girls still have different rules to English girls like they can wear trousers because its against their religion to show their legs but if they are living over here and going to our schools they should obey our rules and treeted the same as us especially as some were born in Britain. I think they should speak English. A load of Pakis own shops round here more than English. If it's our country then we should come first. If it was the other way around they wouldn't do it for us. They also have a lot of our jobs they have such big families that probley why our unemployment is so high. I think it is silly to go rioting because nothing will be gave by the govement because their to soft".

- "I think that there are to many packys and all those foreigners in our country. I think if they were sent out we'de be alot better off and there would be alot more jobs about. The foreigners takes up our houses our jobs our food and sometimes our women. alot of them come from the more poorer countries, maybe if they got out and we got jobs we might be able to send some food and other supplies over because everybody would be better of then. You see these packys riding around in rolls royces and then you see a british family with no car and not being able to hardly afford there food for a week. In Brixton there was alot of riots and it was the coloured people who was doing this, they destroyed alot of things and which wernt even theres to destroy they belonged to the government (british) and british police. How comes our country is so well organized and how comes there country aint".

- "There are millions of immigrants from China pakistan that speak all different languages and I think if they come to this country they should try to speak the language. Alot of these people stay in the own community and speak the own language I think this should not be aloud. I think they should be chucked out".

- "At Brixton the blacks we rioting and should not do this because we let them in and if they do this they should be chucked out for making so many deaths".

- "I think that pakistanis should not be aloud to own shops because so many whites are out of jobs that alot of pakistanis owning all the shops along my way. (For good measure the writer repeated 'so they should all be chucked out' twice more.)"

In a sixth form discussion one black girl was noticeably articulate. Her mother, a white member of staff at the school, said that a number of the teachers at the school complained that she has too much to say. "She's never been naughty, but she questions everything. When she questions things she's described as cheeky". The injustice, she felt, could only be due to prejudice.

School B3

1.   This large co-educational comprehensive school, had a substantial group of Italian pupils many of whom were third generation 'immigrants', a small number of Indians and Pakistanis, some West Indians, and a few other ethnic minorities from Burma, Singapore, Europe and South America. As a group the Pakistanis were considered to be the only ones to give "trouble" and were blamed for "isolating themselves" by language, dress and religion. The Italians were considered to be well integrated and "belonged here" whilst the West Indians made an effort to integrate and were quite popular on account of their "good physique", ability in sport and "carefree attitude".

2.   In Religious Education some attention is given to Islam in the third year and Judaism in the fourth year. The Head of Department was not convinced that the course had much value since he felt that the pupils were incapable of understanding other people's faiths or points of view. For example, they laughed at Muslim rituals and even after being given a picture of Jews' suffering in Nazi Germany they still laughed at their religious practices. This teacher admitted he did nothing and knew nothing about other World Religions – "Islam and Juadism are important but I reserve judgement on the rest". The Head of English admitted that the department had no books by West Indian, Asian or other ethnic minority authors: "We make no nod towards other cultures".

3.   Questionnaires and other materials used with pupils to explore their knowledge of basic facts concerning immigration and the circumstances of ethnic minorities revealed a good deal of ignorance. The large majority of one group of fifth year girls (12 out of 16) thought that 'racial minority groups' (the term was explained) represented between 30% and 65% of the population in Britain. Two pupils omitted to answer and the remaining two gave 10% and 20%. In a class of fourth year pupils a substantial number gave 50% or a higher proportion to the same question. Questions on other related issues exposed similar gross ignorance and irrational and prejudiced views.

4.   The Head provided information about a mock General Election held at the school when the candidates, including a representative of the National Front, addressed the sixth form. In the voting which followed, the National Front candidate took third place and beat the Liberal. The Head expressed the opinion that the substantial vote for the NF was the result of two things – a. some of the students had taken holiday jobs working with Pakistani workers and had acquired some prejudice against them and b. that the vote was a gesture used deliberately as a reaction to the left-wing extremism displayed by some students. "It doesn't mean however that they wouldn't behave that way in certain circumstances", the Head added.

5.   A second year form was referred to as demonstrating serious racial prejudice against Pakistani girls and a tutor group was described by its teacher as 'strong recruits for the National Front'. Such manifestations of racism were attributed to the influences of parents and television on children "few of whom were able to think for themselves" while others were "herd-like". A History teacher included a short course on facts about race in his syllabus for a fifth year group and set questions on immigration. "The ignorance and prejudices which come out in this exercise were appalling"! he said. Another teacher told how a disussion about Race in one class which included a Pakistani boy because very pejorative in its reference to Pakistanis but treated the Pakistani boy in their midst as if he were not there.

6.   A group of sixth form students were brought together for discussion. Feelings of racial prejudice were admitted amongst the group and recognised as present in the school. One described it as 'hatred of black skins'. One reason for it they thought was the threat of large numbers of other ethnic groups: "If you're in a situation where you're outnumbered by blacks then you're wary." The notion that young children were not prejudiced was contradicted by one student's description of the situation in an infants school where her mother worked. "Some

children won't sit next to a black child because their mother objects." There was agreement that prejudice grew out of ignorance and that an understanding of other cultures should be taught from the infant stage when other religions should be included. The students considered that schools could do nothing about prejudice; it must be left to parents. Some thought it was the responsibility of the black person to make friends with others and get himself accepted. "What if he is shy"? was asked. "Tough luck"! was the unsympathetic answer. The group considered it was difficult to treat ethnic minorities in the same way as your own people and that teachers were disinclined to do so. If a black child was made to suffer, they believed it would be resented by the white children if the teacher tried to make it up to him. "If you were walking down the street with a black person in Southall or Birmingham" one student asked another, "how would you feel"? "I'd feel proud that I was showing I'm willing to be on the same level as them", she replied(!).

School B4

1. This medium sized co-educational comprehensive school offered interesting prospects for community involvement but these had not flourished. The Community Association had diminished in membership and activity so that there was "not even a handful of community commitment" at present. The Adult-Tutor said, "Community is a vague notion and abstract thinking is not a commodity found very much about here".

2. The school provides three years of RE for all pupils during which Judaism, Hinduism and Islam are studied. The Head of Department is confident that after three years pupils are beginning to have a better understanding of other people. Those who take certificate examinations include six world religions in their courses. Discussing the need for "example rather than exhortation" in adopting a positive stance against prejudice the Head of RE admitted that in teaching World Religions he realised that he was in danger of reinforcing the children's prejudices and so he decided to introduce work on prejudice. "Finding the ability to deal with prejudice in my own class came by self-examination. I had to look into myself and examine my own fears and prejudices such as against punks and then not to be afraid to use them but admit to pupils that I had them." He admitted "it is not an easy subject to deal with but that does not mean that it should be shelved or avoided".

3. One educational activity being successfully used in this school in the nurturing and changing of attitudes was Drama, – particularly in the form in which it was being developed by a recently trained Drama teacher ie based on role playing. An outline of a lesson observed will illustrate the method used and the effectiveness of the teaching strategy employed in the exploration and formulation of attitudes:

    i.   The teacher discusses with the class the aim of the lesson – to consider attitudes towards people in minority groups. What kind of groups?

        a.   Handicapped, for example in hearing (there's a deaf child in the class).

        b.   Coloured people suffer from other people's prejudice. A black boy says he experiences it and it's worse in school than in his home area.

        c.   Dirty people; a boy who is away from school is named. "He stinks and he has nits, which is why he's away." (The teacher explains that other children are very unkind to him.)

    ii.   The teacher prepared them for a rehearsal warning them not be personal and unkind to members of the class. Groups are asked to choose a scene in which someone is excluded.

    iii. Children go in to their usual groups, move into corners of the room, discuss, prepare their dialogue, rehearse gestures, actions, movements and set up their furniture.

iv. The teacher moves around the groups and discusses what each is going to do. (There is one black boy in one group and a half-caste girl in another.)

v. The groups are left to their own devices to continue their rehearsals.

vi. The class is called to order. One group is asked to come forward and the remainder . sit on the floor as the audience.
Scene 1. In a bus with driver/conductor (the deaf girl). The remainder enter the bus one at a time. The half-caste enters, no-one is willing to make way for her to sit next to them. She is insulted, the others using racist jargon.
Scene 2. Passengers get off the bus and stand in a group at the bus stop. The coloured girl asks a question but she is ignored. The group discuss immigrants in a derogatory way. Busily occupied they miss the bus they intended to catch.

vii. The teacher engages the cast in discussion. Whose idea was it? – the coloured girl's. Why was it chosen? It had happened to her.

Another group was called out and performed their theme which was set in a school playground. A group of boys see a black boy approaching. "Oh look a new kid – and he's black!" They form a group around him and taunt him feeling his hair and rubbing his skin; they look at their hands and rub them on their clothes accompanying the actions with noises of revulsion.
"What's your name? Chalkie?"
"What are you doing here?"
The baiting continues in this way until they are called into school.

The group returns for a discussion with the teacher. The black boy is asked does this happen to him. Sometimes. Today it was treated as a joke; when it happens does he find it funny? Not really. Does he meet with prejudice in his own class? Sometimes – and from the prefects who pick on him and won't allow him to do what others do.

During lunch time some senior members of the Drama Club attended a voluntary session of Drama. They acted out a scene in which two women approached a house gossiping about the daughter of the people they are about to call on. They knock, are admitted by their friend whose husband is in the room reading a paper. In conversation the visitors refer to the 'trouble' the hostess must be suffering: they refer to the daughter's relationship with a black man; the husband's attention is alerted. The visitors leave, the daughter enters and is challenged by her father; daughter admits relationship with black man and announces intention to marry him; father is furious and indulges in racist epithets which are refuted by the daughter. Mother does not contradict the racism but protects her daughter who is old enough to decide for herself. Scene ends with the daughter announcing she is leaving home and father accuses 'blacks' for breaking up his family.

Discussion: the group is asked for reactions to the scene and to an equivalent happening in their own family. They air usual problems about other people's opinions and actions, references to children of a mixed marriage. Asked whether one should try to prevent this happening or try to educate other people to accept or perhaps welcome mixed marriages the group all agreed to the latter. Referring to their own experience members of the group described how parents' attitudes in matters of race are absorbed unconsciously. All members express conviction that people are capable of a change in attitude from one of racism to one of tolerance. The group agreed with the teacher on the value of giving voice to questions of racism, acting them out and discussing them.

4. One teacher, putting forward his views on discussing racial prejudice with a class containing committed racists, described his approach thus: he starts as if no prejudice exists in the class. He continues until the first derogatory remark is made and then stops the lesson and explains the point further seeking to get a wider understanding and acceptance. He awaits a response. A

few are still likely to be sceptical and dismissive. He then concentrates on them and draws them out. At this stage he may set up a role-playing situation so that pupils can work out the issues involved and often themselves verbalize acceptable solutions. This often avoids unpleasant confrontation between pupils and teacher and sublimates the aggression in the problematic situation. The more the pupils are credited with maturity and rationality the more they are likely to achieve it. When they are away from the school setting they are more likely to attain mature behaviour.

5.   The Head of RE commented "Scratch the surface in this school and racial prejudices are there very strongly in some age groups". A group of intelligent and articulate fifth year pupils formed a discussion group under the chairmanship of an experienced teacher. The following were some of the contributions to the discussion about ethnic minorities and education:–

- To learn anything about them is to say they're different. It shouldn't be forced on us in RE. We don't want it; it's boring.
- It makes the gap wider.
- Why did they come here?
- There are such a few coloured people in this school we'd all be looking at them; they'd feel small.
- If they say they're British and live in England they should speak English and be British.
- We're not going to India are we?
- If a coloured family comes here they would keep themselves to themselves.
- They should not all live in one area but mix into the community.
- Because they are black they are discriminated against.
- If we accept them, they'll accept us.
- A German family which came to the village couldn't speak much English and they were not accepted.
- We are the majority and we're being horrible to them.
- What's it got to do with us? They must learn to survive.
- People are saying about a local shop. "It's taken over by Pakis so we won't use it."
- If they're different and don't speak English they must expect 'aggro'.
- We shouldn't let anybody come into the country without having a job to come to.
- Britain is overcrowded; immigration should be controlled.
- They bring all the family – aunts and uncles as well. It's too late now.
- We've got one black in our football team. We've got to go along with him.
- Send them back.
- We should have listened to Enoch Powell.
- They're living off the dole and social security; that's our money.
- Pakis get a house straight away, although there's a long waiting list.
- The older people here are racist, the younger are not.
- My grandmother hates blacks (others made similar statements).
- Whoever is new in this community must be very confident – go out and make friends.
- You never are accepted in a village if you're not an old family – even white families aren't accepted.
- (Speaking about one member of the group) She's against racism; it's built into her isn't it?
- If you went to live in a black community you'd be beaten up.
- I'm against blacks. I can't help it: my parents and grandparents are racist.
- If my parents say racist things I give them a mouthful.

257

(on the question of whether one of their black class members who was not invited to join the discussion should have been):

> – He would be the only black and feel awful.
> – If he's got all pent up he might want to get it out.
> – Do you know his religion? His language? No!
> – It's not important. We should accept him as he is.

The teacher concluded the discussion by asking the group how many were anti-racist. Three out of eleven, all girls, said they were.

6.   An unusual appointment at the school was that of a black African as a Head of Department. After a succession of teaching posts in England (some appointments, he explained, were due to his prowess in cricket and other games), he was made Head of Department at this school. He had been the victim of racist "attacks" of different kinds within the school. Racial expletives and cliches both spoken and written had been directed at him from time to time which upset him initially. Then he tried to ignore them, but they reached a degree which prompted him to tell the Head that if they were allowed to continue he would be obliged to be more outspoken. He found that the less articulate the pupils, the more racist they were in their behaviour. "When I take a low 'set' I have to narrow down the work I do to form-filling and similar routine exercises. The examining of ideas is not on – it would be at my peril. They are victims of propaganda slogans and cliches because they have not other sources – they don't read. They suffer from congenital racism; they have never examined it and are unaware of it." The teacher took great care to resist provocation and reassured himself that incidents were relatively few. "It would be unfair to label the whole institution." He found it more difficult to accept the unintentional racism of colleagues eg the man who greets him in a 'chummy' way: "Hello dere" a West Indian style greeting spoken in a West Indian accent. "I respond in the same accent and walk away leaving him to think out why?" Also he experienced a more sophisticated kind of racism outside school: "You don't speak English too badly." He found this more hurtful.

7.   Provision in the adult department consisted mainly of physical activities. There were day-time classes of adults, mainly women, held on the premises. There was little demand for "questions of the day" such as matters relating to the multi-racial society. A group of women attending an afternoon class in Yoga agreed to stay on and discuss some questions relating to ethnic minorities:

> – On the question of whether local children needed to be prepared for living in a multi-racial society one woman said her son, a former pupil at the school, had gone to live and work in an urban area. He lived next door to Asians and grumbled that they were untidy and he objected to the smell of curry cooking. He also worked with Asians and met a lot of them at other times. His mother commented, "If we don't like some of their ways they don't like our ways either. You have to learn to adjust. We have to tolerate them."
>
> – Another woman whose children were brought up in the village and educated at the local schools said her son and daughter had moved to a local town, the daughter at a college doing 'A' levels and her son at the university. He shared a room with five other students– and he was the only white person; for him this was a totally unfamiliar experience. He was happy and had asked his mother if he could bring them home. She had agreed.
>
> – Members of the group exchanged knowledge of situations in other towns, and also locally, where white people behaved in unkind ways towards ethnic minority neighbours, actions which included moving away. Some had the impression that in some urban areas "there are more coloured people than white. At night there are punch-ups". They concluded that "children are very sheltered here."

- One mother expressed concern about the influence of the TV programme "Grange Hill" in its episodes dealing with racism in school. "My junior aged children found ideas of racism strange and are perplexed by the programme."

- Another woman said, "Schools here don't see the need to question and discuss these matters, but they should". She herself helped with a children's art club in a junior school. The theme 'Indian' was presented to the children. My reaction was that it was not relevant to the children; but now I am beginning to reconsider it: perhaps we should use this theme and help the children about Indian culture."

- The group then went on to consider other positive ways in which children's understanding and appreciation of other cultures could be organised – even limited real experiences of seeing, meeting, hearing, talking to people from ethnic minorities might stimulate projects of work on various cultures.

- All the women were in favour of the appointment of ethnic minority teachers in all-white schools. One woman, however, referred to the report that when "the dark teacher of English came here, girls went home and cried becausee they couldn't understand him."

LEA C

1.   The five schools visited in this LEA had predominantly white pupil populations although they were situated in or near areas of substantial ethnic minority settlement. The local indigenous community had a long history of prejudice against many groups perceived to be 'outsiders' and it was perhaps not surprising therefore to discover evidence of widespread and firmly entrenched racist views amongst pupils. For the most part this racism remained just below the surface and seldom resulted in overt verbal or physical expression. Headteachers and other members of senior management were inclined to understate and even play down this potentially explosive situation.

2.   In the mid 1970s the Chief Education Office had issued a statement to all headteachers concerning 'Education for a Multi-racial Society'. In examining the situation in the Authority's schools this posed the question "Is there a factor of prejudice which affects our attitude towards the young immigrant?". This question was considered by a working party of teachers and community workers who conducted several seminars with fourth year students from local secondary schools. The sessions included a cross-cultural education simulation game which explored the nature of prejudice and a film which examined "commonly believed racist assumptions and solutions to prejudice and racism in modern Britain". One result was seen to be the "questioning of attitudes, even with groups where the majority of students were extremely prejudiced" and in some instances it was claimed that even from a position of extreme racism, there was some shift of attitude in the course of the session. The working party subsequently produced a race relations teaching pack to combat the racism which they felt to be present in schools. The material was used by the Head of Social Studies in one school (School C3 below) as the basis of a course for a fourth year form. At the end of the course a questionnaire was given to the pupils – the responses were illuminating. An analysis of the responses is given at Appendix A.

School C1

1.   This small infants school was an outstanding example of a school which represented family and community character to a marked degree and in a positive sense. When the LEA proposed closing the school because of low numbers, the parents organised themselves into an active pressure group and a public demonstration was staged in the town. The proposal to close the school was reversed. The young Deputy was appointed Headteacher and with several new appointments the school started a new stage of its history. The parents' pride in, and support for, the school was expressed by a group of mothers who were busily engaged in the Parents' Room making costumes for the Christmas nativity play and the school's pantomime. They expressed warm appreciation of the care devoted to the progress and welfare of their children. For them the school also expressed the identity and character of the immediate neighbourhood.

There were few ethnic minority families in the locality. Some of them were referred to as individuals: "I live opposite a West Indian family; the mother is the nicest person you could meet", and from another member of the group, "My son idolized a black boy – they were friends for three years."

2.   There were children attending the school from Indian, Pakistani, Bangladeshi, Turkish Cypriot and Anglo-Indian backgrounds. The English parents said they were prepared to accept ethnic minority children at school "as long as our children are not overpowered and as long as ours are not put aside". They admitted knowing very little about other cultures: "We have no chance to see how others carry on" except that "they tell you about what they cannot eat". It was considered worthy of comment that one member of the group's little boy had been interested in a flag of another nation and had asked her "What country is that, Mum?" because it had been drawn to his attention at school. The mothers were also interested in some Asian wedding clothes which had been shown at school. It was felt that at the age of the children in the school all ethnic groups were friendly with one another but that as they grew up they were influenced by the National Front. The mothers deplored the attacks on Asians which were a fact of life in the area, but, they concluded "They've got to live with it", and they pointed out it was sometimes a case of "blacks set on whites as well as whites set on blacks". They were convinced that there was blame on the side of the black population too. "You can't have a difference of opinion with them because they will say "You only say that because we're black", but if we have a difference with them we don't answer "You said that because we're white". They decided that "the trouble starts when there are too many blacks" and added that "the older people, who had immigrants pushed on to them so that they didn't grow up with them" were the people who did not accept ethnic minorities. These local residents complained that there was little provision for the leisure time of local youths so that they were left to their own devices and formed gangs which walked the streets. Unemployment amongst school-leavers exacerbated the problem. It was not surprising, under the circumstances, that fights broke out between black and white groups of youths. This, they insisted did not directly involve the National Front or the British Movement.

3.   The staff of this school had taken steps to avail themselves of the assistance offered by the National Association for Multi-racial Education. They thought a breakthrough was necessary in schools which were complacent because there were few racial problems. They were engaged in a course of in-service education during the lunch hour when they received visiting speakers on the teaching of English as a Second Language. They particularly appreciated the value of the school-based approach. The head commented,"The most valuable things come out in staff discussion after the speaker has left. Ideas can be incorporated into on-going work in the school. It takes a lot of confidence for a teacher to analyse and revise the content and method of her work. This is more likely to happen if teachers do it together as a staff."

4.   A black nurse accompanying the doctor who was conducting medical examinations at the school emphasized the importance of accepting people of different colour to oneself. "Children should be taught this at home", she said. 'It's wrong to leave it to the school." The nurse quoted an incident she saw on a bus and of which she approved. A young black child asked her mother whether she could go and sit in another seat with a white woman. "Yes, you do that", said the black mother, and released her child's hand. "That black mum had good commonsense", said the nurse, who explained that she was a West Indian, "but my child was born here and is British. I tell my child about back home as best I can but she must accept this country and its culture. I was showing her how to make some West Indian food, and she said, 'I'm not West Indian'." She felt that schools should help all children to know and understand one another's culture. She saw on her visits to schools that a little was being done – but not much. She trained as a nurse in a local Hospital where she experienced some racial prejudice but she insisted "I could stand up for myself even with the tutor. If you do, they say you've got a chip on your shoulder." On the whole she was pleased with the training she received, "I'd do the same again', she concluded.

5.   "Some of the ethnic minority parents attend everything we do", said the Head. "They are very appreciative and want to contribute. They talk about their expectations for the children,

which are different from other mothers' expectations." Members of staff had got to know the three Asian mothers and learnt that they spoke three languages which increased the teachers' appreciation of them. She explained how on one occasion these mothers orally translated into their language the story of the Three Bears. They and the staff all laughed together during this exercise and it broke down barriers between them. "The Asians are now convinced that we are now eager to hear and encourage the use of their languages." A discussion with them about the Royal Wedding led to one of the mothers bringing to school a photograph of her Sikh wedding. In this way the school makes use of opportunities to draw on other cultures, "and so teachers' minds must be constantly geared to the possibilities of bringing in other cultures", said the Head. "We're encouraging Asian mums to tell us about their foods and to produce some dishes". There was some awkwardness at parents' meetings because "there are only a few ethnic minority parents so they feel isolated." The Head therefore liaises between the Asian and White parents.

6.   A black student on a course for nursery nurses at a local college was doing a practice at the school. The course included reference to cultural factors in food and care of the hair but the study of language development did not include English as a second language. She and an 'Asian' student on the course were invited by a tutor, from time to time, to talk to the remainder of the class about their own cultures.

7.   In the staff room teachers expressed their conviction that the local community should learn about the cultures of ethnic minorities living amongst them. "It's an awful thing that people say if they want to live here they must live as we do" and agreed that "unless they understand that Asian culture is valued they won't recognise and accept it. Society is not stable. In time it will absorb parts of these cultures anyway and so we must help to speed up the process."

School C2
1.   At this medium sized primary school approximately 30% of the pupils were of ethnic minority origin – some third generation. The majority were "Asians" although there was a substantial group of West Indians and one family each of the Chinese, Greek and Maltese groups. Many families had a long history of residence in the neighbourhood. The school had the highest degree of multiple deprivation in the Authority: to low income, unemployment, poor communications, inadequate shopping and other social amenities, unstable family relationships, single parents, were added the problems of race relations. On the positive side the more established local families had a strong spirit of devotion to the neighbourhood and were very supportive of the school. The school occupied a central position in the life of the community and the Head was approached as "father confessor, fixer and miracle worker".

2.   The long established inhabitants were also racist. One father said to the head who had appealed to him for tolerance; "tolerance is a middle-class luxury. You don't have black people competing for your jobs." Yet the immediate locality is "reasonably free from organised racism". The National Front was strong in the neighbourhood and some parents with children in the school were members. White boys came to school with National Front leaflets. "The children ask about this and I give the other viewpoint but they slip back to square one." Children were chauvinistic and jingoistic about the Falklands War and wanted to join the forces.

3.   A black student on teaching practice at the school talked about the racial victimisation she had previously experienced at her own secondary school. "Boys called me 'Blackie' and 'Wog face' until I couldn't take any more and reacted: this got me into trouble. One of the teachers of History told us that black people were only interested in Reggae music and were not worth teaching History. He separated us from the white kids and didn't bother with us. We sat in the back of the class and messed about. Blacks didn't take History for exams – we dropped it." The student argued very strongly in favour of schools adopting a multicultural curriculum and especially the need to give an understanding to pupils, from as early a stage as possible, of other religions. She also stressed the need for more black nursery nurses and teachers.

4.   An infant teacher at the school claimed that the children saw themselves as white, eg a picture by a black child in a wall display in her classroom showed five children; they were all

white. The only departure from this would be if a black child nursed a sense of grievance. Most black children were as English as the next person. They had lost any other sense of their own culture. Most of the black children in the school were born locally and had adapted to the English way of life. A few had retained their traditions and customs and brought them to school. Diwali was celebrated in the nursery with the aid of an Asian mother. The Asian children felt happy and for the English children it was a novel experience. In the infants section there were some spontaneous activities as a follow-up to Diwali. This teacher held the view that it was a mistake in a school with comparatively few ethnic minorities "to draw attention to their colour we could do them an injustice. We are here to teach children, not to emphasize their differences." Even young children used the term "that chocolate over there". "It must come from the parents", said the teacher "it's they who need to be educated". Since there was such slight contact with parents it was idealistic to look in that direction for any solution to the problem. Asian women were withdrawn and behaved in a way which made it difficult for them to get to know others. They came to the school and met as a group to chat in the playground.

5.   The Indian woman doctor visiting the school stressed that Asian mothers tended to have large families so that the need to look after them and to clean the house left them with little time to learn English. The doctor recommended the use of Asian language teachers which would permit the use of their own language in the primary school as the medium of teaching non-English speaking Asian children. At later stages Asian languages should not be taught in schools because Asian children at older ages did not want their mother tongue. If they needed to be taught their languages, lessons should be confined to evenings or weekends. Parents would pay for luxuries for their children and so they should pay for language lessons. Other forms of Asian culture should not be encouraged either, eg the exclusion of pork and beef from their diet which was originated and was meaningful only in a hot country. They were "sentimental taboos without intellectual support". The doctor insisted that class differences existed in Britain and were desirable. Integration should take place at one's own intellectual, educational and social level "as water finds its own level". About racism she accepted that human beings had always had their likes and dislikes. There was hope for a solution to the worst forms of racism in ten or twenty years time. Nursery education was essential to achieve this, to provide "community grouping" from early years so that the " mix will blend." She was convinced that "we can't change the adult population"; we must concentrate on "sowing the seed". Meanwhile "we must accept and suffer".

6.   The teacher in the junior section with the most ethnic minority children in his class had found that other cultures were not being maintained to any great extent by the families. He tried to draw on contributions from the Asians for his multi-faith project but got very little from them. He recalled that his college of education gave little guidance in the teaching of ethnic minorities. In his teaching practice school there were non-English speaking Sikhs. He had no idea how to teach them English. The colleges, he said, have too much to do. He noticed that certain white children would be friends with black children in their own class but antagonistic towards those in another class. "There always has been racism and there always will be", he decided. The teacher's role was setting an example; if he showed interest in other cultures the children would become interested but he added "since Christian social values are the ones they're going to live under, they are the main ones we have to teach". The teacher of the fourth year class admitted that as the children passed up through the school their differences became more marked so that by the time they came to her they were very aware of race. "The white children do not see themselves as being one with the ethnic minorities in spite of a lot of talk by me and a lot of discussion. White kids think that Muslims and Hindus are a joke." Some of their parents had said "We don't want that sort of rubbish for our kids". They referred to African music and dance as "them Paki dances!" Even after explanation they remained implacable.

7.   Two welfare assistants on the staff had themselves attended the school as had their children and now their grandchildren. Their husbands had been dockers, had become redundant, moved to factories which had closed and in all had three times become redundant. They remembered

22 years ago the first black woman coming to the small closed community, married to a white man. She was well accepted. Then 17 years ago West Indian families started coming in. They and white families were being rehoused in the neighbourhood – "being dumped on us" and the older inhabitants didn't feel happy about it. The women said the biggest problems at school were between groups of Indians arguing amongst themselves in the playground. "The Jamaicans were more friendly than the Asians", they said. "It's probably because we can understand them more." The main reason for racist feelings is the fear that they are taking over others' homes. "We find that if we visit them they're thrilled. We called on one Asian family a couple of times and another Asian family became jealous: we had to be careful. Perhaps if we understood the differences between them it would be better. In the dining-room it worries us that the Indians don't eat enough. We've had the children crying because they can't get the food they like." These women were clearly eager to learn about other ethnic groups so that they could be more effective in their work. They said they had not heard of any suitable courses. The Head promised to bring up the question of a course for non-teaching staff at a Headteachers' meeting.

8.   An infant teacher who had taught for 12 years in her home area, a country district, applied for this post to gain experience and was surprised to be appointed to the job. It had taken her a year to adapt herself to the work. She found the children interesting and the work challenging and would not now return to an all-white rural area. She related an incident in which she had rebuked a Pakistani child. The father was furious and accused the school of prejudiced behaviour. After a discussion he ended by agreeing with the school and promising support. He explained "everywhere we are picked on and blamed because of our colour. I'm a black man in a white man's world". The teacher commented "that experience brought the situation of blacks home to me and it makes me very depressed".

9.   The Head drew attention to the serious problem of mixed marriages or liaisons in the community and the effect on the children of those relationships. There were several cases of seriously mal-adjusted children in school with very unstable and violent liaisons at home. The parents needed support but it was not available. They lacked cultural support from either a religious or the black or white community. There was no back-up agency. The Head felt strongly that these families had a special need and asked the question "Are they being by-passed by the authorities"?

School C3

1.   The Head of this large co-educational comprehensive school took a count of ethnic minority pupils (17% at the time) for the purpose of the Inquiry. "I don't particularly want to know", he said. "I must not discriminate between boys and girls, the able and less able or between ethnic minorities and between them and others. Perhaps I've been 'innocent' and 'naive' about this, but I don't know how many children in school have blue eyes and red hair. What regard do we have for the ethnic minorities in school? All they want to know at the end of the fifth year is whether they are employable. We drive on the left in this country and it's **not** too comfortable to accomodate the French. The ethnic minorities, too, have tensions; the more they adapt in school the more tension there is at home, eg the mothers are resistant to English as I found when I went to the door of a Pakistani home." He compared the relations between different ethnic groups with that of a marriage of two markedly different people; "one doesn't attempt to alter the other – both have to find a way to live together".

2.   Admission to the school was from an area with a number of small employers in light manufacturing and construction industries and where employment opportunities were some-what better than in other parts of the Authority.

3.   The Deputy Head had recently moved to the school after service in a girls' school which was predominantly black. She was acutely aware of an undercurrent of racial feeling although there were few instances of overt racism. Boys in the upper school were described as "National Front below the surface". The rest of the staff were also aware of this submerged racism but

found it difficult to deal with. She herself was careful not to upset teachers who might not wish to discriminate in favour of a minority. Staff were concerned, but confused, and didn't know how to go about it because they were afraid to offend the white majority. "How was one to root out prejudice"? she asked and quoted a LEA Adviser who had said that by the time a pupil was eleven years of age it was already too late – prejudice was too deeply rooted. The Deputy Head agreed that "unintentional racism in the staff certainly happened in this school because positive action was exremely difficult in a school of this kind." Abusive racist terms were sometimes used by the staff towards ethnic minority pupils in a jocular way, but she suspected that it was sometimes hurtful to them. Relations between staff and ethnic minority parents particulary "Asians" were difficult because of language and cultural barriers.

4. The English teachers in the school considered it their duty to provide a multicultural curriculum since it was a normal part of their work to contribute towards the development of a liberal outlook and a tolerant attitude towards people of other cultures. Although the school claimed that they were providing works by Asian and West Indian writers on the reading shelves for teachers and pupils to make use of, no effort however was made by a teacher to present information unless the question was raised by the class. Pupils rejected books about their own culture and a course offered on African and Indian studies was not taken up. Language problems were experienced by all ethnic groups so no separate provision was made.

5. Religious Education is a part of the core curriculum for three years. A broad approach is adopted throughout the syllabus starting with three different stories of Creation, and in the third year looking at Judaism, Islam, Hinduism, Sikhism, Buddhism and the various forms of Christianity seen on a world basis. Children contribute information about their own religions. Questions are raised and discussed in class concerning world issues of religions in the news.

6. The Head of Lower School believed that the organisation of first year pupils is conducive to the inculcation of sound attitudes. Classes of 30 pupils are split into teams of 15 and further sub-divided into groups of five pupils. The main purpose of the organisation is to launch a determined attack on an enormous problem of underachievement in reading. The pupils inter-relate closely with each other and with teachers in these units of different sizes for different stages of the work. Materials are designed and produced for the purpose by a group of teachers whose qualification is their sympathy for the aims and methods of the scheme, rather than their subject specialism. The emphasis is on a caring relationship and the use of discussion. The success of the organisation has determined its extension into the second year next session and will provide the structure for a Humanities Programme. The organisation, methods and content of this approach is seen by the leader of this team as eminently suitable for a multicultural curriculum and the cultivation of harmonious race relations.

7. In a discussion group, sixth formers were unanimous in recognising that Asians in the school and in the community were generally the objects of strong racial prejudice because their culture was so different but particularly because they were often heard speaking a different language. Local people were also ignorant of the Asian life style which resulted in their withdrawal into their own community. Even in the sixth form the Asians kept to themselves and formed their own clique. One girl in the group said she tried "to bring them in" but they didn't respond. West Indians generally mixed well with the white pupils in school. A West Indian member of the group expressed his belief that ethnic minority parents should be educated to become "British". He thought that if he had been brought up in an area like Brixton he would be a very different person. He hated black ghettoes but recognised that if blacks were more dispersed they would not have a strong voice. People said to him "I don't mind you but I hate Pakis; they stink! Asians do not stand up for themselves. Their temperament is too quiet. Yet when they learn to be more confident they are described as flash Pakis".

8.   A black business studies teacher at the school who was only involved with senior pupils also observed that Asians remained separate from others. They were "polite but not friendly" and she added "I'm surprised that they have not changed by now – still in a little group, not necessarily because they want to be but in response to other pupils. Not one of them has a white friend. There doesn't appear to be much reason. I can't say why – but with racism there is usually not a reason." She had previously worked as manageress in an employment agency where she came up against a great deal of prejudice in employers who discriminated against black people. Often she would make an appointment over the telephone for an employer to interview a West Indian school-leaver. The name would not indicate racial identity. On seeing the black applicant an appointment would not be made. Other applicants would be interviewed until a suitable white person came along and would be appointed. Some employers however openly told the agency they did not want black people. In her experience of employers, Japanese companies were the worst in this respect. Another disadvantage suffered by ethnic minority school-leavers was that if they did not have GCE English and Maths but gained other certificates in subjects such as CSE Home Economics or Social Studies, employers did not understand or accept them. She gave examples of companies who rejected CSE Grade One results out of 'blind ignorance, conservatism and inflexibility'. She emphasised that there was a great need for the education authorities to enlighten the business world about examinations in use.

9.   An Indian teacher spoke appreciatively of the support he received from the head and other staff. There had been occasional National Front signs and slogans directed at him, but otherwise he had experienced little trouble. He claimed that the children were respectful to him. His policy was never to interfere in racial problems amongst the pupils. That was the Head's responsibility. If an Asian pupil complained to him he would not listen. He confined himself to academic responsibilities but was conscious of the importance of his own example. He believed that Indian culture should be a part of the school curriculum in RE, History, Social Studies, Drama, Home Economics, Music, PE and Games. He considered however that other teachers on the staff seemed to have no understanding of the effect of the mono-cultural thinking and practices in the school which he felt led to the exclusion of Asians and to the underachievement of West Indians in school and in society.

10.   The only teacher who appeared to show any real understanding of the way in which other cultures could be embraced within a school curriculum was the peripatetic ESL teacher who was only present at the school on two half-days a week and was restricted to the teaching of nine pupils. She was convinced that the withdrawal of ethnic minority pupils was inadvisable in the face of prejudice against them. Ideally, she felt, the role of an ESL teacher should be as a support to the class teacher with an interest and concern for the progress of all pupils, but it would depend on collaboration from other staff. She found other teachers showed good will and concern for ethnic minority pupils but were extremely nervous about making any concessions towards "multi-culturalism" in the belief that it would provoke antagonism in the white children and not be welcomed by the ethnic minorities. The unanimous view amongst staff and pupils was that the Asians were "persona non grata" in the school and community, that they were disliked and discriminated against but that it was their own fault.

School C4

1.   The stated aim and objectives for this large co-educational comprehensive school, which had only 6% pupils of ethnic minority origin, included the following:-

–to combat both explicitly and implicitly the destructive force of racism;

–to relate the work of the school to the changing nature, needs and demands of society at large;

–to develop in pupils an awareness of the nature of that society.

As a consequence the curriculum of the school made direct reference to racism and, in the words of a senior member of staff "This is an aspect of the work of the school which is ripe for development". A Working Party was being set up to prepare a report to the LEA.

2. Racism is admitted by staff to be rife in the school but apart from in Social Studies there has never been a unified staff attempt to introduce a multicultural curriculum, (parents challenge even the little which is being done about Race in Social Studies). The two year syllabus for RE is circumspect and cosmetic stating in its preamble the aim "to encourage greater sensitivity to the needs of other people . . . and to show the religious basis of compassion", but making no direct reference to other religions. Perhaps the greatest danger of a half-hearted approach was expressed by a black teacher in this school who stressed the danger of pupils regarding this subject as one of low status and only for those not interested in academic subjects so that they switch off. Little money was spent on the subject. The Head of English is sympathetic to the aims of multicultural education but is too enmeshed in the basic difficulties of organising the department to give much time to it. He felt that some novels such as the 'Taste of Honey' were useful in the discussion of prejudice but only an indirect approach was practicable in the classroom.

3. There had been considerable vocal and literary support for the National Front in schools. Physical attacks on Asians ('Paki-bashing') was a "part of the local culture". Pupils therefore regard Pakistanis and Indians as "fair game". Older brothers of school pupils were active and committed members of the National Front. The British Movement used to recruit actively from school pupils but recently it had collapsed. Traditionally the parents and forebears of the children were dock-workers who tenaciously retained 'the ticket' (the right to a job handed down in the family) the concomitant of which was the repulse of everybody else, especially immigrants who were kept out or even literally driven away from the area which in character was like a parochial village. Within school there was a general lack of motivation – "What's the point of doing exams? My father's got a job for me" many would say. School attendance was poor and in the fifth year only about a half of the pupils were present at any time. 30 to 40 pupils were never seen but stayed at home for no particular reason but with the connivance of parents.

4. In the face of the predominant racism in the neighbourhood and therefore in the majority of pupils, the attitudes of the staff were said to fall into one of three positions: a. acceptance of the inevitable b. confrontation on the grounds of and by means of politics c. a reliance on forming good relations with pupils who expected confrontation from staff and who thereby "have the wind taken out of their sails". Any overt racist verbal or physical attacks were treated as violations of school discipline and punished accordingly. A teacher who said "It is essential to combat racism on the ground with kids and colleagues", asked the question "Will every member of staff have the courage to do it?" In such a situation the staff may not get support from the home. An incident was quoted by this teacher who had reproved a boy for racist behaviour in school. The teacher threatened to inform his father but the boy replied "Oh he says the same thing". The same teacher reported that the school employed two Asian teachers as permanent supply teaches. He felt that in a school with pupils for whom racism was 'second nature', Asian teachers should not be placed in the most vulnerable posts which implicitly had little status.

5. A staff Working Party was mainly absorbed with an approach to the problem through the Humanities. Their task was aggravated by the literary impoverishment and the reality of a huge remedial education requirement in the school. Of the present intake, 30% of the children had no reading score, 60% had lower reading ages than chronological ages, leaving only 10% of the children with reading ages equal to or higher than chronological age. One aim therefore was to relate a first year Integrated Studies Syllabus to the improvement of reading skills. Teachers involved in this programme did not criticise the feeder schools which they felt lacked parental support. Ethnic minority parents who had had a number of children at the school were on good

terms with staff and attended Report Evenings but did not join the PTA: special social relations between them and the staff were considered to be too difficult. Also indigenous parents would probably be too unfriendly.

School C5

1.   The catchment area of this medim sized co-educational comprehensive school consisted of a largely white population of labourers. Although situtated close to areas of intensive ethnic minority population, the school had less than 5% ethnic minority pupils, the majority West Indian. The Head described a "strong neighbourhood spirit. It is described as racist by the younger members of staff, but are they jumping at shadows?" he asked. He insisted that there was no racist behaviour in the school. In his view there should be a few ethnic minority children in each school so that 'adaptation' could more easily take place. (The concept in his mind is perhaps more accurately described as 'assimilation' since the 'adaptation' was expected from the ethnic minorities.) "As a school we have not taken much account of being in a multi-ethnic society. This is a neighbourhood school and we do not rub shoulders with other groups." A part of the answer he said was to "try to build up an accepting attitude of others" and he described the results on himself of travelling abroad on holiday to the Far East. He had discovered "how civilised other nationals are. Of course, the trouble comes when they haven't the same level as us of civilisation." He added, "It's a pity that God in his mercy chose to give some a different colour". The Head's aim had always been "to create a school which preserves the dignity and self-esteem of every individual in it". Referring to the pupils he said, "Behaviourwise the spectrum of ethnic minorities is not different from that of whites – just more volatile". The Head was described by several members of staff as 'charismatic' and by others as 'paternalistic'.

2.   The neighbourhood was referred to by the Deputy Head as a "village community which strongly defends its working class traditions and prejudices". He described some long-established black people who had married white wives and were now resentful of, and prejudiced against, more recent immigrants. They felt their status had been lowered by being classed with other immigrants. The resentment was now exacerbated by unemployment for which immigrants were blamed. Another disturbing feature was that because they could usually get jobs white pupils left school at 16. There was also evidence of animosity between Asians and West Indians who identified with whites and proved themselves in sport. Asians "suffered silently and didn't complain". When pupils were rebuked for racism in class, their parents had complained to the school. A white girl, who supported Asians in a discussion, was victimized by class mates and had to be transferred to another class. Thirty per cent of school entrants were described as having reading problems. "The area had become denuded of brighter families and their places taken by 'questionable' families and the community spirit weakened. Housing shortages had created the problem of immigrant multiple occupation", it was claimed.

3.   The Head of Religious Education is hopeful about its success on the basis of a new two-year syllabus dealing with a. Old Testament Stories and b. World Religions. This view was arrived at as a result of two experiences. The first was impressionistic following discussions with parents of some of the second year pupils when they attended a Parents' Evening. "The parent thought it was marvellous that their children went home and discussed the multi-faith lessons often relating what they had learnt to the content of TV News; the parents also said they had learnt from their children." (Not one of this group of pupils ever attended a place of worship.) The second source of evidence was an assessment of the two-year course by means of a questionnaire by which the teacher learned that the children had enjoyed the course and retained a substantial amount of information about a number of the religions studied.

4.   An attempt to deal with race and immigration on a third year course met with open hostility which continued through the course. The Head of Social Studies now avoids any open approach

to the subject. The school intention is to introduce it next year in Integrated Studies for first and second years. Open discussion of prejudice or the consideration of other cultures was felt to be impossible. Extracts from literature and poems are used which are "productive of tolerance" but even then there were some parental objections – "We don't want anything to do with inferior races . . . your books are against the white man". In the light of this, the English department is against any policy which "goes overboard".

5.   There was no staff policy on racist name-calling – eg the Head did not think the term 'Paki' to be defamatory. In fact a significant number of staff did not see "what all the fuss was about". The Head of Senior School insisted that he would not tolerate any overt demonstration of racism so that anyone who wore a National Front emblem would be sent home to change. There were one or two instances of this each term. He blamed television influence as 'pernicious' and following the coverage of the Brixton disorders, "the school had to tidy up the mess". The Head of Middle School was more complacent and expressed a great deal of satisfaction about his area of responsibility: the ethnic minority pupils got on well, there was no segregation of groups. Stress was placed on good pastoral arrangements in the third and fourth years by the organisation of pupils into half-classes under the care of one teacher who was expected to know a great deal about the children. "The organisation provides a caring institution" and this was important for the ethnic minorities, "so we don't have the problems other schools have". Staff often did not understand cultural differences but ethnic minority parents were given a chance to put their point of view and there were 'few confrontations' between staff and parents. Pupils were not expected to wear a school uniform and so were allowed to express their own personality. Also they were not excluded from the premises in out-of-class time, and this freedom was well accepted.

6.   The Head of Lower School stated "We are really concerned about multicultural education in a school like this". He was convinced by his experience in his last school that there was a large proportion of black pupils who had a feeling of being rejected all round. In this school there was a good staff, he said, who cared about the pupils and gave up some of their own time, eg to discuss pupil cases with the visiting psychologist.

7.   An Indian teacher stated that the children of the school were not willing to accept anyone of a difference race from theirs. He had a very difficult time at the beginning, but he persisted with firmness. "Whatever my colour", he said to the pupils, "I am here to teach you; you have to accept me as a teacher". The situation had changed very little. "Children still look at me as an alien who is not supposed to be here", he said. Recently a fifth year girl refused to do any work for him, "because you are a Paki", she announced. The Head excluded her from school. "I have to overcome the difficulty of teaching and also overcome racism." In his last school he had helped to organise a successful Asian evening in which Asian children were involved in various activities. "Here", he said, "It would be disastrous to attempt such an event".

8.   The Head of English confirmed that prejudice was overt and that racist cliches were regularly 'trotted out'. The policy of his department was to "treat all kids the same way". This was helped by the organisation of the school in mixed ability groups which was the way they were regarded in his department, and "not as mixed cultures". There was no arrangement for the teaching of English as a second language.

9.   The Head of Social Studies had come to the school from a school in a black area. On her arrival at this mainly white school she was greeted with Nazi signs and terms such as 'nigger lover' written on the blackboard. It was 'swept under the carpet' by senior management but she was aware of its 'threatening undercurrent'. In connection with her CSE course work, she had raised a question with a class about features of Asian culture and asked the class to do some research on Asian girls in Britain. The mother of a white girl complained, "Now she's doing this thing on Paki". She finds that posters and other visual materials depicting other cultures get defaced. Books receive similar treatment, especially when immigrants are referred to or visually represented as a separate group.

10. The Head of Integrated Studies referred to his use experimentally two years ago with a third year form of materials dealing with race. Whereas normally he would expect the class to be silent on racial matters, in connection with these materials, the white pupils reacted in strong racist terms. They were difficult to manage. As a result the other teachers on the Social Studies staff were frightened and the course was dropped. "I want to put a Race Pack in the library and my aim would be to use it as a part of school policy." He felt however that there was a reluctance in the Head and senior staff to expose the racial prejudice which was present in the school. Also each attempt he made to raise it in the Social Studies Department was met by an admission of fear and so his wishes had been impeded.

III Meetings with the LEAs

Meetings with the three LEAs were arranged in order that officers of the authorities could be informed of the findings of the study. The following notes record the main points raised at the meetings:–

LEA A

1. The report of the visits was discussed at a meeting with the Chief Education Officer and one of the Authority's senior inspectors. Both had some experience earlier in their careers of serving in multi-racial schools and areas and recognised the importance of all pupils in multi-racial Britain being prepared in thinking and in attitude to live in a community and a part of the country which may well be very different from the insular all-white community in which they now lived. Both nevertheless remained cautious about the way the subject of multicultural education was approached, particularly in relation to elected members, school governors, parents and teachers.

2. The Authority's adviser had been instrumental in arranging a regional course of in service education on the theme of "multicultural education in a predominantly indigenous residential area". A pilot project was expected to begin shortly.

3. The LEA had not so far provided any policy or guidance to schools on multicultural education but it was the intention to do so soon.

LEA B

1. A meeting with the Chief Education Officer and several senior colleagues was held to discuss the findings of the study. I told them in general terms about the nature of the findings – appalling ignorance about the facts concerning immigration and ethnic minorities, widespread racial prejudice amongst pupils, the failure of almost all teachers in these schools to adopt strategies or orient their curricula to counter the existence of prejudice or to cultivate in their pupils positive attitudes which will lead to racial harmony. I referred to the few exceptions I found usually in RE and Drama.

2. The officers felt that the appointment of suitable headteachers would be a catalyst in promoting the cause of multicultural education and the subject was now covered in depth in the interviews for headships.

3. It was clear however that although elected members were convinced of the need for, and accepted, the responsibility of providing a suitable multicultural education in multi-racial schools, it was doubtful whether they could be persuaded of the need for it in all white schools.

4. A policy statement on race relations had recently been issued to all schools – responses were awaited at the time of the meeting.

LEA C

1. A meeting with the Chief Education Officer and senior colleagues was held to discuss the findings of the survey. Although the Authority has experience of dealing with the educational

needs of ethnic minority children, the officers were unaware of the prevalent thinking on multicultural education in the mainly all white schools. The Authority's Chief Inspector and the Inspector detailed to have responsibility for multicultural education admitted that they had found little or no time to look into this question. Indeed, whereas a great deal had been and was still being done in providing in-service multicultural education for multi-racials schools (and much of it conducted within schools) the Authority had not applied itself to a consideration of the different needs of the mainly white schools. A full time multicultural adviser was due to take up post soon after the meeting and it was clear that this area would have some priority in his brief.

2. The Chief Education Officer referred to a policy statement on multi-cultural education which had been sent to all primary and secondary schools in 1982 together with a request to each school to formulate its own policy on multicultural education through staff discussions. The schools were asked to forward their statements to the LEA. The Director said that the responses had been very unsatisfactory and one all white Roman Catholic school had expressed indignation at being asked to consider a field which they considered irrelevant. Other schools had responded by asking for more help and guidance in drawing up a statement of their multicultural objectives – some of these showed how much schools were out of touch with current thinking in multicultural matters.

APPENDIX A

Questionnaire completed by a fourth year form at School C2 following the use of a race relations teaching pack.

1.   What was the effect of the British Empire on the economies of countries like Africa and India? Put GOOD or BAD, and give a reason for your answer.

Good	Bad	Don't know or unanswered
20%	12%	68%

Only one reason given: they helped out with jobs and cared for them eg India.

2.   In the last twenty years have more people left Britain, or come into Britain? Put MORE HAVE LEFT or MORE HAVE ENTERED.

Left	Entered	Don't know
80%	4%	16%

3.   Were black people encouraged to come to Britain after the last War? Put YES or NO.

Yes	No	Don't know
96%	4%	nil

4a.   When black people came to Britain after the War they got jobs which white people didn't want. Put YES or No.

Yes	No	Don't know
84%	8%	8%

4b.   Black people are more likely to get the worst kind of housing. YES or NO

Yes	No	Don't know
56%	28%	16%

4c.   Black people are more likely to be unemployed than white people. YES or NO

Yes	No	Don't know
52%	28%	20%

4d.   Are black people discriminated against by the Police? Put YES or NO.

Yes	No	Don't know
40%	28%	32%

5a.   Do you think black people are discriminated against in the fields of housing? Put YES or NO.

Yes	No	Don't know
52%	40%	8%

5b.   Jobs? Put YES or NO.

Yes	No	Don't know
32%	52%	16%

5c.   Education? Put YES or NO.

Yes	No	Don't know
32%	64%	4%

5d. 'A smaller percentage of black people get council houses than white working class people.'
YES or NO.

	Yes	No	Don't know
	60%	28%	12%

6.   Do you think many black people are coming to Britain in the 1980's? Put YES or NO.

	Yes	No	Don't know
	60%	24%	16%

7.   What are your own views about the question of black people and discrimination? Refer to any or all of the topics in Question 5.

Examples:

Critical: blacks are treated well considering they are immigrants.
(5 times)

they must conform to the British way of Life – not bring turbans (twice)

blacks are always complaining so if its better in their own country why dont they all go back there (twice)

I dont like blacks or Asians and even if Asians would all dress and look the same as us they would still be black.

Favourable: they are discriminated against because they are left out (twice)

some of my friends are coloured and I get on well with them

Neutral: some blacks are OK but certain black immigrants I don't like

I don't think in housing and education they are discriminated against – maybe in some areas they are

Ethnic minority responses: all blacks and Asians get discriminated against by whites – with bad housing, in jobs, picked on by whites in school, racial attacks and black teachers get abuse from older pupils;

it's not fair blacks get blamed for everything.

8.   What are the reasons for unemployment in this area in the 1980's.

Responses:

there are not enough jobs to go round because too many blacks have come to our country.

All other answers give economic or other non-racial reasons.

9.   What are the reasons for a shortage of housing, and poor housing in this area in the 1980's?

Examples:

there are too many Pakistanis who take government's money in Social Services so there is not enough for housing (twice)

black people have taken them over (3 times)

All other answers given are neutral.

10.   Why has this area a history of prejudice towards immigrant groups? (The Jews, the Irish). Why were Mosley and the Blackshirts active before the last War?

This area is prejudiced because blacks have slowly pushed white people out.

People believe that blacks shouldn't live in Britain.

272

Teenagers are fed up of them trying to take over the country (3 a load of slum areas (twice).

People believe the country should be white and want it for themselves.

Remainder: dont know or unanswered.

11. Do you think white working class people have problems in common with black people?

Yes	No	Don't know
50%	20%	24%

Example:

Yes, because white people are finding it hard to get jobs and black people have got jobs.

12. What can be done to solve these problems?

Unfavourable:

send all the black people back (5 times).

sack the black people and give jobs to the whites (3 times).

Favourable:

the whole population has to become more friendly

try to find out the truth and trust other people.

Remainder:

dont know or unanswered.

13. Why do you think some white young people join groups like the NF or the British Movement?

Examples:

Support of National Front: to get the blacks out (3 times)

they hate blacks and try to get them out

because they hate blacks as much as we do (twice)

Neutral: they want to look 'hard' in front of their friends

because their parents drum it into them that blacks and Pakis ruin Britain

Ethnic minorities: because they're against us

they think we are taking over their country.

14. Do you think groups like the NF or British Movement should be banned? Put YES or No, give your reasons.

Yes	No	Don't know
56%	20%	24%

Examples:

Support NF and BM: because I'm fed up with black people as much as they are

they are trying to help their country solve its problems (twice)

they are truly English.

273

Opposed to NF and BM: because they start trouble (3 times)

because black people haven't done anything to them so why go around bullying them?

Neutral: they have the same rights as political parties (4 times)

Ethnic minorities: yes, there wouldn't be as many riots

they can't do much just trying to scare us out of the country.

15. What is your opinion of these groups?

Examples:

Support of NF: they're all right it's a British country

groups like this I think are good but I only think that because I dont like blacks. It you are black or you like blacks you would think these groups are sick.

Opposed to NF: I think these groups are terrible

I think they should be banned

Neutral: it's up to them what they do but I wouldn't join them.

16. What would have made the course more interesting?

Examples:

get Asians' and blacks points of view (twice)

more discussions and asking the blacks what they think of whites

have coloured persons to come in and speak on their views.

17. Why do you think the teacher asked you to follow this course?

Example:

to brain-wash us.

The remainder show a general awareness of the need to inform, to help relations, to obtain views about race.

Additional questions.

1. What do you think are the results of racial prejudice in this area?

Examples:

there is misery and a wider gap in understanding each other

there is hatred between black and white and the police, anger and fights and bad housing for blacks and Asians

there are attacks and killings on blacks and Asians and are getting worse

hatred between blacks and whites.

Reminder:

unanswered.

2. Have you learnt anything you did not know before from the course? YES or NO. If yes give an example.

Yes	No	Undecided
40%	16%	44%

Changed:

> Now beginning to understand them more
>
> understand better black person's view but there is not difference between them and us
>
> found out the truth about coloureds and how they really live
>
> I know now they dont take our jobs and houses

Unchanged:

> no it was a waste of time; we should have sent the Pakis back
>
> no I know my own opinion and will not change my mind
>
> no I know what I know and will not change my mind
>
> I have learnt a lot from the course but still my mind is not changed.

Ethnic minorities:

> not much just that we are not the cause of the problems
>
> that we Asians are not the only ones attacked.

3. Have your own views about racial prejudice changed in any way during the course? YES or NO. If yes give an example. If no give your reasons.

Yes	No	Undecided
32%	40%	28%

Examples:

> Unchanged: no but not prejudiced against blacks only against Asians because the country stinks of curry
>
> no but I dont know why
>
> no not in any way at all but many of the things I thought they were the cause of have now gone

> Changed: I've realised they've got feelings like us and had a hard time in this city
>
> they dont take our jobs and dont do the muggings
>
> blacks are not to blame for the situation in our country now I understand them.

4. Have you found this course intresting? YES or NO or PART OF IT.

Yes	No	Part of it
36%	4%	60%

Gratuitous comments

> teacher gave us ideas that blacks are nice but when I gave my own opinion I was called 'big mouth'.
>
> I found it interesting but when I gave my views I was called sick so I kept my thoughts to myself.
>
> the sessions did drag on as I dont like speaking in front of class.

5. Which parts of the course did you find most interesting? Give examples.

Examples:

> no it was not interesting because blacks just cause trouble and that's it
>
> it was interesting that the teacher said that he liked multi-colour culture (twice)
>
> several elements in the course were mentioned.

6.   Which part of the course did you find least interesting? Give examples.

Several items in the course were mentioned eg housing, because I'm not interested in their housing problems; they can fend for themselves. TV films – I did not believe what they were saying. What was coming out of it was rubbish.

7.   Do you think a course like this should be taught to other classes in the school. YES or NO. Give reasons.

Yes	No	Undecided
56%	20%	24%

Examples:

Positive: because it may change the views of people therefore creating better relationships

because they will know what to expect when they get older

because most people do not know the facts about race and cultures

because we took blacks the wrong way so others should know.

Negative: We should be given more freedom in our views because teachers tried too much to make us not prejudiced

most of it was not true

they'd feel as we felt about it – we didn't agree

teacher telling you what to believe and not taking any notice of what we think.

8.   Is there anything you think should be included in a course like this? YES or NO. If yes give an example.

Examples:

marriages of different cultures (5 times)

teachers should let us have our say for once instead of not taking a blind bit of notice.

9.   Is there anything you think should not have been included in the course? Give examples and reasons if necessary.

Examples:

to say that blacks get bad housing is wrong; if they want nice housing they should work for it; they can find jobs if they look really hard; with money from the NHSS and Social Security they should easily be able to afford their own house; if they dont like poor housing they should go back home.

Hitler was boring (twice).

Other items in the course were mentioned.

ANNEX D

A Report of Visits to Schools With Few or No Ethnic Minority Pupils by Laurie Fallows (Formerly County Adviser, Lancashire County Council)

1.   The project set out to ascertain the extent to which a small sample of schools with few or no ethnic minority pupils were responding to the need to prepare all pupils for life in multi-racial Britain. Consideration was to be given to the appropriateness of curriculum content, its presentation and the attitudes conveyed by teachers, text books, visual and auditory aids. It was also hoped to assess among the local community, the pupils and teachers, the nature, degree and origins of prejudice, and to identify reinforcing or modifying agencies.

2.   During the winter of 1982/83 thirteen schools situated in three LEAs were visited. All three LEAs were County Councils; LEAs X and Z were largely rural authorities with few if any ethnic minority children whilst LEA Y had more mixed areas and some ethnic minority children in a number of schools. The schools were chosen from a short list provided by each of the LEAs and were selected to be representative of the full 5-18 age range and to include both county and voluntary schools. The wide range covered by the variety of types of school enabled impressions to be gathered on the earlier stages of prejudice and discrimination and their subsequent reinforcement or modification by natural or contrived processes over a considerable age span. Two full days were spent in each secondary school and one full day in each primary school.

3.   On completion of the visits, arrangements were made to acquaint the LEAs concerned with the findings and to discuss with them the wider issues of multi-cultural education. Notes of these meetings are attached as an appendix to this report.

4.   The notes which follow are not intended to portray a complete picture of the schools visited neither do they seek to pass judgement on them or their respective staffs. Indeed tribute must be paid to all of the Headteachers, teachers, pupils, governors and ancillary workers whom I met for their willingness to discuss their work.

School X1

1.   School X1 is a medium sized infants school in a market town., It is organised into a Reception Unit, and two parallel vertical groups operating in linked units. As a training unit for NNEB students the staff is augmented by at least one other adult. It receives senior pupils from a local secondary school on work experience programmes, and has a regular rota of parental assistance. The adult community of the school is almost exclusively female. The school is situated in a large post-war housing development, but draws its pupils from beyond the town boundaries, including a large over-wintering caravan site for Travellers and Gypsies. There are seven Travellers' children currently on roll. Some will remain over the winter months, but others may leave at short notice. The school has been adopted by the non-Catholic Travellers as "their" school, to which the children are brought by private transport.

2.   The Head's stated philosophy includes: "Within all our work we try to help children to develop a good self-image, to be considerate and caring in their relationships, to grow in self-awareness, to develop an awareness of the needs of others, to be happy in school and contribute to its well-being in so far as they can". These objectives are fully in concord with the principles of multi-cultural education, and it is probably not unfair to say that in part they reflect a response to the special needs of minority group children, Travellers and handicapped, within the school community, into which the Head and other teachers have been involved in extensive study.

277

3.   The curriculum follows traditional lines, but it is noteworthy that in recently changing the reading syllabus, the staff had sought a basic scheme that would help to "broaden the children's horizons." They settled for "Reading 360" (Ginn) that introduced naturally children and adults of other ethnic groups. Some of their back-up readers extend this experience, and the "Terraced House Books" series (Methuen) in which the text are illustrated by colour photographs, often of ethnic minority people living and working in this country, indirectly stress the similarities rather than the differences among them. Nevertheless, the majority of the other reading and library books reflect traditional Anglo-centric values and attitudes.

4.   During the visit the older pupils were seen rehearsing the school's annual Nativity Play. Most knew that it was set in Bethlehem, but had little realisation of where that was. The general impression seemed to be that it was probably somewhere in the South of England. On the surface it appeared that an opportunity to introduce its multicultural aspects had been neglected, but this might also be alleged of its religious significance. The part of Joseph was played by a lively, out-going boy from the Travellers' winter settlement and it was clear that the other children displayed no unhealthy emotions towards him. Another, more withdrawn, Travelling pupil, told me that his only real friend was another Traveller, and that sometimes the others called him names – "Fat Harry" (he was quite slim). The impression gained was that this was a reaction to this child's somewhat serious and withdrawn personality, possibly inculcated by an unsettled nomadic existence often in more hostile environments, rather than a response to the Travelling children in general.

5.   The Head referred to their secure, close-knit social background and averred that as a relatively settled community the Travellers suffered much less from prejudice and discrimination locally than in other places. Because of the relationships built up over twelve years, the Traveller parents were less prejudiced and suspicious towards the teachers. They showed a genuine interest in the school, supported its activities, and ensured that their children were clean, well-dressed, well-spoken and respectful at all times. Easy, friendly relationships had been established between the local and the travelling mothers, and also between their children, although these friendships were apparently limited to school hours. The local children exhibited no hostility towards the Travelling children, each of whom was accepted on a purely personal basis. Sensitive enquiries failed to reveal negative stereotypes on either side. This applied equally to ethnic minorities, although it was apparent that their knowledge of them was very limited.

6.   I took with me some Indian infant school story books written in English, and read stories to small groups of children, showing them the illustrations as the stories developed. Subsequent questioning revealed that they were virtually oblivious of the fact that the names, clothing and scenes were unmistakably Indian. It was the characters and their reactions to universal situations with which the children readily identified that held their attention, illustrating that at this virtually "colour blind" stage they were perceiving similarities, not differences.

7.   The teachers' attitudes towards minority children had been modified over a four-year period when they had had within the school a pupil suffering from terminal cystic fibrosis. They had been greatly exercised in ensuring that the other children, and they themselves, developed positive and helpful attitudes not only to him, but to others who were different from or less fortunate than themselves. I was able to talk to this child's mother, a helper in the school, who spoke feelingly about the hurtful comments of one or two children that had tended to undermine her son's self-image and self-confidence, and the distressing irrational attitudes of some adults towards herself because of his illness.

8.   All the teachers were currently attending in-service courses on different aspects of education. Several had followed courses on handicapped pupils and Travelling children. Course attendance generally reflected a personal concern with practical aspects of their everyday work, into which the concept of multi-racial education had not yet directly entered. Like many other teachers in

278

all-white areas their preoccupation with immediate problems or difficulties appeared to minimise the relevance to them of the principles of multicultural education. Two of the young teachers had received their initial training at colleges in which multicultural education was offered as an option which neither had taken up. Nevertheless they had both undertaken teaching practices in multi-racial schools and their attitudes appeared to be more sympathetic to multicultural principles than some other teachers'.

9. The overall impression of the school was one of a warm, friendly caring community with a conscientious staff dedicated to the social, emotional and educational development of all its pupils, respecting individual differences, fostering positive self-images and inculcating an awareness of the needs of others and positive responses towards them. Racial and cultural stereotypes, prejudice and discrimination are absent from the experience of its pupils, and the school's general philosophy, sense of direction and aura would seem to safeguard their exclusion. Its only deficiency would appear to rest in its failure to portray realistically and accurately, especially in its reading material, its visuals and curriculum content, the multicultural complexity of modern society.

School X2

1. School X2, a large co-educational comprehensive school formed recently by the amalgamation of two single sex secondary modern schools, is situated in a former textile manufacturing town where poverty and deprivation are almost unknown. The working people seldom leave the area, and the conservative "locals", do not easily accept "off-comers." This tends to isolate the teachers socially from the majority of parents. There are virtually no ethnic or foreign national-minorities and, I was informed, stereotypes, prejudice, and even racist attitudes are inherent, especially among the lower socio-economic groups.

2. Few of the teachers are local and several have taught in multi-racial schools or in multi-racial areas. Predictably, their major pre-occupation focusses on creating and developing a dynamic, supportive and caring ethos and learning environment in which to promote the effective academic, intellectual, personal and social development of their pupils. They see this as necessitating a concentration, in the first instance, on the perceived, immediate needs of the pupils and the expectations of the local community, limited though these may be. Considerations like multicultural education are seen as probably important but not immediately germane to the present situation.

3. The curriculum is based on an amalgam of those of the previous schools with additions to cater for the more able pupils, and is under constant review and modification. A number of Department Heads assured me that when future curriculum change was implemented they would endeavour to embrace the principles of multicultural education. They were prepared to accept change from that direction, and some went further to suggest that a national statement (not a directive) on multicultural education from the DES would be welcomed.

Religious Education
4. This subject aims to help pupils recognise and develop personal attitudes, and consider some of the deeper aspects of human experience. For third year pupils it concentrates on comparative religion and involves study of world religions other than Christianity, but in particular Buddhism, Islam, Hinduism and Sikhism. These religions and Judaism are also introduced in the first and second year syllabuses. The staff conceded the indifference of all pupils beyond the first year to the study of religion, whether Christianity or other faiths. The pupils, mostly lacking in faith themselves and without the benefit of family or community

279

religious commitment and tradition, fail to see its relevance either now or in their future lives. Their most positive response is to the study of the lives of religious heroes and martyrs that include Mother Theresa, Martin Luther King and Dietrich Bonnhoeffer. It became apparent that in the main the syllabus related more to the history and philosophy of religions, rather than to their practice and traditions, aspects in which older pupils expressed keen interest.

5. It may, or may not, be significant that none of the RE teachers had ever been visited by, or even met, a specialist RE adviser or HMI. Two of the three had not even received the benefit of a study of comparative religions in their initial training. That RE teachers in this school are totally dependent on their own initiatives and enthusiasm to develop their professional skills and their syllabuses in what must be recognised as a dramatically changing situation is to be greatly deplored and reflects badly on initial and in-service education, and on their LEA's advisory service.

English
6. The Head of English fully accepts the importance of the principles of multicultural education but concedes that they feature only incidentally, if at all, in current English syllabuses. Further, he places them at low priority bearing in mind a primary commitment to building up a strong Department, and a personal conviction that since the majority of pupils will never leave their immediate mono-cultural environment, developing positive attitudes towards ethnic or cultural minorities is irrelevant to their needs.

7. While unable or unwilling to initiate curriculum change within his subject area, he nevertheless acknowledges that change is occurring, largely in multicultural schools and areas, and would happily follow a national lead, particularly if this was implemented through external examination syllabuses. In discussing examination prescribed or suggested literary texts he emphasised the great popularity of such works as "To Kill a Mocking Bird", "Kes", "Cider with Rosie" and "Spring and Port Wine", and the utter rejection of others, of which "Pygmalion" stood out. "To Kill a Mocking Bird" had provided a vehicle for open discussion of some racial issues, and it was interesting to learn that after heart-searching discussion the word "Wogs" and other derogatory racial innuendoes had been expunged from a school performance of "Zigger Zagger". On accent and dialect he had noted that while pupils had commented in scornful amusement at West Indian dialects, they were equally, if not more scornful of, other English regional dialects.

8. Although the school has a very well-stocked Library, it contains very few books about ethnic minorities, and those reflected a dated Anglo-centric view. Many of the books about other countries suffer from a similar stance and over-simplification, very often in terms of want, under-development, and other negative features. The librarian confessed she had never considered the need for the library to reflect the multi-racial constitution of contemporary British society, nor had anyone suggested such a need.

History
9. A traditional approach was the basis of the curriculum, starting with a study of ancient Western civilisation and following a largely chronological development interspersed with wide-range "patch" topics and drawing on a wealth of local historial associations. The fourth and fifth year pupils followed predictable CSE and GCE 'O' level courses in English and European history, but notable exceptions were a CSE course in 20th-Century World History and a joint 16+ GCE/CSE course where the school had opted for a study of Communist China. It was surprising that in a major subject inspection by LEA advisers last year, no mention had been made about multi-racial considerations, and no observations passed about a very Anglo-centric third year study of the British Empire. The Head of Department confessed that he had never thought about the implications of such an approach, and was visibly disturbed about its possible impact on the pupils in the development of their attitudes. Following the inspection, the school had introduced into the third year syllabus a short study of Parliament and democracy, and in this context it was possible if only superficially, to refer to policies on immigration, race relations and kindred issues.

Geography

10. Only a brief discussion was possible with one member of the Department. She claimed that the Department followed courses that, in looking at other countries, endeavoured to depict a balanced view. Nevertheless, it appeared that in considering primarily the economies of the "third world" countries, the overall impression conveyed to pupils might be one of total under-development and deprivation.

11. It is perhaps appropriate at this juncture to record that the school had links with the United Nations Association, of which the Head is local Secretary, the Council for Education in World Citizenship, UNICEF and other charitable organisations that, in order to evoke an emotional, fund-raising response, depict a one-sided aspect of other nations and cultures thereby establishing and reinforcing negative stereotypes. Several of the teachers I spoke to were aware of the potential dangers of a proliferation of such propaganda.

Sixth Form

12. The school maintains an open sixth form divided fairly evenly between 'O' level re-sits or up-gradings, first year 'A' level and second-year 'A' level groups (for which there is a surprisingly wide choice of subjects). Bearing in mind the secondary modern origins, this is not an academic or balanced sixth form.

13. I had the opportunity of conducting a seminar for the Upper Sixth and posed the question: "Has your school education adequately equipped you for adult life?" The quality of discussion was high, and the easy dialogue between boys and girls who up to three years ago were completely segregated, was impressive. The discussion was of necessity discursive, but certain of the pupils' concerns came quickly to the fore. These included a strong feeling that their religious education had been boring and irrelevant. It emerged that had it embraced a consideration of life's great issues and a review of the ways in which different world religions approached them, and study of the practice of other religions, including the many different Christian Sects however extreme, they would have been much happier to accept its compulsory status. The impression was strongly received that they were interested in the beliefs and religious observances of ethnic minority groups in this country as part of a process of understanding and accepting them into a plural society.

14. A very interesting discussion arose from the comment of one perceptive pupil who complained that in 'A' level courses, especially history, she had had to revise the attitudes and values, even some of the facts, that had been implanted throughout the preceding five years in courses leading up to 'O' level. In effect, although they were unable to articulate the fact, it emerged that a narrow Anglo-centric view of the world and its history had been presented to them through text books, teachers and examination courses which they had accepted unquestioningly. Only now, when they were being encouraged to question and challenge all statements and attitudes, had they come to realise that they had been indoctrinated with an outdated, insular, often indefensible set of values and attitudes. That they had been forced to reject many of these values and attitudes implied, if not a rejection, as least a suspicion of all they had been taught. What disturbed them most of all was the thought that while they, representing less than 10 per cent of the year group were in the fortunate position of being able to modify implanted attitudes and values, more than 90 per cent had left school believing implicitly in them, and with little incentive or opportunity to have their opinions altered. A further bone of contention was the fact that they felt that education had denied them access to political ideas, and that they would probably leave school politically illiterate and comparatively easy prey to the first political pressure group that confronted them.

15. The discussion was led towards a consideration of the ethnic minorities in this country, and the general feeling towards them was one of sympathy for their disadvantages and a strong

desire to know more about them, their cultures and traditions in the hope of establishing a mutually-tolerant plural society. They all expected to meet members of ethnic minority groups, and felt that knowledge would help them to forge sound relationships.

Ethnic Minority Pupils

16.   I was able to talk briefly to four ethnic minority pupils, from Africa, Pakistan, Hong Kong and the Caribbean. On the whole they felt they were not discriminated against in any way, although the Carribbean boy admitted that very rarely he had had remarks about his dark colour, to which he had retorted with comments about the physical attributes of his revilers, which effectively terminated the encounters. He seemed quite amused by it. The African girl, a six foot tall, seventeen-year-old, had been the recipient of a number of hurtful remarks, but these had all been about her height, not her colour. They all stressed how happy they were in the school and with their total acceptance by their peers. The second Deputy Head of the school informed me that one of the white pupils had been beaten up, on a visit to a multiracial area, by a small gang of coloured youths. His reaction had been that the colour was coincidental, and that he might equally have received the same treatment from white youths. The experience had not appeared to evoke in him any form of racial reaction.

Conclusion

17.   The over-riding general impression was one of a recently-created organism struggling for survival and recognition, and that until these had been assured in terms of artificial criteria imposed by an insular, cautious community unconvinced as yet of the need for any change, causes such as multicultural education had little hope of recognition save by the initiatives and commitment of dedicated, individual teachers.

School X3

1.   This medium sized co-educational comprehensive school is situated in a small market town, the economy of which is closely linked with agriculture and associated services. Although most of the teachers move into the area from distant parts, it appears that they quickly adopt the local life-style and attitudes, and accept as normal the restricted horizons. Unemployment is well below the national average and most of the school leavers find work locally.

2.   The intake year (11+) is broad-banded into 3 parallel upper-ability forms and 2 lower, and operates as a self-contained community in a unit that physically reflects the informal, often very small primary schools from which the pupils are drawn. The lower school follows a traditional curriculum, with only the more able pupils taking French, the only modern language. In years 4 and 5 all pupils must take English, mathematics, geography and religious education, and 5 options from a range of GCE 'O'-level, CSE and non-examination subjects. The sixth form, at present numbering 50 pupils, offers a small range of subjects to A-level as well as O-level re-sits or CSE conversions.

English

3.   The Head of English has attempted through careful selection of literary studies to extend the pupils' knowledge and experience beyond their immediate environment. Among fairly recent introductions, "The Friends", "My Mate Shofiq", "To Kill a Mockingbird" and "Walkabout" for example, have provided opportunities for the discussion of multi-racial issues in the context of shared experiences. Pupils' responses are reported to reveal sensitivity, empathy and real understanding. Racist works like "The Splendid Journey" are also studied, though to a lesser degree, to enable pupils to recognise negative stereotyping and racial prejudice and to review their own values and attitudes. The Head of English felt that the girls have more firmly-rooted racist attitudes than the boys, and that with both sexes these were more strongly directed towards

Indians and Pakistanis, than towards West Indians or Africans. He considered that television exposure, especially in entertainment and sport, had made the latter appear more conformist, more "human," and therefore more desirable as friends and heroes. He believed that the children are sufficiently sensitive and receptive to be able easily to modify their "feelings" whenever they are able to meet ethnic minority peers.

Geography

4.   The Geography department is committed to a global approach to the subject. The O-level course followed is based on world themes, and the CSE course a series of concentric studies viewed from a British Isles, EEC, then world perspective. They are aware that reference to Empire or Commonwealth evokes uninformed racist responses and therefore make no reference to them.

History

5.   The Head of History did not appear to comprehend the implications of an approach that was fairly traditional and directly geared to O-level British Social and Economic History. Only in the third year do pupils look beyond imperial horizons when they study exploration and discovery, but even this appears to be dominated by Western European attitudes. Bemoaning the dullness and irrelevance of most text books, the Head of History averred that neither he nor his staff had the necessary training, knowledge or experience to incorporate say African and Asian history into the syllabuses. After ten years of teaching in the school he was aware that many pupils have racial prejudices, although he believed that these were now fewer and less firmly held.

Religious Education

6.   Religious education, which does not appear to have any serious tradition in the school, is now taught by a newly-qualified teacher. During her one-year professional course she had taken an optional course on multicultural education. Although she has not yet introduced a new syllabus she has already brought in a consideration of other faiths. She reiterated concern about the inward-looking propensity of the pupils, and saw this reflected in their reluctance to learn about other faiths. She had been concerned about what appeared to be strong prejudice against Jews, but soon realised that this was based on folk mythology and was a superficial and easily modified attitude. She had also experienced strongly held sex roles.

Attitudes

7.   A chemistry teacher had found in his General Studies (4th and 5th year) lessons what he referred to as a pronounced "nigger-hating" attitude. He felt that television contributed to this situation, and wondered if National Front publicity might have been another factor.

8.   Discussions with other teachers reinforced the impression that in this insular community with its inherent stereotyping and antipathy towards all other unfamiliar groups or individuals, racial prejudice is perhaps no stronger than other forms. Its retention of traditional sex roles that undervalue and tend to undermine the credibility of female professionals, even doctors, and inhibit the academic and intellectual aspirations and expectations of girls, further reflects its introspective disposition.

Discussions with Pupils

9.   Seminars with groups of pupils elicited a number of significant factors which were confirmed by further discussion with teachers. It became apparent that the higher ability classes embraced most of the children of mobile, professional and managerial home backgrounds with first-hand experience, and consequently more informed impressions, of ethnic minorities. Many of these were able to cite former close Asian or Caribbean friends. On the whole, however, their attitudes appeared little different from those of the children with only limited, local experience, who avowed that race and colour were of less significance than personality, interests and activities

in choosing friends or accepting others socially. Many were able to name black people they particularly admired and respected, almost exclusively in the spheres of entertainment, sport and athletics, though they all conceded that ethnic minority people were capable of success in all other fields of human endeavour and achievement.

10. Some of the first year pupils confessed to having been admonished at home for referring to "nigger" or "blackies," although one girl conceded that her father was not above using similar terms himself. Fifth and sixth year pupils owned to some racial stereotypes and prejudices, but freely acknowledged that these were irrational and would probably alter on acquaintance. Some appeared to be conforming with assumed peer-group attitudes, and it was sensed that their true feelings were much more neutral, if not more positive, than they would admit. All the pupils believed that they were less prejudiced on racial issues than their parents and grandparents, and stressed that they respected others on the basis of personal qualities. They all felt that in adult life they would be likely to work and seek their recreation alongside ethnic minority people, and would like school to prepare them for this by informing them in some depth about their cultural backgrounds.

11. Opportunities arose to discuss prejudice and racial attitudes with adults associated with the school community. A parent, by profession a nurse but currently working outside nursing maintained that hospital work had helped her to develop positive racial attitudes, but that her husband, without benefit of such experience, held deep-rooted prejudices that neither reason nor persuasion could undermine. She believed that her two daughters shared her attitudes, but considered that the local community was subconsciously apathetic to racial and other minorities both within and beyond their experience. She felt that television and the national press fed this reaction. The school caretaker has enlightened views on race which, he admits, are not common within the area. He confessed to a degree of culture shock when, on a first visit to one urban area, he saw for the first time, coloured people in large numbers. His attitudes have been considerably modified by feelings of gratitude and respect for Asian hospital doctors who, he believes, saved the lives of his wife and one of his children. He likened local prejudices and attitudes towards racial minorities to the local ambivalence towards gypsies where, despite the consciously-modified behaviour of the travelling people, traditional stereotyping still persists. This focusses on attributes of dirt, noise, nuisance, brawling, stealing, cheating, poaching and trespassing, illogically based on folklore despite their contradiction by contemporary experience.

12. The school secretary was not native to the area, although she had lived there for many years. She asserted an adherence to Christian principles, pre-eminent among which was respect for others, whatever their background. Nevertheless, she had felt some racial resentment some years ago when her daughter, after teaching for two years in a multi-racial school, had suffered a total nervous breakdown in attempting to meet the needs and demands of ethnic minority children. She now concedes that the causes may have resided in her daughter, or other agencies, rather than in the pupils, and that the racial attitudes evoked were probably ill-founded and certainly irrational. Like other adults interviewed, she believes that prejudice of all types exists throughout the insular local community, and that most of the racial stereotypes and attitudes held stem from unsympathetic media treatment of ethnic minorities in this country.

13. The chairman of the school governors, whose attitude towards ethnic minorities is strongly influenced by war-time experience, insists that the malaise of modern society stems principally from the collapse of the family structure with its integral discipline and mutual respect, features that he recognises still persist among some ethnic minorities. He believes that colour and race present few direct problems for society; that if social values are restored and economic injustices removed many of the so-called race issues will disappear. While having little comment on the cause of multicultural education, he is convinced that racial attitudes will be enhanced by the employment of more ethnic minority teachers, whom he would be pleased to appoint to the staff of this school.

Conclusion

14. Many of the principles of multicultural education are honoured, albeit indirectly, within the school's general philosophy and practices, and most of the teachers are in total sympathy with those principles. However, they lack awareness of the full range of issues implicit in preparing pupils for life in a multicultural society, and in many cases they are not entirely convinced of their relevance for the pupils of this school. National exhortations appear to have little influence, possibly because of a tendency to presume that multi-cultural considerations are the concern of multi-racial schools alone.

School X4

1. This medium sized co-educational comprehensive school is situated close to towns with long coal-mining traditions. Its physical location distant from sizeable shopping and cultural centres enforces an isolation and insularity that is reflected in local attitudes and life-styles. Unemployment affects 15% of the population, but this figure disguises the relatively high proportion of unemployed school leavers most of whose only resort is to youth opportunity and work creation schemes. For several generations there has been a steady immigration from Ireland which has been accepted as natural and created few difficulties, similarity of life-styles oiling the process of integration. That this is so is reflected in the occasionally expressed allegation that coloured people are taking "our jobs," never in terms of Irish or other white immigrants.

2. The teaching staff has been recruited nationally and consists of many who have taught in multi-racial schools and are sympathetic to the principles of multicultural education. Predominantly working class, the parents have only minimal educational experience themselves and little understanding of the nature and values of education except as a route towards future employment. The school and parents were highly satisfied with last year's (the first comprehensive) O-level results, and are strongly supportive of each other within the community. Few ethnic minority pupils are admitted, and the occasional Chinese, Vietnamese and Polish children recently experienced were warmly welcomed, not least for their novelty interest.

3. The school's educational welfare office with whom I spoke referred to particularly strong inter-estate rivalry and prejudice, and felt that this was more strongly-felt and deeply-rooted than a latent racial prejudice that ignorantly lumps together all coloured peoples into a stereotyped "Packy" on the basis of representations in television programmes like "Grange Hill" and occasional encounters with obsequious itinerant market traders completely unrepresentative of their Indian cultural backgrounds. The existence of an "Andy Capp" like stereotype is confirmed by teachers who have had the opportunity at a residential centre to which they are able to take their classes for a week at a time, to explore pupils' attitudes and values in an unconstrained, constructive and developmental environment. They feel that the children's inherent disposition towards "fairness" quickly enables them, given the opportunity to review their attitudes with the benefit of dispassionate, factual information, to eradicate such views and replace them with more positive and empathetic attitudes.

English

4. The Head of English is fully sensitized to the need for a multicultural approach to her subject, but confesses that this is more coincidental than deliberate. Several of the English teachers have taught in multi-racial schools, contributing to an extensive departmental experience that is again reflected, albeit often subconsciously, in their selection of books and materials and in their treatment of language and literature. Although they have not expressly considered the multicultural implications for their subject, it is noteworthy that the school's library and English text books have been deliberately expurgated of all books representing colonialist values and attitudes or depicting ethnic minorities in a derogatory or insensitive manner. They speak with enthusiasm of the interest and empathy aroused by such books as "To Kill a Mocking Bird", "Walkabout" and "On the Run", and feel that through these and similar

books children's perceptions are heightened in relation to others of different backgrounds, and lead to the realisation that discrimination, even in the form of skitting and name-calling, can be hurtful and uncharitable. Care is taken to ensure that these enlightening processes are not undermined by internal or external influences. There is a belief among the teachers that while "Grange Hill", a very popular television series among pupils of all ages, sometimes compounds existing misapprehensions and stereotypes, television programmes in general are improving pupils' racial awareness and tolerance. Parental attitudes, apparently more prejudiced than the children's, are considered to be the major obstacle to a greater respect and acceptance of ethnic minority people.

Science
5. Members of the science department staff were less convinced about their role in multi-racial understanding. In biology, many opportunities are grasped to show the similarities between ethnic groups, and to present the true facts about skin colour, hair types and physical features, while in some science text books, for example Science 2000, the illustrations featuring coloured as well as white students unaffectedly lead to the implicit recognition of the multi-racial complexity of modern society.

Modern Languages
6. The head of modern language had little to contribute to the ethnic minority discussion, but feels strongly that his department's work is hampered by the deeply implanted stereotyping of the French and the Germans by comics and television. Such stereotypes are always derogatory, portraying the French as dirty, excitable, drunkards who eat "dirty" things like snails and frogs legs, and the Germans as arrogant, aggressive, military minded and our traditional enemies.

Attitudes and Prejudices
7. The sixth form tutor, after only a term in the school, is already aware of the insularity of both parents' and pupils' attitudes. Of particular concern to him is the parents' lack of knowledge and experience of sixth form education, their apparent lack of conviction about its value and a consequent lack of confidence by the pupils. He has found that by normal standards his pupils are very immature in their attitudes and judgements. Their knowledge and experience of life in other parts of the country, far less other parts of the world, is extremely narrow. He has found them naive and undiscriminating in making judgement values, and although relatively innocent of racial discrimination, over-ridden with misapprehensions and folk mythology about racial matters.

8. The head of science voiced local concern over the television exposure of the Brixton and Bristol disorders that implied a purely racial gesture and evoked an equally unbalanced local anti-black reaction. There had also been real fear that local white youths might, for perhaps different reasons, be inspired into "copy-cat" demonstrations. This fear was not allayed until several days after the vivid television reports had been screened. Indirectly they had had the effect of bringing to the surface many of the latent racial stereotypes and prejudices common among the older generation.

9. One of the Heads of House has slightly different views about racial attitudes and prejudice. He is one of the few local teachers who entered teacher training as a mature student. His perception is perhaps heightened by the fact that he and his wife have two adopted West Indian children. He feels that the local people are at least as prejudiced as any in other places, though he believes they are not now as intense as formerly. But they are quick to react among themselves to national political and social issues, when latent anti-black, extreme left wing views come to the surface. He feels that the influence of press and television tends to inflame such prejudices founded on isolated and uninformed impressions and stereotypes. This is reinforced by the accretion of believed confirmatory 'evidence' selected by the individual to justify his attitude.

This teacher feels that such prejudice is almost beyond modification. He is much happier however about the younger generations who, he feels, are certainly less prejudiced, and, given a balanced, objective and factually accurate view of other groups, will develop more positive attitudes of acceptance and respect. His own adopted children have been both the subject and the reciprocators of name-calling, which they regard with amusement and even pleasure. Of course, in a white community, heads have turned when he has been out with his black children, but he imputes this to curiosity or interest, not to any expression of disapproval or disfavour. He does, however, feel that different forms of stereotyping in books or on television, are extremely influential and should be expunged from all children's and adults' experiences.

Discussions with Pupils

10.   When invited to express their feelings towards other groups the comments of a small group of top set, first year pupils are invariably critical or uncomplimentary, eg Scots are arrogant, drunkards, mean; Irish are bad-tempered, drunks, troublemakers; Irish catholics are called "Red Necks," Irish Protestants are referred to as "Prods", "Prodiwogs" or "Golliwogs"; a golliwog may also be anyone, of whatever skin pigmentation, who has curly or frizzy hair; all coloured people are called "Packies"; and Black people, and whites with swarthy complexions, are called "Niggers". One girl had been flattered to be called "Brown Girl in the Ring". (They sensitively exclude from these categories the few minority group children in the school.)

11.   The children have obviously been exposed to many of the folk myths about ethnic minorities, including multiple-family occupation of houses, and taking white people's jobs, but when challenged they readily recognise the possibility that those may be, at worst, exaggerations of the truth. Their preoccupation with "fairness" tempers their attitudes. Towards all minorities they have tolerance and some understanding. They all watch "Grange Hill" on television and their attitude to the Sikh boy's right to wear his turban and to the issue of both arranged and mixed marriages is open and sympathetic. They do, however, appreciate that many of their parents are opposed to mixed race marriages.

Without exception they would all like to learn more in school about ethnic minority religions and cultures, and would be very pleased if, to compensate for their isolation and insularity, exchanges could be arranged with schools in multi-racial areas. Similar views are held by older pupils, especially in the sixth form, who want to grow up in a plural society where individual and group differences are accepted and respected. Among the older pupils is a sense that their obvious political naivety is a reflection of school's apparent unwillingness to expose them to political ideologies and strategies.

Conclusions

12.   The overall impression received was one of a school struggling in the face of severe local constraints to establish in a comprehensive role, a credibility and respectability inevitably founded on academic results but also conscious of a moral responsibility to prepare its pupils in every possible way for adult life in a wider society that is culturally diverse and often more sophisticated than the local community. To these ends the considerable contribution of some teachers, experienced in multi-racial schools elsewhere and totally committed to the principles of multicultural education has to be recognised. But the uneasy feeling remains that the expectations of a majority of teachers, depressed because of stereotyped assumptions about pupil potential and reinforced by modest pupil and parent aspirations, could result in underachievement both in academic standards and in personal development.

School Y1

1.   This large primary school with nursery provision is situated in the centre of a council housing development. Property owned by the Council represents 96% of the accommodation in the area. The unemployment rate in the town is about 25% – that of the council estate exceeds 40%.

2.   On admission to the nursery unit, most children are suffering from severe linguistic deprivation, and find communication difficult. They have no experience of traditional nursery rhymes or fairy tales on which to draw, and social graces can be minimal. Day trips are the only holidays that some children have had.

3.   Most of the children entering the infant department do so from the nursery unit. The initial reading syllabus is based on a variety of commercial schemes, including Ginn 360, Crown, One Two Three and Away and Gay Way, colour coded for degree of difficulty and progression commensurate with the relatively lower overall ability of the children. Many of these reading schemes portray in pictures, characters and stories, a good multi-racial cross section. Library books make a similar contribution.

4.   In addition to linguistic deprivation, a surprisingly high number of infants are treated by visiting specialists for speech defects. While reading is important to the department, perhaps greater priority is accorded to compensatory language development. Approximately 20 pupils from the infant and junior departments have been referred and assessed as suitable for special education but in the absence of special school places for them, they receive additional compensatory teaching from two visiting teachers from a local ESN school.

5.   The junior syllabuses follow fairly traditional patterns, but with frequent injections of multicultural topics and themes. Academic levels throughout the school are lower than average, and the Head believes that had there still been 11+ selection, very few would have attained the standard to qualify for grammar school entry.

6.   Many staff have attended locally-mounted courses in multicultural education, and this is reflected in many ways in the everyday transactions of the school. In addition to following the suggestion of the Schools Council project Education for a Multi-Racial Society, that multicultural principles should permeate the curriculum, a number of initiatives have been started. Many classes use television broadcasts, and when multicultural topics are involved these are followed up and related to the regional context.

7.   In order to evoke empathy and understanding the school is sponsor to a boy in an Indian village, and sends not less that £1.50 a week subscribed voluntarily in odd pennies by the pupils themselves. As part of the overall sponsorship scheme, an Indian teacher and one or two Indian pupils visits this country and the sponsoring schools annually to talk about life in their homes, emphasising the positive aspects and placing local deprivations in a national context.

8.   Periodically, artefacts relating to ethnic minority cultures, received from a variety of sources, are circulated around school to feature in class studies and discussions, again emphasising ingenuity, craftsmanship and appropriateness rather than concentrating on exotic or primitive features. Of particular interest are collections of artefacts and books compiled from contributions by the local ethnic minorities, and therefore guaranteed in authenticity and validity.

9.   Teacher exchanges with multi-racial schools have enabled staff to experience at first-hand the cultures of pupils within them, but of special significance is a new venture now in the final stages of planning. This is a class-exchange scheme, initiated by the Head, that will entail a class of pupils spending a half day at one of four multi-racial schools nearby and experiencing normal lessons paired off with an ethnic minority pupil. They will also sample each other's diets and have opportunities to wear their types of clothing, play their games and possibly meet their parents. The multi-racial school will reciprocate the process shortly afterwards.

10. Of all the other forms of prejudice held, that against racial minorities is second only to the sex role attitude. It differs from the latter principally in the fact that it is less overt, but of its existence, especially among parents, there is no doubt. When it does surface it tends, in this area of high unemployment, to focus on assumed job competition, but is also fuelled by a widespread belief that Asian workers, by their diligence and willingness to work long hours, have somehow undermined trade union "rights" and "perks". Yet dual standards are often applied, the professional Asian – doctor, nurse, teacher – being held in high esteem. This school had, until recently, an Indian teacher on the staff, and the Head is pleased to boast that he was respected and admired by pupils, parents and colleagues alike, never once being the recipient of unkind remarks or any other form of discrimination.

11. The teachers believe that in the nursery unit and infant department children notice colour much less than personality or other physical features, and remain ego-centrically unprejudiced about race. From about seven upwards they are becoming accustomed and tuned-in to parental racial attitudes that, fuelled by television and film impressions harden into personal attitudes. These are believed to be fairly superficial, and are only manifested by name-calling (Nigger, Wog etc). Of the nine children of ethnic minority parents only one has been known to be the butt of other pupils, and this was believed to be a personality-orientated reaction.

12. Discussions with children of junior age revealed irrational attitudes to other groups – gypsies, Scots, Irish, for example – but these were often unjustifiable when asked for reasons. Stereotypes obviously play a part in such attitudes, as occasionally does generalisation from isolated incidents. Several children who said they hated Irish and Scots withdrew their statements when told that two of their teachers were of that descent. They all admitted calling others unkind names, but the examples given related to habits or physical features other than colour.

School Y2

1. This large co-educational comprehensive school is situated in a small market town linked commercially, economically and administratively with nearby industrial areas. Around the nucleus of the old village are situated a number of housing developments mainly of owner-occupied properties accommodating a middle-class community in which social classes 2 and 3 predominate. Unemployment at adult level is well below the regional average, but is just beginning to bite in the school leaving sector. The community preserves a strong local identity and independence. Newcomers, who tend quickly to adopt the values and attitudes of its sub-culture, are readily accepted. Most pupils live near to the school and represent a very wide socio-economic spectrum skewed towards the upper end. The Head and staff are proud to proclaim a strong academic emphasis in the work of the school, but stress that life-skills are not neglected. The school is pervaded with an atmosphere of calm, conscientious industry.

Assemblies and Religious Education

2. School assemblies are held on both year group and house bases and deal with moral and religious topics, often invoking aspects of the faiths, cultures and life-styles of other people in a positive and informative manner. They are led by teachers, whose collective experience, knowledge and commitment afford consideration of a wide range of issues among which questions of race, respect, relationships, stereotypes, prejudice and discrimination are regularly featured. Yet the religious education syllabus, concentrating on Biblical studies and moral education in a narrow, traditional manner, by-passes the whole area of comparative religion. Theology is the least popular subject of the curriculum, and the numbers taking it to external examination level are minimal. At present the department has the temporary benefit of an experienced RE teacher who has unilaterally introduced a multi-faith dimension into the syllabus, which he feels is welcomed by pupils who have a strong aversion to the abstract philosophical

study of Christianity. He deplores the lack of a multi-faith dimension in the syllabus, as well as the sterile manner in which Christianity is treated, and the narrow historical consideration of Judaism, never acknowledged as a valid contemporary faith. Should the syllabus be changed, the problem that will loom largest is the re-education of two senior departmental teachers, whose knowledge of other major religions is very limited. And like the community of their adoption, they equate strangeness with threat. The Head of Humanities, of which religious education is part, is a committed multiculturalist and, convinced that persuasion is more likely to succeed than direction, is gently trying to institute some broadening of the curriculum in Religious Education.

Humanities

3.   As an initial attempt to bring together under a common theme the work of the History, Geography, Social Studies and RE Departments, the Head of Humanities instituted in 1982, Festival of India Year, the school's own Festival of India. A full term was spent considering all aspects of Indian life, culture and history. One significant feature was the in-depth study of an Indian village, showing it in a developing situation and drawing comparisons with similar comparatively recent changes in English villages. But perhaps most important were exchange visits with a school with a high proportion of Indian pupils. Additionally, Sikh, Hindu and Muslim leaders visited the school to talk about their religions and staff visits to a Sikh temple and to the Hindu festival of Diwali helped them to understand more about these faiths. Throughout the project the faculty received generous support from the parent-teacher association and culminated in an ambitious Indian evening in the school. The evening was open to the local community, and public interest and response was so great that the school had never before held so many people at one time. Parents were very warm and positive in their response, and none questioned the validity of such a project. It is hoped to institute similar projects on other ethnic groups in future years. The Head and staff are of the firm opinion that this project did much to correct misconceptions and stereotypes, and to develop more positive attitudes to ethnic minority groups.

Geography

4.   Geography teaching in the lower school is organised on a concentric principle starting with the known and extending frontiers from that base. First year pupils are involved in day visits to nearby villages, towns and industrial centres to experience their atmosphere and significance. Second year pupils are encouraged to join an overseas study trip, usually to the Netherlands, to experience life in a different cultural grouping. In the third year, relating their studies to the previous two years' experience, world topics are considered, including those affecting developing communities. Material from a Multicultural Centre is used to supplement information received from a variety of official sources, many text books on economic geography rapidly becoming out of date as countries begin to exploit new resources, like oil, and new markets. It is interesting to note that this department has abandoned the Geography for the Young School Leaver Programme because it felt that it incorporated racist implications.

History

5.   The Head of Faculty is concerned about the very traditional approach to History. Falling within the umbrella of Environment Studies in years 1 and 2 changes of attitudes and emphasis have been effected. But the entrenched attitudes of History department staff have resisted all attempts to wean it away from an almost exclusively 20th century European preoccupation. It is felt that this war-orientated approach might well be influential in reinforcing anti-German attitudes among many pupils in the school. The LEA has instituted a curriculum review exercise throughout all its schools, and it is hoped that this might influence future curriculum attitudes and approaches. The text books used by the school are unquestionably Euro-centric, if not biased Anglo-centrically.

English

6. Little opportunity presented itself for a review of English teaching in the school, but the impression of a fairly traditional, classically-rooted department was alleviated by the attitude of one department member who also operates the school's bookshop. This lady taught until quite recently in a strongly sectarian school in Belfast, and has first hand experience of sectarian hatred, discrimination and prejudice, through which she empathises with ethnic minority people in England. In her teaching, especially of literature, she tries to convey this sentiment to her pupils whom she feels are apathetic and unresponsive. Within the local community she identifies two distinct groups, a liberal, upper section affecting condescending acceptance of ethnic minorities, and a defensive lower section asserting antipathetic attitudes to all other groups, among which racism is prominent. These attitudes are manifested when pupils are invited to read novels about minority ethnic group characters, but may be accentuated by a lack of interest or empathy in anyone or anything beyond their immediate experience. They completely reject, in the school bookshop, any books portraying black people on dust-covers.

Modern Languages

7. A modern languages teacher believes that in the school there is prejudice against French, German and coloured people, and refers to the difficulties encountered by a black French-Algerian teacher in obtaining a post in the area. Although German is taught in the school and a German language assistant is attached on a half-time basis, the influence of comics, war-films and parental attitudes in implanting stereotypes and prejudice is difficult to overcome. Exchange visits with German schools have tempered adverse attitudes for some children, but since there is no tradition among the parents of overseas travel, the effects of these experiences are short-lived. Similar prejudices are directed towards other groups, and in a sort of prejudicial pecking order it is interesting to note that the Scots are in greater favour than the Southern English. At the other end of the scale are black people, whatever their country of origin, and the abuse directed towards black professional footballers at regional matches is an embarrassment to very many, probably a majority, of fellow-spectators. In addition to these national or racial prejudices, this teacher has noted instances of prejudice across social classes, especially upwards against the more affluent, the better educated, the better spoken; prejudice of various types conditioned by the male chauvinist domination tradition; and prejudice towards aspects of the curriculum conditioned by their perceived value and utility. This last predilection is illustrated by the low take-up of modern language options compared with mathematics, sciences and English. The attitudes of parents are considered to be a very strong influence on the children of this school.

Art

8. The Head of Art, once a commercial designer in London, has been strongly influenced by Rastafarian contributions to art, as well as a specialised interest in Indian art. He makes no attempt to introduce "ethnic art" into his teaching, believing that art has no racial or national frontiers, but in the examples he places before his pupils he draws on a wide range of expression, including eg Japanese screen printing and other techniques often suggesting that these can be superior to British national or European processes.

Careers

9. Like many of his colleagues, the Careers teacher is aware of the strong influence parents have over their children in relation to careers guidance. Within the engineering and light industrial sectors he is conscious of covert sex discrimination, but he has not been aware of any racial discrimination, although his experience here is very limited.

Home Economics

10. The Home Economics teacher who has attended a local course on cookery in multi-racial schools introduces cooking from all over the world into her syllabuses. In other studies, as for

291

example year 1's Home and Family course, she covers overseas home life in such a way as to stress the more positive aspects. Culturally-biased requirements such as table-setting are excluded, and on the practical side presentation is the dominant aim. She finds many of the children conservative in their tastes, often rejecting initially any unusual food on such tenuous grounds as that "it stinks". But she finds consolation and optimism in the extremely well-supported adult evening classes she runs in Indian cookery, believing that this facilitates a two-pronged attack on what must be classed as food prejudice.

The Pupils

11.   Opportunities arose on this visit to conduct seminars with groups of pupils. The first was most disastrous, yet probably most revealing. A group of lowest ability fifth year pupils reported to me in a seminar room. After briefly introducing myself I asked if they knew why they had been sent to me, to be surprised by the aggressive response "we've got to talk to you about niggers and wogs and things" from the dominant member of the group. Of all the groups seen this was the only one where such an attitude had been posed, and caused reflection on the attitudes and sensitivity of the teacher who had sent them. Following the lead of the dominant boy, they all confessed to strong views about ethnic minorities, revelling in the opportunity to display their knowledge of words like nigger, coon, nig-nog and Packy, although the girls disputed some of the more outrageous and patently inaccurate or irrational statements. Gentle probing revealed that their experience was extemely limited. One boy who said he hated the Chinese based his reasons on having been chased out of a Chinese take-away for throwing an apple-core into a boiling pan of food. The dominant one based his proclaimed aversion to "Packies" on his experience in a nearby shop owned and staffed by Pakistanis. He said that when he went into the shop there were a number of Pakistanis standing around and they looked at him and started talking in their own language and laughing. When asked to explain his attitude he responded "Who do they think they are, coming here and taking our jobs?" then more significantly "I'm just as good as they are". Yet this attitude is not directed towards his Indian general practitioner, for whom he has considerable regard and respect. The unmistakable sense of inferiority revealed by this remark was further reflected in the group's equally contemptuous attitudes to other groups, but particularly towards their more affluent and more successful peers, compared with whom they form a small minority.

12.   The middle and upper fifth form pupils at this school share the sentiments and life-styles of the sixth formers, who generally reflect the middle-class values and attitudes of their parents. A survey among lower sixth pupils reveals that newspapers, other than evening issues casually brought in by fathers, are not normally available to them at home. Perhaps surprisingly none received either the Times or Guardian, and only one the Telegraph; the tabloids receiving almost exclusive circulation. The consequences of this phenomenon on attitude formation cannot be ignored. A recent move which introduces a compulsory General Studies component directed towards the development of life-skills and introduces pupils to contemporary social and political issues has only reluctantly been accepted by academically-orientated parents. Within its compass and through the writings of such commentators as Margaret Mead and Leslie Newbiggin, multi-racial and multi-faith topics are studied and debated. Pupils are unconvinced about the relevance of such studies, but are prepared to give them an open hearing. Their knowledge is still very limited, but their repeated desire to learn more about other peoples' beliefs and life-styles offers promise of even better attitudes and stronger conviction. The majority of the upper sixth form pupils bestow greater credibility and respect on personal qualities than on racial, national or sectarian associations. They tend to be embarrassed by their parents' prejudices and insularity, as well as by the low image of the area in which they live. Most of them aspire to higher education and to experience life in an emancipated, heterogeneous society.

Conclusion

13.   It is difficult to summarize the impressions received in this school. In many ways it presents close similarities with other schools in that it perpetuates regional characteristics through an

inward-looking, self-conscious and defensive parochialism that is apathetic to conditions and issues beyond its immediate experience and influence. In others it suggests a desire from its more enlightened members to leap beyond its self-imposed boundaries into an emancipated, more tolerant pluralist society.

School Y3

1.   This large co-educational comprehensive school is situated in a town which despite its proximity to a number of urban centres preserves its own individual traditions and dialect peculiarities within a dogged and narrow local identity. The majority of fathers follow semi-skilled or unskilled occupations, have little personal experience of post 16+ education, and live in either council houses (60%) or on small estates of owner-occupied terraced or semi-detached properties. Despite a 30% unemployment rate, the prevailing impression received is one of affluence and contentment.

Religious Education
2.   Although in its prospectus the school prescribes a Christian education for all its pupils, it is interesting to note that elements of comparative religion are increasingly introduced. The Head of Religious Education, in consultation with department staff has devised a new syllabus that tries to develop concepts of self, truth, morality and causality. Through this approach the recognition and respect for other world religions is facilitated. The fourth and fifth year pupils follow syllabuses leading to GCE 'O' level or CSE examinations. A few non-examination pupils follow courses that concentrate on relationships, and in these the consideration of other religions and ethnic minorities are featured.

English
3.   The Head of English, while recognising the need to remove from the classroom and library those books that portray ethnic minorities in an insulting or derogatory manner or are written from an imperialistic, colonialist viewpoint, expressed mild concern at the possible repercussions against imposing too many multicultural books too quickly. He feels that while the children react favourably towards books like "Walkabout", others like "To Sir With Love" can be so unreal and so far from their experience as to incur rejection both of the story and of the characters. Another teacher is less inhibited towards the introduction of books about or written by ethnic minority people. She feels that the principal attributes of the local community, reflected in their children, are insularity – "self-centred, clannish, inter-related"; apathy rather than antipathy towards minority groups, political issues, or even life outside their home town; and an acquiescence with social and economic relegation. She has not personally encountered discrimination or prejudice, although she has been made aware of strong feelings by some against the Irish, Germans and latterly Argentinians. In these instances she believes that media presentation of political or historical situations have brought to the surface latent prejudices and attitudes that might equally pertain to ethnic minorities. She also considers that band exchanges between this school and German schools have exerted a strong corrective influence and helped to develop positive feelings and relationships towards the German people as a whole. Similarly, she feels that the presence in this school of one or two black children has helped to stress their individuality yet personal similarities, to the benefit of positive attitudes towards ethnic minority groups in general.

Geography
4.   Geography teachers in the school consider that the pupils, like their parents, have a low personal and community image that makes them turn inwards to their familiar and comfortable society that protects them from a potentially hostile world beyond. Despite the school's owner-ship of a coach and minibus, school holidays and field trips are only achieved by strong persuasion. Limited horizons and attitudes discourage curiosity about other places while common misconceptions about people and their life-styles, even in nearby towns, render pupils unsympathetic and uninterested in other people's situations. Hence Geography is a difficult

293

subject to teach and relatively few pupils choose it as an examination option. It is perhaps unfortunate that the world map on permanent display in a geography room proclaiming in bold red all the countries of the British Commonwealth insinuates an outdated British colonialist supremacy, although in fairness, the department has shed a number of text books that portray such an attitude.

History
5.   The Head of History has similar opinions on the pupils and community that he refers to as a "narrow enclave resenting intrusion and interference from without". He feels that this attitude can breed prejudice against anything or anyone that is unfamiliar. Conformity with majority opinion is expected, and individual dissension regarded as betrayal. The only known feeling of antipathy among the community is towards the IRA, but this does not extend to Irish people in general. He believes the pupils, like their parents, to be politically naive, and finds it difficult to arouse their awareness.

The Pupils
6.   Discussions with groups of pupils of all levels of ability confirm many of the teachers' views. Third year children reveal social immaturity and harbour many of the stereotypes and prejudices endemic within the community, among which racial attitudes, in the absence of everyday experience are undeveloped though dormant. A number of children, influenced by war films and comics, display imprinted prejudice against "Krauts" (Germans), although on questioning they deny that this would affect relationships if ever they met one. Only one child admits to dislike of ethnic minority people, referred to collectively as "Packies", influenced by his experience of a single Asian market stall-holder. In response to the protestations of his class mates he is at pains to point out that this attitude does not extend to a well-liked Indian girl in the year group. Older pupils profess a ready welcome and respect for ethnic minority groups, most pupils echoing the sentiment "They were born here, and have as much right to be here as we have", an unexpected comment because of their limited knowledge and experience of them. Among a number of higher ability fifth year boys strong anti-German feeling exists, again attributed to television, probably supplemented by parental observations.

7.   Several pupils in the Lower Sixth form confess somewhat shamefacedly to prejudice of various descriptions, not least to acceptance of the region's adherence to the belief in male superiority and stereotyped sex roles. A small minority also profess antagonistic racial views which, when challenged, they are unable to justify except by cliches like "they're taking our jobs" and irrational counter statements like "send them all back". Their peer group, obviously opposed to these attitudes and embarrassed to be associated with them, confess to very limited knowledge about other ethnic groups and their faiths, and ask that school should redress this ignorance. They also profess similar antagonism towards white groups, including gangs from within and beyond their housing estates, and pupils at other schools. They describe how encounters with such groups consist primarily of trying to assert some form of superiority. Staring, shouting insults, posturing and gesturing reinforced by aggressive clothing and personal appearance are the main armaments in this type of ritual combat, suggesting that such manifestations, like racist comments, stem from primeval reactions to feelings of insecurity, inferiority and assumed threat.

8.   Among the higher ability pupils is a tacit recognition of the enrichment of modern society by minority cultures. While one or two affect a dislike for "foreign" food, the majority welcome the opportunity for greater variety. They are able to name aspects of culture that have been widened, and identify the successes and achievements of a number of ethnic minority person-alities. They recognise that if they move into higher education they are likely to have direct contact with ethnic minority students and staff, and are very open-minded about the sort of relationships they will enjoy together. They make a plea for a broader education in life-skills and an introduction to the cultures, faiths and life-styles of other people. They give the impression

that while they have affection for their home town, they would like school to have facilitated their release from its constraints and its depressed horizons, rather than to have acceded to them.

Conclusions

9. Despite the town's preoccupation with parochial concerns and calculated disinterest in external issues the school, adopting local values and attitudes, develops within its pupils a close identity with the community. Unfortunately its own low image may be transmitted to the pupils' personal self-image, depressing confidence, aspirations and expectations. In doing so it is perpetuating a minority complex that possibly results in a sub-conscious identification with other minorities, including ethnic minorities, hence the apparent absence of antipathy. This is complemented by the school's lack of emphasis on competition, with its implicit notions of challenge or threat. In so far as curriculum content and treatment are concerned, the school, while not consciously striving towards a multicultural education is at worst doing few things of a contrary nature. The greatest concern here, as elsewhere, is the need to make teachers aware of the relevance and implications of multicultural education.

School Y4

Background

1. This large co-educational comprehensive school is situated in a market town transposed in recent times into a dormitory industrial suburb. Most of the parents are more outward-looking than other communities in the region, although some of its traditions, particularly male dominance, are still maintained. The teachers tend to remain for long periods despite poor internal promotion opportunities. Many confess that one of the main reasons for staying is that it is an easy school in which to teach, with comparatively few disciplinary difficulties and a highly motivated pupil community.

English

2. Despite the fact that the Head of English is a traditionalist in his approach to the subject, he has responded to the views of department staff that some of the examinations should be changed. They now work to the regional consortium's Joint 16+ examination in English, but retain allegiance to the JMB 'O'-level Literature examination. CSE pupils take Mode 3 examinations in Language and Literature, the syllabuses being designed by teachers to meet their own pupils' special needs and interests. The Head of English, who feels he understands the multi-racial situation through war-time service in India, agrees without enthusiasm that pupils have studied and some enjoyed "Cry, the Beloved Country", "Walkabout" and "To Kill a Mocking Bird". He owns to a personal preference, shared with pupils, for "Child of China" and "Brother Blackfoot". Nevertheless he is concerned that if too many multi-racial books are introduced or any attempts made to insert a multicultural component into the syllabus they will evoke reactionary attitudes.

Religious Education

3. A much more radical approach to their subject is being adopted by the Religious Education Department and associated Liberal Studies teachers – the multiculturally minded minority of the staff. Several of this group of young teachers are currently attending an in-service course in multicultural education. Religious Education follows a syllabus devised by the school, based loosely on "Learning for Life" (ILEA Agreed Syllabus). For years 1 to 3, where Religious Education is compulsory, a course in comparative religion is followed, which includes a study of the nature of religion; how religion began; 'advanced' religions – Christianity, Judaism, Islam, Hinduism, Buddhism, Sikhism; alternatives to religion; religion and society; and problems of belief and behaviour.

Through this, all pupils gain insight into the religious beliefs and practices of the major ethnic minorities in this country, which they are encouraged to understand and respect. It is significant that in this school, children appear to enjoy their RE lessons. Fourth and fifth year pupils can opt for courses leading to 'O' level or CSE (Mode III) or an unexamined Liberal Studies course with associated community service. All these courses involve further study of the main world religions and their practice by groups in this country; and reinforce the appreciation and respect instilled in the lower school. The relatively high numbers of pupils opting for the examination courses illustrates a positive response by the children to the way in which the subject is approached. Extreme care is taken by the staff to ensure that text-books, visuals and artefacts are authentic, up-to-date, and truly representative of the ways in which religion is conducted and interpreted among ethnic minority groups in Britain. They all express concern about what they consider to be the reactionary attitudes of examining boards, who firmly resist attempts to introduce into their Mode 1 syllabuses the detailed study of any religion other than Christianity and Judaism. But perhaps above all they deplore the apathy and inertia of most of their teaching colleagues in this school who similarly resist any kind of change within their subject areas and are apathetic to multi-racial considerations which they believe are irrelevant to their pupils' needs.

History
4. The Head of History, son of East European immigrants, has personal experience of discrimination and identifies with, and has great empathy with, all other minority groups. He feels, like many other ethnic minority people, that his personal identity lies somewhere between his native and his adoptive culture, a fact seldom acknowledged by either community. He is dedicated multiculturalist, is an active member of the current course attended by other colleagues in the humanities, and attempts to permeate his department's teaching with multi-cultural principles. He has been unable to insinuate his multicultural ideas into the thinking of departmental staff. It is perhaps unfortunate that he is attempting to influence his colleagues with such fervour that resistance appears to be the main response.

5. The Head of History confesses to the department's possession of many ethno-centric or Anglo-centric text books, in which only an English viewpoint is put forward, thereby reinforcing many strongly held stereotypes, and introducing others. He also feels that the teachers, the text books and the external examinations reflect middle class values and attitudes which, with the examination-orientated competitive spirit that is promoted within the school, tend to reinforce social class divisions. His experience in History and Liberal Studies discussion groups persuades him that like their parents and teachers, the pupils are imbued with many prejudices, often based on negative stereotypes that are often difficult to modify. He believes that the not infrequent allegations about coloured people taking white people's jobs stem from parents and television, and to a lesser degree from newspapers, comics and films. The children and teachers look upon coloured pressure groups as anti-white, rather than pro-black, largely because of media presentation. He illustrated the depth of such feelings by the children's reactions to the Brixton disorders and the subsequent Scarman Report. Almost without exception they identify with the (white) police rather than the predominantly black protesters, despite an otherwise strong opposition to the police from many of them. Even the most vehement anti-police pupils, some of whom feel they also suffer police harassment and injustice, fail to identify with the protesters and side with law and order' embodied by the police.

Geography
6. A geography teacher who is also Head of Middle School is attending a current in-service multicultural course. His department is dissatisfied with its current syllabus which is felt to be too discursive and too abstract and therefore of little relevance for the pupils. They feel that many external examination syllabuses inhibit curriculum development within schools, and that some syllabuses actually promote stereotyping while others reflect bias. The geography teacher does not experience racial bias and prejudice in class discussions. Rather, he feels that about

other cultures, and about ethnic minorities in Britain, there is a prevailing ignorance and apathy, usually crystallised in a dismissive "stupid" when unfamiliar life-styles or cultural expressions are encountered. He attempts to influence his colleagues by example and persuasion rather than by confrontation, and the sympathetic response of his colleagues may well be the product of such an approach.

Music

7.   An interesting development in this all-white school is the intention of the Head of Music to set up a steel-drum band in the school to complement existing wind and brass bands and a full orchestra. Her philosophy and teaching have been strongly influenced by experience in a multi-racial school and by "Pop, Rock and Ethnic Music" edited by Vulliamy and Lee. Eventually she hopes to have a gamelin (Javanese) band to further extend pupils' musical experience. She finds that children do not readily respond to the traditional academic approach that concentrates on the classical western idiom, but are willing to respond to other unfamiliar idioms, to which she introduces them through reggae or other popular forms that draw upon oriental instruments and rhythms. Although she encountered initial reaction and refusal for her steel band intentions, she had been allowed to appeal (successfully) to the parent-teacher association for financial support. She feels that through listening to music from other cultures and countries, children can develop respect and tolerance that is transferred into general attitudes. This can apply particularly to African music where, after removing the apparently inevitable stereotyped "jungle" opinions, real appreciation and empathy can be achieved, particularly if performance or involvement are invoked.

The Pupils

8.   Discussion with higher ability pupils reveals tolerant open-minded attitudes to many issues, including racial matters. Pre-occupied with their own academic aspirations they nevertheless reveal concern for social, economic, political and racial injustice. They feel that much of their academic education has little relevance to the hostile situations and pressures they are likely to meet in the outside world of adulthood, and feel that they have not been adequately prepared to face them. Many even feel that the attitudes of adults to teenagers is at best condescending, at worst insulting. One child summarised his received attitude – prevalent throughout education as "We are the British and we are the best", which he and many of his contemporaries feel to be an untenable proposition in a modern, global, multicultural society. It is disturbing to discover that in many ways distrust of political leaders and parties or pressure groups, leads to a resignation and despair that is manifested in apathy and a sense of life's futility, and a depression of idealistic and altruistic motivation to their supersedence by selfish and material standards and values. On contemporary political issues they are both ignorant and fatalistically apathetic.

Conclusion

9.   Concluding thoughts about this school focus on the promising initiatives of a nucleus of committed and energetic multiculturally minded teachers whose contributions through the humanities must be of great importance and value in preparing pupils for life in a multi-racial society, and, by example, showing the way to colleagues in other departments.

School Z1

1.   This medium sized primary school is situated in a residential area, of which owner-occupied houses comprise at least 80% of the total. While it accommodates a fairly broad socio-economic range, lower professional, junior executive and other white-collar workers predominate. Admission to the school is organised on a twice-yearly basis, with the facility of half-time admission for the preceding term for children below statutory age. Four children only have an ethnic minority parent, two having a Jamaican mother, one a Nigerian and one a Chinese father. In each case their other parent is English. Transfer to secondary schools is on a selective basis.

2.   Underlying the curriculum and practices of the school, a philosophy geared towards the development within pupils of a secure self-image allied to a respect for others, often finds positive expression through morning assemblies. On the school day preceding my visit, to highlight the narrowness and irrationality of prejudice the Head had introduced, in the light of a local performance, the stereotyped view that male ballet dancers were somehow effeminate and an object for ridicule. His sensitive treatment of the nature of prejudice had prompted subsequent writings by older pupils on their own prejudices that their teacher had considered to be very perceptive and revealing. Two members of staff confessed that this same theme had caused them to review some of their own attitudes.

3.   Multi-racial aspects have not been overlooked, and their origin and development are worthy of mention. Nearly two years ago an English doctor's child was admitted to the Infant department direct from residence in Nepal. Her mother had brought to the school a number of artefacts, and had been persuaded to talk about them and the Nepalese people to a full school assembly. Its success had prompted this mother to persuade the Head to invite an Indian lady friend of hers, dressed in traditional clothing, to present a similar theme on life in India. This had in turn emboldened a Jamaican mother to make similar and equally impressive contributions. Such insight into the life and customs of other countries are now a regular feature of morning assemblies. Prompted by these external initiatives and subsequent staff discussions, individual teachers have contributed assembly themes based upon minority religions, in particular those of the major immigrant communities in this country. All such themes are underpinned by the aim to engender understanding and respect for other individuals and bodies of people in a mutually tolerant society. It was noteworthy that among five children's portraits on display in a Lower Junior classroom, one represented an attractive black boy with Afro hair style but without any stereotyped exaggeration of features. The teacher informed me that this was one of a number of ethnic minority portraits arising from a painting assignment to illustrate a fictitious "ideal best friend".

4.   The initial reading scheme used by the school is the "One, Two, Three and Away" series, which only recently has introduced one or two ethnic minority characters in supplementary readers. These represent only token inclusion. Nevertheless other back-up readers (eg Breakthrough to Literacy) and Library books, particularly in the Infant department, include multi-racial characters, situations and stories. Once again, a great deal of credit for this situation must go to the Jamaican mother who borrowed a collection of multi-racial library books, brought them to school, discussed their significance and persuaded the staff to purchase copies for school use. Perhaps more important, through her sincerity and conviction she was able to sensitise most of the teachers to the social and cultural needs of all pupils in today's multicultural society. She mounted a similar exhibition on Open Day for the benefit of all the parents. Great interest was shown, and happily there were no adverse reactions.

5.   The Junior department fiction collections, especially in the upper classes, are traditional and almost exclusively Anglo-centric in presentation and attitudes. They contain many out-dated and out-moded books, including a group of books by Willard Price (1964) in which attitudes are often patronising and sometimes insulting (eg "Pygmies resemble monkeys"). Teachers concede the dubious credibility of many of the books but claim they cannot dispose of them until replacement with more appropriate books can be effected. Non-fiction appears to be reasonably accurate and up-to-date in its presentation of overseas countries and peoples.

6.   The mathematics syllabus draws from a number of text book sets, and at least one of these, Nuffield Mathematics 5-11, unaffectedly represents ethnic minority people in its illustrations and by name in its problems.

7.   History is studied from the viewpoint of local connections, and involves frequent museum and site visits. It is therefore essentially British-based, but it is more concerned with social than

political issues. It embraces the successive immigrations into the area from the earliest times onward, and helps to give perspective to contemporary immigration, although this is an issue discussed only incidentally and indirectly. Its consideration, through folk museums, of social history, illustrates that the phenomenon of physical affluence, convenience and sophisticated life-styles are of comparatively recent origin for the majority of people in this country, and may help pupils to recognise that under-development is merely a stage through which any community might quickly progress, thus placing in acceptable perspective the doom-laden "Third World" image often projected by fund-raising charities.

8. Discussion with the teachers, both collectively and individually, revealed a hitherto unconsidered recognition of the racial and cultural diversity of modern society, even though the former was not a feature of the local community. They were agreed about the existence of all forms of prejudice throughout society. While race was not considered to be one of the main areas of prejudice, it was felt that when invoked it could be most firmly and irrationally upheld. It was conceded that prejudice stemmed principally from ignorance and folk mythology, occasionally stoked by assumed challenge, threat or even fear. There was a general belief that it originated in the home, with parental ridicule and criticism being dominant factors. Television, which occupies an apparently increasing amount of children's time, was considered to pose conflicting attitudes, displaying on the one hand positive contributions to society by ethnic minority programme presenters, entertainers and sportspeople, but on the other, perpetuating through situation comedies and similar so-called entertainment the stereotypes and folk myths that display them in a patronising and derogatory manner. All the teachers accepted their role in presenting and developing attitudes of respect for self and for others, but one or two were uncertain about the importance and relevance of multicultural and multi-racial considerations in the local context.

9. With the exception of a single, recently-qualified teacher who had undertaken teaching practice in multi-racial schools, none of the teachers had either in their training or through in-service courses been sensitised to the needs of pupils in a multi-racial society. The teachers considered that there had been no discrimination against the four 'coloured' children in the school, although the Jamaican mother refuted this, averring that her son and daughter had had to suffer name-calling. She recognised that this was a common trait among small children, and that her own indulged in similar, though not racial, habits. She had not been unduly upset about these incidents which she had used to explain the attitudes presented by them as one of the misfortunes of being visibly different from the majority community, and as a preparation for and inoculation against subsequent and more extreme forms of discrimination likely to be encountered. When reported to the teachers, she had been most impressed by the firm and sensitive manner in which they had handled the situations and taken positive steps to avoid their recurrence. Nevertheless, she had found it necessary to dissuade at least one teacher from the stereotyped view that all West Indian children are better at physical than intellectual or academic activities. She stressed that name-calling and other forms of discrimination were practised by only a very small minority of the school population. She had been most impressed by her own acceptance, on equal terms, by the other parents.

School Z2

1. This medium sized 10-30 Middle school is situated in a small market town. It draws its pupils from a number of small first schools serving scattered villages, and its staff are all of secondary school experience or training. A few of the teachers have exclusively local residential and professional experience, but the majority have taught in other areas, some in multi-racial schools.

2. The general feeling of the teachers is that the pupils, reflecting the attitudes of their parents, are very friendly yet suspicious with those from outside their closed community, are insular in

299

their interests and experience, and, in many cases cushioned by an extended family system and an inherent community self-sufficiency, are lacking in motivation and ambition. Attitudes towards other groups are held quite consistently and are strongest against "townies", gypsies and tourists, ambivalence creeping in only as regards "visitors" since while they are accepted as a source of revenue, they are resented for their intrusion. The local weekly paper is the only significant influence on attitudes generally. No strong views appear to exist towards ethnic minorities, the prevailing mutual respect syndrome apparently being unchallenged by any perceived threat or interference.

3. The work of the school is organised on a mixed-ability system that involves some team teaching, particularly in the Humanities department. A topic approach, involving pupil selection and interpretation of source material, field visits and talks/demonstrations by visiting speakers, is the principle instrument of education. The philosophy and strategies are based on the Schools Council Project: Place, Time and Society 8-13. In the absence of external examinations for this age-group, the Richmond Tests of Basic Skills in Humanities are given to the pupils annually.

In years 1 and 2 when topics are derived from the local environment then the industrial revolution, other countries, cultures and faiths are introduced only peripherally. In year 3 there is a positive focus on multicultural issues as shown by this synopsis of the syllabus.

1. Migration: Pupil migration and immigration in the immediate area; Migration to Northern Mill Towns; Irish migration to Britain; Jews to Israel; and West Indians to Britain.

2. Third World: Definitions; Problems of developed countries; Food, agriculture, hunger; Population growth; Trade; Health and disease; and Natural disasters.

3. Farming: at home and abroad, including a study of tropical farming.

4. Energy: uses; conservation; relationships between energy reserves and industry; the poverty of the Third World; coal; oil; gas; and electricity.

For each of these topics study booklets are provided to ensure that pupils' work is structured yet open to individual initiative and research. The teachers have been involved in considerable discussion in compiling these booklets and the planning and industry involved has fostered among them an empathy and understanding of ethnic minorities in this country. The immigration components are complemented by visits to a Synagogue and a Hindu Temple, while family life and customs are explained to the children by visiting Jewish and West Indian speakers. Full use is made of films, video cassettes, television and tape recordings, and the work of the department overlaps into other subject areas including art, craft, English, music and dancing. Interspersed among the art and craft on display in the school are examples of such work, including two memorable pieces, one a painting depicting the capture of slaves, the other a sensitive fabric montage of an African lady's head. The children appear to like this approach and speak with humanity and respect of minority groups so studied. There is no obvious transference of such attitudes to other groups, although the school has become involved in an Action Aid scheme to sponsor a child living in an Indian village, and responds generously to other similar fund-raising appeals. The school also has a health and social education scheme in which relationships play a prominent part, and through role play and informed discussion, reviews issues like race and colour. A good supply of up-to-date and accurate resource books is maintained in the school.

4. The teachers feel that the majority of pupils are open, accepting and honest in their attitudes towards ethnic minorities, although this is not always shared by parents. Some parents refuse to allow their children to visit the synagogue because they cannot see the point of it, but it must also be declared that visits to a town farm draw similar reactions from them.

5.   English teaching in the school does not appear to match the pronounced multicultural input of other departments, the library books following a traditional pattern that is only beginning to entertain science fiction and has not yet considered multi-racial books. The over-riding local pre-occupation with farming and country matters is reflected in the pupils' choice of books, for like most of their parents they are so immersed and involved in their own immediate interests and concerns as to preclude curiosity in other areas. Sex discrimination in book selection is strong, the boys having no inclination to read books about girls or girls' interests. In spoken English there is strong resistance to efforts to replace or modify a pronounced local idiom and dialect.

6.   The only contribution of maths and science to multicultural education is the existence in text books and work cards of portrayals of black as well as white characters.

7.   Individual discussions with third-year pupils reveal only limited and fairly superficial degrees of discrimination. Towards Argentinians (with memories of the Falklands), Australians ("they beat us at cricket"), the French ("dirty people, they eat frogs' legs") and "Blackies" ("they take our jobs") only an insignificant minority express any prejudice, a view confirmed by the school's French assistant. Many talk with pride about their performance of an African slave dance at the school's annual concert, while the musicians and singers declare a positive delight in calypso and other national musical forms. Emotions run highest in relation to "townies" who are believed to be conceited, and "snobs" embracing all who put on airs or assume superiority.

School Z3

1.   This small upper school has close links with Middle School Z2 which is situated in the same town. Its pupils are divided into three year groups of 190 to 200 pupils each, and a sixth form of 90. The teaching staff represents a wide range of expertise and experience, many having worked in multi-racial schools or areas. There are two ethnic minority pupils in the school. In anticipation of my visit the Head Teacher circulated heads of department inviting them to express how they were preparing the pupils for life in a multi-cultural society. As a more detailed description of one school's contribution these are quoted verbatim before recording impressions of the different departments' operations:

English
2.   "English lessons are a part of the curriculum where students are frequently widening their attitudes towards others, and being encouraged to understand the experience of others through imaginative writing, drama and discussion. Inevitably this process focuses at times on the condition of minority groups and the question of racial attitudes is then discussed. This gives pupils an opportunity to express their own views on the subject, share experiences, and listen to the views of others. There is obviously no indoctrination, but I think it would be reasonable to assume that most English teachers would encourage a sympathetic, humane consideration of the rights and privileges of other human beings. In choosing material to read to classes, and in choosing titles for our book boxes, we are always on the lookout for good material irrespective of its country of origin or the ethnic background of its characters. Thus, quite a number of novels, short stories, plays etc contain material which very positively, I feel, helps to promote an understanding of the racial question and the human dimension to the evils of prejudice. None of the above occurs through prescription by me. All good English teaching promotes growth in human understanding and self-awareness. At a number of points in their three-year course students will discuss racial prejudice, from one angle or another, but we do not have a syllabus which prescribes that it should happen at a particular moment in time."

Library
3.   "We have relatively few non-fiction books dealing with race as a subject. I think this reflects a situation where few children in the school at any level display any strong interest in it, and

where few subjects direct children to investigate it as an area of concern. I do not remember any books on race being asked for by children or recommended for purchase by any of the Heads of Department in the two years that I have been running the library. Nor do I remember seeing in publishers' catalogues any particularly good treatments of the area which would be suitable for children of our age range. There are a number of books in the fiction part of the library which have race as part of their concern. One thinks of classics such as "To Kill a Mocking Bird", "Black Boy" by Richard Wright and "Long Journey Home" by Lester. More recent works by people such as Dhondy are also there. I have noticed that these are not particularly easy books to interest our children in. A brown or black face on a cover is often enough to prevent their choosing a book, not because of any racial animosity but because it suggests to them that the concerns of the book will be, in some way, remote to them. We find often that a good deal of pushing of material like the Dhondy books is necessary before they will be read, and while they are then read with interest and some enjoyment, few children want to follow that up with more material of a similar kind. Those children that do are generally those who, because of parental concern and inclination, already have this wider interest. This leads to my being reluctant to buy large amounts of such kinds of material."

Comment
4.   Discussions with teachers confirm the views expressed by these two reports. The general prejudice among boys against any form of reading is considered to be rooted in pragmatic as well as practically-orientated estimation traditional to this type of agriculturally-based society. Girls, who are generally more favourably disposed to all forms of literary activity, still retain preferences although prejudice plays a less significant role in these. The most popular books for pupils in this school are the James Herriot series, the Pig Man Series, and novels, by Cookson, Cormier, Walter and Richter because they portray situations and characters with which it is easy for them to identify. The least popular are those that reflect city life, remote situations, and minorities or individual characters with which they feel unable to empathise. This is considered to be prompted by a desire to read about crises and predicaments relevant to their current needs, rather than to any form of racial or other prejudice. Also prevalent among boys is a self-conscious attitude towards anything of an intellectual nature when attempting to portray an image of practical, physical masculinity.

Careers, Social Education, Religious Education
5.   "One of the major aims of the Careers, Social Education and Religious Education programme is to encourage pupils to think in a tolerant way about other people and to appreciate rather than denigrate other people's differences. We look at multi-racial Britain and often follow communities back to their roots in order to get a clearer understanding of their backgrounds. Films/videos have been shown about Sikhs, Muslims and Jews, and also of Indian cookery and Islamic banking. The films are usually followed by group discussion."

Social Education

6.   "As this course is about 'Education for Life' and the development of 'Life Skills' it is appropriate that the course should prepare youngsters for living in Britain today. A part or section of the course in years 2 and 3 is concerned with religious, moral and social education. Included are such topics as 'Comparative Religions and Cultures'. Some emphasis has been given to ethnic minorities in Britain today. We deal with 'prejudice' as a topic, not merely racialism or colour prejudice, although the emphasis is on these. We promote self-awareness and awareness of others in the community, as well as tolerance of the values of others in society. Other topics include young people and the law, the legal position of young people, and awareness of poverty and deprivation in Britain and in other countries.

Summary of Social education Syllabus

Year 1   (= 3rd year secondary) Personal and social identity.
Smoking, health and safety.

Year 2   (= 4th year secondary) Self awareness. Prejudice. Race.
Work and industry in Britain and abroad.
Major world religions, including Islam, Sikhism, Judaism, Kibbutz life.
Life in multi-racial Britain – Hindus, Jews.
Indian food and cookery.
Personal problems; personal values; others' values; tolerance.
Decision making – influences and choices; values and needs; abilities, skills, qualities, personal style.

Year 3   (= 5th year secondary) Careers education – work experience.
Role play. The law. Counselling agencies.
Personal and group awareness, relationships.
Poverty in Britain and the Third World War.
Contraception, abortion, birth, venereal disease.
Starting married life. Starting a family.

"The syllabus provides a broad framework in which teachers introduce their own approaches according to specialisms and interests."

Comment

7.   It soon becomes apparent that the above programme and statements are genuinely intended and sympathetically carried out, the children responding with genuine interest and sensitivity. Two of the teachers are not wholly convinced about the approach. One, a somewhat disillusioned RE teacher whose inclination would be towards a Christian-based course in religion, is concerned that his own subject is being debased, although he concedes that children appear to enjoy and benefit from the Social Education course, in contrast to the nil response he obtained when he offered a sixth form examination course in Religious Studies. Other teachers concede that pupils, like adults, are constantly categorising people and making value judgements about them on the most tenuous evidence, and that this may apply on occasions to ethnic minorities. But the general feeling is that the thinking pupils are positively inclined towards them, the more inward-looking pupils at worst apathetic. The demeanour, behaviour and disposition of the children, especially in the higher forms, suggest the effectiveness of this approach.

Geography

8.   "As a department our greatest involvement with multi-racial society ideas comes through studying urban geography. Under such a heading we try to deal with topics of immigrant communities and the socio-economic problems related to them. Irish, West Indian and Italian racial groups are discussed. Further abroad, the racial issues of South Africa are dealt with. In general the issues we tackle are seen as racial rather than multi-racial. Though our society as a whole is increasingly cosmopolitan in character, in many ways the short term future for our pupils is unlikely to involve them in direct racial involvement. Other curricular priorities notably those of an environmental nature especially, are of more immediate concern to pupils who live in a rural and relatively isolated community.

It seems likely that recent developments in the field of Social Education in the school would allow this area of the curriculum to better educate pupils in what are essentially personal/moral matters rather than environmental/human ones. We shall continue to see race as an important geographical influence, and assist our pupils to understand its implications."

Comment

9. Two months after making this statement, the Head of the Geography Department's attitudes are now more positive, recognising that simple matters like the selection and presentation of information can be discriminatory. He is concerned about the limited horizons of the pupils, but gratified to find that after the adoption of a new syllabus based on Geography for the Young School Leaver, 130 out of 190 pupils selected geography as an examination option. It appears that this department, now sensitized to the implications of the multi-racial composition of contemporary society and spurred on by the example of other departments, will be reviewing the whole curriculum content and approach before the commencement of the next school year.

History

10. "The implications behind the issue of a multicultural nation are enormously important, not only for those who live in a multicultural community, but also for those whose life has been spent entirely with those of similar culture and background. This whole issue devolves not only an understanding and knowledge of people from different backgrounds, but also, and perhaps more importantly, on the issue of tolerance and acceptance of those different from oneself. In this respect, children living in rural areas like these are in need, not only of an introduction to the values and ideas of people of a different nationality, but also to sensitive guidance towards an acceptance of those coming from areas outside their own immediate environment. I find the children here more insular than any which I have ever taught before, in many different parts of the country (excluding the Highlands of Scotland!), and I therefore feel that our primary task lies in opening their eyes to the habits, values and ways of life which obtain in their own country, and amongst people of their own race. Having said this, I believe that it is also our duty to get pupils to think about the problems of a multicultural society for, though many of them will have met one or two black or Asian or Chinese people, and very many of them will stay in this area for the whole of their lives, some will move elsewhere, and some find the issue challenging enough to pursue it in their careers.

As far as my own department is concerned, one of the foremost objectives is to inculcate a tolerance of peoples and societies other than our own. This is paramount if pupils are to develop any sort of empathy with the people of the societies of the past whom they study, and, by transference we would hope that they would learn to apply this to people of their own times but of different cultures, whether this be in Bradford, Birmingham or Surbiton. Our approach to all aspects of the courses in each year is, of necessity, underpinned by the belief that people of all cultures and all ages are worth respect and consideration, and we hope that pupils can learn that intelligence, for example, is not the preserve of the technological 20th century, but is something which can be found in Neolithic Man as well as in Aborigines, and West Indians living in Handsworth, and which is nothing to do with how much people know or can do. Hence, throughout all our teaching is the underlying objective that pupils should learn that goodness and right and dignity and worthiness are not confined to people whom they understand, but are the inalienable right of the whole of human-kind. This is something which is fundamental to History teaching, irrespective of the content of the course. In specific terms we do study the emergent nations (as the CSE Board calls that part of the syllabus), and have a chance to see the way in which former colonies gain their rightful place within their continents, and cast off their colonial character. Our primary contribution to this issue, however, is in our attempts to make pupils look at their own attitudes towards people who are different from themselves. It is, after all, attitudes which cause the distress which exists in multicultural societies, and though in areas in which there are large numbers of immigrants the problem may well be more practical, here we can only operate on a theoretical level, but hope to encourage our pupils to realise that there is a world beyond their own, and values different from their own."

Comment

11. Such commendable, well-considered and sensitively-expressed sentiments are reflected throughout the attitudes and teaching of this department. The sincere conviction and uncompromising commitment of this teacher to the principles of multicultural understanding is felt to provide a shining example and a thought-provoking catalyst for other teachers. Consistent with her philosophy, she is also dedicated to the removal of other forms of discrimination, particularly sex discrimination, believed to be very strong in this remote rural area where traditionally the strength and stamina of the farmers and other outdoor manual workers has endowed their sex with a superiority that overflows into all aspects of life. She believes sex discrimination to be more strongly implanted and pursued than all other forms of discrimination, and in the approach to her subject attempts to exert in this sphere the same educative and corrective influences as those indicated in her statement towards improving racial attitudes. Curriculum development is severely constrained by the demands and parameters of external examination syllabuses, more significant in a school where they do not receive the pupils until 13+. On arrival at that age they appear to have little historical awareness and no appreciation of historical patterns. The schemes of work therefore comprise a broad framework that allows teachers to insert their individual contributions and introduce wider issues in accordance with their own convictions and specialisms. Examinations are offered at GCE O-level and CSE level in Social and Economic History in Britain since 1760, which involves the consideration of colonialism, exploitation and emancipation, and the emergence of new states and nations, as well as other issues pertinent to multi-racial education.

Modern Languages

12. "i.   Idea of cultural and language differences is fundamental to the course, though specific preparation for life in a multi-racial society is not wholly applicable to children in this area.

    ii.   Department seeks to convey that because another culture/language is different from our own, it has equal value and the people involved in it have equal rights, and are not, in some indefinable way, 'inferior' because they are not English.

    iii.   Through ELS (European Language Studies) the department seeks to show pupils that their own language has been significantly influenced by other languages, races and cultures.

    iv.   Department stresses that other cultures etc have much in common with our own, but that their differences are rich and interesting.

    v.   Children are actively encouraged to go abroad and spend time with people from other countries on their home ground. Exchange visits are also encouraged, together with pen-friends.

Sixth Form. Through sixth form Assembly and General Studies I seek at times to bring inequalities to light or to make known cultural differences. Certain General Studies sessions are particularly geared to the question of race and the society in which we live."

Comment

13. Despite the qualification in i. this teacher, aware of a certain amount of endemic stereotyping and discrimination against other European nationals, feels that it is part of his responsibility to attempt to eradicate such negative attitudes towards all other groups. This is brought into the teaching at any time, but is crystallised in ELS lessons to useful effect.

Biology

14. "I am afraid that we make no special efforts whatsoever to educate pupils for life in a multicultural society, other than the ever-present 'hidden curriculum' represented by teachers' own attitudes to racial problems, ethnic minorities, etc."

Comment

This teacher is obviously aware of the importance of teachers' attitudes and his reference to the hidden curriculum suggests he has studied the literature of multi-racial education. It is interesting to find that he had recently arranged with an Indian school an exchange visit involving 15 fifth and sixth form pupils. Its cancellation because of domestic difficulties at the Indian end only two weeks before the exchange would have commenced, has only slightly dented his enthusiasm for this ambitious project. An avid reader who regularly attends in-service courses over a wide range of topics, he says he was motivated to arrange the exchange, by a social conscience. He is very concerned about the insular background and restricted horizons of so many of the pupils, and feels that only through this type of opportunity can their interest be stimulated and their experience extended towards other people and races.

Conclusion

15. Two things will be immediately apparent from a study of the teachers' statements: first, that in this isolated and insular rural area there exists an unexpected life-giving micro-climate of multicultural awareness and enlightenment; and second, that while the whole staff may not be totally committed to the principles involved, all are inevitably being drawn towards them by the example and dedication of senior colleagues. Discussions persuade me that these are not mere rationalisations calculated to create a favourable impression, but true reflections of their sentiments and commitment. There has been no direction or coercion from above, although the ethos of the school, reflecting the Head's philosophy and style of leadership, has provided a general climate sufficiently benign to encourage and nurture initiatives that stem from personal conviction and professional dedication.

School Z4

1. This small co-educational secondary modern school competes with two other more prestigious secondary modern schools for those pupils not accepted for a grammar school education. For this reason and because it is scheduled to close, it attracts relatively few first choice pupils.

2. Of the school's current roll 60% are boys and 40% girls; all white apart from one Caribbean and three Chinese pupils. The lowest socio-economic groups predominate. There is within the community a rising proportion of split or single-parent families, and a high incidence of maladjustment and relatively minor juvenile delinquency. There are few local facilities for pupil recreation out of school hours, hence an excessive dependency on viewing television, punctuated by occasional visits to discos or amusement arcades in the town. On the whole the children of this virtually mono-cultural society appear to be friendly, acquiescent, lacking in self-confidence and eager for recognition, attention and affection.

3. The Head is a caring, avuncular, person to whom the children respond with respect and affection. In the school's prospectus he declares "The atmosphere within the school depends largely on members of staff and the children are generally very happy and secure because of a policy of reasonableness, firmness and understanding". To these ends academic pretension plays a subordinate role. The teaching staff generally concur with these sentiments although one or two are attempting to elevate pupil aspirations. None of them live within the catchment area of the school, and most have taught in the school for several years or more, despite limited promotion opportunities. Few courses leading to GCE O level are offered, and the results in CSE suggest serious underachievement.

Religious Education

4.   The teacher in charge of religious education is a former crafts teacher who has introduced a syllabus he devised during his training course. Despite the fact that his course was entitled Christianity and World Religion, his syllabus, based on Goldman's Life Themes and Lowkes' experiential approach, makes no direct approach to world religions, their treatment therefore being incidental and usually superficial. Feeling that most of his pupils suffer from an innate sense of insecurity and inferiority, he concentrates on a discussion approach, leaving reading and writing to an absolute minimum. The children appear to like this approach and respond positively to it. They appreciate the discussions about personal problems and personal relationships, but above all "being talked with like adults". This teacher is trying to break down, singlehanded, the school's long tradition of dividing the sexes, the boys and girls normally sitting at opposite sides of the classrooms and having separate playgrounds outside.

5.   The Head who also teaches RE is more traditional in his approach , but more wide-ranging in his content. Combining religious education with education in personal relationships he bases his teaching on 'Life in Our Society': Lambert, which considers community concerns in this country. Drawing on his experience in Birmingham and introducing such topics as Over-Population and World Poverty, Problems of Culture and Race, War, and International Cooperation for Peace, he aims to expose the children to racial considerations in an unemotional contextual manner. He believes that this contributes to a greater respect and understanding towards ethnic minorities in this country.

6.   There is no doubt that there is a consciousness in the school that through religious education better attitudes towards ethnic minorities should be developed, but as yet this consciousness has not been thought through. This was exemplified by one of the two morning assemblies I attended. Devised and conducted by the RE teacher, it consisted of an appropriate introductory song, then a dramatic interpretation of John Bunyan in his Bedford Prison cell reading that portion of Pilgrim's Progress relating to prejudice and racial discrimination. The assembly, after a prayer on the same theme, was concluded by the singing of the hymn "at the name of Jesus, every knee shall bow". Neither the teacher nor the Head had appreciated that in a group of mixed religious persuasions, including in this case three Buddhists, such a title might be inappropriate or even insensitive. While this opinion might well be challenged on the grounds that non-Christians have the right to be excluded from morning assemblies, or even that it is 'nit-picking', it is used to illustrate the limited awareness of some teachers towards multi-racial or multi-faith considerations and the need for much guidance and support to assist them towards such goals.

Humanities

7.   The Head of Humanities is fully aware of the dangers of a colonialist approach to History and a patronising Geographical study of primitive communities. She has already expunged from her resources any books or materials that purvey such attitudes, and selects new material on the basis of strict criteria among which these feature strongly. These same criteria pervade the syllabus.

English

8.   The Head of English has experience of teaching in a multi-racial area and is aware of the need to vary children's literary diet in recognition of the changed composition of contemporary society. Nevertheless, while he is happy to include for examination study such books as 'Walkabout', 'Joby', and 'to Kill a Mocking Bird', he fears that to introduce too many might arouse a backlash that could evoke racist feelings at present unconsidered. He is concerned about the complacency of the children, their very limited knowledge and experience, and their lack of

aspiration or motivation, particularly among the older. Linguistic ability is also limited, although most seem able, though a restricted code, to express themselves adequately for their everyday activities. Language and literature are taught in an integrated way. Most of the pupils' writing is of an imaginative nature. The library has a large but predictable selection of books but with possibly fewer more advanced books than might be necessary to extend the brightest readers.

Discussion with Pupils

9.   The most lively, aware and responsive groups are the first year mixed ability classes, and it is tempting to conclude that they are so inclined because the depreciating influence of the school has not yet stunted their academic and intellectual development. To the surprise of some teachers, a fairly high proportion dislike Germans, largely through the influence of televised war films and documentaries, and through comics and books, some of which are in the school library. Only two pupils express any antipathy towards ethnic minorities, the presence of three Chinese pupils in the school giving some immediate experience and understanding. They both recognise the irrationality of their attitudes, and may well be attitudinizing to draw attention to themselves. All those expressing antipathy to other groups are boys, the girls having much more open attitudes towards others beyond their experience or knowledge. Among the lower ability second-year pupils, who own to parents or grandparents of varied origins including Ireland, Scotland, Wales, France, Poland and China, there are a number of individually-held prejudices, among which feature hatred of the Argentine Junta, not the people; West Indians with thick lips, but not the pupil in this school; slant-eyed Chinese, but not those in this school; Asians, because they keep vicious dogs that don't respond to English commands; and black footballers of opposing sides to those supported. But of greater significance to the boys is the continuous internecine rivalry between neighbouring schools, youth clubs and estates. All accept their traditional sex roles, many of the girls saying they would rather have been boys, and all recognising male superiority.

10.   Similar attitudes, only expressed more aggressively and pontifically, are shared by lower ability third-year pupils. These children acknowledge the value of academic qualifications, especially O-levels in Maths, English and Science, although they know they will never attain them. Several are on probation, and a few receiving Child Guidance, and while they are prejudiced against one or two groups of people they reserve their strongest passions for known groups of which rival gangs feature most prominently. They acknowledge that much of the conflict they have with other gangs is concentrated on displays, rather than acts of aggression. In other areas of prejudice they bow to the principle of fairness and recognise that some of their proclaimed attitudes and opinions are irrational. While accepting the conventions of Western films where the whites are depicted as good and the Indians bad, they can also see how such conventions apply to films like Zulu and German war fiction, recognising that not all Zulus and Germans are bad, or that all English are good. Having been constrained to work and play apart from the opposite sex, the whole of the third year seems awkward and inhibited when boys and girls are asked to do things together in small numbers. Where groups are larger they tend to divide by sex, rather than any other groupings. Yet surprisingly, these pupils do not appear to have any hang-ups about ethnic minorities, possibly recognising sub-consciously that they themselves are a minority in the community at large, and not viewing ethnic minorities in a competitive situation, have very open views towards them.

11.   This attitude also prevails in the forth and fifth years, possibly fostered by the respect in which they hold the school's only black pupil. I am informed that only once had any child called him 'Nigger', and that physical retaliation from this big boy had prevented any possible recurrence. Yet it is fair to say that he is respected for his cheerful out-going personality, rather then feared for his stature and physical prowess. The predominant impression of the older pupils is one of a totally acquiescent, subdued yet unresentful group allowing itself to be swept along towards an adult life which they will enter with few advantages and declining possibilities of

congenial work. But they are not despondent, and this may be because of the caring, supportive, even protective ethos of the school, which they must surely miss when they leave. It is giving them a degree of self-respect and self-confidence, if only within limited horizons, and this is engendering an open-mindedness towards others, and particularly ethnic minorities, that appears to elude many others of similar backgrounds in different schools.

12. The three Chinese pupils in the school, all with a good command of Mandarin Chinese but little English, suffer severe discrimination that is largely beyond the control of the school. They are given tuition in English as a second language for only a few hours a week by a visiting teacher, the remainder of the time being placed at the back of classes and left very much to their own devices because the school has neither the expertise nor staff time to devote to them. The local authority, which employs the visiting ESL teacher, is said to be unable to help further, having similar small-scale ESL commitments scattered over a wide area. This teacher gives help, advice, and work sheets to the teachers who ask for them, but is only able to scratch the surface of their needs.

School Z5

1. School Z5, a sixth form college, is situated in an area where the experience of meeting or seeing anyone of ethnic minority background is extremely rare. In their choices of subjects, traditional sex role attitudes are demonstrated by the 4:1 ratio of boys taking Physics and girls taking Modern Languages. Many more girls than boys take English. Not a single boy is taking Home Economics. Regional sex role presumptions are common throughout the community, as exemplified by the willingness of banks to employ girls as counter or secretarial assistants, but not in higher or professional capacities. Consequently, girls' aspirations are generally lower than boys'.

2. In addition to the prevalent sex discrimination the Principal feels that racial discrimination is rife among his extremely conservative students, many adopting a hard intransigent attitude that maintains equally uncompromising views on capital and corporal punishment. Perhaps it should be noted that in at least one of its contributory secondary schools there is strong National Front support, and that the Principal has found it necessary to proscribe the wearing of its badge and associated insignia among college students. The student community is predominantly middle-class, largely representative of socio-economic groups 1 to 3, and has a wide ability spread skewed towards the upper levels. Half of its leavers are expected to go on to higher education. The almost exclusively graduate staff have served in the school since its inception. With the exception of the Vice Principal and the Heads of English and French, all the senior posts are held by men. Only one teacher is a member of an ethnic minority – an English trained Kenyan Asian.

English

3. The Head of English recongnises the need to introduce more books about ethnic minority characters and situations. She feels that 'To Kill a Mocking Bird' has been well studied in all the contributory secondary schools, and speaks with enthusiasm about racial issues ensuing from the study of 'Othello' and 'Cry the Beloved Country'. She is, however, anxious to introduce new books cautiously since students tend to reject books they feel are preaching to them or are imposed for reasons other than pure enjoyment. Nevertheless, she is convinced of the important role of literature in the indirect shaping of values and attitudes and, with her staff, is constantly attempting to foster this influence. She feels that her students, mainly girls, do not have strong racial attitudes except those of a sympathetic nature generated by Oxfam-type propaganda. One exception she has encountered was occasioned by Indian Consultants sending their children to private schools, not to local secondary schools, which had been interpreted as a form of snobbery, yet generalised into a racial issue. She has experienced ridicule of West Indian dialects, which she counters with allegations that local idiom and dialect can appear equally uncouth and unintelligible outside the region.

Library

4. The teacher responsible for the library, like the Head of English, confesses to a very small multicultural element among the books available to students, but blames their absence on lack of knowledge of their existence. Like many others spoken to, she would very much like to increase the number of multi-racial books, but finds that current capitation allowances are quite inadequate for this purpose except for occasional purchases. She finds the boys generally uninterested in books, but the girls imaginative and exploratory in their selection of books. She confesses to having given no thought previously to the idea of deliberately introducing multicultural works.

Religious Education and General Studies

5. Like many of his counterparts in other schools the Head of Religious Education is depressed by the lack of interest by students in his course, and parental resistance to their opting for it. He believes that pupils and parents alike view the curriculum from pre-vocational considerations, against which criteria Religious Education has low credibility. When pupils opt for RE courses, it is usually as a 'filler' subject, all their energies being directed towards more prestigious subjects in the sciences or humanities. In any case these are usually the lower ability students. This teacher gives the impression that while, as a committed Christian in a Christian country, he feels that the Christian ethic and teaching should dominate the syllabus, there ought to be more room for the study of other major world religions. He blames the lack of this on examination syllabus constraints, although he concedes that these are slowly being eased. On examination boards generally he is disillusioned, having had numerous suggestions for widening syllabuses rejected in the past.

6. He has much greater enthusiasm for General Studies, a compulsory study for all 2-year A-level students. This provides courses in four areas: literature and communication; science with computer studies; politics and ethics; and creative and recreational studies. Within each area students are allowed to select topics of their own choice. Student attitudes to General Studies are summarised by the upper sixth form as "General Studies courses are sometimes interesting". In the politics and ethics course, there is an opportunity for students to consider briefly Hinduism, Buddhism, Islam, Judaism, Chinese religion, and a history of Christianity – all in a 10-week course. Only 20 students have opted for this element, but they have revealed that while resistant of Christian teachings, they are very interested in world religions. The main problem about such a study is its enforced academic approach, based on films, film strips and books of questionable authenticity, access to religious leaders or places of worship being ruled out because none are within reasonable travelling distance. At this stage it would appear that comparative religion is a mere superficial introduction to other faiths, and is as likely to create stereotypes as to destroy them.

7. Throughout local society strong racist undercurrents exist. Press influences tend to reinforce existing attitudes, especially at the extremities. The opportunities of even modifying such extremist attitudes in the short time available are very limited, and the prospects quite daunting. It is reassuring to note that 117 of the 522 A-level students are following examination courses in British Government and Politics, while 55 of the remainder are working for O-level Government and Economics examinations. Both courses deal with issues concerning race in British Society, and enable the factual refutation of racial myths and misapprehensions. In its 'Politics and Ethics' General Studies course, this department is involved in a considerable number of multi-racial issues, including laws (sex and race discrimination, nationality, etc), race relations and Third World studies. This last element which looks at health, food, agriculture, education, trade and aspects of aid is focussed by reference to the Brandt Report to enable students to become more aware of Third World Development in international affairs, but particularly on our own society.

Geography

8.   A similar philosophy underlies the teaching of the Geography department, which through a systematic, rather than a regional approach, relates population to resources, and considers the migration of, for example, workers across Europe, or Mexicans to California. Perhaps more than most others, this department allows itself to be constrained by the requirements of external examinations. The Head of Department confesses freely that an element of 'us' and 'them' pervades part of his teaching, and that he has never considered the principles of multicultural education. Nevertheless, he feels that his approach and the teaching strategies adopted, do help to correct uninformed impressions about other world groups, and that open-mindedness is developed. He seldom uses text books, believing many to be outdated or biased in their approach, basing much of his work on Phillips' Geographical Statistics and other official sources.

History

9.   Like Religious Education, though to a lesser degree, History is viewed by pupils and parents as of little practical or material value, although some are attracted because of an intrinsic interest in the subject. That it fails to attract higher ability pupils is reflected in its comparatively modest examination successes. The examination syllabuses followed, relating to British and European history from the mid-19th century, with an emphasis on political as opposed to social or economic history, is felt to be out-dated and unimaginative. Within current teaching, opportunities exist under the 'decline of Empire', to consider such issues as India under the British Raj but because of students' very limited initial knowledge or understanding, there is insufficient time to cope with this in any depth. Similar feelings exist towards examination requirements concerning Irish immigration, the scramble for Africa, the Spanish Civil War and the emergence of the former colonies.

Economics and Sociology

10.   The endemic introspection and bigotry of the local community is echoed by the Head of Economics and Sociology. Economics is gauged by parents and students as a potentially useful vocational asset, although among many its application, with Sociology, is directed towards nursing and the police force. The A-level economics course deals indirectly, but in some detail, with multicultural issues but particularly with 'underdeveloped' countries, the distribution of wealth, and migrant labour. The O-level sociology has a much more direct approach, particularly in its consideration of the influences of the mass media in building or reinforcing stereotypes, and of social and community life in Britain. Films, newspapers and television are constantly involved in such studies, and the BBC's "Living City" series , and ITV's "A Question of Equality" have proved of particular value. The major influences on student attitudes appear to be the mass media, television entertainment, parental views, and personal experience.

Home Economics

11.   This department offers two major examination courses, 'O' level Home Economics and 'A' level "the Home, the Family and Society", each of which has 12 students, all girls. These courses involve the consideration of ethnic minority cookery, dietary and nutritional requirements, dress and family life, although time seldom permits detailed study of many of these. Towards ethnic minority people, the girl students are equally welcoming and friendly. Cookery, diet, nutrition and crafts also feature in the General Studies course, through which a few boys are persuaded to overcome their imprinted sex roles.

Pre-Vocational Course

12.   Of recent origin within the college is a pre-vocational course geared towards the lower ability, one-year (Foundation) students. Architect of this scheme is the Deputy Principal who

has taught in multi-racial schools in Britain and in a black African school. To the philosophy and principles of multi-cultural education she is totally dedicated, an influential example to all her colleagues. She feels that the students are "nice", with limited ambitions and initiatives often artificially depressed in the contributory secondary schools. Nevertheless, they have a high self-image, exaggerated by the relatively small community in which they live, that often creates problems for them when they advance to highly competitive higher education institutes elsewhere. They are also afflicted with an intellectual lethargy that impairs their ability to think for themselves. Recognising the unreality to such pupils of an academic preparation for life, she has devised a very practical scheme including an element of work experience. Progress is assessed continually, achievement being the basis for detailed references to employers and further education institutions.

13. I was able to talk to a group of 15 students who had recently undertaken a 3-day visit to London as part of the course. Preparation for the visit had begun several weeks ago with the consideration of inner-city deprivation as exemplified by certain districts in London. This led inevitably to a consideration of the disquiet of many people, particularly black youths, towards society in general but focussed on the police. Correspondence with London communities, principally through Youth Clubs, helped them to plan their visit. They decided, because many of them professed to "hate the blacks", to spend a day in Brixton to try to savour the climate. (At least one student brashly boasted that he would like to "get in on the action"). The teacher had spent considerable time and energies outlining the historical, social and economic background to the situation with little sympathetic response from the students. Describing their experiences during the day in Brixton these lower ability, working class students affected an attitude of scornful dismissal towards the black people they met and the problems they had to endure. It was soon apparent, and in one case boastfully confirmed, that National Front opinions and affiliations were maintained at home. Some, mostly boys, echoed the all-too-common "send them back" slogan that was readily challenged, predominantly but not exclusively, by girls. Having adopted their posture the boys would not recant, but grudgingly acknowledged the unfairness and impracticability of such statements. The ensuing discussion on "roots" evoked a number of interesting responses, and one boy who claimed to have a French parent had to endure, albeit amusedly, the affected scorn of some of his peers on the dietary peculiarities of the French people. It became apparent that few of them had any particular interest in their origins, one girl defiantly declaring "We're white, and this is our country and they should all go back where they came from", dismissing as irrelevant the fact that many were second or third gereration British. There was no doubt that some of the students still maintained hard, uncompromising attitudes to all ethnic minorities, yet there was evidence that even the most antagonistic were not entirely convinced of the validity of their standpoints. The experience was still comparatively fresh, and therefore not completely assimilated, but the teachers who accompanied them were insistent that attitudes had been considerably softened. They hope to increase the number and extent of such visits because they are so convinced that only through such experience, however brief and possibly contrived, can such irrational prejudice be modified. An interesting by-product of this visit is an anticipated exchange visit to the town by members of the black youth club in Brixton.

Discussions with Students

14. Discussions with more academic students reveal a strongly-contrasting climate of opinion. Much more articulate and thoughtful, they still reveal prejudice, but are considered less likely to express it in words or actions, and more open to modification, both by logic and experience. As with other sixth formers, they complain that school has neglected many of the life-skills they will need to cope with life in an adult and multi-cultural society. Several had personal experience of different forms of discrimination, including a boy who entered direct from a private school, a girl with an Argentinian mother, and a boy with a French mother. Many of the girls claim to suffer from sex discrimination, a complaint never voiced by the boys. They all confess to

prejudice, their main targets being 'posh', 'snobby' or 'trendy' people – in effect, any who, for one reason or another, impose a feeling of inferiority upon them. They cannot appreciate that to many, because of their own material and intellectual endowments, they could be seen as the targets of similar sentiments.

Having completed the visits to schools and submitted reports to the Committee, it was considered both courteous and politic to acquaint Chief Education Officers of the findings, and discuss with them the wider issues of multicultural education, their present attitudes and possible future initiatives. Their reactions are summarised below:

LEA X

1. The report on the visits was received with extreme interest, especially issues which had previously not been contemplated within the Authority. Within the LEA advisory service there was no one with detailed knowledge and experience of teaching ethnic minority children and whilst most subject specialists were aware of the implications for their own subjects, none had a sufficiently wide grasp of the principles of multicultural education to guide and inform colleagues and schools in their implementation.

2. The lack of multicultural experience extends into the wider educational community and even the colleges of higher education in the area are unable to offer any help. The LEA have to depend on gleanings from the educational press and courses or conferences, picked up almost accidentally and thus lacking cohesion, impetus and direction.

3. The message from this LEA was clear. The principles of multicultural education are still comparatively novel in this rarefied community and the benefit of first hand knowledge and experience is urgently needed to give reality and proportion to the discussion. It is essential that means are devised to make available to remote all-white areas the services of people with expertise in multicultural education.

LEA Y

1. A full day meeting was held at LEA Y and discussions were held with the CEO, and other officers and advisers. After receiving the report of the visits, there followed wide-ranging discussion on the points raised. It was interesting to note that they were occasionally surprised and impressed at a number of praiseworthy initiatives and attitudes of which they had been hitherto unaware.

2. The LEA is currently considering the possible appointment of an adviser for multicultural education. Direction and co-ordination of E2L and mother tongue teaching, as well as other ethnic minority educational and cultural concerns would obviously fall within the responsibility of such an officer. But they are concerned that the wider and more far-reaching issues of multicultural education, particularly as far as the all-white areas of the LEA are concerned, could well be undermined if the post were too narrowly defined and described.

3. It soon became apparent that the LEA, like, they believe, many other authorities with few or no ethnic minority children, is anxious for advice and guidance on a wide range of multicultural education. The activities of the LEA multicultural centre relate mainly to the specific issue of the education of ethnic minority children. As far as the broader issues are concerned, they rely heavily on current literature and occasional courses or conferences that do not always meet their immediate requirements. Unless self supportive cross-territorial arrangements could be agreed between authorities, it would appear that the consultative role of HMI will continue to be of critical importance.

LEA Z

1.   LEA Z believed that multicultural education was beyond its concern and discussion of my report was delegated to the County Adviser responsible for Geography and a primary school headteacher with experience in a multiracial school. Their lack of knowledge and experience of the matters raised permitted little opportunity for dialogue.

2.   The Authority adviser felt that although the LEA had no policy or opinion on multicultural education, certain of his colleagues in the humanities area included a number of multicultural considerations in the approach to their subjects. For example, a recent revision of the authority's agreed syllabus for Religious Education had widened its approach to comparative religion and teachers of geography were retreating slowly from the portrayal of a world simplistically divided into a prosperous West and a relatively primitive undeveloped East. The lack of concern about multicultural education within the schools and the authority was explained by lack of conviction that these matters were of direct concern to themselves, and reflected preoccupation with more immediate organisational and institutional concerns.

3.   To some extent the Authority's lack of initiative may be explained by geographical considerations. Its schools are widely dispersed, often unrelated to recognisable population centres. Its teacher centres are necessarily remote from all but a handful of schools, creating numerous problems for in-service teacher education. Advisers' time was occupied with a great deal of travelling so their contact with teachers in schools was very restricted. In any event, few if any were felt to have any direct knowledge of multicultural education.

4.   Since the onset of this survey the LEA has appointed an administrative officer to co-ordinate the teaching of ESL to the few ethnic minority pupils in the area and presumably, by association, some commitment to multicultural education. the issues raised by the survey would also be raised at the next quarterly meeting of all advisers.

CHAPTER 6

"Education for All": A New Approach

1. **Introduction**

1.1 From our analysis of the evolution of policies in relation to the educational needs of ethnic minority pupils and the broader educational implications of our multi-racial society, we believe that the reasons for the confused and confusing state of provision in this field today are clearly discernible. The absence of clear policy objectives based on firm educational principles, rather than determined by political expediency, from the early days of large-scale immigration has led to the development of piecemeal and *ad hoc* measures around the country varying from those multi-racial schools and areas which are now, in theory at least, committed to their interpretation of "multicultural education", to others which have ignored or rejected the need for any initiatives, in the belief that any problems which may exist will solve themselves given time – a truly "laissez-faire" philosophy. At the same time, areas of the country which as yet have little or no ethnic minority settlement, appear to have remained oblivious to the changed and changing nature of British society and convinced that this has no relevance to the education of their pupils.

1.2 We believe that much of the confusion which exists in the multicultural field derives from the fact that there are two distinct dimensions to the debate – on the one hand, meeting the educational needs of ethnic minority pupils, and, on the other, broadening the education offered to **all** pupils to reflect the multi-racial nature of British society. Whilst these two issues are clearly inter-related and, in our view, complementary, we believe it is now possible and indeed essential to see them within a new and broader perspective – that of offering **all** pupils a good, relevant and up to date education for life in Britain and the world as it is today. Because the early educational responses to the arrival in schools of pupils from a range of cultural backgrounds were, as we have seen, concerned almost exclusively with remedying what were perceived as the "problems" posed by these pupils, it is perhaps understandable that any discussion of the particular educational needs which ethnic minority pupils may experience tends to be regarded, quite mistakenly, as an attempt to "turn the clock back" to the days of assimilationist and intergrationist thinking. Similarly, the fact that attempts to develop educational policies designed to prepare all pupils for life in a multi-racial society often appear to be restricted to schools or authorities with ethnic minority pupils – as though the actual presence of such pupils was the major catalyst for such initiatives rather than any broader **educational** justification – has we believe not only tended to distort discussion of this aspect of educational development, but has also contributed to the generally disappointing degree of progress in this field, especially in "all-white" areas.

1.3   It could of course be suggested that, within our decentralised education system, it is neither appropriate nor desirable to seek to dictate policy too closely to LEAs or schools. Such a view assumes, however, that an appropriate educational response to the multi-racial nature of our society will simply "emerge" without any assistance or direction from the centre. We believe that our review of developments in this field over recent years shows clearly that, far from the various initiatives which have taken place converging into a consensus view of what needs to be done, there seems to have been, if anything, a marked divergence of view as LEAs and schools have continued to develop their own particular "brands" of multicultural education, with little reference to activities in other areas of the country. As long as the underlying climate of racism is allowed to persist unchallenged, it seems likely that, as the report[1] prepared by a staff working party at one multi-racial secondary school we visited put it:

"Multicultural education will not just happen, rather natural prejudice and institutionalised discrimination will dominate."

1.4   At the opening of this report we put forward our view of the kind of pluralist society for which we believe schools should be seeking to prepare children and, more broadly, the part which the education system as a whole can and should play in helping to shape such a society. It will be clear that our view of the role of education in laying the foundations for a genuinely pluralist society is at variance with some of the interpretations which have previously been placed on multicultural education. We believe it is essential to change fundamentally the terms of the debate about the educational response to today's multi-racial society and to look ahead to educating **all** children, from whatever ethnic group, to an understanding of the shared values of our society as a whole as well as to an appreciation of the diversity of lifestyles and cultural, religious and linguistic backgrounds which make up this society and the wider world. In so doing, all pupils should be given the knowledge and skills needed not only to contribute positively to shaping the future nature of British

---

[1] "Multi-cultural Education in the 1980's." Birley High School. Manchester. May 1980.

society but also to determine their own individual identities, free from preconceived or imposed stereotypes of their "place" in that society. We believe that schools also however have a responsibility, within the tradition of a flexible and child-orientated education system, to meet the individual eductational needs of **all** pupils in a positive and supportive manner, and this would include catering for any particular educational needs which an ethnic minority pupil may have, arising for example from his or her linguistic or cultural background.

1.5   In the course of our deliberations we have increasingly been led to reflect on whether the term "multicultural education" is adequate or indeed appropriate to describe the educational process which we envisage, which both caters for the educational needs of **all** children with equal seriousness and sensitivity and which also prepares **all** children, both ethnic minority and majority, through a common educational experience, for life in today's society. As we have already observed, the term "multicultural education" appears to have encouraged schools and LEAs in "all-white" areas to believe that the issues involved are of no concern to them since they see themselves as mono-cultural, and the term seems therefore to have added to the confusion which already exists about the aims and objectives involved. After considerable thought, we feel the simple and straightforward phrase **"Education for All"** describes more accurately the approach to education which we wish to put forward, since it reflects the responsibility which we feel that all those concerned with education share in laying the foundations for the kind of pluralist society which we envisaged at the opening of this report. In this chapter we set out the major principles which we believe should inform and underlie "Education for All" and consider the practical implications of these principles for the curriculum. We then go on to outline our broad strategy for the management of change which we believe to be essential in realising the reorientation of the education system which we have envisaged.

2.   The Principles of "Education for All"

2.1   We believe that the development of a broader approach to the education of **all** pupils is justified, and indeed essential, on straightforward educational grounds. As the DES paper "The School Curriculum[2]" emphasised:

> *"Since school education prepares the child for adult life, the way in which the school helps him to develop his potential must also*

---

[2] "The School Curriculum." DES/Welsh Office. March 1981.

317

be related to his subsequent needs and responsibilities as an active member of our society . . . . It helps neither the children, nor the nation, if the schools do not prepare them for the realities of the adult world."

A "Good" Education

On this basis it is clear that a good education must reflect the diversity of British society and indeed of the contemporary world. As the DES paper drew out, one of the broad aims of education must be:

" – to help pupils understand the world in which they live, and the inter-dependence of individuals, groups and nations."

A recent document from the CNAA Multicultural Working Group amplifies this:

"Education for diversity and for social and racial harmony suggests that the richness of cultural variety in Britain, let alone over the world, should be appreciated and utilised in education curricula at all levels. This can only have beneficial effects for all students in widening cultural awareness and in developing sensitivity towards the cultural identity and practices of various groups."

We firmly believe that the replacement of teaching materials which present an anachronistically Anglo-centric view of the world, and the development, for example, of history and geography syllabuses which are both multicultural in their content and global in their perspective, would remain equally valid from an **educational** point of view whether there were ethnic minority pupils in our schools or not. An out of date and inaccurate text book is indefensible on educational grounds and a history syllabus which presents world history exclusively in terms of British interests, experiences and values could in no way be regarded as "sound" history. Thus, we regard "Education for All" as essentially synonymous with a good and relevant education for life in the modern world – as the Schools Council put it in their evidence to us:

"Whatever the make-up of the locality, the pupils or the staff, however homogeneous or heterogeneous, the interplay of cultures and the world form the backdrop against which we act out our lives, and must be represented fully and compulsively in every facet of the curriculum. A curriculum that is not multicultural would prepare pupils for an unreal society and world; and involve them in a relearning process outside school; it would be an anachronism and an irrelevance since it would fail to prepare pupils for the real world."

318

2.2   We believe that a failure to broaden the perspectives presented to all pupils – particularly those from the ethnic majority community – through their education not only leaves them inadequately prepared for adult life but also constitutes a fundamental **mis**-education, in failing to reflect the diversity which is now a fact of life in this country. As the Assistant Masters and Mistresses Association has emphasised[3]:

> *"Pupils from all backgrounds will one day be voting, decision-making citizens whose views will influence public policies which affect people of all cultural backgrounds. All will contribute to the values of society. It is therefore important that all are made aware of the multicultural nature of British society today, and are encouraged in the attitudes of mutual knowledge, understanding and tolerance which alone can make such a multicultural society a fair and successful one."*

A good education must in our view give every youngster the knowledge, understanding and skills to function effectively as an individual, as a citizen of the wider national society in which he lives and in the interdependent world community of which he is also a member.

2.3   We also see education as having a major role to play in countering the racism which still persists in Britain today and which we believe constitutes one of the chief obstacles to the realisation of a truly pluralist society. We recognise that some people may feel that it is expecting a great deal of education to take a lead in seeking to remedy what can be seen as a social problem. Nevertheless we believe that the education system and teachers in particular are uniquely placed to influence the attitudes of all young people in a positive manner – as one teacher union observed in their evidence to us:

> *"School is the one institution that everyone between the ages of 5 and 16 in Britain has to attend and whilst it cannot alone compensate for the inequities of society it does nevertheless constitute one major area of influence – and one which is susceptible to change."*

Need to Challenge Racism

The need to identify and seek to challenge racism – both the misunderstandings and stereotypes which encourage its persistence, and its many manifestations which deny equality of access and opportunity to all groups – has however only recently been seen as a task for schools. We believe that education has a central role to play

---

[3] "Our Multi-cultural Society: The Educational Response." AMMA. 1983.

319

in preparing all pupils for life in today's multi-racial society, by ensuring that the degree of ignorance which still persists about ethnic minority groups is not allowed to remain uncorrected and that all teachers, pupils and thus the future citizens of this society are much more adequately informed about the range of cultures and lifestyles which are now part of this country. We discussed our views on the theory and practice of racism at some length in Chapter Two, and our attitude is reflected in the following extract from an LEA discussion paper[4]:

"Racism is morally wrong, and therefore contrary to basic principles of social justice since it involves gains and benefits for some members of society at the expense of losses and disadvantages for others. It is also against the long-term interests of the majority, since it is bound to lead in due course to considerable social unrest. It damages and dehumanises white people as well as black, giving them distorted views of their identity, society and history; and in this way too is against their own long-term interests."

A crucial element in developing our aim of "Education for All" is therefore to seek to identify and to remove those practices and procedures which work, directly or indirectly, and intentionally or unintentionally, against pupils from any ethnic group, and to promote, through the curriculum, an appreciation and commitment to the principles of equality and justice, on the part of all pupils. As one multi-racial secondary school put it to us in their "aims and objectives:"

"Our curriculum must acknowledge our multi-ethnic society and also take issue with racism. Therefore it must reflect the diversity of cultures in our society and demonstrate the value to society of cultural diversity .... We should help our pupils overcome assumptions about the superiority of modern, Western society and culture and teach them to approach all societies and cultures with understanding. We must prepare our pupils to live in harmony in a multiracial society by helping them to understand the social and economic origins of prejudice .... We want our pupils to have the power of critical reflection, the ability to explore ideas and attitudes with understanding and detachment, and the ability to challenge information. They should acquire the confidence to question established authorities and to think independently, and should learn to justify opinions in a rational manner."

---

[4] "Education for Equality." A discussion paper prepared in Summer 1982 by the Advisory Committee for Multicultural Education, Berkshire LEA.

As we have stressed in Chapter Two, much of the task in countering and overcoming racism is concerned with attitude change and with encouraging youngsters to develop positive attitudes towards the multi-racial nature of society, free from the influence of inaccurate myths and stereotypes about other ethnic groups. As the authors of the second NFER review of research commented:

> " . . . . surely if it is part of education to develop rationality and critical thinking schools cannot deny their function to assist all pupils to come to have a better appreciation of their own attitudes and emotions – including those towards race and especially other-race pupils in their own school environment. Pupils cannot be forced to like each other . . . . but in coming to see how irrational attitudes and emotions are constitutive of prejudice they may in turn reappraise their own thoughts and feelings which may later have some effect in changed behaviour."

2.4   We believe that such an approach is even more essential in "all-white" areas and schools, and the findings of the study by Mr Matthews and Mr Fallows detailed in the previous chapter illustrate how little progress has yet been made on this front. If youngsters from the ethnic majority community leave school with little if any understanding of the diversity of cultures and lifestyles in Britain today, and with their misunderstandings and ignorance of ethnic minority groups unchallenged or even reinforced, then there is little likelihood of the efforts of multi-racial areas overcoming the climate of racism which we believe exists. Indeed much of the evidence we have received has stressed this view and many of the staff at the multi-racial schools we visited clearly felt that their efforts would be largely in vain, especially in the face of the widespread influence of racism, unless teachers in non multi-racial areas were also prepared to reappraise and where necessary revise their work to reflect a pluralist perspective. As the staff of one multi-racial secondary school put it to us:

> "We recommend that a syllabus recognising the multi-ethnic character of Britain be used in ALL schools, NOT just those with a multi-ethnic population. Ignorance breeds prejudice, especially where there is no opportunity for recognising shared interests."

Not "Teaching Culture" or "Cultural Preservation"   2.5   The role of education cannot be and cannot be expected to be to reinforce the values, beliefs and cultural identity which each child brings to school – indeed such an education would surely be as rooted in one culture as much of the traditional Anglo-centric curriculum is at present. As one Asian teacher we met emphasised, the aim should not be:

> ". . . . the teaching of African or Asian Studies to ethnic minority pupils but rather a sharing and reassessment of one's own culture for all."

In this context we were struck by the comment made to us by a teacher at one school we visited where the pupil population was some 80% of Asian origin, with a majority of pupils sharing the same linguistic and religious background, that her school was as likely as an "all-white" school to offer a **mono**cultural rather than a **multi**cultural education unless great efforts were made to reflect a diversity of cultures, beliefs and lifestyles and not simply those of the majority community in the school. In our view an education which seeks only to emphasise and enhance the ethnic group identity of a child, at the expense of developing both a national identity and indeed an international, global perspective, cannot be regarded as in any sense multicultural. Rather than contributing towards the development of a pluralist society, it may indeed encourage moves towards separatism. As the American writer Professor James A Banks, whom we ourselves met, has proposed[5]:

> "We need to determine the most appropriate educational responses to the different and often conflicting behaviours, values, beliefs and identifications that students bring to school. Our role is certainly not merely to reinforce them. Such an education would be far too limiting and culturally encapsulating. It would also not help students to attain the values, skills, and abilities needed to fully participate in the national civic culture . . . . While the school should not merely reinforce the parochial cultures of students, it should, however, try to avoid teaching students contempt for their primordial cultures and making them ashamed of their behaviour, values and world-views."

Unlike some of those who gave evidence to us, we do not see schools as having a responsibility for cultural **preservation** – indeed, as the policy statement of one LEA we consulted put it:

> ". . . . education is not concerned with teaching children their culture. That is too presumptuous a role for education to attempt to undertake."

---

[5] "Cultural Democracy, Citizenship Education, and the American Dream." Social Education. March 1983.

It must be recognised that seeking to "preserve" a culture is in any case self-defeating since all cultures are dynamic and are continually changing and being changed. The cultures of the countries of origin of ethnic minority communities have indeed often undergone considerable change and development since the original migrants left. It is clear that many British-born ethnic minority youngsters are now developing a cultural identity which is rather different from that of their parents and grandparents, in which elements of their cultural background and their religious and linguistic heritage are blended with, but by no means subsumed by, the influences of the majority community's way of life. In this situation it would in our view be entirely wrong for schools to attempt to impose a predetermined and rigid "cultural identity" on any youngster, thus restricting his or her freedom to decide as far as possible for themselves their own future way of life. We would instead wish to see schools encouraging the cultural **development** of all their pupils, both in terms of helping them to gain confidence in their own cultural identities while learning to respect the identities of other groups as equally valid in their own right.

Not "Separate" Provision or "Tokenism"

2.6   In seeking to reflect the multi-racial nature of today's society within the curriculum and the overall life of a school however there is always a risk that only "token" account will be taken of the presence of ethnic minority pupils – as a paper prepared by one multi-racial LEA observed:

> "Adding "Multicultural Aspects" to an ethnocentric approach does not constitute multicultural education. Multicultural education of the "addition of multicultural aspects" variety (sometimes called the "steelband and Diwali" model) has been ill-conceived, although based on good intentions .... Multicultural education can only develop positively from a serious analysis of the cultural and racial assumptions in the "normal" British education system. The rejection of an ethnocentric approach requires a commitment to equality, which can only come from within each individual. It is a commitment which is either total or non-existent. A lip-service approach to multicultural education is probably more damaging than a declared ethnocentric approach."

We share this view of the need for a multicultural perspective to permeate **all** aspects of the educational experience. We have however been concerned to find the term "tokenism" employed rather too readily by some people to criticise quite genuine initiatives intended to foster mutual understanding between ethnic minority and ethnic majority communities. We have, for example, been present at one

323

school's "ethnic evening" (the type of activity often viewed as token-ism) – a concert featuring Asian, West Indian and "white, indigenous" music and dance, with none being presented as "exotic" or divergent from an assumed "norm" but all being seen as expressions of the pluralist character of the school's population. We believe it is wrong to dismiss such occasions automatically as tokenism; the key issue is whether such provisions are a school's **only** gesture towards the presence of ethnic minority pupils – which would in our view be a form of tokenism – or whether, as in this particular school, this was simply one manifestation of a school's overall attempt to reappraise and revise its practice, both in the curriculum "proper" and in such extra-curricular activities, in response to its pupil population.

Appreciation of Diversity

2.7   In our view "Education for All" should involve more than learning about the cultures and lifestyles of various ethnic groups; it should also seek to develop in **all** pupils, both ethnic majority and minority, a flexibility of mind and an ability to analyse critically and rationally the nature of British society today within a global context. The reality of British society now and in the future, is that a variety of ethnic groups, with their own distinct lifestyles and value systems, will be living together. It is perhaps inevitable that conflicts may arise from time to time between the aspirations and expectations of these groups. It is also possible that there will be some degree of cultural interchange, with individuals adopting or adapting elements of other group's cultural styles as part of their own. The aim of education should be to ensure that from their earliest years children learn to accept the normality and justice of a variety of points of view without feeling threatened, and are indeed encouraged to find this variety of outlook stimulating in itself. Schools should offer their pupils the skills needed to contribute to a resolution of any conflicts which do arise in a positive and constructive way. As the Schools Council put it in their evidence to us:

> *"It would be possible to say that (a multicultural) curriculum existed when: . . . . it was accepted by all sections of society that to draw on a diversity of cultural sources, and to incorporate a world perspective, was proper and unremarkable."*

In many respects therefore we are not concerned in this report primarily with changing the content of the curriculum, but rather with bringing about a fundamental reorientation of the attitudes which condition the selection of curriculum materials and subject matter and which underlie the actual teaching and learning process and the practices and procedures which play such an important part in determining how the educational experience impinges on the lives of pupils.

Educational Needs of Ethnic Minority Pupils

2.8   Within the overall education process which we have outlined, however, it must be recognised that some, but by no means all ethnic minority pupils, both those who have been born in this country and those who are themselves immigrants, have and will continue for the foreseeable future to have certain educational needs which may call for particular responses from schools. As the debate on multicultural education has increasingly come to focus on the broader aspects of provision for all pupils, the development of appropriate policies to respond to the particular educational needs which ethnic minority pupils may experience has tended to be subsumed within this broader context rather than analysed in any depth. Whilst we believe that the development of the kind of pluralist policies towards education which we have discussed above will clearly be of benefit to ethnic minority pupils along with their peers from the majority community, it is also essential that the education system caters for any specific educational needs which these pupils may experience, in order to offer them the true equality of opportunity which we have advocated.

Language Needs

2.9   As we have stressed in Chapter Two, it should never be assumed that ethnic minority pupils will automatically have particular educational difficulties, since this would be establishing a negative stereotype which is precisely what we wish to avoid. Nevertheless, some ethnic minority pupils may, for example, have particular language needs, either because English is not their first language or because they speak a dialect of English which differs from the Standard English of the school. If and when such language needs arise, they should not be regarded negatively simply as "problems", but rather should be seen as just one aspect of that pupil's individual educational needs, which may in any case be similar in nature if not in degree to the linguistic needs of some ethnic majority pupils, and for which it is therefore entirely reasonable and proper to expect schools to cater. An essential distinction must however be drawn between the view taken of catering for ethnic minority pupils' language needs within the assimilationist philosophy and within our pluralist philosophy. Whereas the intention of teaching pupils English was previously seen as enabling them to "settle down" and be absorbed within the majority community, our aim is to accord ethnic minority pupils equality of access and opportunity in a society in which a full command of standard English is and will remain a key factor in success both in academic terms and in adult life.

"Pastoral" Needs

2.10   Looking beyond the language field, if a pupil's parents are not familiar with the British education system and may not be fully fluent in English, this may call for particular sensitivity and appreciation of the situation in the school's arrangements for home/school liaison in order to enable the parents to play their full part in supporting

325

their child's education. An understanding of the home and family background of pupils from different cultural groups, again not based on negative stereotypes or value judgments, may also be necessary for the school to be able to cater for any particular "pastoral" needs which an ethnic minority pupil may experience, for example in relation to intergenerational conflicts or educational aspirations. Similarly we believe that in relation to "pastoral" concerns, schools should take full account of the cultural background from which their pupils come, so that no pupils, nor by extension their parents, are forced into a position of conflict between the requirements of their fundamental religious beliefs and the provisions of the school.

2.11   Thus, schools with ethnic minority pupils should regard any particular educational needs which these pupils may have, as a result of their cultural, religious or linguistic background, as essentially no different from the educational needs which any child may have and which they therefore have a responsibility to meet. The traditional child-centred response of schools should simply be broadened to encompass any particular needs which may derive from the diversity of their pupil population. We believe education must offer ethnic minority pupils not merely acceptance or tolerance – both of which attitudes tend to imply that ethnic minority groups are still regarded by the majority community as outsiders who are here only "on sufferance" – but rather true equality of opportunity and treatment within a framework which regards cultural diversity as a valuable resource to enrich the lives of all and in which all children are able to benefit both from their own cultural heritage and also that of others.

2.12   We hope that the principles which we have put forward here will be accepted by those involved in education at both classroom level and in policy-making at central and local level, and also by the ethnic minority communities. We believe it is only through reaching a consensus on the overall task for education both in meeting the needs of ethnic minority pupils and in preparing **all** pupils, both ethnic minority and ethnic majority, through a common educational experience, for life in today's multi-racial Britain, that our aim of a truly pluralist society can be achieved.

3.   Implications for the Curriculum

3.1   We have outlined above the broad principles which we believe should underlie an education which would prepare all youngsters to live in and to shape the kind of pluralist society which we advocated at the opening of this report. We now turn to the practical implications of such an approach for the curriculum. An increasing amount of attention has been devoted to various aspects of multicultural education during the lifetime of this Committee and a good deal of valid and worthwhile work has undoubtedly taken place. The extent to which our view of the education system's response to today's multi-racial society goes beyond many of these interpretations of multicultural education is we believe self-evident. Not only have we rejected the legacies of the assimilationist and integrationist schools of thought but we have also resisted some of the more recent moves towards encouraging a separatist "solution" to the concerns of ethnic minority communities. The majority of initiatives which have been taken in the multicultural field have still tended to take as their starting point the needs of ethnic minority pupils as something separate and distinct from the mainstream of educational provision. Even when they have gone on to consider the implications of cultural diversity for pupils from the majority community, those developments which have taken place have usually fallen far short of the fundamental reappraisal of what constitutes a good and relevant education for **all** pupils in today's society, which we have advocated. We do not believe therefore that the aims and objectives which we have set out for "Education for All" have yet been fully realised in any of the schools or LEAs from whom we have received evidence. Consequently we are not able to put forward any ready made examples of "good practice", as models for others to emulate. Even where initiatives have been taken in respect of particular areas of the curriculum which go some way towards reflecting the pluralist character of British society today, these have almost always been limited to multi-racial schools and the focus has therefore been primarily on the needs of ethnic minority pupils. We would emphasise again however that in our view the curriculum offered to all pupils, whether in multi-racial or "all-white" schools, must be permeated by a genuinely pluralist perspective which should inform and influence both the selection of content and the teaching materials used.

3.2   We believe there is scope for the whole range of curricular areas to be developed to offer pupils an education more balanced and relevant to the multi-racial nature of today's society. In structuring our own work it was clearly beyond the resources available to us, in either time or specialist expertise, to investigate in depth the various ways in which each and every subject area could contribute to this process. We therefore decided to focus our attention for this report on those aspects of education which emerged clearly from the evidence we received, from the ethnic minority communities, LEAs, schools and teachers, as arousing the greatest interest and anxieties:

327

language and language education, and religion and the role of the school. Accordingly we devote chapters in the next part of this report to these broad areas of educational experience. From Chapter Seven we discuss a range of linguistic issues – the needs of children for whom English is not a first language, the diverse strands of the "mother tongue" debate, the concept of "language across the curriculum", and the general need for enhanced awareness and understanding of the nature of language and of linguistic diversity. From Chapter Eight on we consider not only the implications for "religious education" of the range of religious faiths and belief systems now present in this society, but also the controversial and topical question of the calls from sections of certain ethnic minority communities to establish their own "separate"schools, which derive in the main from essentially religious concerns. In both chapters we put forward specific conclusions and recommendations for progress, reflecting the principles we set out earlier in this chapter. As we emphasised in our interim report, teachers are the key figures in our educational system since any changes in the content, approach, and overall direction of the curriculum can only be achieved with their cooperation and support. In turn, however, teachers are to some extent at least only as good as the training which they receive, both before commencing teaching and in the course of their careers. We have therefore devoted a further chapter to considering in some depth the implications of our view of the task for education, for teacher training at all levels. Whilst some sections of each of these chapters relate specifically to the particular needs which may be experienced by ethnic minority pupils, we seek to take as our starting point throughout the need to enhance the educational experience of **all** pupils. Taken together with the further comments we make here, we believe these chapters illustrate clearly the practical implications of the principles of "Education for All" which we have set out here, and we hope they will serve as exemplars which will enable practitioners in other areas of education to appraise and where necessary revise their work along pluralist lines.

Evaluating the Curriculum

3.3   As we have already emphasised, we are not concerned so much with changing the content of the curriculum as with bringing about a reorientation of the attitudes which inform and condition the selection of teaching materials and the way in which various topics are approached and presented. In seeking to revise the curriculum which they offer their pupils, teachers will, we believe, need to review their work in the light of a range of broad considerations. The following criteria for evaluating the curriculum in this way were suggested in the evidence which we received from the Schools Council:

328

" i. *The variety of social, cultural and ethnic groups and a perspective of the world should be evident in visuals, stories, conversation and information.*

ii. *People from social, cultural and ethnic groups should be presented as individuals with every human attribute.*

iii. *Cultures should be empathetically described in their own terms and not judged against some notion of 'ethnocentric' or 'Euro-centric' culture.*

iv. *The curriculum should include accurate information on racial and cultural differences and similarities."*

We strongly support these criteria but would wish to add a further two, in order to fully reflect the principles of "Education for All":

– All children should be encouraged to see the cultural diversity of our society in a positive light.

– The issue of racism, at both institutional and individual level, should be considered openly and efforts made to counter it.

Developments in the Humanities

3.4 Although progress in developing a pluralist perspective to the school curriculum which reflects these broad criteria has, in our view, been disappointingly slow, it must be acknowledged that increasing attention has been devoted over recent years to the opportunities for reflecting different cultural perspectives in various subject areas, especially within the humanities. Recent curriculum initiatives in the geography field for example have focussed on the need to move away from a perception of other countries, especially those outside Europe, solely in "British" terms, and have emphasised the need to recognise that, as the book "Teaching World Studies"[6] has put it:

"Other nations and cultures have their own validity and should be described in their own terms. Wherever possible they should be allowed to speak for themselves and not be judged exclusively against British or European norms."

The diversity of British society today and the interdependence of the global community also has clear implications for the teaching of history. As the Secretary of State himself observed[7], in discussing the educational justifications for the teaching of history:

---

[6] "Teaching World Studies – an introduction to global perspectives in the curriculum." Ed. Hicks and Townley. Longman. 1982.
[7] Speech to a Conference organised by the Historical Association 10 February 1984.

329

> *"History is . . . . indispensable to understanding the society we live in: to an awareness by pupils of the place of themselves, their families and communities in the developing story of the nation, a story which itself involves other nations and peoples. Our society, like many, is the product of centuries of change, and its history throws light on why things now are as they are".*

On this basis it is clearly essential that an effective history course should concern itself with the patterns of migration which have created today's multi-racial society and consider, in a balanced manner, the factors which have led certain groups, from the time of the Huguenots and earlier, to settle in this country. It must also offer all pupils an understanding of the economic and political relationships which exist in the contemporary world, based on a sensitive appreciation of how and why these have arisen. A pluralist approach to both the national and international dimensions of history can thus enhance a youngster's perception and comprehension of the tide of human experience through history, and ensure that his or her horizons are not limited by an exclusively Anglo- or Euro-centric view, rooted solely in the legacy of Empire, of the world as it is today. As one writer has observed[8], a history syllabus centred entirely on British history:

> *" . . . . will only reinforce . . . . ethnocentric attitudes, and foreigners, who only appear on the scene to be defeated, enslaved and exploited for the glory of one's own group, will hardly be seen more tolerantly when encountered in another context."*

A global perspective to the teaching of history can thus help to counter and overcome the negative stereotypes of ethnic minority groups which lie at the heart of racism.

Books and Teaching Materials

3.5 One of the most important factors in influencing how pupils interpret what they are taught is the selection of the textbooks and teaching materials used in schools. Images, both pictorial and verbal, are among the most powerful influences on how a child perceives the world and thus a major potential source of stereotypes of ethnic minority groups. As one writer[9] has emphasised:

---

[8] "Prejudice and the Teaching of History." C Hannam. Taken from "New Movements in the Study and Teaching of History." Ed M Ballard. Temple Smith. 1970.
[9] "Resources for Multicultural Education: An Introduction." Gillian Klein. Schools Council Programme 4. 1982.

"Neither reading nor writing takes place in a cultural vacuum. All authors bring to their work their own values and attitudes; all readers relate to what they read in the light of their own perceptions. Each early reading experience validates the printed word . . . . It is some years before children learn to question the truth of what they read, and even then they are unlikely to identify and challenge biases which do not immediately threaten them, unless they are actively encouraged to do so. Consider the role of print in shaping children's attitudes towards the world and relate it to the multicultural society into which they are growing up. The population of Britain has changed radically in the past forty years: books have changed little. There is much greater cultural diversity in customs, languages, religious beliefs, skin colours and life-styles, and yet the view of many is of one cultural norm and one way of looking at the world; and prejudice and discrimination remain a reality. Consider next children's reading matter in relation to children in the U.K. and their wide range of life-styles and experiences. Many children see cultural diversity all round them but find little confirmation of it in what they read. Children from ethnic minorities in Britain need to see their culture accurately portrayed and their existence acknowledged in the books they encounter. Children in areas still predominantly white and momocultural are likely to accept without question exclusively monocentric portrayals of other lands and racial stereotypes in books. All these children are growing up into a multicultural society and a shrinking and interdependent world. We who bring them into contact with books have a responsibility to ensure that those books offer not outdated and biased views but accuracy and a multicultural perspective on the world and the people in it."

In our interim report we advocated the review of textbooks and teaching materials in response to today's multi-racial society, and, where resources allowed, the replacement of those which were found to reflect a negative and inaccurate view of any ethnic group. We drew attention to the availability of a number of "checklists" designed to assist teachers in assessing the books they use and indeed reproduced, as an exemplar, the checklist prepared by the NUT drawn from their pamphlet "Guidelines on Racial Stereotyping in Textbooks and Learning Materials". As we stressed in that report, however, even books which portray ethnic minority groups in a negative light can remain valid educational "tools" provided they are used with great skill and sensitivity by the teacher, both as a means of raising the issues of prejudice and stereotyping with pupils, and also, as the interim report observed:

> *" .... (to) provide an insight into the prevailing attitudes and opinions of the time when they were written."*

Relevance to other Curriculum Areas

3.6   As we have already emphasised, we believe that all areas of the curriculum can contribute towards the development of an education which is more appropriate to the contemporary world. It is essential therefore to look beyond those subject areas which have traditionally been seen as open to a broader, pluralist perspective, and to recognise the less obvious relevance of cultural diversity for specialisms such as the sciences and mathematics. The guidelines for reviewing the curriculum prepared by one LEA which submitted evidence to us suggested the following broader perspectives to the teaching of the sciences:

> *"– the development of themes related to conservation and pollution, disease, food and health and population growth needs to be considered in relation to humankind as a whole and the issues of regional or group differences need to be worked out and developed in the context of interdependence and unequal resources;*
>
> *– the issue of 'race' and the origins of humankind needs to be considered carefully in relation to the myths surrounding theories of race;*
>
> *– the question of difference of pigment and physical features and the assumptions made about identities on the basis of pigment needs to be explored more fully;*
>
> *– the history of science, particularly the early history of chemistry and medicine needs to be developed comparatively;*
>
> *– the selection of examples for classroom use needs to take account of the contribution and participation in scientific endeavours of people from a range of backgrounds and cultures;*
>
> *– the question of science as being only a European phenomenon needs to be raised and discussed."*

In relation to mathematics, the Cockcroft Report[10] outlined as follows the various ways in which provision in this field could reflect the diversity of cultural backgrounds and lifestyles now represented in the pupil population:

---

[10] "Mathematics Counts." Report of the Committee of Inquiry into the Teaching of Mathematics in Schools. HMSO. 1982.

"It is possible to make positive use of mathematical ideas drawn from other cultures, especially when discussing shape and space. For example, many of the Rangoli patterns which are used by Hindu and Sikh families to decorate their homes on important occasions have a geometrical basis in which symmetry plays a major part. Practice in drawing patterns of this kind can help to develop geometrical concepts. Again, the intricate patterns which decorate many Islamic buildings are formed by fitting together various geometrical shapes. Patterns of this kind can be examined and discussed and children can then create patterns of their own. As children grow older, it is possible to discuss the ways in which the numerals which we now use have developed from those which were originally used in eastern countries, and the contributions to the development of mathematics which have come from different countries and different cultures."

The creative and peforming arts also lend themselves to the development of an appreciation and awareness of a range of cultures through the study of art forms drawn not only from a European context, and the consideration of music and dance from different cultures and countries. Drama can also play a particularly important part in helping youngsters to reflect on the nature of prejudice and racism through role-playing situations, in which the influence of stereotyping and the ways in which misunderstandings can arise from ignorance about communities other than one's own are explored. There is in fact we believe no area of the curriculum, at either primary or secondary level, which would not be enhanced signficantly in educational terms by the incorporation of a pluralist perspective. It may be worthwhile mentioning here a recent book on "Curriculum Opportunities in a Multicultural Society"[11], based largely on the work undertaken for the Schools Council's Project on "Assessment in a Multicultural Society", which seeks to:

". . . . help teachers visualize multicultural education in terms of their own teaching."

The contributors discuss a number of subject areas, ranging from the humanities and language and literature to mathematics and science and the arts and physical education. In each case the writers, who are themselves teachers or teacher educators, seek to explore three distinct themes:

---

[11] "Curriculum Opportunities in a Multicultural Society." Ed A Craft and G Bardell. Harper and Row Limited. 1984.

> *"– . . . . whether ethnic minority pupils might have particular contributions to make or particular classroom needs in relation to individual curriculum subjects . . . .*
>
> *– . . . . how their subject could contribute to **all** pupils' understanding and acceptance of cultural diversity . . . . (and)*
>
> *– . . . . ways in which their subject could make a more specific and direct contribution towards the combatting of racism."*

Although it does not purport to offer all the answers, we feel that teachers in particular may well find this book of considerable help in considering the practical implications of adopting a broader view of the curriculum for their subject areas.

Political Education

3.7   There is one particular area of the curriculum, to which we have devoted some attention, which we would like to discuss briefly here in the light of our view of the contribution of schools in laying the foundations of a genuinely pluralist society and in countering the influence of racism: political education. Although there has been an increasing amount of discussion in recent years about the theory and practice of political education, this area of the curriculum still tends to be the subject of considerable controversy within and beyond educational circles. Much of the opposition to political education has we believe derived from confusion about its objectives and some of the strongest opponents of its inclusion in the school curriculum have regarded it simply as a form of indoctrination of pupils with clearly defined "party political" beliefs with a view to undermining and destabilising the democratic processes of our society. Far from seeking to dictate or prescribe the political views which pupils should or should not hold, political education should however, in our view, through encouraging pupils to consider how power is exercised and by whom at different levels in our society, how resources are allocated, how policies are determined and implemented, how decisions are taken and how conflicts are resolved, be no more likely to lead them to question and challenge the status quo, other than where this is justified, than to defend and seek to retain it. The essential aim of political education should be to open pupils' minds to a full appreciation of the role which they as adults can and should play in shaping their futures. Political education can thus be described in the simplest terms, in the words of the Thompson Report on the Youth Service,[12] as:

---

[12] "Experience and Participation." Report of the Review Group on the Youth Service in England. Cmnd 8686. HMSO. 1982.

> *. . . . the process whereby a young individual learns how to claim the right of a member of a democratic society and to have a say in how it affects him or her."*

3.8   In broad terms we believe that effective political education should entail a consideration of: the institutional framework of politics in this country; the major contemporary political issues; the role of individuals and various groupings within the political process; and the range of political values and viewpoints present in society. We also regard the intellectual skills which we have already emphasised we feel all schools should be offering their pupils as part of a "good" education – the ability to accept a range of differing and possibly conflicting points of view and to argue rationally and independently about the principles which underlie these, free from preconceived prejudices or stereotypes, and to recognise and resist false arguments and propaganda – as in a sense "political" skills. We believe that effective political education must also help pupils to appreciate the contribution which they as individuals can make to the decision-making process at various levels. Adopting an "active" approach to political education, rather than, as some schools have done, "retreating into knowledge" through an arid study of political machinery, will inevitably influence the way in which the framework of political life in this country is presented to pupils and should mean that existing institutions and procedures are not necessarily regarded as immutable but consideration is given to the possible need for further development or constructive change to meet changing circumstances. Thus, as the authors of the report of the Hansard Society's major Programme for Political Education[13] have put it:

> *"The politically literate person is not merely an informed spectator: he is someone capable of active participation or of positive refusal to participate. At the same time the politically literate person, while tolerating the views of others, is capable of thinking in terms of change and of methods of achieving change."*

3.9   If youngsters are led to reflect critically on the political framework of life in this country, this should involve a consideration of how particular structures and procedures have evolved and their appropriateness to today's multi-racial population. Learning how some long-established practices were originally developed to cater for a relatively homogeneous population should lead youngsters by

---

[13] "Political Education and Political Literacy." Ed Crick and Porter. Longman. 1978.

extension to consider whether such practices are still appropriate to the changed and changing nature of British society today. It should also lead them to consider whether some can now be seen to operate against the interests of certain sections of the community, especially the numerically smaller ethnic minority groups, by depriving them of equality of access to the full range of opportunities open to the majority community. In thus learning how racism can operate, youngsters from both the minority and majority communities may be better able to understand and challenge its influence and to consider positive and constructive changes to reflect the values of a pluralist democracy. This process should not be seen as in any sense posing a threat to democratic principles but rather as a reaffirmation of these principles in response to changing circumstances. Effective political education should also lead youngsters to consider fundamental issues such as social justice and equality and this should in turn cause them to reflect on the origins and mechanism of racism and and prejudice at an individual level. As the Schools Council Report on Social Studies[14] comments:

". . . . courses which stress responsible participation are likely to heighten candidates' awareness of and sensitivity to injustice, prejudice or discrimination."

– and, as HMI observed in their "Red Book":[15]

"Some views and attitudes are arguably unacceptable in our democracy: racism, suppression of opinion, exploitation of the defenceless. These are anathema to most people in our society. Education which identifies the evils we must resist, and suggests how we may resist them, is quite proper and likely to command wide support."

Political education can thus play a major part in countering and overcoming racism at both institutional and individual levels.

3.10 Some educationists have argued that school pupils are insufficiently mature and responsible to be able to comprehend politically sensitive issues such as racism and to cope with them in a balanced and rational manner. Even primary-age pupils however have views and opinions on various "political" issues and are subject to a range of overt and covert political influences based on values and

---

[14] "Assessment in a Multicultural Society. Social Sciences at 16+: a discussion document." A Mukhopadhyay. Schools Council. May 1984.
[15] Chapter on "Political Competence." Taken from "Curriculum 11–16. Working Papers by HM Inspectorate: a contribution to current debate." 1977.

assumptions from their homes, their peers and the media. Our own discussions with secondary pupils from a range of ethnic backgrounds have left us in no doubt that the majority of them have strong views on issues which can be perceived as "political" and have definite opinions on "racial" questions such as immigration, discrimination and the respective "rights and responsibilities" of the ethnic majority community and ethnic minority groups in this society. The more detailed discussions with pupils undertaken by Mr Matthews and Mr Fallows in a range of "all-white" schools (described in Annexes C and D to Chapter Five) confirmed this and highlighted the extent to which pupils' professed attitudes to issues such as the National Front's stance on immigration were far from matched by actual knowledge and understanding of the political arena, being based largely on hearsay and anecdotal sources and derived from family and peer group influences. It must also be recognised that political parties of various persuasions have actively sought to recruit the allegiance of youngsters and a number of school sixth formers are of course already eligible to vote. It is therefore clear that school pupils can in no sense be considered immune to the general political climate. We believe that schools have a clear responsibility to provide accurate factual information and opportunities for balanced and sensitive consideration of political issues in order to enable pupils to reflect upon and sometimes reconsider their political opinions within a broader context. On "racial" issues, as the authors of one article have put it:[16]

> *"The question of race relations permeates our society and one might expect schools, as regulators of society, to do their best to correct misconceptions."*

3.11 We have already emphasised that a central aim of political education should be to equip youngsters with the necessary knowledge and skills for informed and responsible participation in adult life. We believe this objective can be especially important in relation to pupils of ethnic minority origin whose families may be unfamiliar with the institutions and procedures which exist in this country. In Chapter Two we referred to the growing discontent and alienation of an increasing number of ethnic minority youngsters, arising largely from the continuing climate of racism in society and their sense of frustration at what they see as their lack of power to determine their own futures or to influence long-standing practices which they feel fail to take account of their presence here. As Lord Scarman observed in his report:[17]

---

[16] "Teaching for better race relations?" Patricia J Sikes and David J S Sheard. Cambridge Journal of Education. Vol 8 Numbers 2 and 3. 1978.
[17] "The Brixton Disorders." Cmnd 8427. HMSO. November 1981.

"Some young blacks are driven by their despair into feeling that they are rejected by the society of which they rightly believe they are members and in which they would wish to enjoy the same opportunities and to accept the same risks as everyone else. But their experience leads them to believe that their opportunities are less and their risks are greater. Young black people feel neither socially nor economically secure. In addition they do not feel politically secure. Their sense of rejection is not eased by the low level of black representation in our elective political institutions. Their sense of insecurity is not relieved by the liberty our law provides to those who march and demonstrate in favour of tougher immigration controls and "repatriation" of the blacks. Rightly or wrongly, young black people do not feel politically secure, any more than they feel economically or socially secure."

Whilst Lord Scarman was focussing here on the West Indian community, many of these concerns bear equally or more heavily on children from the Asian communities. Lord Scarman's central concern was with the extent to which:

"The accumulation of these anxieties and frustrations and the limited opportunities of airing their grievances at national level in British society .... (might) .... create a predisposition towards violent protest."

This view in itself may well contribute to an unjustifiably negative and stereotyped picture of the attitudes of ethnic minority communities. We believe however that unless urgent and positive efforts are made to counter the growing alienation of many ethnic minority youngsters for the majority community, there is a genuine risk to the long term stability and cohesion of our society through increasing fragmentation along separatist lines, entirely contrary to our aim of a pluralist society. At the broadest level, efforts must be made to involve ethnic minority communities more effectively in policy formulation and decision making in a local and national context. A major step forward can be made in combating racism through the direct involvement of members of ethnic minority communities in positions of power and influence, whether as teachers in the classroom or as Members of Parliament. (At present there are no MPs of Asian or West Indian origin.) The belief that having more ethnic minority teachers, school governors, local authority elected members and MPs would of itself help to counter racism may seem unduly idealistic, but we believe that it is only through ethnic minority communities coming to see themselves in this clear and visible way as having the right and opportunity to shape policies

338

which bear on aspects of their lives, that the present gulf in trust and understanding, which has been deepened by the pervasive influence on racism, can be effectively bridged. We also believe that the political education offered to ethnic minority youngsters can play a major role in countering their sense of alienation, by informing them about the institutions and procedures available within the political framework for making their opinions known, and opening their minds to the possibility that existing practices may, and sometimes should, be altered or replaced. Effective political education can also provide ethnic minority youngsters with the skills necessary to participate in political activities, thus helping to channel their energies into positive rather than negative forms of expression. In this way we believe that political education can be crucial in developing and extending our democratic way of life in the interests of all our citizens. As one writer has put it:[18]

> "It is accepted that education alone cannot significantly alter the basic structure of society but conceivably it could be a powerful and persuasive contributory agent, especially if the alternative is seen as the progressive disintegration of political democracy, a possibility for which the present levels of political ignorance, cynicism and alienation signal a salutary warning . . . . ultimately, the preservation and strengthening of political democracy . . . . can only be achieved if the educational system and other social agencies make a serious effort to heighten the general level of social and political awareness, to increase the possibilities of political involvement and to seek especially to develop in young people attitudes, knowledge and skills which enable them to be politically sensitive and, if they choose to act, politically effective."

3.12 There has been considerable debate amongst the proponents of political education about whether this should be developed as a self-standing curriculum area for all pupils (a limited number of pupils do of course already study for public examinations in subjects such as British Constitution), or whether the essential aims of political education can be achieved through existing subject areas, most notably History or Social Studies. If it is decided to infuse political literacy indirectly through other subjects, we must emphasise the need to identify and develop the political dimension of these subjects explicitly, to ensure that the overall aims and objectives are clearly understood and the contributions of different subject areas are complementary rather than overlapping or contradictory. In view of the role which we believe political education can play in relation to

---

[18] "Political Education and Democracy." Brennan. Cambridge University Press. 1981.

ethnic minority pupils, we hope that multi-racial schools in particular will be prepared to consider the place of political education within their work. There are two final points which we would like to see being taken into account in the further development of political education. Firstly we believe that a start can be made to political education at the primary level in developing the basic "political" skills needed to benefit from more specific provision at secondary level. Secondly it must be recognised that schools are themselves political institutions in the sense that they represent a microcosm of the wider society – as HMI again acknowledged in their "Red Book":

> *"Schools are themselves political institutions in that they involve power and authority, participation, and the resolution of different opinions. Children's perceptions of these are arguably a strong influence in the development of their political attitudes."*

Effective political education must therefore we believe begin **within** schools and the principles which are being developed within the curriculum must be reflected in the day to day life of the school. This can be a particularly important consideration in multi-racial schools where many ethnic minority youngsters rightly or wrongly believe that their needs and concerns are accorded inadequate attention and their opinions are rarely if ever sought and even more rarely heeded. In our own evidence gathering, we were struck by the number of occasions on which, in our discussions with ethnic minority youngsters, we were told that this was the first time in their school careers that anyone had ever sought their views on such relevant and diverse issues as "mother tongue" teaching, the influence of racism on their lives or their attitudes towards teaching as a career. We would like to see senior pupils from both the minority and majority communities far more closely involved by schools, either through school councils or pupils representatives on the governing body, or through informal class discussions, in the consideration of such issues and of the balance and content of the curriculum.

The "Hidden" Curriculum

3.13 Up to now we have focussed primarily on the practical implications of "Education for All" for various areas of the "taught" curriculum. As important, if not more so, in the overall education process is however the "hidden" curriculum offered by schools through the ethos which they present and their attitudes and policies towards what can broadly be termed the "pastoral" needs of their pupils at the interface of the home and the school. We firmly believe that the fundamental principles which we set out earlier in this chapter must equally be seen to be reflected in this aspect of a school's work, especially with regard to the issues which may arise in a multi-racial context, over the concerns of some ethnic minority pupils. As the Schools Council put it in their evidence to us:

"The school must be **seen** *to be welcoming to other cultures, and not confine itself to teaching about them in the classroom while rejecting their manifest expression."*

3.14 We have already emphasised that we regard as one of the principles of "Education for All" that multi-racial schools should take full account, in their "pastoral" provisions, of the cultural background from which their pupils come, so that no pupils, or their parents, are forced into a position of conflict betwen the requirements of their religious beliefs and the rules and practices of the school. We have received a considerable amount of evidence, chiefly, but not exclusively, from the Asian community, expressing concern about the policies of schools in relation to matters such as meals, uniform and dress for physical education, particularly with regard to the education of girls at secondary level. We discuss the points at issue in our consideration of the case for "separate" schools in our Chapter on Religion and the Role of the School, since the establishment of such schools is seen by some sections of the Asian community as the only means of ensuring that their concerns in relation to such matters are adequately met. Nevertheless, even amongst those parents who believe that their children's educational needs can be met within existing schools, there is still considerable strength of feeling about these issues, as we found in our own meetings and discussions with community representatives, and a widespread belief that schools are unable or unwilling to treat such matters seriously. It certainly seems that in some schools Asian parents who have expressed concern about, for example, their daughters having to wear a skirt rather than trousers as part of the school uniform, have been regarded as being "awkward", and their concerns, which may be based on a deep and sincere belief in fulfilling their duties as Muslim parents according to the requirements of their faith, have been dismissed as "petty" and unimportant and the solution has been seen as simply "talking them round". This insensitive and dismissive attitude is clearly shown in the following extract from evidence we received from one multi-racial secondary school:

> *"On the odd occasion we have had an Asian girl's parents of Moslem faith requesting that their daughter should be allowed to wear trousers. With a little pressure from the Headmaster, however, the request has always been dropped. Apart from the above idiosyncracies of uniform, there have been no obvious problems and the same would apply to Physical Education and school meals."*

In some cases which were drawn to our attention, because Heads and teachers failed to treat such parental concerns seriously at first, further

341

misunderstandings and mistrust arose and the incident was allowed to escalate to a point where quite major conflicts between the community and the school authorities, possibly involving whole groups of pupils, resulted. The following "case-study", taken from evidence we received, illustrates this vividly:

> *"Local (Asian) girl was excluded from school ... when her father requested she be allowed not to take part in the once weekly swimming classes (mixed sex) which runs for half an academic year! Despite letters from Islamic authorities to Head teacher and Education Department supporting father in his view, the Head teacher maintained his stance that swimming was "a vital and integral part of the school's curricula", and that the girl "was excluding herself by refusing school discipline". Head refused to admit girl while matter was being resolved "unless she takes part in swimming". Matters eventually taken to MP at same time CRC ensured that Chief Education Officer fully aware that it would make a national campaign of this, and that it considered the Head's actions to be illegal re Race Relations Act and would refer it for action. Head then, presumably, ordered to admit child "while the whole situation being reviewed". Comments to Assistant Community Relations Officer from Head during discussions included "It's the thin end of the wedge" – "These people have got to be shown that they can't have everything to their convenience" and "I will only admit this girl under their conditions if I am ordered to" ... "I will stop swimming for every child in the school if she is excluded from the subject".*

Asian pupils can thus be placed under very strong pressures in being torn between on the one hand their obedience to their parents, their adherence to their faith and their allegiance to their community, and on the other, their desire to comply with the normal practices of the school and the instructions of their teachers. It is important that schools are sensitive to the pressures on children of differing sets of values at school and home resulting from the differing cultural experiences to which child and parent are exposed. Tolerance of and respect for cultural difference at school, may in some cases be in marked contrast to the perhaps more rigid, cultural stance adopted in the home and the problems experienced in this respect may be particularly acute for some ethnic minority girls.

3.15 Illustrations of the way in which such "confrontation" situations can be avoided, as we would wish, through discussions between schools and parents based on an informed understanding of

342

each other's position, were provided in the evidence we received from a number of schools and LEAs. For example, the following reference to school uniform was included in the policy statement of one multi-racial LEA:

"The desire of many Headteachers to have distinctive school uniforms for a variety of reasons is appreciated, but pupils should not be excluded from school because they are not dressed exactly in accordance with school rules. The Authority will not support Heads who exclude pupils and provoke confrontation with parents on this ground alone."

Some LEAs also now make provision for halal meat to be available for Muslim pupils for school dinners. One multi-racial school described their positive and sensitive approach to the issue of dress for physical education, which has also aroused concern, as follows:

"Allowances are made for religious and cultural beliefs regarding dress for physical education, provided always that safety is paramount. Difficulties arise in some instances involving Muslim girls in swimming lessons. These are largely overcome by direct contact with parents, but in a minority of cases it has been decided that the children will miss out on this part of the curriculum. It is believed that the adoption of an inflexible attitude could lead to hostility between home and school, which could be detrimental to all."

We must emphasise again however that we would not regard it as a function of schools to seek to impose a particular cultural identity on any pupil and we cannot accept therefore that, as some Muslim organisations have suggested to us, schools should **assume** that each and every Muslim pupil or parent will necessarily perceive the rquirements of their faith, in relation to such "pastoral" matters, in the same way. We believe however that all parents and pupils should be free to act in accordance with their religious beliefs, unless these are seen to be in direct conflict with the essential **educational** function of schools or to place the physical well-being of any child at risk.

3.16 We have already indicated that it was not our aim in this report to put forward a ready made blueprint for the development of a pluralist approach in all areas of educational experience. We believe however that, from the points which we have raised here, in relation to both the taught and "hidden" curriculum, and the more detailed chapters which follow, individual teachers should be able to interpret and adapt these general principles within their particular subject specialism or levels of provision.

4. The Management of Change

4.1 We believe that the development of the more broadly-based, pluralist approach to education which we have outlined in this chapter, and which is the central theme of this report, constitutes possibly the most urgent and important challenge facing the education system today. One of the major reasons for the hitherto limited and disappointingly slow rate of progress in recognising and responding to this challenge has in our view been the absence of a **coherent overall strategy** for stimulating developments and coordinating initiatives, with, above all, the committed support of central Government in the form of adequate and appropriate resources. In putting forward our philosophy of "Education for All", we therefore believe it is essential for us to set out here our broad strategy for the management of change needed in order to achieve the objectives we have advocated.

Review of the Curriculum

4.2 We have already emphasised that the case for the changes in emphasis and perspective for which we have called is justified on educational grounds, in order to offer all pupils a good and relevant education. It is essential therefore to overcome the still widespread belief that such concerns are peripheral to mainstream curriculum development and to ensure that the issues involved are accorded their rightful place in current educational policy-making. The balance and breadth of the curriculum has of course been the subject of considerable attention by successive Secretaries of State since the mid 1970s, culminating in the 1981 Paper "The School Curriculum" which sought to set out the aims and objectives which should underlie provision at both primary and secondary level. DES Circular 6/81 asked all LEAs to review their policies and the provision made by their schools in the light of these broad principles, and DES Circular 8/83 required them to provide, by April 1984, the following information:

– a report on the progress which has been made in drawing up policies for the curriculum in primary and secondary schools;

– details of the involvement of teachers, governors, parents and the local community in drawing up the policy;

– a description of the ways in which the policy is being given practical effect in the schools;

– details of the steps taken to ensure that the curriculum is balanced, coherent, suited to pupils across the full range of ability, related to what happens outside schools, and that it includes sufficient applied and practical work;

– details of the effect of the availability of resources on putting curriculum policies into practice.

344

LEA Policy Statements

4.3 We urge the Secretary of State, in considering the responses to Circular 8/83, to give particular attention to the approaches which have been adopted by LEAs, both multi-racial and "all-white", to the need for their schools to reflect a pluralist perspective in their work, and to set out his findings on this issue when he publishes his conclusions on the responses. If, as we believe will be the case, the majority of LEAs have not yet given any consideration to the implications of the multi-racial nature of today's society for their schools, we strongly urge the Secretary of State to require them to actively consider their response to the issues which we have raised in this report and to prepare clear policy statements in this field. (There is already a precedent for such a specific request for information by the Secretary of State since Circular 8/83 asked LEAs specifically about their response to the recommendations of the Cockcroft Report on the teaching of mathematics.) We would like to see the Secretary of State acknowledging the need to consider the educational implications of cultural diversity in any further statements that he may make and any agreements that he may seek about the school curriculum. We believe that bringing the issue of the educational response to today's multi-racial society in this way to the fore in the current debate on the curriculum will not only serve to demonstrate the Government's commitment to developments in this area but will also lead all LEAs to appraise their policies in this respect. We believe that all LEAs, whether multi-racial or not, should publicly declare their commitment to the principles underlying "Education for All", especially in terms of developing a broader, multicultural perspective to the curriculum, and seeking to counter the influence of racism. We believe that such policy statements would not only demonstrate visibly to ethnic minority pupils and parents that the education system is prepared to treat their concerns seriously, and is committed to equality of opportunity for all children irrespective of ethnic origin, but would also encourage and "legitimise" the efforts of those individual schools and teachers who may have been seeking to develop their work along pluralist lines but with little interest or support from their LEAs. In drawing up such policy statements it is essential that LEAs involve the teachers in their schools since a policy which is implemented without full prior consultation is unlikely to evoke the commitment of teachers and so is unlikely to be effective in practice. A number of LEAs have of course already adopted policy statements on the implications of today's multi-racial society for education and we attach as Annex A to this chapter the policy statement adopted by Berkshire LEA which reflects many of the points which we have raised in this report. Some policy statements are however unduly influenced by an assimilationist view of the "special needs and problems" of ethnic minority children, or are concerned solely with multi-racial schools and make

345

little if any mention of the relevance of today's multi-racial society to "all-white" schools. We would therefore like to see **all** LEAs being required to review their policies in the light of our findings.

4.4 It must be emphasised however that a policy statement, no matter how positive, is not an end in itself and there is a risk that, as one article[19] has put it:

> ".... these policies become a substitute for action: the destination rather than the launching pad for change."

It is essential therefore that efforts are made to put the principles which may be set out in a policy statement into practice at classroom level. In this process a major influence is clearly the local authority adviser or inspector. In our interim report we saw a particular role for an adviser with specific responsibility for "multicultural education" but also stressed that:

> ".... all .... advisers have a role to play in increasing awareness and understanding of the needs of ethnic minority pupils and in fostering the development of a curriculum relevant to the needs of society."

Multicultural Advisers

We would still advocate this "two-tier" approach. We believe that **all** inspectors and advisers, whatever their specialist areas of concern, must see their work within a pluralist context and the advice which they offer to teachers, whether through in-service courses or visits to schools, should reflect this broader perspective. We also believe however that there is a need for at least one adviser and perhaps a senior officer in every LEA to be designated as having specific responsibility for coordinating and initiating the development of the kind of approach to education which we have advocated. He or she can thus act as a catalyst both in encouraging other advisers to recognise and fulfil their responsibilities in this respect and also in keeping fully informed of new developments. Concerns have of course been expressed in the past that having an identifiable "multicultural adviser" may merely confirm the view that such issues are peripheral to mainstream educational thinking, and may lead other advisers to believe they are absolved from making any efforts to reappraise their own work. If the LEA's stance on "Education for All" is set out clearly and unequivocally in a policy statement, we believe that these risks can be avoided. We must emphasise however that we would not necessarily regard the appointment of a "multicultural" adviser as an end in itself, but rather as a means to an end. One of the leading advisers for multicultural education in the country

---

[19] "Multicultural Education Policies: are they worth the paper they're written on?" B. Troyna and W. Ball. "Times Educational Supplement". 9 December 1983.

said in evidence to us that he saw his long term aim as to "work himself out of a job" since he saw his role chiefly as a catalyst in alerting teachers and other advisers to the opportunities presented by today's multicultural society and to the need to ensure that all pupils were accorded true equality within the education system. Once these objectives were realised and the case for introducing a multi-cultural perspective no longer needed to be made but was accepted and built into the educational principles which informed all curriculum development and classroom teaching, there would no longer remain a need for such a specific appointment. We nevertheless regard multicultural advisers as key figures in the immediate future in achieving the reorientation of educational think-ing which we believe to be essential.

Work of HMI 4.5 In addition to local authority inspectors and advisers, another major influence on curriculum development in schools is of course the work of HM Inspectorate. In our interim report we recommended that:

> *"HM Inspectorate should, within their regular inspections, assess the extent to which schools are responding to the challenges of meeting the special needs of ethnic minority pupils and of preparing all pupils for life in a multi-racial society, and should advise LEAs and teachers accordingly."*

Since early 1983 HMI reports have been published and we have therefore been able to review the extent to which this recommenda-tion has been taken into account. We have been disappointed to find that references in HMI reports to the implications for the curriculum of today's multi-racial society have been few and far between and have been generally limited to only those schools with ethnic minority pupils. In the review of the first six months of published HMI reports[20], the only direct mention of "multicultural" issues was in relation to the lack of attention generally accorded by schools in their religious education work to "our multi-ethnic society". If the development of the broader approach to the curriculum which we have advocated is to be recognised by schools, especially "all-white" schools, as valid on educational grounds, we believe it is essential that HMI adopt a far more positive approach both to evaluating the present activities of schools and to fostering initiatives aimed at developing a more pluralist approach to the curriculum. We would therefore like to see all inspections of schools undertaken in the future giving specific attention to the extent to which the particular institution, whether multi-racial or "all-white", has taken account of the changed and changing nature of society and of the possible need to reappraise both its taught and its "hidden" curriculum. We would

---

[20] "Education Observed." DES. 1984.

like to see HMI's views on this aspect of a school's work referred to explicitly in the published report, in order both to highlight "good" and worthwhile practice and also to draw attention to cases where change or progress is needed. The Secretary of State's original decision to publish HMI reports was coupled with new arrangements to ensure an effective follow-up to all reports. When the DES sends copies of reports on maintained schools to the LEA, the Authority and the Governors are asked to respond within three months on the following points:

– what action they consider is needed in relation to the school inspected;

– what action the LEA and the Governors have taken or propose to take; and

– what application the findings of the report might have for other schools maintained by the LEA.

If concern were to be expressed therefore in an HMI report about the extent to which a school's provision in a particular subject area or indeed across the curriculum failed to take adequate account of the need to reflect a pluralist perspective, both the LEA and the Governors would be required to give active consideration to remedying this situation. Greater attention by HMI to the need to adopt a broader approach throughout the curriculum would also lend added legitimacy and urgency to progress in this field. As a contribution to the debate about the ways in which classroom practice at all levels and in different subject areas can reflect a more broadly-based perspective we would also like to see HMI issuing guidance, possibly in the "Matters for Discussion" series, based on their own expertise and experience, on various approaches which might be adopted by teachers. Efforts should also be made to ensure that a pluralist perspective is reflected in the long and short courses offered by HMI for serving teachers. In addition to offering guidance on the content and balance of the curriculum in the light of today's multi-racial society, we would also like to see HMI adopting a much higher profile in relation to the need to counter the influence of racism on schools. In the autumn of 1983 a discussion paper was prepared by HMI on "Race Relations in Schools"[21]. This paper drew together some interesting, albeit ambivalent, comments by teachers and education administrators relating to the influence of racism on schools – many of which echo our own conclusions in Chapter Two – and concluded that:

---

[21] "Race Relations in Schools: a summary of discussions at meetings in five Local Education Authorities." A Paper prepared by HM Inspectorate. DES. 1983.

"Although it was generally agreed that race relations was a most important issue to which schools and LEAs must respond, there was little reported evidence of consistent and successful practice aimed at tackling the problems."

Having reached this worrying conclusion, HMI failed however to offer any authoritative and detailed guidance on how this unsatisfactory state of affairs might be remedied, presenting their document instead as:

". . . . properly tentative and (going) no further than the current state of the art allows."

We would like to see HMI now following up this paper with a more detailed assessment of existing practice in schools and with a far clearer statement of how progress might be made in effectively countering the influence of racism.

The Role of the School Curriculum Development Committee

4.6 In our interim report we identified the Schools Council as one of the main "agents of change" with regard to the development of multicultural education, and much interesting and valuable work has undoubtedly been carried out under the auspices of the Council. We have for example, in this report, drawn on a number of Schools Council projects ranging from Little and Willey's "Studies in the Multi-Ethnic Curriculum" to the more recent subject-specific reports on "Assessment in a Multicultural Society". Since our interim report the Secretaries of State have established the School Curriculum Development Committee (SCDC) and the Secondary Examinations Council (SEC) to take on these two main areas of responsibility in place of the Schools Council. The SCDC's remit requires it to inform itself of school curriculum development work already being undertaken by other bodies and individuals; to identify on that basis important areas where work is not being undertaken; and to undertake work in these areas or stimulate others to do so. We believe that the SCDC can and must play a leading role in fostering the development of the broader, pluralist approach to the education of **all** children which we have advocated. We are pleased therefore that the Committee itself has already identified "Education for a Multicultural Society" as a priority area for its work and indeed has in hand a preliminary study in this field. The major task for the SCDC is in our view to offer guidance on the practical implications at classroom level of developing a curriculum more appropriate and relevant to the contemporary societal and global context. We would like to see the Committee establish a series of working parties concerned with various subject areas to consider in depth, in

349

consultation with teachers and teacher trainers, the implications for their fields of work of the broad educational principles which we have set out in this report. The aim of these working parties would be to produce subject-specific guidelines and exemplars of content and activities through which various concepts and skills may be taught at varying levels, to assist teachers in both multi-racial and "all-white" schools to put these principles into practice. Clearly such a complex and demanding task cannot be completed overnight, but because of the urgency which we attach to bringing about the overall reorientation of the curriculum, we would hope that guidance relating to all the major curricular areas could be issued by the Committee over the next three years. We should emphasise that we would not regard this as a "once and for all" exercise but rather as part of an ongoing process, since, as we have already pointed out, the educational needs of youngsters do change over time, and it may well be necessary to reappraise provision in particular subject areas as the nature of our multi-racial society continues to evolve. (We understand that for the SCDC to review specific curriculum areas as we have suggested, by commissioning subject specialists to coordinate subject-specific seminars to review work in their areas, would cost of the order of £4,000 per subject area. If a full-time project officer were appointed to coordinate the work of these groups – which would serve to ensure a common approach was adopted in each area – this would cost an additional £25,000 per year.) Alongside this specific role as a catalyst to curriculum development we also believe that the SCDC has a potentially important role to play in the collation and dissemination of existing materials and resources, and also in stimulating the production of new books and teaching materials intended to help teachers to reflect a pluralist perspective in their work. We therefore urge the Committee to give urgent consideration to allocating funds to both these activities.

4.7   In our interim report we expressed the view that:

"Examinations have a major part to play in complementing and reflecting a multicultural approach to the curriculum in schools and the multi-racial nature of today's school population."

Examinations   The various studies undertaken within the Schools Council Project on "Assessment in a Multicultural Society" revealed a generally disappointing response in existing examination syllabuses to the need to develop a broader view of the curriculum. In relation to history, for example, the study[22] found that:

---

[22] "History at 16+." Assessment in a Multicultural Society. Nigel File. Schools Council. 1983.

*"The greatest omission is the lack of any syllabus which . . . .
takes into account, within an international framework, local,
national, and world history . . . . Indeed, it would seem impossible for the majority population to acquire any awareness of
ethnic, national and cultural groups from British history, as
currently offered, beyond the Norman period . . . . very few syllabuses enable teachers to approach questions of stereotyping,
racial prejudice, discrimination directly through reference to
the historical situation, at various times in Britain or the rest
of Europe . . . . most syllabuses do not cover the whole question
of the positive contribution of ethnic minorities to the building
up of the economies of Europe, particularly Britain . . . . in a
significant majority (of syllabuses), non-European cultures do
not feature."*

We hope that the points raised in this study and the others in the
series will be considered seriously by examining boards, and others
concerned with the examinations system, especially the new
Secondary Examinations Council. The Secondary Examinations
Council (SEC) is responsible for promoting improvements in school-
based examinations and other systems of assessment in England and
Wales and for advising the Secretary of State on national examinations policies and their implementation. Uncertainty about the
introduction of a new system of examinations at 16+ may have
resulted in a reluctance to consider or introduce improvements in
examination syllabuses. The recent announcements by the Secretary
of State leading to the introduction of a new system of examinations
at 16+, the General Certificate of Secondary Education (GCSE)
provides the Secondary Education Council, the five new examination
boards and teachers, through subject panels of these boards, with an
opportunity to recognise the multiethnic dimension in our society[23].
We would like to see the SEC establishing links with the subject
working parties which we have recommended should be set up by
the SCDC, in order that parallel developments are fostered and
facilitated within the examinations system. The introduction of the
proposed Certificate of Pre-Vocational Education at 17+ (which also
will produce two year courses for some who leave school at 16)
creates another opportunity for influencing courses and syllabuses.
The Secretary of State's proposals for Advanced Supplementary (AS)
levels (two year half Advanced level equivalents) to be taken by
Advanced level students at 18+ introduces a third examination area
which can be permeated by a pluralist dimension. These opportunities for improving courses and syllabuses throughout the 14-18 age
range do not come frequently and must be grasped.

[23] Examination groups must produce syllabuses by May 1986, the first GCSE examinations will
be taken in May/June 1988.

**Response
by Schools**

4.8 It is clear that the policies which we have advocated have implications for every school in this country whether its pupil population is multi-racial or "all-white", and as part of our overall strategy for change we believe it is important that all LEAs should expect their schools to review their curriculum, both taught and "hidden", in the light of the principles which we have put forward, to prepare appropriate policy statements and monitor their practical implementation. Some schools have of course already begun to appraise their provision in this way and a number of those which submitted evidence to us were in the process of exploring the implications of cultural diversity for different aspects of their work. The great majority of these schools were however multi-racial in character and we would like to see their counterparts in "all-white" areas embarking on similar programmes of self-evaluation. In primary schools such an exercise can usually be undertaken by the staff as a whole, but in secondary schools, with their complex tiers of responsibility and subject divisions, it may be necessary to establish a number of working parties across different departments in order to ensure that all areas of the school's work are covered. Such working parties would be able to consider the implications of cultural diversity for their subject areas and to consider the particular insights and skills which can be developed. It is essential that if any meaningful progress is to be made in bringing about the reorientation of the curriculum along the lines we have suggested, individual teachers are actively involved in this way in reviewing and, where necessary, revising their own work. Little will be achieved if changes in policy are simply dictated from above without such consultation, since teachers may then feel that their professional competence is being questioned or challenged, and are unlikely therefore to feel committed to bringing about any changes which are needed. If on the other hand teachers are encouraged to look critically at their own teaching methods and to reappraise their work in the light of the principles which we have put forward in this report, we believe that they will be led, on straightforward educational grounds, to broaden the curriculum they offer and to revise the aims and objectives which inform their work, along the lines we have proposed. We believe there is a growing feeling among the teaching profession that the education system should respond more positively to the changed and changing nature of British society, and we hope our report will serve as a catalyst in channelling this goodwill into constructive and worthwhile change. If, as we have urged, the Secretary of State focuses particularly on the implications of cultural diversity in the current national review of the school curriculum, this will also serve as a stimulus to progress in this field. Schools are already formulating their own policies for the curriculum as a whole as part of the curriculum exercise and we would wish to see all schools including some reference in their policy statements to the need to reflect today's multi-racial society throughout their work. School Governors and local authority elected members can also play a leading role in formulating policies for the curriculum which reflect cultural diversity and which accord true equality of opportunity to all pupils. We would hope to see parent and pupil representatives on governing bodies, especially those from the ethnic minority communities, encouraged to contribute to such activities. Above all however the support and commitment of the Headteacher is essential if positive progress is to be made. The kind of self-evaluation of a school's work which we have advocated here is closely akin to the objectives and methods involved in much school-based in-service teacher training – an area which we highlight as of particular importance in Chapter Nine – and it must be emphasised that we would not regard this as a "one-off" exercise but rather as part of an ongoing process in which areas of the curriculum, and teaching methods and materials, evolve in response to changing needs.

4.9   We have already identified the broad criteria which can enable a school to evaluate the extent to which its curriculum reflects the essential principles of "Education for All" (see paragraph 3.3 above). We have not attempted to draw up a more detailed list of issues to be considered by a school in reviewing its curriculum since individual teachers are, in our view, best placed to devise their own guidelines according to the particular circumstances of their schools. It may be worthwhile however drawing together some of the major questions which we believe need to be raised by schools. The following "checklist", based largely on guidelines prepared by the Inner London Education Authority[24], indicates some of the broad themes which teachers in all schools, whether multi-racial or "all-white", should consider in appraising their work:

– Are issues related to the multi-racial nature of British society today treated in a coherent and comprehensive way throughout the curriculum?

– Where there are choices to be made about the content of the curriculum, do these take account of the diversity of pupils' cultural experiences?

– Is content provided from a wide range of sources? Is it selected so that it engages pupils' feelings as well as giving them information? Are pupils able to explore and share the ideas, opinions and interests which derive from their particular cultural experiences?

---

[24] "Education in a Multi-Ethnic Society – An aide-memoire for the inspectorate." ILEA. 1981.

353

– Does the curriculum aim to create an understanding of and interest in different environments, societies, systems and cultures across the world?

– Are pupils encouraged to recognise that each society has its own values, traditions and styles of everyday living which should be considered in the context of that society, as well as compared with their own?

– Are opportunities provided to show the contribution that different societies have made to the growing understanding and knowledge of humankind?

– Is the curriculum designed towards developing an understanding and appreciation of the various communities that make up the local and national society?

– Does the content of the curriculum ensure that pupils understand that migration and movement of people – and thus cultural diversity – are underlying themes in history and the contemporary world?

– Have teachers and departments selected the content of courses to help pupils understand how inaccurate and potentially damaging racial and cultural stereotyping can be, and the historical and contemporary processes which encourage this stereotyping?

School Policies on Racism

4.10 We must emphasise again that this checklist cannot be considered in any way comprehensive – it is merely intended to show the kind of questions which we believe schools should be considering in the light of our report. There is however one particular issue on which we should comment further – the need for schools to develop explicit policies to combat racism. We discussed the theory and practice of racism at some length in Chapter Two and emphasised that all schools must accept their responsibility for helping to counter the overall climate of racism by adopting a clear stance against it. In multi-racial schools, where, as we have seen, overt manifestations of racism may impinge very directly on the lives of pupils, the development of school policies on racism can have the added value of helping to regain the confidence of the ethnic minority communities and also ensuring that racially-motivated incidents are treated seriously by the whole school. It must surely have a direct effect on the attitudes of pupils and their parents if their school is committed to such a policy and also encourage those teachers, who might otherwise be inclined to "turn a blind eye" to what they may see as a normal part of the rough edges of school life, to treat such incidents

354

seriously. Racism also however has an influence on the work of "all-white" schools, if less overtly, and here too, staff should give consideration to the need to commit themselves to countering its effects. The following notes[25], prepared by the Inner London Education Authority, give a clear indication of how the development of a school policy on racism can be approached and what such a policy should cover:

> *"Starting Point*
> *Most of the schools and colleges that have developed policies have found it essential to follow a process which includes all the following:*
>
> 1. *Placing the issue firmly on the school/college agenda and making time for discussion and development.*
>
> 2. *Coming to grips with what racism is and its historical context.*
>
> 3. *Considering how racism can and does operate in the school/college's particular circumstances.*
>
> 4. *Analysing both directly conscious racist behaviour and what the Rampton Interim Report terms 'unconscious racism'.*
>
> 5. *Analysing both individual behaviour and the policies and practices of the school/college.*
>
> 6. *Analysing the behaviour and practices of individuals and services that impinge on the life of the school/college.*
>
> 7. *Drawing upon the advice and experience of others, including other schools/colleges and those with specialist knowledge and experience.*
>
> *The Policy*
>
> *Each school or college will finally determine its policy in the light of its own circumstances. However, certain elements are common to all. There will be:*
>
> 1. *A clear, unambiguous statement of opposition to any form of racism or racist behaviour.*
>
> 2. *A firm expression of all pupils' or students' rights to the best possible education.*

---

[25] Taken from "Race, Sex and Class." Booklet 4. "Anti-Racist Statement and Guidelines". ILEA. 1983.

3.   *A clear indication of what is not acceptable and the procedures, including sanctions, to deal with any transgressions.*

4.   *An explanation of the way in which the school or college intends to develop practices which both tackle racism and create educational opportunities which make for a cohesive society and a local school or college community in which diversity can flourish.*

5.   *An outline of the measures by which development will be monitored and evaluated."*

As an indication of the kind of policy statements which have already been adopted by some schools, we attach as Annex B to this chapter, two examples taken from multi-racial schools.

Influence of Our Report

4.11   We have emphasised that we hope this report will itself serve as a catalyst for change and will assist schools in reviewing their work. It was pointed out in evidence to us however that, with financial constraints making it hard for some schools to maintain adequate stocks of textbooks and teaching materials, there was often little money for obtaining documents related less immediately to the classroom situation. At present-day prices this report will undoubtedly be considerably more expensive than was our interim report. The combination of these factors may mean that many schools who might be willing and able to act upon our findings would be unable to obtain a copy of our report. We therefore believe that, as evidence of its commitment to progress in this field, the Government should provide every maintained school in the country with at least a summary of our findings. Whilst there may not be a direct precedent for doing this, it may be worth recalling here that the Government did send copies of the summary of our interim report to all schools, and also that the DES has circulated to schools details of the findings of the Cockcroft Committee on mathematics education. We believe that the issues which we consider in this report are sufficiently urgent and important to justify such action to ensure that no school or its teachers are prevented from studying our findings.

Regional Conferences

4.12   There is one further step which can we believe help teachers to explore the implications of cultural diversity for their work through extending the opportunities for teachers from different schools and different subject areas to meet together and exchange information and ideas. One of the most interesting outcomes of the one-day national conference which we convened in the autumn of 1981 to discuss our interim report, was the way in which the teachers involved welcomed the chance to meet colleagues and to discuss together their views on "multicultural" issues. Staff from "all-white"

356

schools or from areas of the country where LEA policies were still at a very early stage of formulation, particularly valued the opportunity to meet other Heads and teachers from multi-racial schools where the educational implications of a multi-racial society had been considered for some years and specific policies evolved. This was very much a two-way process since many of the staff from multi-racial areas stressed that hearing the views and experiences of individuals from "all-white" areas, served to broaden their horizons and added a further dimension to their perception of the degree of change which was still needed. The success of our conference at this level has led us to believe that the pace of change towards the objectives we have outlined could be accelerated significantly if there were further such opportunities for teachers to discuss the major issues which we have highlighted in this report. We would therefore like to see the DES organising a series of conferences for elected members of LEAs, teachers, and other educationists, to discuss the implications of "Education for All" for their work. We have in mind a programme of one-day conferences, held on a regional basis – possibly adopting the seven divisional areas of HM Inspectorate: Northern, North-Western, Midland, Eastern, Metropolitan and South Midland, Southern, and South-Western – bringing together representatives from both multi-racial and 'all white' areas. These conferences would focus on the challenges posed by our recommendations to LEAs and their schools. We would envisage these conferences being of a 'workshop' nature so as to provide for greater participation by individuals. The conclusions of these conferences might subsequently be drawn to the attention of a wider audience in a conference report. Whilst it would not be possible for these conferences to explore matters in any great depth, they would in our view provide a valuable and visible focus for progress in this field. We would like to see these conferences restricted to a manageable size of something like 150-200 participants. As far as the timing of these conferences is concerned, we recognise that the organisational task is not insignificant. However, in view of the urgency we attach to the realisation of our objectives, we would urge that these conferences should take place as early as possible after the publication of this Report. Thereafter we would envisage that individual LEAs or groups of LEAs, dependent on size, would arrange their own conferences and that every school would have an opportunity to send a representative. The aim of such meetings would be to determine the response of the LEA and its schools to the recommendations in this Report and how both should manage the change towards "Education for All". LEAs with less experience of the issues might look outside their areas for support in arranging such conferences. In addition to the regional conferences mentioned earlier, we recommend that the DES should arrange a series of conferences to consider the implications for initial teacher training of the Report's recommendations.

Resources

4.13 This brings us to the central issue of the availability of the necessary resources to bring about the developments we have advocated. In our interim report we expressed the view that because our major aim was a change in attitude and perspective rather than in actual content, some at least of the cost of the implementation of the policies which we had proposed would be psychological rather than financial. We still believe this to be the case – it is clear for example that additional funds alone cannot effectively counter the pervasive influence of racism or lead to a reorientation of the curriculum. On the other hand, adequate and appropriate resources are we believe essential if any meaningful progress is to be made in realising the objectives we have put forward, not least as a clear manifestation of central and local Government's commitment to this area of concern. We emphasised earlier in this chapter that there can be seen to be two distinct aspects of "Education for All" – on the one hand catering for any particular educational needs which ethnic minority pupils may have, and, on the other, enhancing the education offered to **all** pupils. We believe that developments in these two areas call for rather different forms of funding. Up to now the chief source of funding for activities in the "multicultural" field has been Section 11 of the Local Government Act 1966 which empowers the Home

Section 11

Secretary to pay grants at the rate of 75% in respect of the employment of staff to those local authorities which have to make special provision in the exercise of their functions in consequence of the presence within their areas of substantial numbers of "Commonwealth immigrants" whose language or customs differ from those of the rest of the community. (Although claims may be made in respect of all local authority services, the great majority of claims (about 80%) have related to staff employed in education.) Section 11 is thus the chief source of funding for the "ethnic minority dimension" of "Education for All", although it remains in our view a somewhat imperfect vehicle for progress. As we have already observed in Chapter Four, the origins of Section 11 lie in the assimilationist phase of educational thinking in that the underlying aim appears to be to overcome the perceived "differences" of the ethnic minority groups with a view to their eventual absorption into the majority community. Concern has been expressed for some years about the shortcomings of Section 11 and indeed as long ago as 1978 the then Government published a consultative document setting out proposals for a new form of grant. The resultant Local Government Grants (Ethnic Groups) Bill fell on the dissolution of Parliament in April 1979. In our interim report we concluded that:

". . . . Section 11 provides a valuable source of funding to local authorities. We strongly support, however, the need for the Government to revise its provisions to make it more appropriate to the needs of the ethnic minority communities in our society."

Since then the Home Office have announced various changes in the administrative arrangements for Section 11[26] but these still fall far short of the overall revision of its provisions which is in our view necessary. We have already acknowledged that some, but by no means all, ethnic minority pupils may have certain educational needs which may necessitate particular responses from schools in the form of additional staffing or other support. We believe it is entirely proper that the schools and LEAs which are required to provide such support are able in turn to claim reimbursement from central Government through Section 11. We feel however that the existing legislation does not cater adequately for present-day circumstances and that any new arrangements are bound to be hampered by the terms of the 1966 Act. We believe the time has therefore come for the Government to reconsider the possibility of revising the provisions of Section 11 fully, through new legislation, in order to make it more appropriate to the needs of multi-racial schools and LEAs in Britain today. We have not sought to put forward here detailed proposals for the revision of Section 11 since, as we have already observed, its shortcomings have already been well-rehearsed on a number of occasions, most notably by the Home Affairs Committee in their 1981 Report[27], and were discussed in our interim report. The two main areas in which we believe the existing provisions of Section 11 are deficient are in relation to the ethnic minority communities which are covered and the types of expenditure which are eligible for reimbursement. Section 11 at present relates only to expenditure in relation to the needs of "Commonwealth immigrants", defined as:

"i.   *all immigrants to this country who were born in another country of the Commonwealth (including those born in Pakistan before it left the Commonwealth in 1972), no matter how long their residence in this country; and*

ii.   *all children of the above, whether born in this country or elsewhere, aged 20 or less."[28]*

[26] Home Office Circulars 97/1982 and 94/1983.
[27] "Racial Disadvantage." Fifth Report from the Home Affairs Committee. HMSO.   HC 424-I   July 1981.
[28] Home Office Circular 97/1982.

Not only does this limited definition seek to draw an arbitrary line between the needs of those youngsters who are "immigrant" to this country and those who are settled here and are possibly second- or even third-generation British-born, but it also requires authorities to make artificial distinctions between the educational needs of communities of New Commonwealth origin and the needs of some of the other ethnic minority communities whom we have considered in this report, such as the Vietnamese and the Travellers. We believe that new legislation is needed to cover the needs of **any** group, regardless of when its members settled in this country, which can be perceived as an "ethnic minority community", and which may experience particular needs deriving from distinct cultural or linguistic factors. In addition, Section 11 grant is at present payable only in respect of local authority staff costs. We believe that reimbursement should also be available in respect of any necessary capital expenditure, the running costs of particular projects or the cost of training specialist staff to support and cater for the needs of members of ethnic minority communities.

Other Sources of Funding

4.14 Alongside the costs of catering for the particular needs of ethnic minority youngsters is the expenditure needed to enhance the curriculum offered to **all** pupils to reflect a pluralist perspective. It has been suggested that a revised Section 11 grant might be extended to cover initiatives designed to prepare all youngsters for life in a multi-racial society. We ourselves had some sympathy with this suggestion but now believe that it is more appropriate to look for funding to reflect this broader aspect of "Education for All" from those sources already available to support curriculum initiatives. We have already referred to the need for the SCDC to allocate resources to exploring the practical implications of adopting the principles which we have put forward in this report. We would also like to see far greater use being made of the DES research budget in funding projects related to the "multicultural" field and particularly the hitherto largely neglected "all-white" dimension. We have suggested, in subsequent chapters of this report, a number of specific areas where we would like to see the DES funding research, and we hope that our report as a whole will stimulate bids for other relevant research. The Economic and Social Research Council has indicated to us that it would be glad to consider suitable applications for funding research projects in these areas. In addition to such specific sources of funding we would like to see both local and central Government accord a far higher priority to funding activities related to broadening the curriculum offered to all pupils along the lines we have advocated. We believe a major vehicle for ensuring that this objective is realised is the new Education (Grants and Awards) Act

1984, which allows the Government to pay "education support grants" (ESGs) to LEAs for innovations and improvments in education[29]. The express purpose of these grants is:

". . . . to encourage LEAs to redeploy their expenditure . . . . in accordance with objectives of particular national importance. They will :

– help LEAs to respond swiftly to new demands on the education service;

– promote improvements in the quality of provision in particular areas of the service; and

– assist in the financing of pilot projects within a limited number of authorities, the results of which could be of potential national importance."[30]

The DES announced[31] in June 1984 that 12 activities would be eligible for 70 per cent grant (totalling £21m) in the 1985/1986 financial year, including £1 million for "pilot projects to meet the educational needs of people from ethnic minorities, to promote inter-racial harmony, or in other ways to prepare pupils and students for life in a multi-ethnic society". The Secretary of State subsequently announced[32] that 26 LEAs were to receive grant in respect of projects in this area. We are of course very pleased to see this field of work identified in this way as a priority area for development since we believe that the need for LEAs and schools to reappraise the extent to which the curriculum which they offer to pupils is relevant to the nature of contemporary British society and to explore ways in which a broader, pluralist perspective, which seeks in particular to counter the influence of racism, can be incorporated into existing provision, constitutes an area where progress is fully justified and indeed essential on educational grounds. We hope that in the light of our report the Secretaries of State will consider increasing the proposed expenditure to be supported in this area for 1986/87 and subsequent years. Such a move would not only manifest clearly central Government's commitment to "Education for All" as a priority area for curriculum development but would also provide a further incentive for LEAs to review their spending priorities in the light of our report.

---

[29] The Act limits the total amount in support of which grants can be paid to ½% of Government's plans for local authority expenditure on education. In 1985/86 this will be about £50 million in England.
[30] Taken from DES Press Notice 64/84.
[31] DES Press Notice 95/84. 12 June 1984.
[32] DES Press Notice 208/84. 12 December 1984.

Ethnically-Based Statistics

4.15   In subsequent chapters of this report we have put forward a number of specific recommendations related to particular areas of concern where we believe change is needed. Many of these recommendations can we believe be accommodated within existing expenditure by a reallocation of existing resources or a reordering of priorities, provided the willingness and commitment to change and development is forthcoming. Some recommendations will on the other hand undoubtedly require additional resources. It has not however been possible to prepare a detailed assessment of the costs involved. It is for example impossible to quantify the costs involved in developing a broader, multi-faith approach to religious education provision, or encouraging schools to be more sensitive to the "pastoral" needs of pupils from particular ethnic minority groups. A major contributory factor in the difficulty of costing recommendations has been the continued absence of nationally-agreed educational statistics on an ethnic basis which would at least have enabled us to have quantified accurately the number of ethnic minority pupils from particular groups. In our interim report we recommended the collection of a range of ethnically-based educational statistics on the grounds that these would:

> ".... be of value at all levels and to all parties within education: to central Government, in determining policy; to LEAs in quantifying and locating particular needs; to schools so that they can take full account of the cultural and linguistic backgrounds of pupils and see whether any groups are underachieving or are disproportionately represented in any subject or class and to make an appropriate response; and to parents so that they can assess their child's performance in relation to his peers. We are therefore wholly in favour of the collection of educational statistics on an ethnic basis where they are to be used in establishing facts about how members of the ethnic minorities are faring in the education system."

Our views on the desirability of collecting ethnically-based statistics, provided acceptable categories can be devised and confidentiality safeguarded, have in no way altered, and we hope that the current deliberations of the DES Working Group on the Collection of Educational Statistics on an Ethnic Basis will lead to the implementation of our original recommendations in this field. We were struck by the comment made to us in evidence by one ethnic minority representative who observed that to cater fully and effectively for **any** particular need, it was essential to have a clear indication of the scale and the nature of that need. We certainly believe this to be true and therefore regard the collection of accurate and reliable ethnically-based statistics as an essential element in our overall strategy for achieving the policies we have put forward.

Teacher Education

4.16   It is clear from what we have said in this chapter that we regard teachers as the key figures in putting into practice the policies which we have advocated, since without their full cooperation and support it would be impossible to bring about the reorientation of the curriculum which we have envisaged. The approach which teachers adopt to their work is of course influenced to a very great degree by the training which they receive at initial and in-service level and a central element in seeking to ensure that teachers are both willing and able to play their part in implementing the policies we have set out is clearly therefore to bring about changes and developments within the teacher education field itself. In view of the importance which we attach to the preparation of teachers, and because of the complexity of the teacher training system, we have devoted a major part of Chapter Nine to setting out a distinct strategy for change within teacher training to complement and support the points which we have made here. This strategy for teacher education should therefore be read alongside the other elements which we regard as essential to the management of change, in order to fully comprehend how the objectives of "Education for All" are to be realised.

Government's Response to this Report

4.17   We would finally like to express our hope that the Government will respond positively to this report and to our recommendations **as a matter of urgency,** so that the developments which we have advocated can be set in hand as soon as possible.

4.18   To sum up, the essential steps in the argument for our concept of "Education for All" together with our strategy for implementation are as follows:

The Concept of "Education for All"
   –The fundamental change that is necessary is the recognition that the problem facing the education system is not how to educate children of ethnic minorities, but how to educate **all** children,

   –Britain is a multi-racial and multicultural society and all pupils must be enabled to understand what this means,

   –This challenge cannot be left to the separate and independent initiatives of LEAs and schools: only those with experience of substantial numbers of ethnic minority pupils have attempted to tackle it, though the issue affects all schools and all pupils,

363

–Education has to be something more than the reinforcement of the beliefs, values and identity which each child brings to school,

–It is necessary to combat racism, to attack inherited myths and stereotypes, and the ways in which they are embodied in institutional practices,

–Multicultural understanding has to permeate all aspects of a school's work. It is not a separate topic that can be welded on to existing practices,

–Only in this way can schools begin to offer anything approaching the **equality of opportunity** for all pupils which it must be the aspiration of the education system to provide.

Strategy for Implementation

–The response of schools, both multi-racial and "all-white", to cultural diversity has to be seen as a central feature of the current debate on the balance and breadth of the school curriculum and the Secretary of State should focus on this issue in considering the responses to DES Circular 8/83 and in any further statements that he may make and any agreements that he may seek about the curriculum;

–All LEAs should declare their commitment to the principles of "Education for All", to the development of a pluralist approach to the curriculum and to countering the influence of racism;

–Every LEA should have at least one adviser and perhaps a senior officer with responsibility to promote the policies we have put forward, to act as a catalyst to encourage teachers and other advisers to reflect a pluralist perspective in their work;

–HM Inspectorate should give attention to the extent to which the curriculum takes full account of the multi-racial nature of society and should highlight, in their reports, including reports on individual schools, instances of "good practice" and areas of concern;

–HM Inspectorate should issue clear guidance on the practical implications of adopting a pluralist approach to the curriculum and on ways of countering the influence of racism on schools;

–The School Curriculum Development Committee should establish a series of subject working parties to consider how areas of the curriculum can be made to reflect more fully the diversity of British society, and to offer guidance;

–The School Curriculum Development Committee should review existing materials which reflect a pluralist approach to the curriculum. The Committee should consider how these materials may be made more widely known and how the production of further such resources may be stimulated;

–Examining Boards should reflect cultural diversity in the syllabuses they offer and in their working practices;

–The Secondary Examinations Council should cooperate with the School Curriculum Development Committee to ensure that initiatives to broaden the school curriculum are reflected by parallel developments within the examinations system;

–All LEAs should expect their schools to produce clear policy statements on "Education for All" and monitor their practical implementation;

–All schools, whether multi-racial or "all-white", should review their work in the light of the principles which we have put forward; in secondary schools it may be necessary to establish departmental working parties to appraise provision in different subject areas;

–All schools should adopt clear policies to combat racism;

–The Government should provide every maintained school in the country with a summary of this report;

–The DES should organise a series of regional conferences for elected members of LEAs, teachers and other educationists to consider the implications of this report. The conclusions of these conferences might subsequently be drawn to the attention of a wider audience in a conference report;

–The Government should revise the provisions of Section II of the Local Government Act 1966 to make it more appropriate to the needs of the ethnic minority communities;

–The Secretary of State should include a growing number of initiatives and pilot projects designed to develop a broader, pluralist approach to the curriculum within arrangements for education support grants;

–The DES should implement our interim report recommendations relating to the collection of ethnically-based statistics within education;

ANNEX A

Royal County of Berkshire

Education for Racial Equality: policy paper 1

GENERAL POLICY

Introduction

This paper has three parts. First, Berkshire's formal policy on education for racial equality is stated, and responses concerning its implementation are invited. Second, there are notes about the statement's background and context. Third, there are notes on the definition of its three principal concepts – equality, justice, racism.

1. Formal Statement

> Berkshire County Council requires and supports all its educational institutions and services to create, maintain and promote racial equality and justice.
>
> The Council is opposed to racism in all its forms. It wishes therefore:—
>
> 1) To promote understanding of the principles and practices of racial equality and justice, and commitment to them.
>
> 2) To identify and remove all practices, procedures and customs which discriminate against ethnic minority people and to replace them with procedures which are fair to all.
>
> 3) To encourage ethnic minority parents and communities to be fully involved in the decision-making processes which affect the education of their children.
>
> 4) To increase the influence of ethnic minority parents, organisations and communities by supporting educational and cultural projects which they themselves initiate.
>
> 5) To encourage the recruitment of ethnic minority teachers, administrators and other staff at all levels, and the appointment of ethnic minority governors.
>
> 6) To monitor and evaluate the implementation of County Council policies, and to make changes and corrections as appropriate.

This statement was formally adopted by the Education Committee in January 1983.

Questions

All school and college staffs in Berkshire, and all governing bodies and community organisations, are requested to consider three main questions in relation to the policy statement on education for racial equality:

– What are we already doing to implement this policy?

366

– What improvements and changes do we propose making?
– What additimneed from support services, or directly from the
  education authority?

In order to assist such questioning, the Director has prepared three policy papers, of which this
is the first. The second, entitled **Implications,** is a checklist for schools. It takes each separate
aspect of the formal policy in turn, and notes the main practical questions which may arise. The
third, entitled **Support,** describes the programme of specific projects and measures recommended
by Berkshire's Advisory Committee for Multicultural Education. Financial resources to
implement this programme are available in the 1983/84 budget.

Responses and deadlines
Responses to those three papers will be incorporated by the Director into a series of reports to
the Education Committee in 1983-84.
Responses received by 31 July 1983 will be included in his report in the autumn, and thereafter
the key dates for responses are 31 December 1983 and 31 March 1984.

2. Background and Context

Why was this policy statement created?
The creation of racial equality in Berkshire – as in other parts of Britain – is of urgent importance.
A policy statement emphasises the urgency and importance, and shows the principles according
to which progress is to be measured. It is intended to be a basic signpost and commitment in
Berkshire in all future debates and decisions about expenditure, resources and practical priorities
– in each individual school and college, in relationships between schools and communities, and
in the Education Department.

How was the statement drafted?
In autumn 1981 Berkshire Education Committee set up an Advisory Committee for Multicultural Education. The Advisory Committee had about 40 members – county councillors,
representatives of Afro-Caribbean and Asian organisations, headteachers and teachers, lecturers.
It was chaired by the Director. It met regularly throughout 1982, and in the summer issued a
discussion paper entitled Education for Equality. This was considered at special meetings of
headteachers and community organisations, and at many staff meetings and governors meetings
in individual schools. A policy statement was drafted by the Advisory Committee at the end of
1982 in the light of these extensive discussions and deliberations, and submitted in January
1983 to the Education Committee which made some modifications to the draft before endorsing
it.

The statement refers to 'ethnic minorities'. How is this term to be defined?
Members of an ethnic minority have a shared history and culture, and often a shared language
and religion. Their crucial defining characteristic, however, is that they have a shared experience
of, and relationship to, the power structures of wider society. Ethnic minorities in Britain whose
origins are in the Caribbean, Africa or South Asia have between them a variety of cultures,
languages and religions, but they share one fundamental experience in common: that of being
exposed to racism, both in the past and at the present time.

Therefore policies to oppose and dismantle racism, and to build in its place racial equality and
justice, are necessarily and specifically concerned with relationships between white people and
institutions on the one hand and Afro-Caribbean and Asian people and organisations on the
other.

In addition to Afro-Caribbean and Asian people in Berkshire there are also other ethnic
minorities, for example from Hong Kong, Ireland, Italy, Poland, Portugal, Spain and Vietnam.
The policy statement affects them to the extent that they too experience discrimination and
prejudice against them by the host society. Equally the statement is opposed to anti-semitism

367

Is the policy statement recommending positive discrimination? If so, this is surely unlawful as well as undesirable?

No, the statement is not recommending positive discrimination. That is, it does not envisage that membership of an ethnic minority could ever be a reason, in itself, for treating one individual more favourably than another. The statement does, however, endorse positive action. This has three aspects:

- removing various discriminatory practices and procedures whose effect in practice (though not necessarily also in intention) is to prevent ethnic minority people from competing on equal terms with the host community;

- redressing the effects of previous injustice by taking special steps to attract ethnic minority people to apply for training and appointment as teachers and administrators;

- changing certain policies and practices, such that the creation of racial equality has greater urgency than hitherto, and such that membership of an Asian or Afro-Caribbean community is seen as a relevant and positive advantage for certain appointments.

Is the policy statement saying that changes can be made in education independently of wider society? If so it is surely unrealistic and over ambitious?

Certainly there is a limit to what the education service can do on its own to create greater racial equality and justice, and it is true that many developments in education depend for their success on conditions and complementary developments in the economy and wider society. Greater success at school and college by Afro-Caribbean and Asian young people, for example, must be accompanied by less discrimination in employment. Nevertheless education does have a crucial and urgent role to play, and significant measures can be taken in education without waiting for changes elsewhere.

3. Definitions

The Berkshire policy statement on education for racial equality asks and answers, in very general terms, three main questions: where are we? where do we want to go? how do we get there?

The first question, about our present situation, is provocatively answered with the single word racism. The second, about goals, is answered with two terms: equality and justice. The third, about methods, is answered by the six subsections of the statement.

Few if any readers of this paper would question equality and justice as goals to aim for and stand for. Many, however, would probably wish the terms to be clarified, and many or most white people (but relatively few Asian or Afro-Caribbean people) would question the notion that the term racism adequately summarises, or begins to summarise, the present nature of British society, and of British schools. These three terms – racism, equality, justice – are accordingly discussed and defined here in the next few paragraphs.

The definitions are provisional, and will no doubt be revised and improved in the course of many debates and dialogues in the months and years ahead. They are taken from the report of the Advisory Committee for Multicultural Education, January 1983.

Racism and racialism

First, it is useful to draw a distinction between racism and racialism. The latter refers to explicit negative beliefs, and to intentionally offensive or violent behaviour. It is seen most clearly in the propaganda and policies of extremist organisations such as the National Front and British Movement, and in schools it is seen most clearly in name-calling, insults, and grafitti. The term racism is much wider.

Racism encompasses racialism, but refers also to institutions and routine procedures as well as to the actions of individuals, and to unconscious and unintentional effects as well as to deliberate purposes. It summarises all attitudes, procedures and social patterns whose effect (though not necessarily whose conscious intention) is to create and maintain power, influence and well-being of white people at the expense of Asian and Afro-Caribbean people; and whose further function is simultaneously to limit the latter to the poorest life chances and living conditions, the most menial work, and the greatest likelihood of unemployment and under-employment.

Racism consists of an interaction between three separate components: an uneven distribution of power and influence; discriminatory practices, procedures and customs; and the prejudiced beliefs and attitudes of individuals, both conscious and unconscious. Similarly – it follows – racial equality and justice have three separate components in interaction with each other.

The three components of racism, and also the three components of racial equality and justice, are shown in the table below.

	Racism	Equality and Justice
Power, Participation and Influence	White people control all or most positions of management, government, influence and power; black people are disproportionately involved in menial work, or are unemployed or under-employed	Black people are proportionately represented in management and government at all levels, and are not over-represented in lowest-paid and lowest-status occupations or in unemployment or under-employment.
Practices, Procedures and Customs	Practices, procedures and customs affecting life-chances and the allocation of scarce resources benefit white people rather than black, and work to the disadvantage therefore of black.	Practices, procedures and customs do not discriminate to the advantage of white people and to the disadvantage of black. On the contrary they are fair to all.
Beliefs and Attitudes	White people believe in white superiority, have negative views and expectations of black, and are ignorant or indifferent with regard to the nature of racism. Black people in consequence develop negative views of white.	There is mutual respect and appreciation: black people and white are ready to learn and benefit from each other's history, culture, insights and experience, and to work together cooperatively on the solution of common problems.

Racial Equality

There will be perfect racial equality in Britain if and when Asian and Afro-Caribbean people participate fully in society and the economy, and are therefore proportionately involved in management and government at all levels, and are not disproportionately involved in menial work or in unemployment or under-employment.

There will be racial equality in education, it follows, if and when Asian and Afro-Caribbean people are proportionately involved in teaching and administration at all levels, in higher and further education, and in streams, sets, classes and schools leading to higher and further education.

Racial Justice

There will be perfect racial justice in Britain if and when the practices, procedures and customs determining the allocation of resources do not discriminate, directly or indirectly, against ethnic minority people, and when these practices are on the contrary fair to all.

There will be racial justice in education, it follows, if and when the factors determining successful

369

learning in schools do not discriminate, directly or indirectly, against ethnic minority children.

The relationship between equality and justice is circular. Justice is the means by which equality is both achieved and maintained. Equality is not only the consequence of justice but also its basis and surest guarantee.

A disadvantage of the table is that it does not adequately picture the interaction between the three separate components of racism, nor amongst the three separate components of equality and justice. It does not show, that is to say, that racism is to be understood as a series of vicious circles and spirals, each component both leading to and reinforced by each of the others: uneven power relations and discriminatory procedures are caused not only by prejudice but also by each other, and in addition they themselves generate and maintain prejudice.

To combat racism is to be involved in dismantling vicious circles and spirals, and to replace them with constructive circles and spirals. This idea is shown graphically in the diagram below:

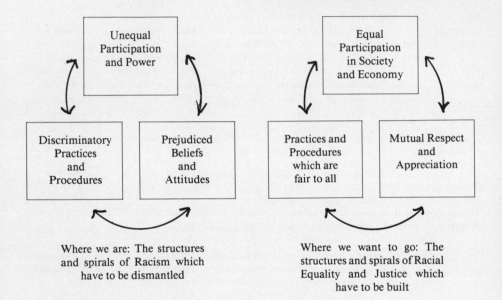

Where we are: The structures and spirals of Racism which have to be dismantled

Where we want to go: The structures and spirals of Racial Equality and Justice which have to be built

There are four separate reasons why racism should be dismantled, and replaced by equality and justice. These are as follows:

(1) Racism is morally wrong, since it involves benefits for some people at the expense of others.

(2) Racism is against the long-term self interest of all, since it is bound to lead eventually to social unrest.

(3) Racism gives to all people a false view of their own identity and history.

(4) Racism prevents ethnic minority people and the host community from learning from each other's cultures, history and experience, and prevents them from genuinely cooperating as equals on the solution of common problems.

This paper is the first of Three. The second, **Implications,** is a checklist for schools outlining some of the practical, everyday questions which the Berkshire policy statement may raise. The third, **Support,** describes the recommendations of the Advisory Committee for Multicultural Education. All three papers are issued by the Director of Education, Shire Hall, Reading, RG2 9XE.

Royal County of Berkshire

Education for Racial Equality: policy paper 2

IMPLICATIONS

Introduction
Berkshire's official policy statement on education for racial equality begins as follows:

> Berkshire County Council requires and supports all its educational institutions and services to create, maintain and promote racial equality and justice. The Council is opposed to racism in all its forms.

The statement then lists six general principles to direct future development. These six general principles are quoted in turn in this paper, and their possible implications are considered through a check-list of questions.

The checklist is a draft for discussion and improvement, not a set of definitive requirements. With every question in the list there is a further question implied between the lines: **is** this an important and relevant question?

In due course the checklist is likely to be revised and considerably expanded, and re-issued in the form of guidelines.

This paper is one of three. The others are entitled **General Policy** (number 1) and **Support** (number 3). The first of these outlines the background to Berkshire's official policy statement, and proposes some provisional definitions of the three key terms equality, justice and racism. The latter paper describes the programme of specific projects and measures recommended by Berkshire's Advisory Committee for Multi-cultural Education.

The checklist in this paper is by and large phrased for schools rather than for other institutions and services. Many of its questions, however, can readily be adapted for colleges and support services, and for adult education and the youth and community service.

Responses to this paper should be sent to the Director by one of the following three dates: 31 July 1983, 31 December 1983, 31 March 1984.

1. To promote understanding of the principles and practices of Racial Equality and Justice, and commitment to them.

1.1 Concepts and themes
Which topics in primary schools, and which subjects and syllabuses in secondary schools, are most relevant for developing understanding of racial equality and justice? For example, when and where at our school are pupils likely to be learning, directly or indirectly, about concepts or themes such as the following:

(i) Diversity: both in Britain and in world society there is a variety of cultures, beliefs, customs, systems, priorities.

Education Department, Shire Hall, Reading RG2 9XE

(ii) **Similarity:** human beings have basic physical needs in common, for example nutrition, shelter and health, and all pursue values such as security, dignity and self-respect.

(iii) **Justice:** relationships and procedures should be fair as distinct from discriminatory, and disputes and conflicts should be resolved on moral and legal principles, not through power alone.

(iv) **Civilisation:** great achievements in law, politics, science, technology, the arts, have been made through history in many different countries and cultures, not in Europe alone.

(v) **Migration:** throughout history human beings have migrated from one country to another, though for different reasons at different times; in 1950s and 1960s migration to Western Europe was required in particular for economic reasons.

(vi) **Racism:** discriminatory systems and practices, and the prejudices which they both reflect and strengthen, need to be identified and understood, and should be opposed both for moral reasons and self-interest reasons.

(vii) **Colonialism:** relationships and beliefs in the contemporary world are of course influenced by the past; it is particularly important in this regard to understand European exploration and expansion from the sixteenth century onwards, and to see these from Third World viewpoints as well as from European ones.

(viii) **Resistance:** struggles and campaigns against injustice take various forms, with regard for example to styles of leadership, the use of existing laws, the use of force, the pace of change, the degree of eventual success.

(ix) **Interdependence:** each neighbourhood and town in modern Britain, as also modern Britain as a whole, is part of 'one world' – a single world society and economy, whose various parts continually influence each other.

1.2 Textbooks
To what extent do our textbooks and other learning materials reflect the concepts and themes mentioned above? Have we systematically reviewed the textbooks and other materials in our classrooms, stores, resource collections and library, in order to remove those which are an actual hindrance to the teaching of these concepts?

1.3 Displays
Do displays of pupils' work in classrooms, corridors and the school foyer reflect recurring attention to these concepts and themes? Do posters and wall-charts in these places similarly reflect these concepts and themes?

1.4 General ethos
In what ways, and to what extents, do learning and teaching methods in classrooms promote and require active cooperation and collaboration amongst pupils as equals? In what ways do pastoral arrangements and general school organisation promote understanding of fairness and equality?

1.5 Combating racialism
Do all staff, both teaching and non-teaching, have an explicit and consistent policy against racialist insults, remarks and assaults by pupils; condemning and removing racialist grafitti and propaganda; and condemning and counteracting the activities of racialist organisations in the school neighbourhood?

1.6 Responsibility
Is there a member of staff, or a staff working party, responsible for ensuring that the curriculum for all pupils includes attention to concepts relating to racial equality and justice?

2. To identify and remove all practices, procedures and customs which discriminate against ethnic minority people, and to replace them with procedures which are fair to all.

2.1 Language and languages

Is the bilingual competence of many ethnic minority pupils recognised and welcomed, as distinct from ignored or rejected?

Is the ability to speak a Caribbean creole similarly seen as a resource to be valued rather than as a hindrance to be regretted?

Are pupils who frequently speak or hear dialect forms of English out of school helped systematically to recognise the relationships and differences between dialect and standard English?

Are pupils for whom English is a second or third language given special assistance with written and academic forms of English?

Are the needs of such pupils recognised by all members of staff who teach them?

2.2 Relevance and Motivation

Do examples and case-study illustrations in syllabuses, topics and schemes of work reflect a broad range of human experience in history and throughout the world, and reflect positively the cultural background and current experience of all pupils in the school?

Do textbooks and other learning materials similarly reflect a wide variety of human achievement and social organisation, as distinct from reflecting only European or Western cultures?

Are teaching methods in the classroom such that all pupils are equally motivated to study, to persevere, to ask questions about topics which they do not understand, to think aloud, to engage in purposeful discussion with each other and the teacher?

Do all pupils have an opportunity to explore their own personal identity and cultural background and critical experiences in their lives?

For example, are Afro-Caribbean and Asian pupils positively supported in their daily moves between two or more cultures, and in their experiences of racism?

2.3 Allocation

Do we ensure, when assigning pupils to sets or streams, that we use criteria, tests and exams which are equally fair and valid for all?

2.4 Religion

Do we ensure that we do not give or permit offence to pupils whose families have a religious allegiance and commitment? Do we enable and encourage such pupils to deepen their understanding of the religious tradition to which they and their family belong?

Is the choice of school lunches such that pupils of all religious backgrounds can have an attractive and nourishing meal?

2.5 Expectations

Do we clearly demonstrate that we have high expectations for all pupils?

3. To encourage ethnic minority parents and communities to be fully involved in the decision-making processes which affect the education of their children

3.1 Are invitations to parents equally welcoming and attractive to all, and are Afro-Caribbean and Asian parents therefore proportionately represented at parents evenings, open days and school functions, and as parent governors and as officers of the parents association?

3.2 If not, what steps is the school taking to correct the imbalance? Do we, for example, arrange:
- for interpreters, and for some of our letters and other communications to be translated?
- meetings with parents on special topics?
- meetings with community leaders?
- publicity through the channels of community organisations?

4. To increase the influence of ethnic minority parents, organisations and communities by supporting educational and cultural projects which they themselves initiate

4.1 What links do we have, both formal and informal, with the supplementary schools and language classes attended by some of our pupils in the evenings and at weekends?

4.2 What measures are taken to ensure that mainstream schools and voluntary classes complement and support each other rather than ignore or hinder each other?

5. To encourage the recruitment of ethnic minority teachers, administrators and other staff at all levels, and the appointment of ethnic minority Governors

5.1 Do advertisements for vacancies emphasise commitment to racial equality and justice, and are they therefore likely to attract applicants from ethnic minorities?

5.2 Is close knowledge and experience of an Asian or Afro-Caribbean community seen as a positive and relevant qualification for certain appointments?

5.3 Are ethnic minority teachers encouraged to apply for promotion and secondment, and do they in fact apply?

5.4 In secondary schools, is teaching specifically commended as a career to be considered by Afro-Caribbean and Asian young people, and by their parents and communities?

5.5 Do the County Council and Minor Authority representatives on the school's governing body reflect the ethnic composition of the community which the school serves? Are the parent governors similarly representative? If not, what steps has the governing body taken to co-opt ethnic minority members, and to inform the County Council and the Minor Authority about the imbalance?

6. To monitor and evaluate the implementation of County Council policies, and to make changes and corrections as appropriate

6.1 Do we monitor the distribution of resources within the school, including teaching time, to ensure that they in practice as well as intention are benefiting all pupils equally?

6.2 Do we systematically examine the extent to which Afro-Caribbean and Asian pupils are proportionately represented amongst pupils obtaining entry to higher and further education, and qualification at O Level and CSE; and amongst pupils in sets, streams and classes leading eventually to higher and further education? What is the pattern over the years?

6.3 Do we similarly monitor the composition of other groupings: for example, pupils who are involved in the school's cultural and sporting activities, and in positions of responsibility and leadership?

6.4 What arrangements do we have for recording changes which have been made in the school curriculum and organisation over the years to build greater racial equality and justice, and for reviewing and evaluating these changes?

Royal County of Berkshire

Education for Racial Equality: policy paper 3

SUPPORT

Introduction
This paper describes a programme of supportive projects and measures recommended by Berkshire's Advisory Committee for Multicultural Education. The programme is intended to assist with the practical implementation of the County's formal policy on education for racial equality.

The paper is the third of three. The first, entitled **General Policy,** states the formal policy and invites responses under three main headings: what are we already doing to implement this policy? what improvements and changes do we intend making? what additional assistance do we need from support services, or directly from the education authority? The second, **Implications,** is a checklist of the main practical questions which the formal policy may raise for schools.

Resources to begin implementing the projects and measures outlined in this paper are in principle available in the 1983/84 budget. It is hoped that many or most of them will start during the current financial year. Governing bodies and others who wish to comment on them before final proposals are drawn up and submitted to the Education Committee for approval should please write to the Director by 31 July 1983. Suggestions and requests for additional projects and measures in 1984-85 should also be submitted by 31 July 1983.

Sixteen separate projects and measures are listed here. They are grouped under six main headings, corresponding to the six subsections of the formal policy statement.

The Advisory Committee which produced these recommendations had about 40 members – county councillors, headteachers and teachers, members of Afro-Caribbean and Asian organisations, lecturers. Their names and affiliations are given in the discussion paper Education for Equality which was distributed to all schools in summer 1982.

The report which recommended the projects and measures outlined in this paper was presented to The Education Committee in January 1983. It contained brief preliminary drafts of job descriptions for the new posts which it was recommending (projects 3,7,8,9,10). Copies of the current drafts of these job descriptions can be obtained from the Education Department.

1. To promote understanding of the principles and practices of racial equality and justice, and commitment to them.

Project 1: curriculum guidelines and inservice
A working party of teachers should be established, similar to the curriculum working parties which already exist in Berkshire, to formulate responses to DES Circular 6/81, to draw up general

Education Department, Shire Hall, Reading RG2 9XE.

guidelines for teaching about racial equality and justice. The guidelines would be submitted to the other working parties, and incorporated as appropriate in their final documents. They would also be published separately, and would be illustrated with examples of good practice in Berkshire schools.

The same working party should also review all inservice courses and programmes in the county in relation to education for racial equality, and should draw up a comprehensive programme for each year.

Project 2: curriculum development
Small teams of teachers should be seconded for a term or half-term each year to Bulmershe College. Each teacher would develop materials on racial equality for use in his or her own classroom, and these would be published in due course for wider use.

Project 3: coordinator of resources
An additional Scale 3 post should be created in the language suport service in Reading, to complement the similar post which already exists in Slough, to engage on three main tasks: (a) to work with teachers to identify and evaluate published materials on equality and justice, and to purchase through existing budgets those which are suitable; (b) to publicise these materials through travelling exhibitions, loan collections, inservice courses and workshops, visits to schools, involvement in team-teaching activities in schools, the publication of a regular newsletter; and (c) to work with teachers to produce original materials geared to their own classrooms.

Project 4: combating racialism
A working party should draw up guidelines on opposing and condemning racialist insults and behaviour by pupils, racialist grafitti and propaganda, and the activities of racialist organisations.

Project 5: general information
A termly newsletter about education for racial equality in Berkshire should be circulated to schools, school governors, community organisations, county councillors, teachers associations, the press and radio, libraries, and other existing channels and networks of communication. Also other forms of communications – exhibitions, displays, audio-visual presentations – should be used.

2.   To identify and remove all practices, procedures and customs which discriminate against ethnic minority people and to replace them with procedures with are fair to all.

Project 6: support services for language and curriculum
The support services in Maidenhead, Reading and Slough which were originally set up to specialise in English as a Second Language should be encouraged and enabled to have a wider brief, as indeed most of their members already wish. This involves attention not only to ESL, both first stage and second stage, but also to the general field of language development and language awareness, bilingualism and support for pupils' home and community languages, and curriculum materials and approaches which reflect, as distinct from ignore, the cultural and linguistic experience of Afro-Caribbean and Asian pupils.

New projects on resources (Project 3), community languages in secondary schools (Project 7), and bilingualism in primary schools (Project 8), should be attached to the language support services.

Project 7: community languages in secondary schools
Community languages such as Hindi, Punjabi and Urdu should be available in the O level and CSE options schemes of secondary schools, and perhaps also elsewhere in the time-table of secondary schools if headteachers and parents wish.

A support service of up to five Scale 2 teachers full-time equivalent, plus a team leader at Scale 3, should be established to provide teaching of community languages in schools whose headteachers and parents request it. The service should be built on the experience which several schools in Reading and Slough already have of teaching community languages.

Project 8: bilingual education in primary schools and nurseries

A support service of up to seven Scale 2 teachers full-time equivalent, plus two Scale 3 teachers as team leaders, should be established to engage in tasks such as the following: (a) provide bilingual teaching to certain pupils, as requested by headteachers and parents; (b) organise the work of volunteers for bilingual teaching; (c) develop materials and approaches for bilingual teaching which can be used by teachers who are not themselves bilingual; (d) contribute to closer cooperation and relationships between schools and parents; (e) assist with liaison between mainstream schools and voluntary classes.

Five of the nine teachers would be based in Slough, three in Reading, one in Maidenhead.

Project 9: advisory teacher for language studies

An additional post on the County's team of advisory teachers should be created, at Group 4 headship equivalent, to assist schools with the development of language policies in relation to linguistic diversity and bilingualism. The person appointed should have particular expertise and interest in Caribbean languages and dialects.

3.   To encourage ethnic minority parents and communities to be fully involved in the decision-making processes which affect the education of their children.

Project 10: a community education team

A team of up to six Scale 2 teachers, plus a team leader and a deputy team leader at Group 4 headship level, should be established, to work on tasks such as the following: (a) to help Afro-Caribbean and Asian parents and communities to solve problems affecting the education of their children; (b) to provide technical and organisational assistance to parents and communities who wish to put their views, concerns and wishes to schools and the Education Department; (c) to provide assistance, as requested, to voluntary classes and schools organised by communities; (d) to assist headteachers and the Education Department in direct consultations with Afro-Caribbean and Asian parents and communities; (e) to assist schools with curriculum development.

If possible, each member of the team would work on a day-to-day basis with one particular community organisation, or with a small number of organisations.

In the first instance only the team leader and deputy would be appointed. They would then assist with the appointment of the rest of the team, and with drawing up detailed job descriptions.

4.   To increase the influence of ethnic minority parents, organisations and communities by supporting educational and cultural projects which they themselves initiate.

Project 11: grants to community organisations

A fund of £12,500 should be created, to be augmented if possible through the Urban Programme of central government to £50,000, for grants to voluntary language classes and supplementary schools and projects run by community organisations

Detailed guidelines about the use of these grants, referring for example to teacher-pupil ratios, rates of pay and management and accountability, should be drawn up, and should be equally applicable to all classes and projects.

5. To encourage the recruitment of ethnic minority teachers, administrators and other staff at all levels, and the appointment of ethnic minority governors.

Project 12: positive action on appointments
A working party should draw up detailed guidelines on positive action for appointments and promotions. The guidelines would emphasise the difference between positive action and positive discrimination, and would describe good practice in relation to advertising, shortlisting, interviewing, record-keeping, and so on.

Project 13: alternative routes to higher education
An access course should be planned and provided at Bulmershe College, to qualify people to enter B.Ed courses and courses leading to the Certificate of Qualification for Social Work, and the Community and Youth Certificate. The course should be for twelve students. There would be costs for discretionary awards, and for tuition and travel.

6. To monitor and evaluate the implementation of County Council policies, and to make changes and corrections as appropriate.

Project 14; evaluation and monitoring
A working party should draw up a list of the main research projects which need to be carried out to evaluate County Council policies, and these should be commissioned. Assistance for the research would presumably be available from the County's Research and Intelligence Unit, and from Bulmershe College.

Project 15: advisory panel
An advisory panel on education for racial equality should be established to report formally to the Education Committee each term. It would itself receive termly reports from the various projects and working parties described in this paper.

The advisory panel should have eighteen members. Three of these would be county councillors, six would be nominated by teachers' associations, and nine would be nominated by community organisations. Five of the latter would be from Slough, three from Reading, one from Maidenhead. Individuals would serve on the committee for a maximum of two years each. In addition the panel would co-opt two consultants from outside Berkshire, and would be served by officers of the Education Department, and the County's Public Relations Unit.

The Director recommends that the advisory panel should have administrative support from an education officer especially appointed for this purpose, and this recommendation is added as Project 16 below.

Project 16: administrative support
In order to administer effectively the various projects described in this paper, and to service the Advisory Panel and the various working parties, the Director wishes to appoint an assistant education officer specialising in education for racial equality. The officer would also be responsible for administering and evaluating Section 11 appointments, and grants under central government's Urban Programme.

A note of finance
It is envisaged that all new appointments will qualify for assistance from central government under Section 11 of the 1966 Local Government Act. The assistance should amount to 75% of the salary costs of each post.

ANNEX B

Examples of anti-racist policy statements adopted by two multi-racial secondary schools

School A – A unified policy for a multicultural school

1. (This) School firmly believes that it is vital for all its pupils to develop, as part of their education, a full understanding of the multicultural society in which they live. Part of that understanding will be a demonstrable respect for all people whatever their race or religion. Because a unified consistent approach is essential, the following procedures should be followed in the event of any racist behaviour in the school.

2. No incident, however apparently trivial, should be ignored, and every opportunity should be taken to teach positively and against racism.

Classroom Incidents

3. A record of any racist incident, however small, which occurs in the classroom should be given to the Head of House concerned. It should be completed on the Serious Incident form in the section entitled 'action taken'.

Corridor Incidents

4. Incidents, including verbal abuse and jostling, should be dealt with by the Heads of House, Deputy Head and Head in that order. The presence of staff with senior posts of responsibility in the school, as well as other teachers, at the change-over of lessons will help if a problem does arise. The Head should be sought immediately in the case of any particularly serious incident.

5. Graffiti and pamphlets must be dealt with promptly. Stickers, badges and any form of appearance which would offend and cause distress to any ethnic group, must be brought to the attention of the Head at once.

6. If the Heads of House receive several reports of a similar nature for particular pupils, it is their responsibility to initiate the next course of action.

7. Action to be taken could include:
    a. writing to parents;
    b. warning of the possibility of suspension; and
    c. in serious situations: suspension.

8. Preventive action is always important. Staff can avert a crush in the corridor by unlocking doors for waiting children. Pupils should be encouraged to move quickly and quietly to lessons.

9. All parents must be informed of any incident involving their child.

10. The whole school and the parents must be made aware of our unified policy so that our commitment to a multicultural society is made clear.

380

School B – Summary of anti-racist policy

1. Overall Policy
We, the teaching and non-teaching staff at (this) School, wish to state our united opposition to any form of racism. We are pleased to be working in a multicultural school for we value and welcome the experiences and opportunities brought to us by our multicultural community.

2. Racism in Teaching and Learning Materials
    a.   The teaching staff will examine our teaching materials including books, films, etc for racist content. We will not buy any text books or other material which in any way express racist attitudes.

    b.   We will do all we can to counteract racism by omission. This means we shall not ignore or neglect the study of various cultures represented in the school community. We will pursue actively multi-ethnic education throughout the school.

3. Racism in Language
We will not use or tolerate in others the conscious or unconscious use of racist language.

4. Racist Attitudes
We will support the exclusion from school, on a temporary basis as a disciplinary measure, of people who openly express in writing, words or other actions, racist views.

Racist attitudes can only harm the education of all. Racist beliefs damage and divide society. As individuals and as a staff we are prepared to oppose racism if ever, and whenever, it occurs.

PART III

Major Areas of Concern

CHAPTER 7

Language and Language Education

1. Introduction

Linguistic Diversity

1.1 The English language is a central unifying factor in "being British", and is the key to participation on equal terms as a full member of this society. There is however a great diversity of other languages spoken amongst British families in British homes. The report from the Linguistic Minorities Project[1] shows, for example, that in Bradford 14,201 pupils spoke between them some 64 languages other than English at home, and in Haringey 7,407 pupils were found to speak a total of 87 "other" languages. In order to lay the foundations for a genuinely pluralist society the education system must we believe both cater for the linguistic needs of ethnic minority pupils and also take full advantage of the opportunities offered for the education of all pupils by the linguistic diversity of our society today. To avoid misunderstandings, it should be said straightaway that this does **not,** as will become apparent, mean that teaching of school subjects in languages other than English, save for one area, the modern languages curriculum – see paragraph 3.19.

The Task for Education

1.2 Language and language education have long been the subject of attention by educationists at all levels. Where there has been a "multicultural" dimension to this debate it has usually been perceived in narrow and discrete terms, initially as concerning the "problem" of teaching English to children for whom it is not a first language, and more recently, as responding to the demands of certain ethnic minority communities for their children to be taught their "mother tongues". We believe that the language needs of an ethnic minority child should no longer be compartmentalised in this way and seen as outside the mainstream of education since language learning and the development of effective communication skills is a feature of every pupil's education. In many respects, ethnic minority children's language needs serve to highlight the need for positive action to be taken to enhance the quality of the language education

[1]"Linguistic Minorities in England." A report by the Linguistic Minorities Project. University of London Institute of Education. 1983. (The Linguistic Minorities Project (LMP) was set up in 1979 at the Institute of Education and was funded by the Department of Education and Science for a period of three and a half years. Its function was to investigate patterns of bilingualism in different parts of England, and to assess the educational implications of linguistic diversity.)

provided for **all** pupils. We feel that a broader approach to language education would be justified even if we did not have in this country substantial communities for whom English is not a first language. Since however we have the additional resource within our society of bilingual, and in many cases, multilingual communities, it is surely right and proper that the education system should seek to build on the opportunities which this situation offers. Linguistic diversity provides the opportunity for all schools, whether monolingual or multilingual, to broaden the linguistic horizons of all pupils by ensuring that they acquire a real understanding of the role, range and richness of language in all its forms.

"Linguistic Prejudice"

1.3   In considering the linguistic needs of ethnic minority pupils and the broader role of language education in relation to all children, it is difficult is isolate factors relating to language from the "climate" of learning which exists in schools. The negative attitudes held towards ethnic minority communities which we discussed in Chapter Two can we believe often manifest themselves in the form of "linguistic prejudice" against the languages of these communities which tend therefore to be regarded as of low status. It is indeed a powerful lesson to those people who claim that Britain is already a just and pluralist society to find how readily "not speaking English" or "not speaking English 'properly' " seems to be taken to indicate that an individual is inadequate and in some way inferior. When such attitudes exist in a school environment, not only on the part of teachers but also ethnic majority pupils, and are left uncorrected, and also permeate much of the policy making in this field, it is inevitable that the educational experience of an ethnic minority pupil for whom English is not a first language may be influenced in a very direct and immediate manner.

This Chapter

1.4   In this chapter, we begin by considering how the educational needs of pupils for whom English is not a first language have been perceived by the education system and the various forms of provision which have been adopted to cater for these needs. We focus particularly on the role of language centres and the extent to which we believe such forms of "separate" provision are in keeping with our philosophy of "Education for All". We then go on to discuss the role of the education system in relation to the maintenance and support of the languages of ethnic minority communities – the "mother tongue debate" – an issue which has become increasingly central to the multicultural field in recent years. Finally, we look at two broader aspects of language education bearing on the needs of all pupils, both ethnic minority and majority – the concept of language across the curriculum, and the need to enhance pupils' awareness of the diversity of languages and language forms now present in our multi-racial society.

2. English as a Second Language

Changing Attitudes

2.1   As we have recalled in Chapter Four, the major response of the education system to the arrival from the late 1950s onwards of growing numbers of ethnic minority pupils was the provision of intensive English teaching for those for whom this was not a first language. The English language was seen as the key to assimilation and to the newcomers "adapting" to the British way of life and it seems to have been assumed that the children's own languages would simply die out and be replaced with English. Whilst it may not have been an explicit aim on the part of schools to eradicate the home languages of ethnic minority pupils this was certainly accepted as a desirable development and it is clear, in retrospect, that the full implications of the policies being pursued were seldom realised. The shift towards integrationist thinking brought about a greater awareness of the backgrounds of ethnic minority pupils including their languages. Whilst this meant that the existing linguistic skills of children were less likely to be ignored entirely, there was still little sign of the education system as a whole actively valuing these skills as of relevance to the pupil's general progress. In recent years, however, with the development of the concept of multicultural education, the emphasis has increasingly been on developing the whole range of a child's linguistic resources and, in the case of those children for whom English is not a first language, on not undermining their existing linguistic resources in teaching them English. This wider view of the role of language in the educational experience of an ethnic minority pupil appears however in some respects to have impinged only marginally on provision for teaching English as a Second Language (E2L), much of which has in fact, in terms of its underlying aims and assumptions, changed little from its early days.

Forms of Provision

2.2   The means by which LEAs have sought to cater for the E2L needs of pupils in their areas have varied widely, ranging from the employment of teams of peripatetic staff serving a number of schools by withdrawing pupils for specialist help, to the establishment of separate language centres catering for children of all ages, either on a part-time basis – having been withdrawn from their normal schools

– or on a full-time basis – before being placed in mainstream schools at all. This pattern was indicated by the findings of a DES Survey[2] which found that in 1983:

> "..... some 104,000 school age children from homes where English is not the first language receive special help with English from the equivalent of 1,900 full-time specialists together with a large number of ordinary class teachers. The provision of such teaching takes a variety of forms .... Reception and language centres still account for 7% of the provision, but most children now receive their English language tuition either in small specialist classes within the school (70%) or by other means within the school (23%)."

Confusion with English as a Foreign Language

2.3   Despite the variety of present day provision, E2L teaching has traditionally been seen as a form of "marginal" provision which is the responsibility of specialist teachers coping with a particular educational need. Non-specialist teachers have been led to believe that they have little or no role to play in the language development of children from homes where English is not the first language. This view that E2L needs are not the responsibility of the ordinary classroom teacher arises in part at least from the fact that many E2L teachers were originally teachers of English as a **Foreign** Language abroad and were thus not seen as part of the mainstream teaching force of this country. It is perhaps understandable that in the early years of large scale immigration such teachers were considered to be best qualified to cater for the language needs of ethnic minority pupils, and full credit must be given to the efforts of many of them in coping with large numbers of children, often with limited resources and support. There is however a marked difference between teaching English as a **Foreign** Language abroad and, as in the case of E2L work, teaching the national language of this country to children who will subsequently have to function in this language throughout their educational experience and their adult lives. It must also be recognised that teachers who have previously taught overseas may be likely to regard ethnic minority children in this country as "foreign" rather than British. These teachers may also be seen as, and indeed may see themselves as, "experts" on the home background of such children and their families, and may, through seeking, for example, to relate their knowledge of life in Pakistan to the needs of a Pakistani

---

[2]DES Memorandum on Compliance with Directive 77/486/EC on the Education of Children of Migrant Workers. February 1983.

family in Bradford, serve, albeit unknowingly, to perpetuate inaccurate and out of date stereotypes of ethnic minority communities.

Language Centres

2.4   The form of E2L provision most in keeping with the assimilationist phase of thinking is clearly separate language centres. Although originally conceived as a form of "positive discrimination" designed to help children whose first language was not English reach the same level of fluency in English as their peers, the thinking behind these centres can we believe in retrospect be seen as an example of institutional racism which, whilst not originally discriminatory in **intent,** is discriminatory in **effect** in that it denies an individual child access to the full range of educational opportunities available – in the case of full-time centres by withdrawing them totally from the mainstream school and with part-time provision by requiring them to miss a substantial part of the normal school curriculum.

2.5   The main arguments in favour of language centres can be seen as organisational and administrative in terms of the convenience of bringing together in one place all children with particular needs so that specialist staffing and resources can be focussed there. The availability of grants under Section 11 of the Local Government Act 1966 may also have encouraged LEAs to establish and retain language centres since they are able to claim grant at a rate of 75% of the salary of every teacher employed in such a centre thus making it cheaper to provide a more generous staffing ratio than if the children were in a number of schools. The arguments against such centres are primarily on socio-educational grounds, as highlighted in the following extract from evidence submitted to us:

> *"The problems of sending pupils to language centres, to my mind, hinge around the questions of peer group relationships and of continuity of timetabling. Children make and consolidate relationships begun in the classroom, in the playground, in registration time, and at lunchtimes. That whole social life is an important part of the pupil's-eye view of the school. The role, presence and interventions of teachers are only part of that view. That is to say, there is a dialectical relationship between the way in which a pupil conducts him or herself in the playground and performance in the classroom; if a child misses half a school day (which includes the morning and afternoon breaks and a large part of the lunch-hour), then this will have a major effect on his or her school life. The feelings of marginality and exhaustion engendered by this kind of language-teaching provision can easily be appreciated by teachers who themselves have worked on a peripatetic basis or in a split-site school. What*

389

is a teacher in the main school to do when a child appears for one lesson and not the next because that's his or her time to go to the language centre? You do not have to be an ill-intentioned teacher to send a child to find a remedial teacher, or similar body, asking for him or her to be taught for that period. Bright, intelligent children can thus be spending the mornings in a language centre and the afternoons in a remedial department . . . . my argument is not that teachers don't care, nor that they are acting deliberately against children's rights to education. Rather that an off-site withdrawal system takes the whole question out of their hands."

Withdrawal Within Schools

2.6 Where the language needs of children from homes where English is not the first language are met within mainstream schools through withdrawal into separate E2L classes, some of the extremes of isolation highlighted above can be avoided. There are nevertheless strong educational arguments against even this degree of segregation, as explained in the following extract from evidence to us:

". . . . second language learners should be in mainstream classes rather than the situation we have more commonly encountered where second language pupils are withdrawn to be taught away from the general run of mainstream activities. This more common situation not only institutionalizes second language pupils to failure but also compounds the difference between second language pupils and other members of the community. Furthermore, on educational grounds, separation of second language learners from the curriculum followed by all the other pupils cannot be theoretically justified since in practice it leads to both their curriculum and social learning being impoverished, and thus both language and intellectual development is held up. It also means that the burden of joining in is always placed on the newcomers and never on those already established in the mainstream."

Concern has been expressed for some years about the possible effects on E2L pupils of providing for their needs through any form of separate "added on" provision and the view that their needs would best be encompassed within the mainstream curriculum has been gaining ground – as the 1975 Bullock Report[3] observed:

". . . . common sense would suggest that the best arrangement is usually one where the immigrant children are not cut off from the social and educational life of a normal school."

---

[3]"A Language for Life." Report of a Committee of Inquiry under the Chairmanship of Sir Alan Bullock. HMSO. 1975

**Status
of E2L**

2.7 One consequence of E2L provision having generally been organised on a withdrawal basis and dealt with by teams of identifiably specialist teachers, often working on a peripatetic basis, has been the effect on the status of the subject, its teachers and its pupils. All the E2L teachers to whom we have spoken, as well as many of the other educationists with whom we have raised this issue, have stressed the low regard in which the subject is held. The teachers have frequently been accused by their colleagues as "taking the easy option" since they generally teach small groups of pupils, and at secondary level a non-examination subject. Peripatetic staff are often regarded as "part-timers" and are not seen as having a role in decision-making since they are not accepted as part of the whole school staff. As one E2L teacher explained to us:

> ". . . . in secondary schools, English departments did not see any relationship between their work and E2L provision which was seen very much as a 'sub-subject' ".

E2L provision often seems to be mistakenly regarded simply as a form of remedial work with lack of English being in effect equated with lack of ability and the pupils themselves being stigmatised as "failures".

**Arguments
Against
"Separate
Provision"**

2.8 The main arguments against E2L provision being made either in language centres or in separate units within schools can be summarised as follows:

– the limitations on the breadth of curriculum which a language centre or unit can offer and the inherent injustice of denying any pupil access to other subjects until he or she has mastered English;

– the absence in many cases of direct links between the language centre or unit and the mainstream of school life which means that the work being done does not mirror that of the school and that the language needs perceived by class teachers are not necessarily met by the E2L specialists;

– the possibly negative effect on a pupil's progress in learning English of mixing primarily or even solely with children for whom English is not a first language;

391

– the possible effects on a child's socialisation and developing maturity of being separated from his or her peers and away from the "social reality" of the school;

– the inevitable trauma for a child of entering the English-speaking environment of the mainstream school, is merely postponed and in no way avoided;

– mainstream school teachers are discouraged from regarding ethnic minority pupils' language needs as their concern and are indeed encouraged to regard E2L work as a whole as of low status.

2.9   In the light of our aim of developing an education system which lays the foundations for a genuinely pluralist society, we believe it is essential to consider carefully how best to cater for the language needs of pupils for whom English is not a first language – as one group of E2L specialists put it to us in their evidence:

> ". . . . the issue we are addressing is not just a question of what is best for second language learners. It is a larger one: that of what organisations and strategies have the best potential for creating for all learners equal access to the starting points of their learning and understanding."

Our View   2.10   We are wholly in favour of a move away from E2L provision being made on a withdrawal basis, whether in language centres or separate units within schools. This view was shared by many of the E2L specialists whom we met who argued strongly for the formulation of coherent policies for meeting the needs of second-language learners through integrated provision within the mainstream school as part of a comprehensive programme of language education for **all** children. We recognise that in the case of pupils of secondary school age arriving in this country with no English some form of withdrawal may at first be necessary. Nevertheless, we believe that this should take place within the mainstream school. We have already emphasised our fundamental opposition to the principle of any form of "separate provision" which seeks to cater only for the needs of ethnic minority children since we believe that such provision merely serves to establish and confirm social and racial barriers between groups. We would therefore hope to see "E2L" being viewed as an extension of the range of language needs for which **all** teachers in schools, should, provided they are given adequate training and appropriate support, be able to cater.

Pre-School Provision

2.11 In our interim report we highlighted the importance of pre-school provision, particularly in the form of nursery education, for the West Indian child and indeed for all children. We urged, for example, that at a time of falling school rolls, LEAs should seek to convert former primary school premises for nursery use and that local authorities should use all available means to inform parents of the nursery education and day care facilities available in their areas. The further evidence we have received since submitting our interim report has we believe confirmed the crucial role of pre-school provision and we make no apology for endorsing our earlier recommendations. For the child from a home where English is not the first language, it is clear that nursery provision can be a particularly valuable stage of the overall educational experience and can we believe serve to ease the sometimes traumatic transition between the home and school.

Primary Level

2.12 As we explain later in this Chapter, we would expect to see all schools developing explicit policies on language education, as advocated in the Bullock Report. Within this overall framework, we would see the E2L needs of pupils in primary school being met within the normal classroom situation by class teachers. To enable these teachers to develop the necessary skills to take on this task, there clearly needs to be an expansion of appropriate in-service provision, preferably school-based. We would also expect the staffing levels of schools with substantial numbers of pupils with E2L needs to be enhanced in order to allow some teachers to develop a particular expertise in language work through further in-service courses and consultation with their LEA's advisory service. These teachers could then work in classes alongside their colleagues to give particular support to 'beginners' in English, not through separate provision but within the framework of the activities being undertaken by the whole class. Such teachers would be able to help not only pupils with E2L needs but also any pupil with language difficulties – a broader role which has not previously been possible within the separate structure of E2L. Clearly existing teachers with skills in the field of language, such as specialist E2L staff or bi-lingual teachers with knowledge of the appropriate mother tongues, would be particularly suited to the role we have in mind. (In areas where specialist language centres are being phased out there may be a need for structured 'staff exchanges' between the centres and mainstream schools during the changeover period as a form of in-service provision for all.) Where the scale of language need is not sufficient to justify enhanced staffing on a permanent basis, an LEA advisory teacher should nevertheless be available to visit schools on a regular basis to work with class teachers.

393

2.13 An indication of the approach outlined above working in practice was provided by a combined First and Middle school we visited:

"In terms of the mother tongues spoken by the majority of the children (Punjabi, Gujerati, Urdu), the school may be said to be one where English is the second language, although for the children English is the principal medium for their learning while they are at school. All the staff are therefore by definition teachers of English as a second language. Seven staff (5 in the First School, 2 in the Middle School) possess an E2L qualification; one member of staff is currently taking the RSA Diploma Course in the Teaching of English as a Second Language in Multicultural Schools; and a further teacher is studying for a post-graduate diploma in Applied Linguistics. While the school has therefore a valuable leavening of staff with special E2L qualifications, all teachers in the school need this kind of expertise and understanding to extend, develop, and enrich the children's language. In the First School . . . . the specialist E2L teacher does not at present have a class of her own. Children in need of specialist E2L language tuition are fully integrated into the 4 vertically-grouped 1st and 2nd Year classes and the teacher is deployed over all 4 classes doing group work, so that as many children as possible can receive her help, while the children themselves benefit through the interaction with other children who provide a more stimulating language environment. In the Middle School, although the E2L Scale post holder has her own class, she is able to offer advice and support to other colleagues, as well as buy in suitable teaching materials."

Secondary Level

2.14 Similarly in secondary schools we believe that pupils with E2L needs should be regarded as the responsibility of **all** teachers, although there is clearly a role for particular language specialists on a school staff who can offer support and advice both to their colleagues and to pupils with language difficulties. Within the broader view of the role of a 'language coordinator' and a school's English department which we envisage later in this Chapter, we would see English departments of schools with substantial numbers of pupils with language needs including E2L specialists who would be able not only to contribute to the development of a general policy on 'language across the curriculum', but, more specifically, to work alongside their subject colleagues in the classroom situation. Such an approach to meeting language needs has already been adopted in a number of schools we have visited and is generally referred to as the

"Team Teach-ing" Approach "co-operative" or "team teaching" method. An indication of the issues which need to be considered in adopting a team teaching approach to E2L provision, together with a "checklist" of aims and objectives for both the specialist teacher and the subject teacher, are provided in a very helpful paper at Annex A, prepared by the staff of one of the schools we visited. The challenge presented to both the mainstream staff and the specialist teacher(s) involved in implement-ing such an approach should clearly not be underestimated and this is illustrated in the further extract from evidence – attached as Annex B to this Chapter – which describes how one school moved from E2L teaching on a withdrawal basis to provision within the "normal" curriculum.

Mainstream Attitudes 2.15 We recognise that there is a considerable way to go before this broader concept of responsibility for language needs gains general acceptance. It would hardly be in the interests of second language learners to lose the specialist help of E2L teachers and to simply be left to "sink or swim" within the mainstream classroom situation without the necessary help and support. In view of the somewhat negative attitudes of some mainstream teachers towards E2L learners, especially the correlation of "lack of English" with "lack of ability", there clearly needs to be major shift in opinion in order to accord these pupils equal opportunities within the mainstream school. We have been very concerned by the number of times that E2L staff in language centres and units have described the hostility, not only of mainstream pupils but also of other teachers, towards their pupils when there have been attempts at joint activities. The broad policies of "language across the curriculum" and the fostering of positive attitudes towards linguistic diversity which we recommend later in this Chapter are clearly essential therefore in creating the positive climate necessary for integrated E2L provision to become a reality.

"Second-Stage" Needs 2.16 In their evidence to us, E2L teachers have often stressed that second language learners are "ordinary" learners and that many of their language needs may in fact be shared, albeit to a lesser degree, by some ethnic majority pupils, especially those in inner urban areas or remote rural areas. This is particularly so in the case of what are generally-termed "second-stage" language needs, ie the need for an E2L learner who has mastered "survival" English to be helped to extend his range and command of the language by applying it to various learning situations. The Bullock Report listed the following uses of language as essential in any child's language development:

"Reporting on present and recalled experiences.

Collaborating towards agreed ends.

Projecting into the future; anticipating and predicting.

Projecting and comparing possible alternatives.

Perceiving casual and dependent relationships.

Giving explanations of how and why things happen.

Expressing and recognising tentativeness.

Dealing with problems in the imagination and seeing possible solutions.

Creating experiences through the use of imagination.

Justifying behaviours.

Reflecting on feelings, their own and other peoples."

The ability to use English in these complex ways lies at the heart of the educational process and without such skills a child, whether ethnic minority or ethnic majority, can be condemned to under-achieve in relation to the academic goals set by the system. As we explain later in this Chapter, we would like to see **all** teachers having a far greater understanding of the role of language in learning, coupled with an awareness of the linguistic demands which they may make of their pupils, especially in a linguistically-mixed classroom. If this heightened language awareness is brought about, we see no reason why mainstream teachers should not be expected to appreciate and indeed cater for second-stage language needs, and given the necessary support, accept their responsibilities even in relation to those pupils who may enter school with little or no English.

Teacher Education

2.17 We deal at length in Chapter Nine with the role of teacher education at all levels in providing teachers with the knowledge and skills necessary to teach in our multi-racial, multi-lingual society. There are however a number of points relating specifically to language which should be drawn out here. In essence, as we have said, we would expect to see appropriate training and support being available to all teachers to enable them to cater for the linguistic needs of all their pupils. It is clear however that teachers in multi-lingual schools, because of the range of languages represented in the classroom, may need additional and specific help. LEAs and individual schools, within the context of a comprehensive programme of induction and in-service training, need to ensure that teachers have an increased awareness of the particular languages used by their pupils including an ability to identify which language an individual child is speaking, to identify various scripts and at the very least to be able to pronounce a child's name correctly. Teachers might also be encouraged to learn some of the basic vocabulary of the languages used by their pupils, and to understand how the structure or intonation of the languages may lie behind a child's difficulty with English. We believe that such information can most effectively be imparted through **school-based** provision so that it can be tailored to the particular circumstances of an individual school and so that teachers can see the issues covered as directly relevant to their own classroom situation.

2.18   In addition to such specific support and guidance there is clearly a need for opportunities for further in-service training for the language specialist and LEA advisory teachers whom we have envisaged (paragraphs 2.12-2.14). We would see the key qualities of such specialist teachers as being flexibility and sensitivity. We would thus expect them to have had a wide range of experience in different teaching situations and to have acquired considerable expertise in the skills needed to help children from a range of backgrounds with their language needs. We feel therefore that in this instance classroom experience is an essential prior qualification for such work and we would not see a direct role for initial training in the preparation of such teachers. Rather, we would see their principal training needs being met through in-service work, on an LEA or regional basis, and the RSA course on "The teaching of English as a second language in multicultural schools" (course details attached as Annex C) seems to us to provide an ideal basis for further course initiatives along these lines, especially in relation to the needs of second language learners. Indeed, this particular course was commended to us by a number of E2L specialists we met as being especially useful in that it is aimed jointly at both prospective language specialists and subject and class teachers wanting to learn about second language needs in order to broaden their own teaching skills. Although we see the preparation of these language specialists as an in-service responsibility we would wish to encourage initial teacher training institutions to offer a range of options for students with a particular interest in the field of language needs.

3.   Mother Tongue Provision

3.1   Of all the various issues relating to language which have been raised with us, the one which has undoubtedly aroused the strongest feelings is the role of the education system in relation to the maintenance and support of the languages of ethnic minority communities, through what is generally referred to as "mother tongue provision". We have indeed received more evidence on this issue than on any other encompassed by our overall remit and in recent years there has been a proliferation of "issue papers", conferences and articles devoted to this area of concern. We believe however that the issue of mother tongue provision cannot be seen in isolation from the whole question of language education and, more importantly, it must be seen in the broader context of an education which responds to and meets the needs of all pupils in today's society.

Range of "Mother Tongues"

3.2 Before considering the "case" for mother tongue provision in its various forms, it is worthwhile recalling the diversity of languages other than English which are now spoken by pupils attending schools in this country, which we emphasised at the opening of this Chapter. The report from the Linguistic Minorities Project (LMP), already referred to, found for example that in Bradford, out of the 14,201 pupils recorded as speaking languages other than English at home, 53% spoke Punjabi, 19% spoke Urdu and 9% spoke Gujerati; in Haringey, of the 7,407 pupils speaking other languages, 34% spoke Greek, 15% spoke Turkish and 9% spoke "Creoles" (defined as English-based and other non-French-based creole languages); in Peterborough, of the 2,408 pupils speaking other languages, 24% spoke Punjabi and the same percentage spoke Italian. Further data from the LMP findings relating to linguistic diversity are reproduced in Annex D to this Chapter.

What is "Mother Tongue"?

3.3 We have used the term "mother tongue" throughout this Chapter to describe the languages of ethnic minority communities in a very particular educational context in which they have been discussed in relation to language education. It must be acknowledged however that this term has been subject to some criticism for its unnecessarily limited connotations of "the language learned at the mother's knee". Where communities are multilingual or speak a markedly distinct dialect, for example, Sylheti Bengali or Sicilian Italian, the languages which parents may wish their children to be taught or to be used within schools may well not be children's "mother tongues" as such but rather standard forms of a particular language, or even different languages entirely which are regarded by the communities as of higher status. As explained in a discussion document[4] produced by the Commission for Racial Equality:

> " Throughout Asian history groups of people have expressed a desire to learn another language which they see functionally more relevant than theirs. Asian children who speak Punjabi at home may well want to learn Urdu instead of Punjabi because this was the traditional language of learning for their parents. Those from the East Punjab may choose to study Hindi for religious reasons. A minority of Cantonese-speaking Chinese children may choose to learn Mandarin which is the national spoken language of the People's Republic of China and Taiwan."

---

[4] "Ethnic Minority Community Languages: A Statement." Commission for Racial Equality. 1982.

In recognition of the range of languages thus under discussion, some educationists now talk of home and/or community or national languages rather than mother tongues. We have however continued to use this term here because it remains most widely used and understood.

Different Forms of Mother Tongue Provision

3.4   As with so many other of the terms used in relation to the education of ethnic minority pupils, there is considerable confusion about what is meant by "mother tongue provision" and several essentially very different activities seem to be embraced by it. We believe it is necessary to distinguish between these different forms of provision and to look carefully at the various factors influencing them. The range of activities can we believe be seen to fall into three main "categories" of provision:

—**Bilingual Education:** the structuring of a school's work to allow for the use of a pupil's mother tongue as a medium of instruction alongside English so that the child may be taught for a set part of the school day in for example Punjabi and for the rest of the time in English;

—**Mother Tongue Maintenance:** the development of a pupil's fluency in his or her mother tongue as an integral part of a primary school's curriculum in order to extend their existing language skills by timetabling a set number of hours each week for the teaching of for example Punjabi;

—**Mother Tongue Teaching:** the teaching of the languages of ethnic minority communities as part of the modern languages curriculum of secondary schools alongside established languages such as French or German.

Making the Case

3.5   The increasing concern about mother tongue provision can be seen as a major consequence of the general rise of consciousness amongst ethnic minority groups in this country. On a broader level, it has been argued that each of the forms of mother tongue provision set out above are important aspects of multicultural education since language is the key to both the religious and cultural heritage of ethnic minority communities and all languages should therefore be valued and maintained as part of our national linguistic resource. Mother tongue provision in all its forms has also been seen as an essential step in according ethnic minority pupils "equality of opportunity" within our education system since it has been pointed out that an ethnic minority child from a home where English may not be spoken may at present be placed at an immediate disadvantage *vis à vis* his peers by being denied the opportunity to build on the linguistic and conceptual skills he has acquired in his early years. It is presented as a form of "natural justice" that all children should receive their education in their own mother tongue and that since pupils whose mother tongue is English have the opportunity to extend and develop their mother tongue within school in specific English lessons, those for whom English is not a first language should be given a similar opportunity to extend and develop **their** mother tongue. The major argument for broadening the modern languages curriculum to include ethnic minority languages is that it is sound educational practice, as well as common sense, for pupils to have the opportunity to study for and obtain a qualification in a language in which they may already have some facility.

Aims of Mother Tongue Provision

3.6   The range of specific aims which have generally been advanced in favour of mother tongue provision are summarised by the authors of the second NFER review of research as follows:

"i.   *To promote cognitive and social growth in the young child whose first language is not English, by the use of the mother tongue as an initial teaching medium in order to counter semi-lingualism.*

ii.   *To increase such a pupil's confidence through the use of his mother tongue so that thereby he will gain psychological and social benefits which will enable him to improve his learning ability and increase motivation which can be applied in connection with other curriculum subjects.*

iii.   *In accordance with the broad objectives of education such a pupil whose first language is not English has a right to have his full potential developed and this includes the development of his ability and competence in his mother tongue.*

iv.   *To enhance the value of such a pupil's culture and the language itself as part of that culture. And by so doing to increase the status of the language, to encourage its maintenance by its speakers and to reduce social and cultural barriers between English speakers and those speaking the minority language.*

v.   *To promote the pride of minority language speakers in their language and hence to promote their own identity through their language.*

vi.   *To facilitate, through a maintenance of linguistic competence in the first language, communication between parents and children and relatives in other countries and hence to preserve religious and cultural traditions.*

vii. *To enrich the cultural life of the country as a whole by means of a diversity of linguistic resources and in particular through the contribution which different language speakers may make to society through their participation in social life and through their linguistic competence as demonstrated by achievements in examinations, to make a contribution to the economic life of the country through industry and commerce."*

Bullock Commitee's View

3.7   Two major catalysts to the development of the mother tongue debate in this country have been the 1975 Bullock Report and the EC Directive on the Education of Children of Migrant Workers (1977). Since we feel that the actual content and intentions of both of these documents have become blurred over time, it may be helpful to recall briefly the actual terms of both. The Bullock Report, in a widely-quoted reference to mother tongue, argued that:

"No child should be expected to cast off the language and culture of the home as he crosses the school threshold (and) ... the school should adopt positive attitudes to its pupils' bilingualism and wherever possible should help maintain and deepen their knowledge of their mother tongues."

Although in retrospect the Bullock Report showed considerable foresight in recognising the opportunities offered for the whole of society by the increasing linguistic diversity of Britain, it gave little guidance as to precisely what it saw schools doing in practice.

EC Directive on the Education of Children of Migrant Workers

3.8   There is clearly widespread misunderstanding as to the acutal content of the 1977 EC Directive on the Education of Children of Migrant Workers as illustrated by the number of occasions on which it is mistakenly referred to as the "Directive on Mother Tongue Teaching". The Directive, the full text of which is reproduced at Annex E, requires that Member States should a. admit migrant workers' children from other member states to school and provide them with tuition in the language of the host country and should b. promote the teaching to these children of the mother tongue and culture of their country of origin:

"... with a view principally to facilitating their possible reintegration into the Member State of origin."

Through an agreement by the Council of Ministers at the time of the Directive's adoption, the UK Government accepted that the benefits of the Directive should be extended to the children of nationals of non-Member States. As the DES Circular 5/81[5] observed however:

" .... *the Directive and accompanying agreement do not address themselves to the position of children whose parents are UK nationals with family origins in other countries."*

– thus excluding the majority of the ethnic minority children in Britain today. This Circular also stressed that the requirement for Member States to "promote" mother tongue and culture teaching did not accord the **right** to such teaching to any individual child. The context in which the EC Directive is being implemented has since been set out further in the DES "Memorandum on Compliance" produced in 1983 (see footnote 2 above).

3.9   We believe that discussion of the provisions of the EC Directive have to a very great extent over-shadowed and indeed distorted the debate about mother tongue provision. It must be recognised that the Directive was explicitly intended to ensure that the children of **Migrant** Workers from EEC countries received an education which would enable them to return to their countries of origin. It is surely illogical therefore to seek to extend such provisions to ethnic minority children, born and brought up in this country, the great majority of whom are unlikely to "return home" and who neither perceive themselves nor wish to be perceived as in any sense "transitory" citizens of this country. In order to justify the need to maintain and foster the linguistic diversity of British society today, it is surely irrelevant for the advocates of mother tongue provision to "pray in aid" a Directive intended to meet an entirely different educational situation. The case for mother tongue provision for ethnic minority pupils in this country is indeed, as we have already indicated above, far more complex than the straightforward intention of the Directive which was simply to enable migrant workers' children to be reintegrated into their home countries—thus as the 1981 Home Affairs Committee Report [6] concluded:

".... any argument in support of (mother tongue) provision must be on the merits of the case."

Mother tongue provision cannot be justified simply by the provisions of the EC Directive. We regret that the DES and many advocates of mother tongue provision have tended to see the arguments for such provision solely in the context of the Directive rather than as an aspect of education which merits consideration in its own right in view of the multi-lingual pupil population of many of our schools.

[5] "Directive of the Council of the European Community on the Education of the Children of Migrant Workers." DES Circular 5/81. 31 July 1981.
[6] "Racial Disadvantage." Fifth Report from the Home Affairs Committee, 1980/81. HC 424 I-III. HMSO.

**Research
Evidence**

3.10 Advocates of mother tongue provision in all its forms have frequently argued that there is a wealth of research evidence which justifies the value of such activities. However the authors of the second NFER review of research concluded on the basis of their work that there was in fact:

> "... . as yet very little research evidence in the field."

They also noted that much of the work which had been done in this field had been undertaken abroad, chiefly in the USA and Scandinavian countries, and concluded that:

> "Whilst such examples of provision and bilingual programmes may indicate ways in which such work may be undertaken, their relevance to a British situation must not automatically be assumed . . . . ."

3.11 In relation specifically to the possible benefits of bilingual education, the findings of much of the research work reviewed by the NFER could hardly be said to provide conclusive evidence as to the value of such provision – for example Mitchell (1978)[7] found that:

> ". . . bilingual education of a pluralist character does not appear either to enhance or to depress the bilingual child's performance in the majority language, English, or in the non-language subjects. It may promote his achievement in the minority first language, particularly in relation to reading and writing skills. But there do not appear to be particularly compelling arguments, on the basis of promoting the academic achievement of the individual minority language child, for choosing between monolingual and bilingual education."

There have been three major research projects in this country on bilingual education:

– the 1976 Council of Europe-funded project in Birmingham;

– the 1977-1981 EC/Bedfordshire pilot project (this project is referred to in greater detail in our Chapter on the Italian community later in this report); and

– the 1978-1980 DES-funded mother tongue and English teaching project in Bradford.

The findings of these projects are considered in some detail in the second NFER review of research, and the authors conclude that:

---

[7] "Bilingual Education of Minority Language Groups in the English Speaking World." Some Research Evidence. Mitchell R. University of Stirling. 1978.

"It would be imprudent to draw any conclusions on the basis of the three different bilingual education programmes which have been undertaken in this country as to implications for establishing the child's mother tongue prior to developing skills in a second language, English. The three projects have been conducted with three different age groups, with different objectives, at different times and in different localities, and whilst the first two were concerned with literacy, the latter project concentrated on fluency, hence they cannot be directly compared. One serious drawback to the evidence which they do supply is the lack of long-term knowledge about the influence of such programmes on various factors, not least of which is the competence of pupils in their mother tongue and in English."

Thus, on the strength of the NFER review, it would not seem possible for the case for any form of mother tongue provision to rest on the research evidence alone.

The Welsh Experience

3.12   Another of the arguments often put forward to support bilingual education is the experience of schools in some parts of Wales in making such provision for their pupils. The linguistic situation in Wales is however we believe far from comparable with that of the ethnic minority communities now present in our society since only one language – Welsh – is involved and this is the **national** language of the country and as such lies at the heart of its culture and traditions. As the then Director of the Centre for Information on Language Teaching and Research recognised in his paper for a Conference on Bilingualism and British Education held in January 1976:

"The issue in Wales is clouded neither by multilingualism nor by any lack of determination of the status (cultural, political or legal) of the languages concerned .. The language policy in Wales originates from a different historical background, and rests on a quite different relationship between the principal minority and majority languages, politically and legally."

We believe similarly that the case for bilingual education for ethnic minority pupils in this country cannot be judged by the bilingual experience of some schools in Wales.

Parental Attitudes

3.13   Another major justification put forward in support of mother tongue teaching and mother tongue maintenance within mainstream schools is pressure from ethnic minority parents for such provision. The authors of the second NFER review of research draw attention to a number of surveys of the attitudes of Asian parents which in

404

the main show considerable, but by no means overwhelming or unequivocal, support for their languages being taught in mainstream schools. They note however that:

> *"Those research studies which do exist are all quite recent, showing that up until the emergence of the EEC Directive few had thought to ask parents what their views would be."*

Alongside the evidence of parental support for mother tongue provision, however, must be set the evidence presented in the NFER reviews and also the views expressed very clearly to us at our various meetings with parents from the whole range of ethnic minority groups that they want and indeed expect the education system to give their children above all a good command of **English** as rapidly as possible, and that any provision for mother tongue should in no way detract from this aim.

Community Based Provision

3.14 Above all, however, the degree of community support for mother tongue provision is claimed to be manifested by the existence of widespread thriving community based language classes. On many occasions it has also been claimed that the only reason why ethnic minority community languages have survived so long in the absence of provision in mainstream schools is the very existence of such community based provision. It may be worth noting however that in many cases the communities would see their own classes continuing in existence even were mother tongue provision in all its forms to be incorporated within mainstream schools, because of the religious and cultural implications of certain languages, and as a positive form of self help which provides a valuable focal point particularly for isolated minority communities. In this connection we have received a considerable amount of evidence from the organisers of community based provision regarding the widely varying degrees of support offered to them by LEAs in different parts of the country, with pleas for a uniformity of approach. The problems faced by the providers of existing community based provision, highlighted in evidence to us from community representatives, can be summarised as follows:

– inadequate and inappropriate accommodation eg in private houses or religious meeting places;

– "teachers" who may in fact not be trained teachers and may not be experienced in using the teaching methods, teaching styles and patterns of discipline of mainstream schools;

– inadequate and inappropriate teaching materials, text books and resources generally;

405

– the timing of such provision – in the evenings and at weekends;

– wide variation in the quality of the provision made; and

– the low status of the provision in the eyes of many people including even the pupils attending.

Our View

3.15   We are conscious that we will be expected to declare ourselves as either "for" or "against" mother tongue. We are without doubt "for" mother tongue in the sense that we regard the linguistic diversity of Britain today as a positive asset in just the same way as everyone welcomes the many dialects and two indigenous languages (Welsh and Gaelic) of the different regions of the United Kingdom. We are also "for" mother tongue in that we see all schools having a role in imparting a broader understanding of our multilingual society to all pupils, and "for" mother tongue in the value which we attach to fostering the linguistic, religious and cultural identities of ethnic minority communities. By like token we applaud the way in which schools in our three National Regions – Scotland, Wales and Northern Ireland – have helped preserve a national identity within a United Kingdom. Where we differ from the view taken by some advocates of mother tongue provision is in the role which we see for mainstream schools in the maintenance and use of ethnic minority community languages. We find we cannot support the arguments put forward for the introduction of programmes of bilingual education in maintained schools in this country. Similarly we would regard mother tongue maintenance, although an important educational function, as best achieved within the ethnic minority communities themselves rather than within mainstream schools, but with considerable support from and liaison with the latter. We are however wholeheartedly in favour of the teaching of ethnic minority community languages, within the languages curriculum of maintained secondary schools, open to all pupils whether ethnic minority or ethnic majority. We now expand on these broad conclusions.

3.16   It is clear that both bilingual education and mother tongue maintenance can only be of relevance to mother tongue speakers of languages other than English, ie to pupils from certain ethnic minority groups. Where such provision has been made therefore it has inevitably meant that ethnic minority pupils have had to be separated from their peers for "special" teaching. As we have stressed throughout this report, we are opposed in principle to the withdrawal of ethnic minority pupils as an identifiable group and to the concept

Concern About "Separate" Provision

of "separate" provision. We cannot accept that such provision can in any sense, as has been suggested, reduce social and cultural barriers between English speakers and ethnic minority pupils. On the contrary, we believe that any form of separate provision catering exclusively for ethnic minority pupils, serves to establish and confirm social divisions between groups of pupils. It also leaves the ethnic majority pupils' education impoverished and monolingual and the negative perceptions of the "strangeness" of ethnic minority groups, which lie at the roots of racism, unaffected. Linguistic barriers between groups can we believe only be broken down effectively by a programme of general language awareness for **all** pupils such as we propose later in this Chapter. Neither can we accept the argument that for ethnic minority pupils to be taught through the medium of their mother tongue accords them equality of opportunity in this society. On the contrary, the key to equality of opportunity, to academic success and, more broadly, to participation on equal terms as a full member of society, is good command of **English** and the emphasis must therefore we feel be on the learning of English. We find the research evidence that the learning of English can be assisted by bilingual education or mother tongue maintenance, unconvincing, since in many instances the most that can be claimed from particular projects is that the child's learning of English is not impaired and **may** in some respects be enhanced. We have also noted with interest the American experience which has led to a current move there away from some of the programmes of bilingual education which had previously been established. Where the languages which parents may wish to see being taught are not their children's "mother tongues" as such, but possibly entirely different languages we would also see the linguistic argument of enhanced development of the "first language" as a basis for learning English, as invalid.

3.17   We accept that, for any child, starting school represents a tremendous upheaval, even where the linguistic, social and cultural context closely mirrors that of his or her home. For a child with little or no English, and with a different cultural frame of reference, the experience can clearly be even more traumatic. It has been suggested that mother tongue provision can help to ameliorate the difficulties facing non-English speaking pupils entering school for the first time. It must however be recognised we believe that such provision can at best serve only to delay rather than overcome the trauma for these

Bilingual Resource

pupils of entering an English speaking environment. We believe however that a particularly important role can be played within primary schools, and in particular in nursery classes, by what we would term a "bilingual resource" to help with the transitional needs of a non-English speaking child starting school. We would see such a resource providing a degree of continuity between the home and school environment by offering psychological and social support for the child, as well as being able to explain simple educational concepts in a child's mother tongue, if the need arises, but always working **within** the mainstream classroom situation and **alongside** the class teacher. We would in no way however see such a situation as meaning that a child's mother tongue should be used as a general medium of instruction or should form a structured part of the curriculum as has traditionally been envisaged in programmes of bilingual education and mother tongue maintenance. Such a role may be undertaken by a bilingual teacher, non-teaching assistant or nursery nurse already on the staff of the school, or even by a parent, or possibly by fifth or sixth formers from local secondary schools as part of their child care courses or community service experience. It should not be assumed however that the bilingual "resource" will as a matter of course relate to pupils from the same linguistic, cultural or ethnic groups when their backgrounds may be entirely different; nor should they be seen as "catering" just for the ethnic minority pupils but rather as an enrichment of the education of all pupils.

Enhanced Support for Community Based Provision

3.18 As far as provision for mother tongue maintenance is concerned we do not believe mainstream schools should seek to assume the role of the community providers for maintaining ethnic minority community languages. Languages are dynamic and are continually being modified and developed by the users according to context and environment. They thrive by being used, not merely taught. If a language is truly the mother tongue of a community and is the language needed for parent/child interaction and for discussions within the immediate and extended family, or for access to the religious and cultural heritage of the community, then we believe it will survive and flourish regardless of the provision made for its teaching and/or usage within mainstream schools. Since the education system does however we believe have a role to play in assisting communities to retain their linguistic heritages, we would see this broad aim best being achieved through the establishment of comprehensive programmes of support by LEAs for existing provision for language maintenance by the "language communities" concerned. In order to overcome some of the difficulties faced by the community providers over matters such as accommodation and teaching resources, we would like to see far more community language classes being held on mainstream school premises. We would like to see LEAs adopting a more uniform approach to this issue in making school premises available **free of charge** and encouraging community providers to use them. By thus bringing the community language classes physically within the mainstream school this will inevitably promote greater interest and understanding, on the part of mainstream teachers, of the activities taking place. We would also hope to see the "community teachers" becoming more involved in mainstream school activities, for example, being able to discuss the progress of a particular child with his or her class teacher. At present the very marked isolation of these community based language classes from mainstream schools is illustrated by the fact that most mainstream teachers to whom we spoke, apart from commenting adversely on the provision made, showed a remarkable lack of knowledge about this part of their pupils' overall education. We would therefore like to see the two providers of a child's education—the community and the school—being brought closer together. Forging this closer link will be made all the easier, and the communities' concerns about the timing of some existing language classes will be overcome, if the classes themselves take place either at lunchtime or immediately at the end of the school day. We would also see LEAs' financial responsibilities for community based classes extending to making grants available to the providers for the purchase of books and the development of teaching materials. Similarly, we would like to see advice and support being offered by LEA advisory services for the community teachers on teaching methods, teaching styles and resources, and possibly even the provision of short *ad hoc* in-service style courses for the teachers, to meet some of the concern felt by the community about the extent to which their teachers are able to provide for this important aspect of their children's education. In order to reassure LEAs that the best possible use is being made of the resources to be provided for these classes, and also to allay the concerns voiced by the community about the variable "quality" of provision, we would expect LEA advisory staff to visit the classes on a regular basis to offer guidance on the work being done.

Mother Tongue Teaching

3.19 The area of mother tongue provision where we believe the greatest shift in attitude is needed is in relation to what we have termed mother tongue teaching and the artificial distinction which has been drawn in secondary schools between what are generally termed modern or foreign languages and ethnic minority community languages. The educational value to an individual of learning a language other than his own is an indisputable component of a full and balanced education. However, the pre-eminence of French and German as the languages offered by schools, whilst perhaps having originally been based on sound educational reasons seems, in today's interdependent world and within our own multilingual environment, somewhat harder to explain and defend. Within the context of "Education for All", we believe it is entirely right for a white English speaking pupil to study an ethnic minority community language as a valid and integral part of his education. For a bilingual pupil, we believe it is only reasonable to expect that he should be able to study for a qualification in a language in which he already has some facility. We believe therefore that the teaching of ethnic minority community languages should form an integral part of the curriculum in secondary schools. Similarly, at LEA level, we would expect to see modern languages advisers having responsibility for the whole range of languages offered, including the languages of ethnic minority communities, rather than, as is usually the case at present, provision for the latter, if recognised at all, falling within the remit of the multicultural adviser or the E2L specialist. We are convinced that a facility, or even a qualification, in a community language should be seen as providing any young person with a skill of direct relevance to work in areas of ethnic minority settlement in fields such as social services, nursing and education, where dealing with people is so important. We would therefore expect to see schools and the careers service emphasising the value of languages in such careers, and employers, particularly local authorities, seeing language skills as one of the criteria to be used when making appointments in these fields.

Attitudes of Pupils

3.20   It is interesting to note that in the schools we visited where ethnic minority community languages were already part of the curriculum, a number of the language speakers had in fact not chosen to study them. In some cases this was clearly because the languages were timetabled against other subjects which the pupils felt were more relevant to their future careers but in one LEA it was simply because the languages had been added to the school curriculum, almost as an afterthought, after the timetables had already been drawn up. To counter this, we would expect to see community languages being built into the school timetable from the start as an integral part of the curriculum. In addition it is clear that some pupils may have been influenced by the albeit sub-conscious negative view of their languages which we still found to be present in these schools which meant they found it difficult to see them as "proper" subjects for study. Of greater significance however may be the attitude of those pupils who seemed to resist the religious and cultural overtones of studying their languages in school which to them seemed to unnecessarily prescribe their future cultural frame of reference. We found this latter reaction particularly interesting since we ourselves would never wish to see an ethnic minority pupil being compelled, whether by the school or his parents, to study his language; simply that the opportunity for him to do so should be there. We recognise of course that for a school to offer these languages there would need to be a viable class size, as with any other subject, but we would like to see schools regularly assessing and reassessing the demand for such provision and, where demand is only limited, considering offering the subjects in conjunction with other schools, on a consortium basis. It is important that schools should **not** assume that the demand for such provision will come solely from "mother tongue" speakers of the languages. We would hope to see a growing number of other pupils, and perhaps more importantly their parents and teachers, seeing these languages as realistic options for them. We have therefore

410

been delighted to find on our visits a number of instances of "white" as well as West Indian pupils studying Asian languages.

Teachers of Ethnic Minority Community Languages

3.21   Since we are looking for ethnic minority community languages to be given their rightful status and for an acceptance of their validity both as media of communication and as subjects for academic study of relevance to all pupils in multilingual Britain, it is vital that the teachers employed to teach them must be demonstrably "good at their jobs" to merit equal status with other subject specialists. We have been concerned, from the evidence which we have received, and from our own visits, about the low status often accorded to teachers of ethnic minority languages at present, which can be seen as a subconscious extension of the negative view which still persists in schools of ethnic minority groups and the languages they speak. We would challenge the assumption often made by schools that any teacher who happens to be bilingual or multilingual can "automatically" teach his language or languages. Language teaching is a highly specialised area of work which requires particular skills, and just as an English speaking science teacher would not be expected to teach English to 'O' level standard neither should a Punjabi speaking teacher of maths necessarily be expected to be able to teach Punjabi at this level. We have been concerned about the limited teaching ability of some of the teachers of ethnic minority languages whom we have met. Indeed some ethnic minority pupils ascribed their reluctance to study the languages to the 'quality' of the teachers. We regard it as important therefore that any teacher employed to teach an ethnic minority language in a mainstream school must hold recognised qualifications in the language concerned, must have received professional training in this country in the techniques needed to teach a language and must be fully proficient in English. Only thus can he or she hope to convince their teaching colleagues and pupils and indeed parents from all groups, of the validity of the subject. At present there are clearly few people, even including many existing teachers of ethnic minority community languages, who, without a good deal of support and preparation could meet these criteria. Remedying this situation represents a tremendous challenge to those responsible for training teachers but one which, we believe, must be met. The time has come for the balance to be redressed to a point where it should be quite possible and acceptable for a specialist in ethnic minority languages to progress to become the head of a secondary school modern languages department or even ultimately a modern languages adviser.

411

Survey of Capacity for Training Teachers of Community Languages

3.22   In an attempt to investigate the extent to which teacher training institutions were responding to this challenge we commissioned a research team based at the University of Nottingham School of Education to undertake a survey of the existing and potential capacity of institutions for preparing students to teach ethnic minority community languages in schools. The results of this survey[8], which are summarised in Annex F, were on the whole rather disappointing if not unexpected. The researchers found that:

> *"PGCE courses in modern languages cater overwhelmingly for graduates in French and German. . . . Nowhere in England and Wales can a graduate in ethnic minority community languages . . . . obtain an appropriate training for teaching . . . . The BEd situation is even weaker, and seems bound to deteriorate as the degree becomes predominantly a primary teaching qualification."*

Looking to the future however the situation was found to be slightly more encouraging. The researchers found evidence of at least some interest or potential expertise in the teaching of ethnic minority community languages spread across some thirty-seven institutions of which eight were significantly ahead of the rest. The task of ensuring that schools are able to recruit teachers of ethnic minority community languages of the quality and indeed the quantity they clearly need is of vital importance. We would urge the Government therefore to respond to the situation by taking measures to ensure that potential teachers of these languages receive the degree of training, support and recognition they are entitled to expect throughout their careers. A useful first step in this direction would, we feel, be for the DES to commission a further in-depth study of the eight teacher training institutions considered by the Nottingham researchers to be "potential centres of growth" in order to identify which have the greatest capacity for development in terms of both initial and in-service provision and to detail the additional resources which would be required to fully realise their present potential. (See paragraph 6(iii) of Annex F.)

Resources and Examinations

3.23   If ethnic minority community languages are to become part of the mainstream languages curriculum, appropriate teaching materials and general resources must be developed. At present, where the languages are being studied, the text books and readers being used have more often than not been produced abroad, often for use in teaching young children their own languages – thus the cultural

---

[8] "Training Teachers of Ethnic Minority Community Languages." a Research Project by Professor M Craft and Dr M Atkins of the University of Nottingham School of Education. 1983.

and social background and the target age group makes them entirely inappropriate to the needs of secondary age pupils born and brought up in this country. We would therefore like to see educational publishers beginning to produce appropriate teaching materials as part of their modern languages output, not only for use in mainstream schools but also in community language classes to bring the curriculum content there closer to that of other language provision. The production of teaching materials is of course closely bound up with examination provision. Those existing examining boards who offer examinations in ethnic minority languages – and we would like to see a considerable expansion of the provision made in public examinations at all levels – do not at present go beyond simply setting the paper as such, and do not prescribe the syllabus to be followed. We would like to see however greater consideration being given to syllabus content in order to bring the provision for these languages in line with other subjects.

4.   Language Across the Curriculum

Bullock Report

4.1   We have argued here for a greater awareness of the language needs of all children and for increased recognition to be given by schools to the positive aspects of the multilingual nature of society today. We have also stressed that we would see all teachers having some responsibility for meeting the linguistic needs of all their pupils, including those for whom English is not a first language. This view that teachers must take their responsibilities in respect of the linguistic development of their pupils more seriously is not of course new, and indeed this was one of the major messages of the Bullock Report which *inter alia* advocated the development of policies for "language across the curriculum" in all schools, in the following terms:

> *"In the primary school the individual teacher is in a position to devise a language policy across the various aspects of the curriculum, but there remains the need for a general school policy to give expression to the aim and ensure consistency throughout the years of primary schooling. In the secondary school, all subject teachers need to be aware of:*
>
> *i.   the linguistic processes by which their pupils acquire information and understanding, and the implications for the teacher's own use of language;*
>
> *ii.   the reading demands of their own subjects, and ways in which the pupils can be helped to meet them."*
>
> *To bring about this understanding every secondary school should develop a policy for language across the curriculum. The responsibility for this policy should be embodied in the organisational structure of the school."*

413

Despite the proliferation of both LEA and school-based in-service courses on the concept of "language across the curriculum" and the number of relevant publications, few schools have been able to translate this vision into effective practice – as the 1979 Secondary Survey[9] found:

> ".... the policies for language across the curriculum in secondary schools recommended by the Bullock Report are difficult to achieve, for a variety of reasons; it may be, indeed, that the phrase itself has not been widely enough understood or that it is not forceful enough to convey the notion of the overall responsibility of all teachers for the development of language essential to learning. In a great majority of schools .... no moves of any significance towards language policies have taken place."

A further discussion paper[10] produced by HMI in June 1982 found a very similar situation and the evidence which we ourselves have received appears to confirm this general lack of progress with the implementation of the Bullock Committee's recommendations in this field.

Ethnic Minority Dimension

4.2   Most people would accept that an important aspect of being a "good" teacher is being able to tailor what you teach to the particular linguistic needs of the class or indeed the individual pupil whom you are teaching and this is indeed the thinking which lies behind the concept of language across the curriculum – as described by HMI in "Bullock Revisited":

> "A teacher of science or geography .... whose concern is simply to impart facts to his pupils, who checks their absorption of these only by questions demanding short factual answers, who dictates quantities of notes without considering whether the vocabulary and structures he uses are intelligible to his pupils, who devises worksheets that take no account of his pupils' language competence .... is using limited and ineffective methods of teaching science or geography. Good teachers of these and other subjects know that pupils learn and understand better if they are able to ask questions, to explore and discuss the matters presented to them, to sift and relate evidence, to speculate, to work towards conclusions, to bring ideas into full understanding by expressing them in their own words, while learning progressively how to express them in ways appropriate to the discipline of the subject."

---

[9] "Aspects of Secondary Education in England." A Survey by HM Inspectors of Schools. HMSO. 1979.
[10] "Bullock Revisited." A Discussion Paper by HMI. DES. 1982.

These broad aims assume added importance and complexity however in schools with a range of pupils for whom English, or at least Standard English, is not a "mother tongue." As explained by Rosen and Burgess in their valuable study of languages and language forms in London[11]:

"There is a growing understanding that the language children are expected to receive in school is often opaque and mystifying and that their learning is hampered accordingly. It faces them in textbooks, worksheets, exercises, examinations and often the teachers' exposition. What should at its best be a liberating experience becomes an imprisoning one. There is often an alarming gap yawning between the language which pupils are expected to comprehend and thelanguage which they bring to school. This takes on new meaning when we consider the range of language repertoires in the classroom and the different ways in which the values, attitudes and concepts are expressed in different cultures. Some of the difficulties arise because the language put before them is inappropriate. It makes assumptions about them as readers and listeners which take no account of their ways of understanding and their language resources. The experienced reader/listener often has similar difficulties and overcomes them by active internal dialogue but many pupils need to have texts mediated for them in discussion with the teacher and with fellow-pupils. In this way the gap can be bridged. Children should not be left to pore uncomprehendingly over texts, left with a sense of failure and defeat. When English is a second language thefailureand defeat are more total."

"Cultural" Context of Language

4.3 Over and above the specific linguistic difficulties of this kind which ethnic minority pupils may face, the vocabulary and terminology used by teachers may also unintentionally present them with particular problems which are in fact related to differences in their home and family background. If a teacher uses unnecessarily complex phraseology or unfamiliar terms which lie outside a child's vocabulary, or more importantly, outside his or her cultural frame of reference, this can put them at an immediate disadvantage *vis-à-vis* their peers. Teachers inevitably seek to enliven their teaching by drawing on examples of "everyday situations" from their pupils' own lives to illustrate particular points. In so doing they often assume a common cultural experience on the part of their pupils. This is perhaps particularly true at primary level where teachers draw heavily on traditional stories, nursery rhymes and songs and where much of the work centres around topics such as "holidays at the seaside", "looking after pets", "picnics in the country", "Church

---

[11] "Languages and Dialects of London School Children." Rosen and Burgess. Ward Lock Educational. 1980.

on Sunday": concepts which may well be 'foreign' to some ethnic minority children. The problems which ethnic minority pupils can face are illustrated by the following extract from the evidence submitted by a secondary school we visited:

"Their (ethnic minority pupils') passive vocabulary is limited not only through lack of reading as with their non-reading indigenous counterparts, but through lack of experience – direct, or through their families and friends – of such familiar concepts as to prune, heather, to parade, porridge, tides etc, expressions such as "tongue in cheek", not to mention more evocative though more narrowly cultural ideas – Sunday joint, vicar, left hook or stately homes. It follows that their active vocabulary is often not adequate to express more than their basic needs. The vague, grey picture they must be left with as a result of half understood reading or hearing may partly account for a general difficulty in writing imaginatively often noticed in children from Asian backgrounds."

Whilst a child may appear to be reasonably fluent in English, it needs considerable sensitivity and expertise on the part of the teacher to help him to extend his skills in English so that he can participate fully in all classroom activities. We are not saying that teachers should avoid using such "culturally weighted" phrases as those mentioned above–on the contrary, since they will be growing up and living as adults in this society, they need to be familiar with them – teachers must however be aware that such phrases may be new to some of their pupils and so must ensure that their meaning and usage is explained and must also, where possible, seek to draw on examples from the broader range of cultures represented in their school.

Our View   4.4 We fully support the principles and objectives of language across the curriculum as important to the education of all pupils in schools and of particular relevance to the needs of ethnic minority pupils. There has been considerable discussion about how the concept of language across the curriculum can best be implemented in schools. The Bullock report of course saw as the key to progress the adoption by schools of formalised policies in this field. In "Bullock Revisited" HMI suggested that:

" . . . . although the importance of language in learning every subject in the curriculum and the contribution the subjects can make to the learning of language can hardly be disputed, the suggested strategy may not have been the best one for all schools. The idea of a policy "embodied in the organisational structure

of the school", desirable at it is, may have been seen by some teachers as a requirement to adapt themselves to a theory derived from a subject discipline other than their own."

We would certainly see the consideration of the language used in the classroom, and at secondary level in the teaching of particular subjects, as being an essential element in the review of the overall education process which we have advocated. In primary schools, the class teacher, who is responsible for all or most of the school work for his class, already has the opportunity to develop his own policy for "language across the curriculum". The need remains however for a coordinated policy across the years of primary schooling. In secondary schools, we would expect this issue to feature on the "agenda" of subject department meetings and where there are pupils from ethnic minority groups in a school we would expect the points relating to "cultural context" mentioned above to be discussed fully and the appropriateness of the course content and teaching resources to be under constant review. However there will inevitably be widespread variations in the way in which heads of department and individual teachers meet their responsibilities in this respect, and we have been struck by the marked reluctance of some teachers of science subjects and mathematics, as compared with their colleagues in the humanities, to look beyond their particular subject disciplines in this way. As HMI have pointed out, many teachers still, regrettably, see the issue of "language" as part of the English curriculum and thus any language problems which their pupils may have as simply the result of the failure of the English department "to teach them English properly". In view of this situation we do not feel that action on language across the curriculum and particularly the ethnic minority dimension of this can be left to the vagaries of the system. As the National Association for the Teaching of English stressed in its evidence to us:

" .... Since a child's sense of confidence is crucial in the business of mastering language, the nature of the school context in which language teaching takes place is important. Essential though it is to get the language procedures right in the English lesson, unless there is a school language and learning policy across the curriculum there will be wastage of effort and often confusion. Again, getting the content right in one subject may be breaking new ground in a commendable way, but there will be little sustained impact until there is a school view of how syllabuses need to change as Britain faces the challenge of developing a harmonious multi-cultural society."

We would endorse this view and firmly believe that in order to bring about the fundamental re-appraisal of language policies which is called for, there needs to be some co-ordination within schools, both primary and secondary, of the efforts of individual teachers and departments.

4.5   The Bullock Report saw a role in every school for:

".... a suitably qualified teacher with responsibility for advising and supporting his colleagues in language and the teaching of reading."

The Role of a "Language Coordinator"

– with, at secondary level, the responsibility for this resting within the English department. Many linguists have subsequently argued for a specific role for a "language coordinator" on the school staff. We would wholeheartedly support the case for an identifiable member of staff to take the lead in fostering a greater awareness and understanding amongst his or her colleagues of the need for progress and initiatives in this field. At primary level, we feel that the Headteacher should have the overall responsibility for this task but where there is a recognised language specialist on the staff (see paragraph 2.12), this teacher would also have a particular role to play in this respect. Within secondary schools, because of the continuing parochialism of many subject departments, we feel it is unrealistic to believe, as did Bullock, that this task can be undertaken by a member of the English department staff or even the Head of English, although they will clearly have a particularly valuable contribution to make. In order to be able to influence heads of all departments and to put into effect the policies necessary for reviewing and revising curriculum content – by for example releasing teachers from teaching commitments in order to evaluate their syllabuses or possibly introducing an English specialist into a subject class alongside the subject teacher with a view to highlighting the role which language in its various forms plays in a lesson (see paragraph 2.14) – we believe this responsibility can only effectively be fulfilled at Deputy Head level. To support this development of language policies in schools, we would like to see LEA advisers and HMI (not just the English specialists) giving far greater prominence to the role of language in learning any subject, through in-service courses, policy documents and advice to teachers generally. The Examining Boards also have a role to play in responding to and fostering, where possible, the use of more appropriate and relevant language throughout education by reviewing syllabuses to ensure that unnecessarily archaic or complex language is avoided. We would see such developments as part of an improvement in education generally but of particular significance and value in schools with ethnic minority pupils.

5. Language Awareness and Linguistic Diversity

5.1 Much of the debate about language education can be seen as a consequence of the concern felt by many in education about the extent to which pupils acquire a real understanding of the role and function of language in all its forms. Within the concept of "Education for All" there is also a need to broaden pupils' concept of language so that they no longer see it solely in terms of "English", and come to appreciate the positive aspects of living in a linguistically diverse society. In a society in which the tradition of monolingualism is deeply entrenched and belief in the "superiority" of the English language has been fostered by its historical relationship with the British Empire and its continuing role as a major international language, the concept of any other languages, even those of our European neighbours, as "strange" and "foreign" is perhaps understandable but hardly defensible. We would see the countering of such attitudes as an important component of "education for all" and the heightening of all pupils' awareness of the range and richness of language as contributing to a better education for all.

Need for Attitude Change

5.2 We have already argued earlier in this chapter for ethnic minority community languages to be accorded their rightful status within the education system and particularly for the modern languages curriculum of secondary schools to be broadened to encompass these languages as realistic options for **all** pupils where the demand justifies this. We recognise that this will require a major shift in attitude not only among teachers but also amongst the ethnic majority community, both pupils and their parents, to move away from the still prevalent view of these languages as inferior and solely of relevance to the ethnic minority communities themselves. A major step in countering this narrow view of languages is we feel for schools, at both primary and secondary levels, to seek to create greater understanding amongst all their pupils of the range of languages which are now a feature of Britain today. In looking to pupils from all groups to consider studying ethnic minority community languages as an integral part of their education it is clearly essential for their earlier educational experience to have set these languages in their proper context. Thus the education service needs to have laid the necessary foundations for the study of them by informing pupils about the various languages which are now spoken in this country and, by implication, about the communities who speak them, both here and in their countries of origin. The remarkable degree of ignorance which exists within the ethnic majority community of the languages of the ethnic minorities was demonstrated to us time and time again on our visits, not only by pupils, but, far more worryingly, by teachers even in schools with considerable numbers of bilingual or multilingual pupils. This situation has been illustrated in many of the surveys which have been conducted of pupils' home languages where teachers and even Heads and their deputies have classified their pupils as speaking "languages" such as African, Indian, "Paki", Cypriot and Swiss![12] It is also revealing that, as the National Association for the Teaching of English commented in its evidence to us:

> *"Teachers often expect that children who speak languages or dialects different from their own will have grave difficulties. Research has shown that it is the teachers' expectation, not the different language or dialect, that causes the difficulties."*

The perpetuation by the education system of such attitudes can in our view be seen as another instance of institutional racism, albeit indirect, and the need for schools to inculcate positive attitudes towards linguistic diversity amongst all their pupils to combat these attitudes accordingly as a matter of crucial importance.

Different Forms of Language

5.3   As a basis for an appreciation of linguistic diversity it is clear that all pupils need to have an insight into the nature of language and its role in our society as well as some knowledge of different forms of language: informal/formal, and standard/non-standard – all equally valid but appropriate to different situations. The concept of "appropriateness of language" was discussed as follows in the Bullock Report:

> *".... a view that has long been held by linguists is that an utterance may be "correct" in one linguistic situation but not in another. Any one person belongs to a number of speech communities, and correctness therefore becomes a matter of conforming to the linguistic behaviour appropriate to the situation in which he is talking. Many people find this notion of relativity hard to accept, but it seems to us far more reasonable to think in terms of appropriateness than of absolute correctness. This is to operate positively rather than negatively, in the sense that one is seeking to extend the child's range of language use, not restrict it. The aim is .... to enlarge his repertoire so that he can use language effectively in other speech situations and use standard forms when they are needed."*

---

[12] The Linguistic Minorities Project Schools Language Survey (see paragraph 1.1) showed that the language label 'Indian' was recorded 134 times in five LEAs, 'Pakistani' was recorded 110 times in Bradford and Waltham Forest and 'Pakistan' 80 times in Bradford, Peterborough and Waltham Forest.

The Linguistic Needs of West Indian Pupils

5.4   One specific issue which has been raised with us in connection with the "appropriateness" of language is the particular language needs of West Indian pupils and the ways in which the education system has responded to these. It may be helpful therefore to consider further the view which we took of West Indian pupils' language needs in our interim report. In that report we introduced this issue by explaining that:

> "West Indian children in this country speak in a variety of ways. Some are able to speak creole and use it on certain occasions; many, regardless of their island of origin, are developing what has been described as "Black English" or "British Jamaican". Other children speak mainly in the local vernacular, with or without creole features, and others again speak mainly in standard English. Children originating from St Lucia and Dominica are sometimes able to understand French Creole. A few are able to use several of these forms. Very few, apart from new arrivals, speak exclusively in creole. In writing, many West Indian children display none of the features of creoles, others fairly commonly use certain forms that are consistent with the rules of creoles; for instance, they may not mark plurals and they may not inflect the verb to show that the past tense is indicated. A few children have more serious difficulties which result in a confusion in structures."

Various Approaches Adopted by Schools

5.5   We then went on to consider the various approaches adopted by schools to West Indian language and the bearing which these might have on the educational experience and overall performance of West Indian pupils. We identified three broad educational positions:

> " i.   *Deficit*
>
> This was the first approach to be put forward and assumed that the language of West Indian children was inadequate for learning, deficient or restricted. This resulted in an effort, from an early age, to change or replace the child's language, with consequent harm to his language development and self image. The evidence that we have received gives no support to this approach, which nevertheless still persists amongst some teachers.
>
> ii.   *Dialect Interference*
>
> Many teachers who would reject the "deficit" approach would still claim that some West Indian children's language, though not inferior is nevertheless sufficiently different from Standard English to cause difficulties.

421

> *Others would go further and claim that the West Indian child's language gives rise to linguistic interference similar to the effect of mother tongue speech habits on foreign language learning . . . .*

> iii.   *Repertoire*

> *The third approach . . . . now recognised as being particularly appropriate to West Indian children is one that values all languages and dialects as an important part of the child's linguistic repertoire. The intention is not to change or replace any particular dialect but to develop a sharper awareness of, and interest in, the different language forms that the child can use, thus avoiding confusion between them . . . . An underlying principle is that whereas both the "deficit" and "dialect interference" approaches focus on what the child cannot do the "repertoire" approach focusses on what the child can do and builds constructively on the considerable linguistic strengths the child brings to the classroom."*

In our interim report we thus expressed our support for the "repertoire" approach to West Indian language needs as well as stressing the particularly damaging effects on a pupil's self concept and motivation of schools simply dismissing his or her language as "bad English". Whilst we have not been able to take our consideration of the language needs of West Indian children as far as we would have wished, the further evidence which we have received for this report has in no way led us to revise this view. It is clear however from some of the comments which we received on our interim report that many teachers are still concerned about the practical implications of adopting a repertoire approach at classroom level. We therefore reproduce as Annex G to this Chapter an extract from a discussion paper prepared by the Inner London Education Authority discussing the repertoire approach in greater detail in the hope that this will stimulate further developments in this field.

Implications for Schools

5.6   Returning to the broader question of promoting all pupils' awareness of language and their appreciation of linguistic diversity, there are considerable differences in the opportunities open to monolingual and multilingual schools in drawing on their pupils' own experiences within the curriculum. We would wish to see pupils in **all** schools acquiring a common grounding in the "nature" of language, its various forms and structures, and the ways in which different language forms have been developed for different purposes, together with some knowledge of the linguistic landscape of Britain today. In multilingual schools however this can be taken further and active use can and must we feel be made of the linguistic skills represented in the pupil population. At primary level we would see all teachers seeking to broaden their pupils' linguistic horizons in this way. At secondary level some linguists have argued that "language" should be introduced as a discrete subject within the curriculum. We believe however that much of what needs to be done can best be achieved by broadening the existing English curriculum to be more relevant to pupils' language needs and by encouraging other subject teachers, through an overall "language across the curriculum" policy, to be more aware of the role of language in learning. It may be suggested that it is expecting a great deal of a monolingual teacher to impart an understanding and appreciation of different languages and language forms to a class of monolingual children especially for example in a part of the country where both teacher and pupil may have had little or no direct contact with members of such other "speech communities". We believe however that the willingness and capacity of the teaching profession to respond with great imagination and enthusiasm to ideas for improving upon the education they are providing for their pupils is too often underestimated.

Examples of Practice

5.7 An illustration of the various aspects of language which we would wish to see being incorporated into the mainstream curriculum of all schools is provided by the "awareness of language" course which has been proposed by Professor Eric Hawkins[13] and we attach the course outline as Annex G to this Chapter. Whilst this is put forward as a secondary school course, there are a number of elements which we believe are equally relevant to a primary context. Although the main emphasis is on language structures, grammar and the "science" of a language, a number of aspects of linguistic diversity are included, notably within theme three – "language in use" – which lend themselves to more extensive coverage within multilingual schools. Another view of how language education can be made more interesting and stimulating for pupils is provided by the "Languages Book" prepared by the Inner London Education Authority[14] which deals with "language and how people use it". Again, although clearly aimed at the early secondary years, many of the themes suggested here are also relevant at primary level. As an indication of the kind of material and the overall approach of this book, we attach some extracts from it as Annex I to this Chapter.

Monolingual Schools

5.8 It is important of course to remember that not all monolingual schools are situated in remote rural areas. Where such schools are situated within reasonable reach of areas of ethnic minority

---

[13] "Modern Languages in the Curriculum." Eric Hawkins. Cambridge University Press. 1981.
[14] "The Languages Book." M Raleigh. ILEA English Centre. 1981.

settlement with multilingual schools, we would expect to see them extending the linguistic resources on which they can draw in teaching about languages through pupil exchanges or possibly joint "language workshops". The role which taped and video-taped material, for example, showing a Liverpool black youngster speaking with a Liverpudlian accent or a schoolboy with a brown skin and a turban from Bradford with a Yorkshire accent, can play in stimulating discussion within a monolingual school about the complex relationship between different languages and dialects and questions of race and ethnicity could also be extended further to diversify the language experience available to the pupils. Needless to say, where secondary schools have, as we have recommended, broadened their modern languages curriculum to incorporate ethnic minority community languages, this in itself will help in extending the ethnic majority pupils' perceptions of these languages simply by them being included in the mainstream curriculum.

Effect On Ethnic Minority Pupils

5.9   A contingent but no less important benefit of giving all pupils in multilingual schools a wider understanding of language and different language forms is of course in the enhanced understanding and respect seen by ethnic minority pupils and their parents as being accorded to their languages. Not only will this help to bring the school and the community closer together through fostering mutual confidence and understanding but also the individual ethnic minority pupil may well feel a greater sense of security and motivation to learn, especially if these pluralist elements are incorporated in the very subject – English – in which he or she may feel least confident and secure. In multilingual primary schools use can be made of stories drawn from different linguistic and cultural contexts – as described by a Scottish teacher in a London primary school quoted in the BBC book on multicultural education[15]:

> "... I try to introduce a multi-ethnic perspective which will also involve the linguistic and cultural variety within the classroom. ... A new Welsh girl joined the class and I encouraged her to talk about Wales and her previous school. This led to a discussion on accent and dialect. I spoke in a Scottish accent and read some poetry in dialect. We also had some examples of other dialects from the children, notably a little piece from two girls of West Indian background. From this we talked about how dialect relates to where we all come from and we should never be ashamed of the way we speak as it is part of ourselves and our personalities. The children also agreed that it is wrong to laugh at or make fun of the way we speak. I am very proud of the bilingual children in my class, and we went on from accent and dialect to different languages. Some of the bilingual children

---

[15] "Multicultural Education: Views from the Classroom." Twitchin and Demuth. BBC 1981.

read out stories in their mother tongue and translated them for us. It was interesting that a story read in Serbo Croat was the familiar story of "The Enormous Turnip" and the Turkish boys read one of Aesop's fables. The point was made that there are similarities as well as differences in the stories read by children all over the world."

LEA Support

5.10 Clearly LEAs will need to play their part in promoting and co-ordinating the kind of developments and initiatives we have discussed above, alongside their overall policies on language. We would expect to see specialist English advisers together with HMI nationally seeking to broaden the expertise of English teachers through the provision of appropriate in-service courses and access to materials. LEAs will also have a role in fostering inter-school exchanges and also contact with other areas of the country thus acting as clearing houses for such initiatives. Examining Boards should also consider matching such developments in the curriculum by broadening the English syllabuses which they offer. Specialist subject associations clearly have a good deal of specialist expertise to offer.

Teacher Education

5.11 As far as the preparation of teachers to enhance their pupils' language awareness is concerned, we discuss in our Teachers Chapter, later in this report, the extent to which we believe all teacher training courses should inform teachers about the linguistic diversity of Britain today. On a more specific level, the survey undertaken for us of the availability of training courses relating to ethnic minority community languages – referred to in paragraph 3.22 above – also obtained some useful data on the coverage of broader aspects of language work in existing initial training courses. Institutions were asked to indicate whether they included reference in their PGCE or BEd courses to the following issues:

(a) conveying an awareness of dialect and language differences, and of a 'repertoire' approach to language learning in schools;

(b) conveying an awareness of the existence and main characteristics of minority community languages in Britain;

(c) conveying an awareness of current professional discussion of mother tongue teaching, bilingualism, etc;

(d) conveying a minimal competence to offer language support across the curriculum in linguistically diverse schools;

(e) developing competencies and strategies for working in multilingual classrooms.

For each of these aspects, respondents were asked to indicate whether it formed part of the 'core' offered to all students, formed an option or appeared in another form. The findings are set out in the following table:

425

(N=97) Type of Provision	Part of core		Option		Other		One or more of these	
	Number of institutions	%	Number of institutions	%	Number of institutions	%	Number of institutions	%
(a)	73	75	40	41	7	7	90	93
(b)	46	47	35	36	10	10	71	73
(c)	53	55	42	43	12	12	81	84
(d)	31	32	29	30	3	3	53	55
(e)	28	29	31	32	6	6	53	55
'Other'	14	14	8	8	3	3	23	24

From these findings the researchers concluded that:

"It is clear .... that a large majority of institutions claim to convey an awareness of language differences to all their students. Conveying an awareness of the existence and main characteristics of minority community languages in Britain, and an awareness of related current professional discussions, feature less prominently in the core; though a substantial majority of institutions in the survey claim to include them somewhere in the training programme. On the other hand, only a little more than half say they seek to develop minimal competencies for offering language support in multilingual classrooms; and even in these institutions, less than one-third place such work in the compulsory core. This can hardly be thought an adequate response to the now widespread presence of ethnic minority languages in the nation's schools, especially in view of the national mobility of newly qualified teachers."

Main Conclusions and Recommendations

General

– We believe that essential to equality of opportunity, to academic success and, more broadly, to participation on equal terms as a full member of society, is a good command of **English** and that first priority in language learning by all pupils must therefore be given to the learning of English (Paragraphs 1.1 and 3.16);

English as a Second Language

– We are wholly in favour of a change from the provision of E2L by withdrawal, whether this has been to language centres or to separate units within schools (Paragraph 2.10);

– The needs of English as a second language learners should be met by provision within the mainstream school as part of a comprehensive programme of language education for **all** children (Paragraph 2.10);

– For the child from a home where English is not the first language pre-school provision can be particularly valuable. We therefore

426

restate the recommendations made on this important stage of the overall educational experience in our interim report. (Paragraph 2.11);

– **All** teachers in schools with substantial numbers of pupils for whom English is not their first language have a responsibility to cater for the linguistic needs of these pupils and should be given appropriate support and training to discharge it (Paragraphs 2.12 and 2.14);

– We believe there is also a role for a language specialist or specialists in primary and secondary schools with substantial numbers of pupils for whom English is not a first language, to work alongside teachers or subject specialists through a "team teaching" approach (Paragraphs 2.12 and 2.14);

– LEAs and individual schools in multilingual areas should seek to provide all teachers, through induction and in-service training, with at least a sufficient acquaintance with minority languages to enable them to recognise the language being spoken, to recognise the various scripts, to pronounce the children's names correctly and to understand enough of the structure of the language to appreciate the nature of the difficulties children may be experiencing with English. (Paragraph 2.16).

Mother Tongue Provision

– Linguistic diversity in Britain is nothing new, and we regard it as a positive asset, whether it be Welsh, Gaelic, dialects or ethnic minority community languages. All schools should impart an understanding of our multilingual society to all pupils (Paragraph 3.15);

– The linguistic, religious and cultural identities of ethnic minority communities should be fostered but we cannot support the arguments put forward for the introduction of programmes bilingual education in maintained schools (Paragraph 3.15);

– We believe that an important role can be played in multilingual primary schools by a "bilingual resource" who is able to offer support to pupils for whom English is not a first language working within the mainstream classroom alongside the class teacher (Paragraph 3.17);

– Mainstream schools should not seek to assume the role of community providers for maintaining ethnic minority community languages (Paragraph 3.18);

– LEAs should offer support for community based language provision by making school premises available free of charge to community providers, by fostering links between community "teachers" and the mainstream school, by offering grants for the

427

purchase of books and the development of teaching materials and by making available to the community their advisory services for short in-service courses (Paragraph 3.18);

- Ethnic minority community languages should be included in the language curriculum of secondary schools where there is likely to be sufficient demand and all pupils in those schools should be encouraged to consider studying them (Paragraphs 3.19 and 3.20);

- Responsibility for ethnic minority community languages should rest with LEA advisers for modern languages (Paragraph 3.19);

- The careers service and employers should emphasise to all youngsters the importance and relevance of a facility in an ethnic minority community language for work in multi-racial areas (Paragraph 3.19);

- Care should be taken to ensure the quality of teachers of ethnic minority community languages. They should hold recognised qualifications in the language concerned, have received professional training in this country in the techniques needed to teach a language and must be fully proficient in English (Paragraph 3.21);

- The Government should take measures to ensure that potential teachers of ethnic minority community languages receive appropriate training, support and recognition. As a first step we recommend that the DES should commission a further qualitative evaluation of the eight teacher training institutions identified by the Nottingham Study (see paragraph 6(iii) of Annex F) as potential centres of growth in relation to ethnic minority community languages (Paragraph 3.22);

- Educational publishers should give consideration to producing teaching materials relating to ethnic minority community languages as part of their modern languages output, not only for use in mainstream but also in community language classes (Paragraph 3.23);

- More examining boards should consider the need to offer examinations in ethnic minority community languages at all levels. Where examinations are already offered in these languages, greater consideration should be given to syllabus content to bring the provision into line with other subjects (Paragraph 3.23).

Language across the curriculum
- We fully support the principles and objectives of 'language across the curriculum' as defined in the Bullock Report of 1975. This concept involves an understanding by teachers of the linguistic processes by which their pupils acquire information and understanding, and the implications for the teacher's own use of

428

language, as well as an awareness of the reading demands of their own subjects, and ways in which pupils can be helped to meet them. We believe that this is important in the education of all children, and of particular relevance to the needs of ethnic minority pupils. (Paragraph 4.4);

– We support the case put forward for each school to have a member of staff designated as a "language coordinator" – at primary level this role could best be fulfilled by the Head and at secondary level by a Deputy Head (Paragraph 4.5);

– We believe that LEA advisers and HMI, through in-service courses, policy documents and advice to teachers generally, should give far greater prominence to the role of language in learning (Paragraph 4.5);

– We believe that examining boards should review their syllabuses for all subjects to ensure that unnecessarily archaic or complex language is avoided (Paragraph 4.5).

Language awareness and linguistic diversity

– We believe that all schools should seek to foster amongst their pupils an awareness of the linguistic diversity of our society and a real understanding of the role and function of language in all its forms (Paragraph 5.1);

– The language of West Indian pupils should not be dismissed simply as bad English but should be catered for in a positive and supportive manner through the repertoire approach (Paragraph 5.5);

– In schools with monolingual pupil populations, distance learning techniques – such as taped and video-taped materials – and pupil or teacher exchanges with multilingual schools should be used to enhance pupils' appreciation of linguistic diversity (Paragraph 5.8);

– We believe that LEA advisers and HMI, through the provision of appropriate in-service courses and access to materials, should seek to broaden the expertise of English teachers (Paragraph 5.10);

– We believe that examining boards should consider the possible need to revise or extend the English syllabuses they offer to enhance pupils' understanding of the nature of language and language forms (Paragraph 5.10).

ANNEX A

Extract from Evidence Submitted by a Multi-Racial Secondary School We Visited Describing Their Approach to Cooperative Teaching

The purpose of the comments below is to serve as a checklist in the cooperative situation, and to help both parties ('subject area' and E.S.L.) work towards a joint approach.

In theory, cooperative teaching offers new possibilities, to the language teacher whose task is to develop the linguistic capabilities of the children, and to the subject teacher who may be faced with a class where language difficulties, a break-down at the written level or just plain numbers hinder progress. In practice, the cooperative teaching situation is considerably harder to work. Sometimes this may be due to personal clashes – and where two teachers have markedly different approaches and styles, the venture is unlikely to succeed. More often, difficulties seem to arise from a lack of definition of roles, a failure to work out what the E.S.L. teacher is present for, so that he/she becomes just another pair of hands – useful, perhaps, but too costly in teacher resource to be justifiable.

During discussions within the E.S.L. department on cooperative teaching, one point that emerged was the variety of aims and objectives which different members saw in the cooperative situation. As a result, we felt it would be useful to draw up a simplified list of aims. It is suggested that teachers about to start a cooperative venture read through the list and decide on areas which they wish to concentrate on. To the list have been added two sets of questions: the first to be considered before starting a cooperative teaching situation, the second after a term or so when we suggest that both E.S.L. and subject teacher should review the exercise. Again, the cooperative situation must be able to justify the use of two teachers in one classroom, though we have found that assessment at too early a stage is pointless: Cooperative teaching needs time to sort out roles and approaches.

Some aims and objectives of cooperative teaching – a checklist with comments and questions

1. Observation/collection of Data
An area which is perhaps too easily neglected since we cannot adequately develop the language within a class without first having an understanding of what that language demand is. Below are some areas which might be considered.

a. Language demand survey – intended to isolate the language needs of a child in a particular subject area by considering the language of the teacher and text books or worksheets. In carrying out such a survey the E.S.L. teacher may consider drawing up a list of vocabulary items specific to the subject teacher, tape recording lessons to look at teacher language in detail and attempting to define any forms of language production particularly relevant to that subject.

b. Language production and error survey. What sort of language are the pupils producing? If errors exist, what causes them? How can they be remedied?

c. Survey of study skills.

d. Survey of conceptual skills.

e. Observation of teacher style and methodology.

f. Observation of teacher-pupil interaction and pupil-pupil interaction.

2. Participation

What role/roles is the E.S.L. teacher to adopt? Sombelow. In a cooperative
teaching situation, the E.S.L. teacher is likely to take on most of them at various times.

a. Teaching the whole lesson – while subject teacher works with a separate group of children,
prepares materials etc.

b. Teaching part of the lesson. Variety of voice can assist pupil concentration.

c. Supporting a group of children: perhaps working in a separate area, allowing the subject
teacher to 'get on' with the rest of the class.

d. Clarifying the lesson; questioning, explaining terms, eliciting comments from the class.

e. Nomadic role; working with individuals or small groups, encouraging talk.

f. Informal chat.

3. Materials Production

Another particularly important aspect of cooperative teaching. The E.S.L. teacher's role might
be to:

a. Adopt existing materials.

b. Produce linguistically appropriate materials.

c. Be involved in the sitting of exams.

Materials produced for one lesson in a single classroom are expensive in time and effort. We
should therefore consider ways of storing materials for future use and also explore ways of
sharing specially written linguistically appropriate materials throughout a department so that
benefits of a cooperative situation are not confined to one class.

4. Miscellania

Some points which need to be discussed at the start of cooperative teaching venture:

a. Marking. Who is to do the marking? Is it to be shared?

b. Discipline. Who takes charge? There is a danger that pupils will see the subject teacher as the
'real' teacher and the cooperative teacher as a helper. Does this matter? If so, how can it be
avoided?

Some questions to consider before starting cooperative teaching.
(for subject and E.S.L. teacher)

1. Do all the pupils in the class cope 'adequately' with all forms of language: oral, written,
reading, understanding?

2. If the answer to the above is no, then which errors produce the most difficulty, and what is
the nature of the difficulty?

3. How do you see the role of the E.S.L. teacher in the 'normal' classroom?

4. How do you feel about another teacher in the classroom,

   a. Watching you?

   b. Interrupting you?

   c. Disagreeing with you?

5. How do you feel about a teacher observing your lesson and making comments on the use of language, linguistic demands on pupils etc?

6. What is your reaction to 'noise' in the classroom? Two teachers in one room each talking to a different group of students, can produce far more noise than one imagines.

7. What do you hope to get from a cooperative teaching situation?

8. What do you hope the pupils will get out of it?

Assessing Cooperative Teaching

A.   For both teachers

1. Do you feel at ease with each other in the classroom?

2. Do you share
   a. the teaching
   b. the marking
   c. the setting of homework
   d. the discipline
   e. the presentation (blackboard or o.h.p. writing)

3. Do you both help individual pupils?

4. Do you discuss teaching or the lesson during the lesson?

5. Do you correct each other's mistakes in front of the pupils?

6. Do you ask each other questions openly during the lesson?

7. Do you plan/discuss lessons jointly in advance?

8. If so, is enough time spent on joint preparation?

9. Do you share the preparation of worksheets and the production of materials?

10. Do you discuss any of the following before a lesson:
    a. the language the pupils will use
    b. the skills and concepts that will be demanded
    c. the subject content
    d. the methodology/best way to present the topic

11. What do you do with materials which are produced?

432

12. Do you both assess lessons afterwards? If so, do you consider
    a. the content
    b. the language

13. Have the lesson content, presentation and materials changed during the venture?

14. What do the pupils think of cooperative teaching?

15. Do you both attend Departmental Meetings?

B. For the Subject Teacher

16. Do you find the E.S.L. teacher a help or a hindrance?

17. Is the E.S.L. teacher 'just another pair of hands'?

18. If not, how do you see his/her role?

19. Has cooperative teaching slowed down or accelerated?
    a. getting through the syllabus
    b. pupil understanding

20. Do you think cooperative teaching benefits
    a. the subject teacher
    b. the pupil

21. Do you think cooperative teaching promotes the teaching of English?

ANNEX B

Extract from evidence submitted to us by a Head of English and an E2L teacher describing how their School moved from E2L teaching on a withdrawal basis to provision within the main-stream curriculum

Until recently the second-language teaching practice in this School was typical of standard practice: withdrawal for language lessons where the focus was on the teaching of structures. Second-language pupils were considered the responsibility of the English as a Second Language Department and their admission to mainstream subjects was held back until such a time as they were adjudged to have attained a 'satisfactory' level of English. Assessment in the first place was made by the special language teachers, but because 'satisfactory' is a shifting, relative description of achievement, this initial assessment was often over-ruled by subject teachers. No matter how 'successful' a pupil had been in the withdrawal class he could be judged never to have achieved a satisfactory level merely by upward changing of the criteria.

The effect of this worrying situation was that children could leave school with an inadequate educational experience and attainment, a low level of language achievement in English, and furthermore, without the experience of positive interaction with their peers in other groups.

Following brief discussion we made a decision to team teach one of our main-stream English classes and to include in it second-language pupils. We argued that the greater range of language that the second-language pupils would be exposed to would enable them to bring their natural learning abilities to bear on the situation, and that this, combined with the fact that the tasks set would present a greater intellectual challenge than the pre-selected language structures (hard to internalise because not learned in use) would, through the struggle for language, create a dynamic language learning environment. In addition, we hoped for a greater social integration, for an increase in confidence in second-language learners' approach to school work, and that they would come to view themselves in a better light.

Our first task was to arrive at a way of working together. It would have been very easy for the specialist language teacher to sit in one corner of the room with the second-language learners, following the lead of the mainstream English teacher, but we could see only how that kind of joint teaching would reinforce differences and even harden attitudes against second-language learners.

We needed to establish a way of working which could act as an example to the pupils. The specialist language teacher had to be seen as equal to the main-stream teacher by the pupils within the classroom. It was therefore important to work towards our roles becoming interchangeable. Planning lessons together (and not just one teacher following the others' lead) was one of the most important factors in enabling us to function within the classroom as equals. As important was the decision taken that second-language pupils would attempt the same tasks as the rest of the mixed ability class. However, if there was to be no special work for the second-language learners to do, then we had to take special care that the tasks set would be accessible to them and that we organised the lessons so that the best support possible was available to them. Such support consists of group work, pair work, talking through with a teacher, being in contact with a range of different models of writing, careful teacher introductions, support lessons.

A third element in our success is the place we give to talk in our work. Talk means interaction and a seeking towards collaboration. What has become salient for us is that this mode of working

434

together, of collaborative learning, is a mode and an attitude of mind that need to permeate not only pupil-pupil interactions, but also those between teacher and pupils, teacher and pupil and teachers and teachers.

Having concluded that second-language learners needed exposure to a greater and richer variety of language than had previously been the case if they were to learn to use it effectively, it was necessary to organise the class so that this richness and variety was available to them both to hear and use. Hence, talk and learning through talk took priority. Working in groups with the teachers acting as consultants as well as leading the class or working in support groups became our principal modes of working. Second-language learners had access then both to pupil-teacher talk and pupil-pupil talk.

We discovered, too, that we had to think hard about the composition of groups if our aims were to be achieved. All the pupils had to be grouped so that the working groups were mixed ability, mixed experience, mixed first and second-language users of English, and, crucially, multi-ethnic. We use the phrase 'crucially multi-ethnic' because we needed to take on the racism present, in this particular classroom, of students from West Indian backgrounds against Asian pupils.

We decided on one way of breaking down racism and suspicion between ethnic groups in the class. We took the risk of composing working groups ourselves; the pupils would not have free choice of who they worked with. Not unnaturally, there was some initial resistance to such an imposition, but our basic relationship with the class was good, and they recognised that this was something about which we were very determined. If not by magic, nevertheless an increasingly notable feature of this class was the growth of good relations and racial harmony. The fact is that the very strategies of openness, interaction and support which we were developing for second-language pupils were equally applicable to the rest of the mixed ability class. It was an unlooked for but critical benefit of what happened when we looked for ways of teaching second-language learners: we have improved our teaching and learning processes to a point where we believe it can play a part not only in school learning but also in countering racism in education.

ANNEX C

RSA Diploma in the Teaching of English as a Second Language in Multicultural Schools: Syllabus (Autumn 1983)

1. Factors Affecting Language Learning

Cultural Context of Education in a Multicultural Society

– Migration as a social phenomenon and historical and political causes of recent migration to this country.

– Socio-economic, cultural and linguistic consequences of migration for communities.

– Host community responses to immigration and their implications:
   i.   attitudes, racism, teacher expectation, etc.
   ii. LEA provision, central government educational funding, central government legislation, school responses, etc.

Individual Differences of Children

– Range of knowledge and experience outside school (including home culture community beliefs and values, etc).

– Previous school learning experience.

– Languages known and to what extent, including degree of literacy.

– Experience of and opportunities for communicating through English.

– Age, sex, status in family.

– Interests and motivation.

– Responses to cultures in contact.

2. Theory

Ways of Looking at Language and Languages

Some knowledge of formal properties of English with contrastive references to other languages: (See 4.3 below)

– Phonology.

– Lexical and grammatical systems.

– Discourse.

– Language in context (Who speaks what, to whom, when, where and how?).

Social and psychological aspects of:

– Language development (including early language development).

– Language and thinking (relativism/universals, concept development, etc).

– Bi-lingualism/bi-culturalism.

– Development of literacy.

Theory Underlying Second Language Learning and Teaching

- Historical development of EF/SL theory reflected by syllabus design.
- Styles of learning and modes of teaching: individual/collaborative aspects of learning.
- The home language(s) and other known languages in relation to ESL learning.
- The integration of skills in language development.
- Theory underlying assessment procedures.

3. Practical Application

Analysis

- Analysing cognitive, linguistic and study skills demands of school work across the curriculum and through the age ranges.
- Analysing (for example, through the use of error analysis) children's developing use of English in order to plan future action: the construction and design of materials, the selection of appropriate published material etc (See 2 above).

Action

Ways of making meanings accessible:

- Building on known cultural experience.
- Aural/Visual support.
- Editing and simplifying texts.
- Use of children's home languages.
- Organisation of learning groups.
- Staging, structure and presentation of tasks.
- Involvement of children in activities.

Learning activities for the development of listening, speaking, reading and writing skills. Construction, design and evaluation of materials for teaching and testing. Assessment of commercially produced teaching and testing materials. Monitoring and recording progress and achievement.

4. The Role of the Teacher

As a Classroom Manager:

Planning for purposeful communication in the classroom.

Devising learning contexts inside and outside school to meet varying needs, ages and previous experience of learners.

Organising classroom resources for independent learning, eg materials, AV aids etc.

As Consultant in the School Context:

In relation to:

- Language across the curriculum.
- Multicultural Education.
- Mother Tongue teaching and bi-lingual education.
- Local and school policy towards ESL provision and organisation.
- Colleagues.
- Forging home-school links.

437

ANNEX D

Extracts from Linguistic Minorities in England: A Report from the Linguistic Minorities Project (LMP) – July 1983

The Schools Language Survey

Aims and Objectives

The Schools Language Survey was developed to assist Local Education Authorities in documenting the range of linguistic diversity among pupils in their schools. It was designed in close collaboration with teachers and advisers to give a broad, overall picture of the number of languages used by pupils in all the schools in a particular area, the numbers of speakers of each language, and the proportions of pupils reading and writing the languages concerned. After piloting in mid-1980, it was administered during 1980-1981 in the Peterborough Division of Cambridgeshire, Coventry, Bradford, Haringey and Waltham Forest.

Context

The function of the collection of data on linguistic diversity among school pupils was intended in part at least to be for the use of the DES and LEAs in developing policy. In addition, certain obligations had been imposed on the U.K. government by the EC Directive of 1977 on the Education of Migrant Workers' Children, whose Article 3 refers directly to the need to "take appropriate measures to promote, in co-ordination with normal education, teaching of the mother tongue and culture of the country of origin". It was clear then that the data collected by the Schools Language Surveys should be such as to assist not only the DES at national level, but also LEAs and individual schools at local level. Administrators, teachers and minority parents were beginning to consider what sort of systematic arrangements might be made to support the maintenance and development of skills in languages other than English, for pupils who already had some of these skills. Some were also asking why these newer minority languages could not be made available more generally throughout the school system.

The overall intention behind our design then was to elicit basic information on:

    a.   the full range of languages spoken at home by pupils in the LEA schools;

    b.   the numbers of pupils speaking each of the languages; and

    c.   the proportions these pupils represented of the totals surveyed.

Findings

Numbers and Proportions of Bilingual Pupils

In the five areas where LMP conducted Schools Language Surveys in 1980 and 1981, the numbers of pupils recorded by their teachers as speaking at least one language at home other than English, for which we use the shorthand expression 'bilingual pupils', are set out in Table 2.1, along with an indication of the proportions that these pupils represented of the total numbers of pupils surveyed.

Most Frequently Mentioned Languages

The languages represented in the different LEAs which we surveyed varied considerably, both in terms of the number of different languages reported, and in terms of the particular languages which were most frequently mentioned.

438

Table 2.1: Number Surveyed and Proportions of Bilingual Pupils

	Bradford	Coventry	Haringey	Peterborough	Waltham Forest
Main Survey Month	March 1981	March 1981	June 1981	November 1980	November 1981
Age Range Surveyed Comprehensively	6—16	6—16	5—15	5—16	6—16
(A) Total Number of Pupils Surveyed	79,758	49,990	24,140	32,662	29,379
(B) Total Number of Pupils Using a Language Other Than English	14,201	7,189	7,407	2,408	5,521
(B) as % of (A)	17·8%	14·4%	30·7%	7·4%	18·8%

439

Table 2.2: Main Languages Reported in Five LEAs

	Bradford	Coventry	Haringey	Peterborough	Waltham Forest
(1) Total Number of Pupils Recorded as Using a Language at Home Other Than English	14,201	7,189	7,407	2,408	5,521
(2) Total Number of Identifiably Distinct Languages Reported	64	50	87	42	65
(3) The Most Frequently Reported Spoken Languages or Language Groupings as % of (1) to Nearest Whole Number	Panjabi 53 Urdu 19 Gujerati 9 Bengali 3 Pushtu 3 Italian 3 Polish 1 Hindi 1 Chinese 1 Creoles* 1 Ukrainian 1	Panjabi 59 Gujerati 16 Urdu 7 Hindi 3 Italian 2 Bengali 2 Polish 2 Chinese 1 Creoles 1	Greek 34 Turkish 15 Creoles* 9 Gujerati 6 Italian 6 French-based Creoles 4 Bengali 3 Urdu 2 Panjabi 2 Spanish 2 Chinese 2 French 1	Panjabi 24 Italian 24 Urdu 18 Gujerati 12 Chinese 4 Polish 2 German 2 Hindi 2 Creoles 1 French 1	Panjabi 31 Urdu 21 Gujerati 8 Greek 8 Creoles* 7 Turkish 4 French-based Creoles 3 Bengali 3 Chinese 2 Italian 2 Hindi 1 French 1
(4) Total of (3) as Cumulative % of (1)	95%	93%	86%	90%	91%

*'Creoles' here means English-based and other non-French-based Creole languages.

ANNEX E

II
(Acts whose publication is not obligatory)
COUNCIL

COUNCIL DIRECTIVE
of 25 July 1977
on the education of the children of migrant workers

(77/486/EEC)

The Council of The European Communities

Having regard to the Treaty establishing the European Economic Community and in particular Article 49 thereof.

Having regard to the proposal from the Commission.

Having regard to the opinion of the European Parliament[1],

Having regard to the opinion of the Economic and Social Committee[2],

Whereas in its resolution of 21 January 1974 concerning a social action programme[3], the Council included in its priority actions those designed to improve the conditions of freedom of movement for workers relating in particular to reception and to the education of their children;

Whereas in order to permit the integration of such children into the educational environment and the school system of the host State, they should be able to receive suitable tuition including teaching of the language of the host State;

Whereas host Member States should also take, in conjunction with the Member States of origin, appropriate measures to promote the teaching of the mother tongue and of the culture of the country of origin of the above mentioned children, with a view principally to facilitating their possible reintegration into the Member State of origin.

Has adopted this directive:

Article 1

This Directive shall apply to children for whom school attendance is compulsory under the laws of the host State, who are dependents of any worker who is a national of another Member State, where such children are resident in the territory of the Member State in which that national carries on or has carried on an activity.

Article 2

Member States shall, in accordance with their national circumstances and legal systems, take appropriate measures to ensure that free tuition to facilitate initial reception is offered in their territory to the children referred to in Article 1, including, in particular, the teaching—adapted to the specific needs of such children—of the official language or one of the official languages of the host State.

Member States shall take the measures necessary for the training and further training of the teachers who are to provide this tuition.

[1] OJ No C 280, 8. 12. 1975, p.48
[2] OJ No C 45, 27.2 1976, p.6
[3] OJ No C 13,12.2 1974, p.1

Article 3

Member States shall, in accordance with their national circumstances and legal systems, and in cooperation with States of origin, take appropriate measures to promote, in coordination with normal education, teaching of the mother tongue and culture of the country of origin for the children referred to in Article 1.

Article 4

The Member States shall take the necessary measures to comply with this Directive within four years of its notification and shall forthwith inform the Commission thereof.

The Member States shall also inform the Commission of all laws, regulations and administrative or other provisions which they adopt in the field governed by this Directive.

Article 5

The Member States shall forward to the Commission within five years of the notification of this Directive, and subsequently at regular intervals at the request of the Commission, all relevant information to enable the Commission to report to the Council on the application of this Directive.

Article 6

This Directive is addressed to the Member States.

Done at Brussels, 25 July 1977.

For the Council
The President
H SIMONET

ANNEX F

Training of Teachers of Ethnic Minority Community Languages

A summary of a Research Project commissioned by the Swan Committee and funded by the Department of Education and Science. The Project was conducted by Professor M Craft and Dr M Atkins of the University of Nottingham.

Introduction
The principal aim of this Project was to map the existing and potential capacity of initial teacher training (ITT) institutions in England and Wales for preparing students to teach ethnic minority community languages in schools. In addition, it was thought desirable to establish the extent to which **all** student teachers were being made aware at a general level of the existence and pedagogic implications of linguistic diversity in British schools. Further, since ITT institutions characteristically also engage in in-service training (INSET), it was considered useful to gather information on existing and potential provision for training in minority community language teaching at the post-experience level. Thus the final objectives of the project were as follows:

a. to establish whether the skills for offering ethnic minority community languages actually exist in ITT institutions in England and Wales, the extent to which such languages are in fact taught and whether institutions would be willing to place them on the curriculum for PGCE/ BEd students if invited to do so.

b. to discover the extent to which broad provision is being made to inform and prepare all students for teaching in linguistically and culturally diverse schools.

c. to map the current and potential INSET provision in minority community languages, both for practising teachers in mainstream schools and for teachers in supplementary schools.

d. to ascertain the extent of additional resourcing required (if any) to enable individual institutions to develop minority community languages at initial or in-service levels.

The research was conducted over a period of 4 months at the end of 1982 by means of a detailed questionnaire sent to all initial teacher training institutions currently offering PGCE and/or BEd degree courses. The data compiled from the responses to the questionnaire was supplemented in two ways. Firstly, in-depth visits were made to five institutions which, on the basis of their questionnaire responses, seemed already to have developed some provision in this area. Secondly in view of the complexity of the field and its interdisciplinary nature, a seminar was held in London, at which leading specialists presented their views in the light of the preliminary findings of the research project.

The response rate to the questionnaire was excellent (90%), and the survey can therefore be regarded as virtually complete. Within the obvious limitations of a preliminary, short-term enquiry, reliability is felt to be generally good, and on the whole the findings were unsurprising.

1. Initial Training: PGCE
Respondents were asked to list all their main and subsidiary teaching method courses in community or modern languages. Basing the figures on the academic year 1982–83, they were also asked to give the actual student numbers following each method course and (for main subject courses) the maximum number of places available. Table A sets out the resulting data.

Table A: PGCE Method Courses in Community or Modern Lanugages

Language	Max places available (main method)	Actual student numbers		Number of institutions offering the language	
		(main)	(subsid)*	(main)	(subsid)
French	420	411	160	36	20
German	172	163	65	21	12
Mod Lang**	275	274	103	18	9
ESL	91	76	140	6	8
TEFL	—	—	50	—	4
Welsh	74	49	21	5	4
Spanish	24	20	38	7	6
Russian	20	18	8	3	4
Italian	1	1	10	2	3

*A small number of students have been counted more than once on subsidiary courses.
**'Mod Lang' refers to those institutions which offered a non-specific language method course. In almost all cases, these courses catered for PGCE students with French, German or combined French/German degrees.

Table A reveals that, as expected, PGCE courses for modern language teaching cater overwhelmingly for graduates in French and German with a handful of institutions offering places in other European languages. Nowhere in England and Wales can a graduate in an ethnic minority community language such as Turkish, Greek, Chinese, Arabic, Portugese, or any Asian language, obtain an appropriate training for teaching. Further, the survey showed that although a tiny minority of institutions make some provision for PGCE students to acquire a new language competence only Spanish and Italian are available among the major community languages in this country. Self-instruction facilities are also severely limited in minority community languages with no more than 3 ITT institutions, for example, holding material for Asian Languages.

It is recognised that the time and curricular constraints acting on PGCE courses can make the introduction of new languages difficult, particularly in the present context of strict subject quotas. Nevertheless, there would appear to be scope for development here both in method work appropriate for community languages and in the provision of opportunities to maintain or acquire a community language, including greater use of strategies such as attachments to urban study centres.

2. Initial Training: B.Ed.

The situation for minority community languages on the B.Ed. at present is even weaker than on the PGCE and seems bound to deteriorate as the B.Ed. becomes a predominantly primary teaching qualification. Very little modern language work is currently taking place, and 75% of all students taking a language as the academic study component of their degree are studying French. A number are studying Welsh, and a sprinkling (12 students in 1982/83) German. This is also true of courses in professional studies except that here, 10 students in a single institution are working on Asian languages. The outlook therefore seems unpromising. On the other hand, the survey revealed that there is work being undertaken in both PGCE and B.Ed. courses in the teaching of English as a second or foreign language. These staff, together with those whose modern language role in the secondary B.Ed. is also now in decline, might form a nucleus for development – perhaps with some re-training – in expanding provision for ethnic minority community languages.

3. Language Across the Curriculum

Respondents were asked to give brief details of the extent to which certain specified aspects of language teaching were included in their institutions' PGCE or B.Ed. courses. The aspects indicated were as follows:

a. conveying an awareness of dialect and language differences, and of a 'repertoire' approach to language learning in schools

b. conveying an awareness of the existence and main characteristics of minority community languages in Britain

c. conveying an awareness of current professional discussion of mother tongue teaching, bilingualism, etc.

d. conveying a minimal competence to offer language support across the curriculum in linguistically diverse schools

e. developing competencies and strategies for working in multilingual classrooms (eg acquisition of a basic vocabulary, learning about the use of aides, etc.)

The questionnaire also included provision for 'other' aspects of language work to be recorded. For each of these aspects, respondents were asked to indicate whether it formed part of the 'core' offered to all students, formed an option or appeared in another form. A summary table of the resulting data follows:

Table B: Language Across the Curriculum

(N = 97) Type of provision	Part of core		Option		Other		One or more of these	
	Number of institutions	%	Number of institutions	%	Number of institutions	%	Number of institutions	%
(a)	73	75	40	41	7	7	90	93
(b)	46	47	35	36	10	10	71	73
(c)	53	55	42	43	12	12	81	84
(d)	31	32	29	30	3	3	53	55
(e)	28	29	31	32	6	6	53	55
'Other'	14	14	8	8	3	3	23	24

It is clear from Table B that a large majority of institutions claim to convey an awareness of language differences to all their students. Conveying an awareness of the existence and main characteristics of minority community languages in Britain, and an awareness of related current professional discussions, feature less prominently in the core; though a substantial majority of institutions in the survey claim to include them somewhere in the training programme. On the other hand, only a little more than half say they seek to develop minimal competencies for offering language support in multilingual classrooms; and even in these institutions, less than one-third place such work in the compulsory core. This can hardly be thought an adequate response to the now widespread presence of ethnic minority languages in the nation's schools, especially in view of the national mobility of newly qualified teachers.

There is in fact considerable variation in modes of presenting this aspect of initial training. Some institutions reported that they were using 'language and literacy' units, or 'multicultural education' options, or options in ESL or 'urban education.' Some claimed that language awareness permeated all their course components, others regretted that it was not possible to do more than present the topic at an introductory level. In some institutions use was being made of study days, conferences or fieldwork. Altogether, the nature and extent of provision appears to be wide ranging and even within the acknowledged constraints of course structure, there is clearly considerable scope for imaginative development.

Overall, then, it would seem that there are very limited initiatives being taken in initial training to prepare teachers in minority community languages. In particular, there appears as yet to be no appropriately tailored training provision either for graduates in these languages seeking to enter the secondary sector, or for students with a mother tongue competency in those languages which could be used in schools, or, finally, for students wishing to acquire a minimal competency in a community language as part of their professional development for work in linguistically diverse classrooms.

4. In-Service Provision

The survey revealed that provision of in-service higher degrees, diplomas and certificates in modern and community languages offered by ITT institutions parallels their provision for initiates: French and German predominate, there is some work in Welsh, a single award in Asian languages (10 students in 1982/83), and one in Spanish (4 students in 1982/83). There is, however, quite a substantial offering in ESL/TEFL an aspect of work which is changing as most ethnic minority pupils are now born here. Much the same is true of short courses offered by ITT institutions, where over 1300 teachers are engaged in work related to French and German, some 227 in Welsh, and 33 in Asian languages, Russian and Italian. None of the many other ethnic minority community languages spoken in our larger towns and cities is represented at all. Although, as the full Report makes clear, these bald figures may conceal the fuller reality, it does appear that, at present, in-service offerings in this field by ITT institutions are very limited indeed, and that they possibly reflect a combination of limited perceptions of need (both in the institutions and their local LEAs) and the corrosive effects of the current resource crisis in ITT and INSET.

It has been pointed out, however, that without a structure of appropriate post-experience courses and higher degrees it may be more difficult for teachers of minority community languages to build attractive career patterns for themselves and to obtain an equality of status with teachers in the more traditional modern languages. It may also be important to develop points of access to professional training for teachers currently working in supplementary schools.

5. Potential Capacity of ITT

An important dimension of the research project was to map the **potential** capacity of the ITT system in this field. Once again French and German predominate, with a far greater number of lecturers potentially available to develop new courses in these languages than in the numerous others mentioned. Table C reports a limited pool of expertise in several significant community languages, but the total number of institutions involved is quite small and they are geographically widespread. Taking account of all the limitations, it must be concluded that although small pockets of potential do exist, the current expertise among teacher trainers would be insufficient on its own for any serious co-ordinated development of community language provision in ITT. On the other hand, it emerged clearly from the survey that there are useful complementary resources in other University and Polytechnic departments as well as in the LEAs, and in the minority communities themselves; future ITT/INSET development seems likely therefore to turn on institutional initiatives in exploring and expanding new collaborative strategies.

Table C: Potential Staff Resources in Education Departments

Language	Total number of staff available	Number of staff fluent in the lang	Number of lecturers who could contribute	
			to language courses	to teaching method courses
Urdu	6	1	4	6
Italian	6	5	5	6
Hindi	5	5	5	5
Welsh	5	5	5	5
Punjabi	4	4	3	3
Gujerati	4	3	3	3
Bengali	2	2	2	1
Creole	1	1	1	1
Spanish	10	6	7	6
Russian	7	7	7	3

Institutions were also asked to indicate their interest in developing new community language units in their PGCE or BEd courses. Responses were sparse, understandably perhaps in the present resource climate. But apart from the continuing predominance of French and German in these proposals, Tables D and E do indicate interest in a wider range of significant community languages. ITT institutions are generally in a state of contraction, especially with respect to the secondary BEd, and they found it difficult to predict the possibilities of future development in this field. But a not insignificant number responded positively (some 32 in all), provided that additional resources were made available, and 7 anticipated that new courses could be developed without additional resources.

Table D: Developing New Community Language Courses in the PGCE

Language	Total number of institutions interested in making some provision	Number of institutions interested in developing **language** courses		Number of institutions interested in developing **teaching methods** courses	
		As main lang	As short course or subsid lang	As main course	As optional/ subsid course
Spanish	1	0	0	1	1
Italian	1	0	1	0	1
Gujerati	3	0	2	1	2
Punjabi	1	0	0	1	1
General Asian Langs	3	2	3	2	3
ESL	4	0	0	2	4
French	5	3	4	3	4
German	6	1	5	2	5
Mod Lang*	4	1	2	3	2

*Defined in Table A

Table E: Developing New Community Language Courses in the BEd

Language	Total number of institutions interested in making some provision	Number of institutions interested in developing **language** courses		Number of institutions interested in developing **teaching methods** courses	
		As main lang	As short course or subsid lang	As main course	As optional/ subsid course
Italian	2	0	2	0	2
Gujerati	1	0	1	0	1
General Asian Langs	4	1	4	2	3
ESL	3	0	0	1	3
French	6	4	5	4	5
German	5	2	4	2	4
Mod Lang*	—	—	—	—	—

*Defined in Table A

A similar picture emerged in respect of potential in-service provision. There was at least one institution interested in mounting a new Named Award course in each of the following minority community languages: Spanish, Italian, Gujerati, Punjabi, Urdu, Welsh, and a slightly larger number of institutions prepared to develop new Short Courses with either language or method components, or both. There were also several institutions prepared to run methods courses for teachers in supplementary schools.

Once again, institutions felt that staff training might be needed before new courses could be run successfully. In particular, designated staff might need time to acquire greater proficiency in an ethnic minority language or to gain expertise in teaching a minority community language in school. This might require short-term staff replacement to cover staff released for a sabbatical term or year to gain or improve the necessary competence and practical experience. This is an important dimension of the key issue of adequate training of trainers in the minority community language field.

6. Key Issues

During the course of the study, a number of significant policy issues emerged from the analysis of the data, from discussions in the institutions visited, and from the DES seminar. Three are briefly considered here: the varying implications for ITT and INSET; the extent to which the problem of training teachers for work in this field is part of a 'vicious circle' in provision; and the possible identification of future 'centres of growth' from among the ITT institutions in England and Wales examined in this survey. Each of these is now considered in turn.

i. Varying National Needs

At present, BEd and PGCE provision in modern languages is very largely concerned with training secondary school specialists who will teach French or German (and occasionally other modern European languages) to children who do not possess them and many of whom are aiming at public examinations. This provision will soon be concentrated mainly in PGCE courses. Future needs, however, in minority community languages will be more diverse. A small number of schools and LEA language centres will continue to need bilingual teachers, (mainly) at the reception level, to work with children (mainly) born here but brought up with a community language. Secondly, there will be a larger need for teachers at primary and secondary levels who possess the skills for working in multilingual classrooms, and for teachers who can help pupils to maintain their mother tongues and acquire a reasonable level of literacy in them. Thirdly, there will be a growing need for secondary school teachers able to offer the main community languages to 'O' and 'A' level, to pupils who in some cases will possess a fluency in the standard language or dialect of it (and, of course, other pupils interested in those languages). Finally, there will be a continuing need for mainstream teachers and ESL specialists to provide English language support at all ages.

Clearly, these are diverse needs, some of which may be met in BEd departments of education and PGCE core units, but much of which must fall to modern language specialists in BEd/PGCE courses. Furthermore, there will be a range of INSET needs in providing for the requirements of mainstream classroom aides, supplementary school teachers, LEA advisers and teacher trainers, as well as for modern language teachers themselves. These courses will be mostly specially tailored; but the present range of relevant award-bearing offerings is in need of review, perhaps by UCET and the CNAA, for it is these courses which will provide the main sources of expertise. It is hoped that the DES will take account of the relatively marginal resource implications of these adjustments in course planning.

ii. The 'Vicious Circle'

This research began with the aim of identifying the existing and latent ITT capacity for producing teachers of ethnic minority community languages. But while ITT appears at first sight to be the obvious avenue for improving the teaching of community languages in the schools, this must in future depend upon the recruitment of those with 'A' level qualifications in these languages (for admission to BEd courses), or with appropriate degrees, in the case of PGCE courses. The 'A' level supply depends on the schools – which lack the capacity; the graduate supply depends upon the output of undergraduate courses – which themselves may be dependent upon 'A' level recruitment: a vicious circle.

But there are several possible points of entry. First, some of the needs of the schools might be met by communicative competence, and not necessarily by the possession of formal qualifications in a community language. Fluency in the language together with some training in the appropriate methodology might be all that is required in some reception and primary school classes, and a number of ethnic minority recruits to BEd/PGCE/INSET courses will possess this fluency. Secondly, ITT courses might offer **subsidiary** level provision for those fluent in community languages but lacking formal qualifications in them, in order to strengthen 'O' and 'A' level teaching in the schools. There is also the RSA Certificate in the Teaching of Community Languages. Clearly, it is important to establish as quickly as possible recognised avenues for young people and others who might be attracted into the teaching of community languages as a career, and to create the appropriate expectations of a career structure including provision of in-service courses. This would strengthen 'O' and 'A' level enrolments in the languages, and strengthen 'A' level recruitment to community language degree courses.

The latter is the third way into the vicious circle and a vitally important one, for the PGCE route is likely to be the main future avenue in this field. This survey was therefore extended, and a brief preliminary survey of undergraduate courses in modern and community languages in the UK was undertaken. The findings are reported in detail in the full research Report, but the essentials are clear:

- provision for French and German is extensive, but there are also numerous undergraduate courses in Italian, Spanish, Arabic and Portugese

- other ethnic minority community languages, however, are far less frequently offered.
  None of the Asian languages could be located in the Polytechnics, and they appear to
  be offered in only 3 Universities.

A more detailed enquiry would be able to describe the nature of these courses and the extent to which they would meet the needs of British students aiming to offer the languages at 'O' and 'A' level, for some may be intended primarily for students from overseas or for those without mother tongue competency. Such an enquiry would need to substantiate the tentative indications of this survey that present undergraduate provision for some of the ethnic minority community languages may be inadequate. Indeed, languages such as Italian have been reported to be under threat as a result of the recent contraction in higher education. However, if on further investigation undergraduate provision proves to be limited, an additional way of breaking into the vicious circle would be to extend the present practice of allowing undergraduates without modern language 'A' levels to commence courses in community languages as initiates.

iii. Potential Centres of Growth

Institutions of higher education have a national (and international) role, and trained teachers, like doctors, architects or engineers, may find employment in any part of the country. It is therefore important that some provision is made in **all** institutions. Nonetheless, the appropriate teaching practice facilities will be localised; and some institutions have already begun to develop an interest in this field. Is it therefore possible to identify, from the findings of the survey, any future centres of growth? A detailed analysis of the questionnaire data was carried out using information on the following: existing language provision, interest in development of new minority community language courses, existing staff expertise, local resources, and complementary curricular developments. From this analysis it emerged that 8 institutions – and two in particular – stand out as potential centres of growth. Since, however, this research project was designed as a preliminary mapping exercise it would be necessary to undertake futher, more qualitative evaluation of institutions before any national policy initiative was implemented through provision of extra resources to certain institutions or in other ways.

ANNEX G

West Indian language: Implications of the repertoire position for practice

(Extract from "Language and Dialect" – A Discussion Paper prepared by the Inner London Education Authority).

1. Valuing Dialect

As a pre-requisite for this position a child's own language must be respected and responded to in the classroom; it must be given status and recognised as an efficient tool for learning (and this is particularly important at the Infants' stage). There is a need not only for a positive attitude towards the children's language on the part of the teacher, but also for the pupils to hear (and sometimes see in print) a range of material along the dialect continuum, to enable them to appreciate more consciously what their dialect can do, and what their people have produced. This is a long term objective, which is only gradually realised. These conditions in themselves have brought forth encouraging results. The Centre for Urban Educational Studies 'Reading Through Understanding' material (mainly for primary school but with possibilities in the secondary school) has resulted in a more positive participation by children and a marked increase in confidence in speaking, which includes young children using their dialect more openly in the classroom. A more positive attitude towards learning and towards school has been noticed in individuals and whole classes in secondary schools. Writing in dialect has sometimes been the starting point for a more lively and committed way of writing which has then been extended to writing in Standard English (which had previously been inadequate and lifeless). And there have been many cases of reluctant readers making a spurt forwards when taking on material in dialect. Confidence is gained by bringing their own expertise to the task and the pleasure of voicing it and entertaining others leads to more meaningful and fluent reading. But there are dangers in this sort of work and some teachers have had unfortunate experiences. Children and young people seem to welcome a genuine interest, and to want to share their language, but if work on dialect is introduced as a novelty, or simply and too obviously for motivation purposes, they may well regard it as an intrusion and resist it.

2. Language Differences

There are many ways of helping older pupils to appreciate how they are using their repertoires not only of dialects but of registers too; small group discussion and reflective pieces of writing have demonstrated how perceptive pupils can be when their own experience is under considera-tion and this thoughtful analysis makes extending the repertoire and refining it much easier. The examination of people's attitudes towards language also makes for fruitful discussion. A consciousness of the difference in dialects and registers is brought out effectively in role play and drama (and one sees here how much of Standard English is already within the pupil's grasp, but often in a passive form until opportunities are found for drawing it out, bringing it into consciousness). Teachers have devised interesting and creative exercises to sharpen children's interest in, and appreciation of, each other's languages. The linguistic diversity found within the multicultural classroom provides ample resources for work of this nature; but for a more objective consideration the speech of characters in stories and of characters and personalities on television, is sometimes used. Some teachers go on from here to teach about the history of the development of languages, and the reasons for the prestige and power of Standard English. Two booklets from the ILEA English Centre, 'Dialect and Language Variety' and 'Languages' are very useful for the range of examples and information and practical classroom suggestions they provide.

450

3. The Development of Written Language

In the English lesson a climate is needed where pupils can express their thoughts and feelings openly, and this means ensuring that the curriculum, or content (topics under discussion and for writing about, reading material) is such that all pupils within a multicultural classroom can relate to it and can feel confident that they have a contribution to make. Where this happens pupils write with commitment, and this demands a more precise (and often more complex and subtle) use of language.

Although Standard English is the usual form for written work, there are occasions when it is beneficial for the children to have a specific option to write in dialect, for instance for writing of a very personal nature, or where it is particularly appropriate because of the topic – or where the impact would be lost without it. This sometimes seems to inspire more vivid and purposeful writing, and often to give hesitant or reluctant children confidence in their writing ability. It is additionally useful in that it helps to make them more conscious of the difference between standard and non-standard forms. (Another useful way of pointing up this difference is to encourage the writing of stories where the narrative is in Standard and the dialogue is in a non-standard dialect. They want to get them both right.)

When it comes to helping children with their writing it is essential to realize that not all written work can be corrected in the same way. For instance, when pupils are feeling their way as they write, writing as an aid to learning, to sorting out their thoughts, they may well move to and fro along the dialect continuum. Teachers need to know that this is happening, that this is a stage they are going through, and they have to decide whether or not it is appropriate or helpful to ask a child to correct his writing. But there are other occasions when they are much more sure of what they want to say, when they are consolidating knowledge that is already fairly clear in their minds – and here it is reasonable to expect them to be able to perform in Standard (depending of course on the individual child). One needs to be aware of opportunities of this sort when the writer is gaining experience in writing in Standard. In the English lesson the re-telling of stories (through the eyes of one of the characters or for a particular audience) serves a similar purpose, and the 'voice' of the original piece is often taken on and helps to unify the writing.

4. Spoken Standard

Although we are more concerned with the ability to write in Standard English than to speak it, we feel that pupils should have the spoken form at their command, should they want to use it. Besides, to be familiar with the handling of the structures orally is of undoubted benefit when it comes to writing. We must emphasise that this does not mean trying to change the way a person speaks, but rather giving him/her experience of using Standard. The following activities are some which prove helpful in this direction: reading aloud to an audience (however small); play-reading; role play and acting; discussing freely in small linguistically mixed groups, where a modified standard will prove to be the common language. It is important too, to find occasions where a more formal speech will seem appropriate – for instance, talking with interested strangers such as visitors to the school.

5. Reading: The Effects of Literature on Language Development

The importance of the place of reading cannot be emphasised too strongly in a discussion of the language development of children in a multi-lingual classroom particularly in relation to the development of their written English. It is experience of stories, novels, poetry and plays that is to a large extent responsible for extending and refining children's written mode of language. It is important that this experience is not used explicitly for the learning of reading (although it inevitably helps that process). We refer rather to fluent private reading, to the reading of stories to children in the home and the primary school and particularly to the reading of a novel or a story to a whole class as a shared experience in the secondary school. In this shared response to a book, if the stories are in themselves well written, and imaginatively involve the children, the children have little difficulty in understanding language that may be different, or may be more complex than they are used to. It does not need to be a barrier. Secondly, the stories will act as powerful language models: the children are receptive to the structures and registers and conventions of the written language, which will be within the framework of their expectations in their own further reading; and their familiarity increases the range of possibilities for them to draw on in their own writing. Some of the results of this are seen immediately in any follow-up work of a creative or imaginative nature, where the 'voice' of the original is often taken on. Because Standard English may seem neutral compared to an oral non-standard dialect it is particularly important that pupils should experience its lively and creative use through literature.

For the language to have a real impact, and for the book to spark off purposeful use of language through discussion and writing, the content must obviously be significant to the children, and this means using material that the children can relate to implicitly; it means symbolically recognising the children.

ANNEX H

Extract from "Modern Languages in the Curriculum" by Professor Eric Hawkins

A suggested outline for the secondary school course in awareness of language

A suggested outline for the secondary school course in awareness of language to be taught as a bridging course in conjunction with mother tongue and foreign language. There are four main themes. Teachers will select topics from the themes in turn to suit the age and interests of pupils.

On the left are some questions to be pursued in classroom discussion and as group or individual projects, based on teachers' worksheets. On the right some typical activities and projects are proposed. The outline is not exhaustive but is offered as a starting-point for discussion by local working parties.

Themes and questions	Typical learning activities
Theme 1	
Forms of language	
a. How do we/could we communicate without language?	a. Pupils in pairs/groups invent messages to be transmitted without language; other groups decipher them
b. What are the possibilities/limitations of sign languages?	b. Compare deaf and dumb alphabet with American deaf and dumb sign language and 'language' of chimpanzees
c. How do birds/animals communicate?	c. Listen to bird-song recordings
d. Codes and secret codes, acronyms etc?	d. Learn and practise Morse code/semaphore Learn signs used on motorways Study rail and shipping signals Design signs that are unambiguous for school purposes Invent secret codes
e. Kinds of language: languages spoken in the UK languages of Europe languages of the world language 'families' dialects registers differences between American and British English	e. Draw language maps for language 'families' Listen to dialect recordings: discuss impressions; explain reactions Translate from one dialect to another Collect American/British contrasts, Creole/standard contrasts

453

Themes and questions

f. Appropriateness of language:
   slang
   jargon
   'in' words

g. Spoken and written language:
   how do they differ?
   the problems of learning to read (see
   Theme 4)

h. Forms of writing:
   pictographic
   hieroglyphic
   syllabic
   alphabetic
   phonetic

Theme 2

Structure of language

a. What is:
   a syllable?
   a vowel/consonant?
   a phoneme?
   a morpheme?
   an allophone, an allomorph, etc?

b. How many words do most speakers know?
   Do we all know the same words?
   Do all languages have the same number of
   words?
   Why not?

c. What does it mean to know a word?
   Who decides (in England) what a word
   means?
   Is it the same in France/Spain/Germany?
   Are we able (like Humpty Dumpty in Alice
   in Wonderland) to decide what meanings
   our own words convey?

Typical learning activities

f. Compose imaginary dialogues in which
   language is used inappropriately (eg
   playground speech on school speech day?
   use first person in science experiment
   report: why inappropriate?)
   List 'in' words for specified groups
   List 'family' words not used outside
   Make glossaries of the vocabulary of games

g. Compare spoken and written forms of
   English
   Attempt to express spoken sounds in
   written form
   Invent new forms of punctuation, diacri-
   tics, etc
   Work out methods of helping slow readers/
   immigrant learners
   Prepare posters for classroom explaining
   key difficulties in the transition to reading

h. Compare examples of writing numerals 1
   to 10/common names/greetings etc)
   Compare American and English spelling
   Work out a phonetic alphabet that is
   simple, unambiguous and uses as many
   familiar symbols as possible (this phonetic
   script can also be used in the Education of
   the Ear programme)

a. Break words up and examine whether the
   bits are 'bound' or 'free' (have meaning in
   isolation)
   Make lists of pairs (a lightship/a light ship):
   discuss how we distinguish them

b. Take ten pages in Oxford English Dictionary and count number of words: how
   many not known to the class? how many of
   romance/germanic origin? Compare length
   of English/French sections of a large
   Anglo-French dictionary

c. List words you know (can say/spell) but
   cannot put a precise meaning to
   List things (parts of bicycle/TV set) that
   you can draw but not put a name to
   List words you know (eg penicillin) but
   about whose meaning others (eg doctor)
   have more detailed knowledge
   Suggest a way of describing different
   degrees of 'knowing' words

454

Themes and questions	**Typical learning activities**
d. How does word order convey meaning? How does word order in English compare with other languages?	d. Study order of subject, verb and object (indirect object) in English sentences and label SVO (SVO + 10), (SV10 + 0), etc Contrast order of words in archaisms (I thee wed, etc) with modern English Contrast order of French/Spanish/ languages of immigrant pupils in the school with English
e. How is meaning affected by changes in sound/spelling? (eg how is singular/plural signalled? how is negative form signalled? how is question form signalled?) How do modifiers (eg a/the/adjectives/adverbs) change meaning of sentences?	e. Make posters and charts to help younger children/immigrant pupils learn plurals/ irregular plurals/position of adjectives/ verb inflections Make coloured charts showing rules for spelling of adjectives in French/Spanish/ German/languages of immigrant pupils in the school
f. How is meaning affected by intonation/ stress? How can/could these be shown in written language?	f. Discrimination games; invent notation to show intonation/stress Compare Spanish syllabic stress patterns with French and English Compare stress patterns of mother tongues of immigrant pupils in school
g. How does grammar convey the time when events happen/the probability of their happening/the place where they happen/ the order of events?	g. Draw charts to help foreigner understand use of simple present and 'progressive' (-ing) tenses in English Compare 'he swam across the river' with 'il traversa la riviere ala nage'; make anthology of similar patterns
h. What is a grammar rule?	h. Practise inducing simple rules from examples of language presented (this may be the most important single activity in this section; the aim should be to challenge pupils with increasingly difficult instances to discover rules by insight into pattern) Collect examples of rules in English that pupils can operate but not describe (eg the use of 'some' and 'any' in affirmative and negative/the preferred order in: he was wearing his { tweed old green cosy } jacket Why is the native speaker so sure his order is best though he cannot state the rule?)

455

Themes and questions	Typical learning activities

Theme 3

Language in use

a. How are sounds produced by the vocal organs?

b. Which sounds in English do not occur in Spanish/French and vice versa?
Which sounds occur in immigrant pupils' languages but not in English as used in the classroom?

c. Compare spoken and written language differences:
in usage
in relative speed of production
in relative speed of comprehension
How do spellings reveal history of word origins (eg science/conscience)?
What would be lost/gained by spelling reform?
What is the difference between learning through eye and ear?
What are the ear's limitations?
What is the effect of short-term memory (STM) on heard messages?; why are meaningless strings of words hard to hold in STM?

a. Use hand mirror in class to study lip/tongue/jaw movements
Draw chart locating positions of vowels and consonants
Contrast position of vowels in English, Spanish, French
Contrast pure vowels in Spanish and French with glides in English

b. Study local regional dialect and find which sounds do not occur in standard English and vice versa
Draw up lists of sounds common to all the languages/dialects studied or peculiar to one language/dialect (here immigrant pupils will be encouraged to play an active part, contributing examples from their mother tongue)
Contrast plosive consonants in French and English using tissue paper in front of lips
Listen to prose/poetry/recitative/church/chant/folksong/lieder/opera and attempt to describe the essential differences between song and speech
Listen to recordings of Welsh/Italian and analyse effect on song
Compare range/pitch in speech/song/selected instruments

c. List spoken usages not met in written form (er/sort of/kind of/like)
Compare speed of speaking and writing/speed of listening to a message and reading the same message
List the activities of reading, speaking, listening, writing in order of speed
Make up simple tests showing limitations of STM for random digits/spoken messages in English/speech in a foreign language known or partially known

456

Themes and questions	Typical learning activities
d. What is 'bad' language? What is bad use of language?	d. Make anthology of 'bad' and 'very bad' language: what is the common factor in the examples studied? Collect examples of language that is ambiguous/based on misunderstanding of common meanings/inappropriate/cliched ("in this day and age")/pretentious, etc Collect examples of 'good' use of language: discuss appropriateness in language Compare regional/social dialect with Standard English Write messages in telegram form conveying information unambiguously using fewest possible words Analyse the omitted words Compare good and bad letters on specified topics Collect/invent clear/ambiguous headlines Collect/compare headlines on the same topic from French/Spanish/English newspapers
e. How are ideas linked by language? What is a clause/sentence/paragraph?	e. Practise adding/opposing/subordinating one idea to another in clause/sentence/paragraph
f. What is it that is tested by gap-filling (cloze) tests? What is meant by a "grammar of expectancy" (Oller, 1973)?	f. Prepare gapped exercises for younger pupils to complete by inserting linking words Given a gapped script, suggest as many fillers as possible for each gap and arrange in order of likelihood Play detective: piece together torn messages, etc
g. What are: riddles and puns? synonyms? homonyms? Why cannot riddles and puns be translated literally into other languages?	g. Learn riddles which play on words (eg "I can jump higher than St Paul's Cathedral" "How's that?" "Because St Paul's Cathedral can't jump at all!") Make posters to warn foreigners of the 'traps' of synonyms/homonyms List other limitations of word-for-word translation
h. How do registers differ?	h. Collect phrases only found in certain registers (eg sports commentary/TV advertising/weather forecasting/playground/school assembly/Party political broadcasts, etc) Try to describe characteristics of each register

457

Themes and questions	Typical learning activities
i. How do dialects differ? Why are some dialects less prestigious than others? What is linguistic prejudice? Why do we make fun of dialects different from our own? How are social class differences reflected in speech?	i. Find patterns of grammar and vocabulary items that are peculiar to a known dialect Contrast American and British English from point of view of class differences/ regional differences and listen to tape recordings Translate from dialect to text-book English, and vice versa
j. How do languages change?	j. Compare Shakespearean English with modern usage and the Authorised Bible with modern translation; list and compare archaisms from the two sources List major pronounciation changes Make place-name map of the region; trace origins of place names Catalogue class surnames by type Collect borrowings from French/Spanish, American/Indian, Chinese/Japanese Show borrowings on world map for classroom wall Compare pupils' language with that of their own parents
k. How do national varieties of English in UK/USA/Australia differ in spoken/ written forms?	k. Collect and display on chart differences of pronunciation/vocabulary/spelling/ syntax List the spelling 'reforms' that Webster introduced (labor, program, etc) and those he failed to perpetuate (korus etc) or those that Caxton failed to launch (gherle, etc) Suggest some more reforms List arguments against spelling reforms

Theme 4

Language acquisition (L1 and L2*)

a. How do babies acquire L1? When do babies speak their first words? What kind of words are they?	a. Listen to recordings, study videotapes, record babies aged 2-3 years, and make list of earliest utterances; arrange these in classes, naming the classes
b. How much do babies understand before they begin to speak?	b. List evidence of babies' understanding in first 2 years Question relatives and compile anthology of opinions/evidence about babies' understanding before they begin to speak

*FOOTNOTE:

NB. Throughout his book Professor Hawkins has used the term 'L1' to describe a child's mother tongue language acquired in the home and the term 'L2' to describe a foreign language learned in school.

Themes and questions	Typical learning activities
d. How does L1 vocabulary expand? How does expansion of L2 vocabulary differ?	d. List babies' words at age 3/4/5 years and put them in boxes: family names/objects/colours/verbs/prepositions/adjectives etc Compare the list with earliest vocabulary in French/Spanish textbooks Compare with immigrant pupils' mother tongues
e. How important is adult dialogue for children? What is the role of 'language games'?	e. As part of 'education for parenthood' course in school, study the dependence of child on parents as models of adult conduct Practise language games with a baby in the classroom (very small groups at any time!) Make posters for mothers' ante-natal clinic showing importance of one-to-one dialogue with baby and of language games
f. What are the main differences between L1 and L2 acquisition?	f. Study children of 5 learning to tell the time; compare with learning to tell time in Spanish/French Make chart showing speech habits in French/Spanish that English pupils find difficult (eg Spanish open vowel [o]; French [y]; nasal vowels, etc) and similar chart of English habits difficult for Spanish/French pupils to acquire; suggest reasons for difficulty Make list of English spellings that give foreigners trouble; suggest reasons
g. How can L2 learning be helped? What makes French/Spanish hard to learn?	g. Make up teaching materials/games to facilitate learning of specific linguistic points Older pupils tutor younger pupils in reading English and in speaking/reading French/Spanish using the materials made in class; tutors write case study describing learners' problems and proposing solutions which are discussed in class seminar Older immigrant pupils prepare lesson notes/games to help younger immigrants acquire English, listing what they consider the main difficulties Draw wall posters and charts to help learners. Senior immigrant pupils form workshop to draft materials for teaching their mother tongue to younger pupils

459

Themes and questions

h. Transition to reading

Typical learning activities

h. Compare spelling of French/Spanish with spelling of English
List points that give most difficulty
Suggest aids to learning
Prepare teaching materials including listening games for matching spelling to sounds, in French/Spanish/German/languages of immigrant pupils

i. Grammatical gender: is gender in French likely to give more or fewer problems to Spanish learners than to English learners? Why?
How do French/Spanish/German children learn the genders of nouns in their mother tongue?

i. Experiment with colour code/spatial code in memorising genders and in mastering concord of adjectives, etc
Study history of disappearance of (Anglo-Saxon) genders from English grammar in aftermath of Norman conquest
List examples in French/Spanish where grammatical gender clarifies meaning, or shows 'constituent' group

j. Other contrasts between English and French/Spanish?
What are the difficulties arising from 'within language' contrasts/'between language' contrasts ('analogical' v. 'transfer' errors)?

j. Compare present tense in French/English/Spanish.

French	English	Spanish
je mange	I eat (I do eat) I am eating	como estoy comiendo

Suggest errors that this contrast might lead English/French/Spanish pupils to make when learning one of the other languages
List 'within-language' and 'between language' contrasts in languages met

The above notes give the barest outline of the scope of the 'awareness of language' course and suggest some typical classroom and homework learning activities. Clearly some of the activities are more suitable for older pupils. This is true of most of Theme 4 (Language acquisition). Teachers will select projects and activities that suit their classes, bearing in mind the objectives of the course:

i   to provide a 'bridge' between English and foreign language learning and between English and the mother tongues of immigrant pupils, encouraging the use of common terminology by teachers and fruitful 'feedback' from one aspect of language study to the other.

ii   to give pupils insight into the role of languages as the distinctive aspect of human behaviour and its importance in learning in the home, and in the school, and an understanding and sympathy for linguistic diversity.

iii   to give all pupils the necessary background on which to build a lifelong interest in language and especially in the responsibility of parents for the language development of children in the pre-school years.

460

This book is about language

This book is about language and how people use it.

It's about:
different languages and dialects
learning to speak
what languages share
playing about with words
how English has changed
special ways of talking
who says what to who
writing and reading
how people learn to read
different kinds of writing
what other people think about the way you speak
and what you think.

But everyone who reads this knows much more about language than can be put in a book. Everyone has managed the amazing job of learning at least one language — and, when you think about it, you use even *one* language in so many different ways that even *one* is a lot. So you're the expert; make sure you tell the others what *you* know about language and the way it works.

COLLECTING LANGUAGES

Speaking another language is not difficult - as long as you're prepared to have a go, make mistakes and enjoy it. There are millions of people in Britain now who have learned to speak another language - because they want to or because they have to.

Mere & Pere

You may be able to find quite a few people in your school or in the place you live who can speak another language as well as English. How about making a collection of words for common things in as many languages as you can?

For example, here's the beginning of a list of words for 'mother' and 'father' in different languages. (The last Russian words have been written in the Roman alphabet to make it easy to pronounce.)

	'MOTHER'	'FATHER'
French	mere	pere
Welsh	mam	tad
Turkish	ana	baba
Russian	mat	otyets

Now see if you can make your own lists of words used in other languages for some of these things:

house	snow	happy	laugh
street	ice-cream	red	cry
family	sky	blue	love
baby	tree	stupid	hate
cat	day	quick	walk
school	night	quiet	sleep

When you've made your list try making up a short poem which uses English words and words from another language together. Here's an English/German poem:

When schnee falls at nacht
the strasse outside the haus
is still, like a picture.

And here's an English/Italian one:

I like rosso gelato
and books that make me ridere
How about you?

What Would You Say?

This next idea is more difficult, and it needs to be done in a pair or a group in which there is at least one person who can speak another language or dialect as well as English.

There are four situations below for a conversation in a pair. 'Person A' in each case speaks in English; 'Person B' speaks in another language or dialect. First go through the conversation with the person who knows the other language or dialect doing 'Person B'. He/she will have to *translate* and teach the others what to say. The 'learner' needs to listen carefully and try to copy what's said.

Then switch it round so that the 'learner' is 'Person B' and uses the other language in the same conversation.

a) Person A wants to know the quickest way from your school to the nearest bus-stop or underground station. How would you give directions?

b) Person B has been asked by his/her mother (Person A) to go to the shops just when he/she was planning to go out to meet a friend. What would you say?

c) A baby brother has scribbled all over Person B's homework. What would you say to the teacher (Person A) next day?

d) Person B has done something really special at school and wants to tell someone (person A) at home about it. What would you say?

Learning Languages In School

Some things to discuss. Which of these statements do you agree with?

* 'There's no point in learning other languages because in 10 years time there will be machines which will translate from one language to another automatically.'

* 'There's no need for people who speak English to learn other languages because English is spoken by millions of people around the world.'

* 'Having French lessons in school for a couple of hours a week is not enough to learn French properly. It would be a good idea if all lessons on one day a week (history, art and so on) were taught in French.'

* 'Instead of spending at least 2 or 3 years on one language like French or German, it would be a good idea if pupils in school had lessons about different languages (say a term on Spanish, a term on Turkish, a term on Chinese and so on).'

SPECIAL WAYS OF TALKING

Even people who speak only one language - English for instance - may find that, when they think about it, they have more than one way of speaking that language. They might speak one kind of English at school, perhaps, another kind at home and yet another kind for a special interest they share with their friends. And when people go to work for the first time they often find that they have to learn a special way of talking for the job.

School

* Think of all the words you use which someone who had never been to school would have to learn. They might know the word but not the school's special meaning for them: form, tutor-set, options, break. Think of as many as you can and make a list of them for someone coming from another country to your school; explain what the words mean.

* Now think of some of the words you use in maths or science or geography. Make a list for someone who doesn't know anything about these subjects and explain the meaning of the words. (Are there any words which have different meanings in different subjects - like the word 'solution'?)

* It's not just the words that can be special in school but the whole way of talking. Try reading this piece aloud: can you get the voice right and work out what's going on?

❛ Wait a minute, wait a minute. Wait a minute, OK, hands up who has got a pen, come on, quickly, hands up, handsup. OK, you're not telling me that out of 37, only six of you? Now look, Marilyn, where's your pen? Well, you should have put your hand up. Why didn't you put up your hand? Billy, where's your pen? Well, get it "off of" him, no not now. Frank, where's yours? Don't talk to me like that. Come on, hurry. Now listen, I'm warning you, this is the last time I give out pens, OK? This school is not a charitable institution. Bring your pens. Bring your books. There'll be trouble otherwise. Now, OK, who hasn't got their book? People with no books raise their hands. OK, I want to see this: who, put up your hands, who hasn't got a pen or a book? Is your hand up or down, Mehmet? No, I don't have your book. OK, this is the last time. Eileen, give the paper out. Wait, not yet. People who want paper put their hands up. OK, Eileen, one piece, one piece, Michael. Victor, give the pens out. No, not to people who've got pencils. Don't throw them, Victor. OK, give them to Errol to give out. Well, do it quietly. Hurry. OK, does everyone have paper? Pauline, why don't you have anything, quick, come and get it. No, sit down, Eileen. OK,

who hasn't got a pen? Not funny, Allen. OK, everybody, I'll write it on the board. Give me that chalk, Neville. Give itto me. If you don't understand what it says, just wait, I'll read it back to you. OK, everybody. Look at the board. ❜

(adapted from OK Now, Tom Lowenstein)

See if you can make up a piece of 'school language' yourself. Use this situation to make up a short play.

A pupil is seen by a teacher coming in late to school for the fourth time in a week. By the end of the conversation he or she has been able to get out of trouble by explaining it all away.

OR write a poem called 'Excuses, Excuses' which makes a list of all the excuses for not doing homework you've ever heard in school. You may have heard some daft excuses . . .

Activities

What topic would people be talking about if you overheard these words in their conversation? A good dictionary might help; look on the checking page if you're stuck.

A.   Ace, fault, volley
B.   Mate, castle, check
C.   Spoke, chain, carrier
D.   Basket, zone, board
E.   Deck, groove, 45
F.   Row, purl, cast off
G.   Cast off, deck, bow

NOW, take something you are interested in (like sport or clothes or fishing or music or cars or bikes) and make a dictionary of some of the special words (and their meanings) which you need to talk about the subject.

463

All kinds of activities have their own special words (or technical terms).

Here is an example of a description of an activity which uses some special words. The person talking here is describing the rules of the game of draughts to someone who doesn't know how to play. What special words (or words used in a special way) can you see here?

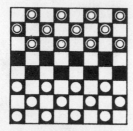

'It's a game for two players. Each player has 12 counters. The counters start off in three ranks at opposite ends of the board but all on black squares.

Each player takes turns to move one counter in a forward diagonal direction only. You make a capture in the same direction. You must make a capture if you can. If you don't you're huffed. If one of your men gets to the other end it's crowned. Then it can move forwards and backwards. The object of the game is to capture or block all your opponent's counters. If neither player can do that, the game is stale.'

If you like you could write a short description of one part of an activity you know a lot about using some of the special words needed. (Drawings or diagrams may help!)

Work

Most jobs have special words for things which are important in the job. These words can be a mystery to outsiders. If you work on the London Tube, for example, you need to know special words like 'iron worm' (train), 'fluffer' (cleaner), or 'wasps' (men in orange jackets who work on the lines).

In this short play the foreman in a factory (Wills) has come to see the boss (Fibbs) to explain why there has been some trouble in the factory. He says that the workers just don't like the things they are making. Fibbs is flabbergasted - and asks Wills which of the factory's products the workers don't like.

FIBBS: But they're beautiful products. I've been in the business a lifetime. I've never seen such beautiful products.

WILLS: There it is, sir.

FIBBS: Which ones don't they like?

WILLS: There's the hemi unibal spherical rod end.

FIBBS: The hemi unibal spherical rod end? Where could you find a finer rod end?

WILLS: There are rod ends and rod ends, Mr. Fibbs.

FIBBS: I know there are rod ends and rod ends. But where could you find a finer hemi unibal spherical rod end?

WILLS: They just don't want to have anything more to do with it.

FIBBS: This is shattering. Shattering. What else? Come on, Wills. There's no point in hiding anything from me.

WILLS: Well, I hate to say it, but they've gone very vicious about the high speed taper shank spiral flute reamers.

FIBBS: The high speed taper shank spiral flute reamers! But that's absolutely ridiculous! What could they possibly have against the high speed taper shank spiral flute reamers?

WILLS: All I can say is they're in a state of very bad agitation about them. And then there's the gunmetal side outlet relief with handwheel.

FIBBS: What!

WILLS: And the one they can't speak about without trembling is the jaw for Jacob's chuck for use on portable drill.

FIBBS: My own Jacob's chuck? Not my very own Jacob's chuck?

WILLS: They've just taken a turn against the whole lot of them, I tell you. Male elbow adaptors, tubing nuts, grub screws, internal fan washers, dog points, half dog points, white metal bushes -

FIBBS: But not, surely not, my lovely parallel male stud couplings.

WILLS: They hate and detest your lovely parallel male stud couplings, and the straight flange pump connectors, and back nuts, and front nuts, and the bronzedraw off cock with handwheel and the bronzedraw off cock without handwheel!

FIBBS: Not the bronzedraw off cock with handwheel?

WILLS: And without handwheel.

FIBBS: Without handwheel?

WILLS: And with handwheel.

FIBBS: Not with handwheel?

WILLS: And without handwheel.

FIBBS: Without handwheel?

WILLS: With handwheel *and* without handwheel.

FIBBS: With handwheel *and* without handwheel?

WILLS: With or without!

Pause.

FIBBS *(broken):* Tell me. What do they want to make in its place?

WILLS: Marshmallows.

(adap. from Trouble in the Works, Harold Pinter)

464

CHAPTER 8

Religion and the Role of the School: Religious Education and the "Separate" Schools Debate

I. Religious Education

**Religious
Diversity**

1. Introduction

1.1 The wide range of religious beliefs which now form part of the overall diversity of religious experience in Britain today is one of the most vivid manifestations of the diversity of our society. Some forty years ago, Christians and Jews were the two main religious communities in this country, together with people without any definite religious belief, some of them nominally Christian, some professedly atheist, and only a few individuals of other faiths. Today there are significant numbers of Muslims, Hindus, Sikhs and members of other faith communities living in many areas. Religious groupings of course cross ethnic divisions, with many West Indian immigrants and their descendants being Christians – including Anglicans, Roman Catholics, Methodists, and members of Pentecostal churches and other denominations – and the Asian community also including Christians as well as adherents of the major Eastern faiths. Of the European minorities, discussed later in this report, the Italians for example are Roman Catholic, the Greek Cypriots Greek Orthodox and the Turkish Cypriots Muslim. It is important to recognise that the faiths of these minority communities are in no sense "minority" religions, but are major faiths which have often played a leading role in shaping world history. One cannot, for example, fully understand the contemporary world without some knowledge of the influence of Islam – as one writer has put it[1]:

> *"The Moslem brush has painted such large tracts of time and space during the last fourteen hundred years that the historical panorama which did not feature them could be nothing but a wild and grotesque distortion of reality."*

**Central
Element in
"Ethnic
Identity"**

1.2 We have already emphasised that one of the major aims of education should, in our view, be to broaden the horizons of *all* pupils to a greater understanding and appreciation of the diversity of value systems and lifestyles which are now present in our society whilst also enabling and

---

[1]"The importance of Islam." J Henderson. World Studies Bulletin No 29 December 1973, quoted in "Assessment in a Multicultural Society: History at 16 + ." N File. Schools Council. 1983.

465

assisting ethnic minority communities to maintain what they regard as the essential elements of their cultural identities. It is clear from the evidence we have received that for many ethnic minority communities, especially those from the various faiths within the Asian community, respect and recognition for their religious beliefs is seen as one of the, and, in some cases, *the* central factor in maintaining their community's strength and cohesiveness. This emphasis is perhaps hardly surprising since, as the Catholic Commission for Racial Justice has observed[2]:

> "Religions and culture are closely interwoven and often religion is the very "soul" of culture."

A major task in preparing *all* pupils for life in the kind of harmonious pluralist society which we outlined at the opening of this report must surely therefore be to enhance their understanding of a variety of religious beliefs and practices thus offering them an insight into the values and concerns of different communities.

Religious Prejudice and Racism

1.3   It is also important to recall that, as we pointed out in Chapter Two, the origins of racism lie to a considerable extent in regarding groups of people as "strange" and thus "inferior". On this basis religious groups within the minority communities which vary from an assumed norm of Christianity and whose religious beliefs are manifested by various forms of dress or behaviour or by the celebration of particular festivals, may be particularly subject to racism if their faiths are neither understood nor accepted in their own right. Bringing about a greater understanding of the diversity of faiths present in Britain today can also therefore we believe play a major role in challenging and overcoming racism.

This Chapter

1.4   In this chapter we discuss the various ways in which the concept of religious education has been perceived and the role which we would see for schools in the context of our multi-faith society within our philosophy of "Education for All". We then go on to consider a particular dimension of the concerns of ethnic minority communities about the contribution of education to the maintenance of their religious beliefs, which has received increasing attention especially over the last few years – the "separate" schools debate. Any consideration of religious education must recognise that there has long been an emotive and often passionate debate about the role of schools in relation to religion in a society which can be seen as increasingly secular in terms of the level of active religious observance amongst the majority of its members: a debate to which the multi-faith character of schools with substantial ethnic minority populations has now added a further dimension. Religious education is of course also

---

[2]"Education and the Multi-racial Society." Report No 5. Catholic Commission for Racial Justice. October 1979.

distinguished from other aspects of a school's work by the unique place which it is accorded in the 1944 Education Act. In this chapter therefore we set our conclusions within the context both of the provisions of the 1944 Education Act and of the ongoing debate about the aims and objectives of religious education.

2.   The principles of Religious Education

2.1   Religious education is an aspect of school life which involves far more than the imparting of a particular body of knowledge to pupils, since it raises complex questions relating to the spiritual and aesthetic development of the individual young person as well as impinging very directly on the essential beliefs and values of his or her family and community. As HMI put it in their "Red Book"[3]:

> ". . . in religious education, the school is operating on the boundary between itself and the local community in that it is dealing with the religious traditions, beliefs and values of the society in which it is set . . . Religious education shares with other subjects the task of helping children to acquire the skills, knowledge and social competence necessary for their personal development and life in society . . . However, religious education also makes a distinctive contribution to the curriculum in directing attention to the religious understanding of human life and to the central values (many of them derived from religion) which society seeks to uphold and to transmit. In this consideration of religion and values, the intention is to help pupils to understand the nature of religious questions and religious affirmations, and to develop a personal and intellectual integrity in dealing with the profoundest aspects of their own experience now and in adult life."

A Contradiction in Terms?

2.2   It must also be recognised however that religious education is seen by many as a particularly difficult aspect of the educational experience to define since the phrase itself seems to be almost a contradiction in terms – the task of education being to teach children to exercise flexibility of mind and to seek rational explanations for situations, whilst the essence of religion is seen by many as belief, and in many faiths, an acceptance of revelation. This inherent paradox has been described in the following terms[4]:

> "There is a deep tension between education on the one hand and the religious and secular ideologies on the other. Education is critical,

---

[3]"Curriculum 11-16. Working Papers by HM Inspectorate: a contribution to current debate." December 1977.
[4]Editorial "Learning for Living" Vol 13 No 5. Ed J Hull. 1974.

sceptical and enquiring. Religion is passionate, committed and adoring."

This apparent "conflict" of intentions has been thrown into even starker relief by the concerns of some of the faith communities within the ethnic minorities, particularly the Muslim community, about the role of maintained schools in relation to their children's religious beliefs and in many ways this is the central issue of the "separate" schools debate which we consider later in this chapter.

Opposition to Religious Education in Schools

2.3 Before considering the various interpretations which have been placed on religious education, it must be acknowledged that the very principle of religion having a place within the school curriculum has been challenged on the grounds that schools exist primarily to equip their pupils with a range of practical skills and factual information and it is beyond their role and responsibility to seek to educate pupils in an area of experience which is uniquely personal and in which there is no single accepted corpus of knowledge. Advocates of this "secularist" viewpoint argue that religious education is the responsibility of the home and the religious communities and has no place, other than on purely historical and social grounds, within the maintained school system, least of all within "secular" county schools. They therefore reject the concept of religious education seeing it as a form of indoctrination which seeks to "impose" religion on young people. The following extract from evidence which we received from a Muslim educational organisation illustrates clearly however a commonly expressed response to the secularists' arguments:

> *"We accept the right of those who do not subscribe to any religion to refuse to be a party to religious education for their children ... But they have no right to deny religious education to those who want it. Imposing the 'humanist' or 'secular' viewpoint on those who do not subscribe to it is as bad as is the imposition of the religious view on the 'humanist'."*

The Case for Religious Education

Educational Grounds

2.4 Turning to the "case" which has been put forward by educationists and theologians for religious education, there appear to be three central reasons why religious education is considered to be a crucial element in the education process. Firstly, it is argued that in order for a young person to be considered fully educated, they must have some understanding of the nature of belief and of different belief systems and of how these have and are still influencing human experience. Such knowledge can by extension help in the formation of pupils' own personal beliefs and values, whether religious or non-religious – as the Durham Report[5] put it:

---

[5] "The Fourth R." The Durham Report on Religious Education. Report of an independent commission set up by the Church of England Board of Education and the National Society for Promoting Religious Education. 1970.

"... religious education has a place in the educational scene on educational grounds, where education is understood as the enriching of a pupil's experience, the opening up of a pupil to all the influences which have coloured his or her environment ... The existence of a religious interpretation of life is a fact of history and of present human experience. There are many millions of men and women throughout the world who find through their religious beliefs a deep meaning and purpose for their lives and a system of values by which their lives can be lived. There appears to be a "spiritual dimension" in man's nature which requires to be expressed by "religion" of one kind or another. By religion we mean some pattern of belief and behaviour related to the questions of man's ultimate concern. For some, it is an Eastern religion; for some it is Christianity; for others it is one of the secular creeds of the West, for example Marxism; for others it is agnostic humanism; for many it may be little more than moral stoicism. Man seems to have to find "a faith to live by", however noble, or simple, or debased. Young people share in the human condition. They should have some opportunity to learn that religion is a feature of this condition, and for some men a deeply significant area of human knowledge and experience."

Contribution to Inter-cultural and International Understanding

2.5   It is also argued that an understanding and appreciation of religious diversity contributes to, and is indeed vital to, the development of a young person's understanding of the motivations, values and outlook of people from a range of religious backgrounds, both within this society and in other societies – as the Berkshire agreed syllabus for religious education[6] puts it:

"Religious education contributes to international understanding in the world as a whole, and to community relations within Britain. Increasingly we live in one world, and increasingly Britain is a multicultural, multi-faith society. It is vital that citizens should be familiar with a variety of beliefs and customs, and that they should have insight into the underlying values and concerns which different cultures and societies have in common."

This can of course be seen as central to our own concern with encouraging an atmosphere of mutual respect and understanding between all the groups in today's multi-racial society and the wider world.

Key to Moral Education

2.6   A further justification often advanced for religious education is that it provides a basis and a context for a school's programme of moral education. Whilst some educationists have argued that moral education

---

[6] "Religious Heritage and Personal Quest. Guidelines for Religious Education." Berkshire Education Department. 1982.

469

can be seen as self-standing and indeed self-justifying in its own right, it is clear that since both areas of education are concerned with attitudes, values and beliefs, as a Schools Council Report[7] has put it:

> ". . . the insights and accumulated wisdom of the great world religions cannot be ignored in any comprehensive scheme of moral education."

The "moral" dimension of religious education also relates directly to some of the fundamental concerns raised by the multi-racial nature of our society, most notably perhaps the need to tackle racism and injustice and to seek to create true equality of opportunity for youngsters from *all* ethnic groups, which we would see as central to "Education for All". As the Berkshire agreed syllabus again explains:

> *"Religious education contributes to moral development: along with other aspects of the school curriculum, it develops consideration for other people, respect for moral and legal obligations, and concern for fairness and justice in society at large."*

Various Approaches to Religious Education

2.7   Turning to the various aims and objectives and forms of provision which have been suggested for religious education in schools, the three main possible approaches were defined as follows in the 1971 Schools Council Report, referred to above, which has influenced much of the subsequent thinking in this field:

> "The 'Confessional' or Dogmatic Approach
> *This begins with the assumption that the aim of religious education is intellectual and cultic indoctrination. It is often linked with a belief that any other kind of religious education is valueless or unworthy of the name . . .*
>
> The Anti-dogmatic Approach
> *This rules out the subjective element from religious education and conceives it as an academic exercise, dispassionate and objective. The National Secular Society, for example, suggests that the study of religion on these terms should be included as part of the history syllabus . . .*
>
> The 'Phenomenological' or Undogmatic Approach
> *This sees the aim of religious education as the promotion of understanding. It uses the tools of scholarship in order to enter into an emphatic experience of the faith of individuals and groups. It does not seek to promote any one religious viewpoint but it recognizes that the study of religion must transcend the merely informative . . ."*

---

[7] "Religious Education in Secondary Schools." Schools Council Working Paper 36. 1971.

The confessional approach to religious education can be seen as the traditional view of the role of the school in relation to religion which was without doubt the approach which the framers of the 1944 Education Act had in mind in requiring schools to provide "religious instruction" (see paragraph 3.2 below) – their terminology indeed indicates clearly that they saw the task for religious education as inculcating young people into a specific religious faith: Christianity. This approach continues to be advocated by some individuals and groups, particularly representatives of some Churches and religious communities, but in general the trend of thinking on religious education has tended increasingly to favour the phenomenological approach as more appropriate to the range of beliefs and unbeliefs now to be found within our society. The anti-dogmatic approach has generally not found favour since it is felt that the true nature of religious belief and its influence on the lives of adherents to particular faiths cannot be adequately understood or appreciated through an entirely objective account of the factual material available.

Distinction Between "Religious" and "Educational" Aspects

2.8 The phenomenological or non-denominational and undogmatic view draws a clear distinction between what can strictly speaking be termed "religious instruction" i.e. instruction in a religion, and "religious education" i.e. education in the concept of religion and in the range of belief systems which exist. It is seen as the function of the home and of the religious community to nurture and instruct a child in a particular faith (or not), and the function of the school to assist pupils to understand the nature of religion and to know something of the diversity of belief systems, their significance for individuals and how these bear on the community. The Durham Report expressed this clear distinction between the "religious" and "educational" aspects of religious education in the following terms:

> *"To press for acceptance of a particular faith or belief system is the duty and privilege of the Churches and other similar religious bodies. It is certainly not the task of a teacher in a county school. If the teacher is to press for any conversion, it is conversion from a shallow and unreflective attitude of life. If he is to press for commitment, it is the commitment to the religious quest, to that search for meaning, purpose, and value which is open to all men."*

The Place of Christianity

2.9 Much attention has been devoted to determining the place of Christianity within such a broader consideration of the nature of religious belief and of world faiths. The phenomenological approach to religious education seeks to move away from the notion of religious education as synonymous with "Christian" education, nevertheless, as a discussion paper prepared by a working party of the Religious Education Council[8] put it:

---

[8]"What future for the agreed syllabus – Now?" Religious Education Council. 1977.

"To say that it is not the duty of the County School to inculcate Christianity is not to deny that the study of Christianity will, on educational grounds, continue to occupy a central place in the syllabus."

If the task of education is to seek to enhance children's understanding and appreciation of the influences which have helped to shape our society, then, as the 1971 Schools Council report observed:

"The tradition of our national life has been largely shaped and sustained by behaviour and ideas closely associated with the practice of religion, and particularly the Christian religion. Since education involves a thorough examination of the environment and the received culture, this source of our national heritage should be studied and appreciated."

The essential distinction between the confessional and the phenomenological approach to Christianity within religious education is, however, that whereas the former approach would tend to present Christianity as the only "true" religion and, if any reference was made to other religions, would present these solely in Christian terms, the latter would more accurately reflect the multiplicity of beliefs and non-beliefs – including Christianity – now present in society. As one writer has put it[9]:

"The Christian vision of the good life can no longer claim to be the only source of belief and value in our society . . . Any attempt by educational institutions to transmit a sectional view as if it were the only publicly defensible one would contradict the value a democracy ascribes to individual judgment and responsibility"

and as the Hampshire agreed syllabus[10] puts it:

". . . it is no part of the responsibility of a county school to promote any particular religious stand-point, neither could an exclusively Christian content do justice to the nature of the subject. A syllabus relevant to the needs of our children must also provide an introduction to other religious commitments and world views found in contemporary British society."

It is regretable that this view of religious education has led to concern in some quarters that Christianity risks being submerged within a "Cook's tour" of the world's religions. This concern has indeed been articulated by the Archbishop of Canterbury in the following terms[11]:

[9]"Problems of RE Syllabus Construction in a Democracy." John Elliott. From "New Directors in Religious Education". Ed. J. Hull. (1982).
[10]"Religious Education in Hampshire Schools." Agreed Syllabus for Religious Education. 1978.
[11]Speech to the National Society. March 1982.

> ". . . while recognising that a truly pluralist society – if such we are –
> should not merely tolerate diversity but value and nurture it, I must
> also express the fear that at times we seem tempted to sacrifice too
> much of our native Christian tradition on the altar of multi-
> culturalism . . . when I read, in one approved syllabus, of the need in
> religious education "to set Christianity alongside other religions", as if
> it were part of some creedal smorgasbord, or that "it should be part of
> an education for life in this country that children come to know
> something of the traditional religion of the land, namely Christianity"
> (as if Christianity was, like Shakespeare, parliamentary democracy or
> roast beef, part of a living heritage rather than a living faith), I wonder
> whether we are not, as Christian educators, selling Christianity short
> by carrying our anti-confessionalism too far."

The intention of the phenomenological approach to religious education is
however in no way to "reduce" Christianity to simply one element in an
arid survey of world religions, but rather to set the consideration of
Christianity, in all its spirital depth and fullness, within a wider context of
the true significance of the religious dimension to life, in all its forms.

**Views of
Ethnic
Minority
Communities**

2.10 Much of the evidence which we have received from ethnic minority
communities has related to the provision of religious education in schools
and particularly to the place accorded to religions other than Christianity.
Many community representatives have emphasised the importance which
their communities attach to their religious beliefs as a key element in their
cultural identity, and it was strongly felt that all the religious communities
in this country had the right to expect the education system to respect and
to reflect their faiths, not by comparing them negatively with Christianity,
but as valid belief systems in their own right – a viewpoint with which we
fully agree. It was pointed out to us that religions such as Islam and
Sikhism are major world faiths in a global context and are in no way
therefore "minority" religions, inferior to Christianity, simply because
they might have fewer adherents in this country. It was also felt that a
better understanding on the part of ethnic majority youngsters of a range
of faiths would not only enhance their understanding of the religious
dimension of life but would also help to counter negative stereotypes of
ethnic minority groups, who were often identifiable as adherents of
particular faiths, and would thus help to challenge and combat racism. As
one Sikh organisation put it in their evidence to us:

> ". . . it seems very much relevant that the children who are born in the
> (Sikh) Faith should have an opportunity to know and understand this
> experience of the Spiritual world. All those children who are born in
> other Faiths should have an opportunity to learn about the
> experience of other peoples and other lands as it is one of the purposes

of education. By providing this opportunity for our children in our schools we will be helping them to broaden their outlook and will make them better citizens of tomorrow's world. In our society . . . there are people who follow different Faiths and have different customs. For better community and race relations it is very appropriate that they should not remain ignorant about each other but better understanding should be developed among all these races and Faiths. School is the right place to give the lead in this field."

At the other end of the spectrum however, some, but by no means all the representatives of the Muslim community whom we met favoured a more confessional approach to religious education – seeing religious *education* as in fact synonymous with religious *instruction* – aimed at developing their children's knowledge and understanding of Islam, and saw no need for a broader approach to religious education. To some extent this attitude within the Muslim community can be seen as a consequence of the world-wide resurgence of Islam over recent years which has led to a greater emphasis on the rights and duties of Muslim parents in relation to their children's education.

Our View
2.11 In the light of our general discussion earlier in this report of the various phases in the development of multicultural education, the confessional approach to religious education can be seen as very much in keeping with the assimilationist tradition since it regards the faiths of ethnic minority communities as inferior to Christianity and seeks therefore, in a "missionary" spirit, to replace these faiths with a commitment to the "superior" Christian religion. The view of religious education mentioned above held by some sections of certain ethnic minority religious communities can be seen, if taken to its logical conclusion of children from a particular faith community being "instructed" only in their own religion, as also in the confessional spirit but, in terms of the nature of the educational provision made – i.e. with different groups of children receiving different forms of religious education – as separatist in effect. We ourselves therefore share the view expressed in the 1971 Schools Council Report that:

". . . the "confessionalist" aim, though perfectly proper within a community of faith, is not appropriate within schools serving a multi-belief society. Moreover, it conflicts at several points with the principles on which education is based."

We find ourselves firmly in favour of the broader phenomenological approach to religious education as the best and indeed the only means of enhancing the understanding of all pupils, from whatever religious background, of the plurality of faiths in contemporary Britain, of

474

bringing them to an understanding of the nature of belief and the religious dimension of human existence, and of helping them to appreciate the diverse and sometimes conflicting life stances which exist and thus enabling them to determine (and justify) their own religious position. This view of the phenomenological approach to religious education as the only response which accords with the fundamental principles underlying the ideal of cultural pluralism was also expressed in a recent Schools Council report on religious education[12] which summarised the implications of various approaches to religious education in tabular form as follows:

The response of Religious Studies to Multiculturalism: A Summary

	ASSIMILATION	SEPARATISM	CULTURAL PLURALISM
Ideology	Total absorption of minority groups into "mainstream" eradication of culture and religion; notion of normativeness	Encapsulation of minority culture; withdrawal of minority groups; self help and separate provision	Minority groups' participation in just society: equal rights with majority; cultural status for all
Emphasis	On the majority.	On minorities.	On the majority and minoritites; currently only an ideal.
Attitude to Religion	*Deficit hypothesis* "true" religion vs "false" religion.	*Avoidance of conflict* religion a "private" matter for individuals and minority communities.	*Interactional approach* religious variability; diversity cele-brated; mutual enrichment; notion of religion in evolution.
Approach to Religious Studies	Neo-confessional*	Confessional	Phenomenological
Curriculum Content	"Fossilised" curriculum; "high culture"; narrowly ethnocentric.	Ethnic studies; traditional scriptures.	Curriculum permeated by openness to all cultural/religious sources. Awareness of stereotyping and religious prejudice.
Organisation of Religious Studies	Christian ideas permeate many school subjects (especially liter-ature, history . . .) Evangelism as a process of socialisation.	Supplementary education: Cheder, Koran schools etc: Religious main-tenance for minorities in state school.	Mixed affiliation classrooms ("all faiths and none") "Specialist" *Reli-gious Studies* teacher.

[12]"Assessment in a Multicultural Society. Religious Studies at 16 + ." Angela Wood. Schools Council. 1984.
*Note: "Neo-confessionalism" is defined by the author as "an attempt to make confessionalism more 'modern' in method and more acceptable in a multicultural society. It tends to be an 'open-ended' form of Christian education which may include some token acknowledgment of 'other world faiths'."

2.12   In order to illustrate further our view of religious education, we reproduce below the general aims of religious education which the 1971 Schools Council Report put forward and which we broadly support:

> "... *religious education seeks to promote awareness of religious issues, and of the contribution of religion to human culture in general; it seeks to promote understanding of religious beliefs and practices, it also aims to awaken recognition of the challenge and practical consequences of religious belief... These general aims can be broken down further and more particularly as follows (and here we also give examples – instances of the kind of objectives the teacher may have when devising a course of study).*

> *1.   Awareness of religious issues*
> > *a.   explicit issues – eg. the capacity to understand the reasons for differences of religious belief, for instance within the Christian tradition.*

> > *b.   implicit issues – eg. the capacity to explore music with a view to seeing whether it can give one new insights into the nature of the world; and, if so, the connexion of these with questions about the 'purpose' of life.*

> *2.   Awareness of the contribution of religion to human culture eg. acquiring knowledge of the ways in which the Christian heritage has influenced social life in different parts of the UK.*

> *3.   Capacity to understand beliefs eg. understanding the Muslim conception of Allah, and the type of language employed to express this.*

> *4.   Capacity to understand practices eg. understanding what worshipping is intended to do, and the use of symbolism in it.*

> *5.   Awareness of the challenge of religious belief eg. the capacity to form a well-infomed judgement about Christian or atheistic belief.*

> *6.   Awareness of the practical consequences of religious belief eg. capacity to understand issues raised by pacifist elements in, for instance, the Christian and Buddhist traditions."*

3.   The practice of religious education

3.1   Having discussed the principles which we see as underlying religious education appropriate to today's multi-faith society, we now consider how these principles are being put into practice. Discussion of the practice of religious education must however take place against the background of the complex legal framework prescribed by the 1944 Education Act. Since some of the evidence we have received suggests that the precise terms of the Act are far from fully understood, we begin by summarising its provisions.

476

**The Legal
Position**

3.2   It is often asserted that "the 1944 Education Act requires all schools to provide religious education". This statement is in fact an over-simplification of the provisions of the Act. Sections 25-30 of the Act are headed "Religious Education in County and Voluntary Schools" but no further explicit references to, or indeed definitions of religious *education* are made in any of these sections. From a reading of the Act however it is clear that "religious education" is seen as an all-embracing term describing an overall process comprising two distinct but inter-related elements:

– *an act of collective worship*; and

– *the provision of religious instruction.*

In order to understand clearly the provisions of the 1944 Act in relation to religious education, it is important therefore to distinguish between the specific requirements laid down in relation to each of these elements. We reproduce as Annex A to this chapter the sections of the Act which relate to Religious Education but the provisions are summarised below.

**Provisions of
the 1944 Act**

3.3   The Education Act 1944 prescribes that religious education should be provided in all maintained schools; that the school day should begin with an act of "collective worship on the part of all pupils in attendance at the school"[13] and that religious instruction should be given to all pupils[14] – the only exception being when a parent requests that his child be "wholly or partly excused" from the act of worship or the religious instruction provided.[15]. Where a parent wishes his child to receive religious instruction of a kind not provided in their school, nor at a neighbouring county or voluntary school, the pupil may be withdrawn from school to receive instruction elsewhere, provided that the LEA is satisfied that this will not interfere with his attendance at school on any day or that it is provided at the beginning or end of the school day[16]. In *county schools* neither the act of worship nor the religious instruction provided may be distinctive of any particular denomination, and the religious instruction must be given in accordance with an agreed syllabus. At secondary level where it has not proved possible to find suitable premises out of school for those children who have been withdrawn from the instruction provided by the school in order that they can receive insruction in a particular denomination, then the LEA, provided that the cost will not fall to them and that there are no special circumstances which would make it unreasonable to do so, must provide facilities for this purpose[17]. (No comparable provision is made for children in primary schools). *In*

[13] Section 25(1) of the Education Act 1944.
[14]Section 25(2).
[15] Section 25(4).
[16] Section 25(5).
[17] Section 26.

477

voluntary controlled schools, the collective act of worship may be distinctive of the denomination which provided the school. The religious instruction provided must be in accordance with an agreed syllabus[18] unless the parents of any pupil attending the school request that their children receive religious instruction in accordance with the provision of the trust deed of the school. In that case, the governors of the school, unless they are satisfied that it would be unreasonable to do so, must arrange for denominational instruction to be provided during not more than two periods a week[19]. *In voluntary aided schools*, the religious instruction provided is determined by the Governors of the school in accordance with the trust deed of the school[20]. If however the parents of any of the pupils attending the school wish them to receive religious education in accordance with an agreed syllabus, and they cannot with reasonable convenience attend a school at which that syllabus is in use, the Governors must make arrangements for such education to be carried out during the times set aside for religious instruction unless the LEA is satisfied that it would be unreasonable to do so. In cases where the Governors are unwilling to make such arrangements the LEA themselves must do so[21]. The Governors of an aided school are free to decide the qualifications they require teachers appointed to give religious instruction to hold (subject to the teachers having DES qualified teacher status) and can dismiss such a teacher (providing they are not solely employed to give instruction in accordance with an agreed syllabus) if he or she "fails to give such instruction efficiently and suitably", without the consent of the LEA[22].

3.4   Although, as we have seen, the Act did not specify that either the act of collective worship or the religious instruction provided in county schools should be explicitly Christian[23], it is clear from the following assurance given by a Government Minister in the House of Lords at the time[24] that this was the intention:

> ". . . *it is the intention of the Government and of the Bill that the religious instruction required to be given shall be Christian instruction, and that the corporate act of worship shall be an act of Christian worship . . .*"

---

[18] Section 27(6).
[19] Section 27(1).
[20] Section 28(1).
[21] Section 28(1).
[22] Section 28(2).
[23] The use of the term "denomination" in saying that Religious Education in schools need not be "distinctive of any particular religious *denomination*" seems to imply however that the framers of the Act had in mind the variety of *Christian* denominations that exist rather than the diversity of religious faiths.
[24] The Earl of Selborne. Hansard. House of Lords 5th series Vol. 132. Col. 366. 21 June 1944.

3.5   Since the 1944 Education Act saw an act of collective worship as an integral part of a school's provision for religious education, we begin by considering the specific issues which have arisen in relation to this aspect of schools' work, before looking at the place of religion within the school curriculum.

Origins and Intentions

The Act of Collective Worship

3.6   In laying down a requirement for a daily act of worship in schools, the 1944 Education Act can be seen as in many respects merely lending statutory support to what was already at that time a recognised procedure in most schools at the time, having its roots in the last Century when the Church played such a central role in education[25]. The philosophy and original intent behind the provision for an act of collective worship are clearly indicated in the following extract from the 1943 White Paper "Educational Reconstruction", which preceded the Act:

> *"There has been a very general wish, not confined to representatives of the Churches, that religious education should be given a more defined place in the life and work of the schools, springing from the desire to revive the spiritual and personal values in our society and in our national tradition. The Church, the family, the local community and the teacher – all have their part in imparting religious instruction to the young. In order to emphasise the importance of the subject, provision will be made for the school day in all primary and secondary schools to begin with a corporate act of worship."*

As we have already indicated, although the provisions of the 1944 Act did not specify that the act of worship should be explicitly Christian, this was undoubtedly the intention. The daily act of worship was seen as providing the context within which the "religious instruction" in the school curriculum would be provided, with both worship and instruction thus constituting complementary elements in a pupil's overall religious education.

Variety of Approaches to Assemblies

3.7   As the aims and content of religious education have come under increasing scrutiny however, and particularly as the situation of schools with pupil populations encompassing a range of beliefs and non-religious belief systems has been raised, the relevance and appropriateness of the collective act of worship has increasingly come to be questioned. In an attempt to respond to the variety of religious backgrounds from which their pupils now come, which it has been claimed makes an act of collective

---

[25] As the Durham Report explains:
"The practice of beginning and sometimes ending the school day with prayers had long been customary and went back to the years before 1870 when public education was almost entirely provided by voluntary schools. In most independent schools, likewise, daily chapel was a well-established tradition by the late nineteenth century."

worship in the spirit of the 1944 Act difficult if not impossible to achieve, many multi-racial schools have in recent years tended to move away from the notion of a spiritual act of worship towards seeing the school assembly as a social and administrative occasion, sometimes, but by no means always, with spiritual overtones[26]. Other multi-racial schools have sought to give some recognition to religions other than Christianity through including references to religious festivals from other faiths in assemblies, while a number of schools have continued with a traditional Christian-oriented act of worship. This range of approaches was reflected in the findings of Young and Connelly's 1981 Study[27] which found that:

> *"The question of assembly in particular has been very largely left to Heads to decide with the result that . . . a remarkable variety of approaches was indicated from more or less traditional Christian assemblies with the occasional reference to Hindu, Sikh or Muslim festivals to what seemed to be a more or less universalistic approach concerned with moral themes . . . In the absence of support, advice and guidance from advisers, Heads were evidently tempted to resolve the religious dilemma by ignoring it."*

Our Own Findings

3.8 The evidence which we obtained from multi-racial schools confirmed this view of the variety of approaches adopted towards assemblies. For example the following extract from evidence from one secondary school was typical of those where the assembly was seen entirely as an "administrative" exercise:

> *"School assembly has ceased to follow precisely the 1944 Act, and is non-denominational. It could be described more as the school's daily news-sheet and magazine, with moral overtones."*

– whereas the following extract from evidence from another school we visited exemplifies a "multifaith" assembly focussing on moral themes and project style studies of famous religious figures:

> *"Daily assemblies take their material from varied sources. Religious festivals from major religions are looked at as are parables from world religions. Prophets and outstanding men connected with particular faiths are quoted and discussed e.g. Gandhi. Themes such as tolerance, love, prejudice, jealousy and war are dealt with. Many contributions come from pupils themselves."*

---

[26] Moves towards more secular style assemblies have not however been confined solely to schools with multi-faith pupil populations, as evidenced by the report of a pilot study "The School Assembly in Hampshire" (Schools Assembly Project Working Paper Two: University of Southampton, Department of Education, 1982), which found that in 49 per cent. of county primary schools assemblies were not specifically linked to a religious education syllabus; for county secondary schools the figures was as high as 86 per cent.

[27] "Policy and Practice in the Multiracial City." PSI. 1981.

It can be seen that neither of these approaches explicitly includes an act of collective worship in accordance with the provisions of the 1944 Education Act. An example of how collective worship can be included in a multi-faith topic based assembly is given in the following extract from evidence we received from a primary school:

> *"(Assemblies) take place each morning as required by the 1944 Act. They are brief and are usually based on a simple topic. Sometimes children bring work to show to others, or a class may perform a short song or poem. All prayers are short and sensitivity to the belief of the Muslim is always shown. Sometimes film strips are shown which centre around themes such as giving, sharing, caring etc. . . . There are no objections from the Asian Community and no child is withdrawn from attendance at assembly. Parents are sometimes invited to join us at the beginning of the day."*

Right of Withdrawal

3.9 The 1944 Act provides for individual parents to withdraw their children from the school's act of worship. Very few multi-racial schools we contacted however mentioned ethnic minority parents making use of this "conscience clause". Whilst schools tended to ascribe this either to the move away from a "religious" towards an administrative assembly which could thus not conflict with parental religious beliefs, or to their attempts to broaden the scope of the faiths encompassed by their assemblies, many community representatives suggested that ethnic minority parents were often simply unaware of their right to withdraw their children. One of the Muslim organisations who gave evidence to us indicated that they had advised parents as follows:

> *". . . in the exercise of their legal rights as granted to them by the law of the land, the Muslim parents should not feel hesitant or embarrassed on their action which is within the scope of the Education Act, Section 25 and is being utilised by other religious groups as well."*

Distinction Between Assemblies and Acts of Worship

3.10 It must be recognised that assemblies which do not contain a collective act of worship are contrary to the spirit and indeed the letter of the law and whilst an *assembly* may include *an act of collective worship* the two terms are neither synonymous nor interchangeable as so often seems to be assumed. Concern about the provisions of the 1944 Act and about whether a revision of the Act in respect of the provision for collective worship might be necessary, was evident from the submissions received by the Select Committee on Education, Science and Arts when it considered this whole issue in 1981. As the Church of England Board of Education put it in their evidence to the Select Committee[28]:

---

[28]"The Secondary School Curriclum and Examinations." Second Report from the Education, Science and Arts Committee. HMSO. HC 116 II.

"The Board accepts the difficulty at the present time of implementing the law relating to a daily act of worship. There are reasons why communities need to assemble and some schools have developed patterns for such assemblies surrounding national, local or school themes. We need to be clear, however, that such assemblies are not necessarily "acts of worship". Some schools disregard the law some perfunctorily observe it, while others have with imagination and pupil participation revolutionised the atmosphere of the assembly . . . This Board would welcome an opportunity to discuss with the Secretary of State a revision of the clauses in the 1944 Act relating to assemblies so that more flexibility both as regards the frequency and the nature of acts of worship might be possible in the future."

A more extreme position was adopted by the National Secular Society which wished to see:

". . . the law prohibit any act of worship taking place within the school timetable."

and the British Evangelical Council which commented:

"Without denying the validity of Christian concerns within the school it does seem wrong to assume that a State school in a pluralist society should be committed to "worship" as if the children were all Christians."

In the light of the evidence which they had received the Select Committee recommended that:

". . . the Secretary of State should now begin discussions with interested bodies, including the church authorities about guidance to schools on the school act of worship. These discussions should also include the possibility that legislative changes may be necessary."

The Government responded as follows[29]:

"The Government recognise that a variety of practice has grown up in the form and content of the act of worship. The Government believe that this reflects the complexity and variety of present-day society and differences in the organisation of schools. They do not believe that it would be helpful to seek to standardise practice in this respect, but they are ready to receive representations about the act of worship from the churches and others at any time."

---

[29]"The Secondary School Curriculum and Examinations: Initial Government observations on the second report from the Education, Science and Arts Committee." Cmnd 8551. HMSO.

**The "Case"
for Agreed
Syllabuses**

The Provision of Religious Instruction

3.11   The provisions of the 1944 Education Act require that in every county school religious "instruction" shall be given in accordance with an "agreed syllabus" drawn up by a local education authority following a complex consultative procedure laid down in the Fifth Schedule to the Act (see Annex A). This requirement adds further to the unique position in which the Act places religious education since it is the only subject in the school curriculum for which a legally supported syllabus is required. The justification for the agreed syllabus procedure is generally held to be that it safeguards denominational interests and also relieves teachers of the direct responsibility for determining what is taught in an area of the curriculum which is particularly sensitive and controversial. As the report of a Religious Education Council Working Party[30] has put it:

"In a society which has many diverse views about religion and has a multiplicity of life-stances, parents and the public generally often wish to know what is supposed to be taught in a subject about which many have strong feelings. Teachers wish to be assured that what they are doing has a measure of public support to safeguard them against unreasonable criticism from a parent or a partisan section of society."

Nevertheless, concern has been expressed for some years over the need for agreed syllabuses and indeed the Durham Report concluded that:

"We do not think that the existing complicated legal machinery for drawing up, adopting, or varying an agreed syllabus should be retained. This is a relic of the ecclesiastical era in religious education, when the content of the curriculum had to be "agreed" between representatives of the Church of England, other Churches in the area which had a claim to be heard, the local education authority, and teachers. We are aware that much creative work was done, and some impressive syllabuses have emerged from it; but we believe this legal machinery to be no longer relevant. Moreover, we see no reason why, in religious education any more than in any other subject, one particular syllabus should be imposed by any local education authority."

**The Content
of Agreed
Syllabuses**

3.12   Although the Act does not state this explicitly, and indeed says nothing about the content or objectives of agreed syllabuses, it is clear that the intention of the requirement for an agreed syllabus was that it would primarily seek to nurture pupils in the Christian faith and this was indeed the approach adopted by LEAs over the next 30 years. A major departure from this interpretation of the role of agreed syllabus came in 1975

[30]"What Future for the Agreed Syllabus?" Religious Education Council Working Party. May 1976.

however with the preparation of a new agreed syllabus by Birmingham LEA. The conference which had prepared this syllabus included representatives of a range of religious communities, as well as taking account of the views of Humanist representatives, and the syllabus itself reflected this variety of view by including for study, alongside Christianity, not only other major world faiths but also other "life stances" such as Humanism and Marxism. The compilers of the Birmingham syllabus justified this radical shift in the following terms:

> *"A generation ago the purpose of religious education in county schools was to nurture pupils into Christian faith, and the agreed syllabus of religious instruction was one of the instruments whereby this was to be achieved. In the present circumstances religious education is seen as an educationally valid component of the school curriculum, subject to the same disciplines as other areas of study. It is thus directed towards developing a critical understanding of the religious and moral dimensions of human experience and away from attempting to foster the claims of particular religious standpoints. The syllabus should thus be used to enlarge and deepen the pupils' understanding of religion by studying world religions, and by exploring all those elements in human experience which raise questions about life's ultimate meaning and value. This involves informing pupils in a descriptive, critical and experiential manner about what religion is, and increasing their sensitivity to the areas of experience from which a religious view of life may arise. It should stimulate within the pupils, and assist them in the search for, a personal sense of meaning in life, whilst enabling them to understand the beliefs and commitments of others."*

– and presented their view of the task for religious education as follows:

> *"The approach to religious education exemplified in this syllabus places it within a wide frame of reference. Whilst in some respects religious education is the task of the specialist teacher, in others it is woven into the pattern of community relationships. The whole life of the school should be one in which the mind can be enlarged and moral responsbility exercised. Those who have prepared this syllabus have been constantly challenged by the need for schools to play their part in the task of preparing young people for life within the community. They have been conscious of the swift rate of social change and of the new Birmingham which is being created, where men and women and boys and girls are having to learn to live and work together in a pluralist situation. This is not to deny that the Christian religion is still a source of guidance and inspiration for many people living in the city, and that Christianity is part of our heritage. They also fully*

acknowledge the presence of significantly large minorities of people committed to other religions and stances for living, and seek to utilise this situation to create new unities and new insights rather than deeply rooted divisions. Prejudice arises from ignorance and fear, evils which can be fought and overcome to some extent within the context of the school community; for here ignorance can be confounded by knowledge and fear may give place to mutual understanding."

The Birmingham syllabus aroused considerable controversy and some criticism – being described for example as:

"initiation into agnosticism . . . an invitation to non-commitment"[31]

– and the issue of whether its approach diverged sufficiently far from the intention of the 1944 Act as to be in breach of its provisions was raised in Parliament in March 1976, when it was suggested that either the syllabus should be declared illegal or the provisions concerning agreed syllabuses should be repealed in order to encourage other authorities to develop similar syllabuses to cater for their multi-faith populations. The Government took the view that since the Birmingham syllabus had been prepared in accordance with the procedures laid down in the Act, and since the letter, if not the spirit of the Act itself did not explicitly require a syllabus to be Christian-oriented, the syllabus was legal and this fact in itself demonstrated that changes did not need to be made to the Act since it was possible to adopt a "pluralist" approach within its provisions.

3.13   Since the appearance of the Birmingham syllabus, a number of other authorities, including Hampshire to which we have already referred, have developed similarly broad agreed syllabuses which focus on developing children's understanding and appreciation of the nature of belief itself and of a range of belief systems, rather than seeking to convert or confirm children into any particular religion or ideology whether Christian or non-Christian. A recent example of such a syllabus, which clearly follows the phenomenological approach to Religious Education, is provided by the 1982 Berkshire agreed syllabus and we reproduce as Annex B to this chapter the statement of aims and objectives put forward in this document. Despite the development of such progressive and broadly-based agreed syllabuses in certain parts of the country, it is important to remember that only a few LEAs have sought to revise their syllabuses in this way and many, including some with substantial non-Christian faith communities, still retain agreed syllabuses, drawn up in the late 1950s, which still focus almost exclusively on Christian education.

---

[31] Initiation into Agnosticism. "Learning for Living." Taylor. 1976.

**Our Evidence
Gathering**

3.14   In the course of our work we have devoted a considerable amount of attention to the issues raised by the teaching of religious education in today's multi-faith context and much of our evidence from ethnic minority communities has related to their concerns about this aspect of education.We have brought together groups of teachers of religious education and other specialists in this field, drawn from local authority advisory services, examining boards and teacher training institutions, to discuss their views on the development of religious education. We also obtained evidence from a range of primary and secondary schools, and in the course of our school visits sought particularly to meet religious education teachers and to observe some lessons in this subject area.

3.15   The majority of religious education teachers whom we met, in schools with multi-faith pupil populations, were in favour of the phenomenological approach to religious education which we ourselves have advocated. It was repeatedly emphasised however that developing an approach to religious education which was appropriate to the needs of all youngsters living in Britain today presented a great challenge to teachers and the amount of work required, in terms of revising syllabuses and developing new material, should not be underestimated. Some of the teachers who favoured broadening the scope of religious education to encompass a range of world faiths expressed doubts to us about covering "non-religious" belief systems, such a Humanism and Marxism, since they regarded this as a "watering down" of the essential religious character of their subject. The majority of teachers whom we met however felt that youngsters should have some understanding of such life stances since they had also been significant in human history. Several of the religious education teachers with whom we discussed this issue stressed that a substantial number of their colleagues, especially those working in "all white" areas, still saw their work strictly in terms of "scripture and Bible studies", and we were therefore only "preaching to the converted" in discussing our views with them. It was strongly felt that, on educational grounds and in the global context, as well as in today's multi-racial Britain, *all* pupils needed to understand and appreciate a wide range of belief systems. Several teachers who had introduced such an approach in their own schools, emphasised how much it had enhanced pupils' (and indeed parents') interest in and enjoyment of the subject, and in some cases had led to increased numbers of pupils studying for examinations. Where there was some parental resistance (usually from the majority community) to studying religions other than Christianity, it was felt that this could best be overcome through "parent education" – explaining to parents what the school was endeavouring to achieve through its religious education programme.

3.16   We discussed with religious education teachers their views on how their own religious convictions could and should affect their teaching. Whilst some teachers took the view that, if asked, they should explain and defend their own beliefs to their pupils, others deliberately avoided expressing their own views in the classroom, in the belief that these would inevitably condition pupils' perception of different religions. Several teachers stressed however that pupils needed to be encouraged to understand and "empathise" with the views of adherents of a range of faith communities, to appreciate why these views were held, and then to seek to assess them personally. Only through this process could they consider what they themselves believed.

3.17 Considerable concern has been expressed to us that religious education, like E2L work, is often seen as a school's "token gesture" towards the presence of ethnic minority pupils and the religious education teacher is therefore regarded as the multicultural "expert". It has been suggested that if the religious education syllabus had been broadened to include some references, however, superficial, to the faiths of ethnic minority communities, then, even though the rest of the curriculum remains untouched, the school is "doing" multicultural education. Several of the religious education teachers felt that they often had a particular insight into the needs and concerns of ethnic minority pupils and their families because of their understanding of the influence of religion on their lives, and were therefore able to act as catalysts within the school to encourage curriculum development on a broader front. Some teachers even felt that they might be able to influence positively the way in which ethnic minority communities were presented in other areas of the curriculum, by for example encouraging their colleagues in the history department to review the way in which events such as the Crusades were dealt with or their colleagues in the geography department to consider how life in developing countries was presented, to avoid creating or adding to a negative stereotype of non-Christian communities. We ourselves would emphasise that the kind of religious education we have advocated here can only be truly effective if the principle of respect and recognition for a range of religious beliefs is seen to permeate all a school's provision within our philosophy of "Education for All". It is obvious for example that little will be achieved by seeking to promote a balanced appreciation of Islam and its influence on the lives of its adherents in the religious education syllabus, whilst at the same time, in the history syllabus, presenting the Crusades solely from a Christian viewpoint. It was regrettably also felt by many teachers that religious education was often accorded a low status by schools and they often had to fight to retain its place in the timetable and for the right to participate in policy discussions alongside their colleagues from other subject areas. This having been said however, many of the religious education specialists whom we met felt that their subject was one of the, if not *the*, most important areas of the school curriculum where positive progress could be made in reflecting and acknowledging the diversity now present in British society, and also in discussing fundamental "moral" issues such as racism.

Teaching Materials and Resources

3.18 Several teachers expressed concern to us about the difficulties of obtaining textbooks and teaching materials which reflected a multi-faith view of religious education and which did not present religions other than Christianity in negative or inaccurate terms. Whilst it was acknowledged that out of date textbooks which misrepresented other religions might cause offence to adherents of these faiths, the view was also expressed that such textbooks might themselves provide a valuable subject for discussion with pupils since they raised issues relating to stereotyping, religious prejudice and how non-believers could perceive other faiths. Since, members of ethnic minority groups were likely to encounter such ill-informed and damaging comments about their religious beliefs in their daily lives, because racism was felt to be a feature of life in Britain, it was felt that such discussions might help them to understand and cope with such reactions, as well as seeking to alter the views of their ethnic majority peers. Several teachers emphasised the value in teaching in multi-faith schools of being able to draw on the experiences of adherents of different faiths within the classroom and from the local community. It was emphasised however that the experiences of individual pupils should be used sensitively and that they should never be presented as "curiosities" thus adding to, rather than countering negative stereotypes. The opportunity for visits to the places of worship of a range of religious groups was seen as a potentially very helpful "living resource" for the teacher, but again it was stressed that such visits should not be presented as, in the words of one teacher, "a zoo trip or a safari into hostile territory", but must form an integral part of an ongoing religious education programme with adequate preparation – to establish the context for the visit – and adequate follow up – to resolve any outstanding misunderstandings or questions. Similarly it was suggested that involving adherents of different religious faiths in speaking to pupils about aspects of their beliefs could prove immensely valuable both in bringing to life the faiths concerned and in enhancing the pupils' appreciation of the presence of a range of faith communities within this society and possibly within the school's own locality. We certainly support the use of both visits and outside speakers from different faiths to illustrate apects of religious education but strongly reiterate the need for careful preparation and sensitivity in using such "living resources".

3.19 Some of the ethnic minority representatives whom we met expressed the opinion that only a teacher who was him or herself an adherent of a particular faith could teach that faith to pupils. When we discussed this viewpoint with teachers, some of whom were themselves of ethnic minority origin, it was pointed out that if this approach were adopted in schools seeking to cover a range of world faiths this would necessitate perhaps four or five teachers "representing" the different religions, which would clearly not be feasible. In addition however, this approach was felt to be justifiable only where a confessional approach was adopted, which sought to bring about a degree of commitment on the part of the pupil to a particular faith. Since the philosophy of the phenomenological approach to religious education was however not to teach children a religion but rather to teach children to understand the nature of belief and a range of belief systems, it was felt that this attitude was unjustified. It was recognised however that considerable skill and sensitivity were required on the part of a teacher, who might well have a personal commitment to a particular faith, in order to present other faiths as valid in their own right and great care needed to be exercised in seeking to "define other people's realities", especially when teaching a class which included pupils who were themselves drawn from particular faith communities. In this context it was again suggested that the use of outside speakers from different communities might prove helpful.

Practice in Schools

3.20   As with other areas of the curriculum, we would not seek to put forward detailed course guidelines and the existence of agreed syllabuses which we have already discussed and to which we return in our conclusion, clearly at present conditions the work which can be undertaken by schools. It may be helpful however to draw together here some comments and examples of classroom practice taken from the evidence which we have received, which serve to illustrate the practical implications of our view of religious education.

Primary Level

3.21   In most primary schools religious education takes place within the time devoted to storytelling and the time set aside for specific projects. It is not generally speaking a distinct subject in the curriculum but rather an integral part of the overall learning situation. At primary level it is of course particularly important for teachers to relate their work directly to the experiences and needs of their pupils. As Dr W Owen Cole has written[32]:

"From the outset it must be recognised that almost all successful primary education derives its effectiveness from beginning where the children are, from capturing their interests and extending and enriching their experiences. Their concern is much more with the tangible and what they can imaginatively experience than with abstract ideas. Consequently theology is out as such, whether it be the Christian doctrine of the life eternal or the Hindu belief in rebirth. Those things which are "in" are those which can become real to the

[32]"World Religions – A handbook for teachers." W Owen Cole. Community Relations Commission. 1976.

*children, how people dress, the foods they eat, how they greet one
another, going to a wedding, where they worship and when, how they
worship. Some of the religious stories may have a place, certainly how
the sacred texts are handled and treated by believers in their homes
and in worship as well as something about the languages they are
written in."*

This approach to religious education can be seen to underlie the practice
followed by one primary school which submitted evidence to us whose
Head wrote as follows:

*"We tell stories from all religions. With older children we compare
and contrast in a friendly way customs, beliefs and rituals. Marriage
ceremonies, for example, provide an excellent opportunity to show
how each in their own way seek to support the concept of family as a
basis for their society."*

3.22   It is important that by the time all children leave their primary
schools they should be aware that there are a range of different "living"
faiths in this society. Religious education at this level should be concerned
with laying the foundations to enable children to develop attitudes
towards all faiths and belief systems based on appreciation, interest and
respect. The extent to which much religious education provision at
primary level still falls short of this aim was highlighted by HMI in their
review of their inspection reports for the first half of 1983[33], which found
that:

*"There is hardly any evidence of work that takes full account of our
multi-ethnic society."*

The objectives set out in the Berkshire agreed syllabus attached as Annex
B, particularly those under the heading of "attitudes", would we feel lend
themselves to being pursued with primary age children and there are skills
within each area which pupils should have mastered by the age of 11. These
objectives can be seen to underlie the approach adopted to religious
education in one multi-racial primary school we ourselves visited whose
syllabus we have reproduced at Annex C. This school had also undertaken
a number of projects in the religious education field and further details of
these, together with some observations by the Head on the background to
them, are also included in Annex C.

**Religious
Education
Coordinator**

3.23   Several of the teachers whom we met expressed the view that the
development of religious education provision at this level, especially with
regard to broadening the syllabus to encompass a multi-faith perspective,

---

[33]"Education Observed – A review of the first six months of published reports by HM Inspectors." DES.
1984.

could be greatly assisted where an individual teacher was nominated to coordinate this field of work. It was suggested that this would help to ensure that the school kept abreast of recent developments on materials and resources and also kept in touch with other schools in its areas. The specific role of such a religious education "coordinator" in a primary school was summarised in evidence to us as follows:

"– *collecting up-to-date information about resources, and advising other teachers about the availability;*

– *attending meetings and courses, and reporting back on them;*

– *maintaining a small collection of handbooks and other materials for use in the school;*

– *ensuring that the school library and other resource collections in the school include books and materials relevant to religious education;*

– *helping colleagues to plan some of their topic and projects;*

– *liaising with other schools, including the secondary schools to which pupils eventually move;"*

We ourselves share the view that the designation of one teacher within a primary school as having responsibility for religious education may well facilitate curriculum development in this field (in the same way in which we have commended, in the previous chapter, the appointment of a language "coordinator").

Secondary Level

3.24   At secondary level, a more explicit approach to religious education is possible. Dr Owen Cole has suggested the following approaches[34]:

"Where We Worship' might provide a first introduction to religious practices other than the domestic and social celebrations which accompany festivals, births and weddings. Visits to places of worship often stimulate eleven-year olds not only to make models or draw pictures, but also to talk and write about their experiences. The visit to any empty synagogue or gurdwara proves interesting because it is different; the value is enhanced if good guides are available (i.e., those who can talk to children), and of course film-strips or slides, accompanied by such sounds as the Muslim call to prayer or the singing of bhajans in a Hindu temple, go far towards providing the

[34]"World Religions in the Multi-Faith School." W Owen Cole in "The School in the Multicultural Society." Ed James and Jeffcoate. Harper and Row Publishers. 1981.

491

authenticity which can only be obtained fully by attending an act of worship. One must remember that for many Hindus or Sikhs a visit to a Christian church is also novel and interesting, and that for the child from a traditional English home it is perhaps no less strange.

From the places of worship, besides moving towards ways of worshipping, it is also natural to progress towards books used in worship (hymn-books as well as sacred texts) and to the people through whom the particular faith was revealed. (For pupils aged 12 and 13 it is) an appropriate time for gathering together the fragmentary knowledge of various kinds, geographical and historical as well as religious, which has been acquired since the age of five.

The upper years, from thirteen to sixteen, are those when the teacher might try to probe as far as possible in assisting the student to understand what it means in terms of practices, belief or commitment to be Jew, a Muslim or a Christian."

3.25   It is clearly neither possible nor desirable to attempt to put forward a single scheme of work as universally appropriate to every school and there will clearly be, as we have indicated, particular areas of religious experience which can be considered more easily in some schools than others, depending on the character of the community they serve. We set out in Annex D however details of the approach adopted to religious education at classroom level by a number of multi-racial secondary schools which submitted evidence to us, in general reflect the broad principles set out above.

The "All-White" Dimension

3.26   It is important to bear in mind that it is not only in multi-racial schools that religious education can play an important role in contributing to a better understanding on the part of all pupils of the variety of faiths in our society and in breaking down racist attitudes. As one writer has put it[35]:

"Too often teachers in predominantly white schools consider themselves fortunate to be spared the "problems" of a multi-racial society. But we do not see cultural pluriformity as being a "problem" . . . The staff of a Cambridgeshire primary school in a mainly white area recently became alarmed by the growth of National Front attitudes among their pupils. A head of department of a school in the more affluent suburbs of Liverpool took a term off to plan projects which would help to counter the unthinkingly prejudiced attitudes which he felt were being ignored in his school. Much unintentional

[35]"Religious Education for a Multi-Racial Society." Louise Pirouet. Cambridge Journal of Education Vol 12 No 2. Easter Term 1982.

racism stems from a lack of information and a failure to question general assumptions.

Some RE teachers in predominantly white as well as racially mixed schools who have adopted a World Religions syllabus have found that this approach has revitalised the whole subject, and that pupils are asking to take CSE and O-Levels. In junior schools and in the first years of secondary school the best approach is thematic. The first introduction to World Religions will be through a study of festivals and sacred places, not through a study of belief or even of the life of the founder (where that is appropriate). A class studying the mosque as part of a scheme of work on sacred places will not only discover how Muslims regard the mosque and what they do there, but will also learn something about the architecture of the building and the designs and calligraphy which adorn it. They may trace out examples of Arabic script, finding the letters of "Allah" and "Muhammad", they may colour Islamic patterns and try to design some of their own; they may learn why it would be inappropriate to include calligraphy in a prayer-mat; they might draw or model a mihrab. Such activities help pupils to get a feel for some aspects of Islamic faith and culture. But then the teacher will at some stage need to find ways of relating what the pupils have learnt about Islam to the existence of Muslim communities in Britain. In schools with no mosque near enough to visit, slides of the Regent's Park mosque might perhaps be shown. Perhaps the class will learn that Muslims from Britain will go on the hajj and visit the mosques of Mecca and Medina. It is important that the study be done in sufficient depth. A swift "conducted tour" round the gurdwara, the mosque, the parish church, the synagogue and the Hindu temple in half a term is not likely to do much to promote imaginative understanding."

4. The supply and training of teachers of religious education

4.1   Clearly a major factor in the development of religious education provision has been the availability of specialist teachers of religious education and the extent to which their training has prepared them to adopt a phenomenological approach to their work which acknowledges the religious diversity of Britain today.

Early Developments

4.2   Looking back, the provisions of the 1944 Education Act created an immediate demand for teachers of religious education in all schools. Not surprisingly there was a serious shortage of such teachers since until the implementation of the Act, religion could not be offered as a qualifying subject for the teacher's certificate. It had therefore become fairly

493

common practice to depute the subject to any teacher willing to teach it
and who had some knowledge of the Bible. As the 1971 Schools Council
Report commented:

*"That inadequate view of the equipment required by an RE teacher is
not uncommon today."*

Implementation of the 1944 Act therefore necessitated the establishment
of religious education departments in many colleges of education and the
appointment of specialists in religious education on the staffs of a number
of university education departments. The supply of teachers of religious
education has not however kept pace with demand – as the Durham
Report commented in 1970:

*"We are impressed by how much has been done in a relatively short
time. But we are even more impressed by how inadequate it all is."*

**Findings of
the HMI
Secondary
Survey**

4.3   An indication of the extent to which the supply of adequately trained
teachers of religious education has failed to keep pace with the
development of the subject, and the difficulties which this situation has
created for schools, was given in the findings of the HMI Secondary
Survey in 1977[36] which found that:

*"Of the 608 teachers (331 men, 277 women) who taught religious
education as their first or only subjct 122 (20 per cent) did not record
this as their first or second subject of study. Of the 486 teachers who
had qualifications in the subject, 213 were graduates and 202
certificated teachers in secondary education. While rather more than
half of the grammar school teachers were graduates, the figure for
comprehensive schools was just over one-third and for modern
schools about one-fifth. 44 (7 per cent) of the 608 teachers were part-
time, 17 per cent were probationary teachers and 43 per cent had had
5 years' teaching experience or less."*

The Secondary Survey also revealed the following distribution of religious
education teachers amongst the schools in the survey, demonstrating the
shortages of staff qualified in the subject:

---

[36]"Aspects of Secondary Education in England – A Survey by HM Inspectors of Schools". HMSO.
1979.

QUALIFICATIONS OF TEACHERS WHO TEACH RELIGIOUS EDUCATION AS FIRST SUBJECT: BY TYPE OF SCHOOL

Percentages

	TYPE OF SCHOOL*					
	Mod	Gram	FR Comp	RR Comp	Trans	All Schools
Teachers with Qualifications in Religious Education						
Level of Qualification:						
Graduate	12	51	30	15	29	28
BEd	8	5	7	12	13	8
Certificated Secondary	38	18	33	41	37	33
Other	22	3	12	10	5	12
TOTAL	80	76	81	76	84	80
Teachers without Qualifications in Religious Education	20	24	19	24	16	20
Percentage Total	100	100	100	100	100	100
Number of Teachers who teach Religious Education as First Subject	100	72	327	71	38	608

```
*Mod      – Modern
 Gram     – Grammar
 FR Comp  – Full Ability Range Comprehensive
 RR Comp  – Restricted Ability Range Comprehensive
 Trans    – Transitional
```

Broader View of Religious Education

4.4   As far as the content of the specialist training received by religious education teachers is concerned, the 1971 Schools Council report which advocated the phenomenological approach to religious education offered the following comments on the adequacy of much of the training available at the time:

> "The study of the main religions of the world has an obvious educational justification in its own right, but the need for deeper understanding of the beliefs and customs of immigrant pupils may urge more concentration on one or two religions instead of a superficial world tour . . . Some theological faculties seem to go on with their traditional questions and problems. The meeting of world religions, the need for dialogue between them, has still no significant place in many theological schools and seminaries. Tutors would be foolish to wait for a lead from such theological faculties rather than to take other steps to equip themselves and their students for the needs of today."

495

Turning to the current situation of the religious education teachers whom we met who were teaching in schools with multi-faith pupil populations, not one felt that their training had prepared them adequately to deal with faiths other than Christianity. Many of these teachers had themselves made the effort, when they found themselves in a multi-racial school, to attend in-service courses or specialist seminars to update their skills and to examine new resources but such activities were felt to be "few and far between" and in several cases teachers had been forced to rely on their own initiative in obtaining relevant material or in devising appropriate schemes of work often in consultation with religious leaders from the ethnic minority communities in their areas. The work of the religious education centres at Westhill College, Birmingham and the West London Institute of Higher Education, and also the activities of the "SHAP" Working Party on World Religions in Education were mentioned by several teachers as having been especially valuable sources of information and advice on resources and materials. We are concerned at the number of religious education teachers who have received no specific training in religious education. In our next chapter we consider the extent to which teacher training courses, at both initial and in-service level, should take account of the diversity of home backgrounds and lifestyles from which the pupils in our schools may come and this would include reflecting the variety of faith communities in our society. In relation to the training received by religious education specialists we believe that far greater efforts should be made by teacher training institutions and LEAs to ensure that their courses reflect the broader view of religious education which we have advocated here.

5. Conclusion

5.1   We believe that religious education can play a central role in preparing all pupils for life in today's multi-racial Britain, and can also lead them to a greater understanding of the diversity of the global community. We feel that religious education of the kind which we have discussed here can also contribute towards challenging and countering the influence of racism in our society. As we have explained, we believe that the phenomenological approach to religious education reflects most closely the aims underlying "Education for All", in laying the foundations for the kind of genuinely pluralist society which we envisaged at the opening of this report. In this chapter we have set out what we regard as the fundamental aims and objectives of religious education, and also considered the practical implications of these principles at classroom level.

5.2   It is important to recognise that the stance which we have adopted in this chapter towards the role of schools in providing religious *education* should in no way be seen as conflicting with the role of individual faith communities to provide religious *instruction* and, as the Durham Report put it:

> ". . . *to nurture a child into a particular faith*".

Indeed, within a truly pluralist society, in which the maintenance of their religious traditions and beliefs is regarded by some groups within it as of great importance in retaining their group identity and cohesiveness, we would see community-based provisions for religious instruction – whether in the form of a Christian Sunday school, an Islamic Mosque school or organised by the Black Churches – as complementing rather than in any sense conflicting with the more broadly based religious education which we believe schools should be offering to *all* children.

5.3   More specifically however, the conclusions which we have reached in this chapter have a direct bearing on the provisions of the 1944 Education Act. As we have already seen, a number of people have suggested that some or all of the sections of the Act relating to religious education should be amended or repealed. During our consideration of religious education we have ourselves found it increasingly difficult to reconcile our own views on religious education with the requirements and the spirit of the Act. Since the Act perceives two distinct elements in religious education, it may be worthwhile considering each of these in turn. With regard to the requirement for a daily act of collective worship in every county and voluntary school, we do not believe that this requirement can continue to be justified with the multiplicity of beliefs and nonbeliefs now present in our society. We would not however wish to restrict the freedom of county schools to make provision for collective worship if it seems appropriate and is acceptable to their pupils and parents. Similarly however we believe the freedom *not* to make such provision should no longer be restricted by law. As we have pointed out, many county schools are in fact already in breach of the provisions of the Act in this respect and this would simply mean therefore regularising their existing practice. Within the existing dual system of education in this country, the trust deeds of some voluntary schools will however still require them to hold an act of collective worship. In relation to school *assemblies*, as opposed to an act of worship, we believe that they can be seen to fulfil a "social" and an administrative function in schools, especially at primary level, and as such are an important aspect of school life.

5.4   In relation to religious education, or in the terms of the Act – religious "instruction" – we have already explained that we regard the study of the nature of belief and of a range of belief systems as an essential and integral part of the educational experience of every child. This is not however to say that provision in this area of the curriculum should necessarily be required by law nor that it should be set within the complex framework established by the Act. Whilst we regard religious education *in the sense in which we have discussed it in this chapter* as an essential aspect of the curriculum we would not see it as any more essential than the other aspects of education which we have discussed in this report. If religious education is indeed regarded as such an important aspect of education, it seems difficult to accept the case for legally providing for pupils to be withdrawn from it. This anomalous position in our view raises serious doubts about the justification for the specific provisions of the Act. Clearly if the provision of religious education (instruction) continues to be required by law, and if there is a likelihood that the provision made may adopt a confessional approach, based on a Christian dominated agreed syllabus, then the right of withdrawal must be retained. If, however, as we wish, religious education is broadened to follow a phenomenological approach which seeks to "inform" rather than to "convert" pupils, and if the position of religious education within the curriculum is acknowledged and accepted on *educational* rather than religious grounds, then we feel that the legal requirement for provision to be made, the legal provision for withdrawal and the requirement for agreed syllabuses, are no longer justified.

5.5   We therefore believe that the Government, in consultation with religious and educational bodies, should look afresh at the relevant provisions of the 1944 Act, to see whether alterations are called for after an interval of 40 years (Paragraphs 5.3 and 5.5).

II.   The "Separate" Schools Debate

1.   Background

1.1   We now turn to considering a rather different dimension of the role of the school in relation to the diversity of today's multi-faith society, and one which has dominated much recent thinking in the "multicultural" field and on which much of our own evidence has focussed – the moves by certain ethnic minority communities, motivated primarily by religious concerns, to establish their own "separate" schools as an alternative to the existing mainstream system. As will become apparent, the term "separate schools" covers a variety of aspirations on the part of members of some ethnic minority communities for the establishment of schools which they feel would provide a more appropriate and acceptable environment for the education of their children. We have however continued to use the umbrella term in this rather imprecise sense because of its widespread usage in this field.

**Voluntary
Aided
Schools**

1.2 Almost without exception, pressure for "separate" schools has focussed on the case for establishing schools for certain ethnic minority communities *within the maintained system* i.e. as voluntary aided[37] schools. (There are of course already a number of "separate" schools catering for particular ethnic minority communities *outside the maintained system* – i.e. independent schools – but it is outside our terms of reference to consider these and the current debate has not really concerned them.) The right of ethnic minority communities to seek to establish their own voluntary aided schools is firmly enshrined in law. Under the provisions of the 1944 Education Act ethnic minority communities, along with any other group of individuals, are entitled to make proposals for the establishment of a voluntary aided school to cater for their children's educational needs. The final decision on whether or not to approve the proposals rests with the Secretary of State for Education and Science. (Further details of the procedure for the establishment of voluntary aided schools are given in the background explanatory notes provided by the DES and attached as Annex E). Where an ethnic minority community which wishes to establish a voluntary aided school is of a distinct religious character, their school would thus be parallel to existing Church of England, Roman Catholic and indeed Jewish schools which are already part of our education system. Where the ethnic minority community concerned does not have a clear religious identity we understand from the DES that proposals to establish a voluntary aided school may be complicated by the provisions of the 1976 Race Relations Act which do not allow for admissions to a maintained school to be limited according to race.

**Contrast with
Existing
Multi-racial
Schools**

1.3 Some advocates of "separate" schools have expressed the view that discussion about their relative advantages and disadvantages has to some extent been overtaken by events in that there are already a number of schools, both primary and secondary, which are already de facto "separate" schools for particular ethnic minority groups in all but name and legal status, since they have a considerable majority of ethnic minority pupils. There are however two essential differences between such schools and true "separate" schools. Firstly, existing multi-racial schools have not been set up expressly to cater for a particular denominational or racial group and we would therefore expect them to be providing an education for their pupils essentially no different from that offered by any school in the country i.e. an education which reflects the pluralist nature of our society and which is not limited to the perspective of any one group, whether minority or majority. They cannot therefore be seen as

---

[37]Voluntary aided schools are established by voluntary bodies, usually a Church or charitable foundation. The voluntary body has to provide the premises for the school and thereafter is responsible for external maintenance, repairs and any major capital expenditure on which it is eligible for grant of up to 85% from the DES. The voluntary body holds a majority on the governing body which enables it to exercise control of admissions and the curriculum.

499

"exemplars" of the kind of "separate" schools which have been proposed which would be very different in character since the nature of their pupil populations would be determined not simply by the make up of their catchment areas (which could of course change over time), but would be intentionally prescribed and enshrined in the school's status. A further difference is that whilst some existing schools may appear to have a majority of pupils from a particular ethnic minority group, this may well be a considerable over-simplification of the various groups represented in the school – for example the description of a school as almost wholly "Asian" would clearly be of little relevance to proposals to establish a Muslim denominational school since the two "groups" are hardly synonymous. Even where there are schools with a majority of pupils sharing the same religious affinity, it must also be recognised that their parents have sent them to a school which they see as part of the mainstream system and as having no explicit "ethnic identity". If the character of the school were to be emphasised however, for example by its establishment as a Muslim school, some parents might well then have reservations about their children's position there, since the communities are by no means united in the belief that "separate" provision is desirable. We believe it is misleading therefore to look on existing multi-racial schools as parallels to the likely situation of any "separate" schools which might be established to cater explicitly for certain ethnic minority groups.

2. The Concerns of the Asian Community

**Religious
Context**

2.1 The debate about the establishment of "separate" schools by ethnic minority communities has focussed in recent years on the pressure from Hindus, Sikhs and above all Muslims within the Asian community in this country to establish their own denominational voluntary aided schools within the maintained system. In 1980 there was an attempt by some of the Sikh community in Southall to acquire an existing secondary school, in 1983 a group of Muslim parents in Bradford sought to purchase a total of five schools – two first schools, two middle schools and an upper school – and Kirklees LEA is currently considering an application from a Muslim group to acquire the premises of an existing school in order to establish a voluntary aided Muslim primary school. Since the groups which have sought to establish these schools are of a clearly religious character it is often argued that their efforts represent nothing more than an attempt to extend the existing dual system of educational provision in this country to embrace other faiths which are now part of British society, and the resistance and antagonism which such attempts have aroused have been seen as manifestations of institutional racism in that the "system" is failing to accord equal treatment to the religions of ethnic minority groups. We believe however that these calls for the establishment of their own denominational schools also need to be seen within the context of the overall concerns of ethnic minority communities about the education of their children and particularly their concerns about the religious education and the general "ethos" provided by existing schools.

The Case for "Separate" Schools

Balance of the Curriculum

Ethnic Minority Teachers

2.2   A range of different objectives have been advanced by those Asian groups which have sought to establish their own voluntary aided schools. Because of their essentially religious character it is hardly surprising that a major reason put forward by these groups has been concern about what they see as the Christian-dominated religious education provided by existing mainstream schools and a consequent desire to give their children the opportunity to learn about the religious traditions of their own faith communities in a positive and accurate manner. (We have of course already referred in the earlier part of this chapter to the widespread concern amongst ethnic minority groups about what they regard as the lack of respect and recognition accorded to their religions by many schools.) This specific concern about religious education provision has also been broadened to encompass other concerns about the balance and bias of much of the rest of the curriculum offered by mainstream schools – for example the lack of attention given to the varied history, literature and culture of the Asian community and the lack of adequate support and encouragement for "mother tongue" languages – which it is again suggested the establishment of their own schools would be able to counter. As an extension of the wish to establish their own schools as an alternative to what they see as the Christian-dominated and Anglo-centric curricular diet of mainstream schools, advocates of "separate" schools have also stressed the contingent benefits of ethnic minority children being taught by teachers who share the same religious and cultural background. We discuss in our Chapter on Teacher Education, later in this report, the importance attached by many ethnic minority groups to increasing the numbers of teachers from their own communities, and we have already mentioned, earlier in this chapter, the view taken by members of some faith communities that their religions can only be effectively taught by a teacher who is an adherent of that faith. It is also worth noting that some groups of Asian teachers to whom we have spoken, concerned about the influence which they see racism as having on their prospects of employment and promotion within the teaching profession, see the potential establishment of Sikh or Muslim schools as offering them the prospect of wider opportunities for career advancement free from such obstacles.

Response to Racism

2.3   A further aspect of the case put forward by the Asian community for establishing its own schools is a response to the influence of racism. Since, as we have already observed, members of the Asian community in this country are subject to some of the most overt manifestations of racism which we have encountered, for example in the form of physical attacks on

501

both pupils and their parents, it is understandable that they may despair of existing schools tackling the issue of racism and seek instead to insulate themselves from racism and to prepare their youngsters for its experience by establishing their own schools. On the broader level, several of the leading Muslim organisations with whom we have discussed the issue of "separate" schools have suggested that they would offer a valuable means of fostering multi-racial understanding by enabling children to become secure in their cultural and religious roots and to have a sense of morality and social responsibility. It is argued that the youngsters would thus not only be good citizens but would have a confident and balanced view of their place in this society, free from the sense of alienation which is experienced by certain other ethnic minorities.

**"External"
Pressures**

2.4   In addition to these issues which have formed the basis of the case put forward for the establishment of "separate" schools, it is also essential to acknowledge the extent to which factors external to the ethnic minority communities may have indirectly contributed to pressure for such schools. It is worth recalling here the background to the moves by the Sikh community in Southall to establish their own school, mentioned in paragraph 2.1, which we believe illustrates vividly how pressures from outside a community can help to fuel the belief that "separate" schools are in fact the only option open to them. In 1979 the Church of England sought to purchase a multi-racial county secondary school in the Southall area and their application was subsequently approved by the then Secretary of State. When the proposal was under consideration, the local Sikh community, which had many children at the school was extremely concerned at its implications, as illustrated by the following comments[38] by an Asian teacher at the school:

> *"It is seen as a tactic by white people to create a school for whites only, using the excuse that it is a Church of England School. We see it as a way of segregating us. The Asian community want the freedom to be able to go on sending their children to . . . and the other schools. Obviously the parents would not particularly want to send their children to a school of another religion . . . Once the school becomes an all white school there will be a strong demand to create a Sikh school. These moves for separate schools (NB a reference to the proposal for a Church of England School) are creating tensions. They go against the spirit of racial harmony. To create a Church of England School in Ealing now is to invite racial trouble."*

In the light of such a climate of opinion it is surely more than a coincidence that the Sikh community in Southall responded to this move with their

---

[38] As reported in the "Teacher." April 13, 1979.

own unsuccessful attempt to purchase another secondary school themselves.

Particular Concerns of the Muslim Community

2.5 Turning to the case which has been put forward by some leading Muslim[39] organisations for the establishment of voluntary aided Muslim schools – which has been very much at the centre of the debate on "separate" schools over the past year or so – we believe that the issues involved here are rather different from those raised by other communities in that they are very specifically related to adherence to Islamic religious and moral principles and represent a clear desire on the part of some members of the Muslim community to remove their children from existing schools. We have already referred to the bearing which the current world-wide resurgence of the Islamic faith appears to have had on the self-awareness and confidence of the Muslim community in this country. Much of the pressure for aided schools from the Muslim community can we believe be seen as a consequence of the moves to reaffirm adherence to Islamic principles in order to counter what is seen as the increasing "westernisation" of Muslim children in this country. We have ourselves received a considerable volume of evidence from Muslim organisations, much of which has been concerned with the religious "rights and duties" of Muslim parents and their children in an educational context, for example in relation to matters such as school uniform, school meals, physical education and religious instruction. Whilst in many cases the emphasis of the Muslim community's concerns has been on seeking to bring about changes in the policies and practices of existing schools in respect of such matters, it is noticable that there is a growing tendency to take the view that no accommodation is in fact feasible or indeed desireable within the existing system and in order to provide a true Islamic education for their children, it is necessary to provide Muslim aided schools.

Influence of Islam

2.6 Whilst the reasons for some members of the Muslim community taking this line are to a certain extent similar to those put forward by other Asian communities, most notaby frustration and dissatisfaction with the failure of existing schools in the past to recognise and respond to their concerns, over and above these common factors there seem to us to be differences in emphasis between the principles inherent in our education system and a strict interpretation of the aims of Islamic education. Much of the evidence which we have received in favour of Muslim schools stresses the need to create an Islamic ethos permeating every aspect of

---

[39] We are aware that in this section we may appear to be referring to "Muslims" as though they can only be seen as a religious sub group within the Asian community. We recognise of course that the Muslim community both in this country and world-wide encompasses people of many races and colours and we ourselves have met, for example West Indian Muslims and Turkish Cypriot Muslims. In numerical terms in this country however, and certainly in the context of the debate on "separate" schools, we are in practice dealing with the concerns of "Asian Muslims". It is worth noting that all the Turkish Cypriot Muslims whom we met disassociated themselves from calls for "separate" schools.

school life. The major aspiration of such a school is seen as educating children to be first and foremost "good Muslims" and all other aspects of education being seen as of secondary concern. With regard to the treatment of religion, the emphasis in many of the submissions which we have received is, as we have already recalled in the first part of this chapter, on the need to *instruct* and confirm the pupils in their Islamic faith through a "confessional" style approach and although it has been suggested that Muslim schools might admit some non-Muslim pupils the intention would still be to offer different religious groups instruction in their own religions.

Educational Aspirations

2.7 In relation to the overall philosophy of education and how this is mediated through the hidden curriculum of the school, there seem to us to be obvious differences of emphasis between secular and religious approaches. Many of these differences of emphasis arise from the apparent irreconcilability of the requirements of a religion, which of its very nature influences every aspect of an individual's life, and the pressures of our secular society. It is widely accepted in this country that education should seek to encourage children to question, to criticise, to investigate, to challenge, to debate, to evaluate and to be able to make decisions and choices about their future adult lives. To some extent at least these objectives can however be seen as in conflict with a faith whose very essence is considered to lie in an aceptance of revelation and adherence to forms of behaviour and conduct. A "conflict of interests" can therefore arise for adherents of other faiths or denominations, such as Roman Catholicism and Islam which deem certain "truths" to be beyond doubt. The dilemma which this apparent conflict poses for Muslims in this country was described thus in evidence to us:

> "A major worry for Muslim parents is the fact that their children soon begin to adopt English standards and ideas. They start to question not only traditional customs but religious ideas which seem to be strangely alien to life in a Western materialistic society. Islam is not something which can be learnt and adhered to overnight. It must be lived, breathed and fostered until it cannot be separated from life itself. It requires constant practice, and it is this fact that creates the dilemma for a Muslim parent in Britain today. Most Muslims acknowledge that Britain is a fair place to live, and in many ways they have come to depend upon it for their livelihood, but it is hard to judge how possible it is to live as a Muslim within the society as a whole."

Single Sex Schools

2.8 Where the concerns of the Muslim community about the "welfare" of their children in relation to the requirements of their faith finds particular expression is in the specific calls which have been made for the establishment of *single sex*[40] Muslim schools. Indeed the fact that in the evidence which we have received the terms "separate" and "single sex" have tended to be used inter-changeably and seen as synonymous is a measure of the extent to which concern about the education of Muslim *girls* lies at the heart of much of the debate on Muslim schools. Before considering this issue further we believe that it is important to recognise that the concept of a single sex school in the Muslim context differs in certain fundamental respects from the philosophy underlying existing single sex schools in the education system. Girls' schools in this country – apart from their pupil populations and to a lesser extent their teacher populations – have in practice differed little from co-educational schools in that the core curriculum has been the same and the same educational standards in terms of public examinations have been sought. Traditional "girls' subjects" such as home economics have of course tended to be included in the curriculum at the expense of "technical" boys' subjects but in recent years even this difference of emphasis has become less clearly defined with the greater acceptance in society as a whole of a broader role for women. From the statements which have been made by spokesmen of the Muslim community however, it is clear that the form of single sex education which at least some of them are advocating for girls would entail a far more central focus in the curriculum on education for marriage and motherhood in a particular Islamic sense, with other subjects receiving less attention and with the notion of careers education being seen as irrelevant to the pattern of adult life which the girls were likely to pursue.

2.9   Advocates of such a pattern of education for girls have argued that it would in no way represent a "second class" education – on the contrary, rather than, as at present requiring girls to study subjects which are unimportant and have little relevance to their future lives, they claim it would give greater respect and recognition to the specific role which Muslim girls can be expected to fulfil within their community. We believe that the following extract from the booklet "Islamic Education and Single Sex Schools" produced by the Union of Muslim Organisations of United Kingdom and Eire is worth quoting at some length here since it serves to illustrate this particular view of the arguments for and against co-educational and single sex schools in the Muslim context:

> *"Many of the arguments in favour of co-educational schools concern social behaviour. Let us look at some of the points for co-education outlined in Mixed or Single Sex Schools? by R R Dale, and consider them in relation to Islamic injunctions.*
>
> 1.   *"It enables each sex to know and learn from the points of view of*

---

[40]*The emphasis is in fact almost exclusively on single sex schools for girls* and less attention is given to the need for parallel provision for boys.

the other, contributing to better mutual understanding between the sexes and avoiding the rather immature attitude of the one sex to the other which is often found in the products of single sex schools."

2.   *"Life at home is living together of father and mother sons and daughters. A co-educational schools is an extension of life at home and can serve as an apprenticeship to becoming an understanding member of society."*

3.   *"The best type of school is that which is a microcosm incorporating within it the essential features of life in the world outside. Segregation of sexes is purely artificial. Education cannot claim to be a training for life unless it prepares the child to take his place naturally in the community of men and women."*

4.   *"The two sexes have an ameliorating effect on the conduct of each other, restraining the extremes of conduct, the boys losing some of their boisterous rudeness and the girls becoming less giggly, simpering, catty."*

5.   *"Friendly rivalry between the two sexes on the standard of work – boys tend to raise the standard of girls in certain subjects, e.g. Mathematics and Science."*

6.   *"There was a lightness which took away much of the drudgery from teaching."*

Such schools produce an "atmosphere" and evoke such phrases as "joie de vivre", "gaiety".

Arguments in favour of co-educational schools on these social aspects would seem to be opposed to basic Islamic principles. Islamic teaching has rejected the idea of free intercourse between the sexes and has encouraged the purity and innocence of adolescence. Segregation of the sexes has been encouraged in Islam and not at all regarded as artificial. A woman is encouraged at all times to behave modestly before men, and not to seek to outrival them in masculine pursuits. It is the job of the home and loving parents, not the school, to develop social awareness and moral judgement.

On the other hand, many arguments against the co-educational school have complete affinity with Islamic principles.

"Different rates of intellectual development of the sexes", "different

*interests", "work suffering from distraction", "the bad effect of
competition on girls" are all linked with the insistence in Islam that
women must play a different role to men, and develop her feminine
qualities rather than merely imitate men, so becoming only a second
rate citizen with no real authority in either the home or in the world
outside the home.*

*Mohammed Mazheruddin Siddiqui, in his "Women in Islam",
questions the basis of co-education thus:*

> *"Co-education is based on the assumption that there are no
> psychological and temperamental differences of any great
> consequence between man and woman, that after completing
> their education they have to pursue like careers and enter
> identical spheres of activity and that no sexual aberrations are
> likely to occur from the herding together of boys and girls in the
> same institution, or if they do occur, their consequences for the
> stability of the family, the happiness of married life and the
> general character formation of men and women are not serious
> enough to warrant social condemnation."*

And concludes thus:

> *"The most vital defect of co-education from the point of view
> of female nature and women's special functions in society, is
> that it prevents the training of women for motherhood. How
> can a common educational instituion run alike for the boys and
> the girls make adequate provision for training women in those
> arts and branches of knowledge which are necessary for her
> future life as a mother? Education for motherhood is the crying
> need of the world today . . . When the whole curriculum of girls
> is hopelessly congested with subjects on the line of boys which
> cost them their mental equilibrium and physical health, their
> essential function in life is allowed to pass on in ignorance."*

*Of course, there are those boys and girls who will study anywhere and
not be influenced but they are in the minority, and for the sake of the
majority who are prone to human weakness it would make more
sense to believe that "prevention is better than cure"."*

Thus, just as we believe that it is misguided to see calls for Sikh or Muslim
schools simply in the context of existing denominational schools, similarly
it is wrong to view pressure from the Muslim community for the
maintenance and establishment of their own single sex schools solely in
relation to existing single sex schools in the education system.

507

**Decline in
Single Sex
Provision**

2.10   As in the case of "separate" schools in general, there seems also to be a strong possibility that factors outside the Muslim community have served to give added impetus to calls for the maintenance and establishment of single sex schools. One of the major changes which has taken place in the education system over the last 10 to 15 years has been the decline[41] in the number of single sex schools, with many such schools having been replaced by, or amalgamated to form, co-educational schools. This move from single sex to co-educational provision seems not to have been as the result of any major policy decision on the part of the Government of the day but rather to have come about largely as a natural concomitant of the reorganisation of secondary education on comprehensive lines which inter alia was thought to necessitate fewer and larger schools. Once established, this trend has continued and we believe that it is perhaps more than a coincidence that the secondary school which Muslim parents in Bradford sought to purchase (see paragraph 2.1 above) was the only remaining girls' school in the Authority and that there had been plans to amalgamate it with the adjacent boys' school. Whilst the move away from single sex education has come about entirely independent of issues relating to the education of ethnic minority children it is clear from this that its consequences bear particularly directly on the interests of the Muslim community. It is certainly evident that reducing and in some cases perhaps removing the option available for parents wishing, for whatever reasons, their children and particularly their daughter to be educated in a single sex environment, can be of especial concern to a community, where some parents as we have seen, have particularly strong views on the education of girls. It may well be therefore that moves away from single sex provision by local education authorities with Muslim populations have served to add weight and urgency to the pressure from these communities to establish their own voluntary aided schools in the belief that this is the only way of preserving the option of single sex education for their children.

**Our
Conclusions**

2.11   Throughout this report we have argued for *all* pupils to share a common educational experience which prepares them for life in a truly pluralist society. We have stressed that, to achieve this aim, *all* schools, both multi-racial schools and those with few or no ethnic minority pupils, will need to reappraise their curricular provision and the attitudes and assumptions which underlie their work, in order to challenge and indeed

---

[41]*Number of Maintained Secondary Schools in England*

	1968	1978	1981
Boys	1066	479	391
Girls	1071	489	415
Co-educational	3085	3743	3848

Source: DES Basic School Statistics

overcome the "barriers", whether physical or psychological, which at present exist between the majority and minority communities in our society. We firmly believe that if the message of this report is accepted by schools and the changes in perspective and emphasis which we have advocated – particularly in relation to religious education, "pastoral" concerns and language needs – are realised, then this will go a considerable way towards meeting the concerns of many ethnic minority parents about their children's education and that many of the particular concerns which have led sections of the Asian community to call for the establishment of their own schools would also be allayed. If schools were seen by parents to be offering a more broadly-based curriculum, which reflected the multi-racial, multi-lingual and multi-faith nature of Britain today we feel this would counter many of the anxieties which have been expressed. If ethnic minority parents were able to exercise some direct influence themselves over policy development and decision making, through greater involvement in governing bodies, this would also, we feel, enhance their confidence in existing schools. Similarly if teachers showed themselves willing to cooperate in a positive way with community-based activities and to respond sensitively to pastoral concerns and to take effective action to tackle all manifestations of racism, whether overt or covert, we believe that much of the mistrust and frustration which lies behind arguments for an alternative to existing schools would be overcome.

2.12   Whilst we fully appreciate the concerns which have led some sections of the Asian Community to press for the establishment of their own schools, we do not believe that creating an artifically separate situation in which groups of children are taught exclusively by teachers from the same ethnic group is desirable from the point of view of the children, the minority community or society as a whole and we are not therefore convinced that "separate" schools can be supported on these grounds. Within our philosophy of "Education for All" we have stressed the role which we see all teachers having in understanding and meeting the needs of all pupils, whether from minority or majority communities, and in addition the particular role which ethnic minority teachers may play in certain situations where they are able to draw on their own experience in supporting children for whom English is not a first language or in pastoral care situations requiring insight into the particular concerns of certain parents for their children. Despite the clearly deeply felt case put forward by many community representatives in evidence to us, we consider that, on the basis of present evidence, the best and perhaps the only way of ensuring that ethnic minority communities in this country are able both to retain their religious, cultural and linguistic heritages, as well as being accorded full equality alongside members of the majority community, is within the broader pluralist context for which we have argued in this report. In many respects we feel that the establishment of "separate" schools could well fail to tackle many of the underlying concerns of the communities and might also exacerbate the very feelings of rejection and of not being accepted as full members of our society, which they were seeking to overcome. By in effect constituting a real and physical manifestation of the psychological barriers and divisions which undoubtedly do exist in our society we believe they might well serve to reinforce and extend these rather than, as we would wish, help to remove them.

Arguments Against "Separate" Provision

2.13   In view of our overall aim of *all* schools offering a full education for *all* our children it is hardly surprising that we find we cannot favour a "solution" to the supposed "problems" which ethnic minority communities face, which tacitly seems to accept that these "problems" are beyond the capacity and imagination of existing schools to meet and that the only answer is therefore to provide "alternative" schools for ethnic minority pupils thus in effect absolving existing schools from even making the attempt to reappraise and revise their practices. Throughout this report we stress our misgivings about the implications and consequences of "separate" provision of any kind, explicitly catering for ethnic minority group pupils. As we have already observed, there is little hope of remedying the inaccurate and misleading stereotypes of ethnic minority groups which persist in the minds of the majority community – an essential element in racism as a whole – by simply seeking to remove some ethnic minority pupils from existing schools thus leaving the educational and social experience of the remaining pupils, both minority and majority, impoverished accordingly.

2.14   As far as the physical security of ethnic minority youngsters is concerned, whilst they may be safer from racial attacks in a "separate" school, the very existence of a visibly identifiable "Asian" school may serve to polarise the attitudes of members of other communities in the area. There will inevitably still be occasions when youngsters from different groups will come into contact with each other – for example travelling to and from school – and if they have had little other experience of meeting one another, then the scope for inter-racial misunderstanding and tension is surely greater and the experience of the racism which the Asian pupils may then face, all the more traumatic for its unexpectedness and their unpreparedness. There is a clear recognition of this inherent risk in pursuing calls for "separate" schools in the following observations made by the President of the National Association of Asian Youth in a newspaper article[42]:

> *"Even if a separate Muslim school can give a good grounding in Islam, it can in one way prepare the pupils for living in a multicultural, multiracial society. How are they to relate to, for example, a skinhead, a West Indian, an elderly white lady? How are they to learn to cope*

---

[42] New Life. April 1983.

with unemployment? If they really want to live as a separate colony, why don't they go back and live in that system? Religiously and culturally they may consider themselves better off, but they'll be at the bottom of the ladder in every other respect in the wider community – where the pressure is likely to increase. They'll just play into the hands of the right wingers and fascists who say "let them have separatism, but not at our expense". If they have separate schools which instil an exclusive culture, religion and education, what aspect of their life will be relevant to the community? they will have no ability to understand or do anything about issues of common concern. Politically they'll be on the losing end too. I would like to see the basic religious or cultural needs of the Muslim communtiy understood and respected by the community at large so that the latter say: "Have your way, traditions – we understand"."

The establishment of "separate" schools could also, we believe, make even harder the task of convincing a teacher in a mainsteam school of the possible need to amend his or her practices in response to the mult-racial nature of the pupil population without inviting the riposte that "They have their own schools for that sort of thing so they know where to go if they want special treatment" – hardly conducive to positive progress.

Retaining the Option of Single Sex Schooling

2.15 There is one particular aspect of the concerns of certain Asian groups, particularly the Muslim community, to which we have referred and which we feel merits further discussion – the issue of single sex provision for girls. We feel that existing co-educational schools with multi-racial pupil populations could do more to ensure that, where there is parental concern about girls participating in certain activities in a mixed group, there is a degree of single sex provision in certain areas of the curriculum. For example some schools already allow for single sex teaching groups for physical education or for sex education, and such provision could, where there is strong concern and if it is felt to be necessary, with sensitivity and imagination, be extended to other aspects of the school's work, such as drama, dance, extra-curricular activities, field trips and even organised school outings and holidays, to encourage the participation of girls. It is clear however that such provision can go only some way towards allaying the concerns of those parents who desire a fully single sex education for girls. In this respect, we are concerned at the extent to which the demise of single sex provision, which we highlighted above, may not only be restricting parental choice in a general sense but may, with particular reference to the Muslim community, be removing the option for some parents of having their daughters educated in what they would see as an acceptable environment. The nature of the pupil population today, in many parts of the country, is very different from that which obtained in the early days of the reorganisation of secondary

511

education and it seems to us that LEAs with multi-racial populations should think very carefully about the implications which following the trend towards co-education many now have for their ethnic minority parents, particularly Muslims. We hope therefore that Authorities will be prepared to consider carefully the value of retaining an option of single sex education as part of their secondary school provision and that the Secretary of State will be similarly sensitive to the wider ramifications of any decision which he might need to make on proposals which could lead to the loss of single sex provision in multi-racial areas. As Muslim representatives have pointed out to us, they are not alone in favouring single sex education and it must be accepted therefore that single sex schools would not draw their pupils exclusively from the Asian community and could be as multi-racial as their co-educational counterparts. In cases where LEAs may either no longer provide for single sex education at all, or may make only very limited such provision, we would hope that if concern was expressed by parents about the education of, in particular, their daughters, the possibility of establishing or re-establishing single sex schools would be given serious consideration. Similarly we hope that the Secretary of State will be sensitive to the wider ramifications of any decisions he may make on proposals which lead to the loss of single sex provision in multi-racial areas. If the position of single sex education was thus preserved and respected, rather than as at present seen as under constant threat, we believe that this would offer considerable reassurance to the Muslim community in that not only would they see that the option of their children being educated in a single sex environment was available to them but it would also offer tangible evidence that their particular concerns about the education of their daughters were being recognised and respected.

Attitude to Girls' Education

2.16 We appreciate that the line we have taken on single sex education may not be accepted as going far enough to meet the demands of those who have argued for a strictly Islamic education for girls but we find ourselves unable to support the kind of education which some members of the Muslim community have proposed. The principle of full equality of opportunity for both boys and girls in terms of access to all aspects of the curriculum and equal rights to be encouraged to think positively about one's place in the world, to be stretched intellectually, and to be equipped with the skills necessary to function as a full member of adult society, is fundamental to the philosophy of education in this country and the notion of equality of opportunity is of course enshrined in law. We therefore have very considerable reservations about the essential desirability of in any way encouraging the establishment, within the maintained education system in this country, of separate Muslim schools explicitly aimed at providing the type of single sex education which has been proposed by some members of the Muslim community. Clearly, a number of the

512

concerns which have led some Muslim parents to adopt a particularly orthodox stance regarding their daughters' education arise from their misgivings about the effect – both moral and physical – of existing school policies in such matters as school uniforms, showers and changing, physical education and swimming. We take these concerns very seriously **"Pastoral"** and believe that far more can be done by schools to respond to the **Concerns** "pastoral" needs of Muslim pupils so that Muslim parents are no longer seen as simply "being awkward". If this is done, it should serve to allay some of the concerns even of the more "extreme" parents and lead them to regain confidence in the fact that existing schools are prepared to respect their wishes. We believe that seeking to meet the communities' concerns on these issues cannot however of itself be seen as necessitating the establishment of Muslim schools. There is much that can and should be done within existing schools to ensure that there is a real respect and understanding by both teachers and parents of each other's concerns and a genuine desire to work together to prepare pupils for life in a pluralist society, whilst not placing any individual child in a position where he or she is in fundamental conflict with the requirements of their faith. We have been struck by a number of instances of schools, mainly at secondary level, where a rigid insistence on long established rules for "pastoral" matters often appears to override educational considerations and even ignore any commonsense approach to differences of opinion between parents and school. Parents are thus, often reluctantly, drawn into a situation of conflict between the requirements of their faith and the rules of the school. Similarly, responding to requests from parents should not be seen by schools as meaning that they should merely seek to talk parents round to their view where such actions may mean that parents are forced into the position of sacrificing some of the basic principles of their faith.

2.17 It is interesting to note that few of the representatives of the Muslim community whom we have met and none of the individual Muslim parents with whom we have discussed the issue of single sex schools have insisted on single sex education solely on religious grounds. It is clearly in no way for us to seek to pass judgement on whether or not Islamic principles do in fact require that the girls are always educated in a single sex environment and indeed there have been differences of opinion on this issue in the evidence which we have received from the various Muslim organisations. It is important however before leaving the issue of single sex schools to point out that many Muslim parents in this country, who we are sure would in no way see themselves as failing in their Islamic duty, do send their children to co-educaional schools even when the option of single sex education is available.

**Future
Developments**

2.18 We recognise that even with the implementation of our recommendations and with the position of single sex provision being safeguarded, there may still be some sections of certain ethnic minority communities who, primarily for reasons of religious conviction, will feel that in order to meet their children's educational needs fully, they need to establish their own voluntary aided schools. As we have emphasised, as the law stands at present, they would have every right to do so. Whilst we hope that the communities who may currently be considering such moves will consider carefully both the points made in this chapter and the message of this report, we trust that if they establish such schools, some of the misgivings we have expressed here will prove to be unfounded and that these schools will provide an education comparable to that offered elsewhere in the maintained system and would adequately prepare pupils for our multicultural society. We hope that in any case, in the interests of multi-racial harmony, all concerned in education will be prepared to adopt a positive and encouraging attitude to such schools and to offer any support and guidance which may help them to succeed. We would also add that if the recommendations which we have made are not implemented effectively and the overall ethos and approach of schools towards the needs of ethnic minority pupils does not change radically, then ethnic minority communities would have considerable justification for the belief that separate schools would offer the only means of meeting their needs.

**Wider
Implications**

2.19 We realise that some of our conclusions about the desirability of denominational voluntary aided schools for Muslims or other groups, by extension seriously call into question the long established dual system of educational provision in this country and particularly the role of the Churches in the provision of education. It is clearly not within our terms of reference to consider and reach a decision on such a fundamental and sensitive question, which has always evoked fervent and passionate views on all sides. Nevertheless, we feel that it is important to acknowledge the real and far-reaching changes which have taken place in the nature of British society particularly in recent years. We believe therefore that the time has come for the DES, in consultation with religious and educational bodies, to consider the relevant provisions of the 1944 Act to see whether or not alterations are required in a society that is now very different.[43]

3. The concerns of the West Indian Community

3.1 Before leaving the issue of "separate" schools we feel we should also comment briefly on a further dimension of the desire by some ethnic minority communities to establish their own schools which, whilst not deriving from essentially religious principles, can also be seen as arising from a particular community's concern about the extent to which existing

514

schools are willing or able to cater for their children's needs: the calls from some West Indians for "Black" schools.

Calls for "Black" Schools

3.2   Calls for "Black" schools can be seen to date back to the late 1960s and early 1970s coinciding with the discussion at that time of the possible need for "Black Studies" courses within the curriculum to enhance the self image of West Indian pupils – see paragraph 3.3.4 of Chapter Four. Some West Indian parents groups and certain leading West Indian educationalists have continued to believe that the only way in which West Indian children can hope to succeed in educational terms is through attending separate "Black" schools since they regard existing schools as irremediably racist and dismiss any moves towards developing multicultural education as merely cosmetic and as in no way tackling the fundamental inequalities and injustices inherent in the system. Advocates of "Black" schools thus see them as the only hope of West Indian children escaping from the "culture of failure". This viewpoint was expressed in the following terms, by a leading member of a West Indian parents association in London who was quoted in evidence to us:

"Multicultural education was continuing to fail Black children and could no longer be expected to achieve genuine equality of opportunity. . . The prospects of Black children were being bargained away while education authorities tinkered with the problem by setting up committees and sending teachers on courses which created a false impression that real progress was being made . . .

---

[43]The following members have dissented from the line taken on this issue: Mr. M. A. Khan-Cheema, Dr. F. S. Hashmi, Mr. T. Carter, Ms. Y. Collymore, Mr. C. G. Duncan and Mr. D. Wong. They have accordingly prepared the following statement:

The right of ethnic minority communities to establish voluntary aided schools is firmly enshrined in British Law.

We believe that it is unjust at the present time not to recommend that positive assistance should be given to ethnic minority communities who wish to establish voluntary aided schools in accordance with the 1944 Education Act.

We recognise the arguments against "separate" schools: that they would not *necessarily* address the underlying concerns of ethnic minority communities for example, and that they might increase the very rejection and marginalisation which the communities are seeking to overcome.

We note at the same time the overwhelming evidence submitted to the Committee, particularly by Muslims, that voluntary aided schools for ethnic minority communities should be established.

We acknowledge that the concerns of ethnic minority communities would, to an extent, be met by LEA provisions of more single-sex schools, and more especially and more significantly, by vigorous and immediate measures, in schools, in LEAs, and at the DES, to implement "Edcuation for All", as outlined in the main body of this report.

If and when Education for All is a reality there will be no need for separate schools. This is no reason however, for not considering the case for such schools at the present time.

On the contrary, an emphasis on an ideal future may be an excuse for inaction in the present, and for failure to meet immediate needs.

It may be impossible to make immediate and valuable progress towards Education for All if the case for voluntary aided schools is merely struck from the agenda.

Finally, we emphasise that a number of separate schools would provide invaluable experience and evidence in the long journey towards the goal of Education for All which all members of the Committee seek.

She called for more all Black and majority Black schools . . . "let us remove the myth that you are doing anything for us" she told a teacher who spoke up against such segregation, "You look after your own, but we are denied that opportunity.""

We have discussed earlier in this report the ways in which we believe the West Indian community has been particularly affected by the racism and rejection which they have faced from the majority community. The resulting alienation has clearly fostered the view that the only way in which the West Indian community can shield its youngsters from racism and its manifestations, both overt and covert, and can instil in them an understanding and pride in their ethnic origins and above all can ensure that they will get a "fair deal" from the education system, is to take that system into their own hands. This reaction can be seen as understandable perhaps when the West Indian community sees so many of its children failing to fulfil their true potential and regards the efforts of schools to remedy this as being little more than tinkering, and of little avail.

3.3   In seeking to show that "Black" schools are not only a feasible proposition but can also be successful in practice, advocates of this way forward have tended to cite the Seventh Day Adventist School which was established in North London in 1979 and which is almost exclusively black in its pupil and teacher make up. Whilst this is an interesting development it is important to bear in mind the obvious risks in generalising from the experience of one school, relatively recently established and which above all is wholly outside the maintained system and has a very selective intake. It is also important to recognise that, as our evidence from the West Indian community has shown, only a small, albeit vociferous, minority of West Indians are in favour of the establishment of "Black" schools, and what pressure there is has not up to now found expression in any firm proposals being made at local or national level in relation to named schools as has been the case with the Asian community.

Main Objectives

3.4   The three main objectives of "Black" schools advanced by their proponents, which in many respects mirror the concerns more latterly expressed by the Asian community, can be summarised as follows:

- to confirm the youngsters in their ethnic identity though broadening the curriculum, for example, to encompass literature by black authors, and to ensure that the history and geography syllabuses present a true and balanced picture of the role and contribution made by black people, both past and present, to this country and to their countries of origin;

- through the employment of staff consisting wholly or at least

516

predominantly of black teachers not only to provide West Indian youngsters with role models of successful black professionals thus enhancing their self image and motivation, but also thereby to ensure that the teachers have some knowledge and understanding of the pupils' ethnic background coupled with personal appreciation of and insight into the experience of racism in our society;

- to protect West Indian youngers from the traumatic experience of racism, both intentional and unintentional, which they may currently face in existing schools, and to prepare them for life in a society in which racism has a profound influence.

Our Concerns 3.5 As with the calls from sections of the Asian community for "separate" schools, we believe that the pressure for "Black" schools cannot be seen as offering a positive way forward in the interests of individual West Indian pupils or indeed the West Indian community as a whole, and the concerns which have been put forward to support the case for their establishment cannot in fact be seen to justify their development. We believe that if the recommendations which we have made in this report for the development of "Education for All' are acted upon, the majority of the concerns of the West Indian community which lie behind the calls for "Black" schools will in fact be allayed. If however our recommendations for broadening the curriculum of all schools and for combating racism within the education system are *not* acted upon, it seems to us likely that increasing numbers of parents of West Indian origin and their children in turn will see "Black" schools as offering the only prospect of receiving what they would regard as a good education. Of even greater concern to us, since it is a far less obvious trend but nevertheless manifests an oblique and insidiously divisive form of racism, is the risk that members of the majority community who may grudgingly tolerate the presence of ethnic minorities in this country may find the prospect of separate "Black" schools attractive as a means of "removing" a group of ethnic minority pupils, who are seen as themselves the cause of problems, from the schools which their own children are attending thus in their view preserving what they would regard as the traditional standards of British education. Just as in the South African situation the establishment of separate development, at least in terms of education, could be presented as the most enlightened way forward. If such a tide of opinion in the majority community were to coincide with the growing pressure from the West Indian community which we have envisaged and "Black" schools were thus to become a reality, we believe that the fragmentation of the education system on racial lines in this way would strongly militate against the harmonious pluralist society for which we have argued.

517

III. Main conclusions and recommendations

Religious Education

- We are in favour of a non denominational and undogmatic approach to religious education as the best and indeed the only means of enabling all pupils, from whatever religious background, to understand the nature of religious belief, the religious dimension of human experience and the plurality of faiths in contemporary Britain; to appreciate the diverse and sometimes conflicting values involved and thus to determine and justify their own religious position (Paragraph 2.11);

- We support the use of both visits and outside speakers from different faiths to illustrate aspects of religious education but stress the need for careful preparation and sensitivity in using such "living resources" (Paragraph 3.18);

- It is important that by the time all children leave their primary schools they should be aware that there are a range of different "living" faiths in this society. Religious education at this level should be concerned with laying the foundations to enable children to develop attitudes towards all faiths and belief systems based on appreciation, interest and respect (Paragraph 3.22);

- The development of religious education at primary level, especially with regard to broadening the syllabus to encompass a multi-faith perspective, can be facilitated by the designation of a teacher to coordinate work in this field (Paragraph 3.23);

- We believe that religious education can play a central role in preparing all pupils for life in today's multi-racial Britain, and can also lead them to a greater understanding of the diversity of the global community (Paragraph 5.1);

- Religious education can also contribute towards challenging and countering the influence of racism in our society (Paragraph 5.1);

- There should be no conflict between the role of the schools in providing religious *education* and the role of community institutions in providing religious *instruction* (Paragraph 5.2);

- Given the multiplicity of beliefs now present in society, it is not surprising that we have received much evidence about the difficulties generated by the requirement in the 1944 Act for a daily act of collective worship and the provision of a particular form of religious education.

We therefore believe that the Government, in consultation with religious and educational bodies, should look afresh at the relevant provisions of the Act to see whether alterations are called for after an interval of 40 years. (Paragraph 5.3 and 5.5);

The "Separate" Schools Debate

- The right of ethnic minority communities to seek to establish their own voluntary aided schools is firmly enshrined in law (Paragraph 1.2);

- We believe that the demand to exercise this right would be much diminished if the policies for "Education for All" which we have advocated in this report are adopted (Paragraph 2.11);

- We do not believe that a situation in which groups of children are taught exclusively by teachers of the same ethnic group is desirable from the point of view of the children, the minority community or society as a whole. We are not therefore convinced that "separate" schools can be supported on these grounds (Paragraph 2.12);

- The establishment of "separate" schools would fail to tackle many of the underlying concerns of the communities and might exacerbate the very feelings of rejection which they are seeking to overcome (Paragraph 2.12);

- Where there is parental concern about the education of girls, existing co-educational schools with multi-racial pupil populations could do more to ensure that in certain specific areas separate provision is offered on a single sex basis as appropriate in the schools' activities (Paragraph 2.15);

- For some ethnic minority parents the demise of single sex provision may mean that there is no acceptable environment for the education of their daughters. We hope that LEAs with multi-racial pupil populations will consider carefully the value of retaining an option of single sex education as part of their secondary school provision and that the Secretary of State will also be sensitive to the wide ramifications of any decisions he may make on proposals which lead to the loss of single sex provision in multi racial areas. In cases where an LEA either no longer provides for single sex education at all, or make only limited provision, we hope that the possibility of establishing or re-establishing single sex schools will be given serious consideration (Paragraph 2.15);

- Far more can and should be done by schools to respond to the

519

"pastoral" needs of Muslim pupils, to ensure that there is a real respect and understanding by both teachers and parents of each other's concerns and that the demands of the school place no child in fundamental conflict with the requirements of his faith (Paragraph 2.16);

- As we have observed earlier, the right of communities to seek to establish their own voluntary aided schools is firmly enshrined in the law. At the same time we do not believe that such "separate" schools would be in the long term interest of the ethnic minority communities. This dilemma leads us to recommend (but see note of dissent on page 361) that the Government, in consultation with religious and educational bodies, should consider the relevant provisions of the 1944 Act, to see whether or not alterations are required in a society that is now very different. (Paragraph 2.19);

- Although we fully understand the reasons underlying the desire for separate "Black" schools we believe that, in the long term they are unlikely to offer the best way forward for individual West Indian pupils or indeed for the West Indian comunity as a whole. On the contrary we believe that if the recommendations of this Report are acted upon, most of the concerns of the West Indian community which lie behind the calls for "Black" schools will be allayed (Pargraph 3.5).

ANNEX A

Extracts from the Education Act 1944

General provisions as to religious education in county and in voluntary schools

Religious Education in County and Voluntary Schools.

25. (1) Subject to the provisions of this section, the school day in every county school and in every voluntary school shall begin with collective worship on the part of all pupils in attendance at the school, and the arrangements made therefor shall provide for a single act of worship attended by all such pupils unless, in the opinion of the local education authority or, in the case of a voluntary school, of the managers or governors thereof, the school premises are such as to make it impracticable to assemble them for that purpose.

(2) Subject to the provisions of this section, religious instruction shall be given in every county school and in every voluntary school.

(3) It shall not be required, as a condition of any pupil attending any county school or any voluntary school, that he shall attend or abstain from attending any Sunday school or any place of religious worship.

(4) If the parent of any pupil in attendance at any county school or any voluntary school requests that he be wholly or partly excused from attendance at religious worship in the school, or from attendance at religious instruction in the school, or from attendance at both religious worship and religious instruction in the school, then, until the request is withdrawn, the pupil shall be excused from such attendance accordingly.

(5) Where any pupil has been wholly or partly excused from attendance at religious worship or instruction in any school in accordance with the provisions of this section, and the local education authority are satisfied:—

(a) that the parent of the pupil desires him to receive religious instruction of a kind which is not provided in the school during the periods during which he is excused from such attendance;

(b) that the pupil cannot with reasonable convenience be sent to another county or voluntary school where religious instruction of the kind desired by the parent is provided; and

(c) that arrangements have been made for him to receive religious instruction during school hours elsewhere,

the pupil may be withdrawn from the school during such periods as are reasonably necessary for the pupose of enabling him to receive religious instruction in accordance with the arrangements:

Provided that the pupil shall not be so withdrawn unless the local education authority are satisfied that the arrangements are such as will not interfere with the attendance of the pupil at school on any day except at the beginning or end of the school session on that day.

(6) No directions shall be given by the local education authority as to the secular instruction to be given to pupils in attendance at a voluntary school so as to interfere with the provision of reasonable facilities for religious

instruction in the school during school hours; and no such direction shall be given so as to prevent a pupil from receiving religious instruction in accordance with the provisions of this section during the hours normally set apart for that purpose, unless arrangements are made whereby the pupil shall receive such instruction in the school at some other time.

(7)   Where the parent of any pupil who is a boarder at a county school or a voluntary school requests that the pupil be permitted to attend worship in accordance with the tenets of a particular religious denomination on Sundays or other days exclusively set apart for religious observance by the religious body to which his parent belongs, or to receive religious instruction in accordance with such tenets outside school hours, the managers or governors of the school shall make arrangements for affording to the pupils reasonable opportunities for so doing and such arrangements may provide for affording facilities for such worship or instruction on the school premises, so however that such arrangements shall not entail expenditure by the local education authority.

Special provisions as to religious education in county schools.

26.   Subject as hereinafter provided, the collective worship required by subsection (I) of the last foregoing section shall not, in any county school, be distinctive of any particular religious denomination, and the religious instruction given to any pupils in attendance at a county school in conformity with the requirements of subsection (2) of the said section shall be given in accordance with an agreed syllabus adopted for the school or for those pupils and shall not include any catechism or formulary which is distinctive of any particular religious denomination:

Provided that, where a county secondary school is so situated that arrangements cannot conveniently be made for the withdrawal of pupils from the school in accordance with the provisions of this Act to receive religious instruction elsewhere, then, if the local education authority are satisfied:—

(a)   that the parents of pupils in attendance at the school desire them to receive religious instruction in the school in accordance with the tenets of a particular religious denomination; and

(b)   the satisfactory arrangements have been made for the provision of such instruction to those pupils in the school and for securing that the cost of providing such instruction to those pupils in the school will not fall upon the authority;

the authority shall, unless they are satisfied that owing to any special circumstances it would be unreasonable so to do, provide facilities for the carrying out of those arrangements

Special provisions as to religious education in controlled schools.

27.   (1)   Where the parents of any pupils in attendance at a controlled school request that they may receive religious instruction in accordance with the provisions of the trust deed relating to the school, or where provision for that purpose is not made by such a deed in accordance with the practice observed in the school before it became a controlled school, the foundation managers or foundation governors shall, unless they are satisfied that owing to special circumstances it would be unreasonable so to do, make arrangements for securing that such religious instruction is given to those pupils at the school during not more than two periods in each week.

(2)   Without prejudice to the duty to make such arrangements as aforesaid whatever the number of the teaching staff of the school, where the number of the teaching staff of a controlled school exceeds two the teaching staff shall include persons (hereinafter referred to as 'reserved teachers') selected for their fitness and competence to give such religious instruction as is required to be given under such arrangements and specifically appointed to do so:

Provided that the number of reserved teachers in any controlled school shall not exceed one-fifth of the number of the teaching staff of the school including the head teacher, so, however, that where the number of the teaching staff is not a multiple of five it shall be treated for the purposes of this subsection as if it were the next higher multiple thereof.

(3)   The head teacher of a controlled school shall not, while holding that position, be a reserved teacher, but before appointing any person to be the head teacher of such a school the local education authority shall inform the managers or governors of the school as to the person whom they propose to appoint and shall consider any representations made by the managers or governors with respect to the proposed appointment.

(4)   Where the local education authority propose to appoint any person to be a reserved teacher in a controlled school, the authority shall consult the foundation managers or foundation governors of the school, and, unless the said managers or governors are satisfied as to that person's fitness and competence to give such religious instruction as is required in pursuance of such arrangments as aforesaid the authority shall not appoint that person to be a reserved teacher.

(5)   If the foundation managers or foundation governors of a controlled school are of opinion that any reserved teacher has failed to give such religious instruction as aforesaid efficiently and suitably, they may require the authority to dismiss him from employment as a reserved teacher in the school.

(6)   Subject to any arrangement made under sub-section (1) of this section, the religious instruction given to the pupils in attendance at a controlled school shall be given in accordance with an agreed syllabus adopted for the school or for those pupils.

Special provisions as to religious education in aided schools and in special agreement schools.

28.   (1)   The religious instruction given to the pupils in attendance at an aided school or at a special agreement school shall be under the control of the managers or governors of the school and shall be in accordance with any provisions of the trust deed relating to the school, or, where provision for that purpose is not made by such a deed, in accordance with the practice observed in the school before it became a voluntary school;

Provided that where the parents of pupils in attendance at the school desire them to receive religious instruction in accordance with any agreed syllabus adopted by the local education authority and cannot with reasonable convenience cause those pupils to attend any school at which that syllabus is in use, then, unless the authority are satisfied that owing to any special circumstances it would be unreasonable so to do, arrangements shall be made for religious instruction in accordance with that syllabus to be given to those pupils in the school during the times set apart for the giving of religious instruction therein, and such arrangements shall be made by the managers or governors of the school, so, however, that if the local education authority are satisfied that the managers or governors are unwilling to make such arrangements, the arrangements shall be made by the authority.

(2)   If a teacher appointed to give in an aided school religious instruction, other than instruction in accordance with an agreed syllabus, fails to give such instruction efficiently and suitably, he may be dismissed on that ground by the managers or governors of the school without the consent of the local education authority.

(3)   Where the special agreement made with respect to any special agreement school provides for the employment of reserved teachers, the local education authority shall, when they propose to appoint any person to be such a teacher in the school, consult the foundation managers or foundation governors of the school, and unless the said managers or governors are satisifed as to that person's fitness and competence to give such religious instruction as aforesaid, the authority shall not appoint that person to be such a teacher.

(4)   If the foundation managers or foundation governors of a special agreement school are of opinion that any such reserved teacher as aforesaid has failed to give, efficiently and suitably, such religious instruction as he was appointed to give, they may require the authority to dismiss him from employment as a reserved teacher in the school.

29.   (1)   The provisions of the Fifth Schedule to this Act shall have effect with respect to the preparation, adoption, and reconsideration, of an agreed syllabus of religious instruction.

Provisions as to religious instruction in accordance with agreed syllabus.

(2)   A local education authority shall have power to constitute a standing advisory council on religious education to advise the authority upon matters connected with religious instruction to be given in accordance with an agreed syllabus and, in particular, as to methods of teaching, the choice of books, and the provision of lectures for teachers.

(3)   The method of appointment of the members of any council constituted under the last foregoing subsection and the term of office and conditions of retirement of the members thereof shall be such as may be determined by the local education authority.

(4)   A local education authority shall have regard to any unanimous recommendations which may be made to them by any conference convened in accordance with the provisions of the said Fifth Schedule with respect to the expediency of constituting such an advisory council as aforesaid or with respect to the method by which the terms and conditions upon which members of any such council should be appointed.

Saving as to position of teachers

30.   Subject as hereinafter provided, no person shall be disqualified by reason of his religious opinions, or of his attending or omitting to attend religious worship, from being a teacher in a county school or in any voluntary school, or from being otherwise employed for the purposes of such a school; and no teacher in any such school shall be required to give religious instruction or receive any less emolument or be deprived of, or disqualified for any promotion or other advantage by reason of the fact that he does or does not give religious instruction or by reason of his religious opinions or of his attending or omitting to attend religious worship:

Provided that, save insofar as they require that a teacher shall not receive any less emolument or be deprived of, or disqualified for, any promotion or other advantage by reason of the fact that he gives religious instruction or by reason of his religious opinions or of his attending religious worship, the provisions of this section shall not apply with respect to a teacher in an aided school or with respect to a reserved teacher in any controlled school or special agreement school.

FIFTH SCHEDULE

Procedure for preparing and bringing into operation an agreed syllabus of religious instruction

(1)   For the purpose of preparing any syllabus of religious instruction to be adopted by a local education authority, the authority shall cause to be convened a conference constituted in accordance with the provisions of this Schedule.

(2)   For the purpose of constituting such a conference as aforesaid, the local education authority shall appoint constituent bodies (hereinafter referred to as "committeees") consisting of persons representing respectively—

(a)   such religious denominations as, in the opinion of the authority, ought, having regard to the circumstances of the area, to be represented;

(b)   except in the case of an area in Wales or Monmouthshire, the Church of England;

(c)   such associations representing teachers as, in the opinion of the authority, ought, having regard to the circumstances of the area, to be represented; and

(d)   the authority:

Provided that where a committee is appointed consisting of persons representing the Church of England, the committee of persons appointed to represent other religious denominations shall not include persons appointed to represent that Church.

(3)   Before appointing a person to represent any denomination or associations as a member of any such committee, a local education authority shall take all reasonable steps to assure themselves that he is representative thereof, but no proceedings under this Schedule shall be invalidated on the ground that a member of such a committee did not represent the denomination or associations which he was appointed to represent unless it is shown that the local education authority failed to take such steps as aforesaid.

(4)   A person so appointed may resign his membership of any such committee or may be withdrawn therefrom by the local education authority if in the opinion of the authority he ceases to be representative of the religious denomination or association which he was appointed to represent, or of the authority, as the case may be; and where a vacancy occurs among the persons so appointed the authority shall fill the vacancy in like manner as they made the original appointment.

(5)   The conference shall consist of the committees aforesaid and it shall be the duty of the conference to seek unanimous agreement upon a syllabus of religious instruction to be recommended for adoption by the local education authority.

(6)   Where the local education authority propose to adopt more than one syllabus of religious instruction for use in schools maintained by them, the authority shall inform the conference as to the schools in which, or in the case of a syllabus intended to be used for certain pupils only, the class or

description of pupils for which, the syllabus to be prepared by the conference is to be used.

(7) Any sub-committee appointed by the conference shall include at least one member of each of the committees constituting the conference.

(8) Upon any question to be decided by the conference or by any sub-committee thereof one vote only shall be given for each of the committees constituting the conference.

(9) If the conference unanimously recommend any syllabus of religious instruction, the authority may adopt it for use in the schools for which, or for the class or description of pupil for which, it was prepared.

(10) If the authority report to the Minister that the conference are unable to reach unanimous agreement as aforesaid, or if it appears to the Minister that an authority have failed to adopt any syllabus unanimously recommended to them by the conference, the Minister shall appoint to prepare a syllabus of religious instruction a body of persons having experience in religious instruction which shall, so far as is practicable, be of the like representative character as is required by paragraph 2 of this Schedule in the case of a conference.

(11) The body of persons appointed:—

(a) shall give to the authority, the conference, and every committee constituting the conference, an opportunity of making representations to it, but, save as aforesaid, may conduct the proceedings in such manner as it thinks fit;

(b) shall, after considering any such representations made to it, prepare a syllabus of religious instruction;

(c) shall transmit a copy of the said syllabus to the authority and to the Minister, and as from such date as the Minister may direct, the syllabus so prepared shall be deemed to be the agreed syllabus adopted for use in the schools for which, or for the class or description of pupils for which, it was prepared until a further syllabus is prepared for use in those schools, or for pupils of that class or description, in accordance with the provisions of this Schedule.

(12) Whenever a local education authority are of opinion (whether upon representations made to them or otherwise) that any agreed syllabus for the time being adopted by them ought to be reconsidered, the authority shall cause to be convened for that purpose a conference constituted in accordance with the provisions of this Schedule. If the conference convened for the reconsideration of any syllabus unanimously recommend that the existing syllabus should continue to be the agreed syllabus or that a new syllabus should be adopted in substitution therefor, the authority may give effect to the recommendation of the conference, but if the authority report to the Minister that the conference are unable to reach unanimous agreement, or if it appears to the Minister that the authority have failed to give effect to the unanimous recommendation of the conference, the Minister shall proceed in accordance with the provisions of paragraph 10 of this Schedule, and paragraph 11 thereof shall apply accordingly.

ANNEX B

Extract from Religious Heritage and Personal Quest — Guidelines for Religious Education – Berkshire LEA 1982

THE AIMS OF RELIGIOUS EDUCATION

Religious Education aims:

– to help pupils understand religious beliefs, practices and insights, in order that they may form their own beliefs and judgments, and their own allegiances and commitments.

OBJECTIVES

ATTITUDES

Curiosity

Pupils should be developing an interest in religious beliefs and practices, and in the main questions and issues with which religions are concerned.

Open-mindedness

Pupils should be developing a preliminary attitude of respect for religious beliefs and practices, and should be ready to change their ideas and judgments as they learn more.

Critical Mind

Pupils should be developing an inclination to examine ideas about religion critically, and to be on their guard against bias, indoctrination, superstition and falsehood.

Tolerance

Pupils should be developing a willingness to maintain and protect the legal right of religious believers to practice their religion, and also the rights of people not to practise a religion.

Self-Confidence

Pupils should be developing confidence in their own capacity to reflect on religious questions, and confidence in their own family and cultural background.

Consideration

Pupils should be developing consideration for other people – each other in school and in friendships, teachers and other adults, their families, and groups and individuals in society at large.

Appreciation

Pupils should be developing a readiness to find religious ideas and practices of value to themselves, as they seek to understand their own experience of life.

Commitment

Pupils should be developing a readiness to identify themselves with a particular religious tradition or philosophy of life, and to explain their views in argument and debate.

SKILLS

Enquiry

Pupils should be developing the ability to find and record information about religion from books of various kinds, including the Bible and other sacred writings, and from audio-visual materials; and they should be able to listen to, and put relevant questions to, religious believers about their faith and practice.

Expression

Pupils should be developing the ability to describe and explain religious ideas and practices, and their own personal views and feelings about religion, in a variety of ways – straightforward written prose, of course, also orally in discussion and conversation, and in poetry, painting, drama, dance and music.

Empathy

Pupils should be developing the ability to imagine the feelings of religious believers, including feelings to do with awe, worship, repentance and grace, and should be able to see events and situations from the point of view of a religious believer.

Interpretation

Pupils should be developing the ability to recognise metaphors and symbols when they are studying religion, and should be able to explain their significance.

Reasoning

Pupils should be developing the ability to compare and contrast religious ideas and practices, to marshal arguments, and to explain their own views with sound reasons and evidence.

Meditation

Pupils should be developing the ability to use some of the approaches to meditation and prayer which are commended in devotional teachings.

KNOWLEDGE

1. Stories and Events

1.1   Describing: Pupils should be developing the ability to describe the main historical and symbolic stories in the Bible, and in the sacred writings of other world religions.

Examples include the creation stories in the Bible and creation stories in other world religions; Noah, Abraham, Moses, the principal kings and prophets of the Old Testament; the life of Jesus; Paul and the early church; the life of Muhammad; Guatama Buddha; Guru Nanak; stories in the sacred scriptures of the Hindus.

1.2   Understanding: Pupils should be developing the ability to explain the claims and insights which religious narratives and stories express for believers.

1.3   Responding: Pupils should be developing the ability to form their own views about religious stories.

2. Festivals and Ceremonies

2.1 Describing: Pupils should be developing the ability to describe the main procedures, customs and ceremonies associated with religious festivals and worship.

Examples include Christmas, Easter, Whitsun, Harvest; ceremonies associated with birth, marriage and death; sacraments; Passover; Eid, Ramadan; Divali; Janam-Ashtmi; procedures and customs at the chapel, church, gurdwara, mosque, shrine, synagogue, temple.

2.2 Understanding: Pupils should be developing the ability to explain the significance which religious festivals and ceremonies have for believers.

2.3 Responding: Pupils should be developing the ability to form their own views about religious festivals and ceremonies.

3. Moral Teachings

3.1 Describing: Pupils should be developing the ability to describe the moral teachings of Christianity and of other great world religions, as outlined in precepts and commandments, and in parables and other stories.

Examples include the Ten Commandments and the Sermon on the Mount; the work of great social reformers; morality in personal relationships; family and marriage; truthfulness, consideration, fairness; love; questions of social justice and community relations; peace and law; care of the environment.

3.2 Understanding: Pupils should be developing the ability to explain how religious believers approach moral issues and dilemmas in the everyday life of individuals and families, and in contemporary society at local, national and international levels.

3.3 Responding : Pupils should be developing the ability to form and apply their own views about moral teachings.

4. Experience and Faith

4.1 Describing: Pupils should be developing the ability to describe the personal experience which believers have of God.

Examples include the religious experience of Abraham, Moses, Jesus, Paul; of the founders of other world religions; of ordinary religious believers over the centuries; the ways in which religious experience is expressed in metaphors, poetry, painting, music.

4.2 Understanding: Pupils should be developing the ability to explain the consequences and implications of religious experience and faith for believers in their daily lives.

4.3 Responding: Pupils should be developing the ability to form and apply their own beliefs, experience and faith.

5. Culture and Organisation

5.1 Describing: Pupils should be developing the ability to describe the historical development of religious traditions; the different kinds of social organisation which religions have adopted; and the art, literature, music and architecture which religions have inspired.

Examples include European art and architecture in the Middle Ages; the Reformation; twentieth century writers and artists; the architecture of local churches and other local religious buildings; the various ways in which religious life is organised; the role of priests, rabbis, imams; monasteries and other religious communities; customs associated with food and clothing.

5.2   Understanding: Pupils should be developing the ability to explain the significance of religious history and culture for believers, and the influence which religion has exerted, and continues to exert, on social and cultural life in general, both in this country and throughout the world.

5.3   Responding: Pupils should be developing the ability to form and express their own views about religious culture and history.

6.   Concepts and Beliefs

6.1   Describing: Pupils should be developing the ability to describe the main beliefs about God and about human nature and destiny which have been developed in the world's religious traditions.

Examples include the main beliefs in the Bible, Torah, Qur'an, Guru Granth, Bhagavad Gita; creation, incarnation, eternal life, the inspiration of scripture, sin, judgment, forgiveness, grace; the creeds of the churches; karma, nirvana; the Five Pillars of Islam; the Four Noble Truths of Buddhism.

6.2   Understanding: Pupils should be developing the ability to explain the significance which religious doctrines and sacred writings have for believers.

6.3   Responding: Pupils should be developing the ability to form and express their own views about religious concepts and beliefs.

7.   Questions and Concerns

7.1   Describing: Pupils should be developing the ability to describe the main questions about human nature and the human condition, and about the personal identity and purpose in life of individuals, to which religions provide answers or responses.

Examples include the question whether there is a God and whether – more generally – human beings can experience the supernatural; if God exists, what he is like, and what he expects or requires of human beings; why the world contains suffering, death and evil; whether there is life after death; how, if there is no God, human beings can nevertheless live with a sense of meaning and purpose.

7.2   Understanding: Pupils should be developing the ability to explain the significance which philosophical and personal questions about the purpose of life have for religious believers.

7.3   Responding: Pupils should be developing the ability to form and express their own views on religious questions.

ANNEX C

Extract from Evidence from a Primary School setting out its aims of Religious Education and describing a number of projects which had been undertaken

The aim of religious education is to provide children with such a width and depth of religious experience and thinking that they have a thorough background knowledge from which they can draw in their quest for the meaning of life. The teacher's positive and sensitive contribution should, together with the other subjects of the curriculum, provide children with a positive appreciation of the beliefs of the whole community in which they live and prepare them with the sense of values and strength of character needed for responsibility in adult life. Religious Education in the classroom should:

– Link with classroom projects.

– Prepare for or follow from Assembly.

– Connect with special occasions and festivals.

– Result from contact with children e.g. birth, weddings, death, suffering etc.

The following syllabus is intended as general guidance:

JUNIOR

FIRST YEAR – CHILDHOOD AND FAMILY LIFE

A.   CHILDHOOD STORIES

     1.   Christmas (Bethlehem, Shepherds, Wise Men, Visit to Jerusalem at 12, life in Nazareth (Christian).

     2.   Rama (Hindu).

     3.   Muhammad (Muslim).

     4.   Nanak (Sikh).

     5.   Buddha (Buddhist).

B.   RELIGION AND CULTURE IN THE FAMILY LIFE OF PEOPLE

     1.   In England.

     2.   From the West Indies.

     3.   From India.

     4.   From Pakistan and Bangladesh.

     5.   From the Punjab.

     6.   From China.

C. BIBLE STORES CONCERNING CHILDREN AND FAMILY LIFE

Abraham and Isaac (or Ishmail), Jacob and Esau, Joseph, Moses' birth, Samuel's call, David and Goliath, David and Jonathan. Naaman the Leper, Healing of Jairus' daughter, Feeding of 5,000, Jesus welcomes the children, Nobleman's Son, John Mark.

SECOND YEAR – CALL TO SERVICE

A. IN DIFFERENT FAITHS

1. Jesus (Christian).

2. Moses (Jewish).

3. Rama and Sita (Hindu).

4. Muhammad (Muslim).

5. Guru Nanak and Guru Gobind Singh (Sikh).

6. Buddha (Buddhist).

B. BIBLE STORIES

Noah, Abraham, Joseph, Ruth, David, Jonah, Annunciation, John the Baptist, Fisherman, Rich Young Ruler, Zacchaeus, Whit-Sunday, St. Paul's Conversion.

C. OTHER STORIES OF CALLS TO SERVICE

Dr. Barnardo, Father Damien, Albert Schweitzer, Gladys Aylward, Mary Slessor, Rahere.

THIRD YEAR – FESTIVAL AND WAYS OF SERVICE

A. FESTIVALS

Christian, Jewish, Hindu, Muslim, Sikh, Chinese, West Indian.

B. STORIES OF THE FAITHS

1. Christian (Lepers, Bartimaeus, Palsied Man, Mary and Martha, Good Samaritan, Rich Fool, Lost Coin, Lost Son, Peter and the Lame Man, Dorcas).

2. Stories of the Hindus.

3. The Life and Work of Muhammad.

4. The Life and Work of Guru Nanak.

C. OTHER STORIES OF SERVICE

Mother Theresa, Edith Cavell, Florence Nightingale, Wilberforce, Shaftesbury, Father Borelli, Marie Curie, Elizabeth Garrett Anderson, Leonard Cheshire, Elisabeth Fry, An Indian Florence Nightingale, Marcus Garvey.

533

FOURTH YEAR – RELIGIOUS PRACTICE AND STORIES OF COURAGE

A.   RELIGIOUS PRACTICE AND PLACES OF WORSHIP

    1.   Christian belief and the church.

    2.   Jewish belief and the synagogue.

    3.   Hindu belief and the temple.

    4.   Muslim, Five Pillars of Islam, and the Mosque.

    5.   Sikh 5 'Ks' and the Gurdwara.

B.   BIBLE STORIES OF COURAGE

Noah, Moses, Gideon, Samson, Daniel, Elijah, Palm Sunday, Garden of Gethsemane, Trial and Death of Jesus, Resurrection, Walk to Emmaus, Thomas, Ascension, Peter, Stephen, St. Paul at Lystra, St. Paul at Philippi, St. Paul's Shipwreck.

C.   OTHER STORIES OF COURAGE

Joan of Arc, Helen Keller, Captain Scott, the Kon Tiki, Flora MacDonald, Grace Darling.

This same primary school had also undertaken a number of projects in the religious education field and further details, together with some observations by the Head of the background to them are set out below.

ISLAM PROJECT

Suggestions for areas of work:—

    Juniors – 4th year – Mosques (purpose-built and house).
                         Worship (attitudes of prayer etc).
                         Qur'an (arabic, reverence etc).

        3rd year – Geography of Muslim countries, especially Pakistan and Bangladesh.
                         Way of Life in these countries.
                         Way Islam is practised in these countries.

        2nd year – 5 Pillars of Islam.
                        1. Submission to the will of Allah.
                        2. Prayer five times a day.
                        3. Almsgiving.
                        4. Fasting.
                        5. Pilgrimage.

Additional areas	– Festivals (Eid-ul-Fitr, Eid-ul-Adha) Arab stories (genies) – drama. Music and musical instruments. Maths-symmetrical patterns, balance, construction.
Infants	– Homes, food, clothes, stories of Arab countries, Festivals in the family and Mosque.
Time	– About two sessions a week on the project, with Art, craft, stories, descriptive writing involved. Use of Team Teaching.
Visual Aids	– Books (schools, local library and Central Library) Pictures (schools and Reference Library). Slides and Film-strips. Artefacts. Outside Speakers.
Assemblies	– General invitation to Parents. Infants, Juniors (First and last to be about the Festivals).
Visits	– Arrange visit to Regents Park Mosque. Local house Mosque visits can be arranged if required.

HINDU PROJECT

Suggestions for areas of work:—

Junior – 4th year	– India (Social – Economic) Religion (images, rivers, temples, death, re-incarnation, holy men, holy books etc.).
3rd year	– Geography (of whole of India or one area). Way of life in village or town. Dance (Temple, Yoga). Famous people (Ghandi).
2nd year	– Festivals (Durga Puja, Diwali, Holi, Janamashtami, Raksha-Bandham). Family Life – clothes, food, Puja Room.
1st year	– Animals of India. Families. Folk Tales (Rama and Sita).
Infants	– Indian homes, food, clothes, animals, folk tales, family festivals.
Time	– About 2 sessions per week on the project, with Art, Craft; Stories. Descriptive writing involved. Use of Team Teaching.
Visual Aids	– Books (Schools, local library, central library). Pictures (Schools and Reference Library). Film-strips and slides. Artefacts. Outside speakers.

Assemblies	– General invitation to parents for class assemblies.
	Hindu Film-strip for Juniors.
Visits	– To Hindu Temples.
	Home Puja rooms – small groups.

OBSERVATIONS BY THE HEAD RELATING TO THE SCHOOLS'S PROJECT WORK

Our aims in undertaking multicultural work were as follows:

– To help children towards a sympathetic understanding of origins and cultures other than their own.

– To give children a pride in and an identity with their own culture.

– To promote contact with and gain the confidence of parents.

— To enable staff to become more familiar with the backgrounds of the children we teach.

Despite the suspicions of certain parents, we were not attempting to make converts, neither were we expressing value judgements. We found that most of us were very ignorant of other people's faiths and cultures. It was agreed in planning the project to involve the whole school and suggested areas of study were put forward for each age group. A timetable was outlined and various approaches discussed. We talked in detail about resources available including books, filmstrips, tape recordings, artefacts and visiting speakers. The initial reaction of staff was perhaps cautious approval but certain individuals expressed considerable reservations and even apprehension. One detected a certain hesitation, doubts, and fear of causing offence through ignorance. To quote one member of staff – 'One felt inadequate dealing with a subject on which more than half the class were expert'. Another teacher, an infant teacher in her probationary year commented – 'I was very interested and keen that the project should be done but totally ignorant of the subject matter and how it should be treated with this age group'.

I placed a tentative limit of two-hour long sessions as the maximum time that should be spent on the project each week. This was sometimes exceeded but since the spin-offs and extensions into other areas were satisfied, in the event most classes extended their area of study beyond the original intention. The infant classes particularly found the response from the children so encouraging that they attempted far more than they had originally planned. Before embarking on the project I wrote to parents informing them of our intention, stressing our aims and inviting co-operation and help in the form of loans of artefacts particularly. We were inundated with items of interest from pictures of the Ka'ba to articles of clothing, prayer beads and the Qur'an. The whole school was decorated with colourful and attractive work produced by children on the theme of the project and exhibitions were mounted in both Infant and Junior Halls.

We invited the parents to Assemblies – we did six in the course of the project. There were a few parents who raised objections. One spread a rumour among the white parents that we were praying to 'Paki-Gods' and didn't want her children to participate. She tried to raise a petition and march of protest. We managed to persuade her to come to the Assemblies and explained our aims of attempting to promote understanding and gradually she was won over and was eventually elected a parent governor, in which capacity she is continuously supportive of all our work.

ANNEX D

Extracts from Evidence submitted by multi-racial Secondary Schools setting out their aims and objectives of Religious Education

1. **Evidence submitted by a multi-racial Middle School (9-13)**

R E Syllabus

Aims:

   i.   To give children the opportunity to become aware of and to learn about the main religious faiths of the world.

   ii.   To encourage respect and understanding of the main religious faiths of the world.

   iii.   To show how religion forms an integral part of peoples lives.

   iv.   To show how various people and groups of people because of their convictions, religious or otherwise, have through their efforts, actions and lives, attempted to change, mould and improve society.

The religious faiths to be studied will be:

   a. Buddhism

   b. Christianity

   c. Hinduism

   d. Islam

   e. Judaism

   f. Sikhism

The above list has been arranged alphabetically and not in order of importance.

First Year Work 9+
Work in the first year will be involved with the study of **festivals** of the major religions. The actual dates of the various festivals can be obtained from the RE Centre, West London Institute of Higher Education, on a yearly basis. The main festivals to be studied are as follows:

Harvest	Christian
Diwali	Hindu
Halloween	
All Saints Day	Christian
Id-ul-Adha	Muslim
Advent	Christian
Guru Nanak Day	Sikh
Christmas	Christian
Chinese New year	
St Valentine's Day	
St David's Day	Christian
St Patrick's Day	Christian
Easter	Christian
St George's Day	Christian
Pesach	Jewish

537

Vesakha	Buddhist
Shevuot	Jewish
Ramadam	Muslim

If possible these festivals should be studied on or as near to the actual date. The reason for the festival and its custom are the two main areas to be studied.

2nd Year 10+

Topics to be covered

Worship	Modes of and special robes
Customs	of birth, maturity, marriage, death
Food	healthy diets, forbidden foods, ceremonial food, fasting.

Worship will be involved with studying the following:

Eucharist
Liwan
Salat
The Sabbath

Customs:

Christening, Circumcision, Naming.
Bar-Mitzvah, Yagyopavit (Sacred Thread).
Confirmation,
Marriage – Ceremonies
Death – Funerals.

Food:

As above.

3rd Year 11+

Topics:

Myth
Holy Books
Saints
Monasteries
Denominations

Myth will deal mainly with the views of creation of the world as seen through the eyes of the Norse people, early Hindus, Chinese, Jews.

Holy books will include a study of the Bible, the Koran, the Hindu Scriptures and the Guru Granth Sahib.

The Saints to be studied:

St Alban
St Columba
St Aidan
St Jerome

Monastic Life – In brief.
Christian Church – In brief.

ANNEX E

The Establishment of Voluntary Aided Schools: Background ExpldDES

1. A body wishing to establish a voluntary aided school must first discuss their proposal with the local education authority to ensure that it can be accommodated with the Authority's plans for education provision in their area. The approval of the Secretary of State must then be sought in accordance with Section 13 of the Education Act 1980.

2. Section 13 requires the voluntary body to publish notices making public their intentions for a period of two months during which time objections to the proposal may be submitted to the Secretary of State to be taken into account in reaching his decision.

3. In addition the factors which the Secretary of State considers before granting voluntary aided status are (a) that an overall need (basic need) for additional maintained school places exists in the locality concerned; or if there is no overall need, that the LEA might consider taking out of use surplus places in existing schools; (b) that where a voluntary aided school of a particular religious or other application is concerned, a 'denominational' justification for the number of extra places planned can also be shown; (c) that any application in respect of a voluntary school has the support of the maintaining local education authority; (d) that the premises to be used for the school will be of accepted standard, and that the teaching and curriculum will be of a standard and type acceptable to the Secretary of State; (e) that if grant is to be claimed for the provision of premises that the LEA concerned has sufficient within its annual voluntary school capital building allocation to cover the cost of provision. (These conditions are required to ensure that the school premises will be physically and educationally satisfactory; that the school will provide efficient education; and that public expenditure will not be necessarily incurred in the provision and maintenance of school places that would be surplus).

CHAPTER 9

Teacher Education and the Employment of Ethnic Minority Teachers

This Chapter

The conclusions which we have reached and the policies which we have advocated in this report clearly place particular responsibilities on the teaching profession, since teachers are the key figures in the education process, and changes and developments in classroom practice and in the overall ethos of schools depend to a very great degree on the co-operation and support of individual teachers. We have already referred in previous chapters to the implications for teachers of our policies in specific areas such as language, and we have devoted considerable attention to the controversial and complex issue of teachers' attitudes towards ethnic minority pupils, and, more generally, towards the changed and changing nature of British society. In this chapter we look more broadly at the preparation and support available to teachers through their training in relation both to the needs of ethnic minority pupils and the wider issues of cultural diversity. As the Home Affairs Committee observed in their 1981 Report[1]:

> *"Teachers cannot reasonably be blamed for failing ethnic minority children if they have not had access to the sort of initial and in-service training which would enable them to perform more successfully."*

After discussing various aspects of teacher education and training, we then go on to consider the recruitment and role of teachers who are themselves of ethnic minority origin – an issue which was frequently raised in evidence to us.

I Teacher Education

Organisation of Teacher Education

1. Introduction

1.1 Teacher education falls into two broad phases – initial (or pre-service) training, and in-service training, incorporating both the induction training of newly qualified teachers or of teachers new to a school and the various forms of continuing in-service provision available to teachers throughout their careers.

– *Initial Teacher Training* is provided by universities, polytechnics and colleges and institutes of higher education. It comprises three or four year

---

[1] "Racial Disadvantage." Fifth Report of the Home Affairs Committee. HC 424 – I. HMSO. July 1981.

courses leading to the Bachelor of Education (BEd) degree, or one year courses for graduates leading to the Postgraduate Certificate in Education (PGCE). There are a limited number of courses offering concurrent teacher training leading to a BA or BSc degree and a Certificate in Education. Initial teacher training courses offered by public sector institutions (polytechnics and colleges and institutes of higher education) are currently validated by some 14 different validating bodies – over half by the Council for National Academic Awards (CNAA) and the remainder by 13 universities. In addition a number of universities offer their own degree level courses. Each teacher training institution and validating body has developed its own style of teacher training and a wide variety of models has evolved. The overall aim of initial teacher training can however be seen as to provide students with an awareness of the academic and professional basis of the education process and an introduction to teaching skills. On completion of a course of initial training a new teacher should have acquired a sound knowledge of the subject or subjects he or she will teach, and should be equipped with the professional skills and competence to begin a career in teaching with confidence.

– *Induction Training*. Initial training cannot however, nor is it intended to, provide teachers with a once and forever training experience. Nor, because of its generalised nature, can it hope adequately to prepare teachers to cope with every classroom and school situation. For this reason local education authorities and schools, to varying degrees, make arrangements for newly qualified teachers to undergo what is usually referred to as "induction training", intended to provide them with specific information about the school and the locality in which they are to teach and to offer them advice, support and possibly an opportunity for further study. Induction training of this character may well be appropriate for *any* teacher joining a school staff for the first time and not only for newly qualified teachers.

– *In-Service Training* is the umbrella term used to describe the wide variety of further training, as well as induction training, which may be available to practising teachers throughout their careers. It is, in its very nature, much more differentiated than initial training and may be provided not only by teacher training institutions but also by schools themselves and by local education authorities through their advisory staff and teachers' centres, and by subject associations, teacher unions and other bodies. It may be relatively formal and structured leading to "named awards" or may consist simply of short courses, conferences, or workshops provided by institutions or by individual schools. In-service training is intended to be responsive to particular needs and especially to changing circumstances and situations and to promote new developments. It is generally a voluntary undertaking – teachers are not required to participate nor are schools obliged to release teachers to attend daytime courses although career advancement is increasingly dependent upon it.

Thus, as is frequently emphasised, teacher education is an indivisible process which can and should continue throughout a teacher's career.

Changing Nature of the Teaching Force

1.2   The pattern of recruitment of new teachers has altered dramatically over recent years in the face of falling school rolls and constraints on public expenditure. DES figures[2] show the number of newly-qualified teachers obtaining full-time permanent appointments in maintained nursery, primary and secondary schools in England and Wales in 1982 was 9,137 (out of a total teaching force of 414,600) compared with a figure of 19,203 for 1978. Against this background of contraction, considerable emphasis in current discussions on teacher training has been placed on the in-service training available to practising teachers already working in schools. This has been seen as potentially the most effective means of directly influencing classroom practice in the short term, since the number of new entrants to the profession who have just undergone initial training is now considered too small to have any significant impact on the work of schools. Whilst we recognise the force of the argument which has led to this focus on in-service training, we believe that the role of initial training in shaping the attitudes and practices of the teaching force in the longer term must also be fully appreciated.

Academic Standards

1.3   We now consider the contribution which we believe each of the stages of teacher education and training can make to the fundamental reorientation of the education system as a whole to incorporate the genuinely pluralist perspective for which we have argued in this report. We must however preface all of our comments in this chapter about the role of teacher training by emphasising our firm belief in the need to preserve and where necessary enhance the academic standard of the teaching force as a whole – as the Government White Paper on "Teaching Quality"[3] put it:

> *"Good teachers need to have a mastery of the subject matter they teach and the professional skills needed to teach it to children of different ages, ability, aptitudes and backgrounds."*

Overall Context

2.   **Initial Training**

2.1   Over the past decade or so the teacher training system in this country has experienced fundamental and far-reaching changes. The expansion of initial training during the 1960s has been followed by a rapid contraction of provision in response both to falling school rolls and public expenditure

---

[2]DES Statistical Bulletin 14/83. "Teachers in service and teacher vacancies 1982-1983." September 1983.
[3]"Teaching Quality." Cmnd 8836. HMSO. March 1983.

543

constraints – whereas, according to the 1983 White Paper on "Teaching Quality", there were in the early 1970s a total of 180 initial teacher training institutions in the public sector in England and Wales, provision is currently we understand offered in some 62 public sector institutions. Alongside this major structural reorganisation, which has involved the amalgamation, diversification or closure of many institutions, there has also been the demise of the former sub-degree Certificate in Education qualification and the expansion of BEd degree and PGCE courses, often with consequent changes in validation arrangements, as a result of the Government's decision to move towards an all-graduate teaching force. Against the background of these major upheavals, and in view of the confusion which exists as to the precise meaning and objectives of "multicultural" education in schools, it is not entirely surprising that the attempts of the teacher training system over recent years to respond to the multi-racial nature of society can perhaps best be seen as characterised by a confusion of aims and a lack of overall coherence.

Assimilation
2.2   During the early years of large scale immigration when, as we have recalled in Chapter Four, the aim of educational policies in relation to immigrant pupils was assimilation, the response of the teacher training system focussed chiefly on developing in-service courses for teachers in multi-racial schools. At initial training level, work was confined almost exclusively to those teacher training institutions actually located in areas of ethnic minority settlement, some of which began to offer specialist options for interested students dealing with what were regarded as the "problems" presented by ethnic minority pupils. The majority of institutions made no response at all to the arrival of ethnic minority pupils, presumably because, in keeping with the thinking of the time, they believed that the difficulties being experienced in multi-racial schools would be relatively short-lived. Institutions in non-multi-racial areas believed in any case that any broader issues arising from changes in the composition of society were irrelevant to their students. A survey undertaken by the former National Committee for Commonwealth Immigrants in 1966[4] indicated that only 15% of institutions, mostly in areas of ethnic minority settlement, were running or intending to run even optional elements in their courses in the field of "immigrant education".

Integration
2.3   With the development of the integrationist view of ethnic minority needs, which attached greater importance to teachers understanding something of the cultural background of their pupils, albeit still as a basis for their eventual absorption into the majority community, specialist options which sought to cover the "lifestyles" of different ethnic minority groups began to be offered, again primarily by institutions in multi-racial areas, and largely through in-service training. The tendency was to focus

---

[4]Quoted in "The Education of Immigrants." Education Survey 13. HMSO. 1971.

on the cultures and religions of different countries and the "problems" which ethnic minority pupils posed thus possibly reinforcing or even establishing negative stereotypes of ethnic minority pupils which could in fact inhibit a teacher's ability to respond positively to such pupils. Overall, developments were still very limited and in their 1972 study[5] Townsend and Brittan found that less than 1 in 5 probationary primary school teachers and only 1 in 16 probationary secondary teachers felt there had been any specific reference to the education of "immigrant" children in their initial training, and the researchers observed that:

". . . there is a valid argument that not all students will become teachers in multi-racial schools. There is an equally valid argument that all students in colleges of education are expected to become teachers in a multi-racial Britain, but this did not seem to have been reflected in the courses of the probationer teachers in the sample."

Development of Multi-Cultural Education

2.4 As doubts began to be expressed about the desirability of assimilation, some attempts began to be made in the teacher training field in the 1970's to broaden the concept of "ethnic minority needs" to "multicultural education". It began to be recognised that the multi-racial nature of society might be of relevance to *all* teachers and thus *all* teacher training institutions. The National Committee for Commonwealth Immigrants had been very much ahead of the general trend of thinking when it had stated in 1967[6] that:

"No Teacher Training Institutions can now contract out from this problem (the multi-racial society and the education of immigrants) and retain an easy conscience . . . All students should be given the opportunity to study this problem during their training."

The emphasis in this statement on "problems" and the clear reference to optional rather than compulsory provision was however characteristic of the period. The Select Committee on Race Relations and Immigration echoed this forward-looking view, and indeed took it further in their 1969 report[7] in stating that:

"We would like to see every college of education in the country teaching its students something about race relations and the problems of immigrants. To say that there is no need to educate all students about such matters because, as one college has said, "very few of our students go into schools where they are likely to meet mixed classes" is

---

[5]"Organisation in Multi-racial Schools." Townsend and Brittan. NFER. 1972.
[6]Extract from a statement issued by the NCCI after a seminar held in January 1967.
[7]"The Problems of Coloured School-leavers." Report from the Select Committee on Race Relations and Immigration. HMSO 413-I. July 1969.

to miss the point . . . Teachers should be equipped to prepare all their children for life in a multi-racial society."

It is regrettable that after this positive statement of the responsibilities of the teacher training system towards the multi-racial nature of society, the DES, in its 1971 report[8], returned to the restricted perception of the role of teacher training in a multi-racial context as relating to only those students who were likely to teach in multi-racial schools:

". . . the proportion of newly qualified teachers likely to meet substantial numbers of immigrant children in their first teaching posts is small, possibly as low as 15%, and . . . many training establishments . . . are remote from areas of immigrant concentration and cannot easily arrange for their students to have contact with immigrant children during teaching practice or otherwise. Many complex demands are made on the training course and it would be impracticable to attempt to ensure that all newly qualified teachers had received a training which would equip them to take charge of classes including a substantial immigrant population immediately on entering schools."

The 1972 James Report on Teaching Training[9] however took a broader view and stated that:

". . . an understanding of the multicultural nature of society should feature in any general (teacher) education."

– and the Select Committee on Race Relations and Immigration reiterated their earlier line of thinking in their 1973 Report[10] and recommended explicitly that:

"All students on initial or postgraduate courses can and should be made aware that, wherever they teach, they will be doing so in a multicultural society. This should be reflected not so much in special courses but throughout the training."

CRC/ATCDE Report 2.5   1974 saw the publication of a joint report [11] prepared by the then Community Relations Commission and Association of Teachers in Colleges and Departments of Education which went into far greater detail than previous publications in considering the implications for teacher training of "an ethnically and culturally diverse society". This has

---

[8]"The Education of Immigrants." Education Survey 13. HMSO 1971.
[9]Report of the Committee on "Teacher Education and Training." HMSO. 1972.
[10]"Education." Report of the Select Committee on Race Relations and Immigration. HMSO 405-I. July 1973.
[11]"Teacher Education for a Multicultural Society." CRC/ATCDE. June 1974.

remained one of the most important and influential documents in this field up to the present day and its findings have been constantly updated and reiterated by the successors to the original sponsoring organisations – the Commission for Racial Equality (CRE) and the National Association of Teachers in Further and Higher Education (NATFHE). This report changed the terms of the debate quite markedly even in its unequivocal starting point that:

> "What happens to (ethnic minorities) in our schools is crucial to the development of a racially just society. The training of teachers and other professionals should equip them to work towards such a society."

The report also stated clearly the responsibilities which it saw for all teachers, explicitly including those working in "all-white" schools, for re-evaluating and, where appropriate, broadening the curriculum they offered.

> "Wherever students eventually teach, regardless of age range or type of child, they will be involved in making curriculum choices. Therefore, all students need to be given an opportunity to consider carefully the inherent attitudes and assumptions contained in the subject matter they teach and its manner of presentation. Highly ethnocentric and implicitly biased views may be transmitted to children, both in obvious ways such as in relation to history or geography teaching about countries from which migrants have come, and also less directly but nevertheless damagingly through the attitudes communicated by other subject specialists. Such teaching can both confirm prejudiced attitudes in all-white classes and aggravate difficulties of identity and confidence for children from minority groups. On the other hand, the curriculum can provide excellent opportunities for presenting other cultures and highlighting the achievement of all human groups. It is therefore important that teachers become sensitive to this function of the curriculum."

The report concluded in terms that we ourselves would endorse:

> "There is nothing new in asking teachers and teacher-trainers to re-examine their work in the light of social change. What is new, however, is the urgent challenge presented by the recent emergence of a society which contains not only the seeds of racial disharmony but also the potential for immense cultural and human enrichment. This is the situation which schools and colleges have to face. Far too many students are inadequately prepared to cope with it. Unless studies are updated to meet it they will become increasingly irrelevant and anachronistic."

**Research
Reports**

2.6   In their evidence to this Committee, NATFHE, reflecting on developments since the 1974 report, observed that:

> *". . . the original Report was more tempered and sanguine than subsequent trends have justified. Worse, the response by institutions to the Report was extremely disappointing."*

It is clearly difficult to assess the response of teacher training institutions over recent years to the need to prepare all their students at initial level to incorporate a pluralist perspective in their work. Whilst there has not been any wholly reliable or comprehensive recent survey of provision in this respect, there have nevertheless been several studies which have sought to examine the current state of affairs. It may be worthwhile therefore drawing together here the finding of these various studies.

– The HMI Report on "Developments in the BEd Degree Course"[12] published in 1979, based on a study of provision in 3 polytechnics and 12 colleges, identified the educational implications of our multi-racial society as:

> *". . . an important area where treatment had been superficial or non-existent."*

and concluded that:

> *"The compulsory elements of most courses did not . . . bring students towards much awareness of the special needs of certain categories of children, in particular those with a cultural background different from that of the majority."*

– Also in 1979 a national survey, funded by the CRE, was undertaken to investigate "multicultural" aspects of teacher training[13]. Since the full findings of this survey have not as yet been made publicly available we reproduce as Annex A to this chapter a paper describing the main findings. In broad terms this study found that roughly half of the colleges, two thirds of the polytechnics and one third of the universities involved claimed to be making at least some provision to help students to teach in a multicultural context. Not all this provision was on a compulsory basis and some courses were concerned primarily with the "special needs" of ethnic minority pupils.

– During 1979/1980 HMI undertook an inspection exercise of the

---

[12]"Developments in the BEd Degree Course – A Study based in 15 Institutions". HMI Matters for Discussion No. 8. 1979.

[13]"Multicultural Teacher Education in the United Kingdom: a Survey of Courses and other Provisions in British Institutions of Higher Education." Cherrington and Giles. CRE. 1979. Unpublished.

coverage of multicultural issues at initial and in-service level in a sample of 46 out of the (then) 69 public sector teacher training institutions in England. Again, because the findings of this study do not appear to be widely known, we reproduce a paper summarising the findings as Annex B to this chapter. The overall picture revealed by this study in relation to initial training was, in the words of HMI:

"... *not a particularly bright one.*"

21 of the institutions expressed the view that the issues of a pluralist society were not immediately relevant to them, and although 30 of the institutions were found to take "some account" of this aspect of education within the basic compulsory programme of professional training, this contrasted strikingly with the PGCE courses, only three of which had an explicit compulsory element on "multicultural education" and only a further five of which had incorporated a reference to ethnic minority groups in school and society within basic educational or professional studies. HMI expressed the view that:

> "*The fact that a third of all the institutions train BEd students who, like the great majority of PGCE students, need take no account, during their preparation for teaching, of education in a multicultural society must be a matter for concern.*"

– In preparing their evidence for the Home Affairs Committee for its 1981 Report on Racial Disadvantage, the National Union of Teachers (NUT) undertook a survey of all teacher training institutions and in their consequent memorandum[14] reported that:

> "*Only 15 replies out of 67 indicated that all students in training would receive some lectures or other form of input to their course which would give them information relevant to teaching in a multicultural society, and even fewer replies mentioned a compulsory element. It is therefore still possible for many teachers to emerge from their training without having covered the subject at all, though a wide range of optional courses and lectures are provided in various College and University departments.*"

– The 1982 HMI Report on "The New Teacher in School"[15] also offered some relevant information in analysing the views of newly trained teachers in a sample of 294 primary and secondary schools in England and Wales about aspects of their initial training. As the following table, taken from the HMI Report, shows, fewer than half of the teachers in the sample

---

[14]Appendix 20. "Racial Disadvantage." Home Affairs Committee Report. HC 424 – IV. HMSO. July 1981.
[15]"The New Teacher in School." HMI Matters for Discussion No. 15. HMSO. 1982.

considered themselves adequately prepared for teaching children with different cultural backgrounds:

PROBATIONERS' VIEWS ABOUT ASPECTS OF THEIR
INITIAL TRAINING
(Expressed in Percentage of Teachers)

Probationers considered that they were:		Rating*			
		1-2	3	4-5	
Well prepared to teach children with different cultural backgrounds	Primary	29	14	55	
	Secondary	28	18	50	Not prepared
	All	29	16	52	

*In the questionnaires the teachers were asked to rate their views on a scale of 1-5: 1 if the statements in the left-hand column reflected their view and 5 if the statements in the right-hand column reflected their view, with the other markings to reflect views between these two extremes.

– A more recent Government survey[16] has reported that in 1981/1982 some 72% of initial teacher training establishments in the UK included tuition about the particular needs of ethnic minority children in their courses. A further 5% were considering introducing such provision.

– The survey undertaken in 1983 for this Committee by Professor Craft and Dr Atkins on the provision for training teachers of ethnic minority community languages, (see Annex F to Chapter Seven) while reporting a dismal picture in that respect, also found that a large majority of institutions now include work on language repertoire and English language support across the curriculum in their courses.

2.7   Thus, looking at the situation overall, as Dr Richard Willey has put it in a draft report on teacher training[17]:

> "Such limited evidence as is available suggests that many schools and teacher education institutions are responding only slowly to the DES's stated pluralist, multicultural aims; there appears to be growing inconsistency between DES rhetoric and the content of much teacher education."

It must be acknowledged that certain teacher training institutions and some other bodies concerned with teacher training, such as the Council for National Academic Awards, have, in recent years, devoted considerable efforts to reappraising their work in the light of the changing nature of

---

[16]Memorandum on Compliance with Directive 77/486/EC on the Education of the Children of Migrant Workers. DES. March 1983.

[17]"Multicultural Britain: The Preparation of Teachers." Dr R Willey. CRE Advisory Group on Teacher Education. Forthcoming.

British society. But even taking these efforts into account, work in this area is still characterised by a lack of clarity and coherence as to essential aims and objectives.

Dual Themes

2.8 What is perhaps most immediately apparent from this consideration of the various recent studies of the "multicultural" aspects of teacher education, apart from the general paucity of provision, is the continuing confusion of two distinct forms of provision – on the one hand, course provision designed specifically to give student teachers the particular knowledge and skills needed to teach in a multi-racial *school*, and, and, on the other hand, the preparation of all students in initial training for teaching pupils in a multi-racial *society*, irrespective of whether the students concerned will be teaching in an "all-white" or multi-racial school. The confusion of these distinct perceptions of multicultural education, as relating either to the immediate multi-racial situation in a particular school or to the broader multi-racial social context, has of course contributed to much of the misunderstanding and lack of progress in this field up to now. As we have already emphasised, we regard a concern for both these complementary elements as equally crucial to our philosophy of "Education for All". Just as we believe however that rather different approaches to the curriculum will be called for in different schools, so within teacher training, distinct approaches will also be needed to cater for different sets of circumstances. There are nevertheless a number of broad principles which we feel must underlie the development of an appropriate teacher training response to the needs of today's society.

The Task for Teacher Education

2.9 We have already made clear that we see *all* schools having a responsibility to offer their pupils an education which reflects the realities of life in today's multi-racial Britain. We regard "Education for All" as essentially synonymous with a "good" education, since an education which is not based on sound educational principles and which fails to take account of the variety of cultural, religious and linguistic backgrounds which now make up British society, and, more broadly, which fails to incorporate a global perspective, would be anachronistic and would prepare pupils, both those from the various minority and the majority communities, for an unreal world. Similarly a curriculum which does not acknowledge and seek to challenge manifestations of racism at both individual and institutional level, through enhancing pupils' political literacy and particularly their appreciation of how power is exercised, and by whom, in this society, would, in our view constitute a fundamental *mis*-education and would certainly fail to lay the foundations for the kind of genuinely pluralist society which we envisaged at the opening of this report. If a genuine pluralist approach to education is thus justified as desirable and indeed essential on *educational* grounds, then it is clear that in order to be equipped, in professional terms, to offer their pupils a full and balanced education *all* teachers must be given the appropriate

551

knowledge and skills for providing such an education. As Dr Richard Willey has again put it in his draft report:

". . . it is the teachers and teacher educators working in the different curriculum areas who must undertake the type of review which follows from the assumption of a multicultural objective, and who face the complex decisions about detailed objectives and priorities. Teacher trainers in particular have a key role to play; in the forum provided by the courses which they already teach, they can stimulate and lead consideration of the implications of cultural pluralism for existing teaching strategies and content . . . The objective of a multicultural society is in the process of closer definition . . . Teachers have a central part to play in this process and they must be given the opportunities to play it. If they are not, not only will minority ethnic and cultural groups become increasingly disillusioned with an education system which is failing to respond adequately to their presence, but there will be a widening gap between society's theoretical aspirations and the reality of what is happening in schools."

2.10   The 1983 HMI discussion paper on Initial Training[18] stressed that the initial training of *all* student teachers should give them an awareness and understanding of the broader context of their work and the responsibility of schools in catering for the aspirations and expectations of society at large:

"No teacher should lack understanding of the purposes of the curriculum and its relationship to the wider society; nor should a teacher lack understanding of the ways in which society and schools are inter-related, ways in which the background of pupils' lives influence what they bring to their learning, and the expectations which they, their families and their teachers have of education. The student's course of training should enable him to place his work within this broader framework of educational meaning and purpose."

We endorse this view of the wider responsibilities of the individual teacher, beyond the immediate concerns of his or her school and subject specialism. *All* student teachers have a responsibility to understand and appreciate the multi-racial social context in which they will be teaching and to prepare their pupils for life in a pluralist society. As the Head of one secondary school put it in a discussion paper prepared for our Conference in November 1981:

"We (teachers) accept the responsibility of fulfilling society's demands

---

[18]"Teaching in Schools: The Content of Initial Training." AN HMI discussion paper. January 1983.

on us, without accepting responsibility for the nature of those demands. We have to accept that society is the product of the education system and we are the custodians of the future. What we are doing in schools today will be reflected in the society of tomorrow. We cannot wait for the world outside school to change, the change begins with us. Tomorrow's multicultural Britain is the pupils we have in school now. The future will be what our pupils make it, and we give them the tools."

The following draft policy statement, which was submitted to us in evidence from one teacher training institution, sets out how one institution envisaged the task for initial teacher training in relation to *all* student teachers and we reproduce it here as a guide to the issues involved:

DRAFT POLICY STATEMENT FOR TEACHER EDUCATION IN A MULTI-RACIAL SOCIETY

1. A STATEMENT OF THE PROFESSIONAL RESPONSIBILITIES OF A TEACHER IN A MULTI-RACIAL SOCIETY

a. It is a teacher's responsibility to know and understand the children he teaches to the best of his ability – in particular to know and understand those social and cultural elements of an individual child's upbringing and experience which contribute to the formation of his distinctive personality, and to accept and to value these distinctive characteristics, so that his understanding of them informs the content and method of his teaching of each child.

b. It is also a teacher's responsibility to develop his understanding throughout his career, of the complex and changing nature of society, and of the knowledge, attitudes and skills needed by children growing up in such a society – so that his understanding of these informs the content and methods of his teaching of all children.

'a.' implies a special responsibility for any teacher who is teaching a child of ethnic minority background (such children are by no means peculiar to the obviously 'multiracial' schools in inner urban areas); 'b.' implies a responsibility for all teachers of all children to prepare those children for life in a multiracial society. Thus these statements entail a common set of objectives for the initial vocational education of all teachers.

2. STATEMENT OF OBJECTIVES ENTAILED BY 1:

a. Affective

On completion of their initial vocational education, all student teachers

553

should accept *and understand the practical implications for teachers of:*

1. *the uniqueness of each human being*

2. *the elements of common experience shared by all human beings.*

3. *the principles of equal rights and of justice.*

4. *the value of the best achievements of all nations, cultures and civilisations.*

5. *diversity and strangeness as sources of interest and stimulus rather than fear and threat.*

6. *the cultural diversity and complexity of British society in the past, the present and the future.*

7. *the dynamic and constantly-evolving character of all living cultures.*

While there are extreme difficulties in translating objectives in the affective domain into operational policies, and possible resistance to the idea of influencing systematically students' (or children's) 'attitudes', it seems undeniable that the attitudes of students towards the children they teach and towards individuals and groups different from themselves are substantially modified for better or worse in the process of teacher-education, that this objective does imply (or rule out) specific teaching policies and practices, and that a student who leaves College without understanding and accepting these propositions lacks *some of the professional qualities required to implement the responsibilities of a teacher (cf 1 above): ie s/he is* not *wholly and adequately qualified to be a teacher.*

b.   Cognitive/Propositional

On completion of their initial teacher education, all student teachers should know, and understand the practical implications for teachers of:

1. *the meaning in scientific usage of the terms 'race', 'culture' and 'community'.*

2a. *the historic reasons for the cultural diversity of modern Britain, and in particular, the reasons for immigration of various ethnic groups during the 20th century.*

2b. *the identity and main distinctive characteristics of major cultural minorities in present-day Britain, including their*

554

religious and social customs, the character and status of their languages, and their moral and cultural values.

2c. *the ethnic composition of the area served by the College.*

2d. *the ethnic composition of their home areas.*

3. *the influences which contribute to the development of attitudes towards self and others in a growing child, and in particular, the special factors influencing the sense of identity of an ethnic minority child, and the factors likely to implant or reinforce hostile attitudes towards groups different from his own in any child, and to cause racial discrimination in practice.*

c. Cognitive/Procedural

On completion of their initial teacher education all student teachers should be able to:

1a. *recognise, and constantly reassess his/her own attitudes, beliefs and understanding.*

1b. *participate in rational discourse, argue for or against a case, change his/her mind in response to evidence, argument or experience.*

1c. *communicate effectively with adults and children whose range of cultural and social experience differs from his/her own.*

1d. *understand and apply the principles of equal rights and justice in his/her dealings with adults and children.*

1e. *evaluate objectively the achievements of any individual, cultural group, nation or civilisation, irrespective of whether s/he identifies with it or not.*

2. *select sources of learning experience for children which:*

2a. *will be intelligible to each child in terms of his own experience and upbringing.*

2b. *will enable each child to draw on the resources of his experience and upbringing in a positive way.*

2c. *will provide all children with accurate information about the*

555

world as it is at present, and in particular the character of British Society.

2d. *will encourage all children to value the diversity of humanity, and in particular, the cultural richness of a multicultural society, as sources of stimulus and interest.*

3. *detect in any materials available for children to see, hear or read:*

3a. *factual inaccuracy, especially in the presentation of information about racial and cultural differences.*

3b. *stereotyping, especially in the presentation of information about distinctive cultural groups (in Britain and overseas).*

3c. *bias, especially in the interpretation of the values, beliefs and cultural achievements of other nations and civilisations.*

4. *plan and organise his/her teaching so that each child:*

4a. *is helped to overcome specific learning difficulties, in particular, difficulties in the use of English.*

4b. *has opportunities to communicate with the teacher and with other children, drawing upon his/her own experience and expressing his own ideas, attitudes and beliefs, in the expectation that these will be received with positive interest and valued in their own terms.*

4c. *has opportunities to hear and read about the experiences, attitudes and beliefs different from his/herself.*

Different Forms of Provision

2.11 The response of the initial teacher training system to "multicultural" concerns has tended to take three main forms – compulsory *"core"studies*, specialist *optional courses*, and, more recently, attempts to develop an implicit *"multicultural awareness"* in all aspects of a course, through what has come to be termed *"permeation"*. We believe that each of these approaches has an essential role to play in preparing *all* students, whether entering teaching through the BEd or the PGCE route, to fulfil their professional responsibilities in today's society and they should be regarded as inter-related and complementary aspects of an overall training process.

Permeation

2.12 The concept of permeation was heralded as long ago as 1974 when the CRC/ATCDE Report argued that the training of students to teach in a multicultural context:

556

". . . cannot be mechanistic, involving merely adding a little here or taking away a little there, whilst leaving the main body of the student's educational experience untouched."

– but that the training which *all* students receive at initial level must reflect the multi-racial nature of today's society. We wholeheartedly endorse this view as in keeping with "Education for All". Just as within the school curriculum we have argued that far more than separate, "added on" provision is called for, so in teacher training we are concerned that reliance on specific courses, whether optional or compulsory, can lend support to the view that the implications of a multi-racial society are peripheral to the mainstream concerns of education. Any course of study is informed and permeated by various assumptions, conscious or unconscious, which condition the selection of subject matter, the approach adopted to it and the emphasis laid upon various parts of it. Existing initial training courses thus already convey to students certain implied values and value judgments. The permeation of an initial training course with the principles underlying a genuinely pluralist approach to education should seek to ensure that all aspects of the course develop an awareness of the multi-racial and culturally diverse nature of British society and of the world as it is today, and of the wide range of information and ideas now required in order to comprehend contemporary issues. It is also important that all existing courses should recognise the diverse cultural context of which the sociology, psychology and philosophy of education should take account. Negative stereotypes of ethnic minority communities should be discussed and challenged and the responsibility of the education system to cater for the needs of *all* pupils and to educate *all* pupils for life in a pluralist society should be recognised. Subject-specific studies may also be permeated with a pluralist perspective for example by discussing the development of scientific and mathematical concepts in different cultures, by broadening the range of literature, music and art drawn upon in subject studies and by moving away from an exclusively Anglo or Euro-centric perception of history and geography. This process will involve not only reviewing the content of courses but also possibly discarding or adapting teaching materials or coursebooks where these present an unreal picture of the world as it is today. Historical understanding, not only in relation to history courses but more generally as the overall perspective through which all study material is seen, may need to be broadened, and the aims of education for the society of the future, and the student's potential role within this, should be analysed and discussed. As the Home Affairs Committee put it in their 1981 Report:

"It is plainly desirable that all teaching should be as broad-minded as possible and so should reflect the diversity of modern Britain, and we recognise the advantage that would accrue to racial harmony were all children made to realise that Britain is a multi-racial society. Teacher

training courses should be permeated by this understanding . . . We recommend . . . that every initial teacher training course should be examined . . . to ensure that it accurately reflects the society in which those who follow the course will be working."

2.13   At the broadest level, a "satisfactorily permeated" course would in our view be one in which:

– All elements in the course are purposefully directed towards the development of the pupils for whom the teachers in training will ultimately be responsible as citizens of a racially just, pluralist democracy.

– Teachers in training come to appreciate the fundamental values of Britain as a pluralist democracy, and can face with confidence the particular professional challenges of teaching in the schools of such a society.

– The fundamental norms within education which students are being trained to present are not those seen to be exclusively based on "white" ethnocentric traditions and values, but are universal in character, being drawn from many cultures and being accorded equal respect as manifestations of the variety of human responses to environmental circumstances.

– The language of "differentiation" on racial grounds would be considered and rejected and the various concepts of "racism": intentional, unintentional, institutionalised, would be understood, and the student equipped to combat such phenomena, as well as the manifestations of personal prejudice in him/herself, in colleagues and in pupils.

– The implications of citizenship of a pluralist society are brought to bear upon the content of the subjects and curriculum areas that the students intend to teach.

The permeation of the training received by a student is thus essential in providing the appropriate context for core courses and optional provision to be fully effective. As Dr Willey has put it in his draft report:

"If there is a contradiction between the theory advanced in a separate course (on multicultural education) and students' experience in most of their other studies, there may be misunderstanding of the need to include multicultural education as a compulsory part of training and a negative reaction or even resentment from some students . . . There is a danger that . . . the theories expounded in specialist multicultural courses, both optional and compulsory, bear little relation to the education provided by the institution's major teaching departments

. . . If the principle of permeation is accepted, it follows that all the subject areas and disciplines contributing to teacher education will need to consider the particular relevance to their own specialisms of a positive attitude to cultural diversity."

2.14   It is important to recognise however that permeation alone cannot be regarded as providing adequate preparation for the kind of teaching which we have advocated and especially for teaching in a multi-racial school, without additional specialist course work, both compulsory and optional. As the NUT put it in their evidence to the Home Affairs Committee:

"Whilst the Union wholly supports the concept of "permeation", and considers that education for a multicultural society should be an integral part of all training courses, there is a danger that it may be possible to pay lip service to ideals which have become fashionable or to respond to growing concern and criticism without much tangible evidence that the ideals are put into practice. This strategy of "permeation" may be effective where the level of awareness and commitment amongst course tutors is high, but without specific, detailed plans for compulsory input to initial courses, backed up by specialist options for those who wish to pursue the issues in more depth and widen their expertise, it may be just a paper promise."

2.15   It will be clear that, in its very nature, it is difficult to seek to present "examples" of a "permeated course" and indeed our impression from the evidence which we received was that little real progress has as yet been made in any but a few institutions to put into practice the rhetoric devoted publicly to the concept of permeation. Nevertheless we draw together in Annex C to this chapter examples of the approach adopted to their work by some teacher training institutions which reflect the underlying principles of permeation.

Core Studies   2.16   If our view of "Education for All" as relevant to every school in the country, whether multi-racial or "all-white", is accepted, it is clear that every student teacher must have at least some opportunity in the course of their training to consider the issues involved. If all initial training courses were already permeated with the broad principles discussed above this would of course ensure that this was so, but it is clear that even if the policies which we have advocated are adopted immediately, it will still be some time before all initial training courses are fully and effectively permeated by a pluralist perspective. We therefore believe there is a strong case in the immediate future for some reference to be made to pluralist issues within the central and compulsory "core" of the initial training received by *all* teachers, as an essential "staging post" and catalyst to overall permeation. Such a core element can also be seen as justified on the grounds of enabling teachers to fulfil their responsibilities in relation to the reality of British society and indeed the modern world today. As the 1982 HMI discussion document on initial training put it (our underlining):

> *"An effective course of training should include for <u>all</u> students practical experience and knowledge of class management and control: <u>knowledge of the variety that constitutes the full range of pupils in terms of ability,</u> behaviour, social background and <u>culture:</u> experience and knowledge of the level of expectation appropriate to the performance of children of differing ages, abilities, aptitudes and backgrounds: awareness of the ethical, spiritual and aesthetic values of society as well as its political, economic and legal foundations: <u>respect for and understanding of the cultural heritage which belongs to the children growing up in our society: sensitivity to the diversity of cultural background in today's school population.</u> This list, while not comprehensive, <u>includes those aspects of the teacher's skill which relate to our multi-cultural society,</u> the recognition of children with special needs in the ordinary classroom and the preparation of pupils for their working and adult lives. While some students may wish to pursue further specialist options in these concerns, they should be part of the basic professional preparation of all teachers in relation to the subjects they will teach to the children of any "normal" classroom."*

2.17 We would not wish to prescribe a "model" core course as appropriate for all institutions and all courses. The main areas which we believe should be covered will be evident from the general comments which we have already offered – at the broadest level all students should be given an informed awareness of the diversity, on many levels, of today's multi-racial society. This would include basic "facts and figures" about the process of immigration to and emigration from this country over the last 150 years; the circumstances which have conditioned the experiences and aspirations of different ethnic minority groups; and also the theory and practice of racism at both institutional and individual level, how this operates, and can be challenged, both in society at large and in the education world. Above all it should be emphasised that the opportunities for broadening and enriching every child's education offered by our multi-racial society are equally relevant should a teacher find him or herself teaching in a rural, "all-white" school or an urban, multi-racial school – all schools and all teachers have a professional responsibility to prepare their pupils for life in a pluralist society and in the wider world which has changed so dramatically over the last 30 years. The changing perceptions of "ethnic minority education" from the early days of assimilationist thinking should also be considered by students and the straightforward *educational* grounds for broadening the curriculum should be discussed alongside questions of justice, equality and the aims of a genuinely pluralist society.

**Needs of
Ethnic
Minority
Pupils**

2.18   We regard an equally important aspect of "Education for All" as meeting the needs of *all* children in a positive manner, which would include catering for any particular educational needs which some ethnic minority pupils may have as a result of their cultural or linguistic background. It has been argued that, since such needs can, by definition, arise only in a multi-racial school, the preparation of teachers to cater for them can only be achieved through in-service provision if a teacher joins a multi-racial school or through specialist options at initial training level in those institutions whose students are likely to be teaching in multi-racial areas. This argument overlooks two important points – firstly, the increasing mobility of the ethnic minority communities which prevents such a rigid dividing line being drawn between multi-racial and "all-white" areas, and secondly, the present teacher employment situation, where it is increasingly difficult for new teachers to choose their first teaching post and to "predict" therefore that any teacher will never teach in a multi-racial school. Multi-racial schools can no longer be regarded as unique to urban areas such as Manchester or Bradford since schools in many other parts of the country now have pupils of ethnic minority origin. On the question of teacher employment, as the Home Affairs Committee observed in their 1981 Report:

> *"Most young teachers will find themselves teaching in a multi-racial school either on starting their teaching career or within 5 years of their induction. Nor are those who train in the West Country or East Anglia any less likely to be teaching in the West Midlands or ILEA than those who trained at Walsall or Goldsmiths. In a mobile and contracting profession, there is every reason why teachers trained at Exeter, for example, may obtain their first teaching post in Leicester, and find themselves unprepared for the experience of teaching Asian children."*

We believe that *all* teachers should receive, as part of the compulsory core of their initial training, an introduction to the particular educational needs which may arise in a multi-racial school. This view was shared by the Home Affairs Committee who concluded that:

> *". . . initial teacher training should not skimp on providing more specialised instruction on the skills needed for teaching English as a second language (E2L); for offering second-stage support for E2L learners, for recognising and coping with other language differences, and for understanding social patterns which may be different from accepted norms . . . it is evident that such instruction is too often regarded as . . . suitable for only those teachers who are likely to be seeking posts in multi-racial areas. Nothing could be more misleading."*

561

We are not suggesting here that such core studies could in any sense fully prepare a student to teach effectively in a multi-racial school with no further specialised induction or in-service training. What we are advocating however is that every student teacher should become familiar with the major issues which arise in relation to the education of ethnic minority pupils and the policies adopted to cater for them, so that if he or she subsequently teaches in a multi-racial school they will be able to respond positively and sensitively to the needs of the pupils and have a "base" of general knowledge on which to build through more specialised in-service training. Care must be taken however in providing such basic understanding not to establish or confirm negative stereotypes of ethnic minority pupils, but rather to convey a positive view of any particular needs which they may have as simply one dimension of their individual education needs and which can often, for example in the language field, be seen as an extension of the needs which any child may have and for which it is entirely reasonable to expect the school to cater. Not only would such an introduction provide teachers with the basic information needed should they find themselves working with ethnic minority pupils, but it would also enable them to make an informed choice as to whether they wished to take up a specialist option course, for example to study language needs in greater depth, within their initial training.

2.19   As an illustration of the various ways in which the areas of work discussed above have been incorporated into the core studies of their BEd courses by various institutions, we attach as Annex D to this chapter two examples of course outlines, taken from the evidence which we have received. Whilst many educationists would accept that the inclusion of the kind of core courses we have advocated is feasible within a 3 or 4 year BEd course, it has been suggested that the time constraints of a PGCE course, even when extended to 36 weeks, are such as to preclude anything other than a very superficial consideration of "multicultural" issues. The view has therefore been expressed that it is prefereable to look to either specialist options at initial level or in-service provision for PGCE-trained entrants. We believe however that the kind of core provision which we have discussed above is equally valid and essential for the overall reorientation of all initial training courses in the immediate future, whether through the BEd or PGCE route. It is important to recognise that the current trend is for an increasing proportion of new teachers to enter the profession through the PGCE route and this adds urgency to the need to incorporate a pluralist perspective within the core studies of such courses. It is likely that few degree courses will have given consideration to issues related to today's multi-racial society and specific questions relating to the role of education in this context will rarely if ever have been raised. The risk that PGCE students will regard specialist optional courses in this field as irrelevant and superfluous is perhaps therefore even greater than for other students, unless a general introduction to the issues involved is provided for *all* students in their core studies. Whilst we recognise that time for the core of a PGCE course is limited, we believe that given appropriate skill and sensitivity it should be possible to avoid creating or confirming stereotypes of ethnic minority groups or focussing only on "problems" and "difficulties", and instead to discuss issues such as the influence of racism and the need for a broader approach to the curriculum for *all* pupils which may lead some students to pursue such questions further through optional studies. Whilst again we would not seek to put forward a "model" PGCE core course, and we have indeed had some difficulty in finding examples which fully reflect our viewpoint, we include in Annex D details of the approach adopted by one University Department of Education which, whilst we would not endorse it wholeheartedly, gives some indication of the range and kind of considerations we have in mind.

Optional Courses

2.20   Much of the provision at initial level in relation to multicultural education has been in the form of optional courses, concerned either with specific topics, such as the language needs of ethnic minority pupils, or more general themes such as race relations. If such issues feature however as simply one or two options in competition with a number of others, students may well feel their career interests are better served by choosing other optional courses – as the HMI survey described in Annex B observed:

> *"The usefulness of a course on slow learners, audio-visual aids or some such topic may well over-ride a student's interest in multicultural issues, as the anxieties of teaching practice draw near. Faced with some sets of options students may feel they have very little choice".*

Optional courses relating to the educational implications of cultural diversity are also likely to attract primarily those students who already have an interest in and some commitment to pluralist principles – in effect "preaching to the converted". They would be less likely to appeal to those students who have little interest or knowledge of "multicultural" issues or who mistakenly see themselves as teaching only in "all-white" schools, which as we stressed in paragraph 2.18, may in fact be far from certain. Above all, however, if these issues are dealt with solely through optional courses, the teacher training system is in effect lending support to the "traditional" view that such matters are not sufficiently important or relevant to mainstream education to warrant a central place in the professional training of all teachers and can simply be relegated to peripheral courses for those students who might wish to specialise in these "problems". Since we believe that such issues are in fact relevant to all pupils, all schools and all teachers, we believe it is entirely inadequate for any teacher training institution to limit its preparation of teachers for a pluralist context to optional courses. It has been suggested that optional provision is in some respects likely to be more effective than compulsory provision since a conscious decision to study a particular issue contributes to a higher degree of motivation and commitment than where students are *required* to cover an area of work. Such an argument assumes however that all students have a basic appreciation and understanding of the importance of cultural diversity for their future role as teachers and can make informed option choices – in other words that "multicultural" issues have been covered specifically through compulsory core studies and more generally elsewhere in the course. As we have seen from the various studies detailed in paragraph 2.6 above however, optional courses seem often, regrettably, to be an institution's only response to such issues and have often been established instead of, rather than alongside, core studies and permeation. In such a situation it is difficult to accept that optional courses alone can effectively support the development of any but the most highly committed and enlightened student.

2.21   This is not to suggest that there is no place for specialist optional courses in initial training. On the contrary, providing such optional courses develop from and build upon a basic understanding of teaching in a culturally pluralist society, received through a student's core studies and ultimately from a fully permeated course, they will continue to play an important role in catering for the particular needs and interests of certain students. The form which such optional courses may take can clearly vary widely from those relating explicitly to the particular linguistic needs which some ethnic minority pupils may have, to those concerned more broadly with the opportunities available to any teacher teaching in a multi-racial school to broaden and enhance their teaching and the need for all teachers to reflect a pluralist perspective in their work. We attach at Annex E some examples of optional provision offered within BEd courses, drawn from the evidence we have received. Such options are however, by no means limited to BEd courses and we received a number of examples of similar options offered within PGCE courses. We attach as Annex F to this chapter a paper prepared by the tutor of such an optional PGCE course on multicultural education, discussing the range of issues covered and raising some interesting points about the reactions of students.

Practical Experience

2.22   Up to now we have focussed primarily on the "taught" elements of initial training courses. However if students, especially those from "all-white" areas, are to be given a genuine awareness of the complexity of British society, it is clear that such course provision should be complemented by appropriate practical experience. As the evidence we received from one teacher training institution put it:

> "... *a genuine synthesis of educational theory, practice and experience needs to be developed in programmes of initial training, and ... the perspectives of multi-racial education offer a genuine and practicable opportunity for such development to be realised. We*

would therefore urge that as many students as is possible should have experience of working in schools of cultural and racial diversity during their period of training in order that this experience might both inform and benefit from College or Institute based programmes."

We hope that efforts will be made by all teacher training institutions to ensure that all their students, whether on BEd or PGCE courses, have an opportunity of gaining some practical experience in a multi-racial school. It might be assumed that this was already customary in those institutions in multi-racial areas, however, the HMI Survey summarised in Annex B found that:

"Whilst one would expect a student's experience of multi-ethnic schools . . . to be related to the proximity of training institutions to areas of settlement by immigrant communities, this was by no means universal. One-third of the institutions offering courses on education in a multi-cultural society did not bring students into sustained contact with multi-ethnic schools or communities, even though some were in areas of substantial ethnic minority populations."

Nevertheless there are we understand a number of institutions which have developed close relationships with multi-racial schools in their areas and which have sought to involve their students with the activities of ethnic minority communities "beyond the school gates" – an approach which we would certainly endorse. It could be suggested that constraints of time and finance may make it difficult for institutions located in "all-white" areas to offer their students experience in multi-racial schools. In our interim report we mentioned as "good practice" the establishment by one teacher training institution situated in a rural area of a residential "urban studies centre" designed to give its students direct experience of a multi-racial environment. Whilst we commend such initiatives, we should emphasise that the main focus should always be on the shared experiences of ethnic majority and ethnic minority communities within our society and on the positive opportunities offered by multi-racial schools, rather than on the "strangeness" or on the "problems" of such schools, which would in our view confirm or establish negative stereotypes rather than create greater awareness and understanding. Even if institutions in "all-white" areas are not able to organise such structured "multi-racial experience" for their students, efforts should still be made to arrange temporary attachments of students to institutions in multi-racial areas or indeed for the "exchange" of students on a regular basis, since it must be recognised that, just as students from "all-white" areas need some experience of multi-racial areas in order to see their work in a truly pluralist context, so students from multi-racial areas would also, in our view, benefit from experience of work in "all-white" schools, as part of broadening their cultural horizons.

Our View   2.23   Thus, to sum up, we would regard core studies, optional courses and permeation as having equally important and complementary roles to play in an overall initial training process which provides students with the essential knowledge and professional skills needed to teach in a pluralist society and to offer their pupils an education which is relevant to the world as it is today. We would envisage permeation setting the appropriate context for all students' work, core studies providing all students with an introduction to the broad issues relevant to a pluralist society as well as developing a basic understanding of the nature of and response to the particular educational needs which may arise in a multi-racial school, and specialist optional courses offering the opportunity for further in-depth study. It is clear that it is the process of permeation that has the most wide-ranging implications for institutions and it is therefore here that we believe the greatest efforts should be directed, through institutions reviewing and evaluating their course provision to incorporate a pluralist perspective throughout. We would endorse the view taken by Dr. Richard Willey in his draft report that:

> *"If the permeation of teacher education programmes is to be made a reality, the teacher education institutions must formally consider the implications of cultural pluralism for the professional training they provide and adopt appropriate policy objectives ... It is only determined initiation of such a process which can eventually produce effective teacher education for a culturally plural society."*

The ways in which an individual teacher training institution can meet these requirements will clearly vary according to particular circumstances and expertise. Some institutions may already have considerable resources, others may have few or none and will need to rely heavily upon outside input. Those institutions offering self-contained BEd courses will have excellent opportunities for ensuring that every aspect of provision is "permeated". In others, where initial teacher training is linked with a BA or BSc degree, difficulties may be experienced as many elements are likely to fall outside the jurisdiction of the teacher trainers, being taken in common with other first degree students. Similar circumstances might be experienced with PGCE courses where the students' first degree studies have frequently been undertaken in another institution entirely. It can be seen therefore that the concept of permeation has implications for the whole of Higher Education provision in this country and we hope that all Higher Education institutions, not just those involved directly in teacher education, will be prepared to incorporate a pluralist perspective in all their provision. We recognise that the reorientation of initial teacher training which we have advocated here will not come about overnight and that it will call for debate and discussion about the specific implications of these broad policy objectives for individual institutions. We hope however that this report will serve as a stimulus and a catalyst to progress.

Role of CATE 2.24 One major current initiative in the field of teacher training which we feel could accelerate the pace of progress towards the incorporation of a pluralist perspective in all initial training courses is the establishment of a Council for the Accreditation of Teacher Education (CATE) to advise the Secretaries of State on the approval of initial teacher training courses in England and Wales[19]. The new Council has been asked to review all existing approved courses of initial training and to scrutinise proposals for new courses in the light of specified criteria designed to ensure a consistent standard of training commensurate with the professional qualities required of a teacher. Since we have argued here that, in order to be professionally equipped to fulfil his or her teaching responsibilities, a teacher must have acquired both the knowledge and skills needed to prepare all pupils for life in a pluralist society, and must also have a basic understanding of the particular educational needs which some ethnic minority pupils may have, we believe it is essential that these considerations are taken into account by the Council in its assessment of course provision. We are encouraged therefore that the criteria laid down by the Government include the following reference to the implications of cultural diversity and to the need to guard against the possible influence of racism:

> "Students should be prepared . . . to teach the full range of pupils whom they are likely to encounter in an ordinary school, with their diversity of ability, behaviour, social background and ethnic and cultural origins. They will need to learn how to respond flexibly to such diversity and to guard against preconceptions based on the race or sex of pupils."

We were concerned to find however that the *draft* criteria originally issued by the Government as a basis for consultation made no explicit reference to the need for all teachers to incorporate a pluralist perspective in their work. Our Chairman therefore wrote to the Secretary of State in February last year suggesting that some reference should be incorporated in the criteria to the need for initial teacher training courses to equip students with an understanding of the multi-racial and culturally diverse nature of British society today in which all their pupils will be living and of how their teaching can help to lay the foundations for a racially just and genuinely pluralist society. We were pleased to find that the final agreed version of the criteria issued by the Government in April took some account of our observations and now include the following reference to these broader concerns:

> "Students should be made aware of the wide range of relationships – with parents and others – which teachers can expect to develop in a

---

[19] DES Circular No 3/84. 13 April 1984.

diverse society, and of the role of the school within a community . . .
They will also need to have a basic understanding of the type of
society in which their pupils are growing up, with its cultural and
racial mix . . ."

We urge the Secretary of State to go further and ask the new Council to pay particular attention to the aims and objectives which we have set out for initial teacher training in this report in undertaking its review of provision. To this end, we consider it important that in their enquiries into initial training courses, HMI should pay specific attention to the provision of training for all students that will prepare them for teaching in a pluralist society and comment on this provision to CATE.

Selection of
Students and
Qualified
Teacher Status

2.25 One of the main messages of the Government's recent pronouncements on teacher training has been a desire for a more stringent selection process of candidates for admission to teacher training, coupled with a wish to ensure that qualified teacher status should not be awarded to any student who, although he or she demonstrates the necessary academic ability, lacks the "professional competence" required of a teacher. Throughout this report we have highlighted the need for all teachers to have positive attitudes towards teaching in a pluralist context and, by extension, this means that we would wish to see such attitudes manifested and developed amongst student teachers. As long ago as 1971, the DES Education Survey 13 stressed that:

> *"A student should honestly examine the premise that a multicultural*
> *society in twentieth century Britain is both right and natural. If his*
> *attitude to a racially mixed class is wrong, no amount of knowledge,*
> *no mastery of techniques will make him effective as a teacher of*
> *immigrant children."*

We would echo this view and indeed go further: if a teacher has negative attitudes towards ethnic minorities and the development of a culturally plural society then he or she will in our view remain an inadequate teacher of *any* child in *any* school in this country. Thus, as observed by HMI in their discussion paper on the content of Initial Training:

> *"Selection of the right students is the first step in providing the right*
> *kind of teachers."*

The criteria used by institutions in selecting students for admission to courses of initial training are therefore extremely important. The DES Circular on the approval of initial teacher training courses reflected the stance taken by the White Paper "Teaching Quality" in respect of the qualities considered suitable for prospective teacher training students in stating that:

"In assessing the personal qualities of candidates, institutions should look in particular for a sense of responsibility, a robust but balanced outlook, awareness, sensitivity, enthusiasm and facility in communication."

We believe an important element in a "balanced and aware outlook" is a positive attitude towards the diversity of British society today. The White Paper on "Teaching Quality" acknowledged that there will inevitably be some students who, although academically able, are temperamentally and professionally unsuited to a career in teaching. We believe that if a student demonstrates by his actions or behaviour during taught studies or teaching practice, deep-seated and openly racist views about ethnic minority groups which materially affect the way he teaches and which do not appear to be open to reason or change through training, that should be an important element in assessing whether he or she is temperamentally suitable to enter the teaching profession. Potential teachers with such views are unlikely to be able to fulfil the professional responsibilities of a teacher in preparing pupils to live harmoniously in today's pluralist society.

Validation 2.26 It is clear that if the developments advocated here are to take place, a leading role must be played by the various validating bodies to exert their influence to encourage all initial training institutions to reappraise and revise their provision. With the ending of college validation by a number of universities a considerable resonsibility in this respect falls on the Council for National Academic Awards (CNAA), and we have therefore been encouraged by the initiatives taken since the establishment of the CNAA Working Group on Multicultural Education. In particular we were impressed by the positive stance adopted by the Working Group in a discussion paper, produced in July 1984, with the following emphasis on the skills needed by student teachers to fulfil their role in a pluralist society:

"Given the wider role that teachers in schools and in further education have to play in (the) recognition of the importance of multicultural and anti-racist education, there is a need to consider the implications for their education and professional preparation. In designing courses of teacher education, institutions should bear in mind the following. Teachers need to:

i. be equipped to prepare all young people for life in a multicultural and racially harmonious society

ii. have an awareness and understanding of racism both historically and in contemporary society and to be conscious of the various forms in which racism can manifest itself

569

iii. have an awareness of intercultural relations and of their social and economic contexts

iv. be able to teach with skill and sensitivity in schools and further education institutions recognising any particular needs of ethnic minority pupils and students.

v. interact effectively with colleagues in the institutional framework in relation to these issues."

We produce the Working Group's paper in full as Annex G to this chapter as an indication of the specific policies advocated to achieve these broad objectives. We hope that the CNAA will continue with its work in this field and that other validating bodies will follow this lead in expressing publicly their support for developing a pluralist perspective throughout teacher education. We also hope that those universities which offer their own degree level courses will seek to ensure that these underlying principles are fully reflected in their teacher education provision.

3. In-Service Training

3.1   We now turn to the varied forms of further training which are offered to teachers in the course of their teaching careers – what can collectively be termed "in-service" provision. This can broadly be divided into, on the one hand, the training offered to newly qualified teachers on taking up a teaching post, or to teachers who are new to a school, and, on the other hand, the bewildering variety of other forms of further training which may be available to any teacher in the course of his or her career. We consider each of these types of in-service training in turn.

Background   *Induction Training*

3.2   Specific programmes aimed at introducing newly qualified staff to an organisation, preparing them for their specific responsibilities and offering them general advice and practical help and support are a feature of most professions. On the face of it the teaching profession is no different from any other in this respect. It has long been accepted that newly qualified teachers in their probationary year can benefit from a programme of professional initiation and support – usually termed "induction training". The James Report emphasised the vital importance of the induction year and this was endorsed by the then Government in their 1972[20] White Paper:

"There is no major profession to which a new entrant, however thorough his initial training, can be expected immediately to make a

---

[20]"Education: A Framework for Expansion." Cmnd 5174. HMSO. 1972.

full contribution. The Government share the view of the James Committee that a teacher on first employment needs, and should be released part-time to profit from, a systematic programme of professional initiation, guided experience and further study."

With the expansion of initial teacher training in the late 1960s and early 1970s some LEAs began to develop provision in the induction field. However few if any LEAs ever reached the level of induction support recommended by the James Report and overall developments in this field were disappointing. With the contraction of provision for initial teacher training in recent years, and the correspondingly smaller number of newly qualified teachers entering schools, even this rather limited development of induction training has generally been curtailed.

3.3   A survey undertaken by the DES in 1979[21] found that:

"In maintained nursery, primary, secondary and special education about 90 per cent of teachers taking up first full-time permanent appointments in 1978-1979 were involved in some sort of induction programme."

Current Situation

A survey undertaken by HMI in 1981 detailed in the Report "The New Teacher in School" considered in detail the provision made by schools and LEAs for induction training for probationary teachers in a sample of 294 schools, both primary and secondary. In relation to the school's role in induction, HMI found that:

"In most cases schools had thought out their role vis-à-vis new teachers in the light of their level of expectation, and this had led to a range of policies from non-intervention to over-protectiveness. Between the two extremes there was evidence in very many schools of a sincere and honest endeavour to incorporate new teachers into the staff team and to help them in their professional development ... There was wide recognition of the importance, for this, of the "right, happy atmosphere in which to work", and a general background of support and encouragement from the staff as a whole. In some schools, both primary and secondary, this was envisaged as a wholly informal and unplanned state of affairs. In others, induction was considered a more purposeful process requiring some level of structure, sometimes a designated member of staff with responsibility for the new teachers, and a clear objective such as "the continuation of the probationer's professional training" or "building on the work of the initial training institution."

---

[21]Detailed in DES Statistical Bulletin 9/80 "Induction and In-service Training of Teachers serving in maintained schools and Further Education establishments in England and Wales: 1979 Survey." August 1980.

The survey found a variety of forms of induction training and support offered to the newly qualified teachers in their schools – only half of the secondary schools and a quarter of the primary schools offered a structured induction programme. The following table, taken from the report of the survey shows the full range of provision made:

ARRANGEMENTS NORMALLY MADE TO ASSIST NEWLY
APPOINTED PROBATIONERS AFTER THEY HAD TAKEN UP THEIR
DUTIES, AS DESCRIBED BY THE SCHOOLS

	Percentage of Schools	
Probationers:	Primary	Secondary
Take part in a structured induction programme in the school	27	52
Observe lessons given by experienced colleagues	60	58
Are observed by experienced colleagues while teaching	97	98
Are given opportunities to visit other schools	55	34
Attend meetings/discussions organised by the school	95	87

In relation to the LEA's role in induction, HMI found that in over half of the schools, the probationers attended planned induction programmes provided by their LEAs and in over 85 per cent. of cases, the probationary teachers attended meetings organised by the authority. Reporting on the views expressed by the heads of the schools about LEA provision for induction, HMI found:

> "A number of heads commented on the abandonment, no doubt in part for financial reasons, of programmes formerly organised by LEAs, while others suggested that current provision was less extensive than it had been. Some authorities had appointed so few probationers in the current year that previous patterns of induction were no longer suitable."

HMI found that the the range of LEA induction provision was very wide, but found it "at its best" to incorporate the following elements:

- introductory meetings with officers, advisers and sometimes members of education committees;

- visits by LEA advisers or inspectors to observe the new teacher at work and to offer advice and help;

- attendance at conferences, courses and workshops; and

- an authority handbook or guidelines on the LEA's work.

572

Taken together, the findings of this HMI survey in relation to induction training were that nearly a half of the secondary teachers and just over three-fifths of the primary teachers appeared to be receiving satisfactory LEA support, and over two-thirds of both primary and secondary schools were providing an environment which encouraged the professional development of new teachers. In relation to the latter figure, as HMI observed:

> ". . . the inadequacies of as many as a third of those (schools) in the sample may lead to the new teachers failing to achieve their potential – or at least in their doing so more painfully and more slowly."

Overall, the findings of this survey show clearly we believe that there is an urgent need for a major expansion in provision for induction training by both LEAs and schools.

General Conclusions

3.4 We believe that a comprehensive and structured programme of induction training provided jointly by the LEA and the school is an essential phase in the career development of a newly qualified teacher – providing a "bridge" between the more generalised emphases of initial training courses and the specific demands of a first teaching post. We are concerned therefore that, in the face of financial constraints, the scale of provision at induction level is declining and we hope that steps will be taken to seek to ensure that adequate and effective induction training is offered to all newly qualified teachers. Induction training is clearly important for new teachers who have entered through the PGCE route in view of the shorter time which they will have been able to devote in their training to developing their practical teaching skills, in comparison with BEd students – as HMI concluded in "The New Teacher in School":

> ". . . a programme of induction, desirable as it is for all new teachers, is particularly necessary for the PGCE-trained teachers, with their much shorter base of training, if they are to acquire an early mastery of a range of teaching skills."

The Multi-Racial Dimension

3.5 Induction training can play a crucial role in preparing teachers to incorporate a pluralist perspective in their work and to educate their pupils for life in today's multi-racial society. Where initial training may have failed to devote sufficient attention to this aspect of a student's development, induction training can, in part at least, serve to set a teacher's work within a school within a broader context. A newly qualified or equally an experienced teacher entering a multi-racial school for the first time, will, in our view, need substantial induction training to provide them with the background knowledge needed to offer *all* pupils an appropriate and relevant education, free from stereotypes of particular minority groups, and to recognise the opportunities offered in a multi-

573

racial situation. It must be emphasised that some new teachers joining multi-racial schools may not have taken a specialist option concerned with the needs of ethnic minority pupils in their initial training and so may be especially in need of such specific provision. Even where a teacher has undertaken such specialist study or where the core of his or her initial training course has incorporated some reference to ethnic minority needs, it is clear that neither of these forms of "introductory" provision can, taken by themselves, have adequately prepared that teacher to teach effectively in a multi-racial school, unless followed up and supported through induction training. At a specific level, any teacher who finds him or herself faced for the first time with a class which inludes a number of pupils for whom, for example, English is not a first language, or whose cultural "frame of reference" is substantially different from their own, will need particular help and support in responding to the needs of these pupils. Induction training should also help a "new" teacher to respond positively to any manifestations of intentional or unintentional racism which may occur within the school, including matters such as racist name-calling or graffiti, and to take account sensitively of the variety of backgrounds and experiences of pupils in the actual teaching situation, for example in the choice of textbooks or course materials. The 1974 CRC/ATCDE Report on "Teacher Education for a Multi-Cultural Society" (see paragraph 2.5 above) set out three broad areas of concern which the induction training of a new teacher working in a multi-racial school should cover. We reproduce these below, since, although some of the materials referred to have since been overtaken, these still summarise the major issues which we too believe should be included in induction training:

" i. *an opportunity to examine and discuss material that may be of use, eg SCOPE Stages one and two, CONCEPT 7-9, Breakthrough to Literacy, or any material evolved in the locality. This material could be discussed with experienced teachers who are actually using it; the local colleges could provide consultants on language and on particular questions, for example the adaptation of the material to different ages and background.*

ii. *an opportunity to study the local social and demographic situation. This will mean looking at the numbers, composition and the movement of immigrant groups and will involve personal contact with the leaders of these groups and those who work with them e.g. community relations councils and youth and community workers. For those working with older pupils the formation of links with detached youth workers may be particularly important. It would be useful for the young teachers to be given insights into patterns of family discipline and religious and socio-political beliefs.*

iii. an opportunity for these young teachers to discuss their problems of discipline and class management in small groups with skilful experienced teachers and tutors present. Perhaps the greatest neec in the first year is for more counselling on how to handle explicit incidents of racial hostility, how to win the confidence of minority group pupils who tend to form groups and support each other."

3.6   Since in order to be fully effective, induction training must relate directly to the specific character of an individual school or LEA, it is impossible to put forward a detailed "model" of an ideal programme. In general terms however induction training in multi-racial areas and schools should we believe cover the following issues:

–   how to avoid ethnocentrism within particular subjects;

–   how to handle manifestations of racism amongst pupils;

–   how to relate to pupils from a wide range of backgrounds and experiences;

–   how to meet the particular needs of some ethnic minority pupils, for example in terms of language;

–   how to support, and be sensitive to any cultural and religious factors which might influence their lives (but without "stereotyping" or placing undue emphasis on "problems");

–   how to utilise positively the range of pupils' experience within a class.

Other In-service Training

3.7   We now consider the range of other forms of in-service training available to teachers in various contexts in the course of their careers. Although we believe that in the longer term we must look to fundamental changes in initial teacher training to bring about the reorientation of education which we have advocated, in view of the limited number of new teachers entering the profession it is clear that in-service training can influence the education offered to pupils now in school in the most direct and immediate way. As HMI has observed[22]:

"Certainly the influence of newly trained teachers is highly important, but they will form only a small minority of the teaching force until well on into the 80s. The quality of work in the secondary

---

[22]"Teacher Training and the Secondary School." HMI. 1981.

schools throughout that period will depend largely upon those who are already teaching. Yet the combined effects of falling rolls and economic stringency will make their task the more difficult. Closure or amalgamation of schools, reduction of promotion prospects, an imbalance of staff specialisms within schools may all put strain upon teachers' morale, dampen their vitality and enthusiasm for change and development, and strengthen the tendency towards traditional styles of teaching. Yet new demands will continue to emerge, as changes in society are mirrored by changes in schools, in the curriculum, and in the subjects which contribute to it. In these circumstances further training becomes a necessity rather than a luxury."

In the context of the multi-racial nature of British society today and of the pupil populations of many of our schools, we believe this latter comment has added force and justification. The majority of teachers in schools today began their careers before the days of Commonwealth immigration and certainly well before the emergence of the debate about the need for the education of *all* children to reflect a pluralist perspective. If ethnic minority pupils were referred to at all in their training this was probably in assimilationist or integrationist terms. Whilst a minority of these teachers have kept pace with the debate in educational circles about "multicultural education" and have updated their knowledge and skills and moved beyond the horizons set for them by their original training, there are inevitably many whose outlook is still determined by a "traditional" view of their responsibilities. Those teachers who have found their schools becoming increasingly multi-racial in character have been particularly anxious to broaden their teaching to incorporate a pluralist perspective, while the majority of their colleagues in "all-white" schools have tended to retain the view that such matters have no bearing on their work. Nevertheless we believe that in-service training has a major role to play in helping *all* teachers wherever they teach to fulfil their professional responsibilities more effectively.

Early Provision

3.8   When the emphasis of educational policy-making in relation to ethnic minority pupils was on assimilationist objectives, the main, and often the only, response of the teacher training system was to offer short in-service courses in multi-racial areas focussing on the "problems" experienced by ethnic minority pupils and intended chiefly for those teachers, especially in the language or "remedial" fields, who were working with these children. Even the provision of such courses, which were often the only support available to teachers who found themselves faced with large numbers of immigrant pupils many of whom spoke no English at all, was relatively limited. Although the available data are at best somewhat patchy, since many of these courses were arranged on an informal, ad hoc basis, DES Education Survey 13 in 1971 found that only one per cent of teachers in English County Boroughs had attended specific courses related to "teaching immigrants" between September 1964 and August 1967, and also reported the findings of an HMI survey undertaken in 1968 that in only half of the 40-50 LEAs with a high concentration of immigrants had such courses been organised.

3.9 In-service provision continued to expand gradually however and Townsend found, in his 1971 survey of LEA support for multi-cultural education[23], that 41 of the then 146 LEAs claimed to be offering in-service courses in this field, although the majority of these were short, part-time courses. LEA-organised courses on the teaching of immigrants in the academic years 1967-1970 were found to have catered for some 5,760 teachers (including of course some "multiple attendances" by the same teachers). The complementary study by Townsend and Brittan in 1972 of practice in multi-racial schools, found that only a total of 7 per cent. of staff in the 230 schools studied had attended relevant in-service courses in the three years prior to the survey as shown in the following table:

STAFF ATTENDING, IN THE PERIOD 1.1.68 TO 31.12.70, COURSES CONCERNING WORK WITH IMMIGRANT PUPILS

	Primary				Secondary			All Schools
Number of schools in the sample	Inf 34	Inf/Jun 55	Jun 43	All 132	Mod 56	Comp 42	All 98	230
Schools having staff attending courses as above	19	22	24	65	30	19	49	114
Number of teachers involved	63	65	83	211	64	53	117	328
Total teaching staff of schools	343	577	532	1,452	1,642	1,759	3,401	4,853
% of teachers involved in courses as above	18	11	16	15	4	3	3	7

3.10 At this time the majority of in-service courses offered were still aimed at specialist teachers and tended to recruit only those teachers who were working directly with "immigrant" pupils such as E2L teachers, rather than their colleagues who were also working in multi-racial schools. Indeed Townsend's 1971 survey of LEA provision referred to:

". . . the considerable difficulty of interesting secondary school teachers in courses on the education of immigrant pupils other than teachers from English or remedial departments."

---

[23]"Immigrant Pupils in England. The LEA Response." H E R Townsend. NFER. 1971.

There was a tendency therefore that even the limited number of courses which were organised were sometimes undersubscribed or even cancelled through lack of interest. It is difficult to ascribe the limited development of in-service training in this field during these early years to any single reason, and clearly the widespread view at the time that the educational needs of these children would be short-lived and could be met quite rapidly through appropriate specialist provision such as language centres, contributed to a feeling that major programmes of in-service provision were unjustified. It may be worth recalling however that the authors of the Institute of Race Relations 1969 report[24] attributed the rather hesitant development of in-service training in this field to:

> ". . . the absence of a concerted drive by DES to get courses set up and attended . . . first of all (through) a serious attempt to persuade the institutes of education and, through them the colleges, to set up courses; and secondly, some effort to impress upon local education authorities that they should release teachers to attend courses."

Needless to say, little thought was given during these early years to the possible need for in-service provision designed, not just to cater for the specific needs of ethnic minority children, but more generally to enable all teachers to broaden their work to reflect the changed and changing nature of British society.

Research Studies

3.11   There are no comprehensive and up-to-date data relating to the provision of in-service training relating to the needs of ethnic minority children or encouraging a broader view of the curriculum for all pupils. There have nevertheless been some studies in this field and we summarise the main findings below, before setting out our own views on the role of in-service training.

– The HMI inspection exercise undertaken during 1979/1980 and detailed in Annex B found:

> ". . . fairly scant treatment of social and cultural issues within in-service provision generally."

with less than half of the institutions studied found to be offering in-service provision and the majority of this concerned specifically with the needs of ethnic minority pupils rather than with the broader implications for education of a multi-racial society. Award-bearing courses were found to be particularly popular with both teachers and institutions although the best examples of good practice in HMI's opinion were found in cases where an institution developed:

---

[24] "Colour and Citizenship – A Report on British Race Relations." E. J. B. Rose et. al. 1969.

". . . a balanced programme of long and short in-service course provision in close co-operation with its Local Authority's advisory service in multicultural education."

– In their memorandum to the Home Affairs Committee for its 1981 Report on Racial Disadvantage, the National Union of Teachers, on the basis of a survey of all teacher training institutions, expressed concern that:

"A very disturbing feature of our survey was the number of institutions which reported a drop in the take-up of in-service courses for serving teachers in multicultural education; this was blamed on the lack of possibilities for secondment by LEA's."

– Professor Maurice Craft, writing in 1981[25], reviewed the provision of in-service courses in "multicultural education" by analysing the courses listed in the DES handbook of long courses for 1981-1982 and found that:

". . . only 4 out of some 80 institutions in England and Wales specifically mention a multicultural element in their programmes for the in-service BEd degree. But many institutions offer courses in the sociology of education, language, urban and community studies, ethical, philosophical and political issues, and curriculum studies in this award, and multicultural perspectives might occur here or elsewhere. As regards advanced Diplomas, only 10 out of 320 currently listed are specifically related to multicultural education . . . As to higher degrees, no single MA/MEd taught course anywhere in England and Wales appears to be devoted to multicultural education."

In relation to short courses, Professor Craft found that, drawing on the 1980 programme of courses to be provided by HMI:

". . . of 91 courses to be mounted in England between April 1981 and March 1982, only five are to be devoted to topics such as 'teaching and learning in multicultural primary schools."

– The Schools Council survey undertaken by Little and Willey in 1978-1980 and published in 1981[26], also provided some data on in-service provision. Of the 94 LEAs who responded to the survey, only 29 (less than a third) claimed to be offering in-service courses explicitly concerned with multicultural issues, all but one of these LEAs being areas with a high or medium concentration of ethnic minority settlement. The great majority

---

[25]"Teaching in a Multicultural Society: The Task for Teacher Education." The Falmer Press. 1981.
[26] "Studies in the Multi-ethnic Curriculum." Little and Willey. Schools Council. 1981.

of the courses offered were on a short (15 weeks or less), part-time basis. A substantial number of authorities claimed however that a "multi-cultural dimension" was included in the other in-service courses which they offered. (Further details of the data obtained in this survey are set out in Annex H to this chapter.) The researchers found that:

> "The difficulty most often mentioned by other authorities was that of attracting to in-service courses teachers who were thought most to need them. Several authorities said that they were concerned that their courses in practice involved 'preaching to the converted'."

40 per cent. of heads in multi-racial secondary schools who responded to the researchers considered school-based courses involving the whole staff of a school to be the most effective form of in-service provision in this field; 30 per cent. gave priority to short courses and 28 per cent. to courses for subject teachers.

– The DES Memorandum on Compliance with the EC Directive on the Education of Children of Migrant Workers (referred to in paragraph 2.6) reported that:

> "... in 1981/1982 over half (53 per cent.) of the establishments providing in-service training made specific provision on meeting the needs of ethnic minority children. A further 7 per cent. were considering introducing such provision for the first time."

– The major source of data relating to the implications of cultural diversity for in-service training is the 1981 report[27] of the DES funded research project undertaken by a research team based at Keele University and led by Professor John Eggleston. The research team based their findings largely on detailed examination of element courses in the multicultural field, chosen as exemplars of the range of provision currently available, including full-time and part-time, award-bearing and non-award-bearing courses of differing types and duration. The central conclusion of the researchers was that:

> "Our investigations have left us in no doubt about the fragmentary and incomplete picture of in-service teacher education for a multicultural society. Indeed it appears non-existent in many areas and in none does it seem wholly adequate."

Whilst the researchers found a good deal of interesting and innovatory work taking place in the in-service field, they observed that:

---

[27] "In-Service Teacher Education in a Multi-Racial Society." Eggleston, Dunn and Purewal. 1981.

". . . the range or provision and its distribution largely arise by the chance incidence of local and even personal initiatives rather than through co-ordinated policy."

In addition to these broad findings the Keele researchers also discussed at some length specific questions related to the demand for courses, course content and organisation, and follow-up, as well as setting in-service training in the multicultural field within the context of the wider society. We would commend the research report as a whole for its thoughtful and thought-provoking insights and reflections on the state of in-service provision and hope particularly that its "conclusions" section will be widely read and discussed. There are however several specific conclusions and comments which we would like to draw out here before moving on to consider our own views on the role of in-service training. The researchers found clear evidence of:

". . . a substantial potential demand for in-service courses for preparing teachers to work in a multicultural society."

This potential demand was not however directly reflected in the actual response to courses, which many course providers considered to be "sluggish", with unfilled or even cancelled courses. The reasons for this apparent mismatch between potential demand and take-up were considered by the researchers to be the poor and "spasmodic" communication network in schools which prevented information about courses reaching teachers; the difficulties some teachers faced in securing release or secondment to attend day-time courses; the lack of official "recognition" given to teachers who had attended these courses, and the failure of course providers to plan courses with teachers. The researchers also found that:

". . . despite the encouragement from HMI and the teachers' organisations the recruitment of teachers from schools and local authorities with relatively few children from minority groups is largely non-existent."

In considering the content of in-service courses in this field, the research team concluded that:

"It is important that courses should not leave participants with any impression of total understanding, rather an informed position which they can maintain and develop. The diverse and changing aspirations among and between sub-groups within each minority are such that participants can almost never be fully in touch with the complexities involved. Courses should also always caution teachers about the danger of encapsulating children within their own perspectives and

perceptions, however sensitive. Courses should also encourage participants to explore alternative styles to learning which may be appropriate to particular children, and to observe successful experiences outside their own classroom which may be incorporated in curricula which develop particular skills. Finally, we reiterate that all those who are concerned with the determination of content and course provision should remember that a keen and sensitive awareness of the needs of all children may be as essential as an awareness of the needs of children from specific ethnic minorities if a sound and well balanced in-service educational provision for a multicultural society is to be developed."

Although the focus of their study was on the in-service provision offered which explicitly dealt with "multicultural" issues, the researchers interpreted their task rather more broadly and reflected in the following terms on the responsibility which they felt *all* in-service provision had to incorporate a pluralist perspective:

"Although there is a clear need for further specific courses of in-service education for multicultural situations both at the award-bearing and short course level, this provision should not be seen as an end in itself. These courses can be regarded as but one essential contribution to the fulfilment of a more pervasive need: to make the consideration of multicultural issues more widely available in the general provision of in-service courses for teachers. It is difficult to believe that any in-service course being offered at the present time could properly avoid some consideration of multicultural education. Obvious cases are courses in educational management, guidance and counselling and curriculum development. A multicultural dimension is an inescapable component of the fabric of contemporary educational provision. Indeed we would hope that such a dimension will come to pervade all courses and equally importantly, that all course tutors will have a proper sensitivity and awareness of the area."

In considering the case for a broader approach to the curriculum, and the task for in-service training in particular, the researchers observed that:

"Teachers in their classrooms have found themselves responsible for an increasing part of society's response. Their need for assistance has never been greater. Yet recent studies continue to demonstrate the dearth of detailed consideration of multicultural issues in most schemes of initial training. And since the flow of recruits to the teaching profession has slowed and, in some schools has ceased altogether the response becomes more and more the responsibility of the existing teaching force."

Our Approach

Permeation of In-Service Provision

3.12   The central message of "Education for All" is that the education offered to *all* pupils should reflect both the diversity of British society and, beyond this, the interdependence of the world community today. It will be clear therefore that just as we see initial teacher training having a major role to play in offering *all* new teachers the skills and background knowledge needed to fulfil their professional responsibilities in a genuinely pluralist context, so we would see in-service training as having an equally important and complementary role to play in relation to those teachers already teaching in schools. We have argued for the permeation of *all* initial training courses with the principles underlying a genuinely pluralist approach to education; we also believe that *all* in-service courses, irrespective of level or subject matter, or the character of the area or institution in which they are provided, must reflect the multiplicity of cultures, faiths and languages in contemporary society. All in-service courses should be informed by the broad principles which we would wish to see underlying all initial training courses and which we set out in paragraph 2.13 above. As the Assistant Masters and Mistresses Association has observed[28]:

> *"In the same way that we believe that multi-cultural perspectives need to inhere in the whole of the school curriculum, they must inform a very wide spectrum of INSET (in-service training), whatever its main purpose. Subject based, pastoral and management courses all need to take account of how their own particular aspects of the education service need to respond to the issues of multi-cultural living. This is an important way of seeing that (a multicultural) approach . . . really does begin to underpin the whole of the school, and also to reach the ears of some teachers who would not choose to go on the more specifically multi-cultural courses, in the hope of awaking their awareness."*

The latter is clearly a particularly important argument in favour of the permeation of all in-service provision, especially in view of our belief that a broader, pluralist approach to education is fully justified on *educational* grounds, quite apart from the presence of ethnic minority pupils in some schools. It can be seen for example that an in-service course offered to teachers in an "all-white" area, relating to aspects of history teaching, religious education or social and political studies, would be unbalanced, incomplete and out of touch with the real world, if it did not incorporate an awareness of the present-day character of British society. All providers of in-service training should ensure that all the courses they offer fully reflect a genuinely pluralist perspective and the broad educational principles which we have set out in this report.

---

[28]"Our Multicultural Society: The Educational Response." AMMA. 1983.

Training of Heads and Senior Staff

3.13   We should perhaps single out for particular emphasis here the courses to be offered by the National Development Centre for School Management Training at Bristol, since it is clear that the attitude and general level of awareness and understanding of Heads and senior staff influences greatly a school's response to this area of development. As the Secretary of State himself observed[29], in announcing the setting up of the National Centre:

> *"The standards of our schools – academic, moral and cultural – are set by the heads and the senior staff within them. It is essential that they should be fully equipped for the difficult tasks that face them."*

We therefore strongly urge that the provision offered by the National Centre, and indeed by other institutions training Heads and their senior colleagues, should incorporate a pluralist perspective.

Specialised In-Service Provision

Award-Bearing Courses

3.14   There is also a range of in-service training provision which is concerned specifically with the educational needs of ethnic minority pupils and the general development of a broader approach to the curriculum. This provision takes a wide variety of forms, ranging from long award-bearing courses leading to higher degrees, options within in-service BEd or MEd degrees and advanced diplomas and certificates offered by universities, polytechnics and colleges, to locally organised short courses and workshops and various school-based activities. Each of these types of provision has a contribution to make in enhancing the knowledge and overall awareness of practising teachers to the implications and opportunities of teaching in a culturally diverse society. However we believe that the area of in-service provision with the greatest potential for influencing the largest number of teachers in the most immediate and practical sense is without doubt the wide range of school-based and school-focussed activities which have developed in recent years and which we discuss in some detail later in this section (see pargraph 3.22 below). High level, award-bearing courses, especially at MEd level, which include options relating to "multicultural education" can however we believe also be valuable in attracting senior post-holders from schools including Heads and deputies and indeed from other teacher training institutions or from LEA advisory services, who, as we have already observed, can play such a major role in influencing their own institution's or organisation's policies. Such individuals can themselves then act as agents of change in bringing about a fundamental reappraisal of policies and practices in their own institutions in accordance with pluralist principles and thus accelerate the pace of the reorientation of educational provision and teacher training which we have advocated. Advanced diplomas and in-service BEd courses can be equally valuable for senior

---

[29]DES Press Notice 283/82. 6 December 1982.

teachers and heads of departments. At present few institutions offer taught Master's degree courses or in-service BEd courses which incorporate specific major or minor options in multicultural issues. The issues covered by these options range from those relating specifically to the multi-racial school – whether in the form of the particular linguistic needs of children for whom English is not a first language, or the approach which can be adopted to certain subject areas in a multi-racial classroom situation – or more broadly to the way in which teaching in any school in this country can and must take account of the multi-racial social context. We would therefore wish to see a general expansion of provision at this level in order to extend the capacity of the teacher training system to influence the senior, key figures within the education service in the manner which we have outlined here. We believe that there is also scope for the further development of Master's degree courses specifically concerned with the broader concept of "Education for All" which we have advocated, rather than simply incorporating options in this field, and we would hope therefore that institutions will give consideration to developing such courses in response to this report

Centres of Specialism

3.15 There are already a few teacher training institutions, such as Bradford College and the University of London Institute of Education, which have developed particular expertise in the multicultural field in relation to the needs of certain ethnic minority groups and which offer a range of long and short in-service courses. Such centres of specialism will clearly continue to attract those practising teachers who wish to acquire particular skills related directly to the character of their own schools, and can offer advice and support to other institutions wishing to develop their provision in this field. Such institutions may also be able to foster curriculum development and support research initiatives in this field. We would hope to see other institutions developing similar expertise in relation to aspects of "Education for All" in the future – for example, the findings of Professor Craft's research project on the capacity of institutions to offer provision relating specifically to ethnic minority community languages, summarised in Annex F to our Language Chapter, drew attention to a number of potential "centres of growth" which we would hope to see develop their provision further.

Short Courses

3.16 A range of specialist short courses has been developed mainly by LEAs and often in collaboration with teacher training institutions to meet the particular needs of teachers working in multi-racial schools. It must be recognised that a course which may last for perhaps only one term part-time can only be regarded as of limited value in itself and should properly be seen as part of a continuing in-service training and curriculum development process. Nevertheless, where a practising teacher wishes to gain further knowledge or skills in a particular aspect of his work, such short courses can be of considerable value. We have already discussed in earlier chapters of this report the particular educational needs which some ethnic minority pupils may experience, and how we feel these needs should best be catered for. For example, we believe that all teachers in schools with substantial numbers of pupils for whom English is not a first language should recognise and accept their responsibility for supporting the linguistic development of these pupils rather than simply regarding this as the role of the language "specialist". Apart from such specific issues, there is also a need for teachers in multi-racial schools to have a particular level of knowledge and understanding of the religious or cultural character of the community or communities which they serve in order to be able to respond sensitively and positively to any "pastoral" needs which may arise and to fulfil their responsibilities in relation to home/school relationships. This would of course be true for any teacher in any school in the country, whether "all-white" or multi-racial, but where the cultural "frame of reference" of a substantial part of a school's pupil population may be markedly different from that of all or most of the staff, it is clear that there may be a particularly pressing need for relevant in-service training of the teachers, and this need can often be met through short course provision. In view of the risks of such "background" courses establishing or reinforcing negative stereotypes of ethnic minority communities, it is essential that great care and sensitivity is exercised in developing such provision. The majority of LEAs now have advisory committees with the specific task of co-ordinating and facilitating in-service provision and we hope that these bodies will be particularly responsive to the need to ensure a recognition of cultural diversity. Since in-service short courses, by definition, need to be related directly to a particular area or school, it is difficult to put forward a "model". Nevertheless there are three broad principles which we believe should inform provision of this type:

– every effort should be made to involve members of the different ethnic minority communities themselves to talk about their life-styles, attitudes towards education and aspirations, to avoid the risks inherent in attempting to "define other people's realities" for them;

– the emphasis should be primarily on the experiences of the communities in *this* country rather than in their countries of origin, since this is the context in which the ethnic minority youngsters now in school are being educated and will be living;

– whilst it is clearly necessary for teachers to gain an understanding of the cultural and religious beliefs and traditions of different communities, it should also be recognised that many British-born ethnic minority youngsters are now developing their own distinct "identities" which may incorporate the central elements of their parents' lifestyles but with a rather different emphasis: it cannot be seen as the task of the school to

586

"enforce" a particular cultural identity on any child, but rather to help him or her evolve their own identity;

Taking account of these broad principles, we would wish to see a general expansion of short course provision relating to the particular educational needs which may arise in multi-racial schools.

Racism Awareness Training

3.17   It is important to mention here the limited but increasing number of short, in-service courses which have been organised by certain multi-racial LEAs and educational organisations in the past few years concerned with what has generally been termed "Racism Awareness". Although the diverse activities which have been organised under this broad heading have varied widely, they have generally derived from the Racism Awareness programmes originally devised in the United States, particularly the programme devised by Judy Katz, whose handbook of "Anti-Racism Training" – "White Awareness" – was published in the USA in 1978. An example of the type of course which has been organised in this country was the Racism Awareness Workshop organised by the National Union of Teachers in March 1983, the aims of which were set out as follows:

> *"The workshop is designed for teachers who wish to develop an awareness of the operation of racism in society in general and in the education system in particular at an institutional and personal level. It will be specifically focused around "white" attitudes and the professional responsibilities of white teachers in a multi-racial, multicultural society. It is hoped that through an exploration of the processes involved in "unlearning" racism, and exercises aimed at strengthening participants' anti-racist understanding and techniques, teachers will be provided with information and skills which will help them to make an effective contribution to anti-racist strategies in their own schools and colleges."*

The objective of Racism Awareness Training is very much in keeping with our own views on the need to acknowledge and challenge manifestations of racism both within education and in society generally at institutional and individual level, and particularly the need for teachers to be prepared to revise their attitudes towards ethnic minorities where these can be seen to be working against the interests of particular pupils or counter to the overall aim of a genuinely pluralist society. It will be clear that we have already stressed the need for in-service training to cover many of the specific elements often involved in Racism Awareness courses – such as studying the origins and operation of racism, the background to today's culturally diverse society and the potential contribution of education to bringing about a racially just, pluralist society – in the rather broader and more positive context of enabling teachers to recognise and fulfil their professional responsibilities in relation to *all* their pupils more effectively.

587

The development of distinct Racism Awareness courses is still at an early stage with little if any work having yet been undertaken in an "all-white" context. The majority of the participants so far have been already "converted" to the aims of multicultural education – the participants in the NUT workshop were for example described as:

> ". . . a self-selected group of volunteers with a positive willingness to learn about racism awareness techniques."

– rather than still remaining to be convinced by the course itself. We find ourselves therefore uncertain as to the value of such courses. It may well be that such a short course – most Racism Awareness courses last no more than 10-15 hours – which is concerned so explicitly and directly with the controversial and complex issue of racism, may stand less chance of effectively influencing the attitudes and behaviour of a teacher who has not previously considered this aspect of his or her work, than would a longer and more broadly-based in-service course or school-based activities which set racism within a wider perspective. It may be interesting to note in this context that we understand from some of those who gave evidence to us about the American situation that the trend there in recent years has been away from specific Racism Awareness courses and towards the incorporation of the underlying aims and objectives involved within rather broader course provision. We believe there is an urgent need for research into the various Racism Awareness training programmes which have been devised so far and we would like to see the DES funding an independent evaluation of the content and effectiveness of such courses.

"All-White" Dimension

3.18   It will be clear that the type of specific in-service provision which we have discussed is designed primarily to meet the needs of those practising teachers who are actually teaching in multi-racial schools. Courses relating to issues such as "teaching in a multilingual classroom", "the pastoral needs of Muslim girls", or to the specific background of certain ethnic minority groups in particular parts of the country, can be seen to be of little relevance to the teacher working in an "all-white" school in an area with little if any ethnic minority settlement. Nevertheless, as we have emphasised throughout this report, the issues raised by "Education for All" are of equal validity and importance for teachers in such "all-white" areas, in offering their pupils a full and balanced education, and in also seeking to counter the misleading and negative stereotypes which ethnic majority pupils may have of ethnic minority groups and which contribute to the overall climate of racism. We have already argued that *all* new teachers should, through their initial training, be brought to an awareness and understanding of the broader multi-racial social context in which they will be teaching and of how to prepare their pupils for life in a pluralist society. It is equally necessary to develop this same degree of awareness and understanding amongst those teachers already in schools, including those in "all-white" areas. As we have seen however, there is virtually no in-service provision currently available which seeks to cater for what is after all still a majority of the existing teaching force – Little and Willey's study reported almost no relevant in-service provision available to teachers in areas with few ethnic minority pupils, and Professor Eggleston and his team found this type of provision "largely non-existent". It could be suggested that this gap in provision could be filled by a major extension of existing in-service courses to LEAs and teacher training institutions in "all-white" areas. This assumes however that the in-service needs of a teacher in an "all-white" school are the same as those of a teacher in a multi-racial school, and, as we have seen, there are in fact clear differences of emphasis and concern in these different contexts. We believe therefore that there is an urgent need to develop appropriate in-service courses across the range of provision, from options in high level, award-bearing courses to part-time, short courses, designed specifically to enable teachers from "all-white" schools to incorporate a pluralist perspective in their work and to bring their pupils to a positive understanding and appreciation of the multi-racial nature of society. Those teachers from "all-white" schools with whom we have discussed the development of courses along these lines have generally expressed themselves willing and indeed anxious to broaden their horizons through such in-service training.

3.19   It is difficult to set out here what we would regard as the ideal content of such courses for teachers in "all-white" areas since the opportunities for detailed study and the emphasis of a course will vary according to type and length. We would nevertheless envisage courses covering the kind of information which we have already indicated we would wish to see included in core studies at both initial and in-service level, which can broadly be summarised as follows:

– an informed awareness of the diversity of contemporary British society, including the basic "facts and figures" about the processes of immigration to and emigration from this country over the last 150 years and the circumstances which have conditioned the experiences and aspirations of different ethnic minority groups;

– the theory and practice of racism at both institutional and individual level and how this operates, and can be challenged, both in society and in education;

– the changing perceptions of "ethnic minority education" and our view of "Education for All";

– the straightforward *educational* grounds for broadening the curriculum to incorporate multicultural and indeed global perspectives and wider questions of justice, equality and the aims of a genuinely pluralist society.

589

Above all it should be emphasised that the opportunities offered by our multi-racial society are equally relevant should a teacher be teaching in a rural, "all-white" school or an urban, multi-racial school, since all schools and all teachers have a professional responsibility to prepare their pupils for life in a pluralist society. Against this general background, it should be possible in some courses to deal with more specific issues which may be of particular relevance or interest to teachers concerned with particular phases of education or with particular subject specialisms – for example the question of enhancing the language skills and awareness of linguistic diversity of pupils in a "monolingual" classroom, which we discussed in Chapter Seven, or developing an appreciation of the tapestry of religious experience in Britian today which we discussed in Chapter Eight. As we have already indicated, we believe that the implications for in-service training of the "all-white" dimension have until very recently been almost entirely overlooked, despite the public pronouncements and exhortations emphasising the relevance of "multicultural education" to all schools and we believe therefore that there is a need for a major central Government initiative to foster the development and expansion of such provision. We urge the Government to establish a series of "pilot projects", involving teacher training institutions, LEAs and schools in "all-white" areas, designed to develop and disseminate good practice in this field. In order to encourage and facilitate the development of such provision, we would also hope to see the emergence, in the longer term, of acknowledged "centres of specialism", comparable to those discussed in paragraph 3.15 above, concerned specifically with the all-white dimension of "Education for All" which could foster further curriculum development and research in this field.

Financial Support

3.20   All that we have said up to now has been intended to bring about an extension and development of in-service provision related to our view of "Education for All". It could be argued that such an expansion of provision is unnecessary and unjustified since one of the few findings to emerge clearly from the limited research available has been that a proportion of the in-service courses already offered in this field are undersubscribed and some have even been cancelled due to lack of support – at first sight hardly a basis on which to press for more such courses to be organised. However it must be recognised that the major factor in this situation, especially in recent years, is not we believe any lack of interest on the part of teachers, but rather the effects of financial constraints which have led many LEAs to reduce substantially the number of teachers whom they are prepared to release for in-service training because of the costs incurred in providing replacements for them. In order to have any chance of effectively enhancing the level of in-service training available to teachers in this field, it is clear that the expansion of course provision which we have advocated here must therefore be matched by appropriate financial support in order to enable teachers and LEAs to take full advantage of the training opportunities available. In March 1983, the DES announced[30] details of a scheme of direct grants for in-service teacher training under which direct financial assistance is offered by central Government to local authorities when serving teachers are released for training on designated courses in any of four priority areas: management training for Headteachers and senior staff; mathematics teaching following the report of the Cockcroft Committee[31]; pre-vocational education in schools; and special educational needs in ordinary schools.[32] The express intention of this move was to bring about an expansion of in-service provision in these areas – as Circular 3/83 explained;

> *"When local authorities are considering the release of teachers for in-service training, a major difficulty can be the costs which would be incurred in providing replacements. It is the Secretary of State's intention under this scheme to secure an increase of in-service training in the ... priority areas. The difficulty referred to above would largely be overcome if, as he expects, the grants paid in respect of eligible teachers attending eligible courses are used towards the salary costs of providing replacements for them."[33]*

We believe that the in-service training of teachers to fulfil their professional responsibilities in relation to their pupil populations, whether multi-racial or "all-white", and to lay the foundations for a genuinely pluralist society is as much a "priority area" within teacher training as are the areas of provision so far included in this scheme. We therefore recommend that the Government should extend the terms of the scheme to allow for grants to be available to authorities in respect of the release of serving teachers for training on courses relating to aspects of "Education for All". Such an extension would require a range of courses to be designated as "eligible" and we hope that, in drawing up such a list, reference would be made to the broad principles and objectives for in-service training which we have set out in this chapter. Whilst the emphasis will initially be on courses related to the needs of teachers teaching in

---

[30]DES Circular 3/83 "The In-Service Teacher Training Grants Scheme." 31 March 1983.

[31]"Mathematics Counts." Report of the Committee of Inquiry into the Teaching of Mathematics in Schools. HMSO. 1982.

[32]The DES subsequently added four new priority areas for inclusion in the scope of the scheme: science education; a special programme of support relating to the introduction of the General Certificate of Secondary Education; craft, design and technology teaching in schools; staff development in further education, and the updating of staff on work-related courses.

[33]The Scheme relates to teachers who are currently in full-time, permanent employment at maintained ordinary or special schools, and who have been so employed for an aggregate period of at least five years. The eligible courses should not involve attendances for longer than a period of 12 months' duration and should involve at least 20 days' attendance on what would normally be working days for the teachers concerned. Circular 4/84 included provisional estimates of the grants allocated to each LEA calculated on the basis of its compulsory school age population. The grants will cover, on average, 90 per cent. of the salary costs of teachers released for in-service training. The remaining 10 per cent. will be met by local education authorities. The Government has issued details of those courses considered eligible for grant aid – Teacher Training Circular Letter 2/84 – although attendance at other courses relating to the priority areas may exceptionally be considered eligible.

multi-racial schools, we should emphasise that we would wish in the longer term to see in-service courses specifically designed for teachers working in "all-white" schools becoming eligible for grant, once these have been developed and their effectiveness evaluated.

School Based Activities

3.21 Up to now we have confined our consideration of in-service training chiefly to the provision of taught courses of varying types and levels but nevertheless all "external" to the individual school. In recent years however, in discussions of in-service training generally, increasing emphasis and attention has come to be devoted to the role of school-based or school-focussed in-service support for teachers, and we ourselves believe that such activities have a crucial part to play in enhancing the knowledge and understanding of serving teachers. In considering the potential role of school-based activities, it is important to appreciate that there are two distinct, although clearly inter-related, purposes of in-service training: on the one hand, as a contribution to the professional development of the individual teacher often as a means of gaining promotion or career advancement, possibly at a new school or elsewhere in the education service, and, on the other hand, as an integral part of the enhancement and development of the policies and practices of a school as a whole. We believe that these two functions of in-service training are both important, however, from the point of view of bringing about the reorientation of the education process which we have advocated in this report, the latter is perhaps the more essential. Whilst we certainly wish to see teachers who have devoted time and effort to gaining additional qualifications being given appropriate recognition, if such teachers subsequently take up posts either at another school or elsewhere in the education service, the in-service training involved has in practice proved of little value to their original schools. There must therefore we believe be a central place in any scheme of in-service provision, for activities which take place on a school basis and which can thus involve a whole school staff working together to enhance and develop the teaching which they offer their pupils. As the James Report observed:

> *"In-service training should begin in the schools. It is here that learning and teaching take place, curricula and techniques are developed and needs and deficiencies revealed. Every school should regard the continued training of its teachers as an essential part of its task, for which all members of staff share responsibility."*

The Cockcroft Committee in their report on mathematics education shared this view of the fundamental importance of school-based support in relation to their particular concerns and outlined the inherent strengths of this form of in-service work as follows:

> *"It can be directed specifically to the needs of the school and its pupils,*

592

so that those who teach mathematics develop professionally as a result of working together to improve the work of the school. Above all, it can and should be a continuing process which is not limited to the length of a lecture, a discussion or a course."

These comments are equally applicable to the broader issues with which we are concerned in this report.

3.22   Many of those who gave evidence to us emphasised that they regarded school-based activities as the most important form of in-service provision and as likely to have the most immediate impact on the greatest number of teachers. School-based activities can be seen as the only effective means of influencing those teachers, who may have received their initial training the longest ago and may therefore be most able to benefit from updating of their knowledge and skills, but are the least likely to attend an out-of-school in-service course although they may be in positions of authority within schools. It is clear that for school-based activities to be effective, they must have the whole-hearted support of Heads and senior staff, Governors and of the LEA, since indirect costs may be involved through the purchase of materials or possibly the closure of the school for an in-service day or the organisation of an in-service weekend. Although we believe that the range of skill and expertise available from within a school's normal staff has generally been underestimated, it is also however necessary to avoid school-based activities becoming either too narrow and inward-looking or too complacent, if any meaningful appraisal of policies and practice is to take place. An outside catalyst to such activities may therefore be needed either in the form of an adviser or outsider "expert" or possibly a teacher from another school, or through a member of the school staff attending an external in-service course and then returning to coordinate activities within the school and to pass on the particular knowledge and skills which he or she has gained. In this way structured in-service course provision and school-focussed activities can be seen as complementary, and the influence and effectiveness of course provision can be extended and developed far beyond the number of teachers who are able to actually attend courses, which, even with the overall expansion of provision for which we have called, will always remain limited in relation to the overall size of the teaching force. The development of continuing school-based activities can also ensure that a school is able to take full advantage of the additional knowledge which a teacher may gain on a course rather than, as may be the case at present, the effectiveness of a course being diluted in the face of a disinterested or unresponsive school staff. As the HMI discussion paper "Teacher Training and the Secondary School" observed

"Experience has shown that the stimulating effect of an in-service course on one or two individuals can be neutralised on their return by

the inability of the school to respond to it and to take advantage of what they have learned."

Thus school-based developments can not only extend the influence of in-service training courses, but can also create the climate of receptivity and openness needed to allow the knowledge and skills gained to have a positive impact in schools.

3.23   It is clear that school-based activities can be especially valuable in fostering the enhanced awareness of multicultural issues and in developing the pluralist perspective which we have advocated here. This was certainly the emphasis of much of the evidence which we received on teacher training – as one teacher training institution put it to us for example:

> *". . . we would see school-based in-service courses as being a necessary and desirable part of any in-service programme. It is essential that all staff in a school are made aware of the need of multi-racial education, and are offered immediate and sustained support in the acquisition of skills and the design of strategies appropriate to meeting these needs."*

One of the clearest findings to emerge from the Schools Council research project (see paragraph 3.11 above) was the very high percentage – 40 per cent. – of heads of multi-racial schools who favoured school-based provision involving the whole school staff as the most effective form of in-service provision in this field. Because school-based activities have to be closely related to the resources and needs of an individual school, it is not possible to put forward a "model" of the kind of programme which we would wish to see schools developing. The issues which all schools, whether multi-racial or "all-white", should consider are however evident from the findings and conclusions which we have reached in this chapter, and we hope that our Report will serve as a catalyst to the self-evaluation and self-appraisal by school staffs of the aims and effectiveness of their work. The following further extract from the HMI discussion paper emphasises the particular role which school-based in-service work can play in focussing teachers' minds on difficult and controversial issues, such as those with which we are concerned, as well as mentioning some of the methods which can be employed in school-based provision:

> *"It is when a school has come to a decision as to what direction it should develop in, and analysed its training needs, that it can absorb and act upon the effects of that training. The school-focussed model will be one of the means by which the institution responds to this self-evaluation. This approach is particularly well fitted to achieve objectives which require a radical change in thinking on the part of the staff. One example is the wider view of the curriculum . . . Heads of*

department can be encouraged to give a lead in forming working groups of teachers from a number of subjects. These might begin by looking at ways in which one subject can provide teaching material for others and draw upon them in turn. They might then work towards identifying particular insights and skills that their subjects have a common interest in developing. Another example is the extension of teaching methods. There are obvious difficulties in persuading experienced teachers that they need to look critically at their own teaching methods. Little will be achieved if school policies to this end are conceived abstractly and handed down as precept. They will fail if they do not take account of the sensitivity of staff who see them as a questioning of their professional competence, or an encroachment upon their autonomy. A school-focussed approach is certainly the best form of in-service training to open up teaching methods to critical scrutiny, but its basis should be inductive. Heads of departments need to cooperate to encourage teachers to look at the demands made upon a pupil in subjects other than their own. This will imply a greater readiness to observe and to be observed and to dicuss openly the outcomes. A third example is the need for the teacher to continue to broaden his experience of pupil performance and keep his standards and expectations under critical review. In-service work in schools should include the opportunity for collective study of work produced by pupils in response to a variety of demands.

Teachers need to be able to look at performance across a wide ability range and in subjects other than their own, and to discuss implications with colleagues. This amounts to a continuous process of self-evaluation on the part of schools, where larger and more general objectives are evolved from evidence and professional judgments accumulated by teachers at individual and group level."

There are two particular types of school-based in-service activities which we would especially like to highlight here as having a potentially very important contribution to make. Firstly we would emphasise the need to develop and extend the use of "distance learning" techniques such as the use by school staffs of taped and video-taped material which can both broaden the expertise available to a school and also widen the horizons of teachers. We are pleased that both the BBC and the IBA have shown an interest in developing appropriate programmes and also that the Open University has already developed some particularly interesting and thought-provoking courses and programmes which would we believe be of great value in stimulating discussion and development within schools. We believe that there is considerable scope for the Open University in particular to further extend its work in this field and we hope that our Report will encourage such an extension. Even more potentially immediate in its impact on schools can however we believe be the development and expansion of schemes for staff exchanges both between schools with similar circumstances and also between schools with widely-different characters, such as an urban multi-racial school and a rural "all-white" school. Much has of course been made of the potential value of teachers from multi-racial schools visiting the countries of origin of their pupils, and the Caribbean Teacher Exchange Scheme has for some years allowed groups of teachers from schools with pupils of West Indian origin to "exchange" jobs for a year with teachers from the West Indies. Such exchanges have undoubtedly served to enhance the awareness and understanding of both the teachers and schools involved. The great majority of ethnic minority pupils now in schools are British-born however and since, as we have stressed, we believe that the role of schools cannot be seen as to "enforce" a particular cultural identity on any child but rather to encourage the development of a child's own identity, which may relate to a British context rather than to their "ethnic" origins, such exchanges may become increasingly irrelevant to the development of the kind of educational processes which we have advocated. We believe however that there is considerable scope for the development of a centrally-funded scheme to facilitate teacher exchanges, possibly organised through the Central Bureau for Educational Visits and Exchanges, *within this country* as part of broadening the horizons of all schools to appreciate the different perspectives and opportunities offered in multi-racial and in "all-white" schools for the development of an overall education process which seeks to prepare *all* pupils for life in a genuinely pluralist society.

In-service Policy Statements and their Implementation

3.24   If the changes we are seeking within schools are to be brought about efficiently, we consider it important that each school should develop, in consultation with the LEA and its advisors, a scheme for the in-service education of its teachers, ranging from award bearing courses to short courses and school based activities as appropriate. Such a scheme could form part of the policy statement on "Education for All" which we consider LEAs should require of each school. To this end, we also consider it necessary that each LEA, in its own policy statement, should commit itself to developing an overall strategy of in-service training for its area which would cover not only the work of teachers but all other members of the education service, for example librarians, careers advisors and educational psychologists. For the implementation of such a policy appropriate funds will need to be allocated to provide not only for the secondment and supply cover for teachers together with related expenses but also for the necessary resources and support services. In each LEA there needs to be provision at teachers' centres of books, materials and facilities together with specialist advice which teachers and LEA personnel can call on as required. In the interests of the economical use of resources it is clear that adequate provision must also be made for the proper evaluation in relation to local needs of the full range of these in-service activities.

Training the Trainers

3.25   It is clear that the task which we have envisaged for teacher education at both initial and in-service level makes great demands on the teacher training institutions and on individual teacher trainers. It may well be necessary therefore for some teacher trainers to become involved in a process of reappraisal, reorientation and even retraining themselves. As the HMI discussion paper on initial training observed:

> "The most carefully planned course of training is still only as good as the people who teach it and the way it is taught . . . The professional element in the student's preparation should be taught by people who are successful and experienced members of the teaching profession, up-to-date in their knowledge of schools and of society, and able to help their students develop an informed empirical approach to their teaching tasks."

The latter point is perhaps even more relevant to the in-service training available to practising teachers since they will clearly be particularly concerned that any provision offered to them relates directly to the realities of the classroom. The contraction of the teacher training system over recent years has however meant that few new lecturers with direct and recent teaching experience, particularly of teaching in multi-racial schools are now joining institutions – a point which we drew out in our interim report. As one teacher training institution explained to us in evidence:

> "Like so many Schools of Education, new recruitment is non-existent. We are a fast ageing staff: most of us have very little experience of recent teaching in inner city (or outer city!) schools."

One of the solutions to this perceived "gap" in the experience of teacher training staff, especially in relation to the multi-racial teaching situation, has been to involve practising teachers on a regular basis to assist trainers in their work. The NUT supported such initiatives in its evidence to the 1981 Home Affairs Committee:

> "The expertise of practising teachers is a valuable resource and colleges should be encouraged in this practice, not only for options and in-service courses, but as a contribution to the "compulsory" element of the initial course, whether BEd or PGCE . . . A more flexible and imaginative use of the secondment of teachers to colleges and college staff to schools, utilising the experience of serving teachers in the training of students, would be beneficial to all concerned."

We would certainly endorse this view, provided the teachers used in this way receive appropriate reward and recognition, since we believe there is a need for far closer links to be developed between schools and teacher training institutions in seeking to complement each other's work. As the HMI discussion document on "Teacher Training and the Secondary School" acknowledged:

> *"It has been strongly argued that the balance of influence and authority in initial training should be shifted towards the schools, leading to a partnership very much more equal than at present. Certainly there is room for more instances of teachers working in colleges with students, for example in subject method courses, and of lecturers regarding a regular school teaching assignment as an essential part of their work. It has been remarked of college and school that "the semi-permeable membrane between them should become wholly permeable"."*

The increasingly widespread opportunities for involving practising teachers in the work of teacher training institutions through Teacher Fellowships and Teacher Associateships can clearly also make an important contribution to relating the provision offered more directly to work in schools and can lend added immediacy to courses. We would therefore wish to see such opportunities further developed and extended in the future. The involvement of individual seconded teachers can however only influence some elements in some courses and there is clearly still a need for teacher trainers themselves to seek to develop a pluralist perspective in their work. In some institutions where progress has been made in developing the kind of course initiatives dicussed here, the major responsibility for this work has tended to fall on particular individuals who already have a commitment to pluralist objectives or who have some experience in multi-racial areas and who have therefore come to be regarded as "experts" in this field. In seeking to ensure that all courses reflect a pluralist perspective we believe *all* teacher trainers have a responsibility to ensure that their work is informed by an awareness of the diversity of experiences which make up British society today, over and above any "specialist" knowledge or skills which certain trainers may need. There is a need for urgent attention to be given to possible ways of providing any additional knowledge or skills, or "reorientation" needed by teacher trainers to enable them to contribute fully to the preparation of their students to offer an education both appropriate and relevant to today's society. Only very recently has much attention been devoted to this area of "training the trainers" and developments are consequently at an early stage. We were interested to learn of a national programme of short courses for lecturers and others involved in both initial and in-service teacher education, organised under the auspices of the University of Nottingham, in six teacher training institutions, aimed at developing participants' awareness of the responsibilities of education in relation to today's multi-racial society and the implications of this for their work as teacher trainers. We attach further details of the courses being offered by the various institutions, together with details of the second phase, as Annex I to this chapter in order to illustrate the type of issues which are being covered. We understand that the DES is funding an evaluation of the impact of these courses and we very much hope that this will enable HM Inspectorate to draw out "good practice" in the field of "training the trainers" and will thus allow for further such course developments in the future. It must be recognised however that, valuable though we believe this initiative is, these courses are somewhat limited in scope and since participation is clearly on a voluntary basis, they can in many ways be likened to specialist optional courses in that they will inevitably attract chiefly those teacher trainers who are already committed to progress in this field and will be unlikely to involve the more senior staff of institutions. Such courses are therefore unlikely, by themselves, to bring about the overall reorientation of teacher training courses which we have advocated here, and it may be necessary in the longer term to look towards the establishment of a designated centre or centres for the retraining of teacher trainers, especially at the more senior level, perhaps along the lines of the recently established National Development Centre for School Management Training.

II The Employment of Ethnic Minority Teachers

1. Background

1.1 There has long been concern amongst both ethnic minority communities and educationists that, as the Assistant Masters and Mistresses Association have put it:

> *"Teachers from ethnic minorities are regrettably and evidently a minority in themselves."*

As long ago as 1973 the Select Committee on Race Relations and Immigration, in discussing the potential contribution of teachers of "immigrant origin", was voicing its agreement with:

> *"... the majority of our witnesses, not least those from local education authorities, that there should be more."*

The need for more teachers drawn from the ethnic minority communities has been a recurring theme in discussion of the development of an education appropriate to today's multi-racial society – with, for example, the National Association of Teachers in Further and Higher Education in its written evidence to the Home Affairs Committee for its 1981 Report, expressing the view that:

> *"There is . . . a desperate urgency to increase as dramatically and quickly as possible the number of black teachers in Britain's schools."*

– and this issue certainly featured prominently in much of the evidence which we ourselves received.

Absence of Statistical Data 1.2 It is clear that ethnic minority groups (by which we would mean the whole range of groups with whom we have been concerned in this report and not only the Asians and West Indians on whom most of the attention in this respect has tended to focus) are disproportionately under-represented in the teaching profession – indeed the DES itself has long accepted this as a legitimate cause for concern. There is however no firm statistical basis for any discussion of the number of teachers of ethnic minority origin and such estimates as have been made in recent years have tended to be both limited in scope and definitionally imprecise – for example, the Commission for Racial Equality (CRE), in its evidence to us, was able only to estimate that:

> *". . . there may be 800 or more teachers of West Indian origins and a rather larger number of Asian origins, but no precise figures are available."*

Pressure has come from many quarters for detailed statistics to be collected by the DES both of the ethnic composition of the teaching force and also of the ethnic breakdown of students training to be teachers, in order to clarify the actual extent of the under-representation of ethnic minorities in these fields. In their 1977 Report on the West Indian Community[34] the Select Committee on Race Relations and Immigration recommended explicitly that:

> *". . . the Department of Education and Science should compile and monitor relevant statistics relating to those students training to be teachers, and teachers in grant-aided establishments, who are of West Indian origin."*

Although the then Government accepted this recommendation in principle in its 1978 White Paper on the West Indian Community[35], no action was in fact taken to implement it. In our own interim report therefore we ourselves recommended, in relation to the whole range of ethnic minority groups, that:

---

[34]"The West Indian Community." HC 180 I. 1977.
[35]"The West Indian Community." Home Office. Cmnd 7186. 1978.

> *"The DES should ask all teacher training institutions to collect statistics on the ethnic origin of all students training to be teachers including students seeking to enter teaching through special access courses."*

and that:

> *"The DES should record and publish statistics on the ethnic origin of all teachers in employment . . . "*

The Secretary of State indicated, in giving evidence to the Home Affairs Committee in July 1982, his approval in principle to the collection of ethnically-based statistics in the education field. As we have already observed in Chapter Four, however, no positive action has yet been taken to implement our recommendations in respect of statistics and the terms of reference of the DES's working group on the collection of ethnic statistics do not cover our recommendations in relation to teachers or teacher training students.

1.3 We firmly believe that the collection of the statistical data which we have previously advocated is an essential element in seeking to tackle the important and often controversial issues of the admission of ethnic minority students to teacher training courses and also the recruitment and career advancement of ethnic minority teachers, since such reliable and up-to-date data would serve to quantify accurately for the first time the extent to which ethnic minorities are under-represented in teaching. We therefore begin this discussion of the role and recruitment of ethnic minority teachers by strongly reiterating our interim report recommendations concerning the collection of statistical data in this field.

2. The Case for More Ethnic Minority Teachers

2.1 Irrespective of the absence of detailed statistical data, it is clear that there are disproportionately low numbers of teachers of ethnic minority origin in our schools. We regard this under-representation of ethnic minority teachers as a matter of great concern which merits urgent attention and positive action. As the authors of the second NFER Review of Research have argued:

> *"If schools are to reflect a multi-ethnic society then not only should their curricula be consciously multicultural but their staff should be conspicuously multi-racial too."*

Equality of Opportunity in Employment

2.2 The specific educational justifications for efforts to be made to increase the number of ethnic minority teachers are many and varied and we discuss these further below. Over and above the educational grounds

601

for action, there is the straightforward question of seeking to bring about true equality of opportunity for members of *all* groups throughout the employment market including the teaching profession. A number of individual teachers of ethnic minority origin as well as the various ethnic minority teachers organisations who gave evidence to us expressed the belief that many qualified ethnic minority teachers have faced racial discrimination in seeking employment and subsequently in gaining career advancement. It has been suggested in particular to us that ethnic minority applicants are less likely than their colleagues from the majority community to obtain permanent posts and are often only able to obtain work as "supply" teachers and that, even once they have joined a school, they have particular difficulty in achieving professional recognition in the eyes of their colleagues and are unlikely to be promoted beyond perhaps Scale 1 or 2 posts even after some years service. Clearly the absence of firm statistical data makes it difficult to establish the extent of such discrimination but, as the CRE observed in their evidence to us:

> "What is most apparent . . . is the widespread sense of frustration and bitterness among ethnic minority teachers about what they see as their subordinate and disadvantaged position in the teaching profession."

2.3   Although evidence of actual discrimination is hard to come by, it is clear that ethnic minority teachers have been and are still subject to racism both in gaining employment and in advancing their careers. On our own visits to schools we have been concerned at the number of fully qualified ethnic minority teachers whom we have met who are "stagnating" in the system, in posts far below both their capabilities and experience. A matter of even greater concern is the number of ethnic minority teachers who, discouraged and disenchanted with the obstacles which they feel have been placed in the way of their progress in the teaching profession, have turned to other forms of employment. We urge both the CRE and all those involved within LEAs and schools in making appointments, to devote far greater efforts to identifying and overcoming racism within the teaching profession. As the CRE itself has commented, in its 1981 guide "Local authorities and the education implications of Section 71 of the Race Relations Act 1976"[36]:

> "The mere fact that allegations of discrimination (direct or indirect)

---

[36]Section 71 of the Race Relations Act, 1976 states that
   "Without prejudice to their obligation to comply with any other provision of this Act, it shall be the duty of every local authority to make appropriate arrangements with a view to securing that their various functions are carried out with due regard to the need:

   a. to eliminate unlawful racial discrimination; and

   b. to promote equality of opportunity, and good relations, between persons of different racial groups."

are made by members of the teaching profession necessitates unequivocal commitments to equality of opportunity from educational employers; if discrimination in the employment of teachers does not exist it must nonetheless be shown not to exist."

In this respect we welcome the efforts made by some LEAs to establish themselves as "equal opportunity employers" and we urge *all* LEAs to follow this lead and adopt similar public "equal opportunities" policies.

Educational Arguments for more Ethnic Minority Teachers

2.4   Turning to the educational arguments for increasing the number of ethnic minority teachers, in its conclusions to a survey published in 1977[37] the then Community Relations Commission put forward the following four reasons for employing more ethnic minority teachers:

"a. It is desirable for people staffing an educational service to be a natural reflection of the make-up of the population.

b. People from ethnic minority groups should have opportunities to become professional workers if they have the desire and the ability to do so.

c. Ethnic minority teachers act as a source of cultural expertise and skill for other staff and children.

d. Ethnic minority parents and children who are unable or unwilling to trust "authority" to understand their needs are reassured by the presence of staff from their own ethnic group."

The Multi-Racial Context

All these reasons appear to us to remain valid to the present day. As we have already stressed elsewhere in this report, it is undoubtedly true that some ethnic minority teachers can play a particularly valuable "pastoral" role within a multi-racial school both directly, through supporting and encouraging pupils and parents drawn from the same ethnic minority group, and indirectly, through advising their colleagues on the background and concerns of certain ethnic minority groups and ensuring that the practices and procedures of the school as a whole take account of the needs of the communities which they serve. As we have emphasised however, it should never be *assumed* that each and every teacher of ethnic minority origin will be able or willing to accept this role. As we have stressed in Chapter Seven, the presence of bilingual or multilingual teachers of ethnic minority origin, who share a common "community language" with pupils for whom English is not a first language, can also

---

[37]"The Education of Ethnic Minority Children. From the perspective of Parents, Teachers and Education Authorities." CRC. 1977.

greatly enhance the capacity of a multi-racial school to respond positively to the linguistic diversity of its pupil population, and can be particularly valuable in a "pastoral" context in relation to developing the school's links with parents and the wider community. It has also been strongly emphasised to us, especially by representatives of the West Indian community, that ethnic minority teachers can serve as valuable "role models" for pupils from the same ethnic background, and can thus have a direct effect on the motivation and even the achievement of these pupils. Such an influence can be particularly powerful where the teacher concerned has been born in this country, like the great majority of ethnic minority pupils, and is thus perceived by them as sharing a common background and as having faced and overcome any educational "hurdles" and succeeded within the system. Against this positive attitude is the view expressed to us by a number of ethnic minority pupils that they felt they had little in common with ethnic minority teachers who had been born and trained overseas and who therefore found it difficult to identify with the problems of identity experienced by British-born ethnic minority youngsters and who tended to be unduly influenced by a rather narrow and stereotyped view of their place in this society. In relation to the multi-racial school context, it is also worth noting that on many of our own visits we were struck by the inherent incongruity of "all-white" teaching staffs, often living well away from the catchment areas of their schools, seeking to meet the needs and respond to the concerns of a multi-racial pupil population.

Potential Contribution to an "All-White" School

2.5   This should not be interpreted as suggesting that we see a role for teachers of ethnic minority origin only where there are ethnic minority pupils. This is far too limited a perception of their potential role and of the contribution which they can make to the education process. We believe that an ethnic minority teacher can be a valuable asset to any school in the country – whether multi-racial or "all-white". Ethnic minority teachers may be "role models" in all-white schools as well as in multi-racial schools, in the sense in which their presence may serve to counter and overcome any negative stereotypes in the minds of pupils, parents or teachers from the majority community about ethnic minorities and their place in our society. Where such teachers are able to bring with them a degree of knowledge and personal experience of other cultures, religions and languages this can also be particularly valuable in enriching the "resources" available in an "all-white" school and in assisting the staff in perceiving how the school's curriculum can be broadened along genuinely pluralist lines. As the Assistant Masters and Mistresses Association have explained in their booklet "Our Multicultural Society":

> "... it could be argued that where a school, because of its mono-cultural population, has been slow to realise the need to take account of the multicultural nature of society outside the school, then the

appointment to it of one or more teachers from ethnic minority groups may well be a useful catalyst. We are not arguing that teachers from minority groups are in any sense automatically experts in, or even enthusiasts for, the sort of multicultural approach that we advocate. Individuals may or may not be. What we do suggest is that the arrival of such a teacher in a previously mono-cultural school may cause white colleagues (and pupils) to ask some questions for the first time."

Thus, given the broader approach to the education of *all* pupils which we have advocated throughout this report, we regard ethnic minority teachers as an integral part of the teaching force in all our schools. Ethnic minority teachers should never be portrayed simply as token figures within a school with just a "curiosity" value or able only to undertake certain specific tasks, but should be regarded as part of the school's staff, on equal terms with their colleagues from the majority community in participation in the development of policies and in the decision-making process.

Recruitment 2.6 We find ourselves in principle opposed to any suggestion of a "quota" system for increasing the number of ethnic minority teachers, which would in any sense bypass or override the desire of LEAs and schools to employ first and foremost the best candidate for a particular job in terms of expertise, experience and ability, since clearly this would run counter to the educational interests of all pupils. We do not wish to see any diminution of standards. We believe however that far more consideration should be given, in making appointments, to the extent to which a particular ethnic, cultural, linguistic or religious background is an additional and desirable feature for a job in any school – whether multi-racial or "all-white". Much of a teacher's influence on pupils is of course indirect rather than direct – through the contribution which he or she makes to the ethos of the school and to the "hidden" curriculum. In any school an ethnic minority teacher may be able to make a particular contribution to the development of policies designed to combat and counter the influence of racism, at both institutional and individual level, by drawing on his or her own personal experience of its effects. Just as we have argued throughout this report for a pluralist approach to be adopted in all schools, an education which seeks to prepare all pupils for life in a pluralist society can surely best be provided by a teaching force which is itself pluralist in character.

3. Sources of Ethnic Minority Teachers

3.1 Having established that it is both desirable and indeed essential to increase the number of ethnic minority teachers in our schools, we now need to consider the question of where such teachers are to be found, since the argument often put forward by LEAs and schools to explain the

605

limited number of such teachers is that ethnic minority candidates simply do not apply for posts and therefore cannot be recruited. Whilst we feel that a major factor in this situation may well be the reluctance of ethnic minority teachers to apply for posts which they feel they will not obtain because of the influence of racism in the appointments procedure which, as we have indicated above, can best be overcome by positive statements by LEAs of policies of equality of opportunity in the employment field, it is also clear that steps need to be taken to encourage more members of ethnic minority groups to enter teaching in the first place. In our view there are three main potential sources for recruiting more teachers of ethnic minority origin:

– Ethnic minority teachers who have qualified and taught overseas;

– Mature individuals from the ethnic minorities who do not hold the appropriate academic qualifications for entry to teacher training but who are keen to become teachers; and

– Ethnic minority youngsters, currently in school, who have or expect to obtain the appropriate qualifications.

Clearly individuals from each of the above categories would require different degrees of support and encouragement in order to become qualified teachers. We therefore consider below the particular needs of each of these groups.

Teachers with Overseas Qualifications

3.2 There are undoubtedly, within the various ethnic minority communities, a number of first generation immigrants who trained, qualified and taught in their respective countries of origin but who have either not sought to or have been unable to resume their teaching careers in this country. At first sight such individuals would appear to offer a valuable source of experienced ethnic minority teachers, although, as we have observed above, it must be recognised that some ethnic minority teachers from overseas may find it particularly difficult to relate to British-born ethnic minority youngsters. It must be borne in mind however that qualifications obtained overseas do not necessarily equate with similar qualifications in this country. The procedure followed by the DES in determining whether to grant qualified teacher status to individuals with overseas qualifications was described to us as follows:

"i. *The regulations governing recognition as a qualified teacher require a course of training completed elsewhere to be comparable to an approved course of initial teacher training undertaken in England and Wales.*

ii.   *Applications are assessed individually. Crucial factors are the age of entry, length, content and standard of the overseas course for comparison with approved courses of initial teacher training in England and Wales.*

iii. *Overseas graduates with degrees obtained before 1974 (when the teacher training requirement came fully into effect) may be acceptable without professional teacher training provided that the standard of the degree equates to that of a first degree of a British University. Untrained graduates are limited to teaching in secondary schools only if the degrees were obtained after 1969.*

iv.   *In line with the policy of improving minimum standards in the teaching profession, evidence of competence in the English language and mathematics will be required from those who are granted qualified teacher status after August 1984. The standard will be GCE 'O' levels or other equivalent qualifications."*

It was emphasised to us that applicants are required to themselves arrange for verification of their overseas qualifications direct from the overseas institutions concerned for the DES. Several of the ethnic minority organisations who gave evidence to us expressed some concern about the fact that the procedure for obtaining qualified teacher status could prove both expensive and time-consuming for the individual applicant, and that the criteria used for evaluating the content and comparability of overseas courses were often unclear. Whilst we fully recognise that it is of the utmost importance to ensure that those gaining qualified teacher status are of an appropriate calibre, we recommend that the DES should clarify the arrangements for granting qualified teachers status to members of ethnic minority communities who possess overseas qualifications with a view to encouraging them to enter the teaching profession, as long as this involves no diminution of standards.

3.3   The 1977 Select Committee Report on the West Indian Community recommended that:

". . . the Department of Education and Science should forthwith consider ways and means of increasing the number of teachers of West Indian origin in maintained schools."

"Special Access" Courses

In 1978, in response to this specific recommendation and to the widespread concern about the shortage of teachers from the whole range of ethnic minority groups, the DES invited seven LEAs to establish what have become known as "special access" courses designed to prepare mature students, particularly but not exclusively from ethnic minority communities, who lacked the normal academic qualifications, to enter training for teaching and other "caring" professions. Six of the LEAs originally approached have felt able to establish access courses and one additional Authority has also since established them. The DES-sponsored evaluation from 1979 to 1983 of these has indicated encouraging results.[39] We understand from the Project Director, Mr. Ken Millins (who was of course also previously a member of this Committee) that during the sessions 1979/1980 – 1983/1984 a total of some 1800 students had been admitted to access courses, of whom 51 per cent. were of West Indian origin and 5 per cent. of Asian origin. A total of 33 institutions are offering access courses, including 17 Colleges of Further Education, 15 Higher Education institutions and 1 Combined Community College, some on a full-time basis and some part-time, with the major emphases being on entry to teacher education or social work and studying the Humanities or Social Sciences. The success rate for all students on access courses preparatory to BEd studies during the sessions 1979/1980 – 1982/1983 was 67.3 per cent., and for all ethnic minority students on these courses during the same period 69.7 per cent. Attached as Annex J is a table taken from the Evaluation Report giving further details of the admission of ethnic minority students from access courses to BEd studies. (It is of course not possible to know how many other former access students may also ultimately enter teacher training through the PGCE route). From these data it can be seen that access courses have enabled a small but nevertheless significant number of ethnic minority students, without the usual entry qualifications, to enter Higher Education and to fulfil a desire to train as teachers. We regard access courses as making an important and valuable contribution not only to offering a "second chance" for access to Higher Education to ethnic minority students and others who may have previously under-achieved and failed to realise their full potential, but also in contributing ultimately to the number of teachers of ethnic minority origin in our schools. We would therefore hope to see an overall expansion of access-style provision to the whole range of Higher Education in the future, not only linked to particular courses or to certain professions but also more generally. We believe that in order to evaluate fully the effectiveness of these courses in the longer term it is essential to monitor closely the continuing progress and performance of those students currently in Higher Education and who may subsequently enter teaching. In April 1984, the Nuffield Foundation agreed to fund a two year follow-up study of the performance of former access students in higher education. We would like to see the DES commission a further project to examine the experience of these students in actually obtaining teaching posts and in fulfilling their responsibilities in schools.

3.4   It is worth mentioning here that we were concerned to learn that

---

[39]"Access Studies to Higher Education. September 1979 – December 1983." A Report to the DES by Mr. P. K. C. Millins. January 1984.

some West Indian students who had entered BEd courses through access courses felt that they were regarded by their fellow students and, even more worryingly, by some of their lecturers as "second-class students" who had entered training through the "backdoor". We strongly deplore such attitudes and urge all those institutions currently training students who have participated in access courses to take steps to ensure that such misguided and negative attitudes, when and if they are found, are firmly countered. A major factor in limiting the development and effectiveness of access courses has been financial constraints since students on these courses are not entitled to mandatory awards and are therefore reliant on discretionary awards. At present only two of the LEAs involved provide major discretionary awards for such students. A number of access courses are, as we have mentioned, being provided on a part-time basis in an effort to minimise this problem, but, as the DES acknowledged in its memorandum on access courses to the Home Affairs Committee for its 1981 report:

> ". . . even in such cases fees and travelling expenses may deter some students."

In expressing our concern about this situation in our interim report, we recommended that:

> "Ways must . . . be found to provide mandatory awards for students on these (access) courses."

Although the Secretary of State indicated at the time that he did not feel able to implement this recommendation, we remain firmly convinced that in order for access courses to cater fully for the needs of all those mature students, from both ethnic minority groups and the ethnic majority community, who could benefit from them, these courses must come within the scope of mandatory awards. We therefore reiterate our earlier recommendation in the hope that the Secretary of State will reconsider the position and that positive action will be taken by the Government in this respect, thus encouraging both the expansion of provision for access courses and the takeup of existing places.

Attitudes of Ethnic Minority Youngsters

3.5 The third, and in our view the most important potential source of ethnic minority teachers in the future are the pupils of ethnic minority origin currently in school who have, or expect to gain, the qualifications needed to go on to Higher Education. Our own discussions with youngsters from a wide range of ethnic minority backgrounds have however revealed that comparatively few of them actually aspire to a career in teaching. The explanations most frequently put forward for this reluctance to consider a future in teaching were that:

– they had experienced racism and negative stereotyping of ethnic

609

minority groups while at school and had no desire therefore to rejoin such an institution;

- they were disenchanted by the somewhat limited role which they felt many ethnic minority teachers were asked to play in the system – as E2L or "mother tongue" teachers or simply as supervisors of ethnic minority pupils – and the restricted career opportunities this presented; and

- they did not regard teaching as offering good career prospects in the current economic situation, especially since they felt their own chances in the jobs market would be hindered by the influence of racism.

It is clear that the general conclusions which we have reached on the need to combat the climate of racism in this country and specifically for tackling individual and institutional racism, both direct and indirect, will help to counter such attitudes and encourage ethnic minority youngsters to consider a career in teaching. We would also however wish to see careers teachers and careers officers, with a strong support of DES and HMI, seeking positively to encourage ethnic minority youngsters to consider the possibility of entering teaching, emphasising particularly that ethnic minority teachers should not be seen as having a role limited solely to catering for the needs of ethnic minority pupils in multi-racial schools but should aspire to playing an integral part within the teaching profession as a whole.

Relationship with Under-Achievement

3.6   The major obstacle to seeking ethnic minority teachers, especially of West Indian origin, from amongst the ethnic minority children now in school is however above all that as long as such pupils continue to under-achieve in academic terms, as is the case at present, they will lack the necessary qualifications for entry to teacher training (other than of course through access courses). As Dr. Willey has quite rightly observed therefore in his draft report on teacher training:

> *"The main continuing need is to ensure that mainstream education provides minority ethnic group pupils with the qualifications and motivation to enter teacher training through the normal channels."*

This adds further weight to the policies which we have advocated in this report to counter the under-achievement of ethnic minority pupils and to seek to ensure that they are able to fulfil their true potential.

III   Main conclusions and recommendations

Teacher Education

- We believe that *all* initial teacher training courses, both PGCE and BEd, should be permeated with the principles underlying a genuinely pluralist approach to education (Paragraph 2.12);

- Consideration should be given to pluralist issues within the central and compulsory "core" of all initial training courses, both PGCE and BEd (Paragraph 2.16);

- Specialist optional courses relating to pluralist issues should continue to be offered within both PGCE and BEd courses (Paragraph 2.21);

- Efforts should be made by all teacher training institutions to ensure that all their students, whether on BEd or PGCE courses, have an opportunity of gaining some practical experience in a multi-racial school (Paragraph 2.22);

- We urge the Secretary of State to ask the new Council for the Accreditation of Teacher Education to pay particular attention to the need to incorporate a pluralist perspective in all initial teacher training courses in their forthcoming review of provision (Paragraph 2.24);

- The CNAA and universities responsible for initial teacher training should continue to support and encourage the development of a pluralist perspective throughout teacher education (Paragraph 2.26);

- We believe that there is an urgent need for a major expansion in provision for induction training. All induction training in multi-racial areas should incorporate the background information and skills needed to respond positively and sensitivity to the particular educational needs which ethnic minority pupils may have and to utilise the opportunities offered by a multi-racial classroom (Paragraph 3.3 and 3.5);

- All in-service courses should reflect the multiplicity of cultures, faiths and languages in present day society. All providers of in-service training should ensure that the courses they offer have this pluralist perspective and embody the essential principals of "Education for All" (Paragraph 3.12);

- The courses offered by the National Development Centre for School Management, and by other institutions training Heads and senior staff, should incorporate a pluralist perspective (Paragraph 3.13);

– The coverage of "multicultural" issues within high level, award-bearing courses should be expanded, in order to extend the capacity of the teacher training system to encourage the senior, key figures within the education service to an understanding of the implications, opportunities and responsibilities of teaching in a culturally-diverse society so that they would be in a position to act as "agents of change" within their own organisations and institutions (Paragraph 3.14);

– We recommend the development of a number of teacher training institutions as "centres of specialism" for work concerned with the needs of ethnic minority pupils and the implications of cultural diversity for "all-white" schools (Paragraphs 3.15 and 3.19);

– Short course provision relating to the particular educational needs which may arise in multi-racial schools should be expanded (Paragraph 3.16);

– We recommend that the DES should fund an independent evaluation of the content and effectiveness of the various Racism Awareness Training programmes which are currently available (Paragraph 3.17);

– The DES should establish a series of "pilot projects", involving teacher training institutions and LEAs and schools in "all-white" areas, designed to develop and disseminate "good practice" across the range of provision from high level, award-bearing courses to part-time, short courses, intended specifically to enable teachers in "all-white" schools to incorporate a pluralist perspective in their work and to bring their pupils to a positive understanding and appreciation of the multi-racial nature of society (Paragraph 3.18);

– We recommend that the In-Service Teacher Training Grants Scheme should be extended to allow for grants to be available to authorities in respect of the release of serving school teachers for training on courses relating to aspects of "Education for All" (Paragraph 3.20);

– Particular attention should be given to the development of school-based in-service support for teachers in developing an enhanced awareness of the implications of cultural diversity for their work (Paragraph 3.23);

– Efforts should be made to develop and extend the use of "distance learning" techniques in relation to in-service teacher training, especially in "all-white" areas. The Broadcasting Authorities and the Open University can play a particularly important role in this regard (Paragraph 3.23);

- The DES should consider initiating the development of a centrally-funded scheme to facilitate teacher exchanges, possibly organised though the Central Bureau for Educational Visits and Exchanges, within this country, especially between multi-racial schools and "all-white" schools, to foster greater understanding and appreciation of the various dimensions of our multi-racial society (Paragraph 3.23);

- We recommend that each school should develop, in consultation with the LEA and its advisors, a scheme for the in-service education of its teachers. Such a scheme could form part of the policy statement on "Education for All" which we consider LEAs should require of each school. (Paragraph 3.24);

- Efforts should be made to develop closer links between schools and teacher training institutions, for example through the secondment of practising teachers to assist teacher trainers in their work, in order to ensure that the training offered takes full account of the realities of the present-day classroom situation, including teaching in a multi-racial context (Paragraph 3.25);

- HM Inspectorate should issue guidance on provision for "training the trainers" in relation to the demands of today's multi-racial society, drawing on the findings of the DES evaluation of the current initiative orgainsed under the auspicies of the University of Nottingham in this field (Paragraph 3.25);

The Employment of Ethnic Minority Teachers

- We reiterate our interim report recommendations that:

  The DES should ask all teacher training institutions to collect statistics on the ethnic origin of all students training to be teachers including students seeking to enter teaching through special access courses.

  The DES should record and publish statistics on the ethnic origin of all teachers in employment . . .

(Paragraph 1.3);

- We regard the under-representation of ethnic minorities in the teaching profession as a matter of great concern which calls for urgent attention. We believe that ethnic minority teachers (and would-be teachers) have been and are still subject to racial prejudice and discrimination, both in gaining employment and in advancing their careers. While we do not support positive discrimination e.g. quotas

613

and do not wish to see any diminution of standards, we urge both the CRE and those involved within LEAs and the schools in making appointments, to devote far greater efforts to identifying and overcoming racist obstacles to the employment and advancement of ethnic minority teachers. (Paragraphs 2.1, 2.3, 2.6);

- We welcome the efforts made by some LEAs to establish themselves as "equal opportunity employers" and we urge *all* LEAs to follow this lead and adopt similar "equal opportunities" policies (Paragraph 2.3);

- We believe that an ethnic minority teacher can be a valuable asset to any school in the country – whether multi-racial or "all-white". In a multi-racial context, some ethnic minority teachers can play a particularly valuable "pastoral" role through supporting and encouraging pupils and parents drawn from the same ethnic minority group, and through advising their colleagues on the background and concerns of certain ethnic minority groups and ensuring that the practices and procedures of the school as a whole take account of the needs of the communities which they serve. The presence of bilingual or multilingual teachers of ethnic minority origin, who share a common "community language" with pupils for whom English is not a first language, can also greatly enhance the capacity of a multi-racial school to respond positively to the linguistic diversity of its pupil population. Ethnic minority teachers can serve as valuable "role models" for pupils from the same ethnic background. Ethnic minority teachers may also be "role models" in "all-white" schools in the sense in which their presence may serve to counter and overcome any negative stereotypes in the minds of pupils, parents or teachers from the majority community about ethnic minorities and their place in our society. Where such teachers are able to bring with them a degree of knowledge and personal experience of other cultures, religions and languages this can also be particularly valuable in enriching the "resources" available to the school (Paragraphs 2.4 and 2.5);

- Ethnic minority teachers should never by portrayed simply as token figures within a school with just a "curiosity" value or able only to undertake certain specific tasks, but should be regarded as an integral part of the school's staff, on equal terms with their colleagues from the majority community in participation in the development of policies and in the overall decision-making process (Paragraph 2.5);

- We recommend that the DES should clarify the arrangements for granting qualified teacher status to members of ethnic minority communities who possess overseas qualifications, with a view to encouraging them to enter the teaching profession, as long as this involves no diminution of standards (Paragraph 3.2);

614

- Access courses make an important and valuable contribution not only to offering a "second chance" for access to Higher Education to ethnic minority students and others but also by contributing to the number of teachers of ethnic minority origin in our schools. We would therefore hope to see an overall expansion of access-style provision to the whole range of Higher Education in the future (Paragraph 3.3);

- We recommend the DES commission a research project to examine the experience of former access students in obtaining teaching posts and in fulfilling their responsibilities in schools (Paragraph 3.3);

- We remain firmly convinced that in order for access courses to cater fully for the needs of all those mature students from both ethnic minority groups and the ethnic majority community, who could benefit from them, these courses must come within the scope of mandatory awards. We therefore reiterate our interim report recommendation that:

  The DES should find ways in which mandatory awards can be given to students on special access courses.

  (Paragraph 3.4)

- In our view the most important potential source of ethnic minority teachers in the future is the ethnic minority pupils currently in school. Careers teachers and careers officers, with the strong support of DES and HMI, should encourage ethnic minority youngsters to consider the possibility of entering teaching (Paragraph 3.5).

Paper* by Derek Cherrington and Ray Giles summarising the Findings of a National Survey of Multicultural Aspects of Teacher Training

In 1979, we conducted a survey in all the Colleges of Higher Education, Polytechnics and Universities offering teacher education in the UK, to obtain information about courses dealing with multicultural education.[1] The survey produced statistical data showing the location, types, level and duration of courses, and also some general information on any current or long term plans for course development, research, publications, staff development, projects or resource centre developments. An additional outcome of the survey is a directory of contact persons who can supply details of courses and other activities in these institutions.

The data in the report should be considered against a background of contraction in higher education and especially in teacher education. This contraction is evidenced by a reduction in recruitment levels, financial cuts which affect staffing levels, staff development programmes, and course development as a whole. Secondly, the majority of higher education institutions are not self-validating, and initiating new courses, in multicultural education for example, can take some time. Similarly, during a period of financial restraint Local Authorities exert some influence over the priorities of the institutions they control, and this can have a deadening effect on course initiatives in such fields of study as multicultural education. However, within that depressing background, there are groups of academics who see themselves as having a role in developing a multicultural curriculum. The authors hope that the survey will enable them and others working in this field of teacher education to extend their network of contacts, and to exchange and develop ideas with a view to new and further course developments.

Obviously, surveys of this kind do of necessity have to operate within a rigid time frame and as a consequence are invariably dated when published. Their long term value lies in creating a reference point from which subsequent progress or otherwise can be charted. Also, by publishing a directory of survey contacts, a potential network is created for use by people active in a field of study, and this can be an invaluable mechanism for the exchange of ideas and information.

Since no other national survey in this field in initial teacher education had been conducted, it was decided that the survey would collect basic data and lay the groundwork for a system of continuous updating of such data should the CRE wish to do it. The project began with an initial letter and a "contact person sheet" which was sent to the heads of all the institutions. The letter and contact sheet were sent out by the CRE as it was felt that such a letter would have more authority coming from the office of the Deputy Chairman, and would greatly enhance the level of returns. Returns from the initial contact letter enabled the researchers to (a) construct the directory of contact persons, and (b) to establish a direct contact for the second phase of the survey. A survey instrument was designed and was sent to each contact person, asking him/her to provide details of any multicultural education programmes or activities being offered in that institution. Follow up procedures were used with all institutions who failed to respond either to the initial contact letter or to the survey instrument. Finally, an analysis of responses to the survey instrument was carried out.

The National Provision of Courses

The following are the findings with reference to each of the 3 broad groups of higher education institutions:

a. *Colleges and Institutes of Higher Education*

14 different Colleges reported having a total of 26 different courses for multicultural education. Of

---

*Originally appeared in Chapter Four of 'Teaching in a Multicultural Society – The Task for Teacher Education'. Ed. M. Craft 1981.
[1]Giles and Cherrington (1981), funded by the Commission for Racial Equality.

these 26 courses only 4 were listed as compulsory. On the other hand, there were 46 different courses which were described as containing elements related to multicultural education. These were the combined offerings of 17 different colleges. Of these the majority were compulsory. It would appear that the majority of students and teachers following programmes offered through colleges which emphasise multicultural education, would receive it through compulsory offerings in the foundations and methods courses.

In these institutions, there does appear to be a growth of activity in the generation of courses which include some element of multicultural education. It would also appear that the main thrust for development is coming from those colleges which are either situated in or serve large urban conurbations. In terms of new developments and plans, it would appear that some colleges are at the stage of re-negotiating the content of courses, especially those validated by the CNAA. The level of new activity does reinforce the view of the researchers that the directory of courses generated by this project should be periodically updated otherwise it will rapidly become outdated.

b. Polytechnics

There were 18 different courses offered by 9 different Polytechnics, and again, only 4 were described as compulsory. There were a number of offerings in the area of multicultural education which were not designated as courses or elements. There were, however, comments to the effect that 14 such units of instruction were compulsory. In these institutions, too, there does appear to be a steady growth of new courses and other developments in the field of multicultural education. It should perhaps be noted that many Colleges of Education merged with Polytechnics in the mid-1970s, and that by now they will be re-negotiating the validation of their CNAA courses for a further 5 years. It is likely that we have identified many of the new proposals, but it is equally likely that many more will be in the pipeline in the next 12 months.

c. Universities

There were only 4 courses on multicultural education offered by 4 different Universities. Only one (offered at Brunel) was designated as compulsory, ("Multicultural Education"). There were also 13 courses identified as having elements related to multicultural education at 9 different institutions. Only 3 were designated as compulsory, most were not designated compulsory or optional.

With some notable exceptions, there appear to be few obvious new initiatives being taken in this sector of higher education. It may well be that economic restraints operated on this sector of higher education first. A number of institutions indicated that as they were not involved in teacher training they would perforce have to send in a nil return, but this did not necessarily mean lack of interest in the area as evidenced by research activities. There would also be a number of general undergraduate courses available, dealing with race and urban problems, but these were often not listed as they did not fit within a teacher education rubric.

Course Design and Content

There were 2 basic approaches for the inclusion of multicultural education into the curricula of various programmes for teacher training. Either multicultural education was offered as a separate *course* of study, as a part of the programme for the BEd or the Diploma in Higher Education or the Post Graduate Certificate in Education; or multicultural education *elements* were included in some of the compulsory or optional courses in the various programmes.

As far as content is concerned, there were 2 different strategies in evidence for both courses and elements of courses. First, there were courses and elements of courses which helped to prepare teachers to understand and teach about Britain as a multicultural society. A number of institutions offered specific courses for this purpose, for example,

617

- "Education for Life in a Multicultural Society" (Bath College)

- "Historical Background to Multicultural Britain" (Bradford College)

- "Education for a Multicultural Society" (Christ's College, King Alfred's College, Edge Hill College, Leeds Polytechnic, Manchester College, Preston Polytechnic, Leeds University, Roehampton Institute)

- "Education in a Multiracial Society" (Derby Lonsdale College, Luton College, Worcester College)

- "Multicultural Education" (Dorset Institute, Roehampton Institute, Keele University, Brunel University)

- "English in a Multiracial Society" (Manchester College)

- "Education in the Multi-ethnic Society" (North London Polytechnic)

- "Education for a Multicultural Britain" (Keele University)

On the other hand, many courses and elements of courses were presented to help teachers and students develop special competencies for teaching in schools or classrooms with racially or culturally diverse pupils populations. For example,

- "Teaching in Multicultural Schools" (Bedford College)

- "The Multiracial School" (Ilkley College)

- "English in the Multiracial School" (Manchester College)

- "Teaching in the Multicultural Classroom" (North London Polytechnic)

- "Community and Race Relations" (Bradford College)

There were also courses and elements of courses designed to address the needs of specific populations. For example,

- "Language Problems of Various Ethnic Groups" (Worcester College)

- "Education of Minority Groups" (Edge Hill College)

- "Education of the Disadvantaged Child" (Manchester College)

- "Education of Children of Ethnic and Racial Minority Groups" (Wolverhampton Polytechnic)

- "Education of Special Cultural Groups" (Bristol University)

Identified Groups or Topics

Looking at the titles of the various courses and the descriptions of the elements of courses categorised as "multicultural", we found a number of specific social groups identified and a variety of themes or issues covered under a number of different disciplines. For example:

618

a. Groups

The following groups were referred to specifically as the topic for courses or elements of courses offered by institutions responding to the survey:

Africans, American Negroes, Asians, the disadvantaged, immigrant peoples, minority groups, religious groups, Welsh.

b. Topics

Among the various issues cited as topics for consideration in courses as a part of multicultural education were the following:

English as a second language, comparative education, race and education, equality of educational opportunity, urban education, Caribbean literature, attitude formation and the nature of prejudice, minority group children in British society, barriers to learning, identity, treatment of minority groups, migration, race relations, religious and moral education, world religions, African studies, Asian studies, the child in the human situation, language across the curriculum, community education, Third World studies, children with special needs, school and community, compensatory and remedial education.

Paper* by HMI Ivor Ambrose summarising the Findings of an Inspection Exercise to Investigate the Coverage of Multicultural Education in Initial and In-Service Teacher Training courses

During the course of 1979/80, an inspection exercise was mounted which aimed at improving the Inspectorate's knowledge of how institutions were taking account, in initial training and in-service courses for teachers, of matters relating to our multicultural society. The exercise was in 2 parts. The first was a largely factual inquiry in 46 of the 69 public sector institutions in England which offer teacher education, ie a two-thirds sample. The purpose of that inquiry was to bring up to date the general picture of kinds of provision and approach found in the Inspectorate's previous national inquiries and in their more informal contacts. The 46 colleges were visited in HMI's normal course of work. The second part of the exercise consisted of visits lasting 2 or 3 days, by either 2 or 3 HMI, to each of 12 of the 46 institutions, with the aim of learning at first hand, and in some detail, about as many aspects as possible of approaches to educational issues concerning the multicultural nature of society. In the selection of the 12 institutions, account was taken of information from the first part of the exercise which suggested where particular kinds of provision might be found. Visits were also paid to schools used by the 12 institutions to see students at work either on teaching practice or in less formal contact with a school. The institutions consisted of 4 polytechnics, 7 colleges of higher education, and one college concerned only with the initial preparation and in-service training of teachers. It is not possible to comment (here) in detail on the 12 institutions in the second part of the exercise. They did however shed useful qualitative light on the largely quantitative information gained in the first part.

It was quite clear from the sample of 46 that there is a very wide range of provision and practice within institutions of teacher training relating to education in a multicultural society. Recent changes associated with the reorganisation of teacher training have undoubtedly had adverse effects on this area of work in some instances, but have afforded new opportunities in others. The overall picture, however, is not a particularly bright one.

Without attempting to invest statistics with undue significance, the fact that in the view of staff concerned only 6 cases of improving provision were in prospect (and these were offset by 6 which had already reduced), 12 were uncertain and 22 probably unchanging, suggests a somewhat dormant state. Since some of the last group had little or no provision anyway, it is clear that the topic does not attract strong support in the planning of new courses within some institutions. Confirmation of this fact may be found in the opinion expressed in 21 cases that the issues of a multicultural society were not immediately relevant.

This widespread view of multicultural issues not being immediately relevant raises the conceptual question of what is commonly meant by "education in a multicultural society". Although some of the institutions expressed clear ideas, well related to the content of their courses, there was a very broad spectrum of views represented across the institutions, ranging from those case study examples to others which limited their consideration to the extent to which pupils from minority ethnic groups were to be found in teaching-practice schools, sometimes ignoring a substantial proportion within the locality. There is a clear need for teacher training institutions to re-examine both their concepts of education in a multicultural society and their courses, to see how they relate.

Staffing of this area of work reflected to some extent the conceptual problem. How should one staff such an ill-defined field which is neither a discipline nor a phase of education, and is multidisciplinary in nature though it is not self-evident which disciplines comprise it? Two attributes tended to identify staff, namely, expertise and commitment. The number of tutors with one of these, and the even smaller

---

* Taken from Chapter Nine - "An HMI Perspective" - of "Teaching in a Multicultural Society - The Task for Teacher Education." Ed. M Craft 1981.

number with both, were not related to the size of the institution, the location of it or the work it was doing. Large polytechnics with only one lecturer in each engaged on this work, and much smaller colleges of higher education with 3 in each, illustrate the diversity. Further diversity in the form of subject expertise, brought to bear by tutors in such fields as English, sociology, religious studies, history, social anthropology, comparative education, curriculum theory, etc served to indicate that the commitment of individual lecturers tended to determine the provision, rather than any overall view of what fields had a contribution to make.

Since most of the BEd degree courses in the 46 institutions were more or less concurrent, they offered a time span of 3 or 4 years in which education in a multicultural society could feature. This had enabled 30 of them to take some account of the topic at an appropriate point within the basic compulsory programme of professional training. Thus, some provision at least was made for all students in those contexts. The contrast with students training to teach by the PGCE route was striking, since only 3 such courses had an explicit compulsory element of education in a multicultural society, and only 5 others had incorporated reference to ethnic minority groups in school and society within basic educational or professional studies. The fact that a third of all the institutions train BEd students who, like the great majority of PGCE students, need take no account, during their preparation for teaching, of education in a multicultural society must be a matter for concern.

There is, however, in teacher training circles a widely held view that the student's course should not be overloaded, and some highly desirable elements, if they are to be given sufficient time and treatment to enable them to be done properly, can only be provided as options. Moreover, it may be argued that by choosing from a range of possible courses, a student comes more highly motivated to the one actually chosen. ''Better to do it well or not at all'', is the essence of this approach.

Most institutions offered an optional course on education in a multicultural society within the BEd, thus enabling an interested student to pursue the topic in the absence of or in addition to any element in the basic education course. The fact that those aspects of this provision which concerned language acquisition, English as a second language, skills and understanding were in general more popular than cultural and social issues such as race relations which aimed at informing and shaping attitudes, is perhaps an indication of the utilitarian and pragmatic predilections of students in a situation of choice.

Options within the PGCE, though much less common, produced a similar pattern of choices on the part of students. Practical usefulness, especially for teaching practice purposes, again seemed to be a major determinant in a course being selected. And it is this very criterion which raises one of the main arguments against making provision for education in a multicultural society available solely through an option system, since so much depends on what other options are offered in competition with it. The usefulness of a course on slow learners, audio-visual aids or some such topic may well over-ride a student's interest in multicultural issues, as the anxieties of teaching practice draw near. Faced with some sets of options students may feel they have very little choice.

In 5 institutions, major study courses corresponding to a traditional main subject were offered which incorporated aspects of the multicultural society. Under titles such as world studies, community studies, urban studies etc, they provided scope for studying in depth a number of issues concerning ethnic minority groups (often groups with which links had been developed) inside a wider academic framework.

Questions as to what aspects of education in a multicultural society should be considered, avoided, ignored or even sought after in a course, are worthy of wide discussion. Whilst one would expect a student's experience of multi-ethnic schools and appropriate course preparation for this to be related to the proximity of the training institutions to areas of settlement by immigrant communities, this was by no means universal. One-third of the institutions offering courses on education in a multicultural society did not bring students into sustained contact with multi-ethnic schools or communities, even though some were in areas of substantial ethnic minority populations. Four others, however, situated far away from any multi-ethnic schools, positively sought and provided more distant fieldwork opportunities for students in such schools and in ethnic minority communities on a systematic basis.

In-Service Provision

In-Service training provision was to be found in fewer than half of the institutions, and the fact that these were located mostly in areas with multi-ethnic schools indicates where teachers perceived their INSET needs to be. The subject matter usually concerned education in a school setting which is multicultural, rather than the wider considerations of education in a society which is multicultural.

There is clearly a relatively high demand for award-bearing courses from those teachers in multi-ethnic schools who are seeking to improve their knowledge and professional skills to meet the particular demand of their work. Questions of teachers' status, career structure and the sheer worthwhileness of their committing time to studying education in its multicultural aspects, are closely related to academically respectable qualifications being available to them. But the predominance of award-bearing courses does not stem solely from this source. The institutions themselves often find them more convenient to mount than shorter courses, which may be regarded as the province of the LEA advisory services. It would, however, be a pity if institutions concentrated unduly on award-bearing courses to the neglect of shorter ones which meet the needs of teachers unable to commit themselves to long-term advanced study. Indeed, the best examples of good practice were to be found in cases where an institution had developed a balanced programme of long and short in-service course provision in close co-operation with its Local Authority's advisory service in multicultural education.

Broad geographical areas remain where there is no provision within the notional two-ninths of resources available for in-service training, the majority of the institutions making no contribution, even where some aspects of education in a multicultural society feature in their initial training courses. This, together with relatively restricted coverage, noted above, arising from the narrow concentration by other institutions on factors relating to teaching in a multi-ethnic school, means that there is fairly scant treatment of social and cultural issues within in-service provision generally.

Evidence from the institutions showed that where good provision exists it has usually been achieved as a result of considerable effort. Institutional reorganisation and the validation of new courses have been the means of negotiating improvements in some courses. There has usually been apparent the strong influence of one or two key tutors with both personal commitment and the facility for involving others with different roles and expertise. Someone with a designated role such as "co-ordinator of multicultural education" has often served a useful function, both as a source of knowledge and also in identifying and harnessing the collective and diverse strengths and resources of colleagues. At this time, when courses of teacher training are continuing to change with the progress of re-validation processes, it is worth remembering that the influence of one competent tutor with a specific responsibility in this area of work can be of exceptional significance.

Given a nuclear group of interested staff, provision certainly has benefited further by the setting up of organisational machinery for close co-operation, either formally or informally, through working groups and committees. The importance of such a structure could be detected in several institutions visited by the qualities of both academic content and practical work within the courses. Moreover some very significant staff development activity on education in a multicultural society was initiated by this means.

Extracts from Evidence received from Two Teacher Training Institutions reflecting the underlying principles of Permeation

A UNIVERSITY SCHOOL OF EDUCATION

The Academic Board recognises the need for all its departments and staff to give active consideration to the relevance of their teaching to a multicultural society, and acknowledges that means must be found to overcome the inertia which inheres in our practices in this respect. We have specified that this will entail staff meetings at departmental level to examine, implement and evaluate changes in practice as well as to provide a supporting structure for these changes. Each department at such staff meetings should:

i. critically appraise its own teaching in order that it becomes conscious of racist content, where it exists, so that any such content can be removed;

ii. review current teaching programmes with the aim of integrating a multicultural perspective within such programmes.

B MULTI-ETHNIC GUIDELINES FOR A FOUR YEAR BEd HONOURS DEGREE - COLLEGE OF HIGHER EDUCATION

Throughout the four years, every single unit of the programme must demonstrate its commitment, in its content and methodology, to the concerns of Britain as a multi-ethnic society. This is embodied in the multi-ethnic guidelines below and also in the aims and objectives of the courses. It is important to recognise that the approach taken encompasses two basic perspectives: the education of ethnic minority children and the education of all children for a multi-ethnic society.

In consequence of the decision to strengthen the multi-ethnic focus of the course programme, the following guidelines have been agreed to assist course units in modifying syllabuses.

By the end of the course students will be able to:

a. demonstrate a working knowledge of the terminology and perspectives employed within the social sciences as applied to ethnic minority groups

b. recognise the political nature of current enquiries into the position of ethnic minority groups

c. situate the current debate on race and ethnicity in the United Kingdom within a social and historical context

d. operationalise this knowledge, awareness and understanding in practical and inter-personal situations within the course

e. demonstrate an awareness of major strategies advanced in relation to the position of ethnic minority groups in the United Kingdom and evaluate their implications for industry and commerce, the education and social services and the wider community, including the ethnic groups themselves.

Extracts from Evidence illustrating the ways in which Multicultural Issues have been incorporated in the Core Studies of various Teacher Training Institutions

A OUTLINE OF BEd EDUCATIONAL STUDIES

a. *Educational Studies*

In Year 1 a course thread for *all* students will consider the developing multi-racial nature of our society from the historical, psychological and sociological viewpoints. This module will be followed up in other years of the course. Details:

i. *Year 1 Module – Course Content*

1. Historical development of immigration

2. Areas of settlement and the consequent organisational problems created

3. Issues posed for schools in terms of the integration of ethnic minorities and curriculum innovation

4. Language acquisition, development, and its effect upon concept formation, thought and communication

5. Cognitive Development: Emphasis in different cultures on factual/conceptual learning, problems in bringing about mutual understanding of the cognitive approach related to different cultural backgrounds

6. Aspects of Personality Development: Differing cultural "norms", dual standards, imitation and identification in two cultures etc

7. Study of contemporary social structure and the socialisation process with specific reference to a multi-racial situation

8. *Community Education Conference:* A one day programme considering the variety of ethnic groups in this country and some practical ways in which multi-racial schools tackle their problems. This conference will be utilized in the continued study of social factors affecting education.

ii. *Development of Year 1 Module in Years 2-4*

1. Intelligence: Cultural differences relating to intelligent behaviour, cross cultural problems of measurement

2. Learning Theory: Cultural differences in conceptual learning to stimulus seeking and stimulus reduction theories of motivation, and in relation to values relating to moral development

3. Motivation: Cultural differences with emphasis on the importance of competence, social motives of affiliation, power, avoidance etc

4. Personality Assessment: Self-concept formation cultural determinants relating to self-esteem, self-image and concept of ideal self

5. Concept of deprivation and disadvantage related to the study of educability

6. Study of home, school and community – links with social services, community relations etc

7. Study of sub-cultures, social construction of reality, related to social construction of urban imagery

8. Ideologies – transmission of cultural values

9. The methodology of all philosophy modules in the course require a dispassionate consideration of issues and a commitment to reason (not to prejudice)

B COMPULSORY CORE COURSE ON EDUCATION FOR A MULTICULTURAL SOCIETY (FOR FIRST AND MIDDLE SCHOOLS)

Within the compulsory education core course which runs throughout the three years of the degree, elements of Education for a Multicultural Society are highlighted as an important part of the total theme under consideration. In year one the theme is human development and studies are made of the relationships existing between maturation and heredity on the one hand, and environmental and cultural influences on the other. Cultural differences are treated specifically by lecture and discussion based upon the series "The Family of Man", and recur in topics such as child-rearing patterns, socialisation, language and cognitive development, adolescence, and educability. In the second year where the theme is essentially the study of learning and teaching and the sociology of school the effects of immigration upon schools and the performance of minority group pupils are treated. A study of curriculum is undertaken in year three and reference is made to two ways in which school curricula may be changed to meet the needs of a changed and changing society. First and middle school students, in their two-year literacy course, deal in a broad manner with issues relating to the language and learning of immigrants. English as a Second Language specialists are represented on the teaching teams and so are able to give appropriate guidance to those students who wish to pursue matters of concern to greater depth. Human movement specialists, in their professional course examine problems which arise in their specialist subject area from the inclusion of minority group pupils in their classes. All students take a half-unit (18 contact hour) course "Teaching in the Multicultural School" in their third year. While minority group backgrounds and the nature of the multicultural society are treated here the main focus will be a professional one – on the language and learning aspect of Education for a Multicultural Society.

C COMPULSORY CORE COURSE ADOPTED BY A UNIVERSITY DEPARTMENT OF EDUCATION

PGCE students take a compulsory course in multicultural education extending over seven weeks in the summer term, two hours per week, during which an attempt is made "through talks, discussions and visits to various educational establishments, to explore important aspects of learning and teaching in a multicultural society". A short course must necessarily be selective, but it is hoped to deal with:

i.   understanding and coming to terms with one's own biases.

ii.   background information on major immigrant groups as a first step to understanding their language in the classroom.

iii. the different uses of language and their importance for pupil achievement.

iv.   difficulties experienced by immigrants and first generation groups in adapting to the general ethos of a school.

v.   the ethnocentric curriculum and the need for change.

vi.   conflict between pupils, and between teacher and pupils.

vii. bringing adult members of minority ethnic groups into educational settings.

viii.   the work of community relations officers.

ix.   development of learning materials – commerically produced and teacher prepared.

Extracts from Evidence relating to Optional Courses offered by various Teacher Training Institutions

A BEd HONOURS COURSE ON "EDUCATION FOR A MULTICULTURAL SOCIETY"

The course is of 50 hours duration and includes fieldwork and practical experience in schools. It forms two units out of nine in the final assessment of the degree.

Objectives

This course develops from the Years 1-3 programme in Educational Studies and Curriculum Studies. Students will be able to:

1. Gain some understanding of the sociological/historical/demographic background to immigration.

2. Analyse some of the key issues concerning the role of education in a multicultural society.

3. Critically examine curriculum development in the multi-racial school from both a theoretical and an empirical perspective.

4. Attempt to identify the special educational needs of multicultural communities.

5. Analyse the role of the teacher in the multi-racial school.

NOTE: The student will supplement the learning process by appropriate fieldwork and the practical experience.

Brief Syllabus

1. The nature, form and structure of multicultural communities in the UK and the development of a multicultural society with its broad implications for education.

2. A critique of the concept of educational disadvantage with special reference to the children of ethnic minority groups.

3. Curriculum development for multicultural education with reference to the following:

   a. philosophical justification,

   b. the concept of cultural pluralism,

   c. the teaching of Race Relations.

4. Language development in a multicultural society, implications for language policy, problems of linguistic diversity.

5. The teacher in the multi-racial school, pre-service and in-service training, careers, self-fulfilling prophecies, stereotypes, ethnocentrism – the psychology of Racialist Prejudice – techniques and problems of attitude change.

6. Planning, innovation and management in a multi-racial school. The role of public bodies (e.g. DES, LEAs, Schools Council) in educational provisions for a multi-racial society.

B MINOR ELECTIVE COURSE ON EDUCATION IN MODERN MULTICULTURAL BRITAIN

Aims

To develop an understanding of differing communities within modern multicultural Britain, and to further an awareness of the implications of cultural differences to education.

Objectives

Students should:

1. acquire a knowledge and understanding of relevant, societal changes in rural/urban communities;

2. have a knowledge and understanding of the expectations of those members of minority groups born in this country and their responses to the economic, social, political and educational provision;

3. reflect on the changes in attitudes by the majority groups towards minority groups in recent years;

4. be encouraged to anticipate the possible trends in British society and to evaluate strategies;

5. have a knowledge of some of the strategies developed both in school organisation and in the curriculum relevant to all people living in modern multicultural Britain.

Content

1. An examination of recent sociological trends in rural/urban communities.

2. A study of changes in patterns of settlement in Britain.

3. Concepts of integration, accommodation, assimilation, aculturation.

4. A knowledge of the hopes, aspirations and fears of second/third generation members of minority groups regarding, for example, such issues as racial attitudes, social mobility, employment, the police, education, parliamentary legislation, local authority provision.

5. An analysis of the changes taking place within society of the attitudes of the majority groups towards minority groups.

6. A critical awareness and appreciation of contemporary and future trends regarding the multicultural scene as reflected in the media.

7. A study of school organisation and curriculum implications for education in a multicultural society.

Teaching Method

Lectures, seminars, visits, guest speakers.

C BEd HONOURS COURSE ON "EDUCATION FOR A MULTICULTURAL SOCIETY"

This course will use sociological, psychological, philosophical, linguistic and historical perspectives. The aim will be to develop a multi-disciplinary approach to the understanding of problems and opportunities presented by the multicultural character of societies such as our own, with particular reference to the role of educational institutions. Lecture, seminar, tutorial work and reading will be supported by visits to relevant institutions, and study of a particular problem or issue will be undertaken through the extended essay which each student is required to complete.

SYLLABUS

The course is designed in two main sections, representing the two main areas of interest; these are relevantly inter-related in the teaching programme, and do not indicate a chronological sequence.

1. *The Multi-Cultural Society*

This section of the course-content is concerned chiefly with the identification and examination of an appropriate theoretical background against which the inter-relationships of race, culture and education may be located and analysed. The nature of a "multicultural" society is analysed in terms of the variety of ways (e.g. racial, cultural, religious, linguistic) in which diversity is manifested. "Race" and "race relations" are interpreted by means of concepts, theories and typologies from the social sciences. An examination is made from the perspectives of sociology, psychology and social psychology of theories of racism and related phenomena (e.g. prejudice, discrimination, ethnocentrism). Specific analysis is undertaken of the issue of race relations in the context of Great Britain.

a. the nature of a "multicultural" society

b. dimensions of diversity (e.g. racial, cultural, religious, linguistic)

c. relevant concepts (e.g. pluralism; minority group; assimilation and integration; economic function; class)

d, theories of prejudice and racism

e. perspectives on imigration and race relations: historical, sociological, demographic, socio-political

f. analysis of the role and scope of legislation and official agencies.

2. *Education and the Multicultural Society*

In this section an attempt is made to bring the perspectives identified above to bear upon issues of educational policy and provision. Through the means of the extended essay in particular, the student will make a synthesis of relevant theory in order to analyse and offer a resolution of a particular educational issue or problem.

a. values and assumptions underlying the ideas of "education for a multicultural society", e.g.

   i. the justification of the promotion of tolerance and inter-cultural respect

   ii. different cultures, languages, etc, and their claims to legitimacy

b. institutional provision: national and local policy; procedures of organisation and assessment, raising in connexion with the latter the "race and intelligence" debate

c. analysis of the role of the teacher; schooling and the socialisation of attitudes; the implications for teacher-education

d. analysis of the role of curriculum and the justification of curriculum innovations; the rationale of major projects, e.g. of the Schools Council; the concept of curriculum permeation; Black Studies

e. language development in a multicultural society: the implications for language policy, organisation and methodology of linguistic diversity.

ANNEX E

Examples of Previous Essay Titles for this Course:

Children's literature in a multicultural society.

Teacher education for a multicultural society.

Under-achievement of pupils of West Indian origin in British schools.

The contribution of IQ tests and teacher-attitudes to the problem of under-achievement in ethnic minorities.

The West Indian experience in British schools – a language problem?

Black Studies and the American and British situation. The development of children's racial attitudes and the school's response.

Cultural and identity problems of second generation Asian and West Indian children in Britain.

The education of gypsy and travelling children.

Cypriots: the education of a minority group in Britain.

Second-phase language teaching in the Secondary School.

Prejudice, its development in the child and the role of education in its eradication.

Assimilation and integration: a review of official policy.

The West Indian child's experience in the British primary school, with particular reference to language.

The Muslim child in the British school with special reference to Religious Education.

Racist textbooks in the British educational system.

A survey of organisational policies for the education of a multicultural society in Britain.

The occurrence and effect of racial bias in Secondary school literature.

Extract from Evidence describing the work undertaken in a PGCE Option Course in Multicultural Education at a University Department of Education

The course was one of twenty special subject seminars offered to students on the Post Graduate Certificate of Education course at a University Department of Educational Studies in the 1980/1981 session. During the academic year there were just eight hour long sessions: the first three at the end of the autumn term and the remaining five in the summer term. During the spring term all students were out of the department on teaching practice in a range of secondary schools, most with a predominantly or entirely white population. As part of the course work a dissertation was required at the end of the summer term.

Eighteen students out of the total of 193 opted for this subject.[1] There were two chemists, a biologist, a physicist and a mathematician, three geographers,[2] two historians, three linguists (French) and five English graduates. Only two (a chemist and a physicist) were men. The other chemist was a black student, born in Jamaica and largely educated in England. In addition, the group was joined by a Guyanese student, who though taking a different option for her dissertation attended all the sessions. They gave a number of reasons for choosing this course:

"I realise that during my time in Birmingham I did not understand what made the people around me tick. I would like to gain more insight into differences between cultures."

"I was struck by the sort of double lives these Asian children (in Burnley) were having to live, in one culture at home and one at school and their ability to cope."

"Having attended a multi-racial school and having experienced racial tension at an early age I want to know more about why such problems arise and what solutions there might be."

"I hope to find out more about the realities of cultural problems, as this seems to be a bigger problem than is made out. (Partly because of my own ignorance coming from a non-immigrant town). The nature of prejudice interests me very much."

"I feel I haven't come to grips with the problems of racism in this country (or in myself) . . . I want to understand other cultures better and by doing this to overcome my own racism."

The course was designed to illuminate these questions, and in doing so to give as much attention to the attitudes and educational needs of pupils in the majority all white schools as to those from minority groups[3]. Ideas, beliefs and misconceptions about black and Asian ethnic groups are widespread and affect the understanding of children far from multi-racial cities. The sessions were intended to tackle problems which students might meet on teaching practice in country areas as well as in city schools. In fact only six of the teaching practice schools had significant numbers of black (Caribbean) and Asian (mainly Muslim pupils).

Autumn Term Sessions

The first two sessions were shared equally between a consideration of the position of some of the

---

[1] Plus one who left at Christmas to take up a research post.
[2] One of the geographers got a job overseas, and so decided to write her dissertation under the directon of the Tutor for seminars on Aspects of Education in Developing Countries. She continued to attend this group's seminars.
[3] West Indian Children in our Schools (HMSO, 1981) (The Rampton Report) Page 28, quotes comments by pupils in an all white secondary school in a rural area. Education for a Multi-racial Society (Schools Council 1981), chapter 9, cites similar evidence.

minority groups of secondary school age and the phenomenon of racial prejudice among the majority white school population. The third session allowed time to discuss ways of gathering impressions and evidence while on teaching practice; this could form a basis for the summer term dissertations.

Although only four of the group had attended multi-racial schools as children, several had at some time lived or studied in towns where minority groups had settled. One of the English graduates had taught in the Caribbean on VSO; another had worked in an immigrant centre and two had been involved with Saturday schools for West Indian children. So they brought a variety of experience to the discussions.

As a framework for considering the range of positions which minority groups might adopt, we used the chart: the assimilation variables (figure 1). This forced students to define terms more precisely instead of using words like "integration" and "assimilation" indiscriminately. It was necessary to look at different aspects of a group's culture and to perceive that a family might change some elements of its life style without breaking with the essential values of its traditions. It enabled us to understand the subtle choices teenageers might be facing and it directed attention to the role of majority attitudes in defining the scope of some of those choices.

Part of this first hour's discussion centred on the students' perception of the problem of inter-generational conflict and the dilemma faced by young people who wanted to conform in some ways to the norms of their white peers, but who were prevented from doing so by their parents. When there is such a conflict, what is the role of the teacher and what are the rights of the family? There was some antagonism to the notion of the right of a family or of a larger kinship group to retain its cultural identity. One student argued that entry into the structure of society depended on adaptation to British norms, and another felt strongly that retention of a separate cultural identity could foster a backward-looking conservatism, an argument that was supported by reference to the Polish community in West London.

How important is ethnic and cultural identity to school children from the various minority groups? This was the major question raised in the first session and it could be approached only by close attention to the behaviour, opinions and wishes of people from the minorities. As a start, students were referred to extracts from writings and transcribed interviews by black children and young people and to a bibliography.

The second session focussed on the attitudes of white people with reference to the incidence of prejudice found among school pupils. The hour took the form of role play, followed by a report back and discussion. In groups of three or four in a simulated staff room conversation, students were faced with quotations taken from children's essays. Supposing these pieces had to be handed back to a class with comments, what would they do?

After an inconclusive debate, the majority felt that an off-the-cuff response might be ineffective or even counter-productive, and that only an all school policy and cross-curriculum development could stand any chance of challenging misconceptions, correcting bias and allaying fears. The major question of how far a teacher should express personal views or try to influence pupils spilled over into the following and final session of the term. This is a subject of controversy in schools. Rob Jeffcoate has argued that it is a mistake to try to suppress racist remarks and National Front literature because "the School is probably the only place in most children's experience where it (the debate) can be undertaken with a semblance of rationality" (Jeffcoate, 1979). The problem had to rest until the summer term when it could be related to policies and practices found in schools. The role play session and ensuing debate had at least given the group the opportunity to talk through some possible responses; one student later reported that it had given her a perspective that helped her to stay cool when faced with fairly acrimonious opinions in a third year classroom.

Finally in this third session we went over a check list of point to look out for during the teaching practice term.

Figure 1

The Assimilation Variables from Milton M Gordon *Assimilation in American Life*, quoted in Taylor, *The Half-Way Generation*, 1976.

THE ASSIMILATION VARIABLES	
Sub Process or Condition	*Type or Stage of Assimilation*
Change of cultural patterns to those of host society.	Cultural or behavioural assimilation (acculturation).
Large-scale entry into cliques, clubs and institutions of host society on primary group level.	Structural assimilation.
Large-scale intermarriage.	Marital assimilation (amalgamation).
Development of sense of peoplehood based exclusively on host society.	Identificational assimilation.
Absence of prejudice.	Attitude receptional assimilation.
Absence of discrimination.	Behavioural Receptional assimilation.
Absence of value and power conflict.	Civic assimilation.

(Note that this analysis lacks reference to economic factors and the vital issue of job availability and opportunity for promotion.)

Summer Term Sessions

Two sessions were devoted to a sharing of experiences and findings: the first in the mainly or all white schools and the second in the multi-racial schools. By sharing these first-hand accounts, the group gained an overall impression of the state of race relations in widely differing schools in both rural and urban areas.

One of the English students had prepared a set of visuals as a stimulus for writing, by cutting out and mounting photographs of people, including some black and Asian characters.[4] Her practice school was in a small market town a good 15 miles from any multi-racial area. She reported that several children had seemed taken aback and nonplussed when faced with photographs of black people. "How do we write about this?" one girl had asked.

In a rural comprehensive, a third year class had spontaneously expressed strong antagonism to "the take-over of (our town) by Asians". This was a medium sized market town where Muslims had experienced difficulty in getting planning permission to convert a terrace house into a mosque. This had been widely reported in the local press.

A few miles away, a geography student had found a concerned and liberal VIth form following a course on development in the third world; and another student teaching French at the same school confirmed the concern among the VIth formers, but found that their benevolent attitudes were not translated into practical help for the Asian children in the school who needed extra language teaching (a fairly normal human failing: to ignore the need on the doorstep). In the junior forms there was some evidence of antagonism.

The most disturbing evidence came from the Guyanese student who had done her teaching practice in a suburban school where there was just a handful of black pupils. After the Brixton riots (April 1981) she had found herself challenged by some of the children and associated with and in a sense blamed for the

[4] Magazines like Ebony and Roots are useful sources of material to use alongside Colour Supplements.

behaviour of West Indians. She is of Asian, not African descent, has lived in a middle class English environment all her married life, and has little or no cultural affinity with British born inner city blacks. The association in the minds of the white children was based solely on skin colour.

She discussed this incident, which involved only a small number of children, with two of the younger staff at the school. They were very sympathetic and one revealed that they had already discussed the riots with pupils, and had tried to rationalise pupils' reactions to them.

Although the student felt that most of the children at the school were not racist, before the incidence of the riots a boy had written in his exercise book, and scored out the first part of the sentence: "Its real crap being taught by a wog".

The black, Jamaican born student had experienced no similar problems with white pupils. But the school where she did her teaching practice was one of the most multi-racial in the city. As a black person she was no rarity; as a black teacher she was. Indeed the black students consulted her over all sorts of matters from careers advice to discipline problems. The fact that the black pupils sometimes referred to her more readily than to their regular teachers at first caused slight friction in the staff room, but her knowledge and understanding of the Rastafarian movement eventually proved valuable in easing some of the difficulties between staff and pupils. She was to be offered a post in the chemistry department but was not able to take it up.

Overall, the picture that emerged was one of a wide range of attitudes and opinions among children, and of a general neglect of the issue in the staff room of both white and multi-racial schools, with a single exception. Apart from extra language teaching, pupils from minority groups were not considered to have any special educational needs, and racist remarks or antagonistic behaviour were disciplined rather than challenged and discussed.

Curriculum development in the area of multicultural education received very little attention. Two of the geographers had found valuable and relevant work and explored the issues in their dissertations. English students were disappointed by the neglect of literature by African, Caribbean and Indian writers. All reported a general lack of interest and awareness. As one student summed it up: "_____ school, situated as it is in a medium sized, prosperous market town, has none of the racial problems of an inner city school and seemed to take a very indifferent attitude to the whole question. Little, if any, of the curriculum had been designed, as far as I could tell in discussions with other members of staff, with a positive attitude towards racial problems as an objective."

But, as the Guyanese student had found to her discomfort, racism could be openly expressed in the most prosperous middle class environment. That school had as great a problem as any in the city; racism was manifest but it was not perceived as a problem by most of the staff and the student herself had not felt able to report the antagonism she had experienced to senior staff or to the head.

After two report back sessions, an anthropologist gave a seminar on her field work with a group of Muslim families settled in the area and their relations in a group of villages in the Punjab area of Pakistan. She described the coherent and continuing culture of the families, their frequent visits to a network of kin living in Glasgow, Rochdale and Newport and their regular contacts with the Punjab. Particularly striking was her recollection of meetings in the villages with pupils educated in city schools, and her perception of the capacity of these teenage girls and boys to span the two cultures without undue strain.

This seminar challenged some of the generalisations, based on more superficial media information that had been voiced in the first session of the autumn term, and showed that continuity and change are not necessarily incompatible, given the strength of the Muslim religion and the persistence of family ties.

In the last two of the five summer term sessions the group split into two so that everyone would have an opportunity to hammer out the most difficult and basic issues: how could racial prejudice be explained and what role, if any, can the school play, both in handling tensions that arise and getting to the roots of racism. For each group one student presented an argument; in each case it was knocked down in favour of a more complex set of inter-related explanations.

In the final session students took a set of objectives and started to work out some of the implications for the curriculum.

Conclusion

This description of the programme of the course may be useful to other institutions planning to introduce courses on issues in multi-racial education. Such courses remain rare and this account may enable students to run their own meetings for discussion.

Obviously there were many deficiencies. We needed more time for detailed case studies to match the seminar on Muslim families, and time for further exploration of our own feelings on race and on the rights of minority groups to find solutions to the dilemmas of adapting to a new society without damaging the essential qualities of their own culture.

In planning a course it is not essential to have access to inner-city multi-racial schools. One of the lessons learned from the students who did their teaching practice in rural and suburban schools was that racial prejudice can manifest itself in the most unexpected places and contexts. The beliefs, assumptions and expectations of white pupils must affect the way they will react to black people. Families move in search of jobs; students from country areas go to study or teach in the cities; the minority groups themselves move into the suburbs as they become able to afford higher house prices. Society is not static. The issues raised here are relevant to all students of education in this country.

635

Council for National Academic Awards
Committee for Education
Multicultural Working Group

Multicultural Education: *Discussion Paper* (1984)

1 INTRODUCTION

1.1   This discussion paper has been prepared by the committee for education's working group on multicultural education, following debate within the group, consultation with boards and panels of the committee, receipt of written responses to an earlier draft from a number of CNAA institutions, and discussions at the DES/CNAA conference of Bedford College of Higher Education ("The Place of Multicultural Education in Teacher Training Institutions", September, 1983).

1.2   The purpose of the paper is to suggest some principles in respect of multicultural and anti-racist education and it contains an agenda or checklist of items which might be included in courses for teachers both in schools and in further education colleges being prepared for or developing their role in a multicultural society.

The paper recognises the need for an education which reflects the reality of our culturally diverse society. It is based upon the view that all education should be multicultural, appropriately reflecting the social, cultural, political and economic complexity of our society. The working group wishes to acknowledge the importance of various sources of cultural, social and economic diversity arising from ethnicity, race, class, gender, religion and region.

1.3   The working group is aware that multicultural education is a sensitive area of concern. Any statement of this kind is certain to be controversial. It is hoped however that this paper, which attempts to suggest the aims and objectives of multicultural and anti-racist education in a teacher education context, will provoke further discussion within institutions among those staff who are involved in the training and education of teachers. The working group hopes that it will engender commitment, interest, and a determination to act, and it urges institutions to consider how aims might be translated into appropriate course structures, contents, and processes.

1.4   The issues raised in this paper are relevant across the spectrum of teacher education, whatever the age phase or subject specialism of the teacher. They are equally germane to both schools and further education institutions, as well as for initial and for inservice courses. The sharply focussed character of some inservice courses, particularly diplomas, may require subtle handling of this dimension.

2 AGENDA FOR MULTICULTURAL AND ANTI-RACIST EDUCATION

2.1   Education for diversity and for social and racial harmony suggests that the richness of cultural variety in Britain, let alone over the world, should be appreciated and utilised in education curricula at all levels. This can only have beneficial effects for all students in widening cultural awareness and in developing sensitivity towards the cultural identity and practices of various groups. At the same time, the serious study of race relations (and of ethnic, religious, class and gender relations) should also be seen as a necessary part of education in our society.

2.2   The paper recognises that without a clear understanding of the importance of achieving equality of opportunity in social and economic life, multicultural education will be of limited value. Awareness of cultural diversity has to be united with awareness of social, economic and political processes in our society.

3 TEACHER EDUCATION COURSES

Given the wider role that teachers in schools and in further education have to play in this recognition of the importance of multicultural and anti-racist education, there is a need to consider the implications for their education and professional preparation. In designing courses of teacher education institutions should bear in mind the following

Teachers need to

i   be equipped to prepare all young people for life in a multicultural and racially harmonious society

ii have an awareness and understanding of racism both historically and in contemporary society and to be conscious of the various forms in which racism can manifest itself

iii have an awareness of intercultural relations and of their social and economic contexts

iv be able to teach with skill and sensitivity in schools and further education institutions recognising any particular needs of ethnic minority pupils and students

v   interact effectively with colleagues in the institutional framework in relation to these issues.

These five areas of professional preparation (each of which is considered below in more detail) should be met by means of a variety of course design approaches, including permeation strategies, core course elements, and special options.

3.1 The multicultural and racially harmonious society

The curriculum of a course of teacher education should be such as to prepare professionals to cater for the needs of all children and students. It is suggested that this would be achieved by

i   permeating all elements of the course with multicultural and anti-racist considerations, in both practical and theoretical components

ii encouraging a critical approach to cultural bias, prejudice, racism and stereotyping in teaching schemes, school and colleges texts and other teaching materials

iii adopting an approach to all subjects in the curriculum of teacher education courses which avoids an ethnocentric view of the world

iv recognising the value of teaching which acknowledges the aspirations of all pupils and students, and which seeks to enhance their chances of realising these aspirations.

v   having knowledge of local education authorities' policy statements of multicultural, multi-ethnic and anti-racist education.

3.2 Intercultural relations and the social and economic context

Teachers should be made aware of the context in which they will work. Courses should provide a broad theoretical framework which encompasses

i   the patterns of living, social customs, religions, attitudes and economic condition of different ethnic and racial groups

ii the sociology of urban change, and of social and economic developments with special reference to inner city areas; segregation, settlement and dispersal and its effect on schools and colleges iii the historical context of empire, migration and the development of a multicultural society

iv the current state of race relations

v legislation and social policies designed to eliminate all forms of discrimination in education and employment

vi the relations among societies throughout the world.

It is recognised that in the time available it will only be possible to study some of these areas among which there has been no attempt here to establish priorities. Courses of inservice training may, however, seek different emphases than those outlined above.

3.3 Awareness of Racism

In the light of the recent comments and definitions in the Rampton Report (1981) on the educational effects of unintentional racism in schools and colleges it is important that all prospective and inservice teachers should be

i sensitive to the presence of unintentional racism in their own expectations, evaluations of and attitudes towards students from ethnic minority groups

ii aware of unintentional racism in for example curriculum materials, the grouping of students, or in vocational and other guidance

iii able to understand racism in its institutional as well as in its individual forms.

The short list above is intended to be illustrative and it is expected that particular institutions will wish to augment it to match their particular needs.

3.4 The school the further education college and the classroom

Teachers should be equipped for their work in schools and further education colleges by recognising

i cultural diversity as a source of social and curriculum enrichment

ii that some ethnic minority pupils and students will have particular needs which should be met through a range of provision, such as education in the mother tongue; the recognition of minority languages at all levels up to and including external examinations; the teaching of English as a second language and English language support across the curriculum

iii the appropriate action to take in the case of students who engage in overt racist behaviour

iv the support through pastoral care and home-school and home-college relations which some ethnic minority pupils and students may require as a result of conflicts in expectations and life plans.

4 INSTITUTIONAL CHANGE AND PROFESSIONAL DEVELOPMENT

In order to move towards the achievement of the measures suggested in this paper, institutions may wish to consider their staffing and staff development policies. In addition to a designated multicultural co-ordinator (already existing in many institutions), some wider institutional mechanisms in the form of a co-ordination committee for multicultural and anti-racist education might be established. Such a committee could include representatives of a comprehensive range of disciplines within the institution. One of its major tasks could be to develop a policy statement for the institution on multicultural and anti-racist education.

Staff development through an appropriate variety of strategies will obviously be desirable as will the development of close working relations with ethnic minority groups and other groups working against discrimination in the local community. This may be of particular significance to teacher education and training institutions in their attempts to afford tutorial staff substantial and recent experience of work in this context.

Data from Little and Willey's Research Report "Studies in the Multi-Ethnic Curriculum" relating to In-Service Training

	Concentration			Total
	"high"	"medium"	"low"*	
1. *LEA courses*				
Number of authorties which reported providing courses:	14	14	1	29
Q 31(a) How many in-service training courses did your authority provide in the academic year 1977-78 on multi-ethnic education for:				
(i) newly appointed teachers, including newly qualified teachers	12	5	0	17
(ii) serving teachers, irrespective of length of service	86	61	3	150
Q 31(b) How long were these courses:				
Part-time courses				
of up to 15 hours	63	41	3	107
over 15 hours	19	11	0	30
Full-time courses				
of less than 4 days	5	7	0	12
of 4-7 days	2	0	0	2
of over 7 days	3	0	0	3
2. *School-based courses*				
Number of authorities which reported providing such courses:	7	4	1	12
Q 31(c) How many school-based courses have been organized on multi-ethnic education in the last year to involve the whole staff of a middle or secondary school?	23	19	3	45
3. *Non-LEA courses*				
Number of authorities which provided information:	13	12	3	28
Q 31(d) How many in-service courses on education in a multi-ethnic society did teachers from your authority attend organized by:				
the DES	30	22	3	55
University Institutes and Departments of Education	26	13	2	41
Colleges of Education and Higher Education	31	15	0	46
Other				
College of Preceptors	2	2	0	4
NAME	2	2	0	4
Centre for Information and Advice on Educationally Disadvantaged	3	1	0	4
ATO/DES	4	0	0	4
LATEL	0	1	0	1
Commonwealth Institute	0	1	0	1
RSA Certificate	0	1	0	1
Association of LEA Advisers	0	1	0	1

*Under the terms of this survey, the LEAs and schools in the sample were categorised according to their estimated ethnic minority populations as:

– ''high''   – 10 per cent. or more births of the total number of births in the area to women from the New Commonwealth;

– ''medium'' – $2\frac{1}{2}$ – 10 per cent. as above

– ''low''   – less than $2\frac{1}{2}$ per cent. as above

National Programme of "Training the Trainers" Courses

The programme was initiated by and is under the overall direction of Professor Maurice Craft, Chairman of the School of Education at Nottingham University. It is funded by the DES, Shell UK Limited and Boots Charitable Trust.

Details of the Course included in the First Phase* of the Programme

Birmingham Polytechnic

Three one-term courses will be mounted during 1984, for lecturers in initial teacher training, and LEA advisers and senior teachers responsible for staff development. Each course will examine the changes in British society which have led to the need for a multicultural perspective in the school curriculum; multicultural education in practice, as well as the underlying rationales; racism awareness programmes; the roles of the various agencies involved in the training and development of teachers, and the ways in which curriculum reform can be implemented. Each course member will develop plans directly related to his/her own particular professional role. Each course will comprise two two-day conferences, with three one-day seminars in between spaced over a period of about twelve weeks. The main emphasis will be on personal development through involvement in the course, and making new contacts with teachers and children in the community.

Liverpool University

A two-term course will be offered in the spring and summer terms, 1984, for teacher educators at both initial and in-service levels, and including senior teachers who have responsibilities for in-service work. The course will be designed to help participants to become more aware of the problems and of the opportunities facing education in a multicultural and multi-racial Britain. That awareness will be promoted by the presentation of information, and by considering strategies for change in relation to participants' roles as teacher educators. The course will have a strong local focus, and it will aim to stimulate discussion and reflection rather than to present any particular viewpoint. The course will be organised from the University of Liverpool Faculty of Education and Extension Studies, and will comprise two whole-day sessions (including a racism awareness workshop) and eight afternoon sessions.

London University Institute of Education

The Institute's training-the-trainers course will be focussing its efforts upon a single institution, rather than recruiting from several. An Institute of Higher Education with significant initial and in-service teacher education programmes will participate over three terms, commencing in October 1983. There will be theoretical inputs on intercultural relations (including prejudice, discrimination and racism), the needs of all children in a plural society, and the particular needs of ethnic minority children. In addition to these studies, there will be practical work in local primary schools. It is therefore envisaged that this model will lead (a) to a greater understanding by the participating teacher educators of both the general and the specific issues relating to education in a culturally diverse society, as well as (b) initiating a piece of useful action research that will be of benefit to both the institution and the schools involved.

Manchester Polytechnic

A two-term course will be mounted during 1983-1984 for lecturers, advisers, and others involved in teacher education. The course will aim to offer participants an opportunity to learn more about the

---

* A second phase of the programme is being planned for 1984–1985 and will establish similar courses in the following six institutions: Bedford College of Higher Education, Bristol Polytechnic, Moray House College of Education, Edinburgh, St Martins College, Lancaster, Southampton University and University College, Cardiff.

context of multicultural education, and to reappraise their own practice. It will examine the changing needs of all children in a multicultural society, as well as the particular needs of those from ethnic minorities. Educational issues such as differences of attainment, language and opportunity will be considered against a wider background of economic and political pressures. Questions of race, racial awareness and prejudice will be explored. There will be subject workshops, contributions by local teachers, and opportunities for participants to develop their own work. Coordination will be provided by a staff team from the Polytechnic and there will be visiting speakers of national standing.

Nottingham University

A two-term course beginning in October 1983 will be offered to lecturers, advisers and senior teachers involved in teacher education. It will have three main features. The first will be an exploration of recent developments in key areas of the field, such as multicultural curriculum and minority language issues. Specialists will lead discussion at two two-day conferences. The second feature will be to encourage members to pursue short, individual study programmes, with tutorial guidance, into multicultural education topics of their own choice, and reflecting their existing training commitment and expertise. The third feature will be the provision of an opportunity for participants to widen their own expertise by observation and practice in schools or other institutions. In addition, two one-day workshops will consider (a) the question of resources, and (b) techniques for working effectively with students/teachers on controversial subject matter.

Sunderland Polytechnic

Three one-term courses will be offered during the 1983-1984 session for teacher educators in the region. The aim of each course will be to work in a collegial fashion with advisers, lecturers and senior staff in schools, to develop knowledge, skills and attitudes which will in turn serve to enhance both the content and approach in their work in multicultural education, with pre- and in-service teachers. A strong element in each course is attachment and practical experience. There will be an action-research dimension which will include the collection of evidence/information about the process of involving colleagues in the development of the field. A central issue in this region will be the need for all schools, whether or not they are ethnically mixed, to appraise educational principles and curriculum content in the light of our recognised membership of a multicultural society.

Admissions of Ethnic Minorities to Teacher Education Studies from Access Courses

1 *Table 1* shows the admissions of ethnic minorities (EMs) to Higher Education Insitutions (HEIs) for the four sessions 1980-81 to 1983-84, in response to the DES Letter of Invitation of 2nd August 1978

2. *Table 1 EM ADMISSIONS FROM PREPARATORY B.Ed. COURSES*

ACCESS STUDIES

Access session	Total intake	EM intake M	W	M&W	Envisaged B.Ed studies Generalist	Specialist(b)
1979-80	49	13	35	48	48	—
1980-81	98	12	62	74	58	16
1981-82	106	13	79	92	74	18
1982-83	131	21	88	109	84	25
	384	59	264	323	264	59
1983-84	159	27	91	118		

EM background

	M	W
Caribbean	17	77
Asian	7	77
Other	3	9

EM ADMISSIONS TO HEIs FOR BEd. COURSES (a)

H E session	Caribbean M	W	Asian M	W	Other M	W
1980-81	3 (4)	19 (21)	—	—	2(2)	—(1)
1981-82	7 (7)	39 (45)	—	2(2)	—(1)	—(1)
1982-83	8 (8)	55 (56)	—	1(1)	—(1)	1(1)
1983-84	11 (14)	43 (53)	—	3(5)	—(-)	1(2)
	29 (33)	156(175)	6(8)	4(4)	2(5)	6(9)
	185(208)		6(8)		6(9)	

Total 197(225)

Notes
(a) Figures in brackets show no. of students who have successfully completed Access studies.
(b) Specialist B.Ed. studies: Home Economics, Mathematics, Youth and Community.

Admissions of Ethnic Minorities to Teacher Education Studies from Access Courses (continued)

3 Table 2   *AGE-RANGES OF CARIBBEAN STUDENTS ON ADMISSION TO PREPARATORY B.Ed. COURSES.*

Access session	18-19 M	18-19 W	20-24 M	20-24 W	25-29 M	25-29 W	30-39 M	30-39 W	40-49 M	40-49 W	50+ M	50+ W	Total
1979-80	—	1	3	11	2	15	5	8	1	2	—	—	
1980-81	1	—	—	18	3	16	5	15	1	2	—	—	
1981-82	—	—	1	18	6	31	3	22	—	4	—	1	
1982-83	—	—	7	24	10	31	3	18	—	1	—	—	
M&W	1	2	11	82	21	114	16	79	2	11	—	1	289
% all Caribbean students		0.7		28.4		39.5		27.3		3.8		0.3	100

4 *Comments*

4.1 The above figures relate only to B.Ed studies. It is not possible to know how many former Access students will later proceed to a PGCE course.

4.2 Very few students have proceeded to B.Ed. studies after completing a multiple-exit course.

4.3 225/323 (69.7%) of EM students successfully completed Access studies. The pass rate for all Access courses during the same period was 67.3%.

The pass rate for each session was:

		%
1979-80	28/48	58.3
1980-81	56/74	75.7
1981-82	67/92	72.8
1982-83	74/109	67.9

4.4 197/225 of the successful students (87.6%) proceeded to B.Ed. courses, virtually all to the linked HEI.

4.5 The proportion of men/women was 33/164 (16.8%/83.2%) who entered Higher Education.

4.6 The proportion of Generalist/Specialist studies envisaged was 264/59 (81.7%/18.3%).

4.7 95% of the Caribbean students entering Access courses were in the 20-39 age-range and 68% in the 20-29 age-range.

PART IV

"Other" Ethnic Minority Groups

INTRODUCTION

The Range of Ethnic Minority Groups

1. It has been clear throughout our work that many people, regard the term "ethnic minority" as simply meaning people of Asian or West Indian origin. This attitude was manifested by those who, after the publication of our interim report, relating to children of West Indian origin, expected that our main report would "complete" our task by dealing solely with the needs of Asian pupils. We have already made clear that we interpreted our task in far broader terms and did not limit our work to looking at any one particular ethnic minority group but attempted to consider the needs of ethnic minority groups within the broader question of the education of *all* children for life in a pluralist society. The central focus of our work has remained the particular educational needs of pupils from ethnic minority groups and this has meant that we have devoted a considerable amount of attention to both Asian and West Indian communities. We were anxious however to also give some consideration to the situation of children from some of the numerically smaller ethnic minority communities which have tended to receive rather less attention than the Asian and West Indian minority groups but which are as much an integral part of British society today.

Communities Considered

2. It was clearly not feasible to attempt to consider separately the experiences of all the many different ethnic minority groups now present in this country. We decided initially therefore to focus our attention on those ethnic minority groups which we saw either as exemplars of particular types of communities or whose needs we considered to be particularly deserving of attention in their own right. These groups were:

— *the Chinese Community:* One of the most numerous "other" ethnic minority groups. A community whose situation has received little attention but whose members often have particular needs because of the widely dispersed nature of their pattern of settlement;

— *the Cypriot Community* (Both Greek Cypriot and Turkish Cypriot): Another of the larger "other" minorities, whose concentrated pattern of settlement presents certain specific educational needs. Also an ethnic minority community where the level of academic achievement of pupils has aroused considerable concern;

— *the Italian Community:* One of the longest established ethnic minority communities in this country and, as a "white", European-derived group, offering a particular insight into ques-

649

tions of "ethnic identity" and links with the majority community. The efforts of the Italian Government to assist with activities such as "mother tongue teaching" also offer an interesting perspective on such issues;

— *the Ukrainian Community:* One of the Eastern European groups who settled in this country following the Second World War as "refugees" rather than as voluntary immigrants. As one of the smaller ethnic minorities at rather greater risk than other, larger groups of being submerged by the majority community and losing their distinct identity;

— *the Vietnamese Community:* The most recent of the refugee groups to come to this country and also one of the ethnic minority communities with perhaps the most tenuous prior ties, in both emotional and cultural terms, with Britain. Also a group whose educational needs have been exacerbated by the traumatic circumstances of their departure from their own country and whose situation has been far more directly controlled by official agencies than other groups.

In addition to these groups, we were also led—by the sheer volume of evidence which we received on their needs—to consider the situation of children from *the Travelling Community,* whose needs have often previously been almost entirely passed over in any consideration of ethnic minority communities. From our consideration of the plight of this community, many of us were led to believe that their needs were if anything even more deserving of attention than the other groups we had considered. In many respects indeed, their situation appears to embody very strikingly many of the issues raised by the educational experiences of other ethnic minorities. We also devoted some attention to considering the *"Liverpool Black"* *Community,* about whom great concern has of course already been expressed on a number of occasions and whose situation also illustrates to an extreme degree many of the problems facing other ethnic minority communities.

Evidence Gathering

3.   In order to assist us with our investigation of these groups, we once again commissioned the NFER to prepare reviews of relevant research data. To supplement this material and the many interesting and valuable submissions of written evidence which we received, we organised a series of meetings, visits and oral evidence sessions around the country in relation to each of these communities. As with the major part of our evidence-gathering, we made particular efforts to meet representatives of the communities themselves, especially parents and young people, and, without exception, the responses we received to our requests for information and to our expressions of

interest were positive and enthusiastic. Above all we were struck by the extent to which members of these groups were both surprised and pleased that a Committee such as this should take the trouble to seek their views on education and on their perceptions of minority/ majority group relationships in this society, rather than, as has almost always happened in the past, simply confining its attention to the "major" ethnic minority groups.

This Part of the Report

4.   In this part of our report we devote chapters to considering the educational needs of pupils from these groups. Since we have already put forward our main findings and conclusions relating to the needs of children from the whole range of ethnic minority groups and our broad strategy for developing "Education for All", we have confined ourselves here to describing the background of these communities and discussing the *particular* educational needs which pupils from them may face. Where very special factors have influenced the experiences of certain groups, as in the case of the Vietnamese and the Travellers, we have put forward some specific recommendations on their behalf. At the end of this part of our report we summarise briefly the conclusions which we feel can be drawn from our findings in relation to these "other" ethnic minorities to further support the conclusions we reached earlier. We must emphasise that the following chapters are not intended to provide a comprehensive picture of the situation of any of these groups. We hope however that they will not only help to inform our readers about the diversity of ethnic minority experience in Britain today, but will also serve to broaden the debate about ethnic minority needs beyond the traditional emphasis on the larger ethnic minority communities. In focussing on these particular groups, we recognise that members of other ethnic minority communities, who may have submitted evidence to us but whose needs we have not considered explicitly in this way, may feel disappointed. We must emphasise however that in preparing this report we have taken full account of the whole range of evidence we have received, and the similarities which have emerged between the experiences, needs and aspirations of all the ethnic minorities whom we have considered in our view lends further weight to the conclusions which we have reached in the interests of all ethnic minority children.

CHAPTER 10

The Educational Needs of Children of Chinese Origin

Background

1. The Chinese community in this country numbers in excess of 100,000 and there are estimated to be some 30,000 children of Chinese origin in UK schools. The educational needs of children from this group have not tended to be the focus of as much attention as the needs of other Asian or West Indian children, and when we began to take evidence relating to their needs we were immediately faced with two very different interpretations of their situation—firstly, that they were "ideal" pupils, who had no problems and represented a "success story" amongst ethnic minority groups, or, alternatively, that they were a "forgotten minority": "invisible" pupils whose needs remained unrecognised and thus unmet by schools. As is often the case, we believe that the truth lies somewhere between these two extremes, but we feel the situation of the Chinese community illustrates clearly the pressures which bear on an ethnic minority community in this country seeking to retain its own individual character, culture and traditions.

Immigration

2. Chinese immigration to Britain developed in the 19th Century when single males came to this country, mainly as seamen, and settled in major ports, chiefly London and Liverpool. Numbers were not large and by 1901 there were thought to be only 545 Chinese people in the whole country. Numbers continued to rise slowly but steadily however, and after the Second World War, with the sudden boom in the Chinese restaurant business, there was a sharp increase in immigration especially from Hong Kong. The pattern of immigration diversified during the 1960s from the traditional single males, with wives and children joining workers already established here, and some 80 per cent of the present Chinese population in this country have arrived within the last 20 years. Immigration to this country from Hong Kong has tended to decline since the late 1970s and a substantial proportion of the Chinese pupils of school age today have been born in this country, although some children are still arriving in schools direct from Hong Kong. The majority of the Chinese population in this country originates from the rural agricultural area of Hong Kong's New Territories.

Settlement

3. The centre of Chinese settlement in Britain is London, with a community of some 35–45,000, concentrated in the central China-

653

town district, but sizeable communities are also to be found in Manchester, Liverpool and Birmingham, and smaller settlements in Southampton, Bristol and other seaports. (Cardiff, Glasgow and Edinburgh are major centres outside England.) London's Chinatown constitutes a cultural and entertainment centre rather than an organisational heart to the community, which functions mainly on the basis of the individual, but extended, family unit. One of the most important factors to bear in mind when considering the Chinese community is the unique extent to which it is dispersed around the country, to all areas in fact where there are Chinese restaurants or "takeaways". Apart from the main areas of settlement mentioned above—and even in these the community is found only in "scattered pockets"—Chinese children are usually therefore found in ones or twos in individual schools, often in isolated, rural areas which otherwise have no experience of providing for the educational needs of ethnic minorities. The scattered nature of the Chinese population also exacerbates the isolation of mothers and children who may not speak English. Quite apart from the educational consequences of this situation, which we consider below, as one witness put it to us:

> "We are therefore not 'visible' in the way that other groups in Brixton or Southall are and there is therefore no political pressure to recognise our needs."

Ethnic Identity

4. Even amongst the British-born Chinese community there seems to be an extremely strong sense of "being Chinese". There is a strong sense of pride in the Chinese heritage, and, to a certain extent at least, a sense of the superiority of the Chinese culture over all others. It is noticeable that Chinese communities around the world have retained their essential "Chineseness" even over centuries of hostility. Whilst the so-called "Chinese community" is in fact very diverse in character, with the clan system and "surname societies" for example still playing important roles for people originating from various regions and with different languages and dialects, the community as a whole therefore presents a strongly unified identity to outside society. The sense of self-reliance and self-help seems to be exceptionally strong both within the Chinese community and within the individual Chinese family—as explained in evidence to us:

> "There is a tendency . . . for the Chinese to take matters in their own hands, rationalised by saying: 'We are all Chinese' and 'Don't let the foreigners despise us'."

The reasons for this overriding sense of "keeping a low profile" and of not "losing face" to outsiders have their roots deep in Chinese culture and philosophy but inevitably as a consequence, in educational terms, parents and children may appear to be "content" and "have no problems" when this is far from the case.

Culture and Religion

5. It is difficult to attempt to summarise the essential nature of Chinese culture briefly, since it embraces many complex philosophical concepts. According to Dr Hugh Baker, however, writing in the Nuffield Foundation's book "Teaching Chinese Children"[1]:

". . . the hallmarks of Chineseness have been a philosophy based on the family, a settled agricultural economy, a universally applicable language, and a strong sense of cultural superiority. . . The Chinese have stressed the importance of the family from earliest times. The Confucian philosphers refined and extended family consciousness through a carefully worked out hierarchy of relationships. Most important was the father-son relationship, the son being expected to obey, to serve, to respect and at all times to defer to the father. . . Ancestor worship was the religion which gave strength and supernatural sanction to the family. . . In this way everyone's position in this life and the after-life was rigidly circumscribed and made subject to the greater welfare of the family unit. The individual counted for little, except as the medium of transmission of the family line. The system made for great security within the family, though it stifled the individual freedom and initiative, and made conservatism an absolute virtue."

6. The essential characteristics of the two great Chinese belief systems—Confucianism and Taoism—bear out these same precepts. As explained by David Ladlow of the Liverpool Language Centre[2]:

"Confucius based his teachings on the concept of 'li'—respectful attitudes towards the ancestors and one's fellow men. He taught the rule 'What you do not want done to yourself, do not do to others' and the significance of Five Relationships in society. . . The concept of filial duty was of paramount importance. . . The Tao (of Taoism) is literally the way, but it is used by philosophers . . . to mean the course of nature, or reason. The Tao Te Ching (the standard work of Taoism) . . . advocates a quietist submission to the course of nature; it preaches humility and compassion and the requiting of good for evil."

Buddhism is also practised in China. In simple terms, as explained in Norman Fitchett's booklet "Chinese Children in Derby"[3]:

"Buddhism is not a religion in the sense that it contains no special references to an eternal God. A Buddhist is simply an enlightened person who is aware of the practical consequences of morality

[1]"Teaching Chinese Children—A Teacher's Guide." The Nuffield Foundation. 1981.
[2]"Aspects of Chinese Culture—Background Information for Teachers." D E Ladlow. Liverpool Language Centre.
[3]"Chinese Children in Derby." Norman Fitchett. 1976.

. . . Although there are many and varied interpretations of the Buddhist 'faith' in different parts of the world, the general principles enshrined in it have influenced much of Chinese thought and culture for many centuries."

There are also of course a minority of Chinese Christians.

These then are the main cultural and religious influences on the Chinese community in this country, many of which appear to have a direct bearing on the educational experiences of Chinese children.

Education

Language 7.   A major issue in relation to the education of Chinese children and young people is the difficulties that they experience in learning English. This is undoubtedly exacerbated by the dispersed nature of Chinese settlement which means that a Chinese child or a small number of Chinese children may be in a school that has no experience of ethnic minority children and more particularly has neither arrangements for, nor access to, E2L support. A reluctance to complain may put these children at particular risk unless teachers exercise sensitivity in identifying language needs, providing for these and monitoring language progress systematically. It is unlikely that individual schools will be able to respond in this way without support from their maintaining authorities.

8.   Particular factors arise when considering the language needs of this group. As mentioned above, the Chinese written language bears very little direct relationship to the spoken language and is common to speakers of a range of Chinese languages which are mutually unintelligible. Chinese characters are basically symbols, similar to ancient Egyptian hieroglyphics. Each character is made up of small pictures or symbols which function very similarly to the suffix and prefix in English. All the Chinese characters, more than 10,000, are constructed in six different ways, of which the most important is the "likeness of shape"—thus 日 means "sun", because the sun comes out each day it also means "day", and every character starting with 日 usually concerns the sun, such as "brightness", "weather", "sky" etc. The symbol for sun would however be read by a Chinese from Peking as "ri" and by a Chinese from Canton as "yat". Because of the complexity of the written language, as explained in evidence to us:

"Chinese education has traditionally laid great emphasis on calligraphy and the memorisation of the written characters. Chinese pupils transfer these skills to English, learning to copy neatly and memorising the spelling of whole words; common

faults however are copying without understanding and failure to see links between sound and spelling."

One of the consequences of the good handwriting of Chinese children because of this tradition of calligraphy, is that teachers are inevitably impressed by a beautifully-presented piece of work and may therefore fail to perceive the lack of understanding which this may mask. As quoted in Anne Garvey and Brian Jackson's research on Chinese children[4]:

> *"'And it's all done' said the head we spoke to, 'in this fantastic handwriting all beautifully laid out. Sort of script writing, but not quite. More like italic writing if you remember that from the old days. It must take hours'."*

9.   As far as the spoken language is concerned, the major Chinese language or dialect, based on the speech of Peking, is Mandarin. The majority of Chinese in Britain however speak Cantonese, the dominant dialect of Hong Kong, and a significant number are Hakka speaking. The following extracts from evidence submitted by one Chinese teacher whom we met, who works in the language unit of a London borough give some indication of the particular difficulties which may be faced by a Chinese child in learning English:

> *"There are no tenses in Chinese. Time is indicated by adverbial phrases of time which are usually put before the verbs, eg. 'I yesterday watch television, I right here watch television, I tomorrow watch television'—word order alone determines whether a Chinese word is functioning as a noun, verb, adjective or adverb in that particular context, eg. 'they run quick', 'a quick lunch' (adjective). The so called pidgin English 'You good?' ('how are you?') is actually a transposition of the Chinese sentence order into English... There are no definite/indefinite articles. Instead, nouns are preceded by 'classifiers' decscribing the shapes of the objects, eg 'flat thin' book 'long thin' pencil... There is no change of form for plural nouns. Numerals like 'one', 'two' or 'a dozen' are used if the meaning of plurality is considered relevant to the message eg. Two 'flat thin' book, three 'long thin' pencil... 'L' and 'n' can be used interchangeably in Cantonese, so students usually confuse the pronunciation of these two sounds in English: eg. 'light' and 'night', 'labour' and 'neighbour'."*

10.   From what we have seen, those Language Centres and peripatetic E2L teachers dealing with numbers of Chinese children seem to have built up adequate resources to meet the particular language

---

[4]"Children Children: research and action project into the needs of Chinese Children." Garvey and Jackson. Cambridge Educational Development Trust. 1974.

difficulties of Chinese children. We would however like to see such materials being more fully used by schools in non-multi-racial areas without specialist E2L support which may nevertheless have one or two Chinese pupils. We feel there is particular scope for greater use to be made of videotaped material which can considerably expand the teaching expertise available to a school, provided it is accompanied by adequate direct support by the class teacher.

11. Further difficulties, resulting from both linguistic and cultural factors, may also arise for schools in relation to the names, relations and ages of Chinese children as explained to us as follows:

"Misunderstanding can easily arise when the teacher tries to obtain from his pupil a. his surname, b. the number of brothers and sisters, and c. his age.

a. **Names.** *The Chinese custom is to put the surname first. Next come either one or two 'given names' or personal names. In many cases where a person has two given names he shares the first of these with other brothers and sisters. However Chinese children take readily to the idea of an English Christian name for use in school. We had two brothers called Wong Chi Dock and Wong Chi Moon. Wong was their surname and Chi a name which they shared. To conform with English usage they soon began to put their surname last, becoming Chi Dock Wong and Chi Moon Wong. They were then given English Christian names and became known as Tony Wong and Robert Wong.*

b. *The question 'How may brothers have you?' may produce the reply 'Two brothers' when the teacher knows that the pupil has only one brother. The pupil is in fact thinking in terms of 'How many brothers are there' since Cantonese uses the same word for 'have' and 'there are'.*

c. **Ages.** *Chinese pupils often give their age as one year older, or possibly two years older, than the teacher expects. According to Chinese tradition a child is one year old at birth (the nine months in the womb) and becomes two years old at the next Chinese New Year."*

Curriculum Content

12. From the evidence which we received, there seems to be little obvious discontent in the Chinese community with the school curriculum, although, as we have noted elsewhere, such apparent satisfaction with the work of schools may mask underlying concerns. However, there is no doubt that children and parents clearly appreciate teachers using elements of their cultural background in teaching since they see this as properly enhancing their culture in the eyes of

the rest of the community. One witness we met felt, for example, that:

> "The teaching of Chinese literature in translation could be a meaningful exercise in erasing cultural barriers. The contribution of Chinese classical drama to the exploration of mask/reality in drama classes is yet another area to be explored. The relationship between calligraphy and the power of abstraction could be a fascinating exercise. In history, the accuracy of the historical Chinese input needs to be seriously examined. More fascinating is the exploration of paradoxes in maths which existed in China 4,000 years ago. Rather than a strict religious education which never has the same significance in the Chinese culture as in the Indian cultures, a course for the senior secondary students on Chinese system of thought and attitudes towards life on a comparative basis may be a useful exercise in sorting out their own values."

Several witnesses stressed to us that all teachers and all children ought to have the opportunity to learn more about Chinese culture. Unfortunately many teachers did not realise how ignorant they in fact were of other cultures. The lack of knowledge about Hong Kong and its economic importance to Britain even amongst leading businessmen and industrialists in this country was felt to be deplorable. It was generally felt that a teacher who was actually of Chinese origin would be best able to draw on Chinese culture, art and history in the general curriculum. Our attention was however drawn to one authority's interesting plans to produce TV programmes and materials which could be used by any teacher to introduce elements of the Chinese heritage into his or her teaching for the benefit of *all* pupils. Those who gave evidence to us generally felt that schools should value Chinese culture in the eyes of all pupils since neglecting their culture merely increased the isolation of Chinese pupils and demotivated them. Usually all that schools offered were token examples of Chinese festivals or cookery rather than introducing elements of Chinese history and geography into the curriculum and, where the number of pupils justified this, the teaching of the Chinese language for both Chinese and non-Chinese pupils. Whilst acknowledging that a British teacher with a traditional training could not be expected to know a great deal about the Chinese cultural heritage, it was suggested that LEAs should build up appropriate resources including videotapes, on which they could draw. The importance of China in the world and the fact that it is one of the world's historic civilisations argue a powerful case for all children knowing something of it.

"Late Arrivals" 13. In considering the educational needs of children of Chinese origin it is important to draw a distinction between those who were born in this country and those who have come to this country later, having already received some education in Hong Kong. In general terms, whereas, for the former group, the problems lie more with the maintenance of their cultural and linguistic background and with resolving possible identity crises and conflicts with parents, for the latter group, there is an overriding need for E2L help. A further dimension of this situation is the fact that, in the past, a number of Chinese parents in this country have sent their children back to Hong Kong for at least some of their education. When such children return to this country, at the age of perhaps 14 or 15, their educational problems can be particularly acute, especially when combined with the problems of readjusting to life in this country with their parents and younger brothers and sisters whom they may never have met before. The particular problems associated with Chinese children arriving in British schools aged 12+ were described thus in evidence to us:

> *"These children fall into two broad groups, namely those who arrive here as first time immigrants accompanying their parents and those who were born in the United Kingdom and were sent at an early age to live with a grandmother or other member of the extended family. This second group arose from the parents' concern for them to 'absorb Chinese culture', and mainly to give the parents the freedom to both work and thereby save enough to start their own independent business. These children, to all intents and purposes, suffer the same disadvantage as those born in Hong Kong and brought here at a later stage. The central problem facing these children is the lack of facility in the English language. Coming as they do from the rural parts of Hong Kong, they invariably attend Chinese schools and have little or no contact with the English language. Their entry into the British school system is often quite a traumatic experience, with the first few months or first year taken up with acquiring a working knowledge of English. It is small wonder that many of them are characterised as quiet and withdrawn, and it is not unknown for teachers to interpret this as an indication of lack of intelligence. Promotion in a typical Chinese school is by achievement. Hence classes usually have students of different ages. Placement in British schools is normally by age. Thus difficulties with the language are compounded by placement in a class unsuited to the child's real attainment. Even in subjects, especially science and mathematics, where the student's knowledge matches that of his classmates, there is difficulty in finding out what the child actually knows and deciding how that child can continue to be effectively taught. There is evidence too that the practice of sending young children to Hong Kong and repatriating them to Britain later on*

is also declining. In recent years the trend has been to send for the grandmother to join the family here. The trend has also been reflected in the increased demand for places in Chinese language classes and the increase in the provision of such classes. Conversely, the availability of such classes has to some extent diminished the need to send children to Hong Kong to learn Chinese and acquire a 'Chinese outlook'."

Teachers'
Attitudes

14.   The most commonly-expressed view of teachers about Chinese children seems to be to see them as having no serious problems and as being generally hard workers and high achievers and especially quiet and well-behaved—in short "ideal pupils". Whilst there may be some truth in this stereotype, as we pointed out in Chapter Two, if teachers allow themselves to react in response to this view of a "typical" Chinese pupil, they may very well underestimate or even overlook educational difficulties, particularly in the field of language, which the child may be experiencing.

Parental
Attitudes

15.   One leading Chinese community representative whom we met summarised the attitudes of Chinese parents towards education as follows:

"It is a truism to say that Chinese parents regard education as a good thing. Education was the traditional means to social betterment, and the high regard for education is reflected in the exalted and esteemed position held by teachers and scholars in Chinese society. However, this enthusiasm for education is tempered by the situation of the parents here. Most of our parents are themselves not educated to any high degree. They therefore cannot take part in any active sense in the education of their children. Their ignorance of the British system and educational methods often leads to misunderstanding and dissatisfaction. As most of the parents are in the catering trade the conditions and hours of their work make it exceedingly difficult for them to be involved with the schools. The language barrier also contributes to the problem of contact between parents and teachers. This lack of contact can give the impression to parents that teachers tend to seek them out only when there is serious trouble afoot."

One Language Centre we visited actively encouraged teachers to visit homes to establish contact with parents, provided proper advance arrangements were made for this and it was made clear that the child was not "in trouble". Community representatives stressed however that teachers should not just "knock on doors" since in traditional Chinese culture guests were entertained in a restaurant rather than at home and it was more acceptable therefore to meet parents through community centres or Chinese language schools. Clearly however the latter approach is only possible in areas where there is a reasonably-sized Chinese population. One witness stressed the need for adult education courses for Chinese parents to help them learn English and about English culture and customs. It was explained that Chinese parents rarely spoke English and did not have the spare time in which to learn it. Some in fact felt strongly that if they gave up Chinese they would lose their cultural heritage and be unable to speak freely. Even where strenuous efforts had been made over the years to encourage parents to learn English they had met with only limited success. One Chinese teacher who had been working with families stressed to us the need for Chinese parents to be taught English by a Chinese teacher since only he could understand the particular linguistic problems they faced. Given the grave problems that Chinese people face in learning English the idea of bilingual teachers deserves careful consideration by LEAs, possibly on a cooperative basis.

Home Environment 16.   One factor which has often been put forward as having a particular bearing on the educational situation of Chinese children is the fact that they may be expected to help in the family's restaurant when they return from school, often until late into the night, making them very tired for school the next day. As one witness explained:

> *"The catering trade involves hard work, and many of the Chinese restaurants are small, not very profitable "take-aways". Workers in the Chinese catering trade are more or less fully employed, and casual part-time labour is difficult to come by. Language problems make it impractical to employ non-Chinese speakers—though in the provinces indigenous part-time workers do serve at the counter. Older children are often recruited to help in the family business where their facility in English (no matter how rudimentary) is an asset. Moreover, the traditional Chinese family concept places an obligation on all members of the family to help whenever and wherever the need arises."*

Whilst the extent of the involvement of Chinese youngsters in family businesses may, we believe, have been unduly emphasised by some writers and has certainly become a feature of the stereotype of the Chinese pupil, the numerous references to this situation in the evidence we received makes it clear that a substantial number of pupils may well face particular pressures as a result of evening and weekend working. It is not for us to criticise or condone this practice by Chinese families but we would hope to see all parents showing a full appreciation of the possible effects which such pressures may have on the educational needs of their children. Again "parent education" may help to bring this about. From an educational viewpoint however, teachers need to be aware of the pressure under which Chinese children may be working and to take full account of this in dealing with their "pastoral needs".

"Mother Tongue" and Community-Based Provision

17. The Committee's general views on the major issue of "mother-tongue" maintenance and teaching in mainstream schools have been dealt with in detail in the Language Chapter of this report but a number of particular points arise in relation to Chinese children which need to be considered in relation to their general educational needs. As explained above, the Chinese written language has a particular role in the Chinese heritage as the single unifying force for Chinese people over the centuries. Many parents may therefore see a command of the language as an essential factor in their children retaining their "Chineseness". The Chinese language is also the key to the Chinese literary heritage and so can be a crucial element in establishing the identity of an isolated Chinese child who may not have the support available to other ethnic minority children living in areas of high ethnic minority settlement or in strong religious communities. Chinese parents may speak little or no English themselves and in restaurants often only the waiters speak English whilst the cooks and other staff speak only Chinese and have no contact with anyone outside the Chinese community. If the children do not speak Chinese this can therefore lead to considerable communication problems and may accentuate the "generation" and "culture" gap which may already exist between them and their parents. As the child learns English at school, conflict may arise when he finds his parents are unable to understand him or the work he is doing and he may simply then reject his parents as "stupid". Clearly this situation, shared by other ethnic minorities, may thus lead to tensions, resentment and frustration. To remedy this the Chinese community around the country has established its own classes where children can learn to speak and write Chinese. Parents are very anxious for their children to attend (although the children we met were generally less enthusiastic) and are therefore willing to pay, and many classes are in fact over-subscribed. When these classes were set up they also had a social purpose in that they relieved parents of what some saw as the need to send their children back to Hong Kong in order to gain some knowledge of Chinese and the Chinese culture. In April 1982 the Hong Kong Government Office in London estimated that there were some 53 such classes (although there may be a few additional classes not recorded officially) with a total enrolment of 6,400 children. The sizes of these classes range from one school in London with a total of 967 pupils to others with perhaps only 20 pupils. The Hong Kong Government Office makes an annual cash grant towards the running costs of most established classes, as well as helping with textbooks. The majority of the textbooks and readers used are those curently in use in schools in Hong Kong itself. Some extracts from a recent article discussing various aspects of the operation of Chinese " mother tongue" classes are attached as an Annex to this chapter.

18.   We discussed at some length with all our witnesses their views on the possibility of teaching Chinese within the curriculum of mainstream schools. There seemed to be general agreement that the majority of the community prefer to retain the responsibility for "mother tongue" provision themselves, seeing it as "their responsibility", and something which their children could readily take on in addition to their normal school. As one Chinese community association put it in evidence to us:

> *"The community feels that as long as our children are able to carry on and have a good education we can carry out their other needs. As far as the maintenance of language and culture we will still carry on with our present provision although we would welcome help in the form of free lettings of school/college premises, educational materials, in-service training and educational training of our non-professional staff. We have the manpower, determination and will to maintain this sort of provision if help could be provided it would be some help."*

This general line of welcoming additional help with the "mechanics" of the classes and regretting the different approaches adopted by LEAs to the letting of premises, but not wishing to hand over fully the responsibility for them to local authorities, seems to be fairly typical. The reasons for this approach, which differs somewhat from the views of other ethnic minority communities, may lie to a certain extent at least with the traditional "self-sufficiency" of the Chinese community. Many Chinese community groups we met also recognised however the particular practical problems presented by the scattered nature of the population when considering the feasibility of introducing Chinese into the curriculum of mainstream schools, even were provision to be made on a regional basis. One representative pointed out that some Chinese children clearly felt that learning Chinese was a waste of time since it was not recognised by the school. He felt that if schools and teachers at least recognised that Chinese children were attending these classes and encouraged them, this might help to change the children's attitudes. Attitudes were changing gradually however and he was now receiving inquiries from teachers about the work of the language schools and when he spoke at conferences he was gaining a positive response. Whilst the organiser of one Chinese language school said he would welcome being able to "hive-off" some of the responsibilities of his school to the maintained system where the facilities might be better, he stressed that his school did not *just* teach the Chinese language—it also sought to encourage the children to respect their cultural heritage. The schools also provided a focal point for the whole community—as explained by the Hong Kong Government Office:

"In many places, particularly in some towns where the Chinese community is relatively small, the organisation of Chinese classes has become the unifying force of the community in the locality and surrounding areas. It has become the regular meeting place for parents, children and overseas students. Friendships are struck up—particularly amongst the mothers, personal or communal problems are brought up for discussion and solutions and assistance found. English lessons for adults come into existence, outings and other social and communal activities are organised. In short, some of the classes have become community centres."

If the LEA took over the functions of the language schools, he felt his teachers would be deprived of a valuable experience. As with most other Chinese language schools, most of his teachers were Chinese university students and working at the school helped overcome the isolation felt by many of them living in a strange society. Arguing for the provision of Chinese in mainstream schools however, another witness stressed the difficulty of the Chinese language and pointed out that it was "glib" to expect children to learn it properly from perhaps one lesson each week. In his experience many of the people running the supplementary schools lacked both the resources and experience to make the work interesting for the children and too much reliance was placed on rote learning. One Chinese teacher from a language unit felt that Chinese children born in this country saw the supplementary classes as leading nowhere and were not interested in learning Chinese as they had no pride in their cultural and linguistic heritage. One way of enhancing their pride in themselves might therefore be to offer Chinese within the maintained system. He also thought that if Chinese was made available in schools then pupils from all groups would be interested in studying it.

19.   Much of our evidence referred to the shortage of suitable teachers to teach Chinese and it was mentioned that there were many well-qualified teachers in Hong Kong who were unable to get work permits to come here because of unemployment in the teaching profession. It was stressed however that teachers of Chinese did not necessarily have to come from Hong Kong since some people had taken degrees in Chinese at British universities and there were also FE courses in Chinese so existing teachers could study this specialism. In this respect it was also mentioned that the "O" level Chinese examination was designed for English speakers learning Chinese and not for native Chinese speakers and some Chinese pupils therefore had difficulty in passing it, not because of their ability in Chinese but because of their command of English. This might therefore militate

against Chinese youngsters who might consider a career in teaching languages.

Achievement   20. As with the other numerically smaller ethnic minority communities whom we have considered, there is a paucity of specific data relating to the educational achievement of Chinese pupils because of the absence of ethnically-based educational statistics. There was a strong impression however, from the majority of teachers and others from whom we received evidence, that, in general, Chinese pupils were doing well in educational terms although there were strong suggestions that they might nevertheless be *under*achieving in relation to their true potential primarily because of a lack of necessary language support, and also because of the general problems of a curriculum which was inappropriate to their background and needs, which we have found bearing on the achievement of ethnic minority pupils in general. Considerable emphasis was placed in the evidence we received on the very positive attitudes of Chinese youngsters and their parents towards education and on their high degree of motivation and aspiration—as one community representative put it to us:

> *"By and large, I find that our children are strongly motivated to do well at school. Their aspirations may be modest (car mechanic, electrician, HND) or ambitious (university and the professions), but generally they share a hopeful attitude towards the future."*

However some witnesses felt that parents often put pressure on youngsters to leave school as soon as possible since they saw academic qualifications as irrelevant to taking over the family business.

Careers   21. As far as careers are concerned, the Chinese community in this country is "locked into" the restaurant and catering trade. In 1978 there were estimated to be some 6,500 Chinese restaurants and takeaways in this country. However we received a lot of evidence about the increasing resistance of British-born youngsters to this limited view of their futures. Some youngsters in Liverpool even spoke of going to Hong Kong to avoid working in the family restaurant. Where a youngster did want to try and break out of the traditional pattern of employment and pursue his or her education further, strong support and guidance was needed from the school. This was particularly so with girls because some Chinese parents still felt strongly that, as evidence from one Chinese organisation put it:

> *"Wives' places are at home, daughters are other people's daughters-in-law and therefore it is not really important that they have any achievements."*

Despite the conflicts which do arise between youngsters and their parents over careers, the general view of those who gave evidence to us was that the youngsters usually bowed ultimately to their parents' wishes since "it was in their nature to be obedient". An important factor at present militating against Chinese youngsters seeking other career opportunities is of course high youth unemployment and we heard of cases where youngsters had left home to find other work but had eventually had to return to work in the family restaurant since they had not been able to find work elsewhere. It seems clear that careers offices and careers teachers need to be particularly supportive in the guidance that they may provide for Chinese young people.

Racism

22. Generally speaking, the Chinese community does not appear to have been subject to racism to the same extent as some other ethnic minority communities. This may be the result of a number of factors including their intentionally low profile, their lack of concentration in any particular area, and also the fact that they are seen to be performing a "useful function" through providing Chinese restaurants and are not competing in the mainstream jobs market (although the latter situation may change in future as mentioned above). As James Watson explained in discussing the Chinese community in "Between Two Cultures"[5], they still exist very much on the "fringe" of majority society in this country and:

> "... the economic niche that the Chinese control allows the migrants to live, work and prosper without changing their way of life to suit British social expectations."

Nevertheless there are some grounds for believing that the extent of racism involving the Chinese community may have been underestimated—as explained in evidence to us:

> "There (is) no systematic discrimination so far against the Chinese at a local level. However individual cases of racial harassment are not unknown; number of known cases are reduced to a less official figure for a few reasons. The Chinese tend to be more tolerant and timid over political issues such as racial discrimination, their belief that it is other people's country and therefore there is no need to fight, the police attitude and their language difficulties also complicate the reporting of these cases."

It is worth mentioning briefly the issue of racism *between* ethnic minority groups in the context of the Chinese. As already observed, the Chinese heritage tends to encourage a sense of "superiority" over other cultures and this seems to have led to some Chinese children

[5] "Between Two Cultures: migrants and minorities in Britain". Ed. James L Watson. 1977.

being prejudiced against other ethnic minority pupils, especially Asians and West Indians, and against indigenous "white" pupils.

Conclusion

23.   We feel that the situation of the Chinese community, and particularly the educational experiences of Chinese children serve to emphasise further the general conclusions which we reached earlier in this report. The fact that Chinese children, because of the dispersed nature of their community are often to be found in otherwise non-multi-racial areas, further highlights the need for schools in such areas to adopt the broader approach to their work which we have already advocated. Throughout our consideration of the Chinese community, we were struck by their very strong sense of "ethnic identity" which is perhaps surprising in a group which is so dispersed around the country and which might therefore be expected to become "submerged" by the influence of the majority community. The fact that there are few signs of this happening lends weight to our view that cultural diversity is and will remain a feature of British society. The importance of the Chinese language in maintaining the community's identity was demonstrated by the firm commitment to community-based language classes which we found. We were concerned at the suggestion that the generally positive stereotype of Chinese pupils which appears to exist might in fact work against their interests in leading teachers to overlook any possible educational difficuties which they might be experiencing—this strengthens further the view which we took in our Racism Chapter of the need to counter stereotyped views of any ethnic minority group in order to ensure that all pupils are regarded on their own merits as individuals with differing needs and problems. In relation to racism, our various consultations with the Chinese community left us with a definite sense that the outward level of racism, both overt and covert, to which the community was subject, represented possibly only the "tip of the iceberg" and that as Chinese youngsters in the future seek to enter the mainstream employment market there is a likelihood of them encountering similar obstacles to those already facing youngsters from other ethnic minority groups.

ANNEX

Extracts from "Community Education: The Unknown Perspective—Chinese Mother Tongue Classes", Ming Tsow[6]

The different kinds of classes could be roughly divided into the following:—

a. Classes organised by Chinese associations and groups.
These groups may have commercial interests, trade orientations, clanmanship, (under the same surname such as the Wong association) based on mutual interest and self-help welfare.

b. Classes attached to Christian denominations.
Anglican and non-conformist groups pre-dominate. In most instances both reading and writing in addition to religious lessons are taught. These religious classes are different from those of the Asian communities in which a different language is taught. In some ways, they are closer to the Greek and Cypriot religious classes as the language remains the same.

c. Newly formed Groups.
These are in the very small minority which may be attached to centres and aided by direct grants from the Government, e.g. in Liverpool, Manchester and in London. This is a pattern which other linguistic groups share as well.

Almost all these classes coincide with the state school terms: 3 terms a year, with an average of 12 weeks per term. There are the very few odd exceptions of 18 week term duration.

Classes are held at various times, with weekends and Wednesdays after school hours, particularly popular. Several classes are held simultaneously from morning to afternoon. The biggest class which is based in London is open from Monday to Sunday. The week-day, after school hours, lessons are normally from 5–7 p.m. The length of each teaching session can be from one hour to two hours.

Classes which are held in the club or centre which are owned by the association, are often limited and inadequate for the purposes of teaching. In church premises, the space may be big but owing to the different levels of teaching taking place, the situation is often one of a village school set-up in that several classes are simultaneously held in little groups. No more than 1/10 of the total Chinese establishments throughout the UK actually use the state school premises. The LEAs attitudes may vary from providing free use of premises to a charge of rent. Some organisers of these classes have tried unsuccessfully to approach LEAs because of the various problems; primarily communication at linguistic and know-how levels and the difficulties of obtaining the co-operation of caretakers. Some attempts have consequently been wild goose chases with no result.

In the privately owned property such as centres, associations, etc. most of these classes will have no more than two to three rooms, the size of an average bedroom. Consequently a shift system is adopted. As many as six classes could be fitted in on Saturday or Sunday. The biggest privately owned premises is also the largest Chinese language class in the country (based in London) which has ten teaching rooms and two toilets. The kind of luxury of space provided here is well beyond the dream of the average or smaller group. No playgrounds are available and toilet facilities are minimal. Most of these establishments complain about the lack of library facilities. In a few instances, the club social room would double as a library more for storage of books than for reading.

[6]Journal of Community Education. Vol.2. No.1. February 1983.

However, even in these cramped quarters where at times forty-five children or more are learning to speak, read and write Chinese, the waiting-list is surprisingly long.

Often the chairs and desks are bought from state schools which are closing down. Audio visual aids are minimal with the exception of pictures and word cards. The usual blackboards, chairs and desks form the rudiments of provisions. The tidying up job is often insisted upon in state school premises, frequently with the help of the children. In the cases of make-shift arrangements such as the church hall, classrooms are set up and dismantled for the length of teaching hours.

Provisions such as crayons, exercise books, pencils, writing-paper/pads are often free for all. In one set up, four exercise books are allocated to one child per year. In others, for the primary-age group, pencils are on loan for the period of attendance. The Hong Kong Government Office has been the prime donator of textbooks for those who chose to use textbooks from Hong Kong. Sometimes in the advanced education age-group, textbooks are self-supplied.

The levels of classes taught are not commensurate with age, and they are not age-related but by ability. Most classes cover the kindergarten to primary groups although some would go into secondary classes and a few teach the GCE "O" and "A" levels.

CHAPTER 11

The Educational Needs of Children of Cypriot[1] Origin

Background

Size of the Community

1. The Cypriot community in this country numbers in the region of 140,000 (including youngsters who have been born here). Whilst this may not at first sight seem a particularly large group, when it is pointed out that, viewed in relation to the actual population of Cyprus itself, *1 in 6 of all Cypriots are living in Britain,* the significance of this community can readily be appreciated.

Immigration

2. The vast majority of Cypriot immigrants have arrived in this country during the last 20–25 years, especially during the 1950s and early 1960s. According to Census data, in 1931 there were some 1,075 people of Cypriot origin in Britain, by 1951 the figure had risen to 10,343 and in 1971 the "immigrant" community numbered some 72,665, although this excluded the increasing number of British-born Cypriots who now comprise a substantial proportion of the community. The peak years of Cypriot migration to Britain were 1960 and 1961 when just over 25,000 Cypriots are estimated to have come here. There has been relatively little migration to Britain since the mid 1960s, partly because of immigration controls and partly because opportunities for economic betterment in this country are seen to have declined. With the renewed inter-ethnic conflict in Cyprus in 1974/1975 some 10,000 Cypriots entered Britain as unofficial "refugees" from the fighting but some of these stayed only a short while and then returned home. The patterns of migration have generally been very similar for Greek and Turkish Cypriots although the Turkish Cypriots were rather later migrants and their numbers increased particularly in the early 1960s.

Reasons for Migration

3. The primary reasons for Cypriot migration to Britain, as with many other groups, were economic, as explained in the following extract from an article by Dr Robin Oakley[2]:

"The post-war emigration from the island must be understood in the context of the extension of Cypriot horizons beginning with

[1] The term "Cypriot" is used here to refer to all children with family origins in Cyprus. There are however, as emphasised in this chapter, some significant differences in the needs and experiences of the *Greek* Cypriot and *Turkish* Cypriot communities and where these are discussed, these more specific terms are used.
[2] "The Cypriot Migration to Britain". Taken from "Minority Families in Britain". Ed V Khan. 1979.

the war-time experiences, and a raising of economic expectations linked to the massive, although in scope limited, economic investment undertaken by the government and military authorities during the 1950s. The inability of this to lead to any self-sustaining economic expansion, combined with the political instability and eventual British Government withdrawal on Independence in 1960, precipitated a mass movement of emigrants seeking to take advantage of employment opportunities in Britain in the late 1950s and early 1960s."

One of our witnesses observed that probably every adult in Cyprus today has at some time weighed up the pros and cons of migration to Britain. In general, many of the original immigrants had not intended to remain in this country. Now that they have become established however and their children have been born here, and since the events in Cyprus of 1974/1975, the vast majority now see their long-term futures here.

Patterns of Settlement

4. Because many of the original immigrants relied on kinship ties both to sponsor their migration and then to find jobs and housing when they first arrived here, the Cypriot community in Britain has tended to reconstruct itself in demographic terms very much along the lines of a Cyprus village. This has meant that the community is very highly concentrated in certain parts of the country: according to the 1971 census data, 70–75 per cent of Cypriots were living in the Greater London area. This focus on London arises from the pre-war concentration of the Cypriot community around the restaurant and clothing trade, particularly in Soho. The geographical distribution of the community today reflects the movement of their economic base gradually northwards from the centre of Haringey and Hackney and out to areas such as Barnet and Enfield as their economic position has improved. This movement has not lessened the degree of concentration however since the community has tended to move as a whole and the Cypriot community remains probably the most concentrated of all Commonwealth-derived immigrant groups. Outside London, the Cypriot community is very widely dispersed throughout the country, as is the Chinese community, through its involvement in the catering industry, to areas such as Wales and Cornwall as well as cities like Birmingham, Leeds and Manchester. The Cypriot population in London is generally mixed, although Turkish Cypriots tend to be concentrated particularly in Hackney, whilst the community outside London is almost entirely Greek Cypriot. The proportion of Greek Cypriots to Turkish Cypriots is generally thought to be 4:1—the same balance as in Cyprus itself—although some of our witnesses felt that this underestimated the size of the Turkish Cypriot community. In relation to school population, the 1981 ILEA

Language Census of school pupils recorded a total of 4,418 Turkish-speakers[3]—the second largest language group in the Authority after Bengali-speakers—and 3,859 Greek-speakers[3]—the third largest group.

Socio-Economic Status

5. In very general terms the Cypriot community can be said to be "successful" from the socio-economic point of view, although it is generally accepted that the Greek Cypriot community is financially more secure than the Turkish Cypriots. In respect of housing and particularly home ownership the Cypriot community seems to be faring well. It is important to recognise however that home ownership, as opposed to council housing, was regarded as of particularly great importance by the orginal immigrants and, as explained in background evidence to us:

"In fact, having a council house or flat carries something of a stigma, since it implies that one has not succeeded in achieving the commonly agreed goals of emigration."

This attitude, rather perhaps than straightforward economic success, must be a major factor in the very high proportion of Cypriots owning their own homes and similarly in the small percentage of Cypriots in public housing. In employment terms, it is important to recognise the changes in work practice which have come about within the Cypriot community as a result of migration. In Cyprus, the majority of the men would probably have worked as craftsmen, labourers or in service trades, whilst their wives would in general not have worked at all. One major shift has therefore been in the economic role of women within the Cypriot community in Britain, in that many of them now work and contribute to the family income. Even those women with pre school age children may do home work, particularly sewing. After migration the men originally remained in service industries, especially catering, in this country but in recent years there has been a noticeable move towards owning their own small businesses and the community as a whole is now characterised by its high occupational mobility. Many of our witnesses stressed the existence of what is often referred to as an "internal economy" within the Cypriot community which allows a Cypriot family to meet all its needs, in terms of goods and services, without ever having to move outside the community. As one witness summed it up:

"Cypriots are, on the whole, extremely hard-working. They came here for economic betterment and material betterment and most work single-mindedly towards these goals."

---

[3] The figures for both Greek and Turkish-speakers include some pupils from families from the respective mainland communities as well as Cypriots, but the great majority in each case were of Cypriot origin.

Religious and Cultural Background

6.   In common with many of the other ethnic minority communities whom we have considered, probably the most important single factor in the cultural and home background of the Cypriot community is the powerful influence of the family. As explained in evidence to us, in the Cypriot community:

> *"Family loyalty is the paramount virtue. This involves, on the one hand, the obligation to put immediate family first, and kin generally before others. On the other, in the competitive and critical atmosphere of village life, it entails the obligation always to maintain and promote the honour and reputation of the family, by discharging one's roles and responsibilities in a manner as near as possible to that prescribed by the gender—differentiated cultural ideals . . . Within traditional Cypriot society, therefore the family is the basic, indeed the sole, solidary group: each family farms its own land, runs its household, travels, celebrates and generally faces the world as a single unit."*

The theme of "living up to the expectations of the community" was further expanded on in the following reference to the Greek Cypriot community[4]:

> *"People judge each other according to strict moral and economic criteria. A commonly heard reason for not carrying through some planned but untypical act is: 'I was embarrassed', or, more properly, 'I was ashamed'. The use of the verb 'shame', a key Greek concept, carries with it the weight of judgment of one's fellows. Greek Cypriots in Britain form, in the anthropological sense, a 'moral community'. This is not of course to say that everybody lives up to the ideal standards, for many do not. Even high status (which for the immigrant is based largely on wealth, education of one's children, and general 'success') does not protect an individual from communal criticism."*

Whilst many of our witnesses emphasised the extent to which such attitudes showed the strength of the Cypriot community, it was admitted that problems were increasingly arising with both Greek and Turkish Cypriot youngsters, especially girls, who had been born in this country and who resented both the individual pressures on them to conform to accepted codes of behaviour, and the tremendous community pressure to "keep up appearances". Whilst many youngsters appreciated the support of the community, others felt stifled by what they regarded as the "surveillance" of all they did. As already mentioned above, there is often a marked gender—differentiation in the community pressures and expectations of youngsters—whereas boys may be afforded considerable licence and be actively encouraged

---

[4] Taken from "Between Two Cultures: Migrants and Minorities in Britain". Ed James L Watson. 1977.

to "go out and seek their fortune", girls are expected to remain in the family circle and to go out chaperoned, and generally to behave with decorum and propriety. One teacher who submitted evidence to us about the behavioural problems she sometimes encountered with Cypriot girls reflected as follows on the firm discipline to which they were accustomed at home:

> *"At school they see much less discipline. They see some lessons being disrupted because of bad behaviour, they see some rudeness to staff, they see girls out of uniform. They do not invariably see this behaviour being corrected. They are also aware that their peers are allowed out with boys, that they often smoke and swear and appear to disregard the rules that the school and their parents make. Some of the Cypriot girls reacted to this stress by showing marked behavioural problems."*

In the majority of cases such traumas appear to be overcome and the youngsters are able to evolve their own identity whilst retaining the strengths of the Cypriot community, and the majority of Cypriot girls for example still marry within their community with the tradition of family "arranged" marriages still strong. In some instances which we heard of however this situation has led to extreme polarisation of the attitudes of both parents and youngsters with a consequent collapse of the traditional family structure and the break up of families.

Cypriot Identity

7. There appear to be few differences between the Greek and Turkish Cypriot communities in cultural terms, except in the major respect of religion—Turkish Cypriots of course being Muslim, whilst Greek Cypriots are part of the Greek Orthodox Church. From the evidence which we have received it would seem that the influence of religion is not seen as central in either community. Both the Greek and Turkish Cypriot communities have retained a strong sense of their "ethnic identities", despite what has been described to us as their "potential invisibility" in that they are not as readily identifiable by the majority community as are, for example, Asians or West Indians. Cypriot parents have generally sought to retain and reinforce an awareness of their origins on the part of their children and, as we mention below, this has led to some strong support for community-based "mother tongue" classes. Although British-born youngsters may to a certain extent resent seeing themselves as in any way "foreign", especially if they are experiencing some family conflict over conforming to the expected community lifestyle, many of our witnesses spoke of the tendency for such youngsters to return to their roots and to acquire a greater interest in their cultural and linguistic heritage as they grew older. The continuing sense of "Cypriot identity" is partly at least sustained by regular visits to Cyprus to see friends and relatives. As explained in background evidence we received:

Visits "Home"

"Visits to Cyprus with their family often have a profound effect, positive or negative, on British-born (Greek) Cypriots. Many feel moved to identify with the beautiful island and the relatives they find there, and are inspired to achieve a better standard of spoken Greek. Others are alienated by language difficulties and the restrictions on their freedom of action required by the relatively strict moral codes of village life."

Such visits home may also have a bearing on the educational progress of Cypriot children. Several Heads and teachers with Cypriot pupils mentioned to us the noticeable effects which extended visits to Cyprus, which often required pupils leaving before the end of the school term, had on the level of English of especially the youngest children.

"Myths of Return"

8. As with the Asian communities, the strong sense of Cypriot identity seems often to be bound up with a "myth of return" to Cyprus, especially amongst the older members of the community, although actual return is in fact relatively rare. The events of 1974/1975 in Cyprus are felt however to have had a direct bearing on this attitude of mind, as well as influencing the Greek Cypriot community in particular, sense of identity, as explained in the following extract from the Chapter "The Greek Cypriots: Factors in the Maintenance of Ethnic Identity" by Pamela Constantinides, again taken from "Between Two Cultures":

"Wherever individual interest may have lain before these events, everyone, including the second generation of immigrants, became acutely conscious of the origins and of the emotional and kinship ties which still bound them to Cyprus ... And yet at the same time as consciousness of specifically Greek Cypriot identity was at its highest point, so too was the awareness that the realities of the future lay in this country. Many had thought of returning to Cyprus to set up in business or to retire and while this was often little more than a daydream, since the actual return to Cyprus has been quite low, it now became for those whose villages were in the occupied areas, a physical impossibility. Before them also was the spectre of the small proportion of Cypriots who had gone back. Several had sold up all they had here and settled in one of the developing tourist areas of Cyprus, only to lose everything in the 1974 invasion and to have to return and try and start again in vastly more difficult economic times than those prevailing when they had first arrived... Thus the paradox is that while ethnic consciousness has probably never been more acute, the immigrants, forced by events to think out the realities of their situation, now accept that they are in Britain to stay. And while

the second generation has, in many cases, been shocked into awareness of its origins, so too this has led to greater social and political participation within the framework of the politics of this country."

Education

Parental Attitudes

9.   The attitudes of Cypriot parents towards education tend, understandably, to derive from their own educational experiences in Cyprus. There is a strong feeling that education is the responsibility of the teacher and that parents should not therefore "interfere". This is combined with a high degree of respect for the teacher's position which can make it a daunting prospect for parents who are not fully fluent in English to approach the school for advice or to discuss their child's progress. Many Cypriot parents are particularly concerned with schools' standards of discipline and behaviour and some clearly feel that there is a general lack of supervision of the "conduct" of girls. There seems also to be a degree of dissatisfaction with the lack of clear and detailed reports from schools on their children's progress and attainment. Some Turkish Cypriot representatives also expressed the view that many parents in their community disliked the informality and flexibility of primary education in this country, which they described as "all play and no work". This opinion was disputed however by other community representatives who stressed that such views were based on a lack of knowledge and understanding of the rationale behind such provision, which they felt it was the schools' responsibility to remedy. The approach adopted by the Head of one infants school we visited, where some 60 per cent of the pupils were of Cypriot origin (both Greek and Turkish), to involving Cypriot parents in the work of the school, was described to us thus:

"She had always encouraged parents to come in to the school but had initially received a poor response. She had however then come to appreciate the difficulties for working parents of visiting during the school day and so she had developed a system where each month parents from two classes at a time were specifically invited to attend morning assembly and then to talk about activities in school with her and the class teachers. This had proved very successful, with c 75% attendances, since the mothers who were often home workers usually brought their children to school anyway and so were able to stay on for a short time. They talked about issues such as the importance of play and games which parents might play with their children for example to help them with the beginnings of mathematics. They also showed parents how to help their children at home. Even where the mothers could not read English themselves they encouraged them to look at books with their children and talk about them in their own lan-

677

guage. At these monthly "teach in" sessions she had always ensured that parents with little or no English sat with other parents who would be able to help them understand what was being discussed. Several ethnic minority parents came in to the school a couple of times each week to read stories and sing songs in the pupils' mother-tongues but suitable books and materials in the mother-tongue were very scarce. The school also had a number of secondary school pupils, including some boys, who were on a child development course who came in to help and were able to talk to the pupils in their mother-tongue. Despite the progress which she thought had been made, she felt that many Cypriot parents still believed that once their children entered the infants school, they should be learning to read and not "just playing". Although the 'teach-ins' helped to a certain extent, she did not feel that they had yet wholly convinced all the parents of the value of the school's approach and many still felt the main emphasis should be on the 'three R's'."

10. We were particularly interested to seek the views of the Turkish Cypriot community on some of the concerns previously expressed to us by Muslims from the various Asian groups about their children's education. None of the Turkish Cypriot representatives with whom we discussed the "rights and duties" of Muslim parents on matters such as religious observance, felt that such concerns would be shared by or indeed would find much sympathy with the majority of Turkish Cypriot parents. (As we mention below however, they were concerned to see greater attention being given within the religious education curriculum to Islam.) Similarly these representatives were unanimous in opposing in principle the concept of a Muslim voluntary aided school—as one group explained to us:

"They felt that it would be a bad thing if it was accepted that those whose predominant concern was religion should be allowed to run schools. There was a fundamental objection to the use of the educational system to promote religious ends. This suspicion was deepened by the association of religion with right-wing political views. Cyprus was a secular society where religion was kept apart from education. They were not in favour of the existing dual system and did not wish to see it extended. Their aim was an international approach with all children mixed together."

One related issue where both the Greek and Turkish Cypriot communities shared the concerns of the Asian community was however in strongly advocating the right of parents to have the option of single-sex education provision for girls. One Turkish Cypriot representative mentioned that he was aware that some parents in his community had consciously taken the decision to send their daughters to a single-sex school rather than to a neighbouring co-educational school, which they believed to have higher educational standards, because of their preference for single-sex provision. Some Greek Cypriot representatives described to us the widespread protests which had taken place amongst Cypriot parents at the proposed discontinuation of single-sex provision in their area and which had led to the retention of the option of such provision because of the community's strength of feeling. (This strong emphasis on the desire for the option of single-sex schooling, especially for girls, to be retained, adds further weight to the conclusions we reached in this respect in our discussion of "the separate schools debate" earlier in this report).

Aspirations   11.   It is clear that in general Cypriot parents are ambitious for their children in educational terms and several of our witnesses commented that this was particularly true of parents who in Cyprus might not have had the opportunity themselves to progress beyond the primary level. Whilst agreeing that Cypriot parents as a rule had high aspirations for their children, the Head of one predominantly Cypriot school we visited felt that there had been a noticeable change over the past 10–12 years in the educational ambitions of Cypriot parents for their children. Whereas they had in the past had very high aspirations and expectations and had tended to "push" their children very hard, it seemed that as the families had become fully established in this country and had gained some financial security, although they were still committed to education, it was now to a markedly lesser degree. A small scale study[5], which was made available to us, covering five schools with Cypriot pupils, 11 Cypriot parents and 13 Cypriot pupils, supported the view of the high aspirations of the Cypriot community, in reaching the following conclusion:

> "Cypriot parents have high expectations of their children ...
> All the parents expected their children to receive an academic
> education at school and go on to Higher Education. Nine wanted
> their children to go on to University whereas two did not mind if
> their children went to another institution. All of them wanted a
> better education for their children so they could get a good job
> and two added that a good education would also turn them into
> better citizens. The children's aspirations coincided very closely
> with the expections of the parents. In fact only two wanted to
> leave school. All the others wanted to stay on at school up to the
> sixth form, and then go on to Higher Education, once again
> mainly to Universities. The replies from the five schools also

[5]"Expectations of Cypriot Parents and Aspirations of their Children, in the Age Group 14—19 years old, of the British Educational System in North London". C Martianou. Unpublished dissertation. 1981.

indicated that the expectations of Cypriot parents and the aspirations of their children are high. Two schools added that in some cases the parents' expectations were unrealistic and they ended up being disappointed when their child did CSEs instead of GCEs. On the children's aspirations, the schools agreed that Cypriot children in general wanted to take CSEs and some not to take any examinations. Some, with no job to go to, were content to stay on in the sixth form to do a CSE course."

Expectations of Boys and Girls

12. Much of the evidence we received on Cypriot parental aspirations for their children referred to marked differences in their educational expectations of boys and girls. It was suggested that whereas parents might be anxious to see their son do well in terms of public examinations and then perhaps go on to higher education, they were far less interested in their daughter's education and might in fact be reluctant to allow her to continue her education beyond compulsory schooling, preferring her instead to leave and get married as soon as possible. A number of witnesses felt however that, whilst this sharp differential might have been true some years ago, there was now a growing acceptance of the need for girls to be accorded full equality of opportunity in educational terms. It was pointed out that the attitudes of the Turkish community in Cyprus towards the education of girls had changed substantially in the past 20 years and girls there were now allowed to go to university in Turkey to continue their studies. It was suggested that many Cypriot parents in this country were now just as interested to see their daughters do well as they were to see their sons succeed and they would certainly be willing to consider a girl going on to higher education if she had the ability and desire to do so, although they might still prefer her to live at home if possible or at least not to be too far away from her family. Even if the family was still primarily concerned to see their daughter make a "good marriage" rather than pursue a career, as one of our witnesses observed, being well educated and perhaps having a university degree might well serve to make her more "marriageable" in any case, since, in the present economic situation, a wife could be seen as having an economic contribution to make to the family.

Language: E2L

13. As with some of the other ethnic minority communities we have considered, although the majority of Cypriot children now entering school have been born in this country, it is likely that many of them will in fact have little if any command of the English language. They will often have spoken only their "mother-tongue"—Greek or Turkish—at home, and because of the scarcity of pre-school places, (and even where these are available Cypriot families are unlikely to "qualify" for them), they may well have been looked after by family or friends within the community. At one Junior School we visited,

where some 50 per cent of the pupil population was of Cypriot origin, together with pupils from a wide range of other ethnic minority groups, we were told that only four children out of the current first year had English as their first language and 19 out of a total of 28 were classified as in need of E2L help. Many of our witnesses expressed concern to us about the nature of E2L provision, criticising the apparent lack of structured and ongoing language support beyond the straightforward "survival" stage, which they felt meant that there was a risk of children being subsequently classified as "slow learners" or even as remedial, when in fact they needed further help with language. It was also suggested that E2L provision for secondary-age pupils was often "over simple" and it could for example be very demotivating for a bright 12-year-old with a good grasp of scientific and mathematical principles, to concentrate on a textbook intended for a six-year-old, without getting frustrated and embarrassed. There was also a clear feeling on the part of the communities that, in the eyes of some teachers, a lack of fluency in English was a sure sign of lack of ability and schools in general were felt to adopt a very negative view of second language learners, which could have a direct bearing on a child's self-image. As one group put it to us in their evidence:

"At the point of entry into formal education the children's language learning may have been hazardous. At best they have achieved only a social grasp of language. Teachers tended to display a punitive attitude to the use of mother-tongue in schools and . . . ignored any approaches by children using mother-tongue in a misconceived attempt to foster early learning of English. This gave children their first direct experience of racism. Similarly mothers were told to speak English to their children at home, despite their own shortcomings in the language. This was the start of "knocking down" children because their backgrounds were not English at the very time when they needed to feel accepted rather than crushed."

Much of the evidence we received relating to E2L provision was critical of the practice of withdrawing pupils for language help, whether within schools or to separate language centres, since this was seen as having a potentially damaging effect on the children's socialisation and general educational progress as well as "categorising" them visibly, in the minds of their peers and teachers, as being "stupid" and "different". The following extract from a report we received from a teacher, based on her discussions with Cypriot pupils at a girls' comprehensive school, illustrates these concerns relating to language, as well as raising points about the unintentionally racist attitudes of some teachers towards Cypriot pupils:

"Some of the girls expressed a certain amount of concern over the lack of appreciation of their language and background. One

681

girl in particular did feel that there was 'a bit of an Us and Them' attitude. She said her English had been criticised as being 'too Greek'! She found that, although she worked hard, she often got poor marks and was given very little help. She consequently feels as if few teachers were ever interested in her. In almost all the cases girls said that their names were misspelt and mis-pronounced. This usually caused concern at first, but they soon learnt to disregard it. Several girls had anglicised their names, Halide calls herself Helen, Sultan is Susan at school. Meryham's school file shows at least 6 different ways of spelling her name. When the records do mention language or background they some-times show lack of appreciation. One primary report read: 'Home background very Cypriot, hinders academic achievement.' Many mention 'poor vocabulary'. It would seem that although at first the girls felt that a part of their identity was being ignored, they soon learnt to put this to the back of their minds. In this way they learn to cope with the ethnocentrism of the school, but only at the expense of merging their own identity with that of the school culture. They learn to accept the school assessment of their educa-tional performance and capability. By withdrawing second lan-guage learners into Language Centres and Remedial groups the school can reinforce this assessment and the self-image of the pupils adjusts accordingly."

Many of these points of course reinforce the views we expressed in the Language Chapter of this report.

Language: "Mother-Tongue"

14.   Both the Greek Cypriot and Turkish Cypriot communities are anxious for their children to be able to speak their "mother-tongue" languages as part of retaining their identity and as a "key" to their religious and cultural heritages, as well as in order to be able to communicate with relatives both in this country or on visits to Cyprus, who might not speak English. The "case" for "mother-tongue" provision is also seen from the point of view of according true equality of opportunity to ethnic minority children on a par with their majority peers. As explained in the following extract from evidence we received from a Turkish Cypriot organisation:

"We feel that the most fundamental reason as to why the Mother Tongues of Ethnic Minority Groups should be taught in the main stream of British Education System should be that the British children have never been deprived of learning their own Mother Tongue throughout history . . . Furthermore, in order that a Migrant child to be able to study his own culture he must have sound knowledge of his own mother tongue . . . This is his birth right . . . Furthermore, the LEAs and the Central Government Education Authorities are under the misconception and/or the

misapprehension that only the conservative Migrant Parents are inclined for the introduction of the Mother Tongue of the Ethnic Minority Workers in the School curriculum . . . This assumption is very wrong and very misleading . . . Even young parents are very conscious of the need of acquiring a working knowledge of their Mother Tongue to be learned by their children so that they may grow up in a multi-racial society without losing touch with his own identity and his National background."

Whilst it was recognised that a range of different ethnic minority communites, notably Asian groups, had advocated "mother-tongue" provision, it was suggested to us by Cypriot representatives that the need for such provision might be particularly acute for smaller groups such as the Greek and Turkish Cypriots, since they were at greater risk of being "swamped" by the influences of the majority community. Strong arguments were put to us in favour of both "mother-tongue maintenance" and "mother-tongue teaching" in mainstream schools; less reference was made to any need for structured programmes of bilingual education, although it was felt that there was a clear need for some bilingual "support"—along the lines we have suggested in Chapter Seven—on the staff of infant and junior schools to help both pupils and their parents who might have little or no English. Reference was made to several secondary schools with Cypriot pupils which currently offered either Modern Greek or Modern Turkish as part of the modern languages curriculum to "O" and "A" level, which had proved popular with the community. We met one Cypriot teacher who taught Modern Greek within a secondary school to both "O" and "A" level as well as after school for some pupils who were studying other options during their mainstream schooling. He currently had a total of 23 pupils including one Turkish Cypriot. Some English pupils had taken an interest in learning Greek but few of these had survived because of the difficulty for them of learning the language from "scratch". It was mentioned however that since Cypriot youngsters spoke distinct dialects of Greek and Turkish, such provision to a certain extent at least also required them to learn a third language, rather than allowing them to rely on their command of their "mother-tongue". It is interesting that, in contrast with the attitudes of the community representatives we met who were strongly in favour of "mother-tongue" teaching in mainstream schools, the Cypriot youngsters (mainly sixth-formers, both Greek and Turkish Cypriots) with whom we discussed this issue were very much against this, saying that they preferred to study other subjects within school in which they might gain an examination qualification and to study Greek or Turkish in their own time and thus to be able to gain an additional qualification. The community representatives suggested however that this reluctance to study their own languages might well spring from the low status accorded to them by schools, which had perhaps subconsciously led the youngsters to regard them as not quite "respectable" subjects to study.

Community-Based Provision

15.   In the absence of widespread "mother-tongue" provision within schools, both the Greek and Turkish Cypriot communities have organised their own community-based language classes which a large number of Cypriot youngsters of all ages attend. Although detailed figures are not available, there are probably about 50 language schools catering for the Greek Cypriot community and 10–15 catering for the Turkish Cypriot community within the London area. These schools receive some help and support from the authorities of their respective communities in Cyprus and on the mainland, and parents also generally pay for the classes. The classes usually operate in the evenings or on Saturdays, and in many cases they are held in hired classrooms in mainstream schools. Although some textbooks are supplied from abroad these do not relate to the experiences and way of life of children in this country and so the schools often have to prepare their own worksheets. Some teachers are also supplied from abroad. As with other communities who run their own language classes, it is acknowledged that some youngsters resent the loss of their free time in attending these classes and may therefore be reluctant to attend and may even turn against their language and reject their community as a result. Parents, whilst valuing the provision, are often concerned about having to send young children out in the evenings at the risk of attack. Racial attacks in one particular area, resulting in the deaths of two young ethnic minority children, had, we were told, in fact led to the discontinuation of one language class. In general the parents would prefer some provision to be made during school hours. Some community representatives expressed reservations about the appropriateness of using teachers who might have come straight from Cyprus or Turkey and who might thus have little knowledge or understanding of English or of life in this country or of the type of education provision which the children were receiving in their mainstream schools. It was also suggested that the fact that the community had no alternative but to send its children to these "separate" schools if they wished them to study their languages, served to exacerbate their sense of alienation from their peers. Several mainstream teachers expressed concern about the strain on very young children of attending such classes in addition to their normal schooling and the "over-tiredness" which this seemed to induce as well as the confusion for a child who was simultaneously attempting to master English. Several of the teachers and representatives from the communities whom we met were themselves involved in running these language classes after school hours on mainstream school premises and they referred to the antagonism of school caretakers

towards them, for example the refusal to open the school gates even 5 minutes early when children were waiting outside in heavy rain.

Curriculum Content

16. Several of those who gave evidence to us stressed the need for the curricular diet offered by *all* schools, not only those with Cypriot or other ethnic minority pupils, to be broadened to reflect a more balanced and less Anglo-centric view of the world. The inherent bias of both geography and history syllabuses was mentioned in particular, for example the way in which the Crusades were traditionally dealt with was hardly fair in its treatment of the Turks. It was also suggested that the range of storybooks and readers used in primary schools, particularly where there were Cypriot pupils, might be broadened to include more traditional Greek and Turkish folk tales with which these pupils might identify. Turkish Cypriot representatives expressed particular concern to us about what they regarded as the Christian-dominated religious education curriculum in schools, with little if any attention being given to other major world religions especially Islam. They also thought that Cypriot parents were generally unaware of their right to withdraw their children from religious education and felt it was the school's duty to inform them of this right.

Teachers

17. Several community representatives expressed concern about the very small number of teachers who were themselves of Cypriot origin since it was felt that such teachers could be very supportive to Cypriot pupils in understanding their home backgrounds and possibly also being able to communicate with them in their "mother-tongue" and also encourage their parents to visit the school. Some of the Cypriot teachers whom we met stressed the great difficulties they felt they faced in gaining promotion and reaching positions of responsibility within schools. These teachers, in describing their own experiences of teacher training in this country, referred to what they saw as the "appalling" absence of any realistic coverage of "multicultural" concerns in their courses and also to what they felt was the hostile atmosphere they had encountered in staffrooms on their teaching practices.

Achievement

18. It is in the area of academic achievement that perhaps the most marked differences in the situation of Greek Cypriot and Turkish Cypriot pupils can be found. Because of the absence of ethnically-based educational statistics, and of course the Cypriots were not covered by our school leavers' survey exercises, there is little firm statistical evidence on achievement levels. (It is interesting to note here that representatives from both the Greek Cypriot and Turkish Cypriot communities, while appreciating the concerns expressed by other ethnic minority groups, were firmly in favour of the collection

of ethnically-based statistics in the education system, on the grounds that "needs could not be met until they were quantified"). Nevertheless data from the ILEA in relation to language (ie English), which is of course a key factor in achievement, gives clear grounds for concern about the performance of Cypriot pupils and particularly Turkish Cypriots who appear to be underachieveing to a considerable degree. The 1980 ILEA Literacy Survey[6] showed the relative reading scores of different ethnic groups as follows:

MEAN READING SCORES AT 8, 10 AND 15 YEARS BY ETHNIC GROUP

AGE IN YEARS	*UK	EIRE	WI	IND	PAK	GC	TC	O
8	98.1	94.8	88.1	89.6	91.1	87.3	85.4	93.2
10	98.3	97.9	87.4	89.6	93.1	87.8	85.0	93.9
15	97.8	96.6	85.9	91.4	94.9	87.6	84.9	95.4
N	12,530	229	1,465	137	74	194	139	502

*UK— United Kingdom; WI—West Indies; IND—India; PAK—-Pakistan; GC—Cyprus, Greek speaking; TC—Cyprus, Turkish speaking; O—all other immigrants.

As can be seen, although no group at any stage was reading at a level expected for its age on the basis of the national sample—since all scores including those of the indigenous were below 100—the Turkish Cypriots had the lowest attainment across the board, falling below the West Indians about whose attainment in this survey we expressed such concern in our interim report. Although their attainment exceeded that of the Turkish Cypriots at all ages, the position of the Greek Cypriots also gives considerable cause for concern and at age 8 they fell below West Indians as the second lowest scoring group. The 1981 ILEA Language Census reflected a considerable differential in the relative fluency in English of Greek and Turkish-speakers (as already mentioned, this data also included some Greeks and Turks from the mainland)—13.4 per cent of Turkish-speakers were classified as "Beginners" (compared with 5.3 per cent of Greek-

---

[6] The survey was based on a cohort of children born between September 1959 and September 1960 numbering over 31,000 when they were tested for reading at 8. They were subsequently also tested on verbal reasoning, and received teachers' assessments on English and mathematics for transfer at 10+. A 10 per cent sample was also tested individually at 11+, and at 8 and 13 when teachers completed questionnaires on the social and educational background of the children.

speakers) and 41.1 per cent of Turkish-speakers were classified as "fluent" (compared with 58.1 per cent of Greek-speakers). Even before the data from the ILEA Literacy Survey and the ILEA Language Census, grounds for concern about the reading attainment of Cypriot children had been given by the findings of the study by Yule, Berger, Rutter and Yule in 1975[7], which showed, *inter alia*, mean reading scores for the Greek Cypriot and Turkish Cypriot children in the sample of 84 and 84, as set against a score of 86 for the West Indian children tested and 95 for the "indigenous" children. In the majority of schools we ourselves visited with Cypriot pupils there was a strong feeling that these pupils as a group were underachieving and the Turkish Cypriots were often singled-out as giving particular cause for concern. It is interesting to note that even where Greek Cypriot pupils were apparently "doing well" ie achieving on a par with their peers from other groups—they were still sometimes regarded as failing to fulfil their true potential since in many of the schools which they attended achievement levels were below the national average and, as one teacher put it to us in evidence:

> *"There is no reason why the intelligence of Cypriots should not show the same spread as the rest of the population. Indeed since it is often the most enterprising families who emigrate one might expect a slight skew towards the higher bands."*

Reasons for Under- Achievement
19. Little in-depth work seems to have been undertaken to establish the factors which might lie behind the apparent underachievement of Cypriot pupils as a whole and the particular problems which might lead Turkish Cypriot children to underachieve in relation to their Greek Cypriot peers with whom they might be expected to share so much in common. Because of our concern about the attainments of Cypriot pupils we discussed with all the teachers and community representatives whom we met how they sought to account for this situation. A number of suggestions were forthcoming, many of them very much in line with our own feelings on factors which can affect the achievement of pupils from the whole range of ethnic minority groups. The points which were raised with us as bearing on the achievement of Cypriot pupils are listed below—not necessarily in order of importance:

— lack of nursery provision which meant that a child's first contact with spoken English could be with their admission to infant/ primary school;

— inadequate E2L provision;

— inappropriate curriculum;

---

[7]"Children of West Indian Immigrants–II. Intellectual Performance and Reading Attainment". J Child Psychol Psychiat, Vol 16, 1975.

— poor home/school links—some Cypriot parents were illiterate even in their own languages and had had little educational experience themselves and so, despite interest, were unable to help and support their children's work; also many parents were uncertain of the aims and purposes of the school and lacked confidence to attend school open evenings: schools needed therefore to "reach out" and involve them in the education process;

— teachers' lack of knowledge and understanding of the background of Cypriot pupils (and also the need for more Cypriot-origin teachers);

— low teacher expectations of Cypriot pupils which, allied with "linguistic prejudice", could be internalised by pupils and thus become a "self-fulfilling prophecy";

— effect of home/school conflict or inter-generational conflict within the family over matters of "conduct", which could put additional pressures on pupils, particularly girls;

— a tendency amongst pupils to "act up" and even become disruptive in the freer atmosphere of the school in contrast to their home environment; and

— influence of racism, direct and indirect, and within schools and in the wider society, on all ethnic minority pupils.

In relation to the apparent differences in the achievement of Greek Cypriot and Turkish Cypriot pupils, a number of interesting and thought-provoking "explanations" were also put forward:

— since the Greek Cypriot community outnumbered the Turkish Cypriot community some 4:1, the former was seen as a more "self confident" group;

— the Greek Cypriot community had generally been better educated and more urbanised in Cyprus, compared with the more rural-orientated Turkish Cypriots, which might make it easier for the former to adapt to the demands of the education system in this country and better able to help and support their children's learning; (NB: This suggestion was *very strongly* refuted by some representatives we met from both the Greek and Turkish Cypriot communities, as presenting an entirely inaccurate picture);

— the greater financial prosperity of the Greek Cypriot community placed them in a better position to support their children's education;

— Turkish Cypriots were in general darker-skinned than Greek Cypriots and whereas the latter might "pass for white", the former could well be seen as "black" and they might therefore be more likely to be subject to racism;

— the stereotypes of the "Turks" and the "Greeks", both in the minds of the majority community, and as conveyed to children through the medium of the school curriculum, were very different: the Greeks being generally regarded and presented as "the great civilisers of the world" and as having made major contributions to art, philosophy etc through the classical tradition, and, above all perhaps, being accepted as "Western"; while the Turks were generally seen as uncivilised and cruel "barbarians" who had threatened civilisation and who were very "Eastern", not least as adherents of a strange, "foreign" faith: Islam. (Powerful negative images of the Turks were for example felt to be created by references in school textbooks to the "massacre" of the Armenians or to Turkey as the "sick man of Europe".) These very different stereotypes were felt to have had a direct bearing on society's and, in particular, teachers' expectations of, and empathy with, Turkish Cypriots. This suggestion was put forward by many of the people we met, from both the Greek and Turkish Cypriot communities, and even though it is clearly very difficult to confirm or refute, it certainly constitutes a powerful argument for the wide-ranging and insidious influence of stereotyping on the experience of different ethnic minority groups.

In one small-scale study[8] which was sent to us concerning the attitudes of a number of Heads of schools with Cypriot pupils, most of the points listed above were mentioned in relation to the perceived "differences" between Greek and Turkish Cypriots:

> *"Some heads did see differences which began to point the way towards Turkish lower achievement—'Turks need more language help—all need E2L help not all Greeks do', 'The top infant reading level of Greeks is high—the Turkish very dodgy' ... Some Turkish Cypriots were leaving the Infants as non-readers. Reasons for this were usually based on social/ethnic criteria 'Turkish have a more impoverished background ... are less educated', 'Turkish are slower starters—their expectations are different', 'Turkish are slower ... more lax discipline', 'Greeks appear to be more intelligent; the Turkish more withdrawn' ... One particular comment sums it up 'The Turkish are not integrat-*

---

[8]"A Study of the Cypriot community in Haringey with special reference to the early years of schooling." Florence S Beetlestone. Unpublished MA dissertation. September 1982.

ing as well as the Greeks . . . they remain in isolation'. Several mentioned the 'difference' of Turkish culture and the influence of the Muslim religion, particularly with regard to the position of women as being 'isolated' and having low status in a male dominated society. Turkish parents were seen as 'not so forthcoming'; "shyer than Greek': 'reluctant to come forward'; sometimes 'aggressive' and 'unco-operative' . . . Most Heads referred to the difficulty in communicating with Cypriot mothers (whom they saw more often than fathers) particularly the Turkish because of the language barrier, and it would seem that fewer Turkish than Greek mothers had a good command of English. (One Greek community leader estimated that 60 per cent of Greeks spoke English whereas only 20 per cent of Turks did) . . . Usually this fact was mentioned as 'most parents don't speak English', without, it would appear, realising the full implication of what this means. The above comments indicate that the Turkish Cypriot has a lower status than the Greek."

School to Work

20.   As we have already mentioned, there is still a tendency for many Cypriot youngsters on leaving school, to work within the Cypriot community. This tie with the traditional "internal economy" of their community seems to some extent to have served to shield Cypriot youngsters from the worst effects of rising youth unemployment as well as meaning that they have perhaps been less subject to racial discrimination in the employment field. As some of the traditional areas of Cypriot employment, notably the "rag trade", are however coming under increasing pressure in the current economic situation, some Cypriot youngsters are now finding themselves in the same situation as their ethnic minority peers. As with the Chinese community, there seems to be a degree of reluctance among some youngsters to work within the community and an attempt therefore to "break away" into the mainstream employment market but the current employment situation often leads them ultimately to fall back on their community. As explained in evidence to us:

"For many youngsters a type of identity crisis seems to occur in the period after they have left school and sought employment. Those who have received their education in overcrowded and poorly staffed schools in the inner city find themselves poor candidates for the more glamorous jobs they have dreamt about. In the case of girls, parental concern for their moral welfare may place restrictions on how far away from home they are allowed to work. However, the ethnic economy is ready and willing to absorb them, particularly when there are family businesses to be maintained. For quite a few rebellious adolescents, this period marks their 're-entry' into their ethnic group."

Racism

21.   We received a considerable amount of evidence from all the community representatives whom we met on the Cypriot community's experiences of racism. We have already referred above to the various comments which were made to us about unintentional racism within the education system, particularly in relation to teachers' attitudes and expectations of Cypriot children. The Head of one school we visited with a substantial proportion of Cypriot pupils recalled the antagonism of some (but by no means all) of the local "white" parents to the changing nature of the pupil population when they had objected to their children attending "a Greek school" and some had actually moved house to avoid this. In the programme "Does School Hurt?" in the BBC series "Multi-Racial Education", a group of Greek Cypriot youngsters, mostly born in Britain, recounted their own experiences of racism and the hostility which they had encountered. Representatives of one community organisation whom we met referred to how telephone enquiries to the DHSS on behalf of clients often resulted in "heavy breathing" once naming of the client had made it clear that they were of Cypriot origin, and evoked comments such as "they will understand when it comes to money" (referring to any mention of language difficulties). In considering the attitudes of the majority community towards Cypriots it is perhaps also worth recalling the feelings which many British held towards Cypriots during the EOKA period in Cyprus.

22.   It is also we feel important to note, in relation to racism, the evidence we received concerning the feelings of the Cypriot community towards other ethnic minority groups—despite events in Cyprus, there seems to be little real antipathy between Greek Cypriots and Turkish Cypriots in this country. In one pre-school centre we visited reference was made to the "outrageous" comments which Cypriot parents made about other ethnic minority groups, predominantly Asians, and the dislike of some other groups for the Cypriots. There had been a number of serious racial attacks on parents in the area and there had been considerable conflict over which group might have been to blame for these. It may be interesting however to bear in mind the suggestions put forward in the following extract from the chapter "The Turkish Cypriots: Ethnic Relations in London and Cyprus" by Sarah Ladbury, taken from "Between Two Cultures" to seek to account for some of the antipathy of Cypriots towards other ethnic minority groups:

> *"Turks[9] have adopted many English racist attitudes towards members of other groups, particularly West Indians and Africans. Pakistanis incite less prejudice, partly because their settlement*

---

[9] NB: In this quote the term "Turk" is used to refer to Turkish Cypriots.

patterns do not coincide with those of Cypriots and they are therefore less visible, partly because they are Moslem, and partly because they are perceived as being 'less black'. . . . It is not that Turkish Cypriots see West Indians or Africans (between whom in any case they do not distinguish) as threatening their own individual interests. They do not occupy the same economic niches and they are not even seen as constituting a moral threat, as are the English on other occasions. Rather it is that in certain situations, notably when working with or simply getting to know English people, it is expedient for Turks to identify with the English majority and the colour difference is the most obvious criterion for creating a common outgroup. Most Turks are also aware of the associations that the term 'immigrant' has for the English. This follows from their reading of the British press, which is mostly confined to the popular dailies—just those which are apt to sensationalise stories concerning immigrants and the Englishman's attitude to them. It is not therefore surprising that the Turkish family, surrounded as it usually is by non-Turkish neighbours, does not like to think it is being classed as 'immigrant'. And again, the most obvious means of getting into the non-immigrant category is to stress that they are white. All the associations the 'black' has for the English working class are then advanced to justify this prejudice and support the ideological and cultural 'Englishness' that they ascribe to themselves. What is interesting here is not so much that group stereotypes are invoked for outsiders who have no particular relevance to Turkish Cypriots as an ethnic group. Rather it is that Turkish Cypriots themselves have adopted those stereotypes already in use by the English majority and, in doing so, differentiate themselves from other minority groups—a status which, from that moment in time, they cease to ascribe to themselves."

Conclusion

23.   In our consideration of the Cypriot community, we were very concerned at the evidence which was put forward to show that children of Cypriot origin, and particularly Turkish Cypriot children, were underachieving in academic terms and we feel it is regrettable that so little attention has previously been paid to this situation. We were particularly interested in the suggestion that the apparent differential in performance between Greek Cypriot and Turkish Cypriot children could, in part at least, be ascribed to the rather different stereotypes which existed of them in the minds of the majority community and particularly teachers. If this suggestion were proven, and we certainly found the case put forward to support it persuasive, this would serve to reinforce directly the conclusions which we ourselves reached, both in our interim report and earlier

in this report, as to the underlying causes of West Indian under-achievement. In relation to language, it was also interesting that the concerns expressed to us by representatives of the Cypriot community about E2L provision reflected many of those which other groups had also raised with us—most notably perhaps the negative view which many mainstream teachers apparently take of second language learners, and the opposition to the withdrawal of children for E2L help—which we have already discussed in Chapter Seven. The views which were expressed about "mother tongue" provision also further emphasise the key role which this plays in the mainten-ance of an ethnic minority group's sense of "identity". We found it interesting to be able to discuss with representatives of the Turkish Cypriot community some of the "pastoral" issues which had pre-viously been raised with us by Asian Muslim community representa-tives and to see the points of similarity and divergence of view which emerged. Concern about the "narrowness" of the religious education curriculum of many schools and the desire for the option of single-sex schooling to be available for girls—both of which we considered at length in Chapter Eight—were emphasised in particular. Some of the points which were raised with us concerning the possible "cultural conflicts" which might face Cypriot youngsters, particularly girls, also further emphasised the difficulties which can arise in this respect. We also found interesting the comparisons which could be drawn between the situations of the Cypriot and the Chinese community, in view of their traditional "internal economies" which had tended perhaps to shield them from the experiences of direct racism which some other ethnic minority groups had faced although there was, as we have observed, still a sense of the Cypriot community being subject to racism. It is clear however that, as we pointed out in the previous chapter, as the current economic pressures come to bear on these previously "self-sufficient" communities, and as youngsters in particular look outside their communities for employment, it seems regrettably inevitable that the level of racism which they encounter will increase.

CHAPTER 12

The Educational Needs of Children of Italian Origin

Background

1. The Italian community in this country, which today numbers in the region of 200,000, is probably one of the longest established and generally accepted of our ethnic minority communities: "Italians" having been coming to this country in fact ever since the Roman invasion! Little attention has however tended to be given to this community in any discussion on "immigrants", and the educational needs of children of Italian origin have only recently come to be considered in the context of "multicultural" education. The reasons for this general lack of attention to Italians have been summarised thus, by Dr Russell King[1]:

> "There are a number of reasons why so little attention has been spotlighted on the Italians. Most obvious is their lack of cospicuousness, the fact that along with other, smaller groups of south Europeans—Spaniards, Portuguese, Cypriots, Maltese etc—they constitute what has been termed the 'invisible immigrants'. But there are other, more subtle reasons too. The long period of Italian immigration has gained the community wide acceptance through a gradual build-up of the Italian presence, particularly in the nineteenth century. There has been no obviously threatening mass influx. A long-established presence has given the community a balanced internal structure which differs from the age, occupational and residential concentrations of more recent migrants to this country. The Italians as a group are also characterised by considerable socio-economic mobility. Yet although stable, the Italian community is also marginal to British society, and this also explains why so little attention is paid to the Italians."

There are, however, a number of interesting and important points which we feel can usefully be made in the context of this report about the Italian community.

Immigration
2. Apart from the Roman influence, Italian immigration to this country can be seen as a virtually continuous process falling into three distinct phases: firstly the arrival of poets, artists, artisans,

---

[1]"Italians in Britain: an idiosyncratic immigration". Article in the Journal of the Association of Teachers of Italian. Number 29. Autumn 1979.

bankers, merchants and scholars through the late Middle Ages and in Elizabethan times; secondly the arrival of "more humble" settlers mainly from Northern Italy, during the nineteenth century, involved in various food trades (this period marked the beginning of the long Italian tradition of involvement in the catering trade in this country); and more recently the post-war influx of unskilled workers, especially from Southern Italy, recruited for work in particular industries. According to Census data, the Italian population in Britain in 1901 numbered 20,332. Numbers remained relatively static during the first half of this century with the more restrictive immigration policy, and with the Italian fascist government's virtual ban on emigration. During the Second World War, many Italians in this country were of course interned and had their property confiscated and, as Dr King again has observed:

> "The fall in status from an accepted minority before 1940 to ipso facto aliens during the war and 'suspected' aliens for a time afterwards was undoubtedly the Italian community's greatest trauma".

In 1951, however, the "Bulk Recruitment Scheme" between the British and Italian Ministries of Labour authorised the "import" of Italian workers for jobs in industries which were unpopular with indigenous workers because of the working conditions. The major industries which recruited Italian workers were the brick industry— which recruited some 15,000 Italians from 1951 onwards —steelworks, coal mining and textiles. Italian immigration to Britain has waned since about 1967, and according to Dr Robin Palmer[2]:

> "... in the 1970s repatriation has greatly exceeded immigration. In 1972 Britain sustained a net loss of 5,000 Italian citizens."

Settlement   3.   The history and nature of Italian immigration to Britain has to a large extent determined the distribution of the Italian community in this country. It is estimated that probably a third of the total community live in Greater London but apart from other traditional centres such as Manchester and of course Bedford—where it is estimated that there are between 6–8,000 Italians (including the British born children of Italian parents):—the community is otherwise very widely dispersed, as a result of its involvement in the restaurant and catering trade, to most parts of the country. (Very similar in fact to the pattern of Chinese settlement).

Ethnic   4.   As with the other ethnic minority communities whom we have
Identity   considered, the Italian community has retained very close links with

---

[2]"The Italians: Patterns of Migration to London." Chapter in "Between Two Cultures." Ed. J Watson. 1977.

its "home" country and there is a strong sense of "being Italian" even amongst youngsters who have been born in this country. The emphasis is however very much on ties to the particular *region* of origin in Italy rather than to the country as a whole and such regional loyalties are generally stronger than straightforward national ties and are maintained by regular visits "home". The "myth of return" noted with other ethnic minority communities is also strong amongst the Italians and many of the original immigrants certainly came with the intention of returning to Italy eventually. Whilst there is some actual "return", in general the practical and economic arguments against returning to areas of Italy which offer little hope of employment, and where children who have been born in this country may find it difficult to integrate, have meant that returning to Italy is on the whole no longer viewed as a realistic option. The Italian community in this country has received a remarkable amount of support from its "home" Government in maintaining itself and its identity—for example there has been an Italian Vice-Consulate in Bedford since 1954, which provides help and advice to the community, and, as we discuss below, there are also arrangements for the teaching of the Italian language, supported directly by the Italian Government, which help the community to retain its distinctive character. The vast majority of the Italian community in this country is of course Roman Catholic and the church also plays a major part in maintaining a cohesive community through the organisation of social and welfare activities and also language teaching.

Home Background

5. Family ties are very strong within the Italian community and there is a marked tendency to see individuals as part of an overall family unit rather than as separate individuals, as illustrated by the following extract from a report of discussions with Italian youngsters in Bedford, quoted in the Open University coursebook "Bedford: Portrait of a Multi Ethnic-Town"[3]:

> *"Time and again it was pointed out . . . that family possessions are 'shared', and the very concept of an individual family member considering something belonged to him alone seemed to be absent. A young man who has commenced employment as an apprentice car mechanic illustrated this by saying, 'If Dad buys a car, it isn't his car, it's our car; I will expect to use it just the same as him when I pass my test."*

Attitudes towards children are based very much on the traditional lifestyle of the home villages in Italy, with boys being allowed almost complete freedom, while girls are expected to conform to fairly strict

---

[3]"Bedford: Portrait of a Multi-Ethnic Town". Open University Coursebook. E354. Block 1. Unit 1. 1982.

controls on their behaviour—for example being chaperoned when attending social functions before they are married. It may be useful here to quote from a letter written by two Italian girls, quoted in the Open University coursebook already referred to, reflecting on such parental attitudes:

"There is no doubt that a great number of Italian parents in Bedford are considerably stricter than English parents but there are two main psychological reasons: fear and ignorance. Fear because they have had to settle in a land alien to their own culture, traditions and language and ignorance for they are unaware of the great changes in their home towns, changes which must come in order to adapt to and keep pace with modern western society. There are also more deeply rooted causes behind this apparent rigidity, One is the belief that to shelter and seclude the daughter who is aproaching the marrying age will subsequently make her more respected, appreciated and inevitably sought after. In most cases, this no longer applies and Italian boys are gradually becoming more aware of more important and fundamental values to be found in the woman they choose to marry, rather than the outdated traditions of chastity and strict upbringing. The Italians are well-known for their great sense of family unity, yet very often parental authority and a child's duty is often masked as respect."

There were some indications in the evidence we received of girls beginning to resent and resist such controls and some instances of the type of inter-generational family conflicts which we have noted with other ethnic minority communities. Nevertheless the majority of Italian youngsters are still likely to marry within their community thus preserving the strong sense of a close-knit and indeed rather inward-looking community which, despite its long settlement in this country, has not yet become to any great extent merged with the majority community.

Socio-Economic Status

6.   In economic terms the Italian community can generally be seen as successful. Despite the decline of some of their traditional types of occupation—for example the ice cream business has declined with the spread of home freezers—the majority of Italian-owned businesses, chiefly in the catering field, are thriving and some 8 per cent of the community are self-employed. The heaviest and most badly-paid jobs in the brickworks in Bedford are no longer dominated by Italians, some of whom have moved on to the lighter, "managerial" jobs, with their places having been taken by later immigrants chiefly Asians and West Indians. The level of home ownership within the Italian community is also high.

Education

7.   The two major educational issues in relation to Italian children are language-related: the teaching of English as a second language, and arrangements for the maintenance and teaching of the "mother tongue" language. Before considering these specific issues in detail however, it is worth noting some of the more general educational points which were made in evidence to us. The Association of Teachers of Italian highlighted the following aspects of "home background" which could have a bearing on an Italian child's education:

**Home/
School
Conflict**

"1. Conflict between the home culture and the English culture assimilated by the child in school and through his English contemporaries;

2. Parents, whilst being ambitious for their children, are often alienated from the school and its teachers through:

a. communication difficulties caused by their limited knowledge of English,

b. little understanding of the educational system and supporting systems from which advice may be sought,

c. the system's failure to conform to the school of their own experience,

d. their own limited education and background."

Other Italian teachers whom we met also emphasised the "conflict of cultures" which could confront Italian children at school and which might be exacerbated by their general lack of socialisation with the majority community. It was also felt that schools gave too little help and support to parents who might be unfamiliar with the education system in this country, in, for example, understanding the examinations system, so that they in turn were better able to help and support their children.

Achievement

8.   Whilst it appears to be generally felt that Italian pupils achieve "reasonably well" in academic terms, there was a wide spread belief amongst the teachers, parents and indeed pupils whom we met that the ability of some Italian children might be under-estimated by schools because of a lack of appreciation of their language needs, and they might therefore be mistakenly placed in remedial streams and thus fail to achieve their full potential—as one group put it to us, "be penalised for life for lack of English".

**The Teaching
of English**

9.   Turning to the specific linguistic issues which were raised with us, we received a considerable amount of evidence from teachers about the need of Italian children, including those who have been born in this country, for continuing help and support with mastering English. Some Italian children were said to be still entering school

with only a very limited knowledge of English—to them, in the words of one teacher:

" the school presents an alien linguistic environment."

—and even where they might appear fluent, this might well mask more complex "second-stage"E2L needs. It was suggested that in respect of language needs, the "invisibility" of Italian children, and the fact that they were often not regarded as ethnic minorities, might lead teachers to fail to recognise the possible difficulties which they might face. Several teachers referred to Italian children who had done well at infant level but who, at primary and secondary level, where they were called upon to apply their knowledge of English to increasingly complex and abstract concepts, had tended to fall behind and who had ultimately found themselves in remedial streams. One language specialist whom we met expressed the view that some Italian children reached a "plateau" in their learning of English, beyond which they made little progress without the right kind of language support so that:

"a. Vocabulary can be extended across the curriculum; and

b. The structural patterns of the language can be mastered."

Another teacher emphasised the risks of relying on Italian children improving their English simply through contact with English-speaking children in the school, rather than through structured language support:

"It would seem . . . that we are in grave danger of over estimating the degree of second language learning that our Italians will achieve simply by being amongst English children. This particularly applies to the Junior School where the 'finer points' of language have been reached, and to all intents and purposes, and as far as the other children are concerned, they can speak English . . . If an English child and an Italian choose one another to talk to, to discuss things with, to share experiences and pool ideas then this can be linguistically invaluable. But . . . it is only in a small minority of cases that they do choose one another."

In general the teachers whom we met were opposed to the withdrawal of children for E2L help and took the view that language support was best provided within the normal classroom situation (the view which we ourselves took in Chapter Seven). It was also stressed to us that language needs should not be seen as the concern solely of specialists and that *all* teachers needed to have a far better understanding of how linguistic difficulties might bear on a child's performance—as part of a full "language across the curriculum" policy, as advocated by the Bullock Report—rather than, as was the case at present with some Italian children, regarding them either as "remedial", or dismissing their needs as " a job for the English department". Several teachers also commented on the extent to which the unnecessarily complex language used in public examinations could militate against second language learners, including Italians, so that they were unable to demonstrate their true ability in a subject and consequently underachieved.

"Mother Tongue" Provision

10.   We also received a considerable amount of evidence relating to the arrangements for maintaining and teaching their "mother tongue" language to children of Italian origin. We have of course already set out, in Chapter Seven, our own views on various forms of "mother tongue" provision. There are however several particular factors relating to the Italian community which we feel it is important to mention here. It may be worth recalling first of all that, unlike the languages of most of the ethnic minority communities whom we have considered, Italian has of course for some time been offered in some schools as a modern language quite irrespective of the presence of "mother tongue" speakers of the language in this country. It has in fact been suggested that Italian is less likely to be offered as a subject for study in those schools which may have Italian pupils. Nevertheless, although the offering of Italian in these circumstances cannot therefore be regarded as "mother tongue" provision, it is a fact that some mainstream secondary schools do include Italian in their normal curriculum and pupils are able to study for public examinations in the language[4]. It is worth noting however that several of the Italian teachers whom we met in fact expressed concern about the appropriateness of the existing 'O' and 'A' level examinations in Italian for "mother tongue" speakers of the language since it was felt that they called for an unnecessarily high level of English, rather than concentrating on a pupil's knowledge of Italian.

11.   As with many other ethnic minority communities, the teaching of their "mother tongue" to their children, especially those born in this country, is seen by many Italian parents as a key factor in preserving the community's "identity" and as a means of strengthening family ties with relations still living in their country of origin and facilitating visits "home". As part of our evidence-gathering in relation to the Italian community we were fortunate in obtaining the co-operation of the Italian Vice-Consulate in Bedford in organising a forum for parents and young people from the Italian community, and the issue which dominated much of the discussion on this occasion was "mother tongue" provision. Several community representa-

---

[4] According to the Joint DES/Welsh Office Consultative Paper "Foreign Languages in the School Curriculum" (May 1983), in the Summer 1981 examinations (English and Welsh Boards) there were a total of 679 CSE entries in Italian, 2,962 'O' level entries in Italian and 652 'A' level entries in Italian.

tives and Italian teachers with whom we discussed this issue, stressed that they regarded some form of "mother tongue support" as an integral part of any plan for "multicultural" education since they saw language and culture as "inextricably entwined".

Italian Government Support

12. A unique factor with the Italian community is the extent to which the "home" Government offers direct support, in the form of teachers and resources, for the teaching of Italian in this country. The provison of Italian classes for the children of Italian emigrants was instituted by the Italian Government in 1971, with the aim of maintaining the Italian language and culture among emigrant communities in order to facilitate their possible return to Italy. These classes—known as "corsi integrativi"—are organised on a regional basis and currently involve some 150 teachers, recruited in Italy and employed by the Italian authorities. They take place in a range of contexts: after school (known as "doposcuola"), on Saturday mornings, or in some cases as part of the normal school day, where the Italian Government-sponsored teachers are attached to a school and pupils are withdrawn from other subjects for teaching (known as "corsi inseriti"). The Association of Teachers of Italian commented thus, in their evidence to us, on these various arrangements for the teaching of Italian:

> "The provision of such classes would seem to help to counteract the problem of developing awareness of a personal cultural identity. Great benefit has been seen to be drawn from the integration of classes in schools, but the system generally is fraught with problems which affect all involved—the children, the Italian authorities and teachers, and the English authorities if they are involved or aware of this activity. The after-school classes have poor support and results as children often have difficulty in maintaining regular attendance, and often regard attendance at classes as an intrusion on their free time and a form of segregation from their contemporaries of other nationalities. The teachers frequently experience problems in finding suitable accommodation for the classes, and consequently their teaching style is severely limited. There is a general lack of continuity, and as the time available is very limited progress is slow. The regional organisers appointed from Italy often have little support from the British authorities, and frequently little knowledge of the British education system. One County Language adviser has reported that a regional organiser who approached him for help knew little or no English and that he himself was unaware of this field of language learning activity in his area until this approach was made. Another Language Adviser reports coming across Italian taught in a school in his area in Corsi Inseriti completely by

chance. Corsi Inseriti seem to be the best form of provision by the Italian authorities and function better when the classes are considered part of the language curriculum in the school and are open to all pupils—as well as children of Italian parentage."

13.   In the course of our evidence-gathering we sat in on several Italian classes taught by Italian Government-sponsored teachers, both after school and within the normal school day, as well as attending a training session organised by one LEA for the Italian teachers working in its area. During the latter session the following points were raised with us by these teachers:

i.   the response of schools to them depended on how the school staff regarded the teaching of Italian. The teachers generally felt "the same" as other teachers but they admitted that they had some problems because they were peripatetic and so were not in any school long enough to build up close links with other teachers, pupils or parents. They felt that they would welcome the opportunity of meeting the other teachers—at present if they taught after-school they might never meet the rest of the staff and were not therefore able to discuss a child's work in relation to his or her progress in other subjects. The teachers did not feel it mattered whether they were employed by the Authority or not; their success depended chiefly on the attitudes of the Head and staff in a school. They admitted however that some problems did arise because of administrative difficulties in Italy. (A number of the teachers were waiting for their contracts to be renewed before they could begin teaching).

ii.   The teachers felt strongly that Italian should be taught during the school day. They felt there were noticeable differences in the response of children whom they taught during the day and those they taught after school—the former were "mentally prepared" to work, whereas the latter saw it as an "imposition" on their time. Some English children studied Italian—in some cases only those who were considered academically successful were able to do so, which enhanced its status. All the pupils wanted to take an examination in the subject if they could.

iii.   The teachers got some feedback from Italian parents but unfortunately many parents did not have much contact with the schools at all because their English was limited and they did not want to "cause ripples". The teachers saw it as part of their role to improve home/school links with Italian families if they could.

iv. The teachers thought that Italian-origin pupils "felt different" even if they had been born in this country, especially the girls, because of the contraints their parents placed upon them. Although they might mix with other pupils when they were younger, after the age of about 13, when the differences between ethnic groups became clearer, they tended to keep together.

v. Several of the teachers felt that Italian children tended to fail to realise their full potential at school, at least partly because their possible language difficulties were not fully understood or recognised, and they were therefore likely to be wrongly classed as "remedial".

Several of the Headteachers of the schools where the Italian Government-sponsored teachers were working stressed that the presence of these teachers had improved the school's links with its Italian parents. Some concern was expressed that the peripatetic nature of the teachers' work meant that they were unable to build up close relationships with other staff members and there was little opportunity therefore to exchange views on the needs of particular pupils. This "separation" between the Italian classes and the mainstream schools seems particularly acute for the "after school" classes where the only link often appears to be the use of the same premises and, in some instances, complaints from mainstream teachers about the untidiness of the classrooms—which arises simply because the classrooms are cleaned before the Italian classes and not afterwards. Certainly in one school we visited, all the mainstream teachers seemed to know about the "after school" Italian class was that "it goes on in that classroom there". In several instances non-Italian children were found to be joining the classes taking place during school hours but Headteachers pointed out that they were not able to adopt Italian as the school's "first" modern language, instead of for example French, in case the Italian Government were to withdraw its support for the teachers. It was felt that some Italian pupils had "rebelled" against studying Italian since they saw it as identified with the authority of the family with which they might be in conflict, and they also resented missing other lessons—in one school we visited, Italian was timetabled against the Humanities and Craft—in which they were more interested. In the majority of classes we visited however, the pupils were pleased to have the opportunity to study their own language, although somewhat less enthusiasm was understandably expressed for "after school" and Saturday classes—at one "after school" class we attended, all but 2 of the 9 pupils said they disliked coming and only did so because of parental pressure.

14. Some concern was expressed to us by Headteachers and community representatives about the different teaching styles adopted by some of the Italian Government-sponsored teachers, who were unfamiliar with the accepted teaching methods and overall approach of the British education system. The majority of these teachers were in fact not qualified in Italy as language teachers which meant that their approach to language teaching differed from, for example, that of mainstream French teachers. (It was in an effort to exchange information about teaching skills and overcome such difficulties, that one authority had, as mentioned above, arranged a series of "in-service" sessions for its Italian teachers.) It is worth noting that only Italian-born teachers are accepted for employment by the Italian Government within this programme and British-born Italians, who would of course be more familiar with our education system as well as more fluent in English, are excluded. Another relevant point worth considering was raised in a submission we received from a British teacher of Italian who complained about the difficulty for teachers like herself in finding jobs, since the Italian teachers were available to Authorities at little or no direct cost.

15. As far as the attitudes of mainstream teachers towards the teaching of Italian are concerned, there was a general feeling amongst the community representatives whom we met that all "mother tongue" languages, including Italian, were seen as of "low status". It was felt that many teachers still believed that the teaching of English to ethnic minority children was of paramount importance and they consequently regarded any "mother tongue" provision as "back pedalling" in educational terms. There was also felt to be a minority of overtly racist teachers who simply felt that all "foreign" children must conform now that they were in this country.

EC Sponsored "Mother Tongue and Culture"

Pilot Project

16. Another particular dimension to the "mother tongue" debate with regard to Italian children, which it is also worth mentioning, is the experience gained during the EC sponsored "Mother Tongue and Culture Pilot Project" which was undertaken in Bedfordshire LEA between 1976 and 1980. A broad outline of the work of this project in relation to Italian children is attached as an Annex to this Chapter. During our consideration of the Italian community we met a number of people who had been directly involved with the work of the project, as well as visiting one of the schools which had participated in it. The former co-ordinator of the project, Dr Arturo Tosi, in giving evidence to us, raised a number of interesting points particularly concerning the attitudes of the Italian community towards the project and its work. For example the Italian parents' differing attitudes towards Standard Italian and the dialect Italian which was actually their "mother tongue", and which was significantly different from

Standard Italian, were especially interesting. All the parents wanted their children to be taught Standard Italian since they regarded their own language form as a "corruption" of "proper" Italian. In fact however, because Italy was only united as a country relatively recently, the Standard form of the language has less of a "pedigree" than the dialect forms which have a far longer history of developing from the original Latin and the various language forms in Italy have thus evolved separately rather than, as is often assumed, the dialect forms developing later. Some doubts have in fact been expressed about the project having focussed on teaching Standard Italian to children to whom it was in effect a third language and not strictly speaking a "mother tongue"—an aspect of the "mother tongue" debate on which we commented in Chapter Seven. Dr Tosi had looked at the differences in attitude between the Italian children involved in the project and those in other schools who learnt Italian in out of school classes. Where Italian had been offered within the school curriculum as part of the project, the children saw it as a normal school activity whereas if they had to study it outside school, they sensed the negative connotations and wondered why it was not thought "good enough" for schools to teach, quite apart from the additional burden of having to attend classes in the evenings and at weekends. Other teachers involved with the project referred to the range of attitudes towards their work amongst the rest of the schools' staffs, varying from those who had seen the project as a positive development, to those who had regarded it as potentially detrimental to the children's education. In one school which had participated in the project—and which had since continued with "mother tongue" maintenance and some bilingual education for its Punjabi-speaking pupils, as well as having a visiting Italian Government sponsored teacher to work with its Italian pupils—the Headteacher felt that the reactions of the other children to the project had been generally positive, with requests for example from them to be allowed to join the Italian classes as well. When asked why they wanted to do this, the children had replied "because you're clever if you can speak another language". There had been some joint activities within the project such as plays and bilingual story-telling so the other children became more aware that the Italian children were not "strange and different" but had some extra abilities. As far as the Italian children were concerned, she felt the project had given them an increased awareness of their own identity as people with "something of value" and had sought, perhaps overtly, to foster their appreciation of their language and culture. The children had not seen it as strange to be taught in their mother tongue and had been quite happy to tell other pupils and teachers what they were doing. Great importance had been attached to involving the parents in the project and the team had visited homes to follow up the children's linguistic backgrounds.

706

This had led to some close contacts with parents who had increasingly then begun to attend school open evenings, sports days etc. Several of the teachers concerned with the project criticised the general lack of interest which the DES had shown during the project's lifetime and also regretted the lack of any follow up work building on the progress which they felt had been made.

Racism

17. It may surprise many of our readers, as indeed it surprised us initially, that we should need to refer to racism in the context of the Italian community, which most people would probably regard as "fully accepted" in this country. Nevertheless several of the teachers whom we met who worked with Italian pupils referred to instances, albeit rare, of what was often termed "racial antagonism" between these pupils and their "English" peers, and in one secondary school we visited, a group of Italian (British-born) fifth and sixth formers explained to us how they felt the need to "group together" in school in the face of name-calling and taunts of "Go home" from the other pupils. Also, at the meeting of Italian parents, to which we have already referred, one parent complained that his children had been "discriminated" against and "called names" at school until he had complained to the school about this.

18. As far as their relationship with other ethnic minority groups is concerned, there is a tendency amongst some of the Italian community to regard themselves very much as "elite" immigrants and thus to disassociate themselves from more recently arrived groups. Some studies of the changing patterns of settlement of Italian communities in particular cities have created a clear impression that as other, mainly "coloured", immigrants have moved into an area, the Italians have tended to move out—as one researcher put it, they have "fled" the new arrivals. One specialist teacher, who worked very closely with the Italian community, suggested to us that this "resistance and resentment" of other ethnic minority groups, especially Asians, had even in her experience led to Italian youngsters becoming involved in "Paki-bashing" alongside their "English" peers.

Conclusion

19. We believe that a number of interesting points emerge from this brief consideration of the educational needs of Italian children. Once again we were struck by the strong sense of "ethnic identity" of the community, further reinforced in this case by very close ties with a particular region of the "home" country. The "mother tongue" language is clearly again regarded as a key factor in maintaining the community's identity and we were particularly interested in the

efforts made by the Italian Government to assist with "mother tongue" teaching and in the comments made to us in the light of the experience gained from the EC sponsored project in Bedford. Some anxiety was again expressed about provision for E2L teaching, particularly in relation to "second stage needs"—an issue which we of course took up in Chapter Seven. The references which were made to the attitude of some mainstream teachers to "mother tongue" teaching—for example seeing it as "backpedalling" in educational terms and, in any case, regarding Italian as of "low status", also echo concerns expressed by other groups. The points raised in relation to the differing perceptions of dialect forms of Italian and the Standard form of the language also provide an interesting comparison with the similar misunderstandings which surround the issue of West Indian dialect. The comments which were made to us about the Italian community's experience of racism, surprising as we found them, perhaps serve to illustrate the extent to which such antagonism towards ethnic minority groups can cross "barriers" of colour, and bear on groups who might have been thought to be "acceptable" to the majority community.

ANNEX

Outline of the EC sponsored project "Mother Tongue and Culture in Bedfordshire"[5]

The Project involves six schools, four primary, one middle and one upper, 127 pupils and parents of those pupils, four project teachers, twenty-four classroom teachers, six heads, three LEA personnel and two/three representatives from the EEC. Two languages are taught—Punjabi and Italian. There are six groups of pupils. Four groups are Punjabi-speaking children and are drawn from three schools. Two groups from one school have 11 and 13 respectively in each. The second school has a group of 22 children and the third a group of 20 making a total of 66 Punjabi-children.

There are two groups of Italian children, one of 15 children from one school, the other of 19 children from two schools totalling 34 Italian children. Taken together, the number of Punjabi and Italian children of age 5–8 involved in the Mother Tongue and Culture Project totals 100. (15 pupils in the middle school and 12 in the upper school make up the total cited earlier of 127.)

Each group of children has approximately five hours of timetabled teaching of their mother tongue each week; each project teacher has approximately ten hours of teaching in addition to their other responsibilities for liaison with schools and parents and preparation of materials.

Aims of the Project
In the description of the Project sent out by the Bedfordshire Education Service the aims were stated thus;

a.　an enhancement of the self-image of the immigrant concerned;

b.　a carefully controlled integration into the English Educational System;

c.　an increase in esteem for the immigrants on the part of the indigenous children in the school;

d.　a greater understanding on the part of the immigrants of the host country's language, culture and education;

e.　general education interest on the part of both indigenous and immigrant groups;

f.　an opportunity to found in Bedford a resources Bank for Italian Language and Culture which is likely to be of interest to other authorities as well as Bedfordshire.

---

[5]Drawn from the second external evaluation report of the project prepared by the Cambridge Institute of Education. September 1978–September 1979.

CHAPTER 13

The Educational Needs of Children of Ukrainian Origin

1. When determining which ethnic minority groups, other than Asians and West Indians, we should consider in this report, we decided that it would be helpful to look briefly at the situation of one of the Eastern European communities which became established in this country at the time of the Second World War. The most obvious such community for us to consider might be thought to be the Polish community. In the absence of much direct evidence from this community, and also in order to put forward a rather different perspective than that which has been the subject of some of the studies which have already been made of the Polish situation, we decided instead to consider the needs of the Ukrainian community, from whom we had received some particularly interesting evidence.

Background

Size and Settlement of the Community

2. Estimates of the size of the Ukrainian community in Britain range between 20-30,000, including descendants of "mixed" marriages. Whilst there are no accurate statistics, it is estimated that probably about one third of the community have been born in this country. The majority of the community is to be found in London, the East Midlands, Yorkshire and Lancashire, with the remainder very widely dispersed around the country.

3. The great majority of the original Ukrainian immigrants came to this country at the end of the 1940s having found themselves in Western Europe at the end of the war and being unwilling to be repatriated to the Soviet Union. The bulk of these Ukrainians being from Western Ukraine which was incorporated into the USSR during the Second World War. Many of the Ukrainians who initially came to this country however subsequently migrated further to the USA and especially to Canada, where there is a sizeable Ukrainian community in the Prairie Provinces. Most of the immigrants to this country were male and the shortage of Ukrainian women led to a significant number of mixed marriages—the wives tending to be other immigrants such as Poles or Italians rather than native British.

Religious and Linguistic Background

4. The religion of the majority of Ukrainians originating from the Western Ukraine is Ukrainian Catholic whilst those from other areas of the Ukraine may be Ukranian Orthodox. Currently only the

711

Orthodox religion is recognised in the USSR so that the Ukrainian Catholic Church is "underground", with the patriarch now residing in Rome. The Ukrainian language has a Slavonic root and may be understood "with difficulty" by Poles and Russians. There is a distinct Ukrainian literature and the Ukrainian language is still spoken in the Ukraine.

Ukrainian Identity

5. As with the other ethnic minority communities we have considered, the Ukrainian community has maintained a very clear sense of its own "ethnic identity" even into the second and third generations. One British-born Ukrainian we met appeared to speak for his community when he remarked:

> "I feel both British and Ukrainian—but 99 per cent Ukrainian."

This sense of being Ukrainian appears to have persisted even through mixed marriages, particularly where the mother is Ukrainian. As one Ukrainian community organisation put it in evidence to us:

> "The Ukrainian community seeks to preserve its identity by passing on to new generations the Ukrainian language, knowledge about Ukraine and its history, and Ukrainian cultural and religious tradition. The objective is to minimise the extent to which people of Ukrainian origin lose their Ukrainian identity through assimilation with the society at large, at the same time encouraging them to be successful members of British society. Assimilation cannot be totally avoided, but it is likely that the community will exist in this country as a distinct entity for the forseeable future."

Education

Achievement

6. Most of the Ukrainians who settled in Britain after the war had modest educational achievements, having been denied access to educational opportunities in the Ukraine. They often had few resources and took menial jobs despite being capable of better things. Today, after some 40 years, the community feels it has established itself and its youngsters are now "succeeding", despite still being regarded rather as "oddities" by the host community. As one community organisation put it to us:

> "If the level of success of Ukrainian children in the British education system is measured in terms of academic performance, then there is no evidence of general underachievement. It is sometimes suggested, in fact, that the proportions of Ukrainian children who gain academic success at the various educational levels are greater than the national averages. This is most likely to be the result of generally strong family life within the Ukrainian community and the particularly keen efforts made by parents to

motivate their children to obtain the education which was not available to many of themselves."

Coupled with the feeling that Ukrainian youngsters are generally "succeeding" in terms of examination results, is a belief that on leaving school they often proceed to Higher Education and are subsequently able to find employment quite readily and are perhaps less affected by the national level of unemployment than some other groups. (Certain employment opportunities—related to security considerations—are of course often not open to them.)

Educational Concerns

7. Despite the apparent achievement of Ukrainian youngsters, there was a major concern amongst the community representatives whom we met that, in their words:

"... the educational environment is not conducive to the development of the children's Ukrainian identity."

The community's specific concerns focussed on two particular issues: the teaching of English, and teachers' knowledge and understanding of factors relating to the children's cultural and home background—both issues of course which have been repeatedly raised with us by other communities. Taking each of these in turn:

English Teaching (E2L)

Since many Ukrainian parents are anxious for their children to learn Ukrainian during their early years (see paragraph 8 below), some children may enter school with limited English. Concern was expressed to us about the common practice of schools, in this situation, to withdraw these children into special language classes which it was felt might in fact hinder rather than aid their progress. It was suggested in evidence to us that Ukrainian children with very little knowledge of English had in fact usually been able to master the basics of the language to a satisfactory level within 3–4 months and did not suffer any subsequent disadvantage *vis-a-vis* their "English" peers. There was unease amongst the community representatives whom we met that some teachers automatically assumed that a lack of fluency in English on the part of a child could be taken as signifying a general lack of ability which was again a cause for considerable concern if the need for separate E2L provision might confirm this view of the children as in some way "remedial".

Teachers' Background Knowledge

Ukrainian representatives expressed great concern to us about what they regarded as the "appalling ignorance" of the great majority of teachers about their community and thus about their children's background. It was pointed out for example that teachers often

713

confused the concept of "Ukrainian" with being either Russian or Polish, which the community considered to be insulting as well as a denial of their particular ethnic identity. This tendency was displayed both in informal contacts with children as well as in the formal curriculum—for example in a geography lesson the Ukraine might be referred to, incorrectly, as part of Russia rather than as part of the USSR, traditional Ukrainian decorated Easter eggs were often called "Russian eggs", and the Ukrainian Orthodox faith was generally assumed to be synonymous with Russian Orthodox. Another aspect of teachers' tendency to, in a sense, seek to deny the community's identity, which was frequently referred to, was the mispronounciation or the "simplification" of children's names. Whilst it was admitted that some Ukrainian names might be difficult for teachers to pronounce, it was felt that they should make the effort to pronounce them correctly since a child's name was clearly an important and integral aspect of his or her whole identity and personality. In addition to these specific points, there was a general feeling that, in relation to all ethnic minority groups, schools should do far more to "recognise" and reflect, in whatever ways were possible, the range of backgrounds from which their pupils now come. The following extract from our evidence expands on this view:

"It is widely accepted that the school plays an important part in many children's development due to its prestige in their eyes. Consequently, if a teacher expresses a sincere interest in the affairs of a child's country of origin, this serves to strengthen the child's positive identification with the country of its parents or ancestors. Conversely, if no interest is shown, a negative attitude could be fostered, and this may even give rise to the development of an inferiority complex vis-a-vis the child's country of origin. The development of a national identity is an important element of the development of a child's personality, and it is therefore desirable that this should be borne in mind in schools with children from national minorities. As well as showing an interest and initiating discussions about pupils' countries of origin, it is important that teachers should make an effort to become familiar with basic facts about the relevant countries and about the reasons why and circumstances in which people from those countries found themselves in Britain. The most appropriate course of action would be to ensure that teacher training courses make teachers aware of the importance of this matter."

"Mother Tongue Teaching" 8. As we have already mentioned above, the learning of the Ukrainian language, especially amongst those children who have been born in this country, is considered to be an essential factor in the maintenance of their Ukrainian identity. In common with the other groups whom we have considered, the Ukrainian community itself has therefore taken steps to organise its own classes to maintain and teach the language and culture. The following extract from evidence from the Association of Ukrainians in Great Britian describes the scale, nature and organisation of this community-based provision:

"Since the 1950s the Ukrainian community has organised kindergartens and Ukrainian Saturday schools for its children. It also encourages sixth formers and students to attend courses in Ukrainian studies held in various countries at various times. Many children and young people are members of one of two Ukrainian youth organisations, where they participate in choirs, folk dancing groups, summer camps, etc. The Educational Affairs Council of the Association of Ukrainians in Great Britain maintains a constant review of the supplementary provision and takes steps to improve or extend it as appropriate. All the work of the Council and the local organisers is voluntary and there are no paid officials. The kindergarten and Saturday school teachers usually receive a small remuneration.

In recent years very few kindergartens have been operational because of the small number of children in the appropriate age group. The number of third generation births is steadily increasing now and renewed effort is being put into planning and organising playgroups and kindergartens. Children attend for two or three hours per week, usually on Saturdays or Sundays. Emphasis is placed on the usual aspects of children's pre-school development, as well as a gradual acquaintance with Ukrainian culture. The language used by teachers and children is Ukrainian.

The number of Saturday schools has also declined in recent years, primarily due to the gap between the second and third generations. There are currently about 20 schools around the country, with between 5 and 70 pupils per school. Children attend the schools from the age of six or seven. The number of classes in each school depends on the available resources, the maximum number of classes being 10. The subjects taught include the Ukrainian language and literature, geography and history of Ukraine, and the history of Ukrainian culture. The practise of Ukrainian folk traditions is greatly encouraged. In some schools additional classes are held specifically to prepare candidates for the GCE Ordinary level examination in Ukrainian. Many of the present teachers, some of whom are also teachers by profession, are second generation Ukrainians."

The majority of the text-books used by these classes derive from the University of Toronto press in Canada. It was mentioned to us that whilst there was already an 'O' level examination available in Ukrainian—with some 40 entrants each year—there was as yet no such provision at 'A' level. The community representatives were therefore anxious to see an 'A' level course being established to provide a stimulus for youngsters to continue their studies 16+.

9.   The Ukrainian representatives whom we met emphasised that their aim was to preserve the Ukrainian language and culture by youngsters having an understanding of the circumstances in which Ukrainian should be used, for example at home and in cultural/social settings when Ukrainians were together. Second generation British-born Ukrainians were having to make a determined effort to speak to each other in Ukrainian in order for their children to experience a consistent language environment at home. There was a danger that parents whilst speaking Ukrainian to their children would speak English to each other—the risk being that children, seeing this "double standard", would then speak English to each other especially when their parents were not present. It was recognised and accepted that outside the home, children would speak together mainly in English. The purpose of the Saturday schools was however to reinforce the home practices. There was no suggestion that the Saturday schools aimed to supplement the normal work of maintained schools.

Possible LEA Support

10.   In response to questions from Committee members, the Ukrainian representatives took the view that, because of the relatively small size of their community, and its dispersed nature, it was neither practical nor feasible for them to expect LEAs to provide for teaching the Ukrainian language within the normal school curriculum. They emphasised however that they would very much welcome some grant support from LEAs towards the running of the classes—along the lines we have recommended in our Language Chapter—and felt that if this required some form of monitoring of the standard of teaching, this could only be a stimulus to improved provision. They also indicated that the voluntary teachers working in their schools would be glad of the opportunity to take part in LEA in-service programmes to assist them with their teaching skills. The community representatives also observed that teachers in mainstream schools might "support" community-based "mother tongue" provision indirectly by encouraging the children and stressing that it was a desirable asset to be able to speak more than one language.

Conclusion

11.   A number of interesting points arise from this brief consideration of the educational needs of the Ukrainian community, which in our view serve to reinforce further the conclusions we have reached

in the main body of this report. The sense of "ethnic identity" is clearly very strong within the Ukrainian community and community-based provision for continuing language and cultural maintenance is considered to be an important element in this. Once again concern was expressed by community representatives about the "withdrawal" approach to E2L teaching and about the negative connotations in the minds of some teachers of a child lacking fluency in English—both of course points which we took up in our Language Chapter. The comments which were made to us about the need for schools to do more to recognise and reflect the range of ethnic groups which are now a part of this society also lend further weight to the case which we have put forward for the development of a broader and more responsive approach to the educational needs of *all* children.

CHAPTER 14

The Educational Needs of Vietnamese Children

1. Because of the outward similarities between their situation and that of the Chinese community, we decided to extend our consideration of the needs of Chinese children to include also a brief look at Vietnamese children. We were however so struck by the situation of the Vietnamese community, particularly the educational consequences of being such a recent refugee group to come to this country, that we subsequently decided to devote a chapter of our report to reviewing their needs and problems.

Background

Size and Nature of the Community
2. Between 1975–1982 some 16,500 refugees from Vietnam entered the United Kingdom (the majority coming from 1978 onwards), including not only those admitted under the quotas agreed by the Government, but also those rescued by British ships and those allowed to rejoin families already here. According to a Home Office study[1], some 70 per cent of the Vietnamese refugee population in this country are ethnic Chinese and over 60 per cent are from North Vietnam. The refugee community is predominantly young, with some 35–45 per cent of pre-school or statutory school age. Admission to this country was not based on as strict selection criteria as it was to other receiving countries and as a result the community here can be seen as relatively disadvantaged in relation for example to the Vietnamese community in the United States, where the majority of refugees are from the elite, professional classes of South Vietnam. The Home Office study found that only some 20 per cent of the refugees currently had a minimum working proficiency in the English language and only 36 per cent of adult males were in employment (the latter figure comparing with an employment rate for Vietnamese refugees in the USA of some 95 per cent for those who have been resident there over 2 years).

3. According to a recent report of the Joint Committee for Refugees from Vietnam (JCRV)[2]:

"The Vietnamese are one of the most disadvantaged groups ever to come to the United Kingdom."

---

[1]"Vietnamese Refugees. A study of their reception and resettlement in the United Kingdom." Peter R Jones. Home Office Research and Planning Unit Paper 13. 1982.
[2]Report of the Joint Committee for Refugees from Vietnam. Home Office. 1982.

719

Particular Problems

The Home Office study highlighted the following particular factors which need to be borne in mind when considering the situation of Vietnamese refugees, compared with the experiences of earlier groups of refugees to this country:

> *"An important feature of the Vietnamese . . . was the almost complete absence of an established ethnic community in the United Kingdom to which the refugees could turn for support. . . . The wide cultural divide between the Vietnamese and the host community . . . was an additional problem which had not been faced in earlier intakes. . . . This cultural divide had implications in terms of language learning, employment (many of the 'skilled' Vietnamese found their skills were not relevant in an industrialised Western economy) and the development of social relationships with British people. These various factors meant the Vietnamese refugees had very much less control over their lives when they came (here) than previous groups and relied to a much greater degree on the efforts of the voluntary agencies."*

"Refugee Trauma"

In addition to these problems which the Vietnamese community face, reference was also made in the evidence we recieved to the particular effect on an ethnic minority group of being refugees rather than immigrants by choice. The 1982 JCRV report described this effect as follows:

> *"This condition, for convenience referred to as refugee trauma, derives from the range of experience and expectations they bring with them to their adopted country. All refugees are vulnerable in this respect, the Vietnamese outstandingly so. They come with a legacy of violence and insecurity from 30 years of war; they have had to face the realisation that the country in which they were born no longer offers security and prospects; they have endured the strains of preparation for covert flight and the flight itself in which large numbers of Vietnamese lost their lives, among whom may be family members and friends. Having reached a country of first asylum they feel guilty at being the ones to get out and survive. They experience a loss of control over the factors that affect their lives, particularly during the processes of selection, rejection and, finally, acceptance by a Western nation. They now become aware that there is no going back, though sometimes a 'myth of return' develops. Expectations of the country of resettlement are unreasonably high. The reality of unemployment, lack of English and isolation, which is the immediate prospect for the Vietnamese in the UK, taken with their earlier experiences and expectation, hits particularly hard."*

Reception

4. On arrival in this country the Vietnamese refugees were placed

in one of some 45 reception centres which were funded by central Government but run by three voluntary bodies: The British Council for Aid to Refugees (later to become the British Refugee Council), the Ockenden Venture, and the Save the Children Fund (later to establish a new charity, Refugee Action, to continue this aspect of its work), each of which had responsibility for a designated zone of the country and for the reception centres and arrangements for resettlement within it. In July 1979, as the refugee numbers increased dramatically, the Joint Committee for Refugees from Vietnam, consisting of representatives of each of the three voluntary bodies under an independent Chairman and with a secretariat seconded from the Home Office, was formed to oversee the coordination of the programme of reception and resettlement. During their stay in the reception centres, which varied considerably in both size (between 18 and 730) and regime, the refugees received some teaching in "survival" English (provided by LEAs but with full reimbursement of costs by central Government) as well as an introduction to life in Britain and any necessary medical treatment. The major responsibility for the **resettlement** of the refugees remained with the voluntary bodies using housing made available by local authorities or housing associations and relying on local volunteers. No special funding was provided for the resettlement stage by central Government and after resettlement the refugees were dependent for financial support on normal statutory entitlements and benefits. Central Government funding for all Vietnamese reception centres ceased on 30 September, 1982 although we understand that the voluntary agencies have themselves funded some centres after this date. A small number of Vietnamese refugees who are living in agency accommodation funded by voluntary bodies still remain to be resettled.

Dispersal

5. In organising the resettlement of the Vietnamese refugees a conscious decision was taken to disperse them throughout the country in small groups. This decision was based partly on administrative convenience—it was felt it would be easier to find housing and to obtain local voluntary support if the "burden" on individual areas was not too great—it was also felt that dispersal would make it easier for the refugees to integrate within the majority community and thus "settle down", and also that the creation of "ghettoes" would be avoided. There has however been some criticism of the dispersal policy for the problems which it poses for the refugees themselves—firstly, by placing them in areas of the country which may be unfamiliar with meeting the needs of "immigrants", for example in terms of education, and secondly, in spreading the refugee community throughout the country the isolation of the refugees may be exacerbated and there is little chance of mutual support within the community. As the JCRV report put it:

721

"The Vietnamese ought to be able to look to their own community for support. However, the dispersal policy has meant that, with the exception of a few urban areas, the numbers settled together are not large enough to provide that support."

The Home Office study reported the following views on the dispersal approach amongst those who have been involved in the refugee programme, both employees of voluntary bodies and local volunteers:

"Attitudes to dispersal were generally positive with respondents balancing the practical short term advantages against the possible longer term problems. The most common reason given in support of dispersal was the need to avoid 'ghettoes'. It was strongly believed that from the point of view of host population response 'it is a good thing that there are not seen to be too many [refugees] in one place'. A second factor was the belief that 'dispersal avoided the statutory resources being overstretched'. Support for dispersal was not limited to purely practical considerations, and several respondents agreed with the view that, though the initial resettlement period is unhappy for some, there are better chances of good integration into the community ultimately. Despite such elements of ideological support the main advantage of dispersal would seem to be the practical one of ease of resettlement. If the refugees had not been dispersed the task of resettlement would have been considerably more difficult and may not have been able to rely so heavily on voluntary local support as much as it did and still continues to do. From the perspective of the refugees the advantages of dispersal are few. 'Dispersal is alright if it means groups of families in different areas of big cities but in country areas it can mean total isolation for old people unable to travel and for young mothers with children'."

We share the concerns reflected here about the social and psychological effects on the refugees of the dispersal policy. We are also troubled by the underlying implications of the policy—firstly, in apparently regarding the concentration of an ethnic minority group in any area as by definition undesirable because of the possible reactions of the majority community, a view which we cannot condone, and secondly, in seeing as its sole aim that the refugees become "integrated", ie "submerged" within British society, rather than retaining their own identity within the kind of pluralist society which we have envisaged in this report. Alongside these concerns however, we must express our admiration for the efforts of the JCRV, the voluntary bodies and the local volunteers for the work which they have done and still do in coping with the care and support of the

Vietnamese refugee community.

Education

6. In relation to the school education of Vietnamese children, the JCRV Report concluded that:

> *"Provided that they come into school at an early age we believe that there is usually sufficient time for total integration of the Vietnamese in the educational stream towards O and A level exams. However, there is no room for complacency. . . . Nor should it be overlooked that although children may absorb formal education, school experience itself can prove traumatic (we have had reports of some able Vietnamese children being placed in classes for the Educationally Sub-Normal)."*

Language Needs

7. From the evidence which we ourselves received, the major issue in relation to the education of Vietnamese youngsters is clearly the acquisition of English, especially for youngsters arriving in the upper secondary age range for whom provision for E2L support may be very limited. Both teachers and community workers working with the Vietnamese referred to the tendency of class teachers to equate lack of English with lack of ability and to categorise able Vietnamese children as "slow" or "remedial" by overlooking the language difficulties which they faced. One language specialist we met, for example, related how a very bright Vietnamese pupil who had shown a definitive talent in science, had asked him to accompany him to a school parents evening where the science teacher had explained that the boy was in a low band because he "couldn't remember things" and this indicated that he lacked the intellect to cope. This science teacher had not realised that it might be difficult for the boy to remember what he might have only partly understood and that his actual knowledge of the subject might "outrun" his proficiency in English. He might thus not only appear slow but his English might seem more incoherent than if he were talking normally. This would inevitably lead to frustration on his part as well as further confirming the school's view of his abilities. (Such incidents serve to reinforce the view we took in our Language Chapter on the need for *all* teachers to have some understanding of E2L needs.) An extract from the booklet "Vietnamese Children in Derby",[3] indicating the more specific language problems which a Vietnamese child may experience in learning English, is attached as Annex A to this chapter.

Effects of Dispersal

8. Several of our witnesses felt that the official policy of dispersing the refugees around the country, especially to areas which had had little previous experience of catering for children for whom English

---

[3]"Vietnamese Children in Derby." Norman Fitchett *et al.* January 1981.

was not a first language, had clearly made the task of teaching English to Vietnamese children considerably harder. (It must be remembered of course that, under the present system, expenditure on special provision related to the needs of the Vietnamese community is not covered by Section 11). A small scale survey, carried out by the Ockenden Venture at the end of 1981, in their "zone" of the country which had few areas of multi-racial settlement, of the E2L provision made by schools for Vietnamese pupils, confirmed this view. For example the following extracts from the school responses to this survey illustrate not only the tendency to equate lack of English with lack of ability, but also the problems associated with some forms of E2L provision:

On the question of the provision made to meet the E2L needs of Vietnamese pupils:

"X attends eight sessions a week with a group of slow-learning English speaking children."

"Remedial English sessions with young children who are slow learners."

"Attached to small remedial group of children of her own age."

On the question of the effects of "inadequate" English on the children's progress:

"X's English is not inadequate, merely eccentric."

"Comprehension of the subtler shades of meaning inherent in some exam/test questions had led to lower scores in mathematics than are a true reflection of X's ability."

"(a hindrance) to some extent although it was masked at first by apparent understanding."

In relation to the desirability of withdrawal for E2L help:

"The withdrawal for extra English, whilst of very great value, does break the continuity of the lessons that are being missed."

"Both X and her sister Y show a (polite) aversion to be singled out from their class groups."
(NB this dislike of being "picked out" from their peers and of thus possibly "losing face" was of course noted also with Chinese pupils.)

Scale of E2L Need

9.   As a general guide to the proficiency in English of Vietnamese youngsters, the following table from the Home Office study indicates the scale of E2L need of secondary age youngsters:

724

Standard of English Assessments for Refugees aged 12 Plus

Standard English:		Spoken	Written	Comprehension
No practical proficiency		7.4	16.7	7.7
Survival proficiency		32.8	39.7	35.2
Limited social proficiency		39.4	29.8	34.9
Minimum working proficiency		15.5	10.0	16.1
Full working proficiency		4.4	3.6	5.6
Bilingual proficiency		0.6	0.3	0.5
Total	%	100.0	100.0	100.0
	n	3,521	3,205	3,474
No Information	n	907	1,223	954

Parental Attitudes to Education

10. As with many other ethnic minority parents, Vietnamese parents tend by tradition to leave the education of their children largely to the teachers and it can often prove difficult to bridge the gap between teachers and parents, not least in linguistic terms, and explain to parents the role which the school wants them to play. All the teachers we met however emphasised the wish of Vietnamese parents to see their children "succeed", although their understanding of what this would actually entail for example in terms of examination results, was often, understandably, somewhat hazy.

Teachers' Attitudes

11. Although some concerns were expressed to us about the effects which the trauma of leaving Vietnam and their arrival in this country had had on the children's behaviour—leaving them sometimes moody and depressed—it was generally agreed that Vietnamese pupils were well-motivated, lively and keen to learn. It was suggested however that, as with Chinese children, there was a risk that such positive "outward" signs might lead teachers to overlook any genuine educational problems which Vietnamese children might experience. As one language teacher we met put it to us:

"The neat and orderly presentation of work, the skills apparent in art and craft, fluency with formal computation and reading, a high level of motivation and concentration, may all be factors which mislead teachers into thinking that the children have no learning problems."

Achievement

12. In relation to achievement, the general feeling amongst the teachers we met was that once they had overcome their linguistic difficulties, Vietnamese children would be "high achievers". Some concern was however expressed about the kind of press reports which highlighted instances of Vietnamese youngsters having obtained examination qualifications after perhaps only 2 years in this country, and the extent to which this probably in fact represented considerable

under-achievement in relation to their true potential. As one teacher put it in his evidence to us:

"In view of the relatively short time of stay in UK it is difficult at present to make any objective assessments of the educational performance of Vietnamese children or make real comparisons with other groups, even if such comparisons are desirable. Pure speculation would foresee that most Vietnamese children would compare favourably with the "better" sub-continent Asian children, and thus be generally lower than the educational performance of indigenous children."

"Late Arrivals"

13. The particular problems of "late arrivals" to this country ie. youngsters arriving aged perhaps 14 or 15, who require probably 4 or 5 years education in order to do themselves justice but whose ages preclude this, was of great concern to our witnesses. We received some evidence concerning an initiative taken by the Save the Children fund to establish a separate residential school for some of these older Vietnamese youngsters. This school, which, we understand, closed with the end of major Government funding for the refugee programme, catered for 50 older Vietnamese pupils offering a specially devised curricular diet of intensive English teaching and with a concentration on maths and science. Provision was also made for teaching by Chinese and Vietnamese teachers in their mother tongues.

Vietnamese Teachers

14. A number of the representatives of the Vietnamese community whom we met referred to the contribution which they felt could be made to the education of Vietnamese children by teachers who were themselves of Vietnamese origin. In this connection, we were interested to learn of the work of one Institute of Higher Education which had run a one year part-time bridging course for teachers from Vietnam, whose qualifications were not accepted in the UK, designed to bring the participants up to a standard that would enable them to gain access to higher education and possibly in due course to enter teaching in this country. Understandably, a substantial part of the course was devoted to improving the fluency, accuracy and confidence of the students in English, and also developing their "cultural awareness" of Britain and the study skills required within higher education, some of which were unfamiliar to them. In a progress report on the course, the course tutor and her head of department offered the following reflections on the students' general progress, which we found particularly revealing in view of the comments which had already been made to us about the psychological pressures on "refugee" groups:

"An interesting progression in the individual tutorials has been

726

the student's willingness and desire to talk about personal problems. At the beginning of the course they still seemed to be suffering from the "grateful refugee" syndrome. They accepted everything passively, thanking people at every stage and seemed as though they could perceive themselves only as Boat People. . . The students now discuss quite freely many of their problems connected with family, health, finance and inter-student relationships. . . From the passive, accepting attitude exhibited by the students at the beginning of the course has developed a marked confidence. The students are now very ready to criticise and question material which is presented to them. It has been heartening to see them argue through their ideas and support them with logical reasoning. . . The students make greater efforts to control their own futures than they did at the beginning of the course. A few have made the conscious decision to pursue a career other than teaching and one has decided to seek employment rather than undertaking any further training course. Such decisions have been reached by individuals after much conscious thought and planning, and without seeking constant 'advice' from other sources."

Of the 12 students who attended this course, we understand that nine subsequently received offers of places in Institutions of Higher Education. In the event, only four actually took up these places—the reasons for the "drop outs" varying from domestic circumstances to other insecurities about being able to cope with the level of English required. Of the four, one was undertaking a BEd degree, two were considering mathematics/computers and one business studies. It remains to be seen whether those taking degrees will go on to Teacher Training. No further such courses were arranged by this Institution because of the lack of funding (previous funding having been provided by one of the voluntary bodies). Nevertheless it is perhaps indicative of the degree of interest amongst the Vietnamese community in such initiatives that some 50 Vietnamese refugees were said to have contacted the Institution after the commencement of this course saying that they had been teachers in Vietnam and would appreciate the opportunity of re-training in this country. Not only did this course demonstrate the existing talent in the teaching field which exists within the Vietnamese community, but also the will to pursue a career in teaching if appropriate means for this can be provided.

Racism

15.   It is regrettable that, despite the tremendous amount of public goodwill originally generated in this country by the plight of the "boat people", much of this seems now to have evaporated as the

refugees have been given public housing, often ahead of those on waiting lists, and have entered the jobs market, which has created some resentment to their presence. The local reactions in the areas where the refugees have been resettled, according to the volunteers working with them, were reported thus in the Home Office study report:

> *"The reaction of the people in the United Kingdom to the refugees has been one of initial goodwill followed by a gradual loss of interest. . . The very favourable media response to the Boat People in this country certainly helped in the initial stages of the programme but local reactions during resettlement have been mixed.*
>
> — *'Initially people were very helpful but now enthusiasm has waned and generally help is now left to a few faithful friends—usually voluntary language teachers.'*
>
> — *'There has certainly been a lot of hostility . . . they have been harassed mainly by groups of young people.'*
>
> — *'Four of my families live very close to me and a general feeling of concern has been expressed by people in this area that no more families be moved in . . .'."*

One of the language specialists whom we met who was teaching Vietnamese children agreed that the refugees had received "very mixed reactions" in the communities where they had settled. He mentioned particularly the resentment which had been felt by some of the volunteers who were supporting the Vietnamese families at these families purchasing hi-fi equipment—he felt there was a need for the majority community to appreciate how such possessions could be seen by a refugee community as tangible and important symbols of security. We ourselves have been particularly concerned to see increasing press reports, such as that attached as Annex B to this chapter, of Vietnamese families being the victims of racial harassment and attacks of the kind which have affected other ethnic minority communities. We feel such occurrences indicate the extent to which the Vietnamese are no longer seen as a special group, deserving of sympathy, and are now coming to be seen as "just more immigrants" to be regarded and treated as those from other ethnic minority groups.

16.   Before leaving the issue of racism, it may be worth noting that we also heard some evidence of antagonism amongst Vietnamese youngsters towards members of other ethnic minority groups, especially Asians, for example the head of one language centre whom we met, referring to his Vietnamese pupils, commented that:

"A few of them seem to have an unfortunate sense of superiority towards people from the Indian sub-continent."

Conclusion

17.   In many ways the experience of the Vietnamese community and the educational needs of Vietnamese children have much in common with the other ethnic minority communities whom we have considered, particularly for example in relation to their language needs and the increasing impact of racism on them. As noted at the beginning of this chapter, however, the very particular circumstances under which the Vietnamese community arrived in this country have meant that their level of self-determination has tended to be very limited and their lives have been very much influenced by external agencies, notably central Government and the voluntary bodies. The clearest manifestation of this external influence was of course the policy of dispersal. As we have explained, we are concerned at the underlying implications of such a policy which appears to be founded on essentially the same principles as were the original assimilationist policies adopted by central Government during the early years of large scale immigration to this country (discussed at some length in Chapter Four) which similarly involved "dispersing" ethnic minority children in order to "spread" a perceived "problem" and cause as little disruption to the majority community as possible. Just as we rejected the legacy of assimilationist thinking in putting forward our philosophy of "Education for All", we are concerned that the approach adopted to the resettlement of the Vietnamese refugees, whilst undoubtedly founded on good intentions, can be seen with hindsight, as misconceived, and as in many respects a manifestation of institutional racism. We strongly urge therefore that, if and when any other groups of refugees come to Britain in the future, central Government and particularly the Home Office will adopt a more enlightened and positive approach to their settlement, which takes greater account of the need for such communities to retain their cohesiveness and cultural identity and which does not exacerbate the already demanding educational challenges which the children from such groups might face.

729

ANNEX A

Language—an Extract from "Vietnamese Children in Derby"

The Vietnamese Alphabet

The original native writing system of Vietnamese was a modification of Chinese characters, and was the sole writing system for the Vietnamese between the 13th and 17th Centuries. In the 17th Century, a Portuguese priest, Alexandre de Rhodes, and other Europeans and Vietnamese, developed a new writing system to further their evangelical work. This writing system was a Roman alphabet modified with diacritics so that it could represent the sounds of Vietnamese, for which there were no Roman symbols. The two writing systems—the Chinese-based and the Roman-based—were used side-by-side for some time, although by different segments of Vietnamese society. Gradually, however, the Roman-based alphabet replaced the Chinese-based writing system, so that today it is the only writing system in general use.

The Vietnamese alphabet is phonetic. There is usually one letter or combination of letters per sound, and only one. The one-sound-one-symbol correspondence sometimes breaks down between one regional dialect and another. Perhaps these differences tend to be academic rather than inhibiting, but it does indicate that some Vietnamese children may differ in their ability to reproduce English sounds.

Pronunciation

Pronunciation of Vietnamese words varies slightly from speaker to speaker depending where in Vietnam the speaker comes from. There are three major dialects—Northern, Central and Southern. Whilst these dialects differ, sometimes very markedly, a speaker of one of them has no great difficulty understanding or communicating with a speaker of another.

The most interesting and difficult to understand aspect of Vietnamese is its tones. Vietnamese, like Chinese, is a tonal language. Every word has a particular "tone" always associated with it, and if a speaker does not use the correct tone for a word, he either mispronounces the word, or pronounces an entirely different word.

English has "tones", but they are associated with sentences rather than words. We call these "intonation patterns", eg consider the difference in meaning between "Now?" and "Now!", or between, "He's a doctor?" and "He's a doctor." There are five tones in the Southern dialect, each of these being represented by a mark (a diacritic) over one of the vowels or syllables, eg:

> The word "ban" spoken with a mid-level tone means "committee": the same word "ban" this time with a diacritic indicating a high-rising tone means "sell"; "ban" with a low-falling tone means "table": "ban" with a mid-rising tone means "copy" and, finally, "ban" with a low-rising tone means "friend".

No doubt, as in English, there are certain contextual clues which will indicate the meaning intended, and it would certainly be an advantage to be able to listen to a native speaker in order to hear the difference between (say) a "low-falling" and a "low-rising" tone.

Vietnamese is also a monosyllabic language—that is, all words consist of only one syllable. Vowels can occur together, but consonants cannot. There are no consonantal clusters in Vietnamese and therefore children have great difficulty in pronouncing English words like "desks", "picture", "crisps" and "skipping".

730

As most Vietnamese children speak either Cantonese, Vietnamese (with regional variations) and Mandarin, they tend to identify English sounds with the sounds with which they are familiar—with confusing and frustrating results.

Here is a table of common difficulties . . .

- ★ l, n and r are confused (hence led for red, can for car).
- ★ final l or ll pronounced as w (hence baw for ball).
- ★ final consonants p, t, k and d are often formed but not sounded.

    (In fact experience has shown that whilst there are considerable pronunciation difficulties with identifying vowel sounds, a major problem has been to teach the children to articulate audibly final consonants. There is a strong tendency to "clip" word endings . . . eg re for red, hou for house, bi for big, gree for green etc . . .).

- ★ s, sh and z are confused (Cantonese for example has no sh or z).
- ★ th is pronounced d (common in Asian sub-continent children) or v.
- ★ the (hard th) unknown in Chinese or Vietnamese.
- ★ f is confused with v or p.
- ★ soft g (as in gentle) does not exist in Vietnamese.
- ★ p is confused with f.
- ★ b is confused with p.
- ★ t as a final consonant sounds like k.
- ★ d (initial) often pronounced as y or z.
- ★ k is always identical with c.
- ★ short vowels are usually easily learned and reproduced, but the children find that long vowels are difficult to distinguish and pronouce . . . eg . . . ee for i and ar for a.

Such difficulties call for very patient listening by the teacher, careful identification of the real problem, some skill in applying basic speech-therapy remediation and consistent and regular use of oral drills and phonic exercises.

731

ANNEX B

Article taken from "The Times"—12/3/82

"Problem Estate is 'Picking on' its Boat People

Vietnamese refugee families in an inner London tower-block estate are being attacked and abused and singled out as scapegoats for the estate's difficulties, it was said yesterday.

Community workers, police and tenants' representatives from the Pepys Estate, in the derelict Deptford dockland, listed a series of attacks on former "boat people" that included muggings, beatings-up, stone-throwing and setting fire to a girl's hair. The refugee families, 36 out of 1,500, are said to be living in a state of siege.

According to Mr Quang Nguyen, a spokesman and interpreter for the boat people, they rarely complain to the police because they are afraid of reprisals.

The British Refugee Council said that the position on the Pepys Estate, although worse than most, was not untypical.

Vietnamese on the estate were brought together yesterday by the Lewisham Council for Community Relations to give their accounts of attacks. The Council said they launched their investigations after a local headmaster asked them why a Vietnamese girl, aged nine, cried all day at school.

Mr Martin Rabstein, a council officer, said: 'We found out that she and her family had been forced into living in one room of their flat because the rest of it was under siege'.

Other examples include a woman aged 50 being beaten up by three teenagers after her hair was deliberately trapped in the lift doors; a mother aged 30 and two small children having to run a gauntlet of sticks and stones; and a man aged 32 who had to crawl back to his flat after being attacked from behind, kicked on the ground and robbed by a gang of about ten teenagers. He has still not fully recovered his sight.

The Pepys Estate has long been plagued by vandalism, high crime rates and tenant discontent, resulting in a high turnover and vacancies. It is now the subject of a 'safe neighbourhood' project run by the National Association for the Care and Resettlement of Offenders with a grant from the Greater London Council.

Mr Nicholas Taylor, Chairman of Lewisham housing committee and a resident on the estate, described security there as an 'absolute disaster'. He added: 'In that situation people look for a scapegoat and the easiest scapegoats are people who cannot easily communicate with others.'

Mr Robert Heagren, Chairman of the Pepys tenants' association, said many residents had resented the allocation of flats to the refugees instead of to British people."

CHAPTER 15

The Educational needs of "Liverpool Blacks"

1. We have included "Liverpool Blacks" in our report for two reasons. Firstly, this group has probably, we believe, fared worse than any other we have described, with the exception of travellers, in its educational and career achievements, and therefore has a particularly strong claim to the consideration and positive action which we hope will arise out of our findings. Secondly, and paradoxically, this group appears to be more closely assimilated, with the "majority" by ancestry, language, culture, and length of residence than any of the others we have looked at. Its experiences therefore lead us to ask new questions, both about this particular group itself and about many of the accepted assumptions concerning ethnicity.

Background

Definition of Liverpool Blacks

2. There is a long-established community in Liverpool of African, mixed African and English, or African and Liverpool-Irish-descent, with some of Asian descent as well. The mixed community characteristic of the modern city grew from the end of the nineteenth century onwards, mainly through the settlement of African seamen. By the late 1940s the ethnic minority population of Liverpool was recorded as coming mainly from West Africa and the West Indies. It it this group of long-established families that we call "Liverpool Blacks". Many are blood relations of Liverpool "whites" and have "black" grandparents and great-greatparents born in Liverpool; they speak "scouse" with a vocabulary, grammar and intonation identical with those of "white" Liverpudlians, and in short there is nothing but their colour and hapless situation to distinguish them from other long-established residents. However, there has been a tendency to lump them together with relatively recent "immigrants", in the strict sense of the word, who have been born abroad, especially those who are non white. Characteristic of "white" Liverpudlian comments are: "I don't know which are West Indians. They're just white or coloured" or "We don't have immigrants here, just coloured." People speaking of "Liverpool Blacks" sometimes mean only the long-established group and sometimes, a larger and more varied set of people. This confusion makes it difficult to give an accurate estimate of the size of the Liverpool Black population. We have received estimates varying from 20,000 to 45,000. It has been estimated by Merseyside Community Relations Council that roughly half the

racial minority population of the city are Liverpool Blacks under the terms of our broad definition.

Location of Group

3.   The great majority of Liverpool Blacks live in Liverpool 8, near the city centre. The Anglican and Roman Catholic cathedrals are both situated here as is the University. It includes broad and beautiful streets, once the place of handsome residences which have now "gone to seed": fine houses stand empty, their facades deteriorating. The most notable landmark to be burnt down in the 1981 disturbances was the Rialto, which had once been a dance-hall that refused admission to "coloureds" and had later been transformed into a factory that did not employ them. Liverpool 8 also houses a "white" population, largely Irish, and as a whole is marked by poverty and lack of opportunity.

4.   It was suggested in evidence to us that:

"Liverpool in the 1980s is a sort of model of what British cities in general may be like in the early 2000s, when the majority of 'immigrants' will not be immigrants at all but British-born."

The city was once very prosperous, but its prosperity, based initially on slavery and sugar, then on shipping and colonial trade, has been declining throughout the present century. The silent docks, waste factory sites and decaying warehouses are a graphic picture of the end of the era of Britain's industrial and commercial dominance; the recession arrived in Liverpool long before it hit most of the country, and many witnesses suggested that other major cities would look just like it in another 20 years' time. Unemployment is the overriding problem. There are men in their 40s in Liverpool who have never had a job, and never expect to. On a visit in 1982, one of our members asked a primary school Head how many of the children's parents were unemployed, and received in reply a look of surprise and the answer: "Oh, there's not many here *working*." It was clear from the secondary schools visited that school leavers face grave difficulty in obtaining any employment.

5.   Appalling though the situation is for all Liverpudlians, it is markedly worse for the ethnic minorities than for "whites", and has been so throughout living memory. In the 1930s, a group of "white" professionals calling themselves the Association for the Welfare of Half-Caste Children, reconstituted in 1937 as the Liverpool Association for the Welfare of Coloured People, appointed a research worker to investigate a range of problems, including employment. Of 119 firms approached, 45 said they would not employ coloured people, and 63 did not reply. (The Association thought the only way to deal with this situation was to stop the settlement of colonial

seamen in Liverpool and to consider returning African British subjects to their native countries.)

Education

6. The 1973 Report of the Select Committee on Race Relations and Immigration on education[1] criticised Liverpool's education system as it found that the Black community was disadvantaged both inside and outside school. Liverpool was criticised for its inability to provide a lead to other LEAs with substantial ethnic minority populations. In the words of the Select Committee's report:

"Liverpool . . . left us with a profound sense of uneasiness."

The Report of the 1980/1981 Home Affairs Committee[2] expressed similar concerns about the City's educational provision and practice.

7. In our visits to various primary and secondary schools in Liverpool 8, we were struck by the teachers' perception of the uncertainty facing their schools. The Heads and their senior colleagues were serving in "acting" capacities whilst the LEA considered various re-organisation options. Despite individual commitment by a number of teachers, the lack of clear policy by the Authority seemed to leave teachers without a sense of direction. It is interesting that the HMI Report in March 1982[3] acknowledged that teachers, especially in primary schools, were trying to establish caring environments even though standards of pupil achievement were not high:

"HMI have seen work that is soundly prepared and shows the dedication of the teachers but it is often limited in range and its expectations of pupils . . . the low attainments noted appear, in some measure, to be a result of low expectations on the part of teachers, parents and the pupils themselves."

In addition to a general failure in educational performance, HMI also noted considerable social aggression between pupils, discipline problems, truancy and cynicism among pupils about examination courses and MSC opportunities. The Report also criticised the LEA for mismanagement, lack of clear guidelines for schools, instability of staffing and low teacher morale, and narrow curriculum policies with few initiatives and commented on:

". . . the apparent inability of elected members to agree on, or

---

[1]"Education." Report of the Select Committee on Race Relations and Immigration. July 1973. HMSO. HC 405. I.
[2]"Racial Disadvantage." Fifth Report from the Home Affairs Committee. July 1981. HMSO. HC 424. I.
[3]"Educational Provision by Liverpool Education Authority in the Toxteth Area." HM Inspectorate. March 1982:

> *pursue any, positive responses to many of the major problems*
> *... leading to feelings of insecurity and uncertainty in every*
> *institution and area of the education service."*

8.   Difficulties have been exacerbated by rapidly falling school rolls and the growing number of small secondary schools has had serious consequences for the curriculum. In the smallest schools some subjects, such as Music and some Modern Languages, have been phased out and others are threatened. Some schools have only one teacher to a department, and some subjects are being taught at secondary level by non-specialists. Many witnesses told the Committee that staff morale was very low in both primary and secondary schools. These difficulties affect all the children in the area but Liverpool Blacks were even worse off than other young people in Liverpool 8. HMI investigated the number of Liverpool 8 students on certain courses in the Further Education colleges nearest to Toxteth. On two full-time catering courses and one hairdressing course, taking about 200 students altogether, teaching staff estimated that only three or four students were "black". The Race Relations Sub-Committee of the Liverpool Teachers' Association produced a pamphlet[4], some months before the disturbances of July 1981, saying it was:

> *"an undisputed fact ... that black children in this city are under-*
> *achieving in education ... "*

What LEA provision there was related to ethnic minorities, the document claimed, was concentrated on the English language needs of recent immigrants.

9.   HMI warned, in their Report, that further cuts in financial and other resources would damage staff morale and effectiveness, both of which were already under strain. They stressed, and our visits confirmed, that some teachers are "resilient and resourceful", and working hard under difficult conditions, including unsuitable buildings and a general atmosphere of city decline, and alienation among many pupils and parents. They found that in one comprehensive school serving the area only 30 per cent of the intake had a reading age of ten or more on entry. Within this general picture of under-achievement by "black" and "white" alike in the area, it was apparent from the written and oral evidence submitted to us that the Liverpool Black children were particularly low in attainment: partly because of the negative attitude towards them of some teachers, and, despite the dedication of other teachers, partly because of their own and their parents' sense of alienation, in a social structure that offers them no hope for the future.

---

[4]"Before the Fire." Liverpool Teachers' Association. 1981.

10.   Recently, some reorganisation of secondary education has scattered some of the Liverpool Black children into new, mainly "white" catchment areas, but not always with happy results. On one of our visits, a girl of 15 described to us how she had been the only "Black" girl in a school and had not liked it because the others "bossed her about". When asked about this, she replied that she had had to go to hospital, once with a broken arm and once with a broken nose. She, and the other pupils present, found it unremarkable, and when the incident was later mentioned at a meeting of teachers and community workers they pointed out that Liverpool schools had always been like that for Liverpool Blacks. Those Liverpool Blacks who find employment are almost all in low-grade jobs, unlike other ethnic minority groups we have considered where there is generally more variety in the spectrum of employment. Expectations too are very low: to be a van-boy, a labourer, a shop assistant, clerical worker or machinist are ambitions; indeed to hope to get a job at all, of any sort, is "flying high". There are few who contemplate the possibility of higher education, and there is a realistic cynicism even about "O" levels: "You just lose time." It is very rare indeed for a Liverpool Black youngster to proceed to University; two who had done so were named at meetings we attended. The University, sited in Liverpool 8, has some black students but not from the locality: they come from overseas or other parts of Britain. Its facilities are a constant reminder of the contrast between what locals can expect and what people from elsewhere receive.

11.   Visiting Liverpool 8 and talking with witnesses there, the observer receives a very vivid impression of how strongly the situation of the Liverpool Black minority is affected by the special character of Merseyside itself. The established social and political structures perpetuate old practices and attitudes formed at different periods of history. The "blacks" are simply left out of the pattern. For example, large firms, when they recruit new employees tend to advertise only within the firm enabling only relatives and friends of existing employees to apply. In cases where there are no "black" employees already, racial inequality is thus perpetuated. A voluntary agency, South Liverpool Personnel, which tries to help young "blacks" get jobs, said in evidence to us:

> *"Local employers claimed there was no discrimination—it was simply that no blacks were employed... Liverpool was a commuter city: all the workers in the city centre travelled in from outlying white areas. Only 5 black people were employed on the buses and there were virtually no blacks in the city centre stores ... The council was a particularly bad employer."*

Liverpool Blacks do not only find it difficult to get work in the city centre: they risk insult or abuse in going there at all, and so their invisibility in the City's social life and power structure has become institutionalised. Until recent years, there was virtually no "Black" involvement in any of the political parties locally.

Conclusion

12. Our consideration of the "Liverpool Black" community highlights the important effect *local* factors can have on the experience and achievement of a particular ethnic minority community. It also illustrates how, despite concern having been expressed by a number of reports and committees over a period of ten years and more about the extreme degree of the problems facing this community, little real progress has yet been made to bring about the necessary changes in education and beyond. As the Home Affairs Committee concluded, in their 1981 Report:

> *"Racial disadvantage in Liverpool is in a sense the most disturbing case of racial disadvantage in the United Kingdom, because there can be no question of cultural problems of newness of language, and it offers a grim warning to all of Britain's cities that racial disadvantage cannot be expected to disappear by natural causes. The Liverpool Black Organisation warned the Sub-Committee, 'what you see in Liverpool is a sign of things to come'. We echo that warning."*

CHAPTER 16

The Educational Needs of Travellers'[1] Children

An Ethnic Minority Group?

1. Many people may be surprised to find not only that we have devoted a chapter of our report to considering the educational needs of children from travelling families, but also that we regard the travelling community as an ethnic minority group at all. There were in fact several factors which led us to decide that this group lay within our terms of reference and that its situation justified consideration. Firstly, from the considerable amount of evidence which we received from traveller organisations and from people working with this community, it was clear that many travellers regarded themselves as an ethnic minority group and were anxious for this Committee to consider their situation—as one group put it in their evidence to us:

> *"Unless your Committee is prepared to consider them (travellers' children), we feel that there is a very real danger that they will slip through the net of existing provision."*

Also, if an ethnic minority group can be seen, in the simplest terms, as an identifiable group of people sharing particular "cultural" characteristics and a way of life which differs markedly from that of the majority community, the travelling community meets these criteria, even without reference to their racial origins—the Gypsies having originated in India and other travellers coming from Scotland and Ireland—and the existence, albeit decreasingly, of their own distinct languages—Romany and Shelta or Gammon. In many ways, in view of the extreme prejudice and hostility they face, Gypsies in particular, can, as one group put it to us in their evidence, be seen as:

> *". . . a group of immigrants still not fully accepted by their host countries after four or five hundred years of occupation."*

A final deciding factor in determing that we should look at the situation of Gypsies and other travellers was the Commission for

---

[1] In this chapter we use the term "traveller" in the sense in which the DES has defined it:

"The term 'traveller' has come to include a number of different groups each with distinctive life-styles and traditions. Common to all is their nomadic life although there are great differences in the amount and range of travelling between groups. Gypsies form the largest group in the traveller community. Other travellers are Irish or Scottish tinkers who have travelled in this country for many years and often still have close links with their country of origin. A third group are the children of fairground and circus families."

(From Notes to Editors in DES Press Notice 191/83).

Racial Equality's statement, in September 1981,[2] that, in their view, Gypsies:

> "... constitute an ethnic minority group and as such are protected against discrimination under the Race Relations Act 1976."

2.   From the findings of our own work, we are convinced that our decision to consider this community was correct, since we have been greatly concerned at the situation of travellers' children, whom the Plowden Report[3] described, in 1967, as:

> "... probably the most severely deprived children in the country."

Whereas, with the other groups of children whom we have considered, we have been chiefly concerned with their needs *within* schools, many of the particular educational needs of travellers' children arise because of difficulties in gaining access to the education system at all. In many respects the situation in which travellers' children find themselves also illustrates to an extreme degree the experience of prejudice and alienation which faces many other ethnic minority children. An appreciation of the educational needs of travellers' children requires some understanding of the complex background factors which impinge on this community as a whole and we therefore begin this chapter by setting the overall context, before going on to consider the educational situation.

Background

Size of the
Community

3.   Estimates of the size of the travelling community are notoriously unreliable and have ranged as high as 50–60,000. Data[4] from the Department of the Environment (DOE), based on their twice-yearly caravan counts,[5] indicate a current total population of approximately 30,000 Gypsies, including up to 12,500 children, out of an estimated world population of perhaps eight million. Some travellers' organisations however regard the DOE figures as a considerable underestimate. Some travelling families lead fully nomadic lives and some travel on a seasonal basis, while others are more or less settled in one place but do not see themselves as having given up the travelling way of life. Even "travellers" who now live in houses—who would not be included in estimates of the size of the travelling community—still

---

[2]"Report of Four Formal Investigations into alleged pressure to discriminate by Brymbo Community Council Councillor K Rogers, Mrs I Stapley, Mrs B Greenaway." CRE. September 1981.
[3]"Children and Their Primary Schools." HMSO. 1967.
[4]DOE Press Notice. 19 October 1982.
[5]In July 1978, the Department of the Environment introduced regular twice-yearly counts of Gypsies and their caravans in England in order to assess the progress made by local authorities in fulfilling their statutory duties under Part II of the Caravan Sites Act 1968 whereby they should provide adequate accommodation for the Gypsies in or resorting to their area. The statistics are provided by District Councils.

retain some very distinctive characteristics and are quite likely to return to the "road" again. About half of the travelling families in England and Wales live on unauthorised and illegal sites because of the severe shortage of official camp sites. This means that, in addition to living, in the majority of instances, in the very deprived circumstances which are inevitable without access to normal services, these families are also under constant threat of eviction and of being moved on by local authorities.

Site Provision 4. The issue of camp site provision was raised time and time again with us as being a crucial factor in considering the education of travellers' children. As one Gypsy representative put it:

"You can't educate a person until you find them a place to live."

The 1968 Caravan Sites Act gave county, county borough and London borough councils a duty to provide caravan sites for Gypsies "residing in or resorting to" their areas. Unfortunately the response to this move was poor and some authorities appear to have set out to reduce, by harassment, the number of travellers in their areas, for whom they might have to make provision rather than seeking to increase site provision. As a result of the 1977 Cripps Report,[6] provision was made for 100 per cent exchequer grant to be made available for the capital costs of site provision and this led to some improvement. We understand however that the 100 per cent grants are now incorporated within "block" allocations for environmental projects and the pace of progress has slowed accordingly. The provision of sites is monitored by the Gypsy Sites Branch of the DOE and according to the most recent survey available to us (January 1983) there were 3,910 caravans on authorised sites, 1,448 caravans on private authorised sites and 3,940 caravans on unauthorised sites—thus only about half of travelling families are settled on official permanent sites.

"Designation" 5. The 1968 Act empowered a Minister to "designate" an authority on application, if adequate provision has been made for the accommodation of travellers in that area. Designation makes it an offence for travellers to place their trailers anywhere in the area other than on an official site and enables the authority to obtain an eviction order from a Magistrates' Court with only 48 hours notice. It was envisaged by the Cripps Report that all designations should be reviewed at least every five years and could be withdrawn. The Report had also seen designation as only one aspect of an overall package of measures which required all authorities to prepare time-related programmes for providing sufficient camp sites and allowed

---

[6]"Accommodation for Gypsies." HMSO. April 1977.

the Secretary of State to use powers of direction where an authority was failing to put forward such a programme. To date over 40 authorities have received designation, some having received it as long ago as 1972. According to the DOE representative whom we met, however, no designation order has ever been reviewed as the DOE saw "no particular need to do so", and no order has ever been revoked. The DOE does not apparently put pressure on authorities to put forward programmes for action and relies on "persuasion" rather than direction. The DOE has in the past employed a national Gypsy Liaison Officer to encourage authorities to provide sites but this post is not currently filled. The DOE stated in its written evidence to us that it:

". . . has not been informed of any example where designation has caused increased hardship to Gypsies occupying unauthorised sites with a designated area."

Much of the evidence we received from the various organisations in this field however claimed that designation had led to an increase in harassment of travelling families and one group spoke of it as running contrary to basic human rights and to the concept of freedom of movement.

6.   Whilst it is not for this Committee to comment in detail on camp site provision, much of what we have heard from representatives of the travelling community seems to cast doubts on the concept of designation and to point to the need for its use by authorities to be far more closely monitored than at present by the DOE. As instances of the type of situation which arises and which should clearly be reviewed:

i.   one authority, which has large numbers of travellers, received designation in 1972 with the provision of one official site. This site is now closed "temporarily for rebuilding" but the designation still applies;

ii.   another authority has designation with *15* pitches on *6* authorised sites and *34* unauthorised encampments.

In neither of these cases would the authorities appear to be making the "adequate provision" required to justify designation.

7.   We would like to see greater efforts being made by central Government to encourage local authorities to establish more official sites and to set up time-related programmes of action, possibly through re-establishment of the Gypsy Liaison Officer post at the DOE. In particular we hope that the travelling community can be

more closely involved in the planning of sites and the provision of appropriate facilities. In addition to more permanent official sites there is also a need for more transit and seasonal sites. It is important to remember however that the facilities and position of official sites often leave much to be desired. Because of political pressures and protests from house dwellers, these sites tend to be established on totally undesirable land for example under motorways or in marshland, well away from other settlement and thus often nowhere near local schools. Whilst we understand the concern of local people about having camp sites placed near them, we also deplore the apparent view of some authorities that "anywhere will do". If placed in such bad conditions, travellers are hardly likely to maintain their sites well and vandalism is to some extent understandable. Undoubtedly if you are living, as many travellers have to, next to a refuse tip or a sewage works, this will show you how society sees you and will only serve to alienate you further from everything it has to offer. One official site we visited in a rural area was in a very deep hollow in the middle of woodland where water collected, the facilities appeared to be completely inadequate and the children, none of whom were attending school, were living in very disadvantaged circumstances indeed. We would be surprised if the circumstances we found there conformed to the advice given in the DOE's "Gypsy Sites Design Guide",[7] and if they did, perhaps this guide itself may need to be reviewed.

Education
8.   While nearly half the travelling population are forced to lead an unstable and unsettled existence on illegal encampments because of the shortage of official sites it is difficult to discuss educational provision for their children. (It is important to recognise however that, as we point out below, by no means all the educational problems of travellers' children would be solved were all travellers to be accommodated on official sites.) One Gypsy representative who was himself illegally camped described vividly to us the need for parents to have security and peace of mind before they could be expected to contemplate sending their children to school. As things were now, there was a very real possibility that a family could be evicted and moved on, possibly over the County boundary, during the day and their child could return home from school to find their trailer gone and no sign of his or her family.

School Attendance
9.   It is difficult to establish precisely how many travellers' children actually attend school. The Plowden Report claimed that less than 10 per cent attended school and a Schools Council study[8] has esti-

---

[7]Gypsy Sites Design Guide. DOE. 1979.
[8]"Education of Travelling Children." C. Reiss. Macmillan. 1975.

mated that between 10 per cent and 25 per cent attended school in 1969–70 but only one third of these had attended on a regular basis and by far the majority of these were of primary age. This widespread non-attendance at school is unique to travellers' children and lies at the heart of their plight. Even where these children are living on an official site and are attending school however, numerous difficulties can arise in meeting their particular educational needs.

Parental Attitudes

10.   In the eyes of most travellers, education is seen solely in terms of literacy and numeracy and the broader concept of education, especially at secondary level, is seen as irrelevant and unnecessary. Many of the travellers have themselves received little or no formal "education", indeed some only learnt to read while on National Service, but as one Gypsy representative put it:

> *"What they lack in education they make up for in common sense."*

The travelling way of life is changing however and there is a growing appreciation amongst parents that, with more and more rules and regulations, for example the need to cope with the taxing of vehicles and tachographs in lorries, education—or at least the ability to read and write—is now crucial to running a business and earning a living.

Non-Attendance

11.   The reasons why traveller parents are reluctant to send their children to school are many and varied. We have already mentioned the particular problems which face a family which is illegally encamped and the understandable tendency to reject a society which so clearly rejects you. Also, as the HMI discussion document on travellers' education[9] explained:

> *"The ambivalence of many traveller parents towards formal education is frequently linked with their own unhappy, unsuccessful and intermittent experiences of school. It is also the case that traveller parents are fearful that their children's presence in school may confirm in others prejudicial cultural stereotypes. Academic backwardness as a result of a previous lack of schooling and unusual behaviour are thought by many parents to be images that would be interpreted in negative terms by schools."*

On a more specific level, many travellers say that they are unable to dress their children well enough to send them to school and that they do not wish them to be "shown up" in this way. Similarly they claim that their children will be ridiculed and subjected to taunting and abuse by the other children, or even by teachers, because of the general hostility towards travellers. Parents also claim to be unwilling

---

[9]"The Education of Travellers' Children." DES. 1983.

to allow their children to walk to school (the family's lorry is of course used for business), if no transport is provided. It sometimes appeared to us however that the latter argument was used as an excuse to avoid sending children to school rather than always a genuine reason. On one site we visited for example this excuse was used by some families while children from another family were in fact walking to school. Clearly it is difficult to contemplate providing transport to school for travelling children in circumstances where it is not available to children in rural areas who may live further away from the school. (The cost of special transport for travelling children is however fully poolable from the "no-area pool"—see paragraph 13 below.) Part of the explanation for the non-attendance of travellers' children at school also undoubtedly lies with the unwillingness of schools to accept them, which may mean that it requires a considerable degree of persistence and understanding of the system for parents to overcome the hurdles which may be placed in the way of their child's admission to school. Many of the problems which arise over parents sending their children to school may be avoided by provision being made on the site. This may be seen by parents as more acceptable since the children do not have to leave the site and do not have to mix with other children. We discuss below however the issues and problems which arise in relation to such on-site provision.

Expectations 12. If their children do go to school, traveller parents tend to expect very rapid results, for example learning to read in a few weeks. When this does not happen they may lose interest in school as a "waste of time" and simply withdraw their children. Traveller children tend to mature faster than other children and may be seen as having a role to play in the family very early on, for example, as one Gypsy representative put it to us, the boys are "little men at eight" and may be expected to help their father in his work then and the girls may be expected to help their mother to look after younger brothers and sisters. Traveller children may be absent from school for many reasons—if there is an illness or a bereavement in the family all the children may be kept at home.

LEA 13. Under the 1944 Education Act, travelling children aged 6 or **Responsibilities** over are required to fulfil only 50 per cent of possible attendances ie. 200 half-day attendances over a 12 month period[10]. The 1980

---

[10] Section 39(3) of the 1944 Education Act states that:

"... *if the parent proves that he is engaged in any trade or business of such a nature as to require him to travel from place to place and that the child has attended at a school at which he was a registered pupil as regularly as the nature of the trade or business of the parent permits, the parent shall be acquitted (of any offence against the requirement for full school attendance): Provided that, in the case of a child who has attained the age of six years, the parent shall not be entitled to be acquitted under this subsection unless he proves that the child has made at least two hundred attendances during the period of twelve months ending with the date on which the proceedings were instituted.*"

745

Education Act unequivocally places a duty on LEAs to ensure that appropriate full-time education is provided for all children residing in their area, whether permanently or temporarily and regardless of the legal status of the camp site where they live. LEA expenditure on provision for travellers' children can be claimed from the "no-area pool" on the following basis:

i.   expenditure on tuition in normal classes may be charged at the full appropriate primary or secondary IAPC rate in proportion to the weeks of their actual attendance;

ii.   expenditure on special provision (eg special units or classes or peripatetic teachers) may be charged at 75 per cent of the recurrent costs; and

iii.   other education expenditure (eg special transport) may be pooled in full.

Unfortunately the pooling arrangements for traveller's children do not appear to be fully understood by some local authority officials and authorities may not therefore be aware of the provision which is covered.

14. Many traveller organisations believe that some LEAs are failing to fulfil their responsibilities in relation to travellers' education and that travellers' children are being intentionally deprived of their right to education. The travelling community take the view that authorities are unwilling to run the risk of provoking hostility from the settled community by allowing travellers' children into schools and that many schools are in any case reluctant to receive these children because of the problems they may present. It was pointed out to us that a local authority which may be seeking to evict a family from an illegal site is unlikely to wish to "complicate" matters by admitting the children from that family into school which may delay the eviction procedure. Although no definite figures are available, very few prosecutions are made by authorities over non-attenance at school and it is not known how many of these are of traveller parents, despite the fact that so many travellers' children clearly do not attend school. The DES acknowledged in evidence to us that some LEAs might not be fulfilling their responsibilities in seeking to ensure that travellers' children attended school. Because of the community's inherent mobility it was pointed out however that it could be difficult for an Education Welfare Officer (EWO) to trace a child's previous educational experience and thus to *prove* that the attendance requirement had not been met and so prosecutions were unlikely. Also many LEAs and EWOs took the view that taking legal proceedings against traveller parents was counterproductive since it simply served to alienate them further from society.

LEA Policies 15. Three broad approaches are adopted by LEAs to providing education for travellers' children:

— no special provision or support—simply expecting them to attend normal schools;

— special support within normal schools or in special units on the school site; and

— special provision in units, usually mobile, on camp sites.

"Open Door" Policy The first of these—often referred to as the "open door" policy—which places all the responsibility for a child attending school on the shoulders of the parent, seems to us to be particularly insensitive in view of the reluctance of many traveller parents to send their children to school and may simply encourage and condone non-attendance, especially if no attempts are made to ensure that the children do attend. As the HMI discussion document put it:

> *"The schools are there, so the policy goes, let the travellers use them; that is if they remain long enough, are bold enough, confident enough, keen enough and persistent enough to seek and gain admission. It is not surprising that in these circumstances many fall at these hurdles, especially if there is an unacknowledged discrimination between those on official and those on unauthorised sites."*

We believe that authorities have a responsibility to reach out to the travelling community to overcome the mistrust and suspicion which understandably exists, and to seek to explain the value and purpose of education. It is in any case in our view unreasonable of authorities to expect a child from a travelling family necessarily to be able to manage in a normal school without particular help and also to expect the school to be able to cope with that child with no additional support or advice.

On-Site Provision 16. Similarly we feel that those authorities which only make provision through mobile units on camp sites, despite the quite remarkable work being done in some of these units (see paragraph 22 below), may also be "abdicating" some of their responsibilities in respect of travellers' children. Obviously, in view of their reluctance to send their children to school, many traveller parents, if offered on-site provision, will consider this to be sufficient. There is no way however in which such a unit can offer a full and balanced curriculum since its resources are limited and the teachers are often dealing with children of widely varying ages and abilities. A mobile unit is unlikely to call at a particular site every day or for a full day—in one case we came across, for example, a unit was calling at a particular site for one hour every 10–14 days and the travellers' children concerned were therefore receiving only periodic teaching on an irregular basis. Where a unit is on a site the lessons are in any case, as we ourselves saw on our visits, liable to be interrupted by parents withdrawing children for meals or errands, and the children may be easily distracted by activities outside. In this situation there are clearly no opportunities for travellers' children to mix with other children and so their isolation from mainstream society is accentuated. Such mobile units were criticised in very strong terms to us by one of the Gypsy organisations as providing sub-standard education and as being designed solely with the purpose of keeping travelling children out of normal schools—as they put it: "segregation on cultural grounds". We ourselves would seriously question the legal position, in the light of the provisions of the 1944 Education Act, of LEAs which, apparently with the knowledge of the DES, provide units offering periodic part time attendance as an alternative to statutory attendance at school. For example, we ourselves visited one such unit which was serving a camp site in an urban area immediately adjacent to a council housing estate and clearly within walking distance of existing schools and where the children appeared to be relatively settled and there seemed little justification for such "special provision" in these circumstances. We would accept however, that on-site provision may have a role to play as part of a comprehensive strategy for travellers' education as a "bridge" into school—as the HMI document put it:

"... an essential first step along the road to normal schooling."

or in relation to "highly mobile" families—most especially fairground and circus children.[11]

Provision Within Schools

17. The other main approach adopted by LEAs to travellers' education is to make provision for travelling children within normal schools but to employ some teachers on a peripatetic basis with responsibility for their needs who can withdraw groups of children for remedial work and can advise the schools and teachers on particular problems. We considered instances of this approach being adopted in two parts of the country. In both cases mobile classrooms were available which could be placed on a school site for withdrawal groups although in areas with falling rolls surplus classroom space within school premises is now becoming available. In one of these areas the specialist team consisted of five peripatetic teachers and one EWO working under the supervision of the multi-ethnic inspectorate.

[11]We were not able ourselves to consider the situation of fairground and circus children. However as an indication of their particular needs and the measures which have been taken to meet them, we reproduce, as an Annex to this chapter, the section relating to their situation taken from the recent HMI document.

The team's function was to make contact with traveller parents and to ease the admission of the children into schools. The teachers assisted schools by teaching travellers' children in small groups prior to integration into normal classes, joining class teachers during normal lessons once the child had been integrated and sometimes continuing to provide special help in withdrawal groups. The EWO acted as a link between the schools and families but all the teachers visited sites some of the time to provide "emergency education" to children whose transit time was too short to bring them into schools. We also considered a regional scheme for travellers' education involving 11 shire counties and metropolitan districts and covering an area of some 10,000 square miles. The scheme's staff comprised three welfare officers, three support staff and thirteen specialist teachers, including one seconded from each of the contributing authorities, working under a central coordinator. The teachers moved between different schools with travelling pupils offering help with remedial problems and advice to other teachers about travellers' needs. Because of the regional structure of the service, teachers were able to move freely across county boundaries in order to "follow" children as they moved to other schools. Whilst we accept the arguments in favour of a regional approach to provision for travelling children, we were concerned that this scheme might in fact be too large to be manageable and to allow for the most economic use of resources. For example we were struck by the fact that two of the teachers we met spoke of driving 100 miles each way to teach in schools for just one hour! We were also somewhat concerned that the authorities which were part of the scheme appeared to take little interest in what was happening in their areas and the scheme seemed to have no clear line of accountability. It seemed possible that, just as with the "open-door" policy mentioned above, LEAs in this case might also be abdicating their responsibilities in respect of travellers' children and that more efficient use could be made of resources if provision were made at LEA level.

Particular Educational Needs of ·Travellers' Children

18.   It would be facile to claim that travelling children do not present schools with considerable problems. When he or she enters school, at whatever age, a travelling child may have had little or no previous educational experience—it is quite possible in respect of travellers' children to talk of the need for "pre-school" education in the literal sense, for youngsters of 12 or 13. Teachers have said to us that travellers' children "dont know how to play" and are unable to settle down in a large building, that they cannot concentrate, have no respect for property especially books, become disruptive if they are frustrated in their work and that the boys in particular do not obey women teachers. Whilst there may be an element of truth in all these assertions, the reasons for these difficulties are understandable if

teachers know something of the children's backgrounds and the life they lead on a camp site. If the children live as a large family in a relatively small trailer they will clearly be intimidated when confronted with a large school building with stairs, corridors and rooms. The family is the central influence in the life of a travelling child and he or she is used to being constantly in the company of relations and especially brothers and sisters. Being surrounded by strange children and adults and being separated from brothers and sisters into age-related classes can therefore be very traumatic. The young child on a camp site may play with oddments of scrap metal which are discarded when finished with and the concept of "looking after" things may therefore be new to him. The children may have no appreciation of the need to care for books and may lack fine motor-skills in using pens and pencils when they first enter school. All these factors clearly affect how a travelling child will respond to school and if they are overlooked or disregarded the education experience may prove unproductive and the child, who will inevitably be conscious of the need to "prove himself" in relation to his peers, may well resort to assertive or possibly disruptive behaviour. There is therefore a need for some form of in-service training to help teachers respond to the needs of travelling children. In view of the relatively small number of such children it is unfortunately impossible to expect normal LEA INSET courses to do more than perhaps refer to the needs of traveller children in the context of "multicultural education". The DES short courses on travelling children have been running since 1973 and are successful in attracting teachers from schools which regularly have pupils from travelling families. There is also a need for informal in-service work through more discussions and exchanges of information and advice between schools with these pupils, more liaison with the Education Welfare Service and more direct contact between teachers and the travelling community including visits to sites. It is only through teachers actually meeting and talking to travelling parents about the aims of education and the work which the school is doing that more positive attitudes towards education can be built up within the travelling community.

Teaching Materials

19. As far as the teaching materials used in schools are concerned, it is clear that reading books which deal only with families living in houses and fathers working in offices or factories will be of little relevance and interest to a child from a travelling family. Since we believe that materials used in schools should reflect the actual make-up of society and the mix of pupils in a school, we would like to see more use being made of materials which reflect the travelling way of life. In view of the numbers of children involved one cannot perhaps expect the commercial development of such materials but a considerable amount of work has been done in certain areas on

developing suitable materials and in particular reading schemes for use with travelling children which deal with trailers, horses, dogs and other features of their way of life. We would like to see such materials being more widely used in all schools with traveller pupils. Also the availability in a school library of just a few books about travellers could have a very positive efect on the motivation of a travelling child to learn to read and may help to improve the attitudes of the house-dwelling community towards this community.

Record-keeping

20. The issue of record-keeping in relation to the progress of travellers' children has been mentioned in much of the evidence we have received. It has been pointed out to us that if a child arrives in a school "off the road", that school needs to be able to establish quickly the educational level the child has reached so he or she can receive appropriate teaching with some continuity from their previous experience. We have seen two main approaches adopted to record-keeping—the teaching team in one LEA relied on folders of work for each traveller child attending school which were held by the team while the child was on the road and were passed onto the the new school when the child arrived. These folders were considered important by the teachers in providing a reference point both for the teacher and also for the child who could see that earlier work was not lost and could see some continuity in the education process. The regional scheme already mentioned had an educational record transfer system based on a detailed record card recording the educational progress of each travelling child in school which was returned to the scheme's headquarters whenever he or she moved on, so that, as the scheme puts it:

> *"Wherever the child next appears, the card can be in the hands of the receiving school in the time it takes to post and deliver."*

Whilst any teacher dealing with any child clearly needs to have some record of that child's progress, we believe that the administrative arrangements needed to run the latter system may not be fully justified. It has been pointed out to us that "ticks on a card" are not a real indication of a child's ability and if a child has been on the road for several months between schools he or she may in any case have regressed educationally. A skilled teacher can assess a child's educational attainment quite rapidly and should be able to plan appropriate programmes of work accordingly.

Secondary Provision

21. Much of what we have said so far about travellers' children in schools has been related to primary schools only, since few travellers' children continue their education after 11 and even fewer continue through to the statutory school-leaving age. On the face of it, this situation should be remedied since these children are being deprived

of the educational opportunities available to their peers, and their parents are in any case in breach of the law in failing to send them to school. The factors involved in non-participation in secondary education are however rather more complex. As we have already said, travellers and their children see little value in education beyond basic literacy and numeracy. The normal secondary school curriculum is generally seen as a "waste of time" and entirely irrelevant and meaningless in the context of the travelling way of life. Any work related to gaining public examinations or employment is for example considered unnecessary if the travellers' children will be working within the travelling community like their parents. It has been suggested to us that travellers' children should be offered a limited, specially-designed curriculum concentrating on relevant practical skills such as cookery, gardening, metalwork, car maintenance and health and first aid. Whilst we appreciate the arguments in favour of this approach, we would not like to see any travellers' child being offered a scheme of work which was so divergent from the norm as to preclude him or her from participating in the normal full curriculum if they were willing and able to do so. Many of the problems experienced by travellers' children entering primary school for the first time are of course also exacerbated at secondary level—the building will normally be far larger, there will be far more children and far more teachers. Whereas travellers' children may have been able to relate to one teacher in a primary school, they are now faced with a range of subject teachers within the compartmentalised secondary structure. The fact that they may be in need of remedial help may be seen as a stigma and there may be more scope for hostility towards them to emerge. There are also likely to be more rules and regulations which the youngsters may find it difficult to abide by and questions such as affording school uniform may present real problems. Also the fact that travellers' children of necessity mature rather earlier than their peers will mean that at 13 or 14 they are likely to consider themselves "too old" for school and frustration and boredom may again lead to disruptive behaviour. Whilst many, if not all, of these factors apply equally to other youngsters, particularly those from other ethnic minority groups, non-attendance—as opposed to truanting in the later years—seems to occur on such a large scale only within the travelling community.

Teachers of Travellers

22. During our visits and discussions we have met a number of teachers working with travellers' children, both in normal schools and in mobile teaching units visiting camp sites. Without exception we have been greatly impressed by their extreme commitment and dedication to their work. Whilst we do not, as we have made clear, favour the use of on-site units, the teachers we met in these units displayed great resourcefulness, sensitivity and imagination in

making the best possible use of the facilities available, often in appalling circumstances on unofficial and official sites. In some cases these teachers appear to have been left to fend for themselves with very little support from their LEAs. They are therefore in a very isolated position both in physical terms and also in terms of links with mainstream schools. We were pleased to learn of the formation of a National Association for Teachers of Travellers (NATT) which could go some way towards remedying this isolation as well as providing a network for the exchange of information and ideas and encouraging regional cooperation. The DES short course on travellers' education also serves to bring together travellers' teachers from all over the country. Travellers' teachers have told us that they often became identified in the eyes of other teachers and the general public with the travelling community and may consequently be subjected to considerable hostility and verbal and even physical attack by the local housed community who see them as encouraging the travellers to stay. These teachers have also spoken of the effect on their career prospects of having worked in what is seen as a professional "backwater" with little relevance to "normal" education. Those peripatetic teachers we spoke to, who visited different schools for a certain time each week and were also allowed time to develop materials and visit sites, were also regarded by the other school teachers as "part-timers" and working a "soft option". This is clearly very far from the truth since all the travellers' teachers we met put a good deal of their own time into their work and because of the daunting problems they faced had in fact very demanding jobs. Since all these teachers had gained so much knowledge and experience from their work, even where they were based in mobile units, we would like to see them involved in any reorganisation of an authority's provision to cater for travellers' children in mainstream schools.

Role of the DES and HMI　23.　Many of the organisations who gave evidence to us referred to the apparent "neglect" of travellers' education by the DES and stressed the need for a lead to be given from the centre in order to encourage local authorities to make better provision for travellers both in terms of sites and education. For some years now, we were told, the DES, under successive Ministers, has stated its intention of issuing guidance on travellers' education. A number of the travellers' representatives whom we met saw the continual delays over issuing such guidance as symptomatic of the DES's lack of concern and commitment to travellers' education. The recent HMI discussion document on the education of travellers' children goes at least some way towards meeting the community's concerns in that it seeks to clarify the legal position as well as discussing various examples of "good practice". It still however falls considerably short of the statement of DES policy for which the community organisations have called and for which they will presumably continue to press in the future. We ourselves have been struck by the reluctance of the DES to be particularly forthcoming in relation to travellers' education and there seems to be a clear desire not to look too closely into a "complex and difficult area" which is invariably troublesome in political terms. We found a guarded approach amongst officials and an apparent lack of concern to improve the present unsatisfactory state of affairs and to ensure that LEAs were fulfilling their responsibilities in respect of travellers' children. This reluctance contrasted notably with the knowledgeable and sensitive comments which we received from the two specialist HMIs concerned with travellers' education, who were clearly deeply concerned about the situation and who were indeed mentioned by a number of the people we met as making valuable contributions to the increasing awareness of the needs and problems of travellers' children.

Racism

24. We have already referred to the particular form of racism which the travelling community faces from the settled community. Much of this hostility surfaces when proposals to establish new camp sites are under discussion in an area and, when seeking evidence, we were overwhelmed by negative references to the travelling community from local newspapers—to quote just one example: a county councillor commenting as follows at a public meeting:

> *"A civilised society can be judged on the way it treats minorities but I don't put the itinerants in that category because they live outside the realms of common decency."*

The roots of such extreme hostility towards travellers can be seen to have much in common with the origins of prejudice and racism towards any group perceived as "outsiders", which we discussed in our Racism Chapter, as the following interesting extract from a recent research report[12] reveals:

> *"Direct contact between travellers and members of the public take place during brief economic exchanges when travellers are selling to the public or offering homeowners a service like tarmacing their driveway. Other direct contacts are restricted to those that occur between travellers and members of various mainstream institutions—the police, hospital staff, environmental health officers, social welfare employees, and similar people. The average member of the public relies for his or her information on what they see—which is usually the squalor of unauthorised encampments that they drive past and from what they read in the*

---

[12]"Special Accommodation Needs of Irish and Other Long Distance Travellers." Smith, Gmelch and Gmelch. DOE. 1982.

newspapers, typically accounts of evictions or public protests to a site proposal. Like all ethnic stereotypes, the negative perceptions held of travellers are exaggerated and unfairly generalized to all members of the group regardless of their individual behaviour. In small communities and established neighbourhoods, residents sometimes distinguish between the bahaviour of the local travellers and that of outsiders who may periodically move into the area. But even, then the hostility and frustration felt when faced with rubbish-strewn encampments is often directed towards all travellers. When an individual or family fails to conform to the expected behaviour (eg, keeps a tidy camp), they are regarded as unique and referred to as 'not being like the rest'. In this way stereotypes and prejudice can exist side by side with a person's positive experience of members of a minority or out-group. This attitude was epitomised by a local newspaper quoting a local resident whose property was close to a proposed permanent site location:

> *'We've nothing against the Gypsy people, but we don't want them on our doorstep.'*

Selective perception and rationalization are also evident in the many statements made by people to the effect that they do not harbour ill-feelings toward the 'proper gypsies' only towards 'tinkers' and 'itinerant scrap merchants'. The negative view most members of the public have of travellers is bolstered by local press coverage which concentrates on provocative episodes. Seldom are the views of travellers taken into account or the root causes of an unsatisfactory situation, (eg, unauthorised encampment due to under-provision of sites), explored. At their worst sensationalist headlines such as: 'Tinkers Causing Bedlam—Claim', 'Clean-up Call on Prostitutes and Gypsies', and 'Tinkers Smash a Dream' help create anti-traveller sentiments. Where local press coverage is informed and responsible, the press can be a great help in promoting understanding between travellers and the public and in breaking down negative stereotypes. Ironically public opposition has been responsible for many sites being built in totally unsuitable locations which seriously affects their chances of success, and when they fail, the public's negative view of travellers is reinforced. Unwitting pawns in somebody else's self-fulfilling prophecies the travellers are also victims of the now fashionable 'Catch 22 situation':

> *'People complain about sites being built but they complain even more if we spend the night on the roadside. You just cannot win.' (Traveller women.)"*

755

25. In the context of education, the degree of hostility towards Gypsies and other travellers' children if they do enter school is quite remarkable even when set alongside the racism encountered by children from other ethnic minority groups. On a visit to a primary school which had a large number of children from a local camp site we were shown cuttings from local papers setting out the fears of parents of other children in the school that the travellers' children would be violent, dirty and diseased and that their admission should be prevented at all costs. (In this particular instance, after a public meeting at which the school's Headmistress spoke in favour of admitting the children, they were admitted to the school and have now settled in well and the original fears of the other parents have proved groundless.) Hostility is not however limited only to parents, since teachers and Heads often seem to resist strongly the admission of travellers' children because of the problems they may present. Travellers' children may also face considerable hostility from the other children in school who may be influenced by their parents' views of "dirty gypsies". As some travellers' teachers pointed out to us, even schools which otherwise showed excellent multicultural practices and had policies on racist name-calling etc, often displayed such hostility and their "tolerance" clearly did not extend to travellers.

Conclusion

26. In many ways the situation of travellers' children in Britain today throws into stark relief many of the factors which influence the education of children from other ethnic minority groups—racism and discrimination, myths, stereotyping and misinformation, the inappropriateness and inflexibility of the education system and the need for better links between homes and schools and teachers and parents. Many of the official attitudes to travelling families tend towards encouraging them to "settle down" and in effect to cease being travellers. Since, as we explained at the opening of this report, we believe that all ethnic minority groups have the right to retain their distinct identities, and to see their way of life and culture respected and valued by the majority community, we believe that, without our overall philosophy of "education for all", ways can and must be found to reconcile the concerns and aspirations of the travelling community and the mainstream education system in a much more positive manner.

27. A central factor in considering the education of travellers' children is clearly site provision, and, as will be evident from our comments, we have been concerned at a number of aspects of the current situation with regard to this issue. We would like to see far greater efforts being made by all concerned to increase the number of sites available and to improve the facitities of existing sites. Educa-

tion should not be presented to travelling families on a "take it or leave it" basis, as seems to be the case in some parts of the country at present, and schools and LEAs should not be able to "turn a blind eye" to travellers' children simply because they may present problems and efforts on their behalf may prove unpopular with the rest of the community. We are concerned that the specific provision in the 1944 Education Act (Section 39(3)) for travellers' children to be required to fulfil only 50 per cent of the school attendances required of all other children (see paragraph 13 above), although presumably intended originally to protect travelling parents from unreasonable prosecution for failing to send their children to school, may in practice serve to deprive travellers' children of equality of access to education; LEAs may see this provision in the Act as offering a convenient excuse for not enforcing school attendance for travellers' children, rather than, as we would wish, striving to achieve full time attendance by all school age children in their areas. In view of the widespread concern about the level of school attendance amongst the travelling community, we therefore urge that Section 39(3) of the 1944 Education Act be repealed, thus removing the present ambiguity over the requirement for school attendance.

28. In relation to specific educational provision, on balance we believe that the approach of any necessary additional educational support being provided *within* the mainstream system offers the only acceptable way of providing education for travellers' children, whilst recognising that some children may require some form of "bridge" into normal schools. Only for the small minority of children from families which are almost continually on the move, staying in one place for perhaps only a couple of weeks, should, we feel, any form of provision on-site be considered in any way desirable. We tend to share the view of one travellers' organisation which gave evidence to us that:

> *"We find it difficult to understand why experimental projects should be set up outside the established system when it is already capable of handling much greater problems than those offered by a comparative handful of Gypsy children."*

We believe that the main aim should be for travellers' children to be educated in normal schools which should be willing and able to cater for their needs, provided LEAs give the appropriate support. There may however be a need for LEAs to have teams of peripatetic advisory teachers who can visit schools with traveller pupils to offer advice to the staff and to work in normal classes with the travellers' children. They could also visit sites to talk to parents and explain the aims and purposes of education, and in certain circumstances provide "emergency help" for individual children who are definitely staying on a site for such a short time that entry into normal schools

757

is not feasible. The costs of this team could be met from the no-area pool.[13] We would like to see each LEA having a "named person" to coordinate work in field of traveller education who could be contacted by any teacher, school or other LEA, for information about any travelling child who had previously received education in that area. All in all, we would like to see the education of travellers' children being considered alongside the needs of children from the whole range of ethnic minority groups, within the overall framework of "Education for All".

---

[13]As indicated in paragraph 13 above, 75 per cent of the cost of such provision could be met from the no-area pool as "exceptional provision" but in addition an Authority could we understand claim 100 per cent of the cost as "expenditure on tuition in normal classes."

ANNEX

**Extract from "The Education of Travellers' Children"—
an HMI Discussion Document. DES. 1983**

Fairground and Circus Children

1. Fairground and circus children experience particular problems in maintaining continuity of education, because their families move so frequently. From October to Easter most fairground children are able to attend local schools in the area in which their winter quarters are located. During the summer season, however, fairground families are on the move for most of the time, often travelling very widely, and many children cease to attend school altogether. Particularly vulnerable are young teenagers who are deemed by the community to have reached adulthood and are of an age to participate fully in the activities of the fair, even though this is precisely the time when they could be taking public examinations. Lost ground is not easily recovered when the children return to normal schooling in the autumn.

2. Some parents have sought to overcome these difficulties by sending their children to boarding school, or by leaving them with friends or relatives during the summer travelling season. However, the idea of family separation is rejected by a majority of parents for whom other ways of maintaining educational continuity must be sought. Where children are able to attend schools for reasonable periods during the summer months, liaison between the "home" and "host" school may be one way of promoting continuity, and some system of pupil profiles or record keeping may be helpful in this respect. Often, however, movement is so frequent that continued attendance at school is impossible, and it is left to parents to take the initiative. There have been several examples of parents obtaining work programmes and books from their children's winter-schools or other sources, and attempting to continue their children's education while on the road. Such an approach may have reasonable success with young children, although it will inevitably become less satisfactory as they grow older.

3. Circus children face similar problems, often accentuated by the even greater mobility of their parents. Circuses may move on every week for most of the year, so that continuous normal education, even when desired, is difficult to achieve, and some circuses have considered establishing their own teaching units. One owner estimated in 1976 that in a single year his circus stopped in over 40 different towns, covering a large number of local education authorities. Subsequently, he appointed a qualified teacher to supervise the education of the 20 or so children attached to his circus. At first they were taught in a tent, but then a single decker coach was converted into a well equipped mobile teaching unit, and some of the resources of the circus, including audio visual aids, were made available to the teacher. For 12 months the financial burden was borne by the circus itself but eventually a local education authority agreed to assume the administrative responsibility for educating the children and the costs incurred became poolable.

Reflections and Conclusions

Common "Ethnic Minority Experience"

1. When we first turned to considering the "other" ethnic minority communities discussed in this part of our report, we expected to find their needs fairly discreet and self-contained with relatively little in the way of common experiences. As is evident from the preceding chapters, however, we found a remarkable number of points of similarity and mutual concerns shared by these groups, many of which had also previously emerged from our consideration of both the West Indian and Asian communities. Taken together, we feel that these shared needs and concerns constitute a clearly defined "ethnic minority experience". By way of conclusion we now seek to draw together some of the key aspects of this common experience.

"Ethnic Identity"

2. One of the major factors which emerged from our consideration of these groups was the very strong sense of their own "ethnic identities" which they shared. This appeared to be just as important for groups, such as the Chinese, where the majority of youngsters were now British-born, as for recent arrivals such as the Vietnamese. With several groups, great efforts were made to maintain the community's identity through regular visits "home", where these were feasible, and through quite extensive programmes of community-based provision for "mother tongue" teaching and other forms of "culture mainten- ance". In the case of the Italian community, and to a lesser extent, the Cypriot and Chinese communities, direct assistance was given by the "home" countries to such activities. Such criticisms as were made of the curricular diet offered by mainstream schools were chiefly concerned with the risk that an exclusively Anglo-centric focus, which appeared neither to respect nor recognise the languages, cultures, histories or religions of ethnic minority communities, might serve to alienate ethnic minority youngsters from their "roots" thus placing in jeopardy the community's integrity. From the point of view of the relationship between the ethnic minority and ethnic majority communities in our society, it seems clear that none of the minority groups whom we considered is looking for "assimilation" within the majority community, other than in terms of being fully accepted as equal members of this society. In fact the continuing strength of ethnic identity within these minority groups in our view reinforces the conclusion which we reached at the opening of this report, that assimilation, in the sense of the "submergence" of minority groups within the majority community, is not only unlooked for but is also likely to impossible to achieve in practice. The only feasible and desirable blue print for our future society is

760

thus, as we have proposed, along pluralist lines.

Influence of Racism

3. Another clear feature of the "ethnic minority experience" shared by these groups is, regrettably, the influence of racism on their lives. We ourselves were initially surprised at the frequency and intensity with which, unprompted by us, representatives of these communities expressed their concerns about racism, and by the extent to which racism appeared to cross the "colour" divide—in that it impinged on the "white" ethnic minorities whom we considered as well as the "non-white". In relation to the "white" ethnic minority groups, we were also concerned at the suggestion that the potential "invisibility" of such groups ie. the fact that they were sometimes not seen as ethnic minorities at all, might lead to any particular, educational difficulties which they might experience being overlooked and therefore remaining unmet. The persistence of racism, even where particular ethnic minority communities have been settled in an area over a long period of time, is evidenced vividly by the situation of the "Liverpool Black" community which, although established over several generations, still experiences extremes of racial prejudice. The forms of racism encountered by different groups encompassed a range of experiences along the continuum of intentional and unintentional racism which we discussed at length in Chapter Two. Included in these were the racial harassment and violence experienced by the Vietnamese community, and ostensibly less serious incidents such as the racist name-calling encountered by the Italians, which we would also regard as indicative of a negative view of these communities. The Cypriot community also offered a particularly interesting illustration of the wide-ranging influence of the stereotypes of different ethnic minority groups, which we see as such a key factor in racism, with the differential achievements of Greek Cypriot and Turkish Cypriot youngsters in part at least appearing to derive from the very different stereotypes of these two groups. The extremely negative stereotype which exists of the Travelling community and the almost universal hostility and hatred which they appear to evoke from most other sections of society also serves to demonstrate the powerful influence of stereotyping. In relation to the Chinese community, as we have seen, even a *positive* stereotype can work against a community if it leads teachers to misinterpret or overlook genuine educational difficulties. One further aspect of racism which was evident from our consideration of these ethnic minority groups was the existence of a degree of racist feeling towards other groups, both minority and majority—a point which we made in Chapter Two. Whilst the factors which may have led to these feelings may be rather different than those which have conditioned the views and attitudes of the majority community towards minority groups—we were for example interested in the suggestion that the Turkish Cypriot community may simply have

adopted and internalised the view held by the majority community of groups such as West Indians—such feelings are nevertheless in our view still very much to be regretted and deplored.

Educational Concerns

4. Many of the points raised with us in relation to the educational needs of pupils from these groups echo the issues to which we have devoted attention earlier in this report. The major educational issue with all groups, except the Travellers, was language—both E2L provision and "mother tongue" maintenance and teaching. In the E2L field a major concern was the extent to which many teachers appeared to regard a child who required E2L help simply as remedial: lack of English being equated with lack of ability. There was general resistance amongst the community representatives to withdrawing children for E2L help, either within school or at separate language centres, which was regarded as having potentially damaging effects on a child's socialisation and self-image and possibly causing them to fall behind in other subjects, thus in effect condemning them to underachieve. It was generally felt that E2L needs were best catered for by offering support within the normal classroom situation—very much along the lines of the cooperative teaching approach which we have endorsed in Chapter Seven. Many of the E2L specialists whom we met during this phase of our work stressed that *all* teachers, and not only language specialists, should have a greater understanding of how language difficulties can influence a child's performance and of the need for a "language across the curriculum" approach in all schools, designed to enhance the language awareness of pupils and teachers. Since many of the children from these minority groups were likely to enter school with at least some knowledge of English, much of the evidence we received focussed on provision to meet "second stage" language needs and to provide continuing language support for pupils, particularly at secondary level, to enable them to cope with the linguistic demands of subject specialisms and of public examinations. In both respects provision was felt to be lacking and it was also felt that examinations in particular tended to use unnecessarily complex and difficult language, thus automatically placing a second language learner at a disadvantage. Inadequately catered for or simply overlooked language needs were generally felt to lead to the possibility of children from these ethnic minority groups underachieving. As we have already noted, the maintenance and teaching of their "mother tongue" languages was regarded by these groups as a key factor in maintaining their community's distinct identity, and community-based provision was in consequence well-developed and thriving. The references in these chapters to the attitude of some mainstream teachers towards "mother tongue" provision, serve to reinforce further the concerns we expressed in our Language Chapter about "linguistic prejudice"—most notably

762

perhaps the perception of the languages of ethnic minority communities as of low status and the belief that any attempt at "mother tongue" teaching constituted "backpedalling" in educational terms.

5. In relation to the rest of the curriculum, as we have already pointed out, concern centred around what was regarded as the Anglo-centric bias of the subject matter and the literature studied, to the virtual exclusion of any references to their own background or experiences with which ethnic minority youngsters could identify. The problems which could result from a lack of contact between the school and ethnic minority parents, and the "cultural conflicts" which can arise for ethnic minority youngsters were also raised by several groups. There seemed to be almost universal criticism of the extent to which teacher training had failed to inform teachers of the backgrounds of ethnic minority groups or to prepare them to adopt a broader approach to their work. Concern about the ability, and in some cases the willingness of teachers to respond to the educational needs of ethnic minority children, had led several of these communities to argue for more teachers from their own communities—an issue which we discussed in Chapter Nine. One final aspect of the educational situation of these groups which is worth drawing out here is the fact that several of these smaller minority communities are dispersed around the country and children are therefore to be found in areas and schools with few, if any, other ethnic minority pupils. The presence of children from such groups in otherwise "all-white" areas lends weight to our view that "multicultural"considerations are of as much relevance to such areas as to other, more evidently multi-racial areas.

6. All in all, we believe that our findings in relation to these "other" ethnic minority communities lend added weight and urgency to the proposals which we have put forward for the development of "education for all" to foster the emergence of a truly pluralist society along the lines we envisaged at the opening of this report.

PART V

Main Conclusions and Recommendations

PART V

Main Conclusions and Recommendations

1.   Introduction

1.1   This report is concerned primarily to change behaviour and attitudes. They need to change throughout Britain, and, while the education system must not be expected to carry the whole burden of that change, schools in particular are uniquely well placed to take a lead role. Britain has evolved, over many centuries, institutions and traditions which, whatever their shortcomings, have been taken as models by many nations, and were indeed an important part of the attraction of this country to the ethnic minorities who are the essential concern of our report. It is because we believe that everyone in Britain has a direct interest in ensuring that those institutions and the attitudes which inform them, change to take full account of the pluralism which is now a marked feature of British life, that we make our recommendations. While we recognise that society and its institutions seldom change rapidly, nevertheless we cannot emphasise too strongly the urgency of the need for change where attitudes to the ethnic minorities are concerned.

1.2   We draw together in this part of the report some of the main conclusions and recommendations which we have reached. Other, more detailed, recommendations will be found elsewhere in the report. Much of the argument upon which our philosophy of what we have termed *"Education for All"* is based, is however, contained in chapters which do not advance specific recommendations and it is important that all of the chapters are studied in depth.

1.3   Although it has not been possible to prepare any detailed costings for our recommendations it is clear that a number will carry resource implications and we would urge the Government to demonstrate its commitment to the development of "Education for All" by ensuring that the necessary additional resources are made available. But as we explained in our interim report, in order to bring about the degree of change of attitude that is needed, we believe that the cost in "psychological terms" will in many instances be far greater than any direct financial outlay.

2.   Achievement and Underachievement—Chapter Three

2.1   West Indian children, on average, are underachieving at school (Section 2). Asian children, by contrast, show on average, a pattern of achievement which resembles that of White children, though there is some evidence of variation between different sub-groups (Section 3). Bangladeshis in particular are seriously underachieving (Annex C). Such evidence as there is suggests that of the smaller ethnic minorities, some are underachieving and some are not (Part IV). Averages, of course, conceal much variation; there are West Indian children who do well, as well as Asian children who are underachieving. We discuss possible causes for the difference in *average* achievement between Asian and West Indian children in Section 6.

2.2   Low average IQ has often been suggested as a cause of underachievement, particularly in the case of West Indians. This has long been disputed, and our own investigations leave us in no doubt that IQ is *not* a significant factor in underachievement (Paragraphs 4.10–4.14 and Annex D).

2.3   School performance has long been known to show a close correlation with Socio-economic status and social class, in the case of all children. The ethnic minorities, however, are particularly disadvantaged in social and economic terms, and there can no longer be any doubt that this extra deprivation is the result of racial prejudice and discrimination, especially in the areas of employment and housing. The resulting deprivation, over and above that of disadvantaged Whites, leads in many instances to an *extra* element of underachievement. A substantial part of ethnic minority underachievement, where it occurs, is thus the result of racial prejudice and discrimination on the part of society at large, bearing on ethnic minority homes and families, and hence, *indirectly*, on children (Paragraphs 4.15–4.22).

2.4   Not all of underachievement, where it occurs, is to be accounted for in these terms, and the rest, we believe, is due in large measure to prejudice and discrimination bearing *directly* on children, within the educational system, as well as outside it. We have received much oral and written evidence on this score, referring in particular to stereotyped attitudes amongst teachers, as well as other factors, and these we discussed in our interim report. See also Chapter Two and Annex A.

2.5   We have examined the research evidence about racial prejudice and discrimination in the educational system and their effects on ethnic minority children. We can only say that the findings are inconclusive when it comes to deciding which factors may be important (Paragraphs 4.23–4.31). We are left in no doubt, however, that the issues involved are complex and ill-understood, and that much more research is needed if we are to understand the problems. We include a section on future research at Annex E.

2.6   It will be evident that society is faced with a dual problem: eradicating the discriminatory attitudes of the white majority on the one hand, and on the other, evolving an educational system which ensures that *all* pupils achieve their full potential.

2.7   In the short term, the first of these problems is a matter for the Law, the Government, Housing Authorities, Employers, Unions, the Commission for Racial Equality, and many others. But in the long run we believe that it is a matter for schools to bring about this much-needed change in attitudes amongst coming generations.

768

2.8   The second problem is specifically one for the educational system. A start has been made in recent years, but there is still a long way to go before schools bring out the full potential of all their pupils, and in this context, particularly their ethnic minority pupils.

2.9   This dual approach to one of Britain's most serious social concerns, leads us to the concept that we have called "Education for All"—an attempt simultaneously to change attitudes amongst the White Majority, and to develop a pattern of education that enables *all* pupils to give of their best. The essential argument of "Education for All" is set out in the next section, and this is followed by our main recommendations.

3.   Education for All—Chapter Six

3.1   The essential steps on the argument for our concept of "Education for All" are as follows:

(a)   The fundamental change that is necessary is the recognition that the problem facing the education system is not how to educate children of ethnic minorities, but how to educate *all* children.

(b)   Britain is a multi-racial and multi-cultural society and all pupils must be enabled to understand what this means.

(c)   This challenge cannot be left to the separate and independent initiatives of LEAs and schools: only those with experience of substantial numbers of ethnic minority pupils have attempted to tackle it, though the issue affects all schools and all pupils.

(d)   Education has to be something more than the reinforcement of the beliefs, values and identity which each child brings to school.

(e)   It is necessary to combat racism, to attack inherited myths and stereotypes, and the ways in which they are embodied in institutional practices.

(f)   Multi-cultural understanding has also to permeate all aspects of a school's work. It is not a separate topic that can be welded on to existing practices.

(g)   Only in this way can schools begin to offer anything approaching the *equality of opportunity* for all pupils which it must be the aspiration of the education system to provide.

4.   A Strategy for Change—Chapter Six

4.1   The response of schools, both 'multi-racial' and 'all white', to cultural diversity has to be seen as a central feature of the current debate on the balance and breadth of the school curriculum. The Secretary of State should focus on this issue when considering responses to DES Circular 8/83 and in any further statements that he may make and any agreements that he may seek about the curriculum;

4.2   All LEA's should declare their commitment to the principles of 'education for all', to the development of a pluralist approach to the curriculum, and to countering the influence of racism;

4.3   Every LEA should have at least one adviser and perhaps a senior officer with responsibility to promote the policies we have put forward, to act as a catalyst to encourage teachers and other advisers to adopt a pluralist perspective in their work;

4.4   HM Inspectorate should give attention to the extent to which the curriculum takes full account of the multi-racial nature of society and should highlight in their reports, including reports on individual schools, instances of 'good practice' and areas of concern;

4.5   HM Inspectorate should issue clear guidance on the practical implications of adopting a pluralist approach to the curriculum and on ways of countering the influence of racism on schools;

4.6   The School Curriculum Development Committee should review existing materials which reflect a pluralist approach to the curriculum. The Committee should consider how these materials may be made more widely known and how the production of further such resources may be stimulated;

4.7   Examining Boards should reflect cultural diversity in the syllabuses they offer and in their working practices;

4.8   The Secondary Examinations Council should co-operate with The School Curriculum Development Committee to ensure that initiatives to broaden the school curriculum are reflected by paralleled developments within the examinations system;

4.9   All LEAs should expect their schools to produce clear policy statements on 'Education for All' and monitor their practical implementation;

4.10   All schools whether multi-racial or 'all white' should review their work in the light of the principles which we have put forward. In secondary schools it may be necessary to establish departmental working parties to appraise provision in different subject areas;

4.11   All schools should adopt clear policies to combat racism;

4.12   The DES should organize a series of regional conferences for elected members of LEAs, teachers and other educationalists to discuss the implications of this Report. The conclusions of these conferences might subsequently be drawn to the attention of a wider audience in a conference report;

4.13   The Government should revise the provisions of Section 11 of the Local Government Act 1966 to make it more appropriate to the needs of the ethnic minority communities;

4.14   The Secretary of State should include a growing number of initiatives and pilot projects designed to develop a broader, pluralist approach to the curriculum within arrangements for education support grants;

4.15   The DES should implement the recommendations of our Interim Report relating to the collection of ethnically-based statistics within education.

5.   Language and Language Education—Chapter Seven

General

5.1   We believe that essential to equality of opportunity, to academic success and, more broadly, to participation on equal terms as a full member of society, is a good command of *English* and that first priority in language learning by all pupils must therefore be given to the learning of English. (Paragraph 3.16).

English as a Second Language

5.2   We are wholly in favour of a change from the provision of E2L by withdrawal, whether this has been to language centres or to separate units within schools. (Paragraph 2.10);

5.3   The needs of learners of English as a second language should be met by provision within the mainstream school as part of a comprehensive programme of language education for *all* children. (Paragraph 2.10);

5.4   For the child from a home where English is not the first language, pre-school provision can be particularly valuable. We therefore restate the recommendations made in our interim report on this important stage of the overall educational experience (Paragraph 2.11);

5.5   *All* teachers in schools with substantial numbers of pupils for whom English is not their first language have a responsibility to cater for linguistic needs of these pupils and should be given appropriate support and training to discharge it. (Paragraphs 2.12 and 2.14);

Mother Tongue Provision

5.6   Linguistic diversity in Britain is nothing new, and we regard it as a positive asset, whether it be Welsh, Gaelic, dialects or ethnic minority community languages. All schools should impart an understanding of our multi-lingual society to all pupils (Paragraph 3.15);

5.7   The linguistic, religious and cultural identities of ethnic minority communities should be fostered but we cannot support the arguments put forward for the introduction of programmes of bilingual education in maintained schools (Paragraph 3.15);

5.8   Mainstream schools should not seek to assume the role of community providers for maintaining ethnic minority community languages (Paragraph 3.18);

771

5.9   LEAs should offer support for community based language provision, by making school premises available free of charge to community providers, by fostering links between community 'teachers' and the mainstream school, by offering grants for the purchase of books and the development of teaching materials, and by making available to the community their advisory services for short in-service courses (Paragraph 3.18);

5.10   Ethnic minority community languages should be included in the languages curriculum of secondary schools where there is likely to be sufficient demand and all pupils in those schools should be encouraged to consider studying them (Paragraphs 3.19 and 3.20);

5.11   Responsibility for ethnic minority community languages should rest with LEA advisers for modern languages (Paragraph 3.19);

5.12   The careers service and employers should emphasize to all youngsters the importance and relevance of facility in an ethnic minority community language for work in multi-racial areas (Paragraph 3.19);

5.13   Care should be taken to ensure the quality of teachers in ethnic minority community languages. They should hold recognised qualifications in the language concerned, have received professional training in this country in the techniques needed to teach a language and must be fully proficient in English (Paragraph 3.21);

5.14   The Government should take measures to ensure that potential teachers of ethnic minority community languages receive appropriate training, support and recognition. As a first step we recommend that the DES should commission a further qualitative evaluation of the eight teacher training institutions identified by the Nottingham Study (see paragraph 6 (iii) of Annex F) as potential centres of growth in relation to ethnic minority community languages (Paragraph 3.22);

5.15   More examining boards should consider the need to offer examinations in ethnic minority community languages at all levels. Where examinations are already offered in these languages greater consideration should be given to syllabus content to bring the provision into line with other subjects (Paragraph 3.23).

6.   Religion and the Role of the School—Chapter Eight

Religious Education

6.1   We are in favour of a non denominational and undogmatic approach to religious education as the best and indeed the only means of enabling all pupils, from whatever religious background, to understand the nature of religious belief, the religious dimension of human experience and the plurality of faiths in contemporary Britain; to appreciate the diverse and sometimes conflicting values involved and thus to determine and justify their own religious position (Paragraph 2.11);

6.2   There should be no conflict between the role of the schools in providing religious *education* and the role of community institutions in providing religious *instruction* (Paragraph 5.2);

6.3   Given the multiplicity of beliefs now present in society, it is not surprising that we have received much evidence about the difficulties generated by the requirement in the 1944 Act for a daily act of collective worship and the provision of a particular form of religious education. We therefore believe that the Government, in consultation with religious and educational bodies, should look afresh at the relevant provisions of the Act to see whether alterations are called for after an interval of 40 years. (Paragraphs 5.3 and 5.5).

The 'Separate' Schools Debate

6.4   The right of ethnic minority communities to seek to establish their own voluntary aided schools is firmly enshrined in law (Paragraph 1.2);

6.5   We believe that the demand to exercise this right would be much diminished if the policies for "Education for All" which we have advocated in this report are adopted (Paragraph 2.11);

6.6   We do not believe that a situation in which groups of children are taught exclusively by teachers of the same ethnic group is desirable from the point of view of the children, the minority community or society as a whole. We are not therefore convinced that 'separate' schools can be supported on these grounds (Paragraph 2.12);

6.7   The establishment of 'separate' schools would fail to tackle many of the underlying concerns of the communities and might exacerbate the very feelings of rejection which they are seeking to overcome (Paragraph 2.12);

6.8   Where there is parental concern about the education of girls, existing co-educational schools with multi-racial pupil populations could do more to ensure that in certain specific areas separate provision is offered on a single sex basis as appropriate in the schools activities (Paragraph 2.15);

6.9   For some ethnic minority parents the demise of single sex provision may mean that there is no acceptable environment for the education of their daughters. We hope that LEA's with multi-racial pupil populations will consider carefully the value of retaining an option of single sex education as part of their secondary school provision and that the Secretary of State will also be sensitive to the wider ramifications of any decisions he may make on proposals which lead to the loss of single sex provision in multi-racial areas. In cases where an LEA either no longer provides for single sex education at all, or make only limited provision, we hope that the possibility of establishing or re-establishing single sex schools will be given serious consideration (Paragraph 2.15);

6.10   Far more can and should be done by schools to respond to the 'pastoral' needs of Muslim pupils, to ensure that there is a real respect and understanding by both teachers and parents of each others concerns and that the demands of the school place no child in fundamental conflict with the requirements of his faith (Paragraph 2.16);

6.11 As we have observed earlier, the right of communities to seek to establish their own voluntary aided schools is firmly enshrined in the law. At the same time we do not believe that such 'separate' schools would be in the long term interest of the ethnic minorities communities. This dilemma leads us to recommend (but see note of dissent on page 361) that the Government, in consultation with religious and educational bodies, should consider the relevant provisions of the 1944 Act, to see whether or not alterations are required in a society that is now very different. (Paragraph 2.19.)

6.12 Although we fully understand the reasons underlying the desire for separate "Black" schools we believe that, in the long term they are unlikely to offer the best way forward for individual West Indian pupils or indeed for the West Indian community as a whole. On the contrary we believe that if the recommendations of this Report are acted upon, most of the concerns of the West Indian community which lie behind the calls for "Black" schools will be allayed (Paragraph 3.5).

7. Teacher Education and the Employment of Ethnic Minority Teachers—Chapter Nine

Teacher Education

7.1 Consideration should be given to pluralist issues within the central and compulsory 'core' of all initial training courses, both PGCE and BEd (Paragraph 2.16);

7.2 Specialist optional courses relating to pluralist issues should continue to be offered within both PGCE and BEd courses (Paragraph 2.21);

7.3 Efforts should be made by all teacher training institutions to ensure that all their students, whether on BEd or PGCE courses, have an opportunity of gaining some practical experience in a multi-racial school (Paragraph 2.22);

7.4 We urge the Secretary of State to ask the new Council for the Accreditation of Teacher Education to pay particular attention to the need to incorporate a pluralist perspective in all initial teacher training courses in their forthcoming review of provision (Paragraph 2.24);

7.5 The CNAA and universities responsible for initial teacher training should continue to support and encourage the development of a pluralist perspective throughout teacher education (Paragraph 2.26);

7.6 We believe that there is an urgent need for a major expansion in provision for induction training. All induction training in multi-racial areas should incorporate the background information and skills needed to respond positively and sensitively to

774

the particular educational needs which ethnic minority pupils may have and to utilise the opportunities offered by a multi-racial classroom (Paragraph 3.5);

7.7 All in-service courses should reflect the multiplicity of cultures, faiths and languages in present day society. All providers of in-service training should ensure that the courses they offer have this pluralist perspective and embody the essential principles of 'Education for All'. (Paragraph 3.12);

7.8 We recommend the development of a number of teacher training institutions as 'centres of specialism' for work concerned with the needs of ethnic minority pupils and the implications of cultural diversity for 'all White' schools. (Paragraphs 3.15 and 3.19);

7.9 We recommend that the DES should fund an independent evaluation of the content and effectiveness of the various Racism Awareness Training programmes which are currently available (Paragraph 3.17);

7.10 We recommend that the In-Service Teacher Training Grants Scheme should be extended to allow for grants to be available to authorities in respect of the release of serving school teachers for training on courses relating to aspects of 'Education for All' (Paragraph 3.20);

7.11 The DES should consider initiating the development of a centrally-funded scheme to facilitate teacher exchanges, possibly organised through the Central Bureau for Educational Visits and Exchanges, within this country, especially between multi-racial schools and 'all White' schools, to foster greater understanding and appreciation of the various dimensions of our multi-racial society (Paragraph 3.24);

The Employment of Ethnic Minority Teachers

7.12 We reiterate our interim report recommendations that:

> "The DES should ask all teacher training institutions to collect statistics on the ethnic origin of all students training to be teachers including students seeking to enter teaching through special access courses.
>
> The DES should record and publish statistics on the ethnic origin of all teachers in employment . . ."

(Paragraph 1.3)

7.13 We regard the under-representation of ethnic minorities in the teaching profession as a matter of great concern, which calls for urgent attention. We believe that ethnic minority teachers (and would-be teachers) have been and are still subject to racial prejudice and discrimination, both in gaining employment and in advancing their careers. While we do not support positive discrimination e.g. quotas and do not wish to see any diminution of standards, we urge both the CRE and those involved within LEAs and the schools in making appointments, to devote far greater efforts to identifying and overcoming racist obstacles to the employment and advancement of ethnic minority teachers. (Paragraphs 2.1, 2.3, 2.6);

7.14 We welcome the efforts made by some LEAs to establish themselves as 'equal

775

opportunity employers' and we urge *all* LEAs to follow this lead and adopt similar 'equal opportunities' policies (Paragraph 2.3);

7.15   We recommend that the DES should clarify the arrangements for granting qualified teacher status to members of ethnic minority communities who possess overseas qualifications, with a view to encouraging them to enter the teaching profession, as long as this involves no diminution of standards (Paragraph 3.2);

7.16   Access courses make an important and valuable contribution not only by offering a 'second chance' for access to Higher Education to ethnic minority students and others but also by contributing to the number of teachers of ethnic minority origin in our schools. We hope to see an expansion of access-style provision to the whole range of Higher Education in the future (Paragraph 3.3);

7.17   We recommend that the DES commission a research project to examine the experience of former access students in obtaining teaching posts and in fulfilling their responsibilities in schools (Paragraph 3.3);

7.18   We remain firmly convinced that in order for access courses to cater fully for the needs of all those mature students from both ethnic minority groups and the ethnic majority community, who could benefit from them, these courses must come within the scope of mandatory awards. We therefore reiterate out interim report recommendation that:

> *"The DES should find ways in which mandatory awards can be given to* *students on special access courses"*
> (Paragraph 3.4).

7.19   In our view the most important potential source of ethnic minority teachers in the future is the ethnic minority pupils currently in school. Careers teachers and careers officers, with the strong support of DES and HMI, should encourage ethnic minority youngsters to consider the possibility of entering teaching. (Paragraph 3.5).

APPENDICES

Appendix A   — Co-opted members to Sub Committees.

Appendix B   — List of Educational Institutions which have submitted evidence to the Committee.

Appendix C   — List of LEAs and organisations which have submitted evidence to the Committee.

Appendix D   — List of individuals who have submitted evidence to the Committee.

Appendix E   — List of open meetings or "forums" arranged to hear the views of parents and young people.

APPENDIX A

CO-OPTED MEMBERS TO SUB COMMITTEES*

Preparation of Interim Report

Ms J Barrow OBE	Lecturer, University of London, Institute of Education.
Mrs E Bernard	Senior Education Welfare Officer, Inner London Education Authority.
Mr F Best	Social Worker, Derbyshire County Council.
Miss E Brittan	Research Officer, London Borough of Harrow.
Mrs W Bushell	Educational Psychologist, London Borough of Croydon.
Mr L Fallows	Formerly County Adviser, Lancashire County Council.
Mrs J Goody	Adviser for Multi-ethnic Education, Inner London Education Authority.
Ms H Hall	Head, Welbourne Infants' School, London Borough of Haringey.
Mr J Jackson	Community Liaison Teacher, Inner London Education Authority.
Mr D Lake	Teacher, Sinfin School, Derby.
Ms J Leitch	Lecturer, North East London Polytechnic.
Mr A D Matthews MBE	Formerly Adviser for Multicultural Education, London Borough of Ealing.
Mr G Myers	Chief Education Welfare Officer, Birmingham Education Authority.

Preparation of Main Report

Professor M Craft	Dean, Faculty of Education, University of Nottingham.
Mr G V I Davis	Adviser for Multicultural Education, London Borough of Brent.
Mrs C K Garcha	Head, Mount Pleasant First School, Southampton.
Mr M E J Hobbs	Formerly Course Director, Birmingham Polytechnic.
Mrs M S Parvaz	Teacher, Farley Junior School, Luton, Bedfordshire.
Mr N Patel	Head of Asian Studies, Everton High School, Blackburn, Lancashire.

* Appointments shown are those held at the time of co-option.

Mrs V Rao	Head, Handsworth Wood Girls School, Birmingham.
Mr R A Richardson	Adviser for Multicultural Education, Berkshire Education Authority.
Kartar Singh Sandhu	Head of Geography, St Pauls's RC School, Leicester.

APPENDIX B

LIST OF EDUCATIONAL INSTITUTIONS WHICH HAVE SUBMITTED EVIDENCE TO THE COMMITTEE

* denotes those institutions which members of the Committee have visited.

i. SCHOOLS, (including language centres, resources centres etc).

AVON LEA

* * Ashley Down Infant School, Bristol.
* * Bannerman Road Junior Mixed and Infant School, Bristol.
* * Hawkesbury Upton Primary School.
* * Kingsweston ESN(M) School, Avonmouth.
* * Lockleaze School, Bristol.
* * Multicultural Centre, Bristol.
* * St George School, Bristol.
* * The Castle School, Thornbury.
* * Whitefield Fishponds School, Bristol.

BEDFORDSHIRE LEA

Beech Hill High School, Luton.
* * Denbigh High School, Luton.
John Bunyan Upper School, Bedford.
Luton Sixth Form College, Luton.
* * Maidenhall Infant School, Luton.
* * Marlborough Lower School, Bedford.
* * Park Wood Middle School, Bedford.
Rotheram High School, Luton.
* * St Bede's RC Middle School, Bedford.
* * The English Language and Resources Centre, Bedford.
Westfield School, Bedford.

BERKSHIRE LEA

St Ethelbert's RC Middle School, Slough.

BIRMINGHAM LEA

* * The Burlington Centre, Birmingham.
Bordesley Green Girls' School, Birmingham.
* * Broadway School, Perry Bar, Birmingham.
The Calthorpe School Youth and Adult Centre, Birmingham.
* * Conway Junior and Infants School, Sparkbrook, Birmingham.
* * Golden Hillock School, Birmingham.
* * Handsworth Wood Girls' School, Birmingham.
* * Holte School, Birmingham.
* * Holyhead School, Birmingham.
* * The Key Centre, Birmingham.

BRADFORD LEA

All Saints Church of England First School, Bradford.
Beckfoot Grammar School, Bingley.
* Belle Vue Girls' School, Bradford.
* Carlton-Bolling School, Bradford.
Fairfax School, Bradford.
* The Grange School, Bradford.
* Green Lane First School, Bradford.
* Green Lane Language Centre, Bradford.
Hollingwood First School, Bradford.
Lidget Green First School, Bradford.
Lidget Green Middle School, Bradford.
* Manningham Lane Sports Centre, Bradford.
Moorfield First School, Bradford.
Parkwood First School, Bradford.
Princeville First School, Bradford.
St Augustine's Church of England First School, Bradford.
St Paul's Church of England First School, Bradford.
Southmere First School, Bradford.
* Thorn Park School for the Deaf, Bradford.
Tyersal First School, Bradford.
Usher Street First School, Bradford.
Utley First School, Keighley.
Wapping First School, Bradford.
Waverley Middle School, Bradford.
Whetley First School, Bradford.

BRENT LEA

* Alperton High School, Wembley.
* Aylestone High School, Brent.
Brent Teachers' Centre.
* Bridge Infants School, Brent.
* Elsley Junior Mixed and Infants School, Brent.
* South Kilburn High School, Brent.
* Sudbury Infants School, Brent.

BROMLEY LEA

St Nicholas School, West Wickham.
Goddington School, Orpington.

BUCKINGHAMSHIRE LEA

* Cheena County Primary School, Chalfont St Peter.
* Jordans County Combined School, Jordans, Beaconsfield.

CAMBRIDGESHIRE LEA

* Brewster Avenue County Infant School, Peterborough.
  Eastholm School, Peterborough.
  Honey Hill Community School, Peterborough.
* Old Fletton County Primary School, Peterborough.
  Peterborugh County Girls' School, Peterborough.
* Resources Centre for Multi-racial Education, Peterborough.
* Stanground School, Peterborough.

COVENTRY LEA

  Broadheath Primary School, Coventry.
* Foxford Comprehensive School, Coventry.
  Minority Group Support Service.
* Sidney Stringer School and Community College, Coventry.

CROYDON LEA

  Lanfranc Travellers' Unit.

DERBYSHIRE LEA

  St James' Church of England (Aided) School, Derby.

EALING LEA

  Acton Green Combined First and Middle School, Acton Green.
* Beaconsfield First and Middle School, Southall.
  Cardinal Newman RC High School, Acton.
* Centre for Reading and Language Development, Greenford.
  Clifton First School, Southall.
  Coston First School, Greenford.
  Derwentwater First School, Acton.
  Dormers Wells First School, Southall.
  Durdans Park First School, Southall.
  Ellen Wilkinson High School, Acton.
  Greenford High School, Greenford.
* Havelock First School, Southall.
* Havelock Middle School, Southall.
  Lady Margaret First School, Southall.
  Little Ealing First School, Ealing.
  Mayfield First School, Hanwell.
  North First and Middle School, Southall.
  Oaklands First School, Hanwell.
* St Anselm's RC First and Middle School, Southall.
  Tudor First School, Southall.
  Twyford High School, Acton.
* Villiers High School, Southall.
* Wolf Fields First School, Southall.

EAST SUSSEX LEA

Sacred Heart Primary School, Hastings.

ENFIELD LEA

St Michael-at-Bowes CE Junior School, Palmers Green.

GLOUCESTERSHIRE LEA

* Chipping Camden Comprehensive School, Chipping Camden.
* Eastville Junior School, Gloucester.
* Linden Secondary Modern School, Gloucester.
* St Benedict's RC Secondary School, Cheltenham.
* St Mary's Church of England Junior School, Tetbury.
* Widden Infants School, Gloucester.
* Widden Junior School, Gloucester.

HAMPSHIRE LEA

Mount Pleasant Middle School, Southampton.
Richard Taunton College, Southampton.

HARINGEY LEA

* Bruce Grove Infants School.
* Coleraine Park Primary School.
* The Drayton School.
* Greenfields School.
* High Cross School.
* Highgate Wood School.
* Lea Valley Primary School.
* Noel Park Infants School.
* Northumberland Park School.
* South Haringey Pre-School Centre.
* South Haringey Infants School.
* South Haringey Junior School.
* Welbourne Junior School.
* William Forster School.
* Wood Green School.

HUMBERSIDE LEA

Bransholme High School, Hull.

INNER LONDON EDUCATION AUTHORITY

* Burrow Hill ESN(M) School.
  Daneford School, E2.
  John Donne Junior Mixed and Infant School, SE15.

    John Milton Primary School, SW8.
    John Stainer Infants School, SE4.
* Lewisham Teachers Centre.
    Oak Lodge School, SW12.
    Pimlico School, SW1.
    Redlands School, E1.
* St. James' and St Peter's Primary School, W1.
* Skinners' Company's School, N16.
    Stepney Green School, E1.
* Teachers for Travellers Team.
    Thomas Buxton Infant School, E1.
* Tower Hamlets School, E1.
* Tulse Hill School, SW2.
    Walsingham School, SW4.
* Westhill Primary School, SW18.
    Woolwich Polytechnic School, SE18.

KENT LEA

    Dover Road County Infant School, Northfleet.
    Dover Road County Junior School, Northfleet.
    Northfleet School for Girls, Northfleet.

KIRKLEES LEA

* Fartown High School, Huddersfield.
* Hopton Language and Resources Centre.
    Mount Pleasant County Junior School, Huddersfield.
* Pentland Infant School, Dewsbury.
* Saville Town Infant School, Dewsbury.
* Saville Town Nursery School, Dewsbury.

LANCASHIRE LEA

    Billinge High School, Blackburn.
* Cedars Infant School, Blackburn.
    Everton High School, Blackburn.
    Frenchwood County Junior School, Preston.
    The Hollins High School, Accrington.
    Northlands High School, Preston.
* Parklands High School, Preston.
    William Temple CE High School, Preston.

LEEDS LEA

* Chapel Allerton Primary School.
* Chapeltown Play Group.
* City of Leeds School.

* Earl Cowper Middle School.
* Elmhurst Middle School.
* Hamilton County Primary School.
* Harehills Middle School.
  Leopold County Primary School.
* Lovell Park Day Nursery.
  Potternewton County Primary School.
* Primrose Hill High School.
  Roundhay School.
  Royal Park Middle School.
  Scott Hall Middle School.
* Scott Hall Day Nursery.
  Westfield Primary School.

LEICESTERSHIRE LEA

* Abbey County Primary School, Leicester.
  Beaumont Leys School, Leicester.
  Burleigh College, Loughborough.
* English Home Tuition Scheme, Leicester.
  Gateway VI Form College, Leicester.
  Judgemeadow School and Community College, Leicester.
  Moat Community College, Leicester.
* Rushey Mead Secondary School, Leicester.
* Rushey Mead Language Centre, Leicester.
  Soar Valley School and Community College, Leicester.
* Uplands Infant School, Leicester.
  Uplands Junior School, Leicester.
  Wyggeston and Queen Elizabeth I College, Leicester.

LIVERPOOL LEA

* Abercromby Nursery School.
* Crown Street Language Centre.
* Morrison County Primary School.
* Multi-Racial Education Centre.
* Paddington Comprehensive School.
* Shorefields Comprehensive School.
* Windsor Street JMI School.

MANCHESTER LEA

* Abraham Moss Centre.
* Birley High School.
* Ducie High School.
* Ethnic Music Faculty.
* Language, Literacy and Numeracy Support Service.
* Manley Park Infant School.

* Travellers' School, c/o Abbott County Primary School.
* Whalley Range High School for Girls.

MERTON LEA

Links Primary School.
Pelham High School.

NEWHAM LEA

* Langdon School.

NOTTINGHAMSHIRE LEA

* Claremont Boys' School, Nottingham.
* Douglas Junior and Infant School, Nottingham.

OXFORDSHIRE LEA

* Slade Park Mobile School, Oxford.

ROTHERHAM LEA

St Anne's New Infant School, Rotherham.
Broom Valley Junior School, Rotherham.

SEFTON LEA

King George V College, Southport.

SHEFFIELD LEA

Park House Comprehensive School, Sheffield.

STAFFORDSHIRE LEA

The Leys Infant School, Tamworth.

WALTHAM FOREST LEA

Whitefield School.

WOLVERHAMPTON LEA

* West Midland Education Service for Travelling Children.

ii. UNIVERSITIES, POLYTECHNICS AND ESTABLISHMENTS OF HIGHER AND FURTHER EDUCATION

* Bedford College of Higher Education.
* City of Birmingham Polytechnic.

University of Birmingham.
* Bradford College.
Bristol Polytechnic.
University of Bristol.
Brixton College.
University of Cambridge.
College of St Mark and St John, Plymouth.
The College of St Paul and St Mary, Gloucester.
Derby Lonsdale College of Higher Education.
Doncaster College of Higher Education.
* Edge Hill College of Higher Education, Ormskirk.
* Goldsmiths College.
Hertfordshire College of Higher Education.
Huddersfield Polytechnic.
Hull College of Higher Education.
Kent College for the Careers Service.
Kingston Polytechnic.
University of Leeds.
Leicester Polytechnic.
City of Liverpool College of Higher Education.
Liverpool Polytechnic.
University of Liverpool.
* University of London, Institute of Education.
University of Manchester.
Manchester Polytechnic.
Middlesex Polytechnic.
Nene College, Northampton.
North Cheshire College of Higher Education.
North East London Polytechnic.
* North London Polytechnic.
North Riding College of Higher Education.
University of Nottingham.
Oxford Polytechnic.
University of Oxford.
* Roehampton Institute of Higher Education.
Sheffield City Polytechnic.
South Devon Technical College.
Sunderland Polytechnic.
Thames Polytechnic.
Westhill College, Birmingham.
West Midlands College of Higher Education.
Worcester College of Higher Education.

APPENDIX C

LIST OF LEAS AND ORGANISATIONS WHICH HAVE SUBMITTED
EVIDENCE TO THE COMMITTEE

* denotes those who have met members of the Committee for discussion

* Advisory Committee for the Education of Romany and other Travellers.
  Afro-Asian Teachers Association, Coventry.
  Afro-Caribbean Education Resource Project.
  Afro-Carribbean Parent Educational Support Group (Waltham Forest) London.
* Afro-Caribbean Teachers Association.
  Afro-West Indian Association.
* Afro-West Indian United Council of Churches.
* All Faiths for One Race (AFFOR), Community Resources Agency, Birmingham.
  Assistant Masters and Mistresses Association.
* Associated Examining Board.
  Associated Lancashire Schools Examining Board.
* Association for Black Educational Advance.
  Association for Religious Education.
  Association for Science Education.
* Association for the Teaching of Caribbean and African Literature.
  Association of Christian Teachers.
* Association of County Councils.
  Association of Directors of Social Services.
  Association of Educational Psychologists.
  Association of Jamaicans (UK) Trust.
* Association of Metropolitan Authorities.
* Association of Teachers of Italian.
* Association of Ukrainians in Great Britain Ltd.
  Association of Yorkshire and Humberside Chambers of Commerce and Trade.
* Avon Educational Authority.

  Bangla Education and Cultural Centre.
  Barking and Dagenham Council for Racial Equality.
  Barnet Community Relations Council.
* Bedfordshire Education Authority.
  Bexley Council for Racial Equality.
* Birmingham Education Authority.
  Black Arrow Organisation.
  Blackburn and District Community Relations Council.
  Black Education Action Group.
* Black Peoples Progressive Association, Redbridge.
* Bradford Education Authority.

Bradford Community Relations Council.
* Brent Education Authority.
Bristol Council for Racial Equality.
Bristol Resource Centre.
Bristol Teachers Association (NUT).
British/American Community Service Institute.
* British Association for Early Childhood Education.
* British Association of Muslims, Birmingham.
* British Association for Teachers of the Deaf.
British Broadcasting Corporation.
British Council of Churches.
* British Refugee Council.
British Youth Council.
Bromley and Bexley Gypsy Support Group.

Calderdale Education Authority.
* Cambridgeshire Education Authority.
Cambridge Community Relations Council.
Camden Committee for Community Relations.
Cardiff Gypsy Support Group.
Careers and Occupational Information Centre.
Caribbean Communications Project.
* Caribbean House Group.
* Caribbean Pastoral Service, Hackney, London.
* Caribbean Teachers Association.
Catholic Commission for Racial Justice.
Central Council for Physical Recreation.
Centre for Advanced Research in Education.
Centre for Information on Language Teaching and Research.
Centre for Urban Educational Studies.
Cheshire Education Authority.
* China Town Chinese Association (London).
* Chinese Action Group, Soho.
Chinese Association, North West.
Chinese Coordinating Committee, Edinburgh.
Circle of Literary Friends, Liverpool.
City of Leicester Teachers Association.
* Commission for Racial Equality.
* Confederation of British Industry.
Council for Education in World Citizenship.
Council for Educational Technology.
* Council of Mosques, Bradford.
Council for National Academic Awards.
* Coventry Education Authority.
Coventry West Indian Assocation.
Croydon Education Authority.
* Cyprus Turkish Association.

* Derbyshire Education Authority.
Devon Education Authority.
Dudley Education Authority.
Dudley Community Relations Council.

* Ealing Education Authority.
* East London Black Womens Organisation.
East London Islamic Centre.
East Sussex Education Authority.
* Elimu Wa Name, Methodist Youth Centre, Liverpool 8.
Essex Education Authority.
Exeter and District Chamber of Commerce and Trade.

* Federation of Bangladesh Associations.
Further Education Curriculum Review and Development Unit.

Geographical Association.
* Greek Cypriot Teachers Association.
Greenwich Council for Racial Equality.

* Hackney Cypriot Association.
* Handsworth Alternate Scheme, Birmingham.
* Handsworth Employment Scheme Limited, Birmingham.
* Haringey Education Authority.
Harrow Community Relations Council.
Headmasters' Conference.
Health Visitors' Association.
Historical Association.
* Hong Kong Government Office.
Hull Harmony Group.
Hyndburn and Rossendale Community Relations Council.

Independent Broadcasting Association.
Indian Workers Association, Leicester.
Indian Workers Association (GB), Wolverhampton.
* Inner London Education Authority.
Inner London NAME Groups Coordinating Committee.
Institute of Careers Officers.
Institute of Directors.
Institute of Race Relations.
Ipswich and District Committee for Community Relations.
Irish Cultural Activities, London.
* Islamic Cultural Centre.

Jamaican Action Group, London.
Joint Council for the Welfare of Immigrants.
* Joint Matriculation Board.

Kensington and Chelsea Community Relations Council.
Kent Education Authority.
* Kirklees Education Authority.

* Labour Party Race Action Group.
* Lancashire Education Authority.
League for the Exchange of Commonwealth Teachers.
* Leeds Education Authority.
* Leeds Community Relations Council.
* Leicestershire Education Authority.
Leicestershire Brahma Samaj.
Leicester Council for Community Relations.
* Lena Gardens Chinese Language School, London.
Lewisham Council for Community Relations.
Library Association.
* Linguistic Minorities Project.
* Liverpool Education Authority.
Liverpool Circle of Literary Friends.
Liverpool Teachers Association.
Local Government Training Board.
London Association for the Teaching of English.
London Regional Examining Board.

* Manchester Chinese Education Cultural Community Centre.
* Merseyside Chinese Advisory Group.
* Minority Rights Group.
* Muslim Education Consultative Committee.
* Muslim Educational Trust.

National Association of Careers and Guidance Teachers.
National Association of Drama Advisers.
* National Association of Head Teachers.
National Association of Inspectors and Educational Advisers.
* National Association for Multi-Racial Education.
National Association for Multi-Racial Education—London and
    Harringay Branches.
* National Association of Nursery and Family Care.
* National Association for Teachers of Travellers.
* National Association of Schoolmasters/Union of Women Teachers.
* National Association of Teachers in Further and Higher Education.
National Association for the Teaching of English.
National Association for Teaching English as a Second Language to
    Adults.
* National Childminding Association.
National Children's Centre, Huddersfield.
National Children's Home.
National Council for Home Economics Education.

* National Council of Hindu Associatons.
* National Deaf Children's Society.
National Institute for Careers Education and Counselling.
* National Gypsy Council.
* National Gypsy Education Council.
National Muslim Education Council for UK.
* National Union of Students.
* National Union of Teachers.
National Union of Teachers (High Wycombe Branch).
Newham Education Authority.
Northamptonshire Education Authority.
* North Kirklees Community Relations Council.
* North West Chinese Association.
North West Regional Conference of the Standing Conference on Inter-
  Faith Dialogue in Education.
North West Regional Examinations Board.
Nottinghamshire Afro-Caribbean Teachers Association.
Nottinghamshire Education Authority.
Nottinghamshire Careers Service.
Nottinghamshire Chamber of Commerce and Industry.
Notting Hill Methodist Church and Ecumenical Group Ministry.

* Ockenden Venture
* One Foundation Organisation, Luton, Bedfordshire.
Oriental Arts and Music Society.
Overseas Chinese Education Centre.
Oxford Delegacy of Local Examinations.
Oxfordshire Council for Community Relations.

Pakistan Workers Association, North West London.
* Professional Association of Teachers.
* Pre-School Playgroups Association.
* Preston and Western Lancashire Council for Community Relations.
Project Fullemploy Trust.

Quaker Social Responsibility and Education Department.

Racism Awareness Programme Unit.
* Redbridge Community Relations Council.
* Refugee Action.
Religious Education Council.
* Romany Guild.
Royal National Institute for the Deaf.
Royal Society of Arts Examinations Board.
Runnymede Trust.

Sahali Group.
Sandwell Council for Community Relations.
* Save the Children Fund.
* Schools Council.
Schools Libraries Association.
Scout Association.
* Secondary Heads Association.
Shali Group.
Sheffield Council for Racial Equality.
Sickle Cell Society.
Sikh Education Council, Leicestershire.
Slough Community Relations Council.
Society for Caribbean Studies.
* Society of Education Officers.
Society of Immigrant Teachers.
* South Kirklees Community Relations Council.
* South London Islamic Centre.
* South Liverpool Personnel Limited.
* Southampton Community Relations Council.
Southern Universities Joint Board.
Standing Conference on Education for International Understanding.
* Steering Committee of Asian Organisations.

Tameside Education Authority.
Teesside and District Chamber of Commerce and Trade.
Thamesdown and District Council for Racial Equality.
The Black Forum, Brent.
The Gujarat Hindu Society, Preston.
* Tower Hamlets Chinese Cooperative Group.
* Turkish Education Group.

* UK Islamic Mission.
* Union of Muslim Organisations.
* United Anglo-Caribbean Society.
United Jewish School.
* University of London, University Entrance and School Examinations
    Council.

* Voluntary Organisations Liaison Council for Under Fives.

Waltham Forest Education Authority.
* Wandsworth Council for Community Relations.
Wellingborough and District Community Relations Council.
* West Indian Concern Ltd.
* Wycombe and District Community Relations Council.

York and District Community Relations Council.
Yorkshire Regional Examinations Board.
Young Mens Christian Association.
Youth at Work Service.

APPENDIX D

LIST OF INDIVIDUALS WHO HAVE SUBMITTED EVIDENCE TO THE
COMMITTEE

* denotes those who have met members of the Committee for discussion.

* Mrs Abji	Head of English as a Second Language, Rotheram High School, Luton, Bedfordshire.
Mr R Ahmed	Parent, Coventry.
* Mr T Ahmed	Editor *'The Asian'*.
Mrs S Ahmed	Training Officer, Social Services Training Centre, Coventry.
Dr Z Ahmed	Parent, Birmingham.
* Mr G Alfonso	West Indian Teacher, on Exchange Visit from Caribbean.
* Mrs C Ajitsingh	Community Education Team, London Borough of Ealing.
Mr D H Ali	Researcher, St Helens, Merseyside.
* Mr M Ali	Careers Officer, Coventry Education Authority.
* Mr F Alkn	Cypriot Liaison Officer, Haringey Social Services Department.
Mrs S Allen	Parent, Kings Lynn, Norfolk.
* Mr M Andrews	Head of Religious Education, The Grange School, Bradford.
Mrs E R Arnold	Teacher, London.
* Dr R Ash	Teacher, Willesden High School, Brent.
Mrs J Atkin	Lecturer in Education, University of Nottingham School of Education.
* Dr M Atkins	Researcher, University of Nottingham.
* Mr M Atkins	Careers Officer, Sheffield Education Authority.
* Dr C Bagley	University of Surrey.
* Ms D Bailey	Head of English as a Second Language, North Westminster Community School, London.
* Mr Bailey	Careers Officer, Manchester Education Authority.
* Dr H Baker	Head, Contemporary China Institute, School of Oriental and African Studies, University of London.
* Dr R Ballard	Lecturer in Race Relations, University of Leeds.
* Mr A Bamforth	Training Manager, Simon Engineering Limited, Stockport.
* Professor J A Banks	University of Seattle, USA.
Dr W Barker	Project Director, Child Development Project, University of Bristol.
* Mr J Barrow	Careers Officer, Inner London Education Authority.
Mrs S Basu	Parent, Sutton.

*	Mr P Batelaan	Department of Teacher Training, Utrecht, Holland.
*	Dr N Beattie	University of Liverpool School of Education.
	Professor C H Bedwell	Department of Visual Function, New Barnet.
	Ms F Beetlestone	Teacher, Haringey.
	Ms A Behchet	Turkish Education Group.
	Dr G Ben-Tovim	Lecturer in Sociology, University of Liverpool.
*	Mr W Best	Senior Community Liaison Officer, Inner London Education Authority.
	Mr R Bhattacharyya	Teacher, Inner London Education Authority.
*	Dr F Bhatti	East London Resource Centre, Inner London Education Authority.
	Mr M R Bhatti	Parent, Nottingham.
	Ms K K Bhavnani	Project Officer, Open University.
*	Mr R Blackman	Nello James Centre, Whalley Range, Manchester.
	Miss H V Birrell	Educational Adviser, Coventry Education Authority.
*	Mr M Bisson	Outreach Careers Officer, Manchester Education Authority.
	Mr D Bloom	Researcher, Manchester Polytechnic.
*	Mrs S Bond	Head of Basic Studies, Soar Valley School and Community College, Leicester.
*	Miss M Boyce	West Indian Teacher, on Exchange Visit from Caribbean.
	Mrs J Bracey	Head, Frankland Junior School, Hoddesdon, Hertfordshire.
*	Mr D Brennan	Religious Education Centre, West London Institute of Higher Education.
*	Mr J Brierley	Personnel Officer, United Biscuits Limited, Manchester.
*	Mrs R Brightmore	Head, Thomas Buxton Infants School, London E1.
	Mrs A Bristow	Head of Italian, Cambridgeshire College of Arts and Technology.
	Mr D Brook	County Adviser for English, Derbyshire Education Authority.
*	Mr P Brown	Careers Officer, Bradford Education Authority.
*	Mr W Brown	Elimu Project Leader, Liverpool and Merseyside Community Relations Council.
	Mrs Brown	Parent, High Wycombe, Buckinghamshire.
*	Mr C Bryant	Director of Coordinating Services, City and East London College.
*	Mr D Burgess	Head of Religious Education, Villiers High School, Southall.
*	Miss B Burthom	Head, Manley Park Infants School, Manchester.
*	Mr Campbell	Westhill College, Birmingham.
*	Ms L Campbell	West Indian Teacher, on Exchange Visit from Caribbean.
	Mr C Carter	Lecturer, London N8.
*	Mr Chan	Businessman, Manchester.

*	Mr A Chan	Tower Hamlets Chinese Cooperative.
	Mr R P Chandaria	Businessman, London.
*	Mr C Chann	Vice Chairman, North West Chinese Association.
*	Mr V Y F Chann	Senior Liaison Officer, Hong Kong Government Office.
	Mr R D Chapman	Adviser for Multicultural Education, Birmingham Education Authority.
*	Ms P Charalambous	Assistant Cypriot Liaison Officer, Haringey Social Services Department.
	Mr E Chatfield	Careers Officer, Inner London Education Authority.
*	Mrs B Chaubhri	Teacher, Warley, West Midlands.
	Mr B K Chaudhari	Parent, Sheffield.
*	Mr D Cherrington	Director, International Centre for Multicultural Education, Birmingham Polytechnic.
*	Mr S M Cheung	Teacher, London.
*	Mrs K Chew	Deputy Head, South Hackney School, London.
*	Miss Y K Chiu	Tower Hamlets Chinese Cooperative.
	Mr H C Chopra	Teacher, Inner London Education Authority.
	Mr D H Chorley	Inspector, Croydon Education Authority.
*	Mrs H Chowdhury	Educational Welfare Officer, Inner London Education Authority.
*	Mr C Chung	Hackney Educational and Development Society, London N16.
*	Sister D Chung	Teacher, Liverpool Language Centre.
	Professor M M Clark	Professor of Education, University of Birmingham.
*	Mr B Clarke	Head, Earl Cowper Middle School, Leeds.
*	Mr H Clarke	Adviser for Multicultural Education, Cambridgeshire Education Authority.
*	Miss C Clough	Examinations Officer, Associated Examining Board.
*	Dr W O Cole	Religious Studies Department, West Sussex Institute of Higher Education, Chichester.
*	Mr R J Collet	Head, Bedford Resources Centre, Bedford.
*	Mr D Collins	Divisional Education Officer, Division 5, Inner London Education Authority.
*	Mrs C Collinson	Head of Religious Education, Cotton Hills School, Wolverhampton.
*	Ms S Constantinides	Cypriot Liaison Officer, Haringey Social Services Department.
*	Mr J Cordwell	Assistant Divisional Education Officer, Division 5, Inner London Education Authority.
	Reverend K Cracknell	Committee for Relations with People of Other Faiths, British Council of Churches.
*	Mrs A Craft	Coordinator for Multicultural Education, Schools Council.
*	Professor M Craft	University of Nottingham, School of Education.
	Mr C T Crellin	Principal Lecturer in Education, Middlesex Polytechnic.
	Mrs P Crellin	Head of Nursery, St Peter's Primary School, St Albans, Hertfordshire.

*	Mr R Cruickshank	Specialist Careers Officer (Ethnic Minorities), Brent Education Authority.
	Mrs J Cubbin	Teacher, Ipswich.
*	Mr Cuddington	Godfrey Davis Limited Training Workshop, Neasden.
	Ms C Dalglish	Head of Continuing Education, West Sussex Institute of Higher Education.
	Mr Dalvi	Head of Biology, Samuel Whitbread Upper School, Shefford, Bedfordshire.
*	Mr G H Dalziel	Head, Thorn Park School for the Deaf, Bradford.
*	Dr A G Davey	Reader in Applied Social Studies, University of Newcastle-upon-Tyne.
*	Miss E Davies	Principal, Pathway Centre, Southall, Ealing.
*	Miss B V Davis	Head of Religious Education, Deanery School, Southampton.
*	Ms D Davis	Teacher, recently on Exchange Visit to Caribbean.
*	Mr G V I Davis	Adviser for Multicultural Education, Brent Education Authority.
*	Mrs R Dennis	Careers Officer, Birmingham Education Authority.
	Mr Y Desai	Parent, Preston, Lancashire.
	Councillor A Devgun	Councillor, London Borough of Waltham Forest.
	Dr B Dickinson	General Practitioner, Hertfordshire.
	Mr A Dorn	Commission for Racial Equality.
*	Dr G Driver	Research Fellow, Applied Anthropology Group, University of Leeds.
*	Miss I Dunkley	Coordinator, Colebrooke Social, Cultural and Welfare Association, Fulham, London.
*	Mr D Dunn	Researcher, University of Keele.
*	Mr R Edwards	Personnel Director, GKN Limited, Warley.
*	Dr V K Edwards	University of Reading.
	Professor S J Eggleston	Head of Department of Education, University of Keele.
	Mr S H Elahi	Parent, Blackburn, Lancashire.
	Ms P Elliott	Polytechnic of North London, School of Librarianship.
*	Mr P Emmett	Head of Religious Education, St Jonathan North Girls School, Leicester.
	Mrs O Entwistle	Teacher, Rickmansworth, Hertfordshire.
	Mrs R Evans	Resources Officer.
*	Mr Exley	Chief Inspector, Manchester Education Authority.
	Mr H I Faryad	Businessman, Croydon.
*	Dr M A Fazal	Principal Lecturer in Law, Trent Polytechnic, Nottingham.
*	Mrs G Feeley	Community Education Project, Coventry Education Authority.
*	Professor J M Figueroa	Visiting Fellow, University of Bradford.
*	Dr P M E Figueroa	Lecturer, University of Southampton.

*	Mr N File	Head of History, Tulse Hill School, London.
	Mr G Fisher	Brunel University.
*	Mr N Fitchett	Warden, Primary English Language Centre, Derby.
	Miss M S Fitter	Community Librarian, Southampton.
	Ms O Foster-Carter	Lecturer in Social Psychology, University of Bradford.
*	Mr S Fowler	Manager, Moss Side Job Centre, Manchester.
*	Mr S F Freeman	Head of Religious Education, Handsworth New Road School, Birmingham.
*	Ms S A M Garvey	Senior Careers Officer, Ealing Education Authority.
	Ms D Gill	Teacher, Inner London Education Authority.
*	Mr J K Gohel	Vice Chairman, Institute of Indian Cultures, London.
*	Mr L Gore	Head of English, John Kelly Boys' School, Brent.
*	Mrs D Gould	Head, Tower Hamlets Secondary School for Girls, London E1.
	Ms M Gravelle	Teacher, Haringey Education Authority.
	Mr E J Griffiths	Staff Inspector (Special Education), Birmingham Education Authority.
*	Dr P A Green	University of Durham.
	Mr C P Gupta	Parent, London.
	Dr R M Gupta	Educational Psychologist, Birmingham Education Authority.
*	Mr P A Hacking	Senior Careers Officer, Nottinghamshire Education Authority.
*	Mrs C Hall	Supplementary School Leader, Coventry.
	Mrs M Halsey	Language Coordinator, Hertfordshire Education Authority.
*	Councillor Hamilton	Chairman, Nursery Committee, Leeds City Council.
*	Mr K Hargreaves	Language Support Service, Bolton, Lancashire.
*	Mr Harris	Careers Officer, Manchester Education Authority.
	Mr C Harrison	Parent, Luton, Bedfordshire.
*	Dr N Hasnie	Chairman, South Kirklees Community Relations Council.
*	Mr R Hedderley	Principal Educational Psychologist, Kirklees Education Authority.
*	Mr B Henry	Black Parents Education Group, Deptford, London.
*	Mr R Henry	West Indian Teacher, on Exchange Visit from Caribbean.
*	Dr J Hewison	Thomas Coram Research Unit, University of London Institute of Education.
*	Mr D Hicks	Education Officer, Minority Rights Group.
*	Mr Hidayettin	Turkish Education Group.
*	Mr D T Hiles	Assistant Education Officer, Kirklees Education Authority.
	Mr M P Holloway	Researcher, Sheffield.
	Mr R Honeyford	Head, Drummond Middle School, Bradford.
	Mrs M Horne	Teacher, Hale, Cheshire.

799

*	Mr Howley	Kilburn Skills Training Workshop.
	Mr S Hoyle	Teacher, Santley Primary School, Brixton.
*	Mrs M E Hoyle	Visiting Teacher of the Deaf, Thorn Park School for the Deaf, Bradford.
	Mrs S Hsia	Researcher, Institute of Phonetics, Free University of Brussels.
*	Mr Hughes	Unemployment Specialist Careers Officer, Brent Education Authority.
	Mr J T R Hull	Bransholme High School, Hull.
*	Miss B Hunt	Adviser for Religious Education, Kirklees Education Authority.
*	Mr R Huntingdon	Deputy Principal, Tower Hamlets Adult Education Institute.
*	Mr R Hurst	Principal Careers Officer, Cleveland Education Authority.
*	Mr M Hussey	Multi-Ethnic Inspectorate, Inner London Education Authority.
*	Miss E Ingel	Outreach Careers Officer, Inner London Education Authority.
	Mr R Jackson	Senior Lecturer, University of Warwick.
*	Mr R Jeffcoate	Faculty of Educational Studies, The Open University.
	Mrs C Job	Teacher of English as a Second Language, Hounslow Education Authority.
	Mr P Jones	Principal Careers Officer, Birmingham.
*	Mr T Jukes	Head of English as a Second Language, Villiers High School, Southall, Ealing.
*	Mr S Kebbie	Roscoe Methodist Church, Chapeltown, Leeds.
	Mrs J Kendrick	School Nurse, Brixton.
*	Mr M Khan	Teacher, Charwood Primary School, Leicester.
*	Mr M H Khan	Vice Principal, Judgemeadow Community College, Leicester.
*	Mr N Khan	Multicultural Adviser, Liverpool Education Authority.
	Mr M C Khular	Teacher, Chatham, Kent.
*	Dr R King	Lecturer, Department of Geography, University of Leicester.
*	Mr Kistan	Teacher, Alameda Middle School, Ampthill, Bedfordshire.
*	Ms D Kleanthous	Assistant Community Relations Officer, Haringey.
*	Ms G Klein	University of London, Institute of Education.
*	Mr R Krawec	Secretary, Educational Affairs Council, Association of Ukrainians in Great Britain Limited.
	Dr S Kushner	Centre for Advanced Research in Education.

*	Mr D Ladlow	Head, Liverpool Language Centre.
	Mr J R Latham	Head of the Division of Philosophy of Education, City of Liverpool College of Higher Education.
*	Professor R Le Page	Department of Language, University of York.
	Dr G Lee	Researcher, University of Aston Sociology Group.
	Mr K Y Lee	Manchester Chinese Christian Fellowship.
*	Mr L Lee	Chinese Education, Culture and Community Centre, Manchester.
	Mr S R Lee	Teacher, Halstead, Essex.
	Mrs J Lee Williams	Blackheath, London.
*	Mrs J Levine	Department of Teaching English (Mother Tongue), University of London Institute of Education.
	Dr S Lewenhak	Research Worker.
*	Mrs S P Lin	Social Worker, Camden Chinese Centre.
	Mr P C D Lines	Hertfordshire College of Higher Education.
*	Professor A Little	Lewisham Professor of Social Administration, Goldsmiths' College, London.
	Miss G M Lloyd	Former Course Tutor, Southlands College.
*	Mrs M Longdon	Head, Noel Park Infants School, Haringey.
*	Miss L Lortie	West Indian Teacher, on Exchange Visit from Caribbean.
*	Dr A S T Lue	China Town Chinese Association and Overseas Chinese Education Centre.
*	Mrs I Lynn	Researcher, Department of Sociology, University of Liverpool.
	Miss E M Maddock	Retired Teacher, Oxford.
	Mr H Malborta	Reporter, Punjab Times, Birmingham.
*	Mr Malik	Home/School Liaison Teacher, Birmingham.
*	Mr Malik	Teacher, Barden High School, Burnley, Lancashire.
	Mrs P Mande	Parent, High Wycombe, Buckinghamshire.
*	Mr Mangat	Teacher, Birmingham.
	Mr M Marland	Head, North Westminster Community School, London.
*	Mr Marshall	Careers Officer, Haringey Education Authority.
	Dr F Master	Researcher, Leeds.
*	Mrs C Martianou	Teacher, Inner London Education Authority.
*	Mr A D Matthews MBE	Formerly Adviser for Multicultural Education, Ealing Education Authority.
*	Dr B Mayall	Thomas Coram Research Unit, University of London, Institute of Education.
*	Mr McBean	Careers Officer, Brent Education Authority.
*	Mr P McCann	Outreach Careers Officer, Liverpool Education Authority.
	Dr G P McGregor	Principal, College of Ripon and York St John, York.
*	Mr K McIntyre	Youth Tutor, Birley High School, Manchester.
*	Ms Mehmet	Turkish Education Group.
*	Ms N Miller	Careers Officer, Leeds Education Authority.

	Mr P K C Millins CBE	Director, DES Evaluation Project on Special Access Courses, Ealing College of Higher Education.
*	Ms G Mitchell	Haringey Multicultural Support Group.
*	Miss P Mitchell	Inspector for Primary Education, Division 5, Inner London Education Authority.
	Mr I Mitchell-Lambert	Head Teacher, Bexley.
*	Reverend D Moore	Head of Religious Education, Tulse Hill School, London.
	Mr J Morgan	Adult Literacy Coordinator Maidstone, Kent.
*	Mr E Morris	Careers Officer, Leicestershire Education Authority.
*	Mr T Mukherjee	Lecturer, Roehampton Institute of Higher Education.
*	Dr C Mullard	Director, Sociological Research Unit, University of London.
*	Mr T Murray	Careers Officer, Inner London Education Authority.
*	Mr D Naylor	Adviser for Religious Education, Hampshire Education Authority.
*	Dr R Ng	Tyne and Wear Community Relations Council.
*	Mr Nixon	Manager, Willesden Employment Office.
*	Dr R Oakley	Department of Sociology, Bedford College, University of London.
	Mr A Obi	
*	Miss T O'Connell	Teacher, recently returned from Exchange Visit to Caribbean.
	Ms M O'Hagan	Course Tutor, North London College.
	Mr I Osborne	Teacher, Slough, Berkshire.
	Mrs S D Pandit	Parent, Hendon, London.
*	Mr N Parr	Head, English Language Resource Centre, Haringey.
	Mrs V Patchett	BEd Student, Kenilworth, Warwickshire.
	Mr M A Patel	Parent, Bolton.
	Mr M S Patel	Dental Surgeon, Southampton.
*	Mr P Patrick	Head of History, Wood Green School, Haringey.
	Mr S Perryman	Parent, Sydenham, London.
*	Mr J W Pidcock	Principal Careers Officer, Manchester Education Authority.
*	Lady Plowden DBE	President, Pre-School Playgroups Association.
*	Mrs S Potesta	Senior Lecturer in Italian, Sheffield City Polytechnic.
	Ms C Poulter	Lecturer, Social Work Education Centre, Bedford College of Higher Education.
*	Mr C Power	Adviser for Multicultural Education, Haringey Education Authority.
	Mr G Power	Lecturer, Birmingham Polytechnic.
	Mr J B Provost	Parent, Inner London Education Authority.
	Mr P D Pumpfrey	Senior Lecturer in Education, University of Manchester.

* Ms A Purewal	Researcher, University of Keele.
Mr R Ramsaran	Student, Hatfield Polytechnic.
* Ms I Raz	Educational Psychologist, Huddersfield.
Mr M A Razak	Parent, Leeds.
Mrs S Reyersbach	Deputy Headmistress, Ellen Wilkinson High School, Ealing.
Mr B J Richardson	Kent Gypsy Support Group.
Mrs M Richardson	Teacher, Warrington, Cheshire.
Mr J Richmond	Teacher, Vauxhall Manor School, London.
* Miss E Roberts	Dorothy Gardner Nursery Centre, Paddington.
* Mr E E Robinson	Principal, Bradford College.
Mr P H Robinson	Community Recreation Officer, Luton, Bedfordshire.
* Miss E Robson	Teacher, recently returned from Exchange Visit to Caribbean.
Ms F G Rodwell	Teacher, Bedford.
Mr C A Rose	Board Member for Personnel, British Railways Board.
Mrs P Rose	Former Teacher, Paddington, London.
* Professor H Rosen	Head of Department of the Teaching of English (Mother Tongue), University of London, Institute of Education.
Dr D J Rostron	Head of Arts Department, Liverpool Polytechnic.
* Mr D Rowlands	Personnel Director, The Littlewoods Organisation Limited, Liverpool.
Mr G Ruffhead	Head of Humanities, Romsey School, Hampshire.
Dr D Ruddell	Multicultural Support Services Unit, Birmingham Education Authority.
* Professor M Rutter	Institute of Psychiatry, University of London.
Mr H A Sair	Parent, London E12.
Mr M Saleem	Madeley Court School, Madeley, Salop.
Mrs V Sarpal	Parent, Maidenhead, Berkshire.
Mr S M Sarwar	Education Secretary, The Islamic Centre, Leicester.
Mr J Savery	Teacher, Avon Multicultural Education Centre, Bristol.
* Mrs S Seth	Teacher, Uplands Infant School, Leicester.
Miss S Shah	
Mr S P Sharad	Parent, Ilford, Essex.
Mr R Sheldrick	Acting Principal Careers Officer, Brent Education Authority.
* Mrs J Sherwin	Head, Language Centre, Rossendale, Lancashire.
Mr M Sherwood	Department of Sociology, Polytechnic of North London.
* Mr Shukla	Teacher, Abbey Primary School, Leicester.
Professor J M Sinclair	Department of English Language and Literature, University of Birmingham.
* Mr A Singhal	Deputy Head, Portway Centre, Bedford.
Mr E D L de Siriwardena	Avon Multicultural Education Centre, Bristol.

*	Mr S Wan	Chairman, North West Chinese Association.
*	Mr B T S Wang	Merseyside Chinese Community Officer.
*	Mr B Watkins	Head of Department of Curricular Studies, Birmingham Polytechnic.
*	Mr G Watkins	Deputy Head, Birley High School, Manchester.
	Dr K Watson	University of Reading, School of Education.
*	Ms S Watts	Secondary Curriculum Development Unit, Inner London Education Authority.
*	Dr D Weikart	President High/Scope Educational Research Foundation, Michigan, USA.
	Mr J Whatmore	Training Manager, Brockhouse Limited, Victoria Works, West Bromwich.
*	Miss K M Whiley	Adviser, Leeds Education Authority.
	Mr S A White	Parent.
*	Mrs D Whitelock	Adviser, Department of Social Services, Leeds City Council.
*	Mr E Whittingham	Lecturer, West Indies.
*	Mr J Wight	Multi-Ethnic Inspectorate, Inner London Education Authority.
*	Miss H Wigmore	National Children's Centre, Huddersfield.
*	Mrs C Wilding	Department of Modern Languages, University of Aston.
	Mr P Wilkinson	Teacher, Chippenham, Wiltshire.
	Dr R Willey	Research Worker.
	Mrs J Williams	Wolverhampton Polytechnic Faculty of Education.
	Mrs S Willsher	Head, George Salter High School, West Bromwich.
*	Mr B Winn	Training Manager, L Gardener and Sons, Barton Hall Engineering Works, Manchester.
*	Mrs Wong	Home/School Liaison Teacher, Liverpool Education Authority.
	Mr E B Wood	Head, Mount Pleasant County Junior School, Huddersfield.
*	Mr B Woodroffe	Senior Inspector for Multi-Ethnic Education Inner London Education Authority.
*	Mr P Woodward	Adviser for Religious Education, Birmingham Education Authority.
	Mr A D Wooster	Lecturer in Education, University of Nottingham, School of Education.
*	Miss M Worrall	Lecturer, University of Oxford, Department of Education.
*	Mr D R Wright	Head of Geography, Keswick Hall College of Education, Norwich.
*	Mr Yashar	Hackney Cypriot Association.
	Ms L Yau	Researcher, Lambeth Community Relations Council.
*	Ms V Yu	Schools Language Unit, Isleworth, Middlesex.
	Mr S A R Zaidi	Parent, Hounslow.

*	Mr G D Skinner	Research Associate, Multicultural Research Unit, University of Manchester.
*	Dr D Smith	Senior Research Fellow, Policy Studies Institute.
	Mr T Smith	Deputy Head ESL Department, North Westminster Community School, London.
	Mrs P Soden	Head, Meon First School, Portsmouth.
	Mrs J Spanswick	Researcher.
*	Mr D Spinney	Head of Careers, Alperton High School, Brent.
*	Mr Stephenson	Multicultural Inspector, Birmingham Education Authority.
\\ *	Ms D Stewart	Careers Officer, Inner London Educational Authority.
*	Mr D Sutcliffe	Researcher, Bedford.
	Mr A Swailes	Head, Parkhead Centre, Ashington, Northumberland.
	Ms J Swann	Researcher.
*	Mr A Syred	Warden, Secondary English Language Centre, Derby.
	Professor I G Taylor	Department of Audiology, University of Manchester.
*	Miss V Taylor	County Staff Teacher for Ethnic Minority Children, Bedfordshire Education Authority.
*	Mr G J Taylor	Head of Religious Education, France Hill School Camberley, Surrey.
*	Mr Tempest	Adviser for Adult and Further Education, Liverpool Education Authority.
	Mr V Thapar	Parent, London N21.
*	Miss M Thompson	Teacher, recently returned from Exchange Visit to Caribbean.
	Mrs B Thomson	Adviser, Bradford Education Authority.
	Mr N Thomson	Postgraduate Student, University of London Institute of Education.
*	Dr A Tjon-a-Ten	Researcher, University of Utrecht.
*	Dr S Tomlinson	Department of Educational Research, University of Lancaster.
*	Miss P Topley	Area Youth Officer, Inner London Education Authority.
*	Dr A Tosi	Modern Languages Department, Oxford Polytechnic.
*	Mr Toufexis	Hackney Cypriot Association.
	Dr J Tough	Schools Council Communication Skills Project.
	Dr K S Trivedi	General Practitioner, Grimsby.
*	Ms M Tsow	Chinese Action Group and Commission for Racial Equality.
*	Mr B Turner	Adviser for Multicultural Education, Lancashire Education Authority.
*	Mr J Twitchin	Producer, BBC Television.
	Ms J Ure	English Studies Department, University of Edinburgh.
	Mr G Varnava	Deputy Head, Pimlico School, London SW1.
*	Mr J Veltman	Head of Upper School, Aylestone High School, Brent.

APPENDIX E

OPEN MEETINGS OR "FORUMS" ARRANGED TO HEAR THE VIEWS OF
PARENTS AND YOUNG PEOPLE

1980

25 February	St Matthew's Meeting Place, Brixton Hill, London.
26 February	Ealing Town Hall. (Organised by The United Anglo-Caribbean Association.)
25 March	All Nations Club, Hackney, London. (Organised by Hackney Community Relations Council.)
28 April	Lozells Social Development Centre, Lozells, Birmingham. (Organised by All Faiths for One Race—AFFOR.)
30 April	Bradford College. (Organised by the Bradford West Indian Parents Association.)
12 May	Caribbean Centre, Liverpool.
13 May	Old Town Hall, Reading, Berkshire. (Organised by Reading Council for Community Relations.)
21 May	Chapeltown Community Centre, Chapeltown, Leeds. (Organised by Leeds Community Relations Council.)
1 June	Tudor House, Spond Street, Coventry. (Organised by Coventry West Indian Association.)
8 June	West Indian Centre, Mosside, Manchester.
17 June	Brent Teachers Centre.
18 July	Cabot Junior Mixed and Infants School, St Pauls, Bristol.
19 July	Luton Central Library Theatre. (Organised by One Foundation Organisation.)
20 September	Sidney Stringer School and Community College, Coventry. (Organised by Coventry Asian Youth Association.)

1981

24 September	Victoria Hall, Harrow. (Organised by Harrow Community Relations Council.)
6 December	North West Chinese Association, Manchester.
7 December	CRC Offices, Huddersfield. (Organised by South Kirklees Community Relations Council.)

1982

7 January	Town Hall, Dewsbury, West Yorkshire. (Organised by North Kirklees Community Relations Council.)
25 March	Eastbrook Hall, Chapel Street, Bradford 1. (Organised by Bradford Metropolitan District Community Relations Council.)

21 April	Town Hall, Preston, Lancashire. (Organised by Preston and Western Lancashire Council for Community Relations.)
19 May	Central Library Hall, Bedford. (Organised by Bedford Community Relations Association.)
17 June	Moat Community College, Leicester. (Organised by Leicester Council for Community Relations.)
11 July	Haringey Social Services Centre. (Organised by the Hackney Cypriot Association and the Turkish Education Group.)
8 September	Resource Centre for Multiracial Education, Peterborough. (Organised by Peterborough Council for Community Relations.)
30 September	St Matthew's Hall, St Mary's Road, Southampton. (Organised by Southampton Community Relations Council.)
19 October	Italian Vice Consulate Offices, Bedford. (Organised by Italian Vice Consulate.)
20 October	Holy Trinity Primary School, Gravesend, Kent. (Organised by Gravesend and District Community Relations Council.)
17 November	London College of the Ukrainian Catholic University. (Organised by the Association of Ukrainians.)
9 December	Pakistan Centre, Liverpool 8. (Organised by Merseyside Community Relations Council.)

1983

15 January	Chinese Language School, London W6. St Paul's Way School, St Paul's, Mile End. (Organised by Tower Hamlets Chinese Co-operative Group.)

Printed for Her Majesty's Stationery Office by Commercial Colour Press, London E7. 4/86, C20, Dd.746581.